THE HISTORY

OF

SLAVERY AND THE SLAVE TRADE,

ANCIENT AND MODERN.

THE FORMS OF SLAVERY THAT PREVAILED IN ANCIENT NATIONS,
PARTICULARLY IN GREECE AND ROME.

THE AFRICAN SLAVE TRADE

AND THE

POLITICAL HISTORY OF SLAVERY

IN THE

UNITED STATES.

COMPILED FROM AUTHENTIC MATERIALS
BY W. O. BLAKE

COLUMBUS, OHIO: J. & H. MILLER
1857

Republished, 1971
Negro History Press – P.O. Box 5129 – Detroit, Michigan 48236

Library of Congress Catalog Card Number: 76-92418
ISBN 0-403-00176-5

CONTENTS.

CHAPTER I.

PRELIMINARY SKETCH.—ANCIENT SLAVERY.

Early existence of Slavery in the world.—The Mosaic institutions in regard to Slavery.—Hebrews, how reduced to servitude.—The Jubilee.—Distinction between native and foreign Slaves.—Voluntary Slaves: the Mercenarii of the Romans; the Prodigals or debtor Slaves; the Delinquents; the Enthusiasts.—Involuntary Slaves; prisoners of war, and captives stolen in peace, with the children and descendants of both.—Voluntary Slavery introduced by decree of the Roman Senate.—Slavery in Rome: condition of the Slaves; cruelty to the old and sick; prisons for Slaves; Sicily: servile war and breaking up of the prisons.—Piracy esteemed honorable by the early Greeks. — Piratical expeditions to procure Slaves.—Causes of the gradual extinction of Slavery in Europe.—Origin of the African Slave Trade by the Portuguese.—Followed by most of the maritime nations of Europe. 17

CHAPTER II.

SLAVERY IN GREECE.—ATHENIAN SLAVES.

Early existence of Slavery in Greece.—Proportion of Slaves to Freemen.—Their numbers in Athens and Sparta.—Mild government of Slaves in Athens—the reverse in Sparta.—Instances of noble conduct of Slaves towards their masters.—Probable origin of Slavery, prisoners of war.—Examples in history of whole cities and states being reduced to Slavery: Judea, Miletos, Thebes.—Slaves obtained by kidnapping and piracy.—The traffic supposed to be attended by a curse.—Certain nations sell their own people into Slavery.—Power of masters over their Slaves; the power of Life and Death.—The Chians, the first Greeks who engaged in a regular Slave-trade.—Their fate in being themselves finally reduced to Slavery.—First type of the Maroon wars.—The Chian Slaves revolt.—The hero slave Drimacos.—His history.—Honors paid to his memory.—Servile war among the Samians.—Athenian laws to protect Slaves from cruelty.—Slaves entitled to bring an action for assault.—Death penalty for crimes against Slaves.—Slaves entitled to purchase freedom.—Privileges of Slaves in Athens.—Revolt of Slaves working in Mines.—The temples a privileged sanctuary for Slaves who were cruelly treated. Tyrannical masters compelled to sell their Slaves.—Slave auctions.—Diogenes.—Price of Slaves.—Public Slaves, their employment.—Educated by the State, and intrusted with important duties.—Domestic Slaves; their food and treatment.—The Slaves partake in the general decline of morals.—History and Description of Athens. 23

CHAPTER III.

SLAVES OF SPARTA, CRETE, THESSALY, &c.—THE HELOTS.

The Helots:—leading events of their History summed up.—Their Masters described.—The Spartans, their manners, customs and constitutions.—Distinguishing traits: severity, resolution and perseverance, treachery and craftiness.—Marriage.—Treatment of Infants.—Physical Education of Youth.—Their endurance of hardships.—The Helots: their origin; supposed to belong to the State; power of life and death over them; how subsisted; property acquired by them; their military service.—Plato, Aristotle, Isocrates, Plutarch and other writers convict the Spartans of barbarity towards them; the testimony of Myron on this point; instances of tyranny and cruelty.—Institution of the Crypteia; annual massacre of the Helots.—Terrible instance of treachery.—Bloody servile wars.—Sparta engaged in contests with her own vassals.—Relies upon foreign aid.—Earthquake, and vengeance of the Helots.—Constant source of terror to their masters.—Other classes of Slaves.—Their privileges and advancement.—Slavery in Crete: classes and condition.—Mild treatment.—Strange privileges during certain Festivals.—Slaves of Syracuse rebel and triumph.—The Arcadians........................ 38

CHAPTER IV.

SLAVERY IN ROME.

Slavery under the kings and in the early ages of the Republic.—Its spread, and effect on the poorer class of Freemen.—The Licinian law.—Prevalence of the two extremes, immense wealth and abject poverty.—Immense number of Slaves in Sicily.—They revolt.—Eunus, their leader.—Their arms.—Horrible atrocities committed by them.—The insurrection crushed.—Fate of Eunus.—Increase of Slaves in Rome.—Their employment in the arts.—Numbers trained for the Amphitheatre.—The Gladiators rebel.—Spartacus, his history.—Laws passed to restrain the cruelty of masters.—Effects of Christianity on their condition.—Their numbers increased by the invasion of northern hordes.—Sale of prisoners of war into slavery.—Slave-dealers follow the armies.—Foreign Slave-trade.—Slave auctions.—The Slave markets.—Value of Slaves at different periods.—Slaves owned by the State, and their condition and occupations.—Private Slaves, their grades and occupations.—Treatment of Slaves, public and private.—Punishment of offenses.—Fugitives and Criminals.—Festival of Saturnus, their privileges.—Their dress.—Their sepulchres.—The Gladiators, their combats 46

CHAPTER V.

SLAVERY IN ROME.—CONTINUED.

Abstract of the laws in regard to Slavery.—Power of Life and Death.—Cruelty of Masters.—Laws to protect the Slave.—Constitution of Antoninus: of Claudius.—Husband and Wife could not be separated; nor parents and children.—Slave could not contract marriage, nor own property.—His peculium, or private property, held only by usage.—Regulations in respect to it.—Master liable for damages for wrongful acts of his Slave.—The murderer of a Slave, liable for a capital offense, or for damages.—Fugitive Slaves, not lawfully harbored: to conceal them, theft.—Master entitled to pursue them.—Duties of the authorities.—Slave hunters. —Laws defining the condition of children born of Slaves.—Laws to reduce free persons to Slavery.—How the state of Slavery might be terminated; by manumission; by special enactments; what Slaves entitled to freedom.—Practice of giving liberty to Slaves in times of civil tumult and revolution.—Effects of Slavery under the Republic, and under the Empire................................ 55

CHAPTER VI.

Christian Slavery in Northern Africa.

Barbary—the Carthaginians, the Romans, the Vandals.— Northern Africa annexed to the Greek Empire.— Conquered by the Saracens.— The Spanish Moors pass over to Africa.—Their expeditions to plunder the coasts of Spain, and carry off the Christian Spaniards into Slavery.—Cardinal Ximenes invades Barbary, 1509, to release the captives.—Barbarossa, the sea-rover, becomes king of Algiers.— The Christian Slaves build the mole.— Expeditions of Charles V. against the Moors.—Insurrection of the Slaves.—Charles releases 20,000 Christians from Slavery, and carries off 10,000 Mohammedans to be reduced to Slavery in Spain.— The Moors retaliate by seizing 6000 Minorcans for Slaves. Second expedition of Charles — its disastrous termination — his army destroyed — prisoners sold into Slavery.—The Algerines extend their depredations into the English Channel.— Condition of the Christian slaves in Barbary—treated with more humanity than African slaves among Christians.—Ransom of the Slaves by their countrymen.— British Parliament appropriates money for the purpose.—The French send bomb vessels in 1688.—Lord Exmouth in 1816 releases 3000 captives, and puts an end to Christian Slavery in Barbary... 68

CHAPTER VII.

African Slave Trade from the Fifteenth to the Eighteenth Century.

Negroland, or Nigritia, described.—Slavery among the Natives.—Mungo Park's estimate of the number of Slaves.—The Portuguese navigators explore the African coast.—Natives first carried off in 1434.—Portuguese establish the Slave-Trade on the Western Coast—followed by the Spaniards.—America discovered—colonized by the Spaniards, who reduce the Natives to Slavery—they die by thousands in consequence.—The Dominican priests intercede for them.—Negroes from Africa substituted as Slaves, 1510.—Cardinal Ximenes remonstrates.—Charles V. encourages the trade.—Insurrection of the Slaves at Segovia.—Other nations colonize America.—First recognition of the Slave-Trade by the English government in 1562, reign of Elizabeth.—First Negroes imported into Virginia in a Dutch vessel in 1620.—The French and other commericial notions engage in the traffic.— The great demand for Slaves on the African coast.—Negroes fighting and kidnapping each other.—Slave factories established by the English, French, Dutch, Spanish, and Portuguese.—Slave factory described.—How Slaves were procured in the interior. 93

CHAPTER VIII.

Slave Traffic of the Levant—Nubian Slaves.

The Mohammedan slave-trade.—Nubian slaves captured for the slave market of the Levant.—Mohammed Ali.—Grand expeditions for hunting.—Annual tribute of

slaves.—The encampment.—Attack upon the villages.—Courage of the Natives.
—Their heroic resistance.—Cruelty of the victors.—Destruction of villages.—The
captives sold into slavery.. 102

CHAPTER IX.

AFRICAN SLAVE TRADE IN THE EIGHTEENTH CENTURY.

England first engages in the Slave-Trade in 1562—Sir John Hawkins' voyages.—
British first establish a regular trade in 1618.—Second charter granted in 1631.
—Third charter in 1662.—Capture of the Dutch Forts.—Retaken by De Ruyter.
—Fourth charter in 1672; the King and Duke of York shareholders.—Monopoly
abolished, and free trade in Slaves declared.—Flourishing condition of the Trade.
—Numbers annually exported.—Public sentiment aroused against the Slave-Trade
in England.—Parliament resolve to hear Evidence upon the subject.—Abstract of
the Evidence taken before a Select Committee of the House of Commons in 1790
and 1791.—Revealing the Enormities committed by the Natives on the persons of
one another to procure Slaves for the Europeans.—War and Kidnapping—imputed Crimes.—Villages attacked and burned, and inhabitants seized and sold.—
African chiefs excited by intoxication to sell their subjects................ 106

CHAPTER X.

AFRICAN SLAVE TRADE IN THE EIGHTEENTH CENTURY, CONTINUED.—THE MIDDLE PASSAGE.

Abstract of Evidence before House of Commons, continued.—The enslaved Africans
on board the Ships—their dejection.—Methods of confining, airing, feeding and
exercising them.—Mode of stowing them, and its horrible consequences.—Incidents of the terrible Middle Passage—shackles, chains, whips, filth, foul air, disease, suffocation.—Suicides by drowning, by starvation, by wounds, by strangling.—Insanity and Death.—Manner of selling them when arrived at their destination.—Deplorable situation of the refuse or sickly Slaves.—Mortality among
Seamen engaged in the Slave-Trade.—Their miserable condition and sufferings
from disease, and cruel treatment... 126

CHAPTER XI.

SLAVERY IN THE WEST INDIES, 1750 TO 1790.

Abstract of Evidence continued.—Slavery in the West Indies from 1750 to 1790.—
General estimation and treatment of the Slaves.—Labor of Plantation Slaves—
their days of rest, food, clothing, property.—Ordinary punishment by the whip
and cowskin.—Frequency and severity of these Punishments.—Extraordinary
Punishments of various kinds, for nominal offenses.—Capital offenses and Punishments.—Slaves turned off to steal, beg, or starve, when incapable of labor.—
Slaves had little or no redress against ill usage. 143

CHAPTER XII.

EARLY OPPONENTS OF AFRICAN SLAVERY IN ENGLAND AND AMERICA.

Period from 1660 to 1760; Godwin, Richard Baxter, Atkins, Hughes, Bishop Warburton.—Planters accustomed to take their Slaves to England, and to carry them back into slavery by force.—Important case of James Somerset decided, 1772.— John Wesley.—Motion in House of Commons against Slave-Trade, 1776.—Case of ship Zong.—Bridgwater Petitions.—The Quakers in England oppose Slavery.— Resolutions of the Quakers, from 1727 to 1760.—They Petition House of Commons.—First Society formed, 1783.—The Quakers and others in America.—Action of the Quakers of Pennsylvania from 1688 to 1788.—Benezet writes tracts against Slavery.—His letter to the Queen.—Sentiment in America favorable to Africans, 1772.—House of Burgesses of Virginia addresses the King.—Original draft of Declaration of Independence.—First Society formed in America " for Promoting Abolition of Slavery," 1774.—Opposition to the Slave-Trade in America.. 158

CHAPTER XIII.

Movements in England to Abolish the Slave Trade.

Thomas Clarkson, the historian of the Abolition of the Slave-Trade.—Devotes his life to the cause, 1785.—Publishes his Essay on Slavery.—His coadjutors.—William Wilberforce, parliamentary leader in the cause.—Middleton, Dr. Porteus, Lord Scarsdale, Granville Sharp.—Clarkson's first visit to a slave-ship.—Association formed——Correspondence opened in Europe and America.—Petitions sent to Parliament.—Committee of Privy Council ordered by the King, 1788.—Great exertions of the friends of the cause.—Clarkson's interview with Pitt............ 179

CHAPTER XIV.

Parliamentary History.—The Twenty Years' Struggle.

Mr. Pitt introduces the subject of the Abolition of the Slave-Trade into the House of Commons, May 9, 1788.—Speech of Mr. Pitt on the occasion.—Parliamentary action in 1789.—Debate of 12th of May.—Speech of William Wilberforce.—Travels and exertions of Clarkson.—Sessions of 1791 and 1792.—Debates in the Commons.—Speeches of Wilberforce, Pitt, Fox, Bailie, Thornton, Whitbread, Dundas, and Jenkinson.—Gradual abolition agreed upon by House of Commons........ 188

CHAPTER XV.

Parliamentary History.—Slave Trade Rendered Illegal.

Action of the House of Lords in 1792.—Clarkson retires from the field from ill health, in 1794.—Mr. Wilberforce's annual motion.—Session of 1799.—Speech of Canning.—Sessions of 1804 and 1805.—Clarkson resumes his labors.—Death of Mr. Pitt, January, 1806.—Administration of Granville and Fox.—Session of 1806. —Debate in the House of Lords.—Speeches of Lord Granville, Erskine, Dr. Porteus, Earls Stanhope and Spencer, Lords Holland and Ellenborough.—Death of Fox, October, 1806.—Contest and triumph in 1807.—Final passage of the Bill for the Abolition of the African Slave-Trade.—Slave-trade declared felony in 1811, and declared piracy in 1824, by England.—England abolishes slavery in her colonies, 1833.—Prohibition of Slave-Trade by European governments.—Slavery abolished in Mexico, 1829—In Guatemala and Colombia.............................. ... 237

CHAPTER XVI.

INDIAN AND AFRICAN SLAVERY IN ST. DOMINGO.—THE INSURRECTIONS.

Discovery and settlement of the island by the Spaniards.—The natives reduced to slavery.—Cruelty of the Spaniards towards them.—Great mortality in consequence.—Their numbers replenished from the Bahamas.—The Dominicans become interested for them.—Las Casas appeals to Cardinal Ximenes, who sends commissioners.—They set the natives at liberty.—The colonists remonstrate against the measure, and the Indians again reduced to slavery.—Las Casas seeks a remedy.—The Emperor allows the introduction of Africans.—Guinea slave-trade established.—The buccaneers.—The French Colony.—Its condition in 1789.—Enormous slave-population.—The Mulattoes.—The French Revolution—its effect on the Colonists.—First Insurrection.—Terrible execution of the leaders.—Second Insurrection—massacre and conflagration—unparalleled horrors.—Burning of Port-au-Prince.—L'Ouverture appears, the spirit and ruler of the storm.—French expedition of 25,000 men sent to suppress the Insurrection.—Toussaint sent prisoner to France—dies in prison.—The slaves establish their freedom.—Independence of Hayti acknowledged by France.................................. 252

CHAPTER XVII.

AFRICAN SLAVE TRADE AFTER ITS NOMINAL ABOLITION.

State of the slave-trade since its nominal abolition.—Numbers imported and losses on the passage.— Increased horrors of the trade.—Scenes on board a captured slaver in Sierra Leone.—The Progresso.—Walsh's description of a slaver in 1829.—The trade in 1820.—The slave-trade in Cuba—officers of government interested in it.—Efforts of Spain insincere.—Slave barracoons near Governor's palace—conduct of the inmates.—The Bozals.—Bryan Edwards' description of natives of Gold Coast—their courage and endurance.—Number of slaves landed at Rio in 1838—barracoons at Rio—government tax.—Slave-trade Insurance—Courts of Mixed Commission—their proceedings at Sierra Leone in 1838.—Joint stock slave-trade companies at Rio.—The Cruisers—intercepted letters.—Mortality of the trade.—Abuses of the American flag.—Consul Trist and British commissioners.—Correspondence of American Ministers to Brazil, Mr. Todd, Mr. Proffit, Mr. Wise.—Extracts from Parliamentary papers.—Full list of Conventions and Treaties made by England for suppression of Slave-trade....................................... 280

CHAPTER XVIII.

EFFORTS TO SUPPRESS THE SLAVE-TRADE.—OPERATIONS OF THE CRUISERS.

Treaty between England and the United States, signed at Washington in 1842.—U. S. African Squadron under the treaty.—The Truxton captures an American slaver, the Spitfire, of New Orleans.—The Yorktown captures the Am. bark Pons, with 896 slaves on board.—Commander Bell's description of the sufferings of the slaves—they are landed at Monrovia and taken care of.—Squadron of 1846.—Capture of the Chancellor.—Slave establishment destroyed by the English and natives.—A slaver's history—embarkation and treatment of slaves.— How disposed of in Cuba.—Natural scenery of Africa.—Excursion to procure slaves—their horror at the prospect of slavery.—Passage from Mozambique—the small-pox on board.—More horrors of the Middle Passage.—The Estrella—revolt of negroes on board.. 303

CHAPTER XIX.

OPERATIONS OF THE CRUISERS UNDER THE ASHBURTON TREATY.

The American Squadrons from 1847 to 1851.—More captures.—U. S. brig Perry cruises off the southern coast.—Capture of a slaver with 800 slaves, by an English cruiser.—Abuses of the American flag.—The Lucy Ann captured.—Case of the Navarre.—Capture by the Perry of the Martha of New York—her condemnation.—Case of the Chatsworth—of the Louisa Beaton.—The Chatsworth seized and sent to Baltimore—is condemned as a slaver. State of the slave-trade on the southern coast.—Importance of the squadron.—The Brazilian slave-trade diminishes 344

CHAPTER XX.

HISTORICAL SKETCH OF SIERRA LEONE AND LIBERIA.

Colony of Sierra Leone founded by the English, 1787.—Free negroes colonized.— Present extent and condition of the colony.—Establishment of English factories on the slave coast.—Treaties with the African chiefs.—Scheme of African Colonization agitated in 1783—by Jefferson and others.—Movements in Va., in 1800 and 1805.—Formation of the American Colonization Society in 1816.—Its object "to colonize the free people of color."—Cape Mesurado purchased and colonized in 1821.—Defense of the infant settlement from an attack by the natives.—Mortality among the early settlers.—Increase of the colony in 1835.—State colonization societies establish settlements.—Consolidation of the state colonies, and establishment of the Commonwealth.—Governor Buchanan's efforts to suppress the slave-trade.—His death, 1841.—Republic of Liberia established in 1847.—Joseph J. Roberts (colored) first President.—Its independence acknowledged by European powers.—The Republic attacks the slave establishments.—Natural resources of Liberia—its climate, soil, productions, exports, schools, churches, &c.—Settlements and population.—The Maryland settlement at Cape Palmas 358

CHAPTER XXI.

HISTORY OF SLAVERY IN THE NORTH AMERICAN COLONIES.

Early existence of Slavery in England.—Its forms.—The Feudal System.—Serfdom.—Its extinction.—African Slavery introduced into the North American Colonies, 1620.—Slavery in Virginia.—Massachusetts sanctions Negro and Indian slavery, 1641 : Kidnapping declared unlawful, 1645.—Negro and Indian slavery authorized in Connecticut, 1650.—Decree against perpetual slavery in Rhode Island, 1652.—Slavery in New Netherland among the Dutch, 1650—Its mild form.— First slavery statute of Virginia, 1662.—In Maryland, 1663, against amalgamation.—Statute of Virginia, conversion and baptism not to confer freedom; other provisions, 1667.—Maryland encourages slave-trade.—Slave code of Virginia, 1682, fugitives may be killed.—New anti-amalgamation act of Maryland, 1681.—Settlement of South Carolina, 1660.—Absolute power conferred on masters.—Law of Slavery in New York, 1665.—Slave code of Virginia, 1692: offenses of slaves, how punishable.—Revision of Virginia code, 1705: slaves made real estate.— Pennsylvania protests against importation of Indian slaves from Carolina, 1705.— New act of 1712 to stop importation of negroes and slaves, prohibition duty of £20.—Act repealed by Queen.—First slave law of Carolina, 1712.—Its remarkable provisions.—Census of 1715.—Maryland code of 1715—baptism not to confer freedom.—Georgia colonized, 1732: rum and slavery prohibited.—Cruel delusion in New York: plot falsely imputed to negroes to burn the city, 1741.—Slavery legalized in Georgia, 1750.—Review of the state of Slavery in all the colonies in 1750.—Period of the Revolution.—Controversy in Massachusetts on the subject of slavery, 1766 to 1773.—Slaves gain their freedom in the courts of Massachusetts.—Court of King's Bench decision.—Mansfield declares the law of England, 1772.—Continental Congress declares against African slave-trade, 1784 369

CHAPTER XXII.

SLAVERY UNDER THE CONFEDERATION.—EMANCIPATION BY THE STATES.

Number of Slaves in the United States at the period of the declaration of Independence.—Proportion in each of the thirteen States.—Declaration against slavery in the State Constitution of Delaware.—Constitutions of Massachusetts and New Hampshire held to prohibit slavery, by Supreme Courts, 1783.—Act of Pennsylvania Assembly, 1780, forbids introduction of slaves, and gives freedom to all persons thereafter born in that State.—A similar law enacted in Connecticut and Rhode Island, 1784.—Virginia Assembly prohibits further introduction of slaves, 1778, and emancipation encouraged, 1782.—Maryland enacts similar laws, 1783.—Opinions of Washington, Jefferson, and Patrick Henry.—New York and New Jersey prohibit further introduction of slaves.—North Carolina declares further introduction of slaves highly impolitic, 1786.—Example of other States not followed by Georgia and South Carolina.—Action of Congress on the subject of the Territories, 1784.—Jefferson's provision excluding slavery, struck out of ordinance.—Proceedings of 1787.—Ordinance for the government of the territory north-west of the Ohio, including Jefferson's provision prohibiting slavery, passed by unanimous vote 388

CHAPTER XXIII.

FORMATION OF THE CONSTITUTION—SLAVERY COMPROMISES.

Convention assembles at Philadelphia, 1787.—Proceedings in reference to the slave basis of representation, the second compromise of the Constitution.—Debate.—Remarks of Patterson, Wilson, King, Gouverneur Morris, and Sherman.—Debate on the Importation of slaves, by Rutledge, Ellsworth, Sherman, C. Pinckney.—Denunciation of slavery by Mason of Virginia.—The third Compromise, the continuance of the African slave-trade for twenty years, and the unrestricted power of Congress to enact Navigation laws 392

CHAPTER XXIV.

POLITICAL HISTORY OF SLAVERY IN THE UNITED STATES FROM 1789 TO 1800.

First session of First Congress, 1789.—Tariff bill—duty imposed on imported slaves.—The Debate—views of Roger Sherman, Fisher Ames, Madison, &c.—Review of the state of slavery in the States in 1790.—Second session.—Petitions from the Quakers of Pennsylvania, Deleware, and New York.—Petition of Pennsylvania Society, signed by Franklin.—Exciting debate—power of Congress over slavery.—Census of 1790.—Slave population.—Vermont the first State to abolish and prohibit slavery.—Constitution of Kentucky—provisions in respect to slavery.—Session of 1791.—Memorials for suppression of slave-trade, from Virginia, Maryland, New York, &c.—The Right of Petition discussed.—First fugitive slave law, 1793.—First law to suppress African Slave Trade, 1794.—The Quakers again, 1797—their emancipated slaves reduced again to slavery, under expost facto law of North Carolina.—Mississippi territory—slavery clause debated.— Foreign slaves prohibited.—Constitution of Georgia—importation of slaves prohibited, 1798—provisions against cruelty to slaves.— New York provides for gradual extinguishment of slavery, 1799.—Failure of similar attempt in Kentucky.— Colored citizens of Pennsylvania petition Congress against Fugitive Slave law and slave-trade—their petition referred to a committee; bill reported and passed, 1800................ 403

CHAPTER XXV.

Political History of Slavery in the United States, from 1800 to 1807.

Slave population in 1800.— Georgia cedes territory—slavery clause.— Territory of Indiana—attempt to introduce Slavery in 1803—Petition Congress—Com. of H. R. report against it.—Session of 1804, committee report in favor of it, limited to ten years.—No action on report.—Foreign slave-trade prohibited with Orleans Territory, 1804.—South Carolina revives slave-trade; the subject before Congress.— New Jersey provides for gradual extinction of slavery, 1804.—Attempt to gradually abolish slavery in District of Columbia, unsuccessful in Congress.—Renewed attempt to introduce slavery into Territory of Indiana, 1806, unsuccessful.—Legislature of Territory in favor of it, 1807—Congressional committee report against it.— Jefferson's Message—recommendation to abolish African slave-trade — the subject before Congress—bill reported—the debate—Speeches of members—Act passed 1807, its provisions 430

CHAPTER XXVI.

Political History of Slavery in the United States from 1807 to 1820.

Slave population in 1810.—Period of the war.—John Randolph's denunciations.— Proclamation of Admiral Cochrane to the slaves.—Treaty of Peace—arbitration on slave property.—Opinions of the domestic slave-trade by southern statesmen. —Constitution of Mississippi—slave· provisions.—The African slave-trade and fugitive law.—Missouri applies for admission—proviso to prohibit slavery.—Debate—speeches of Fuller, Tallmadge, Scott, Cobb, and Livermore.—Proceedings, 1820.—Bill for organizing Arkansas Territory—proviso to prohibit slavery lost.— Excitement in the North.—Public meetings.—Massachusetts memorial.—Resolutions of state legislatures of New York, New Jersey, Pennsylvania, Delaware, and Kentucky.—Congress—the Missouri struggle renewed.—The compromise.— Proviso to exclude slavery in territory north of 36° 30′ carried.—Proviso to prohibit slavery in Missouri lost.—Opinions of Monroe's cabinet.—Reflections of J. Q. Adams.—State Constitution of Missouri—final struggle.—Missouri admitted as a slave state. 447

CHAPTER XXVII.

Period from 1820 to 1825.—Political History of Slavery.

Census of 1820.—Session of 1824-5.—Gov. Troup's demonstrations.—Georgia legislature—Secession threatened.—Slaves in Canada—their surrender refused by England.—Citizens of District of Columbia petition for gradual abolition.—Census of 1830—Anti-slavery societies formed in the north—counter movements north and south.—The mail troubles.—Manifesto of American Anti-slavery Society.—Petitions to congress—Discussion on the disposal of them.—Bill to prohibit the circulation of Anti-slavery publications through the mails.—Calhoun's report—Measure opposed by Webster, Clay, Benton, and others.—Buchanan, Tallmadge, &c., favor it—Bill lost.—Atherton's gag resolutions passed........................ 498

CHAPTER XXVIII.

PERIOD FROM 1835 TO 1842.—POLITICAL HISTORY.

Free territory annexed to Missouri, 1836.—Texas applies for annexation.—Remonstrances.—Preston's resolution in 1838, in favor of it, debated by Preston, John Quincy Adams and Henry A. Wise.—The Amistad—Captives liberated.—Census of 1840.—Session of 1841-2.—Mr. Adams presents petition for dissolution of the Union.—Excitement in the house.—Resolutions of censure, advocated by Marshall.—Remarks of Mr. Wise and Mr. Adams.—Resolutions opposed by Underwood, of Kentucky, Botts, of Virginia, Arnold, of Tennessee, and others.—Mr. Giddings, of Ohio, presents a petition for amicable division of the Union—resolution of censure not received.—Case of the Creole.—Censure of Mr. Giddings ; he resigns, is re-elected.. 511

CHAPTER XXIX.

PERIOD FROM 1842 TO 1849.—ANNEXATION OF TEXAS.

Object of the acquisition set forth by Mississippi, Alabama and Tennessee legislatures, and by Mr. Wise and Mr. Gilmer, 1842.—Tyler's treaty of annexation—rejected by the senate.—Presidential campaign of 1844.—Clay and Van Buren on annexation.—Calhoun's Letter.—Session of 1844-5 ; joint resolution passed, and approved March 1, 1845.—Mexican minister protests.—War with Mexico.—The $2,000,000 bill.—Wilmot Proviso.—Session of 1847-8.—Bill to organize Oregon territory.—Power of Congress over slavery in the territories discussed,—Dix and Calhoun.—Mr. Calhoun controverts the doctrines of the Declaration of Independence.—Cass' Nicholson letter... 531

CHAPTER XXX.

POLITICAL HISTORY OF SLAVERY.—COMPROMISES OF 1850.

Message of President Taylor—Sam. Houston's propositions—Taylor's Special Message. —Mr. Clay's propositions for arrangement of slavery controversy.—His resolutions. Resolutions of Mr. Bell.—The debate on Clay's resolutions, by Rusk, Foote, of Mississippi, Mason, Jefferson Davis, King, Clay, and Butler.—Remarks of Benton, Calhoun, Webster, Seward, and Cass.—Resolutions referred.—Report of Committee.—The omnibus bill.—California admitted.—New Mexico organized.—Texas boundary established.—Utah organized.—Slave-trade in the District of Columbia abolished.—Fugitive Slave law passed................................. 563

CHAPTER XXXI.

REPEAL OF MISSOURI COMPROMISE.—KANSAS AND NEBRASKA ORGANIZED.

The platforms, slavery agitation repudiated by both parties.—Mr. Pierce's Inaugural and Message denounce agitation.—Session of 1853–4 :—the storm bursts forth.—Proposition to repeal the Missouri Compromise.—Kansas-Nebraska bill.—Mr. Douglas' defense of the bill—Mr. Chase's reply—Remarks of Houston, Cass, Seward, and others.—Passage of the bill in the house.—Passed by senate, and approved.—The territories organized... 608

CHAPTER XXXII.

AFFAIRS OF KANSAS.—CONGRESSIONAL PROCEEDINGS.

Session of 1855–6.—The President's special message referred.—Report of committee by Mr. Douglas.—Emigrant Aid Societies.—Minority report by Mr. Collamer.—Special Committee of the House sent to Kansas to investigate affairs.—Report of the Committee.—Armed Missourians enter the territory and control the elections.—Second foray of armed Missourians.—Purposes of Aid Societies defended.—Mob violence.—Legislature assembles at Pawnee.—Its acts.—Topeka Constitutional Convention.—Free State Constitution framed.—Adopted by the people.—Election for State officers.—Topeka legislature.—The Wakarusa war.—Outrages upon the citizens.—Robberies and murders.—Lawrence attacked.—Free state constitution submitted to Congress.—Bill to admit Kansas under free state constitution passes the house.—Douglas' bill before the senate.—Trumbull's propositions rejected.—Amendments proposed by Foster, Collamer, Wilson and Seward, rejected.—Bill passed by senate.—Dunn's bill passed by house.—Appropriation bills.—Proviso to army bill.—Session terminates.—Extra session.—President stands firm, house firmer, senate firmest.—The army bill passed without the proviso.............. 643

CHAPTER XXXIII.

HISTORY OF THE TROUBLES IN KANSAS, CONTINUED.

Judge Lecompte's charge to Grand Jury—Presentments.—Official correspondence.—Attack on Lawrence.—Free State bands organized—attack pro-slavery settlements.—Fights at Palmyra, Franklin, and Ossawattamie.—Murders.—Shannon removed.—Atchison's army retreat.—Geary appointed governor.—Deplorable condition of the territory.—Letter to Secretary Marcy.—Inaugural address and proclamations.—Atchison's call upon the South.—Woodson's proclamation.—Armed bands enter the territory.—Lawrence doomed to destruction.—Gov. Geary's decisive measures.—Army dispersed and Lawrence saved.—Hickory Point—capture of Free State company.—Dispatch to Secretary Marcy.—Murder of Buffum.—Geary and Lecompte in collision.—Official documents.—The Judiciary.—Rumors of Lane's army.—Redpath's company captured—released by governor.—Capture of Eldridge's company.—Official correspondence.—Assembling of Topeka legislature—Members arrested.—Territorial Legislative Assembly convened.—Inaugural—Vetoes of the governor.—The "Census Bill"—its provisions for forming State Constitution.—Constitution not to be submitted to the people.—Gov. Geary's proposition rejected.—He vetoes the bill—Bill passed.—Disturbances in the capital.—Geary's requisition for U. S. troops refused.—His application for money refused.—Difficulties of his situation—he resigns—his farewell address.—Robert J.

Walker appointed his successor. — Secretary Stanton. — Fraudulent apportionment. — Walker's Inaugural — his recommendation to have Constitution submitted
to the people. — This measure denounced at the South. — Convention assembles
September, 1857. — Adjourns to October 26th, 1857 719

CHAPTER XXXIV.

STATISTICAL TABLES CONSTRUCTED FROM THE CENSUS OF 1850.

TERRITORY — Area of Free States ; area of Slave States. — POPULATION — Free colored in
Free States ; Free colored in Slave States ; Slaves. — Amalgamation ; Mulattoes of
Free States ; Mulattoes of Slave States ; Proportion to Whites. — Manumitted Slaves ;
Fugitive Slaves ; Occupation of Slaves ; Number of Slave Holders ; Proportion to
Non-Slave Holders. — REPRESENTATION — Number of Representatives from Slave
States. — Number of Representatives from Free States ; Basis in numbers and
classes. — MORAL AND SOCIAL — Churches, Church Property, Colleges, Public Schools,
Private Schools ; Number of Pupils ; Annual Expenditure ; Persons who cannot
read and write ; Lands appropriated by General Government for Education ; Periodical Press ; Libraries. — CHARITIES — Pauperism in Free States ; in Slave States.
— CRIMINALS — Number of Prisoners. — AGRICULTURE — Value of Farms and Implements in Free and Slave States. — MANUFACTURES, MINING, MECHANIC ARTS — Capital invested ; Annual Product. — RAIL ROADS AND CANALS — Number of Miles ;
Cost. — TOTAL REAL AND PERSONAL ESTATE. — Value of Real Estate in Free States ;
in Slave States ; value of Personal in Free States ; in Slave States, including
and excluding Slaves. — Miscellaneous. 809

APPENDIX — Dred Scott decision 807

PREFACE.

THIS book is intended for general reading, and may also serve as a book of reference. It is an attempt to compile and present in one volume the historical records of slavery in ancient and modern times—the laws of Greece and Rome and the legislation of England and America upon the subject—and to exhibit some of its effects upon the destinies of nations. It is compiled from what are conceded to be authentic and reliable books, documents, and records. In looking up material for that portion of the book which treats of slavery in the nations of antiquity, the compiler found small encouragement among the historians. "There is no class so abject and despised upon which the fate of nations may not sometimes turn;" and it is strange that a system which pervaded and weakened, if it did not ruin, the republics of Greece and the empire of the Cæsars, should not be more frequently noticed by historical writers. They refer, only incidentally, to the existence of slavery. An insurrection or other remarkable event with which the slaves are connected, occasionally reminds the reader of history of the existence of a servile class. The historian of the Decline and Fall of the Roman Empire devotes but two pages to what he describes as "that unhappy condition of men who existed in every province and every family, exposed to the wanton rigor of despotism," and who, according to his own account, numbered, in the age of the Antonines, sixty millions! Yet "slavery was the chief and most direct cause of the ruin of the Roman Empire," if we may credit the assertions made in the legislature of Virginia shortly after an insurrection in that state. How few of the historians of England refer to the existence in that country of a system of unmitigated, hopeless, hereditary slavery. Yet it prevailed throughout England in Saxon and Norman times. In the time of the Heptarchy, slaves were an article of export. "Great numbers were exported, like cattle, from the British coasts." The Roman market was partially supplied with slaves from the shores of Britain. Pope Gregory the Great, struck with the blooming complexions and fair hair of some Saxon children in the slave market, sent over St. Augustine from Rome to convert the islanders to Christianity. In the time of Alfred, slaves were so numerous that their sale was regulated by law. As a general thing, however, feudalism strangled the old forms of slavery, and both disappeared in England in the advancing light of Christianity. The historians of the United States, also, with the exception of Hildreth, seldom refer to the subject of slavery. They perhaps imagine that they descend below the dignity of history if they treat of any thing but "battles and seiges, and the rise and fall of administrations." Yet the printed annals of congress, from the foundation of the government to the present time, are filled with controversies upon the ever prominent "slavery question"; and every important measure seems to have had a "slavery issue" involved in it.

Meantime, and while awaiting the advent of a regular "philosophical" historian of slavery, we present an imperfect, but, we trust, useful compilation. The greater part of the volume is devoted to the Political History of Slavery in the United States. The legislation of congress upon subjects embracing questions of slavery extension or prohibition, has been faithfully rendered from the record; and the arguments used on both sides of controverted questions have been impartially presented. The parliamentary history of the abolition of the African slave-trade has been made to occupy considerable space, chiefly in order to lay before the reader the views upon the subject of slavery entertained by that class of unrivaled statesmen which embraced the names of Pitt, Fox, Burke, and others not unknown to fame. The history of the legislation of our own country upon subjects in which slavery issues were involved, will also bring before the reader another array of eminent statesmen, with whose familiar names he is accustomed to associate the idea of intellectual power. Chapters upon slavery in Greece and Rome have been introduced into the book, as various opinions seem to prevail in regard to the forms, features, laws, extent and effects of ancient slavery. Some point with exultation to the prosperity of imperial Rome with her millions of slaves; others with equal exultation point to her decay as the work of the avenging spirit of slavery. Others, again, contend that slavery was confined to but a small portion of the empire, and had small effect upon its prosperity or adversity.

To gratify a class of readers to whom the relation of exciting incidents is of more interest than the details of legislative action, we have devoted a space to the abominations of the old legalized slave traffic, and to the increased horrors of the trade after it had been declared piracy by Christian nations. It is a fearful chapter of wrong, violence and crime.

"According to an enlightened philosophy," we quote from the Conversations Lexicon, "each human being retains inherently the right to his own person, and can neither sell himself, nor be legally bound by any act of aggression on his natural liberty. Slavery, therefore, can never be a legal relation. It rests entirely on force. The slave being treated as property, and not allowed legal rights, cannot be under legal obligations. Slavery is also inconsistent with the moral nature of man. Each man has an individual worth, significance, and responsibility; is bound to the work of self-improvement, and to labor in a sphere for which his capacity is adapted. To give up this individual liberty is to disqualify himself for fulfilling the great objects of his being. Hence, political societies which have made a considerable degree of advancement do not allow any one to resign his liberty any more than his life, to the pleasure of another. In fact, the great object of political institutions in civilized nations is to enable man to fulfill most perfectly the ends of his *individual* being. Christianity, moreover, lays down the doctrine of doing as we would be done by, as one of its fundamental maxims, which is wholly opposed to the idea of one man becoming the property of another. These two principles of mutual obligation, and the worth of the individual, were beyond the comprehension of the states of antiquity, but are now at the basis of morals, politics, and religion."

HISTORY OF SLAVERY.

CHAPTER I.

Preliminary Sketch.—Ancient Slavery.

Early existence of Slavery in the world.—The Mosaic institutions in regard to Slavery.—Hebrews, how reduced to servitude.—The Jubilee.—Distinction between native and foreign Slaves.—Voluntary Slaves: the Mercenarii of the Romans; the Prodigals or debtor Slaves; the Delinquents; the Enthusiasts.—Involuntary Slaves: prisoners of war, and captives stolen in peace, with the children and descendants of both.—Voluntary Slavery introduced by decree of the Roman Senate.—Slavery in Rome: condition of the Slaves; cruelty to the old and sick; prisons for Slaves; Sicily: servile war and breaking up of the prisons.—Piracy esteemed honorable by the early Greeks.—Piratical expeditions to procure Slaves.—Causes of the gradual extinction of Slavery in Europe.—Origin of the African Slave Trade by the Portuguese.—Followed by most of the maritime nations of Europe.

It is certainly a curious fact, that so far as we can trace back the history of the human race, we discover the existence of Slavery. One of the most obvious causes of this, is to be found in the almost incessant wars which were carried on in the early periods of the world, between tribes and nations, in which the prisoners taken were either slain or reduced to slavery.

The Mosaic institutions were rather predicated upon the previous existence of slavery in the surrounding nations, than designed to establish it for the first time; and the provisions of the Jewish law upon this subject, effected changes and modifications which must have improved the condition of slaves among that peculiar people. There were various modes by which the Hebrews might be reduced to servitude. A poor man might sell himself; a father might sell his children; debtors might be delivered as slaves to their creditors; thieves, who were unable to make restitution for the property stolen, were sold for the benefit of the sufferers. Prisoners of war were subjected to servitude; and if a Hebrew captive was redeemed by another Hebrew from a Gentile, he might be sold by his deliverer to another Israelite. At the return of the year of jubilee all Jewish captives were set free. However, by some writers it is stated that this did not apply to foreign slaves held in bondage; as over these the master had entire control. He might sell them, judge them, and even punish them capitally without any form of legal process. The law of Moses provides that "if a man smite his servant or his maid with a rod, and he die under

2

his hand, he shall be surely punished; notwithstanding if he continue a day or two he shall not be punished, for he is his money." This restriction is said, by some, to have applied only to Hebrew slaves, and not to foreign captives who were owned by Jews. In general, if any one purchased a Hebrew slave, he could hold him only six years. Among other provisions, the Mosaic laws declared the terms upon which a Hebrew, who had been sold, could redeem himself, or be redeemed by his friends, and his right to take with him his wife and children, when discharged from bondage.

Among those who were denominated slaves in the more lax or general use of the term, we may reckon those who were distinguished among the Romans by the appellation of "mercenarii," so called from the circumstances of their hire. These were free-born citizens, who, from the various contingencies of fortune, were under the necessity of recurring for support to the service of the rich. A contract subsisted between the parties, and most of the dependents had the right to demand and obtain their discharge, if they were ill-used by their masters. Among the ancients there was another class of servants, which consisted wholly of those who had suffered the loss of liberty from their own imprudence. Such were the Grecian *prodigals*, who were detained in the service of their creditors, until the fruits of their labor were equivalent to their debts; the *delinquents*, who were sentenced to the oar; and the German *enthusiasts*, mentioned by Tacitus, who were so addicted to gaming, that when they had parted with every thing else, they staked their liberty and their persons. "The loser," says the historian, "goes into a voluntary servitude; and though younger and stronger than the person with whom he played, patiently suffers himself to be bound and sold. Their perseverance in so bad a custom is styled *honor*. The slaves thus obtained are immediately exchanged away in commerce, that the winner may get rid of the scandal of his victory." The two classes now enumerated comprehend those that may be called the Voluntary Slaves, and they are distinguished from those denominated Involuntary Slaves, who were forced, without any previous condition or choice, into a situation, which, as it tended to degrade a part of the human species, and to class it with the brutal, must have been, of all situations, the most wretched and insupportable. The class of involuntary slaves included those who were "prisoners of war," and these were more ancient than the voluntary slaves, who are first mentioned in the time of Pharaoh. The practice of reducing prisoners of war to the condition of slaves existed both among the eastern nations and the people of the west; for as the Helots became the slaves of the Spartans merely from the right of conquest, so prisoners of war were reduced to the same situation by the other inhabitants of Greece. The Romans, also, were actuated by the same principle; and all those nations which contributed to overturn the empire, adopted a similar custom; so that it was a general maxim in their polity, that those who fell under their power as prisoners of war, should immediately be reduced to the condition of slaves. The slaves of the Greeks were generally barbarians, and imported from foreign countries.

"By the civil law the power of making slaves is esteemed a right of nations, and follows, as a natural consequence of captivity in war." This is the first origin of the right of slavery assigned by Justinian. The conqueror, say the civilians, had the right to the life of his captive; and having spared that, has the right to deal with him as he pleases. This position, taken generally, is denied by Blackstone, who observes that a man has a right to kill his enemy, only in cases of absolute necessity for self-defense; and it is plain this absolute necessity did not exist, since the victior did not kill him, but made him prisoner. Since, therefore, the right of making slaves by captivity depends on a supposed right of slaughter, that foundation failing, the consequence drawn from it must fail likewise. Farther, it is said, slavery may begin "jure civili," when one man sells himself to another; but this, when applied to strict slavery, in the sense of the laws of old Rome or modern Barbary, is also impossible. Every sale implies a price, an equivalent given to the seller in lieu of what he transfers to the buyer; but what equivalent can be given for life and liberty, both of which, in absolute slavery, are held to be at the master's disposal? His property, also, the very price he seems to receive, devolves to his master the instant he becomes his slave: and besides, if it be not lawful for a man to kill himself, because he robs his country of his person, for the same reason he is not allowed to barter his freedom;—the freedom of every citizen constitutes a part of the public liberty. In this case, therefore, the buyer gives nothing, and the seller receives nothing; of what validity, then, can a sale be, which destroys the very principle upon which all sales are founded? Lastly, we are told, that besides these two ways, by which slaves may be acquired, they may also be hereditary; the children of acquired slaves being, by a negative kind of birthright, slaves also; but this being founded on the two former rights, must fall together with them. If neither captivity, nor the sale of one's self, can, by the law of nature and reason, reduce the parent to slavery, much less can they reduce the offspring.*

Voluntary slavery was first introduced in Rome by a decree of the senate in the time of the emperor Claudius, and at length was abrogated by Leo. The Romans had the power of life and death over their slaves; which no other nations had. This severity was afterwards modified by the laws of the emperors; and by one of Adrian it was made capital to kill a slave without a cause. The slaves were esteemed the proper goods of their masters, and all they got belonged to them; but if the master was too cruel in his domestic corrections, he was obliged to sell his slave at a moderate price. The custom of exposing old, useless or sick slaves, in an island of the Tiber, there to starve, seems to have been very common in Rome; and whoever recovered, after having been so exposed, had his liberty given him, by an edict of the emperor Claudius, in which it was likewise forbidden to kill any slave merely for old age or sickness. Nevertheless, it was a professed maxim of the elder Cato, to sell his superannu-

---

* Blackstone's Com.: Montesquieu's Spirit of Laws.

ated slaves at any price, rather than maintain what he deemed a useless burden. The dungeons, where slaves in chains were forced to work, were common all over Italy. Columella advises that they be built under ground; and recommends the duty of having a careful overseer to call over the names of the slaves, in order to know when any of them had deserted. Sicily was full of these dungeons, and the soil was cultivated by laborers in chains. Eunus and Athenio excited the servile war, by breaking up these monstrous prisons, and giving liberty to 60,000 slaves.

In the ancient and uncivilized ages of the world, "Piracy" was regarded as an honorable profession; and this was supposed to give a right of making slaves. "The Grecians," says Thucydides, "in their primitive state, as well as the cotemporary barbarians who inhabited the sea coast and islands, addicted themselves wholly to it; it was, in short, their only profession and support." The writings of Homer establish this account, as they show that this was a common practice at so early a period as that of the Trojan war. The reputation which piracy seems to have acquired among the ancients, was owing to the skill, strength, agility and valor which were necessary for conducting it with success; and these erroneous notions led to other consequences immediately connected with the slavery of the human species. Avarice and ambition availed themselves of these mistaken notions; and people were robbed, stolen, and even murdered, under the pretended idea that these were reputable adventures. But in proportion as men's sentiments and manners became more refined, the practice of piracy lost its reputation, and began gradually to disappear. The practice, however, was found to be lucrative; and it was continued with a view to the emolument attending it, long after it ceased to be thought honorable, and when it was sinking into disgrace. The profits arising from the sale of slaves presented a temptation which avarice could not resist; many were stolen by their own countrymen and sold for slaves; and merchants traded on the different coasts in order to facilitate the disposal of this article of commerce. The merchants of Thessaly,—according to Aristophanes, who never spared the vices of the times,—were particularly infamous for this latter kind of depredation; the Athenians were notorious for the former; for they had practiced these robberies to such an extent, that it was found necessary to enact a law to punish kidnappers with death.

From the above statement it appears that there were among the ancients two classes of involuntary slaves: captives taken in war, and those who were privately stolen in peace; to which might be added, a third class, comprehending the children and descendants of the two former.

The condition of slaves and their personal treatment were sufficiently humiliating and grievous, and may well excite our pity and abhorrence. They were beaten, starved, tortured, and murdered at discretion; they were dead in a civil sense; they had neither name nor tribe; they were incapable of judicial process; and they were, in short, without appeal. To this cruel treatment, however, there were some exceptions. The Egyptian slave, though perhaps a greater drudge than any other, yet if he had time to reach the temple of Hercules found a certain retreat from the persecution of his master; and he derived additional comfort from the reflection that his life could not be taken with impunity.* But no place seems to have been so favorable to slaves as Athens. Here they were allowed a greater liberty of speech; they had their convivial meetings, their amours, their hours of relaxation, pleasantry and mirth; and here, if persecution exceeded the bounds of lenity, they had their temple, like the Egyptians, for refuge. The legislature were so attentive as to examine into their complaints, and if founded in justice, they were ordered to be sold to another master. They were allowed an opportunity of working for themselves; and if they earned the price of their ransom, they could demand their freedom forever.

To the honor of Athens and Egypt, and the cities of the Jews, their slaves were considered with some humanity. The inhabitants of other parts of the world seemed to vie with each other in the oppression and debasement of this unfortunate class.

A modern writer, to whom the cause of humanity is under inexpressible obligations, proceeds to inquire by what circumstances the barbarous and inhuman treatment of slaves were produced. The first of these circumstances which he mentions, was "commerce;" for if men could be considered as possessions, if like cattle they might be bought and sold, it will be natural to suppose that they would be regarded and treated in the same manner. This kind of commerce, which began in the primitive ages of the world, depressed the human species in the general estimation; and they were tamed like brutes by hunger and the lash, and the treatment of them so conducted as to render them docile instruments of labor for their possessors. This degradation of course depressed their minds; restricted the expansion of their faculties; stifled almost every effort of genius, and exhibited them to the world as beings endued with inferior capacities to the rest of mankind. But for this opinion of them there seems to have been no foundation in truth and justice. Equal to their fellow men in natural talents, and alike capable of improvement, any apparent, or even real difference between them and others, must have been owing to the treatment they received, and the rank they were doomed to occupy.

This commerce of the human species commenced at an early period. The history of Joseph points to a remote era for its introduction. Egypt seems to have been, at this time, the principal market for the sale of human beings. It was indeed so famous as to have been known, within a few centuries from the time of Pharaoh, to the Grecian colonies in Asia and to the Grecian islands. Homer mentions Cyprus and Egypt as the common markets for slaves, about the time of the Trojan war. Egypt is represented in the book of Genesis as a market for slaves, and in Exodus as famous for the severity of its servitude.

---

*Herodotus.

Tyre and Sidon, as we learn from the book of Joel, were notorious for the prosecution of this trade.

This custom appears also to have existed in other States. It traveled all over Asia. It spread through the Grecian and Roman world. It was in use among the barbarous nations that overturned the Roman empire; and was therefore practised at the same period throughout Europe. However, as the northern nations were settled in their conquests, the slavery and commerce of the human species began to decline, and were finally abolished. Some writers have ascribed this result to the prevalence of the feudal system; while others, a much more numerous class, have maintained that it was the natural effect of Christianity. The advocates of the former opinion allege, that "the multitude of little states which sprung up from one great one at this era occasioned infinite bickerings and matter for contention. There was not a state or seignory that did not want all the men it could muster, either to defend their own right or to dispute that of their neighbors. Thus every man was taken into service: whom they armed they must trust; and there could be no trust but in free men. Thus the barrier between the two classes was thrown down, and slavery was no more heard of in the west."

On the other hand, it must be allowed that Christianity was admirably adapted to this purpose. It taught "that all men were originally equal; that the Deity was no respecter of persons; and that, as all men were to give an account of their actions hereafter, it was necessary that they should be free." These doctrines could not fail of having their proper influence upon those who first embraced Christianity from a conviction of its truth. We find them accordingly actuated by these principles. The greatest part of the charters which were granted for the freedom of slaves, many of which are still extant, were granted "pro amore Dei, pro mercede animæ." They were founded in short on religious considerations, "that they might procure the favor of the Deity, which they had forfeited by the subjugation of those who were the objects of divine benevolence and attention equally with themselves." These considerations began to produce their effects, as the different nations were converted to Christianity, and procured that general liberty at last, which at the close of the twelfth century was conspicuous in the west of Europe.

But still we find that within two centuries after the suppression of slavery in Europe, the Portuguese, in close imitation of those piracies which we have mentioned as existing in the uncivilized ages of the world, made their descents upon Africa, and committing depredations upon the coast, first carried the wretched inhabitants into slavery. This practice, thus inconsiderable in its commencement, soon became general, and we find most of the maritime Christian nations of Europe following the piratical example. Thus did the Europeans, to their eternal infamy, revive a custom, which their own ancestors had so lately exploded from a consciousness of its impiety. The unfortunate Africans fled from the coast, and sought in the interior part of the country a retreat from the persecution of their invaders. But the Europeans still pursued them; they entered their rivers, sailed up into the heart of the country, surprised the Africans in their recesses, and carried them into slavery. The next step which the Europeans found it necessary to take, was that of settling in the country; of securing themselves by fortified posts; of changing their system of force into that of pretended liberality; and of opening, by every species of bribery and corruption, a communication with the natives. Accordingly they erected their forts and factories; landed their merchandize, and endeavored by a peaceable deportment, by presents, and by every appearance of munificence, to allure the attachment and confidence of the Africans. The Portuguese erected their first fort in 1481, about forty years after Alonzo Gonzales had pointed out to his countrymen, as articles of commerce, the southern Africans.

The scheme succeeded. An intercourse took place between the Europeans and Africans, attended with a confidence highly favorable to the views of ambition and avarice. In order to render this intercourse permanent as well as lucrative, the Europeans paid their court to the African chiefs, and a treaty of peace and commerce was concluded, in which it was agreed that the kings, on their part, should sentence prisoners of war, and convicts, to European servitude; and that the Europeans should in return supply them with the luxuries of the north. Thus were laid the foundations of that nefarious commerce, of which, in subsequent chapters, we intend to give the details.*

CHAPTER II.

SLAVERY IN GREECE.—ATHENIAN SLAVES.

Early existence of Slavery in Greece.—Proportion of Slaves to Freemen.—Their numbers in Athens and Sparta.—Mild government of Slaves in Athens—the reverse in Sparta. Instances of noble conduct of Slaves towards their masters.—Probable origin of Slavery, prisoners of war.—Examples in history of whole cities and states being reduced to Slavery: Judea, Miletos, Thebes.—Slaves obtained by kidnapping and piracy.—The traffic supposed to be attended by a curse.—Certain nations sell their own people into Slavery.—Power of masters over their Slaves; the power of Life and Death.—The Chians, the first Greeks who engaged in a regular Slave-trade.—Their fate in being themselves finally reduced to Slavery.—First type of the Maroon wars.—The Chian Slaves revolt.—The hero slave Drimacos.—His history.—Honors paid to his memory. Servile war among the Samians.—Athenian laws to protect Slaves from cruelty.— Slaves entitled to bring an action for assault.—Death penalty for crimes against slaves. Slaves entitled to purchase freedom.—Privileges of Slaves in Athens.—Revolt of Slaves working in Mines.—The temples a privileged sanctuary for Slaves who were cruelly treated.—Tyrannical masters compelled to sell their Slaves.—Slave auctions.—Diogenes. Price of Slaves.—Public Slaves, their employment.—Educated by the State, and intrusted with important duties.—Domestic Slaves: their food and treatment.—The Slaves partake in the general decline of morals.—History and Description of Athens.

IN Greece, slavery existed from the earliest period of her history. Before the days of Homer it generally prevailed. The various states of Greece had

---

*Slavery and Commerce of the Human Species: Encyclopedia Britt.: Antiquities of Greece and Rome.

different codes of laws, but in all of them the slaves were a majority of the people. The proportion of slaves to freemen probably varied in different states, and in the same state at different times. A historian states the proportion to have been at one period as 400 to 30. In Athens, another writer states, there were three slaves to one freeman. In Sparta, the proportion of slaves was much greater than in Athens.

The greatest writers of antiquity were, on this subject, perplexed and undecided. They appear to have comprehended the extent of the evil, but to have been themselves too much the slaves of habit and prejudice to discover that no form or modification of slavery is consistent with justice. Most perplexing of all, however, was the Laconian Heloteia; because in that case the comparatively great number of the servile class rendered it necessary, in the opinion of some, to break their spirit and bring them down to their condition by a system of severity which constitutes the infamy of Sparta.*

The discredit of subsisting on slave labor was, to a certain extent, shared by all the states of Greece, even by Athens. But in the treatment of that unfortunate class, there was as much variation as from the differences of national character might have been inferred. The Athenians, in this respect, as in most others, are represented as the antipodes of the Spartans; inasmuch as they treated their slaves with humanity, and even indulgence.† We read, accordingly, of slaves whose love for their masters exceeded the love of brothers; they have toiled, fought, and died for them; they have sometimes surpassed them in courage, and taught them, in situations of imminent danger, how to die. An example is recorded of a slave, who put on the disguise of his lord, that he might be slain in his stead. These examples, however, do not prove that there is any thing ennobling in servitude. On the contrary, the inference is, that great and noble souls had been dealt with unjustly by fortune.

As soon as men began to give quarter in war, and became possessed of prisoners, the idea of employing them and rendering their labors profitable, naturally suggested itself. When it was found that advantages could be derived from captured enemies instead of butchering them in the field, their lives were spared. At the outset, therefore, it is argued, slavery sprung from feelings of humanity. A distinguished historian remarks: "When warlike people, emerging from the savage state, first set about agriculture, the idea of sparing the lives of prisoners, on condition of their becoming useful to the conquerors by labor, was an obvious improvement upon the practice of former times, when conquered enemies were constantly put to death, not from a spirit of cruelty, but from necessity, for the conquerors were unable to maintain them in captivity, and dared not set them free."‡

---

* Manners and Customs of Ancient Greece.
† Herodes Atticus lamented the death of his Slaves as if they had been his relatives, and erected statues to their memory in woods, or fields, or beside fountains.
‡ Mitford's History of Greece.

Possibly the practice was borrowed from the East, where the mention of slaves occurs in the remotest ages. In later times, the Queen of Persia is represented to have urged Darius into the Grecian war, that she might possess Athenian, Spartan, Argive and Corinthian slaves. The practice was, when a number of prisoners had been taken, to make a division of them among the chiefs, generally by lot, and then to sell them for slaves.

Examples occur in antiquity of whole cities and states being at once subjected to servitude. Thus the inhabitants of Judea were twice carried away captive to Babylon, where their masters, not perhaps from mockery, required of them to sing some of their national songs; to which, as we learn from the prophet, they replied, "How can we sing the songs of Zion in a strange land?" The citizens of Miletos, after the unsuccessful revolt of Aristagoras, were carried into Persia, as were those also of other places. Like the Israelites, those Greeks long preserved in captivity their national manners and language, though surrounded by strangers, and urged by every inducement to assimilate themselves to their conquerors. A similar fate overtook the inhabitants of Thebes, who were sold into slavery by Alexander.

As the supply produced by war seldom equaled the demand, the race of kidnappers alluded to in a former chapter, sprung up, who, partly merchants and partly pirates, roamed about the shores of the Mediterranean, as similar miscreants now do about the slave coasts of Africa. Neither war, however, nor piracy, sufficed at length to furnish that vast multitude of slaves which the growing luxury of the times induced the Greeks to consider necessary. Commerce, by degrees, conducted them to Caria and other parts of Asia Minor, particularly the southern coasts of the Black Sea, those great nurseries of slaves from that time until now. The first Greeks who engaged in this traffic, which even by the Pagans was supposed to be attended by a curse, are said to have been the Chians. They purchased their slaves from the barbarians, among whom the Lydians, the Phrygians and the natives of Pontos, with many others, were accustomed, like the modern Circassians, to carry on a trade in their own people.

Before proceeding farther with the history of the traffic, it may be well to describe the power possessed by masters over their domestics during the heroic ages. Every man appears then to have been a king in his own house, and to have exercised his authority most regally. Power, generally, when unchecked by law, is fierce and inhuman; and over their household, gentlemen, in those ages, exercised the greatest and most awful power, that of life and death, as they afterwards did at Rome. When supposed to deserve death, the slaves were executed ignominiously by hanging. This was regarded as an impure end. To die honorably was to perish by the sword.

The Chians, as before observed, are said to have been the first Grecian people who engaged in a regular slave-trade. For although the Thessalians and Spartans possessed slaves at a period much anterior, they obtained them by different means; the latter by reducing to subjection the ancient Achæan inhabitants; the former by their conquests over other nations. But the Chians possessed only such slaves as they had purchased with money; in which they resembled the slave-holding nations of modern times. Other circumstances strongly suggest the parallel. We have here, perhaps, the first type of the Maroon wars, though on a smaller scale, and marked by fewer outbreaks of atrocity.* It is not, indeed, stated that the females were flogged, though throughout Greece the males were so corrected; but whatever the nature of the severities practiced upon them may have been, the yoke of bondage was found too galling to be borne, and whole gangs took refuge in the mountains. Fortunately for them, the interior of the island abounded in fastnesses, and was in those days covered with forest.

Here, therefore, the fugitives, erecting themselves dwellings, or taking possession of caverns among the almost inaccessible cliffs, successfully defended themselves, subsisting on the plunder of their former owners. Shortly before the time of the writer, to whom we are indebted for these details, a bondsman named Drimacos, made his escape from the city, and reached the mountains, where, by valor and conduct, he soon placed himself at the head of the servile insurgents, over whom he ruled like a king. The Chians led several expeditions against him in vain. He defeated them in the field with great slaughter; but at length, to spare the useless effusion of human blood, invited them to a conference, wherein he observed, that the slaves being encouraged in their revolt by an oracle, would never lay down their arms, or submit to the drudgery of servitude. Nevertheless, the war might be terminated, "for if my advice," said he, "be followed, and we be suffered to enjoy tranquility, numerous advantages will thence accrue to the state."

There being little prospect of a satisfactory settlement of the matter by arms, the Chians consented to enter into a truce, as with a public enemy. Humbled by their losses and defeats, Drimacos found them submissive to reason. He therefore provided himself with weights, measures, and a signet, and exhibiting them to his former masters, said: "When, in future, our necessities require that I should supply myself from your stores, it shall always be by these weights and measures; and having taken the necessary quantity of provisions, I shall be careful to seal your warehouses with this signet. With respect to such of your slaves as may fly and come to me, I will institute a rigid examination into their story, and if they have just grounds for complaint, I will protect them—if not, they shall be sent back to their owners."

To these conditions the magistrates readily acceded; upon which the slaves

---

*Maroons; the name given to revolted negroes in the West Indies and in some parts of South America. The appellation is supposed to be derived from Marony, a river separating Dutch and French Guiana, where larges numbers of the fugitives resided. In many cases, by taking to the forests and mountains, they have rendered themselves formidable to the colonies, and sustained a long and brave resistance against the whites. When Jamaica was conquered by the English, in 1655, about 1500 slaves retreated to the mountains, and were called Maroons. They continued to harass the island till the end of the last century, when they were reduced, by the aid of blood-hounds. (See Dallas's History of the Maroons.)

who still remained with their masters grew more obedient, and seldom took to flight, dreading the decision of Drimacos. Over his own followers he exercised a despotic authority. They, in fact, stood far more in fear of him, than, when in bondage, of their lords; and performed his bidding without question or murmur. He was severe in the punishment of the unruly, and permitted no man to plunder and lay waste the country, or commit any act of injustice. The public festivals he was careful to observe, going round and collecting from the proprietors of the land, who bestowed upon him both wine and the finest victims; but if, on these occasions, he discovered that a plot was hatching, or any ambush laid for him, he would take speedy vengeance.

Observing old age to be creeping upon Drimacos, and rendered wanton apparently by prosperity, the government issued a proclamation, offering a great reward to any one who should capture him, or bring them his head. The old chief, discerning signals of treachery, or convinced that, at last, it must come to that, took aside a young man whom he loved, and said, "I have ever regarded you with a stronger affection than any other man, and to me you have been a brother. But now the days of my life are at an end, nor would I have them prolonged. With you, however, it is not so. Youth, and the bloom of youth, are yours. What, then, is to be done? You must prove yourself to possess valor and greatness of soul: and, since the state offers riches and freedom to whomsoever shall slay me and bear them my head, let the reward be yours. Strike it off, and be happy!"

At first the youth rejected the proposal, but ultimately Drimacos prevailed. The old man fell, and his friend, on presenting his head, received the reward, together with his freedom; and, after burying his benefactor's remains, he sailed away to his own country.

The Chians, however, underwent the just punishment of their treachery. No longer guided by the wisdom and authority of Drimacos, the fugitive slaves returned to their original habits of plunder and devastation; whereupon, the Chians, remembering the moderation of the dead, erected an heroön upon his grave, and denominated him the propitious hero. The insurgents, also, holding his memory in veneration, continued for generations to offer up the first fruits of their spoil upon his tomb. He was, in fact, honored with a kind of apotheosis, and canonized among the gods of the island; for it was believed that his shade often appeared to men in dreams, for the purpose of revealing some servile conspiracy, while yet in the bud; and they to whom he vouchsafed these warning visits, never failed to proceed to his chapel, and offer sacrifice to his manes.

In process of time the Chians themselves were compelled to drain the bitter cup of servitude. For, as we find recorded, they were subjugated by Mithridates, and were delivered up to their own slaves, to be carried away captive into Colchis. This, Athenæus considers the just punishment of their wickedness in having been the first who introduced the slave trade into Greece, when they might have been better served by freemen for hire.

The servile war which took place among the Samians had a more fortunate issue, though but few particulars respecting it have come down to us. It was related, however, by Malacos in his annals of the Siphnians, that Ephesos was first founded by a number of Samian slaves, who, having retired to a mountain on the island to the number of a thousand, inflicted numerous evils on their former tyrants. These, in the sixth year of the war, having consulted the oracle, came to an understanding with their slaves, who were permitted to depart in safety from the island. They sailed away, and became the founders of the city and people of Ephesos.

In Attica the institution of slavery, though attended by innumerable evils is said to have exhibited itself under the mildest form which it any where assumed in the ancient world. With their characteristic attention to the interests of humanity, the Athenians enacted a law, in virtue of which, slaves could indict their masters for assault and battery. Hyperides observed in his oration against Mantitheos, " our laws, making no distinction in this respect between freemen and slaves, grant to all alike the privilege of bringing an action against those who insult or injure them." To the same effect spoke Lycurgus in his first oration against Lycophron. Plato was less just to them than the laws of their country. If, in his imaginary state, a slave killed a slave in self-defense, he was judged innocent; if a freeman, he was put to death like a parricide. But Demosthenes has preserved the law which empowered any Athenian, not laboring under legal disability, to denounce to the Thesmothetæ the person who offered violence to man, woman or child, whether slave or free. Such actions were tried before the court of Heliæa, and numerous were the examples of men who suffered death for crimes committed against slaves. Another privilege enjoyed by the slave class in Attica was that of purchasing their own freedom, as often as, by the careful management of the peculium secured them by law, they were enabled to offer their owners an equivalent for their services.

At Athens, with some exceptions, every temple in the city appears to have been open to them. Occasionally, certain of their number were selected to accompany their masters to consult the oracle at Delphi, when they were permitted, like free citizens, to wear crowns upon their heads, which, for the time, conferred upon them exemption from blows or stripes. Among their more serious grievances was their liability to personal chastisement; which was too much left to the discretion of their owners. In time of war, however, this privilege was not practised, since the flogged slaves could go over to the enemy, as sometimes happened. They are said, besides, to have worked the mines in fetters; probably, however, only in consequence of a revolt, in which they slew the overseers of the mines, and taking possession of the acropolis of Sunium, laid waste, for a time, the whole of the adjacent districts. This took place simultaneously with the second insurrection of the slaves in Sicily, in the quelling of which nearly a million of their number were destroyed.

We find from contemporary writers, that except in cases of incorrigible perverseness, slaves were encouraged to marry; it being supposed they would thus become more attached to their masters, who, in return, would put more trust in slaves born and brought up in the house, than in such as were purchased.

We have seen that slaves were protected by the laws from grievous insults and contumely; but if, in spite of legal protection, their masters found means to render their lives a burden, the state provided them with an asylum in the temple of Theseus and the Eumenides. Having there taken sanctuary, their oppressors could not force them thence without incurring the guilt of sacrilege. Thus in a fragment of Aristophanes' Seasons, we find a slave deliberating whether he should take refuge in the Theseion, and there remain until he could procure his transfer to a new master; for any one who conducted himself too harshly towards his slaves, was by law compelled to sell them. Not only so, but the slave could institute an action against his lord and master, or against any other citizen who behaved unjustly or injuriously towards him. The right of sanctuary was, however, limited, and extended from the time of the slave's flight to the next new moon, when a periodical slave auction appears to have been held.

On this occasion the slaves were stationed in a circle in the market place, and the one whose turn it was to be sold, mounted a table, where he exhibited himself and was knocked down to the best bidder. The sales seem to have been conducted precisely like those of the present day in Richmond, Charleston, New Orleans and other cities of the south. The Greek auctioneer, or slave-broker, however, was answerable at law if the quality of the persons sold did not correspond with the description given of them in the catalogue. It appears that, sometimes, when the articles were lively, or witty, they made great sport for the company, as in the case of Diogenes, who bawled aloud—"whoever among you wants a master, let him buy me."

Diogenes, of Sinope, flourished about the fourth century before Christ, and was the most famous of the Cynic philosophers. Having been banished from his native place with his father, who had been accused of coining false money, he went to Athens, and requested Antisthenes to admit him among his disciples. That philosopher in vain attempted to repel the importunate supplicant, even by blows, and finally granted his request. Diogenes devoted himself, with the greatest diligence, to the lessons of his master, whose doctrines he extended still further. He not only, like Antisthenes, despised all philosophical speculations, and opposed the corrupt morals of his time, but also carried the application of his doctrines, in his own person, to the extreme. The stern austerity of Antisthenes was repulsive; but Diogenes exposed the follies of his contemporaries with wit and humor, and was, therefore, better adapted to be the censor and instructer of the people, though he really accomplished little in the way of reforming them. At the same time, he applied, in its fullest extent, his principle of divesting himself of all superfluities. He taught that a wise man, in order to be happy, must endeavor to preserve himself independent of fortune, of men, and of himself: in order to do this, he must despise riches, power, honor, arts and sciences, and all the enjoyments of life. He endeavored to exhibit, in his own person, a model of Cynic virtue. For this purpose, he subjected himself to the severest trials, and disregarded all the forms of polite society. He often struggled to overcome his appetite, or satisfied it with the coarsest food; practised the most rigid temperance, even at feasts, in the midst of the greatest abundance, and did not even consider it beneath his dignity to ask alms. By day, he walked through the streets of Athens barefoot, without any coat, with a long beard, a stick in his hand, and a wallet on his shoulders; by night, he slept in a tub, though this has been doubted. He defied the inclemency of the weather, and bore the scoffs and insults of the people with the greatest equanimity. Seeing a boy draw water with his hand he threw away his wooden goblet as an unnecessary utensil. He never spared the follies of men, but openly and loudly inveighed against vice and corruption, attacking them with satire and irony. The people, and even the higher classes, heard him with pleasure, and tried their wit upon him. When he made them feel his superiority, they often had recourse to abuse, by which, however, he was little moved. He rebuked them for expressions and actions which violated decency and modesty, and therefore it is not credible that he was guilty of the excesses with which his enemies have reproached him. His rudeness offended the laws of good breeding rather than the principles of morality. Many anecdotes, however, related of this singular person, are mere fictions. On a voyage to Ægina, he fell into the hands of pirates, who sold him as a slave to the Corinthian Xeniades in Crete. The latter emancipated him, and intrusted him with the education of his children. He attended to the duties of his new employment with the greatest care, commonly living in summer at Corinth, and in winter at Athens. It was at the former place that Alexander found him on the road-side, basking in the sun, and, astonished at the indifference with which the ragged beggar regarded him, entered into conversation with him, and finally gave him permission to ask for a boon. "I ask nothing," answered the philosopher, "but that thou wouldst get out of my sunshine." Surprised at this proof of content, the king is said to have exclaimed, "Were I not Alexander, I would be Diogenes." At another time, he was carrying a lantern through the streets of Athens, in the daytime: on being asked what he was looking for, he answered, "I am seeking a man." Thinking he had found, in the Spartans, the greatest capacity for becoming such men as he wished, he said, "Men I have found nowhere; but children, at least, I have seen at Lacedæmon." Being asked, "What is the most dangerous animal?" his answer was, "Among wild animals, the slanderer; among tame, the flatterer." He died 324 B. C., at a great age. When he felt death approaching, he seated himself on the road leading to Olympia, where he died with philosophical calmness, in the presence of a great number of people, who were collected around him.

Slaves of little or no value, were contemptuously called "salt bought," from a custom prevalent among the inland Thracians, of bartering their captives for salt; whence it may be inferred that domestics from that part of the world were considered inferior.

Respecting the price of slaves, a passage occurs in the Memorabilia, where Socrates inquires whether friends were to be valued at so much per head, like slaves; some of whom, he says, were not worth a demimina, while others would fetch two, five, or even ten minæ; that is, the price varied from ten to two hundred dollars. Nicias bought an overseer for his silver mines at the price of a talent, or about twelve hundred dollars.

Exclusively of the fluctuations caused by the variations in the supply and demand, the market price of slaves was affected by their age, health, strength, beauty, natural abilities, mechanical ingenuity, and moral qualities. The meanest and cheapest class were those who worked in the mills, where mere bodily strength was required. A low value was set upon slaves who worked in the mines—a sum equal to about eight dollars. In the age of Demosthenes, ordinary house slaves, male or female, were valued at about the same price. Demosthenes considered two minæ and a half, fifty dollars, a large sum for a person of this class. Of the sword cutlers possessed by the orator's father, some were valued at six minæ, others at five, while the lowest were worth above three. Chairmakers sold for about two minæ, forty dollars. The wages of slaves, when let out for hire by their masters, varied greatly, as did the profit derived from them. Expert manufacturers of fine goods produced their owners much larger returns than miners.

Slaves at Athens were divided into two classes, private and public. The latter, who were the property of the state, performed several kinds of service, supposed to be unworthy of freemen. They were, for example, employed as vergers, messengers, scribes, clerks of public works, and inferior servants of the gods. Most of the temples of Greece possessed a great number of slaves, or serfs, who cultivated the sacred domains, exercised various humbler offices of religion, and were ready on all occasions to execute the orders of the priests. At Corinth, where the worship of Aphrodite chiefly prevailed, these slaves consisted almost exclusively of women, who, having on certain occasions burnt frankincense, and offered up public prayers to the goddess, were sumptuously feasted within the precincts of her fane.*

Among the Athenians, the slaves of the republic, generally captives taken in war, received a careful education, and were sometimes intrusted with important duties. Out of their number were selected the secretaries, who, in time of war, accompanied the generals and treasurers of the army, and made exact minutes of the expenditure, in order that, when, on their return, these officers should come to render an account of their proceedings, their books might be compared with those of the secretaries. In cases of difficulty, these unfortu-

---

* APHRODITE, the Goddess of Love among the Greeks, synonymous with Aphrogeneia, that is, born of the foam of the sea. Aphrodisia was a festival sacred to Venus, which was celebrated in various parts of Greece, but with the greatest solemnity in the island of Cyprus.

nate individuals were subjected to torture, in order to obtain that kind of evidence which the ancients deemed most satisfactory, but which the moderns regard with extreme uncertainty.

Æsop, the oldest Greek fabulist, was a native of Phrygia, and a slave, until he was set free by his last owner. He lived about the middle of the sixth century B. C. He inculcated rules of practical morality, drawn from the habits of the inferior creation, and thus spread his fame through Greece and all the neighboring countries. Crœsus, king of Lydia, invited Æsop to his court, and kept him always about his person. Indeed, he was never absent, except during his journeys to Greece, Persia and Egypt. Crœsus once sent him to Delphi to offer sacrifice to Apollo; while engaged in this embassy, he wrote his fable of the Floating Log, which appeared terrible at a distance, but lost its terrors when approached. The priests of Delphi, applying the fable to themselves, resolved to take vengeance on the author, and plunged him from a precipice. Planudes, who wrote a miserable romance, of which he makes Æsop the hero, describes him as excessively deformed and disagreeable in his appearance, and given to stuttering; but this account does not agree with what his contemporaries say of him. The stories related of Æsop, even by the ancients, are not entitled to credit. A collection of fables made by Planudes, which are still extant under the name of the Grecian fabulist, are ascribed to him with little foundation; their origin is lost in the darkness of antiquity.

A very significant and pleasant custom prevailed when a slave newly purchased was first brought into the house. They placed him before the hearth, where his future master, mistress and fellows ervants poured baskets of ripe fruit, dates, figs, filberts, walnuts, &c., upon his head, to intimate that he was come into the abode of plenty. The occasion was converted by his fellow slaves into a holiday and feast; for custom appropriated to them whatever was cast upon the new comer.

Their food was commonly, as might be expected, inferior to that of their masters. Thus the dates grown in Greece, which ripened but imperfectly, were appropriated to their use; and for their drink they had a thin wine, made of the husks of grapes, laid, after they had been pressed, to soak in water, and then squeezed again. A drink precisely similar is now made in the wine districts of France. They generally ate barley bread; the citizens themselves frequently did the same. To give a relish to their plain meal of bread, plain broth and salted fish, they were indulged with pickles. In the early ages of the commonwealth, they imitated the frugal manner of their lords, so that no slave, who valued his reputation, would be seen to enter a tavern; but in later times they naturally shared largely in the general depravity of morals, and placed their greatest good in eating and drinking. Their whole creed, on this point, has been summed up in a few words by the poet Socian. "Wherefore," exclaims a slave, "dole forth these absurdities; these ravings of sophists, prating up and down the Lyceum, the Academy, and the gates of the Odeion? In all these there is nothing of value. Let us drink—let us drink deeply

Let us rejoice, whilst it is yet permitted us to delight our souls. Enjoy thyself, O Manes! Nothing is sweeter than eating and drinking. Virtues, embassies, generalships, are vain pomps, resembling the plaudits of a dream. Heaven at the fated hour will deliver thee to the cold grasp of death, and thou wilt bear with thee nothing but what thou hast drunk and eaten! All else is dust, like Pericles, Codros and Cimon."

The employment of household slaves necessarily varied according to the rank and condition of their lords. In the dwellings of the wealthy and luxurious, they were accustomed to fan their masters and mistresses, and drive away the flies with branches of myrtle. Among the Roman ladies, it was customary to retain a female slave, for the sole purpose of looking after the Melitensian lap-dogs of their mistresses, in which they were less ambitious than that dame in Lucian, who kept a philosopher for this purpose. Female cup-bearers and ladies' maids were likewise slaves; the latter were initiated in all the arts of the toilet.

There seems to have been a set of men who earned their subsistence by initiating slaves in household labors. In the bakers' business, Anaxarchos, a philosopher, introduced an improvement, by which modern times may profit,— to preserve his bread pure from the touch, and even from the breath of the slaves who made it, he caused them to knead the dough with gloves on their hands, and to wear a respirator of some gauze-like substance over their mouths. Other individuals, who grudged their domestics a taste of their delicacies, obliged them to wear a broad collar like a wheel around their necks, which prevented them from bringing their hands to their mouths. This odious practice, however, could not have been general.

Besides working at the mill and fetching water, both somewhat laborious employments, we find that female slaves were sometimes engaged in wood cutting upon the mountains. Towards the decline of the commonwealth, it became a mark of wealth and consequence to be served by black domestics; as was also the fashion among the Romans and the Egyptian Greeks. Cleopatra had negro boys for torch-bearers; and the Athenian ladies, as a foil, perhaps, liked to be attended by black waiting maids.

When men have usurped an undue dominion over their fellows, they seldom know where to stop. The Syrians, themselves enslaved politically, and often sold into servitude abroad, affected when rich a peculiarly luxurious manner: female attendants waited on their ladies, who, when mounting their carriages, required them to bend on all fours, that they might make a footstool of their backs.

We append to our notice of slavery in Athens, a description of the splendors of that celebrated city, from whence the light of intellectual cultivation has spread for thousands of years down to our own time. This capital of the old kingdom of Attica, and of the more modern democracy, was founded by Cecrops, 1550 years before Christ. The old city was built on the summit of some rocks, which lie in the midst of a wide and pleasant plain, which became

3

filled with buildings as the inhabitants increased; and this made the distinction between Acropolis and Catapolis, or the upper and lower city. The citadel or Acropolis was 60 stadia in circumference, and included many extensive buildings. Athens lies on the Saronic gulf, opposite the eastern coast of the Peloponnesus. It is built on a peninsula formed by the junction of the Cephissus and Ilissus. From the sea, where its real power lay, it was distant about five leagues. It was connected, by walls of great strength and extent, with three harbors—the Piræus, Munychia and Phalerum. The first was considered the most convenient, and was one of the emporiums of Grecian commerce. The surrounding coast was covered with magnificent buildings, whose splendor vied with those of the city. The walls of rough stone, which connected the harbors with the city, were so broad, that carriages could go on their top. The Acropolis contained the most splendid works of art of which Athens could boast. Its chief ornament was the Parthenon, or temple of Minerva. This magnificent building, which, even in ruins, has been the wonder of the world, was 217 feet long, 98 broad, and 65 high. Destroyed by the Persians, it was rebuilt in a noble manner by Pericles, 444 years B. C. Here stood the statue of Minerva by Phidias, a masterpiece of art, formed of ivory, 46 feet high, and richly decorated with gold, whose weight was estimated at from 40 to 44 talents (2000 to 2200 pounds), which, if we reckon, according to Barthelemy, the silver talent at 5700 livres, and the ratio of gold to silver as 1 to 13, would make a sum of 2,964,000, or 3,260,400 livres (523,700, or 576,004 dollars). The Propylæum, built of white marble, formed the entrance to the Parthenon. This building lay on the north side of the Acropolis, close to the Erectheum, also of white marble, consisting of two temples, the one dedicated to Pallas Minerva, and the other to Neptune; besides another remarkable building, called the *Pandroseum*. In the circle of Minerva's temple stood the olive-tree, sacred to that goddess. On the front part of the Acropolis, and on each end, two theatres are visible, the one of Bacchus, the other, the Odeum; the former for dramatic exhibitions, the latter for musical competitions, also built with extraordinary splendor. The treasury is also in the back part of the temple of Minerva. In the lower city were many fine specimens of architecture, viz: the Poikile, or the gallery of historical paintings; besides the temple of the Winds, and the monuments of celebrated men. But the greatest pieces of architecture were without the city—the temples of Theseus and Jupiter Olympius, one of which stood on the north, the other on the south side of the city. The first was of Doric architecture, and resembled the Parthenon. On the metopes of this temple the famous deeds of old heroes and kings were excellently represented. The temple of Jupiter Olympius was of Ionic architecture, and far surpassed all the other buildings of Athens in splendor and beauty. Incalculable sums were spent on it. It was from time to time enlarged, and rendered more beautiful, until, at length, it was finished by Adrian. The outside of this temple was adorned by nearly 120 fluted columns, 60 feet high, and 6 feet in diameter. The inside was nearly half a league in circumference. Here stood the renowned statue of the god made by Phidias, of gold and ivory. The Pantheon (*sacred to all the gods*) must not be forgotten. Of this the Pantheon at Rome is an exact copy. Besides these wonderful works of art, Athens contains many other places which must always be interesting, from the recollections connected with them. The old philosophers were not accustomed, as is well known, to shut up their scholars in lecture-rooms, but mingled with them on the freest and pleasantest terms, and, for this purpose, sought out spots which were still and retired. Such a spot was the renowned academy where Plato taught, lying about six stadia north of the city, forming a part of a place called *Ceramicus*. This spot, originally marshy, had been made a very pleasant place, by planting rows of trees, and turning through it streams of fresh water. Such a place was the Lyceum, where Aristotle taught, and which, through him, became the seat of the Peripatetic school. It lay on the bank of the Ilissus, opposite the city, and was also used for gymnastic exercises. Not far from thence was the less renowned Cynosarges, where Antisthenes, the founder of the Cynic school, taught. The sects of Zeno and Epicurus held their meetings in the city. Zeno chose the well-known Poikile, and Epicurus established himself in a garden within the walls, for he loved both society and rural quiet. Not only literary, but political assemblies gave a particular interest to different places in Athens. Here was the court of areopagus, where that illustrious body gave their decisions; the Prytaneum, or senate-house; the Pnyx, where the free people of Athens deliberated. After 23 centuries of war and devastation, of changes from civilized to savage masters, have passed over this great city, its ruins still excite astonishment. No inconsiderable part of the Acropolis was lately standing. The Turks have surrounded it with a broad, irregular wall. In this wall one may perceive the remains of the old wall, together with fragments of ancient pillars, which have been taken from the ruins of the old to construct new edifices. The right wing of the Propylæum, built by Pericles at the expense of 2012 talents, and which formed the ancient entrance, was a temple of victory. The roof of this building stood as late as 1656, when it was destroyed by the explosion of some powder kept there. In a part of the present wall, there are fragments of excellent designs in *basso relievo*, representing the contest of the Athenians with the Amazons. On the opposite wing of the Propylæum are six whole columns, with gate-ways between them. These pillars, half covered on the front side by the wall built by the Turks, are of marble, white as snow, and of the finest workmanship. They consist of three or four stones, so artfully joined together, that, though they have been exposed to the weather for 2000 years, yet no separation has been observed. From the Propylæum we step into the Parthenon. On the eastern front of this building, also, there are eight columns standing, and several colonnades on the side. Of the pediment, which represented the contest of Neptune and Minerva for Athens, there is nothing remaining but the head of a sea-horse, and the figures of two women without heads; but in all we must admire the highest degree of truth and beauty. The battle between the Centaurs and Lapithæ is better preserved. Of all the statues with which it was adorned, that of Adrian alone remains. The inside of this temple is now changed into a mosque. In the whole of this mutilated building, we find an indescribable expression of grandeur and sublimity. There are also astonishing remains to be seen of the Erectheum (the temple of Neptune Erectheus), especially the beautiful female figures called *Caryatides*, and which form two arch-ways. Of both theatres there is only so much of the outer walls remaining, that one can estimate their former condition and enormous size. The arena has sunk down, and is now planted with corn. In the lower city itself, there are no vestiges to be found of equal beauty and extent. Near a church, sacred to Santa Maria Maggiore, stand three very beautiful Corinthian columns, which support an architrave. They have been supposed to be the remains of a temple of Jupiter Olympius, but the opinion is not well grounded: probably, they are the remains of the old Poikile. The temple of the Winds, built by Andronicus Cyrrhestes, is not entire. Its form is an octagon: on each side it is covered with reliefs, which represent one of the principal winds: the work is excellent. The preservation of this edifice is owing to its being occupied by the dervises as a mosque. Of the monuments of distinguished men, with which a whole street was filled, only the fine one of Lysicrates remains. It consists of a pedestal surrounded by a colonnade, and is surmounted by a dome of Corinthian architecture. This has been supposed to be the spot which Demosthenes used for his study, but the supposition is not well supported. Some prostrate walls are the only remains of the splendid gymnasium built by Ptolemy. Outside of the city, our wonder is excited by the lofty ruins of the temple of the Olympian Jupiter. Of 120 pillars, 16 remain; but none of the statues are in existence. The pedestals and inscriptions are scattered here and there, and partly buried in the earth. The main body of the temple of Theseus has remained almost entire, but much of it, as it now stands, is of modern origin. The figures on the outside are mostly destroyed, but those which adorn the frieze within are well preserved. They represent the actions of the heroes of antiquity. The battle between Theseus and the Centaur is likewise depicted. On the hill where the famous court of areopagus held its sittings, you find steps hewn in the rock, places for the judges to sit, and over against these the stations of the accuser and the accused. The hill is now a Turkish burial-ground, and is covered with monuments. The Pnyx, the place of assembly for the people, not far from the Areopagus, is very nearly in its primitive state. One may see the place from which the orators spoke hewn in the rock, the seats of the scribes, and, at both ends, the places of those officers whose duty it was to preserve silence, and to make known the event of public deliberations. The niches are still to be seen, where those who had any favor to ask of the people deposited their petitions. The paths for running are still visible, where the gymnastic exercises were performed, and which Herodes Atticus built of white marble. The spot occupied by the Lyceum is only known by a quantity of fallen stones. A more modern edifice stands in the garden in the place of the academy. In the surrounding space, the walks of the Peripatetics can be discerned, and some olive-trees of high antiquity still command the reverence of the beholder. The long walls are totally destroyed, though the foundations are yet to be found on the plain. The Piræus has scarcely any thing of its ancient splendor, except a few ruined pillars, scattered here and there : the same is the case with the Phalerum and Munychia. It appears probable, that, in the time of Pausanius, many monuments were extant which belonged to the period before the Persian war ; because so transitory a possession as Xerxes had of the city, scarcely gave him time to finish the destruction of the walls and principal public edifices. In the restoration of the city to its former state, Themistocles looked more to the useful, Cimon to magnificence and splendor ; and Pericles far surpassed them both in his buildings. The great supply of money which he had from the tribute of the other states, belonged to no succeeding ruler. Athens at length saw much of her ancient splendor restored ; but, unluckily, Attica was not an island, and, after the sources of power, which belonged to the fruitful and extensive country of Macedonia, were developed by an able and enlightened prince, the opposing interests of many free states could not long withstand the disciplined army of a warlike people, led by an active, able and ambitious monarch. When Sylla destroyed the works of the Piræus, the power of Athens by sea was at an end, and with that fell the whole city. Flattered by the triumvirate, favored by Adrian's love of the arts, Athens was at no time so splendid as under the Antonines, when the magnificent works of from eight to ten centuries stood in view, and the edifices of Pericles were in equal preservation with the new buildings. Plutarch himself wonders how the structures of Ictinus, of Menesicles and Phidias, which were built with such surprising rapidity, could retain such a perpetual freshness. Probably Pausanius saw Greece yet unplundered. The Romans, from reverence towards a religion approaching so nearly to their own, and wishing to conciliate a people more cultivated than themselves, were ashamed to rob temples where the masterpieces of art were kept as sacred, and were satisfied with a tribute of money, although in Sicily they did not abstain from the plunder of the temples, on account of the prevalence of Carthaginian and Phœnician influence in that island. Pictures, even in the time of Pausanias, may have been left in their places. The wholesale robberies of collectors, the removal of great quantities of the works of art to Constantinople, when the creation of new specimens was no longer possible, Christian zeal, and the attacks of barbarians, destroyed, after a time, in Athens, what the emperors had spared. We have reason to think, that the colossal statue of Minerva Promachos was standing in the time of Alaric. About 420 A. D., paganism was totally annihilated at Athens, and, when Justinian closed even the schools of the philosophers, the recollection of the mythology was lost. The Parthenon was turned into a church of the Virgin Mary, and St. George stepped into the place of Theseus. The manufactory of silk, which had hitherto remained, was destroyed by the transportation of a colony of weavers, by Roger of

Sicily, and, in 1456, the place fell into the hands of Omar. To complete its degradation, the city of Minerva obtained the privilege (an enviable one in the East) of being governed by a black eunuch, as an appendage to the harem. The Parthenon became a mosque, and, at the west end of the Acropolis, those alterations were commenced, which the new discovery of artillery then made necessary. In 1687, at the siege of Athens by the Venetians under Morosini, it appears that the temple of Victory was destroyed, the beautiful remains of which are to be seen in the British museum. September 28, of this year, a bomb fired the powder magazine kept by the Turks in the Parthenon, and, with this building, destroyed the ever memorable remains of the genius of Phidias. Probably, the Venetians knew not what they destroyed; they could not have intended that their artillery should accomplish such devastation. The city was surrendered to them September 29. They wished to send the chariot of Victory, which stood on the west pediment of the Parthenon, to Venice, as a trophy of their conquest, but, in removing, it fell and was dashed to pieces. April, 1688, Athens was again surrendered to the Turks, in spite of the remonstrances of the inhabitants, who, with good reason, feared the revenge of their returning masters. Learned travelers have, since that time, often visited Athens; and we may thank their relations and drawings for the knowledge which we have of many of the monuments of the place.*

CHAPTER III.

SLAVES OF SPARTA, CRETE, THESSALY, &c.—THE HELOTS.

The Helots:—leading events of their History summed up.—Their Masters described.—The Spartans, their manners, customs and constitutions.—Distinguishing traits: severity, resolution and perseverance, treachery and craftiness.—Marriage.—Treatment of Infants.—Physical Education of Youth.—Their endurance of hardships.—The Helots: their origin; supposed to belong to the State; power of life and death over them; how subsisted; property acquired by them; their military service.—Plato, Aristotle, Isocrates, Plutarch and other writers convict the Spartans of barbarity towards them; the testimony of Myron on this point; instances of tyranny and cruelty.—Institution of the Crypteia; annual massacre of the Helots.—Terrible instance of treachery.—Bloody servile wars.—Sparta engaged in contests with her own vassals.—Relies upon foreign aid.—Earthquake, and vengeance of the Helots.—Constant source of terror to their masters.—Other classes of slaves.—Their privileges and advancement.—Slavery in Crete: classes and condition.—Mild treatment.—Strange privileges during certain Festivals.—Slaves of Syracuse rebel and triumph.—The Arcadians.

THERE seems to be a diversity of opinion among modern writers, as to the condition of the Spartan Helots. The American Encyclopedia, in giving

---

* Encyclopedia Americana.

briefly the prominent events of their history, states, that the name is generally derived from the town of Helos, the inhabitants of which were carried off and reduced to slavery by the Heraclidæ, about 1000 B. C. They differed from the other Greek slaves in not belonging individually to separate masters ; they were the property of the state, which alone had the disposal of their freedom. They formed a separate class of inhabitants, and their condition was, in many respects, similar to that of the boors in some countries of Europe. The state assigned them to certain citizens, by whom they were employed in private labors, though not exclusively, as the state still exacted certain services from them. Agriculture and all mechanical arts at Sparta were in the hands of the Helots, since the laws of Lycurgus prohibited the Spartans from all lucrative occupations. But the Helots were also obliged to bear arms for the state, in case of necessity. The barbarous treatment to which they were exposed often excited them to insurrection. Their dress, by which they were contemptuously distinguished from the free Spartans, consisted of cat's-skin, and a leather cap, of a peculiar shape. They were sometimes liberated for their services, or for a sum of money. If their numbers increased too much, the young Spartans, it is said, were sent out to assassinate them. Their number is uncertain, but Thucydides says that it was greater than that of the slaves in any other Grecian state. It has been variously estimated, at from 320,000 to 800,000. They several times rose against their masters, but were always finally reduced.

Before we proceed with the history of the Spartan Helots, it will be well enough to digress, in order to understand the character of their masters, who were, in many respects, a peculiar people.

Sparta, or Lacedæmon, the capital of Laconia and of the Spartan state, lay on the west bank of the river Eurotas, and embraced a circuit of six miles. The ruins are still seen nearly a league to the east of Misistra, and are known by the name of Palæopolis, or "ancient city." The Spartans were distinguished among the people of Greece by their manners, customs and constitution. Their kings ruled only through the popular will, as they had no other privileges than those of giving their opinion first in the popular assemblies, acting as umpires in disputes, and of commanding the army : their only other advantages were a considerable landed estate, a large share of the spoils, and the chief seat in assemblies and at meals. The Spartans, that is, the descendants of the Dorians, who acquired possession of Laconia under the Heraclidæ, were occupied only with war and the chase, and left the agricultural labors to the Helots ; but the Lacedæmonians, or Periœci (the ancient inhabitants of the country), engaged in commerce, navigation and manufactures. Although the Spartan conquerors were superior in refinement and cultivation to the Lacedæmonians, the arts of industry flourished only among the latter. They gradually intermingled with the Spartans, whom they exceeded in number, and formed one people. Both people constituted one state, with a national assembly, to which the towns sent deputies. The military contributions in money and troops formed the principal tribute of the free Lacedæmonians to the

Spartans (Dorians). The former were sometimes divided by jealousy from the latter, and in the Theban war several towns withdrew their troops from the Spartans, and joined Epaminondas. The distinguishing traits of the Spartans were severity, resolution and perseverance. Defeat and reverse never discouraged them. But they were faithless and crafty, as appears from their conduct in the Messenian wars, in which they not only bribed the Arcadian king, Aristocrates, to the basest treachery towards the Messenians, but also corrupted the Delphic oracle, of which they made use to the prejudice of the Messenians. The age at which marriage might be contracted was fixed by Lycurgus at thirty for men and twenty for women. When a Spartan woman was pregnant, it was required that pictures of the handsomest young men should be hung up in her chamber, for the purpose of producing a favorable effect on the fruit of her womb. The other Greeks washed the new-born infants with water, and afterwards rubbed them over with oil; but the Spartans bathed them in wine, to try the strength of their constitution. They had a notion that a wine bath produced convulsions or even death in weakly children, but confirmed the health of the strong. If the infant proved vigorous and sound, the state received it into the number of citizens; otherwise it was thrown into a cave on mount Taygetus. In the other Grecian states, the exposition of children was a matter of custom; in Sparta it was forbidden by law. The Spartan children were early inured to hardship and accustomed to freedom. Stays, which were in use among the other Grecians, were unknown to the Spartans. To accustom the children to endure hunger, they gave them but little food; and, if they stood in need of more, they were obliged to steal it; and, if discovered, they were severely punished, not for the theft, but for their awkwardness. Every ten days, they were required to present themselves before the ephori, and whoever was found to be too fat, received a flogging. Wine was not generally given to girls in Greece, but was commonly allowed to boys from earliest childhood. In Sparta, the boys were obliged to wear the hair short, until they attained the age of manhood, when it was suffered to grow. They usually ran naked, and were generally dirty, as they did not bathe and anoint themselves, like the other Greeks. They took pride in having the body covered with marks of bruises and wounds. They wore no outer garment, except in bad weather, and no shoes at any time. They were obliged to make their beds of rushes from the Eurotas. Till the seventh year, the child was kept in the gynæceum, under the care of the women; from that age to the eighteenth year, they were called *boys*, and thence to the age of thirty, *youths*. In the thirtieth year the Spartan entered the period of manhood, and enjoyed the full rights of a citizen. At the age of seven, the boy was withdrawn from the paternal care, and educated under the public eye, in company with others of the same age, without distinction of rank or fortune. If any person withheld his son from the care of the state, he forfeited his civil rights. The principal object of attention, during the periods of boyhood and youth, was the physical education, which consisted in the practice of various gymnastic exercises — running, leaping, throwing the discus, wrestling, boxing, and the chase. These exercises were performed naked, in certain buildings called *gymnasia*. Besides gymnastics, dancing and the military exercises were practiced. A singular custom was the flogging the boys on the annual festival of Diana Orthia, for the purpose of inuring them to bear pain with firmness : the priestess stood by with a small, light, wooden image of Diana, and if she observed that any boy was spared, she called out that the image of the goddess was so heavy, that she could not support it, and the blows were then redoubled. The men who were present exhorted their sons to fortitude, while the boys endeavored to surpass each other in firmness. Whoever uttered the least cry during the scourging, which was so severe as sometimes to prove fatal, was considered as disgraced, while he who bore it without shrinking was crowned, and received the praises of the whole city. According to some, this usage was established by Lycurgus; others refer it to the period of the battle of Plataeæ. To teach the youth cunning, vigilance and activity, they were encouraged, as has been already mentioned, to practice theft in certain cases; but if detected, they were flogged, or obliged to go without food, or compelled to dance round an altar, singing songs in ridicule of themselves. The fear of the shame of being discovered sometimes led to the most extraordinary acts. Thus it is related that a boy who had stolen a young fox, and concealed it under his clothes, suffered it to gnaw out his bowels, rather than reveal the theft, by suffering the fox to escape. Swimming was considered indispensable among them; they had a proverb to intimate that a man was good for nothing,—He cannot swim. Modesty of deportment was particularly attended to; and conciseness of language was much studied. The Spartans were the only people of Greece who despised learning, and excluded it from the education of youth. Their whole instrutions consisted in learning obedience to their superiors, the endurance of hardships, and to conquer or die in war. The youth were, however, carefully instructed in a knowledge of the laws, which, not being reduced to writing, were taught orally. The education of females was entirely different from that of the Athenians. Instead of remaining at home, as in Athens, spinning, &c., they danced in public, wrestled with each other, ran on the course, threw the discus, &c. This was not only done in public, but in a half-naked state. The object of this training of the women, was to give a vigorous constitution to the children.*

From a valuable work on the manners and customs of ancient Greece, by a distinguished English author, to whom we have been indebted in our description of the Athenian slavery, we gather some interesting particulars relative to the Spartan Helots,† who, he says, were Greeks of the Achaian race, who fell together with the land into the power of the conquerors. He quotes the remark of Ephoros, that "they were, in a certain point of view,

---

* See Muller's History and Antiquities of the Doric race.
† See Smith's Dictionary of Greek and Roman Antiquities. London.

public slaves; their possessor could neither liberate them, nor sell them beyond the borders." His inference is, that they were the property of individuals, but that the state reserved to itself the right of enfranchising them and preventing their emancipation, lest persons should be found, who would sell or give them their liberty when too old to labor. It is true there was an ancient law prohibiting the exportation of the Helots; but we find that there was a regular trade carried on in females, who were exported into all the neighboring countries for nurses. Thus it seems that the state exercised the power to convert its serfs into merchandize. It is stated that over the Helots, "not the state only, but even private individuals, possessed the power of life and death, as well as the right of beating and maiming them."

As the Spartans possessed estates, which personally they never cultivated, the Helots were stationed throughout the country upon those estates, which it was their business to till for the owners. To live, it was of course necessary that they should eat, and therefore a portion of the produce was set aside for them,—one-half, according to Tyrtæos,—a division not over generous, since their numbers were five times greater than those of the Spartans. The learned historian Herodotus remarks upon this, "as the quantity had been definitively settled at a very early period, to raise the amount being forbidden under very heavy imprecations, the Helots were the persons who profited by a good, and lost by a bad harvest, which must have been to them an encouragement to industry and good husbandry; a motive which would have been wanting, if the profit and loss had merely affected the landlords."

There appear to have been instances of Helots becoming comparatively wealthy in spite of the oppressions they endured; as did the Jews of the middle ages, notwithstanding the terrible robberies, persecutions and cruelties they were subject to. This fact proves that no pressure of hardship or ill-usage can entirely destroy the elasticity of the spirit: and no doubt the Helots, like all slaves, sought to soften their miseries by a gratification which the sense of property procures even in bondage. But of what value is property to a man who is himself the property of another? It appears, however, according to Herodotus, that "by means of the rich produce of the land, and in part by plunder obtained in war, they collected a considerable property."

But very little intercourse took place between the Spartans and Helots, at least in earlier times. Afterwards, when the masters quitted the capital, took to husbandry, and went to reside on their estates, the link must necessarily have been more closely drawn. Intercommunion begot more humane feelings in the master, and more attachment in the slave; for the Spartans felt the influence of intimacy, as is proved by their enfranchising the slave companions of their childhood. A certain number of Helots were retained in the city as personal attendants, and these waited at the public tables, and were lent by one person to another.

In the military service of the state, the Helots fought and bled by the side of their masters. The state was, no doubt, reluctant to admit them among the

Hoplitæ, or heavy armed, where the discipline was rigorous, and their weapons would have placed them on a level with their oppressors. But even this was sometimes hazarded, as in the reinforcements forwarded to Gyleppus, at Syracuse, when six hundred Neodomades and picked Helots were complimented with this dangerous distinction. As light troops, however, they almost invariably formed the major part of the Lacedæmonian forces. In other countries, where the subject races were treated more humanely, no fear was entertained at entrusting them with arms. Among the Dardanians, for example, where it was not uncommon for a private individual to possess a thousand slaves, they in time of peace cultivated the land, and in war, filled the ranks of the army.

Plato, Aristotle, Isocrates, Plutarch, and a number of other writers, agree in convicting the Spartans of great barbarity towards their bondmen, differing, however, as to the degree of that barbarity. The following passage occurs in the work of Myron, of Priene, whose testimony, however, is rejected by Müller: "The Helots perform for the Spartans every ignominious service. They are compelled to wear a cap of dog-skin, and a covering of sheep-skin; and are severely beaten every year, without having committed any fault, in order that they might never forget that they are slaves. In addition to this, those amongst them who, either by their stature or their beauty, raise themselves above the ordinary condition of a slave, are condemned to death, and the masters who do not destroy the most manly of them are liable to punishment." Plutarch relates that "the Helots were compelled to intoxicate themselves, and perform indecent dances, as a warning to the Spartan youth." From other authors it appears that it was the constant policy of Sparta to demoralize the Helots. They were commanded to sing obscene songs, and dance indecent jigs, while the Pyrrhic dance, and every warlike lay were forbidden them. It is related, that when the Thebans invaded Laconia and made prisoners a number of Helots, they commanded them to sing some of the songs of Sparta; but the Helots professed their inability, observing that the acquisition of those lays was forbidden them. In short, to adopt the words of Theopompos, they were at all times cruelly and bitterly treated. Critias observes, that, as the freemen of Sparta were of all men the most free, so were the serfs of Sparta of all slaves the most slavish. They were deluded, sometimes, from the protection of sanctuary by perjury, and then assassinated in contempt of oaths and religion. But all this harsh usage was mild, compared with other injuries which the laws of Sparta inflicted on them. We allude to the institution of the Crypteia. Isocrates describes this annual massacre of the Helots, and, with Aristotle, he attributes to the Ephori, magistrates, the direction of this servile war, in which the reins of slaughter were loosed or tightened by their authority. Plutarch says: "According to this ordinance, the Crypteia, the rulers, selecting from among the youths those most distinguished for ability, sent them forth armed with daggers and furnished with the necessary provisions to scour the country, separating and concealing themselves by day, in unfrequented places, but issuing out at night and slaughtering all such of the Helots as they found abroad. Sometimes, indeed, they fell upon them while engaged in the labors of the fields, and then cut off the best and bravest of the race." Flowing from the same policy, and designed to effect the same purpose, were those extensive massacres recorded in history, by one of which more than two thousand of those unhappy men, having been insidiously deluded into the assertion of sentiments conformable to the gallant actions they had performed in the service of the state, were removed in a day. Lulled by the gift of freedom, crowned with garlands, smiled upon, they were conducted to the temples, as if to implicate the very gods in the treachery,—and then they disappeared. Their fate was never revealed.

Every year, on taking office, the magistrates formally declared war against their unarmed and unhappy slaves, "that they might be massacred under pretence of law." It seems reasonable to believe that these oppressions kindled those bloody servile wars which Sparta could not quench without foreign aid. The Spartans were, in fact, during many years, prevented from disputing with the Athenians the supremacy in Greece, by contests with their own vassals. On the occasion of the great earthquake, when nearly every house in Sparta was shaken to the ground, the Helots rejoiced at the calamity, and flocked to the environs of the city from the whole country around, in order to put an end to their tyrants as they were escaping in terror from their tottering habitations.

It is known that the Helots were a constant source of terror to their masters,—that whenever occasion offered, they revolted,—whenever an enemy to the state appeared, they joined him,—that they fled whenever flight was possible,—and were so numerous and so bold, that Sparta was compelled, in her treaties with foreign states, to stipulate "for aid against her own subjects." *

The Spartans appear to have possessed other slaves besides the oppressed Helots, with whom they have often been confounded. These were not viewed with equal dread, since they were brought together from various countries, and had no common bond of union. Many of this class were enfranchised, and rose to the rank of citizens. Another class of persons, commonly ranked among the Laconian slaves, were the Mothaces, whose origin, rank and condition it is difficult to determine. Athenæus observes, that, although not Lacedæmonians, they were *free.* Müller, alluding to this passage, says they are called free in reference to their future, not their past, condition. The words of Philarchos are: "The Mothaces were the brother-like companions of the Lacedæmonians. For every youthful citizen, according to his means, chose one, two, or more of these to be brought up with him; and notwithstanding that they enjoyed not the rank of citizens, they were free, and participated in all the advantages of the national education. Lysander, who defeated the

---

* Muller—Dorians, ii, 43.

Athenians at sea, was one of this class, and was raised for his valor to the rank of citizen." Lycurgus laid much less stress on birth and blood, than on that steadiness and patience of toil, which are the first qualities of a soldier. Whoever from childhood upward gave proof of these, by submitting without a murmur to the rigorous trial he enjoined on the youth of Sparta, was elevated in the end to the rank of a citizen; while they who shrunk from the severity of his discipline, even though they had descended from royal blood, sunk into a state of degradation, or were even confounded with the Helots.

The Thessalians denominated Penestæ, not those who were born in servitude, but persons who were made captives in war. In Crete, the servile caste was divided into many classes: first, those of the cities, who were "bought with gold," as their name implied, and were doubtless barbarians; second, those of the country, who were bound to the estates of the landed gentry; these were the aboriginal tribes reduced to servitude by their foreign conquerors. In condition they resembled the Helots. Thirdly, there existed in every state in Crete, a class of public bondsmen, who cultivated the public lands, upon what conditions is not exactly known. They were sufficiently numerous and powerful to inspire their masters with dread, as is evident by the regulation which excluded them from the gymnasia, and prohibited the use of arms.

In the city of Cydonia during certain festivals of Hermes, the slaves were left masters of the place, into which no free citizen had permission to enter; and if he infringed this regulation, they had the power to chastise him with whips. In other parts of Crete, customs similar to those of the Roman Saturnalia prevailed; for, while the slaves in the Hermæan festival were carousing and taking their ease, their lords, in the guise of domestics, waited upon them at table, and performed in their stead all other menial offices. Something of the same kind took place during the month Gerœstion, at Trœzen, where the citizens feasted their slaves on one particular day of the great annual festival, and played at dice with them. Among the Babylonians we find a similar custom; for, during the Sacæan festival, which lasted five days, the masters waited on their slaves, one of whom, habited in a royal robe, enacted the part of king.

It is stated that the condition and treatment of the Cretan serfs, were better than in any other Doric state; and that the Periœci of Crete never revolted against their masters.

The serfs of the Syracusans were so exceedingly numerous that their numbers became a proverb. They would seem to have dwelt chiefly in the country. In process of time their multitude inspired them with courage; they assaulted and drove out their masters, and retained possession of Syracuse.

Respecting the servile classes in other Grecian states, our information is scanty. The corresponding class among the Arcadians is said to have amounted to three hundred thousand in number. Their treatment was probably more lenient than in some other parts of Greece, as at public festivals we find them sitting at the same table, eating the same food, and drinking from the same cup with their masters.

CHAPTER IV.

SLAVERY IN ROME.

Slavery under the kings and in the early ages of the Republic.—Its spread, and effect on the poorer class of Freemen.—The Licinian law.—Prevalence of the two extremes, immense wealth and abject poverty.—Immense number of Slaves in Sicily.—They revolt. —Eunus, their leader.—Their arms.—Horrible atrocities committed by them.—The insurrection crushed.—Fate of Eunus.—Increase of Slaves in Rome.—Their employment in the arts.—Numbers trained for the Amphitheatre.—The Gladiators rebel.—Spartacus, his history.—Laws passed to restrain the cruelty of masters.—Effects of Christianity on their condition.—Their numbers increased by the invasion of northern hordes. —Sale of prisoners of war into slavery.—Slave-dealers follow the armies.—Foreign Slave trade.—Slave auctions.—The Slave markets.—Value of Slaves at different periods.—Slaves owned by the State, and their condition and occupations.—Private Slaves, their grades and occupations.—Treatment of Slaves, public and private.—Punishment of offenses.—Fugitives and Criminals.—Festival of Saturnus, their privileges.—Their dress.—Their sepulchres.—The Gladiators, their combats.

SLAVES existed at Rome in the earliest times of which we have any record; but they do not appear to have been numerous under the kings and in the earliest ages of the Republic. The different trades and the mechanic arts were chiefly carried on by the clients of the patricians; and the small farms in the country were cultivated for the most part by the labors of the proprietor and of his family. But as the territories of the Roman state were extended, the patricians obtained possession of large estates out of the public domain; since it was a practice of the Romans to deprive a conquered people of a part of their lands. These estates required a larger number of hands for their cultivation than could readily be obtained among the free population, and since the freemen were constantly liable to be called away from their work to serve in the armies, the lands began to be cultivated almost entirely by slave labor. Through war and commerce, slaves could be obtained easily, and at a cheap rate, and their numbers soon became so great, that the poorer class of freemen was thrown almost entirely out of employment. This state of things was one of the chief arguments used by Licinius and the Gracchi for limiting the quantity of public land which a person might possess. In the Licinian Rogations there was a provision that a certain number of freemen should be employed on every estate. This regulation, however, was of little avail, as the lands still continued to be cultivated almost exclusively by slaves. The elder Gracchus, in traveling through Italy, was led to observe the evils which slavery inflicted upon the provinces of his country. The great body of the people were impoverished. Instead of little farms studding the country with their pleasant aspect, and nursing an independent race, he beheld nearly all the lands of Italy monopolized by large proprietors; and the plow was in the hands of slaves. This was one hundred and thirty-four years before the Christian era. The palaces of the wealthy towered in solitary grandeur: the freemen hid themselves in miserable hovels. Deprived of the dignity of proprietors, they were compelled to labor in competition with slaves. Excepting with the immensely rich, and the feeble and decreasing class of independent husbandmen, poverty was extreme. This state of things existed at a time when Rome was considered mistress of the world, and the rulers of Egypt had exalted the Romans above the immortal gods.

In the latest times of the republic, we find that Julius Cæsar attempted a remedy, to some extent, by enacting that of those persons who attended to cattle, a third, at least, should be freemen. In Sicily, which supplied Rome with so great a quantity of corn, the number of agricultural slaves was immense. The oppressions to which they were exposed, drove them twice to rebellion, and their numbers enabled them to defy, for a time, the Roman power. The first of these servile wars began in B. C. 134, and lasted two years; the second commenced thirty years later, and lasted four years. The Sicilians treated their slaves with extraordinary rigor, branding them like cattle, and compelling them to toil incessantly for their masters. The history of the revolt offers numerous points of resemblance to that of Chios, already related; though Eunus, the leader of the Sicilian slaves, cannot be compared with Drimacos, either for character or abilities. Eunus, by visions and pretended prophecies, excited the slaves to insurrection; and his conduct, and that of his followers, when they took possession of the city of Euna, presented a striking contrast to the moderation of the Chian slaves. They pillaged the houses, and, without distinction of age or sex, slaughtered the inhabitants, plucking infants from their mother's breasts, and dashing them on the ground. The number of the insurgents at one time amounted to 60,000 men, who, armed with axes, slings, stakes, and cooking spits, defeated several armies. Pursuing them, however, without relaxation, the state at length prevailed, utterly crushed the insurrection, and carried Eunus a prisoner to Rome, where, according to Plutarch, he was devoured by vermin.

Long after it had become the custom to employ large gangs of slaves in the cultivation of the land, the number of those who served as personal attendants was very small. Persons in good circumstances seem usually to have had only one to wait upon them, who was generally called by the name of the master. But during the latter times of the republic and under the empire, the number of domestic slaves greatly increased, and in every family of importance there were separate slaves to attend to all the duties of domestic life. It was considered a reproach to a man not to keep a considerable number of slaves. The first question asked respecting a person's fortune, was an inquiry as to the number of his slaves. Horace seems to speak of ten slaves as the lowest number which a person in tolerable circumstances ought to keep. The immense number of prisoners taken in the constant wars of the republic, and the increase of wealth and luxury, augmented the number of slaves to a prodigious extent. The statement of Athenæus that very many Romans possessed 10,000 and 20,000 slaves, and even more, is probably an exaggeration; but a freedman under Augustus, who had lost much property in the civil wars, left at his death as many as 4,116.* Two hundred was no uncommon number for a person to keep.†

The mechanic arts, which were formerly in the hands of the clients, were now entirely exercised by slaves : ‡ a natural growth of things, for where slaves perform certain labors, such labor will be thought degrading to freemen. The games of the amphitheatre required an immense number of slaves trained for the purpose. Like the slaves in Sicily, the Gladiators of Italy rose in rebellion against their oppressors,‖ and under the able generalship of Spartacus, defeated a Roman consular army, and were not subdued until after a struggle of two years, and when 60,000 of them had fallen in battle.

Spartacus was a Thracian by birth, and had been compelled, like other barbarians, to serve in the Roman army, from which he had deserted, and, at the head of a body of chosen companions, had carried on a partisan war against the conquerors. Being made prisoner, Spartacus was sold as a slave; and his strength and size caused him to be reserved as a gladiator. He was placed in a gladiatorial school at Capua, with two hundred other Thracian, German and Gaulish slaves, among whom a conspiracy was formed for effecting their escape. Their plot was discovered; but a small body, under Spartacus, broke out, and, having procured arms, and gained some advantages over the Roman forces sent against them, they were soon joined by the slaves and peasantry of the neighborhood, and their numbers amounted to 10,000 men. By the courage and skill of Spartacus, several considerable battles were gained; but his authority was insufficient to restrain the ferocity and licentiousness of his followers, and the cities of the south of Italy were pillaged with the most revolting atrocities. In a few months, Spartacus found himself at the head of 60,000 men; and the consuls were now sent, with two legions, against the revolted slaves. Mutual jealousies divided the leaders of the latter, and the Gauls and Germans formed a separate body under their own leaders, while the Thracians and Lucanians adhered to Spartacus. The former were defeated; but Spartacus skillfully covered their retreat, and successively defeated the two consuls. Flushed with success, his followers demanded to be led against Rome; and the city trembled before the servile forces. In this crisis, Licinius Crassus, who was afterwards a triumvir, was placed at the head of the army. His lieutenant, Mummius, whom he dispatched with two legions to watch the motions of the enemy, was defeated by a superior force, and slain. Crassus, after having made an example of the defeated legions, by executing every tenth man, surrounded Spartacus, near Rhegium, with a ditch six miles in length. Spartacus broke through the enemy by night; but Crassus, who did not doubt that he would march upon Rome, pursued him, and defeated a considerable part of his forces, who had abandoned their general from disaffection. Spartacus now retreated; but his followers compelled him to lead them against the

---

* Pliny.   † Horace.   ‡ Cicero.   ‖ B. C. 73 years.

Romans. His soldiers fought with a courage deserving success; but they were overcome, after an obstinate conflict, and Spartacus himself fell fighting on his knees, upon a heap of his slain enemies. According to the Roman statements, 60,000 rebels fell in this battle, 6000 were made prisoners, and crucified on the Appian way. A considerable number escaped, and continued the war, but were finally destroyed by Pompey.

Under the empire various enactments were made to restrain the cruelty of masters towards their slaves; but the spread of Christianity tended most to ameliorate their condition, though the possession of them was for a long time by no means condemned as contrary to Christian justice. The Christian writers, however, inculcate the duty of acting towards them as we would be acted by; but down to the age of Theodosius, wealthy persons still continued to keep as many as two or three thousand.* Justinian did much to promote the ultimate extinction of slavery; but the number of slaves was again increased by the invasion of the northern barbarians, who not only brought with them their own slaves, who were chiefly Sclavonians, but also reduced many of the inhabitants of the conquered provinces to the condition of slaves. But all the various classes of slaves became merged in the course of time into the serfs of the Middle Ages.

The sources from which the Romans obtained slaves, have already been noticed. Under the republic one of the chief supplies was prisoners taken in war, who were sold by the quæstors† with a crown on their heads, and usually on the spot where they were taken, as the care of a large number of captives was inconvenient. Consequently, slave-dealers generally accompanied an army, and frequently after a great battle had been gained, many thousands were sold at once, when the slave-dealers obtained them for a mere trifle. In the camp of Lucullus on one occasion, slaves were sold for a sum equal to about eighty cents of our money.

The slave trade was also carried on to a great extent, and after the fall of Corinth and Carthage, Delos was the chief mart for this traffic. When the Cilician pirates had possession of the Mediterranean, as many as 10,000 slaves are said to have been imported and sold there in one day.‡ A large number came from Thrace and the countries in the north of Europe, but the chief supply was from Africa, and more especially Asia, whence we read of Phyrgians, Lycians, Cappadocians, &c., as slaves.

The trade of slave-dealers was considered disreputable, and expressly distinguished from that of merchants; but it was very lucrative, and great fortunes were made by it. The slave-dealer Thoranius, who lived in the time of Augustus, was a well-known character.

Slaves were usually sold by auction at Rome; and, as we have observed of the Greek auctions, they were conducted very much like those of our southern cities. They were placed on a raised stone, or table, so that every one might

---

* Chrysost. vol. vii, 633. † Plaut. ‡ Strab. xiv, 668.

4

see and handle them, even if they did not wish to purchase them. Purchasers took care to have them stripped, for slave-dealers had recourse to as many tricks to conceal personal defects, as a horse-jockey of modern times. Sometimes purchasers called in the advice of medical men. Slaves of great beauty and rarity were not exhibited to public gaze in the slave market, but were shown to purchasers in private. Newly imported slaves had their feet whitened with paint;* and those that came from the East had their ears bored,† which was a sign of slavery among many eastern nations.

The slave market, like all other markets, was under the jurisdiction of the aediles, who made many regulations, by edicts, respecting the sale of slaves. The character of the slave to be sold, was set forth on a scroll, hanging around his neck, which was a warranty to the purchaser; the vendor was bound to announce fairly all his defects, and if he gave a false account, had to take him back, any time within six months after he was sold, or make up to the purchaser what the latter had lost by obtaining an inferior article to what had been warranted. The vendor might, however, use general terms of commendation without being obliged to make them good. The chief points which he had to warrant was the health of the slave, especially freedom from epilepsy, and that he had not a tendency to thieving, running away, or committing suicide. The nation of a slave was considered important, and had to be set forth by the vendor. Slaves sold without any warranty, wore at the time a cap upon their head. Slaves newly imported were generally preferred for common work; those who had served long were considered artful.

The value of slaves depended of course upon their qualifications; but under the empire, the increase of luxury, and the corruption of morals, led purchasers to pay immense sums for beautiful slaves, or such as ministered to the caprice or whim of the purchaser. Martial speaks of beautiful boys who sold for as much as 100,000 or 200,000 sesterces each; that is, from 4,000 to 8,000 dollars. A *morio*, or fool, sometimes sold for 20,000 sesterces. Slaves who possessed a knowledge of any art which might bring in profit to their owners, also sold for a large sum. Thus scribes and doctors frequently sold high, and also slaves fitted for the stage, as we see from Cicero's speech in behalf of Roscius. A class of female slaves, who brought in gain to their masters, were also dear. The price of a good ordinary slave, in the time of Horace, was about equal to ninety dollars of our money. In the fourth century, a slave, capable of bearing arms, was valued at 25 aurei, (equal in weight to $125 in gold.) In the time of Justinian, the legal valuation of slaves was as follows: common slaves, both male and female, were valued at 20 solidi, (about $100,) under ten years of age, half that sum; if they were artificers, they were worth fifty per cent. more; if notarii, (short hand writers), they were worth 50 solidi; if medical men or midwives, 60. Female slaves, unless possessed of personal attractions, were generally cheaper than males. Under the republic, and in

---

* Pliny.   † Juvenal.

the early days of the empire, it was found cheaper to purchase than to breed slaves.

Slaves were divided into many various classes : the first division was into public and private. The former belonged to the state and public bodies, and their condition was preferable to that of the common slaves. They were less liable to be sold, and under less control than ordinary slaves. They also possessed the capacity to make a valid will, to the extent of one-half of their property, which shows they were regarded in a different light from other slaves. Scipio, therefore, on the taking of Nova Carthage, promised 2000 artisans, who were taken prisoners, and were consequently liable to be sold as common slaves, that they should become public slaves of the Roman people, with the hope of speedy manumission, if they assisted him in the war.* Public slaves were employed to take care of the public buildings, and to attend upon magistrates and priests. Thus the ædiles and quæstors had great numbers of public slaves at their command, as had also the triumviri nocturni, who employed them to extinguish fires by night. They were also employed as lictors, jailors, executioners, watermen, &c.

A body of slaves belonging to one person was called *familia*. Private slaves were divided into urban and rustic ; but the name of urban was given to those slaves who served in the villa, or country residence, as well as in the town house. When there was a large number of slaves in one house, they were arranged in certain classes, which held a higher or lower rank according to the nature of their occupation.

The ordinarii seem to have been those slaves who had the superintendence of house-keeping. They were always chosen from those who had the confidence of their masters, and they generally had certain slaves under them. They were the stewards and butlers. The vulgares included the great body of slaves in a house who had to attend to any particular duty, and to minister to the domestic wants of their master. These were the bakers, cooks, confectioners, porters, bed-chamber slaves and litter bearers. The literati, or literary slaves, were used for various purposes by their masters, either as readers, copyists or amanuenses.

The treatment of slaves varied of course according to the dispositions of their masters ; but they appear upon the whole to have been treated with greater severity and cruelty than among the Athenians. Originally, the master could use the slave as he pleased : under the republic, the law does not seem to have protected the person or life of the slave at all ; but the cruelty of masters was to some extent restrained under the empire. The general treatment of slaves, however, was probably little affected by legislative enactments. In early times, when the number of slaves was small, they were treated with more indulgence, and more like members of the family. They

---

* Livy, xxvi, 27.

joined their masters in offering up thanksgivings and prayer to the gods,[*] and partook of their meals in common with their masters,[†] though not at the same table with them, but upon benches placed at the foot of the couch. But with the increase of numbers, and of luxury among the masters, the ancient simplicity of manners was changed. A certain quantity of food was allowed them, which was granted either monthly or daily. Their chief food was the grain called *far*, of which the allowance was about one quart per day. They also had an allowance of salt and oil. Meat seems to have been hardly ever given them.

Under the republic, they were not allowed to serve in the army; though after the battle of Canæ, when the state was in such imminent danger, 8000 slaves were purchased by the state for the army, and subsequently manumitted on account of their bravery.[‡]

The offenses of slaves were punished with severity, and frequently with the utmost barbarity. One of the mildest punishments was that of degrading them in rank, and obliging them to work in fetters. They were frequently beaten with sticks or scourged with the whip; but these were such every-day punishments that many slaves ceased to care for them.

Runaway slaves (*fugitivi*) and thieves were branded on the forehead with a mark. Slaves were also punished by being hung up by their hands, with weights attached to their feet, or by being sent to the ergastulum, or private prison, to work in chains. The toilet of the Roman ladies was a dreadful ordeal to the female slaves, who were often barbarously punished by their mistresses for the slightest mistake in the arrangement of the hair or a part of the dress. Masters might work their slaves as many hours in the day as they pleased, but they usually allowed them holidays on the public festivals. At the festival of Saturnus, in particular, special indulgences were granted to all slaves. This festival fell towards the end of December, at the season when the agricultural labors of the year were fully completed. It was celebrated in ancient times by the rustic population as a sort of joyous harvest home, and in every age was viewed by all classes of the community as a period of absolute relaxation and unrestrained merriment. During its continuance no public business could be transacted; the law courts were closed; the schools kept holiday; to commence a war was impious; to punish a malefactor involved pollution. Special indulgences were granted to the slaves of each domestic establishment; they were relieved from all ordinary toils, were permitted to wear the badge of freedom, were granted full freedom of speech, partook of a banquet attired in the clothes of their masters, who waited upon them at table.[||]

There was no distinctive dress for slaves. It was once proposed in the Senate to give slaves a distinctive costume, but it was rejected, as it was considered

---

[*] Horace.   [†] Plutarch.   [‡] Livy, xxii, 57; xxiv 14, 16.
[||] Macrob.: Dion Cass.: Horace: Martial.

dangerous to show them their numbers. Male slaves were not allowed to wear the toga or bulla, nor females the stola, but otherwise they were dressed nearly in the same way as poor people, in clothes of a dark color and slippers.

Gibbon estimates the population of the Roman empire in the time of Claudius at one hundred and twenty millions : sixty millions of freemen and sixty millions of slaves. The proportion of slaves was much larger in Italy than in the provinces, according to Milman. Robertson states that there were twice as many slaves as free citizens, and Blair estimates three slaves to one freeman, between the conquest of Greece, B. C. 146, and the reign of Alexander Severus, A. D. 222, 235. Milman is inclined to "adopt the more cautious suggestions of Gibbon."

As the Romans regarded slavery as an institution of society, death was considered to put an end to the distinction between slaves and freemen. Slaves were sometimes even buried with their masters, and we find funeral inscriptions addressed to the Dii Manes of slaves. In 1726 the burial vaults of the slaves belonging to Augustus and Livia were discovered near the Appian Way, where numerous inscriptions were found, which give us considerable information respecting the different classes of slaves and their various occupations. Other sepulchres of the same time have been discovered in the neighborhood of Rome.

We have already referred to the immense number of slaves trained for gladiators. A more particular description of this class will be interesting to the general reader, and will serve to elucidate the manners, customs and morals of their masters. The gladiators, however, were not all slaves. The term is applied to the combatants who fought in the amphitheatre and other places, for the amusement of the Roman people. They are said to have been first exhibited by the Etruscans, and to have had their origin in the custom of killing slaves and captives at the funeral pyres of the deceased. A show of gladiators was called *munus*, and the person who exhibited it, *editor*, or *munerator*, who was honored during the day of exhibition, if a private person, with the insignia of a magistrate.

Gladiators were first exhibited at Rome in B. C. 264, in the Forum Boarium, by Marcus and Decimus Brutus, at the funeral of their father. They were at first confined to public funerals, but afterwards fought at the funerals of most persons of consequence, and even at those of women. Private persons sometimes left a sum of money in their will to pay the expenses of such an exhibition at their funerals. Combats of gladiators were also exhibited at entertainments, and especially at public festivals by the ædiles and other magistrates, who sometimes exhibited immense numbers with a view of pleasing the people. Under the empire the passions of the Romans for this amusement rose to its greatest height, and the number of gladiators who fought on some occasions appears almost incredible. After Trajan's triumph over the Dacians, there were more than 10,000 exhibited.*

---

* Dion Cass. lxviii,15.

Gladiators consisted either of captives, slaves and condemned malefactors, or of free born citizens who fought voluntarily. Of those who were condemned, some were said to be condemned *ad gladium*, in which case they were obliged to be killed within a year, and others *ad ludum*, who might obtain their discharge at the end of three years. Freemen, who became gladiators for hire, were called *auctorati*. Even under the republic, free born citizens fought as gladiators, but they appear to have belonged only to the lower orders. Under the empire, however, both equites and senators fought in the arena; and even women, which was at length forbidden in the time of Severus. Gladiators were kept in schools, where they were trained by persons called *lanistæ*. They sometimes were the property of the lanistæ, who let them out to persons who wished to exhibit a show of gladiators; but at other times belonged to citizens, who kept them for the purpose of exhibition, and engaged lanistæ to instruct them. The superintendence of the schools which belonged to the emperors, was intrusted to a person of high rank, called curator or procurator. The gladiators fought in these schools with wooden swords. Great attention was paid to their diet, in order to increase the strength of their bodies. They were fed with nourishing food; and a great number were trained at Ravenna on account of the salubrity of the place.

The person who was to exhibit a show of gladiators, published bills containing the numbers and sometimes the names of those who were to fight. When the day came, they were led along the arena in procession, and matched by pairs; and their swords were examined by the exhibitor to see if they were sufficiently sharp. At first there was a kind of sham battle, called *prelusio*, in which they fought with wooden swords; and afterwards, at the sound of the trumpet, the real battle began. When a gladiator was wounded, the people called out *habet*, or *hoc habet;* and the one who was vanquished, lowered his arms in token of submission. His fate, however, depended upon the audience, who pressed down their thumbs if they wished him to be saved, and turned them up if they wished him to be killed, and ordered him to receive the fatal sword, which they usually did with the greatest firmness. If the life of a vanquished gladiator was spared, he obtained his discharge for that day. In some exhibitions, the lives of the conquered were never spared; but this kind was forbidden by Augustus.

Palms were given to the victorious; money was also sometimes given. Old gladiators, and sometimes those who had fought only for a short time, were discharged from the service by the editor at the request of the people, who presented each of them with a wooden sword. If a person was free before he entered the school, he became free again on his discharge; if he was a slave, he became a slave again. A man, however, who had voluntarily become a gladiator, was always considered to have disgraced himself; and consequently it appears he could not attain the equestrian ranks, if he afterwards acquired sufficient property to entitle him to it.

Shows of gladiators were abolished by Constantine, but appear, notwithstanding, to have been generally exhibited until the time of Honorius, by whom they were finally suppressed.

Gladiators were divided into different classes, according to their arms and different mode of fighting, and other circumstances. One class wore helmets without any aperture for the eyes, so that they were obliged to fight blindfold, and thus excited the mirth of the spectators; another class fought with two swords; another on horseback; another from chariots, like the Gauls and Britons. The laqueators used a noose to catch their adversaries. The meridiani fought in the middle of the day, after the combats with the wild beasts in the morning. The retiarii carried only a three-pointed lance, and a net, which they endeavored to throw over their adversaries, and then attack them with the trident while they were entangled. If he missed his aim in throwing the net, he fled and endeavored to prepare his net for another cast, while his adversary followed him round the arena in order to kill him before he could make a second attempt. The Thraces were armed with a round shield, and a short sword or dagger. When a gladiator was killed, the attendants, appointed for the purpose, dragged the body out of the arena with iron hooks.

CHAPTER V.

SLAVERY IN ROME.—CONTINUED.

Abstract of the laws in regard to Slavery.—Power of Life and Death.—Cruelty of Masters.—Laws to protect the Slave.—Constitution of Antoninus: of Claudius.—Husband and Wife could not be separated; nor parents and children.—Slave could not contract marriage, nor own property.—His peculium, or private property, held only by usage.—Regulations in respect to it.—Master liable for damages for wrongful acts of his Slave.—The murderer of a slave, liable for a capital offense, or for damages.—Fugitive Slaves, not lawfully harbored; to conceal them, theft.—Master entitled to pursue them.—Duties of the authorities.—Slave hunters.—Laws defining the condition of children born of Slaves.—Laws to reduce free persons to Slavery.—How the state of Slavery might be terminated; by manumission; by special enactments; what Slaves entitled to freedom.—Practice of giving liberty to Slaves in times of civil tumult and revolution.—Effects of Slavery under the Republic, and under the Empire.

WE now proceed to give an abstract of the laws in regard to Slavery. According to the strict principles of the Roman law, it was a consequence of the relation of master and slave, that the master could treat the slave as he pleased; he could sell him, punish him, or put him to death. Positive morality, however, and the social intercourse that must always subsist between a master and the slaves who are immediately about him, ameliorated the condition of slavery. Still, we read of acts of great cruelty committed by masters in the later republican and earlier imperial periods, and the Lex Petronia was enacted in order to protect the slave. The original power of life and death over a slave, was limited by a constitution of Antoninus, which enacted, that, if a man put his slave to death without sufficient reason, he was liable to the same penalty as if he had killed another man's slave. The same constitution also prohibited the cruel treatment of slaves by their masters, by enacting that, if the cruelty of the master was intolerable, he might be compelled to sell the slave; and the slave was empowered to make his complaint to the proper authority. A constitution of Claudius enacted, that if a man exposed his slaves, who were infirm, they should become free; and the constitution also declared, that if they were put to death, the act should be murder. It was also enacted, that in sales or division of property, slaves, such as husband and wife, parents and children, brothers and sisters, should not be separated.*

A slave could not contract a marriage, and no legal relation between a father and his children was recognized. Still nearness of blood was considered an impediment to marriage after manumission: thus, a manumitted slave could not marry his manumitted sister.

A slave could have no property. He was not incapable of acquiring property, but his acquisitions belonged to his master; which Gaius considers to be a rule of the Jus Gentium, that is, "the law which natural reason has established among all mankind." Slaves were not only employed in the usual domestic offices and in the labors of the field, but also as factors or agents for their masters in the management of business, and as mechanics, artisans, and in every branch of industry. It may be easily conceived, that under these circumstances, especially as they were often intrusted with property to a large amount, there must have arisen a practice of allowing the slave to consider a part of his gains as his own. This was his "peculium;" according to strict law, this was the property of the master, but according to usage, it was considered the property of the slave. Sometimes it was agreed between master and slave, that the slave should purchase his freedom with his peculium, when it amounted to a certain sum. If a slave was manumitted by the owner in his life-time, the peculium was considered to be given with the liberty, unless it was expressly retained. Transactions of borrowing and lending could take place between the master and slave with respect to the peculium, though no right of action arose on either side out of such dealings. In case of the claim of creditors on the slave's peculium, the debt of the slave to the master was first taken into the account, and deducted from the peculium. The master was only bound by the acts and dealings of the slave, when the slave was employed as his agent or instrument.

It is a consequence of the relation of slave and master, that the master acquired no rights against the slave in consequence of his wrongful acts. Other persons might obtain rights against a slave in consequence of his crimes, but their right could not be prosecuted by action until the slave was manumit-

---

* Cod., 3, title 38, s. 11.

ted. They had, however, a right of action against the slave's master for damages, and if the master would not pay the damages, he must give up the slave. The slave was protected against injury from other persons. If the slave was killed, the master might either prosecute the killer for a capital offense, or sue for damages. The master had an action against those who corrupted his slave, and led him into bad practices, and could recover twice the amount of the estimated damage. The female slaves were protected by the master's right of action.

A fugitive slave could not lawfully be received or harbored; to conceal him was theft. The master was entitled to pursue him wherever he pleased; and it was the duty of all authorities to give him aid in recovering his slave. It was the object of various laws to check the running away of slaves in every way, and, accordingly, a runaway slave could not legally be an object of sale. A class of persons made it a business to capture fugitive slaves. The rights of the master over the slave were in no way affected by his running away.

A person was born a slave whose mother was a slave at the time of his birth. At a later period the rule of law was established, that though a woman at the time of the birth might be a slave, still her child was free, if the mother had been free at any time within the nine months preceding the birth. In the cases of children who were the offspring of a free parent and a slave, positive law provided whether the children should be free or slaves.

A person became a slave by capture in war, (also jure gentium.) Captives were sold, as belonging to the public treasury, or distributed among the soldiers by lot. A free person might become a slave in various ways, in consequence of positive law, (jure civili). This was the case with those who refused or neglected to be registered in the census, and those who evaded military service. In certain cases a man became a slave, if he allowed himself to be sold as such in order to defraud the purchaser.

Under the empire the rule was established, that persons condemned to death, to the mines, and to fight with wild beasts, lost their freedom, and their property was confiscated. But this was not the earlier law. A freedman who misconducted himself towards his patron, was reduced to his former state of slavery.

The state of slavery was terminated by manumission. It was also terminated by various positive enactments, either by way of reward to the slave or punishment to the master. Freedom was given to slaves who discovered the perpetrators of certain crimes. After the establishment of Christianity, liberty might be acquired, subject to certain limitations, by becoming a monk or a spiritual person; but if the person left his monastery for a secular life, or rambled about in the towns or the country, he might be reduced to his former servile condition.

In times of revolution under the republic, it was not unusual to proclaim the liberty of slaves to induce them to join in revolt; but these were irregular proceedings, and neither justifiable nor examples for imitation. Lord Dunmore, the last British governor of Virginia, at the commencement of the American Revolution, followed this example.

We have now exhibited to the reader the principal features of slavery in Rome. We have seen the origin, numbers and condition of the slaves, their treatment, and the laws that governed them. We have seen the general prevalence of the institution, but not its effects upon the Romans themselves, and upon many of the prominent events of their history. To such as may feel interested in this branch of the subject, we present the views of an able writer upon the Influence of Slavery on the Revolutions in Rome. We have already referred to the condition of the poorer class of freemen in the time of the elder Gracchus. The writer proceeds:

'Gracchus found the inhabitants of the Roman State divided into three classes. The few wealthy nobles; the many indigent citizens; the still more numerous class of slaves. Reasoning upon the subject, he perceived that it was slavery which crowded the poor freeman out of employment, and barred the way to his advancement. It was the aim of Gracchus, not so much to mend the condition of the slaves, as to lift the brood of idle persons into dignity; to give them land, to put the plow into their hands, to make them industrious and useful, and so to repose on them the liberties of the State. He resolved to increase the number of landed proprietors; to create a Roman yeomanry. This was the basis of his radical reform; the means were at hand. The lands of Italy were of two classes; private estates and the public domain. With private estates he refused to interfere. The public domains, even though they had been usurped by the patricians, were to be reclaimed as public property, and to be appropriated to the use of the people, under restrictions which should prevent their future concentration in the hands of the few. To effect this object required no new order; the proper decree was already engraved among the tablets of the Roman laws. It was necessary only to revive the law of Licinius, which had slumbered for two centuries unrepealed.

In a republic, he that will execute great designs, must act with an organized party. Gracchus took counsel with the purest men of Rome; with Appius Claudius, his father in-law, a patrician of the purest blood; with the great lawyer, Mutius Scævola, a man of consular dignity, and with Crassus, the leader of the priesthood; men of the best learning and character, of unimpeachable patriotism, and friends to the new reform. But his supporters at the polls could be none other than the common people, composed of the impoverished citizens, and the very few husbandmen who had still saved some scanty acres from the grasp of the aristocracy.

The people rallied to the support of their champion; and Gracchus, being elected their tribune, was able to bring forward his Agrarian Law. This law, relating only to the public domain, was distinguished by mitigating clauses. To each of those who had occupied the land without a right, it generously left five hundred acres; to each of their minor children, two hundred and fifty more; and it also promised to make from the public treasury further remuneration for improvements. To every needy citizen it probably allotted not more than ten acres. Thus it was designed to create in Italy a yeomanry; instead of planters and slaves, to substitute free laborers; to plant liberty firmly in the land; to perpetuate the Roman Commonwealth, by identifying its principles with the culture of the soil. No pursuit is more worthy of freemen than agriculture. Gracchus claimed it for the free.

Philanthropy, when it contemplates a slave-holding country, may have its first sympathies excited for the slaves; but it is narrow benevolence which stops there. The indigent freeman is in a worse condition. The slave has his task, and also his home and his bread. He is the member of a wealthy family. The indigent freeman has neither labor, nor house, nor food; and, divided by a broad gulf from the upper class, he has neither hope nor ambition. The poor freeman claims sympathy; he is so abject, that often even the slave despises him. The slave-holder is the competitor of the free laborer, and by the lease of slaves, takes the bread from his mouth. The wealthy Crassus, the richest man in Rome, was the competitor of the poorest free carpenter. The Roman patricians took away the business of the sandal-maker. The existence of slavery made the opulent owners of bondmen the rivals of the poor; greedy after the profits of their labor, and monopolizing those profits through their slaves.

The laws of Gracchus cut the patricians with a double edge. Their fortunes consisted in land and slaves; it questioned their titles to the public land, and tended to force emancipation by making their slaves a burden. In taking away the soil, it took away the power that kept their live machinery in motion.

The moment was a real crisis in the affairs of Rome; such a crisis as hardly occurs to a nation in the progress of many centuries. Men are in the habit of proscribing Julius Cæsar as the destroyer of the Commonwealth. The civil wars, the revolutions of Cæsar, the miserable vicissitudes of the Roman emperors, the avarice of the nobles and the rabble, the crimes of the forum and the palace,—all have their germ in the ill success of the reform of Gracchus.

We pass over the proofs of moderation which the man of the people exhibited, by appearing in the Senate, where he had hoped to obtain from the justice of the patricians some reasonable compromise. The attempt of the aristocracy to check all procedures in the assembly of the people, by instigating another tribune to interpose his veto, was defeated by the prompt decision of the people to depose the faithless representative; and the final success of Gracchus seemed established by the unanimous decision of the commons in favor of his decree. But such delays had been created by his opponents, that the year of his tribuneship was nearly passed; his re-election was needed in order to carry his decree into effect. But the evil in Rome was already too deep to be removed. The election day for tribunes was in mid-summer; the few husbandmen, the only shadow of a Roman yeomanry, were busy in the field, gathering their crops, and failed to come to the support of their champion. He was left to rest his defense on the rabble of the city; and though early in the morning great crowds of people gathered together; and though, as Gracchus appeared in the forum, a shout of joy rent the skies, and was redoubled as he ascended the steps of the Capitol, yet when the aristocracy, determined at every hazard to prevent his election, came with the whole weight of their adherents in a mass, the timid flock, yielding to the sentiment of awe rather than of cowardice, fled like sheep before wolves, and left their defender, the incomparable Gracchus, to be beaten to death by the clubs of senators. Three hundred of his more faithful friends were left lifeless in the market-place. In the fury of triumphant passion, the corpse of the tribune was dragged through the streets, and thrown into the Tiber.

The deluded aristocracy raised the full chorus of victory and joy. They believed that the Senate had routed the democracy, when it was but the avenging spirit of slavery, that struck the first deadly wound into the bosom of Rome.

The murder of Gracchus proved the weakness of the senate; they could defeat the people only by violence. But the blood of their victim, like the blood of other martyrs, cemented his party. It was impossible to carry the Agrarian Law into execution; it was equally impossible to effect its repeal.

Gracchus had interceded for the unhappy indigent freeman, whose independence was crushed by the institution of slavery. The slaves themselves were equally sensible of their wrongs; and in the island of Sicily they resolved on an insurrection. Differing in complexion, in language, in habits, the hope of liberty amalgamated the heterogeneous mass. Eunus, their wise leader, in the spirit of the East, employed the power of superstition to rally the degraded serfs to his banner, and, like Mahomet, pretended a revelation from heaven. Sicily had been divided into a few great plantations; and now the voice of a leader, joining the fanaticism of religion to the enthusiasm for freedom, with the hope of liberty awakened the slaves, not in Sicily only, but in Italy, to the use of arms. What need of dwelling on the horrors of a servile war? Cruel overseers were stabbed with pitchforks; the defenseless were cut to pieces by scythes; tribunals, hitherto unheard of, were established, where each family of slaves might arraign its master, and, counting up his ferocities, adjudge punishment for every remembered wrong. Well may the Roman historian blush as he relates the disgraceful tale. Quis aequo animo ferat in principe gentium populo bella servorum? The Romans had fought their allies, yet had fought with freemen; let the queen of nations blush, for she must now contend with victorious slaves. Thrice, nay, four times, were the Roman armies defeated; the insurrection spread into Italy; four times were even the camps of Roman prætors stormed and taken; Roman soldiers became the captives of their bondmen. The army of the slaves increased to 200,000. It is said, that in this war a million of lives were lost; the statement is exaggerated; but Sicily suffered more from the devastations of the servile, than of the Carthaginian war. Twice were Roman consuls unsuccessful. At length, after years of defeat, the benefits of discipline gave success to the Roman forces. The last garrison of the last citadel of the slaves disdained to surrender, and could no longer resist; they escaped the ignominy of captivity by one universal suicide. The conqueror of slaves, a new thing in Rome, returned to enjoy the honors of an ovation.

The object of Tiberius Gracchus, continued by his eloquent and equally unhappy brother, who moreover was the enlightened and energetic advocate of a system of internal improvement in Italy, aimed at ameliorating the condition of the indigent freemen. The great servile insurrection was designed to effect the emancipation of slaves; and both were unsuccessful. But God is just and his laws are invincible. Slavery next made its attack directly on the patricians, and following the order of Providence in the government of the moral world, began with silent but sure influence to corrupt the virtue of families, and even to destroy domestic life. It is a well ascertained fact, that slavery diminishes the frequency of marriages in the class of masters. In a state where emancipation is forbidden, the slave population will perpetually gain upon the numbers of the free. We will not stop to develop the three or four leading causes of this result, pride and the habits of luxury, the facilities of licentious indulgence, the circumscribed limits of productive industry; some of which causes operate exclusively, and all of them principally, on the free. The position is certain and is universal; no where was the principle more amply exemplified than in Rome. The rich slaveholders preferred luxury and indulgence to marriage; and celibacy became so general, that the aristocracy was obliged by law to favor the institution, which, in a society where all are free, constitutes the solace of labor and the ornament of life. A Roman censor could, in a public address to the people, stigmatize matrimony as a troublesome companionship, and recommend it only as a patriotic sacrifice of private pleasure to public duty. The depopulation of the upper class was so considerable, that the waste required to be supplied by emancipation; and repeatedly there have been periods, when the majority of the Romans had once been bondmen. Emancipation was essential to the preservation of a class of freemen, who might serve as a balance to the slave population. It was this extensive celibacy and the consequent want of succession, that gave a peculiar character to the Roman laws relating to adoption.

The continued and increasing deleterious effects of slavery on Roman institutions, may be traced through the changes in the character of that majority of the citizens, whom it left without the opportunity or the fruits of industry. Even in the time of the younger Gracchus, they retained dignity enough to hope for an amelioration of their condition by the action of laws, and the exercise of their own franchises. . Failing in this end through the firmness of the nobles, the free middling class was entirely destroyed; society soon became divided into the very rich and the very poor; and slaves, who performed all the labor, occupied the intermediate position between the two classes.

The first step in the progress of degradation constituted the citizens, by their own vote, a class of paupers. They called on the state to feed them from the public granaries. But mark the difference between the pauper system of England, or America, and that of Rome. We cheerfully sustain in decent competence the aged, the widow, the cripple, the sick and the orphan; Rome supplied the great body of her citizens. England, who also feeds a large proportion of her laboring class, entrusts to her paupers no elective franchises. Rome fed with eleemosynary corn the majority of her citizens, who retained, even in their condition of paupers, the privileges of electing the government, and the right of supreme, ultimate legislation. Thus besides the select wealthy idlers, here was a new class of idlers, a multitudinous aristocracy, having no estate but their citizenship, no inheritance but their right of suffrage. Both were a burden upon the industry of the slaves; the senate directly from the revenues of their plantations, the commons indirectly, from the coffers of the Commonwealth. It was a burden greater than the fruits of slave industry could bear; the deficiency was supplied by the plunder of foreign countries. The Romans, as a nation, became an accomplished horde of robbers.

This first step was ominous enough; the second was still more alarming. A demagogue appeared, and gaining office, and the conduct of a war, organized these pauper electors into a regular army. The demagogue was Marius; the movement was a revolution. Hitherto the senate had exercised an exclusive control over the brute force of the Commonwealth; the mob was now armed and enrolled, and led by an accomplished chieftain. Both parties being thus possessed of great physical force, the civil wars between the wealthy slaveholders and the impoverished freemen, the select and the multitudinous aristocracy of Rome, could not but ensue. Marius and Sylla were the respective leaders; the streets of Rome and the fields of Italy became the scenes of massacre; and the oppressed bondmen had the satisfaction of beholding the jarring parties, in the nation which had enslaved them, shed each other's blood as freely as water.

This was not all. The slaves had their triumph. Sylla selected ten thousand from their number, and to gain influence for himself at the polls, conferred on them freedom, and the elective franchise.

Of the two great leaders of the opposite factions, it has been asserted that Sylla had a distinct purpose, and that Marius never had. The remark is true, and the reason is obvious. Sylla was the organ of the aristocracy; to the party which already possessed all the wealth, he desired to secure all the political power. This was a definite object, and in one sense was attainable. Having effected a revolution, and having taken vengeance on the enemies of the senate, he retired from office. He could not have retained perpetual authority; the forms of the ancient republic were then too vigorous, and the party on which he rested for support, would not have tolerated the usurpation. He established the supremacy of the senate, and retired into private life. Marius, as the leader of the people, was met by insuperable difficulties. The existence of a slave population rendered it impossible to elevate the character of his indigent constituents; nor were they possessed of sufficient energy to grasp political power with tenacity. He could therefore only embody them among his soldiers, and leave the issue to Providence. His partisans suffered from evils, which it required centuries to ripen and to heal; Marius could have no plan.

Thus the institution of slavery had been the ultimate cause of two political revolutions. The indigence to which it reduced the commons, had led the Gracchi to appear as the advocates of reform, and had encouraged Marius to become their military leader. In the murder of the former, the senate had displayed their success in exciting mobs; and in resistance to the latter, they had roused up a defender of their usurpations. The slaves, also, who had found in Eunus an insurgent leader, were now near obtaining a liberator. The aristocracy was satisfied with its triumphs; the impoverished majority, now accustomed to their abjectness, made only the additional demand of amusements at the public expense; and were also ignobly satisfied. The slaves alone murmured, and in Spartacus, one of their number, they found a man of genius and courage, capable of becoming their leader. Roman legislation had done nothing for them; the legislation of their masters had not assuaged one pain, nor interposed the shield of the law against cruelty. The slaves determined upon a general insurrection, to be followed by emigration. The cry went forth from the plains of Lombardy, and reached the rich fields of Campania, and was echoed through every valley among the Appennines. The gladiators burst the prisons of their keepers; the field-servant threw down his manure-basket; Syrian and Scythian, the thrall from Macedonia and from Carthage, the wretches from South Gaul, the Spaniard, the African, awoke to resistance. The barbarian, who had been purchased to shed his blood in the arena, remembered his hut on the Danube; the Greek, not yet indifferent to freedom, panted for release. It was an insurrection, as solemn in its object, as it was fearful in its extent. Rome was on the brink of ruin. Spartacus pointed to the Alps; beyond their heights were fields, where the fugitives might plant their colony; there they might revive the practice of freedom; there the oppressed might found a new state on the basis of benevolence, and in the spirit of justice. A common interest would unite the bondmen of the most remote lineage, the most various color, in a firm and happy republic. Already the armies of four Roman generals had been defeated; already the immense emigration was on its way to the Alps.

If the mass of slaves could, at any moment, on breaking their fetters, find themselves capable of establishing a liberal government, if they could at once, on being emancipated or on emancipating themselves, appear possessed of civic virtue, slavery would be deprived of more than half its horrors. But the circumstance which more than any other renders the institution execrable, is this: that while it binds the body, it corrupts the mind. The outrages which men commit, when they first regain their freedom, furnish the strongest argument against the system of bondage. The horrible inhumanity of civil war, and slave insurrection, are the topics of the loudest appeal against the condition, which can render human nature capable of committing such crimes. Idleness and treachery and theft, are the vices of slavery. The followers of Spartacus, when the pinnacles of the Alps were almost within their sight, turned aside to plunder; and the Roman army, which could not conquer in open battle the defenders of their personal freedom, was able to gain the advantage, where the fugitive slave was changed from a defender of liberty into a plunderer.

The struggle took place pricisely at a moment when the Roman State was most endangered by foreign enemies. But for the difficulties in the way of communication, which rendered a close coalition between remote armies impossible, the Roman State would have sunk beneath the storm; and from the shattered planks of its noble ruins the slaves alone would have been able to build themselves a little bark of hope, to escape from the desolation. Slaves would have occupied by right of conquest the heritage of the Cæsars. They finally became lords; but it was in a surer, and to human nature and Roman pride, in a more humiliating manner.

The suppression of the great insurrection of Spartacus brings us to the age of the triumvirs, and the approaching career of Julius Cæsar. To form a proper judgment of his designs, and their character, we must endeavor to gain some distinct idea of the condition of the inhabitants of Italy during his time, as divided into the classes of the nobles, the poorer citizens, and the slaves.

The vast capacity for reproduction, which the laws of society secure to capital in a greater degree than to personal exertion, displays itself no where so clearly as in slaveholding states, where the laboring class is but a portion of the capital of the opulent. As wealth consists chiefly in land and slaves, the rates of interest are, from universally operative causes, always comparatively high; the difficulty of advancing with borrowed capital proportionably great. The small land-holder finds himself unable to compete with those who are possessed of whole cohorts of bondmen; his slaves, his lands, rapidly pass, in consequence of his debts, into the hands of the more opulent. The large plantations are constantly swallowing up the smaller ones; and land and slaves soon come to be engrossed by a few. Before Cæsar passed the Rubicon, this condition existed in its extreme in the Roman State. The ARISTOCRACY owned the soil and its cultivators. A free laborer was hardly known. The large proprietors of slaves not only tilled their immense plantations, but also indulged their avarice in training their slaves to every species of labor, and letting them out, as horses from a livery stable, for the performance of every conceivable species of work. Four or five hundred slaves were not an uncommon number in one family; fifteen or twenty thousand sometimes belonged to one master. The wealth of Crassus was immense, and consisted chiefly in lands and slaves; on the number of his slaves we hardly dare hazard a conjecture. Of joiners and masons he had over five hundred. Nor was this the whole evil. The nobles, having impoverished their lands, became usurers, and had their agents dispersed over all the provinces. The censor Cato closed his career by recommending usury, as more productive than agriculture by slave labor; and such was the prodigality of the Roman planters, that, to indulge their fondness for luxury, many of them also mortgaged their estates to the money-lenders. Thus the lands of Italy, at best in the hands of a few proprietors, became virtually vested in the hands of a still smaller number of usurers. No man's house, no man's person, was secure. Nullie est certa domus, nullum sine pignore corpus. Hence, corruption readily found its way into the senate; the votes of that body, not less than the votes of the poorer citizens, were a merchantable commodity. Venalis Curia patrum. The wisdom and the decrees of the senate were for sale to the highest bidder.

Thus there was in all Italy no yeomanry, no free labor, no free manufacturing class; and thus the wealth of the great landed proprietors was wholly unbalanced. The large plantations, cultivated by slave labor, had already ruined Italy. Verum confitentibus, latifundia Italiam perdiderunt.

The FREE CITIZENS, who still elected tribunes and consuls, and were still sometimes convened in a sort of town-meeting, were poor and abject. But the right of suffrage insured them a maintenance. The petty offices in the Commonwealth were filled from their number, and such as retained some capacity for business found many a lucrative job, in return for their influence and their votes. The custom houses, the provinces, the internal police, offered inviting situations to moderate ambition. The rest clamored for bread from the public treasury, for tickets for the theatre at the national expense, for gladiatorial shows, where men were butchered at the cost of the office-seeking aristocracy, for the amusement of the majority. But there existed no free manufacturing establishments, no free farmers, no free laborers, no free mechanics. The state possessed some of the forms of democracy; but the life-giving principle of a democracy, prosperous free labor, was wanting.

The third class was the class of SLAVES. It was three times as numerous as both the others; though, as we have already observed, the whole body belonged almost exclusively to the few very wealthy. Their numbers excited constant apprehension; but care was taken not to distinguish them by a peculiar dress. Their ranks were recruited in various ways. The captives in war were sold at auction. The good Cicero, in the little wars in which he was commander, sold men enough to produce, at half price, half a million dollars. When it was told in Rome that Cæsar had invaded Britain, the people, in the true spirit of robbers, could not but ask one another what plunder he could hope to find there. 'There is not a scruple of silver,' said they, 'in the whole island;' neque argenti scrupulum in illa insula. 'Yes,' it was truly answered, 'but he will bring slaves.'

The second mode of supplying the slave market was by commerce; and this supply was so uniform and abundant, that the price of an ordinary laborer hardly varied very much for centuries. The reason is obvious. The slave merchant gets his cargoes from kidnappers, and the first cost, therefore, is inconsiderable. The great centres of this traffic were in the harbors bordering on the Euxine; and Scythians were often stolen. Caravans penetrated the deserts of Africa, and made regular hunts for slaves. Blacks were in high value; they were somewhat rare, and therefore both male and female negroes were favorite articles of luxury among the opulent Romans. At one period, Delos was most remarkable as the emporium for slavers. It had its harbors, chains, prisons, every thing so amply arranged to favor a brisk traffic, that ten thousand slaves could change hands and be shipped in a single day.

Such was the character of the Italian population over which a government was to be instituted, at the time when Cæsar appeared with his army on the borders of the Rubicon. In the contest which followed, it was the object of Pompey to plunder, to devastate, and to revenge. There did not exist any armed party in favor of a democratic republic. The spirit of the democracy was gone; and its shade only moved, with powerless steps, through the forum and the temples, which had once been the scenes of its glory.

Julius Cæsar was a great statesman, not less than a great soldier. His ambition was in every thing gratified; the noise of his triumphs had filled the shores of England, the swamps of Belgium, and the forests of Germany. Any distinction in the Roman State was within his reach. He was childless; and therefore his ambition hardly seemed to require a subversion of the Roman Commonwealth. And yet, with all this, he deliberately perceived that the continuance of popular liberty was impossible, in the actual condition of the Roman State; that a wasting, corrupt, and most oppressive aristocracy was preparing to assume the dominion of the world; that this aristocracy threatened ruin to the provinces, perpetual cruelty to the slaves, and hereditary, intolerant contempt for the people. Democracy had expired; and the worst form of aristocracy, like that of the Venetian nobles of a later day, could be prevented only by a monarchy. Julius Cæsar coolly resolved on the establishment of a monarchy. This was the third great revolution prepared by slavery.

Slavery having impoverished, but not wholly corrupted the free citizens, Gracchus had endeavored to restore the democracy by creating an independent yeomanry, and had failed from the opposition of the nobles. The nobles, perceiving the increase of the evil, the great degradation of the electors, and the multiplication of slaves, and being firmly resolved on maintaining the system of slave labor, endeavored to effect a revolution, by substituting a strong aristocracy for the democracy. The plan failed, owing to the strength of the democratic forms, which had survived the democratic spirit. Cæsar came, and finding the evil excessive, could devise no cure; but he clearly saw that a monarchical form of government was the only one which would endure in Rome. Had Cæsar possessed the virtues of Washington, the democracy of Jefferson, the legislative genius of Madison, he could not have changed the course of events. The condition of the Roman population demanded monarchy.

There remained no mode of establishing a fixed government in Rome, but by vesting all power in the hands of one man. In Italy, no opposition whatever was made to Cæsar, on the part of the people or of the slaves. The only opposition proceeded from the aristocracy, and they could offer resistance only in the remoter subjected districts, with the aid of hireling troops, sustained by the revenues of the provinces, which were still under the control of the senate. The people conferred on Cæsar all the power which he could desire; he was created dictator for a year, that he might subdue his enemies, and consul for five years, that he might confirm his authority. The inviolability of his person was secured by his election as tribune for life.

What would have been the policy of Julius Cæsar, had he remained in power, cannot be safely conjectured. To say that he had no plan is absurd; every step in his progress was marked by consistency. The establishment of monarchy was already an alternative to slavery. Cæsar did more. He issued an ordinance, not indeed of immediate abolition, but commanding that one-third part of the labor of Italy should be performed by free hands. The command was rendered inoperative by the assassination of Cæsar, the greatest misfortune that could have happened to Rome. For who were his murderers? Not the people, not the insurgent bondmen; but a portion of the aristocracy, to whom the greatest happiness of the greatest number was a matter of supreme indifference.

The great majority of the conspirators have never found a eulogist. Every ancient writer speaks of them with reprobation and contempt. Cassius, one of the chief leaders, was notoriously selfish, violent, and disgracefully covetous, not to say dishonest. He is universally represented as envying injustice rather than abhorring it, and his conduct has ever been ascribed to personal malevolence, and not to patriotism. But Brutus! History never manufactured him into a hero, till he had made himself an assassin. Of a headstrong, unbridled disposition, he never displayed coolness of judgment in any part of his career. It was his misfortune to have been the son of an abandoned woman, and to have been bred in a home which adultery and wantonness had defiled. The vices of early indulgence may be palliated by his youth and the licentiousness of his time; but Brutus, while yet young, was notorious as a merciless and exorbitant usurer, at the rate of four per cent. a month, or forty-eight per cent. a year. When his debtors grew unable to pay, he obtained for his agent an appointment to a military post, and extorted his claims by martial law. The town of Salamis, in the isle of Cyprus, owed him money on the terms we have mentioned. He caused the members of its bankrupt municipal government to be confined in their town-hall, in the hope that hunger would quicken their financial skill; and some of them were starved to death. Such was Brutus at that ingenuous period of life, when benevolence is usually most active. Brutus hated Pompey, yet after deliberating, he joined the party of that leader, and remained true to it, so long as it seemed to be the strongest; but no sooner was the battle of Pharsalia won, than Brutus gave in his adhesion to Cæsar, and to confer a value on his conversion, he betrayed the confidence of the fugitive, whose cause he had abandoned! In the plot against Cæsar, Brutus was the dupe of more sagacious men. The admirer transfers his own enthusiasm for liberty to those who claimed to be the champions of the republic; and reverences the crime of inconsiderate passion, as the exercise of righteous vengeance.

Cæsar had received the senate sitting; this insult required immediate vengeance. They murdered Cæsar, not from public spirit, but from mortified vanity and angry discontent. The people, who had been pleased with the humiliation of their oppressors, were indignant at the assassination, and the assassins themselves had no ulterior plan.

Slavery had poisoned the Roman State to the marrow; and though the conspirators had no fixed line of policy, yet the condition of the population of Italy led immediately to monarchy. The young Octavian owed his elevation, not to his talents, but to the

5

state of the times. Nothing but monarchy was tolerable. The evils that followed servitude made Augustus emperor.

Thus slavery, by impoverishing the majority of the citizens, rendered the reform of Gracchus necessary to the preservation of the democracy, and at the same time rendered that reform impossible. In a word, slavery subverted the Roman democracy. The same cause, corrupting the citizens, occasioned the attempt of Sylla, which Pompey would have renewed, to found an aristocratic government, where there already existed an aristocratic class; a result which the combined interests of the slaves and the people defeated. Slavery was the moving cause of the third revolution; and monarchy was established by the common consent of the people, and to the sure benefit of the slave. In the emperor the slave would have a friend.

Slavery prepared one more revolution, before it expired. It introduced Oriental despotism into Europe; not by force of arms, but by the sure results of causes that were perpetually in action.

Slavery impoverished the soil of Italy. The careless culture wore out even the rich fields of Campania. Large districts were left waste; other large tracts were turned into pastures; and grazing was substituted for tillage. The average crops of Italy hardly ever returned fourfold increase. Nam frumenta majore quidem parte Italiae, quando cum quarto responderint, vix meminisse possumus. It is the confession of the eulogist and the teacher of agriculture. Italy was naturally a very fertile country; but slave labor could hardly wring from it a return one-half, or even one-third, so great as free labor gets from the hills and vales of New England. This impoverishment of the soil impoverished the spirit of its inhabitants. The owners of slaves, disdaining the use of the sickle and the plow, crept within the walls of Rome, abandoning the cares of agriculture to the vilest of their bondmen.

Slavery prepared the way for Oriental despotism by encouraging luxury. The genius of the Romans was inventive; but it was only to devise new pleasures of the senses. The retinue of servants was unexampled; and the caprices, to which men and women were subjected, were innumerable. The Roman writers are so full of it, that it is unnecessary to draw the picture, which would indeed represent humanity degraded by the subserviency of slaves, and by the artificial desires and vices of their masters. This detestable excess extended through the whole upper class. Women ceased to blush for vices which, in other times, render men infamous. Beneficium sexus sui vitiis perdiderunt, et quia foeminam exuerunt, damnatae sunt morbis virilibus. At Rome, the gout was a common disease in the circles of female dissoluteness and fashion. The rage of luxury extended also, in some sort, to the people. For them, tens of thousands of gladiators were sacrificed without concern; for them the enslaved Jews raised the gigantic walls of the Coliseum, the most splendid monument of human infamy; for them actual navies engaged in actual contests; and the sailors, as they prepared for battle, received only an AVETE, on their way to death.

In like manner, the effect of slavery became visible on public morals. Among the slaves there was no such thing as the sanctity of marriage; dissoluteness was almost as general as the class. The slave was ready to assist in the corruption of his master's family. The virtues of self-denial were unknown. But the picture of Roman immorality is too gross to be exhibited. Its excess can be estimated from the extravagance of its remedy. When the Christian religion made its way through the oppressed classes of society, and gained strength by acquiring the affections of the miserable, whose woes it solaced, the abandoned manners of the cities could be forcibly reproved, only by the voice of fanaticism. When domestic life had almost ceased to exist, the universal lewdness could be checked only by the most exaggerated eulogies of absolute chastity. Convents and nunneries grew up, when more than half the world were excluded from the rites of marriage, and condemned by the laws of the empire to promiscuous indulgence. Vows of virginity were the testimony which religion bore against the enormities of the times. Spotless purity could alone put to blush the shamelessness of artificial excess. As in raging diseases, the most violent and unnatural remedies need to be applied for a season, so the transports of enthusiasm and the revolution of fanaticism sometimes appear necessary to stay the infection of a moral pestilence. Thus riot produced asceticism; and monks, and monkish eloquence, and monastic vows grew out of the general depravity of manners. The remedy was demanded, since public vice was threatening the Southern world with depopulation.

The gradual decay of the class of ingenuous freemen had ever been a conspicuous result of slavery. The corruptions of licentiousness spared neither sex of the Roman people; and the consequence was so certain, that emancipation alone could supply the void. Nor was it long before the majority of the cohorts, of the priesthood, of the tribes, of the people, nay of the senate itself, came to consist of emancipated slaves. But the sons of slaves could have no capacity for defending freedom; and despotism was at hand, when, besides the sovereign, there were few who were not bondmen or the children of bondmen. Freedom, to exist securely, must be looked fast in hereditary affections, and confirmed as a mortmain inheritance from long generations.

The government of Rome was sufficiently degraded, when the makers of an emperor, stumbling upon Claudius, the wisest fool of the times, proclaimed him the master of the Roman empire. Slavery now enjoyed its triumph, for a slave became prime minister. Io Saturnalia, shouted the cohorts, as Narcissus attempted to address them. But the consummation of evil had not arrived. The husband of Messalina had, naturally enough, taken up a prejudice against matrimony; but the governors of the weak emperor, who managed him as absolutely as Buckingham managed James I., insisted upon his marrying Agrippina. He did so; and Agrippina, assisted by freedmen and slaves, disinherited his son, murdered her husband, and placed Nero on the throne. Slaves gave Nero the purple.

The accession of Nero is the epoch of the virtual establishment of the fourth revolution. The forms of ancient Rome still continued, but Nero was the incarnation of tyranny; the triumph of human depravity; the very name by which men are accustomed to express the fury of unrestrained malignity. Bad as he was, Nero was not worse than Rome. Rome had no right to complain; Rome had but her due. Nay, when he died, the rabble and the slaves crowned his statues with garlands, and scattered flowers over his grave. And why should they not? Nero never injured the rabble, never oppressed the slave. He murdered his mother, his brother, his wife. But Nero was only the tyrant of the wealthy; the terror of the successful. He rendered poverty sweet, for poverty alone was secure; he rendered slavery tolerable, for slaves alone, or slavish men, were promoted to power. In honoring his tomb, they honored their avenger. The reign of Nero was the golden reign of the populace, and the holiday of the bondman. The death of Gracchus was now avenged on the descendants of his murderers. The streams in Heaven, it is truly said, run up hill; and slavery, in producing its perfect results, had brought the heaviest curse on the heads of its supporters.

Despotism now became the government of the Roman empire. Yet, there was such a vitality in the forms of liberty, that they were still in some degree preserved. Two centuries passed away, before the last vestiges of republican simplicity disappeared; two centuries elapsed, before the Eastern diadem could be introduced with the slavish customs of the East. Up to the reign of Diocletian, a diadem had never been endured in Europe. Hardly had this emblem of servility become tolerated, when language also began to be corrupted; and, within the course of another century, the austere purity of the Greek and Roman tongues, the languages of Demosthenes and of Gracchus, became for the first time familiarized to the forms of Oriental adulation. Your imperial

Highness, your Grace, your Excellency, your Immensity, your Honor, your Majesty, then first became current in the European world; men grew ashamed of a plain name; and one person could not address another without following the custom of the Syrians, and calling him Rabbi, Master.

It is a calumny to charge the devastation of Italy upon the barbarians. We say again, the large Roman plantations, tilled by slave labor, were the ruin of Italy. Verum confitentibus, latifundia Italiam perdidere. From the days of Gracchus, morals, courage, force of character, and agriculture had been declining. The productiveness of the country was constantly diminishing; Italy, for centuries, had not produced corn enough to meet the wants of its inhabitants. Rome was chiefly supplied from Sicily and Africa, and the largest number of its inhabitants had, for centuries, been fed from the public magazines.

The barbarians did not ruin Italy. The Romans themselves ruined it. Slavery had made it a waste and depopulated land, before a Scythian or a Scandinavian had crossed the Alps.

When Alaric led the Goths into Italy, even after the conquest of Rome, he saw that he could not sustain his army in the beautiful but desert territory, unless he could also conquer Sicily and Africa, whence alone daily bread could be obtained. His successor was, therefore, easily persuaded to abandon the unproductive region, and invade the happier France.

Attila had no other object than a roving pilgrimage after plunder; and as his cupidity was little excited, and the climate was ungenial, the wild, unlettered Calmuck was easily overawed by the Roman priesthood, and diverted from the indigent Italy to the more prosperous North. Rome still remained an object for plunderers, but none of the barbarians were tempted to make Italy the seat of empire, or Rome a metropolis. Slavery had destroyed the democracy, had destroyed the aristocracy, had destroyed the empire; and now at last it left the traces of its ruinous power deeply furrowed on the face of nature herself.'

CHAPTER VI.

CHRISTIAN SLAVERY IN NORTHERN AFRICA.

Barbary—the Carthaginians, the Romans, the Vandals.—Northern Africa annexed to the Greek Empire.—Conquered by the Saracens.—The Spanish Moors pass over to Africa —Their expeditions to plunder the coasts of Spain, and carry off the Christian Spaniards into Slavery.—Cardinal Ximenes invades Barbary, 1509, to release the captives.— Barbarossa, the sea-rover, becomes king of Algiers.—The Christian Slaves build the mole.—Expeditions of Charles V. against the Moors.—Insurrection of the Slaves.— Charles releases 20,000 Christians from Slavery, and carries off 10,000 Mohammedans to be reduced to Slavery in Spain.—The Moors retaliate by seizing 6000 Minorcans for Slaves.—Second expedition of Charles—its disastrous termination—his army destroyed —prisoners sold into Slavery.—The Algerines extend their depredations into the English Channel.—Condition of the Christian slaves in Barbary—treated with more humanity than African slaves among Christians.—Ransom of the slaves by their countrymen. —British Parliament appropriates money for the purpose.—The French send bomb vessels in 1688.—Lord Exmouth in 1816 releases 3000 captives, and puts an end to Christian Slavery in Barbary.

BARBARY is the general and somewhat vague denomination adopted by Europeans to designate that part of the northern coast of Africa which, bounded on the south by the desert of Sahara, is comprised between the frontiers of

Egypt on the Mediterranean, and Cape Nun, the western spur of the lofty Atlas range, on the Atlantic. Imperfectly known even at the present day, in ancient legend it was peculiarly the land of mystery and fable. It was there the Grecian poets, giving their airy nothings a local habitation and a name, placed the site of the delightful gardens of Hesperides; whose trees bore apples of the purest gold; there dwelt the terrible Gorgon, whose snaky tresses turned all living things into stone; there the invincible Hercules wrestled and overthrew the mighty Antæus; there the weary Atlas supported the ponderous arch of heaven on his stalwart shoulders. Almost as mythical and mysterious is the little we know of the Phœnicians, the greatest maritime people of antiquity, who planted their most powerful colony, the proud city of Carthage, on these fertile shores of Northern Africa. Of the Carthaginians, we can glean a little from the Greek and Roman historians. We know that in turn becoming the rulers of the seas, they explored and founded colonies and trading-depôts in what were at that time the most distant regions; extending their commercial relations from the tropical banks of the Niger to the frost-bound beach of the Baltic. A powerful people ere Rome was built, they long enjoyed their supremacy; at last, the thirst of territorial conquest brought the two great nations into rivalry, and the rich temples of Carthage fell a prey to the legions of Scipio. For a short period after the destruction of Carthage, the energetic subtlety of Jugurtha prevented the conquerors from extending their dominion; but in a few years, the whole coast, as far as the waves of the Atlantic, became a Roman province. It remained so till about the year 428 of the Christian era, in the reign of the Emperor Honorius, when Genseric, king of the Vandals, crossed over to Africa, conquered the Roman territory, and founded a dynasty which reigned for about 100 years. The Greek emperor Justinian then sent Belisarius to reconquer the country; he defeated the Vandals, made their king prisoner, and added Northern Africa to the Greek Empire.

History presents us with a series of conquering races, following each other as the waves upon the sea-beach, each washing away the impression made upon the sand by its forerunner, and each leaving a fresh impression to be washed out by its successor. The irruption of the Saracens followed hard upon the conquering footsteps of Belisarius. Swarm after swarm of the Arabs came up out of Egypt, till Northern Africa was under the rule of the caliphs, excepting a small part of the sea-coast held by the Spanish Goths. They at last were driven out by Musa, about the year 710; and then Tarik, Musa's lieutenant, crossing the narrow straits, carried the war into Europe, defeated Roderick, the last Gothic king, and laid the foundation of Arab dominion in Spain. The ruthless spirit of religious fanaticism which inspired the followers of Mohammed, destroyed everything it could not change. Romans, Vandals, Greeks, Goths, their laws, literature, and religions, all have disappeared in Northern Africa; the recollection of the most powerful of them is only preserved in the word *Romi*—a term of reproach to the Christians of all nations. Of their more material works, the learned antiquary still finds some traces of Roman edifices, and the remains of a sewer are supposed to indicate the site of Carthage. The warlike enthusiasm of the Saracens was better adapted for making conquests than for preserving them. The great distance from the seat of empire, the revolutions caused by rival houses contending for the caliphate, the ambitious projects of the viceroys inclining them to league with native chiefs, led to a dissolution of the Arabian power in Northern Africa. Consequently, when the dawn of modern history begins to throw a clearer light upon the scene, we find the territory divided into a number of petty sovereignties.

The Saracens in Africa intermixing with the barbarous native tribes, never reached the high position in the arts of peace and civilization attained by their brethren, the conquerors of Spain. The devastating instinct of Islamism seems to have yielded to a more benign influence, as soon as it entered Europe. When Spain was thoroughly subdued, the natives were permitted, with but few restrictions, the full enjoyment of their own laws and religion; and the Arabs, enjoying almost peaceable possession for nearly three centuries after the conquest, devoted their fiery energies to the acquisition of knowledge. Enriched by a fertile soil and prosperous commerce, they blended the acquirements and refinements of intellectual culture with Arabian luxury and magnificence; the palaces of their princes were radiant with splendor, their colleges famous for learning, their libraries overflowing with books, their agricultural and manufacturing processes conducted with scientific accuracy, when all the rest of Europe was buried in midnight barbarism. To those halcyon days of comparative peace succeeded four centuries of bitter conflict between the invaders and the invaded, exhibiting one of the grandest romances of military history on record. It was long doubtful on which side the honors of victory would descend. At last, the ardor and audacity of the Mussulman succumbed to the patriotic courage of the Christian, and the reluctant Moor was compelled to abandon the lovely region he had rendered classical by the exercise of his peculiar taste and genius.

Immediately after the fall of Granada in 1492, about 100,000 Spanish Moors passed over into Africa with their unfortunate king, Boabdil. Some ruined and deserted cities on the sea-coast, the remains of Carthaginian and Roman power and enterprise, were allotted to the exiles; for though of the same religion, and almost of the same race and language as the people they sought refuge amongst, yet they were strangers in a strange land; the African Moors termed them *Tigarins* (Andalucians); they dwelt and intermarried together, and were long known to Europeans, in the *lingua franca* of the Mediterranean, by the appellation of Moriscos. At the period of this forced migration, the Barbary Moors knew nothing of navigation; what little commerce they had was carried on by the ships of Cadiz, Genoa, and Ragusa. But the Moriscos, confined to the sea-coast, and debarred from agriculture, had no sooner rendered the ancient ruins habitable, than they turned their attention to naval affairs. Building row-boats, carrying from fourteen to twenty-six oars, they boldly put to sea, and incited by feelings of the deadliest enmity, revenged themselves on the

AFRICAN SLAVE TRAFIC.

hated Spaniard, at the same time that they plundered for a livelihood. Crossing the narrow channel which separates the two continents, and lying off out of sight of the Spanish coast during the day, they landed at night—not as strangers, but on the shores of their native land, where every bay and creek, every path and pass, every village and homestead, were as well known to them as to the Christian Spaniard. In the morning, mangled bodies and burning houses testified that the Moriscos had been there; while all portable plunder, every captured Christian not too old or too young to be a slave, was in the row-boat, speeding swiftly to the African coast. The harassed Spaniards kept watch and ward, winter and summer, from sunrise to sunset, and sometimes succeeded in cutting off small parties of the piratical invaders; yet such was the audacity of the Moriscos, and so well were their incursions planned, that frequently they plundered villages miles in the interior. Then ensued the hasty flight and hot pursuit; the freebooters retreating to the boats, driving before them, at the lance's point, unfortunate captives, laden with the plunder of their own dwellings; the pursuers, horse and foot, following into the very water, and firing on the retiring row-boats till their long oars swept them out of gunshot. The Barbary Moors soon joined the Moriscos in those exciting and profitable adventures; and thus originated the atrocious practice, which being subsequently recognized in treaties made by various European powers, became, according to the laws of nations, a legally organized system of Christian slavery.

In 1509, Ferdinand the Catholic, anxious to stop the Morisco depredations on the Spanish coast, sent a considerable force, under the celebrated Cardinal Ximenes, to invade Barbary. During this expedition, the Spaniards released 300 captives, and took possession of Oran and a few other unimportant places on the coast. One of those was a small island, about a mile from the main, lying exactly opposite the town since known as Algiers, but previously so little recognized by history, that it is not certain when it received the name. In all probability, it acquired the high-sounding appellation of *Al Ghezire* (The Invincible) at a subsequent period. Carefully fortifying this insulated rock, the Spaniards, by the superiority of their artillery, held possession of it for several years, as a sort of outpost, and a curb upon the piratical tendencies of the native powers.

One of those extraordinary adventurers, who, rising from nothing, carve out kingdoms for themselves with the edge of their sabres, and gleaming at intervals on an astonished world, vanish into utter darkness, like comets in their erratic orbits, appeared at this time, and changed the destinies of the greater part of Northern Africa. The son of a poor Greek potter in the island of Mitylene worked with his father till a younger brother was able to take his place in assisting to support the family; then going on board a Turkish war vessel, he signified his desire to become a Mussulman, and enter the service. His offer was accepted, he received the Turkish name of Aroudje—his previous appellation is unknown—and in a short time, his fierce intrepidity and nautical skill raised him to the command of a vessel belonging to the sultan. Intrusted with a considerable sum of money, to pay the Turkish garrisons in the Morea, he sailed from Constantinople, and having passed the Dardanelles, he mustered his crew, and declared his intentions of renouncing allegiance to the Porte. He told them that, if they would stand by him, he would lead them to the western waters of the Mediterranean, where prizes of all nations might be captured in abundance, where there were no knights of Rhodes to contend against, and where they would be completely out of the power of the sultan. A project so much in unison with the predilections of the rude crew, was received with enthusiastic acclamations of assent. Aroudje then steered for his native island of Mitylene, where he landed, and gave a large sum of money to his mother and sisters; and being joined by his brother, who, becoming a Mohammedan, assumed the name of Hayraddin, he weighed anchor, and turned his prow to the westward. Arriving off the island of Elba, he fell in with two portly argosies under papal colors. Piracy in these western seas having previously been carried on in the Morisco row-boats only, the Christians were not alarmed, but believing Aroudje to be an honest trader, permitted him to run alongside, as he seemed to wish to communicate some information. They were quickly undeceived. Boarding the nearest one, he immediately took possession of her, and then dressing his men in the clothes of the captured crew, he bore down upon her unsuspecting consort. She was captured also, with scarcely a blow; and Aroudje found himself in possession of two ships, each much larger than his own, with cargoes of great value, and some hundreds of prisoners. The fame of this bold action resounded from the southern shores of Europe to the opposite coast of Africa. Such captives as were ransomed, when describing the appearance of Aroudje, did not fail to recount the ferocious aspect of his huge red beard, so unusual an appendage to a native of the south, and thus he obtained the name of Barbarossa (Redbeard), so long the terror of the Mediterranean. Taking his prizes to Tunis, one of the small states that had once been part of the great Saracen Empire in Barbary, Aroudje was well received by the king, who allowed him to use the island and fort of Goleta as a naval depôt, on condition of paying a certain percentage on all prizes. Adding daily to his wealth and fleet, the daring sea-rover had no lack of followers. Turkish and Moorish adventurers eagerly enrolled themselves under his fortunate banner.

The precarious position of the petty Barbary states, threatened by the Berbers and Bedouins of the interior on the land-side, and menaced by the Spaniards on the sea-board, was highly favorable to the ambitious aspirations of the potter's son. The district of Jijil being attacked by famine, he seized the corn-ships of Sicily, and distributed the grain freely and without price among the starving indabitants, who gratefully proclaimed him their king; and in a few years his army equaled in magnitude his still increasing fleet. The fort built by the Spaniards on the island off Algiers was a great annoyance to Eutemi, the Moorish king of that little state. Unwisely, he applied to Barbarossa for aid to evict the Spaniard, and eagerly was the request granted. With 5000 men, the pirate chief marched to Algiers, where the people hailed him as a deliverer; Eutemi was murdered, and Aroudje proclaimed king. The throne thus usurped by audacity, he established by policy; profusely liberal to his friends, ferociously cruel to his enemies, he was loved and dreaded by all his subjects. His reign, however, was short, being defeated and killed in battle by the Spaniards, only two years after he ascended the throne. In such estimation was this victory held, that the head, shirt-of-mail, and gold-embroidered vest of the slain warrior were carried on a lance, in triumphant procession, through the principal cities of Spain, and then deposited as sacred trophies in the church of St. Jerome at Cordova. Hayraddin, who is styled by the old historians, Barbarossa II., succeeded his brother, but, feeling his position insecure, he tendered the sovereignty of Algiers to the Grand Seignior, on condition of being appointed viceroy and receiving a contingent of troops. Sultan Selim, gladly accepting the offer, sent a firman creating Hayraddin pacha, and a force of 2000 janizaries. From that period, the Ottoman supremacy over the Moorish and Morisco inhabitants of Algiers was firmly established.

Piracy upon all Christian nations was still vigorously carried on from Tunis and other ports of Barbary; but the harbor of Algiers being commanded by the island fort in possession of the Spaniards, was deprived of that nefarious source of wealth. This island was long the 'Castle Dangerous' of the Spanish service; nor was it till 1530, that, betrayed by a discontented soldier, it fell into the hands of Hayraddin. Don Martin, the Spanish governor, who had long and nobly defended the isolated rock, was brought a wounded captive before the truculent pacha. "I respect you," said Hayraddin, "as a brave man and a good soldier. Whatever favor you may ask of me, I will grant, on condition that you will accede to whatever I may request."

"Agreed," replied Don Martin. "Cut off the head of the base Spaniard who betrayed his countrymen."

The wretch was immediately brought in, and decapitated on the spot.

"Now," rejoined Hayraddin, "my request is that you become a Mussulman, and take command of my army."

"Never!" exclaimed the chivalrous Don Martin; and immediately, at a signal from the enraged pacha, a dozen yataghans leaped from their sheaths, and the faithful Christian was cut to pieces on the floor of the presence-chamber.

The island, so long a source of danger and annoyance to the Algerines, was now made their safest defense, Hayraddin conceiving the bold idea of uniting it to the mainland by a mole and breakwater. This really great undertaking, which still evinces the engineering and mechanical skill of its promoters, was the work of thousands of wretched Christian slaves, who labored at it incessantly for three years before it was completed. Thus the Algerines obtained a commodious harbor for their shipping, secure against all storms, and, at that time, impregnable to all enemies.

In 1532, the people of Tunis rebelling, deposed their king, and invited the willing Hayraddin to become their ruler. With this increase of power his boldness increased also. Out of his many daring exploits at this period, we need mention only one. Hearing that Julian Gonzago, the wife of Vespasian Colonna, Count of Fondi, was the most beautiful woman in Europe, Hayraddin made a descent in the night on the town of Fondi; scaling the walls, the fierce Moslems plundered the town, and carried off numbers of the inhabitants into slavery. Fortunately, the countess escaped to the fields in her night-dress, and thus evaded the clutches of the pirate, who, to revenge his disappointment, ravaged the whole Neapolitan coast before he returned to Tunis.

The eyes of all Europe were now turned imploringly to the only power considered capable of contending with this 'monstrous scourge of Christendom.' The Emperor Charles V. eagerly responded to the appeal, and summoned forth the united strength of his vast dominions to equip the most powerful armada that had ever plowed the waves of the Mediterranean; the Low Countries, Spain, Italy, Portugal, and Genoa, furnished their bravest veterans and best appointed ships; the Knights of St. John supplied a few vessels, small, yet formidable from the well-known valor of the chevaliers who served in them; the pope contributed his blessing; and the immense armament, inspired with all the enthusiasm of the Crusades, but directed to a more rational and legitimate object, rendezvoused at Cagliari—a convenient harbor of Sardinia.

Hayraddin, aware of the object and destination of this vast armament, energetically prepared to give it a suitable reception. Night and day the miserable Christian slaves, rivetting their own fetters, were employed in erecting new, and strengthening old fortifications; and as a last resource, in case of defeat, the shrewd pacha sent eighteen sail of his best ships to Bona. In July, 1537, the emperor's fleet was descried from the towers of Tunis; and Hayraddin made the last dispositions for defense by placing his treasure, seraglio, and slaves in the citadel, under a strong guard, with the intention of retreating thither if the city and port were taken.

Charles, after landing his troops, commenced a simultaneous attack by land and sea. Hayraddin, with much inferior force, yet greater advantage of position, conducted the defense with skill and determination. But in the heat of the conflict, the Christian slaves, distracted with suspense, and excited to frenzy by the thunder of the cannonade, burst their bonds, overpowered their guards, and turned the guns of the citadel upon their Moslem masters. Hayraddin, then seeing that the day was irrecoverably lost, fled with the remnant of his army to the ships at Bona. Charles reinstated the deposed king of Tunis as his vassal, and on condition, that for the future, all Christians brought as captives to Tunis should be liberated without ransom. With 20,000 Christians released from slavery by the power of his arms—the noblest trophy conqueror ever bore—Charles returned in triumph to Europe. Not only did he restore these unfortunate captives to liberty, but he furnished all of them with suitable apparel, and the means of returning to their respective countries. Such munificence spread the fame of Charles over all the world; for though it entailed on him immense expense, he had personally gained nothing by the conquest of Tunis: disinterestedly he had fought for the honor of the Christian name, for Christian security and welfare. Yet we regret to have to add one fact, highly characteristic of the age : when Charles left Africa, he also carried off 10,000 Mohammedans to be slaves for life, chained to the oars in the galleys of Spain, Italy, and Malta.

We must now return to Hayraddin, the second Barbarossa, whom we left in full retreat to Bona, where he had sagaciously sent his ships to be out of harm's way at Tunis. As soon as he arrived at Bona, he embarked his men, and put to sea.

"Let us go to the Levant," said his officers, "and beg assistance from the sultan."

"To the Levant, did you say ?" exclaimed the incensed pirate. "Am I a man to shew my back ? Must I fly for refuge to Constantinople ? Depend upon it, I am far more likely to attack the emperor's dominions in Flanders. Cease your prating; follow me, and obey orders." Steering for Minorca, he soon appeared off the well-fortified harbor of Port Mahon. The incautious Minorcans believing the pirates utterly exterminated, and that the gallant fleet entering their harbor was returning from the conquest of Tunis, ran to the port to greet and welcome the supposed victors. Not a gun was loaded, not a battery manned, when Hayraddin, swooping like an eagle on its prey, sacked the town, carried off an immense booty in money and military stores, and with 6000 captive Minorcans, returned in triumph to Algiers. This was his last exploit that falls within our province to relate. Earnestly solicited by the sultan, he relinquished the pachalic to take supreme command of the Ottoman fleet. After a life spent in stratagem and war, he died at an advanced age ; and still along the Christian shores of the Mediterranean, mothers frighten their unruly children with the name of Barbarossa.

Hassan Aga, a Sardinian renegade, was next appointed to the vice-royalty. A corsair from his youth, he was well fitted for the office, and during his rule the piratical depredations increased in number and audacity. The continuous line of watch-towers that engirdle the southern coast of Spain, and have so picturesque an effect at the present day, were built as a defense against Hassan's cruisers. Once more all Europe turned to the emperor Charles for relief and protection Pope Paul III. wrote a letter imploring him "to reduce Algiers, which, since the conquest of Tunis, has been the common receptacle of all the freebooters, and to exterminate that lawless race, the implacable enemies of the Christian faith." Moved by such entreaties, and thirsting for glory, Charles equipped a fleet equal in magnitude to that with which he had conquered Tunis. A navy of 500 ships, an army of 27,000 picked men, and 150 Knights of Malta, with noblemen and gentlemen volunteers of all nations, many of them English, sailed on this great expedition. To oppose such a powerful force, Hassan had only 800 Turks and 5000 Moors and Moriscos. On arriving at Algiers, Charles summoned the pacha to surrender, but received a most contemptuous reply. The troops were immediately disembarked, though with great difficulty, owing to stormy weather; and the increasing gale cutting off communication with the fleet, before sufficient stores and camp equipage could be landed, Charles and his army were left with scanty provision, and exposed to torrents of rain. A night passed in this miserable condition. The next day, the tempest increased. The next night, the troops, exhausted by want of food and exposure to the elements, were unable to lie down, the ground being knee-deep in mud. Hassan was too vigilant a warrior not to take advantage of this state of affairs. Before daybreak, on the second morning, with a strong body of horse and foot, he sallied out upon the Christian camp. Weak from hunger and want of rest, benumbed by exposure to the cold and rain, their powder wet, and their matches extinguished, the advanced division of Charles's army were easily defeated by Hassan's fresh and vigorous troops. The main body advanced to the rescue, and after a sharp contest, Hassan's small detachment was repulsed, and driven back into the city. The Knights of Malta, among whom a chivalrous emulation existed with respect to which of them would first stick his dagger in the gate of Algiers, rashly following the retreating Hassan, led the army up to the city, where they were mowed down in hundreds by the fire from the walls. Retreating in confusion from this false position, they were again charged by Hassan's impetuous cavalry, and the Knights of Malta, to save the whole army from destruction, drew up in a body to cover the rear. Conspicuous by their scarlet upper garments, embroidered with a white cross, they served for a short time as a rallying-point; but it was not till Charles, armed with sword and buckler, joined his troops, and stimulated them to fresh exertions by fighting in their ranks, that the Algerines were compelled to return to their strongholds. In this desperate conflict, the Knights of Malta were nearly all killed. Only one of them, Ponce de Salignac, the standard-bearer, had reached and stuck his dagger in the gate, but, pierced with innumerable wounds, he did not live to enjoy the honor of the foolhardy feat. Another night of tempest and privation followed this discouraging battle; hundreds of the debilitated troops were blown down by the violence of the wind, and smothered in the mud. When the day broke, Charles saw 200 of his war-ships and transports, containing 8000 men, driven on shore, and such of their crews as were not swallowed up by the waves, led off into captivity by the exulting enemy. The rest of the fleet sought shelter under a headland four miles off, and thither Charles followed them; but his famished troops, continually harassed by the enemy, were two days in retreating that short distance. With great difficulty, Charles, and a small remnant of his once powerful army, reached the ships, and made sail from the inhospitable coast. So many captives were taken, and such was their enfeebled condition, that numbers were sold by the captors for an onion each. "Do you remember the day when your countryman was sold for an onion?' was for years afterwards a favorite taunt of the Algerine to the Spaniard. Enriched with slaves, valuable military and naval stores, treasure, horses, costly trappings—all brought to their own doors—the pride of the Algerines knew no bounds, and they sneeringly said that

Charles brought them this immense plunder to save them the trouble of going to fetch it. Hassan generously refused to take any part of the spoil, saying that the honor of defeating the most powerful of Christian princes was quite sufficient for his share.

After this great victory, the Algerines, confident of the impregnability of their city, turned their attention to increasing their power on sea. The vessels hitherto used for warlike purposes in the Mediterranean were galleys, principally propelled by oars rowed by slaves; and in quickness of manœuvre and capability of being propelled during a calm, were somewhat analgous to the steam-boat of the present day, and had a decided advantage over the less easily managed sailing-vessels. Not constructed to mount heavy ordnance, the system of naval tactics adopted in the galleys was to close with the enemy, whenever eligible, and then the battle was fought with small-arms—arrows, and even stones, being used as weapons of attack and defense. The Algerines, however, laboring in their vocation, as Falstaff would have said, captured many large ships of Northern Europe, built for long voyages and to contend with stormy seas. Equipping these with cannon, they were enabled to destroy the galleys before the latter could close with them; and thus introducing a new system of naval warfare, they gained a complete ascendancy in the waters of the Mediterranean. Nor did they long confine their depredations to that sea. In 1574, an Algerine fleet surprised the tunny fishery of the Duke of Medina, near Cadiz, and captured 200 slaves; but one of the piratical vessels running ashore, a large number were retaken by their countrymen. In 1585, Morat, a celebrated corsair, landed at night on Lancelote, one of the Canary Islands, and carried off a large booty, with 300 prisoners; among whom were the wife, mother, and daughter of the Spanish governor. Standing out to sea the next morning, until out of gun-range, the pirate hove-to, and showing a flag of truce, treated for the ransom of his captives; and afterwards, eluding, by seamanship and cunning, a Spanish fleet waiting to intercept him at the mouth of the straits, exultingly returned to Algiers. In the following century, pushing their piracies still further, the English Channel became one of their regular cruising-grounds. In 1631, the town of Baltimore, in Ireland, was plundered by Morat Rais, a Flemish renegade, and 237 men, women, and children, "even to the babe in the cradle," carried off into captivity. Aware of the strong family affections of the Irish, we can well believe Pierre Dan, a Redemptionist monk, who saw those poor creatures in Algiers. He says: "It was one of the most pitiable of sights to see them exposed for sale. There was not a Christian in Algiers who did not shed tears at the lamentations of these captives in the slave-market, when husband and wife, mother and child, were separated.* Is it not," indignantly adds the worthy father, "making the Almighty a bankrupt, to sell His most precious property in this manner?" About the same time, two corsairs, guided by a Danish renegade, proceeded as far as

---

* At a later period, the Algerines did not separate slave-families.

Iceland, where they captured no less than 800 persons, a few of whom were ransomed several years afterwards by Christian IV., king of Denmark.

The existence of such an organized system of piracy may well excite our wonder at the present day; but the truth is, that since the time of the Vikings, to the latter part of the last century, the high seas were never clear of pirates belonging to one nation or another. Besides, the commercial jealousies and almost continual wars of the European nations, prevented them from uniting to crush the Barbary rovers. The English and Dutch maintained an extensive commerce with the Algerines, supplying them with gunpowder, arms, and naval stores; and found it more profitable to pay their customers a heavy tribute for a sort of half-peace, than to be at open war with them. De Witt, the famous Dutch admiral and statesman, in his *Interest of Holland*, thus views the question: "Although," he says, "our ships should be well guarded by convoys against the Barbary pirates, yet it would by no means be proper to free the seas from those freebooters—because we should thereby be put on the same footing as the French, Spanish, and Italians; wherefore it is best to leave that thorn in the sides of those nations." An English statesman, in an official paper written in 1671, amongst other objections to the surrender of Tangier, urges the advantage of making it an open port for the Barbary pirates to sell their prizes and refit at, in the same manner as they were permitted to do in the French ports. It is an actual fact that, in the seventeenth century, when England and France were at peace, Algerine cruisers frequently landed their English captives at Bordeaux, whence they were marched in handcuffs to Marseille, and there reshipped in other vessels, and taken to Algiers. This proceeding was to avoid the risk of recapture in the Straits of Gibraltar, and also to allow the pirates to remain out longer on their cruise, enencumbered with prisoners. Numerous instances of the complicity of European powers with this nefarious system might be adduced. Sir Cloudesley Shovel, in 1703, protected a Barbary pirate from receiving a well-merited chastisement from a Dutch squadron; but that need not surprise the reader, for at the same time the gallant admiral had power under the Great Seal to visit Algiers, Tunis, and Tripoli, make the usual presents, and 'if he could prevail with them to make war against France, and that some act of hostility was thereupon committed, he was to give such further presents as he should think proper.'

The political system of the Algerines requires a few words. The authority of the Porte was soon shaken off, and then the janizaries, or soldiers, forming a kind of aristocratic democracy, chose a governor from their own number, under the familiar title of Dey (Uncle); and ruled the native Moors as an inferior and conquered race. Neither Moor nor Morisco was permitted to have any voice in the government, or to hold any office under it; the wealthiest native, if he met a janizary in the street, had to give way to let the proud soldier pass. The janizaries were all either Turks or renegades (slaves who had turned Mohammedans): so strictly was this rule carried out, that the son of a janizary by a Moorish woman was not allowed the privileges of his father, though the offspring of a janizary and a Christian slave was recognized as one of the dominant race. The janizaries were in number about 12,000; their ranks were annually recruited by renegades and adventurous Turks from the Levant; they served by sea as well as by land, and were employed in controlling the tributary native chiefs of the interior, and sailing in the piratical cruisers. Piracy being the basis of this system, the whole foreign policy of the Algerines consisted in claiming the right of maintaining constant war with all Christian nations that did not conciliate them by tribute and treaties. When a European consul arrived at Algiers, he always carried a large present to the dey, and as the latter would, in a short time, quarrel with and send away the consul, in expectation of receiving the usual present with his successor, it was found more convenient to make an occasional present, than incur the trouble and risk of a continual change of consuls. In course of time, these occasional presents became a tribute of 17,000 dollars, regularly paid every two years.

The miseries of Algerine bondage have long been proverbial over all the Christian world, yet they appear light when calmly examined and contrasted with other systems of slavery. Most travelers in Mohammedan countries have remarked the general kindness with which slaves are treated. General Eaton, consul of the United States at Tunis in 1799, writes thus: "Truth and justice demand from me the confession, that the Christian slaves among the barbarians of Africa are treated with more humanity than the African slaves among the Christians of civilized America." John Wesley, when addressing those connected with the negro slave-trade, said: "You have carried them into the vilest slavery, never to end but with life—such slavery as is not to be found with the Turks at Algiers." In fact, the creed of Islam, not recognizing perpetual and unconditional bondage, gave the slave a right of redemption by purchase, according to a precept of the Koran. This right of redemption was daily claimed and acknowledged in Barbary; and though it was only the richer class that could immediately benefit by it, yet it was a great alleviation to the general hardship of the system; and numbers of the poorer captives, by exercise of their various trades and professions, realized money, and were in a short time able to redeem themselves. Again, no prejudice of race existed in the mind of the master against his unhappy bondsman. The meanest Christian slave, on becoming a Mohammedan, was free, and enrolled as a janizary, having superior privileges even to the native Moor or Morisco, and he and his descendants were eligible to the highest offices in the state. Ladies, when captured, were invariably treated with respect, and, till ransomed, lodged in a building set apart for that purpose, under the charge of a high officer, similar to our mayor. The most perfect toleration was extended to the exercise of the Christian religion; the four great festivals of the Roman Church—Christmas, Easter, and the nativities of St. John and the Virgin—were recognized as holidays for the slaves. We read of a large slaveholder purchasing a priest expressly for the spiritual comfort of his bondsmen; and of other masters who regularly, once a week, marched their slaves off to confession. The Algerines were shrewd enough to prefer a religious slave to his less conscientious fellows. "Christianity," they used to say, "was better for a man than no religion at all." Nor were they zealous to make adult converts. "A bad Christian," they said, "can never make a good Mussulman." It was only slaves of known good character and conduct who were received into the Moslem community. Children, however, were brought up Mohammedans, adopted in families, and became the heirs of their adoptors. Captured ecclesiastics were treated with respect, never set to work, but allowed to join the religious houses established in Algiers.

One of the greatest alleviations to the miseries of the captives was the hospital founded for their benefit, by that noble order of monks, the Trinitarian Brothers of Redemption. This order was instituted in 1188, during the pontificate of Innocent III. Its founder, Jean Matha, was a native of Provence, and, according to the old chronicles, a saint from his birth; for when a baby at the breast, he voluntarily abstained every fast-day! Having entered the priesthood, on performing his first mass, an extraordinary vision was witnessed by the congregation. An angelic being, clothed in white raiment, appeared above the altar, with an imploring expression of countenance, and arms crossed; his hands were placed on the heads of two fettered slaves, as if he wished to redeem them. The fame of this miracle soon spread to Rome. Journeying thither, Matha said mass before the pope; and the wonderful apparition being repeated, Innocent granted the requisite concessions for instituting the order of Redemptionists, whose sole object was to collect alms, and apply them to the relief and redemption of Christian slaves. With whatever degree of suspicion such conventual legends may be regarded, it is gratifying to find that the order was truly a blessed charity, and that Englishmen were among the earliest and most zealous of its members. Within a year from its institution, Brother John, of Scotland, a professor at Oxford, and Brother William, of England, a priest in London, departed on the first voyage of redemption, and after many dangers and hardships, returned from the East with 1286 ransomed slaves. It was not, however, till 1551, that the order was enabled to form a regular establishment in Algiers. In that year, Brother Sebastian purchased a large building, and converted it into an hospital for sick and disabled slaves. As neither work nor ransom could be got out of a dead slave, the masters soon perceived the benefit of the hospital, and they levied a tax on all Christian vessels frequenting the port to aid in sustaining it. Among so many captives, there were always plenty of experienced medical men to perform the requisite duties; and no inconsiderable revenue to the funds of the institution was derived by dispensing medicines and advice to the Moslems. A Father Administrator and two brothers of the order constantly resided in Algiers to manage the affairs of the hospital, which from time to time was extended and improved, till it became one of the largest and finest buildings in the city. The owners of slaves who received the benefit of this charity, contributed nothing towards it, but on each slave being admitted, his proprietor paid one dollar to the Father Administrator, which, if the patient recovered, was returned to the master, but if he died, was kept to defray his funeral expenses. For a long period, there was no place of interment allotted to the captives; their dead bodies were thrown outside the city walls, to be devoured by the hordes of street-dogs which infest the towns of Mohammedan countries. At length, by the noble self-denial of a private individual, whose name, we regret to say, we are unable to trace, a slave's burial ground was obtained. A Capuchin friar, the friend and confessor of Don John of Austria, natural son of the Emperor Charles V., was taken captive. Knowing the esteem in which he was held by the prince, an immense sum was demanded for his ransom. The money was immediately forwarded, but instead of purchasing his freedom, the disinterested philanthropist bought a piece of ground for a burial-place for Christian slaves, and, devoting himself to solace the spiritual and temporal wants of his unhappy co-religionists, uncomplainingly passed the rest of his life in exile and captivity.

A few years after the founding of this House of the Spanish Hospital, as it was termed, another Christian religious establishment, the House of the French Mission, was planted in Algiers. A certain Duchess d'Eguillon, at the suggestion of the celebrated philanthropist Vincent de Paul, who had himself been an Algerine captive, commenced this good work by an endowment of 4,000 livres per annum. These two religious houses were exempted from all duties or taxes, and mass was performed in them daily with all the pomp and splendor of the Romish Church. There was also a chapel in each of the six bagnes—the prisons where the slaves were confined at night—in which service was performed on Sundays and holidays. The Greek Church had also a chapel and small establishment in one of the bagnes. Brother Comelin, of the order of redemption, tells us, in his *Voyage*, that they celebrated Christmas in the Spanish Hospital "with the same liberty and as solemnly as in Christendom. Midnight mass was chanted to the sound of trumpets, drums, flutes, and hautboys; so that in the stillness of night the infidels heard the worship of the true God over all their accursed city, from ten at night till two in the morning." Such was Mohammedan toleration in Algiers, at the period, too, we should recollect, of the high and palmy days of the Inquisition. We may easily conceive what would have been the fate of the infidels if they, by any chance, had invaded the midnight silence of Rome or Madrid with the sounds of their worship. The only exceptions to the general good treatment and respect bestowed upon Christian ecclesiastics in Algiers was, when inspired by a furious zeal for martyrdom, they openly insulted the Mohammedan religion; or when the populace were excited by forced conversions and other intolerant cruelties practiced upon Mussulman slaves in Europe. We shall briefly mention two instances of such occurrences.

One Pedro, a brother of Redemption, had traveled to Mexico and Peru, and collected in those rich countries a vast amount of treasure for the order. He then went to Algiers, where he employed half the money in ransoming

6

captives, and the other half in repairing and increasing the usefulness of the hospital, where he resided, constantly attending and consoling the sick slaves. At last, thirsting for martyrdom, he one day rushed into a mosque, and, with crucifix in hand, cursed and reviled the false Prophet Mohammed. In all Mohammedan countries, the penalty of this offense is death. But so much were the piety and good works of Pedro respected by the Algerine government, that they anxiously endeavored to avoid inflicting the punishment of their law. Earnestly they solicited him, with promise of free pardon, to acknowledge that he was intoxicated or deranged when he committed the rash act, but in vain. Pedro was burned; and one of his leg-bones was long carefully preserved as a holy relic in the Spanish Hospital.

In 1612, a young Mohammedan lady, fifteen years of age, named Fatima, daughter of Mehemet Aga, a man of high rank in Algiers, when on her way to Constantinople to be married, was captured by a Christian cruiser, carried into Corsica, and a very large sum of money demanded for her ransom. The distressed father speedily sent the money by two relatives, who were furnished with safe-conduct passes by the brothers of Redemption. On their arrival in Corsica, they were informed that the young lady had become a Christian, was christened Maria Eugenia, and married to a Corsican gentleman; and that the money brought for her ransom must be appropriated as her dowry. The relatives were permitted to see Maria; she declared her name was still Fatima; and that her baptism and marriage were forced upon her. The return of the relatives without either the lady or the money caused great excitement in Algiers. By way of retaliation, the brothers of Redemption were loaded with chains, and thrown into prison, and compelled to pay Mehemet Aga a sum equal to that which he had sent for his daughter's ransom. In a short time, however, they were released, and permitted to resume their customary duties.

When returning from a successful cruise, as soon as an Algerine corsair arrived within sight of the harbor, her crew commenced firing guns of rejoicing and triumph, and continued them at intervals until she came to anchor. Summoned by these signals of success, the inhabitants would flock in numbers to the port, there to learn the value of the prize, the circumstances of its capture, and to congratulate the pirates. Morgan, a quaint old writer, many years attached to the British consulate, says: "These are the times when Algiers very visibly puts on a quite new countenance, and it may well be compared to a great bee-hive. All is hurry, every one busy, and a cheerful aspect succeeds a strange gloom and discontent, like what is to be seen everywhere else, when the complaint of dullness of trade, scarcity of business, and stagnation of cash reigns universal; and which is constantly to be seen in Algiers during every interval between the taking of good prizes." The dey received the eighth part of the value of all prizes, for the service of the government, and had the privilege of selecting his share of the captives, who were brought from the vessel to the court-yard of his palace, where the European consuls attended to claim any of their countrymen who might be considered free in accordance with the terms of previous treaties. In many instances, however, little respect was paid by the strong-handed captors to such documents. The following reply of one of the deys to a remonstrance of the English consul, contains the general answer given on such occasions : "The Algerines being born pirates, and not able to subsist by any other means, it is the Christians' business to be always on their guard, even in time of peace ; for if we were to observe punctilios with all those nations who purchase peace and liberty from us, we might set fire to our shipping, and become degraded to be camel-drivers." When the newly-made captives were mustered in the dey's court-yard, their names, ages, countries, and professions, were minutely taken down by a *hojia*, or government secretary, appointed for the purpose ; and then the dey proceeded to make his selection of every eighth person, and of course took care to choose such as, from their appearance and description, were likely to pay a smart ransom, or those acquainted with the more useful professions and the mechanical arts. After the dey had taken his share, the remainder of the prisoners, being the property of their captors, were taken to the *bestian*, or slave-market, and appraised, a certain value being set upon each individual. From the slave-market the unfortunates were then led back to the court-yard, and there sold by public auction ; and whatever price was obtained higher than the valuation of the slave-market, became the perquisite of the dey.

The government, or, in other words, the dey, was the largest slaveholder in Algiers. All the slaves belonging to the government were termed deylic slaves, and distinguished by a small ring of iron fastened round the wrist or ankle ; and excepting those who were employed in the palace, or hired out as domestic servants, were locked up every night in six large buildings called bagnes. Rude beds were provided in the bagnes, and each deylic slave received three small loaves of bread per day, and occasionally some coarse cloth for clothing. All the carpenters, blacksmiths, masons, ropemakers, and others among the deylic slaves who worked at trades connected with house and ship-building, received a third part of what they earned, when hired out to private persons, and even the same sum was paid to them when employed on government works. Besides, both at the laying down of the keel and launch of a new ship, a handsome gratuity was given to all the slave-mechanics employed upon her. Indeed, all the work connected with ship-building was performed by Christian slaves.

The janizaries never condescended to do any kind of work ; the native Moors were too lazy and too ignorant; and the Moriscos being forbidden, by the jealous policy of the dominant Turkish race, to practice the arts they brought with them from Spain, sank, after the first generation, to a level with the native Moor. Shipwrights were consequently well treated, many of them earning better wages than they could in their own countries. Numbers were thus enabled to purchase their freedom ; but many more, seduced by the sensual debaucheries so prevalent wherever slavery is recognized, preferred remaining in Algiers as slaves or renegades, to returning as freemen to their native lands. Deylic slaves, when hired out as sailors, received one third of their hire, and one-third of a freeman's share in the prize-money. Invariably at the hour of prayer termed *Al Aasar*, all work was stopped for the day, and the remaining three hours between that time and sunset were allowed to the slaves for their own use; on Friday, the Mohammedan Sabbath, they were never set to work; and besides the Christian holidays already mentioned, they had a week's rest during the season of Ramadam. Such of the deylic slaves as were employed at the more laborious work of drawing and carrying timber, stone, and other heavy articles, were divided into gangs, and taken out to work only on alternate days.

Many slaves never did an hour's work during their captivity; for by the payment of a monthly sum, equivalent to about seventy cents of our money, any one might be exempted from labor; and even those who could afford to fee their overseers only with a smaller sum, were put to the lightest description of toil. Slaves when in treaty for ransom were never required to work; and as no person was permitted to leave Algiers in debt, money was freely lent at moderate interest to those whose circumstances entitled them to hope for ransom. Money, also, was readily obtained through the Jews, by drawing bills of exchange on the various mercantile cities of Europe. Many slaves, however, by working at trades and other means, were enabled to pay the tax for immunity from public labor, and support themselves comfortably in the bagnes. Of this latter class were tailors, shoemakers, and, strange to say, a good many managed to live well by theft alone. In each bagne were five or six licensed wine-shops, kept by slaves. This was the most profitable business open to a captive—a wine-shop keeper frequently making the price of his ransom in one year; but, preferring wealth to liberty, these persons generally remained slaves until they were able to retire with considerable fortunes. As there was constantly free ingress and egress to and from all the bagnes during the day, the wine-shops were always crowded with people of all nations; and though nominally for the use of the slaves, yet the renegades, who had not forgotten their relish for wine, drank freely therein; and even many of the "turbaned Turks," forgetting the law of their Prophet, copiously indulged in the forbidden beverage. The Moslem, however, was, like Cassio, choleric in his drink, and frequently, brandishing his weapon, and threatening the lives of all about him, would refuse to pay his shot. As no Christian dare strike a Mussulman, an ingenious device was resorted to on such occasions. A stout slave, regularly employed for the purpose, would, at a signal from the landlord, adroitly drop a short ladder over the reeling brawler's head; by this means, without striking a blow, he was speedily brought to the ground, where he was secured till his senses were restored by sleep; and then, if found to have no money, the landlord was entitled to retain his arms until the reckoning was paid.

The largest private slaveholder in Algiers was one Alli Pichellin, Capitan Pasha, or High-Admiral of the fleet, who flourished about the middle of the seventeenth century, and holds a conspicuous position in the Algerine history of the period. He generally possessed from 800 to 900 slaves, whom he kept in a bagne of his own. Emanuel d'Aranda, a Flemish gentleman, who was for some time Pichellin's slave, gives a curious account of bagne-life as he witnessed it. The bagne resembled a long narrow street, with high gates at each end, which were shut every evening after the slaves were mustered at sunset, and opened at sunrise every morning. Though the deylic slaves each received three loaves of bread per day for their sustenance, Pichellin never gave any food whatever to his slaves, unless they were employed at severe labor; for he said that " a man was unworthy the name of slave, if he could not earn or steal between Al Aasar and Al Magrib," (the three hours before sunset allowed to the slaves,) " sufficient to support him for the rest of the day." We may observe here, that a Moor, Morisco, or Jew, if detected in a theft, was punished by the loss of his right hand, and by being opprobiously paraded through the streets mounted upon an ass. At the same time, neither Moor nor Jew dare even accuse a janizary of so disgraceful a crime. Slaves, however, might steal from Moor or Jew with open impunity; for even if caught in the act, neither dare strike a slave; and if complaint was made to the dey, he would merely order the restitution of the stolen goods, refusing to inflict punishment on the following grounds: " That as the Koran did not condemn a man who stole to satisfy his hunger, and as a slave was not a free agent, but compelled to depend upon his master for food, he could not legally be punished for theft." Under such circumstances, we may readily believe that the bagnes, and especially that of Pichellin, were complete dens of thieves. Every evening, as soon as the gates were closed, the plunder of the day was brought forth and sold by auction; the sale being conducted, to the great amusement of the slaves, with all the Turkish gravity and formality of the slave-market. Articles not thus disposed of were left in the hands of one of the captives, who made it his business, for a small commission, to negotiate between the loser and the thief, and accept ransom for the stolen property. An Italian in Pichellin's bagne, named Fontimana, was so expert and confident a thief, that without possessing the smallest fraction of money in the morning, he would invite a party of friends to sup with him in the evening, trusting to his success in thieving through the day to provide the materials for the feast. Of course no satisfaction was obtained when the sufferers complained to Pichellin. " The Christians," he would say, " are all pilfering rascals. I cannot help it. You must be more careful for the future. Have you yet to learn that all my slaves wear hooks at the ends of their fingers ? " Indeed, he seems to have recognized the slaves' right of theft so fully, that he was not angry when he himself became the victim. On one occasion, Fontimana stole and sold the anchor of his master's galley. " How dare you sell my anchor, you Christian dog ? " said Pichellin. " I thought," replied the thief, " that the galley would sail better without the additional weight." The master laughed at the impudent reply, and said no more on the subject. Another characteristic anecdote is recorded of Pichellin and a Portuguese slave, his confidential steward and chamberlain. One day, when cruising off the coast of Portugal, the Capitan

Pasha ran his vessel close in towards the land, and having ordered the small boat to be lowered, called the slave, and pointing to the beach, said: "There is your native country. You have served me faithfully for seventeen years. I now give you your freedom." The Portuguese, falling on his knees, kissed the hem of his late master's robe, and was profuse in his thanks; but Pichellin stopped him, coolly saying: "Do not thank me, but God, who put it into my heart te restore you to liberty." While the boat was being prepared to land him, the Portuguese, apparently overpowered with feelings of joy, descended into the cabin, as if to conceal his emotions, but in reality to steal Pichellin's most valuable jewels and other portable property, which he quickly concealed round his person. As soon as the boat was ready, Pichellin ordered him to be set ashore, and not long after discovered his loss when the wily Portuguese was far out of his reach. Pichellin had some rough virtues: he prided himself on being a man of his word. A Genoese, who had made a fortune by trade at Cadiz, was returning to his native country with his only child, a girl nine years of age, when his vessel was taken on the coast of Spain by Pichellin's cruiser. Not being far from land, the crew of the Christian vessel escaped to the shore, the terrified Genoese going with them, leaving his daughter in the hands of the pirates. Immediately, when he saw that his child was a captive, he waded into the water, and waved his hat as a signal to the Algerines, who, thinking he might be a Moslem captive about to escape, sent a boat for him. On reaching the cruiser, Pichellin, seeing a Christian, exclaimed: "What madman are you that voluntarily surrenders himself a slave?" "That girl is my daughter," said the Genoese: "I could not leave her. If you will set us to ransom, I will pay it; if not, the satisfaction of having done my duty will enable me to support the hardships of slavery." Pichellin appeared struck, and after musing a moment, said: "I will take fifteen hundred dollars for the ransom of you and your daughter." "I will pay it," replied the Genoese. "Hold, master!" exclaimed one of Pichellin's slaves; "I know that man well: he was one of the richest merchants in Cadiz, and can afford to pay ten times that amount for ransom." "Silence, dog!" said the old pirate. "I have said it: my word is my word." Pichellin was further so accommodating as to take the merchant's bill for the money, and set him and his daughter ashore at once.

Each slave who, from poverty, ignorance of a trade, or want of cunning, was compelled to work in the gangs, always carried a bag and a spoon—the bag, to hold anything he might chance to steal; the spoon, in case any charitable person, as was frequently the case, should present him with a mess of pottage. Only those, however, worked in the gangs who could not by any possibility avoid it; and numberless were the schemes adopted by the slaves to raise money to support themselves and secure their exemption from that description of labor. Some, at the risk of the bastinado, smuggled brandy— a strictly forbidden article—into the bagnes, and sold it out in small quantities to such as wanted it. Scholars were well employed by their less learned fellow-captives, to correspond with friends in Europe. Latin was the language preferred for this correspondence, because it was unintelligible to the masters; and the letters frequently contained allusions to property, family affairs, and other circumstances, which, if known, would raise the price of ransom. The great object of all the captives whose wealth entitled them to hopes of ransom, was to simulate poverty, concealing their real circumstances or station in life as much as possible; and not unfrequently the Algerines, deceived by those professions, permitted persons of wealth and consequence to redeem themselves for a trifling sum. On the other hand, persons in much poorer circumstances were often detained a long time in slavery, ill treated, and held to a high ransom, on the bare suspicion of their being wealthy. The Jews, though not permitted to possess slaves, had, through their commercial ramifications in Europe, means of obtaining correct intelligence respecting the property and affairs of many captives, which they did not fail to profit by, receiving a percentage on the increased ransom gained by their information. In a similar way, some artful old slaves, of various countries, lived well by making friends with new captives, treating them at the wine-shops, and, under the pretext of advising them how to act, inducing them to reveal their true circumstances, which the spy immediately communicated to his master. A grave Spanish cavalier made his living by settling quarrels among his countrymen, and deciding all disputes respecting rank, precedence, and the code of honor; a small fee being paid by each of the parties, and his decision invariably respected. A French gentleman contrived to live, and dress well, and give frequent dinner-parties, by a curious financial scheme he invented and practiced. Knowing many of the French renegades, he borrowed money from them for certain periods at moderate interest; and as one sum fell due he met it by a loan from a new creditor. This system, at first sight, would not appear to be profitable; but the renegades being constantly employed in the cruisers, as in a state of continual warfare, some of the creditors were either killed or captured yearly, and having no heirs, the debts were thus canceled in the French captive's favor. "In fine," says D'Aranda, to whom we are indebted for the preceding peculiarities of bagne-life, "there can be no better university to teach men how to shift for their livelihood; for all the nations made some shift to live save the English, who, it seems, are not so shiftful as others. During the winter I spent in the bagne, more than twenty of that nation died from pure want." It is clear that the unfortunate captives here alluded to must have been persons unfit for labor, and unable to procure ransom; and thus, being of no service to their brutal master, were suffered to live or die as it might happen. There can be no doubt that the English and Dutch captives, of the reformed churches, suffered more privations than any others at that period, ere knowledge and intercourse had dulled the fiery edge of religious bigotry. All the public charities for slaves were founded by the Roman Church, and their bounties exclusively bestowed on its followers. No relief was ever given to a heretic unless he became a convert; and it is an exceedingly curious illustration of this religious hatred, that it was as rife and virulent in the breasts of the renegades who had adopted Mohammedanism, as it was amongst those who remained Christians. Another great disadvantage which the English captives must have labored under, was their ignorance of the language. The *lingua franca* spoken in Algiers was a compound of French, Spanish, and Italian, with a few Arabic words; consequently, any native of those countries could acquire it in a few days, while the unfortunate Briton might be months before he could express his meaning or understand what was said to him.

The hardships of slavery were, in all truth, insufficient to extinguish the religious and national animosities of the captives. Dreadful conflicts frequently occurred between the partisans of the eastern and western churches—Spaniards and Italians uniting to batter orthodoxy into the heads of schismatic Greeks and Russians. Nor were such disturbances quelled until a strong body of guards, armed with ponderous cudgels, vigorously attacking both parties, beat them into peaceful submission. Life was not unfrequently lost in these contests. A most serious one, in which several hundred slaves took part on both sides, occurred during D'Aranda's captivity. At the feast of the Assumption, the altar of one of the churches was decorated with the Portuguese arms, with the motto: "God will exalt the humble, and bring down the haughty." The Spaniards, conceiving this to be an insulting reflection on their national honor, tore down the obnoxious decoration, and trampled it under their feet. The Portuguese immediately retaliated, and a battle ensued between the captives of the two nations, which lasted a considerable time, and cost several lives. The ringleaders were severely bastinadoed by their masters, who tauntingly told them to sell their lands and purchase their freedom, and then they might fight for the honor of their respective countries as long and as much as they liked. It is pleasing, however, after reading of such scenes, to find that the slaves frequently got up theatrical performances. One of their favorite pieces was founded on the history of Belisarius.

The negotiations for ransom were either carried on through the Fathers of Redemption, the European consuls, or by the slaves themselves. When a province of the order of Redemption had raised a sufficiently large sum, the resident Father Administrator in Algiers procured a pass from the dey, permitting two fathers to come from Europe to make the redemption. The rule of the order was, that young women and children were to be released first; then adults belonging to the same nation as the ransomers; and after that, if the funds permitted, natives of other countries. But, in general, the fathers brought with them a list of the persons to be released, who had been recommended to their notice by political, ecclesiastical, or other interest. Slaves, who had earned and were willing to pay part of their ransom, found favor in the eyes of the fathers; and slaves with very long beards, or of singular emaciated appearance, were purchased with a view to future effect, in the grand processional displays made by the Redemptionists on their return to Europe.

From a published narrative of a voyage of Redemption made in 1720, we extract the following amusing account of an interview between two French Redemptionists and the dey. The fathers had redeemed their contemplated number of captives with the exception of ten belonging to the dey, but he, piqued that his slaves had not been purchased first, demanded so high a price for each, that they were unwillingly compelled to ransom only three—a French gentleman, his son, and a surgeon. "These slaves being brought in, we offered the price demanded (3,000 dollars) for them. The dey said he would give us another into the bargain. This was a tall, well-made young Hollander, one of the dey's household, who was also present. We remonstrated with the dey, that this fourth would not do for us, he being a Lutheran, and also not of our country. The dey's officers laughed, and said, he is a good Catholic. The dey said he neither knew nor cared about that. The man was a Christian, and that he should go along with the other three for 5,000 dollars."

After a good deal of fencing, and the dey having reduced his demand by 500 dollars, the father continues: "We yet held firm to have only the three we had offered 3,000 dollars for. 'All this is to no purpose,' said the dey; 'I am going to send all four to you, and, willing or not willing, you shall have them at the price I specified, nor shall you leave Algiers until you have paid it.' But we still held out, spite of all his threats, telling him that he was master of his own dominions, but that our money falling short, we could not purchase slaves at such a price. We then took leave of him, and that very day he sent us the three slaves we had cheapened, and let us know we should have the other on the day of our departure." The reader will not be sorry to learn that the fathers were ultimately compelled to purchase and take away with them the "young Lutheran Hollander."

The primary object of the Redemptionists being to raise money for the ransom of captives, every advantage was taken to appeal successfully to the sympathies of the Christian world, and no method was more remunerative than the grand processions which they made with the liberated slaves on their return to Europe. Father Comelin gives us full particulars of these proceedings. The ransomed captives, dressed in red Moorish caps and white bornouses, and wearing *chains*—they never wore them in Algiers—were met at the entrance of each town they passed through by all the clerical, civil, municipal, and military dignitaries of the place. Banners, wax-candles, music, and "*angels* covered with gold, silver, and precious stones," accompanied them in grand procession through the town; the chief men of the district carrying silver salvers, on which they collected money from the populace, to be applied to future redemptions.

The first general ransom of British captives was made by money apportioned by parliament for the purpose, during the exciting events of the civil war. The first vessel dispatched was unfortunately burned in the Bay of Gibraltar, and the treasure lost. A fresh sum of money was again granted; and in 1646, Mr. Cason, the parliamentary agent, arrived at Algiers. In his official dispatch to the "Committee of the Navy," the agent states that, counting renegades, there were then 750 English captives in Algiers; and proceeds to say that "they come to much more a head than I expected; the reason is, there be many women and children, which cost £50 per head, first penny, and might sell for £100. Besides, there are divers which were masters of ships, calkers, carpenters, sailmakers, coopers, and surgeons, and others who are highly esteemed." The agent succeeded in redeeming 244 English, Scotch, and Irish captives at the average cost of £38 each. From the official record of their several names, places of birth, and prices, it appears that more was paid for the females than the males. The three highest sums on the list are £75, paid for Mary Bruster, of Youghal; £65, for Alice Hayes, of Edinburgh; and £50, for Elizabeth Mancor, of Dundee. The names of several natives of Baltimore—in all probability some of those carried off when that town was sacked fifteen years before—are in this list of redeemed. It will scarcely be believed, that strong opposition was made by the mercantile interest against money being granted by parliament for the ransom of those poor captives—on the ground, as the opposers' petition expresses: "That if the slaves be redeemed upon a public score, then seamen will render themselves to the mercy of the Algerines, and not fight in defense of the goods and ships of the merchants." A more curious instance of wisdom in relation to this subject, occurred during the profligate reign of the second Charles. A large sum of money appropriated for the redemption of captives having been *lost*, somehow, between the Navy Board and the Commissioners of Excise, it was gravely proposed: "That whatever loss or damage the English shall sustain from Algerines, shall be required and made good to the losers out of the estates of the Jews here in England. Because such a law may save a great expense of Christian treasure and blood!"

The first attempt to release English captives by force from Algiers was made in 1621, after the project had been debated in the privy council for nearly four years. With the exception of rescuing about thirty slaves of various nations, who swam off to the English ships, this expedition turned out a perfect failure. In 1662, another fleet was sent, a treaty was made with the dey, and 150 captives ransomed with money raised by the English clergy in their several parishes. In 1664, 1672, 1682, and 1686, other treaties were made with the Algerines: the frequent recurrence of those treaties shows the little attention paid to them by the pirates.

In 1682, Louis XIV. determined to stop the Algerine aggressions on France; and at the same time to try a new and terrible invention in the art of war. Renau d'Elicagarry had just laid before the French government a plan for building ships of sufficient strength to bear the recoil caused by firing bombs from mortars. Louis, accordingly, sent Admiral Duquesne with a fleet and some of the new bomb-vessels to destroy Algiers. The expedition was unsuccessful, the bombs proving nearly as destructive to the French as to their enemies. The next year, Duquesne returned, and, taught by experience, succeeded in firing all his bombs into the pirate city. The terrified dey capitulated, and surrendered 600 slaves to the fleet; but sixty-four of those unfortunate captives being discovered by the French officers to be Englishmen, were sent back to the dey! While a treaty was in preparation, the janizaries, indignant at the loss of their slaves, murdered the dey, elected another, and manning their forts, commenced firing upon the French. Duquesne's bombs being all expended, he was obliged to sheer off and return to France. In 1688, Marshal d'Estrées, with a powerful fleet, arrived off Algiers. The bombs told with terrible effect, and the dey soon sued for peace; but d'Estrées replied that he came not to treat, but to punish. On this occasion, 10,000 bombs were thrown into Algiers; the city was reduced to ruins, and the humbled pirates compelled to sign a treaty dictated by the conqueror. In a few years, however, the demolished fortifications were reërected stronger than ever, and the incorrigible Algerines busy at their old trade of piracy.

Algerine slavery at last came to an end. At the close of the long European war in 1814, the chivalrous Sir Sidney Smith proposed a union of all orders of knighthood for the abolition of white slavery. His plan was to form "an amphibious force, to be termed the Knights Liberators, which, without compromising any flag, and without depending on the wars or political events of nations, should constantly guard the Mediterranean, and take upon itself the important office of watching, pursuing, and capturing all pirates by sea and land." Though Sir Sidney's project fell to the ground, yet it had the good effect of calling the attention of the British nation to the subject; and in 1816, Lord Exmouth, with an English fleet, sailed to Algiers, destroyed the dey's shipping, leveled the fortifications, released altogether about 3,000 captives, and abolished forever the atrocious system of Christian slavery. The subsequent history of Algiers is foreign to our subject; we may merely add, that in 1830 it became, by right of conquest, a French colony.

Limited space compels us to say but little respecting the other piratical states of Barbary—Tunis, Tripoli, and Morocco. They, however, only dabbled in piratical slavery, not making it a systematized profession like the Algerines. When, about the middle of the seventeenth century, there were upwards of 30,000 Christian slaves in Algiers, there were not more than 7,000 in Tunis, 5,000 in Tripoli, and 1,500 in Morocco. In the latter part of the sixteenth century, Tunis and Tripoli fell under the power of the Porte, and for some time were ruled by Turkish viceroys; but in a few years the janizaries, as at Algiers, elected their own rulers; and subsequently the native race, overpowering the janizaries, gained the ascendency over their Ottoman masters. Since Blake humbled the pride of the Tunisians in 1665, and Narbro burned the Tripolitan fleet in 1676, neither of those states has inflicted much injury on British shipping. The treatment of slaves at Tunis and Tripoli was considered to be even milder than at Algiers: the Brothers of Redemption had establishments at both places. It was with Tripoli, in 1796, that the United States, through their envoy, Joel Barlow, made the treaty which caused so much animadversion. In that treaty, Mr. Barlow, to conciliate the Mohammedan powers, declared that "the government of the United States of America is not, in any sense, founded on the Christian religion." Notwithstanding so bold an assertion, the faithless Tripolitans declared war against the United

States in 1801; and after a contest highly creditable to the American navy, then in its infancy, peace was concluded between the two powers, and 200 captives released from slavery. Both Tunis and Tripoli quietly renounced the practice of Christian slavery, when solicited to do so by Lord Exmouth, in 1816

All the territories which formed part of the Roman Empire in Africa, subsequently fell under the sway of Constantinople, except Morocco. Its fertile soil, almost within cannon-shot of Europe, "on the very verge and hem of civilization," has ever attracted European cupidity, and the patriotic energy of its people has ever repelled Christian domination. Almost all the semi-barbarous states of the world have fallen a prey to European ambition and enterprise; not only dynasties, but races have been extinguished; and yet Morocco is still as free from foreign influence as the surf of the Atlantic that thunders on its sands. At one period, indeed, almost subjugated, it was little more than a Portuguese province, when the Cherifs, a family of mendicant fanatics, claiming to be the lineal descendants of Mohammed, expelled the invaders, and founded the present dynasty. Spain, it is true, still holds two fortresses as penal settlements on the coast; but no Spaniard can ever look over an embrasure on the land-side without being saluted with a long Moorish rifle. It is an actual fact, that the governors of those prison forts receive intelligence of what passes in the interior of Morocco, from Madrid.

As in other parts of Barbary, it was the Moriscos, after their expulsion from Spain, that founded the system of piratical slavery in Morocco. Who has not read of the Sallee rovers in *Robinson Crusoe*, and the old ballads? Yet, compared with the Algerine, theirs was, after all, a very petty kind of piracy. The harbor of Sallee, the principal port of Morocco, being only suitable for vessels drawing little water, piracy was carried on in galleys and row-boats, and was formidable only to small unarmed vessels. In 1637, an English fleet, under Admiral Rainborough, took Sallee, and released 290 British captives — "as many as would have cost £10,000." Soon after, the emperor of Morocco sent an ambassador to London, who, on his presentation to Charles I., went to court in procession, taking with him a number of liberated captives dressed in white, and many hawks and Barbary horses splendidly caparisoned. Christian slaves in Morocco were invariably the property of the emperor, and were mostly employed in constructing buildings of *tapia*—a composition somewhat resembling our concrete. In the latter part of the seventeenth century, during the reign of Muley Ishmael, a cruel tyrant to his own subjects, and who had a mania for building, the captives in Morocco were ill-treated, and compelled to work hard. Yet even then, one Thomas Phelps, who made his escape from Mequinez, tells us that the emperor came frequently amongst the slaves when at work, and would "bolt out encouraging words to them, such as: 'May God send you all safe home to your own countries!'" and any captive was excused from work by the payment of a *blanquil*—a sum equivalent to four cents—per day. In 1685, the emperor had 800 Christian slaves, 260 of whom were English; many of those, however, were subsequently

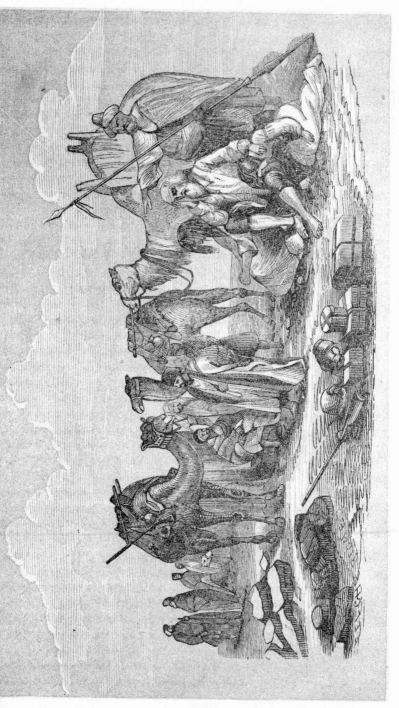

CHRISTIAN SLAVERY IN BARBARY

ransomed. After Muley Ishmael's death, the captives were much better treated. Captain Braithwaite, who accompanied Mr. Russell on a mission from the English government in 1727, thus describes the condition of the Christian captives in Morocco : "Most part of them," he says, " have expectations of getting back to their native country at one time or another. The emperor keeps most of them at work upon his buildings, but not to such hard labor that our laborers go through. The *Canute*, where they are lodged, is infinitely better than our prisons. In short, the captives have a much greater property in what they get than the Moors ; several of them being rich, and many have carried considerable sums out of the country. Several keep their mules, and some their servants, to the truth of which we are all witnesses." Morocco was the first of the Barbary states that gave up the practice of Christian slavery. In a treaty made with Spain in 1799, the emperor declared his desire that the name of slavery might be effaced from the memory of mankind.*

CHAPTER VII.

AFRICAN SLAVE TRADE FROM THE FIFTEENTH TO THE EIGHTEENTH CENTURY.

Negroland, or Nigritia, described.—Slavery among the Natives.—Mungo Park's estimate of the number of Slaves.—The Portuguese navigators explore the African coast.—Natives first carried off in 1434.—Portuguese establish the Slave Trade on the Western Coast—followed by the Spaniards.—America discovered—colonized by the Spaniards, who reduce the Natives to Slavery—they die by thousands in consequence.—The Dominican priests intercede for them.—Negroes from Africa substituted as Slaves, 1510. —Cardinal Ximenes remonstrates.—Charles V. encourages the trade.—Insurrection of the Slaves at Segovia.—Other nations colonize America.—First recognition of the Slave Trade by the English government in 1562, reign of Elizabeth.—First Negroes imported into Virginia in a Dutch vessel in 1620.—The French and other commercial nations engage in the traffic.—The great demand for Slaves on the African coast.—Negroes fighting and kidnapping each other.—Slave factories established by the English, French, Dutch, Spanish, and Portuguese.—Slave factory described.—How Slaves were procured in the interior.

NEGROLAND, or Nigritia, is that part of the interior of Africa stretching from the great desert on the north to the unascertained commencement of Caffreland on the south, and from the Atlantic on the west to Abyssinia on the east. In fact, the entire interior of this great continent may be called the land of the negroes. The ancients distinguished it from the comparatively civilized countries lying along the coast of the Mediterranean and the Red Sea by calling the latter Libya, and the former Ethiopia. It is upon Ethiopia in an especial manner that the curse of slavery has fallen. At first, it bore but a share of the burden ; Britons and Scythians were the fellow-slaves of the Ethiopian : but at last all the other nations of the earth seemed to conspire against the ne-

---

* Chambers' Miscellany.

gro race, agreeing never to enslave each other, but to make the blacks the slaves of all alike. Thus, this race of human beings has been singled out, whether owing to the accident of color, or to their peculiar fitness for certain kinds of labor, for infamy and misfortune; and the abolition of the practice of promiscuous slavery in the modern world, was purchased by the introduction of a slavery confined entirely to negroes.

The nations and tribes of negroes in Africa, who thus ultimately became the universal prey of Europeans, were themselves equally guilty in subjecting men to perpetual bondage. In the most remote times, every Ethiopian man of consequence had his slaves, just as a Greek or Roman master had. Savage as he was, he at least resembled the citizen of a civilized state in this. He possessed his domestic slaves, or bondmen, hereditary on his property; and besides these, he was always acquiring slaves by whatever means he could, whether by purchase from slave-dealers, or by war with neighboring tribes. The slaves of a negro master in this case would be his own countrymen, or at least men o his own race and color; some of them born on the same spot with himself, some of them captives who had been brought from a distance of a thousand miles. Of course, the farther a captive was taken from his home, the more valuable he would be, as having less chance of escape; and therefore it would be a more common practice to sell a slave taken in war with a neighboring tribe, than to retain him as a laborer so near his home. And just as in the cities of the civilized countries, we find the slave population often outnumbering the free, so in the villages of the interior of Africa the negro slaves were often more numerous than the negro masters. Park, in his travels among the negroes, found that in many villages the slaves were three times as numerous as the free persons; and it is likely that the proportion was not very different in more ancient times. In ancient times, the Garamantes used to sell negroes to the Libyans; and so a great proportion of the slaves of the Carthaginians and the Egyptians must have been blacks brought northwards across the desert. From Carthage and Egypt, again, these negroes would be exported into different countries of southern Europe; and a stray negro might even find his way into the more northern regions. They seem always to have been valued for their patience, their mild temper, and their extraordinary power of endurance; and for many purposes negro slaves would be preferred by their Roman masters to all others, even to the shaggy, scowling Picts. But though it is quite certain that negroes were used as slaves in ancient Europe, still the negro never came to enjoy that miserable preëminence which later times have assigned to him, treating him as the born drudge of the human family. White-skinned men were slaves as well as he; and if, among the Carthaginians and Egyptians, negro slaves were more common than any other, it was only because they were more easily procurable.

The Portuguese were the first to set the example of stealing negroes; they were the first to become acquainted with Africa. Till the fifteenth century, no part of Africa was known except the chain of countries on the coast of the Mediterranean and the Red Sea, beginning with Morocco, and ending with

Abyssinia and the adjoining desert. The Arabs and Moors, indeed, traversing the latter, knew something about Ethiopia, or the land of the negroes, but what knowledge they had was confined to themselves; and to the Europeans the whole of the continent to the south of the desert was an unknown and unexplored land. There were traditions of two ancient circumnavigations of the continent by the Phœnicians and the Carthaginians, one down the Red Sea, and round the Cape of Good Hope from the east, the other through the Straits of Gibraltar, and round the same cape from the west; but these traditions were vague and questionable. They were sufficient, however, to set the brains of modern navigators a-working; and now that they were possessed of the mariner's compass, they might hope to repeat the Carthaginian feat of circumnavigating Africa; if, indeed, Africa were circumnavigable. In the year 1412, therefore, a series of attempts was begun by the Portuguese, at the instigation of Prince Henry, to sail southward along the western coast. In every succeeding attempt, the bold navigators got farther and farther south, past the Canaries, past the Cape Verds, along the coast of Guinea, through the Bight of Biafra, down that long unnamed extent of coast south of the equator, until at last the perseverance of three generations succeeded, and the brave Vasco de Gama, in 1497, rounded the great cape itself, turned his prow northward, sailed through the Mozambique Channel, and then, as if protesting that he had done with Africa all that navigator could, steered through the open ocean right for the shores of India. The third or fourth of these attempts brought the Portuguese into contact with the negroes. Before the year 1470, the whole of the Guinea coast had been explored. As early as 1434, Antonio Gonzales, a Portuguese captain, landed on this coast, and carried away with him some negro boys, whom he sold to one or two Moorish families in the south of Spain. The act seems to have provoked some criticism at the time. But from that day, it became customary for the captains of vessels landing on the Gold Coast, or other parts of the coast of Guinea, to carry away a few young negroes of both sexes. The labor of these negroes, whether on board the ships which carried them away, or in the ports to which the ships belonged, being found valuable, the practice soon grew into a traffic; and negroes, instead of being carried away in twos and threes as curiosities, came to form a part of the cargo, as well as gold, ivory, and gum. The ships no longer went on voyages of discovery, they went for profitable cargoes; and the inhabitants of the negro villages along the coast, delighted with the beads, and knives, and bright cloths which they got in exchange for gold, ivory, and slaves, took care to have these articles ready for any ship that might land. Thus the slave-trade, properly so called, began. The Spaniards were the first nation to become parties with the Portuguese in this infamous traffic.

At first, the deportation of slaves from Africa was conducted on a limited scale; but about seventy years after Gonzales had carried away the first negro boys from the Guinea coast, an opening was all at once made for negro labor, which made it necessary to carry away blacks, not by occasional ship-loads, but by thousands annually.

America was discovered in 1492. The part of this new world which was first colonized by the Spaniards, consisted of those islands scattered through the great gap of ocean between North and South America; which, as they were thought to be the outermost individuals of the great Eastern Indies, to which it was the main object of Columbus to effect a western passage, were called the West Indies. When the Spaniards took possession of these islands, they employed the natives, or Indians, as they were called, to do all the heavy kinds of labor for them, such as carrying burdens, digging for gold, &c. In fact, these Indians became slaves of their Spanish conquerors; and it was customary, in assigning lands to a person, to give him, at the same time, all the Indians upon them. Thus, when Bernal Diaz paid his respects to Velasquez, the governor of Cuba, the governor promised him the first Indians he had at his disposal. According to all accounts, never was there a race of men more averse to labor, or constitutionally more unfit for it, than these native Americans. They are described as the most listless, improvident people on the face of the earth, and though capable of much passive endurance, drooped and lost all heart whenever they were put to active labor. Labor, ill-usage, and the small-pox together, carried them off in thousands, and wherever a Spaniard trod, he cleared a space before him, as if he carried a blasting influence in his person. When Albuquerque entered on his office as governor of St. Domingo in 1515, he found that, whereas in 1508 the natives numbered 60,000, they did not then number 14,000. The condition of these poor aborigines under the Spanish colonists became so heart-breaking, that the Dominican priests stepped out in their behalf, asserting them to be free men, and denying the right of the Spaniards to make them slaves. This led to a vehement controversy, which lasted several years, and in which Bartholomew de Las Casas, a benevolent priest, figured most conspicuously as the friend of the Indians. So energetic and persevering was he, that he produced a great impression in their favor upon the Spanish government at home.

Unfortunately, the relaxation in favor of one race of men was procured at the expense of the slavery of another. Whether La Casas himself was led, by his extreme interest in the Indians, to be so inconsistent as to propose the employment of negroes in their stead, or whether the suggestion came from some other person, does not distinctly appear; but it is certain, that what the Spaniards spared the Indians, they inflicted with double rigor upon the negroes. Laborers must be had, and the negroes were the kind of laborers that would suit. As early as 1503, a few negroes had been carried across the Atlantic; and it was found that not only could each of these negroes do as much work as four Indians, but that, while the Indians were fast becoming extinct, the egroes were thriving and propagating wonderfully. The plain inference was, that they should import negroes as fast as possible; and this was accordingly done. "In the year 1510," says the old Spanish historian Herrera, "the king of Spain ordered fifty slaves to be sent to Hispaniola to work in the gold mines, the natives being looked upon as a weak people, and unfit for labor " And this was but a beginning; for, notwithstanding the remonstrances of Cardinal Ximenes, ship-load after ship-load of negroes was carried to the West Indies. We find Charles V. giving one of his Flemish favorites an exclusive right of shipping 4000 negroes to the new world—a monopoly which that favorite sold to some Genoese merchants for 25,000 ducats. These merchants organized the traffic; many more than 4000 negroes were required to do the work; and though at first the negroes were exorbitantly dear, they multiplied so fast, and were imported in such quantities, that at last there was a negro for every Spaniard in the colonies; and in whatever new direction the Spaniards advanced in their career of conquest, negroes went along with them.

. The following extract from the Spanish historian already quoted will show not only that the negroes were very numerous, but that sometimes also they proved refractory, and endeavored to get the upper hand of their masters: "There was so great a number of blacks in the governments of Santa Marta and Venezuela, and so little precaution was used in the management of them, or rather the liberty they had was so great, being allowed the use of arms, which they much delight in, that, prompted by their natural fierceness and arrogance, a small number of the most polished, who valued themselves for their valor and gayety, resolved to rescue themselves from servitude, and become their own masters, believing that they might live at their own will among the Indians. Those few summoning others, who, like a thoughtless brutish people, were not capable of making any reflection, but were always ready at the beck of those of their own color for whom they had any respect or esteem, they readily complied. Assembling to the number of about 250, and repairing to the settlement of New Segovia, they divided themselves into companies, and appointed captains, and saluted one king, who had the most boldness and resolution to assume that title; and he, intimating that they should all be rich, and lords of the country, by destroying the Spaniards, assigned every one the Spanish woman that should fall to his lot, with other such insolent projects and machinations. The fame of this commotion was soon spread abroad throughout all the cities of those two governments, where preparations were speedily made for marching against the blacks, as well to prevent their being joined by the rest of their countrymen that were not yet gone to them, as to obviate the many mischiefs which those barbarians might occasion to the country. In the meantime, the inhabitants of Tucuyo sent succors to the city of Segovia, which was but newly founded; and the very night that relief arrived there, the blacks, who had got intelligence of it, resolved to be beforehand with the Spaniards; and in order that, greater forces thus coming in, they might not grow too strong for them, they fell upon those Spaniards, killing five or six of them, and a clergyman. However, the success did not answer their expectation, for the Spaniards being on their guard, readily took the alarm, fought the blacks courageously, and killed a considerable number. The rest, perceiving that their contrivance had miscarried, retired. The next morning Captain James de Lassado arrived there with forty men from the government of Venezuela, and, judging that no time ought to be lost in that affair, marched against the blacks with the men he had brought, and those

7

who were before at New Segovia. Perceiving that they had quitted the post they had first taken, and were retired to a strong place on the mountain, he pursued, overtook, and attacked them; and though they drew up and stood on their defense, he soon routed and put them all to the sword, sparing none but their women and some female Indians they had with them, after which he returned to Segovia, and those provinces were delivered from much uneasiness."

The Spaniards did not long remain alone in the guilt of this new traffic. At first the Spaniards had all America to themselves; and as it was in America that negro labor was in demand, the Spaniards alone possessed large numbers of negroes. But other nations come to have colonies in America, and as negroes were found invaluable in the foundation of a new colony, other nations came also to patronize the slave trade. The first recognition of the trade by the English government was in 1562, in the reign of Elizabeth, when an act was passed legalizing the purchase of negroes; yet, as the earlier attempts made by the English to plant colonies in North America were unsuccessful, there did not, for some time after the passing of this act, exist any demand for negroes sufficient to induce the owners of English trading vessels visiting the coast of Africa to make negroes a part of their cargo. It was in the year 1620 that the first negroes were imported into Virginia; and even then it was not an English slave-ship which supplied them, but a Dutch one, which chanced to touch on the coast with some negroes on board bound for the Spanish colonies. These negroes the Virginian planters purchased on trial; and the bargain was found to be so good, that in a short time negroes came to be in great demand in Virginia. Nor were the planters any longer indebted to the chance visits of Dutch ships for a supply of negro-laborers; for the English merchants, vigilant and calculating then as they are now, immediately embarked in the traffic, and instructed the captains of their vessels visiting the African coast to barter for negroes as well as wax and elephants' teeth. In a similar way the French, the Dutch, and all other nations of any commercial importance, came to be involved in the traffic; those who had colonies, to supply the demand there; those who had no colonies, to make money by assisting to supply the demand of the colonies of other countries. Before the middle of the seventeenth century, the African slave-trade was in full vigor; and all Europe was implicated in the buying and selling of negroes.

So universal is the instinct for barter, that the immediate effect of the new and great demand for slaves was to create its own supply. Slavery, as we have said, existed in Negroland from time immemorial, but on a comparatively limited scale. The effect of the demand by the European ships gave an unhappy stimulus to the natural animosities of the various negro tribes skirting the west coast; and, tempted by the clasp-knives, and looking-glasses, and wonderful red cloth, which the white men always brought with them to exchange for slaves, the whole negro population for many miles inland began fighting and kidnapping each other. Not only so, but the interior of the continent itself, the district of Lake Tchad, and the mystic source of the fatal Niger, hitherto untrodden by the foot of a white invader, began to feel the tremor caused by the traffic on the coast; and ere long, the very negroes who seemed safest in their central obscurities, were drained away to meet the increasing demand; either led captive by warlike visitants from the west, or handed from tribe to tribe till they reached the sea. In this way, eventually, Central Africa, with its teeming myriads of negroes, came to be the great mother of slaves for exportation, and the negro villages on the coast the warehouses, as it were, where the slaves were stowed away till the ships of the white men arrived to carry them off.

European skill and foresight assisted in giving constancy and regularity to the supply of negroes from the interior. At first the slave vessels only visited the Guinea coast, and bargained with the negroes of the villages there for what quantity of wax, or gold, or negroes they had to give. But this was a clumsy way of conducting business. The ships had to sail along a large tract of coast, picking up a few negroes at one place, and a little ivory or gold at another; sometimes even the natives of a village might have no elephants' teeth and no negroes to give; and even under the most favorable circumstances, it took a considerable time to procure a decent cargo. No coast is so pestilential as that of Africa, and hence the service was very repulsive and very dangerous. As an improvement on this method of trading, the plan was adopted very early of planting small settlements of Europeans at intervals along the slave-coast, whose business it should be to negotiate with the negroes, stimulate them to activity in their slave-hunting expeditions, purchase the slaves brought in, and warehouse them until the arrival of the ships. These settlements were called slave factories. Factories of this kind were planted all along the western coast from Cape Verd to the equator, by English, French, Dutch, and Portuguese traders. Their appearance, the character of the men employed in them, their internal arrangements, and their mode of carrying on the traffic, are well described in the following extract from Mr. Howison's book on "European Colonies":

"As soon as the parties concerned had fixed upon the site of their proposed commercial establishment, they began to erect a fort of greater or less magnitude, having previously obtained permission to that effect from the natives. The most convenient situation for a building of the kind was considered to be at the confluence of a river with the sea, or upon an island lying within a few miles of the coast. In the first case, there was the advantage of inland navigation; and in the second, that of the security and defensibleness of an insular position, besides its being more cool and healthy than any other.

The walls of the fort enclosed a considerable space of ground, upon which were built the necessary magazines for the reception of merchandise, and also barracks for the soldiers and artificers, and a depôt for slaves; so that, in the event of external hostilities, the gates might be shut, and the persons and the property belonging to the establishment placed in security. The quarters for the officers and agents employed at the factory were in general erected upon the ramparts, or at least adjoining them; while the negroes in their service, and any others that might be attracted to the spot, placed their huts outside of the walls of the fort, but under the protection of its guns.

The command of the establishment was vested in the hands of one individual, who had various subordinates, according to the extent of the trade carried on at the place; and if the troops who garrisoned the fort exceeded twenty or thirty, a commissioned officer usually had charge of them.   The most remarkable forts were St. George del Mina, erected by the Portuguese, though it subsequently fell into the hands of the Dutch; Cape Coast Castle, the principal establishment of the English; Fort Louis, at the mouth of the Senegal, generally occupied by the French; and Goree, situated upon an island of the same name, near Cape Verd.   Most of these forts mounted from fifty to sixty pieces of cannon, and contained large reservoirs for water, and were not only impregnable to the negroes, but capable of standing a regular siege by a European force.

The individuals next in importance to the director or governor were the factors, who ranked according to their standing in the company's service.   The seniors generally remained at headquarters, and had the immediate management of the trade there, and the care of the supplies of European merchandise which were always kept in store.   The junior factors were employed in carrying on the traffic in the interior of the country, which they did sometimes by ascending the rivers in armed vessels, and exchanging various articles for slaves, gold-dust, and ivory, with the negroes inhabiting the neighborhood; and sometimes by establishing themselves for several months in a large town or populous district, and, as it were, keeping a shop to which the natives might resort for traffic.

The European subordinates of the establishment consisted of clerks, bookkeepers, warehousemen, artificers, mechanics, gunners, and private soldiers, all of whom had particular quarters assigned for their abode, and lived under military discipline.   The soldiers employed in the service of the different African companies were mostly invalids, and persons who had been dismissed from the army on account of bad conduct.   Destitute of the means of subsistence at home, such men willingly engaged to go to the coast of Africa, where they knew they would be permitted to lead a life of ease, indolence, and licentiousness, and be exposed to no danger except that of a deadly climate, which was in reality the most certain and inevitable one that they could anywhere encounter.   Few of the troops in any of the forts were fit for active duty, which was of the less consequence, because they were seldom or never required to fight except upon the ramparts of the place in which they might be quartered, and not often even there.   Hence they spent their time in smoking, in drinking palm wine, and in gaming, and were generally carried off by fever or dissipation within two years after their arrival in the country.   A stranger, on first visiting any of the African forts, felt that there was something both horrible and ludicrous in the appearance of its garrison; for the individuals composing it appeared ghastly, debilitated, and diseased, to a degree that is unknown in other climates; and their tattered and soiled uniforms, resembling each other only in meanness, and not in color, suggested the idea of the wearers being a band of drunken deserters, or of starved and maltreated prisoners of war.

Each company was in the practice of annually sending a certain number of ships to its respective establishments, freighted with European goods suitable for traffic; while its factors in Africa had in the meantime been collecting slaves, ivory, gumarabic, and other productions of the country; so that the vessels on their arrival suffered no detention, but always found a return cargo ready for them.

Though the forts were principally employed as places of safe deposit for merchandise received from Europe or collected at outposts, they were also generally the scene of a considerable trade, being resorted to for that purpose not only by the coast negroes, but often also by dealers from the interior of the country, who would bring slaves, ivory, and gold-dust for traffic. Persons of this description were always honorably, and even ceremoniously received by the governor or by the factors, and conciliated in every possible way, lest they might carry their goods to another market. They were invited to enter the fort, and were treated with liquors, sweetmeats, and presents, and urged to drink freely; and no sooner did they show symptoms of confusion of ideas, than the factors proposed to trade with them, and displayed the articles which they were disposed to give in exchange for their slaves, &c. The unsuspicious negro-merchant, dazzled by the variety of tempting objects placed before him, and exhilarated by wine or brandy, was easily led to conclude a bargain little advantageous to himself; and before he had fully recovered his senses, his slaves, ivory, and gold-dust were transferred to the stores of the factory, and he was obliged to be contented with what he had in his moments of inebriety agreed to accept in exchange for them."

From this extract, it appears that not only did the managers of these factories receive all the negroes who might be brought down to the coast, but that emissaries, "junior factors," as they were called, penetrated into the interior, as if thoroughly to infect the central tribes with the spirit of commerce. The result of this was the creation of large slave-markets in the interior, where the negro slaves were collected for sale, and where slave-merchants, whether negro, Arabic, or European, met to conclude their wholesale bargains. One of these great slave-markets was at Timbuctoo; but for the most part the slaves were brought down in droves by *Slatees*, or negro slave-merchants, to the European factories on the coast. At the time that Park traveled in Africa, so completely had the negroes of the interior become possessed with the trading spirit, so much had the capture and abduction of negroes grown into a profession, that these native slave-merchants were observed to treat the slaves they were driving to the coast with considerable kindness. The negroes were, indeed, chained together to prevent their escape. Those who were refractory had a thick billet of wood fastened to their ankle; and as the poor wretches quitting their native spots became sullen and moody, their limbs at the same time swelling and breaking out in sores with the fatigue of traveling, it was often necessary to apply the whip. Still, the Slatees were not wantonly cruel; and there was nothing they liked better than to see their slaves merry. Occasionally they would halt in their march, and encourage the negroes to sing their

snatches of song, or play their games of hazard, or dance under the shade of
the tamarind tree. This, however, was only the case with the professional
slave-driver, who was commissioned to convey the negroes to the coast; and
if we wish to form a conception of the extent and intricate working of the
curse inflicted upon the negroes by their contact with white men, we must set
ourselves to imagine all the previous kidnapping and fighting which must have
been necessary to procure every one of these droves which the Slatees carried
down. What a number of processes must have conspired to bring a sufficient
number of slaves together to form a drove! In one case, it would be a negro
master selling a number of his spare slaves; and what an amount of suffering
even in this case must there have been arising from the separation of relatives!
In another case, it would be a father selling his son, or a son selling his old
father, or a creditor selling his insolvent debtor. In a third, it would be a
starving family voluntarily surrendering itself to slavery. When a scarcity
occurred, instances used to be frequent of famishing negroes coming to the
British stations in Africa and begging "to be put upon the slave-chain." In
a fourth case it would be a savage selling the boy or girl he had kidnapped a
week ago on purpose. In a fifth, it would be a petty negro chief disposing
of twenty or thirty negroes taken alive in a recent attack upon a village at a
little distance from his own. Sometimes these forays in quest of negroes to
sell are on a very large scale, and then they are called slave-hunts. The king
of one negro country collects a large army, and makes an expedition into the
territories of another negro king, ravaging and making prisoners as he goes.
If the inhabitants make a stand against him, a battle ensues, in which the
invading army is generally victorious. As many are killed as may be necessary
to decide that such is the case; and the captives are driven away in thousands,
to be kept on the property of the victor till he finds opportunities of selling
them. In 1794, the king of the southern Foulahs, a powerful tribe in Nigritia, was known to have an army of 16,000 men constantly employed in these
slave-hunting expeditions into his neighbors' territories. The slaves they procured made the largest item in his revenue.

CHAPTER VIII.

Slave Traffic of the Levant.—Nubian Slaves.

The Mohammedan slave-trade.—Nubian slaves captured for the slave markets of the
Levant.—Mohammed Ali.—Grand expeditions for hunting.—Annual tribute of slaves.
—The encampment.—Attack upon the villages.—Courage of the natives.—Their heroic
resistance.—Cruelty of the victors.—Destruction of villages. The captives sold into
slavery.

W HILE Central and Eastern Africa were ravaged for slaves to supply the
American market, Nubia and other districts were equally laid under contribu-

tion to supply the slave markets of the Levant, of Egypt, Turkey and the East. The one may be called the Christian, the other the Mohammedan Slave Trade. The main difference between the two trades was, that while the Europeans generally bought slaves after they had been captured, the less fastidious Turks captured slaves for themselves. We have been accustomed to interest ourselves so much in the western or Christian slave-trade, that we have paid but little attention to the other. While the one trade has been legally abolished, the other is carried on as vigorously as ever. A traffic in negroes is at present going on between Negroland and the whole of the East. While it has been declared illegal to carry away a negro from the coast of Guinea, negroes are bought and sold daily in the public slave markets of Cairo and Constantinople.

When Dr. Madden, of England, went to Egypt in 1840, as the bearer of a letter from the Anti-Slavery Convention to Mohammed Ali, the ruler of Egypt, congratulating him upon his having issued an order abolishing the slave hunts, to his great surprise, he found that the order, though issued, had never been enforced, and probably never would be. The truth is, that Mohammed himself had brought the system of hunting slaves to a high degree of perfection. Nubia was his principal hunting ground, into which he permitted no intruder. His own expeditions were conducted on a grand scale; and generally took place after the rainy season. From Dr. Madden's work, we extract a description of these slave hunts: "The capturing expedition consists of from 1000 to 2000 regular foot soldiers; from 400 to 800 mounted Bedouins, armed with guns and pistols; from 300 to 500 militia, half-naked savages on dromedaries, armed with spears, and 1000 more on foot, armed with small lances. As soon as everything is ready, the march begins. They usually take from two to four field-pieces, and only sufficient bread for the first eight days. They take by force on the route such oxen, sheep, and other cattle as they may need, making no reparation and listening to no complaints, as the governor himself is present.

As soon as they arrive at the nearest mountains in Nubia, the inhabitants are asked to give the appointed number of slaves as their customary tribute. This is usually done with readiness, as they are well aware that by an obstinate refusal, they expose themselves to far greater sufferings. If the slaves are given without resistance, the inhabitants of that mountain are preserved from the horrors of an open attack; but as the food of the soldiers begins to fail about that time, the poor people are obliged to procure the necessary provisions as well as the specified number of slaves, and the Turks do not consider whether the harvest has been good or bad. All that is not freely given, the soldiers take by force. Like so many bloodhounds, they know how to discover the hidden stores, and frequently leave these unfortunate people scarcely a loaf for the next day. They then proceed on to the more distant mountains: here they consider themselves to be in the land of an enemy; they encamp near the mountain which they intend to take by storm the following day, or immediately, if it is practicable. But before the attack commences, they endeavor to settle the affair amicably : a messenger is sent to the sheik, in order to invite him to come to the camp, and to bring with him the requisite number of slaves. If the chief agrees with his subjects to the proposal, in order to prevent all further bloodshed, or if he finds his means inadequate to attempt resistance, he readily gives the appointed number of slaves. The sheik then proceeds to procure the number he has promised; and this is not difficult, for many volunteers offer themselves for their brethren, and are ready to subject themselves to all the horrors of slavery, in order to free those they love. Sometimes they are obliged to be torn by force from the embraces of their friends and relations. The sheik generally receives a dress as a present for his ready services.

But there are very few mountains that submit to such a demand. Most villages which are advantageously situated, and lie near steep precipices or inaccessible heights, that can be ascended only with difficulty, defend themselves most valiantly, and fight for the rights of liberty with a courage, perseverance, and sacrifice, of which history furnishes us with few examples. Very few flee at the approach of their enemies, although they might take refuge in the high mountains with all their goods, especially as they receive timely information of the arrival of the soldiers; but they consider such flights cowardly and shameful, and prefer to die fighting for their liberty.

If the sheik does not yield to the demand, an attack is made upon the village. The cavalry and bearers of lances surround the whole mountain, and the infantry endeavor to climb the heights. Formerly, they fired with cannon upon the villages and those places where the negroes were assembled, but, on account of the want of skill of the artillerymen, few shots, if any, took effect ; the negroes became indifferent to this prelude, and were only stimulated to a more obstinate resistance. The thundering of the cannon at first caused more consternation than their effects, but the fears of the negroes ceased as soon as they became accustomed to it. Before the attack commences, all avenues to the village are blocked up with large stones or other impediments, the village is provided with water for several days, the cattle and other property taken up to the mountains ; in short, nothing necessary for a proper defense is neglected. The men, armed only with lances, occupy every spot which may be defended ; and even the women do not remain inactive ; they either take part in the battle personally, or encourage their husbands by their cries and lamentations, and provide them with arms ; in short, all are active, except the sick and aged. The points of their wooden lances are first dipped into a poison which is standing by them in an earthen vessel, and which is prepared from the juice of a certain plant. The poison is of a whitish color, and looks like milk which has been standing ; the nature of the plant, and the manner in which the poison is prepared, is still a secret, and generally known only to one family in the village, who will not on any account make it known to others.

The signal for attack being given, the infantry sound the alarm, and an assault is made upon the mountain. Hundreds of lances, large stones, and pieces of wood, are then thrown at the assailants ; behind every large stone a negro is concealed, who either throws his poisoned lance at the enemy, or waits for the moment when his opponent approaches the spot of his concealment, when he pierces him with his lance. The soldiers, who are only able to climb up the steep heights with great difficulty, are obliged to sling their guns over their backs, in order to have the ⸺ of their hands when climbing, and, consequently, are often in the power of the negroes before they are able to discover them. But nothing deters these robbers. Animated with avarice and revenge, they mind no impediment, not even death itself. One after another treads upon the corpse of his comrade, and thinks only of robbery and murder; and the village is at last taken, in spite of the most desperate resistance. And then the revenge is horrible. Neither the aged nor the sick are spared; women, and even children in the womb, fall a sacrifice to their fury; the huts are plundered, the little possessions of the unfortunate inhabitants carried away or destroyed, and all that fall alive into the hands of the robbers are led as slaves into the camp. When the negroes see that their resistance is no longer of any avail, they frequently prefer death to slavery; and if they are not prevented, you may see the father rip up first the stomach of his wife, then of his children, and then his own, that they may not fall alive into the hands of the enemy. Others endeavor to save themselves by creeping into holes, and remain there for several days without nourishment, where there is frequently only room sufficient to allow them to lie on their backs, and in that situation they sometimes remain for eight days. They have assured me, that if they can overcome the first three days, they may, with a little effort, continue full eight days without food. But even from these hiding-places the unfeeling barbarians know how to draw them, or they make use of means to destroy them: provided with combustibles, such as pitch, brimstone, &c., the soldiers try to kindle a fire before the entrance of the holes, and, by forcing the stinking smoke into them, the poor creatures are obliged to creep out and surrender themselves to their enemies, or they are suffocated with the smoke.

After the Turks have done all in their power to capture the living, they lead these unfortunate people into the camp; they then plunder the huts and the cattle; and several hundred soldiers are engaged in searching the mountain in every direction, in order to steal the hidden harvest, that the rest of the negroes, who were fortunate enough to escape, and have hid themselves in inaccessible caves, should not find anything on their return to nourish and continue their life.

When slaves to the number of 500 or 600 are obtained, they are sent to Lobeid, with an escort of country people, and about fifty soldiers, under the command of an officer. In order to prevent escape, a sheba is hung round the necks of the adults. A sheba is a young tree, about eight feet long, and two inches thick, and which has a fork at the top; it is so tied to the neck of the poor creature, that the trunk of the tree hangs down in the front, and the fork is closed behind the neck with a cross-piece of timber, or tied together with strips cut out of a fresh skin; and in this situation the slave, in order to walk at all, is obliged to take the tree into his hands, and to carry it before him. But none can endure this very long; and to render it easier, the one in advance takes the tree of the man behind him on his shoulder." In this way, the men carrying the sheba, the boys tied together by the wrists, the women and children walking at their liberty, and the old and feeble tottering along leaning on their relations, the whole of the captives are driven into Egypt, there to be exposed for sale in the slave-market. Thus negroes and Nubians are distributed over the East, through Persia, Arabia, India, &c.*

CHAPTER IX.

AFRICAN SLAVE TRADE IN THE EIGHTEENTH CENTURY.

England first engages in the Slave Trade in 1562—Sir John Hawkins' voyages.—British first established a regular trade in 1618.—Second charter granted in 1631.—Third charter in 1662.—Capture of the Dutch Forts.—Retaken by De Ruyter.—Fourth charter in 1672; the King and Duke of York shareholders.—Monopoly abolished, and free trade in Slaves declared.—Flourishing condition of the Trade.—Numbers annually exported.—Public sentiment aroused against the Slave Trade in England.—Parliament resolve to hear Evidence upon the subject.—Abstract of the Evidence taken before a Select Committee of the House of Commons in 1790 and 1791—Revealing the Enormities committed by the Natives on the persons of one another to procure Slaves for the Europeans.—War and Kidnapping—imputed Crimes.—Villages attacked and burned, and inhabitants seized and sold.—African chiefs excited by intoxication to sell their subjects.

SIR John Hawkins was the first Englishman who transported slaves from Africa to America. This was in 1562. His adventures are recorded by Hakluyt, a cotemporary historian. He sailed from England in October, 1562, for Sierra Leone, and in a short time obtained possession of 300 negroes, "partly by the sword and partly by other means." He proceeded directly to Hispaniola, and exchanged his cargo for hides, ginger, sugar, &c., and arrived in England, after an absence of eleven months. The voyage was "very prosperous, and brought great profit to the adventurers."

This success excited the avarice of his countrymen; and the next year, Hawkins sailed for Guinea with three ships. The history of this voyage is related at large in Hakluyt's collections, by a person who sailed with Hawkins. They landed at a small island on the coast to see if they could take any of the inhabitants. Eighty men, with arms and ammunition, started on the hunt; but the natives flying into the woods, they returned without success. A short time after, they proceeded to another island, called Sambula. "In this island," says the narrator, "we staid certain days, going every day on shore to take the inhabitants, with burning and spoiling their towns." Hawkins made a third voyage in 1568, with six ships, which, it seems, "terminated most miserably," and put a stop for some years to the traffic.

---

* Dr. Madden's Egypt and Mohammed Ali.

The first attempt by the British to establish a regular trade on the African coast, was made in the year 1618, when James I. granted an exclusive charter to Sir Robert Rich, and some other merchants of London, for raising a joint stock company to trade to Guinea. The profits not being found to answer their expectations, the charter was suffered to expire.

In 1631, Charles I. granted a second charter to Richard Young, Sir Kenelm Digby, and sundry merchants, to enjoy the exclusive trade to the coast of Guinea, between Cape Blanco and the Cape of Good Hope, for a period of thirty-one years. As the English had by this time began the settlement of plantations in the West Indies, negroes were in general demand; and the company erected on the African coast, forts and warehouses, to protect their commerce. Private adventurers and interlopers of all nations broke in upon them, and forced the trade open, and so it continued until after the restoration of Charles II.

In 1662, a third exclusive company was incorporated, consisting of many persons of high rank and distinction, at the head of whom was the king's brother, the Duke of York. This company undertook to supply the English plantations with 3000 negroes, annually. In 1664, all the Dutch forts on the African coast but two were captured by the English; but in the following year they were retaken by the Dutch Admiral, De Ruyter, who also seized one of the forts belonging to the English company. In 1672, the company surrendered their charter.

The same year, 1672, the fourth and last exclusive company was established. It was dignified by the title of the Royal African Company, and had among the stockholders, the king, the duke of York, and many other persons of high rank. The capital was £111,000, and was raised in nine months. They paid £35,000 for the forts of the old company. Besides the traffic in slaves, they imported into England great quantities of gold. In 1673, 50,000 guineas, (named from the country), were coined. They also imported redwood, ivory, wax, &c., and exported to the value of £70,000, annually, in English goods.

The revolution of 1688 upset the exclusive privileges of this company. By the 1st William and Mary, the African, and all other exclusive companies not authorized by parliament were abolished. The company, however, continued its operations.

The trade to Africa, by the statute, was virtually free, but it was expressly made so in 1698, under certain conditions. A duty of ten per cent. ad valorem, was laid upon the goods exported from England to carry on the trade, to be paid to the collector at the time of clearance. This duty went to the company. A further duty of ten per cent. ad valorem, was laid upon all goods and merchandise imported into England and the colonies, from Africa. This duty was applied to the maintenance of the forts and castles. No duty was to be laid upon negroes, nor upon gold or silver.

Against the provisions of this law, both the company and private traders remonstrated, but without effect. In the course of a few years, the affairs of the company were found in bad condition; and Parliament, in 1739, granted them £10,000, and the like sum annually until 1744, when the grant was doubled for that year. In 1747, no grant was made.

In 1750, the "act for extending and improving the African trade" was passed, and continued in force until the close of the century.

In 1790, the whole number of forts and factories established on the coast, was about forty; fourteen belonged to the English, fifteen to the Dutch, three to the French, four to the Portuguese, and four to the Danes. The value of English goods annually exported to Africa about that time, was estimated at £800,000 sterling.

It is impossible to arrive at any exact conclusion as to the number of negroes annually carried off by the traders of various nations about this time, but there is reason to believe that it did not fall far short of 100,000. It has been estimated, that up to the close of the last century, Africa must have been defrauded of a population of 30,000,000. The principal slave importing places were the West India Islands, the British Colonies of North America, Brazil, and other settlements in South America.

Very early after the commencement of the slave trade, the Africans began to be considered as an inferior race, and even their very color as a mark of it. Under this notion they continued to be transported for centuries, until various persons, taking an interest in their sufferings, produced such a union of public sentiment in their favor in England, that parliament was induced to consider their case by hearing evidence upon it. It is this evidence which we now propose to lay before the reader, in all its sickening and horrible details. It was heard before a select committee of the House of Commons, in the years 1790 and 1791, and we quote it as most reliable proof of the enormities of the African Slave Trade. It was given by persons, some of whom had been engaged in the traffic, and had visited all the principal parts of Africa from the river Senegal to Angola, had been up and down the rivers, and had resided on shore. This testimony covers the period from 1750 to 1790.

ABSTRACT OF EVIDENCE BEFORE HOUSE OF COMMONS.

The trade for slaves, (says Mr. Kiernan), in the river Senegal, was chiefly with the Moors, on the northern banks, who got them very often by war, and not seldom by kidnapping; that is, lying in wait near a village, where there was no open war, and siezing whom they could. He has often heard of villages, and seen the remains of such, broken up by making the people slaves. That the Moors used to cross the Senegal to catch the negroes was spoken of at Fort Louis as notorious; and he has seen instances of it where the persons so taken were ransomed.

General Rooke says, that kidnapping took place in the neighborhood of Goree. It was spoken of as a common practice. It was reckoned disgraceful there, but he cannot speak of the opinion about it on the Continent. He remembers two or three instances of negroes being brought to Goree, who had been kidnapped, but could not discover by whom. At their own request he immediately sent them back.

Mr. Dalrymple found that the great droves (Caffellas or Caravans) of slaves brought from inland, by way of Galam, to Senegal and Gambia, were prisoners of war. Those sold to vessels at Goree, and near it, were procured either by the grand pillage, the lesser pillage, or by robbery of individuals, or in consequence of crimes. The grand pillage is executed by the king's soldiers, from three hundred to three thousand at a time, who attack and set fire to a village, and seize the inhabitants as they can. The smaller parties generally lie in wait about the villages, and take off all they can surprise ; which is also done by individuals, who do not belong to the king, but are private robbers. These sell their prey on the coast, where it is well known no questions as to the means of obtaining it are asked.

As to kidnapping, it is so notorious about Goree, that he never heard any person deny it there. Two men while he was there offered a person, a messenger from Senegal to Rufisco, for sale, to the garrison, who even boasted how they had obtained him. Many also were brought to Goree while he was there, procured in the same manner. These depredations are also practiced by the Moors : he saw many slaves in Africa who told him they were taken by them ; particularly three, one of whom was a woman, who cried very much, and seemed to be in great distress ; the two others were more reconciled to their fate.

Captain Wilson says, that slaves are either procured by intestine wars, or by kings breaking up villages, or crimes real or imputed, or kidnapping. Villages are broken up by the king's troops surrounding them in the night, and seizing such of the inhabitants as suit their purpose. This practice is most common when there is no war with another state. It is universally acknowledged that free persons are sold for real or imputed crimes, for the benefit of their judges. Soon after his arrival at Goree, king Damel sent a free man to him for sale, and was to have the price himself. One of the king's guards being asked whether the man was guilty of the crime imputed to him, answered, that was of no consequence, or ever inquired into. Captain Wilson returned the man.

Kidnapping was acknowledged by all he conversed with, to be generally prevalent. It is the first principle of the natives, the principle of self-preservation, never to go unarmed, while a slave-vessel is on the coast, for fear of being stolen. When he has met them thus armed, and inquired of them, through his interpreter, the reason of it, they have pointed to a French slave-vessel then lying at Portudal, and said their fears arose from that quarter. As a positive instance, he says, a courier of Captain Lacy's, his predecessor, though a Moor, a free man, and one who spoke the French language fluently, was kidnapped as he was traveling on the continent with dispatches on his Britannic Majesty's account, and sold to a French vessel, from which he, Captain Wilson, after much trouble, actually got him back.

When he presided in a court at Goree, a Maraboo swore, with an energy which evinced the truth of his evidence, that his brother, another Maraboo, had been kidnapped in the act of drinking, a moment known to be sacred by their religion, at the instigation of a former governor, who had taken a dislike to him. This was a matter notorious at Goree.

Mr. Wadstrom knows slaves to be procured between Senegal and Gambia, either by the general pillage or by robbery by individuals, or by stratagem and deceit. The general pillage is executed by the king's troops on horseback, armed, who seize the unprepared. Mr. Wadstrom, during the week he was at Joal, accompanying one of those embassies which the French governor sends yearly with presents to the black kings, to keep up the slave trade, saw parties sent out for this purpose, by king Barbesin, almost every day. These parties went out generally in the evening, and were armed with bows and arrows, guns, pistols, sabres, and long lances. The king of Sallum practices the pillage also. Mr. Wadstrom saw twenty-seven slaves from Sallum, twenty-three of whom were women and children, thus taken. He was told also by merchants at Goree, that king Damel practices the pillage in like manner.

Robbery was a general way of taking single slaves. He once saw a woman and a boy in the slave-hold at Goree; the latter had been taken by stealth from his parents in the interior parts above Cape Rouge, and he declared that such robberies were very frequent in his country; the former, at Rufisco, from her husband and children. He could state several instances of such robberies. He very often saw negroes thus taken brought to Goree. Ganna of Dacard was a noted man-stealer, and employed as such by the slave-merchants there. As instances of stratagem employed to obtain slaves, he relates that a French merchant taking a fancy to a negro, who was on a visit to Dacard, persuaded the village, for a certain price, to seize him. He was accordingly taken from his wife, who wished to accompany him, but the Frenchman had not merchandise enough to buy both. Mr. Wadstrom saw this negro at Goree, the day he arrived from Dacard, chained, and lying on the ground, exceedingly distressed in his mind. The king of Sallum also prevailed on a woman to come into his kingdom, and sell him some millet. On her arrival, he seized and sold her to a French officer, with whom Mr. Wadstrom saw this woman every day while at Goree. Mr. Wadstrom was on the island of St. Louis, up the Senegal also, and on the continent near the river, and says that all the slaves sold at Senegal, are brought down the river, except those taken by the robbery of the Moors in the neighborhood, which is sometimes conducted by large parties, in what are called petty wars.

Captain Hills saw, while lying between Goree and the continent, the natives, in an evening, often go out in war dresses, as he found, to obtain slaves for king Damel, to be sold. The reason was, that the king was then poor, not having received his usual dues from us. He never saw the parties that went out return with slaves, but has often seen slaves in their huts tied back to back. He remembers also that some robbers once brought him a man, bound, on board the Zephyr, to sell, but he, Captain Hills, would not buy him, but suffered him to escape. The natives on the continent opposite to Goree all go armed, he imagines for fear of being taken.

When in the river Gambia, wanting servants on board his ship, he expressed a wish for some volunteers. A black pilot in the boat called two boys who were on shore, carrying baskets of shallots, and asked Captain Hills if they would do, in which case he would take them off, and bring them to him. This he declined. From the ease with which the pilot did it, he concludes this was customary. The black pilot said the merchantmen would not refuse such an offer. He apprehends these two boys were free people, from the pilot's mode of speaking, and from his winking, implying that it was an illicit thing. A boy, whom he bought from the merchants in the same river, had been carried in the night from his father's house, where a skirmish had happened, in which he believes he saw both his parents, but he well remembers that one was killed. The boy said many were killed, and some taken.

Mr. Ellison spoke the Mandingo language, in consequence of which he has often conversed with slaves from the Gambia, to which river he made three voyages, and they universally informed him that they had been stolen and sold.

The natives up the river Scaffus informed Mr. Bowman that they had got two women and a girl, whom they then brought him, in a small town which they had surprised in the night; that others had got off, but they expected the rest of the party would bring them in, in two or three days. When these arrived, they brought with them two men whom Mr. Bowman knew, and had traded with formerly; upon questioning them, he discovered the women he had bought to be their wives. Both men and women informed him that the war-men had taken them while asleep. The war-men used to go out, Mr. Bowman says, once or twice in eight or ten days, while he was at Scaffus. It was their constant way of getting slaves, he believed, because they always came to the factory before setting out, and demanded powder, ball, gun-flints, and small shot; also, rum, tobacco, and a few other articles. When supplied, they blew the horn, made the war-cry, and set off. If they met with no slaves, they would bring him some ivory and camwood. Sometimes he accompanied them a mile or so, and once joined the party, anxious to know by what means they obtained the slaves. Having traveled all day, they came to a small river, when he was told they had but a little way farther to go. Having crossed the river, they stopped till dark. Here Mr. Bowman (it was about the middle of the night) was afraid to go farther, and prevailed on the king's son to leave him a guard of four men. In half an hour he heard the war cry, by which he understood they had reached a town. In about half an hour more they returned, bringing from twenty-five to thirty men, women and children, some of the latter at the breast. At this time he saw the town in flames. When they had recrossed the river, it was just daylight, and they reached Scaffus about mid-day. The prisoners were carried to different parts of the town. They are usually brought in with strings around their necks, and some have their hands tied across. He never saw any slaves there who had been convicted of crimes. He has been called up in the night to see fires, and told by the town's people that it was war carrying on.

Whatever rivers he traded in, such as Sierra Leone, Junk, and little Cape Mount, he has usually passed burnt and deserted villages, and learned from the natives in the boat with him, that war had been there, and the natives had been taken in the manner as before described, and carried to the ships.

He has also seen such upon the Coast: while trading at Grand Bassa, he went on shore with four black traders to the town a mile off. On the way, there was a town deserted, (with only two or three houses standing), which seemed to have been a large one, as there were two fine plantations of rice ready for cutting down. A little further on they came to another village in much the same state. He was told that the first town had been taken by war, there being many ships then lying at Bassa: the people of the other had moved higher up in the country for fear of the white men. In passing along to the trader's town, he saw several villages deserted; these, the natives said, had been destroyed by war, and the people taken out and sold.

Sir George Young found slaves to be procured by war, by crimes, real or imputed, by kidnapping, which is called *panyaring*, and a fourth mode was the inhabitants of one village seizing those of another weaker village, and selling them to the ships. He believes, from two instances, that kidnapping was frequently practiced up Sierra Leone river. One was that of a beautiful infant boy, which the natives, after trying to sell to all the different trading ships, came alongside his, (the Phœnix) and threatened to toss overboard, if no one would buy it; saying they had *panyared* it with many other people, but could not sell it, though they had sold the others. He purchased it for some wine. The second was, a captain of a Liverpool ship had got, as a temporary mistress, a girl from the king of Sierra Leone, and instead of returning her on shore on leaving the coast, as is usually done, he took her away with him. Of this the king complained to Sir George Young very heavily, calling this action *panyaring* by the whites.

The term *panyaring* seemed to be a word generally used all along the coast where he was, not only among the English, but the Portuguese and Dutch.

Captain Thompson also says, that at Sierra Leone he has often heard the word *panyaring;* he has heard also that this word, which is used on other parts of the coast, means kidnapping, or seizing of men.

Slaves, says Mr. Town, are brought from the country very distant from the coast. The king of Barra informed Mr. Town, that on the arrival of a ship, he has gone three hundred miles up the country with his guards, and driven down captives to the sea-side. From Marraba, king of the Mandingoes, he has heard that they had marched slaves out of the country some hundred miles; that they had gone wood-ranging, to pick up every one they met with, whom they stripped naked, and, if men, bound; but if women, brought down loose; this he had from themselves, and also, that they often went to war with the Bullam nation, on purpose to get slaves. They boasted that they should soon have a fine parcel for the shallops, and the success often answered. Mr. Town has seen the prisoners (the men bound, the women and children loose) driven for sale to the water-side. He has also known the natives to go in gangs, marauding and catching all they could. In the Galenas river he knew four blacks seize a man who had been to the sea-side to sell one or more slaves. This man was returning home with the goods received in exchange for these, and they plundered him, stripped him naked, and brought him to the trading shallop, which Mr. Town commanded, and sold him there.

He believes the natives also sometimes become slaves, in consequence of crimes, as well as, that it is no uncommon thing on the coast, to impute crimes falsely for the sake of selling the persons so accused. Several respectable persons at Bance Island, and to windward of it, all told Mr. Town that it was common to bring on *palavers* * to make slaves, and he believes it from the information of the slaves afterwards, when brought down the country and put on board the ships.

Off Piccaninni Sestos, farther down on the Windward Coast, Mr. Dove observed an instance of a girl being kidnapped and brought on board by one Ben Johnson, a black trader, who had scarcely left the ship in his canoe, with the price of her, when another canoe with two black men came in a hurry to the ship, and inquired concerning this girl. Having been allowed to see her, they hurried down to their canoe, and hastily paddled off. Overtaking Ben Johnson, they brought him back to the ship, got him on the quarter-deck, and calling him *teefee* (which implies thief) to the captain, offered him for sale. Ben Johnson remonstrated, asking the captain, "if he would buy him whom he knew to be a grand trading man;" to which the captain answered, "if they would sell him, he would certainly buy him, be he what he would," which he accordingly did, and put him into irons immediately with another man. He was led to think, from this instance, that kidnapping was the mode of obtaining slaves upon this part of the coast.

Lieutenant Story says that slaves are generally obtained on the Windward coast by marauding parties, from one village to another in the night. He has known canoes come from a distance, and carry off numbers in the night. He has gone into the interior country, between Bassa and the River Sestos; and all the nations there go armed, from the fear of marauding parties, whose pillages in these countries are termed war. At one time in particular, while Mr. Story was on the coast, a marauding party from Grand Sestos came in canoes, and attacked Grand Cora in the night, and took off twelve or fourteen of the inhabitants. The canoes of Grand Sestos carry twelve or fourteen men, and with these go a marauding among their neighbors. Mr. Story has often seen them at sea out of sight of land in the day, and taking the opportunity of night to land where they pleased.

Mr. Falconbridge supposes the slave trade, on these parts, to be chiefly supplied by kidnapping. On his second voyage, at Cape Mount and the Windward Coast, a man was brought on board, well known to the captain and his officers, and was purchased. This man said he had been invited one evening to drink with his neighbors. When about to depart, two of them got up to seize him; and he would have escaped, but he was stopped by a large dog.

---

* An African word, which signifies conferences of the natives on any public subject, or as in this place, accusations and trials.

He said this mode of kidnapping was common in his country. In the same voyage, two black traders came in a canoe, and stated that there was trade a little lower down. The captain went there, and finding no trade, said he would not be made a fool, and therefore detained one of the canoe-men. In about two hours afterwards a very fine man was brought on board, and sold, and the canoe-man was released. He was informed by the black pilot, that this man had been surrounded and seized on the beach, from whence he had been brought to the ship and sold.

Lieutenant Simpson says, from what he saw, he believes the slave trade is the occasion of wars among the natives. From the natives of the Windward Coast he understood that the villages were always at war; and the black traders and others gave as a reason for it, that the kings wanted slaves. If a trading canoe, alongside Mr. Simpson's ship, saw a larger canoe coming from a village they were at war with, they instantly fled; and sometimes without receiving the value of their goods. On inquiry, he learned their reasons to be, that if taken, they would have been made slaves.

Mr. How states, that when at Secundee, some order came from Cape Coast Castle. The same afternoon several parties went out armed, and returned the same night with a number of slaves, which were put into the repository of the factory. Next morning he saw people, who came to see the captives, and to request Mr. Marsh, the resident, to release some of their children and relations. Some were released and part sent off to Cape Coast Castle. He had every reason to believe they had been obtained unfairly, as they came at an unseasonable time of the night, and from their parents and friends crying and begging their release. He was told as much from Mr. Marsh himself, who said, he did not mind how they got them, for he purchased them fairly. He cannot tell whether this practice subsisted before; but when he has gone into the woods he has met thirty or forty natives, who fled always at his appearance, although they were armed. Mr. Marsh said, they were afraid of his taking them prisoners.

The same Mr. Marsh made no scruple also of shewing him the stores of the factory. They consisted of different kinds of chains made of iron, as likewise an instrument made of wood, about five inches long, of an inch in diameter, or less, which he was told by Mr. Marsh was thrust into a man's mouth horizontally, and tied behind to prevent him from crying out, when transported at night along the country.

Dr. Trotter says, that the natives of these parts are sometimes slaves from crimes, but the greater part of the slaves are what are called prisoners of war. Of his whole cargo he recollects only three criminals : two sold for adultery, and one for witchcraft, whose whole family shared his fate. One of the first said he had been decoyed by a woman who had told her husband, and he was sentenced to pay a slave ; but being poor, was sold himself. Such stratagems are frequent : the fourth mate of Dr. Trotter's ship was so decoyed, and obliged to pay a slave, under the threat of stopping trade. The last said he had had a quarrel with a Cabosheer (or great man) who in revenge accused him of witchcraft, and sold him and his family for slaves.

Dr. Trotter having often asked Accra, a principal trader at Le Hou, what he meant by prisoners of war, found they were such as were carried off by a set of marauders, who ravage the country for that purpose. The bush-men making war to make trade (that is to make slaves) was a common way of speaking among the traders. The practice was also confirmed by the slaves on board, who showed by gestures how the robbers had come upon them; and during their passage from Africa to the West Indies, some of the boy-slaves played a game, which they called slave-taking, or bush-fighting; showing the different manœuvres thereof in leaping, sallying, and retreating. Inquiries of this nature put to women, were answered only by violent bursts of sorrow. He once saw a black trader send his canoe to take three fishermen employed in the offing, who were immediately brought on board, and put in irons, and about a week afterwards he was paid for them. He remembers another man taken in the same way from on board a canoe alongside. The same trader very frequently sent slaves on board in the night, which, from their own information, he found were every one of them taken in the neighborhood of Annamaboe. He remarked, that slaves sent off in the night, were not paid for till they had been some time on board, lest, he thinks, they should be claimed; for some were really restored, one in particular, a boy, was carried on shore by some near relations, which boy told him he had lived in the neighborhood of Annamaboe, and was kidnapped. There were many boys and girls on board Dr. Trotter's ship, who had no relations on board. Many of them told him they had been kidnapped in the neighborhood of Annamaboe, particularly a girl of about eight years old, who said she had been carried off from her mother by the man who sold her to the ship.

Mr. Falconbridge was assured by the Rev. Philip Quakoo, chaplain at Cape Coast Castle, on the Gold Coast, that the greatest number of slaves were made by kidnapping. He has heard that the men on this part of the coast, dress up and employ women, to entice young men, that they may be convicted of adultery and sold.

Lieutenant Simpson heard at Cape Coast Castle, and other parts of the Gold Coast, repeatedly from the black traders, that the slave trade made wars and palavers. Mr. Quakoo, chaplain at Cape Coast Castle, informed him that wars were made in the interior parts, for the sole purpose of getting slaves. There are two crimes on the Gold Coast, which seem made on purpose to procure slaves: adultery and the removal of fetiches.* As to adultery, he was warned against any woman not pointed out to him, for that the kings kept several who were sent out to allure the unwary. As to fetiches, consisting of pieces of wood, old pitchers, kettles, and the like, laid in the path-ways, he was warned to avoid displacing them, for if he should, the natives who were

---

* Certain things of various sorts, to which the superstition of the country has ordered, for various reasons, an attention to be paid.

on the watch would seize him, and, as before, exact the price of a man slave. These baits are laid equally for natives and Europeans; but the former are better acquainted with the law, and consequently more upon their guard.

Mr. Ellison says, that while one of the ships he belonged to, viz : the Briton, was lying in Benin river, Capt. Lemma Lemma, a Benin trader, came on board to receive his customs. This man being on the deck, and happening to see a canoe with three people in it crossing the river, dispatched one of his own canoes to seize and take it. Upon overtaking it, they brought it to the ship. It contained three persons, an old man and a young man and woman. The chief mate bought the two latter, but the former being too old, was refused. Upon this, Lemma ordered the old man into the canoe, where his head was chopped off, and he was thrown overboard. Lemma had many war canoes, some of which had six or eight swivels ; he seemed to be feared by the rest of the natives. Mr. Ellison did not see a canoe out on the river while Lemma was there, except this, and if they had known he had been out, they would not have come. He discovered by signs, that the old man killed was the father of the two other negroes, and that they were brought there by force. They were not the subjects of Lemma.

At Bonny, says Mr. Falconbridge, the greatest number of slaves come from inland. Large canoes, some having a three or four pounder lashed on their bows, go to the up country, and in eight or ten days return with great numbers of slaves : he heard once, to the amount of 1200 at one time. The people in these canoes have generally cutlasses, and a quantity of muskets, but he cannot tell for what use. Mr. Falconbridge does not believe that many of these slaves are prisoners of war, as we understand the word war. In Africa, a piratical expedition for making slaves is termed war. A considerable trader at Bonny explained to him the meaning of this word, and said that they went in the night, set fire to towns, and caught the people as they fled from the flames. The same trader said that this practice was very common. In the same voyage an elderly man brought on board said (through the interpreter) that he and his son were seized as they were planting yams, by professed kidnappers, by which he means persons who make kidnapping their constant practice. On his last voyage, which was also to Bonny, a canoe came alongside his vessel, belonging to a noted trader in slaves, from which a fine stout fellow was handed on board, and sold. Mr. Falconbridge seeing the man amazed and confounded when he discovered himself to be a slave, inquired of him, by means of an interpreter, why he was sold. He replied, that he had had occasion to come to Bonny to this trader's house, who asked if he had ever seen a ship. Replying no, the trader said he would treat him with the sight of one. The man consented, said he was thereupon brought on board, and thus treacherously sold. All the slaves Mr. Falconbridge ever talked to by means of interpreters, said they had been stolen.

Mr. Douglas, when ashore at Bonny Point, saw a young woman come out of the wood to the water-side to bathe. Soon afterwards two men came from the wood, seized, bound, and beat her for making resistance, and bringing her to him, Mr. Douglas, desired him to put her on board, which he did; the captain's orders were, when any body brought down slaves, instantly to put them off to the ship. When a ship arrives at Bonny, the king sends his war canoes up the rivers, where they surprise all they can lay hold of. They had a young man on board, who was thus captured, with his father, mother, and three sisters. The young man afterwards in Jamaica having learned English, told Mr. Douglas the story, and said it was a common practice. These war canoes are always armed. The king's canoes came with slaves openly in the day; others in the evening, with one or two slaves bound, lying in the boat's bottom, covered with mats.

Mr. Morley states, that in Old Calabar persons are sold as slaves for adultery and theft. On pretence of adultery, he remembers a woman sold. He has been told also by the natives at Calabar, that they took slaves in what they call war, which he found was putting the villages in confusion, and catching them as they could. A man on board the ship he was in, showed how he was taken at night by surprise, and said his wife and children were taken with him, but they were not in the same ship. Mr. Morley had reason to think, from the man's words, that they took nearly the whole village, that is, all those that could not get away.

Captain Hall says, when a ship arrives at Old Calabar, or the river Del-Rey, the traders always go up into the country for slaves. They go in their war canoes, and take with them some goods, which they get previously from the ships. He has seen from three to ten canoes in a fleet, each with from forty to sixty paddlers, and twenty to thirty traders and other people with muskets, suppose one to each man, with a three or four pounder lashed on the bow of the canoe. They are generally absent from ten days to three weeks, when they return with a number of slaves pinioned, or chained together. Captain Hall has often asked the mode of procuring slaves inland, and has been told by the traders, that they have been got in war, and sold by the persons taking them.

Mr. J. Parker says, he left the ship to which he belonged at Old Calabar, where being kindly received by the king's son, he staid with him on the continent for five months. During this time he was prevailed upon by the king's son, to accompany him to war.* Accordingly, having fitted out and armed the canoes, they went up the river Calabar. In the day time they lay under the bushes when they approached a village, but at night flew up to it, and took hold of every one they could see; these they handcuffed, brought down to the canoes, and so proceeded up the river till they got to the amount of forty-five, with whom they returned to Newtown, where, sending to the captains of the shipping, they divided them among the ships. About a fortnight after this expedition, they went again, and were out eight or nine days, plundering other

---

* The reader is requested to take notice, that the word war, as adopted in the African language, means in general robbery, or a marauding expedition, for the purpose of getting slaves.

villages higher up the river. They seized on much the same number as before, brought them to Newtown, gave the same notice, and disposed of them as before among the ships. They took man, woman and child, as they could catch them in the houses, and except sucking children, who went with their mothers, there was no care taken to prevent the separation of the children from the parents when sold. When sold to the English merchant they lamented, and cried that they were taken away by force. The king at Old Calabar was certainly not at war with the people up this river, nor had they made any attack upon him. It happened that slaves were very slack in the back country at that time, and were wanted when he went on these expeditions.

Mr. Falconbridge thinks crimes are falsely imputed, for the sake of selling the accused. On the second voyage at the river Ambris, among the slaves brought on board was one who had the craw craw, a kind of itch. He was told by one of the sailors, that this man was fishing in the river, when a king's officer, called Mambooka, wanted brandy and other goods in the boat, but having no slave to buy them with, accused this man of extortion in the sale of his fish, and after some kind of trial on the beach, condemned him to be sold. He was told by the boat's crew who were ashore, when it happened, who told it as of their own knowledge.

Beside the accounts just given, from what the above witnesses saw and heard on the coast of Africa, as to the different methods of making slaves, there are others contained in the evidence, which were learned from the mouths of the slaves themselves, after their arrival in the West Indies.

The Moors, says Mr. Keirnan, have always a strong inducement to go to war with the negroes, most of the European goods they obtain, being got in exchange for slaves. Hence, desolation and waste. Mr. Town observes, that the intercourse of the Africans with the Europeans, has improved them in roguery, to plunder and steal, and pick up one another to sell. Dr. Trotter asking a black trader, what they made of their slaves when the French and English were at war, was answered, that when ships ceased to come, slaves ceased to be taken. Mr. Isaac Parker says, that the king of Old Calabar was certainly not at war with the people up that river, nor had they made any attack on him. It happened that slaves were very slack in the back country at this time, and were wanted when he went on the expeditions, described in a former page.

Mr. Wadstrom says, the king Barbesin, while he, Mr. Wadstrom, was at Joal, was unwilling to pillage his subjects, but he was excited to it by means of a constant intoxication, kept up by the French and mulattoes of the embassy, who generally agreed every morning on taking this method to effect their purpose. When sober, he always expressed a reluctance to harrass his people. Mr. Wadstrom also heard the king hold the same language on different days, and yet he afterwards ordered the pillage to be executed. Mr. Wadstrom has no doubt, but that he also pillages in other parts of his dominions, since it is the custom of the mulatto merchants (as both they and the French officers declare) when they want slaves, to go to the kings, and excite them to pillages which are usually practiced on all that part of the coast. The French Senegal company, also, in order to obtain their complement of slaves, had recourse to their usual method on similar occasions, namely, of bribing the Moors, and supplying them with arms and ammunition, to seize king Dalmammy's subjects. By January 12th, 1788, when Mr. Wadstrom arrived at Senegal, fifty had been taken, whom the king desired to ransom, but they had all been dispatched to Cayenne. Some were brought in every day afterwards, and put in the company's slave-hold, in a miserable state, the greater part being badly wounded by sabres and musket balls. The director of the company conducted Mr. Wadstrom there, with Dr. Spaarman, whom he consulted as a medical man in their behalf. Mr. Wadstrom particularly remembers one lying in his blood, which flowed from a wound made by a ball in his shoulder.

Mr. Dalrymple understood it common for European traders to advance goods to chiefs, to induce them to seize their subjects or neighbors. Not one of the mulatto traders at Goree ever thought of denying it.

Mr. Bowman having settled at the head of Scassus river, informed the king, and others, that he was come to reside as a trader, and that his orders were, to supply them with powder and ball, and encourage them to go to war. They answered, they would go to war in two or three days. By this time they came to the factory, said they were going to war, and wanted powder, ball, rum and tobacco. When these were given them, they went off to the number of from twenty-five to thirty, and in six or seven days, a part of them returned with three slaves.

In 1769, (says Lieut. Storey,) Captain Paterson, of a Liverpool ship, lying off Bristol town, set two villages at variance, and bought prisoners, near a dozen, from both sides.

Mr. Morley owns, with shame, that he has made the natives drunk, in order to buy a good man or woman slave, to whom he found them attached. He has seen this done by others. Captain Hildebrand, commanding a sloop of Mr. Brue's, bought one of the wives of a man, whom he had previously made drunk, and who wished to redeem her, when sober next day, as did the person he (Mr. Morley) bought the man of, but neither of them was given up. He supposes they would have given a third more than the price paid, to have redeemed them.

Sir George Young says, that when at Annamaboe, at Mr. Brue's, (a very great merchant there,) Mr. Brue had two hostages, kings' sons, for payment for arms, and all kinds of military stores, which he had supplied to the two kings, who were at war with each other, to procure slaves for at least six or seven ships, then lying in the road. The prisoners on both sides were brought down to Mr. Brue, and sent to the ships.

Mr. J. Parker has known presents made by the captains, to the black traders, to induce them to bring slaves. Captain Colley in particular gave them some pieces of cannon, which he himself saw landed.

On the subject of Europeans attempting to carry off the natives, General Rooke says that it was proposed to him by three captains of English slave ships, lying under the fort of Goree, to kidnap a hundred, or a hundred and fifty, men, women and children, king Damel's subjects, who had come to Goree in consequence of the friendly intercourse between him and Damel.   He refused, and was much shocked by the proposition.   They said such things had been done by a former governor, but the chief Maraboo at Rufisk did not recollect any such event.

Mr. Wadstrom was informed at Goree, by Captain Wignie, from Rochelle, who was just arrived from the river Gambia, that a little before his departure from that river, three English vessels were cut off by the natives, owing to the captain of one of them, who had his cargo, being tempted by a fair wind to sail away with several of the free negroes, then drinking with the crew.   Soon afterwards the wind changed and he was driven back, seized, and killed, with all his crew, and those of the two other vessels.   Mr. Wadstrom has, by accident, met with the insurer of two of these vessels in London, who confirmed the above facts.

Captain Hills says a man at Gambia, who called himself a prince's brother, had been carried off to the West Indies, by an English ship, but making his case known to the governor, was sent by him to Europe.   Captain Hills was advised not to go on shore at Gambia, by the merchants there, for fear of being taken by the natives, who owed the English a grudge for some injuries received.

Mr. John Bowman says, that when a mate under Captain Strangeways, the ship then lying in the river Sierra Leone, at White Man's Bay, ready to sail, he was sent on shore to invite two traders on board.   They came and were shown into the cabin.   Meantime people were employed in setting the sails, it being almost night, and the land breeze making down the river.   When they had weighed anchor, and got out to sea, Mr. Bowman was called down by the captain, who, pointing to the sail-case, desired him to look into it and see what a fine prize he had got.   To his surprise, he saw lying fast asleep the two men who had come on board with him, the captain having made them drunk, and concealed them there.   When they awoke they were sent upon deck, ironed, and put forward with the other slaves.   On arriving at Antigua they were sold.

The Rev. Mr. Newton has known ships and boats cut off at Sherbro, usually in retaliation.   Once, when he was on shore, the traders suddenly put him into his long-boat, telling him that a ship just passed had carried off two people.   Had it been known in the town, he would have been detained.   He has known many other such instances, but after thirty-six years, he cannot specify them.   It was a general opinion, founded on repeated and indisputable facts, that depredations of this sort were frequently committed by Europeans.   Mr. Newton has sometimes found all trade stopped, and the depredations of European traders have been assigned by the natives as the cause, and he has more than once made up breaches of this kind between the ships and the natives.   He believes several captains of slave ships were honest, humane men ; but he has good reason to think they were not all so.   The taking off slaves by force has

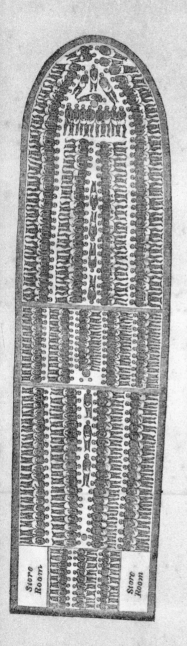
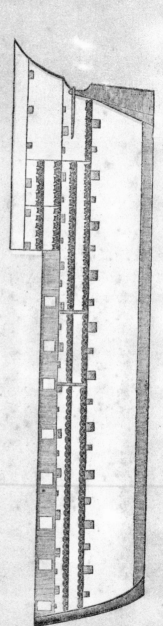

DECKS OF A SLAVE SHIP.

been thought most frequent in the last voyage of captains. He has often heard masters and officers express this opinion. . Depredations and reprisals made to get them were so frequent that the Europeans and Africans were in a spirit of mutual distrust : he does not mean that there were no depredations except in their last voyages. He has known Liverpool and Bristol ships materially injured from the conduct of some ships, from the same ports, that had left the coast. It is a fact that some captains have committed depredations in their last voyages who have not been known to have done it before.

Mr. Towne was once present with part of the crew of his ship, the Sally, at an expedition undertaken by the whites for seizing negroes, and joined by other boats to receive those they could catch. To prevent all alarm, they bound the mouths of the captives with oakum and handkerchiefs. One woman shrieked and the natives turned out in defense. He had then five of them tied in the boat, and the other boats were in readiness to take in what more they could get. All his party were armed, and the men of the town pursued them with first a scattering, and at length a general fire, and several of the men belonging to the boats, he has reason to believe, were killed, wounded, or taken, as he never heard of them afterwards. He was wounded himself. The slaves he had taken were sold at Charleston, South Carolina. The natives had not previously committed any hostilities against any of the ships, whose boats were concerned in this transaction. They owed goods to the captain, for which he resolved to obtain slaves at any rate. He has had several ship-mates, who have themselves told him they have been concerned in similar transactions, and who have made a boast of it, and who have been wounded also.

Mr. Storey believes the natives of the Windward Coast are often fraudulently carried off by the Europeans. He has been told by them that they had lost their friends at different times, and supposed them taken by European ships going along the coast. He has himself taken up canoes at sea, which were challenged by the natives, who supposed the men in them had been taken off the day before by a Dutchman. When once at an anchor, in his boat, between the river Sestos and Settra Crue, he prevented the crew of a long-boat, belonging to a Dutchman then lying off shore, from being cut off by the natives, who gave as a reason for their intentions, that a ship of that country some days before had taken off four men belonging to the place. Afterwards, in 1768, being in a boat, with two other white persons, the natives attacked them. Both the former were killed, and he himself, covered with blood and wounds, was only suffered to escape, by consenting to give up boat and cargo, and to go to Gaboon. The reason the natives gave for this procedure was, that a ship from Liverpool (one Captain Lambert) had, some time before, taken a canoe full of their townsmen, and carried her away. He heard the same thing confirmed afterwards at Gaboon.

Mr. Douglas states that near Cape Coast the natives make smoke as a signal for trade. On board his ship (the Warwick Castle) they saw the smoke and stood in shore, which brought off many canoes. Pipes, tobacco, and brandy were got on deck, to entice the people in them on board. The gratings were unlaid, the slave-room cleared, and every preparation made to seize them; two only could be prevailed on to come up the ship's side, who stood in the main chains, but on the seamen approaching them they jumped off, and the canoes all made for the shore. The Gregson's people, while at Bonny, informed Mr. Douglas, that in running down the coast, they had kidnapped thirty-two of the natives. He saw slaves on board that ship when she came in, and it is not customary for ships bound to Bonny to stop and trade by the way.

Mr. How says that abreast of Cape La Hou, several canoes came alongside of his Majesty's ship Grampus, and on coming on board informed the captain that an English Guinea-trader, a fortnight before, had taken off six canoes with men, who had gone off to them with provisions for trade. On coming to Appolonia he was also told by Mr. Buchanan, the resident there, that a Guinea-man, belonging to one Griffith, an Englishman, and a notorious trader and kidnapper, between Cape La Hou and Appolonia, was then in that latitude.

Captain Hall was told by Captain Jeremiah Smith, that in 1771, a Captain Fox had taken off some people from the Windward Coast. He says also that the boat's crew of the Venus, Captain Smith, which had been sent to Fernando Po for yams from Calabar, enticed a canoe to come alongside that had about ten men in her. As soon as she got near, the boat's crew fired into her, on which they jumped overboard: some were wounded, and one was taken out of the water, and died in less than an hour in the boat: two others were taken up unhurt, and carried to Old Calabar to the ship. Captain Smith was angry at the officer for this procedure, and sent back the two men to the bay from whence they had been taken. Immediately after the boat had committed this depredation, Captain Hall happened to go into the same bay in his own ship's long-boat, and sending on shore two men to fill water, they were surrounded by the natives, who drove three spears into one of the men, and wounded the other with a large stick, in consequence of taking away the two men just mentioned. It was said that the crew had disputed with the natives on shore when trading with them for yams, but the former had not done any of the boat's crew any injury.

Mr. Ellison knew two slaves taken from the island of Fernando Po by the Dobson's boat of Liverpool, and carried to Old Calabar, where the ship lay. He went to the same island for yams, a few days after the transaction, and fired, as the usual signal, for the natives to bring them. Seeing some of them peep through the bushes, he wondered why they would not come to the boat. He accordingly swam on shore, when some of the islanders came round him: an old man showed, by signs, that a ship's boat had stolen a man and woman. He was then soon surrounded by numbers, who presented darts to him, signifying that they would kill him, if the man and woman were not brought back. Upon this, the people in the boat fired some shot, when they all ran into the woods. Mr. Ellison went to Calabar, and told Captain Briggs he could get no yams, in consequence of the two people being stolen; upon which Captain Briggs told the captain of the Dobson there would be no more trade if he did not deliver up the people, which he at length did. As soon as the natives saw their countrymen, they loaded the boat with yams, goats, fowls, honey, and palm-wine: and they would take nothing for them. They had the man and woman delivered to them, whom they carried away in their arms. The Dobson did not stay above eight, ten, or twelve days. This was the last trip her boat was to make, when they carried off the two slaves.

Mr. Morley says, that when off Taboo, two men came in a canoe, alongside his vessel. One of them came up and sat on the netting, but would not come into the ship. The captain at length enticing him, intoxicated him so with brandy and laudanum, that he fell in upon the deck. The captain then ordered him to be put into the men's room, with a sentry over him. The other man in the canoe, after calling in vain for his companion, paddled off fast towards the shore. The captain fired several musket balls after him, which did not hit him. About three or four leagues farther down, two men came on board from another canoe. While they were on board, a drum was kept beating near the man who had been seized, to prevent his hearing them, or they him. He says again, in speaking of another part of the coast, that Captain Briggs's chief mate, in Old Calabar river, lying in ambush to stop the natives coming down the creek, pursued Oruk Robin John, who, jumping on shore, shot the mate through the head. He says also, of another part of the coast, that a Mr. Walker, master of a sloop, was on board the Jolly Prince, Captain Lambert, when the king of Nazareth stabbed the captain at his own table, and took the vessel, putting all the whites to death, except the cook, a boy, and, he believes, one man. Captain Walker, being asked why the king of Nazareth took this step, said it was on account of the people whom Matthews had carried off from Gaboon and Cape Lopez the voyage before. Walker escaped by knowing the language of the country. Mr. Morley sailed afterwards with the same Captain Matthews to Gaboon river, where the chiefs' sons came on board to demand what he had done with their sons, and the boys he had carried off, (the same that Walker alluded to,) and told him that if he dared to come on shore, they would have his head.

As a farther corroboration that such practices as the above take place, it appears in evidence, that the natives of the coast and islands are found constantly hovering in their canoes, at a distance, about such vessels as are passing by, shy of coming on board, for fear of being taken off. But if they can discover that such vessels are not in the slave trade, but are men-of-war, they come on board readily, or without any hesitation, which they would not otherwise have done, and in numbers, and traverse the ships with as much confidence as if they had been on shore.

Mr. Ellison says, when he was lying at Yanamaroo, in the Gambia, slaves were brought down. The traders raised the price. The captains would not give it, but thought to compel them by firing upon the town. They fired red hot shot from the ship, and set several houses on fire. All the ships, seven or eight, fired.

Mr. Falconbridge heard Captain Vicars, of a Bristol ship, say at Bonny, when his traders were slack, he fired a gun into or over the town, to freshen their way. Captain Vicars told this to him and other people there at the time, but he has seen no instance of it himself.

Mr. Isaac Parker says the Guinea captains lying in Old Calabar river, fixed on a certain price, and agreed to lie under a £50 bond, if any one of them should give more for slaves than another; in consequence of which, the natives did not readily bring slaves on board to sell at those prices; upon which, the captains used to row guard at night, to take the canoes as they passed the ships, and so stopping the slaves from getting to their towns, prevent the traders from getting them. These they took on board the different ships, and kept them till the traders agreed to slave at the old prices.

Lieutenant Storey says that Captain Jeremiah Smith, in the London, in 1766, having a dispute with the natives of New Town, Old Calabar, concerning the stated price which he was to give for slaves, for several days stopped every canoe coming down the creek from New Town, and also fired several guns indiscriminately over the woods into the town, till he brought them to his own terms.

Captain Hall says, in Old Calabar river there are two towns, Old Town and New Town. A rivalship in trade produced a jealousy between the towns; so that, through fear of each other, for a considerable time, no canoe would leave their towns to go up the river for slaves. This happened in 1767. In this year, seven ships, of which five were the following—Duke of York, Bevan; Edgar, Lace; Indian Queen, Lewis; Nancy, Maxwell; and Canterbury, Sparkes,—lay off the point which separates the towns. Six of the captains invited the people of both towns on board on a certain day, as if to reconcile them: at the same time they agreed with the people of New Town to cut off all the Old Town people who should remain on board the next morning. The Old Town people, persuaded of the sincerity of the captains' proposal, went on board in great numbers. Next morning, at eight o'clock, one of the ships fired a gun, as a signal to commence hostilities. Some of the traders were secured on board, some were killed in resisting, and some got overboard, and were fired upon. When the firing began, the New Town people, who were in ambush behind the Point, came forward and picked up the people of Old Town, who were swimming, and had escaped the firing. After the firing was over, the captains of five of the ships delivered their prisoners (persons of consequence) to the New Town canoes, two of whom were beheaded alongside the ships. The inferior prisoners were carried to the West Indies. One of the captains, who had secured three of the king's brothers, delivered one of them to the chief man of New Town, who was one of the two beheaded alongside; the other brothers he kept on board, promising, when the ship was slaved, to deliver them to the chief man of New Town. His ship was soon slaved on account of his promise, and the number of prisoners made that day; but he refused to deliver the king's two brothers, according to his promise, and carried them to the West Indies, and sold them. It happened in process of time, that they escaped to Virginia, and from thence, after three years, to Bristol, where

BRANDING SLAVES.

the captain who brought them, fearing he had done wrong, meditated carrying or sending them back, but Mr. Jones, of Bristol, who had ships trading to Old Calabar, and hearing who they were, had them taken from the ship, where they were in irons, by habeas corpus. After inquiry how they were brought from Africa, they were liberated, and put in one of Mr. Jones's ships for Old Calabar, where Captain Hall was, when they arrived in the ship Cato.

So satisfied were the people of Old Town, in 1767, of the sincerity of the captains who invited them, and of the New Town people, towards a reconciliation, that the night before the massacre, the chief man of Old Town gave to the chief man of New Town one of his favorite women as a wife. It was said that from three to four hundred persons were killed that day, in the ships, in the water, or carried off the coast. The king escaped from the ship he was in, by killing two of the crew, who attempted to seize him. He then got into a one-man canoe, and paddled to the shore. A six pounder from one of the ships struck the canoe to pieces; he then swam on shore to the woods near the ships, and reached his own town, though closely pursued. It was said he received eleven wounds from musket shot.

Captain Hall, in his first voyage on board the Neptune, had this account from the boatswain, Thomas Rutter, who, in 1767, had been boatswain to the Canterbury, Captain Sparkes, of London, and concerned in the said massacre. Rutter told him the story exactly as related, and never varied in it. He had it also from the king's two brothers, who agreed exactly with Rutter. Captain Hall also saw at Calabar, in the possession of the king's two brothers, their depositions taken at Bristol, and of Mr. Floyd, who was mate of one of the ships when the transaction happened, but he took no copy. Mr. Millar says that a quarrel happened between the people of Old and New Town, which prevented the ships lying in Calabar river from being slaved. He believes that in June, 1767, Captain S. Sparkes, (captain of his ship, the Canterbury,) came one evening to him, and told him that the two towns, so quarreling, would meet on board the different ships, and ordered him to hand up some swords.

The next day several canoes, as Sparkes had before advertised him, came from both of the towns, on board the Canterbury, Mr. Millar's own ship, and one of the persons so coming on board, brought a letter, which he gave Sparkes, immediately on the receipt of which, he, Sparkes, took a hanger, and attacked one of the Old Town people then on board, cutting him immediately on the arms, head and body. The man fled, ran down the steps leading to the cabin, and Sparkes still following him with the hanger, darted into the boy's room. Mr. Millar is sure this circumstance can never be effaced from his memory. From this room he was, however, brought up by means of a rope, and Sparkes renewing his attack on him, he leaped overboard.

This being concluded, Sparkes left his own ship to go on board some of the other ships then lying in the river. Soon after he was gone, a boy belonging to Mr. Millar's ship came and informed him, Mr. Millar, that he had discovered a man concealed behind the medicine chest. Mr. Millar went and found the man. He was the person before mentioned as having brought a letter on board. On being discovered by Mr. Millar, he begged for mercy, entreating that he might not be delivered up to the people of New Town. He was brought on the quarter-deck, where were some of the New Town people, who would have killed him, had they not been prevented. The man was then ironed, and conducted into the room of the men slaves.

Soon after this transaction, the captain returned, and brought with him a New Town trader, named Willy Honesty. On coming on board, he was informed of what had happened in his absence, and Mr. Millar believes, in the hearing of Willy Honesty, who immediately exclaimed, "Captain, if you will give me that man, to cut off his head, I will give you the best man in my canoe, and you shall be slaved the first ship." The captain upon this looked into Willy Honesty's canoe, picked his man, and delivered the other in his stead, when his head was immediately struck off in Mr. Millar's sight.

Mr. Millar believes that some other cruelties, besides this particular act, were done, because he saw blood on the starboard side of the mizzen-mast, though he does not recollect seeing any bodies from whence the blood might come; and others in other ships, because he heard several muskets or pistols fired from them at the same time. This affair might last ten minutes. He remembers a four-pounder fired at a canoe, but knows not whether any damage was done.

As to other acts of injustice on the part of the Europeans, some consider frauds (says Mr. Newton) as a necessary branch of the slave-trade. They put false heads into powder casks; cut off two or three yards from the middle of a piece of cloth; adulterate their spirits, and steal back articles given. Besides these, there are others who pay in bottles, which contain but half the contents of the samples shown; use false steelyards and weights, and sell such guns as burst on firing, so that many of the natives of the Windward Coast are without their fingers and thumbs on this account.

CHAPTER X.

African Slave Trade in the Eighteenth Century, Continued.—The Middle Passage.

Abstract of Evidence before House of Commons, continued.—The enslaved Africans on board the Ships—their dejection.—Methods of confining, airing, feeding and exercising them.—Mode of stowing them, and its horrible consequences.—Incidents of the terrible Middle Passage—shackles, chains, whips, filth, foul air, disease, suffocation.—Suicides by drowning, by starvation, by wounds, by strangling.—Insanity and Death.—Manner of selling them when arrived at their destination.—Deplorable situation of the refuse or sickly Slaves.—Mortality among Seamen engaged in the Slave Trade. Their miserable condition and sufferings from disease, and cruel treatment.

THE natives of Africa having been made slaves in the modes described in the former chapter, are brought down for sale to the European ships. On being brought on board, says Dr. Trotter, they show signs of extreme distress and despair, from a feeling of their situation, and regret at being torn from their friends and connections; many retain those impressions for a long time; in proof of which, the slaves on board his ship being often heard in the night making a howling melancholy noise, expressive of extreme anguish, he repeatedly ordered the woman who had been his interpreter to inquire into the cause. She discovered it to be owing to their having dreamed they were in their own country again, and finding themselves, when awake, in the hold of a slave-ship. This exquisite sensibility was particularly observable among the women, many of whom, on such occasions, he found in hysteric fits.

The foregoing description, as far as relates to their dejection, when brought on board, and the cause of it, is confirmed by Hall, Wilson, Claxton, Ellison, Towne, and Falconbridge, the latter of whom relates an instance of a young woman who cried and pined away after being brought on board, who recovered when put on shore, and who hung herself when informed she was to be sent again to the ship.

Captain Hall says, after the first eight or ten of them come on board, the men are put into irons. They are linked two and two together by the hands and feet, in which situation they continue till they arrive in the West Indies, except such as may be sick, whose irons are then taken off. The women, however, he says, are not ironed. On being brought up in a morning, says Surgeon Wilson, an additional mode of securing them takes place, for to the shackles of each pair of them there is a ring, through which is reeved a large chain, which locks them all in a body to ring-bolts fastened to the deck. The time of their coming up in the morning, if fair, is described by Mr. Towne to be between eight and nine, and the time of their remaining there to be till four in the afternoon, when they are again put below till the next morning. In the interval of being upon deck they are fed twice. They have also a pint of water allowed to each of them a day, which being divided is served out to them at two different times, namely, after their meals. These meals, says Mr. Falconbridge, consist of rice, yams, and horse-beans, with now and then a little beef and bread. After meals they are made to jump in their irons. This is called *dancing* by the slave-dealers. In every ship he has been desired to flog such as would not jump. He had generally a cat-of-nine-tails in his hand among the women, and the chief mate, he believes, another among the men.

The parts, says Mr. Claxton, (to continue the account,) on which their shackles are fastened, are often excoriated by the violent exercise they are thus forced to take, of which they made many grievous complaints to him. In his ship even those who had the flux, scurvy, and such œdematous swellings in their legs as made it painful to them to move at all, were compelled to dance by the cat. He says, also, that on board his ship they sometimes sung, but not for their amusement. The captain ordered them to sing, and they sung songs of sorrow. The subject of these songs were their wretched situation, and the idea of never returning home. He recollects their very words upon these occasions.

The above account of shackling, messing, dancing,* and singing the slaves, is allowed by all the witnesses, as far as they speak to the same points, except by Mr. Falconbridge, in whose ships the slaves had a pint and a half of water per day.

On the subject of the stowage and its consequences, Dr. Trotter says that the slaves in the passage are so crowded below, that it is impossible to walk through them, without treading on them. Those who are out of irons are locked spoonways (in the technical phrase) to one another. It is the first mate's duty to see them stowed in this way every morning; those who do not get quickly into their places, are compelled by a cat-of-nine-tails.

When the scuttles are obliged to be shut, the gratings are not sufficient for airing the rooms. He never himself could breathe freely, unless immediately under the hatchway. He has seen the slaves drawing their breath with all those laborious and anxious efforts for life, *which are observed in expiring animals, subjected by experiment to foul air, or in the exhausted receiver of an air pump.* He has also seen them, when the tarpaulings have inadvertently been thrown over the gratings, attempting to heave them up, crying out in their own language, " *We are dying !* " On removing the tarpaulings and gratings, they would fly to the hatchway with all the signs of terror and dread of suffocation. Many of them he has seen in a dying state, but some have recovered by being brought hither, or on the deck; others were irrecoverably lost *by suffocation,* having had no previous signs of indisposition.

Mr. Falconbridge also states on this head, that when employed in stowing the slaves, he made the most of the room and wedged them in. They had not so much room *as a man in his coffin,* either in length or breadth. It was impossible for them to turn or shift with any degree of ease. He had often occasion to go from one side of their rooms to the other, in which case he always took off his shoes, but could not avoid pinching them; he has the marks on his feet where they bit and scratched him. In every voyage, when the ship was full, they complained of heat and want of air. Confinement in this situation was so injurious, that he has known them to go down apparently in good health at night, and found dead in the morning. On his last voyage he opened a stout man who so died. He found the contents of the thorax and abdomen healthy, and therefore concludes he died of suffocation in the night. He was never among them for ten minutes below together, but his shirt was as wet as if dipped in water.

One of his ships, the Alexander, coming out of Bonny, got aground on the bar, and was detained there six or seven days, with a great swell and heavy rain. At this time the air ports were obliged to be shut, and part of the gratings on the weather side covered : almost all the men slaves were taken ill with the flux. The last time he went down to see them, it was so hot he took off his shirt. More than twenty of them had then fainted, or were fainting.

---

* The necessity of exercise for health is the reason given for compellng the slaves to dance in the above manner.

He got, however, several of them hauled on deck. Two or three of these died, and most of the rest, before they reached the West Indies. He was down only about fifteen minutes, and became so ill by it that he could not get up without help, and was disabled (the dysentery seizing him also) from doing duty the rest of the passage. On board the same ship he has known two or three instances of *a dead and living slave found in the morning shackled together*.

The crowded state of the slaves, and the pulling off the shoes by the surgeons, as described above, that they might not hurt them in traversing their rooms, are additionally mentioned by surgeons Wilson and Claxton. The slaves are said also by Hall and Wilson to complain on account of heat. Both Hall, Towne, and Morley, describe them as often in a violent perspiration, or dew sweat. Mr. Ellison has seen them faint through heat, and obliged to be brought on deck, the steam coming up through the gratings like a furnace. In Wilson's and Towne's ships, some have gone below well in an evening, and in the morning have been found dead; and Mr. Newton has often seen a dead and living man chained together, and, to use his own words, one of the pair dead.

To come now to the different incidents on the passage. Mr. Falconbridge says that there is a place in every ship for the sick slaves, but there are no accommodations for them, for they lie on the bare planks. He has seen frequently the prominent parts of their bones about the shoulder-blade and knees bare. He says he cannot conceive any situation so dreadful and disgusting as that of slaves when ill of the flux; in the Alexander, the deck was covered with blood and mucus, and resembled a slaughter-house. The stench and foul air were intolerable.

He has known several slaves on board refuse sustenance, with a design to starve themselves. Compulsion was used in every ship he was in to make them take their food. He has known also many instances of their refusing to take medicines when sick, because they wished to die. A woman on board the Alexander was dejected from the moment she came on board, and refused both food and medicine: being asked by the interpreter what she wanted, she replied, nothing but to die—and she did die. Many other slaves expressed the same wish.

The ships, he says, are fitted up with a view to prevent slaves jumping overboard; notwithstanding which he has known instances of their doing so. In the Alexander two were lost in this way. In the same voyage, near twenty jumped overboard out of the Enterprise, Capt. Wilson, and several from a large Frenchman in Bonny River. In his first voyage he saw at Bonny, on board the Emilia, a woman chained to the deck, who, the chief mate said, was mad. On his second voyage, there was a woman on board his own ship, whom they were forced to chain at certain times. In a lucid interval she was sold at Jamaica. He ascribes this insanity to their being torn from their connections and country.

Doctor Trotter, examined on the same subject, says that the man sold with
9

his family for witchcraft, (of which he had been accused, out of revenge, by a Cabosheer,) refused all sustenance after he came on board. Early next morning it was found he had attempted to cut his throat. Dr. Trotter sewed up the wound, but the following night the man had not only torn out the sutures, but had made a similar attempt on the other side. From the ragged edges of the wound, and the blood upon his finger ends, it appeared to have been done with his nails, for though strict search was made through all the rooms, no instrument was found. He declared he never would go with white men, uttered incoherent sentences, and looked wishfully at the skies. His hands were secured, but persisting to refuse all sustenance, he died of hunger in eight or ten days. He remembers also an instance of a woman who perished from refusing food : she was repeatedly flogged, and victuals forced into her mouth, but no means could make her swallow it, and she lived for the four last days in a state of torpid insensibility. A man jumped overboard, at Anamaboe, and was drowned. Another also, on the Middle Passage, but he was taken up. A woman also, after having been taken up, was chained for some time to the mizenmast, but being let loose again made a second attempt, was again taken up, and expired under the floggings given her in consequence.

Mr. Wilson, speaking also on the same subject, relates, among many cases where force was necessary to oblige the slaves to take food, that of a young man. He had not been long on board before he perceived him get thin. On inquiry, he found the man had not taken his food, and refused taking any. Mild means were then used to divert him from his resolution, as well as promises that he should have any thing he wished for : but still he refused to eat. They then whipped him with the cat, but this also was ineffectual. He always kept his teeth so fast, that it was impossible to get any thing down. They then endeavored to introduce a speculum oris between them ; but the points were too obtuse to enter, and next tried a bolus knife, but with the same effect. In this state he was for four or five days, when he was brought up as dead, to be thrown overboard ; but Mr. Wilson finding life still existing, repeated his endeavors, though in vain, and two days afterwards he was brought up again in the same state as before. He then seemed to wish to get up. The crew assisted him, and brought him aft to the fire-place, when, in a feeble voice, in his own tongue, he asked for water, which was given him. Upon this they began to have hopes of dissuading him from his design, but he again shut his teeth as fast as ever, and resolved to die, and on the ninth day from the first refusal he died.

Mr. Wilson says it hurt his feelings much to be obliged to use the cat so frequently to force them to take their food. In the very act of chastisement, they have looked up at him with a smile, and in their own language have said, *"presently we shall be no more."*

In the same ship a woman found means to convey below the night preceding some rope-yarn, which she tied to the head of the armorer's vise, then in the women's room. She fastened it round her neck, and in the morning was found dead, with her head lying on her shoulder, whence it appeared, she must have

PLANTATION SCENE—COFFEE.

used great exertions to accomplish her end. A young woman also hanged her-self, by tying rope-yarns to a batten, near her usual sleeping-place, and then slipping off the platform. The next morning she was found warm, and he used the proper means for her recovery, but in vain.

In the same ship also, when off Annabona, a slave on the sick list jumped overboard, and was picked up by the natives, but died soon afterwards. At another time, when at sea, the captain and officers, when at dinner, heard the alarm of a slave's being overboard, and found it true, for they perceived him making every exertion to drown himself. He put his head under water, but lifted his hands up; and thus went down, as if *exulting that he had got away*.

Besides the above instance, a man slave who came on board apparently well, became afterwards mad, and at length died insane.

Mr. Claxton, the fourth surgeon examined on these points, declares the steerage and boys' room to have been insufficient to receive the sick; they were therefore obliged to place together those that were and those that were not diseased, and in consequence the disease and mortality spread more and more. The captain treated them with more tenderness than he has heard was usual, but the men were not humane. Some of the most diseased were obliged to keep on deck with a sail spread for them to lie on. This, in a little time, became nearly covered with blood and mucus, which involuntarily issued from them, and therefore the sailors, who had the disagreeable task of cleaning the sail, grew angry with the slaves, and used to beat them inhumanly with their hands, or with a cat. The slaves in consequence grew fearful of committing this involuntary action, and when they perceived they had done it would im-mediately creep to the tubs, and there sit straining with such violence, as to produce a prolapsus ani, which could not be cured.

Some of the slaves on board the same ship, says Mr. Claxton, had such an aversion to leaving their native places, that they threw themselves over-board, on an idea that they should get back to their own country. The cap-tain, in order to obviate this idea, thought of an expedient, viz: to cut off the heads of those who died, intimating to them, that if determined to go, they must return without their heads. The slaves were accordingly brought up to witness the operation. One of them seeing, when on deck, the carpenter standing with his hatchet up ready to strike off the head of a dead slave, with a violent exertion got loose, and flying to the place where the nettings had been unloosed, in order to empty the tubs, he darted overboard. The ship brought to, and a man was placed in the main chains to catch him, which he perceiving, dived under water, and rising again at a distance from the ship, made signs, which words cannot describe, expressive of his happiness in escap-ing. He then went down, and was seen no more. This circumstance deterred the captain from trying the expedient any more, and therefore he resolved for the future (as he saw they were determined to throw themselves overboard) to keep a strict watch) notwithstanding which, some afterwards contrived to un-loose the lashing, so that two actually threw themselves into the sea, and were lost; another was caught when about three parts overboard.

All the above incidents, described as to have happened on the Middle Passage, are amply corroborated by the other witnesses. The slaves lie on the bare boards, says surgeon Wilson. They are frequently bruised, and the prominent parts of the body excoriated, adds the same gentleman, as also Trotter and Newton. They have been seen by Morley wallowing in their blood and excrement. Claxton, Ellison, and Hall describe them as refusing sustenance, and compelled to eat by the whip. Morley has seen the pannekin dashed against their teeth, and the rice held in their mouths, to make them swallow it, till they were almost strangled, and they have even been thumb-screwed * with this view in the ships of Towne and Millar. The man stolen at Galenas river, says the former, also refused to eat, and persisted till he died. A woman, says the latter, who was brought on board, refused sustenance, neither would she speak. She was then ordered the thumb-screws, suspended in the mizzen rigging, and every attempt was made with the cat to compel her to eat, but to no purpose. She died in three or four days afterwards. Mr. Millar was told that she had said, the night before she died, " She was going to her friends."

As a third specific instance, in another vessel, may be mentioned that related by Mr. Isaac Parker. There was a child, says he, on board, nine months old, which refused to eat, for which the captain took it up in his hand, and flogged it with a cat, saying, at the same time, "Damn you, I'll make you eat, or I'll kill you." The same child having swelled feet, the captain ordered them to be put into water, though the ship's cook told him it was too hot. This brought off the skin and nails. He then ordered sweet oil and cloths, which Isaac Parker himself applied to the feet; and as the child at mess time again refused to eat, the captain again took it up and flogged it, and tied a log of mango-wood eighteen or twenty inches long, and of twelve or thirteen pounds weight, round its neck, as a punishment. He repeated the flogging for four days together at mess time. The last time after flogging it, he let it drop out of his hand, with the same expression as before, and accordingly in about three quarters of an hour the child died. He then called its mother to heave it overboard, and beat her for refusing. He however forced her to take it up, and go to the ship's side, *where, holding her head on one side, to avoid the sight, she dropped her child overboard, after which she cried for many hours.*

Besides instances of slaves refusing to eat, with the view of destroying themselves, and dying in consequence of it, those of their going mad are confirmed by Towne, and of their jumping overboard, or attempting to do it, by Towne, Millar, Ellison, and Hall.

Other incidents on the passage, mentioned by some of the witnesses in their examination, may be divided into three kinds :

The first kind consists of insurrections on the part of the slaves. Some of these frequently attempted to rise, but were prevented, (Wilson, Towne, Trot-

---

* To show the severity of this punishment, Mr. Dove says, that while two slaves were under the torture of the thumb-screws, the sweat ran down their faces, and they trembled as under a violent ague fit ; and Mr. Ellison has known instances of their dying, a mortification having taken place in their thumbs in consequence of these screws.

ter, Newton, Dalrymple, Ellison,) others rose, but were quelled, (Ellison, Newton, Falconbridge,) and others rose and succeeded, killing almost all the whites:
(Falconbridge and Towne.) Mr. Towne says that, inquiring of the slaves into
the cause of these insurrections, he has been asked what business he had to
carry them from their country. They had wives and children, whom they wanted
to be with. After an insurrection, Mr. Ellison says he has seen them flogged,
and the cook's tormentors and tongs heated to burn their flesh. Mr. Newton
also adds that it is usual for captains, after insurrections and plots happen, to
flog the slaves. Some captains, on board whose ships he has been, added the
thumb-screw, and one in particular told him repeatedly that he had put slaves
to death, after an insurrection, by various modes of torture.

The second sort of incident on the passage is mentioned by Mr. Falconbridge
in the instance of an English vessel blowing up off Galenas, and most of the
men-slaves, entangled in their irons, perishing.

The third sort is described by Mr. Hercules Ross as follows. One instance,
says he, marked with peculiar circumstances of horror, occurs :—About twenty
years ago, a ship from Africa, with about four hundred slaves on board, struck
upon some shoals, called the Morant Keys, distant eleven leagues, S.S.E. off
the east end of Jamaica. The officers and seamen of the ship landed in their
boats, carrying with them arms and provisions. The slaves were left on board
in their irons and shackles. This happened in the night time. The Morant
Keys consist of three small sandy islands, and he understood that the ship had
struck upon the shoals, at about half a league to windward of them. When
morning came, it was discovered that the negroes had got out of their irons,
and were busy making rafts, upon which they placed the women and children,
whilst the men, and others capable of swimming, attended upon the rafts, while
they drifted before the wind towards the island where the seamen had landed.
From an apprehension that the negroes would consume the water and provisions which the seamen had landed, they came to the resolution of destroying
them by means of their fire-arms and other weapons. As the poor wretches
approached the shore, *they actually destroyed between three and four hundred of them.* Out of the whole cargo, only thirty-three or thirty-four were
saved, and brought to Kingston, where Mr. Ross saw them sold at public ven-
due. The ship, to the best of his recollection, was consigned to a Mr. Hugh
Wallace, of the parish of St. Elizabeth's. Mr. Ross says, in extenuation of
this massacre, that the crew were probably drunk, or they would not have acted
so, but he does not know it to have been the case.

When the ships arrive at their destined ports, the slaves are exposed to sale.
They are sold either by scramble, by public auction, or by lots. The sale by
scramble is thus described by Mr. Falconbridge : "In the Emilia, at Jamaica,
the ship was darkened with sails, and covered around. The men-slaves were
placed on the main deck, and the women on the quarter deck. The purchasers
on shore were informed that a gun would be fired when they were ready to open
the sale. A great number of people came on board with tallies or cards in
their hands, with their own names on them, and rushed through the barricado

door with the ferocity of brutes. Some had three or four handkerchiefs tied together, to encircle as many as they thought fit for their purpose. In the yard at Grenada, he adds, (where another of his ships, the Alexander, sold by scramble,) the women were so terrified, that several of them got out of the yard, and ran about St. George's town as if they were mad. In his second voyage, while lying at Kingston, he saw a sale by scramble on board the Tryal, Captain Macdonald. Forty or fifty of the slaves leaped into the sea, all of whom, however, were taken up again." This was a very general mode of sale. Mr. Baillie says it was the common mode in America where he has been. Mr. Fitzmaurice has been at twenty sales by scramble in Jamaica. Mr. Clappeson never saw any other mode of sale during his residence there, and it is mentioned as having been practiced under the inspection of Morley and of Trotter.

The slaves sold by public auction are generally the refuse, or sickly slaves. These were in such a state of health that they sold, says Baillie, greatly under price. Falconbridge has known them sold for five dollars each, Town for a guinea, and Mr. Hercules Ross as low as a single dollar.

The state of such is described to be very deplorable by General Tottenham and Mr. Hercules Ross. The former says that he once observed at Barbadoes a number of slaves that had been landed from a ship. They were brought into the yard adjoining the place of sale. Those that were not very ill were put into little huts, and those that were worse were left in the yard to die, for nobody gave them any thing to eat or drink; and some of them lived three days in that situation. The latter has frequently seen the very refuse (as they are termed) of the slaves of Guinea ships landed and carried to the vendue-masters in a very wretched state; sometimes in the agonies of death; and he has known instances of their expiring in the piazza of the auctioneer.

Mr. Newton says, that in none of the sales he saw was there any care ever taken to prevent such slaves as were relations from being separated. They were separated as sheep and lambs by the butcher. This separation of relations and friends is confirmed by Davison, Trotter, Clapperson, and Towne. Fitzmaurice also mentions the same, with an exception only to infants; but Mr. Falconbridge says that one of his captains (Frazer) recommended it to the planters never to separate relations and friends. He says he once heard of a person refusing to purchase a man's wife, and was next day informed the man had hanged himself.

With respect to the mortality of slaves in the passage, Mr. Falconbridge says, that in three voyages he purchased 1,100, and lost 191; Trotter, in one voyage, about 600, and lost about 70; Millar, in one voyage, 490, and lost 180; Ellison, in three voyages, where he recollects the mortality, bought 895, and lost 356. In one of these voyages, says the latter, the slaves had the small-pox. In this case he has seen the platform one continued scab; eight or ten of them were hauled up dead in a morning, and the flesh and skin peeled off their wrists when taken hold of.

Mr. Morley says that in four voyages he purchased about 1,325, and lost about 313. Mr. Towne, in two voyages, 630, and lost 115. Mr. Claxton, in

one voyage, 250, and lost 132. In this voyage, he says, they were so straighten-
ed for provisions, that if they had been ten more days at sea, they must either
have eaten the slaves that died, or have made the living slaves *walk the plank*,
a term used among Guinea captains for making the slaves throw themselves
overboard. He says, also, that he fell in with the Hero, Captain Withers,
which had lost 360 slaves, or more than half her cargo, by the small-pox
The surgeon of the Hero told him that when the slaves were removed from
one place to another, they left marks of their skin and blood upon the deck, and
it was the most horrid sight he had ever seen.

Mr. Wilson states that in his ship and three others belonging to the same
concern, they purchased among them 2064 slaves, and lost 586. He adds, that
he fell in with the Hero, Captain Withers, at St. Thomas', which had lost 159
slaves by the small-pox. Captain Hall, in two voyages, purchased 550, and
lost 110. He adds, that he has known some ships in the slave-trade bury a
quarter, some a third, and others half of their cargo. It is very uncommon
to find ships without some loss * in their slaves.

Besides those which die on the passage, it must be noticed here that several
die soon after they are sold. Sixteen, says Mr. Falconbridge, were sold by
auction out of the Alexander, all of whom died before the ship left the West
Indies. Out of fourteen, says Mr. Claxton, sold from his ship in an infectious
state, only four lived; and though in the four voyages mentioned by Mr. Wilson, no less than·586 perished on the passage out of 2,064, yet 220 additionally died of the small-pox in a very little time after their delivery in the river
Plate, making the total loss for those ships not less than 836, out of 2,064.

The causes of the disorders which carry off the slaves in such numbers, are
ascribed by Mr. Falconbridge to a diseased mind, sudden transitions from heat
to cold, a putrid atmosphere, wallowing in their own excrements, and being
shackled together. A diseased mind, he says, is undoubtedly one of the causes;
for many of the slaves on board refused medicines, giving as a reason, that
they wanted to die, and could never be cured. Some few, on the other hand,
who did not appear to think so much of their situation, recovered. That
shackling together is also another cause, was evident from the circumstance of
the men dying in twice the proportion the women did; and so long as the
trade continues, he adds, they must be shackled together, for no man will attempt to carry them out of irons.

Surgeon Wilson, examined on the same topic, speaks nearly in the same
manner. He says that of the death of two-thirds of those who died in his
ship, the primary cause was melancholy. This was evident, not only from the
symptoms of the disorder, and the circumstance that no one who had it was
ever cured, whereas those who had it not, and yet were ill, recovered; but
from the language of the slaves themselves, who declared that they wished to
die, as also from Captain Smith's own declaration, who said their deaths were

---

* Total purchased, 7,904, lost, 2,053, exclusive of the Hero, being above one-fourth
of the number purchased. The reader will observe that Mr. Claxton fell in with the
Hero on one voyage, and Mr. Wilson on another.

to be ascribed to their thinking so much of their situation. Though several died of the flux, he attributes their death, primarily, to the cause before assigned ; for, says he, their original disorder was a fixed melancholy, and the symptoms, lowness of spirits and despondency. Hence they refused food. This only increased the symptoms.

Mr. Towne, the only other person who speaks of the causes of the disorders of the slaves, says "they often fall sick, sometimes owing to their crowded state, but mostly to grief for being carried away from their country and friends." This he knows from inquiring frequently (which he was enabled to do by understanding their language) into the circumstances of their grievous complaints.

We make some further extracts from the evidence, to exhibit the disastrous and fatal effects of the trade upon the seamen engaged in it. Such was the despotic character of the discipline on board of the slave-ships, and such the insensibility to suffering acquired by the officers, that the condition of the seamen was not much better than that of the slaves. To exhibit the mortality among the seamen on board these infected ships, a report was made to the House of Commons, giving an abstract of the muster-rolls of such Liverpool and Bristol ships as were returned to the custom houses from September, 1784, to January, 1790. During this period, it appears that in 350 vessels, 12,263 seamen were employed ; of these, only 5,760 returned home of the original crews ; of the remaining 6,503, there had died, *before* the vessels arrived in the West Indies, 2,643. The fate of the 3,860, not accounted for in the muster-rolls, we gather from the witnesses.

The crews of the African slavers, says Captain Hall, when they arrive in the West Indies, are generally (he does not know a single instance to the contrary) in a sickly, debilitated state, and the seamen, who are discharged or desert from those ships in the West Indies, are the most miserable objects he ever met with in any country in his life. He has frequently seen them with their toes rotted off, their legs swelled to the size of their thighs, and in an ulcerated state all over. He has seen them on the different wharves in the islands of Antigua, Barbadoes, and Jamaica, particularly at the two last islands. He has also seen them laying under the cranes and balconies of the houses near the water-side in Barbadoes and Jamaica expiring, and some quite dead.

To confirm the assertion of Captain Hall, of the merchant service, that the crews of Guinea-men generally arrive at their destined ports of sale in a sickly, debilitated state, we may refer to Captain Hall, of the navy, who asserts that in taking men (while in the West Indies) out of merchant ships for the king's service, he has, in taking a part of the crew of a Guinea ship, whose number then consisted of seventy, been able to select but thirty, who could have been thought capable of serving on board any ships of war, and when those thirty were surveyed by order of the admiral, he was reprimanded for bringing such men into the service, who were more likely to breed distemper than to be of any use, and this at a time when seamen were so much wanted, that almost any thing would have been taken. He adds also that this was not a singular instance, but that it was generally the case; for he had many opportunities between the years 1769 and 1773 of seeing the great distresses of crews of Guinea ships, when they arrived in the West Indies.

We may refer also to Captain Smith, of the navy, who asserts that though he may have boarded near twenty of these vessels in the West Indies, for the purpose of impressing men, he was never able to get more than two men. The principal reason was the fear of infection, having seen many of them in a very disordered and ulcerated state.

The assertion also of Captain Hall, of the merchant service, relative to their situation after their arrival at their destined ports of sale, is confirmed by the rest of the witnesses in the minutest manner; for the seamen belonging to the slave-vessels are described as lying about the wharves and cranes, or wandering about the streets or islands full of sores and ulcers. It is asserted by the witnesses, that they never saw any other than Guinea seamen in that state in the West Indies. The epithets also of sickly, emaciated, abject, deplorable objects, are applied to them. They are mentioned again as destitute, and starving, and without the means of support, no merchantmen taking them in because they are unable to work, and men-of-war refusing them for fear of infection. Many of them are also described as lying about in a dying state; and others have been actually found dead, and negroes have been seen carrying the bodies of others to be interred.

It may be remarked here, that this diseased and forlorn state of the seamen was so inseparable from the slave-trade, that the different witnesses had not only seen it at Jamaica, Antigua, and Barbadoes, the places mentioned by Captain Hall, but wherever they have seen Guinea-men arrive, namely, at St. Vincents, Grenada, Dominique, and in North America also.·

The reasons why such immense numbers were left behind in the West Indies, as were found in this deplorable state, are the following: The seamen leave their ships from ill usage, says Ellison. It is usual for captains, say Clappeson and Young, to treat them ill, that they may desert and forfeit their wages. Three others state they were left behind purposely by their captains; and Mr. H. Rose adds, in these emphatical words, "that it was no uncommon thing for the captains to send on shore, a few hours before they sail, their lame, emaciated, and sick seamen, leaving them to perish."

That the seamen employed in the slave-trade were worse fed, both in point of quantity and quality of provisions, than the seamen in other trades, was allowed by most of the witnesses, and that they had little or no shelter night or day from the inclemency of the weather, during the whole of the Middle Passage, was acknowledged by them all. With respect to their personal ill usage, the following extracts may suffice:

Mr. Morley asserts that the seamen in all the Guinea-men he sailed in, except one, were generally treated with great rigor, and many with cruelty. He recollects many instances: Mathews, the chief mate of the Venus, Captain Forbes, would knock a man down for any frivolous thing with a cat, a piece of wood, or a cook's axe, with which he once cut a man down the shoulder, by throwing it at him in a passion.   Captain Dixon, likewise, in the Amelia, tied up the men, and gave them four or five dozen lashes at a time, and then rubbed them with pickle.   Mr. Morley also himself, when he was Dixon's cabin-boy, for accidentally breaking a glass, was tied to the tiller by the hands, flogged with a cat, and kept hanging for some time.   Mr. Morley has seen the seamen lie and die upon the deck.   They are generally, he says, treated ill when sick.   He has known men ask to have their wounds or ulcers dressed; and has heard the doctor, with oaths, refuse to dress them.   .

Mr. Ellison also, in describing the treatment in the Briton, says there was a boy on board, whom Wilson, the chief mate, was always beating.   One morning, in the passage out, he had not got the tea-kettle boiled in time for his breakfast, upon which, when it was brought, Wilson told him he would severely flog him after breakfast.   The boy, for fear of this, went into the lee fore chains.   When Wilson came from the cabin, and called for Paddy, (the name he went by, being an Irish boy,) he would not come, but remained in the fore chains; on which Wilson going forward, and attempting to haul him in, the boy jumped overboard, and was drowned.

Another time on the Middle Passage, the same Wilson ordered one James Allison (a man he had been continually beating for trifles) to go into the women's room to scrape it.   Allison said he was not able, for he was very unwell; upon which Wilson obliged him to go down.   Observing, however, that the man did not work, he asked him the reason, and was answered as before, "that he was not able."   Upon this, Wilson threw a handspike at him, which struck him on the breast, and he dropped down to appearance dead. Allison recovered afterwards a little, but died the next day.

Mr. Ellison relates other instances of ill-usage on board his own ship, and with respect to instances in others, he says, that in all slave ships they are most commonly beaten and knocked about for nothing.   He recollects that on board the Phœnix, a Bristol ship, while lying on the coast, the boatswain and five of the crew made their escape in the yawl, but were taken up by the natives. When Captain Bishop heard it, he ordered them to be kept on shore at Forje, a small town at the mouth of Calabar River, chained by the necks, legs, and hands, and to have each a plantain a day only.   The boatswain, whose name was Tom Jones, and an old shipmate of his, and a very good seaman, died raving mad in his chains there.   The other five died in their chains also.

Mr. Towne, in speaking of the treatment on board the Peggy, Captain Davison, says that their chests were brought upon deck, and staved and burnt, and themselves turned out from lying below; and if any murmurs were heard among them, they were inhumanly beaten with any thing that came in the way, or flogged, both legs put in irons, and chained abaft to the pumps, and there made to work points and gaskets, during the captain's pleasure; and very often beat just as the captain thought proper.   He himself has often seen the captain as he has walked by, kick them repeatedly, and if they have said any thing that he might deem offensive, he has immediately called for a stick to beat them with; they at the same time, having both legs in irons, an iron collar about their necks, and a chain; and when on the coast of Guinea, if not released before their arrival there from their confinement, they were put into the boats, and made to row backwards and forwards, either with the captain from ship to ship, or on any other duty, still both legs in irons, an iron collar about their necks, with a chain locked to the boat, and taken out when no other duty was required of them at night, and locked fast upon the open deck, exposed to the heavy rains and dews, without any thing to lie upon, or any thing to cover them. This was a practice on board the Peggy.

He says, also, that similar treatment prevailed on board the Sally, another ship in which he sailed. One of the seamen had both legs in irons, and a collar about his neck, and was chained to the boat for three months, and very often inhumanly beaten for complaining of his situation, both by the captain and other officers. At last he became so weak that he could not sit upon the thwart or seat of the boat to row, or do anything else. They then put him out of the boat, and made him pick oakum on board the ship, with only three pounds of bread a week, and half a pound of salt beef per day. He remained in that situation, with both his legs in irons, but the latter part of the time without a collar. One evening he came aft, during the middle passage, to beg something to eat, or he should die. The captain on this inhumanly beat him, and used a great number of reproaches, and ordered him to go forward, and die and be damned. The man died in the night. The ill treatment on board the Sally was general.

As another particular instance, a landsman, one Edw. Hilton, was in the boat watering, and complained of his being long in the boat without meat or drink. The boatswain, being the officer, beat him with the boat's tiller, having nothing else, and cut his head in several places, so that when he came on board he was all over blood. Mr. Towne asked him the reason of it. Hilton began to tell him, but before he could properly tell the story, the mate came forward, (by order of the captain) the surgeon and the boatswain, and all of them together fell to beating him with their canes. The surgeon struck him on the side of his eye, so that it afterwards mortified, and was lost. He immediately had both his legs put in irons, after he had been so beat that he could not stand. The next morning he was put into the boat on the same duty as before, still remaining with both legs in irons, and locked with a chain to the boat, until such time as he became so weak that he was not able to remain any longer there. He was then put on board the ship, and laid forwards, still in irons, very ill. His allowance was immediately stopped, as it was the surgeon's opinion it was the only method of curing any one of them who complained of illness. He remained in that situation, after being taken out of the boat, for some weeks after. During this time, Mr. Towne was obliged to go to Junk River, and on his return he inquired for Hilton, and was told that he was lying before the foremast, almost dead. He went and spoke to him, but Hilton seemed insensible. The same day Mr. Towne received his orders to go a second time in the shallop to Junk River. After he had gotten under weigh, the commander of the shallop was ordered to bring to, and take Hilton in, and leave him on shore any where. He lived that evening and night out, and died early the next morning, and was thrown overboard off Cape Mesurado.

Mr. Falconbridge, being called upon also to speak to the ill usage of seamen, said that on board the Alexander, Captain M'Taggart, he has seen them tied up and flogged with the cat frequently. He remembers also an instance of an old man, who was boatswain of the Alexander, having one night some words with the mate, when the boatswain was severely beaten, and had one or two of his teeth knocked out. The boatswain said he would jump overboard; upon which he was tied to the rail of the quarter-deck, and a pump-bolt put into his mouth by way of gagging him. He was then untied, put under the half-deck, and a sentinel put over him all night — in the morning he was released. Mr. Falconbridge always considered him as a quiet, inoffensive man. In the same voyage a black boy was beaten every day, and one day, after he was so beaten, he jumped through one of the gun-ports of the cabin into the river. A canoe was lying alongside, which dropped astern and picked him up. Mr. Falconbridge gave him one of his own shirts to put on, and asked him if he did not expect to be devoured by the sharks. The boy said he did, and that it would be much better for him to be killed at once, than to be daily treated with so much cruelty.

Mr. Falconbridge remembers also, on board the same ship, that the black cook one day broke a plate. For this he had a fish-gig darted at him, which would certainly have destroyed him if he had not stooped or dropped down. At another time also, the carpenter's mate had let his pitch-pot catch fire. He and the cook were accordingly both tied up, stripped and flogged, but the cook with the greatest severity. After that the cook had salt water and cayenne pepper rubbed upon his back. A man also came on board at Bonny, belonging to a little ship, (Mr. Falconbridge believes the captain's name was Dodson, of Liverpool,) which had been overset at New Calabar. This man, when he came on board, was in a convalescent state. He was severely beaten one night, but for what cause Mr. Falconbridge knows not, upon which he came to Mr. Falconbridge for something to rub his back with. Mr. Falconbridge was told by the captain not to give him any thing, and the man was desired to go forward. He went accordingly, and lay under the forecastle. Mr. Falconbridge visited him very often, at which times he complained of his bruises. He died in about three weeks from the time he was beaten. The last words he ever spoke were, after shedding tears, "I cannot punish him," meaning the captain, "but God will." These are the most remarkable instances which Mr. Falconbridge recollects. He says, however, that the ill treatment was so general, that only three in this ship escaped being beaten out of fifty persons.

To these instances, which fell under the eyes of the witnesses now cited, we may add the observations of a gentleman who, though never in the slave-trade, had yet great opportunities of obtaining information upon this subject. Sir George Young remarks, that those seamen whom he saw in the slave-trade, while on the coast in a man-of-war, complained of their ill treatment, bad feeding, and cruel usage. They all wanted to enter on board his ship. It was likewise the custom for the seamen of every ship he saw at a distance, to come on board him with their boats; most of them quite naked, and threatening to turn pirates if he did not take them. This they told him openly. He is persuaded, if he had given them encouragement, and had had a ship-of-the-line to have manned, he could have done it in a very short time, for they would all have left their ships. He has also received several seamen on board his ship from the woods, where they had no subsistence, but to which they had fled for refuge from their respective vessels.

That the above are not the only instances of barbarity contained in the evidence, and that this barbarous usage was peculiar to, or springing out of the very nature of the trade in slaves, may be insisted on the following accounts :

Captain Thompson concludes from the many complaints he received from seamen, while on the coast, that they are far from being well treated on board the slave-ships. One Bowden swam from the Fisher, of Liverpool, Captain Kendal, to the Nautilus, amidst a number of sharks, to claim his protection. Kendal wrote for the man, who refused to return, saying his life would be endangered. He therefore kept him in the Nautilus till she was paid off, and found him a diligent, willing, active seaman. Several of the crew, he thinks, of the Brothers, of Liverpool, Captain Clark, swam towards the Nautilus, when passing by. Two only reached her. The rest, he believes, regained their own ship. The majority of the crew had the day before come on board the Nautilus, in a boat, to complain of ill usage, but he had returned them with an officer to inquire into and redress their complaints. He received many letters from seamen in slave-ships, complaining of ill usage, and desiring him to protect them, or take them on board. He is inclined to think that ships trading in the produce of Africa, are not so ill used as those in the slave-ships. Several of his own officers gave him the best accounts of the treatment in the Iris, a vessel trading for wood, gums, and ivory, near which the Nautilus lay for some weeks.

Lieutenant Simpson says that on his first voyage, when lying at Fort Appolonia, the Fly Guineaman was in the roads. On the return of the Adventure's boat from the fort, they were hailed by some seamen belonging to the Fly, requesting that they might be taken from on board the Guineaman, and put on board the man-of-war, for that their treatment was such as to make their lives miserable. The boat, by the direction of Captain Parry, was sent to the Fly, and one or two men were brought on board him. In his second voyage, he recollects that on first seeing the Albion Guineaman, she carried a press of sail, seemingly to avoid them, but finding it impracticable, she spoke them ; the day after which the captain of the Albion brought a seaman on board the Adventure, whom he wished to be left there, complaining that he was a very riotous and disorderly man. The man, on the contrary, proved very peaceable and well-behaved, nor was there one single instance of his conduct from which he could suppose he merited the character given him. He seemed to rejoice at quitting the Albion, and informed Mr. Simpson that he was cruelly beaten both by the captain and surgeon; that he was half starved; and that the surgeon neglected the sick seamen, alleging that he was only paid for attending the slaves. He also informed Mr. Simpson that their allowance of provisions was increased, and their treatment somewhat better when a man-of-war was on the coast. He recollects another instance of a seaman, with a leg shockingly ulcerated, requesting a passage in the Adventure to England; alleging that he was left behind from a Guineaman. He alleged various instances of ill treatment he had received, and confirmed the account of the sailor of the Albion, that their allowance of provisions was increased, and treatment better, when a man-of-war was on the coast. During Mr. Simpson's stay at Cape Coast Castle, the Adventure's boat was sent to Annamaboe to the Spy Guineaman; on her return, three men were concealed under her sails, who had left the slaveship; they complained that their treatment was so bad that their lives were miserable on board—beaten and half starved. There were various other instances which escaped his memory. Mr. Simpson says, however, that he has never heard any complaints from West Indiamen, or other merchant ships; on the contrary, they wished to avoid a man-of-war; whereas, if the captain of the Adventure had listened to all the complaints made to him from sailors of slaveships, and removed them, he must have greatly distressed the African trade.

Captain Hall, of the navy, speaking on the same subject, asserts that as to peculiar modes of punishment adopted in Guineamen, he once saw a man chained by the neck in the main top of a slave-ship, when passing under the stern of His Majesty's ship Crescent, in Kingston-Bay, St. Vincent's; and was told by part of the crew, taken out of the ship, at their own request, that the man had been there one hundred and twenty days. He says he has great reason to believe that in no trade are seamen so badly treated as in the slave-trade, from their always flying to men-of-war for redress, and whenever they came within reach; whereas men from West Indian or other trades seldom apply to a ship-of-war.

The last witness it will be necessary to cite is the Rev. Mr. Newton. This gentleman agrees in the ill usage of the seamen alluded to, and believes that the slave-trade itself is a great cause of it, for he thinks that the real or supposed necessity of treating the negroes with rigor gradually brings a numbness upon the heart, and renders most of those who are engaged in it too indifferent to the sufferings of their fellow-creatures. If it should be asked how it happened that seamen entered for slave-vessels, when such general ill usage there could hardly fail of being known, the reply must be taken from the evidence, "that whereas some of them enter voluntarily, the greater part of them are trepanned, for that it is the business of certain landlords to make them intoxicated, and get them into debt, after which their only alternative is a Guineaman or a gaol."

CHAPTER XI.

SLAVERY IN THE WEST INDIES, 1750 TO 1790.

Abstract of Evidence continued.—Slavery in the West Indies from 1750 to 1790.—General estimation and treatment of the Slaves.—Labor of Plantation Slaves—their days of rest, food, clothing, property.—Ordinary punishment by the whip and cowskin.—Frequency and severity of these Punishments.—Extraordinary Punishments of various kinds, for nominal offenses.—Capital offenses and Punishments.—Slaves turned off to steal, beg, or starve, when incapable of labor.—Slaves had little or no redress against ill usage.

THE natives of Africa, when bought by European colonists, are generally esteemed, says Dr. Jackson, a species of inferior beings, whom the right of purchase gives the owner a power of using at his will. Consistently with this definition, we find the evidence asserting, with one voice, that they "have no legal protection against their masters," and of course, that "their treatment varies according to the disposition of their masters." If their masters be good men, says the Dean of Middleham, they are well off, but if not, they suffer. The general treatment, however, is described to be very severe. Some speak more moderately than others upon it, but all concur in the general usage as being bad. Mr. Woolrich, examined on this point, says that he never knew the best master in the West Indies use his slaves so well as the worst master his servants in England; that their state is inconceivable; that it cannot be described to the full understanding of those who have never seen it, and that a sight of some gangs would convince more than all words. Others, again, make use of the words, "used with great cruelty,—like beasts, or worse;" and the Dean of Middleham, after balancing in his mind all his knowledge upon this subject, cannot say, (setting aside on one hand particular instances of great severity, and on the other hand particular instances of great humanity,) that treatment altogether humane and proper was the lot of such as he had either observed or heard of.

To come to a more particular description of their treatment, it will be proper to divide them into different classes. The first may be said to consist of those who are bought for the plantation use. These are artificers of various descriptions, and the field slaves. The second consists of what may be termed in-or-out-door slaves. The former are domestics, both in town and country, and the latter, porters, fishermen, boatmen, and the like.

The field-slaves, whose case is the first to be considered, are called out by day-light to their work. For this purpose the shell blows, and they hurry into the field. If they are not there in time, they are flogged. When put to their work, they perform it in rows, and, without exception, under the whip of drivers, a certain number of whom are allotted to each gang. By these means, the weak are made to keep up with the strong. Mr. Fitzmaurice is sorry to say, that from this cause many of them are hurried to the grave; as the able, even if placed with the weakly to bring them up, will leave them behind, and then the weakly are generally flogged up by the driver. This, however, is the mode of their labor. As to the time of it, they begin, as before said, at day-light, and continue, with two intermissions, (one for half an hour in the morn-ing, and the other for two hours at noon,) till sun-set.

The above description, however, does not include the whole of their opera-tions for the day, for it is expected that they shall range about and pick grass for the cattle. It is clear, from the different evidences, that the custom of grass-picking varies, as to the time in which it is to be done, on different estates, for on some it is to be done within the intervals of rest said to be allowed at noon, and on others after the labor of the day. It is complained of, however, in either case, as a great grievance, as it lengthens the time of work; as also, because, particularly in droughts, it is very difficult to find grass at all, and because, if they do not bring it in sufficient quantities, they are punished. Grass-picking, says Captain Smith, is one of the most frequent causes of punishment. He has seen some flogged for not getting so great a quantity of it as others, and that at a time when he has thought it impossible they could have gotten half the quantity, having been upon the spot.

It is impossible to pass over in silence the almost total want of indulgence which the women slaves frequently experience during the operations in the field. It is asserted by Dalrymple, that the drivers, in using their whip, never distinguish sex.

The above accounts of the mode and duration of the labor of the field slaves, are confined to that season of the year which is termed "out of crop," or the time in which they are preparing the lands for the crop. In the crop season, however, the labor is of much longer duration. Weakly handed estates, says Mr. Fitzmaarice, which are far the most numerous, form their negroes in crop into two spells, which generally change at twelve at noon, and twelve at night. The boilers and others about the works, relieved at twelve at noon, cut canes from shell blow (half-past one) till dark, when they carry cane-tops or grass to the cattle pens, and then they may rest till twelve at night, when they re-lieve the spell in the boiling-house, by which they themselves had been relieved at twelve in the day. On all the estates the boiling goes on night and day with-out intermission; but full-handed estates have three spells, and intermissions accordingly.

Mr. Dalrymple, speaking also of their labor in time of crop, says they are obliged to work as long as they can, which is as long as they can keep awake or stand on their legs. Sometimes they fall asleep, through excess of fatigue, when their arms are caught in the mill and torn off. He saw several who had lost their arms in that way. Mr. Cook states, on the same subject, that in crop time they work in general about eighteen hours out of the twenty-four, and are often hurt through mere fatigue and want of sleep. He knew a girl lose her hand by the mill, while feeding it, for being overcome by sleep, she dropped against the rollers. He has heard of several instances of this kind.

To this account of the labor of the slaves, both in and out of crop, it ap-pears by the evidence they have Sunday and Saturday afternoon out of crop, to themselves, that is, to cultivate their own grounds for their support; on others, Sunday only; and on others, Sunday only in part, for some people, says the Dean of Middleham, required grass for the cattle on Sundays to be gathered twice in the day; and Lieutenant Davison says he has known them forced to work on Sundays for their masters. It appears again, that in crop, on no estates, have they more than Sunday for the cultivation of their lands. The Dean of Middleham has known them continue boiling the sugar till late on Saturday night, and in one instance remembers it to have been protracted till sun-rise on Sunday morning: and the care afterwards of setting up the sugar-jars must have required several hours.

The point which may be considered next, is that of the slaves' food. This appears by the evidence to be subject to no rule. On some estates they are allowed land, which they cultivate for themselves at the times mentioned above, but they have no provisions allowed them, except perhaps a small present of salt fish or beef, or salt pork, at Christmas. On others they are allowed provisions, but no land: on others again, they are allowed land and provisions jointly. Without enumerating the different rations mentioned to be allowed them by the different witnesses, it may be sufficient to take the highest. The best allowance is evidently at Barbadoes, and the following is the account of it. The slaves in general, says General Tottenham, appeared to be ill-fed; each slave had a pint of grain for twenty-four hours, and sometimes half a rotten herring, when to be had. When the herrings were unfit for the whites, they were bought up by the planters for the slaves. Mr. Davis says that on those estates in Barbadoes, where he has seen the slaves' allowance dealt out, a grown negro had nine pints of corn, and about one pound of salt fish a week, but the grain of the West Indies is much lighter than wheat. He is of opinion that in general they were too sparingly fed. The Dean of Middleham also mentions nine pints per week as the quantity given, but that he has known masters abridge it in the time of crop. This is the greatest allowance mentioned throughout the whole of the evidence, and this is one of the cases in which the slaves had provisions but no land. Where, on the other hand, they have land and no provisions, all the witnesses agree that it is quite ample for their support, but that they have not sufficient time to cultivate it. Their lands, too, are often at the distance of three miles from their houses, and Mr. Giles thinks the slaves were often so fatigued by the labor of the week, as scarcely to be capable of working on them on Sunday for their own use. It is also mentioned as a great hardship, that often when they had cleared these lands, their master has taken them away for canes, giving them new wood-land in their stead, to be cleared afresh. This circumstance, together with the removal of their houses, many of them have so taken to heart as to have died.

Whether or not their food may be considered as sufficient in general for their support, may be better seen from the following than the preceding account. Mr. Cook says that they have not sufficient food. He has known them to eat the putrid carcasses of animals, and is convinced they did it through want. Mr. J. Terry has known them, on estates where they have been worse fed than on others, eat the putrid carcasses of animals also. Dead mules, horses, and cows, says Mr. Coor, were all burned under the inspection of a white man. Had they been buried, the negroes would have dug them up in the night to eat them through hunger. It was generally said to be done to prevent the negroes from eating them, lest it should breed distempers.

On the subject of their clothing, there is the same variation as to quantity as in their food. It depends on the disposition and circumstances of their masters. The largest allowance in the evidence is that which is mentioned by Dr. Harrison. The men, he says, at Christmas, are allowed two frocks, and two pair of Osnaburgh trowsers, and the women two coats and two shifts apiece. Some also have two handkerchiefs for the head. They have no other clothes than these, except they get them by their own extra labor. Woolrich and Coor agree, that as far as their experience went, the masters did not expend 'or the clothing of their slaves more than half a crown or three shillings a year; and Cook says that they are in general but very indifferently clothed, and th at one-half of them go almost naked in the field.

With respect to their houses and lodging, the accounts of the three following gentlemen will suffice :

Mr. Woolrich states their houses to be small, square huts, built with poles, and thatched at the top and sides with a kind of bamboo, and built by the slaves themselves. He describes them as lying in the middle of these huts before a small fire, but to have no bedding. Some, he says, obtain a board or mat to lie on before the fire. A few of the head-slaves have cabins of boards raised from the floor, but no bedding, except some, who have a coarse blanket. The Rev. Mr. Rees, in describing their houses nearly in the same manner, observes that their furniture consists of stools and benches, that they had no beds or bedding in the houses he was in, but that some of them slept on the ground, and others on a board raised from it. Some of the new slaves, says Dr. Harrison, have a few blankets, but it is not the general practice : for in general they have no bedding at all.

Of the property of the field-slaves, the next article to be considered, the following testimony will give a sufficient illustration :

Many field-slaves, says Mr. Woolrich, have it not in their power to earn any thing, exclusive of their master's work. Some few raise fowls, and some few pigs, and sell them, but their number is very few. Mr. Dalrymple does not say that slaves never become possessed of much property, but he never knew an instance of it, nor can he conceive how they can have time for it. The Dean of Middleham observes, that the quantity of ground allowed to field-slaves for raising provisions does not admit of their frequently possessing any considerable property. It is not likely they can spare much of their produce for sale. Sometimes they possess a pig, and two or three fowls, and if they have also a few plantain trees, these may be the means of supplying them with knives, iron pots, and such other conveniences as their masters do not allow them. The greatest property Mr. M. Terry ever knew a field-slave to possess was two pigs, and a little poultry. A field-slave has not the means of getting much property. Mr. J. Terry has known the field-slaves so poor as not to be able to have poultry. They were not allowed to keep sheep on any estate he knew. On some they might keep two or three goats, but very few allowed it. Some keep pigs and poultry, if able to buy any.

To this testimony it may be added, that all the witnesses, to whom the question has been proposed, agree in answering, that they never knew or heard of a field-slave ever amassing such a sum as enabled him to purchase his own freedom.

With respect to the artificers, such as house-carpenters, coopers, and masons, and the drivers and head-slaves, who form the remaining part of the plantation slaves, they are described as having in general a more certain allowance of provisions, and as being better off.

Having now described the state of the plantation, it will be proper to say a few words on that of the in-and-out-door slaves. The in-door slaves, or domestics, are allowed by all the witnesses to be better clothed and less worked than the others, and invariably to look better. Some, however, complain of their being much pinched for food.

With respect to the out-door slaves, several persons, who have a few slaves, and little work, allow them to work out, and oblige them to bring home three or four bits a day. The situation of these is considered to be very hard, for they are often unable to find work, and to earn the stated sum, and yet, if they fail, they are severely punished. Mr. Clappeson has known them steal grass, and sell it, to make up the sum required.

In this description may be ranked such as follow the occupation of porters. These are allowed to work out, and at the end of the week obliged to bring home to their masters a certain weekly sum. Their situation is much aggravated by having no fixed rates. If, says Foster, on being offered too little for their work they remonstrate, they are often beaten, and receive nothing, and should they refuse the next call from the same person, they are summoned before a magistrate, and punished on the parade for the refusal, and he has known them so punished.

Having now described the labor, food, clothing, houses, property, and different kinds of employment of the plantation, as well as the situation of the in-and-out-door slaves, as far as the evidence will warrant, it may be proper to advert to their punishments; and, first, to those that are inflicted by the cowskin or the whip.

In the towns many people have their slaves flogged upon their own premises, in which case it is performed by a man, who is paid for it, and who goes round the town in quest of the delinquents. But those, says Mr. H. Ross, who do not choose to disturb their neighbors with the slave cries, send them to the wharves or gaol, where they are corrected also by persons paid. At other times they are whipped publicly round the town, and at others tied down, or made to stand in some public place, and receive it there. When they are flogged on the wharves, to which they go for the convenience of the cranes and weights, they are described by H. Ross, Morley, Jeffreys, Towne, and Captain Scott, to have their arms tied to the hooks of the crane, and weights of fifty-six pounds applied to their feet. In this situation the crane is wound up, so that it lifts them nearly from the ground, and keeps them in a stretched posture, when the whip or cow-skin is used. After this they are again whipped, but with ebony bushes (which are more prickly than the thorn bushes in this country) in order to let out the congealed blood.

Respecting the whippings in gaol and round the town, Dr. Harrison thought them too severe to be inflicted on any of the human species. He attended a man, who had been flogged in gaol, who was ill in consequence five or six weeks. It was by his master's order for not coming when he was called. He could lay two or three fingers in the wounds made by the whip.

The punishments in the country by means of the whip and cow-skin appear to differ, except in one instance, from those which have been mentioned of the town.

It is usual for those, says Mr. Coor, who do not come into the field in time, to be punished. In this case a few steps before they join the gang they throw down the hoe, clap both hands on their heads, and patiently take ten, fifteen, or twenty lashes.

There is another mode described by Mr. Coor. About eight o'clock, says he, the overseer goes to breakfast, and if he has any criminals at home, he orders a black man to follow him; for it is then usual to take such out of the stocks and flog them before the overseer's house. The method is generally this : The delinquent is stripped and tied on a ladder, his legs on the sides and his arms above his head, and sometimes a rope is tied round his middle. The driver whips him on the bare skin, and if the overseer thinks he does not lay it on hard enough, he sometimes knocks him down with his own hand, or makes him change places with the delinquent, and be severely whipped. Mr. Coor has known many to receive on the ladder, from one hundred to one hundred and fifty lashes, and some two cool hundreds, as they are generally called. He has known many returned to confinement, and in one, two or three days, brought to the ladder, and receive the same complement, or thereabouts, as before. They seldom take them off the ladder, until all the skin, from the hams to the small of the back, appears only raw flesh and blood, and then they wash the parts with salt pickle. This appeared to him from the convulsions it occasioned, more cruel than the whipping, but it was done to prevent mortification. He has known many after such whipping sent to the field under guard and worked all day, with no food but what their friends might give them, out of their own poor pittance. He has known them returned to the stocks at night, and worked next day, successively. This cruel whipping, hard working, and starving has, to his knowledge, made many commit suicide. He remembers fourteen slaves, who, from bad treatment, rebelled on a Sunday, ran into the woods, and all cut their throats together.

The whip, says Woolrich, is generally made of plaited cow-skin, with a thick strong lash. It is so formidable an instrument in the hands of some of the overseers, that by means of it they can take the skin off a horse's back. He has heard them boast of laying the marks of it in a deal board, and he has seen it done. On its application on a slave's back, he has seen the blood spurt out immediately on the first stroke.

Nearly the same account of its construction is given by other witnesses, and its power and effects are thus described: At every stroke, says Captain Smith, a piece of flesh was drawn out. Dalrymple avers the same thing. It will even bring blood through the clothes, says J. Terry; and such is the effusion of blood on those occasions, adds Fitzmaurice, as to make their frocks, if immediately put on, appear as stiff as buckram; and Coor observes, that at his first going to Jamaica, a sight of a common flogging would put him in a tremble, so that he did not feel right for the rest of the day. It is observed also by Dr. Harrison and the Dean of Middleham, that the incisions are sometimes so deep that you may lay your fingers in the wounds. There are also wheals, says Mr. Coor, from their hams to the small of their backs. These wheals, cuts, or marks, are described by Captain Thompson, Dean of Middleham, Mr. Jeffreys, and General Tottenham, as indelible, as lasting to old age, or as such as no time can erase, and Woolrich has often seen their backs one undistinguished mass of lumps, holes, and furrows.

As farther proofs of the severity of these punishments by the whip or cowskin, the following facts may be adduced. Duncan and Falconbridge have known them so whipped that they could not lie down. He knew also a negro girl die of a mortification of her wounds, two days after the whipping had taken place. A case similar to the last is also mentioned by Mr. Rees. Finding, one day in his walks, a woman lying down and groaning, he understood from her that she had been so severely whipped for running away, that she could hardly move from the place where she was. Her left side, where she had been most whipped, appeared in a mortifying state, and almost covered with worms. He relieved her, as she was hungry, and in a day or two afterwards, going to visit her again, found she was dead and buried. To mention other instances: a planter flogged his driver to death, and even boasted of it to the person from whom Mr. Dalrymple had the account. Captain Hall (of the navy) also knows, by an instance that fell under his eye, that a slave's death may be occasioned by severe punishment. Dr. Jackson thinks, also, severe whippings are sometimes the occasion of their death. He recollects a negro dying under the lash, or soon afterwards; and Captain Ross avers that they often die in a few days after their severe punishments, for having but little food, and little care being taken to keep the sores clean after the whipping, their death is often the consequence.

Having now collected what is said on the punishments by the whip and cowskin, it will be proper to mention those other modes which the evidence presents us. These, however, are not easily subject to a division from the great variety of their kinds.

Captain Cook, speaking of the towns, says he has been shocked to see a girl of sixteen or seventeen, a domestic slave, running in the streets on her ordinary business, with an iron collar, having two hooks projecting several inches, both before and behind.

Captain Ross, speaking of the country, has known slaves severely punished, then put into the stocks, a cattle chain of sixty or seventy pounds weight put on them, and a large collar about their necks, and a weight of fifty-six pounds fastened to the chain when they were drove a-field.

Mr. Cook states that, when runaway slaves are brought in, they are generally severely flogged, and sometimes have an iron boot put on one or both legs, and a chain or collar round their necks. The chain is locked, the collar fastened on by a rivet. When the collar is with three projections, it is impossible for them to lie down to sleep; even with two, they must lie uneasily. He has seen collars with four projections. He never knew any injury from the chain and collar, but severely galling their necks. He has, however, known a negro lose his leg from wearing the iron boot.

Mr. Dalrymple, in June, 1789, saw a negress brought to St. George's, Grenada, to have her fingers cut off. She had committed a fault, and ran away to avoid punishment; but being taken, her master suspended her by the hands, flogged and cut her cruelly on the back, breast and thighs, and then left her suspended till her fingers mortified. In this state Mr. Dalrymple saw her at Dr. Gilpin's house.

Captain Ross has seen a negro woman in Jamaica flogged with ebony bushes, (much worse than our own thorn-bushes) so that the skin of her back was taken off, down to her heels. She was then turned round and flogged from her breast down to her waist, and in consequence he saw her afterwards walking upon all fours, and unable to get up.

Captain Cook being on a visit to General Frere, at an estate of his in Barbadoes, and riding one morning with the General and two other officers, they saw, near a house, upon a dunghill, a naked negro, nearly suspended, by strings from his elbows backwards, to the bough of a tree, with his feet barely upon the ground, and an iron weight round his neck, at least, to appearance, of fourteen pounds weight: and thus, without one creature near him, or apparently near the house, was this wretch left exposed to the noon-day sun. Returning a few hours after, they found him still in the same state, and would have released him, but for the advice of General Frere, who had an estate in the neighborhood. The gentlemen, through disgust, shortened their visit, and returned the next morning.

Lieutenant Davison and Mr. Woolrich mention the thumb-screw, and Mr. Woolrich, Captain Ross, Mr. Clappeson, and Dr. Harrison mention the picket as instruments of punishment. A negro man, in Jamaica, says Dr. Harrison, was put on the picket so long as to cause a mortification of his foot and hand, on suspicion of robbing his master, a public officer, of a sum of money, which, it afterwards appeared, the master had taken himself. Yet the master was privy to the punishment, and the slave had no compensation. He was punished by order of the master, who did not then choose to make it known that he himself had made use of the money.

Jeffreys, Captain Ross, M. Terry, and Coor, mention the cutting off of ears, as another species of punishment. The last gentleman gives the following instance in Jamaica: One of the house-girls having broken a plate, or spilt a cup of tea, the doctor (with whom Mr. Coor boarded) nailed her ear to a post. Mr. Coor remonstrated with him in vain. They went to bed, and left her there. In the morning she was gone, having torn the head of the nail through her ear. She was soon brought back, and when Mr. Coor came to breakfast, he found she had been severely whipped by the doctor, who, in his fury, clipped both her ears off close to her head, with a pair of large scissors, and she was sent to pick seeds out of cotton, among three or four more, emaciated by his cruelties, until they were fit for nothing else.

Mr. M. Cook, while in Jamaica, knew a runaway slave brought in, with part of a turkey with him, which he had stolen, and which, Mr. Cook thinks, he had stolen from hunger, as he was nothing but skin and bone. His master immediately made two negroes hold him down, and, with a hammer and a punch, knocked out two of his upper and two of his under teeth.

Mr. Dalrymple was informed by a young woman slave, in Grenada, who had no teeth, that her mistress had, with her own hands, pulled them out, and given her a severe flogging besides, the marks of which she then bore. This relation was confirmed by several town's people of whom he inquired concerning it.

Mr. Jeffreys has seen slaves with one of their hands off, which he understood to have been cut off for lifting it up against a white man. Captain Lloyd also saw at Mrs. Winne's, at Maumee Bay, in Jamaica, a female slave with but one hand only, the other having been cut off for the same offense. Mrs. Winne had endeavored to prevent the amputation, but in vain, for her indented white woman could not be dissuaded from swearing that the slave had struck her, and the hand was accordingly cut off.

Captain Giles, Dr. Jackson, Mr. Fitzmaurice, and Mr. M. Terry, have seen negroes whose legs had been cut off, by their master's orders, for running away, and Mr. Dalrymple gives the following account: A French planter, says he, in the English island of Grenada, sent for a surgeon to cut off the leg of a negro who had run away. On the surgeon's refusing to do it, the planter took an iron bar, and broke the leg in pieces, and then the surgeon cut it off. This planter did many such acts of cruelty, and all with impunity.

Mr. Fitzmaurice mentions, among other instances of cruelty, that of dropping hot lead upon negroes, which he often saw practiced by a planter of the name of Rushie, during his residence in Jamaica.

Mr. Hercules Ross, hearing one day, in Jamaica, from an inclosure, the cries of some poor wretch under torture, he looked through, and saw a young female suspended by the wrists to a tree, swinging to and fro. Her toes could hardly touch the ground, and her body was exceedingly agitated. The sight rather confounded him, as there was no whipping, and the master was just by, seemingly motionless; but, on looking more attentively, he saw in his hand a stick of fire, which he held, so as occasionally to touch her as she swung. He continued this torture with unmoved countenance, until Mr. H. Ross, calling on him to desist, and throwing stones at him over the fence, stopped it.

Mr. Fitzmaurice once found Rushie, the Jamaica planter before mentioned, in the act of hanging a negro. Mr. Fitzmaurice begged leave to intercede, as he was doing an action that in a few minutes he would repent of. Rushie, upon this, being a passionate man, ordered him off his estate. Mr. Fitzmaurice accordingly went, but returned early the next morning, before Rushie was up, and going into the curing-house, beheld the same negro lying dead upon a board. It was notorious that Rushie had killed many of his negroes, and destroyed them so fast that he was obliged to sell his estate. Captain Ross says, also, that there was a certain planter in the same island, who had hanged a negro on a post, close to his house, and in three years destroyed forty negroes out of sixty by severity. The rest of the conduct of this planter, as described by Captain Ross, was, after a debate, canceled by the committee of the House of Commons who took the evidence, as containing circumstances *too horrible to be given to the world.* On Shrewsbury estate, in Jamaica, says Mr. Coor, the overseer sent for a slave, and in talking with him, he hastily struck him on the head with a small hanger, and gave him two stabs about the waist. The slave said, "Overseer, you have killed me." He pushed him out of the piazza. The slave went home and died that night. He was buried and no more said about it. A manager of an estate, says Mr. Woolrich, in Tortola, whose owner did not reside on the island, sitting at dinner, in a sudden resentment at his cook, went directly to his sword, and ran the negro woman through the body, and she died upon the floor immediately, and the negroes were called in to take her away and bury her.

Mr. Giles recollects several shocking instances of punishment. In particular on the estate where he lived, in Montserrat, the driver at day-break once informed the overseer that one of four or five negroes, chained in the dungeon, would not rise. He accompanied the overseer to the dungeon, who set the others that were in the chain to drag him out, and not rising when out, he ordered a bundle of cane-trash to be put round him and set fire to. As he still did not rise, he had a small soldering iron heated and thrust between his teeth. As the man did not yet rise, he had the chain taken off and sent him to the hospital, where he languished some days and died.

An overseer on the estate where Mr. J. Terry was, in Grenada, (Mr. Coghlan,) threw a slave into the boiling cane-juice, who died in four days. Mr. J. Terry was told of this by the owner's son, by the carpenter, and by many slaves on the estate. He has heard it often.

Mr. Woolrich says a negro ran away from a planter in Tortola, with whom he was well acquainted. The overseer having ordered to take him, dead or alive, a while after found him in one of his huts, fast asleep, in the day time, and shot him through the body. The negro jumping up, said, "What, you kill me asleep?" and dropped dead immediately. The overseer took off his head and carried it to the owner. Mr. Woolrich knew another instance in the same island. A planter, offended with his waiting man, a mulatto, stepped suddenly to his gun, on which the man ran off, but his master shot him through the head with a single ball.

From the above accounts, there are no less than sixteen sorts of extraordinary punishments, which the imagination has invented in the moments of passion and caprice. It is much to be lamented that there are others in the evidence not yet mentioned. But as it is necessary to insert a new head, under which will be explained the concern which the very women take, both in the ordinary and extraordinary punishments of the slaves, and as some of the latter, not yet mentioned, are inseparably connected with it, it was thought proper to cite them under this new division rather than continue them under the old. It will appear extraordinary to the reader, that many women, living in the colonies, should not only order, and often superintend, but sometimes actually inflict, with their own hands, some severe punishments upon their slaves, and that these should not always be women of a low order, but often of respectability and rank.

Lieutenant Davison, Captain Smith and Dr. Jackson, all agree that it was common for ladies of respectability and rank to superintend the punishments of their slaves. Conformably with this, we find Dr. Harrison stating to the committee, that a negro, in Jamaica, was flogged to death by her mistress's order, who stood by to see the punishment. Lieutenant Davison also states, that in the same island he has seen several negro girls at work with the needle, in the presence of their mistresses, with a thumb-screw on their left thumbs, and he has seen the blood gush out from the ends of them. He has also seen a negro girl made to kneel with her bare knees on pebbles, and to work there at the same time ; a sort of punishment, he says, among the domestics, which he knows to be in common use.

On the subject of women becoming the executioners of their own fury, Dr. Jackson observes, that the first thing that shocked him in Jamaica was a creole lady of some consequence, superintending the punishment of her slaves, male and female, ordering the number of lashes, and, with her own hands, flogging the negro driver if he did not punish properly.

Capt. Cook relates that two young ladies of fortune, in Barbadoes, sisters, one of whom was displeased at a female slave belonging to the other, proceeded to some very derogatory acts of cruelty. With their own garters they tied the young woman neck and heels, and then beat her almost to death with the heels of their shoes. One of her eyes continued a long while afterwards in danger of being lost. They, after this, continued to use her ill, confining and degrading her. Capt. Cook came in during the beating, and was an eye witness to it himself.

Lieutenant Davison states, in his evidence, that the clergyman's wife at Port Royal, was remarkably cruel. She used to drop hot sealing wax on her negroes, after flogging them. He was sent for as surgeon to one of them, whose breast was terribly burnt with sealing wax. He lived next door, he states, also, to a washer-woman at Port Royal, who was almost continually flogging her negroes. He has often gone in and remonstrated against her cruelty, when he has seen the negro women chained to the washing-tubs, almost naked, with their thighs and backs in a gore of blood, from flogging. He could mention various other capricious punishments, if necessary.

Mr. Forster, examined on the same subject, says he has known a creole woman, in Antigua, drop hot sealing wax on a girl's back, after a flogging. He and many others saw a young woman of fortune and character flogging a negro man very severely with her own hands. Many similar instances he could relate if necessary. They are almost innumerable among the domestic slaves.

If it should be asked for what offenses the different punishments now cited have taken place, the following answer may be given: The slaves appear to have been punished, as far as can be ascertained from the evidence under the head of ordinary punishments, for not coming into the field in time, not picking a sufficient quantity of grass, not appearing willing to work, when in fact sick and not able, for staying too long on an errand, for not coming immediately when called, for not bringing home (the women) the full weekly sum enjoined by their owners, for running away, and for theft, to which they were often driven by hunger. Under the head of "extraordinary punishments," some appear to have suffered for running away, or for lifting up a hand against a white man, or for breaking a plate, or spilling a cup of tea, or to extort confession. Others, again, in the moments of sudden resentment, and one on a diabolical pretext, which the master held out to the world to conceal his own villainy, and which he knew to be false.

On the subject of capital offenses and punishments, a man and a woman slave are mentioned to have been hanged, the man for running away, and the woman for having secreted him. The Dean of Middleham saw two instances of slaves being gibbetted alive in chains, but he does not say for what, only that this is the punishment for enormous crimes: and Mr. Jeffreys, the only other person who speaks on this subject, says that he was in one of the islands, when some of the slaves murdered a white man, and destroyed some property on the estate. The execution of these he describes as follows:

He was present, he says, at the execution of seven negroes in Tobago, in the year 1774, whose right arms were chopped off: they were then dragged to seven stakes, and a fire, consisting of trash and dry wood, was lighted about them. They were there burnt to death. He does not remember hearing one of them murmur, complain, cry, or do any thing that indicated fear. One of them, in particular, named Chubb, was taken in the woods that morning, was tried about noon, and was thus executed with the rest in the evening. Mr. Jeffreys stood close by Chubb when his arm was cut off. He stretched his arm out, and laid it upon the block, pulled up the sleeve of his shirt with more coolness than he (Mr. Jeffreys) should have done, were he to have been bled. He afterwards would not suffer himself to be dragged to the stake, as the others had been, but got upon his feet and walked to it. As he was going to the stake, he turned about, and addressed himself to Mr. Jeffreys, who was standing within two or three yards of him, and said, "Buckra, you see me now, but to-morrow I shall be like that," kicking up the dust with his foot. (Here Mr.

Jeffreys solemnly added, in his evidence, the words "So help me God.") The impression this made upon his mind, Mr. Jeffreys declared, no time could ever erase. Sampson, who made the eighth, and a negro, whose name Mr. Jeffreys does not recollect, were present at this execution. Sampson, next morning, was hung in chains alive, and there he hung till he was dead, which, to the best of his recollection, was seven days. The other negro was sentenced to be sent to the mines in South America, and, he believes, was sent accordingly. Neither of those two, during the time of the execution, showed any marks of concern, or dismay, that he could observe. A stronger instance of human fortitude, he declared, he never saw.

Having now stated the substance of the evidence on the subject of offenses and punishments, we come to a custom which appears to have been too general to be passed over in silence.

Dalrymple, Forester, Captain Smith, Captain Wilson, and General Tottenham, assert that it is no uncommon thing for persons to neglect and turn off their slaves when past labor. They are turned off, say Captain Wilson, Lieutenant Davison, and General Tottenham, to plunder, beg, or starve. Captain Cook has known some to take care of them; but says others leave them to starve and die. They are often desired, when old, says Mr. Fitzmaurice, to provide for themselves, and they suffer much. Mr. Clappeson knew a man who had an old, decrepit woman slave, to whom he would allow nothing. When past labor, the owner did not feed them, says Giles; and Cook states that, within his experience, they had no food except what they could get from such relations as they might have had. General Tottenham has often met them, and, once in particular, an old woman, past labor, who told him that her master had set her adrift to shift for herself. He saw her about three days afterwards, lying dead in the same place. The custom of turning them off when old and helpless is called in the islands "Giving them free."

As a proof of how little the life of an old slave was regarded in the West Indies, we may make the following extract from the evidence of Mr. Coor. Once, when he was dining with an overseer, an old woman who had run away a few days, was brought home, with her hands tied behind. After dinner, the overseer, with the clerk, named Bakewell, took the woman, thus tied, to the hot-house, a place for the sick, and where the stocks are in one of the rooms. Mr. Coor went to work in the mill, about one hundred yards off, and hearing a most distressful cry from that house, he asked his men what it was. They said they thought it was old Quasheba. About five o'clock the noise ceased, and about the time he was leaving work, Bakewell came to him, apparently in great spirits, and said, "Well, Mr. Coor, Old Quasheba is dead. We took her to the stocks-room; the overseer threw a rope over the beam; I was Jack Ketch, and hauled her up till her feet were off the ground. The overseer locked the door, and took the key with him, till my return just now, with a slave for the stocks, when I found her dead." Mr. Coor said, "You have killed her; I heard her cry all the afternoon." He answered, "She was good for nothing; what signifies killing such an old woman as her?" Mr. Coor said, "Bakewell, you shock me," and left him. The next morning his men told him they had helped to bury her.

But it appears that the aged are not the only persons whose fate is to be commiserated, when they became of no value ; for people in youth, if disabled, were abandoned to equal misery. General Tottenham, about three weeks before the hurricane, saw a youth, about nineteen, walking in the streets, in a most deplorable situation, entirely naked, and with an iron collar about his neck, with five long projecting spikes. His body, before and behind, was almost cut to pieces, and with running sores all over it, and you might put your finger in some of the wheals. He could not sit down, owing to his being in a state of mortification, and it was impossible for him to lie down, from the projection of the prongs. The boy came to the general and asked relief. He was shocked at his appearance, and asked him what he had done to suffer such a punishment, and who inflicted it. He said it was his master, who lived about two miles from town, and that as he could not work, he would give him nothing to eat.

If it be possible to view human depravity in a worse light than it has already appeared in on the subject of the treatment of the slaves when disabled from labor, it may be done by referring to the evidence of Captain Lloyd, who was told by a person of veracity, when in the West Indies, but whom he did not wish to name in his evidence, that it was the practice of a certain planter to frame pretenses for the execution of his old worn out slaves, in order to get the island allowance. And it was supposed that he dealt largely in that way.

Having now cited both the ordinary and extraordinary punishments inflicted upon the slaves, it may be presumed that some one will ask here, whether, under these various acts of cruelty, they were wholly without redress ? To this the following answer may be given : That, with respect to the ordinary punishments by the whip and cowskin, (where they did not terminate in death,) the power of the master or overseer was under little or no control.

As to such of the extraordinary punishments before mentioned as did not terminate in death, such as picketing, dropping hot sealing-wax on the flesh, cutting off ears, and the like, it appears that slaves had no redress whatever, for that these actions also on the part of the masters were not deemed within the reach of the law. In the instance cited of the doctor clipping off the ears of a female slave, no more notice was taken of it, says Coor, than if a dog's ears had been cut off, though it must have been known to the magistrates. In the dreadful instance also cited of a planter's breaking his slave's leg by an iron bar, to induce the surgeon to cut it off, as a punishment, Mr. Dalrymple observes that it was not the public opinion that any punishment was due to him on that account, for though it was generally known, he was equally well received in society afterwards as before ; and in the case also mentioned of the owner torturing his female slave by the application of a lighted torch to her body, Mr. H. Ross states, only that this owner was not a man of character ; with respect to his suffering by the law, he observes that he was never brought to any trial for it ; and he did not know that the law then extended to the punishment of whites for such acts as these.

With respect to such of the punishments as have terminated in death, the reader will be able to collect what power the masters and overseers, and what protection the slaves have had by law, from the following accounts:

There are no less than seven specific instances mentioned in the evidence, in which slaves died in consequence of the whipping they received, and yet in no one of them was the murderer brought to account. One of the perpetrators is mentioned by Mr. Dalrymple as having boasted of what he had done; and Dr. Jackson speaks of the other in these words: "No attempts, says he, were made to bring him to justice: people said it was an unfortunate thing, and were surprised that he was not more cautious, as it was not the first thing of the kind that had happened to him, but they dwelt chiefly on the proprietor's loss."

In such of the extraordinary punishments as terminated in death, there are no less than seven specific instances also in the evidence. In one of them, viz: that of throwing the slave into the boiling cane-juice, we find from Mr. J. Terry that the overseer was punished, but his punishment consisted only of replacing the slave and leaving his owner's service. In that of killing the slave by lighting a fire round him and putting a hot soldering iron into his mouth, the overseer's conduct, says Mr. Giles, was not even condemned by his master, nor in any of the rest were any means whatsoever used to punish the offenders. In the three mentioned by Mr. Woolrich, he particularly says, all the white people in the island were acquainted with these acts. Neither of the offenders, however, were called to an account, nor were they shunned in society for it, or considered as in disgrace.

Such appears to have been, in the experience of the different witnesses cited, the forlorn and wretched situation of the slaves. They often complain, says Dr. Jackson, that they are an oppressed people; that they suffer in this world, but expect happiness in the next; whilst they denounce the vengeance of God on their oppressors, the white men. If you speak to them of future punishments, they say, "Why should a poor negro be punished? he does no wrong; fiery caldrons, and such things, are reserved for white people, as punishments for the oppression of slaves."

Bryan Edwards, the historian of the West Indies, gives the price of new negroes in 1791. An able man, in his prime, £50 sterling; an able woman, £49 sterling; a youth approaching to manhood, £47 sterling; a young girl, £46 sterling; boys and girls, from £40 to £45 sterling; an infant, £5. The annual profit arising to the owner, from each able field negro, employed in cultivating sugar, he estimates at £25 sterling. An opinion prevailed among the planters that it was cheaper to buy than to breed. If a negro lasted a certain time his death was accounted nothing. This time was fixed at seven years by some planters; by others at less. A planter of Jamaica, by name of Yeman, according to Captain Scott's testimony, reduced his calculation to four years, treating his slaves most cruelly, and saying that four years' labor was enough for him, for he then had got his money out of him, and he did not care what became of him afterwards.

CHAPTER XII.

EARLY OPPONENTS OF AFRICAN SLAVERY IN ENGLAND AND AMERICA.

Period from 1660 to 1760: Godwin, Richard Baxter, Atkins, Hughes, Bishop Warburton.—Planters accustomed to take their Slaves to England, and to carry them back into slavery by force.—Important case of James Somerset decided, 1772.—John Wesley.—Motion in House of Commons against Slave-Trade, 1776.—Case of ship Zong.—Bridgwater Petitions.—The Quakers in England oppose Slavery.—Resolutions of the Quakers, from 1727 to 1760.—They Petition House of Commons.—First Society formed, 1783.—The Quakers and others in America.—Action of the Quakers of Pennsylvania from 1688 to 1788.—Benezet writes tracts against Slavery.—His letter to the Queen.—Sentiment in America, favorable to Africans, 1772.—House of Burgesses of Va., addresses the King.—Original draft of Declaration of Independence.—First Society formed in America "for Promoting Abolition of Slavery," 1774.—Opposition to the Slave-Trade in America.

THE first importation of slaves from Africa by the English was in 1562, in the reign of Elizabeth. This great princess seems on the very commencement of the trade to have questioned its lawfulness; to have entertained a religious scruple concerning it, and, indeed, to have revolted at the very thought of it. She seems to have been aware of the evils to which its continuance might lead, or that, if it were sanctioned, the most unjustifiable means might be made use of to procure the persons of the natives of Africa. And in what light she would have viewed any acts of this kind, had they taken place, we may conjecture from this fact; that when Captain (afterwards Sir John) Hawkins returned from his first voyage to Africa and Hispaniola, whither he had carried slaves, she sent for him, and, as we learn from Hill's Naval History, expressed her concern lest any of the Africans should be carried off without their free consent, declaring that "It would be detestable, and call down the vengeance of Heaven upon the undertakers." Captain Hawkins promised to comply with the injunctions of Elizabeth in this respect. But he did not keep his word; for when he went to Africa again, he seized many of the inhabitants, and carried them off as slaves, which occasioned Hill, in the account he gives of his voyage, to use these remarkable words : " Here began the horrid practice of forcing the Africans into slavery, an injustice and barbarity which, so sure as there is vengeance in heaven for the worst of crimes, will some time be the destruction of all who allow or encourage it."

Though the slave-trade commenced so early, there were no united and effective efforts made for its abolition till the year 1787; at which period a number of persons associated themselves in England for this benevolent object. However, for a long time previous to the forming of this important association, individuals were continually rising, who, by their writings and labors rendered valuable service to the cause of humanity, and who are properly considered as forerunners inasmuch as they prepared the way for that extensive and united effort which finally succeeded in rendering illegal the abominable traffic. In giving a history of the Abolition of the slave-trade, it will be proper to notice a few of the more prominent and active of these harbingers in the great cause of humanity.

Morgan Godwyn, a clergyman of the established church, wrote a Treatise upon the subject, which he dedicated to the then archbishop of Canterbury. He gave it to the world, at the time mentioned, under the title of "The Negro's and Indian's Advocate." In this treatise he lays open the situation of these oppressed people, of whose sufferings he had been an eyewitness in the island of Barbadoes. He calls forth the pity of the reader in an affecting manner, and exposes with a nervous eloquence the brutal sentiments and conduct of their oppressors. This seems to have been the first work undertaken in England expressly in favor of the cause.

Richard Baxter, the celebrated divine among the Nonconformists, in his Christian Directory, published about the same time as the Negro's and Indian's Advocate, gives advice to those masters in foreign plantations, who have negroes and other slaves. In this he protests loudly against this trade. He says expressly that they, who go out as pirates, and take away poor Africans, or people of another land who never forfeited life or liberty, and make them slaves and sell them, are the worst of robbers, and ought to be considered as the common enemies of mankind ; and that they, who buy them, and use them as mere beasts for their own convenience, regardless of their spiritual welfare, are fitter to be called demons than christians. He then proposes several queries, which he answers in a clear and forcible manner, showing the great inconsistency of this traffic, and the necessity of treating those then in bondage with tenderness and due regard to their spiritual concerns.

The person who seems to have noticed the subject next was Dr. Primatt. In his "Dissertation on the Duty of Mercy, and on the Sin of Cruelty to Brute-animals," he takes occasion to advert to the subject of the African slave trade. "It has pleased God," says he, "to cover some men with white skins, and others with black; but as there is neither merit nor demerit in complexion, the white man, notwithstanding the barbarity of custom and prejudice, can have no right by virtue of his color to enslave and tyrannize over the black man. For whether a man be white or black, such he is by God's appointment, and, abstractedly considered, is neither a subject for pride, nor an object of contempt."

In the year 1735, Atkins who was a surgeon in the navy, published his voyage to Guinea, Brazil, and the West Indies. In this work he describes openly the manner of making the natives slaves, such as by kidnapping, by unjust accusations and trials, and by other nefarious means. He states also the cruelties practiced upon them by the white people, and the iniquitous ways and dealings of the latter, and answers their argument, by which they insinuated that the condition of Africans was improved by their transportation to other countries.

In the year 1750 the reverend Griffith Hughes, rector of St. Lucy, in Barbadoes, published his Natural History of that island. He took an opportunity, in the course of it, of laying open to the world the miserable situation of the Africans, and the waste of them by hard labor and other cruel means.

Edmund Burke, in his account of the European settlements, complains "that the negroes in our colonies endure a slavery more complete, and attended with far worse circumstances, than what any people in their condition suffer in any other part of the world, or have suffered in any other period of time."

Bishop Warburton preached a sermon in the year 1766, before the Society for the Propagation of the Gospel, in which he took up the cause of the Africans, and in which he severely reprobated their oppressors. The language in this sermon is so striking, that we make an extract from it. " From the free savages," says he, " I now come to the savages in bonds. By these I mean the vast multitudes yearly stolen from the opposite continent, and sacrificed by the colonists to their great idol the god of gain. But what then, say these sincere worshippers of mammon ? They are our own property which we offer up. Gracious God ! to talk, as of herds of cattle, of property in rational creatures, creatures endued with all our faculties, possessing all our qualities but that of color, our brethren both by nature and grace, shocks all the feelings of humanity, and the dictates of common sense ! But, alas ! what is there, in the infinite abuses of society, which does not shock them ? Yet nothing is more certain in itself and apparent to all, than that the infamous traffic for slaves directly infringes both divine and human law. Nature created man free, and grace invites him to assert his freedom.

" In excuse of this violation it hath been pretended, that though indeed these miserable outcasts of humanity be torn from their homes and native country by fraud and violence, yet they thereby become the happier, and their condition the more eligible. But who are you, who pretend to judge of another man's happiness ; that state, which each man under the guidance of his Maker forms for himself, and not one man for another ? To know what constitutes mine or your happiness is the sole prerogative of Him who created us, and cast us in so various and different moulds. Did your slaves ever complain to you of their unhappiness amidst their native woods and deserts ? or rather let me ask, Did they ever cease complaining of their condition under you, their lordly masters, where they see indeed the accommodations of civil life, but see them all pass to others, themselves unbenefited by them ? Be so gracious then, ye petty tyrants over human freedom, to let your slaves judge for themselves, what it is which makes their own happiness, and then see whether they do not place it in the return to their own country, rather than in the contemplation of your grandeur, of which their misery makes so large a part ; a return so passionately longed for, that, despairing of happiness here, that is, of escaping the chains of their cruel task-masters, they console themselves with feigning it to be the gracious reward of heaven in their future state."

Before the year 1700, planters, merchants, and others, resident in the West Indies, but coming to England, were accustomed to bring with them certain slaves to act as servants with them during their stay. The latter, seeing the freedom and the happiness of servants in that country, and considering what would be their own hard fate on their return to the islands, frequently absconded. Their masters of course made search after them, and often had them seized and carried away by force. It was, however, declared by many on these occasions, that the English laws did not sanction such proceedings, for that all persons who were baptized became free. The consequence of this was, that most of the slaves who came over with their masters prevailed upon some pious clergyman to baptize them. They took of course godfathers of such citizens as had the generosity to espouse their cause. When they were seized they usually sent to these, if they had an opportunity, for their protection. And in the result, their godfathers, maintaining that they had been baptized, and that they were free on this account as well as by the general tenor of the laws of England, dared those, who had taken possession of them, to send them out of the kingdom.

The planters, merchants, and others, being thus circumstanced, knew not what to do. They were afraid of taking their slaves away by force, and they were equally afraid of bringing any of the cases before a public court. In this dilemma, in 1729 they applied to York and Talbot, the attorney and solicitor-general for the time being, and obtained the following strange opinion from them: "We are of opinion, that a slave by coming from the West Indies into Great Britain or Ireland, either with or without his master, does not become free, and that his master's right and property in him is not thereby determined or varied, and that baptism doth not bestow freedom on him, nor make any alteration in his temporal condition in these kingdoms. We are also of opinion, that the master may legally compel him to return to the plantations."

This opinion was delivered in the year 1729. The planters, merchants, and others, gave it of course all the publicity in their power. And the consequences were as might easily have been apprehended. In a little time slaves absconding were advertised in the London papers as runaways, and rewards offered for the apprehension of them. They were advertised also, in the same papers, to be sold by auction, sometimes by themselves, and again with horses, chaises, and harness. They were seized also by their masters, or by persons employed by them, in the very streets, and dragged from thence to the ships; and so unprotected now were these poor slaves, that persons in nowise concerned with them began to institute a trade in their persons, making agreements with captains of ships going to the West Indies to put them on board at a certain price.

These circumstances did not fail of producing new coadjutors in the cause. And first they produced that able and indefatigable advocate, Mr. Granville Sharp. This gentleman is to be distinguished from those who preceded him in this particular, that, whereas these were only writers, he was both a writer and an actor in the cause. In fact, he was the first laborer in it in England. The following is a short history of the beginning and of the course of his labors:

In the year 1765, Mr. David Lisle had brought over from Barbadoes, Jonathan Strong, an African slave, as his servant. He used the latter in a bar-

11

barous manner at his lodgings in Wapping, but particularly by beating him over the head with a pistol, which occasioned his head to swell. When the swelling went down, a disorder fell into his eyes, which threatened the loss of them. To this an ague and fever succeeded, and a lameness in both of his legs.

Jonathan Strong, having been brought into this deplorable situation, and being therefore wholly useless, was left by his master to go whither he pleased. He applied accordingly to Mr. William Sharp, the surgeon, for his advice, as to one who gave up a portion of his time to the healing of the diseases of the poor. It was here that Mr. Granville Sharp, the brother of the former, saw him. Suffice it to say, that in process of time he was cured. During this time Mr. Granville Sharp, pitying his hard case, supplied him with money, and he afterwards got him a situation in the family of Mr. Brown, an apothecary, to carry out medicines.

In this new situation, when Strong had become healthy and robust in his appearance, his master happened to see him. The latter immediately formed the design of possessing him again. Accordingly, when he had found out his residence, he procured John Ross, keeper of the Poultry-compter, and William Miller, an officer under the lord mayor, to kidnap him. This was done by sending for him to a public house in Fenchurch street, and then seizing him. By these he was conveyed, without any warrant, to the Poultry-compter, where he was sold by his master, to John Kerr, for thirty pounds.

Strong, in this situation, sent, as was usual, to his godfathers, John London and Stephen Nail, for their protection. They went, but were refused admittance to him. At length he sent for Mr. Granville Sharp. The latter went, but they still refused access to the prisoner. He insisted, however, upon seeing him, and charged the keeper of the prison at his peril to deliver him up till he had been carried before a magistrate.

Mr. Sharp immediately upon this waited upon Sir Robert Kite, the then lord mayor, and entreated him to send for Strong, and to hear his case. A day was accordingly appointed. Mr. Sharp attended, and also William M'Bean, a notary public, and David Laird, captain of the ship Thames, which was to have conveyed Strong to Jamaica, in behalf of the purchaser, John Kerr. A long conversation ensued, in which the opinion of York and Talbot was quoted. Mr. Sharp made his observation. Certain lawyers, who were present, seemed to be staggered at the case, but inclined rather to recommit the prisoner. The lord mayor, however, discharged Strong, as he had been taken up without a warrant.

As soon as this determination was made known, the parties began to move off. Captain Laird, however, who kept close to Strong, laid hold of him before he had quitted the room, and said aloud, "Then I now seize him as my slave." Upon this, Mr. Sharp put his hand upon Laird's shoulder, and pronounced these words: "I charge you in the name of the king with an assault upon the person of Jonathan Strong, and all these are my witnesses." Laird was greatly intimidated by this charge, made in the presence of the lord mayor and others, and fearing a prosecution, let his prisoner go, leaving him to be conveyed away by Mr. Sharp.

Mr. Sharp, having been greatly affected by this case, and foreseeing how much he might be engaged in others of a similar nature, thought it time that the law of the land should be known upon this subject. He applied therefore to Doctor Blackstone, afterwards Judge Blackstone, for his opinion upon it. He was, however, not satisfied with it, when he received it; nor could he obtain any satisfactory answer from several other lawyers, to whom he afterwards applied. The truth is, that the opinion of York and Talbot, which had been made public and acted upon by the planters, merchants, and others, was considered of high authority, and scarcely any one dared to question the legality of it. In this situation, Mr. Sharp saw no means of help but in his own industry, and he determined immediately to give up two or three years to the study of the English law, that he might the better advocate the cause of these miserable people. The result of these studies was the publication of a book, in the year 1769, which he called "A Representation of the Injustice and dangerous Tendency of Tolerating Slavery in England." In this work he refuted, in the clearest manner, the opinion of York and Talbot. He produced against it the opinion of the Lord Chief Justice Holt, who many years before had determined that every slave coming into England became free. He attacked and refuted it again by a learned and laborious inquiry into all the principles of villenage. He refuted it again, by showing it to be an axiom in the British constitution, "That every man in England was free to sue for and defend his rights, and that force could not be used without a legal process," leaving it to the judges to determine whether an African was a man. He attacked, also, the opinion of Judge Blackstone, and showed where his error lay. This book, containing these and other arguments on the subject, he distributed, but particularly among the lawyers, giving them an opportunity of refuting or acknowledging the doctrines it contained.

While Mr. Sharp was engaged in this work, another case offered, in which he took a part. This was in the year 1768. Hylas, an African slave, prosecuted a person of the name of Newton for having kidnapped his wife, and sent her to the West Indies. The result of this trial was, that damages to the amount of a shilling were given, and the defendant was bound to bring back the woman, either by the first ship, or in six months from this decision of the court.

But soon after the work just mentioned was out, and when Mr. Sharp was better prepared, a third case occurred. This happened in the year 1770. Robert Stapylton, who lived at Chelsea, in conjunction with John Malony and Edward Armstrong, two watermen, seized the person of Thomas Lewis, an African slave, in a dark night, and dragged him to a boat lying in the Thames; they then gagged him, and tied him with a cord, and rowed him down to a ship, and put him on board to be sold as a slave in Jamaica. This action took place near the garden of Mrs. Banks, the mother of Sir Joseph Banks. Lewis, it appears, on being seized, screamed violently. The servants of Mrs. Banks, who heard his cries, ran to his assistance, but the boat was gone. On informing their mistress of what had happened, she sent for Mr Sharp, who began now to be known as the friend of the helpless Africans, and professed her willingness to incur the expense of bringing the delinquents to justice. Mr. Sharp, with some difficulty, procured a habeas corpus, in consequence of which Lewis was brought from Gravesend just as the vessel was on the point of sailing. An action was then commenced against Stapylton, who defended himself on the plea, "That Lewis belonged to him as his slave." In the course of the trial, Mr. Dunning, who was counsel for Lewis, paid Mr. Sharp a handsome compliment, for he held in his hand Mr. Sharp's book on the injustice and dangerous tendency of tolerating slavery in England, while he was pleading; and in his address to the jury he spoke and acted thus : "I shall submit to you," says Mr. Dunning, "what my ideas are upon such evidence, reserving to myself an opportunity of discussing it more particularly, and reserving to myself a right to insist upon a position, which I will maintain (and here he held up the book to the notice of those present) in any place and in any court of the kingdom, that our laws admit of no such property." The result of the trial was, that the jury pronounced the plaintiff not to have been the property of the defendant, several of them crying out "No property, no property."

After this, one or two other trials came on, in which the oppressor was defeated; and several cases occurred, in which slaves were liberated from the holds of vessels, and other places of confinement, by the exertions of Mr. Sharp. One of these cases was singular. The vessel on board which a poor African had been dragged and confined had reached the Downs, and had actually got under way for the West Indies. In two or three hours she would have been out of sight; but just at this critical moment the writ of habeas corpus was carried on board. The officer who served it on the captain saw the miserable African chained to the mainmast, bathed in tears, and casting a last mournful look on the land of freedom, which was fast receding from his sight. The captain, on receiving the writ, became outrageous; but, knowing the serious consequences of resisting the law of the land, he gave up his prisoner, whom the officer carried safe, but now crying for joy, to the shore.

Though the injured Africans, whose causes had been tried, escaped slavery, and though many, who had been forcibly carried into dungeons, ready to be transported back into the colonies, had been delivered out of them, Mr. Sharp was not easy in his mind. Not one of the cases had yet been pleaded on the broad ground, "Whether an African slave coming into England became free?" This great question had been hitherto studiously avoided. It was still, therefore, left in doubt. Mr. Sharp was almost daily acting as if it had been determined, and as if he had been following the known law of the land. He wished, therefore, that the next cause might be argued upon this principle. Lord Mansfield, too, who had been biased by the opinion of York and Talbot, began to waver in consequence of the different pleadings he had heard on this subject. He saw also no end of trials like these, till the law should be ascertained, and he was anxious for a decision on the same basis as Mr. Sharp. In this situation the following case offered, which was agreed upon for the determination of this important question.

James Somerset, an African slave, had been brought to England by his master, Charles Stewart, in November, 1769. Somerset, in process of time, left him. Stewart took an opportunity of seizing him, and had him conveyed on board the Ann and Mary, Captain Knowles, to be carried out of the kingdom, and sold as a slave in Jamaica. The question was, "Whether a slave, by coming into England, became free? "

In order that time might be given for ascertaining the law fully on this head, the case was argued at three different sittings. First, in January, 1772; secondly, in February, 1772; and thirdly, in May, 1772. And that no decision otherwise than what the law warranted might be given, the opinion of the Judges was taken upon the pleadings. The result of the trial was, *That as soon as ever any slave set his foot upon English territory, he became free.*

Thus ended the great case of Somerset, which, having been determined after so deliberate an investigation of the law, can never be reversed while the British Constitution remains. The eloquence displayed in it by those who were engaged on the side of liberty, was perhaps never exceeded on any occasion.

Mr. Sharp felt it his duty, immediately after the trial, to write to Lord North, then principal minister of state, warning him, in the most earnest manner, to abolish immediately both the trade and the slavery of the human species in all the British dominions, as utterly irreconcileable with the principles of the British constitution, and the established religion of the land.

In the year 1774, John Wesley, the celebrated divine, to whose pious labors the religious world will be long indebted, undertook the cause of the Africans. He had been in America, and had seen and pitied their hard condition. The work which he gave to the world in consequence, was entitled "Thoughts on Slavery." Mr. Wesley had this great cause much at heart, and frequently recommended it to the support of those who attended his useful ministry.

The year 1776 produced two new friends in England, in the same cause, but in a line in which no one had yet moved. David Hartley, then a member of parliament for Hull, found it impossible any longer to pass over without notice the cause of the oppressed Africans. He had long felt for their wretched condition, and, availing himself of his legislative situation, he made a motion in the house of commons, "That the slave trade was contrary to the laws of God and the rights of men."

Dr. Adam Smith, in his "Theory of Moral Sentiments," had, so early as the year 1759, held the slaves up in an honorable, and their tyrants in a degrading light. "There is not a negro from the coast of Africa, who does not, in this respect, possess a degree of magnanimity which the soul of his sordid master is too often scarce capable of conceiving. Fortune never exerted more cruelly her empire over mankind, than when she subjected those nations of heroes to the refuse of the gaols of Europe, to wretches who possess the virtue neither of the countries they came from, nor of those they go to, and whose levity, brutality, and baseness so justly expose them to the contempt of the vanquished." In 1776, in his "Wealth of Nations," he showed in a forcible manner (for he appealed to the interest of those concerned) the dearness of African labor, or the impolicy of employing slaves.

In the year 1783, we find Mr. Sharp coming again into notice. We find him at this time taking a part in a cause, the knowledge of which, in proportion as it was disseminated, produced an earnest desire among all disinterested persons for the abolition of the slave-trade.

In this year, certain underwriters desired to be heard against Gregson and others of Liverpool, in the case of the ship Zong, captain Collingwood, alleging that the captain and officers of the said vessel threw overboard one hundred and thirty-two slaves alive into the sea, in order to defraud them, by claiming the value of said slaves, as if they had been lost in a natural way. In the course of the trial, which afterwards came on, it appeared that the slaves on board the Zong were very sickly ; that sixty of them had already died, and several were ill and likely to die ; when the captain proposed to James Kelsall, the mate, and others, to throw several of them overboard, stating "that if they died a natural death, the loss would fall upon the owners of the ship, but that if they were thrown into the sea, it would fall upon the underwriters." He selected, accordingly, one hundred and thirty-two of the most sickly of the slaves. Fifty-four of these were immediately thrown overboard, and forty-two were made to be partakers of their fate on the succeeding day. In the course of three days afterwards, the remaining twenty-six were brought upon the deck to complete the number of victims. The first sixteen submitted to be thrown into the sea, but the rest, with a noble resolution, would not suffer the officers to touch them, but leaped after their companions and shared their fate.

The plea which was set up in behalf of this atrocious and unparalleled act of wickedness, was that the captain discovered, when he made the proposal, that he had only two hundred gallons of water on board, and that he had missed his port. It was proved, however, in answer to this, that no one had been put upon short allowance ; and that, as if Providence had determined to afford an unequivocal proof of the guilt, a shower of rain fell and continued for three days immediately after the second lot of slaves had been destroyed, by means of which they might have filled many of their vessels with water, and thus have prevented all necessity for the destruction of the third.

Mr. Sharp was present at this trial, and procured the attendance of a short-hand writer to take down the facts which should come out in the course of it. These he gave to the public afterwards. He communicated them, also, with a copy of the trial, to the Lords of the Admiralty, as the guardians of justice upon the seas, and to the Duke of Portland, as principal minister of state. No notice, however, was taken by any of these of the information which had been thus sent them. But though nothing was done by the persons then in power, in consequence of the murder of so many innocent individuals, yet the publication of an account of it by Mr. Sharp, in the newspapers, made such an impression upon others that new coadjutors rose up.

In the year 1784, Dr. Gregory produced his "Essays Historical and Moral." He took an opportunity of disseminating in these a circumstantial knowledge of the slave-trade, and an equal abhorrence of it at the same time. He explained the manner of procuring slaves in Africa; the treatment of them in the passage, (in which he mentioned the case of the ship Zong,) and the cruel treatment of them in the colonies. He recited and refuted also the various arguments adduced in defense of the trade. He showed that it was destructive to seamen. He produced many weighty arguments also against slavery itself. He proposed clauses for an act of parliament for the abolition of both; showing the good both to England and her colonies from such a measure, and that a trade might be substituted in Africa, in various articles for that which he proposed to suppress.

In the same year, James Ramsay, vicar of Teston in Kent, became also an able, zealous, and indefatigable patron of the African cause. This gentleman had resided nineteen years in the island of St. Christopher, where he had observed the treatment of the slaves, and had studied the laws relating to them. On his return to England, yielding to his own feelings of duty, and the solicitations of some friends, he published a work which he called "An Essay on the Treatment and Conversion of the African Slaves in the British Sugar Colonies." After having given an account of the relative situation of master and slave in various parts of the world, he explained the low and degrading situation which the Africans held in society in the British islands. He showed that their importance would be increased, and the temporal interest of their masters promoted, by giving them freedom, and by granting them other privileges. He showed the great difficulty of instructing them in the state in which they then were, and such as he himself had experienced both in his private and public attempts, and such as others had experienced also. He stated the way in which private attempts of this nature might probably be successful. He then answered all objections against their capacities, as drawn from philosophy, form, anatomy, and observation; and vindicated these from his own experience. And lastly, he threw out ideas for the improvement of their condition, by the establishment of a greater number of spiritual pastors among them; by giving them more privileges than they then possessed; and by extending towards them the benefits of a proper police. Mr. Ramsay had no other motive for giving this work to the public than that of humanity, for he compiled it at the hazard of forfeiting that friendship which he had contracted with many during his residence in the islands, and of suffering much in his private property, as well as subjecting himself to the ill-will and persecution of numerous individuals.

The publication of this book by one who professed to have been so long resident in the islands, and to have been an eye-witness of facts, produced, as may easily be supposed, a good deal of conversation, and made a considerable impression, but particularly at this time, when a storm was visibly gathering over the heads of the oppressors of the African race.

In the year 1785, another advocate was seen in Monsieur Necker, in his celebrated work on the French Finances, which had just been translated into the English language from the original work, in 1784. This virtuous statesman, after having given his estimate of the population and revenue of the French West Indian colonies, proceeds thus: "The colonies of France contain, as we have seen, near five hundred thousand slaves, and it is from the number of these poor wretches that the inhabitants set a value on their plantations. What a dreadful prospect! and how profound a subject for reflection! Alas! how little are we both in our morality and our principles! We preach up humanity, and yet go every year to bind in chains twenty thousand natives of Africa! We call the Moors barbarians and ruffians, because they attack the liberty of Europeans at the risk of their own; yet these Europeans go, without danger, and as mere speculators, to purchase slaves by gratifying the avarice of their masters, and excite all those bloody scenes, which are the usual preliminaries of this traffic!" He goes on still further in the same strain. He then shows the kind of power which has supported this execrable trade. He throws out the idea of a general compact, by which all the European nations should agree to abolish it. And he indulges the pleasing hope that it may take place even in the present generation.

In the same year we find other coadjutors coming before our view, but these in a line different from that in which any other belonging to this class had yet moved. Mr. George White, a clergyman of the established church, and Mr. John Chubb, suggested to Mr. William Tucket, the mayor of Bridgewater, where they resided, and to others of that town, the propriety of petitioning parliament for the abolition of the slave-trade. This petition was agreed upon, and when drawn up, was as follows:

"The humble petition of the inhabitants of Bridgewater showeth: That your petitioners, reflecting with the deepest sensibility on the deplorable condition of that part of the human species, the African negroes, who, by the most flagitious means, are reduced to slavery and misery in the British colonies, beg leave to address this honorable house in their behalf, and to express a just abhorrence of a system of oppression, which no prospect of private gain, no consideration of public advantage, no plea of political expediency, can sufficiently justify or excuse.

"That, satisfied as your petitioners are that this inhuman system meets with the general execration of mankind, they flatter themselves the day is not far distant when it will be universally abolished. And they most ardently hope to see a British parliament, by the extinction of that sanguinary traffic, extend the blessings of liberty to millions beyond this realm, hold up to an enlightened world a glorious and merciful example, and stand foremost in the defense of the violated rights of human nature."

This petition was presented by the honorable members for the town of Bridgewater. It was ordered to lie on the table. The answer which these gentlemen gave to their constituents relative to the reception of it in the house of commons, is worthy of notice: "There did not appear," say they in their common letter, "the least disposition to pay any further attention to it. Every one says that the abolition of the slave-trade must immediately throw the West Indian islands into convulsions, and soon complete their utter ruin."

Amongst others, the amiable and gifted Cowper did not fail to utter his sentiments in regard to the cruel system. Who has not been impressed by the following lines?

> "We have no slaves at home—then why abroad?
> And they themselves once ferried o'er the wave
> That parts us, are emancipate and loos'd.
> Slaves cannot breathe in England; if their lungs
> Receive our air, that moment they are free;
> They touch our country, and their shackles fall.
> That's noble, and bespeaks a nation proud
> And jealous of the blessing. Spread it then,
> And let it circulate through every vein
> Of all your empire—that where Britain's pow'r
> Is felt, mankind may feel her mercy too."

George Fox, the venerable founder of the society of the Quakers, took strong and decided ground against the slave-trade. He was cotemporary with Richard Baxter, being born not long after him, and dying much about the same time. When he was in the island of Barbadoes, in the year 1671, he delivered himself to those who attended his religious meetings in the following manner:

" Consider with yourselves," says he, " if you were in the same condition as the poor Africans are, who came strangers to you, and were sold to you as slaves; I say, if this should be the condition of you or yours, you would think it a hard measure; yea, and very great bondage and cruelty; and therefore consider seriously of this; and do you for them, and to them, as you would willingly have them, or any others do unto you, were you in the like slavish condition."

In the year 1727, we find that the whole society, at a yearly meeting held in London, adopted the following resolution: " It is the sense of this meeting, that the importing of negroes from their native country and relations, by Friends, is not a commendable nor allowed practice, and is therefore censured by this meeting."

In the year 1758, the Quakers thought it their duty, as a body, to pass another resolution upon this subject. At this time the nature of the trade beginning to be better known, we find them more animated upon it, as the following extract will show:

" We fervently warn all in profession with us, that they carefully avoid being any way concerned in reaping the unrighteous profits arising from the iniquitous practice of dealing in negro or other slaves; whereby, in the original purchase, one man selleth another, as he doth the beasts that perish, without any better pretension to a property in him than that of superior force; in direct violation of the Gospel rule, which teacheth all to do as they would be done by, and to do good to all; being the reverse of that covetous disposition which furnisheth encouragement to those poor ignorant people to perpetuate their savage wars, in order to supply the demands of this most unnatural traffic, by which great numbers of mankind, free by nature, are subject to inextricable bondage; and which hath often been observed to fill their possessors with haughtiness, tyranny, luxury, and barbarity, corrupting the minds and debasing the morals of their children, to the unspeakable prejudice of religion and virtue, and the exclusion of that holy spirit of universal love, meekness, and charity, which is the unchangeable nature and the glory of true Christianity. We therefore can do no less than, with the greatest earnestness, impress it upon Friends every where, that they endeavor to keep their hands clear of this unrighteous gain of oppression."

At the yearly meeting of 1761, they agreed to exclude from membership such as should be found concerned in this trade ; and in the meeting of 1763, they endeavored to draw the cords still tighter, by attaching criminality to those who should aid and abet the trade in any manner.

The society was now ready to make an appeal to others, and to bear a more public testimony in favor of the injured Africans. Accordingly, in the month of June, 1783, when a bill had been brought into the house of commons for certain regulations to be made with respect to the African trade, the society sent the following petition to that branch of the legislature :

"Your petitioners, met in this their annual assembly, having solemnly considered the state of the enslaved negroes, conceive themselves engaged, in religious duty, to lay the suffering situation of that unhappy people before you, as a subject loudly calling for the humane interposition of the legislature.

"Your petitioners regret that a nation professing the Christian faith, should so far counteract the principles of humanity and justice, as by the cruel treatment of this oppressed race to fill their minds with prejudices against the mild and benificent doctrines of the Gospel.

"Under the countenance of the laws of this country, many thousands of these our fellow-creatures, entitled to the natural rights of mankind, are held as personal property in cruel bondage; and your petitioners being informed that a bill for the regulation of the African trade is now before the house, containing a clause which restrains the officers of the African company from exporting negroes, your petitioners, deeply affected with a consideration of the rapine, oppression, and bloodshed attending this traffic, humbly request that this restriction may be extended to all persons whomsoever, or that the house would grant such other relief in the premises as in its wisdom may seem meet."

This petition was presented by Sir Cecil Wray, who, on introducing it, spoke very respectfully of the society. He declared his hearty approbation of their application, and said he hoped he should see the day when not a slave would remain within the dominions of this realm. Lord North seconded the motion, saying he could have no objection to the petition, and that its object ought to recommend it to every humane breast; that it did credit to the most benevolent society in the world; but that, the session being so far advanced, the subject could not then be taken into consideration ; and he regretted that the slave-trade, against which the petition was so justly directed, was, in a commercial view, necessary to almost every nation of Europe. The petition was then brought up and read, after which it was ordered to lie on the table. This was the first petition (being two years earlier than that from the inhabitants of Bridgewater) which was ever presented to parliament for the abolition of the slave-trade.

In the same year, 1783, an event occurred which will be found of great importance, and in which only individuals belonging to the society were concerned. This event seems to have arisen naturally out of existing or past circumstances. For the society, as before stated, had sent a petition to parliament in this year, praying for the abolition of the slave-trade. It has also laid the foundation for a public distribution of books, which had been published with a view of enlightening others. The case of the ship Zong had occurred this same year. A letter also had been presented, much about the same time, by Benjamin West, from Anthony Benezet, in America, to the Queen, in behalf of the injured Africans, which she had received graciously. These subjects occupied at this time the attention of many Quaker families, and among others, that of a few individuals who were in close intimacy with each other. These, when they met together, frequently conversed upon them. They perceived, as facts came out in conversation, that there was a growing knowledge and hatred of the slave-trade, and that the temper of the times was ripening towards its abolition. Hence a disposition manifested itself among these, to unite as laborers for the furtherance of so desirable an object. An union was at length proposed and approved of. The first meeting was held on the seventh of July, 1783. At this "they assembled to consider what steps they should take for the relief and liberation of the negro slaves in the West Indies, and for the discouragement of the slave-trade on the coast of Africa."

To promote this object, they conceived it necessary that the public mind should be enlightened respecting it. They had recourse therefore to the public papers, and they appointed their members in turn to write in these, and to see that their productions were inserted. They kept regular minutes for this purpose. It was not, however, known to the world that such an association existed.

This was the first society ever formed in England for the promotion of the abolition of the slave-trade.

The Quakers in America early manifested a deep and compassionate feeling toward the afflicted African. It is true that, at first, they with others became the owners of slaves, the manner in which they were procured not being at that time generally known. Most of them, however, treated their slaves with great kindness. But notwithstanding their mildness toward them, and the consequent content of their slaves, some of the society soon began to entertain doubts in regard to the lawfulness of holding the negroes in bondage at all.

So early as in the year 1688, some emigrants from Krieshiem, in Germany, who had adopted the principles of William Penn, and followed him into Pennsylvania, urged in the yearly meeting of the society there, the inconsistency of buying, selling, and holding men in slavery, with the principles of the Christian religion.

In the year 1696, the yearly meeting for that province took up the subject as a public concern, and the result was advice to the members of it to guard against future importations of African slaves, and to be particularly attentive to the treatment of those who were then in their possession.

In the year 1711, the same yearly meeting resumed the important subject, and confirmed and renewed the advice which had been before given.

In the year 1754, the same meeting issued a pertinent and truly Christian letter to all the members within its jurisdiction. This letter contained exhortations to all in the connection to desist from purchasing and importing slaves, and, where they possessed them, to have a tender consideration of their condition. But that the first part of the subject of this exhortation might be enforced, the yearly meeting for the same provinces came to a resolution, in 1755, that if any of the members belonging to it bought or imported slaves, the overseers were to inform their respective monthly meetings of it, that "these might treat with them as they might be directed in the wisdom of truth."

In the year 1776, the same yearly meeting carried the matter still further. It was then enacted, "that the owner of slaves who refused to execute proper instruments for giving them their freedom, were to be disowned likewise."

In 1778, it was enacted by the same meeting, "that the children of those who had been set free by members should be tenderly advised, and have a suitable education given them."

Whilst the body were thus decisive in their measures, individuals of the society were zealous and devoted in their endeavors to promote the same humane cause. Amongst these Anthony Benezet stands conspicuous. This distinguished philanthropist was born at St. Quintin, in Picardy, of a respectable family, in the year 1713. His father was one of the many protestants who, in consequence of the persecutions which followed the revocation of the edict of Nantz, sought an asylum in foreign countries. After a short stay in Holland, he settled, with his wife and children, in London, in 1715.

Anthony Benezet, having received from his father a liberal education, served an apprenticeship in an eminent mercantile house in London. In 1731, however, he removed with his family to Philadelphia, where he joined in profession with the Quakers. His three brothers then engaged in trade, and made considerable pecuniary acquisitions in it. He himself might have partaken of their prosperity, but he did not feel himself at liberty to embark in their undertakings. He considered the accumulation of wealth as of no importance, when compared with the enjoyment of doing good; and he chose the humble situation of a schoolmaster, as according best with his notion, believing that by endeavoring to train up youth in knowledge and virtue, he should become more extensively useful than in any other way to his fellow-creatures. He had not been long in his new situation before he manifested such an uprightness of conduct, such a courtesy of manners, such a purity of intention, and such a spirit of benevolence, that he attracted the notice, and gained the good opinion, of the inhabitants among whom he lived. He had ready access to them, in consequence, upon all occasions; and if there were any whom he failed to influence at any of these times, he never went away without the possession of their respect.

In the year 1756, when a considerable number of French families were removed from Acadia into Pennsylvania, on account of some political suspicions, he felt deeply interested about them. In a country where few understood their language, they were wretched and helpless; but Anthony Benezet endeavored to soften the rigor of their situation by his kind attention towards them. He exerted himself also in their behalf, by procuring many contributions for them, which, by the consent of his fellow-citizens, were entrusted to his care.

One of the means which Anthony Benezet took to promote the cause in question, (and an effectual one it proved, as far as it went,) was to give his scholars a due knowledge and proper impressions concerning it. Situated as they were likely to be, in after life, in a country where slavery was a custom, he thus prepared many, and this annually, for the promotion of his plans. To enlighten others, and to give them a similar bias, he had recourse to different measures from time to time. In the almanacs published annually in Philadelphia, he procured articles to be inserted, which he believed would attract the notice of the reader, and make him pause, at least for a while, as to the lawfulness of the slave-trade. He wrote, also, as he saw occasion, in the public papers of the day. From small things he proceeded to greater. He collected, at length, further information on the subject, and, winding it up with observations and reflections, he produced several little tracts, which he circulated successively, (but generally at his own expense,) as he considered them adapted to the temper and circumstances of the times. In the course of this employment, having found some who had approved his tracts, and to whom, on that account, he wished to write, and sending his tracts to others, to whom he thought it proper to introduce them by letter, he found himself engaged in a correspondence which much engrossed his time, but which proved of great importance in procuring many advocates for his cause.

In the year 1762, when he had obtained a still greater store of information, he published a larger work. This he entitled, " *A Short Account of that Part of Africa inhabited by the Negroes.*" In 1767, he published "*A Caution and Warning to Great Britain and her Colonies, on the Calamitous State of the enslaved Negroes in the British Dominions :*" and soon after this appeared " *A Historical Account of Guinea, its Situation, Produce, and the General Disposition of its Inhabitants; with an Inquiry into the Rise and Progress of the Slave-trade, its Nature, and Calamitous Effects.*" This pamphlet contained a clear and distinct development of the subject, from the best authorities. It contained also the sentiments of many enlightened men upon it; and it became instrumental, beyond any other book ever before published, in disseminating a proper knowledge and detestation of this trade.

Anthony Benezet may be considered one of the most zealous, vigilant, and active advocates which the cause of the oppressed Africans ever had. He seemed to have been born and to have lived for the promotion of it, and therefore he never omitted any the least opportunity of serving it. If a person called upon him who was going a journey, his first thoughts usually were, how he could make him an instrument in its favor; and he either gave him tracts to distribute, or he sent letters by him, or he gave him some commission on the subject, so that he was the means of employing several persons at the same time, in various parts of America, in advancing the work he had undertaken.

In the same manner he availed himself of every other circumstance, as far as he could, to the same end. When he heard that Mr. Granville Sharp had obtained, in the year 1772, the verdict in the case of Somerset, the slave, he opened a correspondence with him, which he kept up, that there might be an union of action between them for the future, as far as it could be effected, and that they might each give encouragement to the other to proceed.

He wrote also a letter to the Countess of Huntingdon on the following subject: She had founded a college, at the recommendation of George Whitefield, called the Orphan-house, near Savannah, in Georgia, and had endowed it. The object of this institution was to furnish scholastic instruction to the poor, and to prepare some of them for the ministry. George Whitefield, ever attentive to the cause of the poor Africans, thought that this institution might have been useful to them also; but soon after his death, they who succeeded him bought slaves, and these in unusual numbers, to extend the rice and indigo plantations belonging to the college. The letter then in question was written by Anthony Benezet, in order to lay before the countess, as a religious woman, the misery she was occasioning in Africa, by allowing the managers of her college in Georgia to give encouragement to the slave-trade. The countess replied that such a measure should never have her countenance, and that she would take care to prevent it.

On discovering that the Abbé Raynal had brought out his celebrated work, in which he manifested a tender feeling in behalf of the injured Africans, he entered into a correspondence with him, hoping to make him yet more useful to their cause.

Finding, also, in the year 1783, that the slave-trade, which had greatly declined during the war, was reviving, he addressed a pathetic letter to the queen, who, on hearing the high character of the writer of it from Benjamin West, received it with marks of peculiar condescension and attention. The following is a copy of it:

"To CHARLOTTE, QUEEN OF GREAT BRITAIN:

"Impressed with a sense of religious duty, and encouraged by the opinion generally entertained of thy benevolent disposition to succor the distressed, I take the liberty, very respectfully, to offer to thy perusal some tracts, which I believe faithfully describe the suffering condition of many hundred thousands of our fellow-creatures of the African race, great numbers of whom, rent from every tender connection in life, are annually taken from their native land, to endure, in the American islands and plantations, a most rigorous and cruel slavery; whereby many, very many of them, are brought to a melancholy and untimely end.

"When it is considered that the inhabitants of Great Britain, who are themselves so eminently blessed in the enjoyment of religious and civil liberty, have long been, and yet are, very deeply concerned in this flagrant violation of the common rights of mankind, and that even its national authority is exerted in support of the African slave-trade, there is much reason to apprehend that this has been, and, as long as the evil exists, will continue to be, an occasion of drawing down the Divine displeasure on the nation and its dependencies. May these considerations induce thee to interpose thy kind endeavors in behalf of this greatly injured people, whose abject situation gives them an additional claim to the pity and assistance of the generous mind, inasmuch as they are altogether deprived of the means of soliciting effectual relief for themselves; that so thou mayest not only be a blessed instrument in the hand of Him 'by whom kings reign and princes decree justice,' to avert the awful judgments by which the empire has already been so remarkably shaken, but that the blessings of thousands ready to perish may come upon thee, at a time when the superior advantages attendant on thy situation in this world will no longer be of any avail to thy consolation and support.

"To the tracts on this subject to which I have thus ventured to crave thy particular attention, I have added some which at different times I have believed it my duty to publish,* and which, I trust, will afford thee some satisfaction, their design being for the furtherance of that universal peace and good will amongst men, which the gospel was intended to introduce.

"I hope thou wilt kindly excuse the freedom used on this occasion by an ancient man, whose mind, for more than forty years past, has been much separated from the common intercourse of the world, and long painfully exercised in the consideration of the miseries under which so large a part of mankind, equally with us the objects of redeeming love, are suffering the most unjust and grievous oppressions, and who sincerely desires thy temporal and eternal felicity, and that of thy royal consort. ANTHONY BENEZET."

Anthony Benezet, besides the care he bestowed upon forwarding the cause of the oppressed Africans in different parts of the world, found time to promote the comforts and improve the condition of those in the state in which he lived. Apprehending that much advantage would arise both to them and the public, from instructing them in common learning, he zealously promoted the establishment of a school for that purpose. Much of the two last years of his life he devoted to a personal attendance on this school, being earnestly desirous that they who came to it might be better qualified for the enjoyment of that freedom to which great numbers of them had been then restored. To this he sacrificed the superior emoluments of his former school, and his bodily ease also, although the weakness of his constitution seemed to demand indulgence. By his last will he directed, that after the decease of his widow, his whole little fortune, the savings of the industry of fifty years, should, except a few very small legacies, be applied to the support of it. During his attendance upon it he had the happiness to find, and his situation enabled him to make the comparison, that Providence had been equally liberal to the Africans in genius and talents as to other people.

---

* These related to the principles of the religious society of the Quakers.

After a few days illness this excellent man died at Philadelphia in the spring of 1784. The interment of his remains was attended by several thousand of all ranks, professions, and parties, who united in deploring their loss. The mournful procession was closed by some hundreds of those poor Africans, who had been personally benefited by his labors, and whose behavior on the occasion showed the gratitude and affection they considered to be due to him as their own private benefactor, as well as the benefactor of their whole race.

Others in America beside the Quakers, early took the part of the oppressed Africans. In the first part of the eighteenth century, Judge Sewall, of New England, came forward as a zealous advocate for them. He addressed a memorial to the legislature, which he called *The Selling of Joseph*, and in which he pleaded their cause both as a lawyer and a Christian. This memorial produced an effect upon many, but particularly upon those of his own persuasion; and from this time the Presbyterians appear to have encouraged a sympathy in their favor.

In the year 1739, the celebrated George Whitefield became an instrument in turning the attention of many others to their condition, and of begetting in these a fellow-sympathy towards them. This laborious minister, having been deeply affected with what he had seen in the course of his travels in America, thought it his duty to address a letter from Georgia to the inhabitants of Maryland, Virginia, and North and South Carolina. This letter was printed in the year above mentioned, and is in part as follows :

"As I lately passed through your provinces on my way hither, I was sensibly touched with a fellow-feeling for the miseries of the poor negroes. Whether it be lawful for Christians to buy slaves, and thereby encourage the nations from whom they are bought to be at perpetual war with each other, I shall not take upon me to determine. Sure I am it is sinful, when they have bought them, to use them as bad as though they were brutes, nay, worse ; and whatever particular exceptions there may be, (as I would charitably hope there are some,) I fear the generality of you, who own negroes, are liable to such a charge ; for your slaves, I believe, work as hard, if not harder, than the horses whereon you ride. These, after they have done their work, are fed and taken proper care of ; but many negroes, when wearied with labor on your plantations, have been obliged to grind their corn after their return home. Your dogs are caressed and fondled at your table ; but your slaves, who are frequently called dogs or beasts, have not an equal privilege. They are scarce permitted to pick up the crumbs which fall from their master's table ; not to mention what numbers have been given up to the inhuman usage of cruel task-masters, who, by their unrelenting scourges, have plowed their backs, and made long furrows, and at length brought them even unto death. When passing along I have viewed your plantations cleared and cultivated, many spacious houses built, and the owners of them faring sumptuously every day, my blood has frequently almost run cold within me, to consider how many of your slaves had neither convenient food to eat nor proper raiment to put on, notwithstanding most of the comforts you enjoy were solely owing to their indefatigable labors."

The letter, from which this is an extract, produced a desirable effect upon many of those who perused it, but particularly upon such as began to be seriously disposed in those times. And as George Whitefield continued a firm friend to the Africans, never losing an opportunity of serving them, he interested, in the course of his useful life, many thousands of his followers in their favor.

In the year 1772, a disposition favorable to the oppressed Africans became very generally manifest in some of the American Provinces. The house of burgesses of Virginia even presented a petition to the king, beseeching his majesty to remove all those restraints on his governors of that colony, which inhibited their assent to such laws as might check that inhuman and impolitic commerce, the slave-trade : and it is remarkable that the refusal of the British government to permit the colonists to exclude slaves from among them by law, was enumerated afterwards among the public reasons for separating from the mother country.

In allusion to the fact just stated, Mr. Jefferson, in his draft of the Declaration of Independence, said : "He (the king of England) has waged civil war against human nature itself, violating its most sacred rights of life and liberty, in the persons of a distant people, who never offended him; captivating, and carrying them into slavery in another hemisphere, or to incur miserable death in their transportation thither. This piratical warfare, the opprobrium of infidel powers, is the warfare of the Christian king of Great Britain : determined to keep open a market where MEN should be bought and sold, he prostituted his negative for suppressing every legislative attempt to prohibit or to restrain this execrable commerce; and, that this assemblage of horrors might want no fact of distinguished dye, he is now exciting those very people to rise in arms among us, and to purchase that liberty of which he has deprived them, by murdering the people upon whom he also obtruded them, thus paying off former crimes, committed against the liberties of one people, with crimes which he urges them to commit against the lives of another." (See the fac-simile of this draft in Jefferson's *Correspondence.*) But this passage was struck out when the Declaration of Independence was adopted.

But the friendly disposition was greatly increased in the year 1773, by the literary labors of Dr. Benjamin Rush, of Philadelphia. In this year, at the instigation of Anthony Benezet, he took up the cause of the oppressed Africans in a little work, which he entitled *An Address to the Inhabitants of the British Settlements on the Slavery of the Negroes;* and soon afterwards in another, which was a vindication of the first, in answer to an acrimonious attack by a West Indian planter. These publications contained many new observations. They were written in a polished style; and while they exhibited the erudition and talents, they showed the liberality and benevolence of the author. Having had considerable circulation, they spread conviction among many, and promoted the cause for which they had been so laudably undertaken.

12

In the next year, or in the year 1774,* the increased good-will towards the Africans became so apparent, but more particularly in Pennsylvania, where the Quakers were more numerous than in any other state, that they, who considered themselves more immediately as the friends of these injured people, thought it right to avail themselves of it: and accordingly James Pemberton, one of the most conspicuous of the Quakers in Pennsylvania, and Dr. Rush, one of the most conspicuous of those belonging to the various other religious communities in that province, undertook, in conjunction with others, the important task of bringing those into society who were friendly to this cause. In this undertaking they succeeded. This society, which was confined to Pennsylvania, was the first ever formed in America, in which there was a union of persons of different religious denominations in behalf of the African race.

But this society had scarcely begun to act, when the war broke out between England and America, which had the effect of checking its operations. This was considered as a severe blow upon it. But as those things which appear most to our disadvantage turn out often the most to our benefit, so the war, by giving birth to the independence of America, was ultimately favorable to its progress. For as this contest had produced during its continuance, so it left, when it was over, a general enthusiasm for liberty. Many talked of little else but of the freedom they had gained. These were naturally led to the consideration of those among them who were groaning in bondage. They began to feel for their hard case. They began to think that they should not deserve the new blessing which they had acquired, if they denied it to others. Thus the discussions which originated in this contest, became the occasion of turning the attention of many, who might not otherwise have thought of it, toward the miserable condition of the slaves.

Nor were writers wanting, who, influenced by considerations on the war and the independence resulting from it, made their works subservient to the same benevolent end. A work entitled, *A Serious Address to the Rulers of America on the Inconsistency of their Conduct respecting Slavery, forming a Contrast between the Encroachments of England on American Liberty and American Injustice in tolerating Slavery,* which appeared in 1783, was particularly instrumental in producing this effect. This excited a more than usual attention to the case of these oppressed people, and where most of all it could be useful. For the author compared in two opposite columns the animated speeches and resolutions of the members of congress in behalf of their own liberty with their conduct in continuing slavery to others. Hence congress began to feel the inconsistency of the practice; and so far had the sense of this inconsistency spread, that when the delegates met from each state to consider of a federal union, there was a desire that the abolition of the slave-trade should be one of the articles of it. This was, however, op-

---

* In this year, Elhanan Winchester, a supporter of the doctrine of universal redemption, turned the attention of many of his hearers to this subject, both by private conference and by preaching expressly upon it.

posed by the delegates from North and South Carolina, Virginia, Maryland, and Georgia, the five states which had the greatest interest in slaves. But even these offered to agree to the article, provided a condition was annexed to it, which was afterwards done, that such abolition should not commence till the first of January, 1808.

In consequence of these circumstances, the society of Pennsylvania, the object of which was "for promoting the abolition of slavery and the relief of free negroes unlawfully held in bondage," became so popular, that in the year 1787, it was thought desirable to enlarge it. Accordingly, several new members were admitted into it. The celebrated Dr. Franklin, who had long warmly espoused the cause of the injured Africans, was appointed President; James Pemberton and Jonathan Penrose were appointed Vice-Presidents; Dr. Benjamin Rush and Tench Coxe, Secretaries; James Star, Treasurer.*

CHAPTER XIII.

MOVEMENTS IN ENGLAND TO ABOLISH THE SLAVE TRADE.

Thomas Clarkson, the historian of the Abolition of the Slave Trade.—Devotes his life to the cause, 1785.—Publishes his Essay on Slavery.—His coadjutors.—William Wilberforce, parliamentary leader in the cause.—Middleton, Dr. Porteus, Lord Scarsdale, Granville Sharp.—Clarkson's first visit to a slave-ship.—Association formed.—Correspondence opened in Europe and America.—Petitions sent to Parliament.—Committee of Privy Council ordered by the King, 1788.—Great exertions of the friends of the cause.—Clarkson's interview with Pitt.

THE historian of the Abolition of the Slave Trade by the British Parliament was Mr. Thomas Clarkson. He was among the warmest supporters of the sacred cause, and from the year 1785 he devoted his life to it. The various measures pursued to promote it, were registered at the time, either by himself or the committee with whom he acted. Not the shadow of a doubt has ever been expressed as to the authenticity of his work, and we cannot present information on this subject in a more satisfactory manner than by giving the reader a concise abridgement of the work itself.

Besides Mr. Clarkson, there was another individual of whose mind the subject took a deep hold. This was William Wilberforce. In October, 1757, he entered upon his journal that "the Almighty had placed before him the great object of the abolition of the slave-trade." Clarkson and Wilberforce, the twin spirits of the movement, were soon able to form a powerful confederacy, including men of all parties, and to impress the mind of the nation.

Dr. Peckard, master of Magdalen College, in the University of Cambridge,

---

* Abridged from Clarkson's History.

had not only censured the slave-trade in the severest manner, in a sermon preached before the University, but when he became vice-chancellor of it, in 1785, he gave out the following subject for one of the Latin dissertations : "Is it right to make slaves of others against their will ?" At this time Mr. Clarkson, who had obtained the prize for the best essay the preceding year, determined to become again a candidate. He took prodigious pains to make himself master of the subject, as far as the time would allow, both by reading, and conversing with many persons who had been in Africa. Having completed his Latin essay, and sent it in to the vice-chancellor, he soon found himself honored with the first prize. The subject of the essay so entirely engrossed his thoughts that he became seriously affected. He tried to persuade himself that the contents of the essay were not true. The more, however, he reflected upon his authorities, the more he gave them credit, until he finally became convinced that it was the duty of some one to endeavor to mitigate the sufferings of the unhappy Africans. He finally resolved to devote his own life to the cause. When this resolution was formed he was but twenty-four years of age, and he considered his youth and want of knowledge of the world as a great obstacle. He thought, however, that there was one way in which he might begin to be useful; by translating his Latin essay, and publishing it in English.

Of this period of his life and labors he says : "In the course of the autumn of this year (1785), I walked frequently into the woods that I might think on the subject of the slave-trade in solitude. But there the question still occurred, 'Are these things true?' Still the answer followed as instantaneously, 'They are.' Still the result accompanied it, 'Then surely some person should interfere.' I then began to envy those who had seats in parliament, and who had great riches, and widely extended connexions, which would enable them to take up this cause. Finding scarcely any one at that time who thought of it, I was turned frequently to myself. But here many difficulties arose. It struck me, among others, that a young man of only twenty-four years of age could not have that solid judgment, or knowledge of men, manners, and things, which were requisite to qualify him to undertake a task of such magnitude and importance ; and with whom was I to unite ? I believed also that *it looked so much like one of the feigned labors of Hercules, that my understanding would be suspected if I proposed it.* On ruminating, however, on the subject, I found one thing at least practicable, and that this also was in my power. I could translate my Latin dissertation. I could enlarge it usefully. I could see how the public received it, or how far they were likely to favor any serious measures, which should have a tendency to produce the abolition of the slave-trade. Upon this, then, I determined ; and in the middle of the month of November, 1785, I began my work. By the middle of January I had finished half of it, though I had made considerable additions. I now thought of engaging with some bookseller to print it when finished. For this purpose I called upon Mr. Cadell, in the Strand, and consulted him about it. He said that as the original essay had been honored by the University of Cambridge with the first prize, this circumstance would insure it a respectable circulation among persons of taste. I own I was not much pleased with his opinion. I wished the essay to find its way among useful people, and among such as would think and act with me. Accordingly I left Mr. Cadell, after having thanked him for his civility, and determined, as I thought I had time sufficient before dinner, to call upon a friend in the city. In going past the Royal Exchange, Mr. Joseph Hancock, one of the religious society of the Quakers, and with whose family my own had been long united in friendship, suddenly met me. He first accosted me by saying that I was the person whom he was wishing to see. He then asked me why I had not published my prize essay. I asked him in return what had made him think of that subject in particular. He replied, that his own society had long taken it up as a religious body, and individuals among them were wishing to find me out. I asked him who. He answered, James Phillips, a bookseller, in George-yard, Lombard street, and William Dillwyn, of Walthamstow, and others. Having but little time to spare, I desired him to introduce me to one of them. In a few minutes he took me to James Phillips, who was then the only one of them in town, by whose conversation I was so much interested and encouraged, that without any further hesitation I offered him the publication of my work. This accidental introduction of me to James Phillips was, I found afterwards, a most happy circumstance for the promotion of the cause which I had then so deeply at heart, as it led me to the knowledge of several of those who became afterwards material coadjutors in it. It was also of great importance to me with respect to the work itself, for he possessed an acute penetration, a solid judgment, and a literary knowledge, which he proved by the many alterations and additions he proposed, and which I believe I uniformly adopted, after mature consideration, from a sense of their real value. It was advantageous to me also, inasmuch as it led me to his friendship, which was never interrupted but by his death.

" On my second visit to James Phillips, at which time I brought him about half my manuscript for the press, I desired him to introduce me to William Dillwyn, as he had also mentioned him to me on my first visit, and as I had not seen Mr. Hancock since. Matters were accordingly arranged, and a day appointed before I left him. On this day I had my first interview with my new friend. Two or three others of his own religious society were present, but who they were I do not now recollect. There seemed to be a great desire among them to know the motive by which I had been actuated in contending for the prize. I told them frankly that I had no motive but that which other young men in the University had on such occasions, namely, the wish of being distinguished, or of obtaining literary honor; but that I had felt so deeply on the subject of it, that I had lately interested myself in it from a motive of duty. My conduct seemed to be highly approved by those present, and much conversation ensued, but it was of a general nature.

" As William Dillwyn wished very much to see me at his house at Walthamstow, I appointed the thirteenth of March to spend the day with him there.

We talked for the most part, during my stay, on the subject of my essay. I soon discovered the treasure I had met with in his local knowledge, both of the slave-trade and of slavery, as they existed in the United States, and I gained from him several facts, which, with his permission, I afterwards inserted in my work. But how surprised was I to hear, in the course of our conversation, of the labors of Granville Sharp, of the writings of Ramsay, and of the controversy in which the latter was engaged, of all which I had hitherto known nothing. How surprised was I to learn, that William Dillwyn himself had two years before associated himself with five others for the purpose of enlightening the public mind upon this great subject. How astonished was I to find that a society had been formed in America for the same object, with some of the principal members of which he was intimately acquainted. And how still more astonished at the inference which instantly rushed upon my mind, that he was capable of being made the great medium of connection between them all. These thoughts almost overpowered me. I believe that after this I talked but little more to my friend. My mind was overwhelmed with the thought that I had been providentially directed to his house; that the finger of Providence was beginning to be discernible; that the day-star of African liberty was rising, and that probably I might be permitted to become an humble instrument in promoting it.

"In the course of attending to my work, as now in the press, James Phillips introduced me also to Granville Sharp, with whom I had afterwards many interesting interviews from time to time, and whom I discovered to be a distant relation by my father's side. He introduced me also by letter to a correspondence with Mr. Ramsay, who in a short time afterwards came to London to see me. He introduced me also to his cousin, Richard Phillips, of Lincoln's Inn, who was at that time on the point of joining the religious society of the Quakers. In him I found much sympathy, and a willingness to coöperate with me. When dull and disconsolate, he encouraged me. When in spirits, he stimulated me further. Him I am now to mention as a new, but soon afterwards as an active and indefatigable coadjutor in the cause. I shall only now add that my work was at length printed; that it was entitled, An Essay on the Slavery and Commerce of the Human Species, particularly the African, translated from a Latin Dissertation, which was honored with the First Prize in the University of Cambridge, for the year 1785; with Additions; and that it was ushered into the world in the month of June, 1786, or in about a year after it had been read in the senate house in its first form.

"I had long had the honor of the friendship of Mr. Bennet Langton, and I determined to carry him one of my books, and to interest his feelings in it, with a view of procuring his assistance in the cause. Mr. Langton was a gentleman of an ancient family and respectable fortune, in Lincolnshire, but resided then in Queen's-square, Westminster. He was known as the friend of Dr. Johnson, Jonas Hanway, Edmund Burke, Sir Joshua Reynolds, and others. Among his acquaintance indeed were most of the literary, and eminent professional, and public-spirited men of the times. At court, also, he was well known, and had the esteem of his majesty, with whom he frequently conversed. His friends were numerous, also, in both houses of the legislature. As to himself, he was much noted for his learning, but most of all for the great example he gave with respect to the usefulness and integrity of his life. By introducing my work to the sanction of a friend of such high character and extensive connexions, I thought I should be doing great things. And so the event proved. For when I went to him after he had read it, I found that it had made a deep impression upon his mind. As a friend to humanity, he lamented over the miseries of the oppressed Africans, and over the crimes of their tyrants as a friend to morality and religion. He cautioned me, however, against being too sanguine in my expectations, as so many thousands were interested in continuing the trade. Justice, however, which he said weighed with him beyond all private or political interest, demanded a public inquiry, and he would assist me to the utmost of his power in my attempts towards it. From this time he became a zealous and active coadjutor in the cause, and continued so to the end of his valuable life.

"I had now Sir Charles Middleton, who was in the House of Commons. I was sure of Dr. Porteus, who was in the House of Lords. I could count upon Lord Scarsdale, who was a peer also. I had secured Mr. Langton, who had a most extensive acquaintance with members of both houses of the legislature. I had also secured Dr. Baker, who had similar connexions. I could depend upon Granville Sharp, James Phillips, Richard Phillips, Ramsay, Dillwyn, and the little committee to which he belonged, as well as the whole society of the Quakers. I thought, therefore, upon the whole, that, considering the short time I had been at work, I was well off with respect to support. I believed, also, that there were still several of my own acquaintance whom I could interest in the question, and I did not doubt that by exerting myself diligently, persons who were then strangers to me would be raised up in time. I considered next, that it was impossible for a great cause like this to be forwarded without large pecuniary funds. I questioned whether some thousand pounds would not be necessary, and from whence was such a sum to come? In answer to this, I persuaded myself that generous people would be found who would unite with me in contributing their mite towards the undertaking, and I seemed confident that as the Quakers had taken up the cause as a religious body, they would not be behind hand in supporting it. I considered lastly, that if I took up the question I must devote myself wholly to it. I was sensible that a little labor now and then would be inadequate to the purpose, or that where the interests of so many thousand persons were likely to be affected, constant exertion would be necessary. I felt certain that if ever the matter were to be taken up, there could be no hope of success, except it should be taken up by some one who would make it an object or business of his life. I thought, too, that a man's life might not be more than adequate to the accomplishment of the end. But I knew of no one who could devote such a portion of time to it. Sir Charles Middleton, though he was so warm and zealous, was greatly occupied in the discharge of his office. Mr. Langton

spent a great portion of his time in the education of his children.   Dr. Baker
had a great deal to do in the performance of his parochial duty.   The Quakers were almost all of them in trade.   I could look, therefore, to no person
but myself; and the question was, whether I was prepared to make the sacrifice.   In favor of the undertaking I urged to myself, that never was any cause
which had been taken up by man in any country, or in any age, so great and
important; that never was there one in which so much misery was heard to
cry for redress; that never was there one in which so much good could be
done; never one in which the duty of Christian charity could be so extensively
exercised; never one more worthy of the devotion of a whole life towards it;
and that, if a man thought properly, he ought to rejoice to have been called
into existence, if he were only permitted to become an instrument in forwarding it in any part of its progress.   Against these sentiments on the other
hand I had to urge, that I had been designed for the church; that I had
already advanced as far as deacon's orders in it; that my prospects there on
account of my connexions were then brilliant; that by appearing to desert my
profession my family would be dissatisfied, if not unhappy.   These thoughts
pressed upon me, and rendered the conflict difficult.   But the sacrifice of my
prospects staggered me, I own, the most.   When the other objections, which
I have related, occurred to me, my enthusiasm instantly, like a flash of light-
ning, consumed them; but this stuck to me and troubled me.   I had ambition.
I had a thirst after worldly interest and honors, and I could not extinguish it
at once.   I was more than two hours in solitude under this painful conflict.
At length I yielded, not because I saw any reasonable prospect of success in
my new undertaking, (for all cool-headed and cool-hearted men would have pronounced against it,) but in obedience, I believe, to a higher power.   And this
I can say, that both on the moment of this resolution, and for some time afterwards, I had more sublime and happy feelings than at any former period of
my life.

"The distribution of my books having been consigned to proper hands, I
began to qualify myself by obtaining further knowledge for the management
of this great cause.   As I had obtained the principal part of it from reading,
I thought I ought now to see what could be seen, and to know from living
persons what could be known on the subject.   With respect to the first of
these points, the river Thames presented itself as at hand.   Ships were going
occasionally from the port of London to Africa, and why could I not get on
board them and examine for myself?   After diligent inquiry, I heard of one
which had just arrived.   I found her to be a little wood vessel, called the
Lively, captain Williamson, or one which traded to Africa in the natural productions of the country, such as ivory, beeswax, Malaguetta pepper, palm-oil
and dye-woods.   I obtained specimens of some of these, so that I now became possessed of some of those things of which I had only read before.   On
conversing with the mate, he showed me one or two pieces of the cloth made
by the natives, and from their own cotton.   I prevailed upon him to sell me a
piece of each.   Here new feelings arose, and particularly when I considered

that persons of so much apparent ingenuity, and capable of such beautiful work as the Africans, should be made slaves, and reduced to a level with the brute creation. My reflections here on the better use which might be made of Africa by the substitution of another trade, and on the better use which might be made of her inhabitants, served greatly to animate and to sustain me against the labor of my pursuits.

" The next vessel I boarded was the Fly, captain Cooley. Here I found myself for the first time on the deck of a slave vessel. The sight of the rooms below and of the gratings above, and of the barricado across the deck, and the explanation of the uses of all these, filled me both with melancholy and horror. I found soon afterwards a fire of indignation kindled within me. I had now scarce patience to talk with those on board. I had not the coolness this first time to go leisurely over the places that were open to me. I got away quickly. But that which I thought I saw horrible in this vessel had the same effect upon me as that which I thought I had seen agreeable in the other, namely, to animate and to invigorate me in my pursuit.

"But I will not trouble the reader with any further account of my water expeditions, while attempting to perfect my knowledge upon this subject. I was equally assiduous in obtaining intelligence wherever it could be had; and being now always on the watch, I was frequently falling in with individuals from whom I gained something. My object was to see all who had been in Africa, but more particularly those who had never been interested, or who at any rate were not then interested in the trade. I gained, accordingly, access very early to general Rooke; to lieutenant Dalrymple, of the army; to captain Fiddes, of the engineers; to the reverend Mr. Newton; to Mr. Nisbett, a surgeon in the Minories; to Mr. Devaynes, who was then in parliament, and to many others; and I made it a rule to put down in writing, after every conversation, what had taken place in the course of it. By these means things began to unfold themselves to me more and more, and I found my stock of knowledge almost daily on the increase.

While, however, I was forwarding this, I was not inattentive to the other object of my pursuit, which was that of waiting upon members personally. The first I called upon was Sir Richard Hill. At the first interview he espoused the cause. I waited then upon others, and they professed themselves friendly; but they seemed to make this profession more from the emotion of good hearts, revolting at the bare mention of the slave-trade, than from any knowledge concerning it. One, however, whom I visited, Mr. Powys, (the late Lord Lilford,) with whom I had been before acquainted in Northamptonshire, seemed to doubt some of the facts in my book, from a belief that human nature was not capable of proceeding to such a pitch of wickedness. I asked him to name his facts. He selected the case of the hundred and thirty-two slaves who were thrown alive into the sea to defraud the underwriters. I promised to satisfy him fully upon this point, and went immediately to Granville Sharp, who lent me his account of the trial, as reported at large from the notes of the short-hand writer whom he had employed on the occasion. Mr. Powys read the account. He became, in consequence of it, convinced, as, indeed, he could not otherwise be, of the truth of what I had asserted, and he declared at the same time that, if this were true, there was nothing so horrible related of this trade, which might not immediately be believed. Mr. Powys had been always friendly to this question, but now he took a part in the distribution of my books.

"Among those whom I visited, was Mr. Wilberforce. On my first interview with him, he stated frankly, that the subject had often employed his thoughts, and that it was near his heart. He seemed earnest about it, and also very desirous of taking the trouble of inquiring further into it. Having read my book, which I had delivered to him in person, he sent for me. He expressed a wish that I would make him acquainted with some of my authorities for the assertions in it, which I did afterwards to his satisfaction. He asked me if I could support it by any other evidence. I told him I could. I mentioned Mr. Newton, Mr. Nisbett, and several others to him. He took the trouble of sending for all these. He made memoranda of their conversation, and, sending for me afterwards, showed them to me. On learning my intention to devote myself to the cause, he paid me many handsome compliments. He then desired me to call upon him often, and to acquaint him with my progress from time to time. He expressed also his willingness to afford me any assistance in his power in the prosecution of my pursuits."

Mr. Wilberforce finally pledged himself to bring forward the great question of the abolition of the slave-trade, in the House of Commons, as soon as he could prepare himself for so tremendous a task. The matter now assumed a new shape. A parliamentary-leader had been secured, and one whose virtuous life corresponded with the sacredness of the cause he was to advocate. The friends of the cause formed themselves into an association, raised funds, and appointed a committee to procure information and select evidence. Mr. Clarkson was to visit Liverpool, Bristol, and other slave ports, to increase his own knowledge of the subject, and to procure evidence, in case parliament should call for witnesses. He was absent five months, and returned to London in December, 1787. Meantime, the committee had opened an extensive correspondence throughout England, Scotland, and America. They circulated documents, and addressed by letter all the corporate bodies of the kingdom. Tokens of approbation and promises of support flowed in upon them. From France, letters of encouragement were received from the Marquis de La Fayette, and the afterwards celebrated Brissot and Claviere. La Fayette informed the committee that he should attempt the formation of a similar society in France.

Of the indefatigable labors and untiring faithfulness of the committee, the following summary will give some idea : From May, 1787, to July, 1788, they had held no less than fifty-one meetings. These generally occupied them from about six in the evening till about eleven at night. In the intervals between the meetings they were often occupied, having each of them some object committed to his charge. It is remarkable, too, that though they were all, except one, engaged in business or trade, and though they had the same calls as other men for innocent recreation, and the same interruptions of their health, there were individuals who were not absent more than five or six times within this period. In the course of the thirteen months, during which they had exercised this public trust, they had printed, and afterwards distributed, not at random, but judiciously, and through respectable channels, (besides twenty-six thousand five hundred and twenty-six reports, accounts of debates in parliament, and other small papers,) no less than fifty-one thousand four hundred and thirty-two pamphlets, or books.

Thus commenced the great struggle which was destined to last for a period of twenty years; a struggle with the gigantic commercial interest of Liverpool, Bristol, and other ports, and the proprietors of the West India plantations.

Up to the month of February, 1788, thirty-five petitions had been presented to parliament, in favor of abolishing the trade. These proceedings produced such an effect upon the government, that the king was advised to order a committee of privy council to inquire into the nature of the slave-trade. This was dated February 11, 1788, and required the committee "to take into their consideration the present state of the African trade, particularly as far as related to the practice and manner of purchasing or obtaining slaves on the coast of Africa, and the importation and sale thereof, either in the British colonies and settlements, or in the foreign colonies and settlements in America or the West Indies; and also as far as related to the effects and consequences of the trade, both in Africa and in the said colonies and settlements, and to the general commerce of this kingdom; and that they should report to him in council the result of their inquiries, with such observations as they might have to offer thereupon."

An effort was made to enlist Mr. Pitt in the cause, and Mr. Clarkson thus describes his first interview with that great statesman: "My business in London was to hold a conversation with Mr. Pitt previously to the meeting of the council, and to try to interest him, as the first minister of state, in our favor. For this purpose, Mr. Wilberforce had opened the way for me, and an interview took place. We were in free conversation together for a considerable time, during which we went through most of the branches of the subject. Mr. Pitt appeared to me to have but little knowledge of it. He had also his doubts, which he expressed openly, on many points. He was at a loss to conceive how private interest should not always restrain the master of the slave from abusing him. This matter I explained to him as well as I could; and if he was not entirely satisfied with my interpretation of it, he was at least induced to believe that cruel practices were more probable than he had imagined. A second circumstance, the truth of which he doubted, was the mortality and usage of seamen in this trade; and a third was the statement, by which so much had been made of the riches of Africa, and of the genius and abilities of her people; for he seemed at a loss to comprehend, if these things were so, how it had happened that they should not have been more generally noticed before. I promised to satisfy him upon these points, and an interview was fixed for this purpose the next day.

"At the time appointed, I went with my books, papers and African productions. Mr. Pitt examined the former himself. He turned over leaf after leaf, in which the copies of the muster-rolls were contained, with great patience; and when he had looked over above a hundred pages accurately, and found the name of every seaman inserted, his former abode or service, the time of his entry, and what had become of him, either by death, discharge, or desertion, he expressed his surprise at the great pains which had been taken in this branch of the inquiry, and confessed, with some emotion, that his doubts were wholly removed with respect to the destructive nature of this employment; and he said, moreover, that the facts contained in these documents, if they had been but fairly copied, could never be disproved. He was equally astonished at the various woods and other productions of Africa, but most of all at the manufactures of the natives in cotton, leather, gold, and iron, which were laid before him. These he handled and examined over and over again. Many sublime thoughts seemed to rush in upon him at once at the sight of these, some of which he expressed with observations becoming a great and dignified mind. He thanked me for the light I had given him on many of the branches of this great question. And I went away under a certain conviction that I had left him much impressed in our favor."

The first witnesses examined by the council, were persons sent expressly as delegates from Liverpool, who had not only been themselves in the trade, but were at that time interested in it. They endeavored to show that none of the enormities charged belonged to it; that it was attended with circumstances highly favorable to the Africans; that it was so vitally connected with the manufacturing and commercial interests of the country that it would be almost national ruin to abolish it. A few, but highly respectable witnesses upon the other side were called before the council, and contributed to counteract the testimony of the Liverpool delegates. The inquiry continued for four months, during which time the petitions from the people to parliament had increased to one hundred and three.

CHAPTER XIV.

PARLIAMENTARY HISTORY.—THE TWENTY YEARS' STRUGGLE.

Mr. Pitt introduces the subject of the Abolition of the Slave-Trade into the House of Commons, May 9, 1788.—Speech of Mr. Pitt on the occasion.—Parliamentary action in 1789.—Debate of 12th of May.—Speech of William Wilberforce.—Travels and exertions of Clarkson.—Sessions of 1791 and 1792.—Debates in the Commons.—Speeches of Wilberforce, Pitt, Fox, Bailie, Thornton, Whitbread, Dundas, and Jenkinson.—Gradual abolition agreed upon by House of Commons.

MR. WILBERFORCE had been preparing to introduce the subject into the House of Commons when he was taken so ill that his life was despaired of. Under these circumstances, his friend Mr. Pitt, then chancellor of the exchequer and prime minister, undertook to supply his place. On the 9th of May, 1788, he opened the business in the house.

Mr. Pitt arose : He said he intended to move a resolution relative to a subject which was of more importance than any which had ever been agitated in that house. This honor he should not have had, but for a circumstance which he could not but deeply regret, the severe indisposition of his friend Mr. Wilberforce, in whose hands every measure which belonged to justice, humanity, and the national interest, was peculiarly well placed. The subject in question was no less than that of the slave-trade. It was obvious from the great number of petitions which had been presented concerning it, how much it had engaged the public attention, and consequently how much it deserved the serious notice of that house, and how much it became their duty to take some measure concerning it. But whatever was done on such a subject, every one would agree, ought to be done with the maturest deliberation. Two opinions had prevailed without doors, as appeared from the language of the different petitions. It had been pretty generally thought that the African slave-trade ought to be abolished. There were others, however, who thought it only stood in need of regulations. But all had agreed that it ought not to remain as it stood at present. But that measure which it might be the most proper to take, could only be discovered by a cool, patient, and diligent examination of the subject in all its circumstances, relations, and consequences. This had induced him to form an opinion that the present was not the proper time for discussing it ; for the session was now far advanced, and there was also a want of proper materials for the full information of the house. It would, he thought, be better discussed, when it might produce some useful debate, and when that inquiry which had been instituted by his majesty's ministers, (he meant the examination by a committee of privy council,) should be brought to such a state of maturity as to make it fit that the result of it should be laid before the house. That inquiry, he trusted, would facilitate their investigation, and enable them the better to proceed to a decision, which should be equally founded on principles of humanity, justice, and sound policy. As there was not a probability of reaching so desirable an end in the present state of business, he meant to move a resolution to pledge the house to the discussion of the question early in the next session. If by that time his honorable friend should be recovered, which he hoped would be the case, then he (Mr Wilberforce) would take the lead in it ; but should it unfortunately happen otherwise, then he (the chancellor of the exchequer) pledged himself to bring forward some proposition concerning it. The house, however, would observe that he had studiously avoided giving any opinion of his own on this great subject. He thought it wiser to defer this till the time of the discussion should arrive. He concluded with moving, after having read the names of the places from whence the different petitions had come, "That this house will, early in the next session of parliament, proceed to take into consideration the circumstances of the slave-trade complained of in the said petitions, and what may be fit to be done thereupon."

The motion of Mr. Pitt was warmly discussed, and at considerable length.

The principal speakers upon it were Mr. Fox, Mr. Burke, Sir William Dolben, Lord Penrhyn, and Mr. Gascoyn. The two last were members from Liverpool, and were strongly opposed to meddling with the question of the abolition of the slave-trade at any time.

Mr. Fox wished that there might be no delay; he said he was sorry the consideration of the question, but more particularly where so much human suffering was concerned, should be put off to another session, when it was obvious that no advantage could be gained by delay.

At length, when the question was put, the resolution was agreed to unanimously. Thus ended the first discussion that ever took place in the commons on this important subject. This debate, though many of the persons concerned in it abstained cautiously from entering into the merits of the general question, became interesting in consequence of circumstances attending it. Several rose up at once to give relief, as it were, to their feelings by utterance; but by so doing, they were prevented, many of them, from being heard. They who were heard, spoke with peculiar energy, as if warmed in an extraordinary manner by the subject. There was an apparent enthusiasm in behalf of the injured Africans. It was supposed by some that there was a moment in which, if the chancellor of the exchequer had moved for an immediate abolition of the trade, he would have carried it that night.

About this time, Mr. Clarkson brought out his powerful essay on the impolicy of the slave-trade, which was circulated in great numbers by the committee. Their efforts had aroused the feelings of the whole English nation, and had attracted the notice of many distinguished persons throughout Europe and America. As soon as the session was over, Mr. Clarkson again undertook a journey, visiting all the seaports between Kent and Cornwall. His object was to find out new witnesses to strengthen the cause, and form auxiliary committees. The committee, meantime, were indefatigable; they had addressed the rulers of Spain, Portugal, and Sweden; they had circulated five new works, besides the engraving which we have copied of the interior of a slave ship, exhibiting the closely packed bodies of the negroes.

On the 19th of March, 1789, Mr. Wilberforce moved in the House of Commons that the house should, on the 29th of April, take into consideration its resolution of the last session. The motion was agreed to, but it was the signal for all those who supposed themselves interested in the continuance of the trade, such as merchants, planters, manufacturers, mortgagees, and others, to begin a tremendous opposition. Meetings were called, and frightful resolutions passed. The public papers were filled with them; and pamphlets issued, filled with the most bitter invectives against all engaged in the movement. Emancipation was industriously confounded with the abolition of the trade. Compensation was demanded in a monstrous degree. The cry was such that many began to be staggered about the propriety of the total abolition of the trade. Calculations exhibited that the number of slaves in the British West Indies amounted to 410,000, and that to keep up that number the annual importation of 10,000 was required; that the English procured in Africa 30,000 annually, and therefore could sell 20,000 to other nations; that in the prosecution of this trade, English manufactures to the amount of above £800,000 sterling were exported, and above £1,400,000 in value obtained in return, and that the government received £256,000 annually by the slave tax.

The report of the privy council, consisting of the examinations before mentioned, was laid before the house, and that all might have a chance to examine it, Mr. Pitt moved that the consideration of the subject be postponed from the 29th of April to the 12th of May.

At length the 12th of May arrived. Mr. Wilberforce rose up in the commons, and moved the order of the day for the house to resolve itself into a committee of the whole house, to take into consideration the petitions which had been presented against the slave-trade.

This order having been read, he moved that the report of the committee of privy council; that the acts passed in the islands relative to slaves; that the evidence adduced last year on the slave-trade; that the petitions offered in the last session against the slave-trade; and that the accounts presented to the house, in the last and present session, relative to the exports and imports to Africa, be referred to the same committee.

These motions having been severally agreed to, the house immediately resolved itself into a committee of the whole house, and Sir William Dolben was put into the chair.

Mr. Wilberforce began by declaring that when he considered how much discussion the subject, which he was about to explain to the committee, had occasioned not only in that house but throughout the kingdom, and throughout Europe; and when he considered the extent and importance of it, the variety of interests involved in it, and the consequences which might arise, he owned he had been filled with apprehensions, lest a subject of such magnitude and a cause of such weight should suffer from the weakness of its advocate; but when he recollected that in the progress of his inquiries he had every where been received with candor, that most people gave him credit for the purity of his motives, and that, however many of these might then differ from him, they were all likely to agree in the end, he had dismissed his fears and marched forward with a firmer step in this cause of humanity, justice and religion. He could not, however, but lament that the subject had excited so much warmth. He feared that too many on this account were but ill prepared to consider it with impartiality. He entreated all such to endeavor to be calm and composed. A fair and cool discussion was essentially necessary. The motion he meant to offer was as reconcileable to political expediency as to national humanity. It belonged to no party question. It would in the end be found serviceable to all parties; and to the best interests of the country. He did not come forward to accuse the West India planter, or the Liverpool merchant, or indeed any one concerned in this traffic; but, if blame attached any where, to take shame to himself, in common, indeed, with the whole parliament of Great Britain, who, having suffered it to be carried on under their own authority, were all of them participators in the guilt.

In endeavoring to explain the great business of the day, he said he should call the attention of the house only to the leading features of the slave-trade. Nor should he dwell long upon these. Every one might imagine for himself what must be the natural consequence of such a commerce with Africa. Was it not plain that she must suffer from it? that her savage manners must be rendered still more ferocious? and that a trade of this nature carried on round her coasts, must extend violence and desolation to her very centre? It was well known that the natives of Africa were sold as goods, and that numbers of them were continually conveyed away from their country by the owners of British vessels. The question then was, which way the latter came by them. In answer to this question, the privy council report, which was then on the table, afforded evidence the most satisfactory and conclusive. He had found things in it, which had confirmed every proposition he had maintained before, whether this proposition had been gathered from living information of the best authority, or from the histories he had read. But it was unnecessary either to quote the report, or to appeal to history on this occasion. Plain reason and common sense would point out how the poor Africans were obtained. Africa was a country divided into many kingdoms, which had different governments and laws. In many parts the princes were despotic. In others they had a limited rule. But in all of them, whatever the nature of the government was, men were considered as goods and property, and, as such, subject to plunder in the same manner as property in other countries. The persons in power there were naturally fond of our commodities; and to obtain them (which could only be done by the sale of their countrymen) they waged war on one another, or even ravaged their own country when they could find no pretense for quarreling with their neighbors; in their courts of law many poor wretches who were innocent were condemned; and to obtain these commodities in greater abundance, thousands were kidnapped, and torn from their families, and sent into slavery. Such transactions, he said, were recorded in every history of Africa, and the report on the table confirmed them. With respect, however, to these, he should make but one or two observations. If we looked into the reign of Henry the Eighth, we should find a parallel for one of them. We should find that similar convictions took place; and that penalties followed conviction. With respect to wars, the kings of Africa were never induced to engage in them by public principles, by national glory, and least of all, by the love of their people. This had been stated by those most conversant with the subject, by Dr. Spaarman and Mr. Wadstrom. They had conversed with these princes, and had learned from their own mouths, that to procure slaves was the object of their hostilities. Indeed, there was scarcely a single person examined before the privy council, who did not prove that the slave-trade was the source of the tragedies acted upon that extensive continent. Some had endeavored to palliate this circumstance; but there was not one who did not more or less admit it to be true. By one the slave-trade was called the concurrent cause, by the majority it was acknowledged to be the principal motive of the African wars. The same might be said with respect o those instances of treachery and injustice in which individuals were concerned. And here he was sorry to observe that our own countrymen were often guilty. He would only at present advert to the tragedy at Calabar, where two large African villages, having been for some time at war, made peace. This peace was to have been ratified by intermarriages; but some of our captains who were there, seeing the trade would be stopped for a while, sowed dissension again between them. They actually set one village against he other, took a share in the contest, massacred many of the inhabitants, and carried others of them away as slaves. But shocking as this transaction might appear, there was not a single history of Africa to be read, in which scenes of as atrocious a nature were not related. They, he said, who defended this trade, were warped and blinded by their own interests, and would not be convinced of the miseries they were daily heaping on their fellow-creatures. By the countenance they gave it, they had reduced the inhabitants of Africa to a worse state than that of the most barbarous nation. They had destroyed what ought to have been the bond of union and safety among them : they had introduced discord and anarchy among them : they had set kings against their subjects, and subjects against each other : they had rendered every private family wretched : they had, in short, given birth to scenes of injustice and misery not to be found in any other quarter of the globe.

Having said thus much on the subject of procuring slaves in Africa, he would now go to that of the transportation of them. And here he had fondly hoped, that when men with affections and feelings like our own had been torn from their country, and every thing dear to them, he should have found some mitigation of their sufferings; but the sad reverse was the case. This was the most wretched part of the whole subject. He was incapable of impressing the house with what he felt upon it. A description of their conveyance was impossible. So much misery condensed in so little room was more than the human imagination had ever before conceived. Think only of six hundred persons linked together, trying to get rid of each other, crammed in a close vessel with every object that was nauseous and disgusting, diseased, and struggling with all the varieties of wretchedness. It seemed impossible to add any thing more to human misery. Yet, shocking as this description must be felt to be by every man, the transportation had been described by several witnesses from Liverpool to be a comfortable conveyance. Mr. Norris had painted the accommodations on board a slave-ship in the most glowing colors. He had represented them in a manner which would have exceeded his attempts at praise of the most luxurious scenes. Their apartments, he said, were fitted up as advantageously for them as circumstances could possibly admit : they had several meals a day ; some, of their own country provisions, with the best sauces of African cookery ; and, by way of variety, another meal of pulse, according to the European taste. After breakfast they had water to wash themselves, while their apartments were perfumed with frankincense and lime-juice. Before dinner they were amused after the manner of their country : instruments of music were introduced : the song and the dance were promo-

13

ted : games of chance were furnished them : the men played and sang, while the women and girls made fanciful ornaments from beads, with which they were plentifully supplied. They were indulged in all their little fancies, and kept in sprightly humor. Another of them had said, when the sailors were flogged, it was out of the hearing of the Africans, lest it should depress their spirits. He by no means wished to say that such descriptions were wilful misrepresentations. If they were not, it proved that interest or prejudice was capable of spreading a film over the eyes thick enough to occasion total blindness.

Others, however, and these men of the greatest veracity, had given a different account. What would the house think, when by the concurring testimony of these the true history was laid open? The slaves, who had been described as rejoicing in their captivity, were so wrung with misery at leaving their country, that it was the constant practice to set sail in the night, lest they should know the moment of their departure. With respect to their accommodation, the right ankle of one was fastened to the left ankle of another by an iron fetter ; and if they were turbulent, by another on the wrists. Instead of the apartments described, they were placed in niches, and along the decks, in such a manner that it was impossible for any one to pass among them, however careful he might be, without treading upon them. Sir George Yonge had testified, that in a slave-ship, on board of which he went, and which had not completed her cargo by two hundred and fifty, instead of the scent of frankincense being perceptible to the nostrils, the stench was intolerable. The allowance of water was so deficient that the slaves were frequently found gasping for life, and almost suffocated. The pulse with which they had been said to be favored, were absolutely English horse beans. The legislature of Jamaica had stated the scantiness both of water and provisions, as a subject which called for the interference of parliament. As Mr. Norris had said the song and the dance were promoted, he could not pass over these expressions without telling the house what they meant. It would have been much more fair if he himself had explained the word *promoted*. The truth was, that for the sake of exercise, the miserable wretches, loaded with chains and oppressed with disease, were forced to dance by the terror of the lash, and sometimes by the actual use of it. "I," said one of the evidences, "was employed to dance the men, while another person danced the women." Such, then, was the meaning of the word *promoted;* and it might also be observed, with respect to food, that instruments were sometimes carried out in order to force them to eat ; which was the same sort of proof how much they enjoyed themselves in this instance also. With respect to their singing, it consisted of songs of lamentation for the loss of their country. While they sung they were in tears : so that one of the captains, more humane probably than the rest, threatened a woman with a flogging because the mournfulness of her song was too painful for his feelings. Perhaps he could not give a better proof of the sufferings of these injured people, during their passage, than by stating the mortality which accompanied it. This was a species of evidence which was infallible on this occasion. Death was a witness which could not deceive them; and the proportion of deaths would not only confirm, but, if possible, even aggravate our suspicion of the misery of the transit. It would be found, upon an average of all the ships upon which evidence had been given, that, exclusively of such as perished before they sailed from Africa, not less than twelve and a half per cent. died on their passage : besides these, the Jamaica report stated that four and a half per cent. died while in the harbors, or on shore before the day of sale, which was only about the space of twelve or fourteen days after their arrival there ; and one-third more died in the seasoning : and this in a climate exactly similar to their own, and where, as some of the witnesses pretended, they were healthy and happy. Thus, out of every lot of one hundred shipped from Africa, seventeen died in about nine weeks, and not more than fifty lived to become efficient laborers in our islands.

Having advanced thus far in his investigation, he felt, he said, the wickedness of the slave-trade to be so enormous, so dreadful, and irremediable, that he could stop at no alternative short of its abolition. A trade founded on iniquity, and carried on with such circumstances of horror, must be abolished, let the policy of it be what it might; and he had from this time determined, whatever were the consequences, that he would never rest till he had effected that abolition. His mind had indeed been harassed by the objections of the West India planters, who had asserted that the ruin of their property must be the consequence·of such a measure. He could not help, however, distrusting their arguments. He could not believe that the Almighty being, who had forbidden the practice of rapine and bloodshed, had made rapine and bloodshed necessary to any part of his universe. He felt a confidence in this persuasion, and took the resolution to act upon it. Light, indeed, soon broke in upon him. The suspicion of his mind was every day confirmed by increasing information, and the evidence he had now to offer upon this point was decisive and complete. The principle upon which he founded the necessity of the abolition was not policy, but justice : but, though justice were the principle of the measure, yet he trusted he should distinctly prove it to be reconcilable with our truest political interest.

In the first place, he asserted that the number of the slaves in the West India islands might be kept up without the introduction of recruits from Africa ; and to prove this, he would enumerate the different sources of their mortality. The first was the disproportion of the sexes, there being, upon an average, about five males imported to three females : but this evil, when the slave-trade was abolished, would cure itself. The second consisted in the bad condition in which they were brought to the islands, and the methods of preparing them for sale. They arrived frequently in a sickly and disordered state, and then they were made up for the market by the application of astringents, washes, mercurial ointments, and repelling drugs, so that their wounds might be hid These artifices were not only fraudulent, but fatal; but these, it was obvious, would of themselves fall with the trade. A third was, excessive labor joined with improper food ; and a fourth was, the extreme dissoluteness of their manners. These also would both of them be counteracted by the impossibility of getting further supplies; for owners, now unable to replace those slaves whom they might lose, by speedy purchase in the markets, would be more careful how they treated them in future, and better treatment would be productive of better morals. And here he would just advert to an argument used against those who complained of cruelty in our islands, which was, that it was the interest of masters to treat their slaves with humanity; but surely it was immediate and present, not future and distant, interest, which was the great spring of action in the affairs of mankind. Why did we make laws to punish men? It was their interest to be upright and virtuous; but there was a present impulse continually breaking in upon their better judgment, and an impulse which was known to be contrary to their permanent advantage. It was ridiculous to say that men would be bound by their interest, when gain or ardent passion urged them. It might as well be asserted that a stone could not be thrown into the air, or a body move from place to place, because the principle of gravitation bound them to the surface of the earth. If a planter in the West Indies found himself reduced in his profits, he did not usually dispose of any part of his slaves; and his own gratifications were never given up so long as there was a possibility of making any retrenchment in the allowance of his slaves. But to return to the subject which he had left: He was happy to state, that as all the causes of the decrease which he had stated might be remedied, so, by the progress of light and reformation, these remedies had been gradually coming into practice; and that, as these had increased, the decrease of slaves had in an equal proportion been lessened. By the gradual adoption of these remedies, he could prove from the report on the table, that the decrease of slaves in Jamaica had lessened to such a degree, that from the year 1774 to the present it was not quite one in a hundred, and that in fact they were at present in a state of increase; for that the births on that island, at this moment, exceeded the deaths by one thousand or eleven hundred per annum. Barbadoes, Nevis, Antigua, and the Bermudas were, like Jamaica, lessening their decrease, and holding forth an evident and reasonable expectation of a speedy state of increase by natural population. But allowing the number of negroes even to decrease for a time, there were methods which would insure the welfare of the West India islands. The lands there might be cultivated by fewer hands, and this to greater advantage to the proprietors and to this country, by the produce of cinnamon, coffee, and cotton, than by that of sugar. The produce of the plantations might also be considerably increased, even in the case of sugar, with less hands than were at present employed, if the owners of them would but introduce machines of husbandry. Mr. Long himself, long resident as a planter, had proved, upon his own estate, that the plow, though so little used in the West Indies, did the service of a hundred slaves, and caused the same ground to produce three hogsheads of sugar, which, when cultivated by slaves, would only produce two. The division of work, which, in free and civilized countries, was the grand source of wealth, and the reduction of the number of domestic servants, of whom not less than from twenty to forty were kept in ordinary families, afforded other resources for this purpose. But granting that all these suppositions should be unfounded, and that every one of these substitutes should fail for a time, the planters would be indemnified, as is the case in all transactions of commerce, by the increased price of their produce in the British market. Thus, by contending against the abolition, they were defeated in every part of the argument. But he would never give up the point, that the number of slaves could be kept up by natural population, and without any dependence whatever on the slave-trade. He therefore called upon the house again to abolish it as a criminal waste of life; it was utterly unnecessary; he had proved it so by documents contained in the report. The merchants of Liverpool, indeed, had thought otherwise, but he should be cautious how he assented to their opinions. They declared last year that it was a losing trade at two slaves to a ton, and yet they pursued it when restricted to five slaves to three tons. He believed, however, that it was upon the whole a losing concern; in the same manner as the lottery would be a losing adventure to any company who should buy all the tickets. Here and there an individual gained a large prize, but the majority of adventurers gained nothing. The same merchants, too, had asserted that the town of Liverpool would be ruined by the abolition. But Liverpool did not depend for its consequence upon the slave-trade. The whole export tonnage from that place amounted to no less than 170,000 tons, whereas the export part of it to Africa amounted only to 13,000. Liverpool, he was sure, owed its greatness to other and very different causes; the slave-trade bearing but a small proportion to its other trades.

Having gone through that part of the subject which related to the slaves, he would now answer two objections which he had frequently heard started. The first of these was, that the abolition of the slave-trade would operate to the total ruin of our navy, and to the increase of that of our rivals. For an answer to these assertions, he referred to what he considered to be the most valuable part of the report, and for which the house and the country were indebted to the indefatigable exertions of Mr. Clarkson. By the report, it appeared that instead of the slave-trade being a nursery for British seamen, it was their grave. It appeared that more seamen died in that trade in one year than in the whole remaining trade of the country in two. Out of 910 sailors in it, 216 died in the year, while upon a fair average of the same number of men employed in the trades to the East and West Indies, Petersburgh, Newfoundland, and Greenland, no more than 87 died. It appeared also, that out of 3,170, who had left Liverpool in the slave-ships in the year 1787, only 1,428 had returned. And here, while he lamented the loss which the country thus annually sustained in her seamen, he had additionally to lament the barbarous usage which they experienced, and which this trade, by the natural tendency to harden the heart, exclusively produced. He would just read an extract of a letter from Governor Parry, of Barbadoes, to Lord Sydney, one of the secretaries of state. The governor declared that he could no longer contain himself on account of the ill treatment which the British sailors endured at the hands of their savage captains. These were obliged to have their vessels strongly manned, not only on account of the unhealthiness of the climate of Africa, but of the necessity of guarding the slaves, and preventing and suppressing insurrections; and when they arrived in the West Indies, and were out of all danger from the latter, they quarreled with their men on the most frivolous pretenses, on purpose to discharge them, and thus save the payment of supernumerary wages home. Thus many were left in a diseased and deplorable state, either to perish by sickness, or to enter into foreign service; great numbers of whom were forever lost to their country. The governor concluded by declaring that the enormities attendant on this trade were so great as to demand the immediate interference of the legislature.

The next objection to the abolition was, that if we were to relinquish the slave-trade, our rivals, the French, would take it up; so that while we should suffer by the measure, the evil would still go on, and this even to its former extent. This was, indeed, a very weak argument; and, if it would defend the continuance of the slave-trade, might equally be urged in favor of robbery, murder, and every species of wickedness, which, if we did not practice, others would commit. But suppose, for the sake of argument, that they were to take it up, what good would it do them? What advantages, for instance, would they derive from this pestilential commerce to their marine? Should not we, on the other hand, be benefited by this change? Would they not be obliged to come to us, in consequence of the cheapness of our manufactures, for what they wanted for the African market? But he would not calumniate the French nation so much as to suppose that they would carry on the trade if we were to relinquish it. He believed, on the other hand, that they would abolish it also. Mr. Necker, the present minister of France, was a man of religious principle; and, in his work upon the administration of the finances, had recorded his abhorrence of this trade. He was happy also to relate an anecdote of the present king of France, which proved that he was a friend to the abolition; for, being petitioned to dissolve a society, formed at Paris, for the annihilation of the slave-trade, his majesty answered that he would not, and was happy to hear that so humane an association was formed in his dominions. And here, having mentioned the society in Paris, he could not help paying a due compliment to that established in London for the same purpose, which had labored with the greatest assiduity to make this important subject understood, and which had conducted itself with so much judgment and moderation as to have interested men of all religions, and to have united them in their cause.

There was another topic which he would submit to the notice of the house before he concluded. They were, perhaps, not aware that a fair and honorable trade might be substituted in the natural productions of Africa, so that our connection with that continent in the way of commercial advantage need not oe lost. The natives had already made some advances in it; and if they had not appeared so forward in raising and collecting their own produce for sale as in some other countries, it was to be imputed to the slave-trade; but remove the cause, and Africa would soon emerge from her present ignorant and indolent state. Civilization would go on with her as well as with other nations.

Europe, three or four centuries ago, was in many parts as barbarous as Africa at present, and chargeable with as bad practices. For what would be said, if, so late as the middle of the thirteenth century, he could find a parallel there for the slave-trade? Yes. This parallel was to be found even in England. The people of Bristol, in the reign of Henry the Seventh, had a regular market for children, which were bought by the Irish; but the latter having experienced a general calamity, which they imputed as a judgment from heaven on account of this wicked traffic, abolished it. The only thing, therefore, which he had to solicit of the house, was to show that they are now as enlightened as the Irish were four centuries back, by refusing to buy the children of other nations. He hoped they would do it. He hoped, too, they would do it in an unqualified manner. Nothing less than a total abolition of the trade would do away the evils complained of. The legislature of Jamaica, indeed, had thought that regulations might answer the purpose. Their report had recommended that no person should be kidnapped, or permitted to be made a slave, contrary to the customs of Africa. But might he not be reduced to this state very unjustly, and yet by no means contrary to the African laws? Besides, how could we distinguish between those who were justly or unjustly reduced to it? Could we discover them by their physiognomy? But if we could, who would believe that the British captains would be influenced by any regulations made in this country, to refuse to purchase those who had not been fairly, honestly, and uprightly enslaved? They who were offered to us for sale were brought, some of them, three or four thousand miles, and exchanged like cattle from one to another, till they reached the coast. But who could return these to their homes, or make them compensation for their sufferings during their long journeyings? He would now conclude by begging pardon of the house for having detained them so long. He could indeed have expressed his own convictions in fewer words. He needed only to have made one or two short statements, and to have quoted the commandment, "Thou shalt do no murder." But he thought it his duty to lay the whole of the case, and the whole of its guilt before them. They would see now that no mitigations, no palliatives, would either be efficient or admissible. Nothing short of an absolute abolition could be adopted. This they owed to Africa; they owed it, too, to their own moral characters. And he hoped they would follow up the principle of one of the repentant African captains, who had gone before the committee of privy council as a voluntary witness, and that they would make Africa all the atonement in their power for the multifarious injuries she had received at the hands of British subjects. With respect to these injuries, their enormity and extent, it might be alleged in their excuse, that they were not fully acquainted with them till that moment, and therefore not answerable for their former existence; but now they could no longer plead ignorance concerning them. They had seen them brought directly before their eyes, and they must decide for themselves, and must justify to the world and their own consciences the facts and principles upon which their decision was formed.

Mr. Wilberforce having concluded his speech, which lasted three hours and a half, read, and laid on the table of the house, as subjects for their future discussion, nine propositions, which he had deduced from the evidence contained in the privy council report, and of which the following is the abridged substance:

1. That the number of slaves annually carried from the coast of Africa, in British vessels, was about 38,000, of which, on an average, 22,500 were carried to the British islands, and that of the latter, only 17,500 were retained there.

2. That these slaves, according to the evidence on the table, consisted, first, of prisoners of war; secondly, of free persons sold for debt, or on account of real or imputed crimes, particularly adultery and witchcraft; in which cases they were frequently sold with their whole families, and sometimes for the profit of those by whom they were condemned; thirdly, of domestic slaves sold for the profit of their masters, in some places at the will of the masters, and in others, on being condemned by them for real or imputed crimes; fourthly, of persons made slaves by various acts of oppression, violence, or fraud, committed either by the princes and chiefs of those countries on their subjects, or by private individuals on each other; or, lastly, by Europeans engaged in this traffic.

3. That the trade so carried on had necessarily a tendency to occasion frequent and cruel wars among the natives; to produce unjust convictions and punishments for pretended or aggravated crimes; to encourage acts of oppression, violence, and fraud, and to obstruct the natural course of civilization and improvement in those countries.

4. That Africa, in its present state, furnished several valuable articles of commerce which were partly peculiar to itself, but that it was adapted to the production of others, with which we were now either wholly, or in great part, supplied by foreign nations. That an extensive commerce with Africa might be substituted in these commodities, so as to afford a return for as many articles as had annually been carried thither in British vessels; and, lastly, that such a commerce might reasonably be expected to increase by the progress of civilization there.

5. That the slave-trade was peculiarly destructive to the seamen employed in it; and that the mortality there had been much greater than in any British vessels employed upon the same coast in any other service or trade.

6. That the mode of transporting the slaves from Africa to the West Indies necessarily exposed them to many and grievous sufferings, for which no regulations could provide an adequate remedy; and that in consequence thereof a large proportion had annually perished during the voyage.

7. That a large proportion had also perished in the harbors in the West Indies, from the diseases contracted in the voyage and the treatment of the same, previously to their being sold, and that this loss amounted to four and a half per cent. of the imported slaves.

8. That the loss of the newly imported slaves, within the three first years after their importation, bore a large proportion to the whole number imported.

9. That the natural increase of population among the slaves in the islands appeared to have been impeded principally by the following causes: First, by the inequality of the sexes in the importations from Africa. Secondly, by

the general dissoluteness of manners among the slaves, and the want of proper regulations for the encouragement of marriages and of rearing children among them. Thirdly, by the particular diseases which were prevalent among them, and which were in some instances to be attributed to too severe labor, or rigorous treatment, and in others to insufficient or improper food. Fourthly, by those diseases which affected a large proportion of negro children in their infancy, and by those to which the negroes newly imported from Africa had been found to be particularly liable.

These propositions having been laid upon the table of the house, lord Penrhyn rose in behalf of the planters, and next after him, Mr. Gascoyne, (both members for Liverpool,) in behalf of the merchants concerned in the latter place. They both predicted the ruin and misery which would inevitably follow the abolition of the trade. The former said that no less than seventy millions were mortgaged upon lands in the West Indies, all of which would be lost. Mr. Wilberforce therefore should have made a motion to pledge the house to the repayment of this sum before he had brought forward his propositions. Compensation ought to have been agreed upon as a previously necessary measure. The latter said that in consequence of the bill of last year, many ships were laid up and many seamen out of employ. His constituents had large capitals engaged in the trade, and if it were to be wholly done away, they would suffer from not knowing where to employ them. They both joined in asserting that Mr. Wilberforce had made so many misrepresentations in all the branches of this subject, that no reliance whatever was to be placed on the picture which he had chosen to exhibit. They should speak, however, more fully to this point when the propositions were discussed.

The latter declaration called up Mr. Wilberforce again, who observed that he had no intention of misrepresenting any fact. He did not know that he had done it in any one instance; but, if he had, it would be easy to convict him out of the report upon the table.

Mr. Burke then arose : He would not, he said, detain the committee long. Indeed he was not able, weary and indisposed as he then felt himself, even if he had an inclination to do it; but as, on account of his other parliamentary duty, he might not have it in his power to attend the business now before them in its course, he would take that opportunity of stating his opinion upon it.

And, first, the house, the nation, and all Europe were under great obligations to Mr. Wilberforce for having brought this important subject forward. He had done it in a manner the most masterly, impressive, and eloquent. He had laid down his principles so admirably, and with so much order and force, that his speech had equaled any thing he had ever heard in modern oratory, and perhaps it had not been excelled by any thing to be found in ancient times. As to the slave-trade itself, there could not be two opinions about it where men were not interested. A trade, begun in savage war, prosecuted with unheard of barbarity, continued during the transportation with the most loathsome imprisonment, and ending in perpetual exile and slavery, was a trade so horrid in all its circumstances that it was impossible to produce a single argument in its favor. On the ground of prudence, nothing could be said in defense of it, nor could it be justified by necessity. It was necessity alone that could be brought to justify inhumanity; but no case of necessity could be made out strong enough to justify this monstrous traffic. It was therefore the duty of the house to put an end to it, and this without further delay.

With respect to the consequences mentioned by the two members for Liverpool, he had a word or two to offer upon them. Lord Penrhyn had talked of millions to be lost and paid for. But seeing no probability of any loss ultimately, he could see no necessity for compensation. He believed, on the other hand, that the planters would be great gainers by those wholesome regulations which they would be obliged to make if the slave-trade were abolished. He did not, however, flatter them with the idea that this gain would be immediate. Perhaps they might experience inconveniences at first, and even some loss. But what then? With their loss, their virtue would be the greater. And in this light he hoped the house would consider the matter; for, if they were called upon to do an act of virtuous energy and heroism, they ought to think it right to submit to temporary disadvantages for the sake of truth, justice, humanity, and the prospect of greater happiness.

The other member, Mr. Gascoyne, had said that his constituents, if the trade were abolished, could not employ their capitals elsewhere. But whether they could or not, it was the duty of that house, if they put them into a traffic which was shocking to humanity and disgraceful to the nation, to change their application, and not to allow them to be used to a barbarous purpose. He believed, however, that the merchants of Liverpool would find no difficulty on this head. All capitals required active motion. It was in their nature not to remain passive and unemployed. They would soon turn them into other channels. This they had done themselves during the American war; for the slave-trade was then almost wholly lost, and yet they had their ships employed, either as transports in the service of government, or in other ways.

As he now called upon the house not to allow any conjectural losses to become impediments in the way of the abolition of the slave-trade, so he called upon them to beware how they suffered any representations of the happiness of the state of slavery in our islands to influence them against so glorious a measure. Nothing made a happy slave but a degraded man. In proportion as the mind grows callous to its degradation, and all sense of manly pride is lost, the slave feels comfort. In fact, he is no longer a man. If he were to define a man, he would say with Shakspeare,

> "Man is a being holding large discourse,
> Looking before and after."

But a slave was incapable of looking before and after. He had no motive to do it. He was a mere passive instrument in the hands of others, to be used at their discretion. Though living, he was dead as to all voluntary agency. Though moving amidst the creation with an erect form, and with the shape and semblance of a human being, he was a nullity as a man.

Mr. Fox observed, that a trade in human flesh and sinews was so scandalous, that it ought not openly to be carried on by any government whatever, and much less by that of a Christian country. With regard to the regulation of the slave-trade, he knew of no such thing as a regulation of robbery and murder. There was no medium. The legislature must either abolish it, or plead guilty of all the wickedness which had been shown to attend it. He would say a word or two with respect to the conduct of foreign nations on this subject. It was possible that these, when they heard that the matter had been discussed in that house, might follow the example, or they might go before us and set one themselves. If this were to happen, though we might be the losers, humanity would be the gainer. He himself had been thought sometimes to use expressions relative to France which were too harsh, and as if he could only treat her as the enemy of this country. Politically speaking, France was our rival. But he well knew the distinction between political enmity and illiberal prejudice. If there was any great and enlightened nation in Europe, it was France, which was as likely as any country upon the face of the globe to catch a spark from the light of our fire, and to act upon the present subject with warmth and enthusiasm. France had often been improperly stimulated by her ambition; and he had no doubt but that, in the present instance, she would readily follow its honorable dictates.

Aldermen Newnham, Sawbridge, and Watson, though they wished well to the cause of humanity, could not, as representatives of the city of London, give their concurrence to a measure which would injure it so essentially as that of the abolition of the slave-trade. This trade might undoubtedly be put under wholesome regulations, and made productive of great commercial advantages. But if it were abolished, it would render the city of London one scene of bankruptcy and ruin. It became the house to take care, while they were giving way to the goodness of their hearts, that they did not contribute to the ruin of the mercantile interests of their country.

Mr. Martin stated that he was so well satisfied with the speech of the honorable gentleman who had introduced the propositions, and with the language held out by other distinguished members on this subject, that he felt himself more proud than ever of being an Englishman. He hoped and believed that the melancholy predictions of the worthy aldermen would not prove true, and that the citizens of London would have too much public spirit to wish that a great national object, which comprehended the great duties of humanity and justice, should be set aside, merely out of consideration to their own private interests.

Mr. William Smith would not detain the house long at that late hour upon this important subject; but he could not help testifying the great satisfaction he felt at the manner in which the honorable gentleman who opened the debate (if it could be so called) had treated it. He approved of the propositions as the best mode of bringing the decision to a happy issue. He gave Mr. Fox great credit for the open and manly way in which he had manifested his abhorrence of this trade, and for the support he meant to give to the total and unqualified abolition of it; for he was satisfied that the more it was inquired into, the more it would be found that nothing short of abolition would cure the evil. With respect to certain assertions of the members for Liverpool, and certain melancholy predictions about the consequences of such an event, which others had held out, he desired to lay in his claim for observation upon them, when the great question should come before the house.

Soon after this the house broke up ; and the discussion of the propositions, which was the next parliamentary measure intended, was postponed to a future day, which was sufficiently distant to give all the parties concerned time to make the necessary preparations for it.

Of this interval the committee for the abolition availed themselves to thank Mr. Wilberforce for the very able and satisfactory manner in which he had stated to the house his propositions for the abolition of the slave-trade, and for the unparalleled assiduity and perseverance with which he had all along endeavored to accomplish this object, as well as to take measures themselves for the further promotion of it. Their opponents availed themselves of this interval also. But that which now embarrassed them, was the evidence contained in the privy council report. They had no idea, considering the number of witnesses they had sent to be examined, that this evidence, when duly weighed, could by right reasoning have given birth to the sentiments which had been displayed in the speeches of the most distinguished members of the house of commons, or to the contents of the propositions which had been laid upon their table. They were thunder-struck as it were by their own weakness: and from this time they were determined, if possible, to get rid of it as a standard for decision, or to interpose every parliamentary delay in their power.

On the twenty-first of May, the subject came again before the attention of the house. It was ushered in, as was expected, by petitions collected in the interim, and which were expressive of the frightful consequences which would attend the abolition of the slave-trade.

Mr. Wilberforce moved the order of the day, for the house to go into a committee of the whole house on the report of the privy council, and the several matters of evidence already upon the table relative to the slave-trade.

Mr. Alderman Sawbridge immediately arose, and asked Mr. Wilberforce if he meant to adduce any other evidence besides that in the privy council report in behalf of his propositions, or to admit other witnesses, if such could be found, to invalidate them. Mr. Wilberforce replied, that he was quite satisfied with the report on the table. It would establish all his propositions. He should call no witnesses himself : as to permission to others to call them, that must be determined by the house.

This question and this answer gave birth immediately to great disputes upon the subject. Aldermen Sawbridge, Newnham, and Watson ; Lords Penrhyn and Maitland ; Messrs. Gascoyne, Marsham, and others spoke against the admission of the evidence which had been laid upon the table. They contended that it was insufficient, defective, and contradictory ; that it was *ex parte* evidence ; that it had been manufactured by ministers ; that it was founded chiefly on hearsay, and that the greatest part of it was false ; that it had undergone no cross-examination; that it was unconstitutional; and that, if they admitted it, they would establish a dangerous precedent, and abandon their rights. It was urged on the other hand by Mr. Courtenay, that it could not be *ex parte* evidence, because it contained testimony on both sides of the question. The circumstance also of its being contradictory, which had been alleged against it, proved that it was the result of an impartial examination. Mr. Fox observed that it was perfectly admissible. He called upon those who took the other side of the question to say why, if it was really inadmissible, they had not opposed it at first. It had now been a long time on the table, and no fault had been found with it. The truth was, it did not suit them, and they were determined by a side wind as it were to put an end to the inquiry.

In the course of the debate much warmth of temper was manifest on both sides. The expression of Mr. Fox in a former debate, "that the slave-trade could not be regulated, because there could be no regulation of robbery and murder," was brought up, and construed by planters in the house as a charge of these crimes upon themselves. Mr. Fox, however, would not retract the expression. He repeated it. He had no notion, however, that any individual would have taken it to himself. If it contained any reflection at all, it was on the whole parliament who had sanctioned such a trade. Mr. Molyneux rose up, and animadverted severely on the character of Mr. Ramsay, one of the evidences in the privy council report, during his residence in the West Indies. This called up Sir William Dolben and Sir Charles Middleton in his defense, the latter of whom bore honorable testimony to his virtues from an intimate acquaintance with him, and a residence in the same village with him for twenty years. Mr. Molyneux spoke also in angry terms of the measure of the abolition. To annihilate the trade, he said, and to make no compensation on account of it, was an act of swindling. Mr. Macnamara called the measure hypocritical, fanatic, and methodistical. Mr. Pitt was so irritated at the insidious attempt to set aside the privy council report, when no complaint had been alleged against it before, that he was quite off his guard, and he thought it right afterwards to apologize for the warmth into which he had been betrayed. The speaker, too, was obliged frequently to interfere. On this occasion no less than thirty members spoke. And there had probably been few seasons when so much disorder had been discoverable in that house.

The result of the debate was, a permission to those interested in the continuance of the slave-trade to bring counsel to the bar on the twenty-sixth of May, and then to introduce such witnesses as might throw further light on the propositions in the shortest time: for Mr. Pitt only acquiesced in this new measure on a supposition "that there would be no unnecessary delay, as he could by no means submit to the ultimate procrastination of so important a business." He even hoped (and in this hope he was joined by Mr. Fox) that those concerned would endeavor to bring the whole of the evidence they meant to offer at the first examination.

On the day appointed, the house met for the purpose now specified; when Alderman Newnham, thinking that such an important question should not be decided but in a full assembly of the representatives of the nation, moved for a call of the house on that day fortnight. Mr. Wilberforce stated that he had no objection to such a measure, believing the greater the number present, the more favorable it would be to his cause. This motion, however, produced a debate and a division, in which it appeared that there were one hundred and fifty-eight in favor of it, and twenty-eight against it. The business of the day now commenced. The house went into a committee, and Sir William Dolben was put into the chair. Mr. Serjeant Le Blanc was then called in. He made an able speech in behalf of his clients; and introduced John Barnes, esquire, as his first witness, whose examination took up the remainder of the day. By this step they who were interested in the continuance of the trade attained their wishes, for they had now got possession of the ground with their evidence; and they knew they could keep it almost as long as they pleased, for the purposes of delay.

At length, on the ninth of June, by which time it was supposed that new light, and this in sufficient quantity, would have been thrown upon the propositions, it appeared that only two witnesses had been fully heard. The examinations, therefore, were continued, and they went on till the twenty-third. On this day, the order for the call of the house, which had been prolonged, standing unrepealed, there was a large attendance of members. A motion was then made to get rid of the business altogether, but it failed. It was now seen, however, that it was impossible to bring the question to a final decision in this session, for they who were interested in it affirmed that they had yet many important witnesses to introduce. Alderman Newnham, therefore, by the consent of Mr. Wilberforce, moved that "the further consideration of the subject be deferred to the next session."

At the next session, in January, 1790, Mr. Wilberforce carried a motion that witnesses should be examined in future in a committee-room, which should be open to all members. This was important, as the examinations otherwise might have taken up ten years. In the interim, Mr. Clarkson had again traversed the kingdom, and collected a respectable body of witnesses. He had visited over four hundred vessels. By the 20th of April, all the witnesses in favor of the trade had been examined, and an effort was made to have the case argued immediately, without hearing the evidence on the other side; but the eloquence of Wilberforce prevailed, supported powerfully by Pitt and Fox, and the witnesses for their side were also examined. The session closed before half the evidence deemed necessary was heard.

One circumstance occurred to keep up a hatred of the trade among the people in this interval, which, trivial as it was, ought not to be forgotten. The amiable poet Cowper had frequently made the slave-trade the subject of his contemplation. He had already severely condemned it in his valuable poem, The Task. But now he had written three little fugitive pieces upon it. Of these the most impressive was that which he called The Negro's Complaint, and of which the following is a copy:

Forced from home and all its pleasures,
   Afric's coast I left forlorn,
To increase a stranger's treasures,
   O'er the raging billows borne;
Men from England bought and sold me,
   Paid my price in paltry gold;
But, though theirs they have enroll'd me,
   Minds are never to be sold.

Still in thought as free as ever,
   What are England's rights, I ask,
Me from my delights to sever
   Me to torture, me to task?
Fleecy locks and black complexion
   Cannot forfeit Nature's claim;
Skins may differ, but affection
   Dwells in black and white the same.

Why did all creating Nature
   Make the plant, for which we toil?
Sighs must fan it, tears must water,
   Sweat of ours must dress the soil.
Think, ye masters, iron-hearted,
   Lolling at your jovial boards,
Think, how many backs have smarted
   For the sweets your cane affords.

Is there, as you sometimes tell us,
   Is there One, who rules on high?
Has He bid you buy and sell us,
   Speaking from his throne, the sky?
Ask Him, if your knotted scourges,
   Fetters, blood-extorting screws,
Are the means, which duty urges
   Agents of His will to use!

Hark! He answers. Wild tornadoes
   Strewing yonder sea with wrecks,
Wasting towns, plantations, meadows,
   Are the voice with which He speaks.
He, foreseeing what vexations
   Afric's sons should undergo,
Fix'd their tyrant's habitations
   Where his whirlwinds answer—No!

By our blood in Afric wasted,
   Ere our necks receiv'd the chain;
By the miseries, which we tasted
   Crossing, in your barks, the main;
By our sufferings, since you brought us
   To the man-degrading mart,
All sustain'd by patience, taught us
   Only by a broken heart.

Deem our nation brutes no longer,
   Till some reason you shall find
Worthier of regard, and stronger,
   Than the color of our kind.
Slaves of gold ! whose sordid dealings
   Tarnish all your boasted powers,
Prove that you have human feelings,
   Ere you proudly question ours.

This little piece, Cowper presented in manuscript to some of his friends in London ; and these conceiving it to contain a powerful appeal in behalf of the injured Africans, joined in printing it. Having ordered it on the finest hot pressed paper, and folded it up in a small and neat form, they gave it the printed title of " A Subject for Conversation at the Tea-table." After this, they sent many thousand copies of it in franks into the country. From one it spread to another, till it traveled almost over the whole island. Falling at length into the hands of the musician, it was set to music ; and it then found its way into the streets, both of the metropolis and of the country, where it was sung as a ballad, and where it gave a plain account of the subject, with an appropriate feeling to those who heard it.

Nor was the philanthropy of Mr. Wedgwood less instrumental in turning the popular feeling in favor of the cause. He made his manufactory contribute to  this end. He took the seal of the committee for his model ; and he produced a beautiful cameo, of a less size, of which the ground was a most delicate white, but the negro, who was seen imploring compassion in the middle of it, was in his own native color. Mr. Wedgwood made a liberal donation of these, when finished, among his friends. They, to whom they were sent, did not lay them up in their cabinets, but gave them away likewise. They were soon, like the Negro's Complaint, in different parts of the kingdom. Some had them inlaid in gold on the lid of their snuff-boxes. Of the ladies several wore them in bracelets, and others had them fitted up in an ornamental manner as pins for their hair. At length, the taste for wearing them became general ; and thus the fashion, which usually confines itself to worthless things, was seen for once in the honorable office of promoting the cause of justice, humanity, and freedom.

Mr. Clarkson again departed on another tour, and traveled from August, 1790, to February, 1791, and added new and important witnesses to his list. The examinations were resumed, and closed finally on the 4th of April. It is from this body of evidence, thus given, that we have quoted so extensively in former chapters. The evidence having been printed on both sides for the use of the members, the 18th of April was the day fixed upon for deciding the case. By this time every effort had been made to render the question unpopular in the commons. Indemnification, massacre, civil war, ruin, had been vociferated in the ears of members. At this time, unhappily, those sanguinary scenes described in another part of this volume, were taking place in

St. Domingo, in consequence of the revolution which had been effected there, and an insurrection had broken out in the British island of Dominica. All these had been industriously exaggerated in print, and produced a terrific effect upon many members. In this unfavorable frame of mind they went into the house on the day appointed.

On the eighteenth of April, 1791, Mr. Wilberforce made his motion. He began by expressing a hope that the present debate, instead of exciting asperity and confirming prejudice, would tend to produce a general conviction of the truth of what in fact was incontrovertible; that the abolition of the slave-trade was indispensably required of them, not only by morality and religion, but by sound policy. He stated that he should argue the matter from the evidence. He adverted to the character, situation, and means of information of his own witnesses; and having divided his subject into parts, the first of which related to the manner of reducing the natives of Africa to a state of slavery, he handled it in the following manner:

He would begin, he said, with the first boundary of the trade. Captain Wilson and Captain Hills, of his majesty's navy, and Mr. Dalrymple of the land service, had concurred in stating, that in the country contiguous to the river Senegal, when slave-ships arrived there, armed parties were regularly sent out in the evening, who scoured the country, and brought in their prey. The wretched victims were to be seen in the morning bound back to back in the huts on shore, whence they were conveyed, tied hand and foot, to the slave ships. The design of these ravages was obvious, because, when the slave-trade was stopped, they ceased. Mr. Kiernan spoke of the constant depredations by the Moors to procure slaves. Mr. Wadstrom confirmed them. The latter gentleman showed also that they were excited by presents of brandy, gunpowder, and such other incentives; and that they were not only carried on by one community against another, but that the kings were stimulated to practice them in their own territories, and on their own subjects: and in one instance a chieftain, who, when intoxicated, could not resist the demands of the slave-merchants, had expressed, in a moment of reason, a due sense of his own crime, and had reproached his christian seducers. Abundant also were the instances of private rapine. Individuals were kidnapped whilst in their fields and gardens. There was an universal feeling of distrust and apprehension there. The natives never went any distance from home without arms; and when Captain Wilson asked them the reason of it, they pointed to a slave ship then lying within sight.

On the windward coast, it appeared from Lieutenant Story and Mr. Bowman, that the evils just mentioned existed, if possible, in a still higher degree. They had seen the remains of villages which had been burned, whilst the fields of corn were still standing beside them, and every other trace of recent desolation. Here an agent was sent to establish a settlement in the country, and to send to the ships such slaves as he might obtain. The orders he received from the captain were, that "he was to encourage the chieftains by brandy and gunpowder to go to war, to make slaves." This he did. The chieftains perform-

14

ed their part in return. The neighboring villages were surrounded and set on fire in the night. The inhabitants were seized when making their escape; and, being brought to the agent, were by him forwarded to his principal on the coast. Mr. How, a botanist in the service of government, stated that on the arrival of an order for slaves from Cape Coast Castle, while he was there, a native chief immediately sent forth armed parties, who brought in a supply of all descriptions in the night.

All these atrocities, he said, were fully substantiated by the evidence; and here he should do injustice to his cause if he were not to make a quotation from the speech of Mr. Bryan Edwards in the assembly of Jamaica, who, though he was hostile to his propositions, had yet the candor to deliver himself in the following manner there: "I am persuaded," says he, "that Mr. Wilberforce has been rightly informed as to the manner in which slaves are generally procured. The intelligence I have collected from my own negroes abundantly confirms his account; and I have not the smallest doubt, that in Africa the effects of this trade are precisely such as he has represented them. The whole, or the greatest part of that immense continent, is a field of warfare and desolation; a wilderness in which the inhabitants are wolves towards each other. That this scene of oppression, fraud, treachery, and bloodshed, if not originally occasioned, is in part (I will not say wholly) upheld by the slave-trade, I dare not dispute. Every man in the sugar islands may be convinced that it is so, who will inquire of any African negroes, on their first arrival, concerning the circumstances of their captivity. The assertion that it is otherwise is mockery and insult."

It was another effect of this trade that it corrupted the morals of those who carried it on. Every fraud was used to deceive the ignorance of the natives by false weights and measures, adulterated commodities, and other impositions of a like sort. These frauds were even acknowledged by many who had themselves practiced them in obedience to the orders of their superiors. For the honor of the mercantile character of the country, such a traffic ought immediately to be suppressed.

With respect to the miseries of the middle passage, he had said so much on a former occasion, that he would spare the feelings of the committee as much as he could. He would therefore state that the evidence which was before them confirmed all those scenes of wretchedness, which he had then described; the same suffering from a state of suffocation by being crowded together; the same dancing in fetters; the same melancholy singing; the same eating by compulsion; the same despair; the same insanity; and all the other abominations which characterized the trade. New instances, however, had occurred, where these wretched men had resolved on death to terminate their woes. Some had destroyed themselves by refusing sustenance, in spite of threats and punishments. Others had thrown themselves into the sea; and more than one, when in the act of drowning, were seen to wave their hands in triumph, "exulting (to use the words of an eye-witness) that they had escaped." Yet these and similar things, when viewed through the African medium he had mentioned, took a different shape and color. Captain Knox, an adverse witness, had maintained that slaves lay during the night in tolerable comfort. And yet he confessed that in a vessel of one hundred and twenty tons, in which he had carried two hundred and ninety slaves, the latter had not all of them room to lie on their backs. How comfortably, then, must they have lain in his subsequent voyages, for he carried afterwards, in a vessel of one hundred and eight tons, four hundred and fifty, and in a vessel of one hundred and fifty tons, no less than six hundred slaves. Another instance of African deception was to be found in the testimony of Captain Frazer, one of the most humane captains in the trade. It had been said of him that he had held hot coals to the mouth of a slave to compel him to eat.

But upon whom did the cruelties thus arising out of the prosecution of this barbarous traffic fall? Upon a people with feeling and intellect like ourselves. One witness had spoken of the acuteness of their understanding; another of the extent of their memories; a third of their genius for commerce; a fourth of their proficiency in manufactures at home. Many had admired their gentle and peaceable disposition, their cheerfulness, and their hospitality. Even they, who were nominally slaves in Africa, lived a happy life. A witness against the abolition had described them as sitting and eating with their masters in the true style of patriarchal simplicity and comfort. Were these, then, a people incapable of civilization? The argument that they were an inferior species had been proved to be false.

Mr. Wilberforce, after showing in a very lucid manner, and by incontestable arguments, that the abolition of the trade in question, instead of being an injury, would be a lasting benefit to the West India islands, concluded by declaring that, interested as he might be supposed to be in the final event of the question, he was comparatively indifferent as to the present decision of the house upon it. Whatever they might do, the people of Great Britain, he was confident, would abolish the slave-trade when, as would soon happen, its injustice and cruelty should be fairly laid before them. It was a nest of serpents, which would never have existed so long, but for the darkness in which they lay hid. The light of day would now be let in on them, and they would vanish from the sight. For himself, he declared that he was engaged in a work which he would never abandon. The consciousness of the justice of his cause would carry him forward, though he were alone; but he could not but derive encouragement from considering with whom he was associated. Let us not, he said, despair. It is a blessed cause; and success ere long will crown our exertions. Already we have gained one victory. We have obtained for these poor creatures the recognition of their human nature, which for a while was most shamefully denied them. This is the first fruit of our efforts. Let us persevere, and our triumph will be complete. Never, never will we disist till we have wiped away this scandal from the Christian name; till we have released ourselves from the load of guilt under which we at present labor; and till we have extinguished every trace of this bloody traffic, which our posterity, looking back to the history of these enlightened times, will scarcely believe had been suffered to exist so long, a disgrace and a dishonor to our country.

He then moved that the chairman be instructed to move for leave to bring in a bill to prevent the further importation of slaves into the British colonies in the West Indies.

Colonel Tarleton immediately rose up and began by giving an historical account of the trade from the reign of Elizabeth to the present time. He then proceeded to the sanction which parliament had always given it. Hence it could not be withdrawn without a breach of faith. Hence, also, the private property embarked in it was sacred; nor could it be invaded unless an adequate compensation were given in return. They who had attempted the abolition of the trade were led away by a mistaken humanity. The Africans themselves had no objection to its continuance. With respect to the middle passage, he believed the mortality there to be on an average only five in the hundred; whereas in regiments sent out to the West Indies, the average loss in the year was about ten and a half per cent. The slave-trade was absolutely necessary, if we meant to carry on our West India commerce; for many attempts had been made to cultivate the lands in the different islands by white laborers, but they had always failed. It had also the merit of keeping up a number of seamen in readiness for the state. Lord Rodney had stated this as one of its advantages on the breaking out of a war. Liverpool alone could supply nine hundred and ninety-three seamen annually.

He would now advert to the connections dependent upon the African trade. It was the duty of the house to protect the planters, whose lives had been, and were then exposed to imminent dangers, and whose property had undergone an unmerited depreciation, and to what could this depreciation, and to what could the late insurrection at Dominica be imputed, which had been saved from horrid carnage and midnight butchery only by the adventitious arrival of two British regiments? They could only be attributed to the long delayed question of the abolition of the slave-trade; and if this question were to go much longer unsettled, Jamaica would be endangered also. To members of landed property he would observe, that the abolition would lessen the commerce of the country, and increase the national debt and the number of their taxes. The minister, he hoped, who patronized this wild scheme, had some new pecuniary resource in store to supply the deficiencies it would occasion.

Mr. Grosvenor then rose: He complimented the humanity of Mr. Wilberforce, though he differed from him on the subject of his motion. He himself had read only the privy council report; and he wished for no other evidence. The question had been delayed two years. Had the abolition been so clear a point as it was said to be, it could not have needed either so much evidence or time.

He had heard a good deal about kidnapping and other barbarous practices. He was sorry for them. But these were the natural consequences of the laws of Africa; and it became us as wise men to turn them to our own advantage.

The slave-trade was certainly not an amiable trade. Neither was that of a butcher; but yet it was a very necessary one.

There was great reason to doubt the propriety of the present motion. He had twenty reasons for disapproving of it. The first was, that the thing was impossible. He needed not, therefore, to give the rest. Parliament, indeed, might relinquish the trade. But to whom? To foreigners, who would continue it, and without the humane regulations which were applied to it by his countrymen.

He would give advice to the house on this subject in the words which the late Alderman Beckford used on a different occasion: "Meddle not with troubled waters; they will be found to be bitter waters, and waters of affliction." He again admitted that the slave-trade was not an amiable trade; but he would not gratify his humanity at the expense of the interests of his country; and he thought we should not too curiously inquire into the unpleasant circumstances which attended it.

Mr. James Martin succeeded Mr. Grosvenor. He said he had been long aware how much self-interest could pervert the judgment; but he was not apprised of the full power of it till the slave-trade became a subject of discussion. He had always conceived that the custom of trafficking in human beings had been incautiously begun, and without any reflection upon it; for he never could believe that any man, under the influence of moral principles, could suffer himself knowingly to carry on a trade replete with fraud, cruelty, and destruction; with destruction, indeed, of the worst kind, because it subjected the sufferers to a lingering death. But he found now that even such a trade as this could be sanctioned.

It was well observed in the petition from the university of Cambridge against the slave-trade, "that a firm belief in the providence of a benevolent Creator assured them that no system, founded on the oppression of one part of mankind, could be beneficial to another." He felt much concern, that in an assembly of the representatives of a country, boasting itself zealous, not only for the preservation of its own liberties, but for the general rights of mankind, it should be necessary to say a single word upon such a subject; but the deceitfulness of the human heart was such as to change the appearances of truth, when it stood in opposition to self-interest. And he had to lament that even among those whose public duty it was to cling to the universal and eternal principles of truth, justice, and humanity, there were found some who could defend that which was unjust, fraudulent and cruel.

The doctrines he had heard that evening, ought to have been reserved for times the most flagrantly profligate and abandoned. He never expected then to learn that the everlasting laws of righteousness were to give way to imaginary, political, and commercial expediency; and that thousands of our fellow-creatures were to be reduced to wretchedness, that individuals might enjoy opulence, or government a revenue.

This motion, he said, came strongly recommended to them. The honorable member who had introduced it, was justly esteemed for his character. He was the representative, too, of a noble county, which had been always ready to take the lead in every public measure for the good of the community, or for the general benefit of mankind; of a county, too, which had had the honor of producing a Saville. Had his illustrious predecessor been alive, he would have shown the same zeal on the same occasion. The preservation of the unalienable rights of all his fellow-creatures was one of the chief characteristics of that excellent citizen. Let every member in that house imitate him in the purity of their conduct and in the universal rectitude of their measures, and they would pay the same tender regard to the rights of other countries as to those of their own; and, for his part, he should never believe those persons to be sincere, who were loud in their professions of love of liberty, if he saw that love confined to the narrow circle of one community, which ought to be extended to the natural rights of every inhabitant of the globe.

But we should be better able to bring ourselves up to this standard of rectitude, if we were to put ourselves into the situation of those whom we oppressed. This was the rule of our religion. What should we think of those who should say that it was their interest to injure us? But he hoped we should not deceive ourselves so grossly as to imagine, that it was our real interest to oppress any one. The advantages to be obtained by tyranny were imaginary, and deceitful to the tyrant; and the evils they caused to the oppressed were grievous, and often insupportable.

Before he sat down, he would apologize, if he had expressed himself too warmly on this subject. He did not mean to offend any one. There were persons connected with the trade, some of whom he pitied on account of the difficulty of their situation. But he should think most contemptibly of himself as a man, if he could talk on this traffic without emotion. It would be a sign to him of his own moral degradation He regretted his inability to do justice to such a cause; but if, in having attempted to forward it, he had shown the weakness of his powers, he must console himself with the consideration that he felt more solid comfort in having acted up to sound public principles, than he could have done from the exertion of the most splendid talents against the conviction of his conscience.

Mr. Francis instanced an overseer, who, having thrown a negro into a copper of boiling cane-juice for a trifling offense, was punished merely by the loss of his place, and by being obliged to pay the value of the slave. He stated another instance of a girl of fourteen, who was dreadfully whipped for coming too late to her work. She fell down motionless after it, and was then dragged along the ground, by the legs, to a hospital, where she died. The murderer, though tried, was acquitted by a jury of his peers, upon the idea that it was impossible a master could destroy his own property. This was a notorious fact. It was published in the Jamaica Gazette; and it had even happened since the question of the abolition had been started.

Mr. Fox said that he would not believe that there could be found in the house of commons, men of such hard hearts and inaccessible understandings, as to vote an assent to the continuance of this detestable trade, and then go home to their families, satisfied with their vote, after they had been once made acquainted with the subject.

Mr. Matthew Montagu rose, and said a few words in support of the motion; and after condemning the trade in the strongest manner, he declared, that as long as he had life, he would use every faculty of his body and mind in endeavoring to promote its abolition.

Lord John Russell succeeded Mr. Montagu. He said that although slavery was repugnant to his feelings, he must vote against the abolition, as visionary and delusive. It was a feeble attempt without the power to serve the cause of humanity. Other nations would take up the trade. Whenever a bill of wise regulations should be brought forward, no man would be more ready than himself to lend his support. In this way the rights of humanity might be asserted without injury to others. He hoped he should not incur censure by his vote; for, let his understanding be what it might, he did not know that he had, notwithstanding the assertions of Mr. Fox, an inaccessible heart.

Mr. William Smith remarked: That the slaves were exposed to great misery in the islands, was true as well from inference as from facts; for what might not be expected from the use of arbitrary power, where the three characters of party, judge, and executioner were united! The slaves, too, were more capable on account of their passions, than the beasts of the field, of exciting the passions of their tyrants. To what a length the ill treatment of them might be carried, might be learnt from the instance which General Tottenham mentioned to have seen in the year 1780, in the streets of Bridge Town, Barbadoes: "A youth about nineteen, (to use his own words in the evidence,) entirely naked, with an iron collar about his neck, having five long projecting spikes. His body, both before and behind, was covered with wounds. His belly and thighs were almost cut to pieces, with running ulcers all over them; and a finger might have been laid in some of the weals. He could not sit down, because his hinder part was mortified; and it was impossible for him to lie down, on account of the prongs of his collar." He supplicated the general for relief. The latter asked who had punished him so dreadfully? The youth answered his master had done it. And because he could not work, this same master, in the same spirit of perversion which extorts from scripture a justification of the slave-trade, had fulfilled the apostolic maxim, that he should have nothing to eat. The use he meant to make of this instance, was to show the unprotected state of the slaves. What must it be where such an instance could pass not only unpunished, but almost unregarded? If, in the streets of London, but a dog were to be seen lacerated like this miserable man, how would the cruelty of the wretch be execrated, who had thus even abused a brute!

The judicial punishments also inflicted upon the negro showed the low estimation in which, in consequence of the strength of old customs and deep-rooted prejudices, they were held. Mr. Edwards, in his speech to the assembly at Jamaica, stated the following case, as one which had happened in one of the rebellions there. Some slaves had surrounded the dwelling-house of their mistress. She was in bed with a lovely infant. They deliberated upon the means of putting her to death in torment. But in the end one of them reserved her for his mistress; and they killed her infant with an axe before her face. "Now," says Mr. Edwards, (addressing himself to his audience,) "you will think that no torments were too great for such horrible excesses. Nevertheless, I am of a different opinion. I think that death, unaccompanied with cruelty, should be the utmost exertion of human authority over our unhappy fellow-creatures." Torments, however, were always inflicted in these cases. The punishment was gibbeting alive, and exposing the delinquents to perish by the gradual effects of hunger, thirst, and a parching sun; in which situation they were known to suffer for nine days, with a fortitude scarcely credible, never uttering a single groan. But horrible as the excesses might have been, which occasioned these punishments, it must be remembered that they were committed by ignorant savages, who had been dragged from all they held most dear; whose patience had been exhausted by a cruel and loathsome confinement during their transportation; and whose resentment had been wound up to the highest pitch of fury by the lash of the driver.

But he would now mention another instance, by way of contrast, out of the evidence. A child on board a slave-ship, of about ten months old, became sulky and would not eat. The captain flogged it with a cat, swearing that he would make it eat, or kill it. From this and other ill treatment the child's legs swelled. He then ordered some water to be made hot to abate the swelling. But even his tender mercies were cruel; for the cook, on putting his hand into the water, said it was too hot. Upon this the captain swore at him, and ordered the feet to be put in. This was done. The nails and skin came off. Oiled cloths were then put round them. The child was at length tied to a heavy log. Two or three days afterwards, the captain caught it up again, and repeated that he would make it eat, or kill it. He immediately flogged it again, and in a quarter of an hour it died. But, after the child was dead, whom should the barbarian select to throw it overboard but the wretched mother? In vain she started from the office. He beat her till he made her take up the child and carry it to the side of the vessel. She then dropped it into the sea, turning her head the other way that she might not see it.

Now it would naturally be asked, Was not this captain also gibbeted alive? Alas! although the execrable barbarity of the European exceeded that of the Africans before mentioned, almost as much as his opportunities of instruction had been greater than theirs, no notice whatsoever was taken of this horrible action; and a thousand similar cruelties had been committed in this abominable trade with equal impunity: but he would say no more. He should vote for the abolition, not only as it would do away all the evils complained of in Africa and the middle passage, but as it would be the most effectual means of ameliorating the condition of those unhappy persons who were still to continue slaves in the British colonies.

Mr. Courtenay entreated every member to recollect that on his vote that night depended the happiness of millions; and that it was then in his power to promote a measure of which the benefits would be felt over one whole quarter of the globe; that the seeds of civilization might, by the present bill, be sown all over Africa; and the first principles of humanity be established in regions where they had hitherto been excluded by the existence of this execrable trade.

Mr. Pitt rose and said that from the first hour of his having had the honor to sit in parliament down to the present, among all the questions, whether political or personal, in which it had been his fortune to take a share, there had never been one in which his heart was so deeply interested as in the present; both on account of the serious principles it involved, and the consequences connected with it.

The present was not a mere question of feeling. The argument which ought in his opinion to determine the committee, was, that the slave-trade was unjust. It was therefore such a trade as it was impossible for him to support, unless it could be first proved to him that there were no laws of morality binding upon nations; and that it was not the duty of a legislature to restrain its subjects from invading the happiness of other countries, and from violating the fundamental principles of justice.

Several had stated the impracticability of the measure before them. They wished to see the trade abolished; but there was some necessity for continuing in it which they conceived to exist. Nay, almost every one, he believed, appeared to wish that the further importation of slaves might cease, provided it could be made out that the population of the West Indies could be maintained without it. He proposed therefore, to consider the latter point; for, as the impracticability of keeping up the population there appeared to operate as the chief objection, he trusted that, by showing it to be ill founded, he should clear away all other obstacles whatever; so that, having no ground either of justice or necessity to stand upon, there could be no excuse left to the committee for resisting the present motion.

He might reasonably, however, hope that they would not reckon any small or temporary disadvantage which might arise from the abolition to be a sufficient reason against it. It was surely not any slight degree of expediency, nor any small balance of profit, nor any light shades of probability on the one side, rather than on the other, which would determine them on this question. He asked pardon even for the supposition. The slave-trade was an evil of such magnitude that there must be a common wish in the committee at once to put an end to it, if there were no great and serious obstacles. It was a trade by which multitudes of unoffending nations were deprived of the blessings of civilization, and had their peace and happiness invaded. It ought, therefore, to be no common expediency, it ought to be nothing less than the utter ruin of our islands which it became those to plead who took upon them to defend the continuance of it.

He could not help thinking that the West India gentlemen had manifested an over great degree of sensibility as to the point in question; and that their alarms had been unreasonably excited upon it. He had examined the subject carefully for himself; and he would now detail those reasons which had induced him firmly to believe not only that no permanent mischief would follow from the abolition, but not even any such temporary inconvenience as could be stated to be a reason for preventing the house from agreeing to the motion before them ; on the contrary, that the abolition itself would lay the foundation for the more solid improvement of all the various interests of those colonies.

In doing this, he should apply his observations chiefly to Jamaica, which contained more than half the slaves in the British West Indies ; and if he should succeed in proving that no material detriment could arise to the population there, this would afford so strong a presumption with respect to the other islands, that the house could no longer hesitate whether they should or should not put a stop to this most horrid trade.

In the twenty years ending in 1788, the annual loss of slaves in Jamaica, (that is, the excess of deaths above the births,) appeared to be one in the hundred. In a preceding period the loss was greater ; and, in a period before that, greater still ; there having been a continual gradation in the decrease through the whole time. It might fairly be concluded, therefore, that (the average loss of the last period being one per cent.) the loss in the former part of it would be somewhat more, and in the latter part somewhat less than one per cent., insomuch that it might be fairly questioned whether, by this time, the births and deaths in Jamaica might not be stated as nearly equal. It was to be added that a peculiar calamity, which swept away fifteen thousand slaves, had occasioned a part of the mortality in the last mentioned period. The probable loss, therefore, now to be expected was very inconsiderable indeed.

There was, however, one circumstance to be added, which the West India gentlemen, in stating this matter, had entirely overlooked ; and which was so material as clearly to reduce the probable diminution in the population of Jamaica down to nothing. In all the calculations he had referred to of the comparative number of births and deaths, all the negroes in the island were included. The newly imported, who died in the seasoning, made a part. But these swelled, most materially, the number of the deaths. Now as these extraordinary deaths would cease as soon as the importations ceased, a deduction of them ought to be made from his present calculation.

But the number of those who thus died in the seasoning would make up of itself nearly the whole of that one per cent. which had been stated. He particularly pressed an attention to this circumstance ; for the complaint of being likely to want hands in Jamaica arose from the mistake of including the present unnatural deaths, caused by the seasoning, among the natural and perpetual causes of mortality. These deaths, being erroneously taken into the calculations, gave the planters an idea that the numbers could not be kept up. These deaths, which were caused merely by the slave-trade, furnished the very ground, therefore, on which the continuance of that trade had been thought necessary.

The evidence as to this point was clear ; for it would be found in that dreadful catalogue of deaths arising from the seasoning and the passage, which the house had been condemned to look into, that one half died. An annual mortality of two thousand slaves in Jamaica might be therefore charged to the importation; which, compared with the whole number on the island, hardly fell short of the whole one per cent. decrease.

Joining this with all the other considerations, he would then ask, could the decrease of the slaves in Jamaica be such; could the colonies be so destitute of means; could the planters, when, by their own accounts, they were establishing daily new regulations for the benefit of the slaves; could they, under all these circumstances, be permitted to plead the total impossibility of keeping up their number, which they had rested on, as being indeed the only possible pretext for allowing fresh importations from Africa? He appealed, therefore, to the sober judgment of all, whether the situation of Jamaica was such as to justify a hesitation in agreeing to the present motion.

It might be observed, also, that when the importations should stop, that disproportion between the sexes which was one of the obstacles to population, would gradually diminish, and a natural order of things be established. Through the want of this natural order, a thousand grievances were created, which it was impossible to define, and which it was in vain to think that, under such circumstances, we could cure. But the abolition of itself would work this desirable effect. The West Indians would then feel a near and urgent interest to enter into a thousand little details which it was impossible for him to describe, but which would have the greatest influence on population. A foundation would thus be laid for the general welfare of the islands; a new system would rise up, the reverse of the old; and eventually both their general wealth and happiness would increase.

He had now proved far more than he was bound to do; for, if he could only show that the abolition would not be ruinous, it would be enough. He could give up, therefore, three arguments out of four, through the whole of what he had said, and yet have enough left for his position. As to the Creoles, they would undoubtedly increase. They differed in this entirely from the imported slaves, who were both a burthen and a curse to themselves and others. The measure now proposed would operate like a charm; and, besides stopping all the miseries in Africa and the passage, would produce even more benefit in the West Indies than legal regulations could effect.

He would now just touch upon the question of emancipation. A rash emancipation of the slaves would be mischievous. In that unhappy situation, to which our baneful conduct had brought ourselves and them, it would be no justice on either side to give them liberty. They were as yet incapable of it; but their situation might be gradually amended. They might be relieved from every thing harsh and severe; raised from their present degraded state, and put under the protection of the law. Till then, to talk of emancipation was insanity. But it was the system of fresh importations which interfered with these principles of improvement; and it was only the abolition which could establish them. The suggestion had its foundation in human nature. Wherever the incentive of honor, credit, and fair profit appeared, energy would spring up; and when these laborers should have the natural springs of human action afforded them, they would then rise to the natural level of human industry.

From Jamaica he would now go to the other islands. In Barbadoes the slaves had rather increased. In St. Kitts the decrease for fourteen years had been but three-fourths per cent., but here many of the observations would apply which he had used in the case of Jamaica. In Antigua many had died by a particular calamity. But for this, the decrease would have been trifling. In Nevis and Montserrat there was little or no disproportion of the sexes; so that it might well be hoped that the numbers would be kept up in these islands. In Dominica some controversy had arisen about the calculation; but Governor Orde had stated an increase of births above the deaths. From Grenada and St. Vincents no accurate accounts had been delivered in answer to the queries sent them; but they were probably not in circumstances less favorable than in the other islands.

On a full review, then, of the state of the negro population in the West Indies, was there any serious ground of alarm from the abolition of the slave-trade? Where was the impracticability on which alone so many had rested their objections? Must we not blush at pretending that it would distress our consciences to accede to this measure, as far as the question of the negro population was concerned?

Intolerable were the mischiefs of this trade, both in its origin and through every stage of its progress. To say that slaves could be furnished us by fair and commercial means was ridiculous. The trade sometimes ceased, as during the late war. The demand was more or less, according to circumstances. But how was it possible, that to a demand so exceedingly fluctuating, the supply should always exactly accommodate itself? Alas! we made human beings the subject of commerce; we talked of them as such; and yet we would not allow them the common principle of commerce, that the supply must accommodate itself to the consumption. It was not from wars, then, that the slaves were chiefly procured. They were obtained in proportion as they were wanted. If a demand for slaves arose, a supply was forced in one way or other; and it was in vain, overpowered as we then were with positive evidence, as well as the reasonableness of the supposition, to deny that by the slave-trade we occasioned all the enormities which had been alleged against it.

Mr. Fox again rose and observed, that some expressions which he had used had been complained of as too harsh and severe. He had since considered them; but he could not prevail upon himself to retract them; because, if any gentleman, after reading the evidence on the table, and attending to the debate, could avow himself an abettor of this shameful traffic in human flesh, it could only be either from some hardness of heart, or some difficulty of understanding, which he really knew not how to account for.

Some had considered this question as a question of political, whereas it was a question of personal freedom. Political freedom was undoubtedly a great blessing; but, when it came to be compared with personal, it sunk to nothing. To confound the two, served therefore to render all arguments on either perplexing and unintelligible. Personal freedom was the first right of every human being. It was a right, of which he who deprived a fellow-creature was absolutely criminal in so depriving him, and which he who withheld was no less criminal in withholding. He could not therefore retract his words with respect to any, who (whatever regard he might otherwise have for them) should, by their vote of that night, deprive their fellow-creatures of so great a blessing. Nay, he would go further. He would say, that if the house, knowing what the trade was by the evidence, did not by their vote mark to all mankind their abhorrence of a practice so savage, so enormous, so repugnant to all laws, human and divine, they would consign their character to eternal infamy.

That the pretense of danger to our West Indian islands, from the abolition of the slave-trade, was totally unfounded, Mr. Wilberforce had abundantly proved: but if there were those who had not been satisfied with that proof, was it possible to resist the arguments of Mr. Pitt on the same subject? It had been shown, on a comparison of the births and deaths in Jamaica, that there was not now any decrease of the slaves. But if there had been, it would have made no difference to him in his vote ; for, had the mortality been ever so great there, he should have ascribed it to the system of importing negroes, instead of that of encouraging their natural increase. Was it not evident that the planters thought it more convenient to buy them fit for work than to breed them ? Why, then, was this horrid trade to be kept up ? To give the planters, truly, the liberty of misusing their slaves, so as to check population : for it was from ill usage only that in a climate so natural to them, their numbers could diminish. The very ground, therefore, on which the planters rested the necessity of fresh importations, namely, the destruction of lives in the West Indies, was itself the strongest argument that could be given, and furnished the most imperious call upon parliament for the abolition of the trade.

Against this trade innumerable were the charges. An honorable member, Mr. Smith, had done well to introduce those tragical stories, which had made such an impression upon the house. No one of these had been yet controverted. It had indeed been said that the cruelty of the African captain to the child was too bad to be true; and we had been desired to look at the cross-examination of the witness, as if we should find traces of the falsehood of his testimony there. But his cross-examination was peculiarly honorable to his character ; for after he had been pressed, in the closest manner, by some able members of the house, the only inconsistency they could fix upon him was, whether the fact had happened on the same day of the same month of the year 1764, or the year 1765.

But it was idle to talk of the incredibility of such instances. It was not denied that absolute power was exercised by the slave captains; and if this was granted, all the cruelties charged upon them would naturally follow. Never did he hear of charges so black and horrible as those contained in the evidence on the table. They unfolded such a scene of cruelty, that if the house, with all their present knowledge of the circumstances, should dare to vote for its continuance, they must have nerves of which he had no conception. We might find instances, indeed, in history, of men violating the feelings of nature on extraordinary occasions. Fathers had sacrificed their sons and daughters, and husbands their wives; but to imitate their characters, we ought to have not only nerves as strong as the two Brutuses, but to take care that we had a cause as good; or that we had motives for such a dereliction of our feelings as patriotic as those which historians had attributed to these when they handed them to the notice of the world.

But what was our motive in the case before us, to continue a trade which was a wholesale sacrifice of a whole order and race of our fellow-creatures? which carried them away by force from their native country, in order to subject them to the mere will and caprice, the tyranny and oppression of other human beings, for their whole natural lives, them and their posterity for ever! O most monstrous wickedness! O unparalleled barbarity! And, what was more aggravating, this most complicated scene of robbery and murder which mankind had ever witnessed, had been honored by the name of trade.

That a number of human beings should be at all times ready to be furnished as fair articles of commerce, just as our occasions might require, was absurd. The argument of Mr. Pitt, on this head, was unanswerable. Our demand was fluctuating; it entirely ceased at some times; at others it was great and pressing. How was it possible, on every sudden call, to furnish a sufficient return in slaves without resorting to those execrable means of obtaining them which were stated in the evidence? These were of three sorts, and he would now examine them.

Captives in war, it was urged, were consigned either to death or slavery. This, however, he believed to be false in point of fact. But suppose it were true; did it not become us, with whom it was a custom, founded in the wisest policy, to pay the captives a peculiar respect and civility, to inculcate the same principles in Africa? But we were so far from doing this, that we encouraged wars for the sake of taking, not men's goods and possessions, but men themselves; and it was not the war which was the cause of the slave-trade, but the slave-thrade which was the cause of the war. It was the practice of the slave-merchants to try to intoxicate the African kings in order to turn them to their purpose. A particular instance occurred in the evidence of a prince, who, when sober, resisted their wishes; but in the moment of inebriety, he gave the word for war, attacked the next village, and sold the inhabitants to the merchants.

The second mode was kidnapping. He referred the house to various instances of this in the evidence: but there was one in particular, from which we might immediately infer the frequency of the practice. A black trader had kidnapped a girl and sold her; but he was presently afterwards kidnapped and sold himself; and, when he asked the captain who bought him, "What! do you buy me, who am a great trader?" the only answer was, "Yes, I will buy you, or her, or any body else, provided any one will sell you;" and accordingly both the trader and the girl were carried to the West Indies and sold for slaves.

The third mode of obtaining slaves was by crimes committed or imputed. One of these was adultery. But was Africa the place, where Englishmen, above all others, were to go to find out and punish adulterers? Did it become us to cast the first stone? It was a most extraordinary pilgrimage for a most extraordinary purpose! And yet upon this plea we justified our right of carrying off its inhabitants. The offense alleged next was witchcraft. What a reproach it was to lend ourselves to this superstition! Yes: we stood by; we heard the trial; we knew the crime to be impossible, and that the accused must be innocent: but we waited in patient silence for his condemnation; and then we lent our friendly aid to the police of the country, by buying the wretched convict, with all his family, whom, for the benefit of Africa, we carried away, also, into perpetual slavery.

Of the slaves in the West Indies it had been said that they were taken from a worse state to a better. An honorable member, Mr. William Smith, had quoted some instances out of the evidence to the contrary. He also would quote one or two others. A slave under hard usage had run away. To prevent a repetition of the offense his owner sent for his surgeon, and desired him to cut off the man's leg. The surgeon refused. The owner, to render it a matter of duty in the surgeon, broke it. "Now," says he, "you must cut it off, or the man will die." We might console ourselves, perhaps, that this happened in a French island; but he would select another instance which had happened in one of our own. Mr. Ross heard the shrieks of a female issuing from an out-house, and so piercing that he determined to see what was going on. On looking in he perceived a young female tied up to a beam by her wrists, entirely naked, and in the act of involuntary writhing and swinging, while the author of her torture was standing below her with a lighted torch in his hand, which he applied to all the parts of her body as it approached him. What crime this miserable woman had perpetrated he knew not; but the human mind could not conceive a crime warranting such a punishment.

He was glad to see that these tales affected the house. Would they then sanction enormities, the bare recital of which made them shudder? Let them remember that humanity did not consist in a squeamish ear. It did not consist in shrinking and starting at such tales as these; but in a disposition of the heart to remedy the evils they unfolded. Humanity belonged rather to the mind than to the nerves. But if so, it should prompt men to charitable exertion. Such exertion was necessary in the present case. It was necessary for the credit of our jurisprudence at home and our character abroad. For what would any man think of our justice who should see another hanged for a crime which would be innocence itself, if compared with those enormities which were allowed in Africa and the West Indies under the sanction of the British parliament.

With respect to the intellect and sensibility of the Africans, it was pride only which suggested a difference between them and ourselves. There was a remarkable instance to the point in the evidence, and which he would quote. In one of the slave-ships was a person of consequence, a man once high in a military station, and with a mind not insensible to the eminence of his rank. He had been taken captive and sold, and was then in the hold, confined promiscuously with the rest. Happening in the night to fall asleep, he dreamed that he was in his own country, high in honor and command, caressed by his family and friends, waited on by his domestics, and surrounded with all his former comforts in life. But awaking suddenly and finding where he was, he was heard to burst into the loudest groans and lamentations on the miserable contrast of his present state, mixed with the meanest of his subjects, and subjected to the insolence of wretches a thousand times lower than himself in every kind of endowment. He appealed to the house, whether this was not as moving a picture of the miserable effects of the slave-trade as could be well imagined. There was one way by which they might judge of it. Let them make the case their own. This was the Christian rule of judging; and having mentioned Christianity, he was sorry to find that any should suppose that it had given countenance to such a system of oppression. So far was this from being the case, that he thought it one of the most splendid triumphs of this religion, that it had caused slavery to be so generally abolished on its appearance in the world. It had done this by teaching us, among other beautiful precepts, that in the sight of their Maker, all mankind were equal. Its influence appeared to have been more powerful in this respect than that of all the ancient systems of philosophy; though even in these, in point of theory, we might trace great liberality and consideration for human rights. Where could be found finer sentiments of liberty than in Demosthenes and Cicero ? Where bolder assertions of the rights of mankind than in Tacitus and Thucydides ? But alas ! these were the holders of slaves ! It was not so with those who had been converted to Christianity.

He would now conclude by declaring that the whole country, indeed the whole civilized world, must rejoice that such a bill as the present had been moved for. not merely as a matter of humanity, but as an act of justice ; for he would put humanity out of the case. Could it be called humanity to forbear from committing murder ? Exactly upon this ground did the present motion stand, being strictly a question of national justice. He thanked Mr. Wilberforce for having pledged himself so strongly to pursue his object till it was accomplished ; and, as for himself, he declared, that in whatever situation he might ever be, he would use his warmest efforts for the promotion of this righteous cause.

Mr. Stanley (the member for Lancashire) rose, and declared that when he came into the house, he intended to vote against the abolition ; but that the impression made both on his feelings and on his understanding was such, that he could not persist in his resolution. He was now convinced that the entire abolition of the slave-trade was called for equally by sound policy and justice. He thought it right and fair to avow manfully this change in his opinion. The abolition, he was sure, could not long fail of being carried. The arguments for it were·irresistible.

The Honorable Mr. Ryder said that he came to the house, not exactly in the same circumstances as Mr. Stanley, but very undecided on the subject. He was, however, so strongly convinced by the arguments he had heard, that he was become equally earnest for the abolition.

Mr. Smith (member for Pontefract) said that he should not trouble the house at so late an hour further than to enter his protest, in the most solemn manner, against this trade, which he considered as most disgraceful to the country, and contrary to all the principles of justice and religion.

Mr. Burke said he would use but few words. He declared that he had for a long time had his mind drawn toward this great subject. He had even prepared a bill for the regulation of the trade, conceiving at that time that the immediate abolition of it was a thing hardly to be hoped for; but when he found that Mr. Wilberforce had seriously undertaken the work, and that his motion was for the abolition, which he approved much more than his own, he had burnt his papers, and made an offering of them in honor of his nobler proposition, much in the same manner as we read that the curious books were offered up and burnt at the approach of the Gospel. He highly applauded the confessions of Mr. Stanley and Mr. Ryder. It would be a glorious tale for them to tell their constituents, that it was impossible for them, however prejudiced, if sent to hear discussion in that house, to avoid surrendering up their hearts and judgments at the shrine of reason.

Mr. Wilberforce made a short reply to some arguments in the course of the debate; after which, at half-past three in the morning, the house divided. There appeared for Mr. Wilberforce's motion eighty-eight, and against it one hundred and sixty-three; so that it was lost by a majority of seventy-five votes.

Upon the news of this defeat the friends of the cause held a meeting. They passed a vote of thanks to the illustrious minority which had stood forth in the house of commons as the assertors of British justice and humanity; and they resolved not to desist from appealing to their countrymen until the commercial intercourse with Africa should cease to be polluted with the blood of its inhabitants. Mr. Clarkson made an abridgment of the evidence before the house of commons, which was circulated through the kingdom. Great numbers of people left off the use of articles produced by slave labor, and vented their feelings in public meetings to address parliament on the subject; and this they did with so much earnestness and activity, that by the latter end of March, in 1792, no less than 517 petitions were laid on the table of the commons, praying for the total abolition of the slave-trade. Emboldened and supported by the people, Mr. Wilberforce again introduced the question on the 2d of April, 1792, and after a speech of four hours, moved "that it is the opinion of this house that the African slave-trade ought to be abolished." This led to a long and interesting debate. Never in the house of commons was so much splendid oratory displayed as on that night. We extract from the parliamentary records a report of some of the speeches made on that occasion.

Mr. Wilberforce opened the debate in a luminous and impressive speech. After remarking at considerable length upon the evils and the injuries of the

15

slave-trade, he touched upon the argument so often repeated, that other nations would carry on the slave-trade if we abandoned it. But how did we
know this? Had not Denmark given a noble example to the contrary? She
had consented to abolish the trade in ten years; and had she not done this,
even though we, after an investigation of nearly five years, had ourselves hung
back? But what might not be expected if we were to take up the cause in
earnest; if we were to proclaim to all nations the injustice of the trade, and
to solicit their concurrence in the abolition of it! He hoped the representatives of the nation would not be less just than the people. The latter had
stepped forward and expressed their sense more generally by petitions than in
any instance in which they had ever before interfered. To see this great
cause thus triumphing over distinctions and prejudices was a noble spectacle.
Whatever might be said of our political divisions, such a sight had taught us
that there were subjects still beyond the reach of party; that there was a point
of elevation where we ascended above the jarring of the discordant elements
which ruffled and agitated the vale below. In our ordinary atmosphere, clouds
and vapors obscured the air, and we were the sport of a thousand conflicting
winds and adverse currents; but here we moved in a higher region, where all
was pure and clear, and free from perturbation and discomposure.

> "As some tall cliff, that lifts its awful form,
> Swells from the vale, and midway leaves the storm:
> Though round its breast the rolling clouds are spread,
> Eternal sunshine settles on its head."

Here, then, on this august eminence, he hoped we should build the temple
of benevolence; but we should lay its foundation deep in truth and justice;
and that we should inscribe upon its gates, "Peace and good will to men."
Here we should offer the first fruits of our benevolence, and endeavor to compensate, if possible, for the injuries we had brought upon our fellow-men.

He would only observe that his conviction of the indispensable necessity of
immediately abolishing this trade remained as strong as ever. Let those who
talk of allowing three or four years to the continuance of it, reflect on the disgraceful scenes which had passed last year. As for himself, he would wash his
hands of the blood which would be spilled in this horrid interval. He could
not, however, but believe that the hour was come when we should put a final
period to the existence of this cruel traffic. Should he unhappily be mistaken,
he would never desert the cause; but to the last moment of his life he would
exert his utmost powers in its support. He would now move, "That it is the
opinion of this committee that the trade carried on by British subjects, for the
purpose of obtaining slaves on the coast of Africa, ought to be abolished."

Mr. Bailie was in hopes that the friends of the abolition would have been
contented with the innocent blood which had been already shed. The great
island of St. Domingo had been torn to pieces by insurrections. The most
dreadful barbarities had been perpetrated there. In the year 1789, the imports into it exceeded five millions sterling. The exports from it in the same
year amounted to six millions; and the trade employed three hundred thou-

sand tons of shipping, and thirty thousand seamen. This fine island, thus advantageously situated, had been lost in consequence of the agitation of the question of the slave-trade. Surely, so much mischief ought to have satisfied those who supported it; but they required the total destruction of all the West Indian colonies belonging to Great Britain to complete the ruin.

The honorable gentleman who had just spoken, had dwelt upon the enormities of the slave-trade. He was far from denying that many acts of inhumanity might accompany it; but as human nature was much the same every where, it would be unreasonable to expect, among African traders, or the inhabitants of our islands, a degree of perfection in morals which was not to be found in Great Britain itself. Would any man estimate the character of the English nation by what was to be read in the records of the Old Bailey? He himself, however, had lived sixteen years in the West Indies, and he could bear testimony to the general good usage of the slaves.

Before the agitation of this impolitic question, the slaves were contented with their situation. There was a mutual confidence between them and their masters: and this continued to be the case till the new doctrines were broached. But now depots of arms were necessary on every estate, and the scene was totally reversed. Nor was their religious then inferior to their civil state. When the English took possession of Grenada, where his property lay, they found them baptized and instructed in the principles of the Roman Catholic faith. The priests of that persuasion had indeed been indefatigable in their vocation; so that imported Africans generally obtained within twelve months a tolerable idea of their religious duties. He had seen the slaves there go through the public mass in a manner, and with a fervency, which would have done credit to more civilized societies. But the case was now altered; for, except where the Moravians had been, there was no trace in our islands of an attention to their religious interests.

It had been said that their punishments were severe. There might be instances of cruelty, but these were not general. Many of them were undoubtedly ill disposed; though not more, according to their number on a plantation, than in a regiment, or in a ship's crew. Had we never heard of seamen being flogged from ship to ship, or of soldiers dying in the very act of punishment? Had we not also heard, even in this country of boasted liberty, of seamen being seized, and carried away, when returning from distant voyages, after an absence of many years; and this without even being allowed to see their wives and families? As to distressed objects, he maintained that there was more wretchedness and poverty in St. Giles than in all the West Indian islands belonging to Great Britain.

He would now speak of the African and West Indian trades. The imports and exports of these amounted to upwards of ten millions annually; and they gave employment to three hundred thousand tons of shipping, and to about twenty-five thousand seamen. These trades had been sanctioned by our ancestors in parliament. The acts for this purpose might be classed under three heads. First, they were such as declared the colonies and the trade thereof advantageous to Great Britain, and therefore entitled to her protection. Secondly, such as authorized, protected and encouraged the trade of Africa, as advantageous in itself, and necessary to the welfare and existence of the sugar colonies; and, thirdly, such as promoted and secured loans of money to the proprietors of the said colonies, either from British subjects or from foreigners. These acts, he apprehended, ought to satisfy every person of the legality and usefulness of these trades. They were enacted in reigns distinguished for the production of great and enlightened characters. We heard then of no wild and destructive doctrines like the present. These were reserved for this age of novelty and innovation. But he must remind the house that the inhabitants of our islands had as good a right to the protection of their property as the inhabitants of Great Britain. Nor could it be diminished in any shape without full compensation. The proprietors of lands in the ceded islands, which were purchased of government under specific conditions of settlement, ought to be indemnified. They, also, (of whom he was one,) who had purchased the territory granted by the crown to General Monkton in the island of St. Vincent, ought to be indemnified also. The sale of this had gone on briskly, till it was known that a plan was in agitation for the abolition of the slave-trade. Since that period the original purchasers had done little or nothing, and they had many hundred acres on hand which would be of no value if the present question was carried. In fact, they had a right to compensation. The planters generally spent their estates in this country. They generally educated their children in it. They had never been found seditious or rebellious; and they demanded of the parliament of Great Britain that protection which, upon the principles of good faith, it was in duty bound to afford them in common with the rest of his majesty's loyal subjects.

Mr. Henry Thornton remarked, that the manner of procuring slaves in Africa was the great evil to be remedied. Africa was to be stripped of its inhabitants to supply a population for the West Indies. There was a Dutch proverb which said, "My son, get money, honestly if you can; but get money;" or, in other words, "Get slaves, honestly if you can; but get slaves." This was the real grievance; and the two honorable gentlemen, by confining their observations to the West Indies, had entirely overlooked it.

Though this evil had been fully proved, he could not avoid stating to the house some new facts, which had come to his knowledge as a director of the Sierra Leone company, and which would still further establish it. The consideration that they had taken place since the discussion of the last year on this subject, obliged him to relate them.

Mr. Falconbridge, agent to the company, sitting one evening in Sierra Leone, heard a shout, and immediately afterwards the report of a gun. Fearing an attack, he armed forty of the settlers, and rushed with them to the place from whence the noise came. He found a poor wretch, who had been crossing from a neighboring village, in the possession of a party of kidnappers, who were tying his hands. Mr. Falconbridge, however, dared not rescue him, lest, in the defenseless state of his own town, retaliation might be made upon him.

At another time a young woman, living half a mile off, was sold, without any criminal charge, to one of the slave-ships. She was well acquainted with the agent's wife, and had been with her only the day before. Her cries were heard, but it was impossible to relieve her.

At another time a young lad, one of the free settlers who went from England, was caught by a neighboring chief, as he was straggling alone from home, and sold for a slave. The pretext was, that some one in the town of Sierra Leone had committed an offense. Hence, the first person belonging to it, who could be seized, was to be punished. Happily, the free settlers saw him in his chains, and they recovered him before he was conveyed to the ship.

To mark still more forcibly the scenes of misery to which the slave-trade gave birth, he would mention a case stated to him in a letter by king Naimbanna. It had happened to this respectable person, in no less than three instances, to have some branches of his family kidnapped, and carried off to the West Indies. At one time three young men, Corpro, Banna, and Marbrour, were decoyed on board a Danish slave-ship, under pretense of buying something, and were taken away. At another time another relation piloted a vessel down the river He begged to be put on shore, when he came opposite to his own town, but he was pressed to pilot her to the river's mouth. The captain then pleaded the impracticability of putting him on shore, carried him to Jamaica, and sold him for a slave. Fortunately, however, by means of a letter which was conveyed there, the man, by the assistance of the governor, was sent back to Sierra Leone. At another time another relation was also kidnapped. But he had not the good fortune, like the former, to return.

He would mention one other instance. A son had sold his own father, for whom he obtained a considerable price; for, as the father was rich in domestic slaves, it was not doubted that he would offer largely for his ransom. The old man accordingly gave twenty-two of these in exchange for himself. The rest, however, being from that time filled with apprehensions of being, on some ground or other, sold to the slave-ships, fled to the mountains of Sierra Leone, where they now dragged on a miserable existence. The son himself was sold, in his turn, soon after. In short, the whole of that unhappy peninsula, as he learned from eye witnesses, had been desolated by the trade in slaves. Towns were seen standing without inhabitants all over the coast; in several of which the agent of the company had been. There was nothing but distrust among the inhabitants. Every one, if he stirred from home, felt himself obliged to be armed.

Such was the nature of the slave-trade. It had unfortunately obtained the name of a trade, and many had been deceived by the appellation. But it was war and not trade. It was a mass of crimes, and not commerce. It was that which prevented the introduction of a trade in Africa; for it was only by clearing and cultivating the lands, that the climate could be made healthy for settlements; but this wicked traffic, by dispersing the inhabitants, and causing the lands to remain uncultivated, made the coast unhealthy to Europeans. He had found, in attempting to establish a colony there, that it was an obstacle which opposed itself to him in innumerable ways; it created more embarrassments than all the natural impediments of the country; and it was more hard to contend with, than any difficulties of climate, soil, or natural disposition of the people.

Colonel Tarleton repeated his arguments of the last year. In addition to these, he inveighed bitterly against the abolitionists, as a junto of sectaries, sophists, enthusiasts, and fanatics. He condemned the abolition as useless, unless other nations would take it up. He brought to the recollection of the house the barbarous scenes which had taken place in St. Domingo, all of which, he said, had originated in the discussion of this question. He described the alarms in which the inhabitants of the islands were kept, lest similar scenes should occur from the same cause. He ridiculed the petitions on the table. Itinerant clergymen, mendicant physicians, and others had extorted signatures from the sick, the indigent and the traveler. School-boys were invited to sign them, under the promise of a holiday. He had letters to produce which would prove all these things, though he was not authorized to give up the names of those who had written them.

Mr. Whitbread said, that even if he could conceive that the trade was, as some had asserted it to be, founded on principles of humanity; that the Africans were rescued from death in their own country; that, upon being carried to the West Indies, they were put under kind masters; that their labor there was easy; that at evening they returned cheerful to their homes; that in sickness they were attended with care; and that their old age was rendered comfortable; even then he would vote for the abolition of the slave-trade, inasmuch as he was convinced that that which was fundamentally wrong, no practice could justify.

No eloquence could persuade him that the Africans were torn from their country and their dearest connexions, merely that they might live a happier life; or that they could be placed under the uncontrolled dominion of others without suffering. Arbitrary power would spoil the hearts of the best. Hence would arise tyranny on the one side, and a sense of injury on the other. Hence the passions would be let loose, and a state of perpetual enmity would follow.

He needed only to go to the accounts of those who defended the system of slavery, to show that it was cruel. He was forcibly struck last year by an expression of an honorable member, an advocate for the trade, who, when he came to speak of the slaves, on selling off the stock of a plantation, said that they brought less than the common price, because they were damaged. Damaged! What! were they goods and chattels? What an idea was this to hold out of our fellow-creatures! We might imagine how slaves were treated, if they could be spoken of in such a manner. Perhaps these unhappy people had lingered out the best part of their lives in the service of their master. Able then to do but little, they were sold for little; and the remaining substance of their sinews was to be pressed out by another, yet more hardened than the former, who had made a calculation of their vitals accordingly.

Mr. Dundas declared that he had always been a warm friend to the abolition of the slave-trade, though he differed with Mr. Wilberforce as to the mode of effecting it.

The abolitionists, and those on the opposite side of the question, had, both of them, gone into extremes. The former were for the immediate and abrupt annihilation of the trade. The latter considered it as essentially necessary to the existence of the West Indian islands, and therefore laid it down that it was to be continued forever. Such was the vast distance between the parties.

He would say that he agreed with his honorable friend, Mr. Wilberforce, in very material points. He believed the trade was not founded in policy; that the continuation of it was not essential to the preservation of our trade with the West Indian islands; and that the slaves were not only to be maintained, but increased there by natural population. He agreed, too, as to the propriety of the abolition. But when his honorable friend talked of direct and abrupt abolition, he would submit it to him, whether he did not run counter to the prejudices of those who were most deeply interested in the question; and whether, if he could obtain his object without wounding these, it would not be better to do it? Did he not also forget the sacred attention which parliament had ever shown to the private interests and patrimonial rights of individuals?

Mr. Addington (the speaker) professed himself to be one of those moderate persons alluded to by Mr. Dundas. He wished to see some middle measure suggested. The fear of doing injury to the property of others had hitherto prevented him from giving an opinion against the system, the continuance of which he could not countenance.

Mr. Fox said that after what had fallen from the two last speakers, he could remain no longer silent. Something so mischievous had come out, and something so like a foundation had been laid for preserving, not only for years to come, but forever, this detestable traffic, that he should feel himself wanting in his duty, if he were not to deprecate all such deceptions and delusions upon the country.

The honorable gentlemen had called themselves moderate men; but upon this subject he neither felt, nor desired to feel, anything like a sentiment of moderation. Their speeches had reminded him of a passage in Middleton's Life of Cicero. The translation of it was defective, though it would equally suit his purpose. He says: "To enter into a man's house and kill him, his wife and family, in the night, is certainly a most heinous crime, and deserving of death; but to break open his house, to murder him, his wife, and all his children, in the night, may be still right, provided it be done with moderation." Now, was there any thing more absurd in this passage, than to say that the slave-trade might be carried on with moderation; for, if you could not rob or murder a single man with moderation, with what moderation could you pillage and wound a whole nation? In fact, the question of the abolition was simply a question of justice. It was only whether we should authorize by law, respecting Africa, the commission of crimes for which, in this country, we should forfeit our lives; notwithstanding which, it was to be treated, in the opinion of these honorable gentlemen, with moderation.

Upon the whole, he would give his opinion of this traffic in a few words. He believed it to be impolitic, he knew it to be inhuman; he was certian it was unjust; he thought it so inhuman and unjust that if the colonies could not be cultivated without it, they ought not to be cultivated at all. It would be much better for us to be without them, than not to abolish the slave-trade. He hoped therefore that the members would this night act the part which would do them honor. He declared, that whether he should vote in a large minority or a small one, he would never give up the cause. Whether in the house of parliament or out of it, in whatever situation he might ever be, as long as he had a voice to speak, this question should never be at rest. Believing the trade to be of the nature of crimes and pollutions, which stained the honor of the country, he would never relax his efforts. It was his duty to prevent man from preying upon man; and if he and his friends should die before they had attained their glorious object, he hoped there would never be wanting men alive to their duty, who would continue to labor till the evil should be wholly done away. If the situation of the Africans was as happy as servitude could make them, he could not consent to the enormous crime of selling man to man, nor permit a practice to continue, which put an entire bar to the civilization of one quarter of the globe. He was sure that the nation would not much longer allow the continuance of enormities which shocked human nature. The West Indies had no right to demand that crimes should be permitted by this country for their advantage; and if they were wise, they would lend their cordial assistance to such measures as would bring about in the shortest possible time the abolition of this execrable trade.

Mr. Jenkinson admitted that the slave-trade was an evil. He admitted also that the state of slavery was an evil; if the question was, not whether we should abolish, but whether we should establish these, he would be the first to oppose himself to their existence; but there were many evils which we should have thought it our duty to prevent, yet which, when they had once arisen, it was more dangerous to oppose than to submit to. The duty of a statesman was, not to consider abstractedly what was right or wrong, but to weigh the consequences which were likely to result from the abolition of an evil, against those which were likely to result from its continuance. Agreeing then most perfectly with the abolitionists in their end, he differed from them only in the means of accomplishing it. He was desirous of doing that gradually, which he conceived they were doing rashly. He had therefore drawn up two propositions. The first was, that an address be presented to his majesty, that he would recommend to the colonial assemblies to grant premiums to such planters and overseers as should distinguish themselves by promoting the annual increase of the slaves by birth; and likewise freedom to every female slave, who had reared five children to the age of seven years. The second was, that a bounty of five pounds per head be given to the master of every slave-ship, who should import in any cargo a greater number of females than males, not exceeding the age of twenty-five years. To bring forward these propositions, he would now move that the chairman leave the chair.

Mr. Pitt rejoiced that the debate had taken a turn which contracted the question into such narrow limits. The matter then in dispute was merely as to the time at which the abolition should take place. He therefore congratulated the house, the country, and the world, that this great point had been gained; that we might now consider this trade as having received its condemnation; that this curse of mankind was seen in its true light; and that the greatest stigma on our national character, which ever yet existed, was about to be removed! Mankind, he trusted, were now likely to be delivered from *the greatest practical evil that ever afflicted the human race;* from the most severe and extensive calamity recorded in the history of the world.

Mr. Pitt proceeded to remark upon the civilization of Africa; as his eye had just glanced upon a West Indian law, in the evidence upon the table, he said he would begin with an argument, which the sight of it had suggested to him. This argument had been ably answered in the course of the evening; but he would view it in yet another light. It had been said that the savage disposition of the Africans rendered the prospect of their civilization almost hopeless. This argument was indeed of long standing; but last year it had been supported upon a new ground. Captain Frazer had stated in his evidence that a boy had been put to death at Cabenda, because there were those who refused to purchase him as a slave. This single story was deemed by him, and had been considered by others, as a sufficient proof of the barbarity of the Africans, and of the inutility of abolishing the slave-trade. But they, who had used this fact, had suppressed several circumstances relating to it. It appeared, on questioning Captain Frazer afterwards, that this boy had previously run away from his master three several times; that the master had to pay his value, according to the custom of the country, every time he was brought back; and that partly from anger at the boy for running away so frequently, and partly to prevent a repetition of the same expense, he determined to destory him. Such was the explanation of the signal instance which was to fix barbarity on all Africa, as it came out in the cross-examination of Captain Frazer. That this African master was unenlightened and barbarous, he freely admitted; but what would an enlightened and civilized West Indian have done in a similar case? He would quote the law, passed in the West Indies in 1722, which he had just cast his eye upon in the book of evidence, by which law this very same crime of running away was by the legislature of an island, by the grave and deliberate sentence of an enlightened legislature, punished with death; and this, not in the case only of the third offense, but even in the very first instance. It was enacted, "That if any negro or other slave should withdraw himself from his master for the term of six months, or any slave, who was absent, should not return within that time, every such person should suffer death." There was also another West Indian law, by which every negro was armed against his fellow-negro, for he was authorized to kill every runaway slave; and he had even a reward held out to him for so doing.

Let the house now contrast the two cases. Let them ask themselves which of the two exhibited the greatest barbarity; and whether they could possibly vote for the continuance of the slave-trade, upon the principle that the Africans had shown themselves to be a race of incorrigible barbarians!

Something like an opposite argument, but with a like view, had been maintained by others on this subject. It had been said, in justification of the trade, that the Africans had derived some little civilization from their intercourse with us. Yes, we had given them just enough of the forms of justice to enable them to add the pretext of legal trials to their other modes of perpetrating the most atrocious crimes. We had given them just enough of European improvements to enable them the more effectually to turn Africa into a ravaged wilderness. Alas! alas! we had carried on a trade with them from this civilized and enlightened country, which, instead of diffusing knowledge, had been a check to every laudable pursuit. We had carried a poison into their country which spread its contagious effects from one end of it to the other, and which penetrated to its very centre, corrupting every part to which it reached. We had there subverted the whole order of nature; we had aggravated every natural barbarity, and furnished to every man motives for committing, under the name of trade, acts of perpetual hostility and perfidy against his neighbor. Thus had the perversion of British commerce carried misery instead of happiness to one whole quarter of the globe. False to the very principles of trade, misguided in our policy, unmindful of our duty, what almost irreparable mischief had we done to that continent! How shall we hope to obtain forgiveness from heaven if we refused to use those means which the mercy of Providence had still reserved to us for wiping away the guilt and shame with which we were now covered? If we refused even this degree of compensation, how aggravated would be our guilt! Should we delay, then, to repair these incalculable injuries? We ought to count the days, nay, the very hours which intervened to delay the accomplishment of such a work.

On this great subject, the civilization of Africa, which, he confessed, was near his heart, he would yet add a few observations. And first he would say, that the present deplorable state of the country, especially when he reflected that her chief calamities were to be ascribed to us, called for a generous aid, rather than justified any despair, on our part, of her recovery, and still less a repetition of our injuries. On what ground of theory or history did we act, when we supposed that she was never to be reclaimed? There was a time, which it now might be fit to call to remembrance, when human sacrifices, and even this very practice of the slave-trade, existed in our own island. Slaves, as we may read in Henry's history of Great Britain, were formerly an established article of our exports. "Great numbers," he says, "were exported, like cattle, from the British coast, and were to be seen exposed for sale in the Roman market." "Adultery, witchcraft, and debt," says the same historian, "were probably some of the chief sources of supplying the Roman market with British slaves; prisoners taken in war were added to the number; there might be also among them some unfortunate gamesters, who, after having lost all their goods, at length staked themselves, their wives, and their children." Now every one of these sources of slavery had been stated to be at this hour a source of slavery in Africa.   If these practices, therefore, were to be admitted as proofs of the natural incapacity of its inhabitants, why might they not have been applied to ancient Britain ?   Why might not then some Roman senator, pointing to British barbarians, have predicted with equal boldness, that these were a people who were destined never to be free; who were without the understanding necessary for the attainment of useful arts ; depressed by the hand of nature below the level of the human species, and created to form a supply of slaves for the rest of the world ?   But happily, since that time, notwithstanding what would then have been the justness of these predictions, we had emerged from barbarism.   We were now raised to a situation which exhibited a striking contrast to every circumstance by which a Roman might have characterized us, and by which we now characterized Africa.   There was, indeed, one thing wanting to complete the contrast, and to clear us altogether from the imputation of acting even to this hour as barbarians ; for we continued to this hour a barbarous traffic in slaves.   We continued it even yet, in spite of all our great pretensions.   We were once as obscure among the nations of the earth, as savage in our manners, as debased in our morals, as degraded in our understandings as these unhappy Africans.   But in the lapse of a long series of years, by a progression slow, and for a time almost imperceptible, we had become rich in a variety of acquirements.   We were favored above measure in the gifts of Providence, we were unrivaled in commerce, preëminent in arts, foremost in the pursuits of philosophy and science, and established in all the blessings of civil society ; we were in the possession of peace, of liberty, and of happiness ; we were under the guidance of a mild and a beneficent religion; and we were protected by impartial laws, and the purest administration of justice ; we were living under a system of government, which our own happy experience led us to pronounce the best and wisest, and which had become the admiration of the world.   From all these blessings we must forever have been excluded had there been any truth in those principles which some had not hesitated to lay down as applicable to the case of Africa ; and we should have been, at this moment, little superior, either in morals, knowledge, or refinement, to the rude inhabitants of that continent.

If, then, we felt that this perpetual confinement in the fetters of brutal ignorance would have been the greatest calamity which could have befallen us ; if we viewed with gratitude the contrast between our present and our former situation ; if we shuddered to think of the misery which would still have overwhelmed us, had our country continued to the present times, through some cruel policy, to be the mart for slaves to the more civilized nations of the world; God forbid that we should any longer subject Africa to the same dreadful scourge, and exclude that light of knowledge from her coasts which had reached every other quarter of the globe !

He trusted we should no longer continue this commerce ; and that we should no longer consider ourselves as conferring too great a boon on the natives of

Africa, in restoring them to the rank of human beings. He trusted we should not think ourselves too liberal, if, by abolishing the slave-trade, we gave them the same common chance of civilization with other parts of the world. If we listened to the voice of reason and duty this night, some of us might live to see a reverse of that picture, from which we now turn our eyes with shame. We might live to behold the natives engaged in the calm occupations of industry, and in the pursuit of a just commerce. We might behold the beams of science and philosophy breaking in upon their land, which at some happy period in some later times might blaze with full lustre; and joining their influence to that of pure religion, might illuminate and invigorate the most distant extremities of that immense continent. Then might we hope that even Africa, though last of all the quarters of the globe, should enjoy at length, in the evening of her days, those blessings which had descended so plentifully upon us in a much earlier period of the world. Then also would Europe, participating in her improvement and prosperity, receive an ample recompense for the tardy kindness (if kindness it could be called) of no longer hindering her from extricating herself out of the darkness, which, in other more fortunate regions, had been so much more speedily dispelled.

It was in this view, it was as an atonement for our long and cruel injustice towards Africa that the measure proposed by his honorable friend, Mr. Wilberforce, most forcibly recommended itself to his mind. The great and happy change to be expected in the state of her inhabitants was, of all the various benefits of the abolition, in his estimation the most extensive and important. He should vote against the adjournment, and he should also oppose every proposition which tended to prevent or even to postpone for an hour the total abolition of the slave-trade.

Two divisions took place. In the first there were 193 votes for gradual abolition, and 125 for immediate; and in the second there were 230 for gradual, and 85 for no abolition at all. On the 25th of April, Mr. Dundas brought forward a plan conformable with the resolutions of the house above mentioned. He considered that eight years ought to be allowed the planters to stock themselves with negroes, and therefore moved that the year 1800 should be the epoch, after which no more slaves should be imported from Africa in British vessels to the West Indies. Sir Edward Knatchbull proposed the year 1796, which motion was carried by 151 to 132.

After the debate, the committee for the abolition of the slave-trade held a meeting and voted their thanks to Mr. Wilberforce for his motion, and to Mr. Pitt, Mr. Fox, and those other members of the house who had so eloquently supported it. They resolved, also, that a gradual abolition of the slave-trade was not an adequate remedy for its injustice and cruelty; neither could it be deemed a compliance with the general wishes of the people, as expressed in their numerous and urgent petitions to parliament; and they resolved, lastly, to use all constitutional means to obtain its immediate abolition.

CHAPTER XV.

PARLIAMENTARY HISTORY.—SLAVE TRADE RENDERED ILLEGAL.

Action of the House of Lords in 1792.—Clarkson retires from the field from ill health, in 1794.—Mr. Wilberforce's annual motion.—Session of 1799.—Speech of Canning.—Sessions of 1804 and 1805.—Clarkson resumes his labors.—Death of Mr. Pitt, January, 1806.—Administration of Grenville and Fox.—Session of 1806.—Debate in the House of Lords.—Speeches of Lord Grenville, Erskine, Dr. Porteus, Earls Stanhope and Spencer, Lords Holland and Ellenborough.—Death of Fox, October, 1806.—Contest and triumph in 1807.—Final passage of the Bill for the Abolition of the African Slave Trade.—Slave trade declared felony in 1811, and declared piracy in 1824, by England. England abolishes slavery in her colonies, 1833.—Prohibition of Slave Trade by European governments.—Slavery abolished in Mexico, 1829—In Guatemala and Colombia.

THE gradual abolition having been thus agreed upon for 1796, by the house of commons, a committee carried the resolution to the house of lords. On the 8th of May, 1792, the lords met to consider it, when a motion was made by Lord Stormont, on the part of the planters, merchants, and other interested persons, to hear new evidence. On the 5th of June, when only seven witnesses had been examined, all further proceedings were postponed to the next session.

Nothing could be more distressing to the friends of the measure than this determination of the lords; first, because there was no knowing how many years they might prolong the hearing of evidence; and secondly, it involved the necessity of finding out and keeping up a respectable body of witnesses on the side of the opponents of the trade. Mr. Clarkson, therefore, set out again in the month of July on his old errand, and returned in February, 1793. The house of commons was then sitting. The only step to be taken was to bring forward its own vote of the former year, by which the slave-trade was to be abolished in 1796, in order that this vote might be reconsidered and renewed. This motion, made by Mr. Wilberforce, was furiously opposed, and lost by a majority of 61 to 53. By this determination the commons actually refused to sanction their own vote. In the house of lords, but seven witnesses were examined during this session.

Mr. Clarkson once more traversed the kingdom in search of witnesses. He returned in February, 1794, but in such a wretched state of health as to be unable to lend any farther assistance to the committee. The incessant labor of body and mind for so many years, aggravated by anxiety and disappointments, had made a serious inroad upon his constitution. His nervous system had been shattered,—his hearing, voice, and memory were nearly gone. He was therefore obliged, very reluctantly, to be borne out of the field, where he had placed the great honor and glory of his life. Mr. Clarkson says: "These disorders had been brought on by degrees in consequence of the severe labors necessarily attached to the promotion of the cause. For seven years I had a correspondence to maintain with four hundred persons with my own hand. I had some book or other annually to write in behalf of the cause. In this time I had traveled more than thirty-five thousand miles in search of evidence, and a great part of these journeys in the night. All this time my mind had been on the stretch. It had been bent, too, to this one subject; for I had not even leisure to attend to my own concerns. The various instances of barbarity which had come successively to my knowledge, within this period, had vexed, harassed, and afflicted it. The wound which these had produced was rendered still deeper by those cruel disappointments before related, which arose from the reiterated refusal of persons to give their testimony, after I had traveled hundreds of miles in quest of them. But the severest stroke was that inflicted by the persecution begun and pursued by persons interested in the continuance of the trade, of such witnesses as had been examined against them; and whom, on account of their dependent situations in life, it was most easy to oppress. As I had been the means of bringing these forward on these occasions, they naturally came to me, when thus persecuted, as the author of their miseries and their ruin. From their supplications and wants it would have been ungenerous and ungrateful to have fled. The late Mr. Whitbread, to whom one day in deep affliction on this account I related accidentally a circumstance of this kind, generously undertook, in order to make my mind easy upon the subject, to make good all injuries which should in future arise to individuals from such persecution; and he repaired these, at different times, at a considerable expense. I feel it a duty to divulge this circumstance, out of respect to the memory of one of the best of men, and of one whom, if the history of his life were written, it would appear to have been an extraordinary honor to the country to have produced."

In the session of 1795, Mr. Wilberforce moved for leave to bring in a bill for the abolition of the slave-trade. The motion was lost by a small majority. In 1796, Mr. Wilberforce resolved to try the question in a new shape. He moved that the trade be abolished in a limited time, but without assigning to its duration any specific date. He wished the house to agree to this as a general principle. After much opposition, the principle was acknowledged; but when, in consequence of this acknowledgment of it, he brought in a bill and attempted to introduce into one of its clauses, the year 1797, as the period when the trade should cease, he lost it by a majority of 74 to 70. He allowed the next session to pass without any parliamentary notice of the subject, but in 1798 he renewed his motion for a limited time, which was lost.

In the year 1799, undismayed by these different disappointments, he again renewed his motion. Colonel M. Wood, Mr. Petrie, and others, among whom were Mr. Windham and Mr. Dundas, opposed it. Messrs. Pitt, Fox, W. Smith, Sir William Dolben, Sir R. Milbank, Mr. Hobhouse, and Mr. Canning, supported it. Sir R. Milbank contended that modifications of a system fundamentally wrong ought not to be tolerated by the legislature of a free nation. Mr. Hobhouse said that nothing could be so nefarious as this traffic in blood. It was unjust in its principle. It was cruel in its practice. It admitted of no regulation whatever. The abolition of it was called for equally by morality and sound policy.

Mr. Canning exposed the folly of Mr. Dundas, who had said that as parliament had in the year 1787 left the abolition to the colonial assemblies, it ought not to be taken out of their hands. This great event, he observed, could only be accomplished in two ways; either by these assemblies, or by the parliament of England. Now the members of the assembly of Jamaica had professed that they would never abolish the trade. Was it not therefore idle to rely upon them for the accomplishment of it? He then took a very comprehensive view of the arguments which had been offered in the course of the debate, and was severe upon the planters in the house, who, he said, had brought into familiar use certain expressions with no other view than to throw a veil over their odious system. Among these was their right to import laborers. But never was the word "laborers" so prostituted as when it was used for slaves. Never was the word "right" so prostituted, not even when The Rights of Man were talked of, as when the right to trade in man's blood was asserted by the members of an enlightened assembly. Never was the right of importing these laborers worse defended than when the antiquity of the slave-trade, and its foundation on ancient acts of parliament, were brought forward in its support. We had been cautioned not to lay our unhallowed hands on the ancient institution of the slave-trade; nor to subvert a fabric raised by the wisdom of our ancestors, and consecrated by a lapse of ages. But on what principles did we usually respect the institutions of antiquity? We respected them when we saw some shadow of departed worth and usefulness, or some memorial of what had been creditable to mankind. But was this the case with the slave-trade? Had it begun in principles of justice or national honor, which the changes of the world alone had impaired? Had it to plead former services and glories in behalf of its present disgrace? In looking at it we saw nothing but crimes and sufferings from the beginning; nothing but what wounded and convulsed our feelings; nothing but what excited indignation and horror. It had not even to plead what could often be said in favor of the most unjustifiable wars. Though conquest had sometimes originated in ambition, and in the worst of motives, yet the conquerors and the conquered were sometimes blended afterwards into one people; so that a system of common interest arose out of former differences. But where was the analogy of the cases? Was it only at the outset that we could trace violence and injustice on the part of the slave-trade? Were the oppressors and the oppressed so reconciled that enmities ultimately ceased? No. Was it reasonable, then, to urge a prescriptive right, not to the fruits of an ancient and forgotten evil, but to a series of new violences; to a chain of fresh enormities; to cruelties continually repeated; and of which every instance inflicted a fresh calamity, and constituted a separate and substantial crime?

The debate being over, the house divided; when it appeared that there were for Mr. Wilberforce's motion seventy-four, but against it eighty-two.

The question had now been tried and lost in almost every possible shape, but Mr. Wilberforce and the committee resolved to hold themselves in readiness to seize the first favorable opportunity which should present itself of furthering the cause. Four years passed over without action, but the year 1804 was fixed upon for renewed exertion.   Among the reasons for fixing upon this year, one may be assigned, namely, that the Irish members, in consequence of the union which had taken place between the two countries, had then all taken their seats in the house of commons; and that most of them were friendly to the cause.

This being the situation of things, Mr. Wilberforce, on the 30th of March, asked leave to renew his bill for the abolition of the slave-trade within a limited time.   Mr. Fuller opposed it.   A debate ensued.

An amendment having been proposed by Mr. Manning, a division took place upon it, when leave was given to bring in the bill, by a majority of one hundred and twenty-four to forty-nine.

On the 7th of June, the second reading of the bill was moved.   Upon a division, there appeared for the second reading one hundred, and against it forty-two.

On the 27th of June, the bill, though opposed in its last stage, was carried by a majority of sixty-nine to thirty-six.   It was then taken up to the lords; but on a motion of Lord Hawkesbury, then a member of that house, the discussion of it was postponed to the next year.

The session being ended, the committee for the abolition of the slave-trade increased its number by the election of the Right Honorable Lord Teignmouth, Dr. Dickson, and Wilson Birkbeck, as members.

In the year 1805, Mr. Wilberforce renewed his motion of the former year. Colonel Tarleton, Sir William Yonge, Mr. Fuller, and Mr. Gascoyne opposed it.   Leave was given to introduce his bill.

On the second reading of it a serious opposition took place; and an amendment was moved for postponing it till that day six months.   The amendment was opposed by Mr. Fox and Mr. Huddlestone.   The latter could not help lifting his voice against this monstrous traffic in the sinews and blood of man, the toleration of which had so long been the disgrace of the British legislature. He did not charge the enormous guilt resulting from it upon the nation at large; for the nation had washed its hands of it by the numerous petitions it had sent against it; and it had since been a matter of astonishment to all Christendom how the constitutional guardians of British freedom should have sanctioned elsewhere the greatest system of cruelty and oppression in the world.

He said that a curse attended this trade even in the mode of defending it. By a certain fatality, none but the vilest arguments were brought forward, which corrupted the very persons who used them.   Every one of these were built on the narrow ground of interest; of pecuniary profit; of sordid gain; in opposition to every higher consideration; to every motive that had reference to humanity, justice, and religion; or to that great principle which comprehended them all.   Place only before the most determined advocate of this odious traffic the exact image of himself in the garb and harness of a slave, dragged and whipped about like a beast; place this image also before him, and paint it as that of one without a ray of hope to cheer him; and you would extort from him the reluctant confession that he would not endure for an hour the misery to which he condemned his fellow-man for life. How dared he, then, to use this selfish plea of interest against the voice of the generous sympathies of his nature ? But even upon this narrow ground the advocates for the traffic had been defeated. If the unhallowed argument of expediency was worth any thing when opposed to moral rectitude, or if it were to supercede the precepts of Christianity, where was a man to stop, or what line was he to draw ? For any thing he knew, it might be physically true that human blood was the best manure for the land ; but who ought to shed it on that account ? True expediency, however, was, where it ever would be found, on the side of that system which was most merciful and just. He asked how it happened that sugar could be imported cheaper from the East Indies than from the West, notwithstanding the vast difference of the length of the voyages, but on account of the impolicy of slavery, or that it was made in the former case by the industry of free men, and in the latter by the languid drudgery of slaves.

As he had had occasion to advert to the eastern part of the world, he would make an observation upon an argument which had been collected from that quarter. The condition of the negroes in the West Indies had been lately compared with that of the Hindoos. But he would observe that the Hindoo, miserable as his hovel was, had sources of pride and happiness to which not only the West Indian slave, but even his master was a stranger. He was, to be sure, a peasant, and his industry was subservient to the gratifications of an European lord. But he was, in his own belief, vastly superior to him. He viewed him as one of the lowest cast. He would not, on any consideration, eat from the same plate. He would not suffer his son to marry the daughter of his master, even if she could bring him all the West Indies as her portion. He would observe, too, that the Hindoo peasant drank his water from his native well ; that if his meal were scanty, he received it from the hand of her who was most dear to him ; that when he labored, he labored for her and his offspring. His daily task being finished, he reposed with his family. No retrospect of the happiness of former days, compared with existing misery, disturbed his slumber; nor horrid dreams occasioned him to wake in agony at the dawn of day. No barbarous sounds of cracking whips reminded him that, with the form and image of a man, his destiny was that of the beast of the field. Let the advocates for the bloody traffic state what they had to set off on their side of the question against the comforts and independence of the man with whom they compared the slave.

The amendment was supported by Sir William Yonge, Sir William Pulteny, Colonel Tarleton, Mr. Gascoyne, C. Brook, and Hiley Addington. On dividing the house upon it, there appeared for it seventy-seven, but against it only seventy.

This defeat occasioned the severest disappointment. The committee instantly met, when sorrow was seen in the countenances of all present, but they determined to renew the contest with redoubled vigor at the next session. Just at this moment Mr. Clarkson joined them. Eight years of retirement had nearly restored him, and the first moment he found himself able to embark

16

in the cause, he returned to his post.   As it was probable the bill would be passed the next year, by the commons, and if so, that it would go to the lords, and that they might require further evidence, it was judged proper that evidence should be prepared.   The band of witnesses which had been last collected were broken by death and dispersion, and a new one was to be formed. This Herculean task Mr. Clarkson undertook.   He left London immediately, and returned in January, 1806, after having traveled in pursuit of his object 5000 miles.   In this month died Mr. Pitt, who had been one of the great supporters of the cause.

Mr. Clarkson says : "The way in which Mr. Pitt became acquainted with this question, has already been explained.   A few doubts having been removed, when it was first started, he professed himself a friend to the abolition.   The first proof which he gave of his friendship to it is known to but few ; but it is nevertheless true, that so early as in 1788, he occasioned a communication to be made to the French grvernment, in which he recommended a union of the two countries for the prromotion of the great measure.   This proposition seemed to be then new and strange to the court of France, and the answer was not favorable.

"From this time his efforts were reduced within the boundaries of his own powers.   As far, however, as he had scope, he exerted them.   If we look at him in his parliamentary capacity, it must be acknowledged by all that he took an active, strenuous and consistent part, and this, year after year, by which he realized his professions.   In my own private communications with him, which were frequent, he never failed to give proof of a similar disposition.   I had always free access to him.   I had no previous note or letter to write for admission.   Whatever papers I wanted he ordered.   He exhibited also in his conversation with me on these occasions marks of more than ordinary interest in the welfare of the cause.   Among the subjects which were started, there was one which was always near his heart.   This was the civilization of Africa.   He looked upon this great work as a debt due to that continent for the many injuries we had inflicted upon it : and had the abolition succeeded sooner, as in the infancy of his exertions he had hoped, I know he had a plan, suited no doubt to the capaciousness of his own mind, for such establishments in Africa as he conceived would promote in due time this important end."

On the 31st March, 1806, the question was ushered again into parliament, but under new auspices, namely, under the administration of Lord Grenville and Mr. Fox.   It was thought proper that Mr. Wilberforce should be, as it were, in the back ground on this occasion, and that the attorney general, as a conspicuous officer of the government, should introduce it.   The latter accordingly brought in a bill, one of the objects of which was to prevent British merchants and British capital from being employed in the foreign slave-trade. This bill passed both houses of parliament, and was therefore the first that dismembered the traffic.   In the debate it was declared, in substance, both by Lord Grenville and Mr. Fox, in their respective houses, that they would do every thing to effect the abolition, and should they succeed in such a noble work, they would regard their success as entailing more true glory on their administration, and more honor and advantage on the country than any other measure in which they could be engaged.

On the 10th of June, Mr. Fox, in a speech most luminous and pathetic, followed up the victory which had been just gained, by moving a resolution "that this house, considering the African slave-trade to be contrary to the principles of humanity, justice and policy, will, with all practical expedition, take effectual measures for the abolition of it in such manner and at such a period as may be deemed most advisable." This motion produced a strong opposition, and an interesting debate. It was supported by Milbank, Francis, Sir Samuel Romilly, Wilberforce, Petty, Newport, Canning and Smith. It was carried by a majority of 114 to 15. Mr. Wilberforce directly moved an address to the king " praying him to direct a negotiation to be entered into by which foreign powers should be invited to coöperate with his majesty in measures to be adopted for the abolition of the African slave-trade." This was carried, but without a division. On the 24th June, the lords met to consider both the resolution and address. In order to create delay, a proposition was directly made that counsel and evidence should be heard. This was overruled. Lord Grenville then rose up and introduced the subject. His speech was among the masterpieces of eloquence.

Lord Grenville read the resolution of the commons. This resolution, he said, stated first, that the slave-trade was contrary to humanity, justice, and sound policy. That it was contrary to humanity, was obvious; for humanity might be said to be sympathy for the distress of others, or a desire to accomplish benevolent ends by good means. But did not the slave-trade convey ideas the very reverse of this definition ? It deprived men of all those comforts in which it pleased the Creator to make the happiness of his creatures to consist, of the blessings of society, of the charities of the dear relationships of husband, wife, father, son, and kindred ; of the due discharge of the relative duties of these, and of that freedom which in its pure and natural sense was one of the greatest gifts of God to man.

Having shown the inhumanity, he would proceed to the second point in the resolution, or the injustice of the trade. We had two ideas of justice, first, as it belonged to society by virtue of a social compact ; and, secondly, as it belonged to men, not as citizens of a community, but as beings of one common nature. In a state of nature, man had a right to the fruit of his own labor absolutely to himself ; and one of the main purposes for which he entered into society was, that he might be better protected in the possession of his rights. In both cases, therefore, it was manifestly unjust that a man should be made to labor during the whole of his life, and yet have no benefit from his labor. Hence, the slave-trade and the colonial slavery were a violation of the very principal upon which all law for the protection of property was founded. Whatever benefit was derived from that trade to an individual, it was derived from dishonor and dishonesty. He forced from the unhappy victim of it, that which the latter did not wish to give him ; and he gave to the same victim, that which he in vain attempted to show was an equivalent to the thing he took, it being a thing for which there was no equivalent; and which, if he had not obtained by force, he would not have possessed at all. Nor could there be any answer to this reasoning, unless it could be proved that it had pleased God to give to the inhabitants of Britain a property in the liberty and life of the natives of Africa. But he would go further on this subject. The injustice complained of was not confined to the bare circumstance of robbing them of the right to their own labor. - It was conspicuous throughout the system. They who bought them, became guilty of all the crimes which had been committed in procuring them; and, when they possessed them, of all the crimes which belonged to their inhuman treatment. The injustice, in the latter case, amounted frequently to murder. For what was it but murder to pursue a practice which produced untimely death to thousands of innocent and helpless beings? It was a duty which their lordships owed to their Creator, if they hoped for mercy, to do away this monstrous oppression.

With respect to the impolicy of the trade (the third point in the resolution) he would say at once, that whatever was inhuman and unjust must be impolitic. He had, however, no objection to argue the point upon its own particular merits; and, first, he would observe that a great man, Mr. Pitt, now no more, had exerted his vast powers on many subjects to the admiration of his hearers; but on none more successfully than on the subject of the abolition of the slave-trade. He proved, after making an allowance for the price paid for the slaves in the West Indies, for the loss of them in the seasoning, and for the expense of maintaining them afterwards, and comparing these particulars with the amount in value of their labor there, that the evils endured by the victims of the traffic were no gain to the master in whose service they took place. Indeed, Mr. Long had laid it down in his history of Jamaica, that the best way to secure the planters from ruin would be to do that which the resolution recommended. It was notorious that when any planter was in distress and sought to relieve himself by increasing the labor on his estate by means of the purchase of new slaves, the measure invariably tended to his destruction. What, then, was the importation of fresh Africans but a system tending to the general ruin of the islands?

To expose the impolicy of the trade further, he would observe that it was an allowed axiom, that as the condition of man was improved, he became more useful. The history of our own country, in very early times, exhibited instances of internal slavery, and this to a considerable extent. But we should find that precisely in proportion as that slavery was ameliorated, the power and prosperity of the country flourished. This was exactly applicable to the case in question. There could be no general amelioration of slavery in the West Indies while the slave-trade lasted; but, if we were to abolish it, we should make it the interest of every owner of slaves to do that which would improve their condition; and which, indeed, would lead, ultimately, to the annihilation of slavery itself. This great event, however, could not be accomplished at once. It could only be effected in a course of time.

It would be endless, he said, to go into all the cases which would manifest the impolicy of this odious traffic. Inhuman as it was, unjust as it was, he believed it to be equally impolitic; and if their lordships should be of this opinion also, he hoped they would agree to that part of the resolution in which these truths were expressed. With respect to the other part of it, or that they would proceed to abolish the trade, he observed, that neither the time nor the manner of doing it were specified. Hence, if any of them should differ as to these particulars, they might yet vote for the resolution, as they were not pledged to anything definite in these respects, provided they thought that the trade should be abolished at some time or other; and he did not believe that there was any one of them who would sanction its continuance forever.

Lord Hawkesbury said that he did not mean to discuss the question on the ground of justice and humanity, as contradistinguished from sound policy. If it could fairly be made out that the African slave-trade was contrary to justice and humanity, it ought to be abolished. It did not, however, follow because a great evil existed, that therefore it should be removed; for it might be comparatively a less evil than that which would accompany the attempt to remove it. The noble lord who had just spoken, had exemplified this; for, though slavery was a great evil in itself, he was of opinion that it could not be done away but in a course of time.

The Bishop of London (Dr. Porteus) began by noticing the concession of the last speaker, namely, that if the trade was contrary to humanity and justice, it ought to be abolished. He expected, he said, that the noble lord would have proved that it was not contrary to these great principles, before he had supported its continuance; but not a word had he said to show that the basis of the resolution in these respects was false. It followed, then, he thought, that as the noble lord had not disproved the premises, he was bound to abide by the conclusion.

The lord chancellor (Erskine) confessed that he was not satisfied with his own conduct on this subject. He acknowledged, with deep contrition, that during the time he was a member of the other house, he had not once attended when this great question was discussed.

In the West Indies he could say personally, that the slaves were well treated, where he had an opportunity of seeing them. But no judgment was to be formed there with respect to the evils complained of. They must be appreciated as they existed in the trade. Of these he had also been an eye-witness. It was on this account that he felt contrition for not having attended the house on this subject; for there were some cruelties in this traffic which the human imagination could not aggravate. He had witnessed such scenes over the whole coast of Africa; and he could say, that if their lordships could only have a sudden glimpse of them, they would be struck with horror, and would be astonished that they could ever have been permitted to exist. What, then, would they say to their continuance year after year, and from age to age?

From information which he could not dispute, he was warranted in saying that on this continent husbands were fraudulently and forcibly severed from their wives, and parents from their children; and that all the ties of blood and affection were torn up by the roots. He had himself seen the unhappy natives put together in heaps in the hold of a ship, where, with every possible attention to them, their situation must have been intolerable. He had also heard proved, in courts of justice, facts still more dreadful than those which he had seen. One of these he would just mention. The slaves on board a certain ship rose in a mass to liberate themselves; and having advanced far in the pursuit of their object, it became necessary to repel them by force. Some of them yielded; some of them were killed in the scuffle; but many of them actually jumped into the sea and were drowned; thus preferring death to the misery of their situation; while others hung to the ship, repenting of their rashness, and bewailing with frightful noises their horrid fate. Thus the whole vessel exhibited but one hideous scene of wretchedness. They who were subdued and secured in chains were seized with the flux, which carried many of them off. These things were proved in a trial before a British jury, which had to consider whether this was a loss which fell within the policy of insurance, the slaves being regarded as if they had been only a cargo of dead matter. He could mention other instances, but they were much too shocking to be described. Surely their lordships could never consider such a traffic to be consistent with humanity or justice. It was impossible.

That the trade had long existed there was no doubt; but this was no argument for its continuance. Many evils of much longer standing had been done away; and it was always our duty to attempt to remove them. Should we not exult in the consideration that we, the inhabitants of a small island, at the extremity of the globe, almost at its north pole, were become the morning-star to enlighten the nations of the earth, and to conduct them out of the shades of darkness into the realms of light; thus exhibiting to an astonished and an admiring world the blessings of a free constitution? Let us, then, not allow such a glorious opportunity to escape us.

It had been urged that we should suffer by the abolition of the slave-trade. He believed we should not suffer. He believed that our duty and our interest were inseparable: and he had no difficulty in saying, in the face of the world, that his own opinion was that the interests of a nation would be best preserved by its adherence to the principles of humanity, justice, and religion.

The Earl of Westmoreland said that the African slave-trade might be contrary to humanity and justice, and yet it might be politic; at least, it might be inconsistent with humanity, and yet be not inconsistent with justice: this was the case when we executed a criminal or engaged in war.

Lord Holland, in reply, said that the noble earl had made a difference between humanity, justice, and sound policy. God forbid that we should ever admit such distinctions in this country! But he had gone further, and said that a thing might be inhuman and yet not unjust; and he put the case of the execution of a criminal in support of it. Did he not by this position confound all notions of right and wrong in human institutions? When a criminal was justly executed, was not the execution justice to him who suffered and humanity to the body of the people at large?

He wished most heartily for the total abolition of the trade. He was convinced that it was both inhuman, unjust, and impolitic. This had always been his opinion as an individual since he was capable of forming one. It was his opinion then as a legislator. It was his opinion as a colonial proprietor; and it was his opinion as an Englishman, wishing for the prosperity of the British empire.

The Earl of Suffolk contended that the population of the slaves in the islands could be kept up by good treatment, so as to be sufficient for their cultivation. He entered into a detail of calculations from the year 1772 downwards in support of this statement. He believed all the miseries of St. Domingo arose from the vast importation of Africans. He had such a deep sense of the inhumanity and injustice of the slave-trade, that if he ever wished any action of his life to be recorded, it would be that of the vote he should then give in support of the resolution.

Lord Sidmouth said that he agreed to the substance of the resolution, but yet he could not support it. Could he be convinced that the trade would be injurious to the cause of humanity and justice, the question with him would be decided; for policy could not be opposed to humanity and justice. He had been of the opinion for the last twenty years that the interests of the country and those of numerous individuals were so deeply blended with this traffic that we should be very cautious how we proceeded. With respect to the cultivation of new lands, he would not allow a single negro to be imported for such a purpose; but he must have a regard for the old plantations. When he found a sufficient increase in the black population to continue the cultivation already established there, then, but not till then, he would agree to an abolition of the trade.

Earl Stanhope said he would not detain their lordships long. He could not, however, help expressing his astonishment at what had fallen from the last speaker; for he had evidently contessed that the slave-trade was inhuman and unjust, and then he had insinuated that it was neither inhuman nor unjust to continue it. A more paradoxical or whimsical opinion, he believed, was never entertained, or more whimsically expressed in that house. The noble viscount had talked of the interests of the planters; but this was but a part of the subject, for surely the people of Africa were not to be forgotten. He did not understand the practice of complimenting the planters with the lives of men, women, and helpless children by thousands for the sake of their pecuniary advantage; and they who adopted it, whatever they might think of the consistency of their own conduct, offered an insult to the sacred names of humanity and justice.

Earl Grosvenor could not but express the joy he felt at the hope, after all his disappointments, that this wicked trade would be done away. He hoped that his majesty's ministers were in earnest, and that they would, early in the next session, take this great question up with a determination to go through with it ; so that another year should not pass before we extended the justice and humanity of the country to the helpless and unhappy inhabitants of Africa.

Earl Fitzwilliam said he was fearful lest the calamities of St. Domingo should be brought home to our own islands. We ought not, he thought, too hastily to adopt the resolution on that account. He should therefore support the previous question.

Lord Ellenborough said he was sorry to differ from his noble friend, (lord Sidmouth,) and yet he could not help saying that if after twenty years, during which this question had been discussed by both houses of parliament, their lordships' judgments were not ripe for its determination, he could not look with any confidence to a time when they would be ready to decide it.

The question then before them was short and plain. It was, whether the African slave-trade was inhuman, unjust, and impolitic. If the premises were true, we could not too speedily bring it to a conclusion.

Earl Spencer agreed with the noble viscount (Sidmouth) that the amelioration of the condition of the slaves was an object which might be effected in the West Indies ; but he was certain that the most effectual way of improving it would be by the total and immediate abolition of the slave-trade ; and for that reason he would support the resolution. Had the resolution held out emancipation to them, it would not have had his assent ; for it would have ill become the character of this country, if it had been once promised, to have withheld it from them. It was to such deception that the horrors of St. Domingo were to be attributed. He would not enter into the discussion of the general subject at present. He was convinced that the trade was what the resolution stated it to be, inhuman, unjust, and impolitic. He wished, therefore, most earnestly indeed, for its abolition. As to the mode of effecting it, it should be such as would be attended with the least inconvenience to all parties. At the same time he would not allow small inconveniences to stand in the way of the great claims of humanity, justice, and religion.

The resolution and address were both carried by a majority of 41 to 20. After this a belief was generally prevalent that the slave-trade would fall at the next session ; but for fear that it should be carried on in the interior, being as it were the last harvest of the merchants, to a tenfold extent, and with tenfold murder and desolation, a law was passed that no new vessel should be permitted to go to the coast of Africa for slaves. In the month of October after these victories, died Charles James Fox, one of the noblest champions of this noble cause. He had lived to put it in a train for final triumph—this triumph he enjoyed in anticipation—the prospect of it soothed his pains and cheered his spirit in the hours of his last sickness. The hope of it quivered on his lips in the hour of dissolution.

The contest was renewed in January, 1807. Lord Grenville brought the question first before the house of lords in the shape of a bill, which he called "An act for the abolition of the the slave-trade." On the 4th four counsel were heard against it. On the 5th the debate commenced. The bill was carried at 4 o'clock in the morning by a vote of 100 to 36. On the 10th of February it went to the commons. On the 20th counsel were heard against it. On the 23d a debate ensued; and it was finally carried by the vast majority of 283 to 16. On the 6th of March the blanks were filled up. It provided that no vessel should clear out for slaves from any port in the British dominions after May 1, 1807, and that no slave should be landed in the British colonies after March 1, 1808. The bill was sent back to the lords, with the blanks filled up; and in consequence of various amendments, it passed and repassed from one house to the other. On the 24th it passed both houses, and on the 25th it received the royal assent.

Thus passed, after twenty years' hard struggle, during which the field had been disputed inch by inch, this "magna charta for Africa in Britain." The news of the event was received with demonstrations of joy throughout the kingdom, and this joy was heightened by authentic news from the United States that a similar law had been passed by congress.

At first the only punishment for continuing the traffic, now declared illegal, was a penalty in money; but this was found so utterly insufficient, that in 1811 an act was carried by Lord Brougham, making slave-dealing felony, punishable by transportation for fourteen years, or imprisonment with hard labor. Even this was found inadequate, and in 1824 the slave-trade was declared to be piracy, and the punishment death. In 1837, when the number of capital offenses was diminished, the punishment was changed to transportation for life.

On the 28th of August, 1833, ENGLAND ABOLISHED SLAVERY THROUGHOUT THE BRITISH COLONIES, (3 and 4 William IV.) and £20,000,000 were granted by parliament as indemnification to the slave proprietors and other pecuniary sufferers by the act. By this act 770,280 slaves became free.

Although the United States have never relieved themselves from the burden of slavery, they were the first to prohibit the prosecution of the slave-trade. In the year 1794, it was enacted that no person in the United States should fit out any vessel there for the purpose of carrying on any traffic in slaves to any foreign country, or for procuring from any foreign country the inhabitants thereof, to be disposed of as slaves. In 1800 it was enacted that it should be unlawful for any citizen of the United States to have any property in any vessel employed in transporting slaves from one foreign country to another, or to serve on board any vessel so employed. Any of the commissioned vessels of the United States were authorized to seize and take any vessel employed in the slave-trade, to be proceeded against in any of the circuit or district courts, and to be condemned for the use of the officers and crew of the vessel making the capture. In 1807, it was enacted, that after the first of January, 1808, it should not be lawful to bring into the United States, or the territories thereof, from any foreign place, any negro, mulatto, or person of color, with intent to hold or sell him as a slave; and heavy penalties are imposed on the violators of these acts, and others of similar import. In 1820, it was enacted, that if any citizen of the United States, belonging to the company of any foreign vessel engaged in the slave-trade, or any person whatever belonging to the company of any vessel, owned in whole or in part by, or navigated for any citizen of the United States, should land on any foreign shore, to seize any negro, or mulatto, not held to service by the laws of either of the states or territories of the United States, with intent to make him a slave, or should decoy or forcibly carry off such negro, or mulatto, or receive him on board any such vessel, with the intent aforesaid, he should be adjudged a pirate, and, on conviction, should suffer death. The same penalty was extended to those of the ship's company who should aid in confining such negro, or mulatto, on board of such vessel, or transfer him, on the sea or tide-water, to any other ship or vessel, or land him, with intent to sell, or having previously sold him.

In Denmark, king Christian VII., in 1794, declared the slave-trade unlawful after January 1, 1804; and Frederic VI. promised, at the peace of Tilsit, to prohibit his subjects from taking part in the foreign slave-trade. In France, Napoleon, when first consul, promised the continuance of their liberty to the inhabitants of St. Domingo, whilst he praised the inhabitants of Isle de France for not having freed their slaves, and promised that France would never again decree the slavery of the whites by the liberation of the negroes. After the successes of the French on St. Domingo, the slave-trade was once more established. In 1814, Lord Castlereagh obtained from Louis XVIII. a promise that France would abolish the slave-trade; but, by the influence of the chamber of commerce at Nantes, this traffic was permitted for five years more. Public opinion obliged Lord Castlereagh to press upon the congress of Vienna the adoption of general measures for the abolition of the slave-trade; but all that he could effect was that Spain and Portugal promised to give up the slave-trade north of the line.—See the treaty between England and Portugal, Vienna, January 22, 1815. But a paper was drawn up and signed by Castlereagh, Stewart, Wellington, Nesselrode, Lowenhielm, Gomez Labrador, Palmella, Saldanha, Lobo, Humboldt, Metternich and Talleyrand, (Vienna, February 8, 1815,) stating that the great powers would make arrangements to fix a term for the general abolition of the slave-trade, since public opinion condemned it as a stain on European civilization. February 6, 1815, Portugal provided for the total abolition of the slave-trade on January 21, 1823, and England promised to pay £300,000 as an indemnification to Portuguese subjects. Louis XVIII., by the treaty of Paris, November 20, 1815, consented to its immediate abolition. for which Napoleon had declared himself prepared, in April, 1815. Spain promised, by the treaty of September 30, 1817, to abolish the slave-trade entirely, October 31, 1820, in all the Spanish territories, even south of the line; and England, February 9, 1818, paid £400,000 as an indemnification to Spanish subjects. The king of the Netherlands prohibited his subjects from taking part in the slave-trade after the provisions of the treaty of August 13, 1814, had been rendered more precise and extensive by the treaty concluded with England, at the Hague, May 4, 1818. Sweden had already done the same, according to the treaty of March 3, 1813. The United States engaged, in the treaty of Ghent, December 24, 1814, to do all in their power for the entire suppression of the slave-trade. November 23, 1826, a treaty was concluded by England with Brazil, for the abolition of the slave-trade, and it was accordingly prohibited after March, 1830.

The emperor of Austria issued a decree utterly abolishing slavery throughout the Austrian dominions. "Every man," said his imperial majesty, "by the right of nature, sanctioned by reason, must be considered a free person." Every slave becomes free the moment he touches the Austrian soil, or even an Austrian ship.

The rising republics of South America took a stand against slavery and the slave-trade. One of the first acts of the constitutional assembly of Guatemala was the abolition of slavery. The 13th article of their constitution declared every man in the republic free; that no one who took refuge under its laws should be a slave; and that no one should be accounted a citizen who was engaged in the slave-trade.

In 1829, Guerrero, the President of Mexico, issued the following decree :

" Desiring to signalize the year 1829, the anniversary of our independence, by an act of national justice and beneficence that may turn to the benefit and support of such a valuable good; that may consolidate more and more public tranquility; that may coöperate to the aggrandizement of the republic, and return to an unfortunate portion of its inhabitants those rights which they hold from nature, and that the people protect by wise and equitable laws, in conformity with the 30th article of the constitutive act,

" Making use of the extraordinary faculties which have been granted to the executive, I thus decree :

" 1st. Slavery is forever abolished in the republic.

" 2d. Consequently all those individuals who until this day looked upon themselves as slaves, are free.

" 3d. When the financial situation of the republic admits, the proprietors of slaves shall be indemnified, and the indemnification regulated by a law.

" And in order that the present decree may have its full and entire execution, I order it to be printed, published and circulated to all those whose obligation it is to have it fulfilled.

" Given in the federal palace of Mexico, on the 15th of September, 1829."

In Colombia, slave children born after the revolution were to be free at eighteen. In South America, except Brazil, slavery is either abolished or drawing to a close.

The action of the United States government in abolishing the slave-trade, and its efforts to suppress the illegal traffic, are referred to in subsequent chapters. The treaties and conventions of England with foreign nations for the suppression of the slave-trade will also be found in another part of the volume. The practical results of all these labors are exhibited in the chapters relating to the slave-trade after its nominal abolition.

CHAPTER XVI.

INDIAN AND AFRICAN SLAVERY IN ST. DOMINGO.—THE INSURRECTIONS.

Discovery and settlement of the island by the Spaniards.—The natives reduced to slavery. Cruelty of the Spaniards towards them.—Great mortality in consequence.—Their numbers replenished from the Bahamas.—The Dominicans become interested for them. Las Casas appeals to Cardinal Ximines, who sends commissioners.—They set the natives at liberty.—The colonists remonstrate against the measure, and the Indians again reduced to slavery.—Las Casas seeks a remedy.—The Emperor allows the introduction of Africans.—Guinea slave-trade established.—The buccaneers.—The French Colony.—Its condition in 1789.—Enormous slave-population.—The Mulattoes.—The French Revolution—its effect on the Colonists.—First Insurrection—terrible execution of the leaders.—Second Insurrection—massacre and conflagration—unparalleled horrors.—Burning Port au Prince.—L'Ouverture appears, the spirit and ruler of the storm.—French expedition of 25,000 men sent to suppress the Insurrection.—Toussaint sent prisoner to France—dies in prison.—The slaves establish their freedom.—Independence of Hayti acknowledged by France.

HISPANIOLA, St. Domingo, or Hayti, is not only one of the largest but also one of the most beautiful and productive of the West India islands. It is 390 miles long, its breadth is from 60 to 150 miles, and its scenery is diversified by lofty mountains, deep valleys and extensive plains, or savannas, dotted with the luxuriant vegetation of a tropical climate. The sea sweeps boldly into the land, here and there forming commodious harbors and extensive bays. The air on the plains is warm and laden with the perfume of flowers; and the sudden changes from drouth to rain, though trying to an unacclimated constitution, are favorable to the growth of the rich products of the soil.

Columbus and his successors having founded a settlement on the island, it became one of the Spanish colonial possessions, to the great misfortune of the unhappy natives, who were almost annihilated by the labor which the colonists imposed upon them. They soon dwindled away to a mere remnant. Of a population of a million found on the island by Columbus, scarcely twenty-four thousand remained at the time of the governorship of the island by his son, Don Diego Columbus, and these were fast sinking into the grave under the destructive influence of cruelty and hardship. In this emergency expeditions were fitted out to the Bahama islands in order to decoy from their homes the gentle and confiding race which inhabited them, to be sold as slaves in Hispaniola. They were but too successful. Availing themselves of the fond superstition of the natives, that the departed spirits of their friends, after an expiation of their sins by a purgatory of cold in the mountains of the north, passed to more sunny realms, under a more tropical sky, where they enjoyed an indolent paradise forever, the crafty Spaniards alleged that they came from this land of their departed relatives, and invited them to go thither and rejoin them.* The simple Indians trusted to the tale and went to inevitable and deadly servitude. Like their predecessors of Hispaniola, they died at their

---

*Peter Martyr.

tasks, or in despair put an end to their own existence, while new cargoes of their race were arriving daily to the same wretchedness and death.

To the honor of the ecclesiastics of the colony, their exertions were unremitted to ameliorate the condition and retard the ultimate fate of the natives. Of the two orders of clergy to whom the spiritual interests of the colony had been committed, the Dominicans had ever manifested a zeal and unyielding ardor that left their brethren, the Franciscans, far behind. In the ranks of the former was Las Casas, the celebrated bishop of Chiapa. To save the interesting and gentle race of natives from the destructiveness of slavery, was with him more than a passion—it seemed the ruling and guiding principle of his soul. In consequence of his pious appeals to Cardinal Ximines, the regent of Spain, three commissioners were sent out with full powers to adjust the condition of the Indians. There were two parties in the colony. The Dominicans, acting in accordance with what they esteemed a law of Heaven, denounced the right and impugned the justice of enslaving the Indians. The interested colonists, and the Franciscans, who were for a modified servitude, sustained themselves against their opponents on grounds of expediency and the right of conquest. To the deputation appointed by Cardinal Ximines were added a lawyer of distinguished probity, whose name was Zuazo, and Las Casas, upon whom had been conferred the title of Protector of the Indians. The first act of the commissioners was to set at liberty all the Indians that had been granted to the Spanish courtiers, or to any person not residing in the island.

This achievement of the commissioners spread anger and consternation among the colonists. The Spaniards were exasperated or discouraged. The lands could not be cultivated without laborers, and panic, discontent and discouragement were general. The commissioners soon began to doubt the solidity of their policy, and yielded to the storm of passion that was beating on them. The subject was maturely reconsidered, and the question and the colony set at rest by the final decision of the commissioners, that the state of the colony rendered the slavery of the Indians necessary.

The enthusiastic philanthropy of Las Casas had not been turned from its object by the decision of the commissioners. Not discouraged at the obstacles he had to encounter, he now ranged his eye through the whole horizon of possibilities to seek in some quarter for a gleam of hope to illumine the dark destiny of that unhappy people which occupied all his sympathies. A small number of a hardier race, the negroes of Guinea, had been imported into the island. They were found stronger than the Indians, and more capable of enduring labor under the burning heats of the climate; so much so, that it was computed that the labor of one negro was worth that of four Indians. "The Africans," says Herrera, "prospered so much in the colony, that it was the opinion that unless a negro should happen to be hung he would never die, for as yet none had been known to perish from infirmity." Las Casas proposed the substitution of African for Indian laborers in the new world. His representations were listened to with a favorable ear by the emperor, and a patent was granted allowing the introduction of four thousand negroes into Hispaniola and a regular traffic between the Guinea coast and the colony was soon established.*

This statement, however, has been contradicted by the abbé Grégoire, in his Apologie de B. de Las Casas, in the memoirs of the French institute; also by the writer of the article Casas, in the Biographie Universelle, after an examination of all the Spanish and Portuguese historians of that period. This charge, he says, rests solely on the authority of Herrera, an elegant but inaccurate writer. "Negro slavery," says another writer, "was a device struck out in a bold and unconscientious age to meet a great emergency,—the age of Cortes and Pizarro." But by it an evil of fearful magnitude has been entailed upon our hemisphere.

The true sources of wealth in the island were now ascertained, not to consist in digging for gold among the barren mountains, but in cultivating the rich soil of the plains. The sugar-cane was introduced and extensively cultivated. In the hard labor necessary in rearing and manipulating it, the hardiness of the negro was shown infinitely superior to the fragile Indian. Plantation after plantation was brought under cultivation, and yielded a handsome profit. Both Indians and negroes were tasked beyond all reasonable bounds, and the consequence was that the former died and the latter rebelled.

As Spain, however, extended her conquests on the main land, the importance of Hispaniola as a colony began to decline; and at the beginning of the seventeenth century the island had become nearly a desert, the natives having been all but extirpated, and the Spanish residents being few, and congregated in several widely-separated stations round the coast. At this time the West Indian seas swarmed with *buccaneers*, adventurers without homes, families, or country, the refuse of all nations and climes. These men, the majority of whom were French, English, and Dutch, being prevented by the Spaniards from holding any permanent settlement in the new world, banded together in self-defense, and roved the seas in quest of subsistence, seizing vessels, and occasionally landing on the coast of one of the Spanish possessions, and committing terrible ravages. A party of these buccaneers had, about the year 1629, occupied the small island of Tortuga, on the northwest coast of St. Domingo. From this island they used to make frequent incursions into St. Domingo, for the purpose of hunting; the forests of that island abounding with wild cattle, horses and swine, the progeny of the tame animals which the Spaniards had introduced into the island. At length, after various struggles with the Spanish occupants, these adventurers made good their footing in the island of St. Domingo, drove the Spaniards to its eastern extremity, and became masters of its western parts. As most of them were of French origin, they were desirous of placing themselves under the protection of France; and Louis XIV. and his government being flattered with the prospect of thus acquiring a rich possession in the new world, a friendly intercourse between

*Brown's History St. Domingo.

France and St. Domingo began, and the western part of the island assumed the character of a flourishing French colony, while the Spanish colony in the other end of the island correspondingly declined.

From 1776 to 1789, the French colony was at the height of its prosperity. To use the words of a French historian, every thing had received a prodigious improvement. The torrents had been arrested in their course, the marshes drained, the forests cleared; the soil had been enriched with foreign plants; roads had been opened across the asperities of the mountains; safe pathways had been constructed over chasms; bridges had been built over rivers which had formerly been passed with danger by means of ox-skin boats; the winds, the tides, the currents had been studied, so as to secure to ships safe sailing and convenient harborage. Villas of pretty but simple architecture had risen along the borders of the sea, while mansions of greater magnificence embellished the interior. Public buildings, hospitals, acqueducts, fountains, and baths rendered life agreeable and healthy; all the comforts of the old world had been transported into the new. In 1789 the population of the colony was 665,000; and of its staple products, it exported in that year 68,000,000 pounds of coffee, and 163,000,000 pounds of sugar. The French had some reason to be proud of St. Domingo; it was their best colony, and it promised, as they thought, to remain for ages in their possession. Many French families of note had emigrated to the island, and settled in it as planters; and both by means of commerce and the passing to and fro of families, a constant intercourse was maintained between the colony and the mother country.

Circumstances eventually proved that the expectation of keeping permanent possession of St. Domingo was likely to be fallacious. The constitution of society was unsound. In this, as in all the European colonies in the new world, negro slavery prevailed. To supply the demand for labor, an importation of slaves from Africa had been going on for some time at the rate of about 20,000 a year; and thus, at the time at which we are now arrived, there was a black population of between 500,000 and 600,000. These negroes constituted an overwhelming majority of the inhabitants of the colony, for the whites did not amount to more than 40,000. But besides the whites and the negroes, there was a third class in the population, arising from the intermixture of the white and negro races. These were the *people of color*, including persons of all varieties of hue, from the perfect sable of the freed negro, to the most delicate tinge marking remote negro ancestry in a white man. Of these various classes of mulattoes, at the time of which we are now speaking, there were about 30,000 in the colony.

Although perhaps less cruelly treated than others in a state of hopeless servitude, the negroes of St. Domingo were not exempt from the miseries which usually accompany slavery; yet they were not so ignorant as not to know their rights as members of the human family. Receiving occasional instruction in the doctrines of Christianity, and allowed by their masters to enjoy the holidays of the church, they were accustomed to ponder on the principles thus presented to their notice, and these they perceived were at variance with their condition. This dawning of intelligence among the negroes caused no alarm to the planters generally. The French have always been noted for making the kindest slave-owners. Imitating the conduct of many of the old nobility of France in their intercourse with the peasantry, a number of the planters of St. Domingo were attentive to the wants and feelings of their negro dependents—encouraging their sports, taking care of them in sickness, and cherishing them in old age. In the year 1685, likewise, Louis XIV. had published a *code noir*, or black code, containing a number of regulations for the humane treatment of the negroes in the colonies. Still, there were miseries inseparable from the system, and which could not be mitigated; and in St. Domingo, as in all other colonies of the new world, slavery was maintained by the cruelties of the whip and the branding-iron. It was only, we may easily suppose, by a judicious blending of kindness and severity, that a population of upwards of 500,000 negroes could be kept in subjection by 40,000 whites.

The condition of the mulatto population deserves particular attention. Although nominally free, and belonging to no individual master, these mulattoes occupied a very degraded social position. Regarded as public property, they were obliged to serve in the colonial militia without any pay. They could hold no public trust or employment, nor fill any of the liberal professions—law, medicine, divinity, &c. They were not allowed to sit at table with a white, to occupy the same place at church, to bear the same name, or to be buried in the same spot. Offenses which in a white man were visited with scarcely any punishment, were punished with great severity when committed by a mulatto. There was one circumstance, however, in the condition of the mulattoes, which operated as a balance to all those indignities, and enabled them to become formidable in the colony—they were allowed to acquire and to hold property to any amount. Able, energetic, and rendered doubly intent upon the acquisition of wealth by the power it gave them, many of these mulattoes or people of color became rich, purchased estates, and equaled the whites as planters. Not only so, but, possessing the tastes of Europeans and gentlemen, they used to quit St. Domingo and pay occasional visits to what they as well as the whites regarded as the mother country. It was customary for wealthy mulattoes to send their children to Paris for their education. It ought to be remarked also respecting the mulatto part of the population of St. Domingo, that they kept aloof both from the pure whites and the pure negroes. Such was the state of society in the colony of St. Domingo in the year 1789–90, when the French Revolution broke out.

Although situated at the distance of 3500 miles from the mother country, St. Domingo was not long in responding to the political agitations which broke out in Paris in 1789. When the news reached the colony that the king had summoned the States-general, all the French part of the island was in a ferment. Considering themselves entitled to share in the national commotion, the colonists held meetings, passed resolutions, and elected eighteen deputies to be sent home to sit in the States-general as representatives. The eighteen deputies reached Versailles a considerable time after the States-general had commenced their sittings, and constituted themselves the National Assembly; and their arrival not a little surprised that body, who probably never expected deputies from St. Domingo, or who at all events thought eighteen deputies too many for one colony. Accordingly, it was with some difficulty that six of them were allowed to take their seats. At that time colonial gentlemen were not held in great favor at Paris. Among the many feelings which then simultaneously stirred and agitated that great metropolis, there had sprung up a strong feeling against negro slavery. Whether the enthusiasm was kindled by the recent proceedings of Clarkson and Wilberforce in London, or whether it was derived by the French themselves from the political maxims then afloat, the writers and speakers of the revolution made the iniquity of negro slavery one of their most frequent and favorite topics; and there had just been founded in Paris a society called *Amis des Noirs*, or friends of the blacks, of which the leading revolutionists were members.

The intelligence of what was occurring at Paris gave great alarm in St. Domingo. When the celebrated declaration of rights, asserting all men to be "free and equal," reached the island along with the news of the proceedings of the *Amis des Noirs*, the whites, almost all of whom were interested in the preservation of slavery, looked upon their ruin as predetermined. They had no objection to freedom in the abstract, freedom which should apply only to themselves, but they considered it a violation of all decency to speak of black men, mere *property*, having political rights. What disheartened the whites gave encouragement to the mulattoes. Rejoicing in the idea that the French people were their friends, they became turbulent, and rose in arms in several places, but were without much difficulty put down. Two or three whites, who were enthusiastic revolutionists, sided with the insurgents; and one of them, M. de Beaudierre, fell a victim to the fury of the colonists. The negro population of the island remained quiet; the contagion of revolutionary sentiments had not yet reached them.

When the national assembly heard of the alarm which the new constitution had excited in the colonies, they saw the necessity for adopting some measures to allay the storm; and accordingly, on the 8th of March, 1790, they passed a resolution disclaiming all intention to legislate sweepingly for the internal affairs of the colonies, and authorizing each colony to mature a plan for itself in its own legislative assembly, (the revolution having superseded the old system of colonial government by royal officials, and given to each colony a legislative assembly consisting of representatives elected by the colonists,) and submit the same to the national assembly. This resolution, which gave great dissatisfaction to the *Amis des Noirs* in Paris, produced a temporary calm in St. Domingo. For some time nothing was to be heard but the bustle of elections throughout the colony; and at length, on the 16th of April, 1790, the general assembly met, consisting of 213 representatives. All eyes were upon the proceedings of the assembly; and at length, on the 28th of May, it published the results of its deliberations in the form of a new constitution, consisting of ten articles. The provisions of this new constitution, and the language

17

in which they were expressed, were astounding; they amounted, in fact, to the throwing off of allegiance to the mother country. This very unforeseen result created great commotion in the island. The cry rose every where that the assembly was rebelling against the mother country; some districts recalled their deputies, declaring they would have no concern with such presumptuous proceedings; the governor-general, M. Peynier, was bent on dissolving the assembly altogether; riots were breaking out in various parts of the island, and a civil war seemed impending, when in one of its sittings the assembly, utterly bewildered and terrified, adopted the extraordinary resolution of going on board a ship of war then in the harbor, and sailing bodily to France to consult with the national assembly.

In the meantime, the news of the proceedings of the colonial assembly had reached France, and all parties, royalists as well as revolutionists, were indignant at what they called the impudence of these colonial legislators. The *Amis des Noirs* of course took an extreme interest in what was going on; and under their auspices, an attempt was made to take advantage of the disturbances prevailing in the island for the purpose of meliorating the condition of the colored population. A young mulatto named James Ogé was then residing in Paris, whither he had been sent by his mother, a woman of color, the proprietrix of a plantation in St. Domingo. Ogé had formed the acquaintance of the Abbé Gregoire, Brissot, Robespierre, Lafayette, and other leading revolutionists connected with the society of the *Amis des Noirs*, and fired by the ideas which he derived from them, he resolved to return to St. Domingo, and, rousing the spirit of insurrection, become the deliverer of his enslaved race. Accordingly, paying a visit to America first, he landed in his native island on the 12th of October, 1790, and announced himself as the redresser of all wrongs. Matters, however, were not yet ripe for an insurrection; and after committing some outrages with a force of 200 mulattoes, which was all he was able to raise, Ogé was defeated, and obliged, with one or two associates, to take refuge in the Spanish part of the island. M. Blanchelande succeeding M. Peynier as governor-general of the colony, demanded Ogé from the Spaniards; and in March, 1791, the wretched young man was broken alive upon the wheel.

The court convicted Vincent Ogé and Jean Baptiste Chevanne, his associate, of the intent to cause an insurrection of the people of color, and it condemned them to be conducted by the public executioner to the church of Cape François, and there, bare-headed, and *en chemise*, with a rope about their necks—upon their knees, and holding in their hands a wax candle of two pounds weight, to declare that they had wickedly, rashly, and by evil instigation, committed the crimes of which they had been accused and convicted; and then and there they repented of them, and asked forgiveness of God, of the king, and the violated justice of the realm; that they should then be conducted to the Place d'Armes of the said town, and in the place opposite to that appropriated to the execution of white men, to have their arms, legs, hips, and thighs broken alive; that they should be placed upon a wheel, with their faces towards heaven, and there remain so long as God should preserve their lives. After their death, their heads were to be severed from their bodies and placed upon poles—that of Ogé on the road to Dondon, and that of Chevanne on the road to Grand Riviere, and the property of both to be confiscated to the king.*

Chevanne died as he had lived, the stern, unyielding enemy of the whites; but Ogé in that terrible moment lost all his firmness. He implored the pity of his judges, and offered to reveal important secrets if they would spare his life. Twenty-four hours were granted him, and he revealed the existence of a wide-laid conspiracy among the mulattoes and negroes of the island; but as not much importance was attached to his communications, he was ordered back to punishment. Twenty-one of his associates, among whom was his brother, were condemned to be hung, and thirteen others were sent to the galleys for life—the rest were pardoned.

Although the insurrection of Ogé was ill-timed and rash, and his death that of the most degraded criminal, his name and sufferings have ever been hallowed in the memory of his race; and the martyrdom of Ogé was ever afterwards the rallying signal to encourage and unite the mulattoes in deadly hostility against the whites. By this barbarous massacre the breach between these two races was made irreconcilable and eternal. However they were united by the sympathy of relationship, or the ties of interest and property, all these bands were sundered by a hatred, deep, rankling, and inexpiable.†

All this occurred while the eighty-five members of the assembly were absent in France. They had reached that country in September, 1790, and been well received at first; but when they appeared before the national assembly, that body treated them with marked insult and contempt. On the 11th of October, Barnave proposed and carried a decree annulling all the acts of the colonial assembly, dissolving it, declaring its members ineligible again for the same office, and detaining the eighty-five unfortunate gentlemen prisoners in France. Barnave, however, was averse to any attempt on the part of the national assembly to force a constitution upon the colony against its will; and especially he was averse to any direct interference between the whites and the people of color. These matters of internal regulation, he said, should be left to the colonists themselves; all that the national assembly should require of the colonists was, that they should act in the general spirit of the revolution. Others, however, among whom were Gregoire, Brissot, Robespierre, and Lafayette, were for the home government dictating the leading articles of a new constitution for the colony; and especially they were for some sweeping assertion by the national assembly of the equal citizenship of the colored inhabitants of the colony. For some time the debate was carried on between these two parties; but the latter gradually gained strength, and the storm of public indignation which was excited by the news of the cruel death of Ogé gave them the complete victory. Tragedies and dramas founded on the story of Ogé were acted in the theatres of Paris, and the popular feeling against the planters and in favor of

---

* Lacroix.   † Brown's Hist. St. Domingo.

the negroes grew vehement and ungovernable. " Perish the colonies," said Robespierre, " rather than depart, in the case of our colored brethren, from those universal principles of liberty and equality which it is our glory to have laid down." Hurried on by a tide of enthusiasm, the national assembly, on the 15th of May, passed a decree declaring all the people of color in the French colonies born of free parents entitled to vote for members of the colonial judicatures, as well as to be elected to seats themselves. This decree of admission to citizenship concerned, it will be observed, the mulattoes and free blacks only; it did not affect the condition of the slave population.

In little more than a month this decree, along with the intelligence of all that had been said and done when it was passed, reached St. Domingo. The colony was thrown into convulsions. The white colonists stormed and raged, and there was no extremity to which, in the first outburst of their anger, they were not ready to go. The national cockade was trampled under foot. It was proposed to forswear allegiance to the mother country, seize the French ships in the harbors, and the goods of French merchants, and hoist the British flag instead of the French. The governor-general, M. Blanchelande, trembled for the results. But at length the fury of the colonists somewhat subsided ; a new colonial assembly was convened ; hopes began to be entertained that something might be effected by its labors, when lo ! the news ran through the island like the tremor of an earthquake—" The blacks have risen !" The appalling news was too true. The conspiracy, the existence of which had been divulged by Ogé before his execution, had burst into explosion. The outbreak had been fixed for the 25th of August, 1791 ; but the negroes, impatient as the time drew near, had commenced it on the night of the 22d.

The insurrection now burst forth in all its terror and calamity. The slaves of the plantation Turpin, headed by an English negro, set out at 10 o'clock at night, in their way drawing into their ranks the slaves of four or five other plantations, and commenced the horrors of a wide-spread insurrection. They proved to be the veriest tigers in rage and cruelty. The plain of Cape François, that might have rivaled the fabled garden of the Hesperides, both in richness and beauty, was soon in one universal conflagration, the gleams of which painted the sky in lurid horror, while the smoke enveloped the whole country in uncertain gloom. The ranks of the rebels were increased at every step of their progress, and along their march of devastation they murdered every white who fell into their power, without distinction of age or sex, viewing with fiendish delight the agonies and groans of those whom so lately they had not dared to look in the face.

These scenes of destruction were continued through the night, and on the following day the inhabitants of Cape François knew nothing of the disasters around them, but of the smoke that obscured the horizon and the fugitives that were pouring into their gates. Petrified with horror and panic, they quickly fastened themselves in their houses, and locked up their slaves. The troops of the garrison were the only living objects seen in the streets, as they were hurrying to their different posts. An alarm gun soon called the whole population to arms. The people came out of their houses, accosted and questioned each other, and catching courage from the effect of numbers, their former fear was soon changed to an inspiriting cry for vengeance, which, in their determined infatuation, was principally directed against the mulattoes. These were accused of having instigated the blacks to revolt, and on them it was thought immediate and summary vengeance should fall. In the delirium of the moment, a few of that unfortunate race expiated with their lives the suspicion of their being accomplices with the rebels in the plain. To stop this wicked injustice of murdering the innocent for the crimes of the guilty, the provincial assembly hastened to assign places of refuge for this proscribed caste, who ran thither to put themselves under the protection of the military. They demanded arms, especially the mulatto planters, and expressed an eagerness to march against the common enemy ; and such was the blindness of creole prejudice that even the assembly hesitated at first to accept their offer.*

The insurrection spread like a stream of electricity, and within four days one-third part of the plain of Cape François was but a heap of ashes. Many members of the new colonial assembly, in their journey from Leogane to the Cape, were surprised and killed by the rebels, and a detachment of troops was found necessary to guard the route of the president, secretaries and archives of this body. M. Tousard was dispatched against the rebels with a detachment of troops of the line and national guards, together with some grenadiers and chasseurs of the regiment of the Cape ; but nothing, without the courage and veteran skill of this able officer, could have kept the troops in an imposing attitude in such fearful circumstances. On every side, and in every direction, they were beset by swarms of the rebels, who seemed to despise danger and defy the utmost that could be done against them. An order from the governor general, however, recalled the forces of M. Tousard in haste to Cape François, where, from the advance of the negroes on that town, the consternation was heart-rending. The place was now entirely surrounded with blazing plantations, and even the hideous outcries could be heard of those fiends, who were every where triumphant in their march of desolation and massacre. The advance guard established on the plantation Bongars, had been affrighted from its defense of that post, and thus the two most beautiful quarters of the colony, those of Morin and Limonade, were given to the torches of the rebels. They even advanced to the Haut de Cap, and the cannon brought to play upon their huddled masses was scarcely sufficient to check them in their headlong march. The return of Tousard upon their rear dispersed them, but by his retreat they were left in undisputed possession of the country. They immediately extended their ravages from the sea-shore to the mountains, and when nothing more was left for them to destroy, their headlong tumultuousness began to give place in their leisure to a regular organization and a more systematic warfare. Their continuance in the field, notwithstanding the vast amount of plunder to tempt them from their course, and the celerity and skilfulness of their movements,

---

* Lacroix.

had already given rise to the suspicion that they were guided in their enterprise by some being superior to themselves. They no longer exposed themselves in masses to the destructive sweep of cannon and small arms, but by scattering their detachments, by suddenly dispersing to the shelter of hedges and thickets, when occasion required, they often succeeded in surprising or surrounding their enemy, and when neither could be done, in crushing them by a vast superiority in numbers. While the preparations for the attack were in progress, their obies performed the Ouangah, or mysterious rite to their demons, by which the imaginations of the multitude were heated and strained to the utmost degree of tension, and the women and children danced an accompaniment to the ceremony with howlings and outcries that savored of Pandemonium. Amid the excitement of this wild uproar, the attack began with yells and terrific gesticulations. If they met with a firm and effective resistance, the energy of their attack soon slackened; but if the defense was weak and faltering, their boldness and audacity became extreme. They rushed forward to the cannon's mouth, and thrusting in their arms and bodies, purchased the retreat of the enemy by this self-immolation. Contortions and howlings were not the only means they used to intimidate their adversaries—the flames which they applied to the highly inflammable fields of cane, to the houses and mills of the plantations, and to their own cabins, covered the heavens with clouds of smoke by day, and illuminated the horizon by night with gleams that gave to every object the color of blood. After a silence the most profound, there would arise an outcry from their camp the most appalling; this would again be followed by the plaintive cries of their prisoners, whom the savages made it their sport to sacrifice at their advance posts.

The insurgents, in full possession of the plain of Cape François, were reveling amidst the spoils of the vanquished. The colonists, to intimidate them, changed the sluggish and inefficient war they were carrying on to one of extermination. This was ill-timed and impolitic, for the insurrection had grown too strong to yield to fear, and the negroes repaid the cruelty by augmenting the tortures of their own captives. The negro chiefs would have no neutrals among those of their race, and the more faithful slaves, who were found concealing themselves from the rebels, were immediately put to death by their own countrymen. On the other hand, parties of enraged whites were traversing the country, and, with an undiscriminating vengeance, killing every living thing that was black. The faithful slave, who, in this reciprocal destruction, came to claim the protection of his master against those who on either side sought his life, was in many instances put to death by that very master himself. This blind severity served no purpose but to swell the ranks of the rebels, for the peaceable negro could find no security for his life but by assuming arms in the ranks of his countrymen.

In the first moments of the rebellion, the negroes had murdered all their prisoners, but as success increased, the complacency of triumph taught them more clemency, or perhaps they had become glutted with cruelty and crime. They no longer massacred the women and children, and only showed themselves cruel to their prisoners taken in battle, whom they put to death with such studied tortures as cannot be named without a thrill of horror. They tore them with red-hot pincers—sawed them asunder between planks—roasted them by a slow fire—or tore out their eyes with red-hot cork-screws. Their principal leader, Jean François, assumed the title of grand admiral of France, and his lieutenant, Biassou, called himself generalissimo of the conquered country. They were evidently under the guidance and instruction of demons higher in intelligence than they. The rebels stated that they were in arms for their king, whom their enemies and his had cast into prison; but at other times they asserted that their sole object was to save themselves from their tyrants, the planters.

Te Deum was daily sung by both belligerents, in impious thanksgiving to God for what was nothing but a continued massacre. The heads of murdered whites, stuck on poles, surrounded the camp of the rebels, and the hedges that bordered the way conducting to the posts of the whites were filled with the dead bodies of negroes swinging in the wind.

After a long succession of skirmishes which had resulted in nothing but to drive the rebels from the plain to the mountains, whence after the withdrawal of the troops they rushed back again to the plain, the negroes were nearly subdued by a combined movement, which had been ordered by M. Blanchelande, and executed by M. Tousard. Camp Lecoque and Acul were taken by the whites, and a large body of negroes were surrounded upon the plantation Alquier, who were surprised by night, and all who were unable to effect an escape were cut in pieces. M. Tousard was fortunate enough in this expedition to save from the hands of the negroes a great number of white children, and eighty white females, who were found shut up in the church at Limbé.

The rebels ascribed their late disasters to treason in their camp. A negro named Jeannot was of all their chieftains the most ferocious. Suspecting the fidelity of a negro under his orders, who was also accused of having saved his master from the knives of the insurgents, this monster ordered that he should be cut in pieces and thrown into the fire, on the charge that he had drawn the balls from the cartridges of the blacks in their late unsuccessful conflicts with M. Tousard. Other acts of cruelty still more revolting are related of this rebel chief. The plantation of M. Paradole, situated on Grande Riviere, suffered an attack from the insurgents, in which the proprietor himself was made a prisoner. Four of his children, who in the first moments of their panic had fled to places of concealment, came to implore the negro chief to liberate their father. This filial devotion, which was interpreted as defiance by the unfeeling black, irritated him to fury. He ordered that the four young men should be slain separately before the eyes of their parent, who was then himself put to death, the last victim in this domestic tragedy. The atrocity of this action was even too much for Jean François, who had already become jealous of Jeannot's growing ascendency. The latter affected the state and bearing of a monarch, never proceeding to mass but in a chariot drawn by six horses. The envy of Jean François was soon imbodied in action. He attacked his associate chief and overcame him, and the monster was shot at the foot of a tree that had been fitted up with iron hooks upon which to hang his living victims by the middle of the body. Buckman, also, the original leader in the insurrection, fell a sacrifice to the vengeance of the whites during this expedition of M. Tousard, and his head was brought into Cape François and exposed on the gates of the town.

While ruin was thus universal in the north, the mulattoes of the south were seizing the present conjuncture to establish their rights by force. Their leaders showed themselves more skillful than Ogé. Instead of remaining in Port-au-Prince, they made their rendezvous at Croix des Bouquets, and made no demonstration of their design till their organization had been made complete. Port-au-Prince considered itself strong enough to punish this schism, and the military force of the place took up their march immediately for the encampment of the mulattoes. Some detachments of cavalry from both sides had already met in the plain of Cul de Sac, and the advantage was clearly on the side of the mulattoes. On the night of the 1st of September, a body of adventurers and sailors, joined to a force of two hundred troops of the line and a detachment of the national guard, and furnished with a small train of artillery, set off from Port-au-Prince to attack the post of Croix des Bouquets. They continued their march until the break of day, when they found themselves in the grounds of the plantation Pernier, and the fields of cane in flames on every side of their column. A brisk fire of musketry from an ambuscade of mulattoes immediately followed, and the field was strewed with killed and wounded. The whites were thrown into disorder, and their rout soon became complete. The mulattoes, with admirable tact, followed up their advantage by making immediate offers to negotiate, which their defeated opponents accepted without a moment's hesitation. A treaty was made, called a concordat, in which the whites promised to make no farther opposition to the late decree of the national assembly, as well as to recognize the political equality of mulattoes with themselves, and to secure the complete indemnification of all those who had suffered for political offenses, either in property, person or *life*. The mulattoes demanded that the garrison of Port-au-Prince should be composed of whites and mulattoes in equal numbers—that the judges who had condemned Ogé should be consigned to infamy—that the future legislature of the colony should be composed of members chosen conformably to the late decree, and that whenever the principles of this decree were not recognized in the elections, both contracting parties should unite to enforce their execution. The discussions being all finished on the several articles of this treaty, which secured to the mulattoes all that they had ever demanded, it was signed on the 23d of October, 1791.

Meantime the war continued in the plain of Cape François with unmitigated fierceness, and human blood still flowed in torrents amid the cruelty practiced on both sides. It was estimated that within the space of two months, more than two thousand whites had fallen victims to the insurrection—that one hundred and eighty sugar plantations, and nearly nine hundred plantations of coffee, cotton and indigo had been laid waste, and their mills and houses consumed to ashes. The negroes, in the wantonness of their fury, left nothing undestroyed that was not in itself indestructible. The thick walls of edifices, which remained standing after the fire had consumed all enclosed within them, were by painful manual effort razed to the ground. The iron kettles of the boiling houses, and the bells which called them to their labors, were crushed into atoms, as if to destroy from the very face of the earth all memorials of former servitude. Twelve hundred families, once opulent and happy, were reduced to utter poverty, and driven in their destitution to subsist on public charity or private hospitality in their own or foreign countries. More than ten thousand of the rebels also had perished by the sword or by famine, and many hundreds of them had met their fate from the hands of the public executioner.

Meanwhile strange proceedings relative to the colonies were occurring in the mother country. The news of the insurrection of the blacks had not had time to reach Paris; but the intelligence of the manner in which the decree of the 15th of May had been received by the whites in St. Domingo, had created great alarm. "We are afraid we have been too hasty with that decree of ours about the rights of the mulattoes; it is likely, by all accounts, to occasion a civil war between them and the whites; and if so, we run the risk of losing the colony altogether." This was the common talk of the politicians of Paris. Accordingly, they hastened to undo what they had done four months before, and on the 24th of September the national assembly actually repealed the decree of the 15th of May by a large majority. Thus the mother country and the colony were at cross purposes; for at the very moment that the colony was admitting the decree, the mother country was repealing it.

The flames of war were immediately rekindled in the colony. "The decree is repealed," said the whites; "we need not have been in such a hurry in making concessions to the mulattoes." "The decree is repealed," said the mulattoes; "the people in Paris are playing false with us; we must depend on ourselves in future. There is no possibility of coming to terms with the whites; either they must exterminate us, or we must exterminate them."

Hostilities were renewed in the streets of Port-au-Prince. A battery of twenty cannons opened its fire upon the ranks of the armed mulattoes, who retreated from the city and gained the road to the mountains. Scarcely had they departed, when both the north and south portions of the city were discovered to be on fire, and in an incredibly short space of time the whole city was wrapt in conflagration. The fire made such progress that no exertions could arrest it, and it continued to rage for forty-eight hours, when it began to abate for want of further materials to minister to its fury, and twenty-seven out of thirty squares of the town were utterly destroyed.

Affright, disorder and pillage augmented the horrors of the calamity. The fire was of course attributed to the mulattoes; and their wives and children, two thousand in number, found themselves obliged to fly, not only from their burning habitations, but from the sword with which, in the blindness of vengeance, the whites were pursuing them. Driven by this two-fold terror, they fled to the country or rushed toward the sea shore, where, not finding boats enough to contain them, and in their anxiety to escape the death that was following on their footsteps, pressing in crowds upon each other, great numbers of them were forced into the sea, there to find a death as dreadful as that they were escaping. The accusation was afterwards transferred to the merchants, who were charged with having recourse to this means of destroying all documents and securities, as an easy method of ridding themselves from such liabilities. Suspicion was immediately taken for evidence, and executions followed; the mercantile establishments which had escaped the fire, were given up to be pillaged by the mob. A simpler explanation, says Lacroix, is easy. In a town built entirely of wood, and upon a soil where a burning sun dries up every thing not endowed with life, the wadding of a single cartridge would be sufficient to kindle a fire upon the roofs of houses as inflammable as tinder; and that a battle could be fought in such a place without causing a conflagration would be a matter of astonishment. The loss has been estimated at fifty million francs.

The year 1791 was concluded amid scenes of war, pestilence and bloodshed. The whites, collected in forts and cities, bade defiance to the insurgents. The mulattoes and blacks fought on the same side, sometimes under one standard, sometimes in separate bands. A large colony of blacks, consisting of slaves broken loose from the plantations, settled in the mountains under the two leaders, Jean François and Biassou. They planted provisions for their subsistence, and watched for opportunities to make irruptions into the plains.

The national assembly had sent three commissioners to the island to restore peace and subordination to the distracted colony. At the time of their departure they had not been informed of the slave insurrection, nor the vast extent of the calamity that was then desolating the country. On their arrival, the commissioners were struck with horror and astonishment at what they saw. At Cape François they found two wheels and five gibbets in constant employ, to execute the numerous victims that were daily adjudged to death. Horror and loathing made them insensible to the civilities which were proffered them, and despairing of effecting any beneficial measure, they returned to France. Meanwhile the revolution in the mother country was proceeding; the republican party and the *Amis des Noirs* were rising into power; and on the 4th of April, 1792, a new decree was passed, declaring more emphatically than before the rights of the people of color, and appointing three new commissioners, who were to proceed to St. Domingo and exercise sovereign power in the colony. These commissioners arrived on the 13th of September, dissolved the colonial assembly and sent the governor, M. Blanchelande, home to be guillotined. With great appearance of activity, the commissioners commenced their duties; and as the mother country was too busy about its own affairs to attend to their proceedings, they acted as they pleased, and contrived, out of the general wreck, to amass large sums of money for their own use; till at length, in the beginning of 1793, the revolutionary government at home, having a little more leisure to attend to colonial affairs, revoked the powers of the commissioners, and appointed a new governor, M. Galbaud. When M. Galbaud arrived in the island, there ensued a struggle between him and the commissioners, he being empowered to supersede them, and they refusing to submit. At length the commissioners calling in the assistance of the revolted negroes, M. Galbaud was expelled from the island, and forced to take refuge in the United States. While this strange struggle for the governorship of the colony lasted, the condition of the colony itself was growing worse and worse. The plantations remained uncultivated, the whites and the mulattoes were still at war, masses of savage negroes were quartered in the hills, in fastnesses from which they could not be dislodged, and from which they could rush down unexpectedly to commit outrages in the plains.

In daily jeopardy of their lives, and seeing no prospect of a return of prosperity, immense numbers of the white colonists were quitting the island. Many families had emigrated to the neighboring island of Jamaica, many to the United States, and some even had sought refuge, like the royalists of the mother country, in Great Britain. Through these persons, as well as through the refugees from the mother country, overtures had been made to the British government for the purpose of inducing it to take possession of the island of St. Domingo and convert it into a British colony ; and in 1793, the British government, against which the French republic had now declared war, began to listen favorably to the proposals. General Williamson, the lieutenant-governor of Jamaica, was instructed to send troops from that island to St. Domingo, and attempt to wrest it out of the hands of the French. Accordingly, on the 20th of September, 1793, about 870 British soldiers, under Colonel Whitelocke, landed in St. Domingo—a force miserably defective for such an enterprise. The number of troops was afteward increased, and the British were able to effect the capture of Port-au-Prince, and also some ships which were in the harbor. Alarmed by this success, the French commissioners, Santhonax and Polverel, issued a decree abolishing negro slavery, at the same time inviting the blacks to join them against the British invaders. Several thousand did so ; but the great majority fled to the hills, swelling the army of the negro chiefs, François and Biassou, and luxuriating in the liberty which they had so suddenly acquired.

It was at this moment of utter confusion and disorganization, when British, French, mulattoes, and blacks, were all acting their respective parts in the turmoil, and all inextricably intermingled in a bewildering war, which was neither a foreign war nor a civil war, nor a war of races, but a composition of all three—it was at this moment that Toussaint L'Ouverture appeared the spirit and the ruler of the storm.

He was one of the most extraordinary men of a period when extraordinary men were numerous, and beyond all question, the highest specimen of negro genius the world has yet seen. He was born in St. Domingo, on the plantation of the count de Noé, a few miles distant from Cape François, in the year 1743. His father and mother were African slaves on the count's estate. On the plantation there was a black of the name of Pierre-Baptiste, a shrewd, intelligent man, who had acquired much information, besides having been taught the ele-

ments of what would be termed a plain education by some benevolent missionaries. Between Pierre and young Toussaint an intimacy sprung up, and all
that Pierre had learned from the missionaries, Toussaint learned from him.
His acquisitions, says our French authority, amounted to reading, writing,
arithmetic, a little Latin, and an idea of geometry. It was a fortunate circumstance that the greatest natural genius among the negroes of St. Domingo
was thus singled out to receive the unusual gift of a little instruction. Toussaint's qualifications gained him promotion; he was made the coachman of
M. Bayou, the overseer of the count de Noé—a situation as high as a negro
could hope to fill. In this, and in other still higher situations to which he was
subsequently advanced, his conduct was irreproachable, so that while he gained
the confidence of his master, every negro in the plantation held him in respect.
Three particulars are authentically known respecting his character at this period of his life, and it is somewhat remarkable that all are points more peculiarly of moral than of intellectual superiority. He was noted, it is said, for
an exceedingly patient temper, for great affection for brute animals, and for a
strong, unswerving attachment to one female whom he had chosen for his wife.
It is also said that he manifested singular strength of religious sentiment. In
person, he was above the middle size, with a striking countenance, and a robust
constitution, capable of enduring any amount of fatigue, and requiring little
sleep.

Toussaint was about forty-eight years of age when the insurrection of the
blacks took place in August, 1791. Great exertions were made by the insurgents to induce a negro of his respectability and reputation to join them in
their first outbreak, but he steadily refused. It is also known that it was owing
to Toussaint's care and ingenuity that his master, M. Bayou, and his family
escaped being massacred. He hid them in the woods for several days, visited
them at the risk of his own life, secured the means of their escape from the
island, and, after they were settled in the United States, sent them such remit-
tances as he could manage to snatch from the wreck of their property. Such
conduct, in the midst of such barbarities as were then enacting, indicates great
originality and moral independence of character. After his master's escape,
Toussaint, who had no tie to retain him longer in servitude, and who, besides,
saw reason and justice in the struggle which his race was making for liberty,
attached himself to the bands of negroes then occupying the hills, commanded
by François and Biassou. In the negro army Toussaint at once assumed a
leading rank; and a certain amount of medical knowledge, which he had picked
up in the course of his reading, enabled him to unite the functions of army
physician with those of military officer. Such was Toussaint's position in the
end of the year 1793, when the British landed in the island.

It is necessary here to describe, as exactly as the confusion will permit, the
true state of parties in the island. The British, as we already know, were
attempting to take the colony out of the hands of the French republic, and
annex it to the crown of Great Britain; and in this design they were favored
by the few French royalists still resident in the island. The French commis-

sioners, Santhonax and Polverel, on the other hand, men of the republican school, were attempting, with a motley army of French, mulattoes and blacks, to beat back the British. The greater part of the mulattoes of the island, grateful for the exertions which the republicans and the *Amis des Noirs* had made on their behalf, attached themselves to the side of the commissioners and the republic which they represented. It may naturally be supposed that the blacks would attach themselves to the same party—to the party of those whose watchwords were liberty and equality, and who consequently were the sworn enemies of slavery; but such was not the case. Considerable numbers of the negroes, it is true, were gained over to the cause of the French republic by the manifesto the commissioners had published abolishing slavery; but the bulk of them kept aloof, and constituted a separate negro army. Strangely enough, this army declared itself anti-republican. Before the death of Louis XVI., the blacks had come to entertain a strong sympathy with the king, and a violent dislike to the republicans. This may have been owing either to the policy of their leaders, François and Biassou, or to the simple fact that the blacks had suffered much at the hands of republican whites. At all events, the negro armies called themselves the armies of the king while he was alive; and after he was dead, they refused to consider themselves subjects of the republic. In these circumstances, one would at first be apt to fancy they would side with the British when they landed on the island. But it must be remembered that, along with the blind and unintelligent royalism of the negroes, they were animated by a far stronger, and far more real feeling, namely, the desire of freedom and the horror of again being subjected to slavery; and this would very effectually prevent their assisting the British. If they did so, they would be only changing their masters; St. Domingo would become a British colony, and they, like the negroes of Jamaica, would become slaves of British planters. No, it was liberty they wanted, and the British would not give them that. They hung aloof, therefore, not acting consistently with the French, much less with the British, but watching the course of events, and ready, at any given moment, to precipitate themselves into the contest and strike a blow for negro independence.

The negroes, however, in the meantime had the fancy to call themselves royalists, François having assumed the title of grand admiral of France, and Biassou that of generalissimo of the conquered districts. Toussaint held a military command under them, and acted also as army physician. Every day his influence over the negroes was extending; and François became so envious of Toussaint's growing reputation as to cast him into prison, apparently with the further purpose of destroying him. Toussaint, however, was released by Biassou, who, although described as a monster of cruelty, appears to have had some sparks of generous feeling. Shortly after this, Biassou's drunken ferocity rendered it necessary to deprive him of all command, and François and Toussaint became joint leaders, Toussaint acting in the capacity of lieutenant-general, and François in that of general-in-chief. The negro army at this time judged it expedient to enter the service of Spain, acting in coöperation with the governor of the Spanish colony in the other end of the island, who had been directed by his government at home to carry on war against the French commissioners. Toussaint was for some time an officer in the Spanish service, acting under the directions of Joachim Garcia, the president of the Spanish colonial council. In this capacity he distinguished himself greatly. With 600 men, he beat a body of 1500 French out of a strong post which they had occupied near the Spanish town of St. Raphael; and afterwards he took in succession the villages of Marmelade, Henneri, Plaisance, and Gonäives. He was appointed lieutenant-general of the army, and presented at the same time with a sword and a badge of honor in the name of his Catholic majesty. But the Marquis D'Hermona having been succeeded in the command by another, Toussaint began to find his services less appreciated. His old rival, François, did his best to undermine his influence among the Spaniards; nay, it is said, laid a plot for his assassination, which Toussaint narrowly escaped. He had to complain also of the bad treatment which certain French officers, who had surrendered to him, and whom he had persuaded to accept a command under him, had received at the hands of the Spaniards. All these circumstances operated on the mind of Toussaint, and shook the principles on which he had hitherto acted. While hesitating with respect to his next movements, intelligence of the decree of the French convention of the 4th of February, 1794, by which the abolition of negro slavery was confirmed, reached St. Domingo; and this immediately decided the step he should take. Quitting the Spanish service, he joined the French general Laveaux, who—the commissioners Santhonax and Polverel having been recalled—was now invested with the sole governorship of the colony; took the oath of fidelity to the French republic; and being elevated to the rank of brigadier-general, assisted Laveaux in his efforts to drive the English troops out of the island.

In his new capacity, Toussaint was no less successful than he had been while fighting under the Spanish colors. In many engagements, both with the British and the Spaniards, he rendered signal services to the cause of the French. At first, however, the French commander Laveaux showed little disposition to place confidence in him. It is highly creditable, therefore, to this French officer, that when he came to have more experience of Toussaint L'Ouverture, he discerned his extraordinary abilities, and esteemed him as much as if he had been a French gentleman educated in the schools of Paris. The immediate occasion of the change of the sentiments of Laveaux towards Toussaint was as follows: In the month of March, 1795, an insurrection of mulattoes occurred at the town of the Cape, and Laveaux was seized and placed in confinement. On hearing this, Toussaint marched at the head of 10,000 blacks to the town, obliged the inhabitants to open the gates by the threat of a siege, entered in triumph, released the French commander, and reinstated him in his office. In gratitude for this act of loyalty, Laveaux appointed Toussaint lieutenant-governor of the colony, declaring his resolution at the same time to act by his advice in all matters, whether military or civil—a resolution the wisdom of which will appear when we reflect that Toussaint was the only man in the

PLANTATION SCENE—SUGAR.

island who could govern the blacks. A saying of Laveaux is also recorded, which shows what a decided opinion he had formed of Toussaint's abilities:— "It is this black," said he, "this Spartacus, predicted by Raynal, who is destined to avenge the wrongs done to his race."

A wonderful improvement soon followed the appointment of L'Ouverture as lieutenant-governor of the colony. The blacks, obedient to their champion, were reduced under strict military discipline, and submitted to all the regulations of orderly civil government.

Since the departure of the commissioners Santhonax and Polverel, the whole authority of the colony, both civil and military, had been in the hands of Laveaux; but in the end of the year 1795, a new commission arrived from the mother country. At the head of this commission was Santhonax, and his colleagues were Giraud, Raymond, and Leblanc. The new commissioners, according to their instructions, overwhelmed Toussaint with thanks and compliments; told him he had made the French republic his everlasting debtor, and encouraged him to persevere in his efforts to rid the island of the British. Shortly afterwards, Laveaux, being nominated a member of the legislature, was obliged to return to France; and in the month of April, 1796, Toussaint L'Ouverture was appointed his successor, as commander-in-chief of the French forces in St. Domingo. Thus, by a remarkable succession of circumstances, was this negro, at the age of fifty-three years, fifty of which had been passed in a state of slavery, placed in the most important position in the island.

Toussaint now began to see his way more clearly, and to become conscious of the duty which Providence had assigned him. Taking all things into consideration, he resolved on being no longer a tool of foreign governments, but to strike a grand blow for the permanent independence of his race. To accomplish this object, he felt that it was necessary to assume and retain, at least for a time, the supreme civil as well as military command. Immediately, therefore, on becoming commander-in-chief in St. Domingo, he adopted measures for removing all obstructions to the exercise of his authority. General Rochambeau had been sent from France with a military command similar to that which Laveaux had held; but finding himself a mere cipher, he became unruly, and Toussaint instantly sent him home. Santhonax, the commissioner, too, was an obstacle in the way; and Toussaint, after taking the precaution of ascertaining that he would be able to enforce obedience, got rid of him by the delicate pretext of making him the bearer of dispatches to the Directory. Along with Santhonax, several other officious personages were sent to France; the only person of any official consequence who was retained being the commissioner Raymond, who was a mulatto, and might be useful. As these measures, however, might draw down the vengeance of the Directory, if not accompanied by some proofs of good-will to France, Toussaint sent two of his sons to Paris to be educated, assuring the Directory at the same time that, in removing Santhonax and his coadjutors, he had been acting for the best interests of the colony. "I guarantee," he wrote to the Directory, "on my own personal responsibility, the orderly behavior and the good-will to France of my brethren the blacks. You may depend, citizen directors, on happy results; and you shall soon see whether I engage in vain my credit and your hopes."

The people of Paris received with a generous astonishment the intelligence of the doings of the negro prodigy, and the interest they took in the novelty of the case prevented them from being angry. The Directory, however, judged it prudent to send out General Hedouville, an able and moderate man, to superintend Toussaint's proceedings, and restrain his boldness.

The evacuation of St. Domingo by the English in 1798, did not remove all Toussaint's difficulties. The mulattoes, influenced partly by a rumor that the French Directory meditated the reëstablishment of the exploded distinction of color, partly by a jealous dislike to the ascendency which a pure negro had gained in the colony, rose in insurrection under the leadership of Rigaud and Petion, two able and educated mulattoes. The insurrection was formidable ; but, by a judicious mingling of severity with caution, Toussaint quelled it, reducing Rigaud and Petion to extremities ; and the arrival of a deputation from France in the year 1799, bringing a confirmation of his authority as commander-in-chief in St. Domingo by the man who, under the title of first consul, had superseded the Directory, and now swayed the destinies of France, rendered his triumph complete. Petion and Rigaud, deserted by their adherents, and despairing of any further attempt to shake Toussaint's power, embarked for France.

Confirmed by Bonaparte in the powers which he had for some time been wielding in the colony with such good effect, Toussaint now paid exclusive attention to the internal affairs of the island. In the words of a French biographer, " he laid the foundation of a new state with the foresight of a mind that could discern what would decay and what would endure. St. Domingo rose from its ashes ; the reign of law and justice was established ; those who had been slaves were now citizens. Religion again reared her altars ; and on the sites of ruins were built new edifices." Certain interesting particulars are also recorded, which give us a better idea of his habits and the nature of his government than these general descriptions. To establish discipline among his black troops, he gave all his superior officers the power of life and death over the subalterns : every superior officer "commanded with a pistol in his hand." In all cases where the original possessors of estates which had fallen vacant in the course of the troubles of the past nine years could be traced, they were invited to return and resume their property. Toussaint's great aim was to accustom the negroes to industrial habits. It was only by diligent agriculture, he said, that the blacks could ever raise themselves. Accordingly, while every trace of personal slavery was abolished, he took means to compel the negroes to work as diligently as ever they had done under the whip of their overseers. All those plantations the proprietors of which did not reappear, were lotted out among the negroes, who, as a remuneration for their labor, received one-third of the produce, the rest going to the public revenue. There were as yet no civil or police courts which could punish idleness or vagrancy, but the same purpose was served by courts-martial. The ports of the island were opened to foreign vessels, and every encouragement held out to traffic. In consequence of these arrangements, a most surprising change took place : the plantations were again covered with crops ; the sugar-houses and distilleries were re-built ; the export trade began to revive ; and the population, orderly and well-behaved, began to increase. In addition to these external evidences of good government, the island exhibited those finer evidences which consist in mental culture and the civilization of manners. Schools were established, and books became common articles in the cottages of the negro laborers. Music and the theatre were encouraged ; and public worship was conducted with all the usual pomp of the Romish church. The whites, the mulattoes, and the blacks mingled in the same society, and exchanged with each other all the courtesies of civilized intercourse. The commander-in-chief himself set the example by holding public levees, at which, surrounded by his officers, he received the visits of the principal colonists ; and his private parties, it is said, "might have vied with the best regulated societies of Paris."

Successful in all his schemes of improvement, Toussaint had only one serious cause for dread. While he admired, and, it may be, imitated Napoleon Bonaparte, he entertained a secret fear of the projects of that great general. Although Bonaparte, as first consul, had confirmed him in his command, several circumstances had occurred to excite alarm. He had sent two letters to Bonaparte, both headed, "The First of the Blacks to the First of the Whites," one of which announced the complete pacification of the island, and requested the ratification of certain appointments which he had made, and the other explained his reasons for cashiering a French official ; but to these letters Bonaparte had not deigned to return an answer. Moreover, the representatives from St. Domingo had been excluded from the French senate ; and rumors had reached the island that the first consul meditated the reëstablishment of slavery. Toussaint thought it advisable in this state of matters to be beforehand with the French consul in forming a constitution for the island, to supersede the military government with which it had hitherto been content. A draft of a constitution was accordingly drawn up by his directions, and with the assistance of the ablest Frenchmen in the island ; and after being submitted to an assembly of representatives from all parts of St. Domingo, it was formally published on the 1st of July, 1801. By this constitution, the whole executive of the island, with the command of the forces, was to be intrusted to a governor-general. Toussaint was appointed governor-general for life ; his successors were to hold office for five years each ; and he was to have the power of nominating the first of them. Various other provisions were contained in the constitution, and its general effect was to give St. Domingo a virtual independence, under the guardianship of France.

Not disheartened by the taciturnity of Bonaparte, Toussaint again addressed him in respectful terms, and intreated his ratification of the new constitution. The first consul, however, had already formed the resolution of extinguishing Toussaint and taking possession of St. Domingo ; and the conclusion of a treaty of peace with England (1st October, 1801,) increased his haste to effect

18

the execution of his deceitful purpose. The expedition was equipped. It consisted of twenty-six ships of war and a number of transports, carrying an army of 25,000 men, the flower of the French troops, who embarked reluctantly. The command of the army was given to General Leclerc, the husband of Pauline Bonaparte, the consul's sister.

The French squadron reached St. Domingo on the 29th of January, 1802. "We are lost," said Toussaint, when he saw the ships approach; "all France is coming to St. Domingo." The invading army was divided into four bodies. General Kervesau, with one, was to take possession of the Spanish town of St. Domingo; General Rochambeau, with another, was to march on Fort Dauphin; General Boudet, with a third, on Port-au-Prince; and Leclerc himself, with the remainder, on Cape François. In all quarters the French were successful in effecting a landing. Rochambeau, in landing with his division, came to an engagement with the blacks who had gathered on the beach, and slaughtered a great number of them. At Cape François, Leclerc sent an intimidating message to Christophe, the negro whom Toussaint had stationed there as commander; but the negro replied that he was responsible only to Toussaint, his commander-in-chief. Perceiving, however, that his post was untenable, owing to the inclination of the white inhabitants of the town to admit Leclerc, Christophe set fire to the houses at night, and retreated to the hills by the light of the conflagration, carrying 2000 whites with him as hostages.

Although the French had effected a landing, the object of the invasion was yet far from being attained. Toussaint and the blacks had retired to the interior, and in fastnesses where no military force could reach them, they were preparing for future attacks.

The correspondence which Toussaint entered into with Leclerc produced no good result, and the war began in earnest. Toussaint and Christophe were declared outlaws, and battle after battle was fought with varying success. The mountainous nature of the interior greatly impeded the progress of the French. The Alps themselves, Leclerc said, were not nearly so troublesome to a military man as the hills of St Domingo. On the whole, however, the advantage was decidedly on the side of the French; and the blacks were driven by degrees out of their principal positions. The success of the French was not entirely the consequence of their military skill and valor; it was partly owing also to the effect which the proclamations of Leclerc had on the minds of the negroes and their commanders. If they were to enjoy the perfect liberty which these proclamations promised them, if they were to continue free men as they were now, what mattered it whether the French were in possession of the island or not? Such was the general feeling; and accordingly many of Toussaint's most eminent officers, among whom were Laplume and Maurepas, went over to the French. Deserted thus by many of his officers and by the great mass of the negro population, Toussaint, supported by his two bravest and ablest generals, Dessalines and Christophe, still held out, and protracted the war. Dessalines, besieged in the fort of Crete à Pierrot by

Leclerc and nearly the whole of the French army, did not give up the defense until he had caused the loss to his besiegers of about 3000 men, including several distinguished officers; and even then, rushing out, he fought his way through the enemy, and made good his retreat.

The reduction of the fortress of Crete à Pierrot was considered decisive of the fate of the war; and Leclerc, deeming dissimulation no longer necessary, permitted many negroes to be massacred, and issued an order virtually reëstablishing the power of the old French colonists over their slaves. This rash step opened the eyes of the negroes who had joined the French; they deserted in masses; Toussaint was again at the head of an army; and Leclerc was in danger of losing all the fruits of his past labors, and being obliged to begin his enterprise over again. This was a very disagreeable prospect; for although strong reinforcements were arriving from France, the disorders incident to military life in a new climate were making large incisions into his army. He resolved, therefore, to fall back on his former policy; and on the 25th of April, 1802, he issued a proclamation directly opposite in its spirit to his former order, asserting the equality of the various races, and holding out the prospect of full citizenship to the blacks. The negroes were again deceived, and again deserted Toussaint. Christophe, too, despairing of any farther success against the French, entered into negotiation with Leclerc, securing as honorable terms as could be desired. The example of Christophe was imitated by Dessalines, and by Paul L'Ouverture, Toussaint's brother. Toussaint, thus left alone, was obliged to submit; and Christophe, in securing good terms for himself, had not neglected the opportunity of obtaining similar advantages for his commander-in-chief. On the 1st of May, 1802, a treaty was concluded between Leclerc and Toussaint L'Ouverture, the conditions of which were, that Toussaint should continue to govern St. Domingo as hitherto, Leclerc acting only in the capacity of French deputy, and that all the officers in Toussaint's army should be allowed to retain their respective ranks. "I swear," added Leclerc, "before the Supreme Being, to respect the liberty of the people of St. Domingo." Thus the war appeared to have reached a happy close; the whites and blacks mingled with each other once more as friends; and Toussaint retired to one of his estates near Gonáives, to lead a life of quiet domestic enjoyment.

The instructions of the first consul, however, had been precise, that the negro chief should be sent as a prisoner to France. Many reasons recommended such a step as more likely than any other to break the spirit of independence among the blacks, and rivet the French power on the island. The expedition had been one of the most disastrous that France had ever undertaken. A pestilence resembling the yellow fever, but more fatal and terrible than even that dreadful distemper, had swept many thousands of the French to their graves. What with the ravages of the plague, and the losses in war, it was calculated that 30,000 men, 1,500 officers of various ranks, among whom were fourteen generals, and 700 physicians and surgeons, perished in the expedition.

It is our melancholy duty now to record one of the blackest acts committed by Napoleon. Agreeably to his orders, the person of Toussaint was treacherously arrested, while residing peacefully in his house near Gonáives. Two negro chiefs who endeavored to rescue him were killed on the spot, and a large number of his friends were at the same time made prisoners. The fate of many of these was never known; but Toussaint himself, his wife, and all his family, were carried at midnight on board the *Hero* man-of-war, then in the harbor, which immediately set sail for France. After a short passage of twenty-five days, the vessel arrived at Brest (June 1802); and here Toussaint took his last leave of his wife and family. They were sent to Bayonne; but by the orders of the first consul, he was carried to the chateau of Joux, in the east of France, among the Jura mountains. Placed in this bleak and dismal region, so different from the tropical climate to which he had been accustomed, his sufferings may easily be imagined. Not satisfied, however, with confining his unhappy prisoner to the fortress generally, Bonaparte enjoined that he should be secluded in a dungeon, and denied anything beyond the plainest necessaries of existence. For the first few months of his captivity, Toussaint was allowed to be attended by a faithful negro servant; but at length this single attendant was removed, and he was left alone in his misery and despair. It appears a rumor had gone abroad that Toussaint, during the war in St. Domingo, had buried a large amount of treasure in the earth; and during his captivity at Joux, an officer was sent by the first consul to interrogate him respecting the place where he had concealed it. "The treasures I have lost," said Toussaint, "are not those which you seek." After an imprisonment of ten months he was found dead in his dungeon on the 27th of April, 1803. He was sitting at the side of the fire-place, with his hands resting on his legs, and his head drooping. The account given at the time was, that he had died of apoplexy; but some authors have not hesitated to ascribe it to less natural circumstances. "The governor of the fort," observes one French writer, "made two excursions to Neufchâtel, in Switzerland. The first time, he left the keys of the dungeons with a captain whom he chose to act for him during his absence. The captain accordingly had occasion to visit Toussaint, who conversed with him about his past life, and expressed his indignation at the design imputed to him by the first consul, of having wished to betray St. Domingo to the English. As Toussaint, reduced to a scanty farinaceous diet, suffered greatly from the want of coffee, to which he had been accustomed, the captain generously procured it for him. The first absence of the governor of the fort, however, was only an experiment. It was not long before he left the fort again, and this time said, with a mysterious, unquiet air to the captain, 'I leave you in charge of the fort, but I do not give you the keys of the dungeons; the prisoners do not require anything.' Four days after he returned, and Toussaint was dead—starved." According to another account, this miserable victim of despotism, and against whom there was no formal or reasonable charge, was poisoned; but this rests on no credible testimony, and there is reason to believe that Toussaint died a victim only to the severities of confinement in this inhospitable prison. This melancholy termination to his sufferings took place when he was sixty years of age.

The forcible suppression of Toussaint's government, and his treacherous removal from the island, did not prove a happy stroke of policy; and it would have been preferable for France to have at once established the independence of St. Domingo, than to have entered on the project of resuming it as a dependency on the old terms. Leclerc, with all the force committed to his care by Bonaparte, signally failed in his designs. The contemptuous and cruel manner in which the blacks were generally treated, and the attempts made to restore them as a class to slavery, provoked a wide-spread insurrection. Toussaint's old friends and generals, Dessalines, Christophe, Clerveaux, and others, rose in arms. Battle after battle was fought, and all the resources of European military skill were opposed to the furious onsets of the negro masses. All was in vain : before October, the negroes, under the command of Dessalines and Christophe, had driven the French out of Fort Dauphin, Port de Paix, and other important positions. In the midst of these calamities, that is, on the 1st of November, 1802, Leclerc died, and Pauline Bonaparte returned to France with his body. Leclerc was succeeded in the command by Rochambeau, a determined enemy of the blacks. Cruelties such as Leclerc shrunk from were now employed to assist the French arms; unoffending negroes were slaughtered; and bloodhounds were imported from Cuba to chase the negro fugitives through the forests. Rochambeau, however, had a person to deal with who was capable of repaying cruelty with cruelty. Dessalines, who had assumed the chief command of the insurgents, was a man who, to great military talents and great personal courage, added a ferocious and sanguinary disposition. Hearing that Rochambeau had ordered 500 blacks to be shot at the Cape, he selected 500 French officers and soldiers from among his prisoners, and had them shot by way of reprisal. To complete the miseries of the French, the mulattoes of the south now joined the insurrection, and the war between France and England having recommenced, the island was blockaded by English ships, and provisions began to fail. In this desperate condition, after demanding assistance from the mother country, which could not be granted, Rochambeau negotiated with the negroes and the English for the evacuation of the island; and towards the end of November, 1803, all the French troops left St. Domingo.

On the departure of the French, Dessalines, Christophe, and the other generals proclaimed the independence of the island "in the name of the blacks and the people of color." At the same time they invited the return of all whites who had taken no part in the war; but, added they, "if any of those who imagined they would restore slavery return hither, they shall meet with nothing but chains and deportation." On the first of January, 1804, at an assembly of the generals and chiefs of the army, the independence of the island was again solemnly declared, and all present bound themselves by an oath to defend it. At the same time, to mark their formal renunciation of all connection with France, it was resolved that the name of the island be changed from St. Domingo to Hayti, the name given to it by its original Indian inhabitants. Jean Jacques Dessalines was appointed governor-general for life, with the privilege of nominating his successor.

The rule of Dessalines was a sanguinary, but, on the whole, a salutary one. He began his government by a treacherous massacre of nearly all the French who remained in the island trusting to his false promises of protection. All other Europeans, however, except the French, were treated with respect. Dessalines encouraged the importation of Africans into Hayti, saying that since they were torn from their country, it was certainly better that they should be employed to recruit the strength of a rising nation of blacks, than to serve the whites of all countries as slaves. On the 8th of October, 1804, Dessalines exchanged his plain title of governor-general for the more pompous one of emperor. He was solemnly inaugurated under the name of James I., emperor of Hayti; and the ceremony of his coronation was accompanied by the proclamation of a new constitution, the main provisions of which were exceedingly judicious. All Haytian subjects, of whatever color, were to be called *blacks*, entire religious toleration was decreed, schools were established, public worship encouraged, and measures adopted similar to those which Toussaint had employed for creating and fostering an industrial spirit among the negroes. As a preparation for any future war, the interior of the island was extensively planted with yams, bananas, and other articles of food, and many forts built in advantageous situations. Under these regulations the island again began to show symptoms of prosperity. Dessalines was a man in many respects fitted to be the first sovereign of a people rising out of barbarism. Born the slave of a negro mechanic, he was quite illiterate, but had great natural abilities, united to a very ferocious temper. His wife was one of the most beautiful and best educated negro women in Hayti. A pleasant trait of his character is his seeking out his old master after he became emperor, and making him his butler. It was, he said, exactly the situation the old man wished to fill, as it afforded him the means of being always drunk. Dessalines himself drank nothing but water. For two years this negro continued to govern the island; but at length his ferocity provoked his mulatto subjects to form a conspiracy against him, and on the 17th of October, 1806, he was assassinated by the soldiers of Petion, who was his third in command.

On the death of Dessalines, a schism took place in the island. Christophe, who had been second in command, assumed the government of the northern division of the island, the capital of which was Cape François; and Petion, the mulatto general, assumed the government of the southern division, the capital of which was Port-au-Prince. For several years a war was carried on between the two rivals, each endeavoring to depose the other, and become chief of the whole of Hayti; but at length hostilities ceased, and by a tacit agreement, Petion came to be regarded as legitimate governor of the south and west, where the mulattoes were most numerous; and Christophe as legitimate governor in the north, where the population consisted chiefly of blacks. Christophe, trained, like Dessalines, in the school of Toussaint L'Ouverture, was a slave born, and an able as well as a benevolent man; but, like most of the negroes who had arrived at his period of life, he had not had the benefit of any systematic education. Petion, on the other hand, had been educated in the military academy of Paris, and was accordingly as accomplished and well-instructed as any European officer. The title with which Petion was invested, was that of president of the republic of Hayti; the southern and western districts preferring the republican form of government. For some time Christophe bore the simple title of chief magistrate, and was in all respects the president of a republic like Petion; but the blacks have always shown a liking for the monarchical form of government; and accordingly, on the 2d of June, 1811, Christophe, by the desire of his subjects, assumed the regal title of Henry I., king of Hayti. The coronation was celebrated in the most gorgeous manner; and at the same time the creation of an aristocracy took place, the first act of the new sovereign being to name four princes, seven dukes, twenty-two counts, thirty barons, and ten knights.

Both parts of the island were well governed, and rapidly advanced in prosperity and civilization. On the restoration of the Bourbons to the French throne, some hope seems to have been entertained in France that it might be possible yet to obtain a footing in the island, and commissioners were sent out to collect information respecting its condition; but the conduct both of Christophe and Petion was so firm, that the impossibility of subverting the independence of Hayti became manifest. The island was therefore left in the undisturbed possession of the blacks and mulattoes. In 1818 Petion died, and was succeeded by General Boyer, a mulatto who had been in France, and had accompanied Leclerc in his expedition. In 1820, Christophe having become involved in differences with his subjects, shot himself; and the two parts of the island were then reünited under the general name of the republic of Hayti, General Boyer being the first president. In the following year, the Spanish portion of the island, which for a long time had been in a languishing condition, voluntarily placed itself under the government of Boyer, who thus became the head of a republic including the entire island of St. Domingo. In 1825, a treaty was concluded between President Boyer and Charles X. of France, by which France acknowledged the independence of Hayti, in consideration of 150 millions of francs (£6,000,000 sterling,) to be paid by the island in five annual instalments, as a compensation for the losses sustained by the French colonists during the revolution. The first instalment was paid in 1836; but as it was found impossible to pay the remainder, the terms of the agreement were changed in 1838, and France consented to accept 60 millions of francs (£2,400,000,) to be liquidated in six instalments before the year 1867.

As the engagements which Boyer had entered into with the French increased the taxation and bore hard upon the population, an insurrection broke out against his authority in May, 1838. This was suppressed, but was followed by repeated collisions between the president and the representative body. In 1842 a revolution broke out and President Boyer was compelled to flee to Jamaica; and in 1844 the inhabitants of the Spanish portion rose, overpowered their Haytian oppressors, and formed themselves into a republic, under the name of Santo Domingo. After various individuals had, for a short period, occupied the presidential chair of the Haytian republic, the election fell upon General Soulouque, who, in 1849, made an unsuccessful attempt to subjugate the Dominican republic. In the latter part of the same year, however, he ascended the throne of the Haytian republic, under the title of Emperor Faustin I. The independence of the Dominican republic was virtually recognized by Great Britain, by the appointment of a consul to it, in 1849; and it was formally recognized by a treaty of amity and commerce, ratified September 10, 1850. It has also been recognized by France and Denmark; but the Emperor Faustin I. (Soulouque) still refused to recognize its independence.

The present population of the whole island is estimated at 950,000. The effective force of the Haytian army is estimated at 40,000 men, and that of the navy 15 small vessels and 1000 men. Hayti now possesses an established system of government, an established system of education, a literature, commerce, manufactures, a rich and cultivated class in society. In the short space of half a century, it has raised itself from the depths and degradation of servitude to the condition of a flourishing and respectable state. Slavery has been eradicated in the new world from the very spot of its origin.

CHAPTER XVII.

AFRICAN SLAVE TRADE AFTER ITS NOMINAL ABOLITION.

State of the slave-trade since its nominal abolition.—Numbers imported and losses on the passage.—Increased horrors of the trade.—Scenes on board a captured slaver in Sierra Leone.—The Progresso.—Walsh's description of a slaver in 1829.—The trade in 1820.—The slave-trade in Cuba—officers of government interested in it.—Efforts of Spain insincere.—Slave barracoons near Governor's palace—conduct of the inmates. The Bozals.—Bryan Edwards' description of natives of Gold Coast—their courage and endurance.—Number of slaves landed at Rio in 1838—barracoons at Rio—government tax.—Slave-trade Insurance—Courts of Mixed Commission—their proceedings at Sierra Leone in 1838.—Joint stock slave-trade companies at Rio.—The Cruisers—intercepted letters.—Mortality of the trade.—Abuses of the American flag.—Consul Trist and British commissioners.—Correspondence of American Ministers to Brazil, Mr. Todd, Mr. Proffit, Mr. Wise.—Extracts from Parliamentary papers.—Full list of Conventions and Treaties made by England for suppression of Slave-trade.

To import negroes as slaves from Africa is now illegal, according to the laws of civilized nations. Those nations which keep up slavery, such as Brazil, Cuba and the United States, are supposed to breed all the slaves they require, within their own territories. But such is not the fact. The slave-trade is not yet suppressed; and the immese labors of philanthropists and statesmen, the struggles and negotiations of half a century, have not been crowned with per fect success. It is stated, upon good authority, that in 1844, more slaves were carrid away from Africa in ships than in 1744, when the trade was legal and in full vigor. The legal trade, pursued openly, has been changed into a contraband trade, pursued secretly; and the profits, determined from a number of random cases, have averaged from 180 to 200 per cent. Accordingly, a vigorous traffic has been carried on by French, Spanish, Portuguese, British and American crews. Spaniards and Portuguese, however, predominate, and the wages are large. They carry their cargoes to Brazil, Cuba, Porto Rico, &c.; and it has been charged that some are landed secretly in the United States, as there are slaves in the extreme southern States who cannot speak English. But Brazil and Cuba are the principal slave-importing countries. Sir Fowell Buxton, in 1835, calculated that "Brazil imports annually about 80,000, and Cuba about 60,000 slaves. If we add 10,000 for all other places, the annual delivery of negroes into the slave-using countries of America will amount to 150,000." Africa, however, loses far more than America gains. According to his estimates, the whole wastage or tare of the traffic is seven-tenths; that is to say, for every ten negroes whom Africa parts with, America receives only three; the other seven die. This enormous wastage may be divided into three portions—the wastage in the journey from the interior of Africa to the coast, the wastage in the passage across the Atlantic, and the wastage in the process of seasoning after landing. The first is estimated at one-half of the original number brought from the interior, the second at one-fourth of the number shipped, and the third at one-fifth of the number landed. In other words, if 400,000 negroes are collected in the interior of Africa, then of these one-half will die before reaching the coast, leaving only 200,000 to be shipped; of these one-fourth will die in the passage across the Atlantic, leaving only 150,000 to be landed; and of these one-fifth will die in the process of seasoning, leaving only 120,000 available for labor in America.

While the trade was legal, the ships designed for carrying slaves were, in a great measure, constructed like other vessels; though, in order to make the cargo as large as possible, the negroes were packed very closely together. The number of negroes which a vessel was allowed to carry was fixed by law. British vessels of 150 tons and under, were not to carry more than five slaves to every three tons of measurement. In 1789, a parliamentary committee engaged in inquiries connected with Sir W. Dolben's bill, found, by actual measurement of a slave ship, that, allowing every man six feet by one foot four inches, every woman five feet by one foot four inches, every boy five feet by one foot two inches, and every girl four feet six inches by one foot, the ship would hold precisely 450 negroes. The actual number carried was 454; and in previous voyages she had carried more. This calculation, illustrated as it was by an engraving, caused an immense sensation at the time, and assisted in mitigating the miseries of the passage. In order to escape the cruisers, all slave ships now are built on the principle of fast sailing. The risk of being captured takes away all inducement, from mere selfish motives, to make the cargo moderate; on the contrary, it is an object now to make the cargo as

large as possible, for then the escape of one cargo out of three will amply repay the dealer. Accordingly, the negroes now are packed in the slave ships
literally (and this is the comparison always used) like herring in a barrel.
They have neither standing room, nor sitting room, nor lying room ; and as
for change of position during the voyage, the thing is impossible. They are
cooped up anyhow, squeezed into crevices, or jammed up against the curved
planks. The following is a brief description given by an eye-witness of the
unloading of a captured slaver which had been brought into Sierra Leone :
"The captives were now counted ; their numbers, sex, and age, written down,
for the information of the court of mixed commission. The task was repulsive.
As the hold had been divided for the separation of the men and the women,
those on deck were first counted ; they were then driven forward, crowded as
much as possible, and the women were drawn up through the small hatchway
from their hot, dark confinement. A black boatswain seized them one by one,
dragging them before us for a moment, when the proper officer, on a glance,
decided the age, whether above or under fourteen ; and they were instantly
swung again by their arm into their loathsome cell, where another negro boatswain sat, with a whip or stick, and forced them to resume the bent and painful attitude necessary for the stowage of so large a number. The unfortunate
women and girls, in general, submitted with quiet resignation, when absence of
disease and the use of their limbs permitted. A month had made their condition familiar to them. One or two were less philosophical, or suffered more
acutely than the rest. Their shrieks rose faintly from their hidden prison, as
violent compulsion alone squeezed them into their nook against the curve of
the ship's side. I attempted to descend in order to see the accommodation.
The height between the floor and ceiling was about twenty-two inches. The
agony of the position of the crouching slaves may be imagined, especially that
of the men, whose heads and necks are bent down by the boarding above them.
Once so fixed, relief, by motion or change of posture, is unattainable. The
body frequently stiffens in a permanent curve ; and in the streets of Freetown
I have seen liberated slaves of every conceivable state of distortion. One I
remember who trailed along his body, with his back to the ground, by means of
his hands and ankles. Many can never resume the upright posture."

One item of the enormous mortality during the passage consists of negroes
thrown overboard when the slaver is chased, or when a storm arises. Many
thousands perish annually in this way. Very frequently it is decided, upon
trial, that the capture of the vessel has been illegal ; and then the slaver sails
away triumphantly, the poor negroes on board having only been tantalized
with the hope of freedom. A remarkable case of this kind is told by Mr.
Rankin in his account of a visit to Sierra Leone, in 1834 :

"On the morning after my arrival at Sierra Leone," says Mr. Rankin, "I
was indulging in the first view of the waters of the estuary glittering in the
hot sun, and endeavoring to distinguish from the many vessels at anchor the
bark which had brought me from England. Close in-shore lay a large
schooner, so remarkable from the low, sharp cut of her black hull, and the

excessive rake of her masts, that she seemed amongst the other craft as a swallow seems amongst other birds. Her deck was crowded with naked blacks, whose woolly heads studded the rail. She was a slaver with a large cargo. In the autumn of 1833 this schooner, apparently a Brazilian, and named with the liberty-stirring appellation of 'Dona Maria da Gloria,' had left Loando, on the slave coast, with a few bales of merchandise, to comply with the formalities required by the authorities from vessels engaged in legal traffic; for the slave-trade, under the Brazilian flag, is now piracy. No sooner was she out of port than the real object of her voyage declared itself. She hastily received on board four hundred and thirty negroes, who had been mustered in readiness, and sailed for Rio Janeiro. Off the mouth of that harbor she arrived in November, and was captured as a slaver by his majesty's brig Snake. The case was brought in December before the court established there; and the court decided that, as her Brazilian character had not been fully made out, it was incompetent to the final decision of the case. It was necessary to apply to the court of mixed commission at Sierra Leone for the purpose of adjudication. A second time, therefore, the unfortunate dungeon-ship put to sea with her luckless cargo, and again crossed the Atlantic amidst the horrors of a two month's voyage. The Dona Maria da Gloria having returned to Africa, cast anchor at Freetown in the middle of February, 1834, and on arrival, found the number reduced by death from four hundred and thirty to three hundred and thirty-five.

"Continuance of misery for several months in a cramped posture, in a pestilential atmosphere, had not only destroyed many, but had spread disease amongst the survivors. Dropsy, eruptions, abscesses, and dysentery were making ravages, and ophthalmia was general. Until formally adjudicated by the court, the wretched slaves could not be landed, nor even relieved from their sickening situation. With the green hills and valleys of the colony close to them, they must not leave their prison. I saw them in April; they had been in the harbor two months, and no release had been offered them. But the most painful circumstance was the final decision of the court. The slaver was proved to have been sailing under Portuguese colors, not Brazilian; and the treaty with the Portuguesé prohibits slave traffic to the *north* of a certain line only, whereas the Dona Maria had been captured a few degrees to the *south*. No alternative remained. Her capture was decided to have been illegal. She was formally delivered up to her slave-captain; and he received from the British authorities written orders to the commanders of the British cruisers, guaranteeing a safe and free passage back to the Brazils; and I saw the evil ship weigh anchor and leave Sierra Leone, the seat of slave liberation, with her large canvas proudly swelling, and her ensign floating as if in contempt and triumph. Thus, a third time were the dying wretches carried across the Atlantic after seven months' confinement; few probably lived through the passage."

Formerly, the forfeited slave-ships at Sierra Leone used to be sold; and there were frequent instances of a forfeited slaver sold in one year plying the same trade the next. With regard to the crews, Sir Fowell Buxton remarks, that the law by which Great Britain, Brazil, and North America have made slave-dealing piracy, and liable to capital punishment, is, practically, a dead letter, there being no instance of an execution for that crime.

Perhaps never has the inefficacy of all that has yet been done towards the suppression of the slave-trade been more strikingly made out than in the harrowing pamphlet published by the Rev. Pascoe Grenfell Hill, entitled "Fifty Days on Board a Slave-Vessel in the Mozambique Channel, in April and May, 1843." The Progresso, a Brazilian slaver, was captured on the 12th of April, on the coast of Madagascar, by the British cruiser Cleopatra, on board of which Mr. Hill was chaplain. The slaver was then taken charge of by a British crew, who were to navigate her to the Cape of Good Hope. Mr. Hill, at his own request, accompanied her; and his pamphlet is a narrative of what took place during the fifty days which elapsed before their arrival at the Cape. We cannot here quote the details of the description of the treatment of the negroes given by Mr. Hill; but the following account of the horrors of a single night will suffice. Shortly after the Progresso parted company with the Cleopatra, a squall arose, and the negroes, who were breathing fresh air on deck, and rolling themselves about for glee, and kissing the hands and clothes of their deliverers, were all sent below. "The night," says Mr. Hill, "being intensely hot, 400 wretched beings thus crammed into a hold 12 yards in length, 7 feet in breadth, and only 3½ feet in height, speedily began to make an effort to re-issue to the open air. Being thrust back, and striving the more to get out, the after-hatch was forced down on them. Over the other hatchway, in the fore part of the vessel, a wooden grating was fastened. To this, the sole inlet for the air, the suffocating heat of the hold, and perhaps panic from the strangeness of their situation, made them press; and thus a great part of the space below was rendered useless. They crowded to the grating, and clinging to it for air, completely barred its entrance. They strove to force their way through apertures in length 14 inches, and barely 6 inches in breadth, and in some instances succeeded. The cries, the heat—I may say without exaggeration, 'the smoke of their torment'—which ascended, can be compared to nothing earthly. One of the Spaniards gave warning that the consequence would be 'many deaths.'" Next day the prediction of the Spaniard "was fearfully verified. Fifty-four crushed and mangled corpses lifted up from the slave deck have been brought to the gangway and thrown overboard. Some were emaciated from disease, many bruised and bloody. Antonio tells me that some were found strangled, their hands still grasping each other's throats, and tongues protruding from their mouths. The bowels of one were crushed out. They had been trampled to death for the most part, the weaker under the feet of the stronger, in the madness and torment of suffocation from crowd and heat. It was a horrid sight as they passed one by one—the stiff, distorted limbs smeared with blood and filth—to be cast into the sea. Some, still quivering, were laid on the deck to die; salt water thrown on them to revive them, and a little fresh water poured into their mouths. Antonio reminded me of his last night's

warning. He actively employed himself, with his comrade Sebastian, in attendance on the wretched living beings now released from their confinement below;
distributing to them their morning meal of farina, and their allowance of
water, rather more than half a pint to each, which they grasped with inconceivable eagerness, some bending their knees to the deck, to avoid the risk of
losing any of the liquid by unsteady footing; their throats, doubtless, parched
to the utmost with crying and yelling through the night."

On the 12th of April, when the Progresso parted company with the Cleopatra, there were 397 negroes on board. Of these only 222 were landed at the
Cape on the 22d of May; no fewer than 175, a little short of half, having
died. Many also died after being landed. The crew escaped, there being no
court empowered to try them at the Cape.

Walsh, in his notices of Brazil, in 1828 and 1829, says, in describing a slave-
ship, examined by the English man-of-war in which he returned from Brazil,
in May, 1829: "She had taken in, on the coast of Africa, 336 males and 226
females, making in all 562, and had been out seventeen days, during which
she had thrown overboard fifty-five. The slaves were all enclosed under grated
hatchways, between decks. The space was so low, that they sat between each
other's legs, and stowed so close together that there was no possibility of their
lying down, or at all changing their position by night or day. As they belonged to, and were shipped on account of, different individuals, they were all
branded, like sheep, with the owners' marks, of different forms. These were
impressed under their breasts, or on their arms, and, as the mate informed me,
with perfect indifference, 'queimados pelo ferro quento—burnt with the red
hot iron.' Over the hatchway stood a ferocious looking fellow, with a scourge
of many twisted thongs in his hand, who was the slave-driver of the ship; and
whenever he heard the slightest noise below, he shook it over them, and seemed
eager to exercise it. As soon as the poor creatures saw us looking down at
them, their dark and melancholy visages brightened up. They perceived something of sympathy and kindness in our looks, which they had not been accustomed to, and feeling, instinctively, that we were friends, they immediately
began to shout and clap their hands. One or two had picked up a few Portuguese words, and cried out, 'Viva! viva!' The women were particularly excited. They all held up their arms; and when we bent down and shook hands
with them, they could not contain their delight; they endeavored to scramble
upon their knees, stretching up to kiss our hands; and we understood that they
knew we had come to liberate them. Some, however, hung down their heads
in apparently hopeless dejection; some were greatly emaciated, and some,
particularly children, seemed dying. But the circumstance which struck us
most forcibly, was, how it was possible for such a number of human beings to
exist, packed up and wedged together as tight as they could cram, in low cells,
three feet high, the greater part of which, except that immediately under the
grated hatchways, was shut out from light or air, and this when the thermometer, exposed to the open sky, was standing in the shade, on our deck, at 89°.
The space between decks was divided into two compartments, three feet three

inches high; the size of one was sixteen feet by eighteen, and of the other forty by twenty-one; into the first were crammed the women and girls; into the second, the men and boys: 226 fellow creatures were thus thrust into one space 288 feet square, and 336 into another space 800 feet square—giving to the whole an average of twenty-three inches, and to each of the women not more than thirteen inches, though many of them were pregnant. We also found manacles and fetters of different kinds; but it appears they had all been taken off before we boarded. The heat of these horrid places was so great, and the odor so offensive, that it was quite impossible to enter them, even had there been room. They were measured, as above, when the slaves had left them. The officers insisted that the poor suffering creatures should be admitted on deck, to get air and water. This was opposed by the mate of the slaver, who, from a feeling that they deserved it, declared they would murder them all. The officers, however, persisted, and the poor beings were all turned up together. It is impossible to conceive the effect of this eruption—507 fellow creatures, of all ages and sexes, some children, some adults, some old men and women, all in a state of total nudity, scrambling out together to taste the luxury of a little fresh air and water. They came swarming up like bees from the aperture of a hive, till the whole deck was crowded to suffocation, from stem to stern; so that it was impossible to imagine where they could all have come from, or how they could all have been stowed away. On looking into the places where they had been crammed, there were found some children next the sides of the ship, in the places most remote from light and air; they were lying nearly in a torpid state, after the rest had turned out. The little creatures seemed indifferent as to life or death; and when they were carried on deck, many of them could not stand. After enjoying, for a short time, the unusual luxury of air, some water was brought; it was then that the extent of their sufferings was exposed in a fearful manner. They all rushed like maniacs towards it. No entreaties, or threats, or blows, could restrain them; they shrieked and struggled, and fought with one another, for a drop of this precious liquid, as if they grew rabid at the sight of it. There is nothing which slaves, in the mid-passage, suffer from so much as want of water. It is sometimes usual to take out casks filled with sea-water as ballast, and when the slaves are received on board, to start the casks and refill them with fresh. On one occasion a ship from Bahia neglected to change the contents of the casks, and on the mid-passage found, to their horror, that they were filled with nothing but salt water. All the slaves on board perished! We could judge of the extent of their sufferings from the afflicting sight we now saw. When the poor creatures were ordered down again, several of them came and pressed their heads against our knees, with looks of the greatest anguish, at the prospect of returning to the horrid place of suffering below."

The English ship, however, was obliged, though with great reluctance, to release the slaver, as it could not be proved, after a strict examination, that he had exceeded the privilege allowed to Brazilian ships of procuring slaves south of the line

Admiral Sir George Collier, in his report to the lords of admirality, dated September 6, 1820, stated, that "in the last twelve months not less than 60,000 Africans have been forced from their country, principally under the colors of France; most of whom have been distributed between the islands of Martinique, Guadaloupe, and Cuba. The confidence under which vessels navigate, bearing the French flag, has become so great, that I saw at Havana, in July last, no fewer than forty vessels fitting avowedly for the slave-trade, protected equally by the flags and papers of France and Spain. France has certainly issued her decrees against this traffic; but she has done nothing to enforce them. On the contrary, she gives to the trade all countenance short of public avowal.

"On this distressing subject, so revolting to every well regulated mind, I will add, that such is the merciless treatment of the slaves, by the persons engaged in the traffic, that no fancy can picture the horror of the voyage. Crowded together so as not to give the power to move; linked one to the other by the leg, never unfettered while life remains, or till the iron shall have fretted the flesh almost to the bone, forced under a deck, as I have seen them, *not thirty inches in height;* breathing an atmosphere the most putrid and pestilential possible; with little food, and less water; subject also to the most severe punishment at the caprice or fancy of the brute who may command the vessel; it is to me a matter of extreme wonder that any of these miserable people live the voyage through; many of them, indeed, perish on the passage, and those who remain to meet the shore, present a picture of wretchedness language cannot express."

The following singular and distressing circumstance occurred about the same time: The ship Le Rodeur, of 200 tons burthen, left Havre the 24th of January, 1819, for the coast of Africa, and reached her destination on the 14th of March following, anchoring at Bonny, on the river Calabar. The crew, consisting of twenty-two men, enjoyed good health during the outward voyage, and during their stay at Bonny, where they continued till the 6th of April. They had observed no trace of ophthalmia among the natives; and it was not until fifteen days after they had set sail on the return voyage, and the vessel was near the equator, that they perceived the first symptoms of this frightful malady. It was then remarked that the negroes, who, to the number of one hundred and sixty, were crowded together in the hold and between the decks, had contracted a considerable redness of the eyes, which spread with singular rapidity. No great attention was at first paid to these symptoms, which were thought to be caused only by the *want of air* in the hold, and by the *scarcity of water* which had already begun to be felt. At this time they were limited to eight ounces of water a day for each person, which quantity was afterwards reduced to *the half of a wine glass.* By the advice of M. Maignan, the surgeon of the ship, the negroes, who had hitherto remained shut up in the hold, were brought upon deck in succession, in order that they might breathe a purer air. But it became necessary to abandon this expedient, salutary as it was, because many of those negroes, affected with nostalgia, threw themselves into the sea, locked in each others arms.

The disease which had spread itself so rapidly and frightfully among the Africans, soon began to infect all on board, and to create alarms for the crew. The danger of infection, and perhaps the cause which produced the disease, were increased by a violent dysentery, attributed to the use of rain water. The first of the crew who caught the infection was a sailor who slept under the deck, near the grated hatch which communicated with the hold. The next day a landsman was seized with ophthalmia; and, in three days more the captain and almost the whole crew were infected by it.

The sufferings of the people and the number of the blind augmented every day, so that the crew—previously alarmed by the apprehension of a revolt among the negroes—were seized with the further dread of not being able to make the West Indies, if the only sailor who had hitherto escaped the contagion, and on whom their whole hope rested, should become blind like the rest. This calamity had actually befallen the Leon, a Spanish slaver which the Rodeur met with on her passage, and the whole of whose crew, having become blind, were under the necessity of altogether abandoning the direction of their ship. They entreated the charitable interference of the Rodeur; but the seamen of this vessel could not either quit her to go on board the Leon, on account of the cargo of negroes, nor receive the crew in the Rodeur, in which there were scarcely room for themselves. The difficulty of taking care of so large a number of sick in so confined a space, and the total want of fresh meat and of medicines, made them envy the fate of those who were about to become the victims of a death which seemed to them inevitable, and the consternation was general.

The Rodeur reached Gaudaloupe on the 21st of June, 1819, her crew being in a most deplorable condition. Three days after her arrival, the only man who, during the voyage, had withstood the influence of the contagion, and whom Providence appeared to have preserved as a guide to his unfortunate companions, was seized with the same malady. Of the negroes, thirty-nine had become perfectly blind, twelve had lost an eye, and fourteen were affected with blemishes more or less considerable. Of the crew, twelve lost their sight entirely, among whom was the surgeon; five become blind of one eye, one of them being the captain, and four were partially injured.

Such were the miseries of this voyage of iniquity, but the atrocities of it even transcended its miseries. It is stated among other things, that the captain caused several of the negroes who were prevented in the attempt to throw themselves overboard to be shot and hanged in the hope that the example might deter the rest from a similar conduct. But even this severity proved unavailing, and it became necessary to confine the slaves entirely to the hold during the remainder of the voyage. It is further stated, that upwards of thirty of the slaves who became blind *were thrown into the sea and drowned* upon the principle that had they been landed at Guadaloupe no one would have bought them, and that the proprietors would consequently have incurred the expense of maintaining them without the chance of any return; while by throwing them overboard not only was this certain loss avoided, but ground was also laid for a claim on the underwriters by whom the cargo had been insured, and who are said to have allowed the claim and made good the value of the slaves thus destroyed.

In the memorial of the colonization society presented to congress in 1822, it was stated that official documents had been presented to government, from which it appeared that in 1821, two hundred thousand had been carried away from the coast of Africa.

The African institution reported that in 1822, 28,246 slaves were imported into Rio de Janeiro alone from the coast. The number embarked had been 31,240—3,484 having died on the passage.

In 1824, the same society reported that 120,000 were taken from Africa during that year.

In 1825, "there were," says Commodore Bullen, "in the river Bonny alone 2007 tons of shipping, 293 persons and 35 guns, under the flag of the French nation, employed in the speculation of human flesh."

In 1822, four slave vessels were taken on the river Bonny by a squadron under Sir Robert Mends, stationed by the British government on the coast of Africa to prevent the infraction of the laws for the abolition of the slave-trade. The vessels were Spanish and French. They had nearly 1300 slaves on board. A Spanish schooner, when taken possession of, had a lighted match hanging over the open magazine hatch. The match was placed there by the crew, before they leaped overboard and swam for the shore; it was seen by one of the seamen, who boldly put his hat under the burning wick and removed it. The magazine contained a large quantity of powder. One spark from the flaming match would have blown up 325 unfortunate victims lying in irons in the hold. These monsters in iniquity expressed their deep regret after the action that their diabolical plan had failed.

On board another of the vessels, Lieutenant Mildmay, the officer who captured her, observed a slave girl about twelve or thirteen years of age in irons, to which was fastened a thick iron chain, ten feet in length, that was dragged along as she moved. He ordered the girl to be instantly released from this fetter; and that the captain who had treated her so cruelly might not be ignorant of the pain inflicted upon an unprotected and innocent child, the irons were ordered to be put upon him.

The slaves in one of the vessels at the time of the capture, were found in the most wretched condition; some lying on their backs, others sitting on the bottom of the ships. They were chained to each other by the arms and legs; iron collars were placed round their necks. In addition to these provisions for confinement, they were fastened together by a long chain which connected several of the collars for their greater security in that dismal prison. Thumbscrews, to be used as instruments of torture, were also found in the vessel. From their confinement and sufferings, the slaves often injured themselves by beating, and vented their grief upon such as were next to them by biting and

19

tearing their flesh. Some of them were bound by cords, and many had their arms grievously lacerated.

In 1825, on board a schooner's boat of only five tons burthen which was taken, were found seventeen slaves, twenty-three had been taken in, six had already died. The negroes were in a state of complete starvation and approaching dissolution. The space allowed them was no more than eighteen inches between the water casks and the deck.

The Aviso, another captured vessel, had 465 slaves on board; of whom 34 died after their capture, notwithstanding every attention. Such was the filth and crowd that not half could have reached the Brazils alive. Commodore Bullen put the crew on shore in Prince's island. These wretches, as soon as they found that they must be boarded, had stove in their boilers, as a last malignant effort to add to the misery of those whom a few minutes would place beyond their power.

One Oiseau, commander of a French slave-ship called Le Louis, having completed his cargo on the old Calabar, thrust them all between decks, (a height of only three feet,) and closed the hatches on them for the night. Fifty were found dead in the morning. As a matter of course, he only immediately returned on shore to supply their place. Captain Arnaud, of the Louisa, arrived at Guadaloupe with 200 negroes, the remainder of an original cargo of 265. Having by mistake purchased more than he could accommodate, he had thrown the odd 65 into the sea.

A writer in the African Repository, who visited Africa in one of our national vessels, states that the steward of the vessel had been to Africa five times in a slave-ship. On one occasion, when an insurrection was expected, they shot two hundred of the slaves. Out of 400, the number which they carried at each trip, 40 died on every passage. The African Institution in one of their reports publishes the following deed of infernal atrocity: A French slaver having landed part of a cargo of 250 slaves at Guadaloupe, was pursued by an armed French vessel, when, to avoid detection, they threw the remaining sixty-five overboard, all of whom perished.

A writer in a letter from Rio de Janeiro, dated January 11, 1830, says: "I will relate but a single fact at this time to show the dreadful character of the slave-trade. The Brazilian government derives a large revenue from the importation of slaves, by laying a duty of so much per head immediately on their arrival without regard to their health or condition. When vessels, therefore, which have slaves on board arrive off the port, a general survey takes place by the physician, and those poor wretches whose existence is doubtful are *thrown overboard in order to save the duty.*"

Mr. Robert Baird, in his "Impressions of the West Indies and North America," in 1849, speaking of the slave-trade, says: "There can be no doubt of the fact, that during the last year the importation of slaves into the island of Cuba has been carried on in full vigor—so vigorously and extensively that the price of slaves had fallen, in consequence of the plentiful supply, from four hundred and fifty or five hundred, to from two hundred and fifty to three hundred dollars. This fact is notorious, and I heard it authenticated by official authority. It is equally notorious in the island itself that the agent of the queen mother of Spain was and is extensively engaged in the infamous traffic; and it is more than suspected that, directly or indirectly, his royal mistress is a large participator in the heavy gains her agent realizes from this trade in human flesh. Indeed, the traffic is little short of being a legalized one; the amount of dollars payable to the governor or to the government (for there is much difference between these two) being, if not fixed by law or order, at least as well understood as if it were so. All this is, of course, in direct and manifest violation of the engagements and treaties made by Spain with England; and it is an ascertained fact that fully one-half of the slaves in Cuba are there held in abject bondage in violation of these solemn treaties and engagements. Indeed, were it otherwise, it were nearly impossible that the Spanish colonists of Cuba could find slaves to cultivate their fields. Every one who knows Cuba, and the brutal manner in which the great mass of the *agricultural* slaves are treated there, will laugh at the idea of the slave population of Cuba being self-supporting. They also know that it is much cheaper to import slaves than to breed them. The planter in Cuba found this to be the case, even when the vigilance of the British and French cruisers had made slaves so scarce in Cuba that the price of an able-bodied one was fully five hundred dollars. Of course, now that such vigilance had been, for a time, at least, relaxed, and the price of slaves had fallen to from two hundred and fifty to three hundred dollars, the greater economy of keeping up the breed by importation is too plain to be overlooked. Hence it is that the idea of a self-supporting system seems to be quite out of the Cuban's calculations, and that in the barracoons on his estates there are often to be found numerous bands of males and but a very few females, or oftimes none at all. It has been said, and it is generally credited by intelligent parties resident in Cuba, that the average duration of the life of a Cuban slave, after his arrival in the island, does not exceed seven or eight years. In short, that he is worked out in that time. His bodily frame cannot stand the excessive toil for a longer period; and, after that average period, his immortal spirit escapes from the tortured tenement of clay. Ye extenuators of slavery and of the slave-trade, ponder this ascertained fact. Is it not enough to make the flesh creep, and to unite all civilized mankind to put an end at least to the traffic in slaves? 'Nor is it only by treaties that Spain and Brazil are bound to cease their illegal traffic in human flesh. England has paid them large sums of money as the condition of their doing so; and these sums they have received and accepted, under the annexed and expressed condition. It has been unjustly said by some writers on the other side of the Atlantic—writers evidently in the pay of those who think it for their interest to prevent their country from sharing in the glory Great Britain has acquired and will acquire, by her efforts for suppressing and putting an end to the horrors of the slave-trade—that Great Britain has no right to interfere with Spain and Brazil as regards this trade in their own colonies; that slavery is a domestic institution, with which foreign nations have nothing whatever to do; and that, in debarring Spain and Brazil from the conduct of this traffic, the British lion is doing little more than acting the bully. Such writers forget the contract part of the matter. Were England seeking, by threat or force of arms, to promote the emancipation of slaves within any country or any colony, large or small, there might be some foundation for the argument. As it is, there is none. She is only demanding and requiring that Spain and Brazil should do what they have promised and engaged to do, what they have been paid for doing, but what they have hitherto failed to perform. Happy is it for England that, in enforcing these claims, she is fighting in the sacred cause of humanity.

"It is also said, and universally credited, that the present captain-general views the slave-trade with an indulgent eye. At all events, it is indisputable that the importation of slaves into the island, which fell off greatly under the influence of England and the activity of the English cruisers, during the latter years of the dynasty of the late governor, (Count O'Donnel,) has of late years, and since the Count of Alcoy assumed the reins of government, received a fresh impetus, and is now flourishing in fullest vigor. How far the governor is personally concerned in the production of this result, it were next to impossible to ascertain exactly; but assuredly his correspondence with the representative of Britain in the island, as to the landing of slaves, in the course of which the British consul-general offered to give his excellency ocular evidence of the truth of his informant's story—that slaves had been lately landed from a slaver, and were then in course of sale—does not indicate any desire either to suppress the traffic or to keep faith with Britain. Indeed, it is publicly affirmed that a regularly fixed fee (some fifty dollars a-head) is exacted by the governor on each slave that is brought in, besides sundry other fees to the captain of the port or harbor-master, and other officials, who have the power of prevention more or less in their hands. In short, the system is a complete one, and completely inoculated into the principles of Cuban government. No doubt a semblance of respect for the solemn treaties made with Britain, and for the entering into which Spain has been paid, is kept up in the island. The barbarian victims of the inhuman slave-trade are exposed to sale not as slaves, but as 'goods' or 'merchandise,' (*bultos*,) and some such farce is occasionally exhibited as this: A few of the imported slaves—such of them as are sick, disabled, infirm, or likely to die, and of course are of little or no value—are taken possession of by government authority, and an attempt is made to 'throw dust in the eyes of the English,' by making a noise about the matter, and formally delivering up the miserable wretches, thus 'seized,' as slaves imported into Cuba, in violation of the solemn treaties made by Spain with England—much being vaunted, at the time, of Spanish honor and national good faith. If any thing could make matters worse than the real disregard of the treaties, it would be conduct such as this—hypocrisy added to dishonesty, and the whole veiled in high-sounding words. And yet such pretended seizures and deliveries are often taking place. One had occurred only a few days before I reached Cuba, the number then seized being under twenty; while the known number of slaves actually introduced into the island, during that and the previous month, had not been less than four thousand, and while the average rate of present import is not under two thousand per month."

In 1840, Turnbull published his work on "Cuba and Porto Rico." He was a close observer of every thing connected with slavery and the slave-trade, and the greater part of his work is devoted to this subject. From this reliable source we gather some important facts: "As if to throw ridicule on the grave denials of all knowledge of the slave-trade which are forced from successive captains-general of Cuba by the unwearied denunciations of the British authorities, two extensive depots for the reception and sale of newly imported Africans have lately been erected at the further end of the Paseo, just under the windows of his excellency's residence; the one capable of holding 1000 and the other 1500 negroes. These were constantly full during the greater part of the time I remained in Havana. As the barracoon, or depot, serves the purpose of a slave-market as well as a prison, these two have been placed at the point of greatest attraction, where the Paseo ends, and where the grounds of the captain-general begin, and where the railroad passes into the interior. The passengers on the cars are horrified at the unearthly shouts of the thoughtless inmates, who, in their eagerness and astonishment at the passing train, push their arms and legs through the bars of the windows, with the cries, and grimace, and jesticulation, which might be expected from a horde of savages placed in circumstances so totally new and extraordinary. These barracoons are considered by the foreign residents as the lions of the place, and strangers are carried there as to a sight that cannot well be seen elsewhere. On entering you do not find so much misery as an unreflecting visitor might expect. It is the policy of the importer to restore as soon as possible among the survivors, the strength that has been wasted, and the health that has been lost during the horrors of the middle passage. It is his interest to keep up the spirits of his victims, that they may the sooner become marketable, and prevent their sinking under that fatal home-sickness which carries off so many during the first months of their captivity. With this view they are well fed and clothed. Even after leaving the barracoons, the overseer of the plantation finds it for the interest of his master to treat them with lenity for several months, scarcely allowing them to hear the crack of a whip, and breaking them in by slow degrees to the hours and weight of labor which are destined to break them down long before the period which nature prescribes.

"The well understood difficulty of breaking in men and women of mature age to the labors of the field, has produced a demand at the barracoons for younger victims. The range of years in the age of captives appeared to extend from twelve to eighteen, and the proportion of males to females was nearly three to one, as the demand for males was much greater. One motive for the continuation of the slave-trade is the well known fact, that a state of hopeless servitude has the effect of enervating the slave, and reducing the physical powers of his descendants far below the average of his African ancestors. A Bozal African commands a price twenty per cent higher than that of a

Créole, born in slavery on the island. As applied to negroes, the terms Creole and Bozal are nearly antithetical."

Bryan Edwards, the historian of the West Indies, in describing the characteristics of the various tribes of Western Africa, speaks of the natives of the Gold Coast as constituting the genuine and original unmixed negro, both in person and character. He says "the Koromantyn or Gold Coast negroes are distinguished for firmness both of body and mind ; a ferociousness of disposition ; but withal activity, courage, and a stubbornness, or what an ancient Roman would have deemed an elevation of soul, which prompts them to enterprizes of difficulty and· danger, and enables them to meet death in its most horrible forms with fortitude or indifference. They take to labor with great promptitude and alacrity, and have constitutions well adapted for it. It is not wonderful that such men should endeavor, even by means the most desperate, to regain the freedom of which they have been deprived." The historian describes a rebellion of these negroes which occurred in Jamaica in 1760. A band of about one hundred, newly imported, and led by one of their number who had been a chief in Guinea, having revolted and formed themselves into a body, about one o'clock in the morning proceeded to the fort at Port Maria, killed the sentinel, and provided themselves with arms and ammunition. Here they were joined by their countrymen from other plantations, and marched up the high road that led to the interior of the island, carrying death and desolation as they went. They massacred the whites and mulattoes as they went, and literally drank their blood mixed with rum.

Their chief was killed by one of the parties that went in pursuit of them ; and three of the ringleaders were taken. One was condemned to be burnt, and the other two to be hung up alive in irons, and left to perish. The one that was burnt was made to sit on the ground, and his body being chained to an iron stake, the fire was applied to his feet. He uttered not a groan, and saw his legs reduced to ashes with the utmost firmness and composure. After which, one of his arms by some means getting loose, he snatched a brand from the fire that was consuming him, and flung it in the face of the executioner. The two that were hung up alive were indulged at their own request with a hearty meal before they were suspended on the gibbet, which was erected on the Kingston parade. From that time until they expired they never uttered the least complaint, except only of cold in the night, but diverted themselves all day long in discourse with their countrymen, who were permitted to surround the gibbet. The historian says that he visited the gibbet on the seventh day, and while there, he heard them both laugh immoderately at some trifling occurrence. The next morning one of them silently expired, as did the other on the morning of the ninth day.*

The British minister at Rio informed Lord Palmerston in 1838, that 36,974 slaves had been imported into that single harbor during the year 1827, and that

---

*Bryan Edwards' History of the West Indies.

the number would have been greater but for the fact that several of the traders had discharged their vessels at other ports of the empire.

"The system pursued at Rio (says Turnbull), seems, in many respects, to correspond with what I have witnessed at Havana. The receptacles for the Bozal negroes, which serve the double purpose of warehousing and exposing them for sale, are open in both places to public inspection; although perhaps not so closely under the windows of the imperial palace at Rio, as they are under those of the captain-general's residence at Havana. Mr. Ouseley, the British minister, states that no less than 6,000 newly imported Africans have been exposed for sale at one time in the barracoons at Rio. The Brazilian authorities, like those of Cuba, have a direct pecuniary interest in promoting the traffic, by the existence of a sort of capitation tax on the imports, which is divided among the officers of the government.

Two insurance companies were in operation in Havana with a capital of $850,000, for the purpose of covering slave risks. They exacted premiums varying from 25 to 40 per cent., according to the sailing qualities of the ship, and the character of the master for sagacity and courage. The business was also carried on by private underwriters.

In 1837, seventy-eight slavers arrived at Havana under the Portuguese flag, each vessel averaging 300 slaves, making a total of 23,400. For each one of them the captain-general received the usual fee of a doubloon; the levy on the whole yielding $360,000, which sum was divided, as customary, into four equal parts: the captain-general, the captain of the coast guard, the harbor masters where the landing is effected, and the local chiefs of the customs, receiving equal shares. The parties who pay it never obtain any thing in the nature of a receipt, or other written acknowledgment for the money. It will be observed that the captain-general's interest is equal to a whole class of the minor functionaries.

Ninety-three vessels, under the flag of Portugal, are reported to have entered the harbor of Rio de Janeiro alone in 1837, and as many as eighty-four in 1838, from which, in two years, there were landed 78,300 slaves. These calculations do not include the number of slavers which resorted to other places in Cuba besides Havana, nor to other provinces in Brazil besides Rio de Janeiro; neither does it include the number which founder at sea, nor those which were captured and condemned at Sierra Leone. In that settlement there were at the time four courts of mixed commission—the British and Brazilian, the British and Netherlands, the British and Spanish, and the British and Portuguese. In 1838, the number of captured slavers which passed through those courts amounted to thirty. The Dutch and Brazilian commissioners enjoyed a sinecure; but although several of the thirty slavers were condemned in the Spanish court, as being liable under a new interpretation of the *lex mercatoria*, to be treated as Spaniards, and so to be subject to the conditions of the treaty, it is a remarkable fact that every one of them professed to be Portuguese, and was provided with Portuguese papers. Eighteen were condemned in the Portuguese court, because the fact of their being full of slaves at the moment of capture was irresistible; one escaped condemnation; the other eleven were deprived of the shelter of the Portuguese flag and condemned in the Spanish court. Not one of the whole number, however, was really Portuguese: four were Brazilian, and the remaining twenty-six undoubtedly Spanish. Of the eleven condemned in the Spanish court, only one had embarked any slaves previous to her capture; and it was in virtue of the "equipment clause" in the Clarendon treaty with Spain that they were subject to be condemned.

Joint stock companies were organized at Havana and Brazil, with heavy capitals, for the purpose of carrying on the slave-trade. Two of the above vessels belonged to one of these companies, the head-quarters of which were at Pernambuco. From papers found on board one of the vessels, it appeared that the company was composed of twenty members, and the capital invested, $80,000; and that they intended to establish a slave factory in the river Benin, and endeavor to secure a monopoly of the trade with the native princes.

The small number of slavers captured in proportion to the number engaged in the trade, may be accounted for from the fact that the cruisers were engaged in the hopeless task of blockading and watching 8000 miles of coast:—3000 miles of the African continent, embracing those portions only from whence slaves were obtained, and 5000 miles may be estimated for the shores of Brazil, Cuba, and Porto Rico.

From the papers and letters of instruction which occasionally fell into the hands of the captors, some curious facts are obtained. One treasurer of a company in Brazil writes to his agent on the coast, that among his stock in trade, to be sure at all times to have plenty of rum and tobacco, and to estimate all his goods at the highest possible prices; and that as all savages have respect for some kind of religion, the agent must be sure to keep up the exercise of some external forms, which would give a desirable "moral force" to the establishment! The natives were to be treated with the utmost civility, but not the slightest confidence was to be placed in them. Intoxication was to be carefully guarded against by the servants of the company, but the natives were to be encouraged in it. All sorts of contrivances were resorted to in order to cheat the poor negroes. English calico was cut up the middle in order to double its length, and each piece of stripe, or handkerchief, was cut across, making two pieces; the rum was adulterated, and the tobacco packed expressly for deception. From the intercepted correspondence we also gather some particulars in regard to the mortality of the trade. The Salomé had landed a cargo of 253 slaves near Matanzas, of whom seven had died soon after they were landed, and twenty-seven others were sick; seventy-four others had perished during the voyage, "so that we shall with difficulty," the owners pathetically observe to their agent in Africa, "get back the cost of our enterprise." The captain of another vessel writes back to the agent, "There were about 100 of those embarked at your port infected with the putrid fever; all our exertions could not stop the mortality, so that only one half have been saved of the number that ought to have been yielded by our abundant and well assorted barter, calculated to produce more than 400." Another merchant writes, "The business wears a most unfavorable aspect; although the vessel arrived safely, we shall scarcely get back our outlay, for out of the small number embarked, there died eighty-one during the voyage and shortly after landing. The others were sold at Matanzas, at an average of $306. The twenty who were sick brought us $2,304."

The captains of the slavers were generally instructed to fly on the slightest appearance of danger—"if you hesitate, you are lost." In one of the contracts for wages between the owners and crew of a captured slaver, it was stipulated, in order to compel the men to fight, that "wages shall not be due in the event of capture by a vessel of equal force, nor even in the event of capture by one of superior force, unless after an obstinate defense; and in that case the wages of those who will not fight shall be forfeited, and divided among the brave defenders."

The slavers were generally provided with three sets of papers, Spanish, Portuguese, and American, and the American flag was frequently made use of to shield the miscreants. The Venus, a ship of 460 tons, was built in Baltimore in 1838, expressly for a slaver. She arrived at Havana on the 4th of August in that year, and sailed shortly afterwards under American colors. She was owned by a Spaniard and a Frenchman, and was said to have cost them $100,000. She proceeded to the coast of Africa, and embarked the unprecedented number of 1,100 slaves, of whom the survivors, 860 in number, were landed on the coast. She had been absent but four months, and returned into port under Portuguese colors. It was asserted in Havana that $150,000 had been cleared by this single adventure. The arrival of the vessel occasioned a correspondence between the British commissioners and the American consul. The facts which brought about the correspondence were the notoriety with which a large vessel like the Venus, built at Baltimore, had arrived from the United States and sailed on a slaving voyage under the American flag, together with the belief that several American citizens had embarked in her from Havana, and had also returned in her. It was also reported that the Venus had been visited on the coast of Africa, still showing her American colors, by the officers of a British cruiser. It was even a subject of boast that although one of the British cruisers had seen the Venus receive part of her cargo, yet that such was her superiority in sailing that it was found impossible to come up with her on the attempt being made to give chase. While the Venus remained at Havana, she was visited by officers of the British navy. The Portuguese papers with which she returned were those of an old slaver, which had sailed under many a flag, and finally bore the Portuguese name of the Duquesa de Braganza, the name which the Venus assumed in order to have the benefit of her Portuguese papers, without the trouble or expense of going to purchase them.

Under these circumstances, the British commissioners who were sent to Havana for the express purpose of contributing, as far as lay in their power, to the suppression of the slave-trade, felt it their duty to communicate the facts to the consular representative of the American government, and offered some friendly suggestions, such as an appeal to the captain-general, or the introvention of an American sloop of war then lying in Havana. By bringing the culprits to punishment, the American people and government would have been exculpated from all countenance to the disgraceful abuse which had thus been made of the American flag. Mr. Trist, the consul, however, saw the matter in a different light. He had once before been appealed to on the occasion of a similar abuse of his country's flag. The only notice he took of the communication was to return it. On this second occasion he pursued a different course. An answer was returned, in which the former communication is spoken of as an "insult" and an "outrage;" and he informed them that he "could not recognize the right of any agent of any foreign government to interfere in any possible mode or degree in the discharge of his duties."

In afterwards remarking upon this communication, Lord Palmerston desired the commissioners to observe to Mr. Trist, "that the two governments having, by the tenth article of the treaty of Ghent, mutually engaged to each other that they would 'use their utmost endeavors to promote the entire abolition of the slave-trade,' it seems to be perfectly consistent with the respect which the agents of each country must feel for the other country, that they should not only themselves act in strict accordance with the spirit of the engagement which their own government has contracted, but that they should furnish to the agents of the other government any information which may be calculated to enable that other government more effectually to accomplish the common purpose." Mr. Trist also alluded, in his letter, to the manufacture of goods in Great Britain expressly designed for the African trade. Lord Palmerston directed the commissioners to state to that gentleman that "if he can at any time furnish her majesty's government, through them, with any information which may directly or indirectly enable the government to enforce the penalties of the law against British subjects who may be concerned in the slave-trade, her majesty's government will feel most sincerely obliged to him."

Not long after, a similar case occurred with regard to a French vessel, Le Havre, which having sailed from Havana under French colors, and with several French citizens on board, for the coast of Africa, had reëntered the port, after having landed 500 negroes on the shores of the island. The owner was a Frenchman, and his partners were Englishmen. A communication was addressed to the French consul, who applied immediately to the Prince de Joinville, who was then with his ship at Havana. The prince forthwith dispatched a French vessel to capture the slaver, which had put to sea. The cruise was unsuccessful, however, as the Havre was wrecked, as the most efficacious way of silencing further inquiries.

The object of the slavers in hoisting the American flag, is that it protects them from the right of search conceded by other nations to the cruisers engaged in supporting the trade. The laws of the Union declares the slave-trade piracy—the flag of the Union protects the miscreants engaged in it.

In order to obtain the protection of the American flag, a practice arose of sending Spanish vessels to Key West, and after a collusive sale had been effected, the vessels returned to Havana, to be dispatched to the coast of Africa under American colors. In this way, the Spanish schooner which went to Key West as the Espartero, came back as the Thomas, with American papers. A well known Spanish slaver went to New Orleans as the Conchita, and came back as the American schooner Encautadera.

American vessels were privately sold in Havana, the American registers were retained, and the vessels proceded to the coast of Africa under American colors. The buyer generally stipulated that the American captain, or some American citizen to represent him, should remain on board, and the fact of the transfer remain in abeyance until the vessel arrived in Africa. The American captain retained the command, to mislead the commanders of the British cruisers; but he gave it up as soon as the slaves were received on board, so as not to expose himself to the penalty of piracy in case of capture. The American flag and papers protected them from the right of search by the British cruisers—the Portuguese flag and papers shielded them from the penalties of piracy if captured. They were provided with double captains, double papers and double flags.

The American flag thus became involved in the slave traffic. In 1849, the British consul at Rio, in his public correspondence, says : "One of the most notorious slave-dealers in this capital, when speaking of the employment of American vessels in the slave-trade, said, a few days ago : 'I am worried by the Americans, who insist upon my hiring their vessels for slave-trade.' "

Of this there is also abundant and distressing evidence from our own diplomatic officers. Besides a lengthy correspondence from a preceeding mintster near the court of Brazil, the President of the United States transmitted a report from the Secretary of State, in December, 1850, to the Senate of the United States, with documents relating to the African slave-trade. A resolution had previously passed the Senate, calling upon the Executive for this information.

In these documents it is stated that "the number of American vessels which, since the 1st of July, 1844, until the 1st of October last (1849), sailed for the coast of Africa from this city, is ninety-three. . . . Of these vessels, all, except five, have been sold and delivered on the coast of Africa, and have been engaged in bringing over slaves, and many of them have been captured with slaves on board. . . . This pretended sale takes place at the moment when the slaves are ready to be shipped; the American captain and his crew going on shore, as the slaves are coming off, while the Portuguese or Italian *passengers*, who come out from Rio in her, all at once become master and crew of the vessel. Those of the American crew who do not die of coast-fever, get back as they can, many of them being compelled to come over in slave-vessels, in order to get back at all. There is evidence in the records of the consulate, of slaves having started two or three times from the shore, and the master and crew from their vessel in their boat, carrying with them the flag and ship's papers; when, the parties becoming frightened, both retroceded; the slaves were returned to the shore, and the American master and crew again went on board the vessel. The stars and stripes were again hoisted over her, and kept flying until the cause of the alarm (an English cruiser) departed from the coast, and the embarkation was safely effected."

On the other hand, we have the following notice from Brazil: "As in former years, the slave-dealers have derived the greatest assistance and protection for their criminal purposes, from the use of the American flag, I am happy to add that these lawless and unprincipled traders are at present deprived of this valuable protection, by a late determination of the American naval commander-in-chief on this station, who has caused three vessels, illegally using the flag of the United States, and which were destined for African voyages, to be seized on their leaving this harbor. This proceeding had caused considerable alarm and embarrassment to the slave-dealers; and, should it be continued, will be a severe blow to all slave-trading interests."

Mr. David Tod, the American Minister at the court of Brazil, in a letter to the Secretary of State, says: "As my predecessors had already done, I have, from time to time, called the attention of our government to the necessity of enacting a stringent law, having in vew the entire withdrawal of our vessels and citizens from this illegal commerce; and after so much has been already written upon this subject, it may be deemed a work of supererogation to discuss it further. The interests at stake, however, are of so high a character, the integrity of our flag and the cause of humanity being at once involved in their consideration, I cannot refrain from bringing the topic afresh to the notice of my government, in the hope that the President may esteem it of such importance as to be laid before Congress, and that even at this late day, legislative action may be secured."

In this communication, a quotation is made from Mr. Proffit, one of the preceding ministers, to the Secretary of State, February, 1844, in which he says: "I regret to say this, but it is a fact not to be disguised or denied, that the slave-trade is almost entirely carried on under our flag, in American-built vessels, sold to slave-traders here, chartered for the coast of Africa, and there sold, or sold here — delivered on the coast. And, indeed, the scandalous traffic could not be carried on to any great extent, were it not for the use made of our flag, and the facilities given for the chartering of American vessels, to carry to the coast of Africa the outfit for the trade, and the material for purchasing slaves."

Mr. Henry A. Wise, the American Minister, in his dispatch of February 15th, 1845, said to Mr. Calhoun:

"It is not to be denied, and I boldly assert it, that the administration of the imperial government of Brazil is forcibly constrained by its influences, and is deeply inculpated in its guilt. With that it would, at first sight, seem the United States have nothing to do; but an intimate and full knowledge of the subject informs us, that the only mode of carrying on that trade between Africa and Brazil, at present, involves our laws and our moral responsibilities, as directly and fully as it does those of this country itself. Our flag alone gives requisite protection against the right of visit, search, and seizure; and our citizens, in all the characters of owners, consignees, or agents, and of masters and crews of our vessels, are concerned in the business, and partake of the profits of the African slave-trade, to and from the ports of Brazil, as fully as the Brazilians themselves, and others in conjunction with whom they carry it on. In fact, without the aid of our citizens and our flag, it could not be carried on with success at all."

To exhibit additional proof of the state of the slave-trade prior to the equipment clause, we have the following instances from parliamentary papers, and other British authority:

"La Jeune Estelle, being chased by a British vessel, inclosed twelve negroes in casks, and threw them overboard."

"M. Oiseau, commander of *Le Louis*, a French vessel, in completing his cargo at Calabar, thrust the slaves into a narrow space *three feet high*, and closed the hatches. Next morning fifty were found dead. Oiseau coolly went ashore to purchase others to supply their place."

The following extract is from a report by Captain Hayes to the admiralty, of a representation made to him respecting one of these vessels in 1832:

"The master having a large cargo of these human beings chained together, with more humanity than his fellows, permitted some of them to come on deck, but still chained together, for the benefit of the air, when they immediately commenced jumping overboard, hand in hand, and drowning in couples; and (continued the person relating the circumstance) without any cause whatever. Now these people were just brought from a situation between decks, and to which they knew they must return, where the scalding perspiration was running from one to the other. . . . . And men dying by their side, with full in their view, living and dead bodies chained together; and the living, in addition to all their other torments, laboring under the most famishing thirst (being in very few instances allowed more than a pint of water a day); and let it not be forgotten that these unfortunate people had just been torn from their country, their families, their all! Men dragged from their wives, women from their husbands and children, girls from their mothers, and boys from their fathers; and yet in this man's eye (for heart and soul he could have none,) there was no cause whatever for jumping overboard and drowning. This, in truth, is a rough picture, but it is not highly colored. The men are chained in pairs, and as a proof they are intended so to remain to the end of the voyage, their fetters are not locked, but riveted by the blacksmith; and as deaths are frequently occurring, *living men are often for a length of time confined to dead bodies:* the living man cannot be released till the blacksmith has performed the operation of cutting the clinch of the rivet with his chisel; and I have now an officer on board the Dryad, who, on examining one of these slave-vessels, found *not only living men chained to dead bodies, but the latter in a putrid state.*"*

---

* Parliamentary papers presented 1832.

The following TREATIES AND CONVENTIONS for the suppression of the slave-trade were made by England during the period of thirty years, from 1814 to 1845. Some of these treaties have already been referred to.

In 1814 with the United States, the treaty of Ghent, in which the United States agree to do all in their power for the suppression of the slave-trade.

In 1814 with France, engaging that the slave-trade should be abolished by the French government in the course of five years.

In 1814 with the Netherlands, by treaty of London on the 14th of August.

In 1814 with Denmark, treaty of Kiel, stipulating for its abolition.

In 1815 with France, by additional article to Definitive Treaty of Peace.

In 1815 with Portugal, by treaty signed at Vienna.

In 1817 with Portugal, by convention signed at London, prohibiting universally the carrying on of the slave-trade by Portuguese vessels bound to any port not in the dominions of Portugal; also referring to arrangements to be adopted "as soon as the total abolition of the slave-trade, for the subjects of the crown of Portugal, shall have taken place."

In 1817 with Spain, by treaty of Madrid, engaging that the slave-trade shall be abolished throughout the entire dominions of Spain on the 30th of May, 1820; restricting the Spanish trade in the meantime to the south of the equator; and also confining it to the Spanish dominions.

In 1817 with Radama, king of Madagascar and its dependencies, by treaty signed at Tamatave.

In 1818 with the Netherlands, by treaty signed at the Hague, specifying restrictions under which the reciprocal right of search is to be exercised.

In 1820 with Madagascar, by additional articles.

In 1822 with Imaum, of Muscat, by treaty signed at Muscat.

In 1822 with the Netherlands, with explanatory and additional articles. Also with Spain, by explanatory articles.

In 1823 with the Netherlands, by additional article; with Portugal by additional article, and with Madagascar by additional article.

In 1824 with Sweden, by treaty of Stockholm, arranging reciprocal right of search.

In 1826 with Brazil, by treaty of Rio, renewing, on the separation of that empire from Portugal, the stipulations of subsisting treaties with the latter power.

In 1831 with France, by convention at Paris, stipulating mutual right of search within certain seas by a number of ships of war, to be fixed every year by mutual agreement. Also in 1833, further regulating the right of search and visitation.

In 1834 with Denmark, by treaty of Copenhagen, containing the accession of his Danish Majesty to the conventions between Great Britain and France of 1831 and 1833, regulating the mutual right of search.

In 1834 with Sardinia, by additional article respecting place of landing negroes found in vessels with Sardinian flag.

In 1835 with Spain, treaty of Madrid, abolishing slave-trade henceforward on part of Spain totally and finally, in all parts of the world; and regulating right of search reciprocally.

In 1835 with Sweden, by additional article.

In 1837 with Tuscany, containing accession of the Grand Duke to the French conventions of 1831 and 1833.

In 1837 with Hanse Towns, to the same effect.

In 1838 with kingdom of the Two Sicilies, to the same effect.

In 1839 with Republic of Venezuela, by treaty signed at Caracas, abolishing forever the African slave-trade; expressing the determination of Venezuela to enforce the provisions of a law passed in 1825, declaring Venezuelans found engaged in that trade to be pirates, and punishable with death; also regulating the mutual right of visitation and search.

In 1839 with Chili, by treaty signed at Santiago; with Uruguay, by treaty signed at Montevideo; with the Argentine Confederation, by treaty signed at Buenos Ayres; and with Hayti, by convention signed at Port-au-Prince.

In 1840 with Bolivia, by treaty signed at Sucre; and with Texas, by treaty signed at London.

In 1841 with Mexico, by treaty signed at Mexico; and with Austria, Russia and Prussia, by treaty signed at London, 16th November.

In 1842 with United States, by treaty signed at Washington, stipulating that each party shall maintain on the coast of Africa a naval force of not less than 80 guns, "to enforce, separately and respectively, the laws, rights, and obligations of each of the two countries for the suppression of the slave-trade; the said squadrons to be independent of each other, but to act in concert and co-operation, upon mutual consultation, as exigencies may arise."

In 1842 with Portugal, by treaty signed at Lisbon. Also, same year, with Argentine Republic and Hayti.

In 1845 with Brazil.

In 1845 with France, by a convention signed at London, by which each power is to keep up an equal naval force on the western coast of Africa, and the right of visitation is to be exercised only by cruisers of the nation whose flag is carried by the suspected vessel.

CHAPTER XVIII.

EFFORTS TO SUPPRESS THE SLAVE-TRADE.—OPERATIONS OF THE CRUISERS

Treaty between England and the United States, signed at Washington in 1842.—U. S. African Squadron under the treaty.—The Truxton captures an American slaver, the Spitfire, of New Orleans.—The Yorktown captures the Am. bark Pons, with 896 slaves on board.—Commander Bell's description of the sufferings of the slaves—they are landed at Monrovia and taken care of.—Squadron of 1846.—Capture of the Chancellor.—Slave establishment destroyed by the English and natives.—A slaver's history —embarkation and treatment of slaves.—How disposed of in Cuba.—Natural scenery of Africa.—Excursion to procure slaves—their horror at the prospect of slavery.— Passage from Mozambique—the small-pox on board.—More horrors of the Middle Passage.—The Estrella—revolt of negroes on board.

THE question of the abuse of the American flag was discussed by the British and American diplomatists in 1842. In the same year a treaty between the two governments was signed at Washington. The treaty stipulates that each nation shall maintain on the coast of Africa a force of naval vessels "of suitable numbers and description to carry in all not less than eighty guns, to enforce separately and respectively the laws, rights, and obligations of each of the two countries for the suppression of the slave-trade." This stipulation was limited to the term of five years from the date of the exchange of the ratifications of the treaty, "and afterwards, until one or the other party shall signify a wish to terminate it." The United States have continued to maintain a squadron on that coast for the protection of its commerce, and for the suppression of the slave-trade, so far as it may be carried on in American vessels, or by American citizens.

Great Britain conceded, during the discussion referred to, as the slave-trade by the United States had only been declared piracy in a municipal sense, that although a vessel was fully equipped for the trade, and even had slaves on board, if American, she was not amenable to British cruisers.

The question is still open, How is a vessel to be ascertained to be American? The United States do not claim that their flag shall give immunity to those who are not American; but any vessel which claims to be American, and hoists the American flag, may be boarded and examined by an American cruiser; but the right is not conceded to any other cruiser; and if such vessel be really an American, the boarding officer will be regarded in the light of a trespasser, and the vessel will have all the protection which that flag supplies. If the vessel proves to be not an American, the flag affords no protection. A foreign officer boarding a vessel under the American flag does it upon his own responsibility for all consequences.*

These principles not being clearly understood, led to some mistakes on the part of the British cruisers; and occasionally a genuine American slaver was captured and condemned by an English admiralty court, which had no legal jurisdiction over her. In commenting on these proceedings, Dr. Hall, of the Maryland colony at Cape Palmas, says: "No stronger incentive could be given to the commission of outrageous acts on the part of the British cruisers, than the course pursued by the United States government in declaring the slave-trade piracy, and then taking no effective steps to prevent its prosecution under their own flag" Again he says: "If our force is not increased, and we continue to disregard the prostitution of our flag, annoyances to our merchantmen will more frequently occur. We shall no longer receive the protection of British cruisers, which has ever been rendered to American vessels, and without which the whole coast would be lined with robbers and pirates."

In 1843 the United States African squadron was established under the treaty, and placed under the command of Commodore Perry. It consisted of the Macedonian frigate, the sloops of war Saratoga and Decatur, and the brig Porpoise. The squadron was actively employed in protecting legal commerce and checking the slave-trade carried on in American vessels. It was relieved in 1845 by the arrival of Commodore Skinner with the sloops of war Jamestown, Yorktown, and Preble, and the brig Truxton. An officer of the Truxton, under date of March 29, 1845, off Sierra Leone, says:

"Here we are in tow of her Britannic Majesty's steamer Ardent, with an American schooner, our prize, and a Spanish brigantine, prize to the steamer, captured in the Rio Pongas, one hundred miles to the northward. We had good information when we left Monrovia, that there was a vessel in the Pongas, waiting a cargo; and on our arrival off the river, finding an English man-of-

---

* A. H. Foote, Commander, U. S. Navy.

war steamer, arrangements were made to send a combined boat expedition to make captures for both vessels." The American boats were in charge of lieutenant Blunt.

"On coming in sight, our little schooner ran up American colors to protect herself from any suspicion, when our boats, after running alongside of her, produced the stripes and stars, much to the astonishment of those on board. She proved to be the Spitfire, of New Orleans, and ran a cargo of slaves from the same place last year. Of only about one hundred tons; but though of so small a size, she stowed three hundred and forty-six negroes, and landed near Matanzas, Cuba, three hundred and thirty-nine.

"Between her decks, where the slaves are packed, there is not room for a man to sit, unless inclining his head forward; their food, half a pint of rice per day, with one pint of water. No one can imagine the sufferings of slaves on their passage across, unless the conveyances in which they are taken are examined. Our friend had none on board, but his cargo of three hundred were ready in a barracoon, waiting a good opportunity to start. A good hearty negro costs but twenty dollars, or thereabouts, and is purchased for rum, powder, tobacco, cloth, &c. They bring from three to four hundred dollars in Cuba. The English are doing everything in their power to prevent the slave-trade; and keep *a force of thirty vessels on this coast, all actively cruising.* The British boats also brought down a prize; and the steamer is at this moment towing the Truxton, the Truxton's prize, and her own, at the rate of six miles an hour.

"It is extremely difficult to get up these rivers to the places where the slavers lie. The whole coast is intersected by innumerable rivers, with branches pouring into them from every quarter, and communicating with each other by narrow, circuitous and very numerous creeks, bordered on each side with impenetrable thickets of mangroves. In these creeks, almost concealed by the trees, the vessels lie, and often elude the strictest search. But when they have taken on board their living cargo, and are getting out to sea, the British are very apt to seize them, except, alas! when they are *protected by the banner of the United States.*"

On the 30th of November, the Yorktown, Commander Bell, captured the American bark "Pons," off Kabenda, on the south coast, with eight hundred and ninety-six slaves on board. This vessel had been at Kabenda about twenty days before, during which she had been closely watched by the British cruiser "Cygnet." The Cygnet, leaving one morning, the master of the Pons, James Berry, immediately gave up the ship to Gallano, the Portuguese master. During the day, so expeditious had they been, that water and provisions were received on board, and nine hundred and three slaves were embarked; and at eight o'clock the same evening, the Pons was under way. Instead of standing out to sea, she kept in with the coast during the night, and in the morning discovering the British cruiser, furled sails, and drifted so close to the shore that the negroes came down to the beach in hopes of her being wrecked. She thus

20

eluded detection. When clear of the Cygnet, she stood out to sea, and two days afterwards was captured by the Yorktown.

Commander Bell says: "The captain took us for an English man-of-war and hoisted the American colors; and no doubt had papers to correspond." These he threw overboard. "As soon as the slaves were recaptured, they gave a shout that could have been heard a mile."

During the night, eighteen of the slaves had died, and one jumped overboard. The master accounted for the number dying from the necessity of his sending below all the slaves on deck, and closing the hatches, when he fell in with the Yorktown, in order to escape detection. Ought not every such death be regarded as murder?

Commander Bell says: "The vessel has no slave-deck, and upwards of eight hundred and fifty were piled, almost in bulk, on water-casks below. As the ship appeared to be less than three hundred and fifty tons, it seemed impossible that one-half could have lived to cross the Atlantic. About two hundred filled up the spar-deck alone when they were permitted to come up from below; and yet the captain assured me that it was his intention to have taken *four hundred more* on board if he could have spared the time.

"The stench from below was so great that it was impossible to stand more than a few minutes near the hatchways. Our men who went below from curiosity, were forced up sick in a few minutes: then all the hatches were off. What must have been the sufferings of those poor wretches when the hatches were closed! I am informed that very often in these cases, the stronger will strangle the weaker; and this was probably the reason why so many died, or rather were found dead the morning after the capture. None but an eye-witness can form a conception of the horrors these poor creatures must endure in their transit across the ocean.

"I regret to say that most of this misery is produced by our own countrymen. They furnish the means of conveyance in spite of existing enactments; and although there are strong circumstances against Berry, the late master of the Pons, sufficient to induce me to detain him, if I should meet him, I fear *neither he nor his employers can be reached by our present laws.*"

In this letter to the Secretary of the Navy, Commander Bell adds: "For twenty days did Berry wait in the roadstead of Kabenda, protected by the flag of his country, yet closely watched by a foreign man-of-war, who was certain of his intention; but the instant that cruiser is compelled to withdraw for a few hours, he springs at the opportunity of enriching himself and owners, and disgracing the flag which had protected him."

The prize "Pons" was taken to Monrovia. There the slaves were landed, and gave the people a practical exhibition of the trade by which their ancestors had been torn from their homes. In the fourteen days intervening between the capture and arrival of the vessel at Monrovia, one hundred and fifty had died.

"The slaves," says the Monrovia Herald of December 28th, "were much emaciated, and so debilitated that many of them found difficulty in getting out of the boats. Such a spectacle of misery and wretchedness, inflicted by a lawless and ferocious cupidity, so excited our people, that it became unsafe for the captain of the slaver, who had come to look on, to remain on the beach. Eight slaves died in harbor before they were landed, and their bodies were thrown overboard."

The slaves, who were from eight to thirty years of age, came starved and thirsting from on board. Caution was required in giving them food. "When it was supposed that the danger of depletion was over, water was poured into a long canoe, into which they plunged like hungry pigs into a trough—the stronger faring the best."

Still, the kindness of human nature had not altogether been obliterated by length and intensity of suffering. Two boys, brothers, had found beside them a younger boy of the same tribe, who was ill. They contrived to nestle together on the deck, under such shelter as the cover of the long-boat offered them—a place where the pigs, if they are small enough, are generally stowed. There they made a bed of some oakum for their dying companion, and placed a piece of old canvas under his head. Night and day one was always awake to watch him. Hardship rendered their care fruitless: the night after the vessel anchored he died, and was thrown overboard.

The recaptured slaves were apprenticed out to the Liberians, and kindly treated and cared for. An American who visited Monrovia a few years after, found many of them admitted to the churches as members, and others attending the Sabbath schools. The squadron also captured several empty slavers and sent them to the United States.

In 1846 this squadron was relieved, and the sloop of war Marion, brigs Dolphin and Boxer, with the flag-ship United States, Commodore Read, were sent out.

The Dolphin was lying at Cape Mount, watching the American bark Chancellor, which was trading with the suspected Captain Canot, since extensively known throughout the United States by his "Life of an African Slaver." The British cruiser Favorite was stationed off the cape, and the officers stirred up the chiefs, who were bound by treaty to suppress the slave-trade, to attack and destroy the extensive trading establishment of Canot, who they said was making preparations for slaving. The premises were burnt, together with a large stock of goods he had shipped from New York. Captain Canot states in his book, that his brigantine, stores and dwellings, were fired by the officers and crew of the cruiser, and that he was then engaged in a legitimate business.

We leave the narrative of the operations of the cruisers for the present, in order to present some scenes in the life of a slave-trader. This Captain Canot had been engaged for twenty years in the traffic. After his downfall, as related, he embraced, with zeal, the first opportunity to mend his fortunes by honorable industry, and succeeded. His journals and papers were placed in the hands of Brantz Mayer, who wrote out the history of his life. Dr. Hall, the distinguished founder and first governor of the Maryland colony, pronounced him, setting aside his career as a slaver, a man of unquestionable integrity. The N. A. Review, upon sufficient grounds, pronounced the work truthful and reliable as to the events described. While the genius of Mayer has imparted a pleasant coloring to some of the incidents, it has also portrayed with fidelity the repelling horrors of a traffic, which, in the language of a gallant naval officer, "for revolting, heartless atrocity, might make the devil wonder, and hell recognize its own likeness."

A correct idea of the crew of a slaver may be formed from Canot's description of his first voyage : "Our crew consisted of twenty-one scamps, Spaniards, Portuguese, Frenchmen and mongrels, the refuse of the press-gang and jail-birds. The Areostatico cleared at Havana for the Cape de Verde isles, but in truth bound for the Rio Pongo. Accustomed as I had been to wholesome American seamanship and discipline, I trembled not a little when I discovered the amazing ignorance of the master and the utter worthlessness of the crew. Forty-one days, however, brought us to the end of our voyage at the mouth of the Rio Pongo. While we were slowly drifting between the river banks, and watching the gorgeous vegetation of Africa, which that evening first burst upon my sight, I fell into a chat with the native pilot, who had been in the United States, and spoke English remarkably well. Berak very soon inquired whether there was any one else on board who spoke the language besides myself, and when told that the cabin-boy alone knew it, he whispered a story which, in truth, I was not the least surprised to hear.

"That afternoon one of our crew had attempted the captain's life, while on shore, by snapping a carbine behind his back! Our pilot learned the fact from a native who followed the party from the landing along the beach, and its truth was confirmed, in his belief, by the significant boasts made by the *tallest* of the boatmen who accompanied him on board. He was satisfied that the entire gang contemplated our schooner's seizure.

"The pilot's story corroborated some hints I received from our cook during the voyage. It struck me instantly, that if a crime like this was really designed, no opportunity for its execution could be more propitious than the present. I determined, therefore, to omit no precaution that might save the vessel and the lives of her honest officers. On examining the carbines brought back from shore, which I had hurriedly thrown into the arm-chest on deck, I found that the lock of this armory had been forced, and several pistols and cutlasses abstracted.

"Preparations had undoubtedly been made to assassinate us. As night drew on, my judgment, as well as *nervousness*, convinced me that the darkness would not pass without a murderous attempt. There was an unusual silence. On reaching port, there is commonly fun and merriment among crews; but the usual song and invariable guitar were omitted from the evening's entertainment. I searched the deck carefully, yet but two mariners were found above the hatches, apparently asleep. Inasmuch as I was only a subordinate officer, I could not command, nor had I any confidence in the nerve or judgment of the chief mate, if I trusted my information to him. Still I deemed it a duty to tell him the story, as well as my discovery about the missing arms. Accordingly, I called the first officer, boatswain, and cook, as quietly as possible, into the cabin, leaving our English cabin-boy to watch in the companion way. Here I imparted our danger, and asked their assistance in *striking the first blow.* My plan was to secure the crew, and give them battle. The mate, as I expected, shrank like a girl, declining any step till the captain returned. The cook and boatswain, however, silently approved my movement; so that we counseled our cowardly comrade to remain below, while we assumed the responsibility and risk of the enterprise.

"It may have been rather rash, but I resolved to begin the rescue, by shooting down, like a dog, and without a word, the notorious Cuban convict who had attempted the captain's life. This, I thought, would strike panic into the mutineers, and end the mutiny in the most bloodless way. Drawing a pair of large horse-pistols from beneath the captain's pillow, and examining the load, I ordered the cook and boatswain to follow me to the deck. But the craven officer would not quit his hold on my person. He besought me not to commit murder. He clung to me with the panting fear and grasp of a woman. He begged me, with every term of endearment, to desist; and, in the midst of my scuffle to throw him off, one of the pistols accidentally exploded. A moment after, my vigilant watch-boy screamed from the starboard a warning 'look-out!' and peering forward in the blinding darkness as I emerged from the lighted cabin, I beheld the stalwart form of the ringleader, brandishing a cutlass within a stride of me. I aimed and fired. We both fell: the mutineer from two balls in his abdomen, and I from the recoil of an over-charged pistol.

"My face was cut and my eye injured by the concussion; but as neither combatant was deprived of consciousness, in a moment we were both on our feet. The Spanish felon, however, pressed his hand on his bowels, and rushed forward, exclaiming he was slain; but in his descent to the forecastle he was stabbed in the shoulder with a bayonet by the boatswain, whose vigorous blow drove the weapon with such trmendous force that it could hardly be drawn from the scoundrel's carcass.

"I said I was up in a moment; and feeling my face with my hand I perceived a quantity of blood on my cheek, around which I hastily tied a handkerchief, below my eyes. I then rushed to the arm-chest. At that moment, the crack of a pistol and a sharp, boyish cry, told me that my pet was wounded beside me. I laid him behind the hatchway and returned to the charge. By this time I was blind with rage, and fought, it seems, like a *madman.* I confess that I have no personal recollection whatever of the following events, and only learned them from the subsequent reports of the cook and the boatswain.

"I stood, they said, over the arm-chest like one spell-bound. My eyes were fixed on the forecastle; and, as head after head loomed up out of the darkness above the hatch, I discharged carbine after carbine at the mark. Every thing that moved fell by my aim. As I fired the weapons, I flung them away to grasp fresh ones; and, when the battle was over, the cook aroused me from my mad stupor, still groping wildly for arms in the emptied chest.

"As the smoke cleared off, the fore part of our schooner seemed utterly deserted; yet we found two men dead, one in mortal agony on the deck, while the ringleader and a colleague were gasping in the forecastle. Six pistols were fired against us from forward; but, strange to say, the only efficient ball was the one that struck my English boy's leg.

"When I came to my senses, my first quest was for the gallant boatswain, who, being unarmed on the forecastle when the unexpected discharge took place, and seeing no chance of escape from my murderous carbines, took refuge over the bows.

"Our cabin-boy was soon quieted. The mutineers needed but little care for their hopeless wounds, while the felon chief, like all such wretches, died in an agony of despicable fear, shrieking for pardon. My shriving of his sins was a speedy rite! Such was my *first* night in Africa!

"There are casual readers who may consider the scene described unnatural. It may be said that a youth, whose life had been checkered by trials and disasters, but who preserved a pure sensibility throughout them, is sadly distorted when portrayed as expanding, at a leap, into a desperado. I have but little to say in reply to these objections, save that *the occurrences are perfectly true as stated*, and, moreover, that I am satisfied that they were only the natural developments of my character.

"From my earliest years I have adored nobility of soul, and detested dishonor and treachery. I have passed through scenes which will be hereafter told, that the world may qualify by harsh names; yet I have striven to conduct myself throughout them, not only with the ideas of fairness current among reckless men, but with the truth that, under all circumstances, characterizes an honorable nature.

"Now the tragedy of my first night on the Rio Pongo was my transition from pupilage to responsible independence. I do not allege in a boastful spirit that I was a man of courage; because courage, or the want of it, are things for which a person is no more responsible than he is for the possession or lack of physical strength. I was, moreover, always a man of what I may style *self-possessed passion*. I was endowed with something more than cool energy; or, rather, cool energy was heightened and sublimated by the fire of an ardent nature. Hitherto I had been tempered down by the habitual obedience to which I was subjected as a sailor under lawful discipline. But the events of the last six months, and especially the gross relaxation on the voyage to Africa, the risks we had run in navigating the vessel, and the outlaws that surrounded me, not only kept my mind for ever on the alert, but aroused my dormant nature to a full sense of duty and self-protection.

"Is it unnatural, then, for a man whose heart and nerves have been laid bare for months, to quiver with agony and respond with headlong violence when imperiled character, property and life, hang upon the fiat of his courageous promptitude? The doubters may cavil over the philosophy, but I think I may remain content with the fact. *I did my duty*—dreadful as it was.

"Let me draw a veil over our gory decks when the gorgeous sun of Africa shot his first rays through the magnificent trees and herbage that hemmed the placid river. Five bodies were cast into the stream, and the traces of the tragedy obliterated as well as possible. The recreant mate, who plunged into the cabin at the report of the first pistol from the forecastle, reäppeared with haggard looks and trembling frame, to protest that *he* had no hand in what he called "the murder." The cook, boatswain, and African pilot recounted the whole transaction to the master, who inserted it in the log-book, and caused me to sign the narrative with unimplicated witnesses. Then the wound of the cabin-boy was examined and found to be trifling, while mine, though not painful, was thought to imperil my sight. The flint lock of a rebounding pistol had inflicted three gashes just beneath the eye on my cheek.

"There was but little appetite for breakfast that day. After the story was told and recorded, we went sadly to work unmooring the vessel, bringing her slowly like a hearse to an anchorage in front of Bangalang, the residence and factory of Mr. Ormond, better known by the country name of "Mongo John." This personage came on board early in the morning with our returned captain, and promised to send a native doctor to cure both my eye and the boy's leg, making me pledge him a visit as soon as the vessel's duties would permit.

"When the runners returned from the interior with the slavés required to complete the Areostatico's cargo, I considered it my duty to the Italian grocer of Regla to dispatch his vessel personally. Accordingly, I returned on board to aid in stowing *one hundred and eight boys and girls, the eldest of whom did not exceed fifteen years of age!* As I crawled between decks, I confess I could not imagine how this little army was to be packed or draw breath in a hold but *twenty-two inches high!* Yet the experiment was promptly made, inasmuch as it was necessary to secure them below in descending the river, in order to prevent their leaping overboard and swimming ashore. I found it impossible to adjust the whole of them in a sitting posture; but we made them lie down in each other's laps, like *sardines* in a can, and in this way obtained space for the entire cargo. Strange to tell, when the Areostatico reached Havana, but *three* of these "passengers" had paid the debt of nature."

Capt. Canot remained on the coast, first as secretary to Ormond, and finally established himself as a regular "trader." The first vessel consigned to him was the Fortuna, which he promptly dispatched with 220 human beings packed in her hold. The vessel arrived safe at Matanzas, yielding a "clear profit to the owners of $41,000." The Areostatico again returned and was dispatched with a "choice cargo of Mandingoes" for house servants in Havana. This vessel went to the bottom in a gale.

Of the embarkation and treatment of slaves he says: "As I am now fairly embarked in a trade which absorbed so many of my most vigorous years, I suppose the reader will not be loth to learn a little of my experience in the alleged "cruelties" of this commerce; and the first question, in all likelihood, that rises to his lips, is a solicitation to be apprised of the embarkation and treatment of slaves on the dreaded voyage.

"An African factor of fair repute is ever careful to select his human cargo with consummate prudence, so as not only to supply his employers with athletic laborers, but to avoid any taint of disease that may affect the slaves in their transit to Cuba or the American main. Two days before embarkation, the head of every male and female is neatly shaved; and, if the cargo belongs to several owners, each man's *brand* is impressed on the body of his respective negro. This operation is performed with pieces of silver wire or small irons fashioned into the merchant's initials, heated just hot enough to blister without burning the skin. When the entire cargo is the venture of but one proprietor, the branding is always dispensed with.

"On the appointed day, the *barracoon*, or slave-pen, is made joyous by the abundant "feed" which signalizes the negro's last hours in his native country. The feast over, they are taken alongside the vessel in canoes; and as they touch the deck, they are entirely stripped, so that the women as well as men go out of Africa as they came into it—*naked.* This precaution, it will be understood, is indispensable; for perfect nudity, during the whole voyage, is the only means of securing cleanliness and health. In this state, they are immediately ordered below, the men to the hold and the women to the cabin, while boys and girls are, day and night, kept on deck, where their sole protection from the elements is a sail in fair weather, and a *tarpaulin* in foul.

"It is the duty of a guard to report immediately whenever a slave refuses to eat, in order that his abstinence may be traced to stubbornness or disease. Negroes have sometimes been found in slavers who attempted voluntary starvation; so that, when the watch reports the patient to be "shamming," his appetite is stimulated by the medical antidote of a 'cat.'

"At sundown the process of stowing the slaves for the night is begun. The second mate and boatswain descend into the hold, whip in hand, and range the slaves in their regular places; those on the right side of the vessel facing forward, and lying in each other's lap, while those on the left are similarly stowed with their faces towards the stern. In this way each negro lies on his right side, which is considered preferable for the action of the heart. In allotting places, particular attention is paid to size, the taller being selected for the greatest breadth of the vessel, while the shorter and younger are lodged near the bows. When the cargo is large and the lower deck crammed, the supernumeraries are disposed of on deck, which is securely covered with boards to shield them from moisture. The *strict* discipline of nightly stowage is, of course, of the greatest importance in slavers, else every negro would accommodate himself as if he were a passenger.

"In order to insure perfect silence and regularity during night, a slave is chosen as constable from every ten, and furnished with a 'cat' to enforce commands during his appointed watch. In remuneration for his services, which, it may be believed, are admirably performed whenever the whip is required, he is adorned with an old shirt or tarry trowsers. Now and then billets of wood are distributed among the sleepers, but this luxury is never granted until the good temper of the negro is ascertained, for slaves have often been tempted to mutiny by the power of arming themselves with these pillows from the forest.

"But *ventilation* is carefully attended to. The hatches and bulkheads of every slaver are grated, and apertures are cut about the deck for ampler circulation of air. Wind-sails, too, are constantly pouring a steady draft into the hold, except during a chase, when, of course, every comfort is temporarily sacrificed for safety. During calms or in light baffling winds, when the suffocating air of the tropics makes ventilation impossible, the gratings are always removed, and portions of the slaves allowed to repose at night on deck, while the crew is armed to watch the sleepers.

"Handcuffs are rarely used on shipboard. It is the common custom to secure slaves in the *barracoons* and while shipping, by chaining *ten* in a gang; but as these platoons would be extremely inconvenient at sea, the manacles are immediately taken off and replaced by leg-irons, which fasten them in pairs by the feet. Shackles are never used but for *full-grown men*, while *women* and *boys* are set at liberty as soon as they embark. It frequently happens that when the behavior of *male* slaves warrants their freedom, they are released from all fastenings long before they arrive. Irons are altogether dispensed with on many *Brazilian* slavers, as negroes from Anjuda, Benin and Angola, are mild, and unaddicted to revolt like those who dwell east of the Cape or north of the Gold Coast. Indeed, a knowing trader will never use chains but when compelled, for the longer a slave is ironed the more he deteriorates; and, as his sole object is to land a healthy cargo, pecuniary interest as well as natural feeling, urges the sparing of metal.

"In old times, before treaties made slave-trade piracy, the landing of human cargoes was as comfortably conducted as the disembarkation of flour. But now, the enterprise is effected with secrecy and hazard. A wild, uninhabited portion of the coast, where some little bay or sheltering nook exists, is commonly selected by the captain and his confederates. As soon as the vessel is driven close to the beach and anchored, her boats are packed with slaves, while the craft is quickly dismantled to avoid detection from sea or land. The busy skiffs are hurried to and fro incessantly till the cargo is entirely ashore, when the secured gang, led by the captain, and escorted by armed sailors, is rapidly marched to the nearest plantation. There it is safe from the rapacity of local magistrates, who, if they have a chance, imitate their superiors by exacting "*gratifications.*"

"In the meantime, a *courier* has been dispatched to the owners in Havana, Matanzas, or Santiago de Cuba, who immediately post to the plantation with clothes for the slaves and gold for the crew. Preparations are quickly made through brokers for the sale of the blacks; while the vessel, if small, is disguised, to warrant her return under the coasting flag to a port of clearance. If the craft happens to be large, it is considered perilous to attempt a return with a cargo, or "*in distress*," and, accordingly, she is either sunk or burnt where she lies.

"Many of the Spanish governors in Cuba have respected treaties, or, at least, promised to enforce the laws. Squadrons of dragoons and troops of lancers have been paraded with convenient delay, and ordered to gallop to plantations designated by the representative of England. It generally happens, however, that when the hunters arrive the game is gone. Scandal declares that, while brokers are selling the blacks at the depot, it is not unusual for their owner or his agent to be found knocking at the door of the captain-general's secretary. It is even said that the captain-general himself is sometimes present in the sanctuary, and, after a familiar chat about the happy landing of 'the contraband,' as the traffic is amiably called, the requisite *rouleaux* are insinuated into the official desk under the intense smoke of a fragrant *cigarillo*. The metal is always considered the property of the captain-general, but his scribe avails himself of a lingering farewell at the door, to hint an immediate and pressing need for 'a very small darkey!' Next day, the diminutive African does not appear; but, as it is believed that Spanish officials prefer gold even to mortal flesh, his algebraic equivalent is unquestionably furnished in the shape of shining ounces!"

The following extract will be read with satisfaction, exhibiting as it does one of the native tribes in a very favorable aspect: "During the rainy season, which begins in June and lasts till October, the stores of provisions in establishments along the Atlantic coast become sadly impaired. The Foulah and Mandingo tribes of the interior are prevented by the swollen condition of intervening streams from visiting the beach with their produce. In these straits, the factories have recourse by canoes to the small rivers, which are neither entered by sea-going vessels, nor blockaded for the caravans of interior chiefs.

"Among the tribes or clans visited by me in such seasons, I do not remember any whose intercourse afforded more pleasure, or exhibited nobler traits, than the BAGERS, who dwell on the solitary margins of those shallow rivulets, and subsist by boiling salt in the dry season and making palm oil in the wet. I have never read an account of these worthy blacks, whose civility, kindness, and honesty will compare favorably with those of more civilized people.

"The Bagers live very much apart from the great African tribes, and keep up their race by intermarriage. The language is peculiar, and altogether devoid of that Italian softness that makes the Soosoo so musical.

"Having a week or two of perfect leisure, I determined to set out in a canoe to visit one of these establishments, especially as no intelligence had reached me for some time from one of my country traders who had been dispatched thither with an invoice of goods to purchase palm oil. My canoe was comfortably fitted with a water-proof awning, and provisioned for a week.

"A tedious pull along the coast and through the dangerous surf, brought us to the narrow creek through whose marshy mesh of *mangroves* we squeezed our canoe to the bank. Even after landing, we waded a considerable distance through marsh before we reached the solid land. The Bager town stood some hundred yards from the landing, at the end of a desolate savanna, whose lonely waste spread as far as the eye could reach. The village itself seemed quite deserted, so that I had difficulty in finding 'the oldest inhabitant,' who invariably stays at home and acts the part of chieftain. This venerable personage welcomed me with great cordiality; and having made my *dantica*, or, in other words, declared the purpose of my visit, I desired to be shown the trader's house. The patriarch led me at once to a hut, whose miserable thatch was supported by four posts. Here I recognized a large chest, a rum cask, and the grass hammock of my agent. I was rather exasperated to find my property thus neglected and exposed, and began venting my wrath in no seemly terms on the delinquent clerk, when my conductor laid his hand gently on my sleeve, and said there was no need to blame him. 'This,' continued he, 'is his house; here your property is sheltered from sun and rain; and, among the Bagers, whenever your goods are protected from the elements, they are safe from every danger. Your man has gone across the plain to a neighboring town for oil; to-night he will be back; in the meantime, look at your goods.'

"I opened the chest, which, to my surprise, was unlocked, and found it nearly full of the merchandise I had placed in it. I shook the cask, and its weight seemed hardly diminished. I turned the spiggot, and lo! the rum trickled on my feet. Hard-by was a temporary shed, filled to the roof with hides and casks of palm oil, all of which, the gray-beard declared, was my property.

"Whilst making this inspection, I have no doubt the expression of my face indicated a good deal of wonder, for I saw the old man smile complacently as he followed me with his quiet eye. 'Good!' said the chief, 'it is all there, is it not? We Bagers are neither Soosoos, Mandingoes, Foulahs, nor *Whitemen*, that the goods of a stranger are not safe in our towns! We work for a living; we want little; big ships never come to us, and we neither steal from our guests nor go to war to sell one another!'

"The conversation, I thought, was becoming a little personal; and, with a gesture of impatience, I put a stop to it. On second thoughts, however, I turned abruptly round, and shaking the noble savage's hand with a vigor that made him wince, presented him with a piece of cloth. Had Diogenes visited Africa in search of his man, it is by no means unlikely that he might have extinguished his lamp among the Bagers!

"It was about two o'clock in the afternoon when I arrived in the town, which, as I before observed, seemed quite deserted, except by a dozen or two ebony antiquities, who crawled into the sunshine when they learned the advent of a stranger. The young people were absent gathering palm nuts in a neighboring grove. A couple of hours before sundown, my trader returned; and, shortly after, the merry gang of villagers made their appearance, laughing, singing, dancing, and laden with fruit As soon as the gossips announced the arrival of a white man during their absence, the little hut that had been hospitably assigned me was surrounded by a crowd, five or six deep, of men, women, and children. The pressure was so close and sudden that I was almost stifled. Finding they would not depart until I made myself visible, I emerged from concealment and shook hands with nearly all. The women, in particular, insisted on gratifying themselves with a *sumboo* or smell at my face—which is the native's kiss—and folded their long black arms in an embrace of my neck, threatening peril to my shirt with their oiled and dusty flesh. However, I noticed so much *bonhommie* among the happy crew that my heart would not allow me to repulse them; so I kissed the youngest and shunned the crones. In token of my good will, I led a dozen or more of the prettiest to the rum-barrel, and made them happy for the night.

"When the town's-folks had comfortably nestled themselves in their hovels, the old chief, with a show of some formality, presented me a heavy ram-goat, distinguished for its formidable head ornaments, which, he said, was offered as a *bonne-bouche* for my supper. He then sent a crier through the town, informing the women that a white stranger would be their guest during the night; and, in less than half an hour, my hut was visited by most of the village dames and damsels. One brought a pint of rice; another some roots of *cassava;* another, a few spoonsful of palm oil; another a bunch of peppers; while the oldest lady of the party made herself particularly remarkable by the gift of a splendid fowl. In fact, the crier had hardly gone his rounds before my mat was filled with the voluntary contributions of the villagers; and the wants, not only of myself but of my eight rowers, completely supplied.

"There was nothing peculiar in this exhibition of hospitality, on account of my nationality. It was the mere fulfillment of a Bager law; and the poorest *black stranger* would have shared the rite as well as myself. I could not help thinking that I might have traveled from one end of England or America to the other without meeting a Bager *welcome.*

"These Bagers are remarkable for their honesty, as I was convinced by several anecdotes related, during my stay in this village, by my trading clerk. He took me to a neighboring lemon-tree, and exhibited an English brass steelyard hanging on its branches, which had been left there by a mulatto merchant from Sierra Leone, who died in the town on a trading trip. This article, with a chest half full of goods, deposited in the 'palaver house,' had been kept securely more than twelve years in expectation that some of his friends would send for them from the colony. The Bagers, I am told, have no *jujus, feitiches,* or *gregrees;* they worship no god or evil spirit; their dead are buried without tears or ceremony; and their hereafter is eternal oblivion.

"The males of this tribe are of middling size and deep black color; broad shouldered, but neither brave nor warlike. They keep aloof from other tribes, and by a Fullah law, are protected from foreign violence in consequence of their occupation as salt-makers, which is regarded by the interior natives as one of the most useful trades. Their fondness for palm oil and the little work they are compelled to perform, make them generally indolent. Their dress is a single handkerchief, or a strip of country cloth four or five inches wide, most carefully put on.

"The young women have none of the sylph-like appearance of the Mandingoes or Soosoos. They work hard and use palm oil plentifully, both internally and externally, so that their relaxed flesh is bloated like blubber. Both sexes shave their heads, and adorn their noses and lower lips with rings, while they penetrate their ears with porcupine quills or sticks. *They neither sell nor buy each other*, though they acquire children of both sexes from other tribes, and adopt them into their own, or dispose of them if not suitable. Their avails of work are commonly divided ; so the Bagers may be said to resemble the Mormons in polygamy, the Fourierites in community, but to exceed both in honesty."

As a contrast to our gloomy picture of the wrongs of Africa, we present a glimpse of its gorgeous natural scenery. It will be a relief to turn away for a moment from the contemplation of violence and crime, of wretchedness and despair—the foul exhalations of the reeking slave-deck, the charnel house of corruption, disease, and death.

"As the traveler along the coast turns the prow of his canoe through the surf, and crosses the angry bar that guards the mouth of an African river, he suddenly finds himself moving calmly onward between sedgy shores, buried in mangroves. Presently the scene expands in the unruffled mirror of a deep majestic stream. Its lofty banks are covered by innumerable varieties of the tallest forest trees, from whose summits a trailing net-work of vines and flowers floats down and sweeps the passing current. A stranger who beholds this scenery for the first time is struck by the immense size, the prolific abundance, and gorgeous verdure of every thing. Leaves large enough for garments lie piled and motionless in the lazy air. The bamboo and cane shake their slender spears and pennant leaves as the stream ripples among their roots. Beneath the massive trunks of forest trees the country opens; and, in vistas through the wood, the traveler sees innumerable fields lying fallow in grass, or waving with harvests of rice and *cassava*, broken by golden clusters of Indian corn. Anon, groups of oranges, lemons, coffee-trees, plantains, and bananas are crossed by the tall stems of cocoas, and arched by the broad and drooping coronals of royal palm. Beyond this, capping the summit of a hill, may be seen the conical huts of natives, bordered by fresh pastures dotted with flocks of sheep and goats, or covered with numbers of the sleekest cattle. As you leave the coast, and shoot round the river-curves of this fragrant wilderness, teeming with flowers, vocal with birds, and gay with their radiant plumage, you plunge into the interior, where the rising country slowly expands into hills and mountains.

"The forest is varied. Sometimes it is a matted pile of tree, vine and bramble, obscuring every thing, and impervious save with knife and hatchet. At others it is as a Gothic temple. The sward spreads openly for miles on every side, while, from its even surface, the trunks of straight and massive trees rise to a prodigious height, clear from every obstruction, till their gigantic limbs, like the capitals of columns, mingle their foliage in a roof of perpetual verdure.

"At length the hills are reached, and the lowland heat is tempered by mountain freshness. The scene that may be beheld from almost any elevation is always beautiful, and sometimes grand. Forest, of course, prevails ; yet with a glass, and often by the unaided eye, gentle hills, swelling from the wooded landscape, may be seen covered with native huts, whose neighborhood is checkered with patches of sward and cultivation, and inclosed by massive belts of primeval wildness. Such is commonly the westward view; but north and east, as far as vision extends, noble outlines of hill and mountain may be traced against the sky, lapping each other with their mighty folds, until they fade away in the azure horizon.

"When a view like this is beheld at morning, in the neighborhood of rivers, a dense mist will be observed lying beneath the spectator in a solid stratum, refracting the light now breaking from the east. Here and there, in this lake of vapor, the tops of hills peer up like green islands in a golden sea. But ere you have time to let fancy run riot, the 'cloud compelling' orb lifts its disc over the mountains, and the fogs of the valley, like ghosts at cock-crow, flit from the dells they have haunted since night-fall. Presently the sun is out in his terrible splendor. Africa unveils to her master, and the blue sky and green forest blaze and quiver with his beams."

The account of an excursion made into the interior of the country for the purpose of procuring slaves and opening trade with the native chiefs, exhibits the horror of the people at the prospect of being sold into slavery.

"Timbo lies on a rolling plain. North of it a lofty mountain range rises at the distance of ten or fifteen miles, and sweeps eastwardly to the horizon. The landscape, which declines from these slopes to the south, is in many places bare; yet fields of plentiful cultivation, groves of cotton-wood, tamarind, and oak, thickets of shrubbery and frequent villages stud its surface and impart an air of rural comfort to the picturesque scene.

"I soon proposed a gallop with my African kindred over the neighborhood; and one fine morning, after a plentiful breakfast of stewed fowls, boiled to rags with rice, and seasoned with delicious 'palavra sauce,' we cantered off to the distant villages. As we approached the first brook, but before the fringe of screening bushes was passed, our cavalcade drew rein abruptly, while Amah-de-Bellah cried out, 'Strangers are coming!' A few moments after, as we slowly crossed the stream, I noticed several women crouched in the underwood, having fled from the bath. This warning is universally given, and enforced by law to guard the modesty of the gentler sex.

"In half an hour we reached the first suburban village; but fame had preceded us with my character, and as the settlement was cultivated either by serfs or negroes liable to be made so, we found the houses bare. The poor wretches had learned, on the day of my reception, that the principal object of my journey was to obtain slaves, and, of course, they imagined that the only object of my foray in their neighborhood was to seize the gang and bear it abroad in bondage. Accordingly, we only tarried a few minutes in Findo, and dashed off to Furo; but here, too, the blacks had been panic-struck, and escaped so hurriedly that they left their pots of rice, vegetables, and meat boiling in their sheds. Furo was absolutely stripped of inhabitants; the veteran chief of the village did not even remain to do the honors of his affrighted brethren. Amah-de-Bellah laughed heartily at the terror I inspired; but I confess I could not help feeling sadly mortified when I found my presence shunned as a pestilence.

"The native villages through which I passed on this excursion manifested the great comfort in which these Africans live throughout their prolific land, when unassailed by the desolating wars that are kept up for the slave-trade. It was the height of the dry season, when every thing was parched by the sun, yet I could trace the outlines of fine plantations, gardens, and rice-fields. Every where I found abundance of peppers, onions, garlic, tomatoes, sweet potatoes, and cassava, while tasteful fences were garlanded with immense vines and flowers. Fowls, goats, sheep, and oxen stalked about in innumerable flocks, and from every domicil depended a paper, inscribed with a charm from the Koran to keep off thieves and witches.

"My walks through Timbo were promoted by the constant efforts of my entertainers to shield me from intrusive curiosity. Whenever I sallied forth, two townsfolk in authority were sent forward to warn the public that the Fur-too desired to promenade without a mob at his heels. These lusty criers stationed themselves at the corners with an iron triangle, which they rattled to call attention to the king's command; and in a short time the highways were so clear of people, who feared a *bastinado*, that I found my loneliness rather disagreeable than otherwise. *Every person I saw, shunned me.* When I called the children or little girls, they fled from me. My reputation as a slaver in the villages, and the fear of a lash in the town, furnished me much more solitude than is generally agreeable to a sensitive traveler.

"Towards night-fall I left my companions, and wrapping myself closely in a Mandingo dress, stole away through by-ways to a brook which runs by the town walls. Thither the females resort at sunset to draw water; and choosing a screened situation where I would not be easily observed, I watched, for more than an hour the graceful children, girls, and women of Timbo as they performed this domestic task of eastern lands.

"I was particularly impressed by the general beauty of the sex, who, in many respects, resembled the Moor rather than the negro. Unaware of a stranger's presence, they came forth as usual in a simple dress which covers their body from waist to knee, and leaves the rest of the figure entirely naked. Group after group gathered together on the brink of the brook in the slanting sunlight and lengthening shadows of the plain. Some rested on their pitchers and water vessels; some chatted, or leaned on each other gracefully, listening to the chat of friends; some stooped to fill their jars; others lifted the brimming vessels to their sisters' shoulders, while others strode homeward singing, with their charged utensils poised on head or hand. Their slow, stately, swinging movement under the burden was grace that might be envied on a Spanish *paseo*. I do not think the forms of these Fullah girls, with their complexions of freshest bronze, are exceeded in symmetry by the women of any other country. There was a slender delicacy of limb, waist, neck, hand, foot, and bosom, which seemed to be the type that moulded every one of them. I saw none of the hanging breast; the flat, expanded nostrils; the swollen lips, and fillet-like foreheads that characterize the Soosoos and their sisters of the coast. None were deformed, nor were any marked by traces of disease. I may observe, moreover, that the male Fullahs of Timbo are impressed on my memory by a beauty of form which almost equals that of the women ; and, in fact, the only fault I found with them was their minute resemblance to the feminine delicacy of the other sex. They made up, however, in courage what they lacked in form, for their manly spirit has made them renowned among all the tribes they have so long controlled by distinguished bravery and perseverance.

"The patriarchal landscape by the brook, with the Oriental girls over their water-jars, and the lowing cattle in the pastures, brought freshly to my mind many a Bible scene I heard my mother read when I was a boy at home.

"My trip to Timbo, I confess, was one of business rather than pleasure or scientific exploration. I did not make a record, at the moment, of my 'impressions de voyage,' and never thought that, a quarter of a century afterwards, I would feel disposed to chronicle the journey in a book, as an interesting *souvenir* of my early life. Had I supposed that the day would come when I was to turn author, it is likely I might have been more inquisitive ; but being only 'a slaver,' I found Ahma, Sulimani, Abdulmomen, the Ali-Mami, and all the quality and amusements of Timbo, dull enough, *when my object was achieved.* Still, while I was there, I thought I might as well see all that was visible. I strolled repeatedly through the town. I became excessively familiar with its narrow streets, low houses, mud walls, cul-de-sacs, and mosques. I saw no fine bazaars, market-places, or shops. The chief wants of life were supplied by peddlers. Platters, jars, and baskets of fruit, vegetables, and meat, were borne around twice or thrice daily. Horsemen dashed about on beautiful steeds toward the fields in the morning, or came home at night-fall at a slower pace. *I never saw man or woman bask lazily in the sun.* Females were constantly busy over their cotton and spinning wheels when not engaged in household occupations ; and often I have seen an elderly dame quietly crouched in her hovel at sunset reading the Koran. Nor are the men of Timbo less thrifty. Their city wall is said to hem in about ten thousand individuals, representing all the social industries. They weave cotton, work in leather, fabricate iron from the bar, engage diligently in agriculture, and, whenever not laboriously employed, devote themselves to reading and writing, of which they are excessively fond.

"These are faint sketches, which, on ransacking my brain, I find resting on its tablets. But I was tired of Timbo ; I was perfectly refreshed from my journey ; and I was anxious to return to my factory on the beach. Two 'moons' only had been originally set apart for the enterprise, and the third was already waxing toward its full. I feared the Ali-Mami was not yet prepared with *slaves* for my departure, and I dreaded lest objections might be made if I approached his royal highness with the flat announcement. Accordingly, I schooled my interpreters, and visited that important personage. I made a long speech, as full of compliments and blarney as a Christmas pudding is of plums, and concluded by touching the soft part in African royalty's heart—*slaves!* I told the king that a vessel or two, with abundant freights, would be waiting me on the river, and that I must hasten thither with his choicest gangs if he hoped to reap a profit.

"The king and the royal family were no doubt excessively grieved to part with the Furtoo Mongo, but they were discreet persons and 'listened to reason.' War parties and scouts were forthwith dispatched to blockade the paths, while press-gangs made recruits among the villages, and even in Timbo. Sulimani-Ali himself sallied forth, before day-break, with a troop of horse, and at sundown came back with forty-five splendid fellows, captured in Findo and Furo!

"The personal dread of me in the town itself was augmented. If I had been a Pestilence before, I was Death now! When I took my usual morning walk the children ran from me screaming. Since the arrival of Sulimani with his victims, all who were under the yoke thought their hour of exile had come. The poor regarded me as the devil incarnate. Once or twice, I caught women throwing a handful of dust or ashes towards me, and uttering an invocation from the Koran to avert the demon or save them from his clutches. Their curiosity was merged in terror. *My popularity was over!*"

The captain takes command of the schooner La Esperanza, whose chief officer had died of the fever, resolved to make a visit to his friends in Cuba, for a little relaxation from the monotony of a slave-trader's life in Africa. The slave cargo was duly stowed, and the schooner put to sea, but the British bull-dogs soon scented the foul slaver on the tainted breeze and were on his track.

"When the land breeze died away, it fell entirely calm, and the sea continued an unruffled mirror for three days, during which the highlands remained in sight, like a faint cloud in the east. The glaring sky and the reflecting ocean acted and reacted on each other until the air glowed like a furnace. During night a dense fog enveloped the vessel with its clammy folds. When the vapor lifted on the fourth morning, our look-out announced a sail from the mast-head, and every eye was quickly sweeping the landward horizon in search of the stranger. Our spies along the beach had reported the coast clear of cruisers when I sailed, so that I hardly anticipated danger from men-of-war; nevertheless, we held it discreet to avoid intercourse, and, accordingly, our doubled-manned sweeps were rigged out to impel us slowly toward the open ocean. Presently, the mate went aloft with his glass, and, after a deliberate gaze, exclaimed: 'It is only the Dane,—I see his flag.' At this my crew swore they would sooner fight than sweep in such a latitude; and, with three cheers, came aft to request that I would remain quietly where I was until the Northman overhauled us.

"We made so little headway with oars that I thought the difference trifling, whether we pulled or were becalmed. Perhaps it might be better to keep the hands fresh, if a conflict proved inevitable. I passed quickly among the men, with separate inquiries as to their readiness for battle, and found all—from the boy to the mate—anxious, at every hazard, to do their duty. Our break-

21

fast was as cold as could be served in such a climate, but I made it palatable with a case of claret.

When a sail on the coast of Africa heaves in sight of *a slaver*, it is always best for the imperiled craft, especially if gifted with swift hull and spreading wings, to take flight without the courtesies that are usual in mercantile sea-life. At the present day, fighting is, of course, out of the question, and the valuable prize is abandoned by its valueless owners. At all times, however,—and as a guard against every risk, whether the cue be to fight or fly,—the prudent sla-ver, as soon as he finds himself in the neighborhood of unwholesome canvas, puts out his fire, nails his forecastle, sends his negroes below, and secures the gratings over his hatches.

"All these preparations were quietly made on board the Esperanza; and, in addition, I ordered a supply of small arms and ammunition on deck, where they were instantly covered with blankets. Every man was next stationed at his post, or where he might be most serviceable. The cannons were spunged and loaded with care; and, as I desired to deceive our new acquaintance, I ran up the Portuguese flag. The calm still continued as the day advanced; indeed, I could not perceive a breath of air by our dog-vane, which veered from side to side as the schooner rolled slowly on the lazy swell. The stran-ger did not approach, nor did we advance. There we hung—

'A painted ship upon a painted ocean!'

I cannot describe the fretful anxiety which vexes a mind under such circum-stances. Slaves below; a blazing sun above; the boiling sea beneath; a withering air around; decks piled with materials of death; escape unlikely; a phantom in chase behind; the ocean like an unreachable eternity before; un-certainty every where; and, within your skull, a feverish mind harassed by doubt and responsibility, yet almost craving for any act of desperation that will remove the spell. It is a living night-mare, from which the soul pants to be free.

"With torments like these, I paced the deck for half an hour beneath the awning, when, seizing a telescope and mounting the rigging, I took deliberate aim at the annoyer. He was full seven or eight miles away from us, but very soon I saw, or fancied I saw, a row of ports, which the Dane had not: then sweeping the horizon a little astern of the craft, I distinctly made out three boats, fully manned, making for us with ensigns flying.

"Anxious to avoid a panic, I descended leisurely, and ordered the sweeps to be spread once more in aid of the breeze, which, within the last ten minutes, had freshened enough to fan us along about a knot an hour. Next, I imparted my discovery to the officers; and, passing once more among the men to test their nerves, I said it was likely they would have to encounter an angrier cus-tomer than the Dane. In fact, I frankly told them our antagonist was un-questionably a British cruiser of ten or twelve guns, from whose clutches there was no escape, unless we repulsed the boats.

"I found my crew as confident in the face of augmented risk as they had been when we expected the less perilous Dane. Collecting their votes for fight or surrender, I learned that all *but two* were in favor of resistance. I had no doubt in regard *to the mates*, in our approaching trials.

"By this time the breeze had again died away to utter calmness, while the air was so still and fervent that our sweltering men almost sank at the sweeps. I ordered them in, threw overboard several water-casks that encumbered the deck, and hoisted our boat to the stern-davits to prevent boarding in that quarter. Things were perfectly ship-shape all over the schooner, and I congratulated myself that her power had been increased by two twelve pound carronades, the ammunition, and part of the crew of a Spanish slaver, abandoned on the bar of Rio Pongo a week before my departure. We had in all three guns, and abundance of musketry, pistols and cutlasses, to be wielded and managed by thirty-seven hands.

"By this time the British boats, impelled by oars alone, approached within half a mile, while the breeze sprang up in cat's paws all around the eastern horizon, but without fanning us with a single breath. Taking advantage of one of these slants, the cruiser had followed her boats, but now, about five miles off, was again as perfectly becalmed as we had been all day. Presently, I observed the boats converge within the range of my swivel, and lay on their oars as if for consultation. I seized this opportunity, while the enemy was hundled together, to give him the first welcome ; and, slewing the schooner round with my sweeps, I sent him a shot from my swivel. But the ball passed over their heads, while, with three cheers, they separated—the largest boat making directly for our waist, while the others steered to cross our bow and attack our stern.

"During the chase my weapons, with the exception of the pivot gun, were altogether useless, but I kept a couple of sweeps ahead and a couple astern to play the schooner, and employed the loud-tongued instrument as the foe approached. The larger boat, bearing a small carronade, was my best target, yet we contrived to miss each other completely until my sixth discharge, when a double-headed shot raked the whole bank of starboard oar-blades, and disabled the rowers by the severe concussion. This paralyzed the launch's advance, and allowed me to devote my exclusive attention to the other boats ; yet, before I could bring the schooner in a suitable position, a signal summoned the assailants aboard the cruiser to repair damages. I did not reflect until this moment of reprieve, that, early in the day, I had hoisted the Portuguese ensign *to deceive the Dane*, and imprudently left it aloft in the presence of *John Bull*. I struck the false flag at once, unfurled the Spanish, and refreshing the men with a double allowance of grog and grub, put them again to the sweeps. When the cruisers reached their vessels, the men instantly reëmbarked, while the boats were allowed to swing alongside, which convinced me that the assault would be renewed as soon as the rum and roast-beef of Old England had strengthened the heart of the adversary. Accordingly, noon had not long passed when our pursuers again embarked. Once more they approached, divided as before, and again we exchanged ineffectual shots. I kept them at bay with grape and musketry until near three o'clock, when a second signal of retreat was hoisted on the cruiser, and answered by exultant *vivas* from my crew. It grieved me, I confess, not to mingle my voice with these shouts, for I was sure that the lion retreated to make a better spring, nor was I less disheartened when the mate reported that nearly all the ammunition for our cannons was exhausted. Seven kegs of powder were still in the magazine, though not more than a dozen rounds of grape, cannister, or balls remained in the locker. There was still an abundance of cartridges for pistols and musketry, but these were poor defenses against resolute Englishmen whose blood was up and who would unquestionably renew the charge with reinforcements of vigorous men. Fore and aft, high and low, we searched for missils. Musket balls were crammed in bags, bolts and nails were packed in cartridge paper, slave shackles were formed with rope yarns into chain-shot, and, in an hour, we were once more tolerably prepared to pepper the foe.

"When these labors terminated, I turned my attention to the relaxed crew, portions of whom refused wine, and began to sulk about the decks. As yet, only two had been slightly scratched by spent musket balls; but so much discontent began to appear among the passenger-sailors of the wrecked slaver, that my own hands could with difficulty restrain them from revolt. I felt much difficulty in determining how to act, but I had no time for deliberation. Violence was clearly not my *role*, but persuasion was a delicate game in such straits among men whom I did not command with the absolute authority of a master. I cast my eye over the taffrail, and seeing that the British boats were still afar, I followed my first impulse, and calling the whole gang to the quarter-deck, tried the effect of African palaver and Spanish gold. I spoke of the perils of capture and of the folly of surrendering *a slaver* while there was the slightest hope of escape. I painted the unquestionable result of being taken after such resistance as had already been made. I drew an accurate picture of a tall and dangerous instrument on which piratical gentlemen have some times been known to terminate their lives; and finally, I attempted to improve the rhythm of my oratory by a couple of golden ounces to each combatant, and the promise of a slave apiece at the end of our *successful* voyage.

"My suspense was terrible, as there—on the deck of a slaver, amid calm, heat, battle, and mutiny, with a volcano of three hundred and seventy-five imprisoned devils below me—I awaited a reply, which, favorable or unfavorable, I must hear without emotion. Presently, three or four came forward and accepted my offer. I shrugged my shoulders, and took half a dozen turns up and down the deck. Then turning to the crowd, I *doubled my bounty*, and offering a boat to take the recusants on board the enemy, swore that I would stand by the Esperanza with my unaided crew in spite of the *dastards!*

"The offensive word with which I closed the harangue seemed to touch the right string of the Spanish guitar, and in an instant I saw the dogged heads spring up with a jerk of mortified pride, while the steward and cabin-boy poured in a fresh supply of wine, and a shout of union went up from both divisions. I lost no time in confirming my converts; and, ramming down my eloquence with a wad of doubloons, ordered every man to his post, for the enemy was again in motion.

"But he did not come alone. New actors had appeared on the scene during my engagement with the crew. The sound of the cannonade had been heard, it seems, by a consort of his Britannic Majesty's brig, and, although the battle was not within her field of vision, she dispatched another squadron of boats under the guidance of the reports that boomed through the silent air.

"The first division of my old assailants was considerably in advance of the reinforcement, and in perfect order approached us in a solid body, with the apparent determination of boarding on the same side. Accordingly, I brought all my weapons and hands to that quarter, and told both gunners and musketeers not to fire without orders. Waiting their discharge, I allowed them to get close; but the commander of the launch seemed to anticipate my plan by the reservation of his fire till he could draw mine, in order to throw his other boat-loads on board under the smoke of his swivel and small arms. It was odd to witness our mutual forbearance, nor could I help laughing, even in the midst of danger, at the mutual checkmate we were trying to prepare. However, my Britons did not avoid pulling, though they omitted firing, so that they were already rather perilously close when I thought it best to give them the contents of my pivot, which I had crammed almost to the muzzle with bolts and bullets. The discharge paralyzed the advance, while my carronades flung a quantity of grape into the companion boats. In turn, however, they plied us so deftly with balls from swivels and musketry, that five of our most valuable defenders writhed in death on the deck.

"The rage of battle at closer quarters than heretofore, and the screams of bleeding comrades beneath their feet, roused to its fullest extent the ardent nature of my Spanish crew. They tore their garments; stripped to their waists; called for rum; and swore they would die rather than yield!

"By this time the consort's reinforcement was rapidly approaching; and, with hurrah after hurrah, the five fresh boats came on in double column. As they drew within shot, each cheer was followed with a fatal volley, under which several more of our combatants were prostrated, while a glancing musket ball lacerated my knee with a painful wound. For five minutes we met this onset with cannon, muskets, pistols, and enthusiastic shouts; but in the dispairing cosfusion of the hour, the captain of our long gun rammed home his ball before the powder, so that when the priming burnt, the most reliable of our weapons was silent forever. At this moment a round shot from the launch dismounted a carronade—our ammunition was wasted—and in this disabled state the Britons prepared to board our crippled craft. Muskets, bayonets, pistols, swords, and knives, for a space kept them at bay, even at short quarters; but the crowded boats tumbled their enraged fighters over our forecastle like surges from the sea, and, cutlass in hand, the victorious furies swept everything before them. The cry was to 'spare no one!' Down went sailor after sailor, struggling with the frenzied passion of despair. Presently an order went forth to split the gratings and release the slaves. I clung to my post and cheered the battle to the last; but when I heard this fatal command, which, if obeyed, might bury assailant and defender in common ruin, I ordered the remnant to throw down their arms, while I struck the flag and warned the rash and testy Englishman to beware.

"The senior officer of the boarding party belonged to the division from the cruiser's consort. As he reached the deck, his clement eye fell sadly on the scene of blood, and he commanded 'quarter' immediately. It was time. The excited boarders from the repulsed boats had mounted our deck brimming with revenge. Every one that opposed was cut down without mercy; and in another moment, it is likely I would have joined the throng of the departed.

"All was over! There was a hushed and panting crowd of victors and vanquished on the bloody deck, when the red ball of the setting sun glared through a crimson haze and filled the motionless sea with liquid fire. For the first time that day I became sensible of personal sufferings. A stifling sensation made me gasp for air as I sat down on the taffrail of my captured schooner, and felt that I was—a prisoner!"

The night after the capture the captain made his escape in one of the boats, and again reached the coast and his establishment at Kambia. Shortly afterwards the "Feliz" arrived from Matanzas, consigned to him for a cargo of slaves.

"Slaves dropped in slowly at Kambia and Bangalang, though I still had half the cargo of the Feliz to make up. Time was precious, and there was no foreigner on the river to aid me. In this strait I suddenly resolved on a foray among the natives on my own account; and equipping a couple of my largest canoes with an ample armament, as well as a substantial store of provisions and merchandise, I departed for the Matacan river, a short stream, unsuitable for vessels of considerable draft. I was prepared for the purchase of fifty slaves.

"I reached my destination without risk or adventure, but had the opportunity of seeing some new phases of Africanism on my arrival. Most of the coast negroes are wretchedly degraded by their superstitions and *sauvagerie*, and it is best to go among them with power to resist as well as presents to purchase. Their towns did not vary from the river and bush settlements generally. A house was given me for my companions and merchandise; yet such was their curiosity to see the 'white man,' that the luckless mansion swarmed with sable bees both inside and out, till I was obliged to send for his majesty to relieve my sufferings.

"After a proper delay, the king made his appearance in all the paraphernalia of African court-dress. A few fathoms of check girded his loins, while a blue shirt and red waistcoat were surmounted by a dragoon's cap with brass ornaments. His countenance was characteristic of Ethiopia and royalty. A narrow forehead retreated rapidly till it was lost in the crisp wool, while his eyes were wide apart, and his prominent cheek-bones formed the base of an inverted cone, the apex of which was his braided beard coiled up under his chin. When earnest in talk, his gestures were mostly made with his head, by straining his eyes to the rim of their sockets, stretching his mouth from ear to ear, grinning like a baboon, and throwing out his chin horizontally with a sudden jerk. Notwithstanding these personal oddities, the sovereign was kind, courteous, hospitable, and disposed for trade. Accordingly, I 'dashed,' or presented him and his head-men a few pieces of cottons, with some pipes, beads and looking-glasses, by way of whet for the appetite of to-morrow.

"Next day we proceeded to formal business. His majesty called a regular 'palaver' of his chiefs and head-men, before whom I stated my *dantica* and announced the terms. Very soon several young folks were brought for sale, who, I am sure, never dreamed at rising from last night's sleep that they were destined for Cuban slavery! My merchandise revived the memory of peccadilloes that had been long forgotten, and sentences that were forgiven. Jealous husbands, when they tasted my rum, suddenly remembered their wives' infidelities, and sold their better halves for more of the oblivious fluid. In truth, I was exalted into a magician, unroofing the village and baring its crime and wickedness to the eye of *justice*. Law became profitable, and virtue had never reached so high a price! Before night the town was in a turmoil, for every man cudgeled his brain for an excuse to kidnap his neighbor, so as to share my commerce. As the village was too small to supply the entire gang of fifty, I had recourse to the neighboring settleménts, where my 'barkers,' or agents, did their work in a masterly manner. Traps were adroitly baited with goods to lead the unwary into temptation, when the unconscious pilferer was caught by his ambushed foe, and an hour served to hurry him to the beach as a slave for ever. In fact, five days were sufficient to stamp my image permanently on the Matacan settlements, and to associate my memory with any thing but blessings in at least fifty of their families!

"In 1829, vessels were publicly sold, and, with very little trouble, equipped for the coast of Africa. The captures in that region were somewhat like playing a hand—taking the tricks, reshuffling the same cards, and dealing again to take more tricks! Accordingly, I fitted a schooner to receive a cargo of negroes immediately on quitting port. My crew was made up of men from all nations, captured in prizes; but I guardedly selected my officers from Spaniards exclusively.

"We were slowly wafting along the sea, a day or two out of the British colony, when the mate fell into a chat with a clever lad who was hanging lazily over the helm. They spoke of voyages and mishaps, and this led the sailor to declare his recent escape from a vessel, then in the Rio Nunez, whose mate had poisoned the captain to get possession of the craft. She had been fitted, he said, at St. Thomas with the feigned design of coasting; but, when she sailed for Africa, her register was sent back to the island in a boat to serve some other vessel, while she ventured to the continent *without* papers.

"I have cause to believe that the slave-trade was rarely conducted upon the honorable principles between man and man, which, of course, are the only security betwixt owners, commanders and consignees whose commerce is exclusively contraband. There were men, it is true, engaged in it, with whom the 'point of honor' was more omnipotent than the dread of law in regular trade. But innumerable cases have occurred in which the spendthrifts who appropriated their owners' property on the coast of Africa, availed themselves of such superior force as they happened to control, in order to escape detection, or assure a favorable reception in the West Indies. In fact, the slaver sometimes ripened into something very like a pirate !

"In 1828 and 1829, severe engagements took place between Spanish slavers and this class of contrabandists. Spaniards would assail Portuguese when the occasion was tempting and propitious. Many a vessel has been fitted in Cuba for these adventures, and returned to port with a living cargo, purchased by cannon-balls and boarding-pikes exclusively.

"Now, I confess that my notions had become at this epoch somewhat relaxed by my traffic on the coast, so that I grew to be no better than folks of my cloth. I was fond of excitement; my craft was sadly in want of a cargo; and, as the mate narrated the helmsman's story, the Quixotic idea naturally got control of my brain that I was destined to become the *avenger* of the poisoned captain. I will not say that I was altogether stimulated by the noble spirit of justice; for it is quite possible I would never have thought of the dead man had not the sailor apprised us that his vessel was half full of negroes !

"As we drifted slowly by the mouth of my old river, I slipped over the bar, and, while I fitted the schooner with a splendid nine-pounder amidships, I dispatched a spy to the Rio Nunez to report the facts about the poisoning, as well as the armament of the unregistered slaver. In ten days the runner verified the tale. She was still in the stream, with one hundred and eighty-five human beings, but would soon be off with two hundred and twenty-five.

"The time was extraordinarily propitious. Every thing favored my enterprise. The number of slaves would exactly fit my schooner. Such a windfall could not be neglected; and, on the fourth day, I was entering the Rio Nunez under the Portuguese flag, which I unfurled by virtue of a pass from Sierra Leone to the Cape de Verde islands.

"I cannot tell whether my spy had been faithless, but when I reached Fucaria, I perceived that my game had taken wing from her anchorage. Here was a sad disappointment. The schooner drew too much water to allow a further ascent, and, moreover, I was unacquainted with the river.

"As it was important that I should keep aloof from strangers, I anchored in a quiet spot, and seizing the first canoe that passed, learned, for a small reward, that the object of my search was hidden in a bend of the river at the king's town of Kakundy, which I could not reach without the pilotage of a certain mulatto, who alone was fit for the enterprise.

"I knew this half-breed as soon as his person was described, but I had little hope of securing his services, either by fair means or promised recompense. He owed me five slaves for dealings that took place between us at Kambia, and had always refused so strenuously to pay, that I felt sure he would be off to the woods as soon as he knew of my presence on the river. Accordingly,

I kept my canoemen on the schooner by an abundant supply of 'bitters,' and at midnight landed half a dozen, who proceeded to the mulatto's cabin, where he was seized *sans ceremonie.* The terror of this ruffian was indescribable when he found himself in my presence—a captive, as he supposed, for the debt of flesh. But I soon relieved him, and offered him a liberal reward for his prompt, secret and safe pilotage to Kakundy. The mulatto was willing, but the stream was too shallow for my keel. He argued the point so convincingly, that in half an hour I relinquished the attempt, and resolved to make 'Mahomet come to the mountain.'

"The two boats were quickly manned, armed, and supplied with lanterns ; and, with muffled oars, guided by our pilot—whose skull was kept constantly under the lee of my pistol—we fell like vampyres on our prey in the darkness.

"With a wild hurrah and a blaze of our pistols in the air, we leaped on board, driving every soul under hatches without striking a blow ! Sentries were placed at the cabin door, forecastle and hatchway. The cable was slipped, my launch took her in tow, the pilot and myself took charge of the helm, and, before daylight, the prize was alongside my schooner, transhipping one hundred and ninety-seven of her slaves, with their necessary supplies.

"Great was the surprise of the captured crew when they saw their fate ; and great was the agony of the poisoner, when he returned next morning to the vacant anchorage, after a night of debauch with the king of Kakundy. First of all, he imagined we were regular cruisers, and that the captain's death was about to be avenged. But when it was discovered that they had fallen into the grasp of *friendly slavers,* five of his seamen abandoned their craft and shipped with me.

"We had capital stomachs for breakfast after that night's romance. Hardly was it swallowed, however, when three canoes came blustering down the stream, filled with negroes and headed by his majesty. I did not wait for a salutation, but, giving the warriors a dose of bellicose grape, tripped my anchor, sheeted home my sails, and was off like an albatross !

"The feat was cleverly achieved ; but, since then, I have very often been taxed by my conscience with doubts as to its strict morality. The African slave-trade produces singular notions of *meum and tuum* in the minds and hearts of those who dwell for any length of time on that blighting coast ; and it is not unlikely that I was quite as prone to the infection as better men, who perished under the malady, while I escaped !

"It was a sweltering July, and the 'rainy season' proved its tremendous power by almost incessant deluges. In the breathless calms that held me spellbound on the coast, the rain came down in such torrents that I often thought the solid water would bury and submerge our schooner. Now and then, a south-wester and the current would fan and drift us along ; yet the tenth day found us rolling from side to side in the longitude of the Cape de Verdes.

"Day broke with one of its customary squalls and showers. As the cloud lifted, my look-out from the cross-trees announced a sail under our lee. It was invisible from deck, in the folds of the retreating rain, but, in the dead calm that followed, the distant whistle of a boatswain was distinctly audible. Before I could deliberate, all my doubts were solved by a shot in our main-sail, and the crack of a cannon. There could be no question that the unwelcome visitor was a man-of-war.

"It was fortunate that the breeze sprang up after the lull, and enabled us to carry everything that could be crowded on our spars. We dashed away before the freshening wind like a deer with the unleashed hounds pursuing. The slaves were shifted from side to side—forward or aft—to aid our sailing. Headstays were slackened, wedges knocked off the masts, and every incumbrance cast from the decks into the sea. Now and then, a fruitless shot from his bow-chasers reminded the fugitive that the foe was still on his scent. At last, the cruiser got the range of his guns so perfectly that a well-aimed ball ripped away our rail and tore a dangerous splinter from the foremast, three feet from deck. It was now perilous to carry a press of sail on the same tack with the weakened spar, whereupon I put the schooner about, and, to my delight, found we ranged ahead a knot faster on this course than the former. The enemy 'went about' as quickly as we did, but her balls soon fell short of us, and, before noon, we had crawled so nimbly to windward that her top-gallants alone were visible above the horizon.

"Our voyage was uncheckered by any occurrence worthy of recollection save the accidental loss of the mate in a dark and stormy night, until we approached the Antilles. Here, where everything on a slaver assumes the guise of pleasure and relief, I remarked not only the sullenness of my crew, but a disposition to disobey or neglect. The second mate—shipped in the Rio Nunez, and who replaced my lost officer as chief mate of the schooner—was noticed occasionally in close intercourse with the watch, while his deportment indicated dissatisfaction, if not mutiny.

"A slaver's life on shore, as well as at sea, makes him wary when another would not be circumspect, or even apprehensive. The sight of land is commonly the signal for merriment, for a well-behaved cargo is invariably released from shackles, and allowed free intercourse between the sexes during the daytime on deck. Water tanks are thrown open for unrestricted use. 'The cat' is cast into the sea. Strict discipline is relaxed. The day of danger or revolt is considered over, and the captain enjoys a new and refreshing life till the hour of landing. Sailors, with proverbial generosity, share their biscuits and clothing with the blacks. The women, who are generally without garments, appear in costume from the wardrobes of tars, petty officers, mates, and even captains. Sheets, table-cloths, and spare sails are torn to pieces for raiment, while shoes, boots, caps, oil-cloths, and monkey-jackets contribute to the gay masquerade of the 'emigrants.'

"It was my sincere hope that the first glimpse of the Antilles would have converted my schooner into a theatre for such a display; but the moodiness of my companions was so manifest that I thought it best to meet rebellion half way, by breaking the suspected officer, and sending him forward at the same time that I threw his 'dog-house' overboard.*

" I was now without a reliable officer, and was obliged to call two of the youngest sailors to my assistance in navigating the schooner. I knew the cook and steward—both of whom messed aft—to be trustworthy ; so that, with four men at my back, and the blacks below, I felt competent to control my vessel. From that moment, I suffered no one to approach the quarter-deck nearer than the mainmast.

" It was a sweet afternoon when we were floating along the shores of Porto Rico, tracking our course upon the chart. Suddenly, one of my new assistants approached, with the sociability common among Spaniards, and, in a quiet tone, asked whether I would take a *cigarillo*. As I never smoked, I rejected the offer with thanks, when the youth immediately dropped the twisted paper on my map. In an instant, I perceived the *ruse*, and discovered that the *cigarillo* was, in fact, a *billet* rolled to resemble one. I put it in my mouth, and walked aft until I could throw myself on the deck, with my head over the stern, so as to open the paper unseen. It disclosed the organization of a mutiny, under the lead of the broken mate. Our arrival in sight of St. Domingo was to be the signal of its rupture, and for my immediate landing on the island. Six of the crew were implicated with the villain, and the boatswain, who was ill in the slave-hospital, was to share my fate.

" My resolution was promptly made. In a few minutes, I had cast a hasty glance into the arm-chest, and seen that our weapons were in order. Then, mustering ten of the stoutest and cleverest of my negroes on the quarter-deck, I took the liberty to invent a little strategic fib, and told them, in the Soosoo dialect, that there were bad men on board, who wanted to run the schooner ashore among the rocks and drown the slaves while below. At the same time, I gave each a cutlass from the arm-chest, and supplying my trusty whites with a couple of pistols and a knife a-piece, without saying a word, I seized the ringleader and his colleagues ! Irons and double-irons secured the party to the mainmast or deck, while a drum-head court-martial, composed of the officers, and presided over by myself, arraigned and tried the scoundrels in much less time than regular boards ordinarily spend in such investigations. During the inquiry, we ascertained beyond doubt that the death of the mate was due to false play. He had been wilfully murdered, as a preliminary to the assault on me, for his colossal stature and powerful muscles would have made him a dangerous adversary in the seizure of the craft.

" There was, perhaps, a touch of the old-fashioned Inquisition in the mode of our judicial researches concerning this projected mutiny. We proceeded very much by way of 'confession,' and whenever the culprit manifested reluctance or hesitation, his memory was stimulated by a 'cat.' Accordingly, at the end of the trial, the mutineers were already pretty well punished ; so that

---

* The forecastle and cabin of a slaver are given up to the living freight, while officers sleep on deck in kennels, technically known as "dog-houses."

we sentenced the six accomplices to receive an additional flagellation, and continue ironed till we reached Cuba. But the fate of the ringleader was not decided so easily. Some were in favor of dropping him overboard, as he had done with the mate; others proposed to set him adrift on a raft, ballasted with chains; but I considered both these punishments too cruel, notwithstanding his treachery, and kept his head beneath the pistol of a sentry till I landed him in shackles on Turtle Island, with three days food and abundance of water.

"After all these adventures, I was very near losing the schooner before I got to land, by one of the perils of the sea, for which I blame myself that I was not better prepared. It was the afternoon of a fine day. For some time I had noticed on the horizon a low bank of white cloud, which rapidly spread itself over the sky and water, surrounding us with an impenetrable fog. I apprehended danger; yet, before I could make the schooner snug to meet the squall, a blast—as sudden and loud as a thunderbolt—prostrated her nearly on her beam. The shock was so violent and unforeseen that the unrestrained slaves, who were enjoying the fine weather on deck, rolled to leeward till they floundered in the sea that inundated the scuppers. There was no power in the tiller to 'keep her away' before the blast, for the rudder was almost out of water; but, fortunately, our mainsail burst in shreds from the bolt-ropes, and, relieving us from its pressure, allowed the schooner to right under control of the helm. The West Indian squall abandoned us as rapidly as it assailed, and I was happy to find that our entire loss did not exceed two slave-children, who had been carelessly suffered to sit on the rail.

"The reader knows that my voyage was an *impromptu* speculation, without papers, manifest, register, consignees, or destination. It became necessary, therefore, that I should exercise a very unusual degree of circumspection, not only in landing my human cargo, but in selecting a spot from which I might communicate with proper persons. I had never been in Cuba, save on the occasion already described, nor were my business transactions extended beyond the Regla Association, by which I was originally sent to Africa.

"The day after the 'white squall,' I found our schooner drifting with a leading breeze along the southern coast of Cuba, and as the time seemed favorable, I thought I might as well cut the gordian knot of dilemma by landing my cargo in a secluded cove that indented the beach about nine miles east of Sant Iago. If I had been consigned to the spot, I could not have been more fortunate in my reception. Some sixty yards from the landing, I found the comfortable home of a *ranchero* who proffered the hospitality usual in such cases, and devoted a spacious barn to the reception of my slaves, while his family prepared an abundant meal.

"As soon as the cargo was safe from the grasp of cruisers, I resolved to disregard the flagless and paperless craft that bore it from Africa, and being unacquainted in Sant' Iago, to cross the island towards the capital, in search of a consignee. Accordingly, I mounted a spirited little horse, and with a *montero* guide, turned my face once more towards the 'ever faithful city of Havana.'

" My companion had a thousand questions for 'the captain,' all of which I answered with so much *bonhommie* that we soon became the best friends imaginable, and chatted over all the scandal of Cuba. I learned from this man that a cargo had recently been 'run' in the neighborhood of Matanzas, and that its disposal was most successfully managed by a Señor * * *, from Catalonia.

" I slapped my thigh and shouted *eureka!* It flashed through my mind to trust this man without further inquiry, and I confess that my decision was based exclusively upon his *sectional* nationality. I am partial to the Catalans. Accordingly, I presented myself at the counting-room of my future consignee in due time, and 'made a clean breast' of the whole transaction, disclosing the destitute state of my vessel. In a very short period, his excellency the captain-general was made aware of my arrival, and furnished a list of 'the Africans,' by which name the Bosal slaves are commonly known in Cuba. Nor was the captain of the port neglected. A convenient blank page of his register was inscribed with the name of my vessel as having sailed from the port six months before, and this was backed by a register and muster-roll, in order to secure my unquestionable entry into a harbor.

" Before nightfall everything was in order with Spanish dispatch, when stimulated either by doubloons or the smell of African blood; and twenty-four hours afterwards, I was again at the landing with a suit of clothes and a blanket for each of my 'domestics.' The schooner was immediately put in charge of a clever pilot, who undertook the formal duty and *name* of her commander, in order to elude the vigilance of all the minor officials whose conscience had not been lulled by the golden anodyne.

" In the meanwhile every attention had been given to the slaves by my hospitable *ranchero*. 'The head-money' once paid, no body—civil, military, foreign, or Spanish—dared interfere with them. Forty-eight hours of rest, ablution, exercise and feeding, served to recruit the gang and steady their gait. Nor had the sailors in charge of the party omitted the performance of their duty as '*valets*' to the gentlemen, and '*ladies' maids*' to the females; so that when the march towards Sant Iago began, the procession might have been considered as 'respectable as it was numerous.'

" The brokers of the southern emporium made very little delay in finding purchasers at retail for the entire venture. The returns were, of course, in cash; and so well did the enterprise turn out, that I forgot the rebellion of our mutineers, and allowed them to share my bounty with the rest of the crew. In fact, so pleased was I with the result on inspecting the balance sheet, that I resolved to divert myself with the *dolce far niente* of Cuban country life for a month at least.

" But while I was making ready for this delightful repose, a slight breeze passed over the calmness of my mirror. I had given, perhaps imprudently, but certainly with generous motives, a double pay to my men in recompense of their perilous service on the Rio Nunez. With the usual recklessness of their craft, they lounged about Havana, boasting of their success, while a Frenchman of the party, who had been swindled of his wages at cards, appealed to his consul for relief. By dint of cross questions, the Gallic official extracted the tale of our voyage from his countryman, and took advantage of the fellow's destitution to make him a witness against a certain Don Téodore Canot, who *was alleged to be a native of France!* Besides this, the punishment of my mate was exaggerated by the recreant Frenchman into a most unjustifiable as well as cruel act.

"Of course the story was promptly detailed to the captain-general, who issued an order for my arrest. But I was too wary and flush to be caught so easily by the guardian of France's lilies. No person bearing my name could be found in the island; and as the schooner had entered port with Spanish papers, Spanish crew, and was regularly sold, it became manifest to the stupefied consul that the sailor's ' yarn' was an entire fabrication. That night a convenient press-gang, in want of recruits for the royal marine, seized the braggadocio crew, and as there were no witnesses to corroborate the consul's complaint, it was forthwith dismissed.

"Things are managed very cleverly in Havana—*when you know how!*"

The following extract presents a new phase of the slave-trade; as the ordinary horrors of the middle passage were increased by that terrible disease, the small-pox. The narrator had shipped as a sailing master on board the San Pablo. The vessel was disguised as a French cruiser; her officers wore the French uniform, and on all occasions, except in the presence of a genuine French cruiser, she hoisted the Bourbon lilies, and the vessel was conducted in every way as if she belonged to the royal navy. She proceeded to the Mozambique channel, took on board eight hundred victims, and started on the return voyage: "We had hardly reached the open sea before the captain was prostrated with an ague which refused to yield to ordinary remedies, and finally ripened into fever, that deprived him of reason. Other dangers thickened around us. We had been several days off the cape of Good Hope, buffeting a series of adverse gales, when word was brought me after a night of weary watching, that several slaves were ill of small-pox. Of all calamities that occur in the voyage of a slaver, this is the most dreaded and unmanageable. The news appalled me. Impetuous with anxiety, I rushed to the captain, and regardless of fever or insanity, disclosed the dreadful fact. He stared at me for a minute as if in doubt; then opening his bureau and pointing to a long coil of combustible material, said that it communicated through the decks with the powder magazine, and ordered me to—' *blow up the brig!*'

"The master's madness sobered his mate. I lost no time in securing both the dangerous implement and its perilous owner, while I called the officers into the cabin for inquiry and consultation as to our desperate state.

"The gale had lasted nine days without intermission, and during all this time with so much violence that it was impossible to take off the gratings, release the slaves, purify the decks, or rig the wind-sails. When the first lull occurred, a thorough inspection of the eight hundred was made, and *a death announced.* As life had departed during the tempest, a careful inspection of the body was made, and it was this that first disclosed the pestilence in our midst. The corpse was silently thrown into the sea, and the malady kept secret from crew and negroes.

"When breakfast was over on that fatal morning, I determined to visit the slave deck myself, and ordering an abundant supply of lanterns, descended to the cavern, which still reeked horribly with human vapor, even after ventilation. But here, alas! I found nine of the negroes infected by the disease. We took counsel as to the use of laudanum in ridding ourselves speedily of the sufferers—a remedy that is seldom and secretly used in *desperate* cases to preserve the living from contagion. But it was quickly resolved that it had already gone too far, when nine were prostrated, to save the rest by depriving them of life. Accordingly, these wretched beings were at once sent to the forecastle as a hospital, and given in charge to the vaccinated or inoculated as nurses. The hold was then ventilated and limed; yet before the gale abated, our sick list was increased to thirty. The hospital could hold no more. Twelve of the sailors took the infection, and fifteen corpses had been cast into the sea!

"All reserve was now at an end. Body after body fed the deep, and still the gale held on. At last, when the wind and waves had lulled so much as to allow the gratings to be removed from our hatches, our consternation knew no bounds when we found that nearly all the slaves were dead or dying with the distemper. I will not dwell on the scene or our sensations. It is a picture that must gape with all its horrors before the least vivid imagination. Yet there was no time for languor or sentimental sorrow. Twelve of the stoutest survivors were ordered to drag out the dead from among the ill, and though they were constantly drenched with rum to brutalize them, still we were forced to aid the gang by reckless volunteers from our crew, who, arming their hands with tarred mittens, flung the fœtid masses of putrefaction into the sea!

"One day was a counterpart of another; and yet the love of life, or, perhaps, the love of gold, made us fight the monster with a courage that became a better cause. At length death was satisfied, but not until the eight hundred beings we had shipped in high health had dwindled to four hundred and ninety-seven skeletons!

"The San Pablo might have been considered entitled to a 'clean bill of health' by the time she reached the equator. The dead left space, food, and water for the living, and very little restraint was imposed on the squalid remnant. None were shackled after the outbreak of the fatal plague, so that in a short time the survivors began to fatten for the market to which they were hastening. But such was not the fate of our captain. The fever and delirium had long left him, yet a dysenteric tendency, the result of a former malady, suddenly supervened, and the worthy gentleman rapidly declined. His nerves gave way so thoroughly that from fanciful weakness he lapsed into helpless hypochondria. One of his pet ideas was that a copious dose of calomel would insure his restoration to perfect health.

"But there was no balm in calomel for the captain. Physic could not save him. He declined day by day; yet the energy of his hard nature kept him alive when other men would have sunk, and enabled him to command even from his sick bed.

"It was always our Sabbath service to drum the men to quarters and exercise them with cannons and small arms. One Sunday, after the routine was over, the dying man desired to inspect his crew, and was carried to the quarter-deck on a mattrass. Each sailor marched in front of him and was allowed to take his hand; after which he called them around in a body, and announced his apprehension that death would claim him before our destination was reached. Then, without previously apprising us of his design, he proceeded to make a verbal testament, and enjoined it upon all as a duty to his memory to obey implicitly. If the San Pablo arrived safely in port, he desired that every officer and mariner should be paid the promised bounty, and that the proceeds of the cargo should be sent to his family in Nantz. But if it happened that we were attacked by a cruiser, and the brig was saved by the risk and valor of a defense, then he directed that one-half the voyage's avails should be shared between officers and crew, while one-quarter was sent to his friends in France, and the other given to me. His sailing-master and Cuban consignees were to be the executors of this salt-water document.

"We were now well advanced north-westwardly on our voyage, and in every cloud could see a promise of the continuing trade-wind, which was shortly to end a luckless voyage. From deck to royal—from flying-jib to ring-tail, every stitch of canvas that would draw was packed and crowded on the brig. Vessels were daily seen in numbers, but none appeared suspicious till we got far to the westward, when my glass detected a cruising schooner, jogging along under easy sail. I ordered the helmsman to keep his course; and tautening sheets, braces, and halyards, went into the cabin to receive the final orders of our commander.

"He received my story with his usual bravery, nor was he startled when a boom from the cruiser's gun announced her in chase. He pointed to one of his drawers and told me to take out its contents. I handed him three flags, which he carefully unrolled, and displayed the ensigns of Spain, Denmark, and Portugal, in each of which I found a set of papers suitable for the San Pablo. In a feeble voice he desired me to select a nationality; and, when I chose the Spanish, he grasped my hand, pointed to the door, and bade me not to surrender.

"When I reached the deck, I found our pursuer gaining on us with the utmost speed. She outsailed us—two to one. Escape was altogether out of the question; yet I resolved to show the inquisitive stranger our mettle, by keeping my course, firing a gun, and hoisting my Spanish signals at peak and main.

"At this time the San Pablo was spinning along finely at the rate of about six knots an hour, when a shot from the schooner fell close to our stern. In a moment I ordered in studding-sails alow and aloft, and as my men had been trained to their duty in man-of-war fashion, I hoped to impose on the cruiser by the style and perfection of the manœuvre. Still, however, she kept her way, and, in four hours after discovery, was within half gun-shot of the brig. Hitherto I had not touched my armament, but I selected this moment to load under the enemy's eyes, and, at the word of command, to fling open the ports and run out my barkers. The act was performed to a charm by my well-drilled gunners; yet all our belligerent display had not the least effect on the schooner, which still pursued us. At last, within hail, her commander leaped on a gun, and ordered me to 'heave to, or take a ball!'

" Now, I was prepared for this arrogant command, and, for half an hour, had made up my mind how to avoid an engagement. A single discharge of my broadside might have sunk or seriously damaged our antagonist, but the consequences would have been terrible if he boarded me, which I believed to be his aim. Accordingly, I paid no attention to the threat, but tautened my ropes and surged ahead. Presently, my racing chaser came up *under my lee* within pistol-shot, when a reiterated command to heave to or be fired on, was answered for the first time by a faint '*no intiendo,*'—'I don't understand you,'—while the man-of-war shot ahead of me. *Then I had him!* Quick as thought, I gave the order to 'square away,' and putting the helm up, struck the cruiser near the bow, carrying away her foremast and bowsprit. Such was the stranger's surprise at my daring trick that not a musket was fired or boarder stirred, till we were clear of the wreck. It was then too late. The loss of my jib-boom and a few rope-yarns did not prevent me from cracking on my studding-sails, and leaving the lubber to digest his stupid *forbearance!*

" This adventure was a fitting epitaph for the stormy life of our poor commander, who died on the following night, and was buried under a choice selection of the flags he had honored with his various nationalities. A few days after the blue water had closed over him forever, our cargo was safely ensconced in the *hacienda* nine miles east of St. Jago de Cuba, while the San Pablo was sent adrift and burned to the water's edge."

In a former chapter of this work the natives of the Gold Coast are described as remarkable for ferocity, courage and endurance. Four hundred and eighty of these negroes were embarked on board the Estrella at Ayudah, and the incidents of the voyage are thus related : " I have always regretted that I left Ayudah on my homeward voyage without interpreters to aid in the necessary intercourse with our slaves. There was no one on board who understood a word of their dialect. Many complaints from the negroes that would have been dismissed or satisfactorily adjusted, had we comprehended their vivacious tongues, and grievances were passed over in silence or hushed with the lash. Indeed, the whip alone was the emblem of La Estrella's discipline ; and in the end it taught me the saddest of lessons.

"From the beginning there was manifest discontent among the slaves. I endeavored at first to please and accommodate them by a gracious manner ; but manner alone is not appreciated by untamed Africans. A few days after our departure, a slave leaped overboard in a fit of passion, and another choked himself during the night. These two suicides, in twenty-four hours, caused much uneasiness among the officers, and induced me to make every preparation for a revolt.

"We had been at sea about three weeks without further disturbance, and there was so much merriment among the gangs that were allowed to come on deck, that my apprehensions of danger began gradually to wear away. Suddenly, however, one fair afternoon, a squall broke forth from an almost cloudless sky; and as the boatswain's whistle piped all hands to take in sail, a simultaneous rush was made by the confined slaves at all the after-gratings, and amid the confusion of the rising gale, they knocked down the guard and poured upon deck. The sentry at the *fore-hatch* seized the cook's axe, and sweeping it around him like a scythe, kept at bay the band that sought to emerge from below him. Meantime, the women in the cabin were not idle. Seconding the males, they rose in a body, and the helmsman was forced to stab several with his knife before he could drive them below again.

"About forty stalwart devils, yelling and grinning with all the savage ferocity of their wilderness, were now on deck, armed with staves of broken water-casks, or billets of wood, found in the hold. The suddenness of this outbreak did not appal me, for, in the dangerous life of Africa, a trader must be always admonished and never off his guard. The blow that prostrated the first white man was the earliest symptom I detected of the revolt; but in an instant I had the arm-chest open on the quarter-deck, and the mate and steward beside me to protect it. Matters, however, did not stand so well forward of the mainmast. Four of the hands were disabled by clubs, while the rest defended themselves and the wounded as well as they could with handspikes, or whatever could suddenly be clutched. I had always charged the cook, on such an emergency, to distribute from his coppers a liberal supply of scalding water upon the belligerents; and, at the first sign of revolt, he endeavored to baptize the heathen with his steaming slush. But dinner had been over for some time, so that the lukewarm liquid only irritated the savages, one of whom laid the unfortunate 'doctor' bleeding in the scuppers.

"All this occurred in perhaps less time than I have taken to tell it; yet, rapid as was the transaction, I saw that, between the squall with its flying sails, and the revolt with its raving blacks, we would soon be in a desperate plight, unless I gave the order *to shoot*. Accordingly, I told my comrades to *aim low and fire at once*.

"Our carbines had been purposely loaded with buck-shot, to suit such an occasion, so that the first two discharges brought several of the rebels to their knees. Still, the unharmed neither fled nor ceased brandishing their weapons. Two more discharges drove them forward among the mass of my crew, who had retreated to the bowsprit; but, being reinforced by the boatswain and carpenter, we took command of the hatches so effectually, that a dozen additional discharges among the ebony legs, drove the refractory to their quarters below.

"It was time; for sails, ropes, tacks, sheets, and blocks, were flapping, dashing and rolling about the masts and decks, threatening us with imminent danger from the squall. In a short time, everything was made snug, the vessel put on her course, and attention paid to the mutineers, who had begun to fight among themselves in the hold.

"I perceived at once, by the infuriate sounds proceeding from below, that it would not answer to venture in their midst by descending through the hatches. Accordingly, we discharged the women from their quarters under a guard on deck, and sent several resolute and well-armed hands to remove a couple of boards from the bulk-head that separated the cabin from the hold. When this was accomplished, a party entered, on hands and knees, through the aperture, and began to press the mutineers forward towards the bulk-head of the forecastle. Still, the rebels were hot for fight to the last, and boldly defended themselves with their staves against our weapons.

"By this time, our lamed cook had rekindled his fires, and the water was once more boiling. The hatches were kept open, but guarded, and all who did not fight were suffered to come singly on deck, where they were tied. As only about sixty remained below engaged in conflict, or defying my party of sappers and miners, I ordered a number of auger-holes to be bored in the deck, as the scoundrels were forced forward near the forecastle, when a few buckets of boiling water, rained on them through the fresh apertures, brought the majority to submission. Still, however, two of the most savage held out against water as well as fire. I strove as long as possible to save their lives, but their resistance was so prolonged and perilous, that we were obliged to disarm them *for ever* by a couple of pistol shots.

There was very little comfort on board La Estrella, after the suppression of this revolt. We lived with a pent-up volcano beneath us, and, day and night, we were ceaselessly vigilant. Terror reigned supreme, and the lash was its sceptre.

"At last, we made land at Porto Rico, and were swiftly passing its beautiful shores, when the inspector called my attention to the appearance of one of our attendant slaves, whom we had drilled as a sort of cabin-boy. He was a gentle, intelligent child, and had won the hearts of all the officers. His pulse was high, quick and hard; his face and eyes read and swollen; while, on his neck, I detected half a dozen rosy pimples. He was sent immediately to the forecastle, free from contact with any one else, and left there, cut off from the crew, till I could guard against pestilence. It was small-pox!

"The boy passed a wretched night of fever and pain, developing the malady with all its horrors. It is very likely that I slept as badily as the sufferer, for my mind was busy with his *doom*. Daylight found me on deck in consultation with our veteran boatswain, whose experience in the trade authorized the highest respect for his opinion. Hardened as he was, the old man's eyes filled, his lips trembled, and his voice was husky, as he whispered the verdict in my ear. I guessed it before he said a word; yet I hoped he would have counseled against the dread alternative. As we went aft to the quarter-deck, all eyes were bent upon us, for every one conjectured the malady and feared the result, yet none dared ask a question. I ordered a general inspection of the slaves, yet when a *favorable* report was made, I did not rest content, and descended to examine each one personally. It was true; the child *alone* was infected! For half an hour, I trod the deck to and fro restlessly, and caused the crew to subject themselves to inspection. But my sailors were as healthy as the slaves. There was no symptom that indicated approaching danger. I was disappointed again. A single case—a single sign of peril in any quarter, would have spared the poison!

"That evening, in the stillness of night, a trembling hand stole forward to the afflicted boy with a potion that knows no waking. In a few hours, all was over. Life and the pestilence were crushed together; for a necessary murder had been committed, and the poor victim was beneath the blue water!

"I am not superstitious, but a voyage attended with such calamities could not end happily. Incessant gales and head winds, unusual in its season and latitude, beset us so obstinately, that it became doubtful whether our food and water would last till we reached Matanzas. To add to our risks and misfortunes, a British corvette espied our craft, and gave chase off Cape Maize. All day long she dogged us slowly, but, at night, I tacked off shore, with the expectation of eluding my pursuer. Day dawn, however, revealed her again on our track, though this time we had unfortunately fallen to leeward. Accordingly, I put La Estrella directly before the wind, and ran till dark with a fresh breeze, when I again dodged the cruiser, and made for the Cuban coast. But the Briton seemed to scent my track, for sunrise revealed him once more in chase.

"The wind lulled that night to a light breeze, yet the red clouds and haze in the east betokened a gale from that quarter before meridian. A longer pursuit must have given considerable advantage to the enemy, so that my best reliance, I calculated, was in making the small harbor near St. Jago, now about twenty miles distant, where I had already landed two cargoes. The corvette was then full ten miles astern.

"My resolution to save the cargo and lose the vessel was promptly made; orders were issued to strike from the slaves the irons they had constantly worn since the mutiny; the boats were made ready; and every man prepared his bag for a rapid launch.

"On dashed the cruiser, foaming at the bows, under the impetus of the rising gale, which struck him some time before it reached us. We were not more than seven miles apart when the first increased pressure on our sails was felt, and every thing was set and braced to give it the earliest welcome. Then came the tug and race for the beach, three miles ahead. But, under such circumstances, it was hardly to be expected that St. George could carry the day. Still, every nerve was strained to effect the purpose. Regardless of the gale, reef after reef was let out while force pumps moistened the sails; yet nothing was gained. Three miles against seven were too much odds;—and, with a slight move of the helm, and 'letting all fly,' as we neared the line of surf, to break her headway, La Estrella was fairly and safely *beached*.

"The sudden shock snapped her mainmast like a pipe-stem, but, as no one was injured, in a twinkling the boats were overboard, crammed with women and children, while a stage was rigged from the bows to the strand, so that the males, the crew and the luggage were soon in charge of my old *hacien-dado.*

"Prompt as we were, we were not sufficiently so for the cruiser. Half our cargo was ashore when she backed her top-sails off the mouth of the little bay, lowered her boats, filled them with boarders, and steered towards our craft. The delay of half a mile's row gave us time to cling still longer to the wreck, so that, when the boats and corvette began to fire, we wished them joy of their bargain over the remnant of our least valuable negroes. The rescued blacks are now, in all likelihood, citizens of Jamaica; but, under the influence of the gale, La Estrella made a very picturesque bonfire, as we saw it that night from the *azotéa* of our landlord's domicil."

On a subsequent voyage, the captain fell into the hands of the Philistines. While loading his fast-sailing Baltimore clipper in the Rio Salum, the vessel was seized by the boats of a French corvette, and the captain and crew, after being tried at San Luis, were sentenced to imprisonment in France, the captain for ten years. When two years had elapsed, he obtained a pardon, and sailed immediately from Marseilles to the coast of Africa, to recruit his fortunes. He entered the service of the noted Don Pedro, the prince of African slave-merchants. This extract is given to exhibit the enormous wealth which could be accumulated in the slave traffic by a man of superior ability.

"Our concern is now with Gallinas. Nearly one hundred miles northwest of Monrovia, a short and sluggish river, bearing this well-known name, oozes lazily into the Atlantic; and, carrying down in the rainy season a rich alluvion from the interior, sinks the deposit where the tide meets the Atlantic and forms an innumerable mesh of spongy islands. To one who approaches from sea, they loom up from its surface, covered with reeds and mangroves, like an immense field of *fungi*, betokening the damp and dismal field which death and slavery have selected for their grand metropolis. A spot like this, possessed, of course, no peculiar advantages for agriculture or commerce; but its dangerous bar, and its extreme desolation, fitted it for the haunt of the outlaw and slaver.

"Such, in all likelihood, were the reasons that induced Don Pedro Blanco, a well educated mariner from Malaga, to select Gallinas as the field of his operations. Don Pedro visited this place originally in command of a slaver; but failing to complete his cargo, sent his vessel back with one hundred negroes, whose value was barely sufficient to pay the mates and crew. Blanco, however, remained on the coast with a portion of the Conquistador's cargo, and, on its basis, began a trade with the natives and slaver-captains, till, four years after, he remitted his owners the product of their merchandise, and began to flourish on his own account. The honest return of an investment long given over as lost, was perhaps the most active stimulant of his success, and for many years he monopolized the traffic of the Vey country, reaping enormous profits from his enterprise.

"Gallinas was·not in its prime when I came thither, yet enough of its ancient power and influence remained to show the comprehensive mind of Pedro Blanco. As I entered the river, and wound along through the labyrinth of islands, I was struck, first of all, with the vigilance that made this Spaniard stud the field with look-out seats, protected from sun and rain, erected some seventy-five or hundred feet above the ground, either on poles or on isolated trees, from which the horizon was constantly swept by telescopes, to announce the approach of cruisers or slavers. These telegraphic operators were the keenest men on the islands, who were never at fault in discriminating between friend and foe. About a mile from the river's mouth we found a group of islets, on each of which was erected the factory of some particular slave-merchant belonging to the grand confederacy. Blanco's establishments were on several of these marshy flats. On one, near the mouth, he had his place of business or trade with foreign vessels, presided over by his principal clerk, an astute and clever gentleman. On another island, more remote, was his residence, where the only white person was a sister, who, for a while, shared with Don Pedro his solitary and pestilential domain. Here this man of education and refined address surrounded himself with every luxury that could be purchased in Europe or the Indies, and dwelt in a sort of oriental but semi-barbarous splendor, that suited an African prince rather than a Spanish grandee. Further inland was another islet, devoted to his seraglio, within whose recesses each of his favorites inhabited her separate establishment, after the fashion of the natives. Independent of all these were other islands, devoted to the barracoons or slave prisons, ten or twelve of which contained from one hundred to five hundred slaves each. These barracoons were made of rough staves or poles of the hardest trees, four or six inches in diameter, driven five feet in the ground, and clamped together by double rows of iron bars. Their roofs were constructed of similar wood, strongly secured and overlaid with a thick thatch of long and wiry grass, rendering the interior both dry and cool. At the ends, watch-houses—built near the entrance—were tenanted by sentinels, with loaded muskets. Each barracoon was tended by two or four Spaniards or Portuguese; but I have rarely met a more wretched class of human beings, upon whom fever and dropsy seemed to have emptied their vials.

"Such were the surroundings of Don Pedro in 1836, when I first saw his slender figure, swarthy face, and received the graceful welcome which I had hardly expected from one who had passed fifteen years without crossing the bar of Gallinas! Three years after this interview, he left the coast forever, with a fortune of near a million. For a while he dwelt in Havana, engaged in commerce; but I understood that family difficulties induced him to retire altogether from trade; so that, if still alive, he is probably a resident of 'Genova la Superba,' whither he went from the island of Cuba.

"The power of this man among the natives is well known; it far exceeded that of any one with whom I became acquainted. Resolved as he was to be successful in traffic, he left no means untried, with blacks as well as whites, to secure prosperity. I have often been asked what was the character of a mind

PLANTATION LIFE—BRAZIL.

which could voluntarily isolate itself for near a lifetime amid the pestilential swamps of a burning climate, trafficking in human flesh, exciting wars, bribing and corrupting ignorant negroes; totally without society, amusement, excitement or change; living, from year to year, the same dull round of seasons and faces; without companionship, save that of men at war with law; cut loose from all ties except those which avarice formed among European outcasts who were willing to become satellites to such a luminary as Don Pedro? I have always replied to the question, that this African enigma puzzled me as well as those orderly and systematic persons, who would naturally be more shocked at the tastes and prolonged career of a resident slave-factor in the marshes of Gallinas.

"I heard many tales on the coast of Blanco's cruelty, but I doubt them quite as much as I do the stories of his pride and arrogance. I have heard it said that he shot a sailor for daring to ask him for permission to light his cigar at the *puro* of the Don. Upon another occasion, it is said that he was traveling the beach some distance from Gallinas, near the island of Sherboro, where he was unknown, when he approached a native hut for rest and refreshment. The owner was squatted at the door, and, on being requested by Don Pedro to hand him fire to light his cigar, deliberately refused. In an instant Blanco drew back, seized a carbine from one of his attendants, and slew the negro on the spot. It is true that the narrator apologized for Don Pedro, by saying that to deny a Castilian *fire for his tobacco* was the gravest insult that can be offered him; yet, from my knowledge of the person in question, I cannot believe that he carried etiquette to so frightful a pitch, even among a class whose lives are considered of trifling value *except in market*. On several occasions, during our subsequent intimacy, I knew him to chastise with rods, even to the brink of death, servants who ventured to infringe the sacred limits of his seraglio. But, on the other hand, his generosity was proverbially ostentatious, not only among the natives, whom it was his interest to suborn, but to the whites who were in his employ, or needed his kindly succor. I have already alluded to his mental culture, which was decidedly *soigné* for a Spaniard of his original grade and time. His memory was remarkable. I remember one night, while several of his *employés* were striving unsuccessfully to repeat the Lord's prayer in Latin, upon which they had made a bet, that Don Pedro joined the party, and taking up the wager, went through the petition without faltering. It was, indeed, a sad parody on prayer to hear its blessed accents fall perfectly from such lips on a bet; but when it was won, the slaver insisted on receiving *the slave which was the stake,* and immediately bestowed him in charity on a captain who had fallen into the clutches of a British cruiser!

"Such is a rude sketch of the great man-merchant of Africa, the Rothschild of slavery, whose bills on England, France, or the United States, were as good as gold in Sierra Leone and Monrovia!"

The great slave-mart of Gallinas has since been destroyed by the colonists and cruisers, as narrated in a subsequent chapter.

CHAPTER XIX.

Operations of the Cruisers under the Ashburton Treaty.

The American Squadrons from 1847 to 1851.—More captures.—U. S. brig Perry—cruises
off the southern coast.—Capture of a slaver with 800 slaves, by an English cruiser.—
Abuses of the American flag.—The Lucy Ann captured.—Case of the Navarre.—Capture by the Perry of the Martha of New York—her condemnation.—Case of the
Chatsworth—of the Louisa Beaton.—The Chatsworth seized and sent to Baltimore—
is condemned as a slaver.—State of the slave-trade on the southern coast.—Importance of the squadron.—The Brazilian slave-trade diminishes.

WE now return to the operations of the American cruisers. In 1847, the
sloop-of-war Jamestown proceeded to the African station, under Commodore
Bolton, and the frigate United States was relieved. The year following, the
commodore was relieved by the Yorktown, Commodore Cooper. In 1849, the
squadron was assigned to Commodore Gregory, and consisted of the sloops-of-
war Portsmouth, John Adams, Dale, Yorktown, and the brigs Bainbridge,
Porpoise and Perry. Three or four slavers were captured, and the entire
coast closely watched.

In 1851, the Germantown, Commodore Lavalette, relieved Commodore
Gregory. He made an active cruise for two years, when the frigate Constitution, Commodore Mayo, arrived to take command of the squadron, consisting of the sloops-of-war Marion and Dale and the brig Perry.

Of these squadrons, that of 1850 and 1851 contributed largely toward suppressing the trade and the abuses of the American flag. The efficient commander of the Perry, Andrew H. Foote, in his work entitled "Africa and the
American Flag," published in 1854, has given the results of his cruising operations on the southern coast, a region seldom before visited by American
cruisers. We are also indebted to his work for reliable information in regard
to Liberia, the Maryland Colony, and other subjects connected with Africa.

The object of the cruise was "to protect the lawful commerce of the United
States, and to prevent the flag and citizens thereof from being engaged in
the slave-trade, to carry out in good faith the treaty stipulations with England,
and to act in concert with British cruisers, so far as instructions permitted."

Information was received at Benguela, that five days previous to the arrival
of the Perry, an English cruiser had captured, near this place, a brig, with
eight hundred slaves on board. In this case, it appeared that the vessel came
from Rio de Janeiro, under American colors and papers, with an American
captain and crew; and had been, when on the coast, transferred to a Brazilian captain and crew, the Americans having gone on shore with the papers.
The captured slaver was sent to the island of St. Helena for adjudication.

After remaining three days at Benguela, where neither fresh water nor provisions could be procured, the Perry weighed anchor and ran down the coast,
examining all intermediate points and boarding several vessels during the

passage to Loanda. This city is the capital of Loango, and the most flourishing of the Portuguese establishments on the African coast.

In a letter announcing the arrival of the vessel, and her reception by the authorities, the Navy Department was informed that an English steamer had arrived, having recently captured a slaver, the bark Navarre, which had sailed from Rio de Janeiro to St. Catharine's, where she had fitted up for a slave cargo, and received a Brazilian captain and crew. When boarded by the English steamer, the slaver had American colors flying; and on being told by the commander that her papers were forged, and yet that he could not search the vessel, but must send her to an American cruiser, the captain then ordered the American colors to be hauled down, and the Brazilian to be hoisted, declaring that she was Brazilian property, sent the Brazilian captain and crew on deck, and gave up the vessel.

The commander of the Perry also informed the Navy Department that, soon after his arrival at Loanda, he had received from various sources information of the abuse of the American flag in connection with the slave-trade; and inclosed copies of letters and papers addressed to him by the British commissioner, and the commander of an English cruiser, which gave authentic information on the subject.

He suggested that as the legitimate commerce of the United States exceeded that of Great Britain and France, on the coast south of the equator, and the American flag had been used to cover the most extensive slave-trade, it would seem that the presence of one or two men-of-war, and the appointment of a consul, or some public functionary at that place, were desirable.

In reference to vessels ostensibly American, which had been engaged in the slave-trade, a British officer, on the 21st of March, 1850, in a letter inclosing a list of American vessels which had been boarded by the cruiser under his command, stated that all the vessels had afterwards taken slaves from the coast, and, with the exception of the "Lucy Ann,"* captured with five hundred slaves on board by a British steamer, had escaped. The registers, or sea-letters, of these vessels appeared to be genuine; and he being unable to detect any inaccuracies in their papers, his duty to the American flag had ceased. The vessels in his list had been boarded by himself; but the senior officer of the division was referred to, "who could give a list of many more, all of which would have been good prizes to an officer having the right of search;" for he was well assured that they went over to that coast, fully fitted and equipped for the slave-trade.

On the 25th of March, the commander requested the English captain to

---

* The "Lucy Ann," when captured, was boarded fifty or sixty miles to leeward, or north of Loanda. She had an American flag flying, although her papers had been deposited in the consul's office at Rio. The English boarding officer, who was not allowed to see any papers, suspecting her character, prolonged his visit for some time. As he was about leaving the vessel, a cry or stifled groan was heard issuing from the hold. The main hatches were apparently forced up from below, although a boat was placed over them, and the heads of many people appeared. Five hundred and forty-seven slaves were found in the hold, almost in a state of suffocation. The master then hauled down the American flag, declared the vessel to be Brazilian, and gave her up.

give him a detailed account of the circumstances attending the capture of the bark Navarre, by her B. M. steamer Fire Fly.

He asked for this information, as the Navarre was boarded when under American colors, although displaying Brazilian colors when captured.

In reply, the English captain informed him that the slave bark Navarre, seized under the Brazilian flag, on the 19th instant, had the American ensign flying at the time she was boarded. The boarding officer having doubts of her nationality, in consequence of her papers not appearing to be regular, he himself, although ill at the time, considered it his duty to go on board, when, being convinced that her papers were false, he informed the person calling himself master of her, that it was his duty to send him to the American squadron, or in the event of not falling in with them, to New York. The master immediately went on deck and ordered the mate to haul down the American ensign—to throw it overboard—and to hoist their proper colors. The American ensign was hauled down and thrown overboard by the mate, who immediately hoisted the Brazilian ensign. A man then came on deck from below, saying that he was captain of the vessel; that she was Brazilian property, and fully fitted for the slave-trade; which the person who first appeared acknowledged, stating that he himself was a Brazilian subject. Having obtained this from them in writing, the person who first called himself captain having signed it, and having had the signing of the document witnessed by two officers, he opened her hatches, found all the Brazilian crew below, slave-deck laid, water filled, provisions for the slaves, and slave-shackles.

On the 6th of June, 1850, at three o'clock in the afternoon, a large ship with two tiers of painted ports was made to windward, standing in for the land toward Ambriz. At four o'clock the chase was overhauled, having the name " Martha, New York," registered on her stern. The Perry had no colors flying. The ship, when in range of the guns, hoisted the American ensign, shortened sail, and backed her main-topsail. The first lieutenant, Mr. Rush, was sent to board her. As he was rounding her stern, the people on board observed, by the uniform of the boarding officer, that the vessel was an American cruiser. The ship then hauled down the American, and hoisted Brazilian colors. The officer went on board, and asked for papers and other proofs of nationality. The captain denied having papers, log, or any thing else. At this time something was thrown overboard, when another boat was sent from the Perry, and picked up the writing-desk of the captain, containing sundry papers and letters, identifying the captain as an American citizen; also indicating the owner of three-fifths of the vessel to be an American merchant, resident in Rio de Janeiro. After obtaining satisfactory proof that the ship Martha was a slaver, she was seized as a prize.

The captain at length admitted that the ship was fully equipped for the slave-trade. There were found on board the vessel one hundred and seventy-six casks filled with water, containing from one hundred to one hundred and fifty gallons each; one hundred and fifty barrels of farina for slave-food; several sacks of beans; slave-deck laid; four iron boilers for cooking slave-provisions; iron bars, with the necessary wood-work, for securing slaves to the deck; four hundred spoons for feeding them; between thirty and forty muskets, and a written agreement between the owner and captain, with the receipt of the owner for two thousand milreis.

There being thirty-five persons on board this prize, many of whom were foreigners, it was deemed necessary to send a force of twenty-five men, with the first and second lieutenants, that the prize might be safely conducted to New York, for which place she took her departure that evening.

Soon after the Martha was discovered, she passed within hailing distance of an American brig, several miles ahead of the Perry, and asked the name of the cruiser astern; on being told, the captain, in despair, threw his trumpet on deck. But on a moment's reflection, as he afterwards stated, he concluded, notwithstanding, that she must be an English cruiser, not only from her appearance, but from the knowledge that the Perry had left for Porto Praya, and could not in the mean time have returned to that part of the coast. Therefore, finding when within gun-shot of the vessel, that he could not escape, and must show his colors, ran up the American ensign, intending under his nationality to avoid search and capture. The boarding-officer was received at the gangway by a Brazilian captain, who strongly insisted that the vessel was Brazilian property. But the officer, agreeably to an order received on leaving the Perry, to hold the ship to the nationality first indicated by her colors, proceeded in the search. In the mean time, the American captain, notwithstanding his guise as a sailor, being identified by another officer, was sent on board the Perry. He claimed that the vessel could not lawfully be subjected to search by an American man-of-war, while under Brazilian colors. But on being informed that he would be seized as a pirate for sailing without papers, even were he not a slaver, he admitted that she was on a slaving voyage; adding, that had he not fallen in with the Perry, he would, during the night, have shipped *eighteen hundred slaves*, and before daylight in the morning been clear of the coast.

Possession was immediately taken of the Martha, her crew put in irons, and both American and Brazilian captains, together with three or four cabin passengers, (probably slave-agents,) were given to understand that they would be similarly served, in case of the slightest evidence of insubordination. The accounts of the prize crew were transferred, the vessel provisioned, and in twenty-four hours after her capture, the vessels exchanged three cheers, and the Martha bore away for New York.

She was condemned in the U. S. District Cou t. The captain was admitted to bail for the sum of five thousand dollars, which was afterwards reduced to three thousand: he then escaped justice by its forfeiture. The American mate was sentenced to the penitentiary for the term of two years; and the foreigners, who had been sent to the United States on account of the moral effect, being regarded as beyond our jurisdiction, were discharged.

The writing-desk thrown overboard from the Martha, soon after she was boarded, contained sundry papers, making curious revelations of the agency of some American citizens engaged in the slave-trade. These papers implicated a number of persons who are little suspected of ever having participated in such a diabolical traffic.

After parting company with the Martha, the Perry proceeded to Loanda, and found English, French, and Portuguese men-of-war in port. The John Adams, having exhausted her provisions, had sailed for the north coast, after having had the good fortune to *capture a slaver*. The British commissioner called aboard, and offered his congratulations on the capture of the Martha, remarking that she was the largest slaver that had been on the coast for many years; and the effect of sending all hands found in her to the United States, would prove a severe blow to the iniquitous traffic. The British cruisers, after the capture of a vessel, were in the practice of landing the slave-crews, except when they are British subjects, at some point on the coast. This is believed to be required by the governments with which Great Britain has formed treaties.

On boarding traders, the masters, in one or two instances, when sailing under a foreign flag, had requested the boarding-officer to search, and, after ascertaining her real character, to indorse the register. This elicited the following order to the boarding officer :

"If a vessel hoists the American flag; is of American build; has her name and place of ownership in the United States registered on her stern; or if she has but part of these indications of American nationality, you will, on boarding, ask for her papers, which papers you will examine and retain, if she excites suspicion of being a slaver, until you have searched sufficiently to satisfy yourself of her real character. Should the vessel be American, and doubts exist of her real character, you will bring her to this vessel; or, if it can be done more expeditiously, you will dispatch one of your boats, communicating such information as will enable the commander to give specific directions, or in person to visit the suspected vessel.

"If the strange vessel be a foreigner, you will, on ascertaining the fact, leave her; declining, even at the request of the captain, to search the vessel, or to indorse her character, as it must always be borne in mind that our government does not permit the detention and search of American vessels by foreign cruisers; and, consequently, is scrupulous in observing towards the vessels of other nations the same line of conduct which she exacts from foreign cruisers towards her own vessels."

On the 18th of August, the captain of an English cruiser entered Loanda with his boat, leaving the vessel outside, bringing the information that a suspected American trader was at Ambriz. The captain stated that he had boarded her, supposing she might be a Brazilian, but on ascertaining her nationality, had left her, and proceeded to Loanda for the purpose of communicating what had transpired.

On receiving this information, the commodore ordered the Perry to proceed to Ambriz and search the vessel, and in case she was suspected of being engaged in the slave-trade, to bring her to Loanda. In the meantime, a lieutenant who was about leaving the squadron as bearer of dispatches to the government, volunteered his services to take the launch and proceed immediately to Ambriz, as the Perry had sails to bend, and make other preparations previous to leaving. The launch was dispatched, and in five hours afterwards the Perry sailed. Arriving on the following morning within twelve miles of Ambriz, the commander, accompanied by the purser and the surgeon, who volunteered their services, pulled for the suspected vessel, which proved to be the American brigantine "Chatsworth," of Baltimore. The lieutenant, with his launch's crew, was on board. He had secured the papers and commenced the search. After taking the dimensions of the vessel, which corresponded to those noted in the register, examining and comparing the cargo with the manifest, scrutinizing the crew list, consular certificate, port clearance, and other papers on board, possession was taken of the Chatsworth, and the boarding officer directed to proceed with her, in company with the Perry, to Loanda.

Both vessels having arrived, a letter to the following purport was addressed to the commodore : "One hundred bags of farina, a large quantity of plank, sufficient to lay a slave-deck, casks and barrels of spirits, in sufficient quantity to contain water for a large slave-cargo, jerked beef, and other articles, were found on board the Chatsworth. These articles, and others on board, corresponded generally with the manifest, which paper was drawn up in the Portuguese language. A paper with the consular seal, authorizing the shipment of the crew, all foreigners, was also made out in the Portuguese language. In the register, the vessel was called a brig, instead of a brigantine. A letter of instructions from the reputed owner, a citizen of Baltimore, directed the American captain to leave the vessel whenever he should be directed to do so by the Italian supercargo. These, together with the report that the vessel on her last voyage had shipped a cargo of slaves, and her now being at the most notorious slave-station on the coast, impressed the commander of the Perry so strongly with the belief that the Chatsworth was a slaver, that he considered it his duty to direct the boarding officer to take her in charge, and proceed in company with the Perry to Loanda, that the case might undergo a more critical examination by the commander-in-chief."

The commodore, after visiting the Chatsworth in person, although morally certain she was a slaver, yet as the evidence which would be required in the United States courts essential to her condemnation, was wanting, conceived it to be his duty to order the commander of the Perry to surrender the charge of that vessel, and return all the papers to her master, and withdraw his guard from her.

The Chatsworth still in port, and suspected of the intention of shipping a cargo of slaves at Ambriz, the Perry sailed, the day on which her orders were received, without giving any intimation as to her cruising-ground. When outside of the harbor, the vessel was hauled on a wind to the southward, as if bound up the coast, and continued beating until out of sight of the vessels in the harbor. She was then kept away to the northward, making a course for Ambriz, in anticipation of the Chatsworth's soon sailing for that place.

The cruising with the English men-of-war was resumed. A few days after leaving Loanda, when trying the sailing qualities of the vessel with a British cruiser, a sail was reported, standing down the land towards Ambriz. Chase was immediately made, and, on coming within gun-shot, a gun was fired to bring the vessel to. She was then boarded, and again searched, without finding any additional proof against the vessel's character.

On returning towards Ambriz, soon after, the steamer Cyclops, with another British cruiser, was observed; and also the Chatsworth, with an American brigantine lying near her. A boat from the Cyclops, with an English officer, pulled out several miles, while the Perry was in the offing, bringing a packet of letters and papers marked as usual, " On Her Britanic Majesty's Service." These papers were accompanied by a private note from the British commander of the division, expressing great regret at the occurrence, which was officially noticed in the accompanying papers, and the earnest desire to repair the wrong.

The official papers were dated September the ninth, and contained statements relating to the *chasing, boarding* and *detention* of the American brigantine Louisa Beaton, on the seventh and eighth instant.

The particulars of the seizure of the vessel were given in a letter from the commander of the English cruiser Dolphin, directed to the British commander of the division, as follows : " I have the honor to inform you, that at daylight on the 7th instant, being about seventy miles off the land, a sail was observed on the lee bow, while her majesty's brigantine, under my command, was steering to the eastward. I made all possible sail in chase : the chase was observed making more sail and keeping away. Owing to light winds, I was unable to overtake her before 0h. 30m. a. m. When close to her and no sail shortened, I directed a signal gun to be fired abeam, and hailed the chase to shorten sail and heave to. Chase asserted he could not, and requested leave to pass to leeward; saying, if we wanted to board him, we had better make haste about it, and that ' we might fire and be damned.'

" I directed another gun to be fired across her bows, when she immediately shortened sail and hove to : it being night, no colors were observed flying on board the chase, nor was I aware of her character.

" I was proceeding myself to board her, when she bore up again with the apparent intention of escaping. I was therefore again compelled to hoist the boat up and to close her under sail. I reached the chase on the second attempt, and found her to be the American brig Louisa Beaton. The master produced an American register, with a transfer of masters; this gave rise to a doubt of the authenticity of the paper, and on requesting further information, the master refused to give me any, and declined showing me his port clearance, crew-list, or log-book.

" The lieutenant who accompanied me identified the mate as having been in charge of the slave-brig Lucy Ann, captured by her majesty's steam-sloop Rattler. Under these suspicious circumstances, I considered it my duty, as the Louisa Beaton was bound to Ambriz, to place an officer and crew on board of her, so as to confer with an American officer, or yourself, before allowing her, if a legal trader, to proceed on her voyage."

The British commander of the division, in his letter, stated, that immediately on the arrival of the vessels, he proceeded with the commander of the Dolphin and the lieutenant of the Rattler to the brigantine Louisa Beaton. Her master then presented the register, and also the transfer of masters made in Rio, but refused to show any other documents.

On examining the register, and having met the vessel before on that coast, he decided that the Louisa Beaton's nationality was perfect; but that the conduct pursued by her master, in withholding documents that should have been produced on boarding, had led to the unfortunate detention of the vessel.

The British commander further stated, that he informed the master of the Louisa Beaton that he would immediately order his vessel to be released, and that on falling in with the commander of the Perry, all due inquiry into the matter for his satisfaction should be made; but that the master positively refused to take charge again, stating that he would immediately abandon the vessel on the Dolphin's crew quitting her; and, further, requested that the vessel might be brought before the American commander.

That, as much valuable property might be sacrificed should the master carry his threat into execution, he proceeded in search of the Perry, that the case might be brought under consideration while the Dolphin was present; and on arriving at Ambriz, the cutter of the Perry was found in charge of one of her officers.

On the following morning, as he stated, accompanied by the officer in charge of the Perry's cutter, and the commander of the Dolphin, he proceeded to the Louisa Beaton, and informed her master that the detention of his vessel arose from the refusal, on his part, to show the proper documents to the boarding-officer, authorizing him to navigate the vessel in those seas; and from his mate having been identified by one of the Dolphin's officers as having been captured in charge of a vessel having on board five hundred and forty-seven slaves, which attempted to evade search and capture by displaying the American ensign; as well as from his own suspicious manœuvering in the chase. But as he was persuaded that the Louisa Beaton was an American vessel, and her papers good, although a most important document was wanting, namely, the *sea-letter*, usually given by consular officers to legal traders after the *transfer of masters*, he should direct the commander of the Dolphin to resign the charge of the Louisa Beaton, which was accordingly done; and, that on meeting the commander of the Perry, he would lay the case before him; and was ready, if he demanded it, to give any remuneration or satisfaction, on the part of the commander of the Dolphin, for the unfortunate detention of the Louisa Beaton, whether engaged in *legal or illegal trade*, that the master might in fairness demand, and the commander of the Perry approve.

After expressing great regret at the occurrence, the British commander stated that he was requested by the captain of the Dolphin to assure the commander of the Perry, that no disrespect was intended to the flag of the United

States, or even interference, on his part, with traders of America, be they legal or illegal; but the stubbornness of the master, and the identifying of one of his mates as having been captured in a Brazilian vessel, trying to evade detection by the display of the American flag, had led to the mistake.

A postscript to the letter added, "I beg to state that the hatches of the Louisa Beaton have not been opened, nor the vessel or crew in any way examined."

On the Perry's reaching the anchorage, the Louisa Beaton was examined. The affidavit of the master, which differs not materially from the statements of the British officers, was taken. A letter by the commander of the Perry was then addressed to the British officer, stating that he had in person visited the Louisa Beaton, conferred with her master, taken his affidavit, examined her papers, and found her to be in all respects a legal American trader. That the *sea-letter*, which had been referred to, as being usually given by consular officers, was only required when the vessel changes owners, and not, as in the present case, on the appointment of a new master. The paper given by the consul authorizing the appointment of the present master, was, with the remainder of the vessel's papers, strictly in form.

The commander also stated that he respectfully declined being a party concerned in any arrangement of a pecuniary nature, as satisfaction to the master of the Louisa Beaton, for the detention and seizure of his vessel, and if such arrangement was made between the British officers and the master of the Louisa Beaton, it would be his duty to give the information to his government.

The commander added, that the government of the United States did not acknowledge a right in any other nation to visit and detain the vessels of American citizens engaged in commerce : that whenever a foreign cruiser should venture to board a vessel under the flag of the United States, she would do it upon her own responsibility for all consequences : that if the vessel so boarded should prove to be American, the injured party would be left to such redress, either in the tribunals of England, or by an appeal to his own country, as the nature of the case might require.

He also stated that he had carefully considered all the points in the several communications which the commander of the British division had sent him, in relation to the seizure of the Louisa Beaton, and he must unqualifiedly pronounce the seizure and detention of that vessel wholly unauthorized by the circumstances, and contrary both to the letter and the spirit of the eighth article of the treaty of Washington; and that it became his duty to make a full report of the case, accompanied with the communications which the British commander had forwarded, together with the affidavit of the master of the Louisa Beaton, to the government of the United States.

This letter closed the correspondence.

The British commander-in-chief then accompanied the commander of the Perry to the Louisa Beaton, and there wholly disavowed the act of the commander of the Dolphin, stating, in the name of that officer, that he begged pardon of the master, and that he would do anything in his power to repair the wrong; adding, "I could say no more, if I had knocked you down."

The Louisa Beaton was then delivered over to the charge of her own master, and the officer of the cutter took his station alongside of the Chatsworth.

On the 11th of September this brigantine was seized as a slaver. During the correspondence with the British officers in relation to the Louisa Beaton, an order was given to the officer of the cutter to prevent the Chatsworth from landing the remaining part of her cargo. The master immediately called on board the Perry with the complaint that his vessel had been seized on a former occasion, and afterwards released by the commodore, with the indorsement of her nationality on the log-book. Since then she had been repeatedly searched, and now was prevented from disposing of her cargo; he wished, therefore, that a definite decision might be made. A decision was made by the instant seizure of the vessel.

Information from the master of the Louisa Beaton, that the owner of the Chatsworth had in Rio acknowledged to him that the vessel had shipped a cargo of slaves on her last voyage, and was then proceeding to the coast for a similar purpose—superadded to her suspicious movements, and the importance of breaking up this line of ostensible traders, but real slavers, running between the coasts of Brazil and Africa—were the reasons leading to this decision.

On announcing the decision to the master of the Chatsworth, a prize crew was immediately sent on board and took charge of the vessel. The master and supercargo then drew up a protest challenging the act as illegal, and claiming the sum of fifteen thousand dollars for damages. The supercargo, on presenting this protest, remarked that the United States Court would certainly release the vessel; and the *procuro* of the owner, with other parties interested, would then look to the captor for the amount of damages awarded. The commander replied, that he fully appreciated the pecuniary responsibility attached to this proceeding.

The master of the Louisa Beaton, soon after the supercargo of the Chatsworth had presented the protest, went on shore for the purpose of having an interview with him, and not coming off at the time specified, apprehensions were entertained that the slave-factors had revenged themselves for his additional information—leading to the seizure of the Chatsworth. At nine o'clock in the evening, three boats were manned and armed, containing thirty officers and men—leaving the Perry in charge of one of the lieutenants. When two of the boats had left the vessel, and the third was in readiness to follow, the master of the Louisa Beaton made his appearance, stating that his reception on shore had been anything but pacific. Had the apprehensions entertained proved correct, it was the intention to have landed and taken possession of the town; and then to have marched out to the barracoons, liberated the slaves, and made, at least for the time being, "free soil" of that section of country.

In a letter to the commodore, dated September 14th, information was given to the following purport:

"Inclosed are affidavits, with other papers and letters, in relation to the

23

seizure of the American brigantine Chatsworth. This has been an exceedingly complicated case, as relating to a slaver with two sets of papers, passing alternately under different nationalities, eluding detection from papers being in form, and trading with an assorted cargo.

"The Chatsworth has been twice boarded and searched by the commander, and on leaving for a short cruise off Ambrizette, a boat was dispatched with orders to watch her movements during the absence of the Perry. On returning from Ambrizette, additional evidence of her being a slaver was procured. Since then the affidavits of the master of the Chatsworth and the mate of the Louisa Beaton have been obtained, leading to further developments, until the guilt of the vessel, as will be seen by the accompanying papers, is placed beyond all question."

The Italian supercargo, having landed most of the cargo, and his business being in a state requiring his presence, was permitted to go on shore, with the assurance that he would return when a signal was made. He afterwards came within hail of the Chatsworth, and finding that such strong proofs against the vessel were obtained, he declined going on board, acknowledging to the master of the Louisa Beaton that he had brought over Brazilian papers.

The crew of the Chatsworth being foreigners, and not wishing to be sent to the United States, were landed at Ambriz, where it was reported that the barracoons contained four thousand slaves, ready for shipment; and where, it was said, the capture of the Chatsworth, as far as the American flag was concerned, would give a severe and unexpected blow to the slave-trade.

After several unsuccessful attempts to induce the supercargo of the Chatsworth to come off to that vessel, a note in French was received from him, stating that he was "an Italian, and as such could not be owner of the American brig Chatsworth, which had been seized, it is true, but unjustly, and against the laws of all civilized nations. That the owner of the said brig would know how to defend his property, and in case the judgment should not prove favorable, the one who had been the cause of it would always bear the remorse of having ruined his countryman."

After making the necessary preliminary arrangements, the master, with a midshipman aud ten men, was placed in charge of the Chatsworth; and on the 14th of September, the following order was sent to the commanding officer of the prize: "You will proceed to Baltimore, and there report yourself to the commander of the naval station, and to the Secretary of the Navy. You will be prepared, on your arrival, to deliver up the vessel to the United States marshal, the papers to the judge of the United States District Court, and be ready to act in the case of the Chatsworth as your orders and circumstances may require."

After a protracted trial, the Chatsworth was at length condemned as a slaver, in the U. S. District Court of Maryland.

After a trip to St. Helena and the Cape de Verds, the Perry again proceeded to the south coast. She anchored in Loango, and the commander addressed a letter to the British commodore, April 4, 1851, asking whether any suspected vessels had been seen on the south coast; also requesting his views of the present state of the slave-trade on the coast. In reply, the commodore writes:

"On the second subject, my view of the present state of the slave-trade on the south coast: It is formed on my own observations of the line of coast from Cape St. Paul's to this port, and from the reports which I have received from the captains of the divisions, and the commanders of the cruisers under my orders, as well as from other well-informed persons on whom I can rely, that it has never been in a more depressed state, a state almost amounting to suppression; and that this arises from the active exertions of her majesty's squadron on both sides of the Atlantic, and the cordial coöperation which has been established between the cruisers of Great Britain and the United States on this coast, to carry out the intention of the Washington treaty; and latterly from the new measures of the Brazilian government.

"Factories have been broken up at Lagos, in the Congo, and at Ambriz; although of this I need hardly speak, because your own observation during the past year must satisfy you of the present state of depression there.

"The commencement of last year was marked by an unusual number of captures by her majesty's cruisers, both in the bights and on the south coast, and also by those by the cruisers of the United States. This year, the capture of only one vessel equipped in the bights, and one with slaves (a transferred Sardinian,) on the south coast, have been reported to me—a striking proof of my view.

"The desperate measures also adopted by the slave-dealers in the last few months to get rid of their slaves by the employment of small vessels, formerly engaged in the legal and coasting trade, as marked by the capture of several (named) slavers, prove the difficulty to which they have been driven.

"The barracoons, however, along the whole line of coast, are still reported to me to contain a great number of slaves, to ship whom, I have little doubt further attempts will be made.

"Most satisfactory, on the whole, as this state of things may be considered, still I hope it will not lead to any immediate relaxation either of our efforts or of our coöperation; but that a vigilance will be observed for a time sufficient to enable a legal trade to replace the uprooted slave-traffic, and to disperse the machinery (I may say) of the merchants connected with it, and prevent any resumption of it by them."

In answer to the charge frequently made that the American squadron had been unsuccessful in their efforts to prevent the slave-trade, commander Foote replies that "it has been shown that the African squadrons, instead of being useless, have rendered *essential service*. For much as colonization has accomplished, and effectual as Liberia is in suppressing the slave-traffic within her own jurisdiction, these means and these results have been established and secured by the presence and protection of the naval squadrons of Great Britain, France, and the United States. And had no such assistance been rendered, the entire coast, where we now see legal trade and advancing civiliza-

tion, would have been at this day, in spite of any efforts to colonize, or to establish legal commerce, the scene of unchecked, lawless slave-trade piracy.

"Strange and frightful maladies have been engendered by the cruelties perpetrated within the hold of a slaver. If any disease affecting the human constitution were brought there, we may be sure that it would be nursed into mortal vigor in these receptacles of filth, corruption and despair. Crews have
been known to die by the fruit of their own crime, and leave ships almost helpless. They have carried the scourge with them. The coast fever of Africa,
bad enough where it has its birth, came in these vessels, and has assumed perhaps a permanent abode in the western regions of the world. No fairer sky
or healthier climate were there on earth, than in the beautiful bay, and amid
the grand and picturesque scenery of Rio de Janeiro, in Brazil. But it became a haunt of slavers, and the dead of Africa floated on the glittering waters, and were tumbled upon the sands of its harbor. The shipping found, in
the hot summer of 1849, that death had come with the slavers. Thirty or forty
vessels were lying idly at their anchors, for their crews had mostly perished.
The pestilence swept along the coast of that empire with fearful malignity.

"Cuba for the same crime met the same retribution. Cargoes of slaves
were landed to die, and brought the source of their mortality ashore, vigorous
and deadly. The fever settled there in the beginning of 1853, and came to
our country, as summer approached, in merchant vessels from the West Indies.
At New Orleans, Mobile, and other places it spread desolation, over which the
country mourned. Let it be remembered that it is never even safe to disregard crime.

"Civilized governments are now very generally united in measures for the
suppression of the slave-trade. The coast of Africa itself is rapidly closing
against it. The American and English colonies secure a vast extent of sea-
coast against its revival. Christian missions, at many points, are inculcating
the doctrines of divine truth, which, by its power upon the hearts of men, is
the antagonist of such cruel unrighteousness.

"The increase of commerce, and the advance of Christian civilization, will
undoubtedly, at no distant date, render a naval force for the suppression of
the African slave-trade unnecessary; but no power having extensive commerce
ought ever to overlook the necessity of a naval force on that coast. The Secretary of the Navy, it is to be hoped, has, in his recent report, settled the
question as to the continuance of the African squadron.

"The increasing influence of Liberia and Cape Palmas will prove a powerful protection everywhere. With them Sierra Leone will unite in feeling and
purposes. Their policy will always be the same. It must necessarily happen
that a close political relationship in interests and feelings will unite them all
in one system of action. Their policy will be that of uncompromising hostility to the slave-trade."

The pestilence which swept the coast of Brazil in 1849, had its effect in inducing the government to adopt more vigorous efforts to put down the slave-
trade. In September, 1850, a law was passed declaring the slave-trade piracy,

and several vessels were afterwards captured by the Brazilian men-of-war. According to a report of the Brazilian government, there were 60,000 slaves imported from Africa in 1848, 54,000 in 1849. In 1851, the number had been reduced to 3,287, of which 1,006 were captured by a Brazilian cruiser; and in 1852 but one slave vessel is known to have landed on the coast.

Cuba is still the great mart of the slave-trade, as appears by the occasional capture of slavers bound for that island. Witness the statements of the captain of a captured vessel, as given in the following letter, dated Jamaica, April 23, 1857 : "The newspapers which I send you will inform you of the slaver captured by the Arab off the coast of Cuba. On the day of her arrival, after the landing of her wretched cargo, I paid a visit to the vessel, and thus witnessed the horrible manner in which the negroes had been stowed. The slave deck was exactly two feet six inches in height, in a vessel of one hundred and fifty tons, and water casks were stowed beneath. Is it any wonder that out of five hundred human beings, one hundred and thirty-eight, including those the brutal captain shot, should have died in a passage of fifty-three days from Africa? Forty died in one day between Cuba and St. Ann's Bay, on this island, showing at what fearful rate the mortality was increasing. When captured, they had but one biscuit to each person on board.

"The captain states that he has run nine successful cargoes, and been captured six times, and that he has lost £6,000 by this trip, but he does not mind it, as, if he had succeeded in landing the cargo, he would have received £37,000 for the adventure. What mercantile speculation can compete with this hellish traffic? and is it any wonder that Spain has been cursed beyond all the nations upon the earth?

"On landing at Fort Augusta, where the slaves are kept until they recruit, I never saw such a picture of woe. In a large room, nearly twice the size of the slaver, were three hundred and twenty-two young men and boys, and in an adjoining one more than forty women and girls, all naked living spectres, with wasted limbs, and thighs about the circumference of a large walking-stick—in fact, mere skin and bone, eaten up with scurvy and the itch. Yet, strange to say, on a black soldier informing them that they were free, their eyes danced with delight, and with feeble strength they clapped their emaciated hands and shouted for joy. When their food was distributed, the whip had of necessity to be used, to save the weakest from being crushed to death in the scramble, so ravenously hungry were they.

"Although the room in which they were placed is so much larger than the vessel, I could scarcely walk amongst them, as they occupied the whole space, and it seems impossible that they could have been packed in the slave deck. It is stated that each individual had to sit down with wide extended legs, and another was then stowed in, and so on until the vessel was full; and thus they remained, with the rare exception of being aired in detachments, for the space of fifty-four days."

CHAPTER XX.

Historical Sketch of Sierra Leone and Liberia.

Colony of Sierra Leone founded by the English, 1787.—Free negroes colonized.—Present extent and condition of the colony.—Establishment of English factories on the slave coast.—Treaties with the African chiefs.—Scheme of African Colonization agitated in 1783—by Jefferson and others.—Movements in Va., in 1800 and 1805.—Formation of the American Colonization Society in 1816.—Its object " to colonize the free people of color."—Cape Mesurado purchased and colonized in 1821.—Defense of the infant settlement from an attack by the natives.—Mortality among the early settlers.—Increase of the colony in 1835.—State colonization societies establish settlements.—Consolidation of the state colonies, and establishment of the Commonwealth.—Governor Buchanan's efforts to suppress the slave-trade.—His death, 1841.—Republic of Liberia established 1847.—Joseph J. Roberts (colored) first President.—Its independence acknowledged by European powers.—The Republic attacks the slave establishments.—Natural resources of Liberia—its climate, soil, productions, exports, schools, churches, &c.—Settlements and population.—The Maryland settlement at Cape Palmas.

IN connection with the subject of the slave-trade, the English and American colonies deserve notice. Sierra Leone was founded by the English, May 9th, 1787, as a colony for free negroes. At the close of the American war, several hundred were discharged from the army and navy, and were wandering about in a desolate condition. There were others who had gained their freedom under the decision of Lord Mansfield. Granville Sharp had noticed the condition of these negroes in the streets of London, and formed the plan of transporting them to Africa. He obtained the aid of government, and in the year mentioned about four hundred were landed upon a district purchased of the king of Sierra Leone. In 1792, about twelve hundred more were landed from Nova Scotia. These last were those who had been seduced from their masters in the States during the revolutionary war. Some five hundred Maroons from Jamaica, were also sent to the colony a few years afterwards. In 1807, the colony was surrendered to the crown. After the employment of British cruisers on the coast to suppress the slave-trade, the vessels which were captured were taken to the colony and the slaves liberated. They were provided with a daily allowance for the first six months, after which lands were assigned them.

The colony at the present time comprises about 25,000 square miles. The soil is very fertile, growing excellent crops of rice, Indian corn, yams, plantains and cassadas. Many of the West India products have been introduced, and sugar, coffee, indigo, ginger and cotton thrive well. The principal fruits are the cocoa, banana, pine-apples, orange, lime, guava, pomegranate and plum. The annual exports, chiefly to Great Britain, amount to about $500,000. Its population, chiefly of native Africans, is being brought under the influence of religious education, and thus fitted to become an important lever in promoting the civilization of their native regions.

For a distance of twelve hundred miles along the coast from Cape Palmas to the Gaboon, English factories and agents are established, for commercial purposes and for the suppression of the slave-trade. These establishments are supported by the government; and its authorized commissioners enter into negotiations with the powerful chiefs of the interior on the subject of the slave-trade. The Danish ports on the coast have recently been sold to the English. A treaty has been formed with the powerful king of Dahomey, whose chief revenue was derived from incursions against his neighbors and seizing and selling them to the slavers. He had kept an army of men and women trained for the purpose, and his victims numbered about nine thousand annually. An annual stipend from England supplies the deficiency in his revenue, and the trade is abolished in his dominions. Human sacrifices have also been to a great extent abolished in the two great states of Dahomey and Ashantee, and both are opened to missionary influences.

The scheme of colonizing the free people of color was agitated in the United States shortly after the close of the revolutionary war. Dr. Thornton, of Washington, in 1783, suggested the establishment of a colony in Africa. Mr. Jefferson, as secretary of state, made an application to the Sierra Leone company, but without success. The Portuguese government was sounded for the acquisition of territory in South America for the purpose. The legislature of Virginia, in 1800, 1805, and 1816 discussed the subject. The Rev. Dr. Finley, of New Jersey, matured a plan for the purpose, and proceeded to Washington. On the 25th of December, 1816, a meeting was called, over which Henry Clay presided, and Andrew Jackson, William H. Crawford, Dr. Finley and others were elected vice-presidents. The American Colonization Society was formed. "Its objects is, to promote and execute a plan for colonizing, with their consent, the free people of color residing in our country, either in Africa, or such other places as Congress shall deem expedient;" to prepare the way for the interference of the government by proving that a colony can be established and maintained without the opposition of the natives, that an important commerce might be thus established, and the slave-trade in consequence discouraged. The gradual emancipation of slaves, as favored by Jefferson and others in earlier days, was discussed. The work of forming an African nation in Africa, with republican institutions and Christian influences, was commenced.

In 1817, two agents were sent by the society to examine the western coast for a suitable place for a colony. They selected the island of Sherboro, about sixty miles S. S. E. from Sierra Leone, and then sailed for the United States. Mr. Mills, one of the agents, died on the passage.

On the 3d of March, 1819, Congress passed an act by which the President was authorized to restore to their own country any Africans captured from American or foreign vessels attempting to introduce them into the United States; and to provide, by the establishment of a suitable government agency on the coast, for their subsistence and comfort. It was determined to make the site of the government agency, that of the colonial also, and to incorporate into the settlement all the Africans delivered by our men-of-war to the government agent.

Rev. Samuel Bacon was appointed both government and colonial agent; two society's agents were associated with him. In February, 1820, they sailed for the coast of Africa, accompanied by eighty emigrants. They found Sherboro an unhealthy spot; the fever made its appearance among them, and about twenty died, including Mr. Bacon. Lieutenant Townsend, of the sloop-of-war Cyane, which accompanied the emigrant vessel, also died of the fever. After this disastrous attempt, Sherboro was abandoned, and the emigrants removed to Sierra Leone.

In 1821, Cape Mesurado, with a large tract of country, was purchased of the native chiefs. Mr. Jehudi Ashmun took charge of the colony in 1822, previous to which forty more emigrants had been sent out. For more than six years this able man devoted all his powers to the establishment of the colony on a firm foundation. His defense of the infant settlement in November and December, 1822, against the united forces of the natives, exhibited great courage and talent.

"On the 11th November the attack was commenced by a force of eight hundred warriors. The picket, contrary to orders, had left their station in advance of the weakest point of defense; the native force, already in motion, followed close in the rear of the picket, and as soon as the latter had joined the detachment of ten men stationed at the gun, the enemy, presenting a front, opened their fire, and rushed forward to seize the post; several fell, and off went the others, leaving the gun undischarged. This threw the small reserve in the centre into confusion, and had the enemy followed up their advantage, victory was certain; but such was their avidity for plunder, that they fell upon the booty in the outskirts of the town. This disorded the main body. Mr. Ashmun, who was too ill to move at any distance, was thus enabled, by the assistance of one of the colonists, Rev. Lot Carey, to rally the broken forces of the settlers. The brass field-piece was now brought to bear, and being well served did good execution. A few men, commanded by Elijah Johnson, passed round on the enemy's flank, which increased their consternation, and soon after the front of the enemy began to recoil. The colonists now regained the post which had at first been seized, and instantly brought the long-nine to bear upon the mass of the enemy; eight hundred men were in a solid body, and every shot literally spent itself among them. A savage yell was raised by the enemy, and the colonists were victors.

"In the assault, the colonists, (who numbered but thirty-five capable of bearing arms) had fifteen killed and wounded. It is impossible to estimate the loss of the natives, which must have been very great. An earnest but ineffectual effort was made by the agent to form with the kings a treaty of peace.

"Notwithstanding this disastrous result, the natives determined upon another attack. They collected auxiliaries from all the neighboring tribes who could be induced to join them. The colonists, on the other hand, under Ashmun, the agent, were busily engaged in fortifying themselves for the decisive battle, upon which the fate of the settlement was suspended. On the 2d of December the enemy attacked simultaneously the three sides of the fortifications. The colonists received them with that bravery and determination which the danger of total destruction, in case of defeat, was calculated to inspire. The main body of the enemy being exposed to a galling fire from the battery, both in front and flank, and the assault on the opposite side of the town having been repulsed, a general retreat immediately followed, and the colonists were again victorious.

"Mr. Ashmun received three musket-balls through his clothes; three of the men stationed at one of the guns were dangerously wounded; and not three rounds of ammunition remained after the action. Had a third attack been made, the colony must have been conquered; or had the first attack occurred before the arrival of Mr. Ashmun, it would have been extirpated. But its foundations were now secured by a firm and lasting peace."

Mr. Ashmun, during his administration, made important acquisitions of territory; established schools and built churches; destroyed slave-factories, and made treaties with the natives. In 1828, his health failed, from excessive labors, and he sailed for home in the hope of recruiting it; but died at New Haven on the 25th of August. He found the colony on the brink of ruin—he left it in peace and prosperity.

Dr. Richard Randall was appointed successor to Ashmun, and accompanied by Dr. Mechlin, a colored surgeon, arrived in December, 1828. Dr. Randall died four months after his arrival. The agency devolved upon Mechlin. In 1829, Dr. Anderson was appointed physician and assistant agent, and took with him sixty emigrants. Ninety recaptured slaves were added to the colony about the same time. Dr. Mechlin was induced to return home from ill health, and the government devolved upon Dr. Anderson, who soon afterwards died. A. D. Williams, the vice-agent, filled the vacancy. Five Christian missionaries arrived from Switzerland, and took charge of the schools; and two more emigrant vessels and two missionaries from the United States, had a favorable influence upon the colony. The Liberia Herald was established; and the colonial exports reached the sum of ninety thousand dollars. In 1832, the colonists again took the field and were successful against a combination of the native tribes. In 1834, Rev. J. B. Pinney, as agent, and Dr. Todson, as physician, arrived in the colony, accompanied by nine missionaries. After a short but efficient administration, Dr. Pinney was compelled, from ill health, to retire. Dr. Skinner succeeded him. In 1835, nine vessels arrived from the United States with emigrants, which produced a great sensation among the natives, who supposed that rice had given out in America. Dr. Skinner returned home, suffering from ill health, and the vice-agent, A. D. Williams, took charge of the colony.

Meantime, state societies had been establishing settlements in Liberia. In 1837 there were: Monrovia, under the American colonization society; Bassa Cove, of the New York and Pennsylvania societies; Greenville, of the Mississippi society, and Cape Palmas, of the Maryland society—embracing twelve towns and five thousand emigrants. From this chaotic entanglement of interests and jurisdictions sprung the commonwealth of Liberia, and Thomas H. Buchanan became its governor. The friends of the American Colonization

Society, and of the state societies, had forseen the necessity of a union, and a committee met at Washington City and drew up a common constitution for the colonies. Elisha Whittlesey moved, and the motion was adopted, that no white man should become a landholder in Liberia, and that full rights of citizenship should be enjoyed only by colored men. The American Colonization Society retained the right to veto the acts of the colonial legislature.

In April, 1839, Governor Buchanan landed with the new constitution, which was approved by the Monrovians, and subsequently by the state colonies. He arrived with a large supply of guns and ammunition, furnished by the navy department, and a quantity of agricultural implements and machinery, including a sugar mill.

Governor Buchanan seems to have been indefatigable in his efforts to diminish the slave-trade. His appeals and strong-handed measures had their effect in calling the attention of our government to the abuse of the American flag. He armed the colonists and marched to attack the slave-factories on the coast. He captured the slavers, and liberated the slaves from the barracoons. One of the native tribes attacked an outpost of the colony; they were driven off, and Governor Buchanan promptly marshaled his forces to "carry the war into Africa." For this purpose a force of two hundred effective men, with a field-piece and a body of followers, assembled at Millsburg, on the St. Paul's river. About thirty miles from this, by the air-line, in the swampy depths of the forest, was the point aimed at. Many careful arrangements were necessary to baffle spies, and keep the disaffected at bay during this desperate incursion, which the governor was about to make into the heart of the enemy's country. The fine conception had this redeeming characteristic, that it was quite beyond the enemy's understanding.

"The force left Millsburg on Friday, 27th of March. Swamps and thickets soon obliged him to leave the gun behind. Through heavy rains, drenched and weary, they made their way, without any other resistance, to a bivouac in an old deserted town. Starting at daylight next morning, they forced their way through flooded streams and ponds, 'in mud up to their knees, and water up to the waist.' After a halt at ten o'clock, and three hours' march subsequently, they learnt that the enemy had become aware of their movements, and was watching them. About six miles from their destination, after floundering through the mud of a deep ravine, followed by a weary pull up a long hill, a sharp turn brought them in front of a rude barricade of felled trees. A fire of musketry from it brought to the ground Captain Snetter, of the riflemen, who was in advance of his men. The men made a dash on the enemy so suddenly that soon no body was in front of them. The line moved on without stopping, and met only a straggling fire here and there, as they threaded their narrow path through the bushes in single file. A few men were wounded in this disheartening march. At length those in advance came to a halt before the fortress, and the rear closed up. There the line was extended, and the party advanced in two divisions. The place was a kind of square, palisaded

PLANTATION—COTTON PICKING.

inclosure, having outside cleared patches here and there, intermingled with clumps of brush.

"The assailants were received with a sharp fire from swivels and muskets, which was warmly returned. Buchanan ordered Roberts (afterwards president) to lead a reserved company round from the left, so as to take in reverse the face attacked. This so confounded Gaytumba's garrison that they retreated, leaving everything behind. The hungry colonists became their successors at the simmering cooking-pots. So rapid had the onslaught been, that the second division did not reach in time to take a hand in it. The operation was thus completely successful, with the ultimate loss of only two men.

"The place was burnt, and a lesson given which established beyond all future challenge the power of civilization on that coast. The banks of the St. Paul's river, with its graceful meanderings, palm-covered islands, and glorious basin spreading round into the eastward expanse of the interior, were secured for the habitations of peace and prosperity."

The commonwealth flourished under the administration of Buchanan. Every district was supplied with a free school, and lyceums were established. Alms-houses were erected, with manual labor schools attached. Rules were established for the treatment of apprentices, or recaptured Africans who were not able to take care of themselves.

We are compelled to add the name of Buchanan to the catalogue of victims to the African fever. He died September 3, 1841.

Joseph J. Roberts, a colored man, was his successor as governor of the commonwealth. The early part of his administration was signalized by an expedition far into the interior, for the purpose of making treaties and establishing commercial intercourse. Taking a small number of men with him, he proceeded up the St. Paul's river, visited the Camwood country, about seventy miles inland, and found the forests greatly wasted, and the main source of supply, at that time, about one hundred miles farther back. Kings were visited and relieved of their fears, although not of their wonder, that the "governor should be at that distance from home without engaging in war." The party had left the canoe, and after a circuit round to the eastward, they reached "Captain Sam's" town, one hundred and twenty miles east of Monrovia.

Several kings met with the president in his excursion, with whom a conversation was held, "on the subject of trade, the course and extent of the river, native wars, religion, &c." One, "who was seated in state, on a sofa of raised earth, gave us a hearty shake of the hand, and said he was glad to see us;" adding, "this country be your country, all this people be your countryman, you be first king." This king was informed by the president, "that he and his people must agree to abandon the slave-trade, to discontinue the use of sassy-wood, engage in no war except by permission of the colonial government." On one occasion, "Ballasada, the principal war-man of the Golah tribe, made his appearance; he entered the gate of the barricade, at the head of some twenty or thirty armed warriors, with drums beating, horns blowing, dressed in a large robe, and stepping with all the majesty of a great monarch." At

Yando's town, arrangements were made for establishing a school. At Gelby, one of the missionaries preached to a large congregation—the king with most of his people being present. The audience was attentive, and, with the king, gave "a nod of the head at almost every word uttered by the interpreter."

At "Captain Sam's town," a place of great trade, they met three strangers from different tribes, anxious to have a question settled, viz: "whether, if they carried their produce to the American settlement for sale, the colonists would beat them, take their property away, and put them in jail." Their intermediate friends had persuaded them that such would be the case, and consequently had themselves, in the meantime, become their agents, and plundered them at discretion. They had, at that time, brought a considerable quantity of produce for sale, and some of them had been kept waiting for many months. All this was fully cleared up to their satisfaction, and great extension of trade was promised. The governor says: "I have traveled considerably in the United States, but have never seen anywhere a more beautiful country than the one passed through, well timbered and watered, and the soil, I venture to assert, equal to any in the world."

In order to obtain exclusive and complete jurisdiction over the territory of Liberia, it was a necessary measure to establish a national independence. The leading men saw the necessity of making the experiment. A constitution was framed, borrowed from that of the United States, and a declaration of independence was drawn up and proclaimed. On the 24th day of August, 1847, the flag of the Republic of Liberia was displayed, and Joseph J. Roberts was elected first president of the republic. England, France, Belgium, Prussia, and Brazil acknowledged its independence. England presented the republic with a man-of-war schooner, with armament and stores complete, and France presented it with a large quantity of arms. Treaties of amity and commerce were formed with both nations.

On the 22d of February, 1849, the French flag steam frigate Penelope, accompanied by another cruiser, arrived at Monrovia. On the following day, the commander, with the officers and two hundred men, landed for the purpose of saluting the flag of the republic. They were received by three uniform companies of Monrovia, in front of Colonel Yates's residence, where three field-pieces had been placed. The procession was then formed and moved up Broad street to the president's house, where the flag-staff, bearing the Liberian colors, was standing. A salute of twenty-one guns was fired from the field-pieces, which was repeated by the French cruisers, and returned by the Liberian guns. Refreshments were provided for the men, and the officers dined with the president.

In March, 1849, several English and French cruisers placed themselves at the disposal of President Roberts for an expedition against the slave establishments at New Sestos. Roberts embarked 400 men in the cruisers, and accompanied by the U. S. sloop-of-war Yorktown, proceeded to the scene of action. Some of the native chiefs had been induced to defend the slavers, but a shell from the French steamer bursting over their heads, the natives made tracks for the jungle. Roberts marched his men upon the barracoons. The defense was abandoned and the buildings fired. The slaves were liberated and New Sestos annexed.

In the north, along the Gallinas river, the slave-trade lingered. President Roberts, by the aid of Mr. Gurney, Lord Ashley, and benevolent individuals in the United States and England, purchased the territory for nine thousand dollars. By the annexation of this territory, and in May, 1852, of the Cassa territory, Liberia virtually extends its dominion over six hundred miles of sea coast, exterminating the slave-trade from near Cape Palmas to Sierra Leone.

Liberia is well watered, and its natural resources are immense. Cotton is indigenous, and yields two crops a year. Coffee thrives well; a single tree at Monrovia yielding thirty pounds at one gathering. Sugar-cane grows in unrivaled luxuriance, and cam-wood in unlimited quantities; red-wood, bar-wood, and other dyes, are likewise plentiful; the oil-palm is abundant; and indigo, caoutchouc, ginger, arrow-root, cocoa, cocoa-nuts, pine-apples, castor-nuts, yams, plantains, bananas, figs, olives, tamarinds, limes, oranges, lemons, &c., may be added to the list of vegetable products, many of which are exported to a greater or less extent. Ivory is easily obtainable; and rich metallic veins also exist. An important export and import trade is now carried on; and a large number of the inhabitants of the interior depend upon Liberia for their supplies of imported goods.

The exports amount to about eight hundred thousand dollars per annum, and are on the increase. The soil is capable of sustaining an immense population, but the want of agricultural industry has been felt. As the country becomes settled, and the character of its diseases better understood, the acclimating fever is less dreaded, and now rarely proves fatal. This having been passed through, the colored emigrants enjoy far better health than they did in most parts of the United States. The statistics of President Roberts exhibit about three per cent. less number of deaths than among the same class of people in Canada and New England. The thermometer ranges from 70° to 85°; seldom higher or lower.

A thirst for education has been awakened among the surrounding aborigines of Liberia, many of whom send their children 400 and 500 miles, to be educated in the republic. The Liberians have built for themselves above thirty churches of brick and stone; and possess numerous schools, and a considerable number of printing-presses. More than 20,000 natives have requested to be taken under the protection of the state, while not less than 100,000 live on its territory, and 350,000 are bound to it by treaties to abolish the slave-trade. At different times, ten buildings, erected by slave-traders for the storage of slaves, have been burned down by the Liberians, and hundreds of their fellow-creatures, therein confined, liberated; and they at all times afford refuge to the weak and the oppressed. Monrovia, the capital and port of the colony, is situated on Cape Mesurado. There are, besides, above twenty towns and villages in the territory. The government of the country is precisely on the American model; consisting of a president, a vice-president, a senate, and a house of representatives ; the number of members in the former being six, and in the latter twenty-eight. A company has recently been organized in the United States for establishing steam communication between Liberia and this country. Population in 1850, 250,000.*

The yearly income of the American Colonization Society, it appears, has only ranged from $3,000 to $50,000. The annual average of the first six years was $3,276. A liberal bequest of $25,000 per annum for forty years was made to the society by Mr. M'Donough, of New Orleans. From a table published in the Colonization Herald for April, 1857, it appears that since the first settlement of the colony, 9,502 emigrants have been sent out. Of these, 3,676 were born free ; 326 purchased their own liberty ; and the remaining 5,500 were emancipated for emigration. Of the whole number, 3,315 have gone from Virginia.

The Maryland Colonization Society established its colony at Cape Palmas in 1834. A tract extending about twenty miles along the sea coast, and as many inland, was purchased of the natives by Dr. James Hall, the agent of the society. Fifty-three emigrants commenced the settlement, but vessels continued to arrive with more settlers. An additional tract was procured in 1836, and in succeeding years new settlers arrived. The state had voted $20,000 per annum for twenty years. In 1837, Mr. Russworm, a colored man, was appointed governor of the colony, and fulfilled the high expectations formed of him. Six chiefs ceded to him their territories, which became incorporated in the colony. Every treaty contained an absolute prohibition of the slave-trade. A line of packets was established in 1846, to carry out emigrants and bring home produce. It is now contemplated to erect the colony into an independent state.

From an address put forth by the colonists of Liberia to the free people of color of the United States, we make a few extracts :

" The first consideration which caused our voluntary removal to this country, and the object which we still regard with the deepest concern, is liberty—liberty in the sober, simple, but complete sense of the word ; not a licentious liberty, nor a liberty without government, or which should place us without the restraint of salutary laws ; but that liberty of speech and conscience which distinguishes the free enfranchised citizens of a free state. We did not enjoy that freedom in our native country ; and from causes which, as respects ourselves, we shall soon forget forever, we were certain it was not there attainable for ourselves or our children. This, then, being the first object of our pursuit in coming to Africa, is probably the first subject on which you will ask for information ; and we must truly declare to you that our expectations and hopes, in this respect, have been realized. Our constitution secures to us, so far as our condition allows, ' all the rights and privileges enjoyed by the citizens of the United States,' and these rights and privileges are ours. We are proprietors of the soil we live on, and possess the rights of freeholders. Our suf-

---

* Lippincott's Gazetteer of the World.

frages, and what is of more importance, our sentiments and our opinions, have their due weight in the government we live under. Our laws are altogether our own; they grow out of our circumstances, are framed for our exclusive benefit, and administered by officers of our own appointment, and as such possess our confidence. We have a judiciary chosen from among ourselves; we serve as jurors in the trials of others, and are liable to be tried only by juries of our fellow-citizens ourselves. We have all that is meant by *liberty of conscience*. The time and mode of worshiping God, as prescribed to us in His word, and dictated by our conscience, we are not only free to follow, but are protected in following.

"Forming a community of our own in the land of our forefathers; having the commerce, and the soil, and the resources of the country at our disposal, we know nothing of that debasing inferiority with which our very color stamped us in America. There is nothing here to create the feeling of caste —nothing to cherish the feeling of superiority in the minds of foreigners who visit us. It is this moral emancipation, this liberty of the mind from worse than iron fetters, that repays us ten thousand times over for all that it has cost us, and makes us grateful to God and our American patrons for the happy change which has taken place in our situation. We are not so self-complacent as to rest satisfied with our improvement, either as regards our minds or our circumstances. We do not expect to remain stationary—far from it. But we certainly feel ourselves, for the first time, in a state to enjoy either to any purpose. The burden is gone from our shoulders. We now breathe and move freely, and know not (in surveying your present state) for which to pity you most, the empty name of liberty which you endeavor to content yourselves with, in a country that is not yours, or the delusion which makes you hope for ampler privileges in that country hereafter.

"We solicit none of you to emigrate to this country; for we know not who among you prefers rational independence, and the honest respect of his fellow-men, to that mental sloth and careless poverty which you already possess, and your children will inherit after you in America. But if your views and aspirations rise a degree higher—if your minds are not as servile as your present condition, we can decide the question at once; and with confidence say that you will bless the day, and your children after you, when you determined to become citizens of Liberia.

"But we do not hold this language on the blessings of liberty for the purpose of consoling ourselves for the sacrifice of health, or the sufferings of want, in consequence of our removal to Africa. We enjoy health, after a few months' residence in this country; and a distressing scarcity of provisions, or any of the necessaries of life, has of late been entirely unknown, even to the poorest persons in this community. On these points there are, and have been, much misconception and some malicious misrepresentations in the United States.

"The true character of the African climate is not well understood in other countries. Its inhabitants are as robust, as healthy, as long-lived, to say the least, as those of any other country. Nothing like an epidemic has ever appeared in this colony; nor can we learn from the natives, that the calamity of a sweeping sickness ever yet visited this part of the continent. But the change from a temperate to a tropical country is a great one—too great not to affect the health more or less, and in the cases of old people, and very young people, it often causes death. In the early years of the colony, want of good houses, the great fatigues and dangers of the settlers, their irregular mode of living, and the hardships and discouragements they met with, greatly helped the other causes of sickness, which prevailed to an alarming extent, and were attended with great mortality. But we look back to those times as a season of trial long past, and nearly forgotten. Our houses and circumstances are now comfortable; and for the last two or three years not one person in forty, from the middle and southern states, has died from the change of climate.

"A more fertile soil, and a more productive country, so fas as it is cultivated, there is not, we believe, on the face of the earth. Its hills and its plains are covered with a verdure which never fades; the productions of nature keep on in their growth through all seasons of the year. Even the natives of the country, almost without farming tools, without skill, and with very little labor, make more grain and vegetables than they can consume, and often more than they can sell.

"Add to all this, we have no dreary winter here, for one-half the year, to destroy the products of the other half. Nature is constantly renewing herself, and is also constantly pouring her treasures all the year round in the laps of the industrious. We could say on this subject more, but we are afraid of exciting too highly the hopes of the imprudent. Such persons, we think, will do well to keep their rented cellars, and earn their twenty-five cents a day at their wheelbarrow, in the commercial towns of America, and stay where they are. It is only the industrious and virtuous that we can point to independence, and plenty, and happiness in this country.

" Truly, we have a goodly heritage; and if there is any thing lacking in the character or condition of the people of this colony, it can never be charged to the account of the country; it must be the fruit of our own mismanagement, or slothfulness, or vices. But from all these evils we confide in Him to whom we are indebted for our blessings, to preserve us. It is the topic of our weekly and daily thanksgiving to Almighty God, both in public and private, and He knows with what sincerity we were conducted, by His providence, to this shore. Such great favors, in so short a time, and mixed with so few trials, are to be ascribed to nothing but His special blessing. This we acknowledge. We only want the gratitude which such signal favors call for. Nor are we willing to close this paper, without adding a heartfelt testimonial to the deep obligations we owe to our American patrons and best earthly benefactors, whose wisdom pointed us to this home of our nation, and whose active and persevering benevolence enabled us to reach it. Judge, then, of the feelings with which we hear the motives and doings of the Colonization Society traduced—and that, too, by men too ignorant to know what the society has already accomplished; too weak to look through its plans and intentions; or too dishonest to acknowledge either. But, without pretending to any prophetic sagacity, we can certainly predict to that Society the ultimate triumph of their hopes and labors ; and disappointment and defeat to those who oppose them. Men may theorize and speculate upon their plans in America, but there can be no speculation here. The cheerful abodes of civilization and happiness which are scattered over this verdant mountain—the flourishing settlements which are spreading around it—the sound of Christian instruction, and scenes of Christian worship, which are heard and seen in this land of brooding pagan darkness—a thousand contented freemen united in founding a new Christian empire, happy themselves, and the instrument of happiness to others—every object, every individual, is an argument, is a demonstration, of the wisdom and goodness of the plan of colonization."

CHAPTER XXI.

HISTORY OF SLAVERY IN THE NORTH AMERICAN COLONIES.

Early existence of Slavery in England.—Its forms.—The Feudal System.—Serfdom.—Its extinction.—African Slavery introduced into the North American Colonies, 1620.—Slavery in Virginia.—Massachusetts sanctions Negro and Indian slavery, 1641: Kidnapping declared unlawful, 1645.—Negro and Indian slavery authorized in Connecticut, 1650.—Decree against perpetual slavery in Rhode Island, 1652.—Slavery in New Netherland among the Dutch, 1650—Its mild form.—First slavery statute of Virginia, 1662.—In Maryland, 1663, against amalgamation.—Statute of Virginia, conversion and baptism not to confer freedom ; other provisions, 1667.—Maryland encourages Slave-trade.—Slave code of Virginia, 1682, fugitives may be killed.—New anti-amalgamation act of Maryland, 1681.—Settlement of South Carolina, 1660.—Absolute power conferred on masters.—Law of Slavery in New York, 1665.—Slave code of Virginia, 1692 : offenses of slaves, how punishable.—Revision of Virginia code, 1705 : slaves made real estate.—Pennsylvania protests against importation of Indian slaves from Carolina, 1705.—New act of 1712 to stop importation of negroes and slaves, prohibiting duty of £20.—Act repealed by Queen.—First slave law of Carolina, 1712.—Its remarkable provisions.—Census of 1715.—Maryland code of 1715—baptism not to confer freedom.—Georgia colonized, 1732 : rum and slavery prohibited.—Cruel delusion in New York ; plot falsely imputed to negroes to burn the city, 1741.—Slavery legalized in Georgia, 1750.—Review of the state of Slavery in all the colonies in 1750.—Period of the Revolution.—Controversy in Massachusetts on the subject of slavery, 1766 to 1773.—Slaves gain their freedom in the courts of Massachusetts.—Court of King's Bench decision.—Mansfield declares the law of England, 1772.—Continental Congress declares against African Slave-trade, 1784.

SLAVERY existed in England in early times, and slaves became an article of export. Prisoners of war were reduced to slavery ; criminals and debtors were added to the number, and unfortunate gamesters who had staked their liberty.* There were also hereditary slaves, who derived their condition from their parents, and who were sold and transferred from hand to hand. This

---

* Henry's History of England.

form of slavery was gradually extinguished by the feudal system, which sub-stituted villeinage. To the serfs, who were the lowest grade of vassals, was committed the task of tilling the lands which the soldier gained or protected. There were grades even among the serfs, though probably there were not in-stances in which one held another as vassal and superior. The peculiarity of the class was, that they were astricted to the domain, and went with it when it changed hands. Some, however, had rights and privileges which they might maintain in the court of the manor of their lord. Some held small estates, which, however, they could not dispose of. The lowest class were abject and unprivileged.*

At the time of the first English emigration to America, but few faint traces were left of that system of villeinage once so universal throughout Europe, and still prevalent in Russia. In England it had disappeared, not by any for-mal legislative act, but as the joint result of private emancipations and by the discouragement long given by the English courts to claims so contrary to nat-ural right. It became an established opinion throughout western Europe that Christians could not be held as slaves—but the immunity did not extend to in-fidels or heathen.

We have mentioned in a former chapter that slavery was first introduced into the North American colonies in 1620, by a Dutch vessel which landed a por-tion of her human merchandise at Jamestown, Virginia. The event was al-most simultaneous with the landing of the Pilgrims on Plymouth Rock, Dec. 22d, 1620. In buying and holding negro slaves, the Virginians did not sup-pose themselves to be violating any law, human or divine. Whatever might be the case with the law of England, the law of Moses, in authorizing the en-slavement of "strangers," seemed to give to the purchase of negro slaves an express sanction. The number of negroes in the colony, limited as it was to a few cargoes, brought at intervals by Dutch traders, was long too small to make the matter appear of much moment, and more than forty years elapsed before the colonists thought it necessary to strengthen the system of slavery by any express enactments.

In the colony of Massachusetts a body of fundamental laws was established in 1641. One of the articles, based on the Mosaic code, provides that "there shall never be any bond slavery, villeinage, nor captivity among us, unless it be lawful captives, taken in just wars, and such strangers as willingly sell them-selves or are sold unto us, and these shall have all the liberties and Christian usages which the law of God established in Israel requires. This exempts none from servitude who shall be judged thereto by authority." This article sanctions the slave-trade and the holding of negroes and Indians in bondage. This seems to be the first positive enactment in the colonies on the subject of slavery.

About this time a transaction occurred, (1645,) which some consider a pro-test on the part of Massachusetts against the African slave-trade. We state

---

* Chambers' History of Laws.

the facts, and the reader can judge whether the inference is warranted or not: The ships which took cargoes of staves and fish to Madeira and the Canaries were accustomed to touch on the coast of Guinea "to trade for negroes," who were carried generally to Barbadoes or the other English islands in the West Indies, the demand for them at home being but small. In the case above referred to, instead of buying negroes in the regular course of traffic, which, under a fundamental law of Massachusetts already quoted, would have been perfectly legal, the crew of a Boston ship joined with some London vessels on the coast, and, on pretense of some quarrel with the natives, landed a "murderer"—the expressive name of a small piece of cannon—attacked a negro village on Sunday, killed many of the inhabitants, and made a few prisoners, two of whom fell to the share of the Boston ship. In the course of a lawsuit between the master, mate, and owners, all this story came out, and Saltonstall, who sat as one of the magistrates, thereupon presented a petition to the court, in which he charged the master and mate with a threefold offense, murder, man-stealing, and Sabbath-breaking; the two first capital by the fundamental laws of Massachusetts, and all of them "capital by the law of God." The magistrates doubted their authority to punish crimes committed on the coast of Africa; but they ordered the negroes to be sent back, as having been procured not honestly by purchase, but unlawfully by kidnapping.

A code of laws for Connecticut was compiled in 1650 and adopted by the general court, as the legislative assembly was then called. On the subject of the Indians this code exhibits much anxiety. The militia law is full and precise. Every town is to have a store of powder, and on Sundays and lecture days to be furnished with an armed guard, to prevent sudden surprises. Trade with the Indians in arms of any kind, or in dogs, is strictly forbidden. White men leaving the colony and joining the Indians are liable to three years' imprisonment. Every band of Indians resident near any plantation is to have some sachem or chief to be personally responsible for all depredations committed by the band; and, in conformity with a recommendation of the commissioners for the united colonies, if satisfaction for injuries is refused or neglected, the Indians themselves may be seized; " and, because it will be chargeable keeping them in prison," they may be delivered to the injured party, "either to serve, or to be shipped out and exchanged for negroes, as the case will justly bear." It thus appears that negro slavery was authorized in Connecticut as well as in Massachusetts. It was only the heretics of Providence who prohibited perpetual servitude by placing "black mankind" on the same level with regard to limitation of service as white servants. Unfortunately for the honor of Rhode Island, this regulation, enacted during a temporary disruption of the province, never extended to the other towns, and never obtained the force of a general law.*

Slaves were introduced into New Netherland by the Dutch West India Company, about the year 1650. Most of them remained the property of the company, and the more trusty and industrious, after a certain period of labor, were allowed little farms, paying a stipulated amount of produce. This emancipation did not extend to the children, a circumstance inexplicable and highly displeasing to the Dutch commonalty, who could not understand "how any one born of a free Christian mother could nevertheless be a slave."

At a session of the Virginia legislature, in December, 1662, an act was passed, being the first statute of Virginia which attempts to give a legislative basis to the system of hereditary slavery. It was enacted that children should be held bond or free "according to the condition of the mother."

In 1663, the subject of slavery also attracted the notice of the Maryland legislature. It was provided, by the first section of an act now passed, that "all negroes and other slaves within this province, and all negroes and other slaves to be hereafter imported into this province, shall serve during life ; and all children born of any negro or other slave, shall be slaves, as their *fathers* were, for the term of their lives." The second section recites that "divers free-born English women, forgetful of their free condition, and to the disgrace of our nation, do intermarry with negro slaves ;" and for deterring from such "shameful matches," it enacts that, during their husbands' lives, white women so intermarrying shall be servants to the masters of their husbands, and that the issue of such marriages shall be slaves for life.

In 1667, the assembly of Virginia enacted that negroes, though converted and baptized, should not thereby become free. At the same session, in re-markable deviation from the English law, it was also enacted, that killing slaves by extremity of correction should not be esteemed felony, "since it can not be presumed that prepense malice should induce any man to destroy his own estate." The prohibition against holding Indians as slaves was also re-laxed as to those brought in by water, a new law having enacted "that all ser-vants, *not being Christians*, imported by shipping, shall be slaves for life." About this period, and afterward, a considerable number of Indian slaves seem to have been imported into Virginia and New England from the West Indies and the Spanish main.

As a necessary pendent to the slave code, the system now also began of subjecting freed slaves to civil disabilities. It had already been enacted that female servants employed in field labor should be rated and taxed as tithable. Negro women, though free, were now subjected to the same tax. Free ne-groes and Indians were also disqualified to purchase or hold white servants.

Some replies of Berkeley to a series of questions submitted to him by the plantation committee of the privy council, give quite a distinct picture of the colony as it was in 1671. The population is estimated at 40,000, including 2,000 "black slaves," and 6,000 "Christian servants," of whom about 1,500 were imported yearly, principally English. Since the exclusion of Dutch ves-sels by the acts of navigation, the importation .of negroes had been very lim-ited ; not above two or three ship loads had arrived in seven years. The Eng-lish trade to Africa, a monopoly in the hands of the Royal African Company, does not seem to have been prosecuted with much spirit ; and such supply of slaves as that company furnished was chiefly engrossed by Jamaica and other sugar colonies.

In 1671 an act was passed by Maryland encouraging the importation of slaves.

In 1682 the slave code of Virginia received some additions. Slaves were prohibited to carry arms, offensive or defensive, or to go off the plantations of their masters without a written pass, or to lift hand against a Christian even in self-defense. Runaways who refused to be apprehended might be lawfully killed. The condition of slavery was imposed upon all servants, whether negroes, Moors, mulattoes, or Indians, brought into the colony by sea or land, whether converted to Christianity or not, provided *they were not of Christian parentage or country*, or Turks or Moors in amity with his majesty. An unsuccessful attempt was made in the council, whether dictated by humanity, by policy, or by a wish to promote the interests of the Royal African company, to reënact the old law prohibiting the enslavement of Indians.

The attempt in Maryland to prevent the intermarriage of whites and blacks seems not to have proved very successful. The preamble to a new act on this subject recites that such matches were often brought about by the "instigation, procurement, or connivance of the master or mistress," who thus availed themselves of the provisions of the former law to prolong the servitude of their female servants, and, at the same time, to raise up a new brood of slaves. To remedy this evil, all white female servants intermarrying with negro slaves were to be declared free at once, and their children also ; but the minister celebrating the marriage, and the master or mistress promoting or conniving at it, were subjected to a fine of ten thousand pounds of tobacco.

The settlement of South Carolina commenced about 1660. In the scheme of government for this colony, drafted by the afterwards celebrated metaphysician, John Locke, there was inserted a provision that "every freeman of South Carolina shall have absolute power and authority over his negro slaves, of what opinion and religion whatsoever."

In the code of laws known as the "Duke's laws," enacted for the government of New York in 1665, there is a provision that "no *Christian* shall be kept in bond slavery, villeinage, or captivity, except such who shall be judged thereunto by authority, or such as willingly have sold or shall sell themselves," in which case a record of such servitude shall be entered in the court of sessions, "held for that jurisdiction where the master shall inhabit." This provision, borrowed, with some modifications, from the "Massachusetts Fundamentals," did not exempt heathen negroes and Indians from slavery.

In Virginia, in 1692, an "act for suppressing outlying slaves," after setting forth in a preamble that "many times negroes, mulattoes, and other slaves unlawfully absent themselves from their masters' and mistresses' service, and lie hid, and lurk in obscure places, killing hogs, and committing other injuries to the inhabitants of this dominion," authorizes any two justices, one being of the quorum, to issue their warrant to the sheriff for the arrest of any such outlying slaves. Whereupon the sheriff is to raise the necessary force, and if the slaves resist, run away, or refuse to surrender, they may be lawfully killed and destroyed "by guns, or any other way whatsoever," the master, in such cases, to receive from the public four thousand pounds of tobacco for the loss of his slave.

Individual runaways seem at times to have made themselves formidable. We find, a few years later, an act setting forth that one Billy, a negro, slave to John Tillet, "has several years unlawfully absented himself from his master's service, lying out, and lurking in obscure places, supposed within the counties of James City, York, and Kent, devouring and destroying the stocks and crops, robbing the houses of, and committing and threatening other injuries to several of his majesty's good and liege people within this his colony and dominion of Virginia, in contempt of the good laws thereof;" wherefore the said Billy is declared by the act guilty of a capital offense; and "whosoever shall kill and destroy the said negro slave Billy, and apprehend and deliver him to justice," is to be rewarded with a thousand pounds of tobacco; and all persons entertaining him, or trading and trucking with him, are declared guilty of felony; his master, if he be killed, to receive as compensation from the public four thousand pounds of tobacco.

The same statute above cited for suppressing outlying slaves, contains the first provision to be found in the Virginia laws on the subject of the intermixture of the races : " For the prevention of that abominable mixture and spurious issue which hereafter may increase in this dominion, as well by negroes, mulattoes, and Indians intermarrying with English or other white women, as by their unlawful accompanying with one another," any free white man or woman intermarrying with a negro, mulatto, or Indian, was to be forever banished—a punishment changed a few years after to six months' imprisonment and a fine of ten pounds. White women having mulatto children without marriage were to pay fifteen pounds sterling, or be sold for five years, that period, if they were servants, to take effect from the expiration of their former term, the child to be bound out as a servant till thirty years of age.

Another clause of this act placed a serious restraint upon emancipation, by enacting that no negro or mulatto slave shall be set free, unless the emancipator pay for his transportation out of the country within six months. Yet the manumission was not void. The idea of reducing again to slavery persons once made free was not yet arrived at. A violation of the act exposed to a penalty of ten pounds, to be appropriated toward the transportation out of the colony of the freed slave.

The practice of special summary tribunals for the trial of slaves charged with crimes was now first introduced—another remarkable deviation from the English law. Any slave guilty of any offense punishable by the law of England with death or loss of member, was to be forthwith committed to the county jail, there to be kept "well laden with irons," and upon notice of the fact, the governor was to issue a commission to any persons of the county he might see fit, before whom the prisoner was to be arraigned, indicted, tried "without the solemnity of a jury," and on the oath of two witnesses, or one witness "with pregnant circumstances" or confession, was to be found guilty and sentenced. The same act, by another section, forbade slaves to keep horses, cattle, or hogs. It also provided that the owner should be liable for damage done "by any negro or other slave living at a quarter where there is no Christian overseer."

These laws indicate the start which the slave-trade had recently received, and the rapid increase in Virginia of slave population.

A fifth revision of the Virginia code, in progress for the last five years by a committee of the council and burgesses, was completed in 1705. This code provided that "all servants imported or brought into this country by sea or land, *who were not Christians in their native country*, (except Turks and Moors in amity with her majesty, and others who can make due proof of their being free in England or any other Christian country before they were shipped in order to transportation thither,) shall be accounted, and be slaves, notwithstanding a conversion to Christianity afterward," or though they may have been in England ; "all children to be bond or free, according to the condition of their mothers."

By a humane provision of this code, slaves are made real estate, and thus, as it were, attached to the soil. Nor can it be said that the sole object was to shield them from seizure for debt—they remained liable to that as before. They were also to descend like personal property, but provision was made by which the heir of the plantation could buy out the inherited interest of others in the slaves. Such continued to be the law so long as Virginia remained a British colony.

The export of Indian slaves from Carolina had been a subject of complaint in Pennsylvania. The importation of Indian slaves into that province, except such as had been a year domiciled in the family of the importer, had been prohibited, in 1705, by an act especially referring to this Carolina traffic, "as having given our neighboring Indians of this province some umbrage for suspicion and dissatisfaction." A new act, in 1712, "to prevent the importation of negroes and slaves," alleging plots and insurrections, and referring in terms to a recent plot in New York, imposed a prohibitory duty of £20 upon all negroes and Indians brought into the province by land or water, a drawback to be allowed in case of reëxportation within twenty days. Indulgence was also to be granted for a longer time, not exceeding six months, "to all gentlemen and strangers traveling in this province who may have negro or Indian slaves to attend them, not exceeding two for one person." Runaways from the neighboring provinces, if taken back within twenty days after identification, were to be free of duty ; otherwise, or if not claimed within twelve months, they were to be sold, and the proceeds paid into the treasury, the owner being entitled only to what remained after paying the duty and expenses. Very large powers were given to the collector to break all doors, and seize and sell all slaves suspected to be concealed with intent to evade the duty. This act, however, within a few months after its passage, was disallowed and repealed by the queen.

A Massachusetts act on the same subject, August, 1712, recites "that divers conspiracies, outrages, barbarities, murders, burglaries, thefts, and other notorious crimes and enormities, at sundry times, and especially of late, have been perpetrated and committed by Indians and other slaves within several of her majesty's plantations in America, being of a surly and revengeful spirit, rude and insolent in their behavior, and very ungovernable, the over great number and increase whereof within this province is likely to prove of pernicious and fatal consequences to her majesty's subjects and interest here unless speedily remedied, and is a discouragement to the importation of white Christian servants, this province being differently circumstanced from the plantations in the islands, and having great numbers of the Indian natives of the country within and about them, and at this time under the sorrowful effects of their rebellion and hostilities;" in consideration of all which, the further import of Indian slaves is totally prohibited, under pain of forfeiture to the crown.

Cotemporaneously with these prohibitory acts of Pennsylvania and Massachusetts, the first extant slave law of South Carolina was enacted, June, 1712, the basis of the existing slave code of that state. "Whereas," says the preamble of this remarkable statute, "the plantations and estates of this province can not be well and sufficiently managed and brought into use without the labor and service of negro and other slaves; and forasmuch as the said negroes and other slaves brought unto the people of this province for that purpose are of barbarous, wild, savage natures, and such as renders them wholly unqualified to be governed by the laws, customs, and practices of this province; but that it is absolutely necessary that such other constitutions, laws, and orders should in this province be made and enacted for the good regulation and ordering of them as may restrain the disorders, rapine, and inhumanity to which they are naturally prone and inclined, and may also tend to the safety and security of the people of this province and their estates," it is therefore enacted that "all negroes, mulattoes, mestizoes, or Indians, which at any time heretofore have been sold, and now are held or taken to be, or hereafter shall be bought or sold for slaves, are hereby declared slaves; and they and their children are hereby made and declared slaves to all intents and purposes, excepting all such negroes, mulattoes, mestizoes, and Indians which heretofore have been or hereafter shall be, for some particular merit, made and declared free, either by the governor and council of this province, pursuant to any act of this province, or by their respective masters and owners, and also excepting all such as can prove that they ought not to be sold for slaves."

Every person finding a slave abroad without a pass was to arrest him if possible, and punish him on the spot by "moderate chastisement," under a penalty of twenty shillings for neglecting it. All negro houses were to be searched once a fortnight for arms and stolen goods. A slave guilty of petty larceny, for the first offense was to be "publicly and severely whipped;" for tne second offense was to have "one of his ears cut off," or be "branded in the forehead with a hot iron, that the mark thereof may remain;" for the third offense was to "have his nose slit;" for the fourth offense was "to suffer death, or other punishment," at the discretion of the court. Any justice of the peace, on complaint against any slave for any crime, from "chicken stealing" up to "insurrection" and "murder," was to issue his warrant for the slave's arrest, and, if the accusation seemed to be well founded, was to associate with himself another justice, they two to summon in three freeholders. The five together, or, by an additional act, the majority of them, satisfactory evidence of guilt appearing, were to sentence the culprit to death, or such lesser punishment as the offense might seem to deserve. In case of lesser punishment, "no particular law directing such punishment" was necessary. In case of death, "the kind of death" was left to "the judgment and discretion" of the court, execution to be forthwith done on their sole warrant, the owner to be indemnified at the public charge. This summary form of procedure in the trial of slaves remains in force in South Carolina to this day, and a very similar form was also adopted, and still prevails, in North Carolina.

He who enticed a slave, "by specious pretense of promising freedom in another country," or otherwise, to leave the province, if successful, or if caught in the act, was to suffer death; and the same extreme penalty was to be inflicted on slaves "running away with intent to get out of the province." Any slave running away for twenty days at once, for the first offense was to be "severely and publicly whipped." In case the master neglected to inflict this punishment, any justice might order it to be inflicted by the constable, at the master's expense. For the second offense the runaway was to be branded with the letter R on the right cheek. If the master omitted it, he was to forfeit £10, and any justice of the peace might order the branding done. For the third offense, the runaway, if absent thirty days, was to be whipped, and have one of his ears cut off; the master neglecting to do it to forfeit £20; any justice, on complaint, to order it done as before. For the fourth offense, the runaway, "if a man, was to be gelt," to be paid for by the province if he died under the operation; if a woman, she was to be severely whipped, branded on the left cheek with the letter R, and her left ear cut off. Any master neglecting for twenty days to inflict these atrocious cruelties, was to forfeit his property in the slave to any informer who might complain of him within six months. Any captain or commander of a company, "on notice of the haunt, residence, and hiding-place of any runaway slaves," was "to pursue, apprehend, and take them, either alive or dead," being in either case entitled to a premium of from two to four pounds for each slave. All persons wounded or disabled on such expeditions were to be compensated by the public. If any slave under punishment "shall suffer in life or member, which," says the act, "seldom happens, no person whatsoever shall be liable to any penalty therefor." Any person killing his slave out of "wantonness," "bloody-mindedness," or "cruel intention," was to forfeit "fifty pounds current money," or, if the slave belonged to another person, twenty-five pounds to the public, and the slave's value to the owner. No master was to allow his slaves to hire their own time, or, by a supplementary act two years after, "to plant for themselves any corn, peas, or rice, or to keep any stock of hogs, cattle, or horses."

"Since charity and the Christian religion which we profess," says the concluding section of this remarkable act, "obligates us to wish well to the souls of men, and that religion may not be made a pretense to alter any man's property and right, and that no person may neglect to baptize their negroes or slaves for fear that thereby they should be manumitted and set free," "it shall be and is hereby declared lawful for any negro or Indian slave, or any other slave or slaves whatsoever, to receive and profess the Christian faith, and to be thereunto baptized; but, notwithstanding such slave or slaves shall receive or profess the Christian religion, and be baptized, he or they shall not thereby be manumitted or set free."*

In the quarter of a century from the English Revolution to the accession of the house of Hanover, the population of the English colonies had doubled. The following table, compiled for the use of the Board of Trade, though probably somewhat short of the truth, will serve to exhibit its distribution in 1715:

	Whites.	Negroes.	Total.
New Hampshire	9,500	150	9,650
Massachusetts	94,000	2,000	96,000
Rhode Island	8,500	500	9,000
Connecticut	46,000	1,500	47,000
New York	27,000	4,000	31,000
New Jersey	21,000	1,500	22,500
Pennsylvania and Delaware	43,300	2,500	45,800
Maryland	40,700	9,500	50,200
Virginia	72,000	23,000	95,000
North Carolina	7,500	3,700	11,200
South Carolina	6,250	10,500	16,750
	375,750	58,850	434,600

By a revisal of the Maryland code, in 1715, "all negroes and other slaves already imported, or hereafter to be imported, and all children now born, or hereafter to be born of such negroes and slaves, shall be slaves during their natural lives"—an act construed as sanctioning in Maryland, though without any express provision to that effect, the Virginia rule of determining the condition of the child by that of the mother. It was expressly provided that baptism should not confer freedom. The provisions, in a long act on the subject of slaves and servants, bear a very strong resemblance to those of the Virginia code; but there were some peculiarities. "Any person whatsoever" traveling out of the county of his residence without a pass under the seal of the county, might be apprehended and carried before a magistrate, and if not sufficiently known, or unable to give a good account of himself, might, at the magistrate's discretion, be committed to jail for six months, or until the procurement of "a certificate or other justification that he or she is not a servant." Notwithstanding this certificate, no discharge was to be had till the jailor was paid ten pounds of tobacco, or one day's service for each day of imprisonment, and the person making the arrest, as a reward for his trouble, two hundred pounds of

*Hildreth's History United States.

tobacco, or twenty days' service! What is much more remarkable than the passage of this statute, it remains unrepealed to this day.

On the banks of the Savannah a new colony was planted. Its founder was James Edward Oglethorpe, an officer of the English army, and member of the House of Commons. Desirous to provide a place in America for such discharged prisoners and others of the suffering poor as might be willing to commence there a life of industry and sobriety, Oglethorpe, in conjunction with several others, petitioned the king for a grant of territory. The charter was issued June 9, 1732. The right of legislation for the province was vested in a board of trustees. Oglethorpe superintended in person the planting of the colony. The use of rum was prohibited; and, the better to exclude this source of demoralization, all trade with the West Indies was forbidden. The trustees did not wish to see their province " void of white inhabitants, filled with blacks, the precarious property of a few, equally exposed to domestic treachery and foreign invasion." They prohibited negro slavery, not only as unjust and cruel—for so it was beginning to be esteemed by all the more intelligent and humane—but as fatal to the interests of the poor white settlers, for whose special benefit the colony had been projected.

The city of New York became, in 1741, the scene of a cruel and bloody delusion, less notorious, but not less lamentable than the Salem witchcraft. That city then contained some seven or eight thousand inhabitants, of whom twelve or fifteen hundred were slaves. Nine fires in rapid succession, most of them, however, merely the burning of chimneys, produced a perfect insanity of terror. An indented servant woman purchased her liberty and secured a reward of £100 by pretending to give information of a plot formed by a low tavern-keeper, her master, and three negroes, to burn the city and murder the whites. This story was confirmed and amplified by an Irish prostitute convicted of a robbery, who, to recommend herself to mercy, reluctantly turned informer. Numerous arrests had been already made among the slaves and free blacks. Many others followed. The eight lawyers who then composed the bar of New York all assisted by turns on behalf of the prosecution. The prisoners, who had no counsel, were tried and convicted upon most insufficient evidence. The lawyers vied with each other in heaping all sorts of abuse on their heads, and chief-justice Delancey, in passing sentence, vied with the lawyers. Many confessed to save their lives, and then accused others. Thirteen unhappy convicts were burned at the stake, eighteen were hanged, and seventy-one transported.

The slow progress of Georgia for twenty years, furnished new proofs, if such were needed, that the colonization of a wilderness, even with abundant facilities for it, is, for the most part, a tedious process; and, when undertaken by a company or the public, very expensive.

The results of their own idleness, inexperience, and incapacity, joined to the inevitable obstacles which every new settlement must encounter, were obstinately ascribed by the inhabitants of Georgia to that wise but ineffectual prohibition of slavery, one of the fundamental laws of the province. The convenience of the moment caused future consequences to be wholly overlooked.   Every means was made use of to get rid of this prohibition.   Even Whitfield and Haber-sham, forgetful of their former scruples, strenuously pleaded with the trustees in favor of slavery, under the old pretense of propagating in that way the Christian religion.   "Many of the poor slaves in America," wrote Haber-sham, "have already been made freemen of the heavenly Jerusalem."   The Salzburgers for a long time had scruples, but were reässured by advice from Germany : "If you take slaves in faith, and with intent of conducting them to Christ, the action will not be a sin, but may prove a benediction."   Thus, as usual, the religious sentiment and its most disinterested votaries were made tools of by avarice for the enslavement of mankind.   Habersham, however, could hardly be included in this class.   Having thrown off the missionary, and established a mercantile house at Savannah, the first, and for a long time the only one there, he was very anxious for exportable produce.   The counselors of Georgia—for the president was now so old as to be quite incapacitated for business—winked at violations of the law, and a considerable number of negroes had been already introduced from Carolina as hired servants, under indentures for life or a hundred years.   The constant toast at Savannah was, " The one thing needful," by which was meant negroes.   The leading men both at New Inverness and Ebenezer, who opposed the introduction of slavery, were tra-duced, threatened, and persecuted.

Thus beset, the trustees yielded at last, in 1750, on condition that all masters, under " a mulct of £5," should be obliged to compel their negroes "to attend at some time on the Lord's day for instruction in the Christian religion "—the origin, doubtless, of the peculiarly religious character of the negroes in and about Savannah.

By custom, or by statute, says Hildreth, whether legal or illegal, slavery ex-isted as a fact in every one of the Anglo-American colonies.   The soil and climate of New England made slaves of little value there except as domestic servants.   In 1701, the town of Boston had instructed its representatives in the General Court to propose "putting a period to negroes being slaves."   About the same time, Sewall, a judge of the Superior Court, aftewards chief-justice of Massachusetts, published " The Selling of Joseph," a pamphlet tending to a similar end.   But these scruples seem to have been short-lived.   With the increase of wealth and luxury, the number of slaves increased also.   There were in Massachusetts in 1754, as appears by an official census, twenty-four hundred and forty-eight negro slaves over sixteen years of age, about a thousand of them in Boston—a greater proportion to the free inhabitants than is to be found at present in the city of Baltimore.   Connecticut exceeded Massachusetts in the ratio of its slave population, and Rhode Island exceeded Connecticut.   Newport, grown to be the second commercial town in New England, had a proportion of slaves larger than Boston.   The harsh slave-laws in force in the more southern colonies were unknown, however, in New England.   Slaves were regarded as possessing the same legal rights as appren-tices ; and masters, for abuse of their authority, were liable to indictment.

Manumissions, however, were not allowed except upon security that the freed slaves should not become a burden to the parish.

In the provinces of New York and New Jersey, negro slaves were employed to a certain extent, not only as domestic servants, but as agricultural laborers. In the city of New York they constituted a sixth part of the population. The slave code of that province was hardly less harsh than that of Virginia.

In Pennsylvania, the number of slaves was small, partly owing to the ample supply of indented white servants, but partly, also, to scruples of conscience on the part of the Quakers. In the early days of the province, in 1688, some German Quakers, shortly after their arrival, had expressed the opinion that slavery was not morally lawful. George Keith had borne a similar testimony: but he was disowned as schismatic, and presently abandoning the society, was denounced as a renegade. When Penn, in 1699, had proposed to provide by law for the marriage, religious instruction, and kind treatment of slaves, he met with no response from the Quaker legislature. In 1712, to a petition in favor of emancipating the negroes, the Assembly replied, "that it was neither just nor convenient to set them at liberty." They imposed, however, a heavy duty, in effect prohibitory, and intended to be so, on the importation of negroes. This act, as we have seen, was negatived by the crown. The policy, however, was persevered in. New acts, passed from time to time, restricted importations by a duty first of five, but lately reduced to two pounds per head. The Quaker testimony against slavery was renewed by Sandiford and Lay, who brought with them to Pennsylvania a strong detestation of the system of servitude which they had seen in Barbadoes in all its rigors. The same views began presently to be perseveringly advocated by Woodman and Benezet, whose labors were not without effect upon the Quakers, some of whom set the example of emancipating their slaves. Franklin was also distinguished as an early and decided advocate for emancipation. The greater part of the slaves of Pennsylvania were to be found in Philadelphia. A fourth part of the inhabitants of that city were persons of African descent, including many, however, who had obtained their freedom.

In the tobacco growing colonies, Maryland, Virginia, and North Carolina, slaves constituted a third part or more of the population. In South Carolina, where rice was the principal produce, they were still more numerous, decidedly outnumbering the free inhabitants.

The slave code of South Carolina, as revised and reënacted in a statute still regarded as having the force of law, had dropped from its phraseology something of the extreme harshness of the former act. It contained, also, some provisions for the benefit of the slaves, but, on the whole, was harder than before. "Whereas," says the preamble to the act of 1740, "in his majesty's plantations in America, slavery has been introduced and allowed, and the people commonly called negroes, Indians, mulattoes, and mestizoes have been deemed absolute slaves, and the subjects of property in the hands of particular persons, the extent of whose power over such slaves ought to be settled and limited by positive laws, so that the slaves may be kept in due subjection and obedience, and the owners and other persons having the care and government of slaves may be restrained from exercising too great rigor and cruelty over them, and that the public peace and order of this province may be preserved," it is therefore enacted that "all negroes, Indians, mulattoes, and mestizoes (free Indians in amity with this government, and negroes, mulattoes, and mestizoes who are now free, excepted,) who now are or shall hereafter be in this province, and all their issue and offspring born and to be born, shall be, and they are hereby declared to be and remain forever hereafter absolute slaves, and shall follow the condition of the mother, and shall be claimed, held, taken, reputed, and adjudged in law to be chattels personal." This provision, which deprives the master of the power of manumission, and subjects to slavery the descendant of every slave woman, no matter how many degrees removed, nor who may have been the male ancestor, nor what the color, was subsequently adopted in the same terms by the Georgia Legislature as the law of that province. A suit for freedom might be brought by any white man who chose to volunteer for that purpose on behalf of any person claimed as a slave. But in all such suits, " the burden of proofs shall lay upon the plaintiff, and it shall always be presumed that every negro, Indian, mulatto, and mestizo is a slave, unless the contrary can be made to appear, the Indians in amity with this government excepted, in which case the burden of proof shall lie on the defendant." Masters were forbidden to allow their slaves to hire their own time ; to let or hire any plantation ; to possess any vessel or boat ; to keep or raise any horses, cattle, or hogs ; to engage in any sort of trade on their own account; to be taught to write ; or to have or wear any apparel (except livery servants) "finer than negro cloth, duffils, kerseys, osnaburgs, blue linen, check linen, or coarse garlix or calicoes, checked cotton or Scotch plaid ; " and any constable seeing any negro better clad, might seize the clothes and appropriate them to his own use. It was forbidden to work slaves on Sundays, under a penalty of five pounds ; for working them more than fifteen hours daily in summer, and fourteen in winter, a like penalty was imposed. Upon complaint to any justice that any master does not provide his slaves with sufficient " clothing, covering, or food," the justice might make such order in the premises as he saw fit, and fine the master not exceeding £20. "And whereas cruelty is not only highly unbecoming those who profess themselves Christians, but odious in the eyes of all men who have any sense of virtue and humanity," the fine for the willful murder of a slave was increased to £700 currency, with incapacity to hold any office, civil or military, and in case of inability to pay the fine, seven years' labor in a frontier garrison or the Charleston work-house. For killing a slave in the heat of passion, for maiming, or inflicting any other cruel punishment " other than by whipping or beating with a horsewhip, cowskin, switch, or small stick, or by putting in irons or imprisonment," a fine of £350 was imposed ; and in case of slaves found dead, maimed, or otherwise cruelly punished, the masters were to be held guilty of the act unless they make the contrary appear.

No statute of North Carolina seems ever to have declared who were or might be held as slaves in that province, the whole system being left to rest on usage or the supposed law of England. But police laws for the regulation of slaves were enacted similar to those of Virginia, and the Virginia prohibition was also adopted of manumissions, except for meritorious services, to be adjudged by the governor and council.

Among the ten acts of the Virginia revision rejected by the king in 1751, was one "concerning servants and slaves," a consolidation and reënactment of all the old statutes on that subject, the substance of which has been given in former pages. It appears from the address of the Assembly to the king on the subject of this veto, to have been a standing instruction to the governor not to consent to the reënactment of any law once rejected by the king, without express leave first obtained upon representation of the reasons and necessity for it. Such a representation was accordingly made by the Assembly as to eight of the ten rejected laws. The act concerning servants and slaves was not of this number, yet we find it reënacted within a year after in the very same words. Why the royal assent had been refused does not appear. It could hardly have been from any scruples on the subject of slavery; for among the acts expressly approved was one "for the better government of Indians, negroes, and mulattoes," which provided that the death of a slave under extremity of correction should not be esteemed murder, unless it were proved by the oath of at least one "lawful and credible witness" that the slave was willfully and maliciously killed; persons indicted for the murder of a slave, and found guilty of manslaughter only, to "incur no forfeiture or punishment." Slaves set free without leave from the governor and council might be sold at auction by the church-wardens of any parish in which such freed slave might reside for the space of a month. The same statute also continued the authority formerly given to the county courts to "dismember" disorderly slaves "notoriously guilty of going abroad in the night, or running away and laying out," and not to be reclaimed by the common methods—an authority very much abused, if we may judge by a subsequent statute, 1769, which declares this dismembering "to be often disproportioned to the offense, and contrary to the principles of humanity," and prohibits the castration of slaves except on conviction of an attempt to ravish a white woman.

The negroes imported from the African coast, whose descendants now constitute a sixth part of the population of the United States, were not by any means of one nation, language, or race. A single slave-ship often brought to America a great variety of languages and customs, a collection of unfortunate strangers to each other, or perhaps of hereditary enemies, with no common bond except that of servitude. Hence a want of union and sympathy among the slaves, which, joined to their extreme ignorance and simplicity, prevented coöperation, and rendered it easy to suppress such outbreaks as occasionally occurred. Even in complexion and physiognomy, the most obvious characteristic of the negroes, there were great differences. Some were of a jet black, often with features approaching the European standard; others of a mahogany or reddish black, with features less shapely and regular; and others yet of a tawny yellow, with flat noses and projecting jaws—an ugliness often, but erroneously, esteemed characteristic of all the African races, but which seems to have been principally confined to the low and swampy grounds about the delta of the Niger.   The negroes marked by these shapeless features were noted also for indomitable capacity of endurance, and were esteemed, therefore, the best slaves.   Intermixture among themselves, and a large infusion of European blood, have gradually obliterated these differences, or made them less noticeable.

Contrary to what happened in the West Indies, in the Anglo-North American provinces the natural increase of the slave population was rapid.   The women were seldom put to the severer labors of the field.   The long winter secured to both sexes a season of comparative rest.   Such was the abundance of provisions, that it was cheaper to breed than to buy slaves.   Those born in America, and reared up on the plantations, evidently surpassed the imported Africans both physically and intellectually.   Of the imported slaves a few were Mohammedans, among whom were occasionally found persons of some education, who knew Arabic, and could read the Koran.   But the great mass were pagans, in a condition of gross barbarism.   They brought with them from Africa many superstitions, but these, for the most part, as well as the negro languages, very soon died out.

Zealous for religion as the colonists were, very little effort was made to convert the negroes, owing partly, at least, to a prevalent opinion that neither Christian brotherhood nor the law of England would justify the holding Christians as slaves.   Nor could repeated colonial enactments to the contrary entirely root out this idea, for it was not supposed that a colonial statute could set aside the law of England.   What, precisely, the English law might be on the subject of slavery, still remained a matter of doubt.   Lord Holt had expressed the opinion, in 1697, that slavery was a condition unknown to English law, and that every person setting foot in England thereby became free. American planters, on their visits to England, accompanied by their slaves, seem to have been annoyed by claims of freedom set up on this ground, and that, also, of baptism.   To relieve their embarrassments, the merchants concerned in the American trade had obtained a written opinion from Yorke and Talbot, in 1729, the attorney and solicitor general of that day.   According to this opinion, which passed for more than forty years as good law, not only was baptism no bar to slavery, but negro slaves might be held in England just as vell as in the colonies.   The two lawyers by whom this opinion was given, rose afterward, one of them to be chief justice of England, and both to be chancelors.   Yorke, sitting in the latter capacity with the title of Lord Hardwicke, had recognized the doctrine of that opinion as sound law in 1749.   He objects to Lord Holt's doctrine of freedom, secured by setting foot on English soil, that no reason could be found "why slaves should not be equally free when they set foot in Jamaica or any other English plantation."   "All our colonies are subject to the laws of England, although as to some purposes they have laws of their own."   His argument is, that if slavery be contrary to

English law, no local enactments in the colonies could give it any validity. To avoid overturning slavery in the colonies, it was absolutely necessary to uphold it in England. At a subsequent period, as stated in a former chapter, the law of England was definitively settled in favor of liberty, the extra-judicial opinion of Talbot and Hardwicke being set aside by a solemn decision of the King's Bench.

The remaining exclusive privileges of the Royal African Company having expired, the English government undertook to maintain, at their own expense, the forts and factories on the African coast; and thus the slave-trade was thrown open to free competition. The recent introduction of the cultivation of coffee into the West Indies, and the increasing consumption in Europe of colonial produce, gave fresh impulse to this detestable traffic, and it now began to be carried on to an extent which soon roused against it the indignant humanity of an enlightened age. The West Indies were the chief market; but the imports to Virginia and the Carolinas were largely increased. New England rum, manufactured at Newport, was profitably exchanged on the coast of Africa for negroes, to be sold in the southern colonies; and vessels sailed on the same business from Boston and New York. The trade, however, was principally carried on by the English merchants of Bristol and Liverpool. Except in Pennsylvania, the colonial duties levied on the import of slaves were intended chiefly for revenue. They were classed in the instructions to the royal governors with duties on British goods, as impediments to British commerce not to be favored. On this ground several of these acts received the royal veto. Yet Virginia was allowed to impose such duties as she pleased, on the sole condition of making them payable by the buyer.

The position of the Africans in the colonies was disastrous. Not only were they servants for life, which possibly the law of England might have countenanced, but by colonial statute and usage this servitude descended to their children also. The few set free by the good will or the scruples of their masters seemed a standing reproach to slavery, and an evil example in the eyes of the rest. They became the objects of a suspicious legislation, which deprived them of most of the rights of freemen, and reduced them to a social position very similar, in many respects, to that which inveterate prejudice in many parts of Europe has fixed upon the Jews. Hence, too, legislative restraints on the bounty or justice of the master in manumitting his slave.

Intermarriage with the inferior race, whether bond or free, was prohibited by religion as a sin, by public opinion as a shame, and by law as a crime. But neither law, gospel, nor public opinion could prevent that amalgamation which, according to all experience, inevitably and extensively takes place whenever two races come into that close juxtaposition which domestic slavery of necessity implies. Falsehood and hypocrisy took the place of restraint and self-denial. The Dutch, French, Spanish, and Portuguese colonists, less filled with pride of race, and less austere and pretending in their religious morality, esteemed that white man mean and cruel who did not, so far as his ability permitted, secure for his colored children emancipation and some pecuniary pro-

25

vision. Laws were even found necessary, in some of those colonies, to limit what was esteemed a superfluity of parental tenderness. In the Anglo-American colonies. colored children were hardly less numerous   But conventional decorum, more potent than law, forbade any recognition by the father. They followed the condition of the mother. They were born, and they remained slaves. European blood was thus constantly transferred into servile veins; and hence, among the slaves sold and bought to-day in our American markets, may be found the descendants of men distinguished in colonial and national annals.—*Hildreth's History United States.*

In Massachusetts a controversy arose as to the justice and legality of negro slavery, which was conducted by able writers. It began about 1766 and was continued until 1773, when the subject was very warmly agitated. In 1767 and afterwards, attempts were made in the legislature to restrict the further importation of slaves. It was even questioned whether, under the laws of Massachusetts, any person could be held as a slave. This point was carried before the superior court in a suit by a negro to recover wages from his alleged master. The negroes collected money among themselves to carry on the suit, and it terminated favorably. Other suits were instituted between that time and the revolution, and the juries invariably gave their verdict in favor of freedom. The pleas on the part of the masters were, that the negroes were purchased in open market, and bills of sale were produced in evidence; that the laws of the province recognized slavery as existing in it, by declaring that no person should manumit his slave without giving bond for his maintenance, &c. On the part of the blacks, it was pleaded that the royal charter expressly declared all persons born or residing in the province to be as free as the king's subjects in Great Britain; that, by the law of England, no subject could be deprived of his liberty but by the judgment of his peers; that the laws of the province respecting an evil, and attempting to mitigate or regulate it, did not authorize it; and on some occasions the plea was, that though the slavery of the parents were admitted, yet no disability of that kind could descend to the children.[*]

The view taken by the Massachusetts juries, was sanctioned about the same time in England by a solemn decision of the court of king's bench, in the celebrated case of James Somersett, mentioned in a former chapter. Being brought before Lord Mansfield on a writ of habeas corpus, his case was referred to the full court. After the argument, Lord Mansfield said: "In five or six cases of this nature, I have known it accommodated by agreement between the parties. On its first coming before me I strongly recommended it here. But if the parties will have it decided, we must give our opinion. Compassion will not on the one hand, nor inconvenience on the other, be to decide, but the law." "The question now is, whether any dominion, authority, or coercion can be exercised in this country on a slave according to the American laws. The difficulty of adopting the relation, without adopting it in all

---

[*] Belknap in Massachusetts Historical Collections.

its consequences, is indeed extreme; yet many of those consequences are absolutely contrary to the municipal law of England. On the other hand, should we think the coercive power cannot be exercised, it is now about fifty years since the opinion" to the contrary "by two of the greatest men of their own or any time." This referred to the opinion of Yorke and Talbot, subsequently recognized as law by Lord Hardwicke, sitting as chancelor. "The setting fourteen or fifteen thousand men"—the estimated number of negro slaves in England—"at once loose by a solemn opinion, is very disagreeable in the effects it threatens." But "if the parties will have judgment, *fiat justitia ruat cœlum*, let justice be done, whatever be the consequence. Fifty pounds may not be a high price; then a loss follows to the proprietors of above £700,000 sterling. How would the law stand in respect to their settlement—their wages? How many actions for any slight coercion by the master? We can not in any of these points direct the law, the law must direct us."

Afterward, in giving judgment, June 22, 1772, Lord Mansfield said: "The only question before us is whether the cause on the return is sufficient. If it is, the negro must be remanded; if it is not, he must be discharged. The return states that the slave departed, and refused to serve, whereupon he was kept to be sold abroad. So high an act of dominion must be recognized by the law of the country where it is used. The power of a master over his slave has been exceedingly different in different countries. The state of slavery is of such a nature that it is incapable of being introduced on any reasons moral or political, but only by positive law, which preserves its force long after the reasons, occasions, and time itself from whence it was created is erased from memory. It is so odious that nothing can be suffered to support it but positive law. Whatever inconveniences, therefore, may follow from the decision, I can not say this case is allowed or approved by the law of England, and therefore the black must be discharged."

The continental congress which assembled in Philadelphia in 1784, made a declaration of colonial rights. As means of enforcing this claim of rights, fourteen articles were agreed to to form the basis of an "American Association," and in one of these articles the slave-trade was especially denounced; and entire abstinence from it, and from any trade with those concerned in it, formed a part of the association.

CHAPTER XXII.

SLAVERY UNDER THE CONFEDERATION.—EMANCIPATION BY THE STATES.

Number of Slaves in the United States at the period of the declaration of Independence.—Proportion in each of the thirteen States.—Declaration against slavery in the State Constitution of Delaware.—Constitutions of Massachusetts and New Hampshire held to prohibit slavery, by Supreme Courts, 1783.—Act of Pennsylvania Assembly, 1780, forbids introduction of slaves, and gives freedom to all persons thereafter born in that State.—A similar law enacted in Connecticut and Rhode Island, 1784.—Virginia Assembly prohibits further introduction of slaves, 1778, and emancipation encouraged, 1782.—Maryland enacts similar laws, 1783.—Opinions of Washington, Jefferson, and Patrick Henry.—New York and New Jersey prohibit further introduction of slaves.—North Carolina declares further introduction of slaves highly impolitic, 1786.—Example of other States not followed by Georgia and South Carolina.—Action of Congress on the subject of the Territories, 1784.—Jefferson's provision excluding slavery, struck out of ordinance.—Proceedings of 1787.—Ordinance for the government of the territory north-west of the Ohio, including Jefferson's provision prohibiting slavery, passed by unanimous vote.

THE number of slaves in the United States at the time of the Declaration of Independence has been estimated at half a million. The following table exhibits their numbers in each state. It appears that slavery existed in all of the thirteen states at the commencement of the revolutionary war; but shortly after its close, as we shall see hereafter, slavery and the slave-trade were abolished in some of the states:

NUMBER OF SLAVES IN THE UNITED STATES IN 1776.

Massachusetts	3,500	Delaware	9,000
Rhode Island	4,373	Maryland	80,000
Connecticut	5,000	Virginia	165,000
New Hampshire	629	North Carolina	75,000
New York	15,000	South Carolina	110,000
New Jersey	7,600	Georgia	16,000
Pennsylvania	10,000		

No distinct provision on the subject of slavery appears in any of the state constitutions of the period, except in that of Delaware, which provided "that no person hereafter imported from Africa ought to be held in slavery under any pretense whatever;" and that "no negro, Indian, or mulatto slave ought to be brought into this state for sale from any part of the world."

Legal proceedings commenced in Massachusetts prior to the revolution to test the legality of slavery there, and though resulting in favor of the claimants of freedom, failed, however, to produce a general emancipation. Some attempts made at the commencement of the revolution to introduce the subject into the provincial Congress of Massachusetts were defeated; and that body seemed to recognize the legality of slavery by a resolution that no negro slave should be enlisted in the army. In 1777, a prize ship from Jamaica, with several slaves on board, was brought into Salem by a privateer. The slaves were advertised for sale; but the General Court interfered, and they were set at liberty. The declaration, presently inserted into the Massachusetts Bill of

Rights, that "all men are born free and equal," was *held by the supreme court of that state to prohibit slavery.* So it was *decided* in 1783, upon an indictment for assault and battery against a master for beating his alleged slave. A similar clause in the second constitution of New Hampshire was *held to guarantee personal freedom* to all born in that state after its adoption.

An act of the Pennsylvania Assembly of 1780, passed principally through the efforts of George Bryan, and a little prior in date to the ratification of the constitution of Massachusetts, *forbade the further introduction of slaves,* and *gave freedom to all persons thereafter born in that state.* Moderate as it was, this act did not pass without a good deal of opposition. Several members of Assembly entered a protest against it, acknowledging, indeed, "the humanity and justice of manumitting slaves in time of peace," but denouncing the present act as "imprudent" and "premature," and likely to have, by way of example, a most dangerous effect on the southern states, whither the seat of war seemed about to be transferred. In 1784, *laws similar to that of Pennsylvania* were enacted in Connecticut and Rhode Island.

The Virginia Assembly, on the motion of Jefferson, *prohibited,* in 1778, *the further introduction of slaves.* In 1782, the old colonial statute was repealed, which forbade emancipations except for meritorious services, to be adjudged by the governor and council. This repeal remained in force for ten years, during which period *private emancipations were very numerous.* But for the subsequent reënactment of the old restrictions, the free colored population of Virginia might now have exceeded the slaves. Maryland *followed the footsteps of Virginia* both in prohibiting the further introduction of slaves and in removing the restraints on emancipation.

That feeling which led in New England and Pennsylvania to the legal abolition of slavery, was strongly responded to by the most illustrious and enlightened citizens of Maryland and Virginia. JEFFERSON denounced the whole system of slavery, in the most emphatic terms, as fatal to manners and industry, and endangering the very principles on which the liberties of the state were founded—"a perpetual exercise of the most unremitting despotism on the one part, and degrading submission on the other." Similar sentiments were entertained and expressed by PATRICK HENRY. "Would any one believe," he wrote, "that I am a master of slaves of my own purchase? I am drawn along by the general inconvenience of living here without them. I will not—I can not justify it! I believe a time will come when an opportunity will be offered to abolish this lamentable evil. Every thing we can do is to improve it, if it happens in our day; if not, let us transmit to our descendants, together with our slaves, a pity for their unhappy lot, and an abhorrence of slavery." WASHINGTON avowed to all his correspondents "that it was among his first wishes to see some plan adopted by which slavery may be abolished by law." But these generous sentiments were confined to a few liberal and enlightened men. The uneducated and unreflecting mass did not sympathize with them. JEFFERSON, in his old age, in a letter on this subject, says: "From those of a former generation, who were in the fullness of age when I came into public life, I soon saw that nothing was to be hoped. Nursed and educated in the daily habit of seeing the degraded condition, both bodily and mental, of those unfortunate beings, not reflecting that that degradation was very much the work of themselves and their fathers, few had yet doubted that they were as legitimate subjects of property as their horses and cattle. The quiet and monotonous course of colonial life had been disturbed by no alarm and little reflection on the value of liberty, and when alarm was taken at an enterprise on their own, it was not easy to carry them the whole length of the principles which they invoked for themselves. In the first or second session of the legislature after I became a member, I drew to this subject the attention of Colonel Bland, one of the oldest, ablest, and most respectable members, and he undertook to move for certain moderate extension of the protection of the laws to these people. I seconded his motion, and, as a younger member, was more spared in the debate; but he was denounced as an enemy to his country, and was treated with the greatest indecorum." With the advance of the revolution, the sentiments of Jefferson made a certain progress, resulting in the prohibition of the slave-trade and the freedom of emancipations, already mentioned; yet, though the constitution of Virginia declared life, liberty, and property to be unalienable rights, no legal restraint was placed upon the exorbitant and despotic power hitherto exercised over those held as slaves; and Washington, in 1785, complained in a letter to La Fayette that some "petitions for the abolition of slavery, presented to the Virginia Legislature, could scarcely obtain a hearing."

New York and New Jersey followed the example of Virginia and Maryland in *prohibiting the further introduction of slaves*—a prohibition extended to the domestic as well as to the African slave trade. Neither of these states, however, declared a general emancipation until many years thereafter. Slavery did not wholly cease in New York until about 1830, and in New Jersey a few years later.

The same generous sentiments had penetrated also into North Carolina, especially among the Quaker population; but the legislators of that state did not fully sympathize with them. Complaining of the frequency and danger of freedom given to slaves, the Assembly of 1777 reënacted the old restrictive law on the subject, with this modification, that, instead of the governor and council, the consent of the county court was made necessary to emancipations; and all negroes emancipated without that consent were ordered to be resold into slavery. Yet in 1786, by an act which declared the introduction of slaves into the state to be "*of evil consequences and highly impolitic,*" a duty of £5 per head was imposed upon all future importations. South Carolina and Georgia omitted to follow the example of the other states in enacting laws to prevent or restrict the further introduction of slaves. So long, however, as the war lasted, an effectual stop, so far as importations from Africa were concerned, was put to that detestable traffic. Congress, indeed, never abrogated that part of the American Association by which the African slave-trade was totally renounced.

The disposition of the territories belonging to the thirteen recent colonies, now confederated as independent states, became a subject of solicitude in the states and in Congress. By the terms of their charters, some of the colonies had an indefinite extension westwardly, and were only limited by the power of the grantor. Many of these charters conflicted with each other—the same territory being included within the limits of two or more totally distinct colonies. As the expenses of the revolutionary struggle began to bear heavily on the resources of the states, it was keenly felt by some that their share in the advantages of the expected triumph would be less than that of others. Massachusetts, Connecticut, New York, Virginia, North Carolina, and Georgia, laid claim to spacious dominions outside of their proper boundaries: while New Hampshire, (save in Vermont,) Rhode Island, New Jersey, Maryland, Delaware, and South Carolina, possessed no such boasted resources to meet the war-debts constantly augmenting. They urged, therefore, with obvious justice, that these unequal advantages ought to be surrendered, and all the lands within the territorial limits of the Union, but outside of the proper and natural boundaries of the several states, respectively, should be ceded to, and held by, Congress, in trust for the common benefit of all the states, and their proceeds employed in satisfaction of the debts and liabilities of the Confederation. This reasonable requisition was ultimately, but with some reservations, responded to. Virginia reserved a sufficiency beyond the Ohio to furnish the bounties promised to her revolutionary officers and soldiers. Connecticut, a western reserve, since largely settled from the parent state. Massachusetts reserved five millions of acres, located in Western New York, which she claimed to be entitled by her charter to own. In either of these cases, the fee only was reserved, the sovereignty being surrendered.

The cessions were severally made during, or directly after the close of the revolutionary war. And one of the most obvious duties devolved on the Continental Congress, which held its sessions in Philadelphia directly after the close of that exhausting struggle, was the framing of an act or ordinance for the government of the vast domain thus committed to its care and disposal.

The responsible duty of framing this ordinance was devolved by Congress on a select committee, consisting of Mr. Jefferson of Va., (chairman,) Chase of Md., and Howell of R. I.; who in due time reported a plan for the government of the western territory, contemplating the whole region included within our boundaries west of the old thirteen states, and as far south as our 31st degree of north latitude; territory as yet partially ceded to the Confederation, but which was expected to be so, and embracing several of our present slave states. This plan contemplated the ultimate division of this territory into seventeen states, eight of them situated below the parallel of the Falls of the Ohio, (now Louisville,) and nine above it. Among other rules reported from this committee by Mr. Jefferson, for the government of this vast region, was the following:

"That after the year 1800, of the Christian era, there shall be neither slavery nor involuntary servitude in any of the said *states*, otherwise than in punishment of crimes, whereof the party shall have been convicted to be personally guilty."

Congress having the aforesaid report under consideration, April 19, 1784, Mr. Spaight, of N. C., moved the striking out of the above paragraph. Mr. Read, of S. C., seconded the motion. The ayes and nays, being required by Mr. Howell, were ordered, and put in this form—" Shall the words moved to be stricken out stand ?"

The question was lost, and the words were struck out, although six states voted aye to only three nay ; and though of the members present, fifteen voted for, to six against, Mr. Jefferson's proposition. But the articles of confederation required a vote of nine states to carry a proposition ; and, failing to receive so many, this comprehensive exclusion of slavery from the federal territories was defeated. The ordinance, thus depleted, after undergoing some further amendments, was finally approved, April 23d—all the delegates, but those from South Carolina, voting in the affirmative.

In 1787, the last Continental Congress, sitting in New York simultaneously with the Convention at Philadelphia which framed our Federal Constitution, took up the subject of the government of the western territory, raising a committee thereon, of which Nathan Dane, of Massachusetts, was chairman. That committee reported (July 11th) " An Ordinance for the government of the Territory of the United States, *Northwest of the Ohio* "—the larger area contemplated by Mr. Jefferson's bill not having been ceded by the southern states claiming dominion over it. This bill embodied many of the provisions originally drafted and reported by Mr. Jefferson, but with some modifications, and concludes with six unalterable articles of perpetual compact, the last of them as follows :

" There shall be neither slavery nor involuntary servitude in the said territory, otherwise than in punishment of crimes, whereof the parties shall be duly convicted."

To this was added, prior to its passage, the stipulation for the delivery of fugitives from labor or service, soon after embodied in the Federal Constitution ; and in this shape, the entire ordinance was adopted (July 13th) by a unanimous vote, Georgia and the Carolinas concurring.

CHAPTER XXIII.

FORMATION OF THE CONSTITUTION—SLAVERY COMPROMISES.

Convention assembles at Philadelphia, 1787.—Proceedings in reference to the slave basis of representation, the second compromise of the Constitution.—Debate.—Remarks of Patterson, Wilson, King, Gouverneur Morris, and Sherman.—Debate on the Importation of slaves, by Rutledge, Ellsworth, Sherman, C. Pinckney.—Denunciation of slavery by Mason of Virginia.—The third Compromise, the continuance of the African slave-trade for twenty years, and the unrestricted power of Congress to enact Navigation laws.

THE convention of delegates from the several states to revise the Articles of Confederation, was legally assembled at Philadelphia, in 1787, and appointed George Washington its President. The result of its labors was the formation of the present Constitution of the United States, though some amendments were afterwards made.

The fourteenth of May was the day appointed for the meeting of the convention; but seven states were not present till eleven days later, when the convention assembled in the chamber of the State House in Philadelphia, in which the Continental Congress, while resident in that city, had been accustomed to hold its sessions, and in which the independence of the United States had been declared. Washington was a member, and so was Franklin, for the two years since his return from Europe president of Pennsylvania. As Franklin could be the only competitor for the place of president of the convention, the nomination of Washington came gracefully from Robert Morris, on behalf of the Pennsylvania delegation. A secretary was chosen, and a committee appointed to report rules of proceeding.

Upon the report of this committee rules were adopted, copied chiefly from those of Congress. As in Congress, each state was to have one vote; seven states were to constitute a quorum; all committees were to be appointed by ballot; the doors were to be closed, and an injunction of secrecy, never removed, was placed on the debates. The members were not even allowed to take copies of the entries on the journal.

Eleven states were soon represented by about fifty delegates from among the most illustrious citizens of the states—men highly distinguished for talents, character, practical knowledge, and public services. The aged Franklin had sat in the Albany convention of 1754, in which the first attempt had been made at colonial union. Dickinson, who sat in the present convention as one of the members from Delaware, William S. Johnson, of Connecticut, and John Rutledge, of South Carolina, had participated in the Stamp Act Congress of 1765. Besides Washington, Dickinson, and Rutledge, who had belonged to the Continental Congress of 1774, there were also present, from among the members of that body, Roger Sherman, of Connecticut, William Livingston, governor of New Jersey, George Read, of Delaware, and George Wythe, of Virginia; and of the signers of the Declaration of Independence—besides Franklin, Read, Wythe, and Sherman—Elbridge Gerry, of Massachusetts, and Robert Morris, George Clymer, and James Wilson, of Pennsylvania. Eighteen members were at the same time delegates to the Continental Congress; and of the whole number there were only twelve who had not sat at some time in that body. The officers of the revolutionary army were represented by Washington, Mifflin, Hamilton, and Charles Cotesworth Pinckney, who had been colonel of one of the South Carolina regiments, and at one time an aid-de-camp to Washington. Of those members who had come prominently forward since the declaration of independence, the most conspicuous were Hamilton, Madison, and Edmund Randolph, who had lately succeeded Patrick Henry as governor of Virginia. The members who took the leading part in the debates were Madison, Mason, and Randolph, of Virginia; Gerry, Gorham, and King, of Massachusetts; Wilson, Gouverneur Morris, and Franklin, of Pennsylvania; Johnson, Sherman, and Ellsworth, of Connecticut; Hamilton and Lansing, of New York; Charles Cotesworth Pinckney and Charles Pinckney, of South Carolina—the latter chosen governor of that State the next year; Patterson, of New Jersey; Martin, of Maryland; Dickinson, of Delaware; and Williamson, of North Carolina.

In settling a rule of apportionment, several questions were to be considered. What should be the number of representatives in the first branch of the legislature? Ought the number from each state to be fixed, or to increase with the increase of population? Ought population alone to be the basis of apportionment? or should property be taken into account? Whatever rule might be adopted, no apportionment founded upon population could be made until an enumeration of the inhabitants should have been taken. The number of representatives was, therefore, for the time being, fixed at sixty-five, and apportioned as directed by the constitution, Art. I. sec. 2.

In establishing a rule of future apportionment, great diversity of opinion was expressed. Although slavery then existed in all the states except Massachusetts, the great mass of the slave population was in the southern states. These states claimed a representation according to numbers, bond and free, while the northern states were in favor of a representation according to the number of free persons only. This rule was forcibly urged by several of the northern delegates. Mr. Patterson, of New Jersey, regarded slaves only as property. They were not represented in the states; why should they be in the general government? They were not allowed to vote; why should they be represented? It was an encouragement of the slave-trade. Said Mr. Wilson, of Pennsylvania: "Are they admitted as citizens? then why not on an equality with citizens? Are they admitted as property? then why is not other property admitted into the computation?" A large portion of the members of the convention, from both sections of the Union, aware that neither extreme could be carried, favored the proposition to count the whole number of free citizens and three-fifths of all others.

Prior to this discussion, a select committee, to whom this subject had been referred, had reported in favor of a distribution of the members on the basis of wealth and numbers, to be regulated by the legislature. Before the question was taken on this report, a proviso was moved and agreed to, that direct taxes should be in proportion to representation. Subsequently a proposition was moved for reckoning three-fifths of the slaves in estimating taxes, and making taxation the basis of representation, which was adopted; New Jersey and Delaware against it, Massachusetts and South Carolina divided; New York not represented, her three delegates being all absent.

To render the constitution acceptable to the southern states, which were the principal exporting states, the committee of detail had inserted a clause, providing that no duties should be laid on exports, or on slaves imported; and another, that no navigation act might be passed, except by a two-thirds vote. By depriving congress of the power of giving any preference to American over foreign shipping, it was designed to secure cheap transportation to southern exports. As the shipping was principally owned in the eastern states, their delegates were equally anxious to prevent any restriction of the power of congress to pass navigation laws. All the states, except North Carolina, South Carolina, and Georgia, had prohibited the importation of slaves; and North Carolina had proceeded so far as to discourage the importation by heavy duties. The prohibition of duties on the importation of slaves was demanded by the delegates from South Carolina and Georgia, who declared that, without a provision of this kind, the constitution would not receive the assent of these states. The support which the proposed restriction received from other states, was given to it from a disposition to compromise, rather than from an approval of the measure itself. The proposition not only gave rise to a discussion of its own merits, but révived the opposition to the apportionment of representatives according to the three-fifths ratio, and called forth some severe denunciations of slavery.

Mr. King, of Massachusetts, in reference to the admission of slaves as a part of the representative population, remarked : " He had not made a strenuous opposition to it heretofore, because he had hoped that this concession would have produced a readiness, which had not been manifested, to strengthen the general government. The report of the committee put an end to all those hopes. The importation of slaves could not be prohibited ; exports could not be taxed. If slaves are to be imported, shall not the exports produced by their labor supply a revenue to help the government defend their masters? There was so much inequality and unreasonableness in all this, that the people of the northern states could never be reconciled to it. He had hoped that some accommodation would have taken place on the subject ; that at least a time would have been limited for the importation of slaves. He could never agree to let them be imported without limitation, and then be represented in the national legislature. Either slaves should not be represented, or exports should be taxable."

Gouverneur Morris, of Pa., pronounced slavery " a nefarious institution. It was the curse of Heaven on the states where it prevailed. Compare the free regions of the middle states, where a rich and noble cultivation marks the prosperity and happiness of the people, with the misery and poverty which overspread the barren wastes of Virginia, Maryland, and the other states having slaves. Travel through the whole continent, and you behold the prospect continually varying with the appearance and disappearance of slavery. The admission of slaves into the representation, when fairly explained, comes to this, that the inhabitant of Georgia and South Carolina, who goes to the coast of Africa in defiance of the most sacred laws of humanity, tears away his fellow-creatures from their dearest connections, and damns them to the most cruel bondage, shall have more votes in a government instituted for the protection of the rights of mankind, than the citizen of Pennsylvania or New Jersey, who views with a laudable horror so nefarious a practice. And what is the proposed compensation to the northern states for a sacrifice of every principle of right, every impulse of humanity ? They are to bind themselves to march their militia for the defense of the southern states, against those very slaves of whom they complain. The legislature will have indefinite power to tax them by excises and duties on imports, both of which will fall heavier on them than on the southern inhabitants ; for the Bohea tea used by a northern freeman, will pay more tax than the whole consumption of the miserable slave, which consists of nothing more than his physical subsistence and the rag which covers his naked-ness. On the other side, the southern states are not to be restrained from im-porting fresh supplies of wretched Africans, at once to increase the danger of attack and the difficulty of defense ; nay, they are to be encouraged to it by an assurance of having their votes in the national government increased in pro-portion, and, at the same time, are to have their slaves and their exports ex-empt from all contributions to the public service." Mr. Morris moved to make the free population alone the basis of representation.

Mr. Sherman, of Ct., who had on other occasions manifested a disposition to compromise, again favored the southern side. He " did not regard the ad-mission of the negroes as liable to such insuperable objections. It was the freemen of the southern states who were to be represented according to the taxes paid by them, and the negroes are only included in the estimate of the taxes."

After some farther discussion, the question was taken upon Mr. Morris' mo-tion, and lost, New Jersey only voting for it.

With respect to prohibiting any restriction upon the importation of slaves, Mr. Martin, of Maryland, who moved to allow a tax upon slaves imported, remarked: " As five slaves in the apportionment of representatives were reck-oned as equal to three freemen, such a permission amounted to an encourage-ment of the slave-trade. Slaves weakened the union which the other parts were bound to protect; the privilege of importing them was therefore unrea-sonable. Such a feature in the constitution was inconsistent with the principles of the revolution, and dishonorable to the American character."

Mr. Rutledge, of S. C., " did not see how this section would encourage the importation of slaves. He was not apprehensive of insurrections, and would readily exempt the other states from every obligation to protect the south. Religion and humanity had nothing at all to do with this question. Interest alone is the governing principle with nations. The true question at present is, whether the southern states shall or shall not be parties to the union. If the northern states consult their interest, they will not oppose the increase of slaves, which will increase the commodities of which they will become the car-riers."

Mr. Ellsworth, of Ct., said : " Let every state import what it pleases. The morality or wisdom of slavery is a consideration belonging to the states. What enriches a part enriches the whole, and the states are the best judges of their particular interests."

Mr. C. Pinckney said : " South Carolina can never receive the plan if it prohibits the slave-trade. If the states be left at liberty on this subject, South

Carolina may perhaps, by degrees, do of herself what is wished, as Maryland and Virginia already have done."

Mr. Sherman, of Ct., concurred with his colleague, (Mr. Ellsworth.) "He disapproved the slave-trade; but as the states now possessed the right, and the public good did not require it to be taken away; and as it was expedient to have as few objections as possible to the proposed scheme of government, he would leave the matter as he found it. The abolition of slavery seemed to be going on in the United States, and the good sense of the several states would probably, by degrees, soon complete it."

Mr. Mason, of Va., said: "Slavery discourages arts and manufactures. The poor despise labor when performed by slaves. They prevent the immigration of whites, who really enrich and strengthen a country. They produce a pernicious effect on manners. Every master of slaves is born a petty tyrant. They bring the judgment of heaven on a country. He lamented that some of our eastern brethren, from a lust of gain, had embarked in this nefarious traffic. As to the states being in possession of the right to import, that was the case of many other rights now to be given up. He held it essential, in every point of view, that the general government should have power to prevent the increase of slavery."

Mr. Ellsworth, not well pleased with this thrust at his slave-trading friends at the north, by a slave-holder, tartly replied: "As I have never owned a slave, I can not judge of the effects of slavery on character; but if slavery is to be considered in a moral light, the convention ought to go further, and free those already in the country." The opposition of Virginia and Maryland to the importation of slaves he attributed to the fact that, on account of the rapid increase in those states, "it was cheaper to raise them there than to import them, while in the sickly rice swamps foreign supplies were necessary. If we stop short with prohibiting their importation, we shall be unjust to South Carolina and Georgia. Let us not intermeddle. As population increases, poor laborers will be so plenty as to render slaves useless. Slavery, in time, will not be a speck in our country."

Delegates from South Carolina and Georgia repeated the declaration that, if the slave-trade were prohibited, these states would not adopt the constitution. Virginia, it was said, would gain by stopping the importation, she having slaves to sell; but it would be unjust to South Carolina and Georgia to be deprived of the right of importing. Besides, the importation of slaves would be a benefit to the whole union. The more slaves, the more produce, the greater carrying trade, the more consumption, the more revenue.

Williamson, of N. C., expressed his conviction that the two southern states, if prohibited to import slaves, would not become members of the union. Wilson, of Pa., suggested that, if negroes were the only imports not subject to a duty, such an exception would amount to a bounty. Gerry, of Mass., thought the convention had nothing to do with the conduct of the states as to slavery; but they ought to be careful not to give any sanction to it. Dickinson and Langdon, of New Hampshire, maintained that neither honor, safety, nor good conscience would allow permission to the states to continue the slave-trade. King thought the subject should be considered in a political light only. If two southern states would not consent to the prohibition, neither would other states to the allowance. "The exemption of slaves from duty while every other import was subject to it, was an inequality that could not fail to strike the commercial sagacity of the northern and middle states."

This hint about a tax was not thrown away. Charles Pinckney, of S. C., would consent to a tax equal to that imposed on other imports, and he moved a commitment with that view. Rutledge seconded the motion. Gouverneur Morris proposed that the whole article, including the clauses relating to navigation laws and taxes on exports, should be referred to the same committee. "These things," he remarked, "may form a bargain among the northern and southern states." Sherman suggested that a tax on slaves imported would make the matter worse, since it implied they were property. Randolph supported the commitment in hopes that some middle ground might be hit upon. He would rather risk the constitution than support the clause as it stood. Ellsworth advocated the article as it was. "This widening of opinions had a threatening aspect. He was afraid we should lose two states, with such others as might be disposed to stand aloof, should fly into a variety of shapes and directions, and most probably into several confederations—not without bloodshed." The motion for reference prevailed, and the article was referred to a grand committee of one from each state. The report of this committee retained the prohibition of export duties, but struck out the restriction on the enactment of navigation laws. Until the year 1800 it allowed the unrestrained migration or importation of such persons as the states might see fit to receive, subject, however, to the imposition of a duty by congress, the maximum of which was presently fixed at ten dollars.

Williamson, of N. C., declared himself, both in opinion and practice, against slavery; but he thought it more in favor of humanity, from a view of all circumstances, to let in South Carolina and Georgia on these terms, than to exclude them from the union. Sherman, of Ct., again objected to the tax as acknowledging men to be property. Gorham, of Mass., replied that the duty ought to be considered, not as implying that men are property, but as a discouragement to their importation. Sherman said the duty was too small to bear that character. Madison thought it "wrong to admit, in the constitution, the idea that there could be property in a man," and the phraseology of one clause was subsequently altered to avoid any such implication. Gouverneur Morris objected that the clause gave congress power to tax freemen imported; to which Mason replied that such a power was necessary to prevent the importation of convicts. A motion to extend the time from 1800 to 1808, made by C. C. Pinckney and seconded by Gorham, was carried against the votes of New Jersey, Pennsylvania, Delaware and Virginia; Massachusetts, Connecticut, and New Hampshire voting this time with Georgia and South Carolina. That part of the report which struck out the restriction on the enactment of navigation acts was opposed by Charles Pinckney in a set speech, in which he enumerated five distinct commercial interests: the fisheries and West India trade, belonging to New England; the interest of New York in a free trade; wheat and flour, the staples of New Jersey and Pennsylvania; tobacco, the staple of Maryland and Virginia, and partly of North Carolina; rice and indigo, the staples of South Carolina and Georgia. The same ground was taken by Williamson and Mason, and very warmly by Randolph, who declared that an unlimited power in congress to enact navigation laws "would complete the deformity of a system having already so many odious features that he hardly knew if he could agree to it." Any restriction of the power of congress over commerce was warmly opposed by Gouverneur Morris, Wilson, and Gorham. Madison also took the same side. C. C. Pinckney did not deny that it was the true interest of the south to have no regulation of commerce; but, considering the commercial losses of the eastern states during the revolution, their liberal conduct toward the views of South Carolina (in the vote just taken, giving eight years' further extension to the slave-trade), and the interest of the weak southern states in being united with the strong eastern ones, he should go against any restrictions on the power of commercial regulation. "He had himself prejudices against the eastern states before he came here, but would acknowledge that he had found them as liberal and candid as any men whatever." Butler and Rutledge took the same ground, and the amended report was adopted, against the votes of Maryland, Virginia, North Carolina, and Georgia.

Thus, by an understanding, or, as Gouverneur Morris called it, "a bargain," between the commercial representatives of the northern states and the delegates of South Carolina and Georgia, and in spite of the opposition of Maryland and Virginia, the unrestricted power of congress to enact navigation laws was conceded to the northern merchants, and to the Carolina rice planters, as an equivalent, twenty years' continuance of the African slave-trade. This was the third great compromise of the constitution. The other two were the concession to the smaller states of an equal representation in the senate, and, to the slave-holders, the counting three fifths of the slaves in determining the ratio of representation. If this third compromise differed from the other two by involving not merely a political, but a moral sacrifice, there was this partial compensation about it, that it was not permanent, like the others, but expired at the end of twenty years by its own limitation.*

When the article came up providing for the mutual delivery of fugitives from justice, a motion was made by Butler, seconded by C. Pinckney, that fugitive slaves and servants be included. Wilson objected that this would require a delivery at the public expense. Sherman saw no more propriety in the public seizing and surrendering a servant than a horse. Butler withdrew his motion; but the next day he introduced a clause substantially the same with that now found in the constitution, which provides that "no person held to service or labor in one state, under the laws thereof, escaping into another,

---

* Secret Debates. Hildreth's History of U. S. Political History of U. S.

shall, in consequence of any law or regulation therein, be discharged from such service or labor, but shall be delivered up on claim of the party to whom such service or labor may be due."

The constitution bears date the 17th of September, 1787. It was immediately transmitted to congress, with a recommendation to that body to submit it to state conventions for ratification, which was accordingly done. It was adopted by Delaware, December 7; by Pennsylvinia, December 12; by New Jersey, December 18; by Georgia, January 2, 1788; by Connecticut, January 9; by Massachusetts, February 7; by Maryland, April 28; by South Carolina, May 23; by New Hampshire, June 21; which being the ninth ratifying state, gave effect to the constitution. Virginia ratified June 27; New York, July 26; and North Carolina, conditionally, August 7. Rhode Island did not call a convention.

In Massachusetts, Virginia and New York, the constitution encountered a most formidable opposition, which rendered its adoption by these states for a time extremely doubtful. In their conventions were men on both sides who had been members of the national convention, associated with others of distinguished abilities. In Massachusetts there were several adverse influences which would probably have defeated the ratification in that state, had it not been accompanied by certain proposed amendments to be submitted by congress to the several states for ratification. The adoption of these by the convention gained for the constitution the support of Hancock and Samuel Adams; and the question on ratification was carried by one hundred and eighty-seven against one hundred and sixty-eight.

In the Virginia convention, the constitution was opposed by Patrick Henry, James Monroe, and George Mason, the last of whom had been one of the convention framers. On the other side were John Marshall, Mr. Pendleton, Mr. Madison, George Wythe, and Edmund Randolph, the three last also having been members of the national convention. Mr. Randolph had refused to sign the constitution, but had become one of its warmest advocates. In the convention of this state, also, the ratification was aided by the adoption of a bill of rights and certain proposed amendments; and was carried, eighty-eight yeas against eighty nays.

In the convention of New York, the opposition embraced a majority of its members, among whom were Yates and Lansing, members of the general convention, and George Clinton. The principal advocates of the constitution were John Jay, Robert R. Livingston, and Mr. Hamilton. Strong efforts were made for a conditional ratification, which were successfully opposed, though not without the previous adoption of a bill of rights, and numerous amendments. With these, the absolute ratification was carried, thirty-one to twenty-nine.

The ratification of North Carolina was not received by congress until January, 1790; and that of Rhode Island, not until June of the same year.

The injunction of secrecy as to the proceedings of the convention was never removed. At the final adjournment, the Journal, in accordance with a previous vote, was intrusted to the custody of Washington, by whom it was afterward deposited in the department of state. It was first printed by order of congress in 1818. Yates, one of the members from New York, took short notes of the earlier debates, which were publishad after his death in 1821. The more perfect notes of Madison, recently published, with the official Journal, the notes of Yates, and a representation to the legislature of Maryland, made by Luther Martin, furnish materials for a view, tolerably complete, of the conflicting opinions by which the convention was divided, and of the process which gradually matured and brought into shape the federal consititution.

The following are the provisions of the constitution which are presumed to relate to the subject of slavery :

Preamble. "We, the people of the United States, in order to form a more perfect Union, establish justice, insure domestic tranquility, provide for the common defense, promote the general welfare, and secure the blessings of liberty to ourselves and our posterity, do ordain and establish this constitution for the United States of America.

"Art. 1. Sec. 1. All legislative powers herein granted, shall be vested in a congress of the United States, which shall consist of a senate and house of representatives.

" Sec. 2. * * * Representatives and direct taxes shall be apportioned among the several states which may be included within this Union, according to their respective numbers, which shall be determined by adding to the whole number of free persons, including those bound to servitude for a term of years, and excluding Indians not taxed, three-fifths of all other persons.

" Sec. 9. The migration or importation of such persons as any of the states now existing shall think proper to admit, shall not be prohibited by the congress prior tó the year 1808 ; but a tax or duty may be imposed, not exceeding ten dollars on each person.

" The privilege of the writ of *habeas corpus* shall not be suspended, unless when, in the cases of rebellion or invasion, the public safety may require it.

" No bill of attainder, or *ex post facto* laws, shall be passed.

"Art. III. Sec. 3. Treason against the United States shall consist only in levying war against them, or in adhering to their enemies, giving them aid and comfort.

"Art. IV. Sec. 2. The citizens of each state shall be entitled to all the privileges of citizens, in the several states.

" No person held to service or labor in one state, under the laws thereof, escaping into another, shall, in consequence of any law or regulation therein, be discharged from such service or labor, but shall be delivered up on claim of the party to whom such service or labor may be due.

Sec. 3. New states may be admitted by the congress into this Union ; but no new state shall be formed or erected within the jurisdiction of any other state ; nor any state be formed by the junction of two or more states, or **parts**

26

of states, without the consent of the legislatures of the states concerned, as well as of the congress.

"The congress shall have power to dispose of, and make all needful rules and regulations respecting the territory or other property belonging to the United States; and nothing in this constitution shall be so construed as to prejudice any claims of the United States, or of any particular state.

"Sec. 4.   The United States shall guarantee to every state in this Union a republican form of government, and shall protect each of them against invasion; and on application of the legislature, or of the executive when the legislature cannot be convened, against domestic violence.

"Art. VI.   This constitution, and the laws of the United States, which shall be made in pursuance thereof, and all the treaties made, or which shall be made, under the authority of the United States, shall be the supreme law of the land; and the judges in every state shall be bound thereby, anything in the constitution or laws of any state to the contrary notwithstanding."

The above are all the clauses of the constitution that have been quoted, on one side or the other, as bearing upon the subject of slavery.

It will be noted that the word "slave," or "slavery," does not appear therein.   Mr. Madison, who was a leading and observant member of the convention, and who took notes of its daily proceedings, affirms that this silence was designed—the convention being unwilling that the constitution of the United States should recognize property in human beings.   In passages where slaves are presumed to be contemplated, they are uniformly designated as "persons," never as property.   Contemporary history proves that it was the belief of at least a large portion of the delegates that slavery could not long survive the final stoppage of the slave-trade, which was expected to (and did) occur in 1808.

The following among the amendments to the constitution proposed by the ratifying convention of one or more states, and adopted, are supposed by some to bear on the questions now agitated relative to slavery:

"Art. I.   Congress shall make no law respecting an establishment of religion, or prohibiting the free exercise thereof; or abridging the freedom of speech, or of the press; or of the rights of the people peacefully to assemble, and to petition the government for a redress of grievances.

"Art. II.   A well-regulated militia being necessary to the security of a free state, the right of the people to keep and bear arms shall not be infringed.

"Art. V.   No person shall be * * * deprived of life, liberty, or property, without due process of law; nor shall private property be taken for public use without just compensation."

CHAPTER XXIV.

Political History of Slavery in the United States from 1789 to 1800.

First session of First Congress, 1789.—Tariff bill—duty imposed on imported slaves.—
The Debate—views of Roger Sherman, Fisher Ames, Madison, &c.—Review of the
state of slavery in the States in 1790.—Second session.—Petitions from the Quakers
of Pennsylvania, Delaware, and New York.—Petition of Pennsylvania Society, signed
by Franklin.—Exciting debate—power of Congress over slavery.—Census of 1790.—
Slave population.—Vermont the first State to abolish and prohibit slavery.—Constitution of Kentucky—provisions in respect to slavery.—Session of 1791.—Memorials
for suppression of slave-trade, from Virginia, Maryland, New York, &c.—The Right of
Petition discussed.—First fugitive slave law, 1793.—First law to suppress African Slave
Trade, 1794.—The Quakers again, 1797—their emancipated slaves reduced again to
slavery, under expost facto law of North Carolina.—Mississippi territory — slavery
clause debated.—Foreign slaves prohibited.—Constitution of Georgia—importation of
slaves prohibited, 1798—provisions against cruelty to slaves.—New York provides for
gradual extinguishment of slavery, 1799.—Failure of similar attempt in Kentucky.—
Colored citizens of Pennsylvania petition Congress against Fugitive Slave law and
slave-trade—their petition referred to a committee ; bill reported and passed, 1800.

THE first session of the new Congress was held in the city of New York in
1789. A quorum was obtained for business on the 6th of April. A tariff bill
having been reported, and being under discussion in the house on the question
of its second reading, Parker, of Virginia, moved to insert a clause imposing a
duty of ten dollars on every slave imported. "He was sorry the constitution prevented Congress from prohibiting the importation altogether. It was
contrary to revolution principles, and ought not to be permitted." The only
state which seemed to have a direct pecuniary interest in this question was
Georgia. In all the other states at present represented on the floor, the importation of slaves, whether from Africa or elsewhere, was prohibited. Even
South Carolina, just before the meeting of the federal convention, had passed
an act, as she had been accustomed to do occasionally in colonial times, when
the prices of produce were too low to be remunerative, prohibiting, for one
year, the importation of slaves—a prohibition since renewed for three years.
But, notwithstanding this temporary prohibition, the same jealousy as to her
right of importation, so strongly manifested in the federal convention, was now
exhibited on the floor of the house. Smith, the representative from the Charleston district, "hoped that such an important and serious proposition would not
be hastily adopted. It was rather a late moment for the first introduction of
a subject so big with serious consequences. No one topic had been yet introduced so important to South Carolina and the welfare of the Union." Sherman, of Connecticut, threw out some suggestions similar to those he had offered in the federal convention. He "approved the object of the motion, but did
not think it a fit subject to be embraced in this bill. He could not reconcile
himself to the insertion of human beings, as a subject of impost, among goods,
wares, and merchandise. He hoped the motion would be withdrawn for the
present, and taken up afterwards as an independent subject."

Jackson, of Georgia, "was not surprised, however others might be so, at the quarter whence this motion came. Virginia, an old settled state, had her complement of slaves, and the natural increase being sufficient for her purpose, she was careless of recruiting her numbers by importation. But gentlemen ought to let their neighbors get supplied before they imposed such a burden. He knew this business was viewed in an odious light at the eastward, because the people there were capable of doing their own work, and had no occasion for slaves. But gentlemen ought to have some feeling for others. Surely they do not mean to tax us for every comfort and enjoyment of life, and, at the same time, to take from us the means of procuring them! He was sure, from the unsuitableness of the motion to the businsss now before the house, and the want of time to consider it, the gentleman's candor would induce him to withdraw it. Should it ever be brought forward again, he hoped it would comprehend the white slaves as well as the black, imported from all the jails of Europe; wretches convicted of the most flagrant crimes, who were brought in and sold without any duty whatever. They ought to be taxed equally with Africans, and he had no doubt of the equal constitutionality and propriety of such a course."

In reply to the suggestions of Sherman, Jackson, and others, Parker declared "that, having introduced the motion on mature reflection, he did not like to withdraw it. The gentleman from Connecticut had said that human beings ought not to be enumerated with goods, wares, and merchandise. Yet he believed they were looked upon by African traders in that light. He hoped congress would do all in their power to restore to human nature its inherent privileges; to wipe off, if possible, the stigma under which America labored; to do away the inconsistency in our principles justly charged upon us; and to show, by our actions, the pure beneficence of the doctrine held out to the world in our Declaration of Independence."

Sherman still "thought the principles of the bill and the principles of the motion inconsistent. The principle of the bill was to raise revenue; it was the principle of the motion to correct a moral evil. Considering the proposed duty as having revenue for its object, it would be unjust, because two or three states would bear the burden. He should therefore vote against the present motion, though he had no objection to taking up the subject by itself on the principles of humanity and policy." Ames, of Massachusetts, "detested slavery from his soul; but he had some doubts whether imposing a duty on their importation would not have an appearance of countenancing the practice." "It is the fashion of the day," said Jackson, "to favor the liberty of slaves. He believed them better off as they were, and better off than they had been in Africa. Experience had shown that liberated slaves would not work for a living. Thrown upon the world without property or connections, they can not live but by pilfering. Will Virginia set her negroes free? When the practice comes to be tried there, the sound of liberty will lose those charms which make it grateful to the ravished ear."

Madison supported Parker's motion in an elaborate speech, in which he replied to all the various objections urged against it. "The confounding men with merchandise might be easily avoided by altering the title of the bill; it was, in fact, the very object of the motion to prevent men, so far as the power of congress extended, from being confounded with merchandise. The clause in the constitution allowing a tax to be imposed, though the traffic could not be prohibited for twenty years, was inserted, he believed, for the very purpose of enabling congress to give some testimony of the sense of America with respect to the African trade. By expressing a national disapprobation of that trade, it is to be hoped we may destroy it, and so save ourselves from reproaches, and our posterity from the imbecility ever attendant on a country filled with slaves. This was as much the interest of South Carolina and Georgia as of any other states. Every addition they received to their number of slaves tended to weakness, and rendered them less capable of self-defense. In case of hostilities with foreign nations, their slave population would be a means, not of repelling invasions, but of inviting attack. It was the duty of the general government to protect every part of the Union against danger, as well internal as external. Every thing, therefore, which tended to increase this danger, though it might be a local affair, yet, if it involved national expense or safety, became of concern to every part of the Union, and a proper subject for the consideration of those charged with the general administration of the government." Bland was equally decided with Madison and Parker in support of the motion. Burke, of South Carolina, suggested that gentlemen were contending about nothing; for if not particularly mentioned, slaves would still fall under the general five per cent. ad valorem duty on all unenumerated articles, a duty just about equivalent to the one proposed. Madison replied that no collector of the customs would presume to apply the terms goods, wares, and merchandise to persons; and in this he was supported by Sherman, who denied that persons were recognized any where in the constitution as property. He thought that the clause in the constitution on which the present motion was founded applied as much to other persons as to slaves, and that there were other persons to whom it ought to be applied, as convicts, for instance; but the whole subject ought to be taken up by itself. Finally, upon Madison's suggestion, Parker consented to withdraw his motion, with the understanding that a separate bill should be brought in. A committee was appointed for that purpose; but there the matter was suffered to rest.

At the next session, 1790, the House became involved in an exciting discussion in reference to slavery and the slave-trade. Slavery still existed in every state of the Union except in Massachusetts. A clause in the constitution of that state, declaring all men to be born free and equal, inserted for the express purpose of tacitly abolishing slavery, had been judicially decided (1783) to have that effect. A few months previously to the final adoption of the constitution of Massachusetts, the state of Pennsylvania had passed an act (1780) introducing a system of gradual emancipation, prohibiting the further importation of slaves, (and by a subsequent act their exportation,) and assuring freedom to all persons thereafter born in that state, or brought into it, except runaways from other states and the servants of travelers and others not remaining above six months. This Pennsylvania system of gradual emancipation had been imitated in the states of Connecticut, Rhode Island and New Hampshire. The other eight states retained their old colonial slave-holding systems. But New York, New Jersey, Delaware, Maryland, and Virginia had prohibited the further importation of slaves, and in Virginia and Maryland the old colonial restrictions on emancipation had been repealed, leaving thereby full play, and not without considerable results, to the conscience and generosity of the slave-holders. Jefferson and Wythe, as commissioners to revise the statute law of Virginia, had agreed upon a bill for gradual emancipation; but when the revision of the statutes came before the House of Delegates (1785), Jefferson was absent as minister at Paris, those who shared his opinions thought that the favorable moment had not arrived, and the bill was not brought forward. Even in New York, an attempt (1785) to pass an act for the gradual abolition of slavery had failed to succeed. Yet in all the states, from North Carolina northward, warm opponents of slavery and ardent advocates for emancipation were more or less numerous, including many distinguished citizens. Influenced, perhaps, by the sarcasms thrown out in the federal convention, Rhode Island, shortly after the adjournment of that body, had passed a law (Oct., 1787) forbidding its citizens to engage in the slave-trade. The kidnapping of three colored persons at Boston, enticed on board a vessel and carried to the West Indies, where they were sold as slaves, produced a great excitement in Massachusetts, and occasioned (1788) a similar prohibitory act there—an example speedily imitated by Connecticut and Pennsylvania. But as the federal constitution gave to congress the exclusive regulation of commerce, it had become very questionable whether these laws retained any force.

Nor was the opposition to slavery confined to legislative acts alone. The united synod of New York and Philadelphia, while constituting themselves as the General Assembly of the Presbyterian Church in America, had issued a pastoral letter (1788), in which they strongly recommended the abolition of slavery and the instruction of the negroes in letters and religion. The Methodist Episcopal Church, lately introduced and rapidly increasing, especially in Maryland and Virginia, had even gone so far as to disqualify slave-holders to be members of their communion. Coke, the first bishop, was exceedingly zealous on this subject; but the rule was afterwards relaxed. In consequence of the efforts and preaching of Woolman and others, opposition to slavery had come to be a settled tenet of the Quakers.

The same opinions had been taken up as matters of humanity and policy as well as of religion. A society "for promoting the abolition of slavery, for the relief of free negroes unlawfully held in bondage, and for improving the condition of the African race," had been organized in Philadelphia (1787), of which Franklin was president, and Dr. Rush and Tench Coxe secretaries. A similar society had been formed in New York, of which Jay was an active member; and this example already had been or soon was imitated in all the states form Virginia northward.*

---

*Hildreth's History of the United States.

A petition from the yearly meeting of the Quakers of Pennsylvania and Delaware, seconded by another from the Quakers of New York, had been laid before the House, in which it was suggested whether, notwithstanding "seeming impediments," occasioned by "the influence and artifice of particular persons, governed by the narrow, mistaken views of self-interest," it was not within the power of congress "to exercise justice and mercy, which, if adhered to," the petitioners could not doubt, "must produce the abolition of the slave-trade."

Hartley moved the reference of this memorial to a special committee. Supported by Madison and his colleagues, Parker, Page, and White, by Lawrence, Sedgwick, Boudinot, Sherman, and Gerry, this motion was violently opposed by Smith of South Carolina, Jackson, Tucker, Baldwin, and Burke, not without many sneers at "the men in the gallery"—the Quaker deputation appointed to look after the petition—"who had come here to meddle in a business with which they had nothing to do." Finally, on a suggestion of Clymer's, supported by one of the rules of the House, the memorial was suffered to lie over till the next day.

At the opening of the session that next day, Feb. 12, another petition was presented relating to the same subject, coming from the Pennsylvania society for the abolition of slavery. It was signed by Franklin as president—one of the last public acts of his long and diversified career. He died within a few weeks afterward. "That mankind," said this memorial, "are all formed by the same Almighty Being, alike objects of his care, and equally designed for the enjoyment of happiness, the Christian religion teaches us to believe, and the political creed of Americans fully coincides with that position. Your memorialists, particularly engaged in attending to the distresses arising from slavery, believe it their indispensable duty to present this subject to your notice. They have observed, with real satisfaction, that many important and salutary powers are vested in you for promoting the welfare and securing the blessings of liberty to the people of the United States; and as they conceive that these blessings ought rightfully to be administered, without distinctions of color, to all descriptions of people, so they indulge themselves in the pleasing anticipation that nothing which can be done for the relief of the unhappy objects of their care will be either omitted or delayed.

"From a persuasion that equal liberty was originally the portion, and is still the birthright of all men, and influenced by the strong ties of humanity and the principles of the constitution, your memorialists conceive themselves bound to use all justifiable endeavors to loosen the bonds of slavery, and promote a general enjoyment of the blessings of freedom. Under these impressions, they earnestly entreat your serious attention to the subject of slavery, that you will be pleased to countenance the restoration of liberty to those unhappy men who alone, in this land of freedom, are degraded into perpetual bondage, and who, amid the general joy of surrounding freemen, are groaning in servile subjection; that you will devise means for removing this inconsistency from the character of the American people; that you will promote mercy and justice toward this distressed race; and that you will step to the very verge of the power vested in you for discouraging every species of traffic in the persons of our fellow-men."

Immediately after the reading of this petition, which could not have much tended to soothe the excitement of the day before, Hartley called up the Quaker memorial, and moved its commitment. In opposition to this motion, Tucker and Burke took the ground that the memorial contained an unconstitutional request, as congress had no power to meddle with the slave-trade for twenty years to come. Tucker pronounced it "a mischievous attempt, an improper interference, at the best, an act of imprudence." Burke was certain that the commitment "would sound an alarm and blow the trumpet of sedition through the southern states."

"I cannot entertain a doubt," said Scott of Pa., in reply, "that the memorial is strictly agreeable to the constitution. It respects a part of the duty particularly assigned to us by that instrument. We can at present lay our hands on a small tax of ten dollars. I would take that; and if that is all we can do, we must be content. I am sorry the framers of the constitution did not go further, and enable us to interdict the slave-trade altogether, for I look upon it to be one of the most abominable things on earth; and if there were neither God nor devil, I should oppose it on principles of humanity and the law of nature. For my part, I cannot conceive how any person can be said to acquire a property in another. The petitioners view the subject in a religious light; but I stand not in need of religious motives to induce me to reprobate the traffic in human flesh. Perhaps, in our legislative capacity, we can go no further than to impose a duty of ten dollars; but I do not know how far I might go if I was one of the judges of the United States, and these people were to come before me and claim their emancipation. I am sure I would go as far as I could." Jackson maintained, in reply, "the qualified property of the master in his slaves;" he referred to the example of the republics of antiquity; and relied "on the whole current of the Bible, from Genesis to Revelations," as proving that religion was not against slavery.

Sherman "could see no difficulty in committing the memorial. It was probable the committee would understand their business, and perhaps they might bring in such a report as would be satisfactory to gentlemen on both sides of the House." Baldwin "was sorry that a subject of so delicate a nature, as respected some of the states, had been brought before congress. Such gentlemen as had been present at the formation of the constitution could not but recollect the pain and difficulty which this subject had then occasioned. So tender were the southern members on this point, that the convention had wellnigh broken up without coming to any determination. From extreme desire to preserve the Union and to establish an efficient government, mutual concessions had resulted, concessions which the constitution had jealously guarded. The moment we go to jostle on that ground, I fear we shall feel it tremble under our feet. The clause in the constitution, that no capitation or direct tax should be laid, except in proportion to the census, was intended to prevent congress from laying any special tax upon slaves, lest they might in that way so burden the owners as to bring about a general emancipation. Gentlemen have said that this petition does not pray for the abolition of the slave-trade; I think, sir, it prays for nothing else, and that, consequently, we have nothing more to do with it, than if it prayed us to establish an order of nobility or a national religion."

The same ground, the unconstitutionality of the object prayed for, was relied upon by Smith of South Carolina, as a reason for not committing the memorial. "Notwithstanding all the calmness with which some gentlemen have viewed the subject, they will find that the mere discussion of it will create alarm. We have been told that, if so, we should have avoided discussion by saying nothing. But it was not for that purpose we were sent here. We look upon this measure as an attack upon property; it is, therefore, our duty to oppose it by every means in our power. When we entered into a political connection with the other states, this property was there. It had been acquired under a former government conformably to the laws and constitution, and every attempt to deprive us of it must be in the nature of an ex post facto law, and, as such, forbidden by our political compact." Like the other speakers on that side, Smith indulged in a good many slurs on the Quakers. "His constituents wanted no lessons in religion and morality, and least of all from such teachers." Madison, Page, Gerry, and Boudinot advocated the commitment. As to the alarm which it was said would be produced by committing the memorial, Page thought there might be greater ground for alarm should they refuse to commit it. "Placing himself in the case of a slave, on hearing that congress had refused to listen to the decent suggestions of a respectable part of the community, he should infer that the general government, from which great good was expected to every class, had shut their ears against the voice of humanity. If anything could induce him to rebel, it must be a stroke like this, impressing on his mind all the horrors of despair. Were he told, on the other hand, that application was made in his behalf, and that congress were willing to hear what could be urged in favor of discouraging the importation of his fellow-wretches, he would still trust in their justice and humanity, and patiently await their decision. Presuming that these unfortunate people would reason in the same way, he thought that to commit the petition was the likeliest means to avert danger. He lived in a state which had the misfortune to have in her bosom a great number of slaves. He held many himself, and was, he believed, as much interested in the business as any gentleman in South Carolina or Georgia. Even were he determined to hold them in eternal bondage, he should feel no uneasiness at the reference of the memorial, relying on the virtue of congress, and their disinclination to exercise any unconstitutional power." "Though congress were restricted by the constitution from immediately abolishing the slave-trade, yet there were a variety of ways," so Madison remarked, "by which they might countenance the abolition of that traffic. They might, for example, respecting the introduction of slaves into the new states to be formed out of the western territory, make regulations such as were beyond their power in relation to the old settled states, an object which he thought well worthy of consideration."

Gerry "never contemplated this subject without reflecting what his own feelings would be were himself, his children, or his friends placed in the same deplorable circumstances. He thought the subject-matter of the memorial clearly within the powers of congress. They had the power to lay at once a duty of ten dollars per head on imported slaves. They had the right, if they saw proper, to propose to the southern states to purchase the whole of their slaves, and their resources in the western territory might furnish them with the means. He did not intend to propose any scheme of that kind, but only referred to it, to show that congress had a right to deal with the matter."

The question being taken by yeas and nays, the reference was carried, forty-three to eleven. Of these eleven, six were from Georgia and South Carolina, being all the members present from those two states, two were from Virginia, two from Maryland, and one from New York. North Carolina was not yet represented.

The special committee to whom the memorial was referred, consisting of one member from each of the following states, New Hampshire, Massachusetts, Connecticut, New York, New Jersey, Pennsylvania, and Virginia, after a month's delay, brought in a report consisting of seven resolutions : 1st. That the general government was expressly restrained, until the year 1808, from prohibiting the importation of any persons whom any of the existing states might till that time think proper to admit. 2d. That, by a fair construction of the constitution, congress was equally restrained from interfering to emancipate slaves within the states, such slaves having been born there, or having been imported within the period mentioned. 3d. That congress had no power to interfere in the internal regulation of particular states relative to the instruction of slaves in the principles of morality and religion, to their comfortable clothing, accommodation, and subsistence, to the regulation of marriages or the violation of marital rights, to the separation of children and parents, to a comfortable provision in cases of age or infirmity, or to the seizure, transportation, and sale of free negroes ; but entertained the fullest confidence in the wisdom and humanity of the state legislatures that, from time to time, they would revise their laws, and promote these and all other measures tending to the happiness of the slaves. The fourth asserted that congress had authority to levy a tax of ten dollars, should they see fit to exact it, upon every person imported under the special permission of any of the states. The fifth declared the authority of congress to interdict or to regulate the African slave-trade, so far as it might be carried on by citizens of the United States for the supply of foreign countries, and also to provide for the humane treatment of slaves while on their passage to any ports of the United States into which they might be admitted. The sixth asserted the right of congress to prohibit foreigners from fitting out vessels in the United States to be employed in the supply of foreign countries with slaves from Africa. The seventh expressed an intention on the part of congress to exercise their authority to its full extent to promote the humane objects aimed at in the Quakers' memorial.

After a warm speech against the injustice and unconstitutionality of meddling with the question of slavery in any shape, Tucker moved to strike out the whole report, and substitute for it a simple resolution, refusing to take the memorial into consideration " as unconstitutional, and tending to injure some of the states of the Union." Jackson seconded the motion in a speech equally warm, to which Vining replied. But this motion of Tucker's, after a good deal of time spent upon that point, was declared out of order.

White, of Virginia, moved to strike out the first resolution, as containing a definition of the powers of congress, a subject not referred to the committee. His colleague, Moore, passing by the report, attacked the memorial and its authors, accusing the Quakers of harboring runaway slaves. He hoped emancipation would take place at a proper time, but he wished to have it brought about by other means than by the influence of people who had been inimical to independence. Burke was not an advocate for slavery, but he wished to preserve the tranquility of the Union, which this unnecessary and impolitic measure bade fair to throw into a state of confusion. The memorial was a reflection on the southern states. The negroes there lived better and in more comfortable houses than the poor of Europe. He referred to an advertisement which he had lately seen in a New York paper of a woman and child to be sold. That, he declared, was a species of cruelty unknown in the southern states. There the negroes have property, horses, cattle, hogs, and furniture. With respect to their ceremony of marriage, they took each other from love and friendship. Though eastern gentlemen expressed so great an antipathy to this species of property, many of them who settled in the south became as fond of it as any others—a fling to which Gerry subsequently replied that the eastern states could not be held responsible for the misdoings of their emigrant citizens, since it was no uncommon thing, even in the animal world, for exotics to degenerate.

Smith, of South Carolina, exerted his utmost efforts in an elaborate defense of slavery and the slave-trade, the objections to which he considered to spring from a "misguided and misinformed humanity." The southern states required slaves to cultivate their lands, which could not be done by white people. A white laborer from the northern states asks two dollars per day when employed in any of the southern states. The low countries, in which rice and indigo are cultivated, would be deserted if emancipation took place; and what would then become of the revenue? To set the slaves loose would be a curse to them. A plan had been thought of in Virginia of shipping them off as soon as they were freed, and this was called humanity! Jefferson's scheme for gradual emancipation, as set forth in his Notes upon Virginia, was derided as impracticable. Emancipation would probably result in an exterminating war. If, on the other hand, a mixture of blood should take place, we should all be mulattoes! The very advocates of manumission held the blacks in contempt, and refused to associate with them. No scheme could be devised to stop the increase of the blacks, except a law to prevent the intercourse of the sexes, or Herod's scheme of putting the children to death. The toleration of slavery was said to bring down reproach upon America, but that reproach belongs only to those who tolerate it, and he was ready to bear his share. It was said, also, that slavery vitiates and debases the mind of the slave-holder; but where is the proof? Do the citizens of the south exhibit more ferocity in their manners, more barbarity in their dispositions, than those of the other states? Slavery was first introduced into the West Indies by Las Casas from motives of humanity. The French promote the slave-trade by premiums; and are not the French a polished people, sensible of the rights of mankind, and actuated by just sentiments? The Spaniards encourage slavery, and they are people of the nicest honor, proverbially so. The Greeks and Romans held slaves, and are not their glorious achievements still held up as incitements to great and magnanimous actions? Sparta teemed with slaves at the time of her greatest fame as a valiant republic. Much had been said of the cruel treatment of slaves in the southern states and the West Indies. As to the southern states, from experience and information, he denied the fact; he believed in his conscience that the slaves in South Carolina were a happier people than the lower order of whites in many countries he had visited. As to the West Indies, Lord Rodney and Admiral Barrington, both of whom had spent some time there, had lately declared in the house of commons that they had never heard of a negro being cruelly treated, and that they should rejoice exceedingly if the English day-laborers were half as happy.

The abolition of the slave-trade would cause an African massacre, for it was *well known to be the custom* to put to death all such slaves as were brought to the coast and not sold. The cruelty of the method of transportation was alleged as a motive for abolishing the traffic; but surely the merchants would so far attend to their own interests as to preserve the lives and health of the slaves on the passage. All voyages must be attended with inconveniences, and those from Africa to America not less than others. The confinement on board was no more than was necessary. The space allowed was more than to soldiers in a camp; for the cubical measurement of air breathed by encamped soldiers fell below that allowed in the slave-ships, in the ratio of seventeen to thirty.

Baldwin "was in hopes that the experience of the house had convinced them of the impropriety of entering at all on this business. It was a reckless wandering without guidance, and the longer it was continued, the more inextricable their perplexities would become. The same memorial, he was informed, had been presented to the senate, but they had taken no notice of it. They had even negatived a motion that it should lie upon the table; they would not blot their paper with the subject at all. He hoped this house would imitate the wisdom of the senate, and pursue the subject no further. The most important business of the Union, the plan for the support of the public credit, the division of North Carolina into collection districts, the post-office act, additional revenue act, on which nearly half the resources of the year depended, were all pressing for early attention, and had all been laid aside as of no account, had all been made to yield to this report. And yet no bill was brought forward to be enacted into a law; nothing but a string of propositions in exposition of different articles of the constitution, but which, in fact, concluded nothing.

"Another reason for pursuing this business no further was the influence it manifestly had on the temper of the members. For several days the house had been in a constant storm. This subject contained materials of the most combustible character; it had always been among the most contentious in the government of the country. In different parts of the Union there was a well known clashing of feelings and interests on this subject. It was long a doubt whether it would not form an insuperable bar to our union as one people, under one government. In the constitution that difficulty had been surmounted, and, so far as he had been informed, almost to universal satisfaction. The strength and violence of majority had been expected on this subject; and as it was not unknown on which side the majority was, security against it was settled deep among the pillars of the government. He had not felt the least alarm that the rights of his constituents would be disturbed. The house, from its constitution, would be in some respects a mirror to reflect all the passions of the people. It was wise that the feelings of the people should have an opportunity to bear a part in legislation; and, though sometimes inconvenient, it would not be dangerous, since there was another branch of the legislature whose concurrence was necessary in all public measures. From the manner in which that body was constituted, and from the experience already had, he doubted not the senate would give to our government that wisdom and firmness which otherwise it would not possess. Acts of congress must also have the approbation of the man whom the people, in the remotest regions of the country, regard as their father. After all, should there be any doubt of the constitutionality of the measures of congress, they cannot be carried into effect without the approval of the supreme court of the United States, composed of six of our most venerable sages, forming one of the most respectable courts upon earth, possessing our confidence as well from the independence of their position as from the long experience we have had of their wisdom. On this, as on all other occasions, he should see the effects of majority and of public passion on this subject totally unconcerned. The uproar of contending waves was not pleasant, but they were dashing against a rock."

This speech of Baldwin's was on a motion of Benson's, which Baldwin had seconded, to recommit the report, with a view to give the whole matter the go-by. But the majority were not thus to be driven from their purpose. The motion to recommit was voted down, and the report was then taken up article by article. The three first resolutions (those relating to the power of congress over slavery in the states) were adopted, the second and third being compressed into one, dropping the somewhat offensive details, but retaining the substance. Upon the fourth resolution—that relating to the ten dollar tax on slaves imported—the struggle was renewed. Tucker moved to strike it out, in which he was supported by Baldwin, apparently on the ground that the resolution did not fairly express the sense of the constitution. Hartley took this occasion to defend the committee against some strictures of Burke's; but Burke still insisted that every clause in the report was drawn in ambiguous words, so as to involve in some measure such an interpretation as the Quakers wished. He acquitted the committee of any bad intention; yet he could not but think that, throughout the whole business, the southern members had been very hardly dealt by. The demand of the Quakers, as iniquitous as it was impolitic, had been referred to a committee. The southern members dragged, as it were, in spite of their remonstrances, to the bar of the house, had been set to defend their reputation and property against the Quakers, for whose right to offer such petitions gentlemen had strenuously contended. He hoped not to be out of order in offering another remark. The southern states were able to defend, and he hoped would defend, their property. No doubt those states would pass laws punishing as incendiaries any Quakers or others who should be found exciting their domestics to conspiracies or insurrections.

Page, of Virginia, was in favor of the ten dollar duty, not only as a proper regulation of commerce, but to show that congress, as far as lies in their power, were disposed to discourage a shameful traffic. He was willing, however, to strike out the resolution, and that for two reasons. Without any such resolution, congress would still have the power to lay the tax. Should the power be asserted, and then the tax not be laid, it would look too much like temporizing, like seeming to yield to the demand of the Quakers, while in heart the house was still as much against it as those by whom the Quakers and their memorial had been so heartily abused.

Smith, of South Carolina, believed that the committee had been desirous so to frame this report as to please all parties. Some clauses were meant to allay the fears of the southern members, others were calculated to gratify the memorialists. The clause now under consideration seemed to be intended for that purpose ; yet he was persuaded it would not be agreeable to the Quakers. Their nice feelings would not be gratified by a tax of this kind, the imposition of which would make slaves an article of commerce. He and his colleagues had been censured for making this business so serious. But was it reasonable to require them to give up the right to be heard ? Had the southern members been silent on this occasion, and not expressed themselves as they had done, they would have betrayed the charge intrusted to them.

On the question of striking out the fourth resolution, the committee was equally divided, but the motion was carried by the casting vote of Benson, the chairman.

The fifth resolution, affirming the power of congress to regulate the slave-trade, was vehemently opposed by Jackson, Tucker, and Smith, as was also a modification of it offered by Madison. It was said that, under pretense of regulating the trade, congress might, in fact, prohibit it entirely. They might insist, for instance, on such expensive accommodations and such costly provisions as would deter merchants from engaging in it. They might prohibit vessels of less than six hundred tons burden to engage in the traffic, whereas no vessel of that size could get across Charleston bar.

The patience of some of the northern members began at length to give way. Vining, of Delaware, thought the southern gentlemen ought to be satisfied with the alterations already made to please them. Some respect was due to the committee which had framed the report, and to the prevailing sentiment of the country. All the states, from Virginia to New Hampshire, had passed laws against the slave-trade. He entered also into a defense of the Quakers, many of whom were still present in the gallery, and whose treatment, by several gentlemen, he thought cruel and unjustifiable. Baldwin thought the regulation of the slave-trade had better be left to the states that tolerate it. He insinuated some doubts, though he would not venture to express a decided opinion, how far the power to regulate commerce gave to congress the right to pursue an individual citizen in his business between one foreign nation and another. Tucker pushed this argument to a much greater extent, denying the right of congress over citizens trading out of their jurisdiction, any further than to deprive vessels so employed of their American character. But, in spite of all the objections urged against it, the resolution, as modified by Madison, was adopted.

On the sixth resolution, that relating to the foreign slave-trade carried on from ports of the United States, Scott made an elaborate speech. " This was a subject," he remarked, "which had agitated the minds of most civilized nations for a number of years, and therefore what was said, and more particularly what was done in congress at this time, would, in some degree, form the political character of America on the subject of slavery.

"Most of the arguments advanced had gone against the emancipation of such as were slaves already. But that question was not before the committee. The report under consideration involves no such idea. It was granted on all hands that congress have no authority to intermeddle in that business. I believe that the several states with whom that authority really rests will, from time to time, make such advances in the premises as justice to the master and slave, the dictates of humanity and sound policy, and the state of society will require or admit, and here I rest content.

"An advocate for slavery in its fullest latitude, in this age of the world, and on the floor of the American congress too, seems to me a phenomenon in politics. Yet such advocates have appeared, and many argumentative statements have been urged, to which I will only answer by calling on those who heard them to believe them if they can. With me they defy, yea, mock all belief."

But while conceding that slavery within the states was out of the constitutional reach of congress, Scott was not inclined to admit any limitation to the power of that body over the importation of slaves from abroad. " The clause relative to the free migration or importation, until 1808, of such persons as any of the states might see proper to admit, had indeed been urged as intended to cover this very case of the slave-trade, and the 'persons' referred to in that clause were said to be slaves. He could not think it satisfactory to be told that there was an understanding on this subject between the northern and southern members of the national convention. He trusted there was no trafficking in the convention. When considering our constitutional powers, we must judge of them by the face of the instrument under which we sit, and not by the certain understandings which the framers of that instrument may be supposed to have had with each other, but which never transpired. At any rate, the constitution was not obligatory until ratified by a certain number of state conventions, which can not be supposed to have been acquainted with the understanding in the national convention, but must be taken to have ratified the constitution on its own merits, as they appear on the face of the instrument. He had the honor of a seat in one of those conventions, and gave his assent to the constitution on those principles. He did then, he did now, and he ever should, judge of the powers of congress by the words of the constitution, with as much latitude as if it were a thousand years old, and every man in the convention that framed it long since in his grave.

"I acknowledge," he added, "that by this clause of the constitution congress is denied the power of prohibiting, for a limited period, the importation or migration of persons, but may impose a tax or duty; and I say, as well on the white as on the black person. But some certain inadmissible qualities may be adherent to persons which, from the necessity of things, must and will, notwithstanding this provision, justify the exclusion of the persons themselves, such as a plague, or hostile designs against the union by armed immigrants. In such a case, if the importation were not prevented, I should be more inclined to impute it to want of physical than of constitutional power. In consistency with this mode of reasoning, I believe that if congress should at any time be of opinion that a state of slavery attached to a person is a quality altogether inadmissible into America, they would not be bound by the clause above cited from prohibiting that hateful quality. As in the first case the plague, and in the second the enmity and arms, so in the third the state of slavery may, notwithstanding any thing in this clause, be declared by congress qualities, or conditions, or adherents, or what you please to call them, which, being attached to any person, the person himself can not be admitted.

"By another clause of the constitution, congress have power to regulate trade. Under that head not only the proposition now under consideration, but any other or further regulation which to congress may seem expedient, is fully in their power. Nay, sir, if these wretched Africans are to be considered as property, as some gentlemen would have it, and, consequently, as subjects of trade and commerce, they and their masters so far lose the benefit of their personality, that congress may at pleasure declare them contraband goods, and so prohibit the trade altogether.

"Again, sir, congress have power to establish a rule of naturalization. This rule, it is clear, depends on the mere pleasure of congress. Whenever they may declare, by law, that any and every person, black or white, who from foreign ports can only get his or her foot on the American shore, within the territory of the United States, shall, to all intents and purposes, be not only free persons, but free citizens. And that congress has such power is clearly proved by the very bill read this morning on the subject of naturalization, in which it is provided that the applicant shall be a "free white person," plainly implying that, but for that restriction, the slave black man, as well as the free white man, might avail himself of that law by fulfilling its conditions.

"Moreover, congress have power to define and punish piracies and felonies on the high seas. Under this head, congress may, when they please, declare by law that an American going to the coast of Africa, and there receiving on board of any vessel any person in chains or fetters, or in any manner under confinement, or carrying such person, whether sold as a slave or not, to any part of the world, without his own free will and consent, to be certified as congress may direct, shall be guilty of piracy and felony on the high seas, and, on conviction thereof, shall suffer death without benefit of clergy; and congress may, perhaps, go equally far with respect to foreigners who land slaves within the territory of the United States, in contravention of any regulation they may please to make.

"So much as to the powers of congress. I desire that the world should know, I desire that those people in the gallery, about whom so much has been said, should know, that there is at least one member on this floor who believes that congress have ample powers to do all they have asked respecting the African slave-trade. Nor do I doubt that congress will, whenever necessity or policy dictate the measure, exercise those powers. I believe that the importation of one cargo of slaves would go far toward inducing such action; but I believe, also, that this necessity is not likely to happen. The states, I think, will severally do what is right in the premises.

"If the question were, what will congress do? not a member from the south is more ready than I to say, nothing. I think that as yet there is no necessity for acting. But the question being as to the powers of congress, those powers, if expressed at all, should be fully expressed."

Jackson, who rose in reply to Scott, after laboring to establish the divine origin of slavery by quotations from Moses, and its moral and political rectitude by the example of the Greeks and Romans, addressed himself then to the constitutional question. "The gentleman trusted there was no trafficking in the convention. What he called trafficking I believe was necessary. In order that the constitution might be made agreeable to all parties, interests were to be mutually given up. In suffering a bare majority of congress to decide on laws relative to navigation, the south admitted what was injurious to them, in order to obtain security for their slave property; and without it I believe the union would never have been completed. Break this tie, and you now dissolve it. Suppose congress were to forbid the eastern fishery, or to put restrictions upon it; would the eastern states submit? Affect the southern property, and gentlemen may assure themselves of the same tendency. The gentleman is willing to let this business rest till it appears what the states will do. His alternative is, if you will not abolish slavery, we will. He hoped

27

the house would be cautious how they adopted this language, how they destroyed that constitution which had been so happily established."

Smith, of South Carolina, wished to see an end of this disagreeable business, and had determined to say nothing more on the subject, because he lamented the waste of time already occasioned by it, and the ill humor it had
produced among gentlemen heretofore accustomed to treat each other with
politeness. But the observations made by the gentleman from Pennsylvania
(Scott) required some answer. He agreed that congress had no greater right
to levy a duty of ten dollars on slaves imported than on freemen, for the constitution made no difference. It spoke of migration as well as importation.
But this remark he could not reconcile with another made by the gentleman,
that, as congress had power to regulate trade, they might, therefore, regulate
the trade in slaves; for, if there was nothing in the constitution which held
out the idea of slavery, how could these Africans be viewed in a light different
from any other class of beings?

"But the gentleman had insisted that congress might prohibit the importation of any species of persons of an inadmissible quality; as, for instance,
persons affected with a pestilential disorder; and, as slavery was as bad as
the plague, they might interdict the importation of slaves. The argument
was new and ingenious, and, if well founded, would go much further; for, if
congress could interdict the bringing of a plague into the country, they had
equal authority to drive a plague out of it; and as the Quaker memorialists
had been a great plague to them, and as sore a plague to the southern states
as any whatever, these Quakers, under this power, might be exterminated.

" The respectable name of Dr. Franklin had been mentioned as giving countenance to these memorials, one of which was signed by him as president of
the abolition society. It was astonishing to see that gentleman's name to an
application which called upon congress, in explicit terms, to break a solemn
compact to which he had himself been a party. The gentleman from Massachusetts (Gerry) had declared that it was the opinion of the select committee,
of which he was a member, that the memorial from the Pennsylvania society
asked congress to violate the constitution. And it was no less astonishing
that Dr. Franklin had taken the lead in a business which looked so much like
a persecution of the southern inhabitants, especially when he recollected the
parable the doctor had written some time ago with a view to show the impropriety of one set of men persecuting others for a difference of opinion."

Boudinot "agreed to the general doctrines of Scott, but could not go so
far as to say that the clause in the constitution relating to the importation or
migration of such persons as the states now existing shall think proper to admit, did not include the case of negro slaves. Candor required him to acknowledge that this was the express design of the constitution. He had been
informed that the tax or duty of ten dollars was agreed to instead of five per
cent. ad valorem, and that it was so expressly understood by all parties in the
convention. It was, therefore, the interest and duty of congress to impose the
tax, or it would not be doing justice to the states or equalizing the duties

throughout the union. The gentlemen in opposition were justifiable in supporting the interests of their constituents, but their warmth had been excessive. Yet even that warmth was not without excuse. It was an arduous task, in this enlightened age, to prove the legality of slavery. When gentlemen attempt to justify this unnatural traffic, or to prove the lawfulness of slavery, they ought to advert to the genius of our government and to the principles of the revolution. 'If it were possible for men who exercise their reason to believe,' says the declaration of 1775, setting forth the causes and necessity for taking up arms, 'that the divine author of our existence intended a part of the human race to hold an absolute power in and an unbounded property over others, marked out by his infinite goodness and wisdom as the objects of a legal domination never rightfully resistible, however severe and oppressive, the inhabitants of these colonies might at least require from the parliament of Great Britain some evidence that this dreadful authority over them had been granted to that body.' By the declaration of independence, in 1776, congress declare 'these truths to be self-evident, that all men are created equal, that they are endowed by their creator with certain inalienable rights, and that among these are life, liberty, and the pursuit of happiness.' Such was the language of America in the day of her distress.

" But there was a wide difference between justifying the African slave-trade and supporting a claim vested at the adoption of the constitution and guaranteed by it; nor would he be understood as contending for any right in congress to give freedom to those who are now held as slaves, or, at the present time, to prohibit the slave-trade. It would be a piece of inhumanity to turn these unhappy people loose, to murder each other or to perish for want of the necessaries of life. He never was an advocate for conduct so extravagant."

After an elaborate vindication of the Quakers, Boudinot denied that the petition signed by Franklin asked any thing contrary to the constitution. The request "was to go to the utmost verge of the constitution," not to go beyond it.

Jackson was by no means satisfied with the distinction attempted to be set up between the African slave-trade and the case of the slaves already in the country. " I am for none of these half-way consciences; if I was disposed to do any thing, I should be for total abolition. Let charity and humanity begin at home; let the gentlemen in the northern states who own slaves and advocate their cause, set the example of emancipation. Let them prove their own humanity; let them pull the beam out of their own eye previous to discovering the mote in their neighbor's. That is an argument that would speak for itself. Gentlemen have talked of our raising alarms; but it is at a reality, not at a bug-bear. The whole tenor of the resolutions has been contrary to southern interests; and manumission, emancipation, and abolition have been their intention. I give the gentleman from Pennsylvania (Scott) credit; I admit his candor; he has boldly spoken out. I wish the same might be done by other members, who appear to me to conceal their real designs under the specious pretext of concern for the interests of the southern states."

Williamson thought the time of congress badly employed in passing abstract resolutions as to what they could or could not do, and still worse in discussing, what appeared to be the general subject of debate, whether the Quakers were the worst or the best of all religious societies. As to their conduct in the present case, he believed they held themselves bound in conscience to bear a testimony against slavery. He revered all men who respect the dictates of conscience at the expense of time and money : such men are seldom bad members of society. "We, too, must regard the dictates of conscience ; we are bound to support the constitution, and to protect the property of our fellow-citizens ; and we are expressly prohibited by the constitution from giving liberty to a single slave. That business remains with the individual states ; it is not committed to congress, who have no right to intermeddle with it." He was therefore opposed to all the resolutions.

After some further debate, in which the merits of the Quakers continued to hold a large place, the sixth resolution was agreed to. The seventh, pledging congress to exert their full powers for the restriction of the slave-trade—and, as it might also be understood, for the discountenancing of slavery—was struck out. The committee then rose, and reported the resolutions to the house.

The next day, March 23d, as soon as the preliminary business had been disposed of, it was moved to take up this report. Ames expressed the opinion that the subject might rest at the stage it had reached. He regretted the time consumed, and the manner also in which the debate had been conducted. He reprobated the idea of a declaration of abstract propositions. Let the report lie on the files of the house, where it might be occasionally referred to.

Ames was highly complimented by Jackson, who wished that more of the members from the eastward had acted in the same spirit. Madison thought the suggestion of Ames a good one, with this modification, that the report of the committee of the whole should be entered on the journals for the information of the public, and to quiet the fears of the south, by showing that congress claimed no power to prohibit the importation of slaves before 1808, and no power of manumission at any time.

Burke "complained of this as an uncandid method of disposing of the business. He would rather it should pass regularly through the forms of the house. It was smuggling the affair to let it rest here, as it deprived the people of the counsel of their senate." Smith took the same ground. The precedents quoted of memorials entered on the journals were not applicable to the present question, which involved a discussion of the powers of congress. On a question as to those powers, the senate, composing one branch of the legislature, should certainly be consulted. Both reports were now to be entered on the journals, without any declaration to show which had been approved and which rejected. They were precluded from having the yeas and nays on the report, and yet it would be called the act of the house. Madison contended that, as it was impossible to shut the door altogether upon this business, the method proposed was the most conciliatory, and the best adapted to the present situation of things. The motion finally prevailed by a vote of twenty-nine to twenty-five, and the report was entered on the journal as follows :

" That the migration or importation of such persons as any of the states now existing shall think proper to admit, can not be prohibited by congress prior to the year 1808.

" That congress have no right to interfere in the emancipation of slaves, or in the treatment of them, in any of the states, it remaining with the several states alone to provide any regulations therein which humanity and true policy require.

" That congress have authority to restrain the citizens of the United States from carrying on the African slave-trade for the purpose of supplying foreigners with slaves, and of providing by proper regulations for the humane treatment, during their passage, of slaves imported by the said citizens into the said states admitting such importation.

"That congress have also authority to prohibit foreigners from fitting out vessels in any port of the United States for transporting persons from Africa to any foreign port." *

On the 22d of December, 1789, North Carolina passed an act ceding, on certain conditions, all her territory lying west of her present limits, to the United States. Among the conditions is the following :

" Provided always, that no regulations, made or to be made, by congress, shall tend to emancipate slaves."

The conditions exacted were acceded to by congress in an act approved April 2, 1790. No report of the debate on the passage of the act exists.

SLAVE POPULATION.—CENSUS OF 1790.

Connecticut	2,759	North Carolina	100,572
Delaware	8,887	Pennsylvania	3,737
Georgia	29,264	Rhode Island	952
Kentucky	11,830	South Carolina	107,094
Maryland	103,036	Vermont	17
New Hampshire	158	Virginia	293,427
New Jersey	11,423	Territory south of Ohio	3,417
New York	21,324	Aggregate,	697,897.

Vermont was admitted into the Union Feb. 18, 1791. The constitution under which she came in was originally adopted in 1777, and had been slightly altered in 1785. The first article of the Bill of Rights declared that "no male person born in this country, or brought from over sea, ought to be bound by law to serve any person as a servant, slave, or apprentice after he arrives at the age of twenty-one years, nor female, in like manner, after she arrives at the age of twenty-one years, unless they are bound by their own consent after they arrive at such age, or are bound by law for the payment of debts, damages, fines, costs, or the like " This provision was contained in the constitu-

---

* Annals of Congress. Hildreth's Hist. U. S.

tion of 1777, so that to Vermont the honor belongs of having been the first American state to abolish and prohibit slavery.

Kentucky was admitted into the Union, by act of congress, Feb. 4, 1791, before any constitution had been formed for the state. In 1792, however, a constitution was framed. An article on the subject of slavery provided that the legislature should have no power to pass laws for the emancipation of slaves without the consent of their owners, nor without paying therefor, previous to such emancipation, a full equivalent in money; nor laws to prevent immigrants from bringing with them persons deemed slaves by the laws of any one of the United States, so long as any persons of like age and description should be continued in slavery by the laws of Kentucky. But laws might be passed prohibiting the introduction of slaves for the purpose of sale, and also laws to oblige the owners of slaves to treat them with humanity, to provide them with necessary clothing and provisions, and to abstain from all injuries extending to life or limb; and provision might be made, in case of disobedience to such laws, for the sale of the slave to some other owner, the proceeds to be paid over to the late master. The legislature was also required to pass laws giving to owners of slaves the right of emancipation, saving the rights of creditors, and requiring security that the emancipated slaves should not become a burden to the county.

During the congressional session of 1791, the abolition society of Pennsylvania presented a memorial, calling upon congress to exercise, for the suppression of the slave-trade, those powers which, by the report of the committee of the whole, entered on the journals of the house, congress had been declared to possess. Reënforced by others from the abolition societies of Rhode Island, Connecticut. New York, Virginia, and from several local societies in Maryland, that memorial was referred to a special committee. As that committee made no report, memorials were presented at the next session from the abolition societies of New Hampshire and Massachusetts, recalling the attention of congress to the subject; but these were suffered to lie upon the table without reference. Afterward a separate petition was presented from Warner Mifflin, a philanthropic Quaker of Delaware, on the general subject of negro slavery, its injustice, and the necessity of its abolition. At the time of its presentation, this document was read and laid upon the table without comment. Two days after, Nov. 26, 1792, Steele, of North Carolina, called attention to it by observing " that, after what had passed at New York, he had hoped the house would have heard no more of that subject. To his surprise, he found the business started anew by a fanatic, who, not content with keeping his own conscience. undertook to be the keeper of the consciences of other men, and, in a manner not very decent, had obtruded his opinion on the house." After some complaints that such a petition should have been presented, Steele moved that it be returned to the petitioner by the clerk, and that the entry of it be erased from the journal. The petition, it chanced, had been presented by Ames. to whom Mifflin had applied for that purpose, as the Delaware member happened to be absent. Ames hastened to renew the declaration of his opinion, expressed in the debate two years before, that congress could take no steps as to the matter to which the memorial related. Having been requested to present it, he had done so on the general principle that every citizen had a right to petition the legislature, and to apply to any member as the vehicle to convey his petition to the house.

In seconding Steele's motion, Smith, of South Carolina, "admitted, to its full extent, the right of every citizen to petition for redress of grievances, and the duty of the house to consider such petitions. But the paper in question was not of that description. It was a mere rant and rhapsody of a meddling fanatic, interlarded with texts of Scripture, and without any specific prayer. The citizens of the southern states, finding that a paper of this sort had been received by the house, and formally entered on their journals, might justly be alarmed, and led to believe that doctrines were countenanced destructive of their interests. The gentleman who presented it, and who, he observed with regret, had not on this occasion displayed his usual regard for the southern states, had stated its contents to relate only to the slave-trade. Had he stated its real objects, namely, to create disunion among the states, and to excite the most horrible insurrections, the house would undoubtedly have refused its reception. After the proceedings at New York, his constituents had a right to expect that the subject would never be stirred again. These applications were not calculated to meliorate the condition of those who were their objects, and who were at present happy and contented. On the contrary, by alienating their affections from their masters, and exciting a spirit of restlessness, they tended to make greater severities necessary. He therefore earnestly called upon the house, by agreeing to the present motion, to convince this troublesome enthusiast, and others who might be disposed to communicate their ravings and wild effusions, that they would meet the treatment they justly deserved. As the present application was disrespectful to the house, insulting to the southern members, and a libel on their constituents, it ought no longer to remain on the table, but should be returned to its author with marked disapprobation." That part of the motion relating to the return of the petition was agreed to; the part respecting the erasure of the journal was withdrawn by the mover.

An important act regulating the surrender of fugitives from justice and the restoration of fugitives from service, as provided for in the constitution, was passed in 1793.

Fugitives from justice, on the demand of the executive of the state whence they had fled upon the executive of any state in which they might be found, accompanied with an indictment or affidavit charging crime upon them, were to be delivered up and conveyed back for trial. This part of the act still remains in force.

In case of the escape out of any state or territory of any person held to service or labor under the laws thereof, the person to whom such labor was due, his agent, or attorney, might seize the fugitive and carry him before any United States judge, or before any magistrate of the city, town, or county in which the arrest was made; and such judge or magistrate, on proof to his satisfaction, either oral or by affidavit before any other magistrate, that the person seized was really a fugitive, and did owe labor as alleged, was to grant a certificate to that effect to the claimant, this certificate to serve as sufficient warrant for the removal of the fugitive to the state whence he had fled. Any person obstructing in any way such seizure or removal, or harboring or concealing any fugitive after notice, was liable to a penalty of $500, to be recovered by the claimant.

This act, which originated with the senate, seems to have passed the house without any debate. At the time of its passage, and for many years after, the above provisions attracted little attention. At a later period, they were denounced not only as exceedingly harsh and peremptory, opening a door to great abuses, but as unconstitutional, in subjecting that most important of all juridical questions, the right of personal liberty, to a summary jurisdiction, without trial by jury, or any appeal on points of law. Availing themselves of a decision of the supreme federal court as to the want of power in congress to impose duties on state officers, most of the free states passed acts forbidding their magistrates, under severe penalties, to take any part in carrying this law into execution ; and it was thus substantially reduced to a dead letter.*

In 1794, a convention was held in Philadelphia of delegates from all the abolition societies in the country. A memorial was drawn up by this convention in such a manner as to avoid constitutional objections, praying congress to do whatever they could for the suppression of the slave-trade. This memorial, with several Quaker petitions, was referred to a select committee, and the bill which they reported passed with little opposition. It prohibited the fitting out of vessels in the United States for supplying any foreign countries with slaves, under penalty of forfeiture of the vessel and a fine of $2,000.

In 1797, the subject of slavery was again brought before congress, by the presentation of a petition from the yearly meeting at Philadelphia of the Quakers. Among other matters, the memorial complained that certain persons of the African race, to the number of one hundred and thirty-four, set free by the Quakers, besides others whose cases were not so particularly known, had been reduced again into cruel bondage under the authority of an ex post facto law passed for that purpose by the state of North Carolina, in 1777, authorizing the seizure and resale, as slaves, of certain emancipated negroes.

Any action upon this petition was vehemenently opposed by Harper, of S. C., who complained that this was not the first, second, nor third time that the house had been troubled by similar applications, which had a very dangerous tendency. This and every other legislature ought to set their faces against memorials complaining of what it was impossible to alter.

Thacher, of Massachusetts, suggested, in reply, that where persons considered themselves injured, they would not be likely to leave off petitioning till the house took some action upon their petitions. If the Quakers considered

---

*Hildreth's History United States.

themselves aggrieved, it was their right and their duty to present their memorial, not three, five, or seven times only, but seventy times seven, until redress was obtained; therefore, gentlemen who wished not to be troubled again ought to be in favor of reading and reference.

Lyon, of Vermont, observed that a grievance was complained of which ought to be remedied, namely, that a certain number of black people who had been set at liberty by their masters were now held in slavery contrary to right; he thought that ought to be inquired into.

Rutledge, of South Carolina, would not oppose a reference if he were sure the committee would report as strong a censure as the memorial deserved; such a censure as a set of men ought to meet who attempt to seduce the servants of gentlemen traveling to the seat of government, and who are incessantly importuning congress to interfere in a business with which, by the constitution, they have no concern. At a time when other communities were witnesses of the most horrid and barbarous scenes, these petitioners were endeavoring to excite a certain class to the commission of like enormities here. Were he sure that this conduct would be reprobated as it deserved, he would cheerfully vote far a reference; but not believing that it would be, he was for laying the memorial on the table or under the table, that the house might have done with the business, not for to-day, but forever.

Gallatin, of Pennsylvania, by whom the memorial had been offered, maintained that it was the practice of the house, whenever a petition was presented, to have it read a first and second time, and then to commit, unless it were expressed in such indecent terms as to induce the house to reject it, or related to a subject upon which it had been recently determined by a large majority not to act. It was not best to decide under the influence of such passion as had just been exhibited, and that furnished an additional reason for a reference. He also vindicated the character of the Quakers against the aspersions in which Rutledge had very freely indulged.

Sewall, of Massachusetts, suggested a third case, applicable, as he thought, to the present memorial, in which petitions might be rejected without a commitment, and that was when they related to matters over which the house had no cognizance, especially if they were of a nature to excite disagreeable sensations in a part of the members possessed of a species of property held under circumstances in themselves sufficiently uncomfortable. The present memorial seemed to relate to topics entirely within the jurisdiction of the states.

Macon declared that there was not a man in North Carolina who did not wish that there were no blacks in the country. Negro slavery was a misfortune; he considered it a curse; but there was no means of getting rid of it. And thereupon he proceeded to inveigh against the Quakers, whom he accused not only of unconstitutional applications to congress, but of continually endeavoring to stir up in the southern states insurrection among the negroes.

Against these assaults on the petitioners, Livingston, of New York, warmly protested. There might be individuals such as had been described; but as against the body of the Quakers these charges were false and unjust.

Parker, of Virginia, and Blount, of North Carolina, warmly opposed the reference of the memorial. Nicholas, of Virginia, felt as much as other southern gentlemen on this subject, but as he thought the holders of slaves had nothing to fear from inquiry, he was in favor of a reference. So, also, was Smith, of Maryland. Finally, after a very warm debate, the reference was carried, and a special committee was appointed, of which Sitgreaves was chairman, Dana, Smith, of Maryland, Nicholas, and Schureman, of New Jersey, being members. This committee, after hearing the petitions, subsequently reported leave to withdraw, in which the house concurred, on the ground, as set forth in the report, that the matter complained of was exclusively of judicial cognizance, and that congress had no authority to interfere.

At the same session a bill was introduced for erecting all of that portion of the late British province of West Florida within the jurisdiction of the United States into a government to be called the Mississippi Territory; to be constituted and regulated in all respects like the territory north-west of the Ohio, with the single exception that slavery would not be prohibited.

While this section of the act was under discussion, Thacher, of Massachusetts, having first stated that he intended to make a motion touching the rights of man, moved to strike out the exception as to slavery, so as to carry out the original project of Jefferson, as brought forward by him in the Continental Congress, of prohibiting slavery in all parts of the western territory of the United States, south as well as north of the Ohio.

Rutledge, of South Carolina, hoped that this motion would be withdrawn; not that he feared its passing, but he hoped the gentleman would not indulge himself and others in uttering philippics against a usage of most of the states merely because his and their philosophy happened to be at war with it. Surely, if his friend from Massachusetts had recollected that the most angry debate of the session had been occasioned by a motion on this very subject, he would not again have brought it forward. Such debates led to more mischief in certain parts of the Union than the gentleman was aware of, and he hoped, upon that consideration, the motion would be withdrawn. The allusion, doubtless, was to the advantage taken of these debates by the opposition to excite hostility against the federal government in those southern states in which its friends were at best but too weak.

Otis, of Massachusetts, very promptly responded to Rutledge in hoping that the motion would not be withdrawn; he wanted gentlemen from his part of the country to have an opportunity to show by their votes how little they were disposed to interfere with the southern states as to the species of property referred to.

Thacher remarked, in reply, "that he could by no means agree with his colleague (Otis.) In fact, they seldom did agree, and to-day they differed very widely indeed. The true interest of the Union would be promoted by agreeing to the amendment proposed, of which the tendency was to prevent the increase of an evil, acknowledged to be such by the very gentlemen themselves who held slaves. The gentleman from Virginia (Nicholas) had frequently told the house that slavery was an evil of very great magnitude. He agreed with that gentleman that it was so. He regarded slavery in the United States as the greatest of evils—an evil in direct hostility to the principles of our government; and he believed the government had a right to take all due measures to diminish and destroy that evil, even though in doing so they might injure the property of some individuals; for he never could be brought to believe that an individual could have a right in any thing that went to the destruction of the government—a right in a wrong. Property in slaves is founded in wrong, and never can be right. The government must, of necessity, put a stop to this evil, and the sooner they entered upon the business the better. He did not like to hear much said about the rights of man, because of late there had been much quackery on that subject. But because those rights and the claim to them had been abused, it did not follow that men had no rights. Where legislators are chosen from the people and frequently renewed, and in case of laws which affect the interest of those who pass them, the rights of man are not likely to be often disregarded. But when we take upon us to legislate for men against their will, it is very proper to say something about those rights, and to remind gentlemen, at other times so eloquent upon this subject, that men, though held as slaves, are still men by nature, and entitled, therefore, to the rights of man—and hence his allusion to those rights in making the motion.

"We are about to establish a government for a new country. The government of which we form a part originated from, and is founded upon, the rights of man, and upon that ground we mean to uphold it. With what propriety, then, can a government emanate from us in which slavery is not only tolerated, but sanctioned by law? It has indeed been urged that, as this territory will be settled by emigrants from the southern states, they must be allowed to have slaves; as much as to say that the people of the south are fit for nothing but slave-drivers—that, if left to their own labor, they would starve!

"But if gentlemen thought that those now holding slaves within the limits of the proposed territory ought to be excepted from the operation of his amendment, he would agree to such exception for a limited period."

Thacher's amendment was lost. Only twelve votes were given in favor of it. A day or two after, Harper, of South Carolina, offered an amendment, which was carried without opposition, prohibiting the introduction into the new Mississippi territory of slaves from without the limits of the United States.

In this year, 1798, the constitution of Georgia was revised. Following the example already set by the assembly of the two Carolinas, the further importation of slaves "from Africa or any foreign place" was expressly prohibited. By a further provision, any person maliciously killing or dismembering a slave, was to suffer the same punishments as if the acts had been committed on a free white person, except in cases of insurrection, or "unless such death should happen by accident, in giving such slave moderate correction." But while these concessions were made to the antipathy to slavery, that institution was sustained by a clause copied from the constitution of Kentucky, but still more stringent, by which the legislature was forbidden to pass laws for the emancipation of slaves, except with the previous consent of the individual owners; nor were immigrants to be prohibited from bringing with them " such persons as may be deemed slaves by the law of any one of the United States."

In 1799, the legislature of New York passed a law for the gradual extinguishment of slavery, a measure which Governor Jay had much at heart, and which, after three previous unsuccessful attempts, was now at last carried. Those who were slaves at the passage of the act were to continue so for life; but all their children born after the 4th of July then following were to be free, to remain, however, with the owner of the mother as apprentices, males till the age of twenty-eight, and females till the age of twenty-five. The exportation of slaves was forbidden under a pecuniary penalty, the slave upon whom the attempt was made to become free at once. Persons removing into the state might bring with them slaves whom they had owned for a year previously; but slaves so brought in could not be sold.

In 1799, a convention met in Kentucky to revise the constitution of that growing state. An attempt was made to introduce a provision for the gradual abolition of slavery, which was supported by Henry Clay, a recent immigrant from Virginia, a young lawyer, who commenced a political career of half a century by holding a seat in this convention. The attempt met, however, with very feeble support, and, so far as related to the subject of slavery, the constitution underwent no change.

A similar proposition for the gradual abolition of slavery had been introduced a short time before into the Maryland assembly, but it found so little encouragement there as to be withdrawn by the mover. Even in Pennsylvania, a proposition introduced into the assembly for the immediate and total abolition of slavery, though supported by the earnest efforts of the Pennsylvania abolition society, failed of success. The contemporaneous act of the state of New York for the gradual abolition of slavery has been already mentioned.

On the 2d of January, 1800, a petition from certain free colored inhabitants of the city and county of Philadelphia was presented to congress by Waln, the city representative, setting forth that the slave-trade to the coast of Guinea, for the supply of foreign nations, was clandestinely carried on from various ports of the United States; that colored freemen were seized, fettered, and sold as slaves in various parts of the country; and that the fugitive law of 1793 was attended in its execution by many hard and distressing circumstances. The petitioners, knowing the limits of the authority of the general government, did not ask for the immediate emancipation of all those held in bondage; yet they begged congress to exert every means in its power to undo the heavy burdens, and to prepare the way for the oppressed to go free. Attention had recently been drawn to slavery and the slave-trade, not only by alleged violations of the act forbidding American vessels to assist in the supply of foreign slave-markets, but much more forcibly by a recent conspiracy, or alleged conspiracy, in Virginia, which had produced a great alarm, resulting in the execution of several slaves charged as having been concerned in it. A great clamor was excited by Waln's motion to refer this petition to a committee already raised on the subject of the slave-trade ; a reference vehemently opposed, not only by Rutledge, Harper, Lee, Randolph, and other southern members, on the ground that the petition intermeddled with matters over which congress had no control, but also by Otis, of Boston, and Brown, of Rhode Issland, whose vehemence was even greater, if possible, than that of the members from the south. Waln, Thacher, Smilie, Dana, and Gallatin argued, on the other hand, that, as parts of the petition were certainly within the jurisdiction of congress, it ought to be received and acted upon.   The particulars of this debate are very imperfectly preserved ; but, as usual on this subject, it was a very warm one. Rutledge called for the yeas and nays, wishing, as he said, to show by how decisive a majority all interference had been declined, and so to allay any fear that the matter would ever again be agitated in congress.   Waln, however, anticipated the vote by withdrawing his motion, and substituting another, for the reference of such parts of the petition as related to the laws of the United States touching fugitives from service, and the supply of foreign countries with slaves.   Rutledge raised a point of order as to the reference of a part of a petition, but the speaker decided against him.   Gray, of Virginia, then moved to amend by adding a declaration that the unreferred parts of the petition, inviting congress to legislate on subjects over which the general government has no jurisdiction, "have a tendency to create disquiet and jealousy, and ought, therefore, to receive the pointed disapprobation of this house."   Objections being stated to this amendment by Dana and Thacher, Gray agreed to modify it by substituting for the last clause, "ought therefore to receive no encouragement or countenance from this house."   Against the amendment thus modified but one vote was given in the negative, that of Thacher, who had represented the district of Maine ever since the adoption of the constitution, and who had lost no opportunity to signalize his hostility to slavery.   In the course of the session, the committee to whom the petition was referred brought in a bill which passed to be enacted, restricting, by more stringent provisions, the supply of slaves to foreign countries by ships of the United States.*

---

* Hildreth's Hist. U. S.

CHAPTER XXV.

POLITICAL HISTORY OF SLAVERY IN THE UNITED STATES, FROM 1800 TO 1807.

Slave population in 1800.—Georgia cedes territory—slavery clause.—Territory of Indiana
—attempt to introduce Slavery in 1803—Petition Congress—Com. of H. R. report
against it.—Session of 1804, committee report in favor of it, limited to ten years.—No
action on report.—Foreign slave-trade prohibited with Orleans Territory, 1804.—South
Carolina revives slave-trade ; the subject before Congress.—New Jersey provides for
gradual extinction of slavery, 1804.—Attempt to gradually abolish slavery in District
of Columbia, unsuccessful in Congress.—Renewed attempt to introduce slavery into
Territory of Indiana, 1806, unsuccessful.—Legislature of Territory in favor of it,
1807—Congressional committee report against it.—Jefferson's Message—recommendation to abolish African slave-trade—the subject before Congress—bill reported—the
debate—Speeches of members—Act passed 1807, its provisions.

THE total population of the United States in 1800, was 5,305,925 persons,
of whom 893,041 were slaves. The following table exhibits the number of
slaves in each State :

CENSUS OF 1800—SLAVE POPULATION.

District of Columbia..	3,244	New Hampshire.......	8
Connecticut..........	951	New York	20,343
Delaware	6,153	North Carolina........	133,296
Georgia..............	59,404	Pennsylvania	1,706
Indiana Territory.....	135	Rhode Island	381
Kentucky............	40,343	South Carolina........	146,151
Maryland	105,635	Tennessee	13,584
Mississippi Territory..	3,489	Virginia..............	345,796
New Jersey	12,422	Aggregate, 893,041.	

Georgia, in 1802, April 2d, ceded the territory lying west of her present
limits, now forming the states of Alabama and Mississippi. Among the conditions exacted by her, and accepted by the United States, is the following :
"That the territory thus ceded shall become a state, and be admitted into
the Union as soon as it shall contain sixty thousand free inhabitants, or, at an
earlier period, if congress shall think it expedient, on the same conditions and
restrictions, with the same privileges, and in the same manner, as provided in
the ordinance of congress of the 13th day of July, 1787, for the government
of the western territory of the United States : which ordinance shall, in all its
parts, extend to the territory contained in the present act of cession, the article
only excepted which forbids slavery."

When Ohio was made a state in 1802–3, the residue of the territory conveyed by the ordinance of 1787, was called the Indiana Territory, and William
Henry Harrison was appointed governor. The new territory made repeated
efforts to procure a relaxation in her favor of the restrictive clause of the ordinance of 1787, one of them through the instrumentality of a convention assembled in 1802–3, and presided over by the territorial governor ; so he, with

the great body of his fellow-delegates, memorialized congress, among other things, to suspend, temporarily, the operation of the sixth article of the ordinance aforesaid. This memorial was referred in the house to a select committee of three, two of them from slave states, with the since celebrated John Randolph as chairman. On the 2d of March, 1803, Mr. Randolph made what appears to have been a unanimous report from this committee, of which we give so much as relates to slavery, as follows :

"The rapid population of the state of Ohio sufficiently evinces, in the opinion of your committee, that the labor of slaves is not necessary to promote the growth and settlement of colonies in that region. That this labor—demonstrably the dearest of any—can only be employed in the cultivation of products more valuable than any known to that quarter of the United States ; that the committee deem it highly dangerous and inexpedient to impair a provision wisely calculated to promote the happiness and prosperity of the northwestern country, and to give strength and security to that extensive frontier. In the salutary operations of this sagacious and benevolent restraint, it is believed that the inhabitants of Indiana will, at no very distant day, find ample remuneration for a temporary privation of labor, and of emigration."

The committee proceed to discuss other subjects set forth in the prayer of the memorial, and conclude with eight resolves, whereof the only one relating to slavery is as follows :

" *Resolved,* That it is inexpedient to suspend, for a limited time, the operation of the sixth article of the compact between the original states and the people and states west of the river Ohio."

This report, having been made at the close of the session, was referred at the next to a new committee, whereof Cæsar Rodney, a new representative from Delaware, was chairman. Mr. Rodney, from this committee, reported, (February 17, 1804)—

" That, taking into their consideration the facts stated in the said memorial and petition, they are induced to believe that a qualified suspension, for a limited time, of the sixth article of compact between the original states and the people and states west of the river Ohio, might be productive of benefit and advantage to said territory."

The report goes on to discuss the other topics embraced in the Indiana memorial, and concludes with eight resolves, of which the first (and only one relative to slavery) is as follows :

" That the sixth article of the ordinance of 1787, which prohibited slavery within the said territory, be suspended in a qualified manner, for ten years, so as to permit the introduction of slaves, born within the United States, from any of the individual states ; *provided,* that such individual state does not permit the importation of slaves from foreign countries : *and provided further,* that the descendants of all such slaves shall, if males, be free at the age of twenty-five years, and if female, at the age of twenty-one years."

On this report no action was had ; but the subject, as we shall presently see, was not allowed to rest here, being repeatedly urged on congress by the inhabitants of Indiana. Had the decision rested with them, both Indiana and Illinois would have come into the Union as slave states.

The annual convention of delegates from the state societies for promoting the abolition of slavery and improving the condition of the African race, then in session at Philadelphia, presented a memorial, early in the session of 1804–5, praying congress to prohibit the further importation of slaves into the newly acquired region of Louisiana. The memorial was referred to the committee on the government of Louisiana, and a provision was inserted into the act organizing the territory of Orleans, that no slaves should be carried thither, except from some part of the United States, by citizens removing into the territory as actual settlers. This provision not to extend to negroes introduced into the United States since 1798. The intention of the latter clause was to guard against the effect of a recent act of South Carolina reviving the African slave-trade, after a cessation of it as to that state for fifteen years. This act of South Carolina, if not guarded against, might open the way for introducing an indefinite number of slaves from Africa into the new territories of Mississippi and Orleans.

In order to express the sense of the nation upon this act of South Carolina, Bard, of Pennsylvania, introduced at this session a resolution to impose a tax of ten dollars on every slave imported. In opposing this resolution in committee of the whole, Lowndes, of S. C., apologized for the conduct of his state on the ground of an alleged impossibility of enforcing the prohibition. " Such was the nature of their coast, deeply penetrated by navigable rivers, that the people of South Carolina, especially as they had stripped themselves of means by giving up to the general government the duties on imports, could not restrain their 'eastern brethren,' who, in defiance of the authority of the general government, allured by the excitement of gain, had been engaged in this trade. The repeal had become necessary to remove the spectacle of the daily violation of the law."

Lowndes added that, personally, he was opposed to the slave-trade, and that he wished the time were already arrived when it might be constitutionally prohibited by act of congress ; but the imposition of the proposed tax, so far from checking the traffic, would, he thought, rather tend to its increase, by seeming to give to it a congressional sanction. Another effect of the duty would be to lay so much additional and special taxation on South Carolina, which he thought very unjust.

Bard defended his resolution on two grounds. The proposed tax was a constitutional and fair source of revenue. Since the African slave-trade made men articles of traffic, they must be subject to impost like other merchandise. The value of an imported slave being $400, a duty of ten dollars was only two and a half per cent. on the value. While this duty would add to the revenue, it would also accomplish a more important end, by showing the world that the general government was opposed to slavery, and ready to exercise its powers as far as they would go for preventing its extension. "We owe it indispensably to ourselves," said Bard, "and to the world whose eyes are upon us, to maintain the republican character of our government." As additional reasons in favor of his resolution, he dwelt at length on the cruelty and immorality of the slave-trade, and the danger of slave insurrections, of which St. Domingo had furnished so striking an example, and two or three alarms of which had recently occurred in Virginia.

Mr. Speaker Macon expressed the opinion that the morality or immorality of the slave-trade had nothing to do with the question before the house. "The question is not whether we shall prohibit the trade, but whether we shall tax it. Gentlemen think that South Carolina has done wrong in permitting the importation of slaves. That may be, and still this measure may also be wrong. Will it not look like an attempt in the general government to correct a state for the undisputed exercise of its constitutional power? It appears to be something like putting a state to the ban of the empire."

Lucas, of Pennsylvania, denied that South Carolina had any right to complain of the proposed duty. If she had the right, under the constitution, to permit the importation, congress, under the same constitution, had the right to impose the tax. If she chose to exercise her constitutional authority, why complain of a like exercise of it on the part of congress? If she wished to avoid paying the tax, let her prohibit the importation. Nor did he admit that, by taxing the importation, congress legalized or countenanced the traffic. The importation was not legalized by congress, but by South Carolina, congress not yet having the power to prohibit it. The tax would tend to check a traffic which, in four years, might add a hundred thousand slaves to those already in the Union. The thirst for gain was more alive in the country than ever, and the opening of the trade by South Carolina would virtually amount to a general opening; for, African slaves once introduced into one state, would find their way into all others in which slavery was allowed.

Smilie wished to steer clear of the question of morality; at the same time, he could not but think that the whole Union had a direct interest in the measure adopted by South Carolina, inasmuch as it tended to weaken the common defense of the country. Every slave brought in must be regarded in the light of an imported enemy.

Stanton, of Rhode Island, insisted strenuously on the tax. Nor did he confine his reprobation to the foreign slave-trade merely; he described, in very strong terms, his emotions at meeting, on his way to the seat of government, twenty or thirty negroes chained together and driven like mules to market.

Eppes, the son-in-law of Jefferson, zealously supported the resolution; and, notwithstanding an attempt at postponement, on the ground that perhaps South Carolina would reënact her old prohibitory law, it was finally agreed to by the house, and was referred to a committee, to bring in a bill. That bill was reported, read twice, and referred to a committee of the whole. But the entreaties of the South Carolina members, and their promises of what the state would do, arrested any further action.

Just previous to the commencement of this debate, New Jersey, the seventh and the last of the old confederation to do so, had joined the circle of the free

28

states, by an act, passed by an almost unanimous vote, securing freedom to all persons born in that state after the fourth of July next following; the children of slave parents to become free, males at twenty-five, and females at twenty-one—a law which gave great satisfaction to Governor Bloomfield, who had been from the beginning a zealous member of the New Jersey society for the abolition of slavery. A new effort was also made in Pennsylvania to hasten the operation of the old act for gradual abolition, by giving immediate freedom to all slaves above the age of twenty-eight years; but this attempt failed as before.

In January, 1805, a proposition was brought before congress by Sloan, of New Jersey, that all children born of slaves within the District of Columbia, after the ensuing fourth of July, should become free at an age to be fixed upon. This proposition was refused reference to the committee of the whole, by a vote of sixty-five to forty-seven, and was then rejected, seventy-seven to thirty-one.

At the session of 1805–6, the renewed African slave-trade with South Carolina being carried on with great vigor, the question of a tax on slaves imported was again revived by Sloan. After some debate, in which the blame of the traffic was bandied about between South Carolina, by which the importation was allowed, and Rhode Island, accused of furnishing ships for the business, a bill was ordered by a decided majority. But the subject was passed over to the next session, when it would be competent for congress to provide for abolishing the trade altogether.

At the same session, the original memorial from Indiana, to suspend temporarily the operation of the sixth article of the ordinance of 1787, with several additional memorials of like purport, was again referred by the house to a select committee, whereof Mr. Garnett, of Virginia, was chairman, who, on the 14th of February, 1806, made a report in favor of the prayer of the petitioners, as follows:

"That, having attentively considered the facts stated in the said petition and memorials, they are of opinion that a qualified suspension, for a limited time, of the sixth article of compact between the original states and the people and states west of the river Ohio, would be beneficial to the people of the Indiana territory. The suspension of this article is an object almost universally desired in that territory.

"It appears to your committee to be a question entirely different from that between slavery and freedom; inasmuch as it would merely occasion the removal of persons, already slaves, from one part of the country to another. The good effects of this suspension, in the present instance, would be to accelerate the population of that territory, hitherto retarded by the operation of that article of compact, as slave-holders emigrating into the western country might then indulge any preference which they might feel for a settlement in the Indiana territory, instead of seeking, as they are now compelled to do, settlements in other states or countries permitting the introduction of slaves. The condition of the slaves themselves would be much ameliorated by it, as it is evident, from experience, that the more they are separated and diffused, the more care and attention are bestowed on them by their masters—each proprietor having it in his power to increase their comforts and conveniences, in proportion to the smallness of their numbers. The dangers, too, (if any are to be apprehended,) from too large a black population existing in any one section of country, would certainly be very much diminished, if not entirely removed. But, whether dangers are to be feared from this source or not, it is certainly an obvious dictate of sound policy to guard against them, as far as possible. If this danger does exist, or there is any cause to apprehend it, and our western brethren are not only willing but desirous to aid us in taking precautions against it, would it not be wise to accept their assistance ? We should benefit ourselves, without injuring them, as their population must always so far exceed any black population which can ever exist in that country, as to render the idea of danger from that source chimerical."

After discussing other subjects embodied in the Indiana memorial, the committee close with a series of resolves, which they commend to the adoption of the house. The first is as follows :

"Resolved, That the sixth article of the ordinance of 1787, which prohibits slavery within the Indiana territory, be suspended for ten years, so as to permit the introduction of slaves, born within the United States, from any of the individual states."

This report and resolve were committed and made a special order on the Monday following, but were never taken into consideration.

At the next session, a fresh letter from Governor William Henry Harrison, inclosing resolves of the legislative council and house of representatives in favor of suspending, for a limited period, the sixth article of compact aforesaid, was received January 21st, 1807, and referred to a select committee, whereof Mr. B. Parke, delegate from said territory, was made chairman. The committee consisted of Messrs. Alston, of North Carolina, Masters, of New York, Morrow, of Ohio, Parke, of Indiana, Rhea, of Tennessee, Sanford, of Kentucky, and Trigg, of Virginia.

Mr. Parke, from this committee, made February 12th, a *third* report to the house in favor of granting the prayer of the memorialists. It is as follows :

"The resolutions of the legislative council and house of representatives of the Indiana territory, relate to a suspension, for the term of ten years, of the sixth article of compact between the United States and the territories and states northwest of the river Ohio, passed the 13th of July, 1787. That article declares that there shall be neither slavery nor involuntary servitude in the said territory.

"The suspension of the said article would operate an immediate essential benefit to the territory, as emigration to it will be inconsiderable for many years, except from those states where slavery is tolerated.

"And although it is not considered expedient to force the population of the territory, yet it is desirable to connect its scattered settlements, and, in admitted political rights, to place it on an equal footing with the different states.

From the interior situation of the territory, it is not believed that slaves could ever become so numerous as to endanger the internal peace or future prosperity of the country. The current of emigration flowing to the western country, the territories should all be opened to their introduction. The abstract question of liberty and slavery is not involved in the proposed measure; as slavery now exists to a considerable extent in different parts of the Union, it would not augment the number of slaves, but merely authorize the removal to Indiana of such as are held in bondage in the United States. If slavery is an evil, means ought to be devised to render it least dangerous to the community, and by which the hapless situation of the slaves would be most ameliorated; and to accomplish these objects, no measure would be so effectual as the one proposed. The committee, therefore, respectfully submit to the house the following resolution:

"*Resolved*, That it is expedient to suspend, from and after the 1st day of January, 1808, the sixth article of compact between the United States and the territories and states northwest of the Ohio, passed the 13th day of July, 1787, for the term of ten years."

This report, with its predecessors, was committed, and made a special order, but never taken into consideration.

The same letter of General Harrison, and resolves of the Indiana legislature, were submitted to the senate January 21st, 1807. They were laid on the table "for consideration," and do not appear to have even been referred at that session; but at the next, or first session of the fourth congress, which convened October 26th, 1807, the President, November 7th, submitted a letter from General Harrison and his legislature—whether a new or old one does not appear—and it was now referred to a select committee, consisting of Messrs. J. Franklin, of North Carolina, Kitchel, of New Jersey, and Tiffin, of Ohio.

November 13th, Mr. Franklin, from said committee, reported as follows:

"The legislative council and house of representatives, in their resolution, express their sense of the propriety of introducing slavery into their territory, and solicit the congress of the United States to suspend, for a given number of years, the sixth article of compact in the ordinance for the government of the territory northwest of the Ohio, passed the 13th day of July, 1787. That article declares: 'There shall be neither slavery nor involuntary servitude within the said territory.'

"The citizens of Clark county, in their remonstrance, express their sense of the impropriety of the measure, and solicit the congress of the United States not to act on the subject, so as to permit the introduction of slaves into the territory; at least, until their population shall entitle them to form a constitution and state government.

"Your committee, after duly considering the matter, respectfully submit the following resolution:

"*Resolved*, That it is not expedient at this time to suspend the sixth article of compact for the government of the territory of the United States northwest of the river Ohio."

Here ended the effort, so long and earnestly persisted in, to procure a suspension of the restriction in the ordinance of 1787, so as to admit slavery, for a limited term, into the territory lying between the Ohio and Mississippi rivers.

The following is a copy of the resolutions above referred to, passed by the legislative council and house of representatives of the territory of Indiana, and laid before congress :

Resolved, unanimously, by the legislative council and house of representatives of the Indiana Territory, That a suspension of the sixth article of compact between the United States and the territories and states northwest of the river Ohio, passed the 13th day of July, 1787, for the term of ten years, would be highly advantageous to the said territory, and meet the approbation of at least nine-tenths of the good citizens of the same.

Resolved, unanimously, That the abstract question of liberty and slavery is not considered as involved in a suspension of the said article, inasmuch as the number of slaves in the United States would not be augmented by the measure.

Resolved, unanimously, That the suspension of the said article would be equally advantageous to the territory, to the states from whence the negroes would be brought, and to the negroes themselves. To the territory, because of its situation with regard to the other states; it must be settled by emigrants from those in which slavery is tolerated, or for many years remain in its present situation, its citizens deprived of the greater part of their political rights, and, indeed, of all those which distinguish the American from the citizens and subjects of other governments. The states which are overburdened with negroes would be benefited by their citizens having an opportunity of disposing of the negroes which they cannot comfortably support, or of removing with them to a country abounding with all the necessaries of life; and the negro himself would exchange a scanty pittance of the coarsest food for a plentiful and nourishing diet; and a situation which admits not the most distant prospect of emancipation, for one which presents no considerable obstacle to his wishes.

Resolved, unanimously, That the citizens of this part of the former northwestern territory consider themselves as having claims upon the indulgence of congress in regard to a suspension of the said article, because at the time of the adoption of the ordinance of 1787, slavery was tolerated, and the slaves generally possessed by the citizens then inhabiting the country, amounting at least to one-half the present population of Indiana, and because the said ordinance was passed in congress when the said citizens were not represented in that body, without their being consulted, and without their knowledge and approbation.

Resolved, unanimously, That from the situation, soil, climate, and productions of the territory, it is not believed that the number of slaves would ever bear such proportion to the white population as to endanger the internal peace and prosperity of the country.

The remaining resolutions require copies of the above to be laid before congress, and instruct the delegate of the territory to use his best endeavors to obtain a suspension of the article.

In his message, at the commencement of the session of 1806–7, President Jefferson suggested to congress the interposition of its authority for the abolition of the African slave-trade. He says :

"I congratulate you, fellow-citizens, on the approach of the period at which you may interpose your authority, constitutionally, to withdraw the citizens of the United States from all further participation in those violations of human rights which have so long been continued on the unoffending inhabitants of Africa, and which the morality, the reputation, and the best interests of our country have long been eager to proscribe."

This portion of the message was referred to a select committee of the house, consisting of Messrs. Early, of Georgia, T. M. Randolph, of Va., J. Campbell, of Md., Thomas Kenan, of N. C., Cook, of Mass., Kelly, of Pa., and Van Ransellaer, of New York.

The committee reported a bill "to prohibit the importation or bringing of slaves into the United States or the territories thereof after the 31st day of December, 1807."

As originally reported by the committee, of which Early, of Georgia, was chairman, the bill provided that all negroes, mulattoes, and persons of color illegally introduced, "should be forfeited and sold for life for the benefit of the United States." Sloan, of N. J., moved to substitute "shall be entitled to his or her freedom," an amendment very violently opposed by the southern members. Early maintained with great earnestness that the persons so illegally introduced must not only be forfeited, but must be sold as slaves and continued as such. "What else can be done with them? We of the south consider slavery a dreadful evil, but the existence of large numbers of free blacks among us as a greater evil ; and yet you would by this amendment turn loose all who may be imported. You can not execute such a law, for no man will inform who loves himself or his neighbor."

The same view, the impossibility of enforcing the law, if negroes illegally imported were to become free, was urged by Macon, the speaker. Other arguments were added by his colleague, Willis Alston. "Should a state by law forbid the freeing of any slaves, congress could not contravene such a law." "Slaves being property by the laws of a state, congress could not, in opposition to those laws, consider them otherwise."

On the other hand, Smilie, of Pa., called attention to the inconsistency of laying severe penalties, as this bill did, upon all concerned in buying or selling imported slaves, while, at the same time, the United States set themselves up as sellers ! Barker, of Massachusetts, argued that the United States ought not only to declare all illegally imported Africans free, but to convey them safely back to their native country. That, Macon thought, would be impracticable. Quincy opposed the amendment, because it was not right to say that a certain class of people should be free, who could not be so according to the laws of the state where they might be, and whose freedom might produce a fatal, injurious, or disagreeable effect. Only nineteen members voted in favor of Sloan's amendment ; but the next day, Pitkin, of Connecticut, urged some very strong objections against forfeiting imported Africans, and selling them at public auction like bales of goods. He admitted the inconvenience that might arise in some of the states from setting them free ; but that might be obviated by binding them out for terms of years, and appointing some proper officer to look after them. As the bill now stood, it authorized the selling of forfeited slaves even in Massachusetts, where slavery was totally prohibited. He moved to recommit the bill, and after an animated debate, that motion prevailed.

When the bill came back from the select committee to which it had been referred, some debate arose upon the punishment of death to be inflicted on those engaged in the slave-trade. This, Early said, had been introduced to gratify some of the committee, and test the sense of the house. He moved to strike it out, with a view to substitute imprisonment ; and, after some debate, that motion was carried.

When the disposal of the forfeited negroes was again resumed, Findley advocated binding them out for terms of years. Bidwell strongly opposed the forfeiture, as implicating the United States in the same crime with the traders. He hoped the statute book would never be disgraced by such a law. This verbal implication of the United States being, however, avoided, he was quite willing to leave the imported Africans to the laws of the states, whatever they might be. Quincy, of Mass., in reply, insisted on the forfeiture, not only because the southern gentlemen regarded it as the only means of enforcing the law, but because it was also the only means by which the United States could obtain a control over these unfortunate creatures, so as to be certain that the best was done for them that circumstances would admit. It did not follow that they must be sold because they were forfeited. "May you not do with them what is best for human beings in that condition—naked, helpless, ignorant of our laws, character, and manners ? You are afraid to trust the national government, and yet, by refusing to forfeit, you will throw them under the control of the states, all of which may, and some of which will and must retain them in slavery. The great objection to forfeiture is that it admits a title. But this does not follow. All the effect of forfeiture is, that whatever title can be acquired in the cargo shall be vested in the United States. If the cargo be such that, from the nature of the thing, no title can be acquired in it, then nothing vests in the United States. The only operation of the forfeiture is to vest the importer's color of title by the appropriate commercial term, perhaps the only term we can effectually use, to this purpose, without interfering with the rights of the states. Grant that these persons have all the rights of man : will not those rights be as valid against the United States as against the importer ? And, by taking all color of title out of the importer, do we not place the United States in the best possible situation to give efficiency to the rights of man in the case of the persons imported ?

"But let us admit that forfeiture does imply a species of title lost on one side and acquired on the other, such as we can not prevent being recognized in those states into which these importations will most frequently take place: which is best? which is most humane? To admit a title, gain it for the United States, and then to make these miserable creatures free, under such circumstances and at such time as the condition into which they are forced permits, or, by denying the possibility of title, to leave them to be slaves? But my colleague has a sovereign specific for this. We do not make them slaves, he says, we only leave them to the laws of the states. But if the laws of all the states may, and if some of them do and will make them slaves, by leaving them to the operation of the laws of those states, do we not as absolutely make them slaves as though we voted them to be so in express terms? To my mind, if, when we have the power, we fail to secure to ourselves the means of giving freedom to them under proper modifications, we have an agency in making them slaves. To strike out the forfeiture, as it seems to me, will defeat the very end its advocates have in view."

Fiske, of Vermont, denied that, in order to give the United States the desired control over Africans or others illegally imported, any forfeiture was necessary. It was never thought that shipwrecked people belonged to the finder. Just so with the alleged slaves brought here. It was our duty to take them into our custody, and, if they needed assistance, to provide for them; and this might be done without seeming to recognize any title in the importer. He was inclined to the apprenticeship plan.

Clay, of Philadelphia, and Macon, strongly urged the bill as it stood, on the ground that it was only as a commercial question that congress had any jurisdiction over the slave-trade. Smilie, of Pa., insisted that this was something more than a mere commercial question, and that the bill could not be passed with this clause of forfeiture in it without damage to the national character. He quoted the declaration of independence; to which Clay replied that the declaration of independence must be taken with great qualifications. It declared that men have an inalienable right to life—yet we hang criminals; to liberty—yet we imprison; to the pursuit of happiness—and yet men must not infringe on the rights of others. If that declaration were to be taken in its fullest extent, it would warrant robbery and murder, for some might think even these crimes necessary to their happiness. Hastings, of Massachusetts, hoped the general government would never be disgraced by undertaking to sell human beings like goods, wares and merchandise. Yet, in spite of all these objections, the house refused to strike out the forfeiture, sixty-three to thirty-six.

The debate then turned upon the punishment to be inflicted on the masters and owners of vessels engaged in the slave-trade. The substitution, which had been adopted in committee of the whole, of imprisonment for death, was warmly opposed by the greater part of the northern members, a few excepted, who professed scruples at inflicting capital punishment at all. "We have been repeatedly told," said Mosely, of Connecticut, "and told with an air of triumph, by gentlemen from the south, that their citizens have no concern in this infamous traffic; that people from the north are the importers of negroes, and thereby the seducers of southern citizens to buy them. We have a right to presume, then, that the citizens of the south will entertain no particular partiality for these wicked traffickers, but will be ready to subject them to the most exemplary punishment. So far as the people of Connecticut are concerned, I am sure that, should any citizen of the north be convicted under this law, so far from thinking it cruel in their southern brethren to hang them, such a punishment of such culprits would be acknowledged with gratitude as a favor."

The southern members all opposed the punishment of death as too severe to be carried into execution. "A large majority of the people in the southern states," said Early, "do not consider slaveholding as a crime. They do not believe it immoral to hold men in bondage. Many deprecate slavery as an evil—a political evil—but not as a crime. Reflecting men apprehend incalculable evils from it some future day, but very few consider it a crime. It is best to be candid on this subject. If they considered the holding men in slavery as a crime, they would necessarily accuse themselves. I will tell the truth, a large majority of people in the southern states do not consider slavery even an evil. Let gentlemen go and travel in that quarter of the union, and they will find this to be the fact."

Holland, of North Carolina, gave a similar account of the public sentiment of the south : "Slavery is generally considered a political evil, and, in that point of view, nearly all are disposed to stop the trade for the future. But has capital punishment been usually inflicted on offenses merely political? Fine and imprisonment are the common punishments in such cases. The people of the south do not generally consider slaveholding as a moral offense. The importer might say to the informer, I have done no worse than you, nor even so bad. It is true, I have brought these slaves from Africa; but I have only transported them from one master to another. I am not guilty of holding human beings in bondage ; you are. You have hundreds on your plantation in that miserable condition. By your purchase you tempt traders to increase that evil which your ancestors introduced into the country, and which you yourself contribute to augment. And the same language the importer might hold to the judge or jury who might try him. Under such circumstances, the law inflicting death could not be executed. But if the punishment should be fine and imprisonment only, the people of the south will be ready to execute the law." Holland, like all the other southern speakers on this subject, wished to place the prohibition of the slave-trade on political, and not on moral grounds. The negroes, he said, brought from Africa were unquestionably brought from a state of slavery. All admitted that, as slaves, they were infinitely better off in America than in Africa. How, then, he argued, could the trade be immoral?

The infliction of capital punishment was also objected to by Stanton, one of the democratic members from Rhode Island. "Some people of my state," he remarked, "have been tempted by the high price offered for negroes by the southern people to enter into this abominable traffic. I wish the law made strong enough to prevent the trade in future, but I can not believe that a man ought to be hung for only stealing a negro!"—a declaration received by the house with a loud laugh. "Those who buy are as bad as those who import, and deserve hanging just as much."

"We are told," said Theodore Dwight, of Connecticut, "that morality has nothing to do with this traffic; that it is not a question of morals, but of politics. The president, in his message at the opening of the session, has expressed a very different opinion. He speaks of this traffic as a violation of human rights, which those who regarded morality, and the reputation and best interests of the country, have long been eager to prohibit. The gentleman from North Carolina has argued that, in importing Africans, we do them no harm; that we only transfer them from a state of slavery at home to a state of slavery attended by fewer calamities here. But by what authority do we interfere with their concerns? Who empowered us to judge for them which is the worse and which is the better state? Have these miserable beings ever been consulted as to their removal? Who can say that the state in which they were born, and to which they are habituated, is not more agreeable to them than one altogether untried, of which they have no knowledge, and about which they can not even make any calculations? Let the gentleman ask his own conscience whether it be not a violation of human rights thus forcibly to carry these wretches from their home and their country?"

Clay insisted that capital punishment under this law could not be carried into execution even in Pennsylvania, of which state it had been the policy to dispense with the penalty of death in all cases except for murder in the first degree. But on this point Findley and Smilie expressed very decidedly an opposite opinion. This was a crime, they said, above murder; it was man-stealing added to murder. In spite, however, of all efforts, the substitution of imprisonment for death prevailed by a vote of sixty-three to fifty-two.

Another attempt was afterwards made by Sloan, of New Jersey, to strike out the forfeiture clause; but he could not even succeed in obtaining the yeas and nays upon it. Three days after, the bill having been engrossed and the question being on its passage, the northern members seemed suddenly to recollect themselves. Again it was urged that by forfeiting the slaves imported, and putting the proceeds into the public treasury, the bill gave a direct sanction to the principle of slavery, and cast a stain upon the national character. In order that some other plan might be devised, consistent at once with the honor of the Union and the safety of the slave-holding states, it was moved to recommit the bill to a committee of seventeen—one from each state. This motion, made by Bedinger, of Kentucky, was supported not only by Sloan, Bidwell, Findley, and Smilie, but also by Quincy, of Boston, and Clay, of Philadelphia, who seemed at length to have taken the alarm at the extent to which they had been playing into the hands of the slaveholders. It was urged, on the other side, that the bill, as it stood, was satisfactory to nearly or quite all the members from the southern states, who alone were interested in the matter, and that to recommit a bill at this stage was very unusual. The motion to recommit was carried, however, seventy-six to forty-nine.

The committee of seventeen proposed that all persons imported in violation of the act should be sent to such states as had prohibited slavery, or had enacted laws for its gradual abolition, and should there be bound out as apprentices for a limited time, at the expiration of which they were to become free.

When this report came up for discussion, a very extraordinary degree of excitement was exhibited by several of the southern members. Early declared that the people of the south would resist this provision with their lives; and he moved, by way of compromise, as he said, to substitute for it a delivery of the imported negroes to the state authorities, to be disposed of as they might see fit—the same, in substance, with Bidwell's suggestion. This Smilie pronounced a new scene indeed! Was the house to be frightened by threats of civil war? Early denied having made any such threats. He merely meant to intimate that troops would be necessary to enforce the act. The whole day, thus commenced, was consumed in a very violent debate, of which no detailed report has been preserved.

While this subject had been under discussion in the house, the senate had passed and sent down a bill having the same object in view. The house bill, with the report of the committee, having been laid upon the table, the senate bill was taken up. That bill provided that neither the importer, nor any purchaser under him, should "have or gain " any title to the persons illegally imported, leaving them to be disposed of as the states might direct. Williams, of South Carolina, moved to substitute the word "retain " instead of the words "have or gain." The motion to strike out prevailed, but, instead of "retain," the word "hold " was substituted; whereupon Williams declared, in a very vehement speech, that he considered this word "hold " as leading to the destruction and massacre of all the whites in the southern states; and he attacked Bidwell with great violence as the author of this calamity. The punishment of death was also stricken from the bill, and, thus amended, it was reported to the house. These amendments being concurred in, the bill was passed, one hundred and thirteen to five, and was sent back to the senate.

But, notwithstanding this concession to the south, the trouble was not yet over. Among other precautions against the transportation coastwise of imported slaves, the senate bill had forbidden the transport, for the purpose of sale, of any negro whatever on board any vessel under forty tons burden. A proviso had been added by the house, excluding from the operation of this section the coastwise transportation of slaves accompanied by the owner or his agent. The refusal of the senate to concur in this amendment called out John Randolph, who hitherto had hardly spoken. " If the bill passed without this proviso, the southern people," he said, "would set the act at defiance. He would set the first example. He would go with his own slaves, and be at the expense of asserting the rights of the slaveholders. The next step would be to prohibit the slaveholder himself going from one state to another. The bill without the amendment was worse than the exaction of ship-money. The proprietor of sacred and chartered rights was prevented from the constitutional use of his property."

Other speeches were made in the same high strain, and finally a committee of conference was appointed, by which an amended proviso was agreed to, allowing the transportation of negroes, not imported contrary to the provisions of the act, in vessels of any sort on any river or inland bay within the jurisdiction of the United States. This, however, was far from satisfying the more violent southern members. Randolph still insisted "that the provisions of the bill, so far as related to the coastwise transportation of slaves, touched upon the right of private property," and he expressed a fear lest at any future period this claim of power might be made the pretext for a general emancipation. "He would rather lose all the bills of the session, every bill passed since the establishment of the government, than submit to such a provision. It went to blow the constitution into ruins. If disunion should ever take place, the line of disseverance would not be between the east and the west, lately the topic of so much alarm, but between the slaveholding and the non-slaveholding states." Early and Williams joined in these demonstrations; but the report of the committee of conference was agreed to, sixty-three to forty-nine.*

The act, as finally passed, imposed a fine of $20,000 upon all persons concerned in fitting out any vessel for the slave-trade, with the forfeiture of the vessel; likewise a fine of $5,000, with forfeiture also of the vessel, for taking on board any negro, mulatto, or person of color in any foreign country, with the purpose of selling such person within the jurisdiction of the United States as a slave. For actually transporting from any foreign country and selling as a slave, or to be held to service or labor within the United States, any such person as above described, the penalty was imprisonment for not less than five nor more than ten years, with a fine not exceeding $10,000 nor less than $1,000. The purchaser, if cognizant of the facts, was also liable to a fine of $800 for every person so purchased. Neither the importer nor the purchaser were to hold any right or title to such person, or to his or her service or labor; but all such persons were to remain subject to any regulations for their disposal, not contrary to the provisions of this act, which might be made by the respective states and territories. Coasting vessels transporting slaves from one state to another were to have the name, age, sex, and description of such slaves, with the names of the owners, inserted in their manifests, and certified also by the officers of the port of departure; which manifests, before landing any of the slaves, were to be exhibited and sworn to before the officer of the port of arrival, under pain of forfeiture of the vessel, and a fine of $1,000 for each slave as to whom these formalities might be omitted. No vessel of less than forty tons burden was to take any slaves on board except for transportation on the inland bays and rivers of the United States; and any vessel found hovering on the coast with slaves on board, in contravention of this act, was liable to seizure and condemnation; for which purpose the president was authorized to employ the ships of the navy, half the proceeds of the captured vessels and their cargoes to go to the captors. The masters of vessels so seized were lia-

---

* Annals of Congress, 1806-7: Gales & Seaton.—Hildreth's Hist. U. S.

ble to a fine of $10,000, and imprisonment for not less than two nor more than four years. The negroes found on board were to be delivered to such persons as the states might respectively appoint to receive them, or, in default of such appointment, to the overseers of the poor of the place to which they might be brought; and if, under state regulations, they should be " sold or disposed of," the penalties of this act upon the seller and purchaser were not to attach in such cases.

" The importation of Africans into South Carolina," says Hildreth, " during the four years from the reöpening of the traffic up to the period when the law of the United States went into effect, amounted to about 40,000, of whom half were brought by English vessels. A very large proportion of the remainder seem to have been introduced by Rhode Islanders. The English act for the abolition of the slave-trade, and especially the commercial restrictions which went into operation simultaneously with the American act, contributed to give it an efficacy which otherwise it might not have had. At a subsequent period, after the reëstablishment of freedom of navigation, additional provisions, as we shall see, became necessary.

" The convention of delegates from the various abolition societies had continued, since its institution in 1793, to meet annually at Philadelphia; but of late the delegations from the south had greatly fallen off, and the convention of the present year resolved that its future meetings should be only triennial. That spirit, twin-born with the struggle for liberty and independence, which had produced in three states (Massachusetts, Vermont, and Ohio,) the total prohibition of slavery, in six others provisions for its gradual abolition, and, in spite of the efforts of the people of Indiana for its temporary introduction, (efforts renewed again at the present session, but again, notwithstanding the favorable report of a committee, without success,) its continued prohibition in the territories northwest of the Ohio, culminating now in the total prohibition of the foreign slave-trade, seems to have become, for a considerable interval, less active, or at least, less marked in its manifestations. The greater part of the societies whence the delegates came gradually died out, and even the triennial convention presently ceased. Jefferson preserved, with all his zeal on this subject, a dead silence. In his private letters he sometimes alluded to the necessity of steps for getting rid of the evil of slavery; but he took good care not to hazard his popularity at the south by any public suggestions on the subject.

" That dread of and antipathy to free negroes which had been evinced in the debate on the slave-trade prohibition act had not been without its influence upon the legislation of the states. Indeed, it had led to some serious infractions of these alleged rights of property, but a very distant approach to which by the general government had thrown Randolph into such excitement. In 1796, North Carolina had reënforced and reënacted her law prohibiting emancipation except for meritorious services and by allowance of the county courts. South Carolina, in 1800, had prohibited emancipation except by consent of a justice of the peace and of five indifferent freeholders. Another South Carolina act of the same year had declared it unlawful for any number of slaves, free negroes, mulattoes, or mestizoes to assemble together, even though in the presence of white persons, "for mental instruction or religious worship." The same influences were felt in Virginia, aggravated, perhaps, by two successive alarms of insurrection, one in 1799, the other in 1801. The freedom of emancipation allowed by the act of 1782 was substantially taken away in 1805, by a provision that thenceforward emancipated slaves remaining in the state for twelve months after obtaining their freedom should be apprehended and sold for the benefit of the poor of the county—a forfeiture given afterward to the literary fund. Overseers of the poor, binding out black or mulatto orphans as apprentices, were forbidden to require their masters to teach them reading, writing, or arithmetic. Free blacks coming into the state were to be sent back to the places whence they came. The legislature of Kentucky presently (1808) went so far as to provide that free negroes coming into that state should give security to depart within twenty days, and on failure to do so should be sold for a year—the same process to be repeated if, twenty days after the end of the year, they were still found within the state. 'Such is the fate,' exclaims Marshall, the historian of Kentucky, indignant at this barbarous piece of legislation, 'of men not represented, at the hands of law-makers, often regardless of the rights of others, and even of the first principles of humanity.' Yet this statute remains in force to the present day, and many like ones, in other states, have since been added to it. Whether the excessive dread of the increase of free negroes, which still prevails, and which seems every day to grow more and more rabid throughout the southern states, has any better foundation than mere suspicion and fear, is not so certain. In Delaware and Maryland the free colored population is far greater in proportion than elsewhere; yet life and property are more secure in those than in any other slaveholding states, nor are they inferior in wealth and industry." *

---

* Hildreth.

CHAPTER XXVI.

POLITICAL HISTORY OF SLAVERY IN THE UNITED STATES FROM 1807 TO 1820.

Slave population in 1810.—Period of the war.—John Randolph's denunciations.—Proclamation of Admiral Cochrane to the slaves.—Treaty of Peace—arbitration on slave property.—Opinions of the domestic slave-trade by southern statesmen.—Constitution of Mississippi—slave provisions.—The African slave-trade and fugitive law.—Missouri applies for admission—proviso to prohibit slavery.—Debate—speeches of Fuller, Tallmadge, Scott, Cobb, and Livermore.—Proceedings, 1820.—Bill for organizing Arkansas Territory—proviso to prohibit slavery lost.—Excitement in the North.—Public meetings.—Massachusetts memorial.—Resolutions of State Legislatures of New York, New Jersey, Pennsylvania, Delaware, and Kentucky.—Congress—the Missouri struggle renewed.—The compromise.—Proviso to exclude slavery in territory north of 36° 30′ carried.—Proviso to prohibit slavery in Missouri lost.—Opinions of Monroe's cabinet. Reflections of J. Q. Adams.—State Constitution of Missouri—final struggle.—Missouri admitted as a slave state.

IN the period between 1800 and 1810, the slave population of the states and territories increased 298,323, exhibiting a total in 1810 of 1,191,364, a rate of increase of about 33 per cent.

CENSUS OF 1810.—SLAVE POPULATION.

District of Columbia	5,395	Georgia	105,218
Rhode Island	108	Maryland	111,502
Connecticut	310	North Carolina	168,824
Pennsylvania	795	South Carolina	196,365
Delaware	4,177	Virginia	392,518
New Jersey	10,851	Mississippi Territory	17,088
New York	15,017	Indiana Territory	237
Louisiana	34,660	Louisiana Territory	3,011
Tennessee	44,535	Illinois Territory	168
Kentucky	80,561	Michigan Territory	24

About this period the foreign relations of the country absorbed the attention of congress, and the subject of slavery was only incidentally alluded to. John Randolph, of Virginia, in a speech in opposition to the contemplated war with England, in his usual discursive style, thus denounces the slavery agitation and the "infernal principles" of the French democracy, as inconsistent with the safety of the south :

"No sooner was the present report laid on the table, than the vultures came flocking round their prey—the carcass of a great military establishment. Men of tainted reputation, of broken fortunes (if they ever had any), of battered constitutions, 'choice spirits, tired of the dull pursuits of civil life,' seeking after agencies and commissions, and wishing to light the public candle at both ends.

"Such a war might hold out inducements to gentlemen from Tennessee and Genesee (Grundy and Porter). Western hemp would rise in the market, and western New York might grow rich by provisioning our armies ; not to mention the political interest which that state had in the acquisition of Canada. But how absurd to commence a war for maritime rights by invading that province, while our whole sea-coast lay exposed to the enemy; not a spot on all the shores of Chesapeake bay, the city of Baltimore alone excepted, safe from attack or capable of defense!

"If it were true that Britain had stimulated the late Indian hostilities, that might justify the proposed invasion; but that was a rash charge, with no foundation beyond suspicion and surmise. There was, indeed, an easy and natural solution of the events on the Wabash, without resort to any such conjecture. It was our own thirst for territory, our want of moderation that had driven those sons of nature to despair.

"But this Canadian campaign, it seems, is to be a holiday matter. There is to be no expense of blood or treasure on our part. Canada is to conquer herself—is to be subdued by the principles of French fraternity! We are to succeed by this French method! Our whole policy, indeed, is French! But how dreadfully might not this sort of warfare be retorted on our own southern states!

"During the war of the revolution, so fixed among the slaves was the habit of obedience, that while the whole country was overrun by the enemy, who invited them to desert, no fears were entertained of insurrection. But should we therefore be unobservant spectators of the progress of society with the last twenty years? Even the poor slaves have not escaped. The French revolution has polluted even them. Nay, there have not been wanting members of this house—witness our legislative Legendre, the butcher—[this referred to Sloan, who had proposed the abolition of slavery in the District of Columbia] to preach upon this very floor the doctrine of imprescriptible rights to a crowded audience of blacks in the galleries; teaching them that they are equal to their masters; in other words, advising them to cut their masters' throats! Similar doctrines are spread throughout the south by Yankee peddlers; and there are even owners of slaves so infatuated, as by the general tenor of their conversation, by contempt of order, morality, and religion, unthinkingly to cherish these seeds of destruction. And what has been the consequence? Within the last ten years repeated alarms of slave insurrections, some of them awful indeed. By the spreading of this infernal doctrine, the whole south has been thrown into a state of insecurity. Men dead to the operation of moral causes have taken from the poor slave those habits of loyalty and obedience which lightened his servitude by a double operation, beguiling his own labors and disarming his master's suspicions and severity; and now, like true empirics in politics, you propose to trust to the mere physical strength of the shackle that holds him in bondage. You have deprived him of all moral restraint; you have tempted him to eat of the tree of knowledge just enough to perfect him in wickedness; you have opened his eyes to his nakedness; you have roused his nature against the hand that has fed him, and has clothed him, and has cherished him in sickness—that hand which, before he became a pupil in your school, he was accustomed to press to his lips with respectful affection; you have done all this—and now you point him to the whip and the gibbet as incentives to a sullen, reluctant obedience. God forbid that the southern states should ever see an enemy on their shores with these infernal principles of French fraternity in the van ! While talking of Canada, we have too much reason to shudder for our own safety at home. I speak from facts when I say that the night-bell never tolls for fire in Richmond that the frightened mother does not hug her infant the more closely to her bosom, not knowing what may have happened. I have.myself witnessed some of the alarms in the capital of Virginia."

The infernal principles spoken of by Randolph, were, it seems, reduced to practice in 1814 by admiral Cochrane, of the Chesapeake blockading squadron, who issued a proclamation, addressed to the slaves, under the denomination of "persons desirous to emigrate." They were offered a reception, with their families, on board the British vessels of war, with the choice of entering into the service, or of being sent to the British possessions as free settlers. "Then is reason, indeed, to believe," says Hildreth, "that a plan suggested by s of the British officers, for taking possession of the peninsula between Delaware and Chesapeake bays, and then training a black army, was only rejected because the British, being then slaveholders themselves, did not like to encourage insurrection elsewhere."

Subsequent to the ratification of the treaty of peace, a question arose whether the United States were entitled, under the treaty, to compensation for slaves within the territory or places occupied by the British forces at the time of the making of the treaty, and directed by that treaty to be restored to the United States. The question was referred, by agreement, to the emperor of Russia, who gave his decision as follows :

"That the United States were entitled to indemnification for all the slaves carried away by the British forces from places and territories which the treaty stipulated to restore, in quitting these same places and territories : That all slaves were to be considered as having been so carried away, who had been transferred from these territories to British vessels within the said territories, and who for this reason had not been restored : But that for slaves carried away from territories which the treaty did not stipulate to restore, the United States are not entitled to indemnification. The emperor also appointed two of his privy councilors, Count Nesselrode and Count Capodistrias, together with Henry Middleton, the American minister at St. Petersburgh, and Charles Bagot, the British minister at the same place, to provide the mode of ascertaining the value of the slaves, and of other private property unlawfully carried away, and for which indemnification was to be made.

The settlement of the southwest proceeded rapidly after the war. The great profits derived from the cultivation of cotton, kept the African slave-trade alive in spite of the prohibitory laws. The domestic slave-trade increased, and Washington became a great resort of the traders, who were engaged in buying up slaves in Maryland and Virginia for transportation to the southwest John Randolph, of Virginia, in congress denounced this new traffic as heinous and abominable, inhuman and illegal, and moved a committee of inquiry, whose report justified some of the epithets. Governor Williams, of South Carolina, in a message to the legislature, denounced "this remorseless and merciless traffic, this ceasless dragging along the streets and highways of a crowd of suffering victims to minister to insatiable avarice," as condemned alike by "enlightened humanity, wise policy and the prayers of the just." The legislature accordingly passed an act forbidding the introduction of slaves from abroad; which was repealed, however, in two years.

About this time the American Colonization Society sprung into existence, as related in a former chapter.

The new state of Mississippi was admitted into the Union December 10, 1817. By one of the provisions of its constitution, grand juries were dispensed with in the indictment of slaves; and slaves were not allowed trial by jury except in capital cases.

At the session of 1817–18, the Maryland Quakers sent in a petition to congress praying further provisions for the security of free persons of color against the increased danger of being kidnapped, growing out of the domestic slave-trade. The Quaker memorial was referred, and Burrell, of Rhode Island, moved instructions to the committee, also to inquire into the expediency of additional provisions for the suppression of the African slave-trade, and especially of concert with other nations for that purpose.

At this session, Pindall, of Virginia, obtained a committee, which brought in a bill to give new stringency to the old fugitive slave act. The bill provided for assimilating the proceedings in the case of fugitives from labor to those in the case of fugitives from justice. The claimant, having made out a title before some judge of his own state, was then to be entitled to an executive demand on the governor of the state where the fugitive was, with the imposition of heavy penalties upon those who refused to aid in the arrest.

Strong, Fuller, and Whitman, of Massachusetts, Williams, of Connecticut, Livermore, of New Hampshire, and several Pennsylvania representatives, warmly opposed this bill, as going entirely beyond the constitutional provision on the subject of fugitives from labor. The old law, in their opinion, went quite far enough already. The personal rights of one class of citizens were not to be trampled upon to secure the rights of property of other citizens. The question of servitude ought to be tried in the state where the fugitive was. A motion was made by Sergeant to modify the bill in accordance with this idea; but it did not succeed. On the other hand, the bill was supported by Cobb, of Georgia, as a right of the slaveholders secured by the constitution, by Mr. Speaker Clay, and by Baldwin, of Pennsylvania. The bill was also supported by Holmes, of Massachusetts, by Storrs, of New York, who thought that, for the sake of union and harmony, northern men must learn to sacrifice their prejudices; and by Mason, the new Boston representative, who professed, indeed, a personal interest in the question, from his fear lest, if the bill failed to pass, his own town of Boston might be inconveniently infested by southern runaways. Thus sustained, the bill passed the house, 84 to 69. Among the yeas were ten from New York, still a slaveholding state, five from Massachusetts, four from Pennsylvania, and one from New Jersey, that of the late governor and general, Bloomfield, in his earlier days a most zealous member of the New Jersey society for the abolition of slavery.

Having reached the senate, this bill was referred to a committee, of which Crittenden was chairman. He reported it back with several amendments, one of which provided that the identity of the alleged fugitive, after being carried back, should be established by some testimony other than that of the claimant. Thus amended, the bill was carried in the senate; but not without a very warm debate, of which, however, not a syllable has been preserved. The vote stood 17 to 13, the Delaware senators against it; Otis, of Massachusetts, Sanford, of New York, and Taylor, of Indiana, for it. But by the time the bill got back to the house, its northern supporters seem to have taken some alarm; and, in spite of repeated efforts of its authors to get some action upon it, it was suffered to lie and to die on the table.

Burrell's resolution in the senate, especially that part of it relating to cooperation with foreign nations, was strongly opposed by Barbour and Troup, as leading to foreign entanglements, and involving a pledge which congress had no right to give. Morrell, a new democratic senator from New Hampshire, launched out, in reply, into a most emphatic denunciation of slavery. King defended the resolution, since the concert which it suggested was one, not of arms, but of opinion, example, and influence, to prevail on Spain and Portugal to join in the abolition of the traffic; but he suggested that the debate had taken quite too wide a range, the subject of the resolution being, not slavery in general, a topic, as he remarked, always alluded to in the senate with very great reserve, but the abolition of the slave-trade, as to which they were all agreed. The resolution was adopted; and the committee to which it was referred reported a bill, which became a law, throwing the burden of proof, in all cases where negroes were found on board a ship, on those in possession; and extending the penalties of the prohibitory act to the fitting out of vessels for the slave-trade, or the transporting slaves to any country whatever.

At the session of 1818–19, an act was passed allowing a premium of fifty dollars to the informer for every illegally-imported African seized within the United States, and half as much for those taken at sea; with authority to the president to cause them to be removed beyond the limits of the United States, and to appoint agents on the coast of Africa for their reception. An attempt was also made to punish slave-trading with death, as had been contended for at the time of the original abolition act. Such a provision passed the house, but was struck out in the senate.

In March, 1818, the delegate from Missouri presented petitions from sundry inhabitants of that territory, praying for the admission of Missouri into the Union as a state. These petitions were referred to a select committee, which reported a bill to authorize the people of that territory to form a constitution and state government, and for the admission of such state into the Union on an equal footing with the original states. The bill was read the first and second time and sent to the committee of the whole, where it slept the remainder of the session. At the next session, on the 13th February, 1819, the house went into committee of the whole, Gen. Smith, of Maryland, in the chair, and took up the Missouri bill, which was considered through that sitting, and also on Monday, the 15th. Gen. Tallmadge, of New York, moved the following amendment:

"And provided that the introduction of slavery, or involuntary servitude, be prohibited, except for the punishment of crimes, whereof the party has been duly convicted, and that all children born within the said state, after the admission thereof into the Union, shall be declared free at the age of twenty-five years."

Mr. Fuller, of Massachusetts, said, that in the admission of new states into the Union, he considered that congress had a discretionary power. By the 4th article and 3d section of the constitution, congress are *authorized* to admit them; but nothing in that section, or in any part of the constitution, enjoins the admission as imperative, under any circumstances. If it were otherwise, he would request gentlemen to point out what were the circumstances or *conditions precedent*, which being found to exist, congress *must* admit the new state. All discretion would, in such case, be taken from congress, Mr. Fuller said, and deliberation would be useless. The honorable speaker (Mr. Clay) has said that congress has no right to prescribe any condition whatever to the newly-organized states, but must admit them by a simple act, leaving their sovereignty unrestricted. [Here the speaker explained—he did not intend to be understood in so broad a sense as Mr. Fuller stated.] With the explanation of the honorable gentleman, Mr. Fuller said, I still think his ground as untenable as before. We certainly have a right, and our duty to the nation requires, that we should examine the actual state of things in the proposed state; and, above all, the constitution expressly makes a REPUBLICAN *form of government* in the several states a fundamental principle, to be preserved under the sacred guarantee of the national legislature.—[Art. 4, sec 4.] It clearly, therefore, is the duty of congress, before admitting a new sister into the Union, to ascertain that her constitution or form of government is republican. Now, sir, the amendment proposed by the gentleman from New York, Mr. Tallmadge, merely requires that slavery shall be prohibited in Missouri. Does this imply anything more than that its constitution shall be republican? The existence of slavery in any state is, *so far*, a departure from republican principles. The Declaration of Independence, penned by the illustrious statesman then, and at this time, a citizen of a state which admits slavery, defines the principle on which our national and state constitutions are all professedly founded. The second paragraph of that instrument begins thus: "We hold these truths to be self-evident—that *all men are created equal*—that they are endowed by their Creator with certain inalienable rights; that among these are life, LIBERTY, and the pursuit of happiness." Since, then, it cannot be denied that slaves are *men*, it follows that they are, in a *purely* republican government, born *free*, and are entitled to *liberty* and the pursuit of happiness. [Mr. Fuller was here interrupted by several gentlemen, who thought it improper to question in debate the republican character of the slaveholding states, which had also a tendency, as one gentleman (Mr. Colston, of Virginia,) said, to deprive those states of the right to hold slaves as property, and he adverted to the probability that there might be slaves in the gallery, listening to the debate.] Mr. Fuller assured the gentleman that nothing was farther from his thoughts, than to question on that floor, the right of Virginia and other states, which held slaves when the constitution was established, to continue to hold them. With that subject the national legislature could not interfere, and ought not to attempt it. But, Mr. Fuller continued, if gentlemen will be patient, they will see that my remarks will neither derogate from the constitutional rights of the states, nor from a due respect to their several forms of government. Sir, it is my wish to *allay*, and not to excite local animosities, but I shall never refrain from advancing such arguments in debate as my duty requires, nor do I believe that the reading of our Declaration of Independence or a discussion of republican principles on any occasion, can endanger the rights, or merit the disapprobation of any portion of the Union.

My reason, Mr. Chairman, for recurring to the Declaration of our Independence, was to draw from an authority admitted in all parts of the Union, a definition of the basis of republican government. If, then, all men have equal rights, it can no more comport with the principles of a free government to exclude men of a certain color from the enjoyment of " liberty and the pursuit of happiness," than to exclude those who have not attained a certain portion of wealth, or a certain stature of body, or to found the exclusion on any other capricious or accidental circumstance. Suppose Missouri, before her admission as a state, were to submit to us her constitution by which no person could elect, or be elected to any office, unless he possessed a clear annual income of twenty thousand dollars; and suppose we had ascertained that *only five*, or a very small number of persons had such an estate, would this be anything more or less than a *real aristocracy*, under a form nominally republican ? Election and representation, which some contend are the only essential principles of republics, would exist only in name—a shadow without substance, a body without a soul. But if all the other inhabitants were to be made slaves, and mere property of the favored few, the outrage on principle would be still more palpable. Yet, sir, it is demonstrable that the exclusion of the black population from all political freedom, and making them the property of the whites, is an equally palpable invasion of right, and abandonment of principle. If we do this in the admission of *new states*, we violate the constitution, and we have not now the excuse which existed when our national constitution was established. Then, to effect a concert of interests, it was proper to make concessions. The states where slavery existed not only claimed the right to continue it, but it was manifest that a general emancipation of slaves could not be asked of them. Their political existence would have been in jeopardy ; both masters and slaves must have been involved in the most fatal consequences.

To guard against such intolerable evils, it is provided in the constitution "that the migration or importation of such persons, as any of the *existing* states think proper to admit, shall not be prohibited till 1808."—Art. 1, sec. 9. And it is provided elsewhere, that persons held to service by the laws of any state, shall be given up by other states, to which they may have escaped, etc.—Art. 4, sec. 2.

These provisions effectually recognized the right in the states, which at the time of framing the constitution held the blacks in slavery, to *continue* so to hold them until they should think proper to meliorate their condition. The constitution is a compact among all the states then existing, by which certain principles of government are established for the whole, and for each individual state. The *predominant* principle in both respects is, that ALL MEN are FREE, and have an EQUAL RIGHT TO LIBERTY, and all other privileges; or, in other words, the predominant principle is REPUBLICANISM, in its largest sense. But, then, the same compact contains certain exceptions. The states then holding slaves are *permitted*, from the necessity of the case, and for the sake of union, to exclude the republican principle so far, and *only* so far, as to retain their slaves in servitude, and also their progeny, as had been the usage, until they think it proper or safe to conform to the pure principle, by abolishing slavery. The compact contains on its face the *general* principle and the *exceptions*. But the attempt to extend slavery to the *new states*, is in direct violation of the clause, which guarantees a republican form of government to all the states. This clause, indeed, must be construed in connection with the exceptions before mentioned; but it cannot, without violence, be applied to any other states than those in which slavery was allowed at the formation of the constitution.

The honorable speaker cites the first clause in the 2d section of the 4th article, "the citizens of each state shall be entitled to all the privileges and immunities of citizens of the several states," which he thinks would be violated by the condition proposed in the constitution of Missouri. To keep slaves, to make one portion of the population the property of another, hardly deserves to be called a *privilege*, since what is gained by the masters must be lost by the slaves. But, independently of this consideration, I think the observations already offered to the committee, showing that holding the black population in servitude is an exception to the general principles of the constitution, and can not be allowed to extend beyond the fair import of the terms by which that exception is provided, are a sufficient answer to the objection. The gentleman proceeds in the same train of reasoning, and asks if congress can require one condition, how many more can be required, and where these conditions will end? With regard to a republican constitution, congress are *obliged* to require that condition, and that is enough for the present question; but I contend, further, that congress has a right, at their discretion, to require any other reasonable condition. Several others were required of Ohio, Indiana, Illinois and Mississippi. The state of Louisiana, which was a part of the territory ceded to us at the same time with Missouri, was required to provide in her constitution for trials by jury, the writ of habeas corpus, the principles of civil and religious liberty, with several others, peculiar to that state. These, certainly, are none of them more indispensable ingredients in a republican form of government than the equality of privileges of all the population; yet these have not been denied to be reasonable, and warranted by the national constitution in the admission of new states. Nor need gentlemen apprehend that congress will set no reasonable limits to the conditions of admission. In the exercise of their constitutional discretion on this subject, they are, as in all other cases, responsible to the people. Their power to levy direct taxes is not limited by the constitution. They may lay a tax of one million of dollars, or of a hundred millions, without violating the letter of the constitution; but if the latter enormous and unreasonable sum were levied, or even the former, without evident necessity, the people have the power in their own hands—a speedy corrective is found in the return of the elections. This remedy is so certain, that the representatives of the people can never lose sight of it; and consequently, an abuse of their powers to any considerable extent can never be apprehended. The same reasoning applies to the exercise of *all* the power entrusted to congress, and the admission of new states into the Union is in no respect an exception.

One gentleman, however, has contended against the amendment, because it abridges the rights of the slaveholding states to transport their slaves to the new states, for sale or otherwise. This argument is attempted to be enforced in various ways, and particularly by the clause in the constitution last cited. It admits, however, of a very clear answer by recurring to the 9th section of article 1st, which provides that "the *migration* or importation of such persons as any of the states then existing shall admit, shall not be prohibited by congress till 1808." This clearly implies that the *migration* and importation may be prohibited *after* that year. The importation has been prohibited, but the migration has not hitherto been restrained; congress, however, may restrain it when it may be judged expedient. It is, indeed, contended by some gentlemen, that migration is either synonymous with importation, or that it means something different from the transportation of slaves from one state to another. It certainly is not synonymous with *importation*, and would not have been used had it been so. It cannot mean *exportation*, which is also a definite and precise term. It cannot mean the reception of *free* blacks from foreign countries, as is alleged by some, because no possible reason existed for regulating their admission by the constitution; no free blacks ever came from Africa, or any other country to this; and to introduce the provision by the side of that for the importation of slaves, would have been absurd in the highest degree. What alternative remains but to apply the term "migration" to the transportation of slaves from those states where they are admitted to be held, to other states? Such a provision might have in view a very natural object. The price of slaves might be affected so far by a sudden prohibition to transport slaves from state to state, that it was as reasonable to guard against that inconvenience as against the sudden interdiction of the importation. Hitherto it has not been found necessary for congress to prohibit migration or transportation from state to state. But now it becomes the right and duty of congress to guard against the further extension of the intolerable evil and the crying enormity of slavery.

The expediency of this measure is very apparent. The opening of an extensive slave market will tempt the cupidity of those who, otherwise, perhaps, might gradually emancipate their slaves. We have heard much, Mr. Chairman, of the colonization society; an institution which is the favorite of the humane gentlemen in the slaveholding states. They have long been lamenting the miseries of slavery, and earnestly seeking for a remedy compatible with their own safety and the happiness of their slaves. At last the great desideratum is found—a colony in Africa for the emancipated blacks. How will the generous intentions of these humane persons be frustrated if the price of slaves is to be doubled by a new and boundless market? Instead of emancipation of the slaves, it is much to be feared that unprincipled wretches will be found kidnapping those who are already free, and transporting and selling the hapless victims into hopeless bondage. Sir, I really hope that congress will not contribute to discountenance and render abortive the generous and philanthropic views of this most worthy and laudable society. Rather let us hope that the time is not very remote, when the shores of Africa, which have so long been a scene of barbarous rapacity and savage cruelty, shall exhibit a race of free and enlightened people—the offspring, indeed, of cannibals or slaves; but displaying the virtues of civilization and the energies of independent freemen. America may then hope to see the development of a germ, now scarcely visible, cherished and matured under the genial warmth of our country's protection, till the fruit shall appear in the regeneration and happiness of a boundless continent.

One argument still remains to be noticed. It is said that we are bound, by the treaty of cession with France, to admit the ceded territory into the Union "as soon as possible." It is obvious that the president and the senate, the treaty-making power, cannot make a stipulation with any foreign nation in derogation of the constitutional powers and duties of this house, by making it imperative on us to admit the new territory according to the literal tenor of the phrase; but the additional words in the treaty, "according to the principles of the constitution," put it beyond all doubt that no such compulsory admission was intended, and that the republican principles of our constitution are to govern us in the admission of this, as well as all the new states in the national family.

Mr. Tallmadge, of New York, rose: Sir, said he, it has been my desire and my intention to avoid any debate on the present painful and unpleasant subject. When I had the honor to submit to this house the amendment now under consideration, I accompanied it with a declaration that it was intended to confine its operation to the newly acquired territory across the Mississippi; and I then expressly declared that I would in no manner intermeddle with the slaveholding states, nor attempt manumission in any one of the original states in the Union. Sir, I even went further, and stated that I was aware of the delicacy of the subject, and that I had learned from southern gentlemen the difficulties and the dangers of having free blacks intermingling with slaves; and, on that account, and with a view to the safety of the white population of the adjoining states, I would not even advocate the prohibition of slavery in the Alabama territory; because, surrounded as it was by slaveholding states, and with only imaginary lines of division, the intercourse between slaves and free blacks could not be prevented, and a servile war might be the result. While we deprecate and mourn over the evils of slavery, humanity and good morals require us to wish its abolition, under circumstances consistent with the safety of the white population. Willingly, therefore, will I submit to an evil which we cannot safely remedy. I admitted all that had been said of the danger of having free blacks visible to slaves, and therefore did not hesitate to pledge myself that I would neither advise nor attempt coercive manumission. But, sir, all these reasons cease when we cross the banks of the Mississippi, into a territory separated by a natural boundary—a newly acquired territory, never contemplated in the formation of our government, not included within the compromise or mutual pledge in the adoption of our constitution—a new territory acquired by our common fund, and ought justly to be subject to our common legislation.

Sir, when I submitted the amendment now under consideration, accompanied with these explanations, and with these avowals of my intentions and of my motives, I did expect that gentlemen who might differ from me in opinion would appreciate the liberality of my views, and would meet me with moderation, as upon a fair subject for general legislation. I did expect, at least, that the frank declaration of my views would protect me from harsh expressions, and from the unfriendly imputations which have been cast out on this occasion. But, sir, such has been the character and the violence of this debate, and expressions of so much intemperance and of an aspect so threatening have been used, that continued silence on my part would ill become me who had submitted to this house the original proposition. While this subject was under debate before the committee of the whole, I did not take the floor, and I avail myself of this occasion to acknowledge my obligations to my friends (Mr. Taylor and Mr. Mills) for the manner in which they supported my amendment, at a time when I was unable to partake of the debate. I had only on that day returned from a journey, long in extent and painful in its occasion; and from an affection of my breast I could not then speak. I cannot yet hope to do justice to the subject; but I do hope to say enough to assure my friends that I have not left them in the controversy, and to convince the opponents of the measure that their violence has not driven me from the debate.

Sir, the hon. gentleman from Missouri, (Mr. Scott,) who has just resumed his seat, has told us of the ides of March, and has cautioned us to "beware of the fate of Cæsar and of Rome." Another gentleman, (Mr. Cobb,) from Georgia, in addition to other expressions of great warmth, has said that if we persist, the Union will be dissolved; and with a look fixed on me, has told us, "we have kindled a fire which all the waters of the ocean cannot put out, which seas of blood can only extinguish."

Language of this sort has no effect on me; my purpose is fixed, it is interwoven with my existence; its durability is limited with my life; it is a great and glorious cause, setting bounds to a slavery the most cruel and debasing the world has ever witnessed; it is the freedom of man; it is the cause of unredeemed and unregenerated human beings.

If a dissolution of the Union must take place, let it be so! If a civil war, which gentlemen so much threaten, must come, I can only say, let it come! My hold on life is probably as frail as that of any man who now hears me; but while that hold lasts, it shall be devoted to the service of my country—to the freedom of man. If blood is necessary to extinguish any fire which I have assisted to kindle, I can assure gentlemen, while I regret the necessity, I shall not forbear to contribute my mite. Sir, the violence to which gentlemen have resorted on this subject will not move my purpose, nor drive me from my place. I have the fortune and the honor to stand here as the representative of freemen, who possess intelligence to know their rights—who have the spirit to maintain them. Whatever might be my own private sentiments on this subject, standing here as the representative of others, no choice is left me. I know the will of my constituents, and, regardless of consequences, I will avow it—as their representative, I will proclaim their hatred to slavery in every shape—as their representative, here will I hold my stand, till this floor, with the constitution of my country which supports it, shall sink beneath me—if I am doomed to fall, I shall, at least, have the painful consolation to believe that I fall, as a fragment, in the ruins of my country.

Sir, the gentleman from Virginia (Mr. Colston) has accused my honorable friend from New Hampshire (Mr. Livermore) of "speaking to the galleries," and by his "language endeavoring to excite a servile war;" and has ended by saying, "he is no better than Arbuthnot and Ambrister, and deserves no better fate." When I hear such language uttered upon this floor, and within this house, I am constrained to consider it as hasty and unintended language, resulting from the vehemence of debate, and not really intending the personal indecorum the expression would seem to indicate. [Mr. Colston asked to explain, and said he had not distinctly understood Mr. T. Mr. Livermore called on Mr. C. to state the expressions he had used. Mr. C. then said he had no explanation to give.] Mr. T. said he had none to ask—he continued to say, he would not believe any gentleman on this floor would commit so great an indecorum against any member, or against the dignity of this house, as to use such expressions, really intending the meaning which the words seem to import, and which had been uttered against the gentleman from New Hampshire. [Mr. Nelson, of Virginia, in the chair, called to order, and said no personal remarks would be allowed.] Mr. T. said he rejoiced the chair was at length aroused to a sense of its duties. The debate had, for several days, progressed with unequaled violence, and all was in order; but now, when at length this violence on one side is to be resisted, the chair discovered it is out of order. I rejoice, said Mr. T., at the discovery, I approve of the admonition, while I am proud to say it has no relevancy to me. It is my boast that I have never uttered an unfriendly personal remark on this floor; but I wish it distinctly understood, that the immutable laws of self-defense will justify going to great lengths, and that, in the future progress of this debate, the rights of defense would be regarded.

Sir, has it already come to this, that in the congress of the United States— that, in the legislative councils of republican America, the subject of slavery has become a subject of so much feeling, of such delicacy, of such danger, that it cannot safely be discussed ? Are members who venture to express their sentiments on this subject to be accused of talking to the galleries, with intention to excite a servile war; and of meriting the fate of Arbuthnot and Ambrister ? Are we to be told of the dissolution of the Union, of civil war, and seas of blood ? And yet, with such awful threatenings before us, do gentlemen in the same breath insist upon the encouragement of this evil—upon the extension of this monstrous scourge of the human race ? An evil so fraught with such dire calamities to us as individuals, and to our nation, and threatening, in its progress, to overwhelm the civil and religious institutions of the country, with the liberties of the nation, ought at once to be met, and to be controlled. If its power, its influence, and its impending dangers have already arrived at such a point that it is not safe to discuss it on this floor, and it cannot now pass under consideration as a proper subject for general legislation, what will be the result when it has spread through your widely-extended domain? Its present threatening aspect, and the violence of its supporters, so far from inducing me to yield to its progress, prompt me to resist its march. Now is the time. It must now be met, and the extension of the evil must now be prevented, or the occasion is irrecoverably lost, and the evil can never be controlled.

Sir, extend your view across the Mississippi, over your newly-acquired territory—a territory so far surpassing, in extent, the limits of your present country, that that country which gave birth to your nation, which achieved your revolution, consolidated your Union, formed your constitution, and has subsequently acquired so much glory, hangs but as an appendage to the extended empire over which your republican government is now called to bear sway. Look down the long vista of futurity; see your empire, in extent unequaled, in advantageous situation without a parallel, and occupying all the valuable part of one continent. Behold this extended empire, inhabited by the hardy sons of American freemen, knowing their rights, and inheriting the will to protect them—owners of the soil on which they live, and interested in the institutions which they labor to defend; with two oceans laving your shores, and tributary to your purposes, bearing on their bosoms the commerce of our people; compared to yours, the governments of Europe dwindle into insignificance, and the whole world is without a parallel. But, sir, reverse this scene; people this fair domain with the slaves of your planters; extend *slavery*, this bane of man, this abomination of heaven, over your extended empire, and you prepare its dissolution; you turn its accumulated strength into positive weakness; you cherish a canker in your breast; you put poison in your bosom; you place a vulture preying on your heart—nay, you whet the dagger and place it in the hands of a portion of your population, stimulated to use it by every tie, human and divine. The envious contrast between your happiness and their misery, between your liberty and their slavery, must constantly prompt them to accomplish your destruction. Your enemies will learn the source and the cause of your weakness. As often as external dangers shall threaten, or internal commotions await you, you will then realize, that by your own procurement, you have placed amidst your families, and in the bosom of your country, a population producing at once the greatest cause of individual danger, and of national weakness. With this defect, your government must crumble to pieces, and your people become the scoff of the world.

Sir, we have been told, with apparent confidence, that we have no right to annex conditions to a state, on its admission into the Union; and it has been urged that the proposed amendment, prohibiting the further introduction of slavery, is unconstitutional. This position, asserted with so much confidence, remains unsupported by any argument, or by any authority derived from the constitution itself. The constitution strongly indicates an opposite conclusion, and seems to contemplate a difference between the old and the new states. The practice of the government has sanctioned this difference in many respects.

The third section of the fourth article of the constitution says, "*new states may be admitted by the congress into this Union,*" and it is silent as to the terms and conditions upon which the new states may be so admitted. The fair inference from this is, that the congress which might admit, should prescribe the time and the terms of such admission. The tenth section of the first article of the constitution says, "*the migration or importation of such persons as any of the states* NOW EXISTING *shall think proper to admit, shall not be prohibited by the congress prior to the year* 1808." The words "*now existing*" clearly show the distinction for which we contend. The word *slave* is no where mentioned in the constitution; but this section has always been considered as applicable to them, and unquestionably reserved the right to prevent their importation into any *new state* before the year 1808.

Congress, therefore, have power over the subject, probably as a matter of legislation, but more certainly as a right, to prescribe the time and the condition upon which any new state may be admitted into the family of the Union. Sir, the bill now before us proves the correctness of my argument. It is filled with conditions and limitations. The territory is required to take a census, and is to be admitted only on condition that it have 40,000 inhabitants. I have already submitted amendments preventing the state from taxing the lands of the United States, and declaring that all navigable waters shall remain open to the other states, and be exempt from any tolls or duties. And my friend (Mr. Taylor) has also submitted amendments prohibiting the state from taxing soldiers' lands for the period of five years. And to all these amendments we have heard no objection—they have passed unanimously. But now, when an amendment prohibiting the further introduction of slavery is proposed, the whole house is put in agitation, and we are confidently told it is unconstitutional to annex conditions to the admission of a new state into the union. The result of all this is, that all amendments and conditions are proper, which suit a certain class of gentlemen, but whatever amendment is proposed, which does not comport with their interests or their views, is unconstitutional, and a flagrant violation of this sacred charter of our rights. In order to be consistent, gentlemen must go back and strike out the various amendments to which they have already agreed. The constitution applies equally to all, or to none.

Sir, we have been told that this is a new principle for which we contend, never before adopted, or thought of. So far from this being correct, it is due to the memory of our ancestors to say, it is an old principle, adopted by them as the policy of our country. Whenever the United States have had the right and the power, they have heretofore prevented the extension of slavery. The states of Kentucky and Tennessee were taken off from other states, and were admitted into the Union without condition, because their lands were never owned by the United States. The territory northwest of the Ohio is all the land which ever belonged to them. Shortly after the cession of those lands to the Union, congress passed, in 1787, a compact, which was declared to be unalterable, the sixth article of which provides that *"there shall be neither slavery nor involuntary servitude in the said territory, otherwise than in the punishment for crimes, whereof the parties shall have been duly convicted."* In pursuance of this compact, all the states formed from that territory have been admitted into the Union upon various conditions, and, amongst which, the sixth article of this compact is included as one.

Let gentlemen also advert to the law for the admission of the state of Louisiana into the Union; they will find it filled with conditions. It was required not only to form a constitution upon the principles of a republican government, but it was required to contain the "fundamental principles of civil and religious liberty." It was even required, as a condition of its admission, to keep its records, and its judicial and its legislative proceedings in the English language; and also to secure the trial by jury, and to surrender all claim to unappropriated lands in the territory, with the prohibition to tax any of the United States' lands.

After this long practice and constant usage to annex conditions to the admission of a state into the Union, will gentlemen yet tell us it is unconstitutional, and talk of our principles being novel and extraordinary? It has been said that if this amendment prevails, we shall have a union of states possessing unequal rights. And we have been asked, whether we wished to see such a *"checkered union?"* Sir, we have such a union already. If the prohibition of slavery is a denial of a right, and constitutes a checkered union, gladly would I behold such rights denied, and such a checker spread over every state in the Union. It is now spread over the states northwest of the Ohio, and forms the glory and the strength of those states. I hope it will be extended from the Mississippi to the Pacific ocean.

Sir, we have been told that the proposed amendment cannot be received, because it is contrary to the treaty and cession of Louisiana. "Article 3. The inhabitants of the ceded territory shall be incorporated in the Union of the United States, and admitted as soon as possible, according to the principles of the federal constitution, to the enjoyment of all the rights, advantages and immunities of citizens of the United States, and in the mean time they shall be maintained and protected in the free enjoyment of their liberty, their property, and the religion which they profess." I find nothing, said Mr. T., in this article of the treaty incompatible with the proposed amendment. The rights, advantages, and immunities of citizens of the United States are guaranteed to the inhabitants of Louisiana. If one of them should choose to remove into Virginia, he could take his slaves with him; but if he removes to Indiana, or any of the states northwest of the Ohio, he cannot take his slaves with him. If the proposed amendment prevail, the inhabitants of Louisiana, or the citizens of the United States, can neither of them take slaves into the state of Missouri. All, therefore, may enjoy equal privileges. It is a disability, or what I call a blessing, annexed to the particular district of country, and in no manner attached to the individual. But, while I have no doubt that the treaty contains no solid objection against the proposed amendment, if it did, it would not alter my determination on the subject. The senate, or the treaty-making power of our government, have neither the right nor the power to stipulate by a treaty, the terms upon which a people shall be admitted into the Union. This house have a right to be heard on the subject. The admission of a state into the Union is a legislative act, which requires the concurrence of all the departments of legislative power. It is an important prerogative of this house, which I hope will never be surrendered.

The zeal and the ardor of gentlemen, in the course of this debate, have induced them to announce to this house, that, if we persist and force the state of Missouri to accede to the proposed amendment, as the condition of her admission into the Union, she will not regard it, and, as soon as admitted, will alter her constitution, and introduce slavery into her territory. Sir, I am not prepared, nor is it necessary, to determine what would be the consequence of such a violation of faith—of such a departure from the fundamental condition of her admission into the Union. I would not cast upon a people so foul an imputation, as to believe they would be guilty of such fraudulent duplicity. The states northwest of the Ohio have all regarded the faith and the conditions of their admission; and there is no reason to believe the people of Missouri will not also regard theirs. But, sir, whenever a state admitted into the Union shall disregard and set at naught the fundamental conditions of its admission, and shall, in violation of all faith, undertake to levy a tax upon lands of the United States, or a toll upon their navigable waters, or introduce slavery, where congress have prohibited it, then it will be in time to determine the consequence. But, if the threatened consequence were known to be the certain result, yet would I insist upon the proposed amendment. The declaration of this house, the declared will of the nation to prohibit slavery would produce its moral effect, and stand as one of the brightest ornaments of our country.

Sir, it has been urged with great plausibility, that we should spread the slaves now in our country, and thus spread the evil, rather than confine it to its present districts. It has been said we should thereby diminish the dangers from them, while we increase the means of their living, and augment their comforts. But, you may rest assured, that this reasoning is fallacious, and that, while slavery is admitted, the market will be supplied. Our coast, and its contiguity to the West Indies and the Spanish possessions, render easy the introduction of slaves into our country. Our laws are already highly penal against their introduction, and yet it is a well-known fact, that about fourteen thousand slaves have been brought into our country this last year.

Since we have been engaged in this debate, we have witnessed an elucidation of this argument, of bettering the condition of slaves, by spreading them over the country. A slave-driver, a trafficker in human flesh, as if sent by providence, has passed the door of your capitol, on his way to the west, driving before him about fifteen of these wretched victims of his power, collected i the course of his traffic, and by their removal, torn from every relation from every tie which the human heart can hold dear. The males, who might raise the arm of vengeance, and retaliate for their wrongs, were hand-cuffed and chained to each other, while the females and children were marched in their rear, under the guidance of the driver's whip! Yes, sir, such has been the scene witnessed from the windows of congress hall, and viewed by members who compose the legislative councils of republican America!

In the course of the debate on this subject, we have been told that, from the long habit of the southern and western people, the possession of slaves has become necessary to them, and an essential requisite in their living. It has been urged, from the nature of the climate and soil of the southern countries, that the lands cannot be occupied or cultivated without slaves. It has been said that the slaves prosper in those places, and that they are much better off there than in their own native country. We have ever been told that if we succeed and prevent slavery across the Mississippi, we shall greatly lessen the value of property there, and shall retard, for a long series of years, the settlement of that country.

Sir, said Mr. T., if the western country cannot be settled without slaves, gladly would I prevent its settlement till time shall be no more. If this class of arguments is to prevail, it sets all morals at defiance, and we are called to legislate on this subject as a matter of mere personal interest. If this is to be the case, repeal all your laws prohibiting the slave-trade; throw open this traffic to the commercial states of the east; and if it better the condition of these wretched beings, invite the dark population of benighted Africa to be transplanted to the shores of republican America. But I will not cast upon this or upon that gentleman an imputation so ungracious as the conclusion to which their arguments would necessarily tend. I do not believe any gentleman on this floor would here advocate the slave-trade, or maintain in the abstract the principles of slavery. I will not outrage the decorum, nor insult the dignity of this house, by attempting to argue in this place, as an abstract proposition, the moral right of slavery. How gladly would the *"legitimates of*

Europe chuckle," to find an American congress in debate on such a question! As an evil brought upon us without our own fault, before the formation of our government, and as one of the sins of that nation from which we have revolted, we must, of necessity, legislate upon this subject. It is our business so to legislate as never to encourage, but always to control this evil; and, while we strive to eradicate it, we ought to fix its limits, and render it subordinate to the safety of the white population, and the good order of civil society.

Sir, on this subject the eyes of Europe are turned upon you. You boast of the freedom of your constitution and your laws; you have proclaimed, in the Declaration of Independence, *"that all men are created equal; that they are endowed by their Creator with certain inalienable rights—that amongst these are life, liberty, and the pursuit of happiness;"* and yet you have slaves in your country. The enemies of your government, and the legitimates of Europe, point to your inconsistencies, and blazon your supposed defects. If you allow slavery to pass into territories where you have the lawful power to exclude it, you will justly take upon yourself all the charges of inconsistency; but confine it to the original slaveholding states, where you found it at the formation of your government, and you stand acquitted of all imputation.

This is a subject upon which I have great feeling for the honor of my country. In a former debate upon the Illinois constitution, I mentioned that our enemies had drawn a picture of our country, as holding in one hand the Declaration of Independence, and with the other brandishing a whip over our affrighted slaves. I then made it my boast that we could cast back upon England the accusation—that she had committed the *original sin* of bringing slaves into our country. I have since received, through the post-office, a letter postmarked in South Carolina, and signed *"A native of England,"* desiring that, when I had occasion to repeat my boast against England, I would also state that she had atoned for her original sin by establishing in her slave-colonies a system of humane laws, meliorating their condition, and providing for their safety, while America had committed the secondary sin of disregarding their condition, and had even provided laws by which it was not murder to kill a slave. Sir, I felt the severity of the reproof; I felt for my country. I have inquired on the subject, and I find such were formerly the laws in some of the slaveholding states; and that even now, in the state of South Carolina, by law, the penalty of death is provided for stealing a slave, while the murder of a slave is punished with a trivial fine. Such is the contrast and the relative value which is placed, in the opinion of a slaveholding state, between the property of the master and the life of a slave.

Sir, gentlemen have undertaken to criminate, and to draw odious contrasts between different sections of our country—I shall not combat such arguments; I have made no pretense to exclusive morality on this subject, either for myself or my constituents; nor have I cast any imputations on others. On the contrary, I hold that mankind under like circumstances are alike, the world over. The vicious and unprincipled are confined to no district of country; and it is for this portion of the community we are bound to legislate. When honorable gentlemen inform us we overrate the cruelty and the dangers of slavery, and tell us that their slaves are happy and contented, and would even contribute to their safety, they tell us but very little; they do not tell us that, while their slaves are happy, the slaves of some depraved and cruel wretch in their neighborhood may be stimulated to revenge, and thus involve the country in ruin. If we had to legislate only for such gentlemen as are now embraced within my view, a law against robbing the mail would be a disgrace upon the nation; and, as useless, I would tear it from the pages of your statute book; yet sad experience has taught us the necessity of such laws—and honor, justice, and policy teach us the wisdom of legislating to limit the extension of slavery.

In the zeal to draw sectional contrasts, we have been told by one gentleman, that gentlemen from one district of country talk of their morality, while those of another practice it. And the superior liberality has been asserted of southern gentlemen over those of the north, in all contributions to moral institutions, for bible and missionary societies. Sir, I understand too well the pursuit of my purpose, to be decoyed and drawn off into the discussion of a collateral subject. I have no inclination to controvert these assertions of comparative liberality. Although I have no idea that they are founded in fact, yet, because it better suits the object of my present argument, I will, on this occasion, admit them to the fullest extent. And what is the result? Southern gentlemen, by their superior liberality in contributions to moral institutions, justly stand in the first rank, and hold the first place in the brightest page in the history of our country. But turn over this page, and what do you behold? You behold them contributing to teach the doctrines of Christianity in every quarter of the globe. You behold them legislating to secure the ignorance and stupidity of their own slaves! You behold them prescribing, by law, penalties against the man that dares teach a negro to read. Such is the statute law of the state of Virginia. [Mr. Bassett and Mr. Tyler said that there was no such law in Virginia.]

No, said Mr. T., I have mis-spoken myself; I ought to have said, such is the statute law of the state of Georgia. Yes, while we hear of a liberality which civilizes the savages of all countries, and carries the gospel alike to the *Hottentot* and the *Hindoo*, it has been reserved for the republican state of Georgia, not content with the care of its overseers, to legislate to secure the oppression and the ignorance of their slaves. The man who there teaches a negro to read is liable to a criminal prosecution. The dark, benighted beings of all creation profit by our liberality—save those of our own plantations. Where is the missionary who possesses sufficient hardihood to venture a residence to teach the slaves of a plantation? Here is the stain! Here is the stigma! which fastens upon the character of our country; and which, in the appropriate language of the gentleman from Georgia, (Mr. Cobb,) *all the waters of the ocean cannot wash out; which seas of blood can only take away.*

Sir, there is yet another, and an important point of view, in which this sub-

30

ject ought to be considered. We have been told by those who advocate the extension of slavery into the Missouri, that any attempt to control this subject by legislation is a violation of that faith and mutual confidence upon which our Union was formed, and our constitution adopted. This argument might be considered plausible if the restriction was attempted to be enforced against any of the slaveholding states which had been a party in the adoption of the constitution. But it can have no reference or application to a new district of country recently acquired, and never contemplated in the formation of government, and not embraced in the mutual concessions and declared faith upon which the constitution was adopted. The constitution provides that the representatives of the several states to this house shall be according to their number, including *three-fifths* of the slaves in the respective states. This is an important benefit yielded to the slaveholding states, as one of the mutual sacrifices for the Union. On this subject, I consider the faith of the Union pledged, and I never would attempt coercive manumission in a slaveholding state.

But none of these causes which induced the sacrifice of this principle, and which now produce such an unequal representation on this floor, of the free population of the country, exist as between us and the newly-acquired territory across the Mississippi. That portion of country has no claims to such an unequal representation, unjust in its results upon the other states. Are the numerous slaves in extensive countries, which we may acquire by purchase, and admit as states into the Union, at once to be represented on this floor, under a clause of the constitution, granted as a compromise and a benefit to the southern states which had borne part in the revolution? Such an extension of that clause in the constitution would be unjust in its operations, unequal in its results, and a violation of its original intention. Abstract from the moral effects of slavery, its political consequences in the representation under this clause of the constitution, demonstrate the importance of the proposed amendment.

Sir, I shall bow in silence to the will of the majority, on whichever side it shall be expressed; yet I confidently hope that majority will be found on the side of an amendment, so replete with moral consequences, so pregnant with important political results.

Mr. Scott, of Missouri, said he trusted that his conduct, during the whole of the time in which he had the honor of a seat in the house, had convinced gentlemen of his disposition not to obtrude his sentiments on any other subjects than those on which the interest of his constituents, and of the territory he represented, were immediately concerned. But when a question such as the amendments proposed by the gentlemen from New York, (Messrs. Tallmadge and Taylor,) was presented for consideration, involving constitutional principles to a vast amount, pregnant with the future fate of the territory, portending destruction to the liberties of that people, directly bearing on their rights of property, their state rights, their all, he should consider it a dereliction of his duty, as retreating from his post, nay, double criminality, did he not raise his voice against their adoption. After the many able and luminous views that had been taken of this subject, by the speaker of the house, and other honorable gentlemen, he had not the vanity to suppose that any additional views which he could offer, or any new dress in which he could clothe those already advanced, would have the happy tendency of inducing any gentleman to change his vote. But, if he stood single on the question, and there was no man to help him, yet, while the laws of the land and the rules of the house guaranteed to him the privilege of speech, he would redeem his conscience from the imputation of having silently witnessed a violation of the constitution of his country, and an infringement on the liberties of the people who had intrusted to his feeble abilities the advocation of their rights. He desired, at this early stage of his remarks, in the name of the citizens of Missouri territory, whose rights on other subjects had been too long neglected and shamefully disregarded, to enter his solemn protest against the introduction, under the insidious form of amendment, of any principle in this bill, the obvious tendency of which would be to sow the seeds of discord in, and perhaps eventually endanger the Union.

Mr. S. entertained the opinion that, under the constitution, congress had no the power to impose this, or any other restriction, or to require of the people of Missouri their assent to this condition, as a pre-requisite to their admission into the Union. He contended this from the language of the constitution itself, from the practice in the admission of new states under that instrument, and from the express terms of the treaty of cession. The short view he intended to take of those points would, he trusted, be satisfactory to all those who were not so anxious to usurp power as to sacrifice to its attainment the principles of our government, or who were not desirous of prostrating the rights and independence of a state to chimerical views of policy or expediency. The authority to admit new states into the Union was granted in the third section of the fourth article of the constitution, which declared that "new states may be admitted by the congress into the Union." The only power given to the congress by this section appeared to him to be that of passing a law for the admission of the new state, leaving it in possession of all the rights, privileges, and immunities enjoyed by the other states; the most valuable and prominent of which was that of forming and modifying their own state constitution, and over which congress had no superintending control, other than that expressly given in the fourth section of the same article, which read, "the United States shall guarantee to every state in this Union a republican form of government." This end accomplished, the guardianship of the United States over the constitutions of the several states was fulfilled; and all restrictions, limitations, and conditions beyond this, was so much power unwarrantably assumed. In illustration of this position, he would read an extract from one of the essays written by the late President Madison, contemporaneously with the constitution of the United States, and from a very celebrated work : "In a confederacy founded on republican principles, and composed of republican members, the superintending government ought clearly to possess authority to defend the system against aristocratic or monarchical innovations. The more intimate the nature of such a union may be, the greater interest have the members in the political institutions of each other, and the greater right to insist that the forms of government under which the compact was entered into, should be substantially maintained. But this authority extends no further than to a *guarantee of a republican form* of government, which supposes a preëxisting government of the form which is to be guaranteed. As long, therefore, as the existing republican forms are continued by the states, they are guaranteed by the federal constitution. Whenever the states may choose to substitute other republican forms, they have a right to do so, and to claim the federal guarantee for the latter. The *only restriction* imposed on them is, that they shall not exchange republican for anti-republican constitutions ; a restriction which, it is presumed, will hardly be considered as a grievance."

Mr. S. thought that those two clauses, when supported by such high authority, had they been the only ones in the constitution which related to the powers of the general government over the states, and particularly at their formation and adoption into the Union, could not but be deemed satisfactory to a reasonable extent ; but there were other provisions in the constitution, to which he would refer, that beyond all doubt, to his mind, settled the question. One of those was the tenth article in the amendments, which said that "the powers not delegated to the United States by the constitution, nor prohibited by it to the states, are reserved to the states respectively or to the people." He believed that, by common law and common usage, all grants giving certain defined and specific privileges or powers, were to be so construed as that no others should be intended to be given but such as were particularly enumerated in the instruments themselves, or indispensably necessary to carry into effect those designated. In no part of the constitution was the power proposed to be exercised, of imposing conditions on a new state, given, either in so many words, or by any justifiable or fair inference ; nor in any portion of the constitution was the right prohibited to the respective states to regulate their own internal police, of admitting such citizens as they pleased, or of introducing any description of property that they should consider as essential or necessary to their prosperity ; and the framers of that instrument seem to have been zealous, lest, by implication or by inference, powers might be assumed by the general government over the states and people, other than those expressly given : hence they reserve in so many terms to the states and the people, all powers not delegated to the federal government. The ninth article of the amendments to the constitution still further illustrated the position he had taken ; it read that " the enumeration in the constitution of certain rights shall not be construed to deny or disparage others retained by the people." Mr. S. believed it to be a just rule of interpretation, that the enumeration of powers delegated to congress weakened their authority in all cases not enumerated ; and that beyond those powers enumerated they had none, except they were essentially necessary to carry into effect those that were given. The second section of the fourth article of the constitution, which declared that "the citizens of each state shall be entitled to all the privileges and immunities of citizens in the several states," was satisfactory, to his judgment, that it was intended the citizens of each state, forming a part of one harmonious whole, should have, in all things, *equal privileges;* the necessary consequence of which was, that every man, in his own state, should have the same rights, privileges, and powers, that any other citizen of the United States had in his own state; otherwise discontent and murmurings would prevail against the general government who had deprived him of the equality.

For example, if the citizens of Pennsylvania, or Virginia, enjoyed the right, in their own state, to decide the question whether they would have slavery or not, the citizens of Missouri, to give them the same privileges, must have the same right to decide whether they would or would not tolerate slavery in their state; if it were otherwise, then the citizens of Pennsylvania and Virginia would have more rights, privileges, and powers in their respective states, than the citizens of Missouri would have in theirs. Mr. Scott said he would make another quotation from the same work he had before been indebted to, which he believed had considerable bearing on this question. "The powers delegated by the proposed constitution to the federal government, are few and defined; those which are to remain in the state governments, are numerous and indefinite; the former will be exercised principally on external objects, as war, peace, negotiation, and foreign commerce, with which last the powers of taxation will, for the most part, be connected. The powers reserved to the several states will extend to all the objects, which in the ordinary course of affairs concern the lives, liberties, and properties of the people, and the internal order, improvement, and prosperity of the state." The applicability of this doctrine to the question under consideration was so obvious, that he would not detain the house to give examples, but leave it for gentlemen to make the application. He would, however, make one other reference to the constitution, before he proceeded to speak of the practice under it; in the second section of that instrument it was provided, that "representatives, and direct taxes, shall be apportioned among the several states which may be included within this Union, according to their respective numbers, which shall be determined by adding to the whole number of free persons, including those bound to service for a term of years, and excluding Indians not taxed, three-fifths of all other persons." This provision was not restricted to the states then formed, and about to adopt the constitution; but to all those states which *might* be included within this Union, clearly contemplating the admission of new states thereafter, and providing, that to them, also, should this principle of representation and taxation equally apply. Nor could he subscribe to the construction, that as this part of the constitution was matter of compromise, it was to be limited in its application to the original states only, and not to be extended to all those states that might after its adoption become members of the federal Union; and a practical exposition had been made by congress of this part of the constitution, in the admission of Kentucky, Louisiana, and Mississippi states, all of whom were slaveholding states, and to each of them this principle had been extended.

Mr. Scott believed, that the practice under the constitution had been different from that now contended for by gentlemen; he was unapprised of any similar provision having ever been made, or attempted to be made, in relation to any other new state heretofore admitted. The argument drawn from the states formed out of the territory northwest of the river Ohio, he did not consider as analogous; that restriction, if any, was imposed in pursuance of a compact, and only, so far as congress could do, carried into effect the disposition of Virginia in reference to a part of her own original territory, and was, in every respect, more just, because that provision was made and published to the world at a time when but few, if any, settlements were formed within that tract of country; and the children of those people of color belonging to the inhabitants then there have been, and still were, held in bondage, and were not free at a given age, as was contemplated by the amendment under consideration, nor did he doubt but that it was competent for any of those states admitted in pursuance of the ordinance of 1787, to call a convention, and so to alter their constitution as to allow the introduction of slaves, if they thought proper to do so. To those gentlemen who had in their argument, in support of the amendments, adverted to the instance where congress had, by the law authorizing the people of Louisiana to form a constitution and state government, exercised the power of imposing the terms and conditions on which they should be permitted to do so, he would recommend a careful examination and comparison of those terms with the constitution of the United States, when, he doubted not, they would be convinced that these restrictions were only such as were in express and positive language defined in the latter instrument, and would have been equally binding on the people of Louisiana had they not been enumerated in the law giving them authority to form a constitution for themselves.

Mr. Scott said he considered the contemplated conditions and restrictions, contained in the proposed amendments, to be unconstitutional and unwarrantable, from the provisions of the treaty of cession, by the third article of which it was stipulated, that "the inhabitants of the ceded territory shall be incorporated in the Union of the United States, and admitted as soon as possible, according to the principles of the federal constitution, to the enjoyment of all the rights, advantages, and immunities of citizens of the United States, and, in the mean time, they shall be maintained and protected in the free enjoyment of their liberty, property, and the religion which they profess."

This treaty having been made by the competent authority of government, ratified by the senate, and emphatically sanctioned by congress in the acts making appropriations to carry it into effect, became a part of the supreme law of the land, and its bearings on the rights of the people had received a practical exposition by the admission of the state of Louisiana, part of the same territory, and acquired by the same treaty of cession, into the Union. It was in vain for gentlemen to tell him that, by the terms of the treaty of cession, the United States were not bound to admit any part of the ceded territory into the Union as a state; the evidence of the obligation congress considered they were under, to adopt states formed out of that territory, is clearly deducible from the fact that they had done so in the instance of Louisiana. But, had no state been admitted, formed of a part of the territory acquired by that treaty, the obligation of the government to do so would not be the less apparent to him. "The inhabitants of the ceded territory shall be incorporated in the Union of the United States." The people were not left to the wayward discretion of this, or any other government, by saying that they *may be incorporated* in the Union. The language was different and imperative : "*they shall be incorporated.*" Mr. Scott understood by the term *incorporated,* that they were to form a constituent part of this republic ; that they were to become joint partners in the character and councils of the country, and in the national losses and national gains; as a territory, they were not an essential part of the government; they were a mere province, subject to the acts and regulations of the general government in all cases whatsoever. As a territory, they had not all the *rights, advantages and immunities* of citizens of the United States. Mr. Scott himself furnished an example, that, in their present condition, they had not all the rights of the other citizens of the Union. Had he a vote in this house ? And yet these people were, during the war, subject to certain taxes imposed by congress. Had those people any voice to give in the imposition of taxes to which they were subject, or in the disposition of the funds of the nation, and particularly those arising from the sales of the public lands, to which they already had, and still would largely contribute ? Had they a voice to give in selecting the officers of this government, or many of their own? In short, in what had they equal *rights, advantages and immunities* with the other citizens of the United States, but in the privilege to submit to a procrastination of their rights, and in the advantage to subscribe to your laws, your rules, your taxes, and your powers, even without a hearing ? Those people were also "to be admitted into the Union as soon as possible." Mr. Scott would infer from this expression, that it was the understanding of the parties, that so soon as any portion of the territory, of sufficient extent to form a state, should contain the number of inhabitants required by law to entitle them to a representative on the floor of this house, that they then had the right to make the call for admission, and this admission, when made, was to be, not on conditions that gentlemen might deem expedient, not on conditions referable to future political views, not on conditions that the constitution the people should form should contain a clause that would particularly open the door for emigration from the north or from the south, not on condition that the future population of the state should come from a slaveholding or non-slaveholding state, "*but according to the principles of the federal constitution,*" and none other. The people of Missouri were, by solemn treaty stipulation, when admitted, to enjoy all the rights, advantages, and immunities of citizens of the United States. Can any gentleman contend, that, laboring under the proposed restriction, the citizens of Missouri would have all the rights, advantages, and immunities of other citizens of the Union ? Have not other new states, in their admission, and have not all the states in the Union, now, privileges and rights beyond what was contemplated to be allowed to the citizens of Missouri ? Have not all other states in this government the right to alter, modify, amend, and change their state constitutions, having regard alone to a republican form ? And was there any existing law, or any clause in the federal constitution, that prohibited a total change from a slaveholding to a non-slaveholding state, or from a non-slaveholding to a slaveholding state ? Mr. Scott thought that if this provision was proper, or within the powers of congress, they also had the correlative right to say that the people of Missouri should not be admitted as a state, unless they provided, in the formation of their state constitution, that slavery should be tolerated. Would not those conscientious gentlemen startle at this, and exclaim, *what !* impose on those people slaves, when they do not want them ? This would be said to be a direct attack on the state independence. Was it in the power of congress to annex the present condition, Mr. Scott deemed it equally within the scope of their authority to say what color the inhabitants of the proposed state should be, what description of property, other than slaves, those people should or should not possess, and the quantity of property each man should retain, going upon the agrarian principle. He would even go further, and say that congress had an equal power to enact to what religion the people should subscribe; that none other should be professed, and to provide for the excommunication of all those who did not submit.

The people of Missouri were, if admitted into the Union, to come in on an equal footing with the original states. That the people of the other states had the right to regulate their own internal police, to prescribe the rules of their own conduct, and, in the formation of their constitution, to say whether slavery was or was not admissible, he believed was a point conceded by all. How, then, were the citizens of Missouri placed on an equal footing with the other members of the Union ? Equal in some respects—a shameful discrimination in others. A discrimination not warranted by the constitution, nor justified by the treaty of cession, but founded on mistaken zeal, or erroneous policy. They were to be bound down by onerous conditions, limitations, and restrictions to which he knew they would not submit. That people were brave and independent, and willing to risk their own happiness and future prosperity on the legitimate exercise of their own judgment and free will. Mr. Scott protested against such a guardianship as was contemplated now to be assumed over his constituents. The spirit of freedom burned in the bosom of the freemen of Missouri, and if admitted into the national family, they would be equal, or not come in at all. With what an anxious eye have they looked to the east, since the commencement of this session of congress, for the good tidings, that on them you had conferred the glorious privilege of self-government and independence. What seeds of discord will you sow, when they read this suspicious, shameful, unconstitutional inhibition in their charter ? Will they not compare it with the terms of the treaty of cession, that bill of their rights, emphatically their magna charta ? And will not the result of that comparison be a stigma on the faith of this government ? It had been admitted by some gentlemen, in debate, that, were the people of Missouri to form a constitution conforming to this provision, so soon as they were adopted into the Union it would be competent for them to call a convention and alter their constitution on this subject. Why, then, he would ask gentlemen, would they legislate, when they could produce no permanent, practical effect ? Why expose the imbecility of the general government to tie up the hands of the state, and induce the people to an act of chicanery, which he knew from principle they abhorred, to get clear of an odious restriction on their rights ? Mr. Scott had trusted that gentlemen who professed to be actuated by motives of humanity and principle would not encourage a course of dissimulation, or, by any vote of theirs, render it necessary for the citizens of Missouri to act equivocally to obtain their rights. He was unwilling to believe that political views alone led gentlemen on this or any other occasion; but from the language of the member from New York, (Mr. Taylor,) he was compelled to suspect that they had their influence upon him. That gentleman has told us, that if ever he left his present residence, it would be for Illinois or Missouri ; at all events, he wished to send out his brothers and his sons. Mr. Scott begged that gentleman to relieve him from the awful apprehension excited by the prospect of this accession of population. He hoped the house would excuse him while he stated, that he did not desire that gentleman, his sons, or his brothers, in that land of brave, noble, and independent freemen. The member says that the latitude is too far north to admit of slavery there. Would the gentleman cast his eye on the map before him, he would there see that a part of Kentucky, Virginia, and Maryland, were as far north as the northern boundary of the proposed state of Missouri. Mr. Scott would thank the gentleman if he would condescend to tell him what precise line of latitude suited his conscience, his humanity, or his political views, on this subject. Could that member be serious, when he made the parallel of latitude the measure of his good will to those unfortunate blacks ? Or was he trying how far he could go in fallacious argument and absurdity, without creating one blush even on his own cheek, for inconsistency ? What ! starve the negroes out, pen them up in the swamps and morasses, confine them to southern latitudes, to long, scorching days of labor and fatigue, until the race becomes extinct, that the fair land of Missouri may be tenanted by that gentleman, his brothers, and sons? He expected from the majority of the house a more liberal policy, and better evidence that they really were actuated by humane motives.

Mr. S. said he would trouble the house no longer ; he thanked them for the attention and indulgence already bestowed ; but he desired to apprise gentlemen, before he sat down, that they were sowing the seeds of discord in this Union, by attempting to admit states with unequal privileges and unequal rights ; that they were signing, sealing, and delivering their own death-warrant ; that the weapon they were so unjustly wielding against the people of Missouri, was a two-edged sword. From the cumulative nature of power, the day might come when the general government might, in turn, undertake to dictate to *them* on questions of internal policy ; Missouri, now weak and feeble, whose fate and murmurs would excite but little alarm or sensibility, might become an easy victim to motives of policy, party zeal, or mistaken ideas of power ; but other times and other men would succeed; a future congress might come, who, under the sanctified forms of constitutional power, would dictate to *them* odious conditions; nay, inflict on their internal independence a wound more deep and dreadful than even this to Missouri. The house had seen the force of precedent, in the mistaken application of the conditions imposed on the people of Louisiana anterior to their admission into the Union. And, whatever might be the ultimate determination of the house, Mr. S. considered this question big with the fate of Cæsar and of Rome.

Mr. Cobb, of Georgia, observed that he did not rise for the purpose of detaining the attention of the house for any length of time. He was too sensible of the importance of each moment which yet remained of the session, to obtrude many remarks upon their patience. But, upon a measure involving the important consequences that this did, he felt it to be an imperious duty to express his sentiments, and to enter his most solemn protest against the principle proposed for adoption by the amendment. Were gentlemen aware of what they were about to do? Did they foresee no evil consequence likely to result out of the measure if adopted? Could they suppose that the southern states would submit with patience to a measure, the effect of which would be to exclude them from all enjoyment of the vast region purchased by the United States beyond the Mississippi, and which belonged equally to them as to the northern states? He ventured to assure them that they would not. The people of the *slaveholding states*, as they are called, *know* their rights, *and will insist* upon the enjoyment of them. He should not now attempt to go over ground already occupied by others, with much more ability, and attempt to show that, by the treaty with France, the people of that territory were secured in the enjoyment of the property which they held in their slaves. That the proposed amendment was an infraction of this treaty, had been most clearly shown. Nor would he attempt to rescue from slander the character of the people of the southern states, in their conduct towards, and treatment of, their black population. That had also been done with a degree of force and eloquence, to which he could pretend no claim, by the gentleman from Virginia (Mr. Barbour), and the honorable speaker. He was, however, clearly of opinion that *congress possessed no power under the constitution* to adopt the principle proposed in the amendment. He called upon the advocates of it to point out, and lay their fingers upon that clause of the constitution of the United States, which gives to this body the right to legislate upon the subject. Could they show in what clause or section this right was *expressly given*, or from which it could be inferred? Unless this authority could be shown, congress would be *assuming* a power, if the amendment prevailed, not delegated to them, and most dangerous in its exercise. What is the end and tendency of the measure proposed? It is to impose on the state of Missouri conditions not imposed upon any other state. It is to deprive her of one branch of sovereignty not surrendered by any other state in the Union, not even those beyond the Ohio; for all of them had legislated upon this subject; all of them had decided for themselves whether slavery should be tolerated, at the time they framed their several constitutions. He would not now discuss the propriety of admitting slavery. It is not now a question whether it is politic or impolitic to tolerate slavery in the United States, or in a particular state. It was a discussion into which he would not *permit himself* to be dragged. Admit, however, its *moral impropriety*, yet there was a vast difference between moral impropriety and political sovereignty. The people of New York or Pennsylvania may deem it highly immoral and politically *improper* to permit slavery, but yet they possess *the sovereign right and power* to permit it, if they *choose*. They can to-morrow so alter their constitutions and laws as to admit it, if they were so disposed. It is a branch of sovereignty which the old thirteen states never surrender in the adoption of the federal constitution. Now, the bill proposes that the new state shall be admitted upon an *equal footing* with the other states of the Union. It is in this way only that she can be admitted under the constitution. These words can have no other meaning than that she shall be required *to surrender no more* of her rights of sovereignty than the other states, into a union with which she is about to be admitted, have surrendered. But if the proposed amendment is adopted, will not this new state be *shorn of one* branch of her sovereignty, *one right*, which the other states *may and have* exercised, (whether properly or not, is immaterial,) and *do now* exercise whenever they think fit ?

Mr. C. observed that he did conceive the principle involved in the amendment pregnant with danger. It was one, he repeated, to which he believed the people of the region of country which he represented, *would not quietly* submit. He might, perhaps, subject himself to ridicule, for attempting the display of a spirit of prophecy which he did not possess, or of zeal and enthusiasm for which he was entitled to little credit. But he *warned* the advocates of this measure against the certain effects which it must produce—effects destructive of the peace and harmony of the Union. He believed that they were kindling a fire which all the waters of the ocean could not extinguish. It could be extinguished only in *blood !*

Mr. Livermore, of New Hampshire, said : I am in favor of the proposed amendment. The object of it is to prevent the extension of slavery over the territory ceded to the United States by France. It accords with the dictates of reason, and the best feelings of the human heart; and is not calculated to interrupt any legitimate right arising either from the constitution or any other compact. I propose to show what slavery is, and to mention a few of the many evils which follow in its train; and I hope to evince that we are not bound to tolerate the existence of so disgraceful a state of things beyond its present extent, and that it would be impolitic and very unjust to let it spread over the whole face of our western territory. Slavery in the United States is the condition of man subjected to the will of a master, who can make any disposition of him short of taking away his life. In those states where it is tolerated, laws are enacted, making it penal to instruct slaves in the art of reading, and they are not permitted to attend public worship, or to hear the gospel preached. Thus the light of science and of religion is utterly excluded from the mind, that the body may be more easily bowed down to servitude. The bodies of slaves may, with impunity, be prostituted to any purpose, and deformed in any manner by their owners. The sympathies of nature in slaves are disregarded ; mothers and children are sold and separated ; the children wring their little hands, and expire in agonies of grief, while the bereft mothers commit suicide in despair. How long will the desire of wealth render us blind to the sin of holding both the bodies and souls of our fellow-men in chains ! But, sir, I am admonished of the constitution, and told we cannot emancipate slaves. I know we may not infringe that instrument, and therefore do not propose to emancipate slaves. The proposition before us goes only to prevent our citizens from making slaves of such as have a right to freedom. In the present slaveholding states, let slavery continue, for our boasted constitution connives at it ; but do not, for the sake of cotton and tobacco, let it be told to future ages that, while pretending to love liberty, we have purchased an extensive country, to disgrace it with the foulest reproach of nations. Our constitution requires no such thing of us. The ends for which that supreme law was made, are succinctly stated in its preface. They are, first, to form a more perfect Union, and insure domestic tranquility ? Will slavery effect this ? Can we, sir, by mingling bond with free, black spirits with white, like Shakspeare's witches in Macbeth, form a more perfect Union, and insure domestic tranquility ? Secondly, to establish justice. Is justice to be established by subjecting half mankind to the will of the other half ? Justice, sir, is blind to colors, and weighs in equal scales the rights of all men, whether white or black. Thirdly, to provide for the common defense, and secure the blessings of liberty. Does slavery add anything to the common defense ? Sir, the strength of a republic is in the arm of freedom. But, above all things, do the blessings of liberty consist in slavery ? If there is any sincerity in our profession, that slavery is an ill, tolerated only from necessity, let us not, while we feel that ill, shun the cure, which consists only in an honest avowal that liberty and equal rights are the end and aim of all our institutions, and that to tolerate slavery beyond the narrowest limits prescribed for it by the constitution, is a perversion of them all.

Slavery, sir, I repeat, is not established by our constitution ; but a part of the states are indulged in the commission of a sin from which they could not at once be restrained, and which they would not consent to abandon. But, sir, if we could, by any process of reasoning, be brought to believe it justifiable to hold others to involuntary servitude, policy forbids that we should increase it. Even the present slaveholding states have an interest, I think, in limiting the extent of involuntary servitude ; for, should slaves become much more numerous, and, conscious of their strength, draw the sword against their masters, it will be to the free states the masters must resort for an efficient power to suppress servile insurrection. But we have made a treaty with France, which, we are told, can only be preserved by the charms of slavery.

Sir, said Mr. L., until the ceded territory shall have been made into states, and the new states admitted into the Union, we can do what we will with it.

We can govern it as a province, or sell it to any other nation. A part of it is probably at this time sold to Spain, and the inhabitants of it may soon not only enjoy the comforts of slavery, but the blessings of the holy inquisition along with them. The question is on the admission of Missouri, as a state, into the Union. Surely it will not be contended that we are bound by the treaty to admit it. The treaty-making power does not extend so far. Can the president and senate, by a treaty with Great Britain, make the province of Lower Canada a state of this Union? To be received as a state into this Union, is a privilege which no country can claim as a right. It is a favor to be granted or not, as the United States may choose. When the United States think proper to grant a favor, they may annex just and reasonable terms: and what can be more reasonable than for these states to insist that a new territory, wishing to have the beneffts of freedom extended to it, should renounce a principle that militates with justice, morality, religion, and every essential right of mankind? Louisiana was admitted into the Union on terms. The conditions, I admit, were not very important, but still they recognize the principles for which I contend.

An opportunity is now presented, if not to diminish, at least to prevent the growth of a sin which sits heavily on the soul of every one of us. By embracing this opportunity, we may retrieve the national character, and, in some degree, our own. But if we suffer it to pass unimproved, let us at least be consistent, and declare that our constitution was made to impose slavery, and not to establish liberty. Let us no longer tell idle tales about the gradual abolition of slavery; away with colonization societies, if their design is only to rid us of free blacks and turbulent slaves; have done also with bible societies, whose views are extended to Africa and the East Indies, while they overlook the deplorable condition of their sable brethren within our own borders; make no more laws to prohibit the importation of slaves, for the world must see that the object of such laws is alone to prevent the glutting of a prodigious market for the flesh and blood of man, which we are about to establish in the west, and to enhance the price of sturdy wretches, reared, like black cattle and horses, for sale on our own plantations.

On coming out of the committee, the yeas and nays were called on the question of agreeing to the first part of the amendment, which reads,

"And provided also, that the further introduction of slavery or involuntary servitude be prohibited, except for the punishment of crimes, whereof the party shall be duly convicted;"

Yeas, 87; only one from a slave state, the state of Delaware—nays, 76; ten from free states, and sixty-six from slave states. The house proceeded to vote on the residue of the proposed amendment, which reads,

—"and that all children of slaves, born within the said state, after the admission thereof into the Union, shall be declared free at the age of twenty-five years."

Yeas, 82; one vote from Maryland—nays, 78; fourteen from free states. So the whole amendment—as moved by Gen. Tallmadge in committee of the whole, and there carried—was sustained when reported to the house.

Mr. Storrs, of New York, (opposed to the restriction,) now moved the striking out of so much of the bill as provides that the new state shall be admitted into the Union " on an equal footing with the original states "—which, he contended, was nullified by the votes just taken. The house negatived the motion.

Messrs. Desha, of Ky., Cobb, of Ga., and Rhea, of Tenn., declared against the bill as amended.

Messrs. Scott, of Mo., and Anderson, of Ky., preferred the bill as amended to none.

The house ordered the bill, as amended, to a third reading; yeas, 98; nays, 56. The bill thus passed the house next day, and was sent to the senate.

The house bill thus passed, reached the senate Feb. 17th, when it was read twice and sent to a select committee already raised on a like application from Alabama, consisting of Messrs. Tait, of Ga., Morrow, of Ohio, Williams, of Miss., Edwards, of Ill., Williams, of Tenn.

On the 22d, Mr. Tait, from this committee, reported the bill with amendments, striking out the anti-slavery restrictions inserted by the house. The bill was taken up in committee of the whole on the 27th, when Mr. Wilson, of N. J., moved its postponement to the 5th of March—that is, to the end of the session—negatived: yeas, 14; nays, 23.

The senate then proceeded to vote on agreeing to the amendments reported by the select committee, viz. : 1. to strike out of the house bill the following :

" And that all children of slaves born within the said state, after the admission thereof into the Union, shall be free, but may be held to service until the age of twenty-one years."

This clause was struck out, by a vote of 27 to 7 ; eleven free state senators voting in favor of striking it out; the seven senators who voted for the restriction were all from free states. The senate then proceeded to vote on the residue of the house restriction, as follows :

" And provided also, that the further introduction of slavery or involuntary servitude be prohibited, except for the punishment of crimes, whereof the party shall have been duly convicted."

For striking out this restriction, 22—five of whom were from free states: against striking out, 16—all from free states.

The bill thus amended was ordered to be engrossed, and was (March 2d—last day but one of the session) read a third time, and passed without a division. The bill was on that day returned to the house, and the amendments of the senate read; whereupon, Mr. Tallmadge, of N. Y., moved that the bill be postponed indefinitely. Yeas, 69; nays, 74.

The vote was then taken on concurring in the senate's amendments, as aforesaid, and the house refused to concur Yeas, 76 ; nays, 78.

The bill was now returned to the senate, with a message of non-concurrence; when Mr. Tait moved that the senate adhere to its amendment, which was carried without a division The bill being thus remanded to the house, Mr. Taylor, of N. Y., moved that the house adhere to its disagreement, which prevailed. Yeas, 78; nays, 66. So the bill fell between the two houses, and was lost.

The southern portion of the then territory of Missouri was excluded from the proposed state of Missouri, and organized as a separate territory, and entitled the Arkansas territory. This bill being under consideration, Mr. John W. Taylor, of New York, moved that the foregoing restriction be applied to it also. In the course of the debate, Mr. Taylor said: " How often and how eloquently have I heard southern gentlemen deplore the existence of slavery ! What willingness, nay, what solicitude have they not manifested to be relieved from this burden ! How have they wept over the unfortunate policy that first introduced slaves into this country ! How have they disclaimed the guilt and shame of that original sin, and thrown it back on their ancestors ! I have heard with pleasure this avowal of regret, I have confided in its sincerity, and have hoped to see its effects in the advancement of the cause of humanity. Gentlemen have now an opportunity of putting their professions into practice. If they have tried slavery, and found it to be a curse; if they desire to dissipate the gloom with which it covers their land, I call upon them to exclude it from the territory in question. Plant not its seeds in this uncorrupt soil ! Let not our children, in looking back to the proceedings of this day, say of them, as we have been constrained to say of our fathers, we wish their decision had been different; we regret the existence among us of this unfortunate population; but we found them here; we know not what to do with them; it is our misfortune; we must bear it with patience !

"To the objection that the amendment, if adopted, will diminish the value of a species of property in one portion of the Union, and thereby operate unequally, I reply, that if, by depriving slaveholders of the Missouri market, the business of raising slaves should become less profitable, it would be, not the object of this measure, but an effect incidentally produced. The law prohibiting the importation of foreign slaves was not passed to enhance the value of those then in the country, yet it incidentally produced that effect to a very great degree. The exclusion of slavery from Missouri may operate, perhaps, to some extent, to retard a further advance. But surely, when gentlemen consider the present demand, and the vast extent of country in Louisiana, Mississippi, and Alabama requiring a supply, they ought not to oppose its exclusion from the territory in question.

" But it is further objected that the amendment is calculated to disfranchise our brethren from the south by discouraging their emigration to the country west of the Mississippi. If it were proposed to discriminate between citizens of the different sections of our Union, and to allow a Pennsylvanian to hold slaves there while that power was denied to a Virginian, the objection might very properly be made. But when we place all upon an equal footing, denying to all what we deny to one, I am unable to discover the injustice or inequality of which honorable gentlemen have thought proper to complain. The description of immigrants may in some measure be affected by the amendment. If slavery shall be tolerated, the country will be settled by rich planters with their slaves. If it shall be rejected, the emigrants will chiefly consist of the poorer and more laborious classes of society. If it be true that the prosperity and happiness of a country ought to constitute the great object of its legislators, I can not hesitate for a moment which species of population deserves most to be encouraged. In their zeal to oppose the amendment, gentlemen seem to have considered but one side of the case. If the prohibition of slavery will tend to discourage migration from the south, will not its admission have the same effect with relation to the north and east? Whence came the people, who, with a rapidity never before witnessed, have changed the wilderness between the Ohio and the Mississippi into fruitful fields, erecting there, within a period almost too short for the credence of future ages, three of the freest and most flourishing states of the Union? They came, sir, from the eastern hive, from that source of population, which, in the same time, has added more than a hundred thousand inhabitants to my own native state, besides furnishing seamen for a large portion of the navigation of the world; seamen who have unfurled your banner in every port to which the enterprise of man has gained admittance, and who, though poor themselves, have drawn rich treasures for the nation from the bosom of the deep. Do you believe that these people will settle in a country where they must take rank with negro slaves? Having neither the will nor the ability to hold slaves themselves, they labor cheerfully while labor is honorable. Make it disgraceful, they will despise it. You can not degrade it more effectually than by establishing a system whereby it shall be performed principally by slaves. The business in which slaves are principally engaged, be it what it may, soon becomes debased in public estimation. It is considered low, and unfit for freemen. Can I better illustrate this truth than by referring to a remark of the gentleman from Kentucky (Clay)? I have often admired the liberality of his sentiments. He is governed by no vulgar prejudices. Yet with what abhorrence did he speak of the performance by our wives and daughters of those domestic duties which he was pleased to call servile! What comparison did he make between the black slaves of Kentucky and the white slaves of the north, and how instantly did he strike the balance in favor of the condition of the former! If such opinions and expressions can fall, even in the ardor of debate, from that gentleman, what ideas do you suppose are entertained of laboring men by the generality of slaveholders? A gentleman from Virginia replies that they are treated with confidence and esteem, and their rights respected. I did not imagine that they were put out of the protection of the law. Their persons and property are doubtless secure from violence, or, if injured, the courts of justice are open to them. But in a country like this, where the people are sovereign, and every citizen is entitled to equal rights, the mere exemption from flagrant wrongs is no great privilege. No class of freemen should be excluded in this country, either by law, or by the ostracism of public opinion, more powerful than law, from competing for offices and political distinctions. A humane master will respect the rights of his slave, and, if worthy, will honor him with confidence and esteem. And it is this same measure, as I apprehend, that is dealt out in slaveholding states to the laboring class of their white population. But whom of that class have they ever called to fill stations of any considerable responsibility? When have we seen a representative on this floor from that section of our Union who was not a slaveholder? Who but slaveholders are elected to their state legislatures? Who but they are appointed to fill their executive or judicial offices? I appeal to gentlemen whether the selection of one who labors with his own hands, however well educated, would not be considered an extraordinary event? For this I do not reproach my brethren of the south. They doubtless choose those to represent them in whom they most confide, and far be it from me to intimate that their confidence is ever misplaced. But my objection is to the introduction of a system which can not but produce the effect of rendering labor disgraceful."

The clause proposing that slaves born in the territory after the passage of the act shall be free at twenty-five years of age, was carried, February 17, by a vote of 75 yeas to 73 nays. The clause providing against the farther introduction of slaves into the territory was lost by a vote of 70 yeas to 71 nays. On the next day, however, the clause adopted was stricken out, and the bill finally passed without any allusion to slavery. When the bill reached the senate, Roberts, of Pennsylvania, moved to insert a prohibition of slavery, which failed by a vote of 19 to 14. Arkansas became a slave territory and ultimately a slave state in 1836.

The discussions in congress on the extension of slavery beyond the Mississippi aroused the anti-slavery sentiment of the north. Public meetings were held in Trenton, Philadelphia, New York, Boston, Salem, and other northern cities and towns, democrats and federalists coöperating, and committees were appointed to address the people. The state legislatures freely expressed their opinions. Pennsylvania made a solemn appeal to the states "to refuse to covenant with crime," and by a declaration that it was the duty as well as the right of congress to prohibit slavery west of the Mississippi. New Jersey and Delaware followed, both also unanimously. New York, Ohio, and Indiana indorsed the same doctrine. The New England legislatures remained silent, but memorials were sent to congress from towns and cities in favor of freedom. Virginia, Kentucky, and Maryland were as earnest on the other side. The city of Baltimore, however, memorialized congress against the extension of slavery, at a meeting over which the mayor presided.

At a meeting of the citizens of Boston and vicinity, held at the state house, in December, 1819, a vote was passed to memorialize congress on the subject of "restraining the increase of slavery in new *states* to be admitted into the Union." In pursuance of the vote the following memorial, drawn up by Daniel Webster, was presented to congress:

" *To the senate and house of representatives of the United States in congress assembled:*

"The undersigned, inhabitants of Boston and its vicinity, beg leave most respectfully and humbly to represent: that the question of the introduction of slavery into the new states to be formed on the west side of the Mississippi

31

river, appears to them to be a question of the last importance to the future welfare of the United States. If the progress of this great evil is ever to be arrested, it seems to the undersigned that this is the time to arrest it. A false step taken now, cannot be retraced; and it appears to us that the happiness of unborn millions rests on the measure which congress on this occasion may adopt. Considering this as no local question, nor a question to be decided by a temporary expediency, but as involving great interests of the whole United States, and affecting deeply and essentially those objects of common defense, general welfare, and the perpetuation of the blessings of liberty, for which the constitution itself was formed, we have presumed, in this way, to offer our sentiments and express our wishes to the national legislature. And as various reasons have been suggested against prohibiting slavery in the new states, it may perhaps be permitted to us to state our reasons, both for believing that congress possesses the constitutional power to make such prohibition a condition, on the admission of a new state into the Union, and that it is just and proper that they should exercise that power.

"And in the first place, as to the constitutional authority of congress. The constitution of the United States has declared 'that congress shall have power to dispose of and make all needful rules and regulations respecting the territory or other property belonging to the United States; and nothing in this constitution shall be so construed as to prejudice the claims of the United States or of any particular state.' It is very well known that the saving in this clause of the claims of any particular state was designed to apply to claims by the then existing states, of territory which was also claimed by the United States as their own property. It has, therefore, no bearing on the present question. The power, then, of congress over its own territories, is, by the very terms of the constitution, unlimited. It may make all 'needful rules and regulations,' which of course include all such regulations as its own views of policy or expediency shall, from time to time, dictate. If, therefore, in its judgment it be needful for the benefit of a territory to enact a prohibition of slavery, it would seem to be as much within its power of legislation as any other act of local policy. Its sovereignty being complete and universal as to the territory, it may exercise over it the most ample jurisdiction in every respect. It possesses, in this view, all the authority which any state legislature possesses over its own territory; and if any state legislature may, in its discretion, abolish or prohibit slavery within its own limits, in virtue of its general legislative authority, for the same reason congress also may exercise the like authority over its own territories. And that a state legislature, unless restrained by some constitutional provision, may so do, is unquestionable, and has been established by general practice.   *   *   *   *   *

"The creation of a new state is, in effect, a compact between congress and the inhabitants of the proposed state. Congress would not probably claim the power of compelling the inhabitants of Missouri to form a constitution of their own, and come into the Union as a state. It is as plain, that the inhabitants of that territory have no right of admission into the Union, as a state, without the consent of congress. Neither party is bound to form this connection. It can be formed only by the consent of both. What, then, prevents congress, as one of the stipulating parties, to propose its terms? And if the other party assents to these terms, why do they not effectually bind both parties? Or if the inhabitants of the territory do not choose to accept the proposed terms, but prefer to remain under a territorial government, has congress deprived them of any right, or subjected them to any restraint, which, in its discretion, it had no authority to do? If the admission of new states be not the discretionary exercise of a constitutional power, but in all cases an imperative duty, how is it to be performed? If the constitution means that congress *shall* admit new states, does it mean that congress shall do this on every application and under all circumstances? Or if this construction cannot be admitted, and if it must be conceded that congress must in some respects exercise its discretion on the admission of new states, how is it to be shown that that discretion may not be exercised in regard to this subject as well as in regard to others?

"The constitution declares, 'that the migration or importation of such persons as any of the states *now existing* shall think proper to admit, shall not be prohibited by the congress prior to the year 1808.' It is most manifest that the constitution does contemplate, in the very terms of this clause, that congress possesses the authority to prohibit the migration or importation of slaves; for it limits the exercise of this authority for a specific period of time, leaving it to its full operation ever afterward. And this power seems necessarily included in the authority which belongs to congress, 'to regulate commerce with foreign nations *and among the several states.*' No person has ever doubted that the prohibition of the foreign slave-trade was completely within the authority of congress since the year 1808. And why? Certainly only because it is embraced in the regulation of *foreign commerce;* and if so, it may for the like reason be prohibited since that period between the states. Commerce in slaves, since the year 1808, being as much subject to the regulation of congress as any other commerce, if it should see fit to enact that no slave should ever be sold from one state to another, it is not perceived how its constitutional right to make such provision could be questioned. It would seem to be too plain to be questioned, that congress did possess the power, before the year 1808, to prohibit the migration or importation of slaves into the territories (and in point of fact it exercised that power) as well as into any *new states;* and that its authority, after that year, might be as fully exercised to prevent the migration or importation of slaves into any of the old states. And if it may prohibit new states from importing slaves, it may surely, as we humbly submit, make it a condition of the admission of such states into the Union, that they shall never import them. In relation, too, to its own territories, congress possesses a more extensive authority, and may, in various other ways, effect the object. It might, for example, make it an express condition of its grants of soil, that its owners shall never hold slaves; and thus prevent the possession of slaves from ever being connected with the ownership of the soil.

"As corroborative of the views which have been already suggested, the memorialists would respectfully call the attention of congress to the history of the national legislation, under the confederation as well as under the present constitution, on this interesting subject. Unless the memorialists greatly mistake, it will demonstrate the sense of the nation, at every period of its legislation, to have been, that the prohibition of slavery was no infringement of any just rights belonging to free states, and was not incompatible with the enjoyments of all the rights and immunities which an admission into the Union was supposed to confer.

" The memorialists, after this general survey, would respectfully ask the attention of congress to the state of the question of the right of congress to prohibit slavery in that part of the former territory of Louisiana which now forms the Missouri territory. Louisiana was purchased of France by the treaty of the 30th of April, 1803. The third article of that treaty is as follows : ' The inhabitants of the ceded territory shall be incorporated into the Union of the United States, and admitted as soon as possible, *according to the principles of the federal constitution,* to the enjoyment of all the *rights, advantages,* and *immunities of the citizens of the United States;* and in the mean time they shall be maintained and protected in the free enjoyment of their liberty, property, and the religion which they profess.'

"Although the language of this article is not very precise or accurate, the memorialists conceive that its real import and intent cannot be mistaken. The first clause provides for the admission of the ceded territory into the Union, and the succeeding clause shows this must be *according to the principles of the federal constitution; and this very qualification necessarily excludes the idea that congress were not to be at liberty to impose any conditions upon such admission which were consistent with the principles of that constitution, and which had been, or might justly be, applied to other new states.* The language is not by any means so pointed as that of the resolve of 1780 ; and yet it has been seen that that resolve was never supposed to inhibit the authority of congress, as to the introduction of slavery. And it is clear, upon the plainest rule of construction, that in the absence of all restrictive language, a clause, merely providing for the admission of the territory into the Union, must be construed to authorize an admission in the manner, and upon the terms, which the constitution itself would justify. This construction derives additional support from the next clause. The inhabitants ' shall be admitted as soon as possible, according to the principles of the federal constitution, to the enjoyment of all the *rights, advantages,* and *immunities of citizens of the United States.*' The rights, advantages, and immunities here spoken of, must, from the very force of the terms of the clause, be such as are recognized or communicated by the constitution of the United States ; such as are common to all citizens, and are uniform throughout the United States. The clause cannot be referred to rights, advantages, and immunities derived exclusively from the state government, for these do not depend upon the federal constitution. Besides, it would be impossible that all the rights, advantages, and immunities of citizens of the United States, could be at the same time enjoyed by the same persons. These rights are different in different states; a right exists in one state which is denied in others, or is repugnant to other rights enjoyed in others. In some of the states, a freeholder alone is entitled to vote in the elections; in some a qualification of personal property is sufficient; and in others, age and freedom are the sole qualifications of the electors. In some states, no citizen is permitted to hold slaves; in others, he possesses that power absolutely; in others, it is limited. The obvious meaning, therefore, of the clause is, that the rights derived under the federal constitution, shall be enjoyed by the inhabitants of Louisiana in the same manner as by the citizens of other states. The United States, by the constitution, are bound to guarantee to every state in the Union a republican form of government; and the inhabitants of Louisiana are entitled, when a state, to this guarantee. Each state has a right to two senators, and two representatives according to a certain enumeration of population, pointed out in the constitution. The inhabitants of Louisiana, upon their admission into the Union, are also entitled to these privileges. The constitution further declares, 'that the citizens of each state shall be entitled to all the privileges and immunities of citizens *in* the several states.' It would seem as if the meaning of this clause could not well be misinterpreted. It obviously applies to the case of the removal of a citizen of one state to another state; and in such a case it secures to the migrating citizen all the privileges and immunities of citizens *in* the state to which he removes. It cannot surely be contended, upon any rational interpretation, that it gives to the citizens of each state all the privileges and immunities of the citizens of every other state, at the same time, and under all circumstances. Such a construction would lead to the most extraordinary consequences. It would at once destroy all the fundamental limitations of the state constitutions upon the rights of their own citizens; and leave all those rights to the mercy of the citizens of any other state, which should adopt different limitations. According to this construction, if all the state constitutions, save one, prohibited slavery, it would be in the power of that single state, by the admission of the right of its citizens to hold slaves, to communicate the same right to the citizens of all the other states within their own exclusive limits, in defiance of their own constitutional prohibitions; and to render the absurdity still more apparent, the same construction would communicate the most opposite and irreconcilable rights to the citizens of different states at the same time. It seems, therefore, to be undeniable, upon any rational interpretation, that this clause of the constitution communicated no rights in any state which its own citizens do not enjoy; and that the citizens of Louisiana, upon their admission into the Union, in receiving the benefit of this clause, would not enjoy higher or more extensive rights than the citizens of Ohio. It would communicate to the former no right of holding slaves except in states where the citizens already possessed the same right under their own state constitutions and laws.

" Upon the whole, the memorialists would most respectfully submit that the terms of the constitution, as well as the practice of the government under it, must, as they hnmbly conceive, entirely justify the conclusion that congress may prohibit the further introduction of slavery into its own territories, and also make such prohibition a condition of the admission of any new state into the Union.

"If the constitutional power of congress to make the proposed prohibition be satisfactorily shown, the justice and policy of such prohibition seem to the undersigned to be supported by plain and strong reasons. The permission of slavery in a new state, necessarily draws after it an extension of that inequality of representation, which already exists in regard to the original states. It cannot be expected that those of the original states, which do not hold slaves, can look on such an extension as being politically just. As between the original states, the representation rests on compact and plighted faith; and your memorialists have no wish that that compact should be disturbed, or that plighted faith in the slightest degree violated. But the subject assumes an entirely different character, when a new state proposes to be admitted. With her there is no compact, and no faith plighted; and where is the reason that she should come into the Union with more than an equal share of political importance and political power? Already the ratio of representation, established by the constitution, has given to the states holding slaves twenty members of the house of representatives more than they would have been entitled to, except under the particular provision of the constitution. In all probability, this number will be doubled in thirty years. Under these circumstances, we deem it not an unreasonable expectation that the inhabitants of Missouri should propose to come into the Union, renouncing the right in question, and establishing a constitution prohibiting it for ever. Without dwelling on this topic, we have still thought it our duty to present it to the consideration of congress. We present it with a deep and earnest feeling of its importance, and we respectfully solicit for it the full consideration of the national legislature.

"Your memorialists were not without the hope that the time had at length arrived when the inconvenience and the danger of this description of population had become apparent in all parts of this country, and in all parts of the civilized world. It might have been hoped that the new states themselves would have had such a view of their own permanent interests and prosperity as would have led them to prohibit its extension and increase. The wonderful increase and prosperity of the states north of the Ohio is unquestionably to be ascribed, in a great measure, te the consequences of the ordinance of 1787; and few, indeed, are the occasions, in the history of nations, in which so much can be done, by a single act, for the benefit of future generations, as was done by that ordinance, and as may now be done by the congress of the United States. We appeal to this justice and to the wisdom of the national councils to prevent the further progress of a great and serious evil. We appeal to those who look forward to the remote consequences of their measures, and who cannot balance a temporary or trifling convenience, if there were such, against a permanent, growing, and desolating evil. We cannot forbear to remind the two houses of congress that the early and decisive measures adopted by the American government for the abolition of the slave-trade, are among the proudest memorials of our nation's glory. That slavery was ever tolerated in the republic is, as yet, to be attributed to the policy of another government. No imputation, thus far, rests on any portion of the American confederacy. The Missouri territory is a new country. If its extensive and fertile fields shall be opened as a market for slaves, the government will seem to become a party to a traffic which, in so many acts, through so many years, it has denounced as impolitic, unchristian, inhuman. To enact laws to punish the traffic, and, at the same time, to tempt cupidity and avarice by the allurements of an insatiable market, is inconsistent and irreconcilable. Government, by such a course, would only defeat its own purposes, and render nugatory its own measures. Nor can the laws derive support from the manners of the people, if the power of moral sentiment be weakened by enjoying, under the permission of government, great facilities to commit offenses. The laws of the United States have denounced heavy penalties against the traffic in slaves, because such traffic is deemed unjust and inhuman. We appeal to the spirit of these laws; we appeal to this justice and humanity; we ask whether they ought not to operate, on the present occasion, with all their force? We have a strong feeling of the injustice of any toleration of slavery. Circumstances have entailed it on a portion of our community, which cannot be immediately relieved from it without consequences more injurious than the suffering of the evil. But to permit it in a new country, where yet no habits are formed which render it indispensable, what is it, but to encourage that rapacity, and fraud, and violence, against which we have so long pointed the denunciations of our penal code? What is it, but to tarnish the proud fame of the country? What is it, but to throw suspicion on its good faith, and to render questionable all its professions of regard for the rights of humanity and the liberties of mankind?

"As inhabitants of a free country—as citizens of a great and rising republic—as members of a Christian community—as living in a liberal and enlightened age, and as feeling ourselves called upon by the dictates of religion and humanity, we have presumed to offer our sentiments to congress on this question, with a solicitude for the event far beyond what a common occasion could inspire."

On the 17th January, 1820, the legislature of New York passed the following resolutions unanimously:

"WHEREAS, The inhibiting the further extension of slavery in these United States is a subject of deep concern among the people of this state; and whereas, we consider slavery as an evil much to be deplored; and that every constitutional barrier should be interposed to prevent its further extension; and that the constitution of the United States clearly gives congress the right to require of new states, not comprised with the original boundaries of these United States, the prohibition of slavery, as a condition of its admission into the Union: therefore,

"*Resolved*, That our senators be instructed, and our representatives in congress be requested, to oppose the admission, as a state, into the Union, any territory not comprised as aforesaid, without making the prohibition of slavery therein an indispensable condition of admission : therefore,

"*Resolved*, That measures be taken by the clerks of the senate and assembly of this state, to transmit copies of the preceding resolution to each of our senators and representatives in congress."

The following resolutions of the state of New Jersey were communicated to congress, by Mr. Wilson, of N. J., on the 24th January, 1820 :

"WHEREAS, A bill is now depending in the congress of the United States, on the application of the people in the territory of Missouri for the admission of that territory as a state into the Union, not containing provisions against slavery in such proposed state, and a question is made upon the right and expediency of such provision.

" The representatives of the people of New Jersey, in the legislative council and general assembly of the said state, now in session, deem it a duty they owe to themselves, their constituents, and posterity, to declare and make known the opinions they hold upon this momentous subject : and,

"1. *They do resolve and declare*, That the further admission of territories into the Union, without restriction of slavery, would, in their opinion, essentially impair the right of this and other existing states to equal representation in congress (a right at the foundation of the political compact), inasmuch as such newly-admitted slaveholding state would be represented on the basis of their slave population ; a concession made at the formation of the constitution in favor of the then existing states, but never stipulated for new states, nor to be inferred from any article or clause in that instrument.

"2. *Resolved*, That to admit the territory of Missouri as a state into the Union, without prohibiting slavery there, would, in the opinion of the representatives of the people of New Jersey aforesaid, be no less than to sanction this great political and moral evil, furnish the ready means of peopling a vast territory with slaves, and perpetuate all the dangers, crimes, and pernicious effects of domestic bondage.

"3. *Resolved*, As the opinion of the representatives aforesaid, that inasmuch as no territory has a right to be admitted into the Union, but on the principles of the federal constitution, and only by a law of congress, consenting thereto on the part of the existing states, congress may rightfully, and ought to refuse such law, unless upon the reasonable and just conditions, assented to on the part of the people applying to become one of the states.

"4. *Resolved*, In the opinion of the representatives aforesaid, that the article of the constitution which restrains congress from prohibiting the migration or importation of slaves, until after the year 1808, does, by necessary implication, admit the general power of congress over the subject of slavery, and concedes to them the right to regulate and restrain such migration and importation after that time, into the existing, or any newly to be created state.

"5. *Resolved*, As the opinion of the representatives of the people of New

Jersey aforesaid, that inasmuch as congress have a clear right to refuse the admission of a territory into the Union, by the terms of the constitution, they ought, in the present case, to exercise that absolute discretion in order to preserve the political rights of the several existing states, and prevent the great national disgrace and multiplied mischiefs which must ensue from conceding it, as a matter of right, in the immense territories yet to claim admission into the Union, beyond the Mississippi, that they may tolerate slavery.

"6. *Resolved*, (with the concurrence of council), That the governor of this state be requested to transmit a copy of the foregoing resolutions to each of the senators and representatives of this state in the congress of the United States."

The following preamble and resolutions were unanimously adopted in the legislature of Pennsylvania, Dec. 16, 1819:

"The senate and house of representatives of the commonwealth of Pennsylvania, while they cherish the right of the individual states to express their opinion upon all public measures proposed in the congress of the Union, are aware that its usefulness must in a great degree depend upon the discretion with which it is exercised; they believe that the right ought not to be resorted to upon trivial subjects or unimportant occasions; but they are also persuaded that there are moments when the neglect to exercise it would be a dereliction of public duty.

"Such an occasion, as in their judgment demands the frank expression of the sentiments of Pennsylvania, is now presented. A measure was ardently supported in the last congress of the United States, and will probably be as earnestly urged during the existing session of that body, which has a palpable tendency to impair the political relations of the several states; which is calculated to mar the social happiness of the present and future generations; which, if adopted, would impede the march of humanity and freedom through the world; and would transfer from a misguided ancestry an odious stain and fix it indelibly upon the present race—a measure, in brief, which proposes to spread the crimes and cruelties of slavery from the banks of the Mississippi to the shores of the Pacific. When a measure of this character is seriously advocated in the republican congress of America, in the nineteenth century, the several states are invoked by the duty which they owe to the Deity, by the veneration which they entertain for the memory of the founders of the republic, and by a tender regard for posterity, to protest against its adoption, to refuse to covenant with crime, and to limit the range of an evil that already hangs in awful boding over so large a portion of the Union.

"Nor can such a protest be entered by any state with greater propriety than by Pennsylvania. This commonwealth has as sacredly respected the rights of other states as it has been careful of its own; it has been the invariable aim of the people of Pennsylvania to extend to the universe, by their example, the unadulterated blessings of civil and religious freedom; and it is their pride that they have been at all times the practical advocates of those improvements and charities among men which are so well calculated to enable them to answer the purposes of their Creator; and above all, they may boast that they were foremost in removing the pollution of slavery from among them.

"If, indeed, the measure against which Pennsylvania considers it her duty to raise her voice, were calculated to abridge any of the rights guaranteed to the several states; if, odious as slavery is, it was proposed to hasten its extinction by means injurious to the states upon which it was unhappily entailed, Pennsylvania would be among the first to insist upon a sacred observance of the constitutional compact. But it cannot be pretended that the rights of any of the states are at all to be affected by refusing to extend the mischiefs of human bondage over the boundless regions of the west, a territory which formed no part of the Union at the adoption of the constitution; which has been but lately purchased from an European power by the people of the Union at large; which may or may not be admitted as a state into the Union at the discretion of congress; which must establish a republican form of government, and no other; and whose climate affords none of the pretexts urged for resorting to the labor of natives of the torrid zone; such a territory has no right, inherent or acquired, such as those states possessed which established the existing constitution. When that constitution was framed in September, 1787, the concession that three-fifths of the slaves in the states then existing should be represented in congress, could not have been intended to embrace regions at that time held by a fereign power. On the contrary, so anxious were the congress of that day to confine human bondage within its ancient home, that on the 13th of July, 1787, that body unanimously declared that slavery or involuntary servitude should not exist in the extensive territories bounded by the Ohio, the Mississippi, Canada and the Lakes; and in the ninth article of the constitution itself, the power of congress to prohibit the emigration of servile persons after 1808, is expressly recognized; nor is there to be found in the statute book a single instance of the admission of a territory to the rank of a state in which congress have not adhered to the right, vested in them by the constitution, to stipulate with the territory upon the conditions of the boon.

"The senate and house of representatives of Pennsylvania, therefore, cannot but deprecate any departure from the humane and enlightened policy pursued not only by the illustrious congress which framed the constitution, but by their successors without exception. They are persuaded that to open the fertile regions of the west to a servile race, would tend to increase their numbers beyond all past example, would open a new and steady market for the lawless venders of human flesh, and would render all schemes for obliterating this most foul blot upon the American character useless and unavailing.

"Under these convictions, and in the full persuasion that upon this topic there is but one opinion in Pennsylvania—

"*Resolved by the senate and house of representatives of the commonwealth of Pennsylvania,* That the senators of this state in the congress of the United States be, and they are hereby instructed, and that the representatives of this state in the congress of the United States be, and they are hereby requested, to vote against the admission of any territory as a state into the

Union, unless said territory shall stipulate and agree that 'the further introduction of slavery or involuntary servitude, except for the punishment of crimes,
whereof the party shall have been duly convicted, shall be prohibited; and
that all children born within the said territory, after its admission into the
Union as a state, shall be free, but may be held to service until the age of
twenty-five years.'

"*Resolved,* That the governor be, and he is hereby requested to cause a
copy of the foregoing preamble and resolution to be transmitted to each of the
senators and representatives of this state in the congress of the United States."

In the senate of the United States, early in 1820, Mr. Van Dyke communicated the following resolutions of the legislature of the state of Delaware,
which were read:

"*Resolved, by the senate and house of representatives of the state of Delaware, in general assembly met,* That it is, in the opinion of this general assembly, the constitutional right of the United States, in congress assembled, to
enact and establish, as one of the conditions for the admission of a new state
into the Union, a provision which shall effectually prevent the further introduction of slavery into such state; and that a due regard to the true interests of
such state, as well as of the other states, require the same should be done.

"*Resolved,* That a copy of the above and foregoing resolution be transmitted, by the speaker of the senate, to each of the senators and representatives
from this state in the congress of the United States."

In senate, January 24th, 1820, Mr. Logan communicated the following preamble and resolutions of the legislature of the state of Kentucky, which were read:

"WHEREAS, The constitution of the United States provides for the admission of new states into the Union, and it is just and proper that all such states
should be established upon the footing of original states, with a view to the
preservation of state sovereignty, the prosperity of such new state, and the
good of their citizens; and whereas, successful attempts have been heretofore
made, and are now making, to prevent the people of the territory of Missouri
from being admitted into the Union as a state, unless trammeled by rules and
regulations which do not exist in the original states, particularly in relation to
the toleration of slavery.

"WHEREAS, also, if congress can thus trammel or control the powers of a
territory in the formation of a state government, that body may, on the same
principle, reduce its powers to little more than those possessed by the people of
the District of Columbia; and whilst professing to make it a sovereign state,
may bind it in perpetual vassalage, and reduce it to the condition of a province; such state must necessarily become the dependent of congress, asking
such powers, and not the independent state, demanding rights. And whereas,
it is necessary, in preserving the state sovereignties in their present rights, that
no new state should be subjected to this restriction, any more than an old one,
and that there can be no reason or justice why it should not be entitled to the
same privileges, when it is bound to bear all the burdens and taxes laid upon
it by congress.

"In passing the following resolution, the general assembly refrains from expressing any opinion either in favor or against the principle of slavery; but to support and maintain state rights, which it conceives necessary to be supported and maintained, to preserve the liberties of the free people of these United States, it avows its solemn conviction, that the states already confederated under one common constitution, have not a right to deprive new states of equal privileges with themselves. Therefore,

"*Resolved, by the general assembly of the commonwealth of Kentucky,* That the senators in congress from this state be instructed, and the representatives be requested, to use their efforts to procure the passage of a law to admit the people of Missouri into the Union, as a state, whether those people will sanction slavery by their constitution or not.

"*Resolved,* That the executive of this commonwealth be requested to transmit this resolution to the senators and representatives of this state in congress, that it may be laid before that body for its consideration."

A new congress had assembled on the 6th of December, 1819. Mr. Clay was again chosen speaker. On the 8th, Mr. Scott, delegate from Missouri, moved that the memorial of her territorial legislature, as also of several citizens, praying her admission into the Union as a state, be referred to a select committee. Carried, and Messrs. Scott, of Mo., Robertson, of Ky, Terrell, of Ga., Strother, of Va., and De Witt, of N. Y., were appointed said committee.

Mr. Strong, of N. Y., that day gave notice of a bill "to prohibit the further extension of slavery in the United States."

On the 14th, Mr. Taylor, of N. Y., moved a select committee on this subject, which was granted; and the mover, with Messrs. Livermore, of N. H., P. P. Barbour, of Va., Lowndes, of S. C., Fuller, of Mass., Hardin, of Ky., and Cuthbert, of Ga., were appointed such committee. A majority of this committee being pro-slavery, Mr. Taylor could do nothing; and on the 28th the committee was, on motion, discharged from the further consideration of the subject.

On the same day, Mr. Taylor moved "that a committee be appointed with instructions to report a bill prohibiting the further admission of slaves into the territories of the United States west of the river Mississippi."

On motion of Mr. Smith, of Md., this resolve was sent to the committee of the whole, and made a special order for Jan. 10th; but it was not taken up, and appears to have slept the sleep of death.

In the senate, the memorial of the Missouri territorial legislature, asking admission as a state, was presented by Mr. Smith, of S. C., Dec. 29th, and referred to the judiciary committee.

The bill authorizing Missouri to form a constitution, etc., came up in the house as a special order, Jan. 24th. Mr. Taylor, of N. Y., moved that it be postponed for one week: lost; yeas, 87; nays, 88. Whereupon the house adjourned. It was considered in committee the next day, as also on the 28th and 30th, and thence debated daily until the 19th of February, when a bill came down from the senate "to admit the state of *Maine* into the Union," but with a rider authorizing the people of Missouri to form a state constitution, etc., without restriction on the subject of slavery.

The house, very early in the session, passed a bill providing for the admission of Maine as a state. This bill came to the senate, and was sent to its judiciary committee aforesaid, which amended it by adding a provision for Missouri as above. After several days' debate in senate, Mr. Roberts, of Penn., moved to recommit, so as to strike out all but the admission of Maine, which was defeated, (Jan. 14th, 1820;) yeas, 18 ; nays, 25. Hereupon, Mr. Thomas, of Ill., (who voted with the majority, as uniformly against any restriction on Missouri,) gave notice that he should " ask leave to bring in a bill to prohibit the introduction of slavery into *the territories of the United States north and west of the* contemplated *state of Missouri*," which he accordingly did on the 19th, when it was read and ordered to a third reading.*

The Maine admission bill, with the proposed amendments, was discussed through several days, until, Feb. 16th, the question was taken on the judiciary committee's amendments, (authorizing Missouri to form a state constitution, and saying nothing of slavery,) which were adopted by the following vote: Yeas, 23 against restriction—20 from slave states, 3 from free states. Nays, 21 in favor of restriction—19 from free states, 2 from Delaware.

Mr. Thomas, of Ill., then proposed his amendment, as follows :

" And be it further enacted, that the sixth article of compact of the ordinance of congress, passed July 13th, 1787, for the government of the territory of the United States northwest of the river Ohio, shall, to all intents and purposes, be, and hereby is, deemed and held applicable to, and shall have full force and effect in and over, all that tract of country ceded by France to the United States under the name of Louisiana, which lies north of thirty-six degrees and thirty minutes, north latitude, excepting only such part thereof as is included within the limits contemplated by this act."

On the following day, Mr. Thomas withdrew the foregoing and substituted the following :

" And be it further enacted, that in all the territory ceded by France to the United States under the name of Louisiana which lies north of thirty-six degrees thirty minutes, north latitude, excepting only such part thereof as is included within the limits of the state contemplated by this act, slavery and involuntary servitude, otherwise than in the punishment of crime, whereof the party shall have been duly convicted, shall be and is hereby forever prohibited. Provided always, that any person escaping into the same, from where labor or

---

* Great confusion and misconception exists in the public mind with regard to "the Missouri restriction," two totally different propositions being called by that name. The original restriction, which Mr. Clay vehemently opposed, and Mr. Jefferson in a letter characterized as a "fire-bell in the night," contemplated the limitation of slavery in its exclusion from the state of Missouri. This was ultimately defeated, as we shall see. The second proposed restriction was that of Mr. Thomas, just cited, which proposed the exclusion of slavery, not from the state of Missouri, but from the territories of the United States north and west of that state. This proposition did not emanate from the original Missouri restrictionists, but from their adversaries, and was but reluctantly and partially accepted by the former.—GREELEY'S SLAVERY EXTENSION.

service is lawfully claimed in any state or territory of the United States, such fugitive may be lawfully reclaimed and conveyed to the person claiming his or her labor or service as aforesaid."

Mr. Trimble, of Ohio, moved a substitute for this, somewhat altering the boundaries of the region shielded from slavery, which was rejected. Yeas, 20, (northern;) nays, 24, (southern, with Noble, Edwards, and Taylor.)

The question then recurred on Mr. Thomas's amendment, which was adopted as follows : Yeas, for excluding slavery from all the territory north and west of Missouri, 34—20 from free states, 14 from slave states. Nays, against such restriction, 10—2 from Indiana.

The bill, thus amended, was ordered to be engrossed for a third reading, by a vote of 24 to 20.

The bill was thus passed, (Feb. 18th) without further division, and sent to the house for concurrence. In the house, Mr. Thomas's amendment (as above) was at first rejected by both parties, and defeated by the strong vote of 159 to 18. Prior to this vote, the house disagreed to the log-rolling of Maine and Missouri, into one bill, by the strong vote of 93 to 72.

The house also disagreed to the remaining amendments of the senate (striking out the restriction on slavery in Missouri) by the strong vote of 102 yeas to 68 nays. Nearly or quite every representative of a free state voted in the majority of this division, with four from slave states.

So the house rejected all the senate's amendments, and returned the bill with a corresponding message.

The senate took up the bill on the 24th, and debated it till the 28th, when, on a direct vote, it was decided *not* to recede from the attachment of Missouri to the Maine bill : yeas 21 (19 from free states and 2 from Delaware) ; nays 23, (20 from slave states, with Messrs. Taylor, of Indiana, Edwards and Thomas, of Illinois.)

The senate also voted not to recede from its amendment prohibiting slavery west of Missouri, and north of 36° 30′ north latitude. (For receding, 9 from slave states, with Messrs. Noble and Taylor, of Indiana;) against it 33 ; (22 from slave states, 11 from free states.) The remaining amendments of the senate were then insisted on without division, and the house notified accordingly.

The bill was now returned to the house, which, on motion of Mr. John W. Taylor, of New York, voted to insist on its disagreement to all but section 9 of the senate's amendments, by yeas 97 to nays 76 ; all but a purely sectional vote : Hugh Nelson, of Virginia, voting with the north ; Baldwin, of Pennsylvania, Bloomfield, of New Jersey, and Shaw, of Massachusetts, voting with the south.

Section 9, (the senate's exclusion of slavery from the territory north and west of Missouri,) was also rejected—yeas 160, nays 14, (much as before.) The senate thereupon (March 2nd) passed the house Missouri bill, striking out the restriction of slavery by yeas 27 to nays 15, and adding without a division the exclusion of slavery from the territory west and north of said state. Mr.

Trimble again moved the exclusion of slavery from Arkansas also, but was again voted down, yeas 12, nays 30.

The senate now asked a conference, which the house granted without a division. The committee of conference was composed of Messrs. Thomas, of Illinois, Pinkney, of Maryland, and Barbour, of Virginia, (all anti-restrictionists), on the part of the senate, and Messrs. Holmes, of Massachusetts, Taylor, of New York, Lowndes, of South Carolina, Parker, of Massachusetts, and Kinsey, of New Jersey, on the part of the house. John Holmes, of Massachusetts, from this committee, reported that, 1. The senate should give up the combination of Missouri in the same bill with Maine. 2. The house should abandon the attempt to restrict slavery in Missouri. 3. Both houses should agree to pass the senate's separate Missouri bill, with Mr. Thomas's restriction or compromising proviso, excluding slavery from all territory north and west of Missouri. The report having been read, the first and most important question was put, viz : "Will the house concur with the senate in so much of the said amendments as proposes to strike from the fourth section of the [Missouri] bill the provision prohibiting slavery or involuntary servitude in the contemplated state, otherwise than in the punishment of crimes ? " On which question the yeas and nays were demanded and were as follows :

YEAS, *for giving up restriction on Missouri.*—Massachusetts, 4 ; Rhode Island, 1 ; Connecticut, 2 ; New York, 2 ; New Jersey, 3 ; Pennsylvania, 2 ; Delaware, 1 ; Maryland, 9 ; Virginia, 22 ; North Carolina, 12 ; South Carolina, 9 ; Georgia, 6 ; Alabama, 1 ; Mississippi, 1 ; Louisiana, 1 ; Kentucky, 8 ; Tennessee, 5. Total from free states, 14 ; from slave states, 76—in all 90.

NAYS, *against giving up the restriction on slavery in Missouri.*—New Hampshire, 6 ; Massachusetts, including Maine, 16 ; Rhode Island, 1 ; Connecticut, 4 ; Vermont, 6 ; New York, 22 ; New Jersey, 3 ; Pennsylvania, 21 ; Ohio, 6 ; Indiana, 1 ; Illinois, 1. Total 87—all from free states.

Mr. Taylor, of New York, now moved an amendment, intended to include Arkansas territory under the proposed inhibition of slavery west of Missouri ; but this motion was cut off by the previous question, and the house proceeded to concur with the senate in inserting the exclusion of slavery from the territory west and north of Missouri, instead of that just stricken out, by 134 yeas to 42 nays, (the nays being from the south). So the bill was *passed* in the form indicated above ; and the bill admitting Maine as a state, (relieved, by a conference, from the Missouri rider,) passed both houses without a division, on the following day.

Thus was consummated a measure which, while it opened the door to slavery in Missouri, was to exclude it "FOREVER" from all that territory lying north of 36° 30′ north latitude. Randolph, the leader of the ultra southern party, indignantly denounced it as a "dirty bargain," and the northern men who voted for it, as "dough-faces." Before signing the bill, President Monroe submitted the question to his cabinet, "Has congress the constitutional power to prohibit slavery in a territory ? " All the cabinet declared themselves in the affirmative, though neither Crawford, Calhoun, nor Wirt could see any express authority. The president submitted another question: Was the term "forever" in the prohibition clause of the Missouri bill to be understood as referring only to the territorial condition of the district, or was it intended to extend the prohibition of slavery to such states as might be erected therefrom? Adams thought that the term "forever" must be understood to mean forever, and that the prohibition would extend to any states that might at any time be erected from the territory. The others, including Thompson, of New York, were all of opinion that the term "forever" was only a territorial forever, not interfering with the right of any state that might at any time be organized within the district referred to, to establish or prohibit slavery. The second question was modified into the inquiry, Was the proviso, as it stood in the bill, constitutional? To this they all replied, yes, and Monroe signed the bills. This account is from the unpublished diary of John Quincy Adams, quoted by Hildreth.

"The impression produced on my mind," so Adams wrote at the time in his diary, "by the progress of this discussion is, that the bargain between freedom and slavery contained in the constitution of the United States is morally and politically vicious, inconsistent with the principles upon which alone our revolution can be justified; cruel and oppressive, by riveting the chains of slavery, in pledging the faith of freedom to maintain and perpetuate the tyranny of the master; and grossly unequal and impolitic, by admitting that slaves are at once enemies to be kept in subjection, property to be secured and restored to their owners, and persons not to be represented themselves, but for whom their masters are privileged with nearly a double share of representation. The consequence has been, that this slave representation has governed the Union. Benjamin, portioned above his brethren, has ravined as a wolf, in the morning he has devoured the prey, and at night he has divided the spoil. It would be no difficult matter to prove, by reviewing the history of the Union under this constitution, that almost every thing which has contributed to the honor and welfare of the nation has been accomplished in despite of them; and that every thing unpropitious and dishonorable, including the blunders and follies of their adversaries, may be traced to them."

Governor Wolcott, in his address shortly after to the Connecticut legislature, in reference to a very elaborate disquisition on state rights in their bearing on the Missouri question, which the Virginia legislature had sent, in the form of a circular, to all the states, thus expressed himself: "It can not have escaped your attention, that a diversity of habits and principles of government exist in this country; and I think it is evident that slavery is gradually forming those distinctions, which, according to invariable laws of human action, constitute the characteristic difference between aristocratical and democratical republics.

"Where agricultural labor is wholly or chiefly performed by slaves, it must constitute the principal revenue of the community. The owners of slaves must necessarily be the chief owners of the soil, and those laborers who are too poor to own slaves, though nominally free, must be dependent on an aristocratical order, and remain without power or political influence. It has been urged, as a compensation for the admitted evils of slavery, that the spirit of liberty is more elevated and persevering among the masters of slaves, than in states where liberty is a common blessing. We may admit that our southern brethren are as firmly attached to liberty as ourselves, but we can not concede that they are in any respect our superiors, without submitting to humiliation and reproach. Probably the claim has no other just foundation than in the well known ardor, tenacity of opinion, and strict concert of action with which the members of a privileged order invariably pursue a separate and exclusive interest. Even a tacit admission of inferiority by habitual concessions would imply, on our part, a secret preference of aristocratical over democratical institutions."

On the 16th of November, 1820, Missouri applied for admission into the Union, with a state constitution containing the following provisions :

"The general assembly shall have no power to pass laws, first, for the emancipation of slaves without the consent of their owners, or without paying them, before such emancipation, a full equivalent for such slaves so emancipated ; and, second, to prevent bona fide emigrants to this state, or actual settlers therein, from bringing from any of the United States, or from any of their territories, such persons as may there be deemed to be slaves, so long as any persons of the same description are allowed to be held as slaves by the laws of this state.

"It shall be their duty, as soon as may be, to pass such laws as may be necessary,

"First, to prevent free negroes and mulattoes from coming to, and settling in, this state, under any pretext whatever."

The last requirement was considered a palpable violation of that clause of the constitution which gives to the citizens of each state the rights of citizens in every state. In several of the free states the class referred to were considered citizens, and not only a determined resistance to any such exclusion was manifested in congress, but a portion of the northern members evinced a disposition to renew the struggle against the further introduction of slaves into Missouri. The first vote in the house on her admission, stood yeas, 79 ; nays, 93. A second attempt was made to admit her, on condition that she would expunge the last quoted obnoxious clause of her constitution, which was voted down by a vote of 156 to 6.

The house now rested, until a joint resolve, admitting her with but a vague and ineffective qualification, came down from the senate, where it was passed by a vote of 26 to 18—six senators from free states in the affirmative. Mr. Clay, who had resigned in the recess, and been succeeded, as speaker, by John W. Taylor, of New York, now appeared as the leader of the Missouri admissionists, and proposed terms of compromise, which were twice voted down by the northern members, aided by John Randolph and three others from the south, who would have Missouri admitted without condition or qualification At last, Mr. Clay proposed a joint committee on this subject, to be chosen by ballot—which the house agreed to by 101 to 55 ; and Mr. Clay became its chairman. By this committee it was agreed that a solemn pledge should be required of the legislature of Missouri, that the constitution of that state should not be construed to authorize the passage of any act, and that no act should be passed, " by which any of the citizens of either of the states should be excluded from the enjoyment of the privileges and immunities to which they are entitled under the constitution of the United States." The joint resolution, amended by the addition of this proviso, passed the house by 86 yeas to 82 nays ; the senate concurred (February 27th, 1821,) by 26 yeas to 15 nays ; (all northern but Macon, of North Carolina,) Missouri complied with the condition, and became an accepted member of the Union. Thus closed the last stage of the fierce Missouri controversy which seemed at times to threaten the existence of the Union. " So true it is," says Hildreth, "and let it not be forgotten, that no class can exist in any community so helpless and despised that it may not become the very hinge on which the fate of the nation shall turn."

CHAPTER XXVII.

PERIOD FROM 1820 TO 1835.—POLITICAL HISTORY OF SLAVERY.

Census of 1820.—Session of 1824–5.—Gov. Troup's demonstrations.—Georgia legislature—Secession threatened.—Slaves in Canada—their surrender refused by England.—Citizens of District of Columbia petition for gradual abolition.—Census of 1830.—Antislavery societies formed in the north—counter movements north and south.—The mail troubles.—Manifesto of American Anti-slavery Society.—Petitions to congress—Discussion on the disposal of them.—Bill to prohibit the circulation of anti-slavery publications through the mails.—Calhoun's report—Measure opposed by Webster, Clay, Benton and others.—Buchanan, Tallmade, &c., favor it—Bill lost.—Atherton's gag resolutions passed.

THE census of 1820 exhibits a slave population of 1,538,038, being an increase of 346,674 for the ten years since 1810, a rate of about 30 per cent.

CENSUS OF 1820—SLAVE POPULATION.

Alabama	41,879	Missouri	10,222
District of Columbia	6,377	New Jersey	7,557
Connecticut	97	New York	10,088
Delaware	4,509	North Carolina	205,017
Georgia	149,654	Pennsylvania	211
Illinois	917	Rhode Island	48
Indiana	190	South Carolina	258,475
Kentucky	126,732	Tennessee	80,107
Louisiana	69,064	Virginia	425,153
Maryland	107,397	Arkansas Territory	1,617
Mississippi	32,814	Aggregate, 1,538,038.	

Slavery was fast decreasing in what are now the free states, except in Illinois ; it had also decreased in Maryland. The increase in Virginia for the last decade had been only 8 per cent.; in North Carolina 21, and in South Carolina 31 per cent. The rapid settlement of the southwest had stimulated the domestic slave-trade, and the market was supplied chiefly from Maryland and Virginia, which accounts for the decrease in the former, and the small increase in the latter state. Slavery in Tennessee had increased 79 per cent.; in Mississippi 92, and in Louisiana 99 per cent.

At the session of 1824–5, Mr. King, senator from New York, offered a resolution proposing to appropriate, after the payment of the public debt, the proceeds of the sales of public lands, to aid in the emancipation of slaves, and also the colonizing of free people of color without the limits of the United States. This resolution was never called up by the mover, being intended, as was supposed, merely for record as his opinion. Similar propositions were sent to congress by state legislatures in the form of resolutions. About the same time, Mr. Wirt, attorney-general of the United States, gave an official opinion that a law of South Carolina, authorizing the imprisonment of colored mariners, was unconstitutional. These acts took place at the time of the famous controversy between governor Troup, of Georgia, and the general government, in reference to the removal of the Creek Indians; and the governor, in convening a special session of the legislature, directed attention to them in his message. As the proceedings of the governor and his legislature were not productive of any brilliant results, they are only referred to as to something especially ludicrous.

These acts of Mr. King and Mr. Wirt, were pronounced by the governor in his message, "officious and impertinent intermeddlings with our domestic concerns." The doctrine of the attorney-general, if sanctioned by the supreme court, "would make it quite easy for congress, by a short decree, to divest this entire interest, without cost to themselves of one dollar, or of one acre of public land. If the government of the United States wishes a principle established which it dare not establish for itself, a cause made before the supreme court, and the principle once settled, the act of congress follows of course. One movement of congress unresisted by you, and all is lost. Temporize no longer, make known your resolution, that this subject shall not be touched by them but at their peril. If this matter (slavery) be an evil, it is our own; if it be a sin, we can implore the forgiveness of it. To remove it we ask not either their sympathy or assistance. It may be our physical weakness—it is our moral strength. If, like the Greeks and Romans, we cease to be masters, we are slaves. I entreat you most earnestly, now that it is not too late, to step forth, and, *having exhausted the argument, to stand by your arms.*"

This subject was referred to a select committee, who presented to the house a report responding to the feelings and sentiments of the governor. "The hour is come," says the committee, "or is rapidly approaching, when the states, from Virginia to Georgia, from Missouri to Louisiana, must confederate, and, as one man, say to the Union: We will no longer submit our retained rights to the sniveling insinuations of bad men on the floor of congress—our constitutional rights to the dark and strained construction of designing men upon judicial benches; that we detest the doctrine, and disclaim the principle, of unlimited submission to the general government.

"Let our northern brethern, then, if there is no peace in union, if the compact has become too heavy to be longer borne, in the name of all the mercies, find peace among themselves. Let them continue to rejoice in their self-righteousness; let them bask in their own elysium, while they depict all south of the Potomac as a hideous reverse. As Athens, as Sparta, as Rome was, we will be: they held slaves; we hold them. Let the north, then, form national roads for themselves; let them guard with tariffs their own interest; let them deepen their public debt until a high-minded aristocracy shall arise out of it. We want none of all those blessings. But in the simplicity of the patriarchal government, we would still remain master and servant under our own vine and our own fig tree, and confide for safety upon Him who, of old time, looked down upon this state of things without wrath."

The committee concluded their report with two resolutions, declaring their concurrence in the sentiments of the governor, and for the support of their determination to "stand by their arms," pledging their lives, their fortunes, and their sacred honor; and requesting the governor to forward copies of the resolutions to the governors of the several states, and to their own senators and representatives in congress.

On the next day, (June 7th, 1825,) another message was communicated, in which the governor again reverted to the resolutions of the state legislatures on the subject of slavery, and the acts of the individuals before mentioned; complained of the efforts that had been made to render unavailing the guaranties of the constitution; and concluded thus:

"The attorney-general, representing the United States, says before the supreme court, in a ripe and splendid argument, that slavery, being inconsistent with the laws of God and nature, can not exist. Do we want more? or shall we wait until the principle being decided against us, the execution issues, and the entire property is bought in from the proceeds of our public lands? This is left to your decision. The United States can choose between our enmity and our love; and when you offer them the choice, you perform the last and holiest of duties. They have adopted a conceit; and if they love that more than they love us, they will cling to it and throw us off; but it will be written in your history, that you did not separate from your household without adopting the fraternal language: choose ye this day between our friendship and that worthless idol you have set up and worshiped."

Here the matter seems to have been dropped, as the subject of the Indian difficulties took the precedence, and kept the governor in a comfortable sweat until the close of 1827.

An attempt was made during Mr. Adams' administration to effect an arrangement with Great Britain for the surrender of fugitive slaves taking refuge in the Canadian provinces. By a resolution of the house of representatives, May 10, 1828, the president was requested to open a negotiation with the British government for this purpose. On the 15th of December, in compliance with a resolution of the 8th, the president transmitted to the house the correspondence between the secretary of state and Mr. Gallatin, our minister at London, and Mr. Barbour, his successor. The following is an extract from the instructions of Mr. Clay to Mr. Gallatin :

"If it be urged that Great Britain would make, in agreeing to the proposed stipulation, a concession without an equivalent, there being no corresponding class of persons in her North American continental dominions, you will reply :

"1st. That there is a similar class in the British West Indies, and, although the instances are not numerous, some have occurred of their escape, or being brought, contrary to law, into the United States.

"2dly. That Great Britain would probably obtain an advantage over us in the reciprocal restoration of military and maritime deserters, which would compensate any that we might secure over her in the practical operation of an article for the mutual delivery of fugitives from labor.

"3dly. At all events, the disposition to cultivate good neighborhood, which such an article would imply, could not fail to find a compensation in that, or in some other way, in the already immense and still increasing intercourse between the two countries. The states of Virginia and Kentucky are particularly anxious on this subject. The general assembly of the latter has repeatedly invoked the interposition of the government of the United States with Great Britain. You will, therefore, press the matter whilst there exists any prospect of your obtaining a satisfactory arrangement of it. Perhaps the British government, whilst they refuse to come under any obligation by treaty, might be willing to give directions to the colonial authorities to afford facilities for the recovery of fugitives from labor ; or, if they should not be disposed to disturb such as have heretofore taken refuge in Upper Canada, they might be willing to interdict the entry of any others in future."

These considerations were not deemed sufficiently weighty to induce the English government to make the desired concession.

A petition from the citizens of the District of Columbia was presented to congress at the session of 1827–28, praying for the prospective abolition of slavery in the district, and for the repeal of those laws which authorize the selling of supposed runaways for their prison fees or maintenance. The petitioners declare slavery among them to be "an evil of serious magnitude, which greatly impairs the prosperity and happiness of the district, and to cast the reproach of inconsistency upon the free institutions established among us." They represent the domestic slave-trade at the seat of the national government as "scarcely less disgraceful in its character, and even more demoralizing in its influence," than the foreign slave-trade, which is declared piracy, and punishable with death. "Husbands and wives are separated ; children are taken from their parents without regard to the ties of nature, and the most endearing bonds of affection are broken for ever."

It was mentioned also as a special grievance, that "some who were entitled to freedom had been sold into unconditional slavery." And they gave the case of a colored man who had been taken up as a runaway slave, imprisoned, and advertised; and no one appearing to claim him, he was sold for life at public auction for the payment of his jail fees, and taken to the south. A stronger anti-slavery document has not in later years been presented to congress; nor did it receive any more efficient action than similar petitions have since received.

CENSUS OF 1830.—SLAVE POPULATION.

District of Columbia.....	6,119	Mississippi..............	65,659
Delaware...............	3,292	Missouri................	25,091
Florida..................	15,501	New Jersey.............	2,254
Georgia	217,531	North Carolina..........	245,601
Illinois.............	747	South Carolina..........	315,401
Kentucky	165,213	Tennessee..............	141,603
Louisiana..............	109,588	Virginia	469,757
Maryland...............	102,994	Arkansas...............	4,576
Alabama	117,549	Aggregate, 2,009,043.	

In 1833, the National Anti-Slavery Society was formed. Societies were also formed in all the northern states; in some of them, in almost every county. Meetings were held at the south denouncing these movements; and in the north attempts were made to suppress the anti-slavery meetings by violence. Meetings were also held in the north to express sympathy for the south, and to censure the "abolitionists." These anti-abolition meetings were gratifying to the people of the south. The proceedings of the Albany meeting were thus noticed by the Richmond Enquirer: "Amid these proceedings, we hail with delight the meeting and resolutions of Albany. They are up to the hub. They are in perfect unison with the rights and sentiments of the south. They are divested of all the metaphysics and abstractions of the resolutions of New York. They are free from all qualifications and equivocation—no idle denunciations of the evils of slavery—no pompous assertions of the right of discussion. But they announce in the most unqualified terms that it is a southern question, which belongs, under the federal compact, exclusively to the south. They denounce all discussions upon it in the other states, which, from their very nature, are calculated to 'inflame the public mind,' and put in jeopardy the lives and property of their fellow-citizens, as at war with every rule of moral duty, and every suggestion of humanity; and they reprobate the incendiaries who will persist in carrying them on, 'as disloyal to the Union.' They pronounce these vile incendiaries to be 'disturbers of the public peace.' They assure the south 'that the great body of the northern people entertain opinions similar to those expressed in these resolutions;' finally, 'that we plight to them our faith to maintain, in practice, so far as lies in our power, what we have thus solemnly declared.'

"We hail this plighted faith to arrest, by 'all constitutional and legal means,' the movements of these incendiaries. We hail these pledges with pleasure; and should it become necessary, we shall call upon them to redeem them in good faith, and to act, and to put down these disturbers of the peace."

"The Albany resolutions," said the Richmond Whig, "are far more acceptable than those of New York. They are unexceptionable in their general expressions towards the south, and in their views of the spirit and consequences of abolition; and they omit any specific recognition of the right of agitation. Nothing is wanting, indeed, but that which, *being wanting*, all the rest, we fear, is little more than a 'sounding brass and a tinkling cymbal.' We mean the recognition of the power of the legislature to suppress the fanatics, and the recommendation to do so. This is the substance asked of the north by their brethren of the south; and the recent manifesto of Tappan & Co. makes it plain that without it, nothing effective can be done; that without it, urgent remonstrances to these madmen to desist, and warm professions towards the south, avail not a whit. Up to the mark the north must come, if it would restore tranquility and preserve the union.

"The failure of the Albany meeting to enforce the expediency of legislative enactments, is ominous. There is reason to believe that strong appeals were made to the leaders from various points, perhaps from Richmond itself, to go as far as possible, and to adopt a resolution, conceding to the south its demand for legislative enactment. Political importance was attached to it from the circumstance that the immediate friends of Mr. Van Buren and his party leaders were to preside at the meeting, and thus that an intelligent sign might be given to the south, that *he* sustained her claim. We infer nothing against Mr. Van Buren himself from the failure; but we do infer this, either that his Albany partisans reject the claim, or fear to encounter public opinion by adopting it. Either way it may be regarded as decisive of the fate of the demand itself, and as conclusive that nothing will be done by the state of New York to suppress the fanatics *by law*. New York is the hotbed of the sect; and nothing being done there, what may be done elsewhere will avail nothing."

The Philadelphia Inquirer said: "The south has called upon the north for action in relation to Garrison and his co-workers: Philadelphia, at least, has responded to this call in a spirit of the utmost liberality. The resolutions adopted at the town meeting of Monday last not only denounce the recent movements of the abolitionists, but they expressly disclaim any 'right to interfere, directly or indirectly, with the subject of slavery in the southern states,' and aver that any action upon it by the people of the north would be not only a violation of the constitution, but a presumptuous infraction of the rights of the south; and further, one of them recommends to the legislature of this commonwealth to enact, at the next session, certain provisions to protect our fellow-citizens of the south from any incendiary movements within our borders, should any such hereafter be made. Are not these declarations to the point? Do they not cover the whole ground? Do they not go even farther than many of the resolutions passed at public meetings in the south?"

Despairing of seeing the progress of anti-slavery sentiment arrested by legislation, the south suggested the remedy of non-intercourse and disunion. In the resolutions of a public meeting in South Carolina, it was declared "that when the southern states are reduced to the alternative of choosing either union without liberty, or disunion with liberty and property, be assured they will not hesitate which to take, and will make the choice promptly, unitedly, and fearlessly." And it was unanimously resolved, "that should the non-slaveholding states omit or refuse, at the ensuing meeting of their respective legislatures, to put a final stop to the proceedings of their abolition societies against the domestic peace of the south, and effectually prevent any further interference by them with our slave population, *by efficient penal laws*, it will then become the solemn duty of the whole south, in order to protect themselves and secure their rights and property against the unconstitutional combination of the non-slaveholding states, and the murderous designs of their abolitionists, to withdraw from the union."

In relation to the suspension of commercial intercourse, the Richmond Whig said : " The suggestion of acting upon fanaticism by withholding the profits of southern commerce from those engaged, either actively or by countenance, in propagating its designs, is obtaining extensive popularity. A general persuasion prevails of its efficacy. It is an argument which will carry more weight than appeals to justice, humanity, and fraternal affection. It is never lost to mankind. Through the purse is the surest road to the understandings of men ; especially, so we have been taught to believe, to the understandings of those with whom the south is now contending. Southern commerce is essential to the north. Can the south be blamed for cutting off the resources employed to disturb its tranquility, and overthrow its institutions ? Where is the illiberality ? Where is the injustice ? That all should suffer where a part only are guilty, is to be deplored but not avoided. When the innocent feel the consequences, they will be stimulated to more active steps for the suppression of the wretches who have wrought so much mischief and engendered so much bad feeling

" The merchants are well disposed to the experiment ; but they say its success depends upon the country, not the cities. Without the coöperation of the country citizens—without they put their shoulders to the wheel, and discourage the custom of buying goods in the north—they can do nothing. They are ready to promise, and to fulfill the promise, that, if the country will buy their goods, they shall have them as cheap and as good as the northern markets now supply. Let none be alarmed by the silly and traitorous clamor put up about the *Union*. The articles of Union, we presume, do not inhibit the south from caring for its own safety, or promoting its own prosperity."

Application was made to the postmaster-general to interpose his authority to prevent the transmission, by mail, of anti-slavery papers and documents. In answer to a request of a meeting in Petersburg, Virginia, to adopt in his department some regulation to this effect, Mr Kendall, under date of August 20, 1835, said it was not in his power, by any lawful regulation, to obviate the evil. Such a power, if any necessity for it existed, ought not to be vested in the head of the executive department. He, however, regarded the transmission, through the mail, of papers "tending to promote discontent, sedition, and servile war, from one state to another, as a violation of the spirit, if not the letter, of the federal compact, which would justify, on the part of the injured states, any measure necessary to effect their exclusion." For the present, the only means of relief was "in responsibilities voluntarily assumed by the postmasters." He hoped congress would, at the next session, put a stop to the evil, and pledged his exertions to promote the adoption of a measure for that purpose.

Conceiving the principles and objects of anti-slavery associations to be misunderstood, the officers of the American anti-slavery society published in its defense the following address "TO THE PUBLIC :"

"In behalf of the American anti-slavery society, we solicit the candid attention of the public to the following declaration of our principles and objects. Were the charges which are brought against us, made only by individuals who are interested in the continuance of slavery, and by such as are influenced solely by unworthy motives, this address would be unnecessary; but there are those who merit and possess our esteem, who would not voluntarily do us injustice, and who have been led by gross misrepresentations to believe that we are pursuing measures at variance, not only with the constitutional rights of the south, but with the precepts of humanity and religion. To such we offer the following explanations and assurances :

"1st. We hold that congress has no more right to abolish slavery in the southern states, than in the French West India islands. Of course we desire no national legislation on the subject.

"2d. We hold that slavery can only be lawfully abolished by the legislatures of the several states in which it prevails, and that the exercise of any other than moral influence to induce such abolition is unconstitutional.

"3d. We believe that congress has the same right to abolish slavery in the District of Columbia, that the state governments have within their respective jurisdictions, and that it is their duty to efface so foul a blot from the national escutcheon.

"4th. We believe that American citizens have the right to express and publish their opinions of the constitution, laws, and institutions of any and every state and nation under heaven ; and we mean never to surrender the liberty of speech, of the press, or of conscience—blessings we have inherited from our fathers, and which we intend, as far as we are able, to transmit unimpaired to our children.

"5th. We have uniformly deprecated all forcible attempts on the part of the slaves to recover their liberty. And were it in our power to address them, we would exhort them to observe a quiet and peaceful demeanor, and would assure them that no insurrectionary movements on their part would receive from us the slightest aid or countenance.

"6th. We would deplore any servile insurrection, both on account of the calamities which would attend it, and on account of the occasion which it might furnish of increased severity and oppression.

"7th. We are charged with sending incendiary publications to the south. If by the term *incendiary* is meant publications containing arguments and facts to prove slavery to be a moral and political evil, and that duty and policy require its immediate abolition, the charge is true. But if this charge is used to imply publications encouraging insurrection, and designed to excite the slaves to break their fetters, the charge is utterly and unequivocally false. We beg our fellow-citizens to notice that this charge is made without proof, and by many who confess that they have never read our publications, and that those who make it, offer to the public no evidence from our writings in support of it.

"8th. We are accused of sending our publications to the slaves, and it is asserted that their tendency is to excite insurrections. Both the charges are false. These publications are not intended for the slaves, and were they able to read them, they would find in them no encouragement to insurrection.

"9th. We are accused of employing agents in the slave states to distribute our publications. We have never had one such agent. We have sent no package of our papers to any person in those states for distribution, except to five respectable resident citizens, at their own request. But we have sent, by mail, single papers addressed to public officers, editors of newspapers, clergymen, and others. If, therefore, our object is to excite the slaves to insurrection, the masters are our agents.

"We believe slavery to be sinful, injurious to this and every other country in which it prevails; we believe immediate emancipation to be the duty of every slaveholder, and that the immediate abolition of slavery by those who have the right to abolish it, would be safe and wise. These opinions we have freely expressed, and we certainly have no intention to refrain from expressing them in future, and urging them upon the consciences and hearts of our fellow-citizens who hold slaves, or apologize for slavery.

"We believe the education of the poor is required by duty, and by a regard for the permanency of our republican institutions. There are thousands and tens of thousands of our fellow-citizens, even in the free states, sunk in abject poverty, and who, on account of their complexion, are virtually kept in ignorance, and whose instruction in certain cases is actually prohibited by law! We are anxious to protect the rights, and to promote the virtue and happiness of the colored portion of our population, and on this account we have been charged with a design to encourage intermarriages between whites and blacks. This charge has been repeatedly, and is now again denied, while we repeat that the tendency of our sentiments is to put an end to the criminal amalgamation that prevails wherever slavery exists.

"We are accused of acts that tend to a dissolution of the Union, and even of wishing to dissolve it. We have never 'calculated the value of the Union,' because we believe it to be inestimable, and that the abolition of slavery will remove the chief danger of its dissolution; and one of the many reasons why we cherish and will endeavor to preserve the constitution is, that it restrains congress from making any law abridging the freedom of speech or of the press.

"Such, fellow-citizens, are our principles; are they unworthy of republicans and Christians? Or are they in truth so atrocious, that in order to prevent their diffusion you are yourselves willing to surrender, at the dictation of others, the invaluable privilege of free discussion—the very birthright of Americans? Will you, in order that the abominations of slavery may be concealed from public view, and that the capital of your republic may continue to be, as it now is, under the sanction of congress, the great slave mart of the American continent, consent that the general government, in acknowledged defiance of the constitution and laws, shall appoint throughout the length and breadth of your land, ten thousand censors of the press, each of whom shall have the right to inspect every document you may commit to the post-office, and to suppress every pamphlet and newspaper, whether religious or political, which in his sovereign pleasure he may adjudge to contain an incendiary article ? Surely we need not remind you, that if you submit to such an encroachment on your liberties, the days of our republic are numbered, and that although abolitionists may be the first, they will not be the last victims offered at the shrine of arbitrary power."

Petitions from the free states praying for the abolition of slavery and the slave-trade in the District of Columbia were daily presented in congress. Southern members objected to receiving the petitions, as praying for an act that was unconstitutional—interference with the right of property without the consent of the owners ; and also that such interference would be a violation of good faith with the states of Maryland and Virginia, which ceded the territory of the district to the general government. The discussion resulted in the adoption, by a large majority, February 8, 1836, of the following resolution of Mr. Pinckney, of South Carolina :

"*Resolved,* That all the memorials which have been offered, or which may hereafter be presented to this house, praying for the abolition of slavery in the District of Columbia, and also the resolutions offered by an honorable member from Maine, (Mr. Jarvis,) with the amendment thereto proposed by an honorable member from Virginia, (Mr. Wise,) and every other paper or proposition that may be submitted in relation to that subject, be referred to a select committee, with instructions to report that congress possesses no constitutional authority to interfere in any way with the institution of slavery in any of the states of this confederacy ; and that, in the opinion of this house, congress ought not to interfere in any way with slavery in the District of Columbia, because it would be a violation of the public faith, unwise, impolitic, and dangerous to the Union."

On the 18th of May, Mr. Pinckney, from the select committee appointed on his motion, reported three resolutions ; the first denying the power of congress over slavery in the states ; the second, declaring that congress ought not to interfere with it in the District of Columbia. The third, which was not contemplated by the instructions to the committee, required all petitions and papers relating to the subject, to be at once laid upon the table, without being printed or referred, and without any other action on them. On the 25th of May, the vote was taken on the first resolution, under the pressure of the previous question. Mr. Adams said, if the house would allow him five minutes, he would prove the resolution to be false. Eight members were understood to have voted in the negative : Messrs. Adams, Jackson and Phillips, of Mass., Everett and

Slade, of Vt., Clark, Denny and Potts, of Penn. The second resolution was adopted the next day, 132 to 45; the third 117 to 68.

In the senate, the principal discussion on the disposal of abolition petitions was upon one from the society of the "Friends" in the state of Pennsylvania, adopted at the Caln quarterly meeting. It was presented the 11th of January, by Mr. Buchanan, who said he was in favor of giving the memorial a respectful reception; but he wished to put the question at rest. He should therefore move that the memorial be read, and that the prayer of the memorialists be rejected. The question on receiving the petition was, on the 9th of March, decided in the affirmative : ayes, 36 ; noes, 10; the latter all from southern senators. On the 11th, the whole subject, including the rejection of the petition, was agreed to, 34 to 6. Those who voted in the negative, were Messrs. Davis and Webster, from Mass., Prentiss, of Vt., Knight, of R. I., and Southard, of New Jersey.

But the most important action of the senate was upon a bill to prohibit the circulation of abolition publications by mail. The president had in his annual message called the attention of congress to the subject. He said : "I must also invite your attention to the painful excitement produced in the south, by attempts to circulate, through the mails, inflammatory appeals addressed to the passions of the slaves, in prints, and in various sorts of publications, calculated to stimulate them to insurrection, and to produce all the horrors of a servile war." He said it was "fortunate for the country, that the good sense and generous feeling of the people of the non-slaveholding states" were so strong "against the proceedings of the misguided persons who had engaged in these unconstitutional and wicked attempts, as to authorize the hope that these attempts will no longer be persisted in." But if these expressions of the public will should not effect the desirable result, he did "not doubt that the non-slaveholding states would exercise their authority in suppressing this interference with the constitutional rights of the south." And he would respectfully suggest the passing of a law that would "prohibit, under severe penalties, the circulation in the southern states, through the mail, of incendiary publications, intended to instigate the slaves to insurrection."

This part of the message was, on motion of Mr. Calhoun, referred to a select committee, which, in accordance with his wishes, was composed mainly of senators from the slaveholding states. They were Messrs. Calhoun, King, of Georgia, Mangum, Linn, and Davis ; the last alone being from the free states. The report of the committee was made the 4th of February. Notwithstanding four-fifths of its members were southern, only Messers. Calhoun and Mangum were in favor of the entire report. The accompanying bill prohibited postmasters from knowingly putting into the mail any printed or written paper or pictorial representation relating to slavery addressed to any person in a state in which their circulation was forbidden ; and it prohibited postmasters in such state from delivering such papers to any person not authorized by the laws of the state to receive them. And the postmasters of the offices where such papers were deposited, were required to give notice of the same from time to time; and if the papers were not, within one month withdrawn by the person depositing them, they were to be burnt or otherwise destroyed. Mr. Linn, though dissenting from parts of the report, approved the bill.

Mr. Calhoun, in his report, reiterated his favorite doctrine of state sovereignty; from which he deduced the inherent right of a state to defend itself against internal dangers; and he denied the right of the general government to assist a state, even in case of domestic violence, except on application of the authorities of the state itself. He said it belonged to the slaveholding states, whose institutions were in danger, and not to congress, as the message supposed, to determine what papers were incendiary; and he asserted the proposition, that each state was under obligation to prevent its citizens from disturbing the peace or endangering the security of other states; and that, in case of being disturbed or endangered, the latter had a right to demand of the former the adoption of measures for their protection. And if it should neglect its duty, the states whose peace was assailed might resort to means to protect themselves, as if they were separate and independent communities.

As motives to suppress by law the efforts of the abolitionists, the report mentioned the danger of their accomplishing their object, the abolition of slavery in the southern states, and the consequent evils which would attend it. It would destroy property to the amount of $950,000,000, and impoverish an entire section of the Union. By destroying the relation between the two races, the improvement of the condition of the colored people, now so rapidly going on, and by which they had been, both physically and intellectually, and in respect to the comforts of life, elevated to a condition enjoyed by the loboring class in few countries, and greatly superior to that of the free people of the same race in the non-slaveholding states, would be arrested; and the two races would be placed in a state of conflict which must end in the expulsion or extirpation of one or the other.

The bill, reported by Mr. Calhoun, sustained by the combined influence of his own report and the executive recommendation, made its way nearly through the senate. Mr. Webster opposed the bill, because it was vague and obscure, in not sufficiently defining the publications to be prohibited. Whether for or against slavery, if they "touched the subject," they would come under the prohibition. Even the constitution might be prohibited. And the deputy postmaster must decide, and decide correctly, under pain of being removed from office! He must make himself acquainted with the laws of all the states on the subject, and decide on them, however variant they might be with each other. The bill also conflicted with that provision of the constitution which guarantied the freedom of speech and of the press. If a newspaper came to him, he had a property in it; and how could any man take that property and burn it without due form of law? And how could that newspaper be pronounced an unlawful publication, and having no property in it, without a legal trial? He argued against the right to examine into the nature of publications sent to the post-office, and said that the right of an individual in his papers was secured to him in every free country in the world.

Mr. Clay said the papers, while in the post-office or in the mail, did no harm ; it was their circulation—their being taken out of the mail, and the use made of them—that constituted the mischief; and the state authorities could apply the remedy. The instant a prohibited paper was handed out, whether to a citizen or a sojourner, he was subject to the law which might compel him to surrender or to burn it. The bill was vague and indefinite, unnecessary and dangerous. It applied to non-slaveholding as well as to slaveholding states ; to papers touching slavery, as well for as against it; and a non-slaveholding state might, under this bill, prohibt publications in defense of slavery. But the law would be inoperative : the postmaster was not amenable, unless he delivered the papers *knowing* them to be incendiary ; and he had only to plead ignorance to avoid the penalty of the law. Mr. Clay wished to know whence congress derived the power to pass this law. The senator from Pennsylvania had asked if the post-office power did not give the right to say what should be carried in the mails. There was no such power as that claimed in the bill. If such doctrine prevailed, the government might designate the persons, or parties, or classes, who should have the exclusive benefit of the mails.

Before the question was taken on the engrossment of the bill, a motion by Mr. Calhoun to amend it so as to prevent the withdrawal of the prohibited papers, was negatived, 15 to 15. An amendment offered by Mr. Grundy, restricting the punishment of deputy-postmasters to removal from office, was agreed to ; and the bill was reported to the senate. Mr. Calhoun renewed his motion in senate, and it was again lost, 15 to 15. In committee of the whole, the vice-president did not vote in the case of a tie. The question being then taken on the engrossment, there was again a tie, 18 to 18. The vice-president having temporarily left the chair, returned, and gave the casting vote in the affirmative. Of the senators from the free states voting in the affirmative, wefe Messrs. Buchanan, Tallmadge and Wright. Those who voted in the negative from the slave states, were Messrs. Benton, Clay, and Kent, of Maryland.

This casting vote of Mr. Van Buren, and the several votes of Mr. Wright, who voted with Mr. Calhoun on this subject, have been justified by their friends on the ground that Mr. Calhoun (to use the language of Mr. Benton,) "had made the rejection of the bill a test of alliance with northern abolitionists, and a cause for the secession of the southern states ; and if this bill had been rejected by Mr. Van Buren's vote, the whole responsibility of its loss would have been thrown upon him and the north, and the south inflamed against those states and himself—the more so, as Mr. White, of Tennessee, the opposing democratic candidate for the presidency, gave his votes for the bill." The several successive tie votes have been ascribed to design—that of placing Mr. Van Buren in this position. With this intent, other senators voted for the bill, and still others absented themselves, knowing it would not finally pass. This supposition was strengthened by the full vote given on the question of its final passage : yeas, 19; noes, 25; only four absent; the three senators from the free states, Buchanan, Tallmadge and Wright, again voting in the affirmative ; and Benton, Clay, Crittenden, Goldsborough and Kent, of Maryland, Leigh, Naudain, of Delaware, in all seven, from slave states, in the negative.

On the 11th of December, 1838, Mr. Artherton, of New Hampshire, offered a series of resolutions, denouncing petitions for the abolition of slavery in the District of Columbia, and against the slave-trade between the states, as a plan indirectly to destroy that institution within the several states ; declaring that congress has no right to do that indirectly which it can not do directly ; that the agitation of this question for the above purpose, is against the true spirit and meaning of the constitution, and an infringement of the rights of the states affected, and a breach of the public faith on which they entered into the confederacy ; and that every petition, memorial, or paper relating in any way to slavery as aforesaid, should, on presentation, without further action thereon, be laid on the table without being debated, printed or referred.

After the close of a speech in support of these resolutions, Mr. Atherton moved the previous question, which was seconded, 103 to 102. A motion to adjourn, that the resolutions might be printed, so that the house might vote understandingly, was objected to by Mr. Cushman, of New Hampshire ; and the main question was ordered, 114 to 107. The resolutions were subsequently all adopted by different votes. That which related to the reception of petitions was adopted by a vote of 127 to 78. These resolutions, as well as their author, obtained considerable notoriety, being generally referred to by the friends of the right of petition, as "Atherton's gag resolutions." Although the fifth resolution, like one adopted at a former session, prevented a formal reception of petitions, it did not apparently affect their presentation. They were daily offered as usual ; indeed, an additional object of petition was furnished ; numerous petitions being presented for the abolition of the gag resolutions.*

CHAPTER XXVIII.

PERIOD FROM 1835 TO 1842.—POLITICAL HISTORY.

Free territory annexed to Missouri, 1836.—Texas applies for annexation.—Remonstrances —Preston's resolution in 1838, in favor of it, debated by Preston, John Quincy Adams and Henry A. Wise.—The Amistad—Captives liberated.—Census of 1840.—Session of 1841-2.—Mr. Adams presents petition for dissolution of the Union.—Excitement in the house.—Resolutions of censure, advocated by Marshall.—Remarks of Mr. Wise and Mr. Adams.—Resolutions opposed by Underwood, of Kentucky, Botts, of Virginia, Arnold, of Tennessee, and others.—Mr. Giddings, of Ohio, presents petition for amicable division of the Union—resolution of censure not received.—Case of the Creole.—Censure of Mr. Giddings ; he resigns, is re-elected.

THE state of Missouri, as originally organized, was bounded on the west by a line which excluded a triangle west of said line, and between it and the Missouri, which was found, in time, to be exceedingly fertile and desirable. It

---

* Young's Political History.

was free soil by the terms of the Missouri compact, and was also covered by Indian reservations, not to be removed without a concurrence of two-thirds of the senate. Messrs. Benton and Linn, senators from Missouri, undertook the difficult task of engineering through congress a bill including this triangle (large enough to form seven counties) within the state of Missouri; which they effected, at the long session of 1835–6, so quietly as hardly to attract attention The bill was first sent to the senate's committee on the judiciary, where a favorable report was procured from Mr. John M. Clayton, of Delaware, its chairman; and then it was floated through both houses without encountering the perils of a division. The requisite Indian treaties were likewise carried through the senate; so Missouri became possessed of a large and desirable accession of territory, which has since become one of her most populous and wealthy sections, devoted to the growing of hemp, tobacco, &c., and cultivated by slaves. This is the most pro-slavery section of the state.

In 1837, the republic of Texas applied for annexation to the United States Remonstrances against it, and resolutions passed by state legislatures for and against annexation, were sent to congress and presented at the session of 1837–8. On the 4th of January, 1838, Mr. Preston, senator of South Carolina, offered the following preamble and resolution :

"WHEREAS, the just and true boundary of the United States under the treaty of Louisiana, extended on the southwest to the Rio Grande del Norte, which river continued to be the boundary line until the territory west of the Sabine was surrendered to Spain by the treaty of 1819.

"And whereas such surrender of a portion of the territory of the United States is of evil precedent and doubtful constitutionality.

"And whereas many weighty considerations of policy make it expedient to re-establish the said true boundary, and to re-annex to the United States the territory occupied by the state of Texas, with the consent of the said state :

"Be it therefore resolved, that, with the consent of the said state previously had, and whenever it can be effected consistently with the faith and treaty stipulations of the United States, it is desirable and expedient to re-annex the said territory to the United States."

On the 24th of April, 1838, the resolution was taken up for consideration, and supported by a speech, which is valuable for the historical information which it contains :

Mr. Preston said his proposition was not indecorous or presumptuous, since the lead had been given by Texas herself. The question of annexation, on certain terms, had been submitted to the people of the republic, and decided in the affirmative; and a negotiation had been proposed for effecting the object. Nor did his resolution give just cause of offense to Mexico. Its terms guarded our relations with that republic. Our intercourse with Mexico should be characterized by fair dealing, on account of her unfortunate condition, resulting from a long continued series of intestine dissensions. As long, therefore, as she should attempt to assert her pretensions by actual force, or as long as there was a reasonable prospect that she had the power and the will to resubjugate Texas, he would not interfere. He believed that period had already

passed. In this opinion he differed, perhaps, from the executive. The negotiation had been declined by the secretary of state, because it would involve
our relations with Mexico. Admitting that the executive had more extensive
and exact information upon this question than he (Mr. Preston) could have,
the resolution therefore expressed an opinion in favor of the annexation only
when it could be done without disturbing our relations with Mexico.

The acquisition of territory, Mr. Preston said, had heretofore been effected
by treaty; and this mode of proceeding had been proposed by the Texan minister, General Hunt. But he believed it would comport more with the importance of the measure, that both branches of the government should concur;
the legislature expressing a previous opinion; which being done, all difficulties
might be avoided by a treaty tripartite, between Mexico, Texas, and the United
States, in which the consent and confirmation of Mexico (for a pecuniary consideration, perhaps,) might be had without infringing the acknowledged independence and free agency of Texas.

Mr. P. proceeded to show that "the Texan territory was once a part of the
United States. In 1762, France ceded Louisiana to Spain. In 1800, Spain
re-ceded it to France. In 1804, France ceded it to the United States. The
extent of the French claim, therefore, determined ours, and included Mississippi and all the territories drained by its western tributaries. It rested upon
the discovery of La Salle, in 1683, who penetrated from Canada by land, descended the Mississippi, and established a few posts on its banks. Soon afterwards, endeavoring to enter the mouth of that river from the gulf, he passed
it unperceived, and sailing westward, discovered the bay of St. Bernard, now
called Matagorda, whence, a short distance in the interior, he established a
military post on the bank of the Guadaloupe, and took possession of the country in the name of his sovereign. The western limits of the territory, enuring
to the French crown by virtue of this discovery, was determined by the application of a principle recognized by European powers making settlements in
America, viz: that the dividing line should be established at a medium distance
between their various settlements. At the time of La Salle's settlement, the
nearest Spanish possession was a small post called Panuco, at the point where
a river of that name falls into the bay of Tampico. The medium line between
Panuco and the Guadaloupe was the Rio Grande, which was assumed as the
true boundary between France and Spain. France asserted her claim to that
boundary from 1685, the period of La Salle's discovery, up to 1762, when, by
the cession of Louisiana to Spain, the countries were united and the boundaries obliterated."

Mr. P. referred to Mr. Adams' letter to Don Onis, of March, 1818, in which
he recapitulated the testimony in favor of the French title. Mr. Jefferson expressed the same opinion. Messrs. Monroe and Pinckney, in 1805, in obedience to instructions from Mr. Madison, then secretary of state, asserted our
claim west to the Rio Grande, in their correspondence with the Spanish commissioner. Mr. Monroe, when president, held equally strong language, through

33

Mr. Adams, his secretary of state. General Jackson entertained the same opinion.

To the testimony of these presidents, he added the authority of the senator from Kentucky. During the delay on the part of Spain, in ratifying the treaty of 1819, that senator, then in the other house, taking the same view of the treaty which he (Mr. P.) was now urging—that it was a cession of a part of our territory to which the treaty-making power was incompetent—offered the following resolutions :

"1. *Resolved*, That the constitution of the United States vests in congress no power to dispose of the territory belonging to them; and that no treaty purporting to alienate any portion thereof is valid, without the concurrence of congress.

"2. *Resolved*, That the equivalent proposed to be given by Spain to the United States, for that part of Lousiana west of the Sabine, was inadequate, and that it would be inexpedient to make a transfer thereof to any foreign power."

" The author of these resolutions, in advocating them, said : ' He presumed the spectacle would not be presented of questioning, in this branch of the government, our title to Texas, which had been constantly maintained by the executive for more than fifteen years past, under three successive administrations.' And he said : ' In the Florida treaty, it was not pretended that the object was simply a declaration of where the western line of Louisiana was ; it was, on the contrary, the case of an avowed cession of territory from the United States to Spain. The whole of the correspondence manifested that the respective parties to the negotiation were not engaged so much in an inquiry where the limit of Louisiana was, as where it should be. We find various limits discussed. Finally the Sabine is fixed, which neither of the parties ever contended was the ancient limit of Louisiana. And the treaty itself proclaims its purpose to be a cession of the United States to Spain.' Such, Mr. P. said, were the opinions of the senator in 1820, and he trusted the wisdom and patriotism which warred against that rash treaty of 1819, would now be exerted against its great and growing evils, by the reännexation of Texas.

" But he took higher ground than this. Mr. Clay rested the constitutional objection upon the incompetency of the treaty-making power to alienate territory ; he (Mr. P.) considered it incompetent to the whole government. The constitution vests in congress the power "to dispose of the territory or other property of the United States." This clause was inserted to give power to effect the objects for which the states had granted these lands to the general government ; and the true exposition of the clause was found in our vast and wise land system. It was never dreamed that congress could dispose of the sovereignty of territory to a foreign power. The south, he said, had gone blindly into this treaty. The importance of Florida had led them precipitately into a measure by which we threw a gem away that would have bought ten Floridas. Under any circumstances, Florida would have been ours in a short time ; but our impatience had induced us to purchase it by a territory ten times as large, a hundred times as fertile, and to give five millions of dollars into the bargain. He acquiesced in the past ; but he proposed to seize the present fair and just occasion to remedy the mistake made in 1819; to repair, as far as possible, the evil effect of a breach of the constitution, by getting back into the Union that fair and fertile province which, in an evil hour, we severed from the confederacy.

"This proposition which now inflamed the public mind was not a novel policy. It was strange that a measure which had been urged for twelve years past should be met by a tempest of opposition ; and very strange that he should be riding upon and directing the storm, who was first to propose the annexation of Texas, as one of the earliest measures of his administration after he was made president. He had endeavored to repair the injury inflicted upon the country by the treaty of 1819. As secretary of state in 1819, he negotiated the treaty of transfer; in 1825, as president of the United States, he instituted a negotiation for the reännexation. Through his secretary of state, Mr. Clay, he instructed Mr. Poinsett, minister to Mexico, to urge a negotiation for the reäcquisition of Texas and the establishment of the southwest line of the United States at the Rio Grande del Norte. Jackson and Van Buren had continued the effort; and why it had failed, it was useless now to inquire. It was certain, that president Jackson never lost sight of it, and that he continued to look to its accomplishment as one of the greatest events of his administration, to the moment when the title of Mexico·was extinguished forever by the battle of San Jacinto.   ٠

" Mr. P. considered the boundary line established by the treaty of 1819, as an improper one, not only depriving us of an extensive and fertile territory, but winding with 'a deep indent' upon the valley of the Mississippi itself, running upon the Red river and the Arkansas. It placed a foreign nation in the rear of our Mississippi settlements, within a stone's throw of that great outlet which discharged the commerce of half the Union. The mouths of the Sabine and the Mississippi were of a dangerous vicinity. The great object of the purchase of Louisiana was to remove all possible interference of foreign states in the vast commerce of the outlet of so many states. By the cession of Texas, this policy had been to a certain extent compromised. He also referred to the instructions of secretary Van Buren to Mr. Poinsett, saying : ' The line proposed as the most desirable to us would constitute a most natural separation of the resources of the two nations.'

"Mr. P. next considered the report of a committee of the Massachusetts legislature, which said : ' The committee do not believe that any power exists in any branch of this government, or in all of them united, to consent to such a union, (viz. with the *sovereign* state of Texas,) nor, indeed, does such authority pertain, as an incident of sovereignty, or otherwise, to the government, however absolute, of any nation.' Both of these propositions he controverted. As to the powers of this government, the mistake of the committee laid in considering it, as to its nature and powers, a consolidated government. The states originally came together as sovereign states, having no power of reciprocal control. North Carolina and Rhode Island stood off for a time, and at length came in by the exercise of a sovereign discretion. So Missouri and other new states were fully organized and perfect, and self-governed, before they came in ; and so might Texas be admitted. The power to admit new states was expressly given ; and by the very terms of the grant they must be *states* before they were admitted. The power granted to congress was, not to *create*, but to *admit* new states ; the states created themselves. Missouri and Michigan had done so, and exercised all the functions of self-government, while congress deliberated whether they should be admitted. In the meantime, the territorial organization was abrogated, and the laws of congress superseded."

After some further discussion of the question, Mr. P. said: " There is no point of view in which the proposition for annexation can be considered, that any serious obstacle in point of form presents itself. If this government be a confederation of states, then it is proposed to add another state to the confederation. If this government be a consolidation, then it is proposed to add to it additional territory and population. That we can annex, and afterwards admit, the cases of Florida and Louisiana prove. We can therefore deal with the people of Texas for the territory of Texas ; and the people can be secured in the rights and privileges of the constitution, as were the subjects of Spain and France."

Having considered these " formal difficulties," he next adverted to those which exercised a more decisive influence over that portion of the Union which was offering such determined opposition to this measure. He regarded this joint movement of the northern states as a " combination conceived in a spirit of hostility towards one section, for the purpose of aggrandizing the political power of another." It could not fail to make a deep and mournful impression upon the south, that the opposition to the proposed measure was contemporaneous with the recent excitement on the subject of abolition. He said: "All men, of all parties, from all sections, in and out of office, Mr. Adams most conspicuous amongst them, desired the aquisition of Texas, until the clamorous interference in the affairs of the south was caught up in New England from old England. Then, for the first time, objections were made to this measure ; then those very statesmen who were anxious for the acquisition of Texas for their glory, found out that it would subvert the constitution and ruin the country. You are called upon to declare that the southern portion of your confederacy, by reason of certain domestic institutions, in the judgment of your petitioners wicked and detestable, is to be excluded from some part of the benefits of this government. The assumption is equally insulting to the feelings and derogatory to the constitutional rights of the south. We neither can nor ought—I say it, Mr. President, in no light mood or wrong temper—we neither can nor ought to continue in political union on such terms."

" Mr. P. spoke of the diminution of the comparative political power of the south. The sceptre, he said, had passed from them, and forever. All that was left them was to protect themselves. All they asked was some reasonable check upon an acknowledged power ; some approach to equipoise in the senate. All the power they coveted was the power to resist incursions. He suspected that the idea of checking the extension of domestic slavery was but a hollow and hypocritical pretext to cover political designs. He did not think the extension of slave territory and the increase of the slaveholding population would increase the number of slaves. Instead of this, annexation would rather prevent such increase. We stand entirely on the defensive ; we desire *safety*, not power, and we must have it. Give us safety and repose, by doing what all your most trusted and distinguished statesmen have been so long anxious to do. Give them to us by restoring what you wantonly and unconstitutionally deprived us of. Give us this just and humble boon, by repairing the violated integrity of your territory, by augmenting your wealth and power, by extending the empire of law, liberty, and Christianity."

In the house of representatives, on the 12th of December, 1837, Mr. Adams presented a large number of memorials against the annexation of Texas, and moved that these and all others presented by himself and his colleagues at the extra session, be referred to a select committee. His colleagues had assented to approve the motion. Mr. Howard, of Maryland, having moved their reference to the committee on foreign affairs, Mr. Adams expressed his views on the question of annexation in a manner which subjected him to several interruptions.

Mr. Adams said he and his colleagues viewed this question as one which involved even the integrity of the union—a question of the most deep, abiding and vital interest to the whole American nation. "For," said he, "in the face of this house, and in the face of Heaven, I avow it as my solemn belief that the annexation of an independent foreign power to this government would, *ipso facto*, be a dissolution of this Union. And is this a subject for the peculiar investigation of your committee on foreign affairs ?" Mr. A. said the question involved was, whether a foreign nation—acknowledged as such in a most unprecedented and extraordinary manner, by this government, a nation ' damned to everlasting fame ' by the reïnstitution of that detestable system, slavery, after it had once been abolished within its borders—should be admitted into union with a nation of freemen. "For, sir," said Mr. A., " that name, thank God, is still ours ! And is such a question as this to be referred to a committee on *foreign* affairs ?"

Mr. A. said the exact grounds upon which the memorialists based their prayer were not officially known to the house. He had presented one hundred and ninety petitions upon this subject, signed by some twenty thousand persons, and his colleagues had presented collectively a larger number. Members from other states had also presented similar memorials ; but his colleagues had thought it fitting to move the reference to a select committee of those only which he and they had presented. All had the same object ; and they contained nothing that had the least connection with the foreign affairs of the country.

These memorialists from Massachusetts, Mr. A. said, had observed with alarm and terror the conduct of the government towards Mexico, during the last, and as far as it had gone, of the present administration, in relation to the affairs of Texas.   One strong reason of the remonstrance, on the part of his constituents, was, that the nation sought to be annexed to our own had its origin in violence and fraud; an impression by no means weakened by the impulses given by the late and present administrations to push on this senseless and wicked war with Mexico.   They had seen the territory of that republic invaded by the act of the executive of this government, without any action of congress; and they had seen conspirators coming here, and contriving and concerting their plans of operations with members of our own government! Amidst all these demonstrations, they had heard the bold and unblushing pretense that the people of Texas were struggling for freedom, and that the wrongs inflicted upon them by Mexico had driven them into insurrection, and forced them to fight for liberty !

There had been recent evidence afforded the country as to the real origin of the insurrection.   A citizen of Virginia, (Dr. Mayo,) who for years had held offices under the late administration, had just issued a pamphlet in this city, giving a copy of a letter by himself, in December, 1830, to the President of the United States, in which he declared that, in February, 1830, the person now called *President Houston* did in this city disclose to himself, the author of this letter, all his designs as to this then state of the republic of Mexico— Texas.   What that letter contained as to the disclosure of a scheme to be executed, was now a matter of history.   It disclosed the particulars of a conversation which detailed the plan of the conspiracy, since consummated, to rob Mexico of the province of Texas.

Mr. A. then inquired what were the pretenses upon which the disseverment of Texas from Mexico were justified.   As early as 1824, the legislature of the republic of Mexico, to its eternal honor, passed an act for the emancipation of slaves, and the abolition of slavery; and the only real ground of rebellion was that very decree ; the only object of the insurrection, the revival of the detested system of slavery; and she had adopted a constitution *denying to her legislature even the power of ever emancipating her slaves!*

Mr. Adams did not wish to refer the memorials to the committee on foreign affairs, because it was not properly constituted.   Its chairman, (Mr. Howard,) was himself a slaveholder, and, it was feared, entertained a widely different opinion as to the morality of slavery from that held by the mass of the memorialists; and that a majority of the committee were in favor of annexing Texas to this government.   It was conformable with the parliamentary rule to appoint a majority of the committee in favor of the prayer of the memorialists. This seemed to him as one of the incidents of freedom of petition itself.   Six out of nine of the committee on foreign affairs were slaveholders; and he took it for granted that every member of the house who was a slaveholder, was ready for the annexation of Texas ; and its accomplishment was sought, not for the acquisition of so much new territory, but as a new buttress to the tottering institution of slavery.

After a brief interruption by southern members, Mr. A. proceeded :

He said discussion must come ; though it might for the present be delayed, he believed it would not forever be smothered by previous questions, motions to lay on the table, and all the other means and arguments by which the institution of slavery was wont to be sustained on that floor—the same means and arguments, in spirit, which in another place have produced murder and arson. Yes, sir, the same spirit which led to the inhuman murder of Lovejoy at Alton——

The chair remarked that Mr. A. was straying from the question of reference; and some conversation ensued as to his right to proceed, which he was at length permitted to do.

In the course of his remarks, he said that he and his colleagues had seen, in reading the late message of the executive, how much was *not* in that document as well as how much *was* in it. It contained much allusion to the grievances of this government at the hands of Mexico, and none to our relation with Texas. The annexation of Texas and the proposed war with Mexico were one and the same thing, though expressed in different forms. The message was adverse to the prayer of the memorialists. Under the decision of the chair, he should reserve what he had to say further on this point until the mouths of members inclined to advocate the cause of freedom upon that floor, should be permitted to be opened more widely; if, indeed, there was any hope that that time should ever arrive.

Mr. Wise said there was no need, at present, of any such reference as had been proposed. Texas had attempted to open a negotiation for admission; but her overture had been declined on the ground of our relations with Mexico. No memorial in favor of such a measure had ever been before the house. It would be time enough to discuss the subject dwelt upon with so much feeling by the gentleman from Massachusetts, when it should come up regularly for discussion. He therefore moved to lay the motions of reference on the table; and having refused to withdraw his motion at the request of Mr. Rhett and Mr. Dawson to enable them to reply to Mr. Adams, the question was taken, and decided in the affirmative. Yeas, 127; nays, 68.

On the 13th of June, 1838, the committee on foreign affairs reported that there was no proposition pending in the house either for the admission of Texas as a state, or for its territorial annexation to the United States. And in October it was announced in the official paper (Globe) that, since the proposition submitted by Texas for admission into the Union had been declined, the Texan minister had communicated to our government the formal and absolute withdrawal of that proposition.

In August, 1839, a vessel lying near the coast of Connecticut, under suspicious circumstances, was captured by Lieut. Gedney, of the brig Washington, and taken into New London. This vessel was a schooner, called L'Amistad, bound from Havana to Guanaja, Port Principe, with fifty-four blacks and two passengers on board. The former, four nights after they were out, rose and murdered the captain and three of the crew; then took possession of the vessel with the intention of returning to Africa. The two passengers were Jose Ruiz and Pedro Montez, the former owning forty-nine of the slaves, and most of the cargo; the latter claiming the remaining five, all children from seven to twelve years of age, and three of them females. These two men were saved to navigate the vessel. Instead, however, of steering for the coast of Africa, they navigated in a different direction, whenever they could do so without the knowledge of the Africans. It appeared that the slaves had been purchased at Havana, soon after their arrival from Africa. Cingues, who was the son of an African chief, and leader of the revolt, with thirty-eight others of the revolters, was committed to trial; and the three girls were put under bonds to appear and testify.

A demand was soon after made upon our government by the acting Spanish minister in this country, for the surrender of the Amistad, cargo, and alleged slaves, to the Spanish authorities.

The children were brought before the circuit court of the United States, held at Hartford, in September, on a writ of *habeas corpus*, with a view to their discharge, on the ground that they were not slaves; proof of which was given by two of the prisoners who testified that the children were native Africans. The discharge was resisted by Mr. Ingersoll, counsel for the Spanish claimants, who stated that the persons were libeled in the district by Capt. Gedney, his officers and crew, as property; they were also libeled by the Spanish minister as the slave property of Spanish subjects, and as such ought to be delivered up; and they were libeled by the district attorney, that they might be delivered up to the executive, in order to their being sent to their native country, if it should be found right that they should be so sent. The counsel presumed that this (circuit) court would not, under this writ, take this case out of the legitimate jurisdiction of the district court, as, if the decision of that court should not be satisfactory, the matter could be brought before this court by appeal.

It was maintained by Mr. Baldwin, counsel for the children, that they had been feloniously and piratically captured in Africa—contrary to the laws of Spain—consequently, they were not property, and therefore the district court was ousted of its jurisdiction. The district judge had not issued his warrant to take these individuals. This he could not do without first judicially finding that they were property. The warrant issued by his honor to the marshal was to take the vessel and other articles of *personal property*. These children were not, and never could become personal property. They formed a part of a number of persons, who, born free, were captured and reduced to slavery. They had come here, not as slaves, but as free; and we are asked first to make them slaves, and then give them up to the Spaniards. But we can only deliver up *property;* and before they can be delivered up, they must be proved to be *property.* Mr. Staples, associate counsel for the Africans, said Montez had the hardihood to come into a court of justice in our free country, and in contravention of our treaty with Spain, to ask the surrender of these human beings, when the very act he desired us to countenance, would, by his own sovereign's decree, have subjected him to forfeiture of all his goods and to transportation and he would himself have become a slave. This was a case of felony; and felony could not confer property.

The next day, a second writ of *habeas corpus* having been issued, all the Africans were before the court. The counsel recapitulated the facts of the case, and again denied the jurisdiction of the district court. As a court of admiralty, it could do nothing with them but as property; and the applicant must first prove them to be property. Some of them were taken on shore; these were within the jurisdiction of the common law.

As to the libel of the district attorney at the suit of the Spanish minister, what had the minister to do with it? The parties claimed were neither fugitives or criminals. The district attorney libels them and prays that they may be kept in custody, that, if at some future time it should appear that they had been brought hither illegally, they might be delivered up to the president to be sent back to their own country. The counsel then asked their discharge. He said they should be taken care of (as it was right they should be) by the state of Connecticut.

The counsel for the claimants followed in support of the jurisdiction of the district court; and the district attorney in support of his libel on behalf of the executive.

The decision of the court (Judge Thompson) in relation to the motion of the prisoners' counsel to discharge the Africans, was to *deny the motion*, as the question before the court was simply as to the jurisdiction of the district court over this subject. If the seizure was made upon the high seas—and the grand jury said it was made a mile from the shore—then the matter was right —fully before the court for this district. If, as was supposed by the counsel on both sides, the seizure was made within the district of New York, the court could endeavor to acertain the locality. To pass upon the question of property, belonged to the district court. Should either party be dissatisfied with the decision of that court, an appeal could be taken to the circuit court, and afterwards to the supreme court of the United States.

The court said the question now disposed of had not been affected by the manner in which the grand jury had disposed of the case upon the directions of the court. They had only found that there had been no criminal offense committed which was cognizable by the courts of the United States. Murder committed on board a foreign vessel with a foreign crew and foreign papers, was not such an offense; but an offense against the laws of the country to which the vessel belonged. But if the offense had been against the law of nations, this court would have jurisdiction. The murder of the captain of the Amistad was not a crime against the law of nations.

The district court was opened; and the judge said he should order the district attorney to investigate the facts to ascertain where the seizure was made; and then adjourned the court to November.

At the adjourned term of the court in November, it was pleaded in behalf of the Africans, that neither the constitution, laws, or any treaty of the United States, nor the law of nations, gave this court any jurisdiction over their persons; they therefore prayed to be dismissed. The counsel for Captain Gedney denied that the Africans had anything to do with the question now before the court. It was a claim for salvage; and the parties were the libelants, (Gedney and the other officers and crew of the Washington,) and Ruiz and Montez, owners of the vessel and cargo. Gedney and others claimed salvage for saving the property of these Spaniards, who did not resist the claim.

The district attorney presented a claim in behalf of the United States for the vessel, cargo and negroes, with a view to their restoration to their owners, who were Spanish subjects, without hindrance or detention, as required by our treaty with Spain.

The interpreter being absent and sick, the court adjourned to New Haven in January next.

In January, the decision of Judge Judson was given. The blacks who murdered the captain and others on board the schooner, were set free. But if they had been whites, they would have been tried and executed as pirates. The schooner having been proved to have been taken on the "high seas," the jurisdiction of the court was established. The libel of Gedney and others had been properly filed, and the seizers were entitled to salvage. Ruiz and Montez had established no title to the Africans, who were undoubtedly Bozal negroes, or negroes recently imported from Africa in violation of the laws of Spain. The demand of restoration made by the Spanish minister, that the question might be tried in Cuba, was refused, as by Spanish laws the negroes could not be enslaved; and therefore they could not properly be demanded for trial. One of them a Creole, and legally a slave, and wishing to be returned to Havana, a restoration would be decreed under the treaty of 1795. These Africans were to be delivered to the president, under the act of 1819, to be transported to Africa.

An appeal was taken from the decree of the district judge to the circuit court, judge Thompson presiding, who affirmed that decree. And the government of the United States, at the instance of the Spanish minister, here appealed to the supreme court of the United States. That court affirmed the judgment of the district court of Connecticut in every respect, except as to sending the negroes back to Africa: they were discharged as free men.

A deep interest seems to have been taken by the British government in the case of these Africans. Their minister in this country, Mr. Fox, was instructed to intercede with our government in their behalf; and their minister in Spain was directed to ask for their liberty if they should be delivered to the Spaniards at the request of the Spanish minister at Washington, and should be sent to Cuba; and to urge Spain to enforce the laws against Montez and Ruiz and any other Spanish subjects concerned in the transaction in question.

A disposition was manifested on the part of our government to effect the delivery of the captives to the Spanish authorities, at Cuba, to be there dealt with according to the laws of Spain. The friends of the Africans in this country deprecated such event, apprehending that the freedom of the negroes might not be obtained through the Spanish tribunals.

On the 10th of February, 1840, probably suspecting unfairness on the part of the administration, a resolution was offered, requesting the president to communicate to the house copies of any demand by the Spanish government for the surrender of the Africans, and of the correspondence between the state department and the Spanish minister and the district attorney of the United States in the judicial district of Connecticut.

On the 20th of January, 1841, while the question of the prisoners was still pending in the supreme court of the United States, the British minister addressed to Mr. Forsyth, secretary of state, a letter representing the interest felt by his government in the case of the African negroes, mentioning the obligation of Spain, by treaty with Great Britain, to prohibit the slave trade from the 30th of May, 1820, and the mutual engagements of the United States and Great Britain, by the 10th article of the treaty of Ghent, to use their endeavors for the entire abolition of the slave trade. And as the freedom of the negroes may depend upon the action of the United States government, he expresses the hope that the president will find himself empowered to take such measures in their behalf, as should secure them their liberty.

Mr. Forsyth, in his answer of the 1st of February, says, in substance, that the introduction of the negroes into this country did not proceed from the wishes or direction of our government The vessel and the negroes had been demanded by the Spanish minister, and the grounds of that demand were before the judicial tribunals. He tells Mr. Fox that our government is not willing to erect itself into a tribunal between Spain and Great Britain ; that he, (Mr. Fox,) had doubtless observed from the correspondence published in a congressional document, that the Spanish minister intended to restore the negroes, should their delivery to his government be ordered, to the island of Cuba, to be placed under the protection of the government of Spain. There was the proper place, and there would be a full opportunity, to discuss questions arising under the Spanish laws and the treaties of Spain with Great Britain.

The decision of the supreme court was awaited with deep interest by all who sympathized with the negroes. Mr. Adams, who had not argued a case for thirty or forty years before that court, made a very elaborate as well as able argument in their behalf. The opinion of the court was pronounced by Mr. Justice Story, early in March, 1841, affirming the decision of the district court in every particular, except that which ordered the negroes to be delivered to the president to be transported to Africa. The court reversed this part of the decree, and ordered the cause to be remanded to the circuit court which had affirmed the same, with directions to enter in lieu thereof, that the negroes be declared free, and be discharged from suit.*

[The word *libel* used in the above case signifies, in courts of admiralty, "a declaration or charge in writing, exhibited in court, particularly against a ship or goods, for a violation of the laws of trade or revenue ;" also when a prize is brought into port, the captors make a writing called *libel.*]

*Young's Political History.

CENSUS OF 1840.—SLAVE POPULATION.

Alabama	253,532	Mississippi	195,211
Arkansas	19,935	Missouri	58,240
District of Columbia	4,694	New Jersey	674
Delaware	2,605	New York	4
Florida	25,717	Pennsylvania	64
Georgia	280,944	North Carolina	245,817
Illinois	331	South Carolina	327,038
Kentucky	182,258	Tennessee	183,059
Louisiana	168,452	Virginia	449,087
Maryland	89,737	Aggregate,	2,487,455.

In the ten years between 1830 and 1840, the aggregate increase amounted to 478,412. Slavery had decreased in the District of Columbia, Delaware, Maryland and Virginia.

On the 24th of January, 1842, Mr. Adams presented a petition to the house, signed by forty-six citizens of Haverhill, Massachusetts, for the adoption of measures peaceably to dissolve the Union, assigning as one of the reasons the inequality of benefits conferred upon different sections, one section being annually drained to sustain the views and course of the other without adequate return. Mr. Adams moved its reference to a select committee, with instructions to report an answer showing the reasons why the prayer of the petitioners should *not* be granted.

This matter produced considerable excitement, questions and motions followed. Mr. Gilmer, of Virginia, submitted as a question of privilege the following : "Resolved, that in presenting to this house a petition for the dissolution of the Union, the member from Massachusetts has justly incurred the censure of this house." The resolution was objected to as out of order ; the speaker decided that being a question of privilege it was in order. Mr. Adams hoped the resolution would be received and debated, desiring the privilege of addressing the house in his own defense. A motion to lay Gilmer's resolution on the table was negatived, 94 to 112, Mr. Adams himself voting in the negative.

Mr. Marshall, of Kentucky, then offered as a substitute for Gilmer's resolution, a preamble and two resolutions, declaring a proposition to the representatives of the people to dissolve the constitution which they were sworn to support, to be " a high breach of privilege, a contempt offered to the house, a direct proposition to each member to commit perjury, and involving necessarily in its consequences the destruction of our country, and the crime of high treason ; " that Mr. Adams, in presenting the petition, had "offered the deepest indignity to the house, and insult to the people," and would, if "unrebuked and unpunished, have disgraced his country in the eyes of the world." It was farther resolved, that this insult, the first of the kind ever offered, deserved expulsion ; but, as an act of grace and mercy they would only inflict upon him "their severest censure, for the maintenance of their own purity, and dignity ; and for the rest, they turn him over to his own conscience and the indignation of all true American citizens."

A debate then ensued, which continued, with little intermission, until the 7th of February. The nature of the subject of the resolutions, the serious charges which they contained, and the individual accused, as well as certain incidental topics which it embraced, imparted to this debate a surpassing interest throughout the country. For several days Mr. Marshall, Mr. Wise, and Mr. Adams, were the chief participators. Mr. Wise undertook to show, in the course of his speeches, that there was a combination of pretended philanthropists of Great Britain and the abolitionists of this country to overthrow slavery in the southern states; and he charged Mr. Adams with being an ally of British emissaries in the furtherance of this object.

Mr. Wise said he should at the proper time ask to be excused from voting for the resolution of censure. Personally, he had not censured him; politically, he had. He said: "The gentleman was honored, time honored, hoary—but he could not add, with wisdom. The gentleman had immense power, the power of station, the power of fame, the power of age, the power of eloquence, the power of the pen; and any man was greatly mistaken who should say or think, that the gentleman was MAD. The gentleman might say with an apostle, 'I am not mad, most noble Festus,' though he could not add, 'but speak forth the words of truth and soberness.' All who knew him would say he was not mad. In a political, not in a personal sense, Mr. Wise would say, and with entire sincerity of heart, the gentleman was far more wicked than weak. A mischief might be done by him. Mr. Wise believed he was disposed to do it, and would wield his immense intellectual, moral, and political power to effect it. That mischief was the dissolution of this Union, and the agent of that dissolution, should it ever be effected, Mr. Wise did in his heart believe, would be the gentleman from Massachusetts. Governed by his reputation, by his habits, by all considerations arising from the belief of personal wrongs, his passions were roused, and his resentment and his vengeance would be wreaked on the objects of his hatred, if he could reach them. If this state of mind were monomania, then it was hereditary; no matter what might be its cause, it was dangerous—deadly. The gentleman was astute to design, obstinate and zealous in power, and terrible in action, and an instrument well fitted to dissolve the Union."

Mr. Adams questioned the right of the house to entertain the resolutions of Mr. Mashall, because they charged him with crimes of which the house had no jurisdiction; and because, if it entertained the jurisdiction, it deprived him of rights secured to him by the constitution. All that the house could try him for, was a contempt of the house, under the resolution of Mr. Gilmer. "But," said Mr. Adams, " there was a trial in this house, about four or five years ago, of a member of the house for crime. [Mr. Wise had had connection with the duel between Messrs. Graves and Cilley, in which the latter was killed.] There came into this house then a man with his hands and face dripping with the blood of murder, the blotches of which were yet hanging upon him; and the question was put, upon the proposition of those very democrats to whom he has this day rendered the tribute and homage of his thanks, that he should be tried by this house for that crime, the crime of murder. I opposed the trial of that crime by this house. I was willing that the parties to that atrocious crime should be sent to their natural judges, to have an impartial trial; and it is very probable that *I* saved that blood-stained man from the censure of the house at the time."

Mr. Wise, interrupting Mr. Adams, inquired of the speaker whether his character or conduct was involved in the issue before the house, and whether it was in order to charge him with the crime of murder; a charge made by a man who had at the time defended him from the charge on that floor; and who had, as he was informed by one of Mr. Adams' own colleagues, defended him before thousands of people in Massachusetts.

Mr. Adams said he never had defended the man on the merits of the case; and never did believe but what he was the guilty man, and that the man who pulled the trigger was but an instrument in his hands. He repeated, that the house had no power to try and punish him for the crimes charged against him. The constitution provides, that "in all criminal prosecutions the accused shall enjoy the right of a speedy and public trial by an impartial jury." The house was not an impartial tribunal. "I wish," said Mr. Adams, "to speak of the slaveholders of this house and of the Union with respect. There are three classes of persons included in the slave interest as representatives here. As to the slaveholder, I have nothing to say against him, except if I am to be tried by him, I shall not have an impartial trial. I challenge him for partiality—for preädjudication upon this question, as a question of contempt, which I repeat, is the only charge on which I can be made to answer here, I say he is not impartial. Every slaveholder has not only an interest, but the most sordid of all interests—a personal, pecuniary interest—which will govern him. I come from a portion of the country where slavery is known only by name; I come from a soil that bears not the foot of a slave upon it. I represent here the descendants of Bedford, and Winslow, and Carver, and Alden—the first who alighted on the rock of Plymouth. And am I, the representative of the descendants of these men—of the *free* people of the state of Massachusetts, that bears not a slave upon it—am I to come here and be tried for high treason because I presented a petition—*a petition*—to this house, and because the fancy or imagination of the gentleman from Kentucky supposes that there was anti-slavery or the abolition of slavery in it? The gentleman charges me with subornation of perjury and of high treason, and he calls upon this house, *as a matter of mercy and grace,* not to expel me for these crimes, but to inflict upon me the severest censure they can; and to decide upon that, there are one hundred members of this house who are slaveholders. Is any one of them impartial? No. I trust they will not consider themselves as impartial men; I trust that many of them will have those qualms of conscience which the gentleman from Accomac (Mr. Wise) assigns as his reason for being ex cused, and that they will not vote upon a question on which their personal, pecuniary, and most sordid interests are at stake."

Mr. Underwood, of Kentucky, also maintained that the house was not the proper tribunal before which Mr. Adams, if guilty of the crimes alleged, ought to be arraigned. He defended the right of petition. He believed where there was no power to grant the prayer of the petitioners, there was no right to petition. But he had voted against the 21st rule, because by that petitioners were excluded who had a right to be heard. As a slaveholder, he had differed from his brethren in reference to the whole gag proceedings. In reference to all gag rules, he said, away with them. Let those who wish, discuss this topic as much as they please. He attempted to show that the proceeding against Mr. Adams was to punish him for an imputed motive. What had he been guilty of? Had he sanctioned the petition? How could they judge his motive? Nor had he violated the rules of order. He had simply presented a petition; and they were attemptiog to punish him for the manner in which he had considered it his duty to represent a portion of the people of Massachusetts. He told gentlemen to beware how they put it into the power of the gentleman from Massachusetts to go home and tell his constituents that he was a martyr to the right of petition.

Mr. Botts, of Virginia, also defended Mr. Adams. "He did not approve all that he had said on that floor. But he would not wound the feelings of that venerable gentleman. He believed he had expressed many sentiments in the irritability of the weight of years that hung on him, which his own calm reflection would condemn. There was enough passing under his immediate observation to provoke the gentleman, and if he might use the expression, to 'bedevil' him. But what was the offense with which he stood charged? He had presented a petition; and he had asked permission to present a remonstrance, and appeal to the petitioners against the folly of their course. This was not the first time the house had heard of the dissolution of the Union. A gentleman from South Carolina, now a member of this body, (Mr. Rhett,) had three or four years ago actually drawn up a resolution, asking congress to appoint a committee, to consist of one member from each state, to devise measures for the dissolution of the Union. [This called out Mr. Rhett in explanation. It was not his wish to dissolve the Union; he intended it as an amendment to a motion to refer with instructions to report a bill for abolishing slavery in the District of Columbia. He expected it to be laid on the table with the original motion. His design was to place before congress and the people what he believed to be the true issue upon this great and vital question. The resolution proposed a committee of two from each state.] It was, said Mr. Botts, not only the doctrine of the gentleman, but of the majority of his state. They held that a state had a right to secede from the Union. If one state had such right, others had."

Mr. Botts "considered this affair a great farce—a storm in a tea-pot. Talk of censuring the gentleman from Massachusetts! Look at the other end of this avenue. A man at the head of the right arm of the defense of this nation—the secretary of the navy, (Mr. Upshur,)—the last time he had had conversation with him, was an open, avowed advocate of the immediate dissolution of the Union. [Mr. Wise: I deny it.] Mr. Botts repeated the declaration, and said, when the secretary denied it, he would undertake to prove his statement. If there were to be any charges for high treason, the secretary of the navy should be put on his trial."

Mr. Arnold, of Tennessee, spoke at length in opposition to the resolutions, and in defense of Mr. Adams. " He could have no possible motive for desiring the dissolution of the Union. He had presented this petition, because he wanted, as the last and most glorious act of a long life, to send forth, in these times of general confusion and political degeneracy, a paper with healing in its wings—a report adverse to the prayer of the petition, and which should state, in a luminous and convincing manner, all the strong arguments in favor of union. He would like to see such a paper from the able pen of that venerable patriot. It would dissipate all doubts as to the purity and patriotism of its author.

" But for the crime of presenting a petition with such an object in view, the house was to put on record against him a charge of aiding in high treason, and in suborning the members of that house to the commission of perjury; and he was to consider it as a great favor that the house did not expel him, but contented itself with giving him a reprimand. Mr. Arnold should like to witness the spectacle. He should like to see that gentleman standing at the bar, with his palsied hand, his bare head, and whitened locks, to be rebuked by the speaker, comparatively a mere boy, after having been visited with the vituperation and vindictive persecution of another, as much a boy in comparison. What a spectacle ! Mr. Arnold turned from the thought with loathing and disgust, and so would the nation. So far from helping the cause of the south, it would kindle up against her a blaze high as the very heavens. He was against it—utterly and totally against it—from principle and from policy too."

Mr. Adams demanded that before the house came to the conclusion on the motives assumed in this charge, they should send him out to be tried before a tribunal of the country. Then he should have the benefit secured by the constitution. And he wanted, in that case, to have two or three calls made on the departments for information necessary for his defense ; and for this purpose he sent several resolutions to the chair. The first of these resolutions requested the president to communicate copies of the correspondence relating to an act of South Carolina directing the imprisonment of colored persons arriving from abroad in the ports of that state ; also, copies of the act or acts, and of any official opinions given by judge Johnson of the unconstitutionality of the said acts. [The act here referred to, subjects *any* colored person landing from a vessel in any port of South Carolina, to be arrested and imprisoned, and in case of inability to pay the costs incurred by such imprisonment, to be sold for the same as a slave.] One of the other resolutions called for a copy of any letter or letters from the president to a certain member of the house, relating to the rule of the house excluding from reception anti-slavery petitions, or to any agency of the said member in introducing the rule. The first two resolutions, after considerable further debate, were adopted. Upon the two relating to the " 21st rule," the vote was not then taken.

Mr. A. maintained that he was guilty of no offense; he had, on presenting the petition, declared it was the last thing he would ever vote for. He also repeated what he had said on former occasions, that he had given notice to the house, the petitioners, and the whole country, and his constituents among them, that if they sent to him their petitions for abolishing slavery in the District of Columbia, because they expected him to support them, they were mistaken.

After Mr. Adams had occupied two or three days more in his defense, a disposition was manifested to get rid of the subject, by laying it on the table. He was willing to acquiesce in such a proposition, provided it should never be taken up again. The subject was thereupon laid on the table, by a vote of 106 to 93; and the reception of the petition was refused, 40 to 106.

On the 28th of February, 1842, Mr. Giddings, of Ohio, presented a petition from upwards of eighty citizens of Austinburg, in his district, of both political parties, it was said, praying for an amicable division of the Union, separating the free and slave states. Mr. G. moved a reference of the petition to a select committee, with instructions to report against the prayer of the petitioners, and to assign reasons why their prayer should not be granted. Mr. Triplett, of Kentucky, considering the petition disrespectful both to the house and the man who presented it, moved that it be not received. The question on receiving the petition was decided in the negative: yeas 24, nays 116.

Mr. Kennedy, of Maryland, offered a resolution declaring that all such petitions should thereafter be deemed offensive, and the member presenting them liable to censure. The resolution, however, was not received. For a different act, however, Mr. Giddings, at a later period of the session, incurred a formal censure of the house.

In October, 1841, the brig Creole left Richmond, for New Orleans, with a cargo consisting principally of tobacco and slaves, about 135 in number. On the 7th of November, the slaves rose upon the crew, killed a man on board named Hewell, part owner of the negroes, and severely wounded the captain and two of the crew. Having obtained command of the vessel, they directed her to be taken into the port of Nassau, in the British island of New Providence, where she arrived on the 9th. An investigation was made by British magistrates, and an examination by the American consul. Nineteen of the negroes were imprisoned by the local authorities as having been concerned in the mutiny and murder. Their surrender to the consul, to be sent to the United States for trial, was refused, until the advice of the government of England could be had. A part of the remaining slaves were liberated and suffered to go beyond the control of the master of the vessel and the consul.

Mr. Webster, secretary of state, in a letter dated January 29th, 1842, instructed Mr. Everett, our minister at London, to present the case to the British government, "with a distinct declaration, that, if the facts turn out as stated, this government think it a clear case for indemnification."

A different view of the question was taken by England. Lord Brougham stated in the house of lords, others concurring and and none dissenting, that "the only treaty by which England or America could claim any refugees,

34

either from the other, related exclusively to murderers, forgers, and fraudulent bankrupts; and even that treaty had expired. There was no international law by which they could claim, or we give up, the parties who had taken possession of the Creole; and those persons must stand or fall by British laws only." All agreed that there was no authority to surrender the fugitives, nor hold in custody the mutineers; and it was stated that orders had been sent for their liberation.

On the 21st of March, 1842, Mr. Giddings submitted a series of resolutions on a subject which, he said, had excited some interest in the other end of the capitol, and in the nation, and which he wished to lay before the country. These resolutions declared jurisdiction over slavery to belong exclusively to the states; that by the 8th section of the first article of the constitution, the states had surrendered to the federal government jurisdiction over commerce and navigation upon the high seas; that slavery, being an abridgment of the natural rights of man, can exist only by force of *positive municipal law*, and is necessarily confined to the territorial jurisdiction of the power creating it; that when the brig Creole left the territorial jurisdiction of Virginia, the slave laws of that state ceased to have jurisdiction over the persons on board the said brig, who became amenable only to the laws of the United States, and who, in resuming their natural rights of personal liberty, violated no law of the United States; and that all attempts to reënslave the said persons, or to exert our national influence in favor of the coastwise slave-trade, or to place the nation in an attitude of maintaining a "commerce in human beings," were subversive of the rights and injurious to the feelings and the interests of the free states, unauthorized by the constitution, and incompatible with our national honor.

Mr. Ward, of New York, moved the previous question on these resolutions. Mr. Everett, of Vermont, with a view, probably, to their discussion, moved to lay them on the table. This motion was rejected: yeas 52, nays 125. The previous question having been seconded, and the main question ordered, Mr. Giddings, in the midst of the confusion and excitement which ensued, withdrew his resolutions.

Mr. Botts then offered a resolution, upon the adoption of which he intended to move the previous question. The preamble to the resolution deprecated the resolutions of Mr. Giddings, "touching a subject of negotiation between the United States and Great Britain of a most delicate nature," and as possibly "involving those nations and the whole civilized world in war;" declared it to be the duty of every good citizen, and especially of every representative of the people, to discountenance all efforts to create excitement and division among the people under such circumstances; and denounced them as justifying mutiny and murder, in terms shocking to all sense of law, order and humanity: therefore,

"*Resolved,* That this house hold the conduct of said member as altogether unwarranted and unwarrantable, and deserving the severe condemnation of the people of this country, and of this body in particular."

An excited debate ensued, which continued during the remainder of that day and the next, and in which sundry questions of order, appeals, and of privilege were discussed. Several members having expressed a desire that Mr. Giddings should be heard in his defense, he rose and said: "I stand before the house in a peculiar situation." Mr. Cooper, of Georgia, objected to his proceeding, but at the request of his colleagues withdrew his objection. But Mr. G. did not resume the floor. He, however, addressed to the reporter of the National Intelligencer a note stating, that when he was called to order the last time, he had written and desired to state to the house as follows :

"Mr. Speaker: I stand before the house in a peculiar situation. It is proposed to pass a vote of censure upon me, substantially for the reason that I differ in opinion from a majority of the members. The vote is about to be taken without giving me time to be heard. It would be idle for me to say that I am ignorant of the disposition of a majority to pass the resolution. I have been violently assailed in a personal manner, but have had no opportunity of being heard in reply. I do not now stand here to ask for any favor or to crave any mercy at the hands of the members. But in the name of an insulted constituency—in behalf of one of the sovereign states of this Union—in behalf of the people of these states and the federal constitution—I *demand* a hearing, agreeably to the rights guaranteed to me, and in the ordinary mode of proceeding. I accept of no other privilege ; I will receive no other courtesy."

The resolution of Mr. Botts was adopted by a vote of 125 to 69; the preamble, 129 to 66.

Mr. Giddings then addressed to the speaker a letter of resignation, which was the next day laid before the house. He immediately departed for his residence in Ohio—was reëlected on the 26th of April, at a special election called by the governor of the state, by a majority of about 3,500 votes over his opponent—and returned to his seat in the house on the 5th of May.*

CHAPTER XXIX.

Period from 1842 to 1849.—Annexation of Texas.

Object of the acquisition set forth by Mississippi, Alabama and Tennessee legislatures, and by Mr. Wise and Mr. Gilmer, 1842.—Tyler's treaty of annexation—rejected by the senate.—Presidential campaign of 1844.—Clay and Van Buren on annexation.—Calhoun's Letter.—Session of 1844-5; joint resolution passed, and approved March 1, 1845.—Mexican minister protests.—War with Mexico.—The $2,000,000 bill.—Wilmot Proviso.—Session of 1847-8.—Bill to organize Oregon territory.—Power of Congress over slavery in the territories discussed.—Dix and Calhoun.—Mr. Calhoun controverts the doctrines of the Declaration of Independence.—Cass' Nicholson letter.

THE project for the annexation of Texas had not been abandoned. The *object* to be attained by the acquisition is thus set forth in the report of a committee of the Mississippi legislature :

---

* American Statesman.

"But we hasten to suggest the importance of the annexation of Texas to this republic, upon grounds somewhat local in their complexion, but of an import infinitely grave and interesting to the people who inhabit the southern portion of this confederacy, where it is known that a species of domestic slavery is tolerated and protected by law, whose existence is prohibited by the legal regulations of other states of this confederacy; which system of slavery is held by all, who are familiarly acquainted with its practical effects, to be of highly beneficial influence to the country within whose limits it is permitted to exist.

"The committee feel authorized to say that this system is cherished by our constituents as the very palladium of their prosperity and happiness, and whatever ignorant fanatics may elsewhere conjecture, the committee are fully assured, upon the most diligent observation and reflection on the subject, that the south does not possess within her limits a blessing with which the affections of her people are so closely entwined and so completely enfibered, and whose value is more highly appreciated, than that which we are now considering.

"It may not be improper here to remark, that during the last session of congress, when a senator from Mississippi proposed the acknowledgment of Texan independence, it was found, with a few exceptions, the members of that body were ready to take ground upon it, as upon the subject of slavery itself.

"With all these facts before us, we do not hesitate in believing that these feelings influenced the New England senators, but one voting in favor of the measure; and, indeed, Mr. Webster has been bold enough, in a public speech recently delivered in New York, to many thousand citizens, to declare that the reason that influenced his opposition was his abhorrence to slavery in the south, and that it might, in the event of its recognition, become a slaveholding state. He also spoke of the efforts making in favor of abolition; and that being predicated upon, and aided by the powerful influence of religious feeling, it would become irresistible and overwhelming.

"This language, coming from so distinguished an individual as Mr. Webster, so familiar with the feelings of the north, and entertaining so high a respect for public sentiment in New England, speaks so plainly the voice of the north as not to be misunderstood.

"We sincerely hope there is enough good sense and genuine love of country among our fellow-countrymen of the northern states, to secure us final justice on this subject; yet we cannot consider it safe or expedient for the people of the south to entirely disregard the efforts of the fanatics, and the opinions of such men as Webster, and others who countenance such dangerous doctrines.

"The northern states have no interests of their own which require any special safeguards for their defense, save only their domestic manufactures; and God knows they have already received protection from government on a most liberal scale; under which encouragement they have improved and flourished beyond example. The south has very peculiar interests to preserve—interests already violently assailed and boldly threatened.

"Your committee are fully persuaded that this protection to her best interests will be afforded by the annexation of Texas; an equipoise of influence in the halls of congress will be secured which will furnish us a permanent guarantee of protection."

The states of Alabama and Tennessee had also adopted resolutions in favor of annexation. Hon. Henry A. Wise, in a speech in congress, Jan. 26, 1842, said:

"True, if Iowa be added on the one side, Florida will be added on the other. But there the equation must stop. Let one more northern state be admitted, and the equilibrium is gone — gone forever. The balance of interests is gone—the safeguard of

American property—of the American constitution—of the American Union, vanished into thin air. This must be the inevitable result, unless by a treaty with Mexico, the south can add more weight to her end of the lever! Let the south stop at the Sabine, (the eastern boundary of Texas,) while the north may spread unchecked beyond the Rocky Mountains, and the southern scale must kick the beam!"

Mr. Gilmer, member of congress and formerly governor of Virginia, wrote to a friend in January, 1842:

"You ask if I have expressed the opinion that Texas would be annexed to the United States. I answer, yes; and this opinion has not been adopted without reflection, or without a careful observation of causes, which I believe are rapidly bringing about this result. I do not know how far these causes have made the same impression on others; but I am persuaded that the time is not distant when they will be felt in all their force. The excitement which you apprehend may arise; but it will be temporary, and, in the end, salutary.

"I am, as you know, a strict constructionist of the powers of our federal government; and I do not admit the force of mere precedent to establish authority under written constitutions. The power conferred by the constitution over our foreign relations, and the repeated acquisitions of territory under it, seem to me to leave this question open as one of expediency.

"But you anticipate objections with regard to the subject of slavery. This is indeed a subject of extreme delicacy, but it is one on which the annexation of Texas will have the most salutary influence. Some have thought that the proposition would endanger our Union. I am of a different opinion. I believe it will bring about a better understanding of our relative rights and obligations.

"Having acquired Louisiana and Florida, we have an interest and a frontier on the Gulf of Mexico, and along our interior to the Pacific, which will not permit us to close our eyes or fold our arms with indifference to the events which a few years may disclose in that quarter. We have already had one question of boundary with Texas; other questions must soon arise, under our revenue laws, and on other points of necessary intercourse, which it will be difficult to adjust. The institutions of Texas, and her relations with other governments, are yet in that condition which inclines her people (who are our countrymen) to unite their destinies with ours. This must be done soon or not at all."

Texas was also making movements for annexation; resolutions and a bill for the purpose were introduced into the legislature. A Texas paper announced that Mr. Upshur, our secretary of state, had proposed to Mr. Van Zandt, the Texas chargé at Washington, to open a negotiation for annexing Texas to the Union. This proved to be true. A treaty was concluded at Washington on the 12th of April, 1844, by John C. Calhoun, secretary of state, on the part of the United States, and Isaac Van Zandt and J. Pinckney Henderson on the part of Texas. This treaty was communicated to the senate on the 22d, and ordered to be printed in confidence for the use of the senators. On the 27th of April, notwithstanding the injunctions of secrecy upon the action of the senate, the New York Post announced the conclusion of the treaty, and published the president's message and documents which accompanied it.

On the 8th of June, the question was taken in the senate on the ratification of the treaty, a majority of two-thirds being necessary to ratify. Only 16 sen-

ators voted in the affirmative, and 25 in the negative.   Of the senators from
the free states who voted for the treaty, were Messrs. Buchanan and Sturgeon,
of Pennsylvania, Mr. Breese, of Illinois, and Mr. Woodbury, of New Hampshire.   Of the democrats from the free states who voted against the treaty,
were Mr. Fairfield, of Maine, Mr. Atherton, of New Hampshire, Mr. Niles,
of Connecticut, Mr. Wright, of New York, Messrs. Allen and Tappan, of
Ohio; also, Mr. Benton, of Missouri, a slave state.

The vote on the question of ratification does not, however, indicate the views
of senators on the abstract question of annexation.   One objection to the
treaty was, that it would involve the United States in a war with Mexico.
Another was, that Texas claimed disputed territory; and to receive Texas
would compel our government to defend the claim against Mexico.   It was
also objected, that the annexation was unconstitutional.

In the debate in secret session on the ratification, a large number of senators took part; among whom were Messrs. Benton, Choate, Wright, Walker,
and M'Duffie; the two last in favor of the treaty, the others in opposition.

Mr. Benton's great speech was delivered on the 16th, 17th, and 20th of
May, and was in support of resolutions offered by him on the 13th, declaring,

1st. That the ratification of the treaty would be the adoption of the Texan
war with Mexico, and would devolve its conclusion upon the United States.

2d. That the treaty-making power does not extend to the power of making
war, and that the president and senate have no right to make war, either by
declaration or by adoption.

3d. That Texas ought to be reünited to the American union, as soon as it
can be done with the consent of a majority of the people of the United States
and of Texas, and when Mexico shall either consent to the same, or acknowledge the independence of Texas, or cease to prosecute the war against her,
(the armistice having expired,) on a scale commensurate to the conquest of the
country.

Mr. Benton contended that the treaty proposed to annex much more territory than originally belonged to Texas; and therefore the proposition for the
" reännexation of Texas " was a fraud in words.   It was not pretended, even
by those who used that word, that the province of Texas, when it was ceded
in 1819 to Spain, extended farther than the boundaries included between the
Sabine and the Rio del Norte, and the Gulf of Mexico and the Red River,
whilst the republic of Texas, as defined in the treaty, included the whole extent of the Rio del Norte, and embraced portions of the department of New
Mexico, with its capital, being many hundred miles of a neighbor's dominion,
with whom we had treaties of peace and friendship and commerce—a territory
where no Texan force had ever penetrated, and including towns and villages
and custom-houses now in the peaceful possession of Mexico.

In a message to the senate subsequent to that accompanying the treaty, the
president has asserted the doctrine that the treaty signed by him was ratified
from that moment; and, consequently, that part of Mexico above mentioned

must be and remain "reännexed," until the acquisition should be rejected by the senate. In relation to this, Mr. Benton speaks thus :

"The president in his special message of Wednesday last informs us that we have acquired a title to the ceded territory by his signature to the treaty, wanting only the action of the senate to perfect it; and that, in the mean time, he will protect it from invasion, and for that purpose has detached all the disposable portions of the army and navy to the scene of action. This is a caper about equal to the mad freaks with which the unfortunate emperor Paul, of Russia, was accustomed to astonish Europe about forty years ago. By this declaration, the thirty thousand Mexicans in the left half of the valley of the Rio del Norte are our citizens, and standing, in the language of the president's message, in a hostile attitude towards us, and subject to be repelled as invaders. Taos, the seat of the custom-house, where our caravans enter their goods, is ours; governor Armijo is our governor, and subject to be tried for treason if he does not submit to us; twenty Mexican towns and villages are ours, and their peaceful inhabitants, cultivating their fields and tending their flocks, are suddenly converted, by a stroke of the president's pen, into American citizens, or American rebels. This is too bad : and, instead of making themselves party to its enormities, as the president invites them to do, I think rather that it is the duty of the senate to wash its hands of all this part of the transaction by a special disapprobation. The senate is the constitutional adviser of the president, and has the right, if not the duty, to give him advice when the occasion requires it. I therefore propose, as an additional resolution, applicable to the Rio del Norte boundary only—the one which I will read and send to the secretary's table—and on which, at the proper time, I shall ask the vote of the senate. This is the resolution :

'Resolved, That the incorporation of the left bank of the Rio del Norte into the American union, by virtue of a treaty with Texas, comprehending as the said incorporation would do, a part of the Mexican departments of New Mexico, Chihuahua, Coahuila, and Tamaulipas, would be an act of direct aggression on Mexico ; for all the consequences of which the United States would stand responsible.'

Having shown the effect of the treaty on the Rio Grande frontier, Mr. B. took up the treaty itself, under all its aspects and in its whole extent, and assumed four positions in relation to it, namely :

1. That the ratification of the treaty would be, of itself, war between the United States and Mexico.

2. That it would be unjust war.

3. That it would be war unconstitutionally made.

4. That it would be war upon weak and groundless pretext."

Mr. M'Duffie, on the 23d of May, replied to Mr. Benton. The question as to boundary, he said, had been exhausted by the conclusive argument of Mr. Walker, of Mississippi, and he would not discuss it. It had been contended by senators that the ratification of the treaty would subject us to the charge of a violation of the public faith. In answer to this objection, Mr. M'Duffie referred to the case of France, in 1778. When the United States were waging an unequal war with Great Britain, she came to our aid, recognized our independence, and formed with us a treaty of alliance, offensive and defensive. Had any historian mentioned this as a breach of national faith on the part of France? Had our government contracted such an alliance with Texas when Santa Anna was marching to meet a disgraceful defeat at San Jacinto, it would have violated no national faith, nor any dictate of international law. He contended that she had maintained her independence; we had recognized it : so had Great Britain, France, Holland, and Belgium. She possessed all the attributes of national sovereignty, and the elements of self-government, more so than Mexico herself. Texas, he said, had a right to enter into a treaty of annexation if she chose; and who would deny her that right? Could she not dispose of herself as she pleased? And did it not follow that the United States had a corresponding and an equal right to receive her? The right of property implied the right of the proprietor to sell, and the correlative right of every other person to purchase.

But it was said the ratification would involve us in a war with Mexico. So he himself thought in 1836, when Texas was a "rebellious province;" but since the battle of San Jacinto, Mexico had not made a single military movement toward recovering her lost dominions. She had done nothing that deserved the name of war. Appealing to the gasconading proclamation of Mexico, the senator from Missouri had asked, "Is this peace?" The orders to the home squadron, and the army of observation sent to the Sabine, to watch the movements of Mexico, should any be made, and promptly report them to headquarters, that they might as promptly be reported to congress, the senator had pronounced an act of war. If to employ a corps of observation was to make war, then we were at war with the powers in the West Indies, on the Mediterranean, and on the coast of Africa; for we had squadrons in every sea to protect our commerce, and to make war on pirates. The proclamation of Mexico, and the counter proclamations and defiances of Texas, he did not consider war, as did the senators on the other side.

Mr. M'Duffie referred to the proposition to Mexico made by Mr. Clay, when secretary of state under Mr. Adams, in 1825, to purchase Texas, when the war between Spain and Mexico was still in existence. So in 1829, when Mexico was invaded by a large army, and her ports were blockaded, Mr. Van Buren, by order of Gen. Jackson, made to Mexico a proposition to purchase Texas.

Having advocated the *right* to receive Texas, he proceeded to show the duty of making the treaty. Great Britain should not be allowed to obtain the control of Texas by a treaty of guaranty stipulating for extensive commercial privileges. He had never till now realized the justice of Mr. Monroe's declaration, that no European power must ever be permitted to establish a colony on this continent. And he urged the danger to the slave property of the south, if Great Britain should get control of Texas. They had a right to demand from the government protection to their property. Annexation, too, would operate as a safety-valve to let off their superabundant slave population, which would render them more happy, and the whites more secure. And with regard to the time of annexation, he adopted the language of Gen. Jackson, "now or never."

Immediately after the treaty was rejected, Mr. Benton gave notice of a bill for the annexation of Texas, with the consent of Mexico. On the 10th of April, pursuant to notice, he brought in the bill, which authorized and advised the president to open negotiations with Mexico and Texas for adjusting boundaries and annexing Texas to the United States, on the following bases :

1st. The boundary to be in the desert prairie west of the Nueces, and along the highlands and mountain heights which divide the waters of the Mississippi from those of the Rio del Norte, and to latitude 42 degrees north.

2d. The people of Texas, by a legislative act or otherwise, to express their assent to annexation.

3d. A state to be called "Texas," with boundaries fixed by herself, and an extent not exceeding that of the largest state in the union, to be admitted into the union by virtue of this act, on an equal footing with the original states.

4th. The remainder of the territory, to be called "the Southwest Territory," and to be held and disposed of by the United States as one of their territories.

5th. Slavery to be forever prohibited in the northern half of the annexed territory.

6th. The assent of Mexico to such annexation and boundary to be obtained by treaty, or to be dispensed with when congress may deem such assent unnecessary.

7th. Other details to be adjusted by treaty so far as they may come within the scope of the treaty-making power.

On presenting his bill, Mr. Benton spoke nearly two hours. He said his was not a new burst of affection for the possession of the country, as his writings a quarter of a century ago would testify. He disapproved the course of the executive in not having first consulted congress. The rejection of the treaty having wiped out all cause of offense to Mexico, he thought it best to commence again, and at the right end—with the legislative branch, by which means we should proceed regularly and constitutionally. As to the boundary, he had followed the basis laid down by Jefferson, fixing, as the limit to be adopted in settling the boundary with Spain, all the territory watered by the tributaries to the Mississippi, and made it applicable to Mexico and Texas. He did not attach so much importance to the consent of Mexico as to make it an indispensable condition, yet he regarded it as something to be respectfully sought for. But if it were not obtained, it was left to the house to say when that consent became necessary. He wished to continue in amity with Mexico. Those who underrated the value of a good understanding with her, knew nothing of what they spoke. Mexico took the products of our farms, and returned the solid silver of her mines. Our trade with her was constantly increasing. In 1821, the year in which she became independent, we received from her $80,000 ; in 1835, $8,500,000. When we began to sympathize with Texas, this trade rapidly fell off, until it got down to one million and a half. As the earliest and most consistent friend of Texas, he desired peace with Mexico, in order to procure the ultimate annexation of Texas. If Mexico, blind to her interests, should refuse to let Texas take her natural position as a part of the valley of the Mississippi, let congress say in what case the consent of Mexico might cease to be necessary.

Mr. Benton severely censured that party, who, while an armistice was sub-sisting between Mexico and Texas, which bid fair to lead to peace, rushed in with a firebrand to disturb these relations of amity. For this act they must stand condemned in the eyes of Christendom. Every wise man must see that Texas and Mexico were not naturally parts of a common country. The set-tlements of Mexico had never taken the direction of Texas. In a northeast-ern direction, they had not extended much over the Rio Grande ; they had come merely to the pastoral regions, but had never professed strength enough to subdue the sugar and cotton sections. He alluded to his own far back prophecies and writings concerning Texas. Messrs. Walker and Woodbury he termed " Texas neophytes," who had been so anxious to make great demon-strations of love for Texas. For himself, he had no such anxiety, because his sentiments had always been known. With him it was not a question " now or never," but Texas then, now, and always

Mr. Benton said he had provided against another Missouri agitation. For those who regarded slavery as a great moral evil, in which he, perhaps, did not differ much from them, there was a provision which would neutralize the slave influence. He would not join the fanatics on either side—those who were running a muck for or against slavery.

The senator from South Carolina, in his zeal to defend his friends, goes be-yond the line of defense and attacks me ; he supposes me to have made anti-annexation speeches ; and certainly, if he limits the supposition to my speeches against the treaty, he is right. But that treaty, far from securing the annexa-tion of Texas, only provides for the disunion of these states. The annexation of the whole country as a territory, and that upon the avowed ground of laying it all out into slave states, is an open preparation for a Missouri question and a dissolution of the union. I am against that ; and for annexation in the mode pointed out in my bill. I am for Texas—for Texas with peace and hon-or, and with the union. Those who want annexation on these terms should support my bill ; those who want it without peace, without honor, and without the union, should stick to the lifeless corpse of the defunct treaty."

The president, having been foiled in his scheme of annexation by treaty, ap-pealed to the house of representatives, in a message, dated the 10th of June, two days after the rejection of the treaty, accompanied by the rejected treaty with the correspondence and documents which had been submitted to the senate. The president says in the message, that he does not perceive the force of the objections of the senate to the ratification. Negotiations with Mexico, in ad-vance of annexation, would not only prove abortive, but might be regarded as offensive to Mexico and insulting to Texas. We could not negotiate with

Mexico for Texas, without admitting that our recognition of her independence was fraudulent, delusive, or void. Only after acquiring Texas, could the question of boundary arise between the United States and Mexico, a question purposely left open for negotiation with Mexico, as affording the best opportunity for the most friendly and pacific arrangements. He asserted that Texas no longer owed allegiance to Mexico; she was, and had been for eight years, independent of the confederation of Mexican republics. Nor could we be accused of violating treaty stipulations. Our treaty with Mexico was merely commercial, intended to define the rights and secure the interests of the citizens of each country. There was no bad faith in negotiating with an independent power upon any subject not violating the stipulations of such treaty.

In view of the importance of the subject, he invited the immediate attention of the representatives of the people to it; and for so doing he found a sufficient apology in the urgency of the matter, as annexation would encounter great hazard of defeat, if something were not *now* done to prevent it. He transmitted to the house a number of private letters on the subject from citizens of Texas entitled to confidence.

Much had occurred to confirm his confidence in the statements of General Jackson, and of his own statement in a previous message, that "instructions had already been given by the Texan government to propose to the government of Great Britain forthwith, on the failure of the treaty, to enter into a treaty of commerce, and an alliance offensive and defensive." He also referred the house to a letter from Mr. Everett from London, which he seemed to construe into an intention to interfere with the contemplated arrangement between the United States and Texas. Although he regarded annexation by treaty as the most suitable form in which it could be effected, should congress deem it proper to resort to any other expedient compatible with the constitution, and likely to accomplish the object, he was ready to yield his prompt and active coöperation. He says: "The question is not as to the manner in which it shall be done, but whether it shall be accomplished or not. The responsibility of deciding this question is now devolved upon you."

The message was communicated at too late a day for deliberation and action at this session. Congress adjourned on the 17th of June.

During the presidential campaign of 1844, the annexation of Texas constituted a leading issue between the two great political parties. Before the meeting of the nominating conventions, public sentiment had designated Clay and Van Buren as candidates for the presidency. Accordingly, letters were addressed to them to obtain an expression of their views upon the annexation of Texas.

The letters of Messrs. Clay and Van Buren, taking ground against annexation, without the consent of Mexico, as an act of bad faith and aggression, which would necessarily result in war, which appeared in the spring of 1844, make slight allusions to the slavery aspect of the case. In a later letter, Mr. Clay declared that he did not oppose annexation on account of slavery, which he regarded as a temporary institution, which, therefore, ought not to stand in the way of a permanent acquisition. And, though Mr. Clay's last letter on the subject, prior to the election of 1844, reiterated and emphasized all his objections to annexation under the existing circumstances, he did not include the existence of slavery.

In his first letter Mr. Clay said, "there were those who favored and those who opposed the annexation of Texas, from its supposed effect upon the balance of political power between two great sections of the union. He discountenanced the motive of acquiring territory for the purpose of strengthening one part of the union against another. If to-day Texas should be obtained to strengthen the south, to-morrow Canada might be acquired to add strength to the north. In the progress of this spirit of universal dominion, the part of the union now the weakest, would find itself still weaker from the impossibility of securing new theaters for those peculiar institutions which it is charged with being desirous to extend. But he doubted whether Texas would really add strength to the south. From the information he had of that country, he thought it susceptible of a division into five states of convenient size and form; three of which he thought would be unfavorable to the employment of slave labor, and would be free states, while only two of them would be slave states. This might serve to diminish the zeal both of those who oppose and those who urge annexation "

In conclusion, he thus sums up his opinions : He "considers the annexation of Texas, at this time, without the assent of Mexico, as a measure compromising the national character, involving us certainly in war with Mexico, probably with other foreign powers, dangerous to the integrity of the union, inexpedient to the present financial condition of the country, and not called for by any general expression of public opinion."

The sentiments expressed in the following extracts from Mr. Van Buren's letter are worthy of observation : "We must look to this matter as it really stands. We shall act under the eye of an intelligent, observing world ; and the affair cannot be made to wear a different aspect from what it deserves if even we had the disposition (which we have not) to throw over it disguises of any kind. We should consider whether there is any way in which the peace of the country can be preserved, should an immediate annexation take place, save one—and that is, according to present appearances, the improbable event that Mexico will be deterred from the farther prosecution of the war by the apprehension of our power. The question then recurs, if, as sensible men, we cannot avoid the conclusion that the immediate annexation of Texas would, in all human probability, draw after it a war with Mexico, can it be expedient to attempt it ? Of the consequences of such a war, the character it might be made to assume, the entanglements with other nations which the position of a belligerent almost unavoidably draws after it, and the undoubted injuries which might be inflicted upon each—notwithstanding the great disparity of their respective forces, I will not say a word. God forbid that an American citizen should ever count the cost of any appeal to what is appropriately denominated the last resort of nations, whenever that resort becomes necessary either for the safety or to vindicate the honor of his country. There is, I trust, not one so base as not to regard himself and all he has to be forever and at all times subject to such a requisition. But would a war with Mexico, brought on under such circumstances, be a contest of that character? Could we hope to stand justified in the eyes of mankind for entering into it; more especially if its commencement is to be preceded by the appropriation to our own uses of the territory, the sovereignty of which is in dispute between two nations, one of which we are to join in the struggle? This, sir, is a matter of the gravest import, one in respect to which no American statesman or citizen can possibly be indifferent."

It was not long after this letter appeared, before it was apparent that Mr. Van Buren was to be abandoned. Movements were soon made in many places to prevent his nomination. Annexation was to southern democrats an object for which even Mr. Van Buren was not deemed too great a sacrifice. Meetings were held for the purpose of revoking the instructions which had been given to delegates to support Mr. Van Buren; and resolutions were passed recommending to them to cast their votes for men known and pledged to be in favor of annexation. In New York and other northern states, the "democracy" protested against these southern movements to defeat Mr. Van Buren.

Notwithstanding Mr. Clay's hostility to the annexation of Texas, he was nominated unanimously in the whig convention. Mr. Van Buren did not fare so well in the democratic convention. He received a clear majority on the first ballot, but a rule of the convention required two-thirds. He was eventually sacrificed to make room for James K. Polk, who was in favor of the annexation.

Of course many of the northern democrats who had deprecated annexation, now became ardent advocates of the "great American measure," but there were some who still protested against it. The organ of this class was the New York Evening Post, whose editor, with six other gentlemen, issued a private circular to some of their friends in different parts of the state. The letter explains its object:

"SIR—You will, doubtless, agree with us, that the late Baltimore convention placed the democratic party at the north in a position of great difficulty. We are constantly reminded that it rejected Mr. Van Buren, and nominated Mr. Polk, for reasons connected with the immediate annexation of Texas—reasons which had no relation to the principles of the party. Nor was that all. The convention went beyond the authority delegated to its members, and adopted a resolution on the subject of Texas (a subject not before the country when they were elected, upon which, therefore, they were not instructed,) which seeks to interpolate into the party creed a new doctrine, hitherto unknown among us, at war with some of our established principles, and abhorrent to the opinions and feelings of a great majority of northern freemen. In this position, what was the party of the north to do? Was it to reject the nominations, and abandon the contest? Or should it support the nominations, rejecting the untenable doctrine interpolated at the convention, and taking care that their support should be accompanied by such an expression of their opinion as to prevent its being misinterpreted? The latter alternative has been preferred, and we think wisely; for we conceive that a proper expression of their opinion will save their votes from misconstruction, and that proper efforts will secure the nomination of such members of congress as will reject the unwarrantable scheme now pressed upon the country."

About this time the following official dispatch was addressed by Mr. Calhoun, Mr. Tyler's secretary of state, to the American Minister at Paris, the Hon. Wiliam R. King:

"DEPARTMENT OF STATE, ⎱
WASHINGTON, August 12, 1844. ⎰

"SIR—I have laid your dispatch, No. 1, before the president, who instructs me to make known to you that he has read it with much pleasure, especially the portion which relates to your cordial reception by the king, and his assurance of friendly feelings toward the United States. The president, in particular, highly appreciates the declaration of the king, that, in no event, would any steps be taken by his government in the slightest degree hostile, or which would give to the United States just cause of complaint. It was the more gratifying from the fact, that our previous information was calculated to make the impression that the government of France was prepared to unite with Great Britain in a joint protest against the annexation of Texas, and a joint effort to induce her government to withdraw the proposition to annex, on condition that Mexico should be made to acknowledge her independence. He is happy to infer from your dispatch that the information, so far as it relates to France, is, in all probability, without foundation. You did not go further than you ought, in assuring the king that the object of annexation would be pursued with unabated vigor, and in giving your opinion that a decided majority of the American people were in its favor, and that it would certainly be annexed at no distant day. I feel confident that your anticipation will be fully realized at no distant period.

"Every day will tend to weaken that combination of political causes which led to the opposition of the measure, and to strengthen the conviction that it was not only expedient, but just and necessary.

"You were right in making the distinction between the interests of France and England in reference to Texas—or rather, I should say, the apparent interests of the two countries. France cannot possibly have any other than commercial interests in desiring to see her preserve her separate independence, while it is certain that England looks beyond, to political interests, to which she apparently attaches much importance. But, in our opinion, the interest of both against the measure is more apparent than real; and that neither France, England, nor even Mexico herself, has any in opposition to it, when the subject is fairly viewed and considered in its whole extent, and in all its bearings. Thus viewed and considered, and assuming that peace, the extension of commerce, and security, are objects of primary policy with them, it may, as it seems to me, be readily shown that the policy on the part of those powers which would acquiesce in a measure so strongly desired by both the United States and Texas, for their mutual welfare and safety, as the annexation of the latter to the former, would be far more promotive of these great objects than that which would attempt to resist it.

" It is impossible to cast a look at the map of the United States and Texas, and to note the long, artificial and inconvenient line which divides them, and to take into consideration the extraordinary increase of population and growth of the former, and the source from which the latter must derive its inhabitants, institutions, and laws, without coming to the conclusion that it is their destiny to be united, and of course, that annexation is merely a question of time and mode. Thus regarded, the question to be decided would seem to be, whether it would not be better to permit it to be done now, with the mutual consent of both parties, and the acquiescence of these powers, than to attempt to resist and defeat it.

" If the former course be adopted, the certain fruits would be the preservation of peace, great extension of commerce by the rapid settlement and improvement of Texas, and increased security, especially to Mexico. The last, in reference to Mexico, may be doubted; but I hold it not less clear than the other two.

" It would be a great mistake to suppose that this government has any hostile feelings toward Mexico, or any disposition to aggrandize itself at her expense. The fact is the very reverse.

" It wishes her well, and desires to see her settled down in peace and security ; and is prepared, in the event of the annexation of Texas, if not forced into conflict with her, to propose to settle with her the question of boundary, and all others growing out of the annexation, on the most liberal terms. Nature herself has clearly marked the boundary between her and Texas by natural limits, too strong to be mistaken. There are few countries whose limits are so distinctly marked; and it would be our desire, if Texas should be united to us, to see them firmly established, as the most certain means of establishing permanent peace between the two countries, and strengthening and cementing their friendship. Such would be the certain consequence of permitting the annexation to take place now, with the acquiescence of Mexico ; but very different would be the case if it should be attempted to resist and defeat it, whether the attempt should be successful for the present or not. Any attempt of the kind would not improbably lead to a conflict between us and Mexico, and involve consequences, in reference to her and the general peace, long to be deplored on both sides, and difficult to be repaired. But, should that not be the case, and the interference of another power defeat the annexation for the present, without the interruption of peace, it would but postpone the conflict, and render it more fierce and bloody when it might occur.

" Its defeat would be attributed to enmity and ambition on the part of that power by whose interference it was occasioned, and excite deep jealousy and resentment on the part of our people, who would be ready to seize the first favorable opportunity to effect by force what was prevented from being done peaceably by mutual consent. It is not difficult to see how greatly such a conflict, come when it might, would endanger the general peace, and how much Mexico might be the loser by it.

" In the mean time, the condition of Texas would be rendered uncertain, her settlement and prosperity in consequence retarded, and her commerce crippled; while the general peace would be rendered much more insecure. It could not but greatly affect us. If the annexation of Texas should be permitted to take place peaceably now, (as it would without the interference of other powers,) the energies of our people would, for a long time to come, be directed to the peaceable pursuits of redeeming and bringing within the pale of cultivation, improvement, and civilization, that large portion of the continent lying between Mexico on one side and the British possessions on the other, which is now, with little exception, a wilderness, with a sparse population, consisting, for the most part, of wandering Indian tribes.

" It is our destiny to occupy that vast region; to intersect it with roads and canals; to fill it with cities, towns, villages, and farms; to extend over it our religion, customs, constitution, and laws, and to present it as a peaceful and splendid addition to the domains of commerce and civilization. It is our policy to increase by growing and spreading out into unoccupied regions, assimilating all we incorporate: in a word, to increase by accretion, and not through conquest, by the addition of masses held together by the adhesion of force.

" No system can be more unsuited to the latter process, or better adapted to the former, than our admirable federal system. If it should not be resisted in its course, it will probably fulfill its destiny without disturbing our neighbors, or putting in jeopardy the general peace; but if it be opposed by foreign interference, a new direction would be given to our energy, much less favorable to harmony with our neighbors, and to the general peace of the world.

" The change would be undesirable to us, and much less in accordance with what I have assumed to be primary objects of policy on the part of France, England, and Mexico.

" But, to descend to particulars: it is certain that while England, like France, desires the independence of Texas, with the view to commercial connections, it is not less so that one of the leading motives of England for desiring it is the hope that, through her diplomacy and influence, negro slavery may be abolished there, and ultimately, by consequence, in the United States and throughout the whole of this continent. That its ultimate abolition throughout the entire continent is an object ardently desired by her, we have decisive proofs in the declaration of the Earl of Aberdeen, delivered to this department, and of which you will find a copy among the documents transmitted to congress with the Texan treaty. That she desires its abolition in Texas, and has used her influence and diplomacy to effect it there, the same document, with the correspondence of this department with Mr. Packenham, also to be found among the documents, furnishes proof not less conclusive. That one of the objects of abolishing it there is to facilitate its abolition in the United States, and throughout the continent, is manifest from the declaration of the abolition party and societies both in this country and in England. In fact, there is good reason to believe that the scheme of abolishing it in Texas, with a view to its abolition in the United States, and over the continent, originated with the prominent members of the party in the United States; and was first broached by them in the (so called) world's convention, held in London in the year 1840, and through its agency brought to the notice of the British government.

" Now, I hold, not only that France can have no interest in the consummation of this grand scheme, which England hopes to accomplish through Texas, if she can defeat the annexation, but that her interests, and those of all the continental powers of Europe, are directly and deeply opposed to it.

" It is too late in the day to contend that humanity or philanthropy is the great object of the policy of England in attempting to abolish African slavery on this continent. I do not question but humanity may have had a considerable influence in abolishing slavery in her West India possessions, aided, indeed, by the fallacious calculation that the labor of the negroes would be at least as profitable, if not more so, in consequence of the measure. She acted on the principle that tropical products can be produced cheaper by free African labor and East India labor, than by slave labor. She knew full well the value of such products to her commerce, navigation, navy, manufactures, revenue, and power. She was not ignorant that the support and maintenance of her political preponderance depended on her tropical possessions, and had no intention of diminishing their productiveness, nor any anticipation that such would be the effect, when the scheme of abolishing slavery in her colonial possessions was adopted. On the contrary, she calculated to combine philanthropy with profit and power, as is not unusual with fanaticism. Experience has convinced her of the fallacy of her calculations. She has failed in all her objects. The labor of her negroes has proved far less productive, without affording the consolation of having improved their condition.

" The experiment has turned out to be a costly one. She expended nearly one hundred million of dollars in indemnifying the owners of the emancipated slaves. It is estimated that the increased price paid since, by the people of Great Britain, for sugar and other tropical productions, in consequence of the measure, is equal to half that sum ; and that twice that amount has been expended in the suppression of the slave-trade ; making together two hundred and fifty millions of dollars as the cost of the experiment. Instead of realizing her hope, the result has been a sad disappointment. Her tropical products have fallen off to a vast amount. Instead of supplying her own wants, and those of nearly all Europe with them, as formerly, she has now, in some of the most important articles, scarcely enough to supply her own. What is worse, her own colonies are actually consuming sugar produced by slave-labor, brought direct to England, or refined in bond, and exported and sold in her colonies as cheap, or cheaper, than can be produced there ; while the slave-trade, instead of diminishing, has been in fact carried on to a greater extent than ever. So disastrous has been the result, that her fixed capital invested in tropical possessions, estimated at the value of nearly five hundred millions of dollars, is said to stand on the brink of ruin.

" But this is not the worst ; while this costly scheme has had such ruinous effects on the tropical productions of Great Britain, it has given a powerful

35

stimulus, followed by a corresponding increase of products, to those countries which had had the good sense to shun her example. There has been vested, it has been estimated by them, in the production of tropical products, since 1808, in fixed capital, nearly $4,000,000,000, wholly dependent on slave-labor. In the same period, the value of their products has been estimated to have risen from about $72,000,000, annually, to nearly 220,000,000 ; while the whole of the fixed capital of Great Britain, vested in cultivating tropical products, both in the East and West Indies, is estimated at only about $830,000,000, and the value of the products annually at about $50,000,000. To present a still more striking view of three articles of tropical products (sugar, coffee, and cotton), the British possessions, including the East and West Indies, and Mauritius, produced in 1842, of sugar, only 3,995,771 pounds; while Cuba, Brazil, and the United States, excluding other countries having tropical possessions, produced 9,600,000 pounds; of coffee, the British possessions produced only 27,393,003 pounds, while Cuba and Brazil produced 201,590,125 pounds; and of cotton, the British possessions, including shipments to China, only 137,443,-446 pounds, while the United States alone produced 790,479,275 pounds.

" The above facts and estimates have all been drawn from a British periodical of high standing and authority,* and are believed to be entitled to credit.

" The vast increase of the capital and production on the part of those nations who have continued their former policy toward the negro race, compared with that of Great Britain, indicates a corresponding relative increase of the means of commerce, navigation, manufactures, wealth, and power. It is no longer a question of doubt, that the great source of wealth, prosperity, and power of more civilized nations of the temperate zone (especially Europe, where the arts have made the greatest advance), depends, in a great degree, on the exchange of their products with those of the tropical regions. So great has been the advance made in the arts, both chemical and mechanical, within the few last generations, that all the old civilized nations can, with but a small part of their labor and capital, supply their respective wants ; which tends to limit within narrow bounds, the amount of the commerce between them, and forces them all to seek for markets in the tropical regions, and the more newly settled portions of the globe. Those who can best succeed in commanding those markets, have the best prospect of outstripping the others in the career of commerce, navigation, manufactures, wealth, and power.

This is seen and felt by British statesmen, and has opened their eyes to the errors which they have committed. The question now with them is, how shall it be counteracted ? What has been done cannot be undone. The question is, by what means can Great Britain regain and keep a superiority in tropical cultivation, commerce, and influence ? Or, shall that be abandoned, and other nations be suffered to acquire the supremacy, even to the extent of supplying British markets, to the destruction of the capital already vested in their pro-

*Blackwood's Magazine for June, 1841.

duction? These are the questions which now profoundly occupy the attention of her statesmen, and have the greatest influence over her councils.

"In order to regain her superiority, she not only seeks to revive and increase her own capacity to produce tropical productions, but to diminish and destroy the capacity of those who have so far outstripped her in consequence of her error. In pursuit of the former, she has cast her eyes to her East India possessions—to Central and Eastern Africa—with the view of establishing colonies there, and even to restore, substantially, the slave-trade itself, under the specious name of transporting her free laborers from Africa to her West India possessions, in order, if possible, to compete successfully with those who have refused to follow her suicidal policy. But these all afford but uncertain and distant hopes of recovering her lost superiority. Her main reliance is on the other alternative—to cripple or destroy the productions of her successful rivals. There is but one way by which it can be done, and that is by abolishing African slavery throughout this continent; and that she openly avows to be the constant object of her policy and exertions. It matters not how, or from what motive, it may be done—whether it be by diplomacy, influence, or force; by secret or open means; and whether the motive be humane or selfish, without regard to manner, means, or motive. The thing itself, should it be accomplished, would put down all rivalry, and give her the undisputed supremacy in supplying her own wants, and those of the rest of the world; and thereby more than fully retrieve what she lost by her errors. It would give her the monopoly of tropical productions, which I shall next proceed to show.

"What would be the consequence if this object of her unceasing solicitude and exertions should be effected by the abolition of negro slavery throughout this continent, some idea may be formed from the immense diminution of productions, as has been shown, which has followed abolition in her West India possessions. But, as great as that has been, it is nothing compared with what would be the effect, if she should succeed in abolishing slavery in the United States, Cuba, and Brazil, and throughout this continent. The experiment in her own colonies was made under the most favorable circumstances. It was brought about gradually and peaceably by the steady and firm operation of the parent country, armed with complete power to prevent or crush at once all insurrectionary movements on the part of the negroes, and able and disposed to maintain to the full, the political and social ascendency of the former masters over their former slaves. It is not at all wonderful that the change of the relation of master and slave took place, under such circumstances, without violence and bloodshed, and that order and peace should have been since preserved. Very different would be the result of abolition should it be effected by her influence and exertions in the possessions of other countries on this continent—and especially in the United States, Cuba, and Brazil, the great cultivators of the principal tropical products of America. To form a correct conception of what would be the result with them, we must look, not to Jamaica, but to St. Domingo, for example. The change would be followed by unforgiving hate between the two races, and end in a bloody and deadly struggle between them for the superiority. One or the other would have to be subjugated, extirpated, or expelled ; and desolation would overspread their territories, as in St. Domingo, from which it would take centuries to recover. The end would be, that the superiority in cultivating the great tropical staples would be transferred from them to the British tropical possessions.

"They are of vast extent, and those beyond the Cape of Good Hope, possessed of an unlimited amount of labor, standing ready, by the aid of British capital, to supply the deficit which would be occasioned by destroying the tropical productions of the United States, Cuba, Brazil, and other countries cultivated by slave-labor on this continent, as soon as the increased prices, in consequence, would yield a profit. It is the successful competition of that labor which keeps the prices of the great tropical staples so low as to prevent their cultivation with profit in the possessions of Great Britain, by what she is pleased to call free-labor.

"If she can destroy its competition, she would have a monopoly of these productions. She has all the means of furnishing an unlimited supply—vast and fertile possessions in both Indies, boundless command of capital and labor, and ample power to suppress disturbances and preserve order throughout her wide domain.

"It is unquestionable that she regards the abolition of slavery in Texas as a most important step toward this great object of policy, so much the aim of her solicitude and exertions; and the defeat of the annexation of Texas to our Union as indispensable to the abolition of slavery there. She is too sagacious not to see what a fatal blow it would give to slavery in the United States, and how certainly its abolition with us will abolish it over the whole continent, and thereby give her a monopoly in the productions of the great tropical staples, and the command of the commerce, navigation, and manufactures of the world, with an established naval ascendency and political preponderance. To this continent, the blow would be calamitous beyond description. It would destroy, in a great measure, the cultivation and productions of the great tropical staples, amounting annually in value to nearly $300,000,000, the fund which stimulates and upholds almost every other branch of its industry, commerce, navigation, and manufactures. The whole, by their joint influence, are rapidly spreading population, wealth, improvement and civilization over the whole continent, and vivifying, by their overflow, the industry of Europe, thereby increasing its population, wealth, and advancement in the arts, in power, and in civilization.

"Such must be the result, should Great Britain succeed in accomplishing the constant object of her desire and exertions—the abolition of negro slavery over this continent—and toward the effecting of which she regards the defeat of the annexation of Texas to our Union so important.

"Can it be possible that governments so enlightened and sagacious as those of France and the other great continental powers, can be so blinded by the plea of philanthropy as not to see what must inevitably follow, be her motive what it may, should she succeed in her object ? It is little short of mockery to talk of philanthropy, with the example before us of the effects of abolishing negro slavery in her own colonies, in St. Domingo, and in the northern states of our Union, where statistical facts, not to be shaken, prove that the free negro, after the experience of sixty years, is in a far worse condition than in the other states, where he has been left in his former condition. No: the effect of what is called abolition, where the number is few, is not to raise the inferior race to the condition of freemen, but to deprive the negro of the guardian care of his owner, subject to all the depression and oppression belonging to his inferior condition. But, on the other hand, where the number is great, and bears a large proportion to the whole population, it would be still worse. It would be to substitute for the existing relation a deadly strife between the two races, to end in the subjection, expulsion, or extirpation of one or the other; and such would be the case over the greater part of this continent where negro slavery exists. It would not end there; but would, in all probability, extend, by its example, the war of races over all South America, including Mexico, and extending to the Indian as well as the African race, and make the whole one scene of blood and devastation.

"Dismissing, then, the stale and unfounded plea of philanthropy, can it be that France and the other great continental powers—seeing what must be the result of the policy, for the accomplishment of which England is constantly exerting herself, and that the defeat of the annexation of Texas is so important towards its consummation—are prepared to back or countenance her in her efforts to produce either? What possible motives can they have to favor her cherished policy? Is it not better for them that they should be supplied with tropical products in exchange for their labor from the United States, Brazil, Cuba, and this continent generally, than to be dependent on one great monopolizing power for their supply? Is it not better that they should receive them at the low prices which competition, cheaper means of production, and nearness of market, would furnish them by the former, than to give the high prices which monopoly, dear labor, and great distance from market would impose? Is it not better that their labor should be exchanged with a new continent, rapidly increasing in population and capacity for consuming, and which would furnish, in the course of a few generations, a market nearer to them, and almost of unlimited extent, for the products of their industry and arts, than with old and distant regions, whose population has long since reached its growth?

"The above contains those enlarged views of policy which, it seems to me, an enlightened European statesman ought to take, in making up his opinion on the subject of the annexation of Texas, and the grounds, as it may be inferred, on which England vainly opposes it. They certainly involve considerations of the deepest importance, and demanding the greatest attention. Viewed in connection with them, the question of annexation becomes one of the first magnitude, not only to Texas and the United States, but to this continent and Europe. They are presented that you may use them on all suitable occasions where you think they may be with effect, in your correspondence, where it can be done with propriety, or otherwise. The president relies with confidence on your sagacity, prudence, and zeal. Your mission is one of the first magnitude at all times, but especially now; and he feels assured that nothing will be left undone on your part to do justice to the country and the government in reference to this measure.

"I have said nothing as to our right of treaty with Texas, without consulting Mexico. You so fully understand the grounds on which we rest our right, and are so familiar with all the facts necessary to maintain them, that it was thought unnecessary to add anything in reference to it.

"I am, sir, very respectfully, your obedient servant,

"WILLIAM R. KING, Esq., &c., &c.   J. C. CALHOUN."

The presidential contest of 1844 resulted in the election of Jas. K. Polk. The second session of the 28th congress commenced Dec. 2d, to terminate with the close of Mr. Tyler's presidential term. On the 19th of December, Mr. John B. Weller, of Ohio, introduced a joint resolution providing for the annexation of Texas to the United States, which he moved to the committee of the whole. Mr. Hamlin, of Ohio, moved its reference to a committee of one from each state, with instructions to report to the house,

"1st. Whether congress has any constitutional power to annex a foreign, independent nation to this government; and if so, by what article and section of the constitution it is conferred; whether it is among the powers expressly granted, or among those which are implied; whether it is necessary to carry into effect any expressly-granted power; and if so, which one.

"2d. Whether annexation of Texas would not extend and perpetuate slavery in the slave states, and also the internal slave-trade; and whether the United States government has any constitutional power over slavery in the states, either to perpetuate it there, or to do it away.

"3d. Whether the United States, having acknowledged the independence of Texas, Mexico is thereby deprived of her right to reconquer that province.

"4th. That they report whether Texas is owing any debts or not; and if she is, what is the amount, and to whom payable; and whether, if she should be annexed to the United States, the United States government would be bound to pay them all.

"5th. That they report what treaties are in existence between Texas and foreign governments; and, if she should be annexed to the United States, whether the United States government would be bound, by the law of nations, to fulfill those treaties."

The question was first taken on Mr. Weller's motion, and carried. Yeas, 109, democrats; nays, 61, whigs; whereupon it was held that Hamlin's amendment was defeated, and the original proposition alone committed.

On the 10th of January, 1845, John P. Hale, of New Hampshire, proposed the following as an amendment to any act or resolve contemplating the annexation of Texas to the Union:

"Provided, that immediately after the question of boundary between the United States of America and Mexico shall have been definitively settled by the two governments, and before any state formed out of the territory of Texas shall be admitted into the Union, the said territory of Texas shall be divided as follows, to wit: beginning at a point on the Gulf of Mexico, midway between the northern and southern boundaries thereof on the coast; and thence by a line running in a northwesterly direction to the extreme boundary thereof, so as to divide the same as nearly as possible into two equal parts; and in that portion of said territory lying south and west of the line to be run as aforesaid, there shall be neither slavery nor involuntary servitude, otherwise than in the punishment of crimes, whereof the party shall have been duly convicted.

"And provided further, that this provision shall be considered as a compact between the people of the United States and the people of the said territory, and forever remain unalterable, unless by the consent of three-fourths of the states of the Union."

Mr. Hale asked for a suspension of the rules to enable him to offer it now, and have it printed and committed. Refused by a vote of yeas 92, not two-thirds; nays, 81. All the whigs and most of the democrats from the free states voted aye; all the members from slave states except three, and 17 democrats from free states, voted nay. On the 12th of January, Mr. Ingersoll, of Pa., from the committee on foreign affairs, reported a joint resolution for the annexation of Texas, which was discussed in committee of the whole, and on the 25th reported to the house in the following form; that portion relating to slavery having been added in committee, on motion of Milton Brown, of Tennessee :

"Resolved by the senate and house of representatives in congress assembled, That congress doth consent that the territory properly included within, and rightfully belonging to, the republic of Texas, may be erected into a new state, to be called the state of Texas, with a republican form of government, to be adopted by the people of said republic, by deputies in convention assembled, with the consent of the existing government, in order that the same may be admitted as one of the states of this Union.

" 2. And be it further resolved, That the foregoing consent of congress is given upon the following conditions and with the following guaranties, to wit :

"First. Said state to be formed, subject to the adjustment by this government of all questions of boundary that may arise with other governments ; and the constitution thereof, with the proper evidence of its adoption by the people of said republic of Texas, shall be transmitted to the President of the United States, to be laid before congress for its final action, on or before the 1st day of January, 1846.

"Second. Said state, when admitted into the Union, after ceding to the United States all public edifices, fortifications, barracks, ports, and harbors, navy and navy-yards, docks, magazines, arms, armaments, and all other property and means pertaining to the public defense, belonging to the said republic of Texas, shall retain all the public funds, debts, taxes, and dues of every kind which may belong to, or be due or owing said republic ; and shall also retain all the vacant and unappropriated lands lying within its limits, to be applied to the payment of the debts and liabilities of said republic of Texas ; and the residue of said lands, after discharging said debts and liabilities, to be disposed of as said state may direct ; but in no event are said debts and liabilities to become a charge upon the United States.

"Third. New states of convenient size, not exceeding four in number, in addition to said state of Texas, and having sufficient population, may hereafter, by the consent of said state, be formed out of the territory thereof, which shall be entitled to admission under the provisions of the federal constitution. And such states as may be formed out of that portion of said territory lying south of thirty-six degrees thirty minutes north latitude, commonly known as the Missouri compromise line, shall be admitted into the Union, with or without slavery, as the people of each state asking admission may desire ; and in such state or states as shall be formed out of said territory north of said Missouri compromise line, slavery or involuntary servitude (except for crime) shall be prohibited."

Cave Johnson, of Tenn., moved the previous question, which the house seconded—yeas, 113; nays, 106—and then the amendment was agreed to; yeas, 118; nays, 101. The yeas comprised 114 democrats and 4 southern whigs; the nays, all the whigs present but the four just mentioned, and 23 democrats from free states. The house then ordered the whole proposition to a third reading forthwith; and passed it by yeas 120 to 98 nays. Sent to the senate for concurrence, where, on the 24th February, it was taken up for consideration. Mr. Walker, of Wis., moved to add an alternative proposition contemplating negotiation as the means of effecting the meditated end. Several amendments were moved and rejected. Walker's was carried by a vote of 27 to 25. The resolution, as amended, was adopted; yeas, 26, all democrats but three; nays, 25, all whigs. The senate amendment was agreed to by the house, and the annexation of Texas decreed. The resolutions were the next day, March 2, approved by the President. Mr. Tyler seized upon the last moment of his official existence to exercise the power conferred by the resolutions. Almonte, the Mexican minister, protested against the act, and asked for his passports.

The following is the joint resolution for the annexation of Texas:

" *Resolved by the senate and house of representatives of the United States in congress assembled,* That congress doth consent that the territory properly included within, and rightfully belonging to, the republic of Texas, may be erected into a new state, to be called the state of Texas, with a republican form of government, to be adopted by the people of said republic, by deputies in convention assembled, with the consent of the existing government, in order that the same may be admitted as one of the states of this Union.

" SEC. 2. *And be it further rseolved,* That the foregoing consent of congress is given upon the following conditions, and with the following guaranties, to wit:

" *First.* Said state to be formed, subject to the adjustment by this government of all questions of boundary that may arise with other governments; and the constitution thereof, with the proper evidence of its adoption by the people of said republic of Texas, shall be transmitted to the President of the United States, to be laid before congress for its final action, on or before the first day of January, one thousand eight hundred and forty-six.

" *Second.* Said state, when admitted into the Union, after ceding to the United States all public edifices, fortifications, barracks, ports, and harbors, navy and navy-yards, docks, magazines, arms, armaments, and all other property and means pertaining to the public defense, belonging to the said republic of Texas, shall retain all the public funds, debts, taxes, and dues of every kind which may belong to, or be due or owing said republic; and shall also retain all the vacant or unappropriated lands lying within its limits, to be applied to the payment of the debts and liabilities of said republic of Texas; and the residue of said lands, after discharging said debts and liabilities, to be disposed of as said state may direct; but in no event are said debts and liabilities to become a charge upon the United States.

" *Third.* New states of convenient size, not exceeding four in number, in addition to the said state of Texas, and having sufficient population, may hereafter, by the consent of said state, be formed out of the territory thereof, which shall be entitled to admission under the provisions of the federal constitution ; and such states as may be formed out of that portion of said territory lying south of thirty-six degrees thirty minutes north latitude, commonly known as the Missouri compromise line, shall be admitted into the Union with or without slavery, as the people of each state asking admission may desire ; and in such state or states as shall be formed out of said territory north of said Missouri compromise line, slavery or involuntary servitude, (except for crime,) shall be prohibited.

" *And be it further resolved,* That if the President of the United States shall, in his judgment and discretion, deem it most advisable, instead of proceeding to submit the foregoing resolution to the republic of Texas, as an overture on the part of the United States, for admission, to negotiate with that republic ; then,

" *Be it resolved,* That a state to be formed out of the present republic of Texas, with suitable extent and boundaries, and with two representatives in congress, until the next apportionment of representation, shall be admitted into the Union by virtue of this act, on an equal footing with the existing states, as soon as the terms and conditions of such admission, and the cession of the remaining Texan territory to the United States, shall be agreed upon by the governments of Texas and the United States.

" *And be it further enacted,* That the sum of one hundred thousand dollars be, and the same is hereby appropriated to defray the expenses of missions and negotiations, to agree upon the terms of said admission and cession, either by treaty to be submitted to the senate, or by articles to be submitted to the two houses of congress, as the president may direct.

" Approved March 2, 1845."

Texas having been annexed in pursuance of the foregoing joint resolution of the two houses of congress, a portion of the United States army, under Gen. Taylor, was, early in the spring of 1846, moved down to the east bank of the Rio Grande del Norte, claimed by Texas as her western boundary, but not so regarded by Mexico. A hostile collision ensued, resulting in war between the United States and Mexico.

It was early thereafter deemed advisable that a considerable sum should be placed by congress at the president's disposal, to negotiate an advantageous treaty of peace and limits with the Mexican government. A message to this effect was submitted by President Polk to congress, August 8th, 1846, and a bill in accordance with its suggestions laid before the house, which proceeded to consider the subject in committee of the whole. The bill appropriating $30,000 for immediate use in negotiations with Mexico, and placing $2,000,000 more at the disposal of the president, to be employed in making peace, Mr. David Wilmot, of Pa., after consultation with other northern democrats, offered the following proviso, in addition to the first section of the bill :

"Provided, that an express and fundamental condition to the acquisition of any territory from the republic of Mexico by the United States, by virtue of any treaty which may be negotiated between them, and to the use by the executive of the moneys herein appropriated, neither slavery nor involuntary servitude shall ever exist in any part of said territory, except for crime, whereof the party shall first be duly convicted."

This proviso was carried in committee by a vote of 84 to 63. The bill was then reported to the house, and the previous question moved on its engrossment, which was carried, and the bill sent to the senate. Mr. Lewis, senator from Alabama, moved that the proviso be struck out, on which debate arose, and Mr. John Davis, of Mass., was speaking, when twelve o'clock, August 10th, arrived, the time fixed for adjournment, and both houses adjourned without day.

The 30th congress assembled Dec. 6, 1847. On the 28th February, Mr. Putnam, of New York, moved the following resolution :

"WHEREAS, In the settlement of the difficulties pending between this country and Mexico, territory may be acquired in which slavery does not now exist :

"And whereas, Congress, in the organization of a territorial government, at an early period of our political history, established a principle worthy of imitation in all future time, forbidding the existence of slavery in free territory ; therefore,

"Resolved, That in any territory that may be acquired from Mexico, over which shall be established territorial governments, slavery or involuntary servitude, except as a punishment for crime, whereof the party shall have been duly convicted, shall be forever prohibited ; and that in any act or resolution establishing such governments, a fundamental provision ought to be inserted to that effect."

The resolution was ordered to lie on the table by a vote of 105 to 93. This terminated all direct action on the Wilmot proviso for that session.

A bill for the establishment of a territorial government for Oregon was reported in the senate early in the session, and the question of slavery furnished matter for a protracted debate. The power of congress to legislate on the subject of slavery in the territories was discussed in the senate by Mr. Dix, of New York, who maintained the affirmative, and Mr. Calhoun the negative.

Mr. Dix stated certain positions which he thought constituted a proper basis for the settlement of the question ; positions, the correctness of which a majority of the friends of free territory, it is believed, do not concede. They are these : 1. All external interference with slavery in the states is a violation of the compromises of the constitution, and dangerous to the harmony and perpetuity of the federal union. 2. Territory acquired by the United States should, in respect to slavery, be received as it is found. If slavery exists therein at the time of the acquisition, it should be left to remain undisturbed by congress. If it does not exist therein at the time of the acquisition, its introduction ought to be prohibited while the territory continues to be governed as such. 3. All legislation by congress in respect to slavery in the territory, ceases to be operative when the inhabitants are permitted to form a state government ; and the admission of a state into the Union carries with it, by force of the sovereignty such admission confers, the right to dispose of the whole question of slavery at its discretion, without external interference.

Mr. Calhoun denied the existence of the power of congress to exclude the south from a free admission into the territories with its slaves. He denied what had been by many assumed, that congress had an absolute right to govern the territories. The clause of the constitution which gives "power to dispose of and make all needful rules and regulations respecting the territory and other property belonging to the United States," did not, he said, convey such a right: "it conferred *no governmental power whatever;* no, not a particle." It only referred to territory as public lands—*as property*—and gave to congress the right to dispose of it as such, but not to exercise over it the power of government. Mr. Calhoun thought the best method of settling the slavery question was by *non-action*—by leaving the territories free and open to the emigration of all the world, and when they became states, to permit them to adopt whatever constitution they pleased.

Mr. Calhoun considered the interference on the subject dangerous to the Union. If the Union and our system of government were ever doomed to perish, the historian who should record the events ending in so calamitous a result, would devote his first chapter to the ordinance of 1787; his next to the Missouri compromise; and the next to the present agitation. Whether there would be another beyond, he knew not. He reviewed and controverted the doctrines of the declaration of independence. The proposition that "all men are created free and equal," he called a "hypothetical truism." Literally, there was not a word of truth in it. This assertion he supported with the singular argument, that "Men are not born free. Infants are born. They grow to be men. They were not born free. While infants, they are incapable of freedom; they are subject to their parents." Nor was it less false that they are born "equal." But in the declaration of independence the word "free" did not occur. Still the expression was erroneous. "All men are not created. Only two, a man and a woman, were created, and one of these was pronounced subordinate to the other. All others have come into the world by being born, and in no sense, as I have shown, either free or equal." This expression, Mr. C. said, had been inserted in the declaration without any necessity. It made no necessary part of our justification in separating ourselves from the parent country. Nor had it any weight in constructing the governments which were to be substituted in the place of the colonial. They were formed from the old materials, and on practical and well established principles, borrowed, for the most part, from our own experience, and that of the country from which we sprang.

Mr. Calhoun argued, that, instead of liberty and equality being born with men, and instead of all men and all classes being entitled to them, they were high prizes to be won; they were rewards bestowed on mental and moral development. The error which he was combating had done more to retard the cause of liberty and civilization, and was doing more at present, than all other causes combined. It was the leading cause which had placed Europe in its present state of anarchy, and which stood in the way of reconstructing good governments. He concluded as follows:

"Nor are we exempt from its disorganizing effects. We now begin to experience the danger of admitting so great an error to have a place in the declaration of our independence. For a long time it lay dormant; but in process of time it began to germinate, and produce its poisonous fruits. It had strong hold on the mind of Jefferson, the author of that document, which .caused him to take an utterly false view of the subordinate relation of the black to the white race in the south; and to hold, in consequence, that the latter, though utterly unqualified to possess liberty, were as fully entitled to both liberty and equality as the former; and that to deprive them of it was unjust and immoral. To this error, his proposition to exclude slavery from the territory northwest of the Ohio may be traced, and to that the ordinance of 1787, and through it the deep and dangerous agitation which now threatens to engulf, and will certainly engulf, if not speedily settled, our political institutions, and involve the country in countless woes."

The house bill providing a government for Oregon was passed by that body on the second of August, 129 to 71. It contained a provision for extending the ordinance of 1787 over the territory. The bill passed the senate on the 13th August—the session closing the next day.

The following letter from Gen. Cass to A. O. P. Nicholson, appeared during the winter of 1847–8. It is regarded as the first well considered enunciation of squatter sovereignty:

WASHINGTON, December 24, 1847.

DEAR SIR: I have received your letter, and shall answer it as frankly as it is written.

You ask me whether I am in favor of the acquisition of Mexican territory, and what are my sentiments with regard to the Wilmot proviso.

I have so often and so explicitly stated my views of the first question, in the senate, that it seems almost unnecessary to repeat them here. As you request it, however, I shall briefly give them.

I think, then, that no peace should be granted to Mexico, till a reasonable indemnity is obtained for the injuries which she has done us. The territorial extent of this indemnity is, in the first instance, a subject of executive consideration. There the constitution has placed it, and there I am willing to leave it: not only because I have full confidence in its judicious exercise, but because, in the ever-varying circumstances of a war, it would be indiscreet, by a public declaration, to commit the country to any line of indemnity, which might otherwise be enlarged, as the obstinate injustice of the enemy prolongs the contest, with its loss of blood and treasure.

It appears to me, that the kind of metaphysical magnanimity which would reject all indemnity at the close of a bloody and expensive war, brought on by a direct attack upon our troops by the enemy, and preceded by a succession of unjust acts for a series of years, is as unworthy of the age in which we live, as it is revolting to the common sense and practice of mankind. It would conduce but little to our future security, or, indeed, to our present reputation, to declare that we repudiate all expectation of compensation from the Mexican government, and are fighting, not for any practical result, but for some vague, perhaps philanthropic object, which escapes my penetration, and must be defined by those who assume this new principle of national intercommunication. All wars are to be deprecated, as well by the statesman as by the philanthropist. They are great evils; but there are greater evils than these, and submission to injustice is among them. The nation which should refuse to defend its rights and its honor, when assailed, would soon have neither to defend; and, when driven to war, it is not by professions of disinterestedness and declarations of magnanimity that its rational objects can be best obtained, or other nations taught a lesson of forbearance—the strongest security for a permanent peace. We are at war with Mexico, and its vigorous prosecution is the surest means of its speedy termination, and ample indemnity the surest guaranty against the recurrence of such injustice as provoked it.

The Wilmot proviso has been before the country for some time. It has been repeatedly discussed in congress, and by the public press. I am strongly impressed with the opinion, that a great change has been going on in the public mind upon this subject, in my own as well as others; and that doubts are resolving themselves into convictions, that the principle it involves should be kept out of the national legislature, and left to the people of the confederacy in their respective local governments.

The whole subject is a comprehensive one, and fruitful of important consequences. It would be ill-timed to discuss it here. I shall not assume that responsible task, but shall confine myself to such general views as are necessary to the fair exhibition of my opinions.

We may well regret the existence of slavery in the southern states, and wish they had been saved from its introduction. But there it is, not by the act of the present generation; and we must deal with it as a great practical question, involving the most momentous consequences. We have neither the right nor the power to touch it where it exists; and if we had both, their exercise, by any means heretofore suggested, might lead to results which no wise man would willingly encounter, and which no good man could contemplate without anxiety.

The theory of our government presupposes that its various members have reserved to themselves the regulation of all subjects relating to what may be termed their internal police. They are sovereign within their boundaries, except in those cases where they have surrendered to the general government a portion of their rights, in order to give effect to the objects of the Union, whether these concern foreign nations or the several states themselves. Local institutions, if I may so speak, whether they have reference to slavery or to any other relations, domestic or public, are left to local authority, either original or derivative. Congress has no right to say that there shall be slavery in New York, or that there shall be no slavery in Georgia; nor is there any other human power, but the people of those states, respectively, which can change the relations existing therein; and they can say, if they will, 'we will have slavery in the former, and we will abolish it in the latter.'

In various respects, the territories differ from the states. Some of their rights are inchoate, and they do not possess the peculiar attributes of sovereignty. Their relation to the general government is very imperfectly defined by the constitution; and it will be found, upon examination, that in that instrument the only grant of power concerning them is conveyed in the phrase, "congress shall have the power to dispose of and make all needful rules and regulations respecting the territory and other property belonging to the United States." Certainly this phraseology is very loose, if it were designed to include in the grant the whole power of legislation over persons, as well as things. The expression, the "territory and other property," fairly construed, relates to the public lands, as such; to arsenals, dockyards, forts, ships, and all the various kinds of property which the United States may and must possess.

But surely the simple authority *to dispose of and regulate* these does not extend to the unlimited power of legislation; to the passage of all *laws*, in the most general acceptation of the word; which, by-the-by, is carefully excluded from the sentence. And, indeed, if this were so, it would render unnecessary another provision of the constitution, which grants to Congress the power to legislate, with the consent of the states, respectively, over all places purchased for the "erection of forts, magazines, arsenals, dock-yards," etc. These being the *property* of the United States, if the power to make "needful rules and regulations concerning" them includes the general power of legislation, then the grant of authority to regulate "the territory and other property of the United States" is unlimited, wherever subjects are found for its operation, and its exercise needed no auxiliary provision. If, on the other hand, it does not include such power of legislation over the "other property" of the United States, then it does not include it over their "*territory;*" for the same terms which grant the one, grant the other. "*Territory*" is here classed with property, and treated as such; and the object was evidently to enable the general government, as a property-holder—which, from necessity it must be—to manage, preserve and "*dispose of*" such property as it might possess, and which authority is essential almost to its being. But the lives and persons of our citizens, with the vast variety of objects connected with them, cannot be controlled by an authority which is merely called into existence for the purpose of making *rules and regulations for the disposition and management of property*.

Such, it appears to me, would be the construction put upon this provision of the constitution, were this question now first presented for consideration, and not controlled by imperious circumstances. The original ordinance of the congress of the confederation, passed in 1787, and which was the only act upon this subject in force at the adoption of the constitution, provided a complete frame of government for the country north of the Ohio, while in a territorial condition, and for its eventual admission in separate states into the Union. And the persuasion that this ordinance contained within itself all the necessary means of execution, probably prevented any direct reference to the subject in the constitution, further than vesting in congress the right to admit the states formed under it into the Union. However, circumstances arose which required legislation, as well over the territory north of the Ohio as over other territory, both within and without the original Union, ceded to the general government, and, at various times, a more enlarged power has been exercised over the *territories*—meaning thereby the different territorial governments—than is conveyed by the limited grant referred to. How far an existing necessity may have operated in producing this legislation, and thus extending, by rather a violent implication, powers not directly given, I know not. But certain it is that the principle of interference should not be carried beyond the necessary implication which produces it. It should be limited to the creation of proper governments for new countries, acquired or settled, and to the necessary provision for their eventual admission into the Union; leaving, in the meantime, the people inhabiting them, to regulate their internal concerns in their own way. They are just as capable of doing so as the people of the states; and they can do so, at any rate as soon as their political independence is recognized by admission into the Union. During this temporary condition, it is hardly expedient to call into exercise a doubtful and invidious authority, which questions the intelligence of a respectable portion of our citizens, and whose limitation, whatever it may be, will be rapidly approaching its termination—an authority which would give to congress despotic power, uncontrolled by the constitution, over most important sections of our common country. For, if the relation of master and servant may be regulated or annihilated by its legislation, so may the regulation of husband and wife, of parent and child, and of any other condition which our institutions and the habits of our society recognize. What would be thought if congress should undertake to prescribe the terms of marriage in New York, or to regulate the authority of parents over their children in Pennsylvania? It would be vain to seek an argument justifying the interference of the national legislature in the cases referred to in the original states of the Union. I speak here of the inherent power of congress, and do not touch the question of such contracts as may be formed with new states when admitted into the confederacy.

Of all the questions that can agitate us, those which are merely sectional in their character are the most dangerous, and the most to be deprecated. The warning voice of him who from his character and services and virtue had the best right to warn us, proclaimed to his countrymen, in his farewell address, that monument of wisdom for him, as I hope it will be of safety for them, how much we had to apprehend from measures peculiarly affecting geographical sections of our country. The grave circumstances in which we are now placed make these words words of safety; for I am satisfied, from all I have seen and heard here, that a successful attempt to engraft the principles of the Wilmot proviso upon the legislation of this government, and to apply them to new territory, should new territory be acquired, would seriously affect our tranquility. I do not suffer myself to foresee or to foretell the consequences that would ensue; for I trust and believe there is good sense and good feeling enough in the country to avoid them, by avoiding all occasions which might lead to them.

Briefly, then, I am opposed to the exercise of any jurisdiction by congress over this matter; and I am in favor of leaving to the people of any territory, which may be hereafter acquired, the right to regulate it for themselves, under the general principles of the constitution. Because—

1. I do not see in the constitution any grant of the requisite power to congress; and I am not disposed to extend a doubtful precedent beyond its necessity—the establishment of territorial governments when needed—leaving to the inhabitants all the rights compatible with the relations they bear to the confederation.

2. Because I believe this measure, if adopted, would weaken, if not impair, the union of the states; and would sow the seeds of future discord, which would grow up and ripen into an abundant harvest of calamity.

3. Because I believe a general conviction that such a proposition would succeed, would lead to an immediate witholding of the supplies, and thus to a dishonorable termination of the war. I think no dispassionate observer at the seat of government can doubt this result.

4. If, however, in this I am under a misapprehension, I am under none in the practical operation in this restriction, if adopted by congress, upon a treaty of peace, making any acquisition of Mexican territory. Such a treaty would be rejected as certainly as presented to the senate. More than one-third of that body would vote against it, viewing such a principle as an exclusion of the citizens of the slaveholding states from a participation in the benefits acquired by the treasure and exertions of all, and which should be common to all. I am repeating—neither advancing nor defending these views. That branch of the subject does not lie in my way, and I shall not turn aside to seek it.

In this aspect of the matter, the people of the United States must choose between this restriction and the extension of their territorial limits. They cannot have both; and which they will surrender must depend upon their representatives first, and then, if these fail them, upon themselves.

5. But after all, it seems to be generally conceded that this restriction, if carried into effect, could not operate upon any state to be formed from newly-acquired territory. The well-known attributes of sovereignty, recognized by us as belonging to the state governments, would sweep before them any such barrier, and would leave the people to express and exert their will at pleasure. Is the object, then, of temporary exclusion for so short a period as the duration of the territorial governments, worth the price at which it would be purchased?—worth the discord it would engender, the trial to which it would expose our union, and the evils that would be the certain consequence, let the trial result as it might? As to the course, which has been intimated, rather than proposed, of engrafting such a restriction upon any treaty of acquisition, I persuade myself it would find but little favor in any portion of this country. Such an arrangement would render Mexico a party, having a right to interfere in our internal institutions in questions left by the constitution to the state governments, and would inflict a serious blow upon our fundamental principles. Few, indeed, I trust, there are among us who would thus grant to a foreign

power the right to inquire into the constitution and conduct of the sovereign states of this union; and if there are any, I am not among them, nor never shall be. To the people of this country, under God, now and hereafter, are its destinies committed; and we want no foreign power to interrogate us, treaty in hand, and to say, "why have you done this, or why have you left that undone?" Our own dignity and the principles of national independence unite to repel such a proposition.

But there is another important consideration, which ought not to be lost sight of, in the investigation of this subject. The question that presents itself is not a question of the increase, but of the diffusion of slavery. Whether its sphere be stationary or progressive, its amount will be the same. The rejection of this restriction will not add one to the class of servitude, nor will its adoption give freedom to a single being who is now placed therein. The same numbers will be spread over greater territory; and, so far as compression, with less abundance of the necessaries of life, is an evil, so far will that evil be mitigated by transporting slaves to a new country, and giving them a larger space to occupy.

I say this in the event of the extension of slavery over any new acquisition. But can it go there? This may well be doubted. All the descriptions which reach us of the condition of the Californias and of New-Mexico, to the acquisition of which our efforts seem at present directed, unite in representing those countries as agricultural regions, similar in their products to our middle states, and generally unfit for the production of the great staples which can alone render slave labor valuable. If we are not grossly deceived—and it is difficult to conceive how we can be—the inhabitants of those regions, whether they depend upon their plows or their herds, cannot be slaveholders. Involuntary labor, requiring the investment of large capital, can only be profitable when employed in the production of a few favored articles confined by nature to special districts, and paying larger returns than the usual agricultural products spread over more considerable portions of the earth.

In the able letter of Mr. Buchanan upon this subject, not long since given to the public, he presents similar considerations with great force. "Neither," says the distinguished writer, "the soil, the climate, nor the productions of California south of 36° 30′, nor indeed of any portion of it, north or south, is adapted to slave labor; and beside, every facility would be there afforded for the slave to escape from his master. Such property would be entirely insecure in any part of California. It is morally impossible, therefore, that a majority of the emigrants to that portion of the territory south of 36° 30′, which will be chiefly composed of our citizens, will ever reëstablish slavery within its limits.

"In regard to New Mexico, east of the Rio Grande, the question has already been settled by the admission of Texas into the Union.

"Should we acquire the territory beyond the Rio Grande and east of the Rocky Mountains, it is still more impossible that a majority of the people would consent to reëstablish slavery. They are themselves a colored popula-

36

tion, and among them the negro does not belong socially to a degraded race."
With this last remark, Mr. Walker fully coincides in his letter written in
1844, upon the annexation of Texas, and which everywhere produced so favorable an impression upon the public mind, as to have conduced very materially to the accomplishment of that great measure. "Beyond the Del Norte,"
says Mr. Walker, " slavery will not pass; not only because it is forbidden by
law, but because the colored race there preponderates in the ratio of ten to one
over the whites ; and holding, as they do, the government and most of the offices in their possession, they will not permit the enslavement of any portion of
the colored race, which makes and executes the laws of the country."

The question, it will be therefore seen on examination, does not regard the
exclusion of slavery from a region where it now exists, but a prohibition
against its introduction where it does not exist, and where, from the feelings of
the inhabitants and the laws of nature, "it is morally impossible," as Mr.
Buchanan says, that it can ever reëstablish itself.

It augurs well for the permanency of our confederation, that during more
than half a century, which has elapsed since the establishment of this government, many serious questions, and some of the highest importance, have agitated the public mind, and more than once threatened the gravest consequences;
but that they have all in succession passed away, leaving our institutions unscathed, and our country advancing in numbers, power and wealth, and in all
the other elements of national prosperity, with a rapidity unknown in ancient
or in modern days. In times of political excitement, when difficult and delicate questions present themselves for solution, there is one ark of safety for us;
and that is, an honest appeal to the fundamental principles of our Union, and a
stern determination to abide their dictates. This course of proceeding has
carried us in safety through many a trouble, and I trust will carry us safely
through many more, should many more be destined to assail us. The Wilmot
proviso seeks to take from its legitimate tribunal a question of domestic policy, having no relation to the Union, as such, and to transfer it to another, created by the people for a special purpose, and foreign to the subject matter involved in this issue. By going back to our true principles, we go back to the
road of peace and safety. Leave to the people, who will be affected by this
question, to adjust it upon their own responsibility, and in their own manner,
and we shall render another tribute to the original principles of our government, and furnish another guaranty for its permanence and prosperity. I am,
dear sir, respectfully, your obedient servant,   LEWIS CASS.

A. O. P. NICHOLSON, Esq., Nashville, Tenn.

CHAPTER XXX.

POLITICAL HISTORY OF SLAVERY.—COMPROMISES OF 1850.

Message of President Taylor.—Sam Houston's propositions.—Taylor's Special Message
—Mr. Clay's propositions for arrangement of slavery controversy.—His resolutions.—
Resolutions of Mr. Bell.—The debate on Clay's resolutions, by Rusk, Foote, of Mississippi, Mason, Jefferson Davis, King, Clay, and Butler.—Remarks of Benton, Calhoun, Webster, Seward, and Cass.—Resolutions referred.—Report of Committee.—
The omnibus bill.—California admitted.—New Mexico organized.—Texas boundary established.—Utah organized.—Slave-trade in the District of Columbia abolished.—
Fugitive Slave law passed.

THE slave population of the United States amounted, in 1850, to 3,204,313; exhibiting an increase, for the last decade, of 716,858. Of the slaves in 1850, 2,957,657 were black, or of unmixed African descent, and 246,656 were mulatto. The free colored population in 1850 amounted to 434,495; of whom 275,400 were black, and 159,095 mulattoes. The total number of families, holding slaves, was, by the same census, 347,525.

CENSUS OF 1850.—SLAVE POPULATION.

Alabama	342,844	Mississippi	309,878
Arkansas	47,100	Missouri	87,422
District of Columbia	3,687	New Jersey	236
Delaware	2,290	North Carolina	268,548
Florida	39,310	South Carolina	384,984
Georgia	381,682	Tennessee	239,459
Kentucky	210,981	Texas	58,161
Louisiana	244,809	Virginia	472,528
Maryland	90,368	Utah Territory	26

The first session of the thirty-first congress commenced on the third day of December, 1849. Much time was spent in unsuccessful efforts to organize, until the 23d, when Mr. Howell Cobb, of Georgia, was elected speaker, by a plurality vote.

On the 24th, President Zachary Taylor transmitted to both houses his first annual message. In reference to the new territories, he says:

"No civil government having been provided by congress for California, the people of that territory, impelled by the necessities of their political condition, recently met in convention, for the purpose of forming a constitution and state government; which, the latest advices give me reason to suppose, has been accomplished; and it is believed they will shortly apply for the admission of California into the Union, as a sovereign state. Should such be the case, and should their constitution be conformable to the requisitions of the constitution of the United States, I recommend their application to the favorable consideration of congress.

" The people of New Mexico will also, it is believed, at no very distant period, present themselves for admission into the Union. Preparatory to the admission of California and New Mexico, the people of each will have instituted for themselves a republican form of government, laying its foundation in such principles, and organizing its power in such form, as to them shall seem most likely to effect their safety and happiness.

"By awaiting their action, all causes of uneasiness may be avoided, and confidence and kind feeling preserved. With a view of maintaining the harmony and tranquility so dear to all, we should abstain from the introduction of those exciting topics of a sectional character which have hitherto produced painful apprehensions in the public mind ; and I repeat the solemn warning of the first and most illustrious of my predecessors, against furnishing any ground for characterizing parties by geographical discriminations."

On the 4th of January, 1850, General Sam Houston, of Texas, submitted the following proposition to the senate :

"WHEREAS, The congress of the United States, possessing only a delegated authority, have no power over the subject of negro slavery within the limits of the United States, either to prohibit or to interfere with it in the states, territories, or district, where, by municipal law, it now exists, or to establish it in any state or territory where it does not exist; but as an assurance and guarantee to promote harmony, quiet apprehension, and remove sectional prejudice, which by possibility might impair or weaken love and devotion to the Union in any part of the country, it is hereby

"RESOLVED, That, as the people in territories have the same inherent rights of self-government as the people in the states, if, in the exercise of such inherent rights, the people in the newly-acquired territories, by the annexation of Texas and the acquisition of California and New Mexico, south of the parallel of 36 degrees and 30 minutes of north latitude, extending to the Pacific Ocean, shall establish negro slavery in the formation of their state governments, it shall be deemed no objection to their admission as a state or states into the Union, in accordance with the constitution of the United States."

In answer to a resolution of inquiry, General Taylor sent a message to the house stating that he had urged the formation of state governments in California and New Mexico, and adds :

"In advising an early application by the people of these territories for admission as states, I was actuated principally by an earnest desire to afford to the wisdom and patriotism of congress the opportunity of avoiding occasions of bitter and angry discussions among the people of the United States.

"Under the constitution, every state has the right to establish, and, from time to time, alter its municipal laws and domestic institutions, independently of every other state and of the general government, subject only to the prohibitions and guarantees expressly set forth in the constitution of the United States. The subjects thus left exclusively to the respective states, were not designed or expected to become topics of national agitation. Still as, under the constitution, congress has power to make all needful rules and regulations respecting the territories of the United States, every new acquisition of territory has led to discussions on the question whether the system of involuntary servitude, which prevails in many of the states, should or should not be prohibited in that territory. The periods of excitement from this cause, which have heretofore occurred, have been safely passed; but, during the interval, of whatever length, which may elapse before the admission of the territories ceded by Mexico, as states, it appears probable that similar excitement will prevail to an undue extent.

"Under these circumstances, I thought, and still think, that it was my duty to endeavor to put in the power of congress, by the admission of California and New Mexico as states, to remove all occasion for the unnecessary agitation of the public mind.

"It is understood that the people of the western part of California have formed the plan of a state constitution, and will soon submit the same to the judgment of congress, and apply for admission as a state. This course on their part, though in accordance with, was not adopted exclusively in consequence of, any expression of my wishes, inasmuch as measures tending to this end had been promoted by officers sent there by my predecessor, and were already in active progress of execution, before any communication from me reached California. If the proposed constitution shall, when submitted to congress, be found to be in compliance with the requisitions of the constitution of the United States, I earnestly recommend that it may receive the sanction of congress.

"Should congress, when California shall present herself for incorporation into the Union, annex a condition to her admission as a state affecting her domestic institutions contrary to the wishes of the people, and even compel her temporarily to comply with it, yet the state could change her constitution at any time after admission, when to her it should seem expedient. Any attempt to deny to the people of the state the right of self-government, in a matter which peculiarly affects themselves, will infallibly be regarded by them as an invasion of their rights; and, upon the principles laid down in our own Declaration of Independence, they will certainly be sustained by the great mass of the American people. To assert that they are a conquered people, and must, as a state, submit to the will of their conquerors, in this regard, will meet with no cordial response among American freemen. Great numbers of them are native citizens of the United States, and not inferior to the rest of our countrymen in intelligence and patriotism; and no language of menace to restrain them in the exercise of an undoubted right, substantially guarantied to them by the treaty of cession itself, shall ever be uttered by me, or encouraged and sustained by persons acting under my authority. It is to be expected that, in the residue of the territory ceded to us by Mexico, the people residing there will, at the time of their incorporation into the Union as a state, settle all questions of domestic policy to suit themselves."

On the 29th of January, Mr. Clay submitted to the senate of the United States the following propositions for an amicable arrangement of the whole slavery controversy:

"1. Resolved, That California, with suitable boundaries, ought, upon her application, to be admitted as one of the states of this Union, without the imposition by congress of any restriction in respect to the exclusion or introduction of slavery within those boundaries.

"2. Resolved, That as slavery does not exist by law, and is not likely to be introduced into any of the territory acquired by the United States from the republic of Mexico, it is inexpedient for congress to provide by law either for its introduction into, or exclusion from, any part of the said territory: and that appropriate territorial governments ought to be established by congress in all the said territory, not assigned as within the boundaries of the proposed state of California, without the adoption of any restriction or condition on the subject of slavery.

"3. Resolved, That the western boundary of the state of Texas ought to be fixed on the Rio del Norte, commencing one marine league from its mouth, and running up that river to the southern line of New Mexico; thence with that line eastwardly, and so continuing in the same direction to the line as established between the United States and Spain, excluding any portion of New Mexico, whether lying on the east or west of that river.

"4. Resolved, That it be proposed to the state of Texas, that the United States will provide for the payment of all that portion of the legitimate and bona fide public debt of that state contracted prior to its annexation to the United States, and for which the duties on foreign imports were pledged by the said state to its creditors, not exceeding the sum of ——— dollars, in consideration of the said duties so pledged having been no longer applicable to that object after the said annexation, but having thenceforward become payable to the United States; and upon the condition, also, that the said state of Texas shall, by some solemn and authentic act of her legislature, or of a convention, relinquish to the United States any claim which she has to any part of New Mexico.

"5. Resolved, That it is inexpedient to abolish slavery in the District of Columbia whilst that institution continues to exist in the state of Maryland, without the consent of that state, without the consent of the people of the district, and without just compensation to the owners of slaves within the district.

"6. But Resolved, That it is expedient to prohibit, within the district, the slave-trade in slaves brought into it from states or places beyond the limits of the district, either to be sold therein as merchandise, or to be transported to other markets without the District of Columbia.

"7. Resolved, That more effectual provision ought to be made by law, according to the requirement of the constitution, for the restitution and delivery of persons bound to service or labor in any state, who may escape into any other state or territory in the Union. And

"8. Resolved, That congress has no power to prohibit or obstruct the trade in slaves between the slaveholding states, but that the admission or exclusion of slaves brought from one into another of them, depends exclusively upon their own particular laws."

Among the propositions to dispose of the territorial and slavery questions in both houses was a series of resolutions offered by Mr. Bell, of Tenn., in the senate, on the 28th of February, providing for the future division of Texas, and the admission of the different portions as states; also, by consent of Texas, that portion of lands claimed by Texas, lying west of the Colorado, and north of latitude 42, was to be ceded to the United States for a sum not exceeding ——— millions of dollars. California to be admitted as a state; but in future the formation of state constitutions by the inhabitants of the territories was to be regulated by law, and the inhabitants were to have power "to regulate and adjust all questions of internal state policy of whatever nature they may be." The following are Mr. Bell's resolutions:

"Whereas, Considerations of the highest interest to the whole country demand that the existing and increasing dissensions between the north and the south, on the subject of slavery, should be speedily arrested, and that the questions in controversy be adjusted upon some basis which shall tend to give present quiet, repress sectional animosities, remove, as far as possible, the causes of future discord, and secure the uninterrupted enjoyment of those benefits and advantages which the Union was intended to confer in equal measure upon all its members;

"And whereas, It is manifest, under present circumstances, that no adjustment can be effected of the points of difference unhappily existing between the northern and southern sections of the Union, connected with the subject of slavery, which shall secure to either section all that is contended for; and that mutual concessions upon questions of mere policy, not involving the violation of any constitutional right or principle, must be the basis of every project affording any assurance of a favorable acceptance;

"And whereas, The joint resolution for annexing Texas to the United States, approved March 1, 1845, contains the following condition and guarantee—that is to say: 'New states of convenient size, not exceeding four in number, in addition to said state of Texas, and having sufficient population, may hereafter, by the consent of said state, be formed out of the territory thereof, which shall be entitled to admission under the provisions of the federal constitution; and such states as may be formed out of that portion of said territory lying south of thirty-six degrees thirty minutes north latitude, commonly known as the Missouri compromise line, shall be admitted into the Union with or without slavery, as the people of each state asking admission may desire; and in such state or states as shall be formed out of said territory north of said Missouri compromise line, slavery or involuntary servitude, (except for crime,) shall be prohibited;' therefore,

"1. Resolved, That the obligation to comply with the condition and guarantee above recited in good faith be distinctly recognized; and that, in part compliance with the same, as soon as the people of Texas shall, by an act of their legislature, signify their assent by restricting the limits thereof, within the territory east of the Trinity and south of the Red river, and when the people of the residue of the territory claimed by Texas adopt a constitution, republican in form, they be admitted into the Union upon an equal footing in all respects with the original states.

"2. Resolved, That if Texas shall agree to cede, the United States will accept, a cession of all the unappropriated domain in all the territory claimed by Texas, lying west of the Colorado and extending north to the forty-second parallel of north latitude, together with the jurisdiction and sovereignty of all the territory claimed by Texas north of the thirty-fourth parallel of north latitude, and to pay therefor a sum not exceeding —— millions of dollars, to be applied in the first place to the extinguishment of any portion of the existing public debt of Texas, for the discharge of which the United States are under any obligation, implied or otherwise, and the remainder as Texas shall require.

"3. Resolved, That when the population of that portion of the territory claimed by Texas lying south of the thirty-fourth parallel of north latitude and west of the Colorado, shall be equal to the ratio of representation in congress, under the last preceding apportionment, according to the provisions of the constitution, and the people of such territory shall, with the assent of the new state contemplated in the preceding resolution, have adopted a state constitution, republican in form, they be admitted into the Union as a state, upon an equal footing with the original states.

"4. Resolved, That all the territory now claimed by Texas lying north of the thirty-fourth parallel of north latitude, and which may be ceded to the United States by Texas, be incorporated with the territory of New Mexico, except such part thereof as lies east of the Rio Grande and south of the thirty-fourth degree of north latitude, and that the territory so composed form a state, to be admitted into the Union when the inhabitants thereof shall adopt a state constitution, republican in form, with the consent of congress;

but, in the mean time, and until congress shall give such consent, provision be made for the government of the inhabitants of said territory suitable to their condition, but without any restriction as to slavery.

"5. Resolved, That all the territory ceded to the United States, by the treaty of Guadaloupe Hidalgo, lying west of said territory of New Mexico, and east of the contemplated new state of California, for the present, constitute one territory, and for which some form of government suitable to the condition of the inhabitants be provided, without any restriction as to slavery.

"6. Resolved, That the constitution recently formed by the people of the western portion of California, and presented to congress by the president on the 13th of February, 1850, be accepted, and that they be admitted into the Union as a state, upon an equal footing in all respects with the original states.

"7. Resolved, That, in future, the formation of state constitutions, by the inhabitants of the territories of the United States, be regulated by law ; and that no such constitution be hereafter formed or adopted by the inhabitants of any territory belonging to the United States, without the consent and authority of congress.

"8. Resolved, That the inhabitants of any territory of the United States, when they shall be authorized by congress to form a state constitution, shall have the sole and exclusive power to regulate and adjust all questions of internal state policy, of whatever nature they may be, controlled only by the restrictions expressly imposed by the constitution of the United States.

"9. Resolved, That the committee on territories be instructed to report a bill in conformity with the spirit and principles of the foregoing resolutions."

A debate of unusual duration, earnestness, and ability ensued, mainly on Mr. Clay's resolutions. Mr. Clay having read and briefly commented on his propositions, *seriatim*, he desired that they should be held over without debate, to give time for consideration, and made a special order for Monday or Tuesday following. Mr. Rusk rose at once to protest against that portion of them which called in question the right of Texas to so much of New Mexico as lies east of the Rio del Norte. Mr. Foote, of Miss., spoke against them generally, saying :

"If I understand the resolutions properly, they are objectionable, as it seems to me,

"1. Because they only assert that it is not *expedient* that congress should abolish slavery in the District of Columbia ; thus allowing the implication to arise that congress has power to legislate on the subject of slavery in the district, which may hereafter be exercised, if it should become expedient to do so ; whereas, I hold that congress has, under the constitution, no such power at all, and that any attempt thus to legislate would be a gross fraud upon all the states of the Union.

"2. The resolutions of the honorable senator assert that slavery does not now exist by law in the territories recently acquired from Mexico ; whereas, I am of opinion that the treaty with the Mexican republic carried the constitution, *with all its guaranties*, to all the territory obtained by treaty, and secured the privilege to every southern slaveholder to enter any part of it, attended by his slave property, and to enjoy the same therein, free from all molestation or hindrance whatsoever.

"3. Whether slavery is or is not likely to be introduced into these territorfes, or into any of them, is a proposition too uncertain, in my judgment, to be at present positively affirmed; and I am unwilling to make a solemn legislative declaration on the point. *Let the future provide the appropriate solution of this interesting question.*

"4. Considering, as I have several times heretofore formally declared, the title of Texas to all the territory embraced in her boundaries, as laid down in her law of 1836, full, complete, and undeniable, I am unwilling to say any thing, by resolution or otherwise, which may in the least degree draw that title into question, as I think is done in one of the resolutions of the honorable senator from Kentucky.

"5. I am, upon constitutional and other grounds, wholly opposed to the principle of *assuming state debts*, which I understand to be embodied in one of the resolutions of the honorable senator from Kentucky. If Texan soil is to be bought, (and with certain appropriate *safeguards*, I am decidedly in favor of it,) let us pay to the sovereign state of Texas the value thereof in money, to be used by her as she pleases. It will be, as I think, more delicate and respectful to let her provide for the management of this matter, which is strictly *domestic* in its character, in such manner as she may choose—presuming that she will act wisely, justly, and honorably towards all to whom she may be indebted.

"6. As to the abolition of the *slave-trade* in the District of Columbia, I see no particular objection to it, provided it is done in a delicate and judicious manner, and is not a concession to the menaces and demands of factionists and fanatics. If other questions can be adjusted, this one will, perhaps, occasion but little difficulty.

"7. The resolutions which provide for the restoration of fugitives from labor or service, and for the establishment of territorial governments, free from all restriction on the subject of slavery, have my hearty approval. The last resolution, which asserts that congress has no power to prohibit the trade in slaves from state to state, I equally approve.

"8. If all other questions connected with the subject of slavery can be satisfactorily adjusted, I can see no objection to admitting all California, above the line of 36° 30', into the Union; *provided another new slave state can be laid off within the present limits of Texas*, so as to keep the present *equiponderance* between the slave and free states of the Union; and provided further, all this is done by way of *compromise*, and in order to save the Union, as dear to me as to any man living."

Mr. Mason, of Va., after expressing his deep anxiety to "go with him who went furthest, but within the limits of strict duty, in adjusting these unhappy differences," added: "Sir, so far as I have read these resolutions, there is but one proposition to which I can give a hearty assent, and that is the resolution which proposes to organize territorial governments at once in these territories, without a declaration one way or the other as to their domestic institutions. But there is another which I deeply regret to see introduced into this senate, by a senator from a slaveholding state; it is that which assumes that slavery does not now exist by law in those countries.   I understand one of these propositions to declare that, by law, slavery is now abolished in New Mexico and California.   That was the very proposition advanced by the non-slaveholding states at the last session ; combated and disproved, as I thought, by gentlemen from the slaveholding states, and which the compromise bill was framed to test. So far, I regarded the question of law as disposed of, and it was very clearly and satisfactorily shown to be against the spirit of the resolution of the senator from Kentucky.   If the contrary is true, I presume the senator from Kentucky would declare that if a law is now valid in the territories abolishing slavery, that it could not be introduced there, even if a law was passed creating the institution, or repealing the statutes already existing ; a doctrine never assented to, as far as I know, until now, by any senator representing one of the slaveholding states.   Sir, I hold the very opposite, and with such confidence, that at the last session I was willing and did vote for a bill to test this question in the supreme court.   Yet this resolution assumes the other doctrine to be true, and our assent is challenged to it as a proposition of law.

"I do not mean to detain the senate by any discussion ; but I deemed it to be my duty to enter a decided protest, on the part of Virginia, against such doctrines.   They concede the whole question at once, that our people shall not go into the new territories and take their property with them ; a doctrine to which I never will assent, and for which, sir, no law can be found.   There are other portions of the resolution, for which, if they could be separated, I should be very willing to vote.   That respecting fugitive slaves, and that respecting the organization of governments in these territories, I should be willing to vote for ; and I am happy to declare the gratification I experience at finding the senator from Kentucky differing so much, on this subject, from the executive message recently laid before the senate.   I beg not to be understood as having spoken in any spirit of unkindness towards the senator from Kentucky, for whom I entertain the warmest and most profound respect ; but I cannot but express also my regret that he has felt it to be his duty, standing as he does before this people, and representing the people he does, to introduce into this body resolutions of this kind."

Mr. Jefferson Davis, of Miss., said : " Sir, we are called upon to receive this as a measure of compromise !   As a measure in which we of the minority are to receive nothing.   A measure of compromise !   I look upon it as but a modest mode of taking that, the claim to which has been more boldly asserted by others ; and, that I may be understood upon this question, and that my position may go forth to the country in the same columns that convey the sentiments of the senator from Kentucky, I here assert, that never will I take less than the Missouri compromise line extended to the Pacific ocean, with the specific recognition of the right to hold slaves in the territory below that line ; and that, before such territories are admitted into the Union as states, slaves may be taken there from any of the United States at the option of the owners. I can never consent to give additional power to a majority to commit further aggressions upon the minority in this Union ; and will never consent to any proposition which will have such a tendency, without a full guaranty or counteracting measure is connected with it."

Mr. Clay, in reply, said : "I am extremely sorry to hear the senator from Mississippi say that he requires, first, the extension of the Missouri compromise line to the Pacific, and also that he is not satisfied with that, but requires, if I understood him correctly, a positive provision for the admission of slavery south of that line. And now, sir, coming from a slave state, as I do, I owe it to myself, I owe it to truth, I owe it to the subject, to state that no earthly power could induce me to vote for a specific measure for the introduction of slavery where it had not before existed, either south or north of that line. Coming as I do from a slave state, it is my solemn, deliberate, and well-matured determination that no power—no earthly power—shall compel me to vote for the positive introduction of slavery either south or north of that line. Sir, while you reproach, and justly, too, our British ancestors for the introduction of this institution upon the continent of America, I am, for one, unwilling that the posterity of the present inhabitants of California and of New Mexico shall reproach us for doing just what we reproach Great Britain for doing to us. If the citizens of those territories choose to establish slavery, I am for admitting them with such provisions in their constitutions; but then, it will be their own work, and not ours, and their posterity will have to reproach them, and not us, for forming constitutions allowing the institution of slavery to exist among them. These are my views, sir, and I choose to express them ; and I care not how extensively or universally they are known. The honorable senator from Virginia has expressed his opinion that slavery exists in these territories, and I have no doubt that opinion is sincerely and honorably entertained by him; and I would say with equal sincerity and honesty, that I believe that slavery nowhere exists within any portion of the territory acquired by us from Mexico. He holds a directly contrary opinion to mine, as he has a perfect right to do; and we will not quarrel about that difference of opinion."

Mr. William R. King, of Ala., on the question of slavery in the new territories, said : "With regard to the opinions of honorable senators, respecting the operation of the laws of Mexico in our newly-acquired territories, there may be, and no doubt is, an honest difference of opinion with regard to that matter. Some believe that the municipal institutions of Mexico overrule the provisions of our constitution, and prevent us from carrying our slaves there. That is a matter which I do not propose to discuss ; it has been discussed at length in the debate upon the compromise bill, putting it on the ground of a judicial decision. Sir, I know not—nor is it a matter of much importance with me—whether that which the honorable senator states to be a fact, and which, as has been remarked by the senator from Mississippi, can only be conjectural, be in reality so or not—that slavery never can go there. This is what is stated, however. Well, be it so. If slave labor be not profitable there, it will not go there; or, if it go, who will be benefited ? Not the south. They will never compel it to go there. We are misunderstood—grossly, I may say—by honorable senators, though not intentionally ; but we are contending for a principle, and a great principle—a principle lying at the very foundation of our constitutional rights—involving, as has been remarked, our property; in one word, involving our safety, our honor, all that is dear to us, as American freemen. Well, sir, for that principle we will be compelled to contend to the utmost, and to resist aggression at every hazard and at every sacrifice. That is the position in which we are placed. We ask no act of congress—as has been properly intimated by the senator from Mississippi—to carry slavery anywhere. Sir, I believe we have as much constitutional power to prohibit slavery from going into the territories of the United States, as we have to pass an act carrying slavery there. We have no right to do either the one or the other. I would as soon vote for the Wilmot proviso as I would vote for any law which required that slavery should go into any of the territories."

Mr. Downs, of Louisiana, said: "I must confess, that in the whole course of my life, my astonishment has never been greater than it was when I saw this (Mr. Clay's) proposition brought forward as a compromise; and I rise now, sir, not for the purpose of discussing it at all, but to protest most solemnly against it. I consider this compromise as no compromise at all. What, sir, does it grant to the south? I can see nothing at all. The first resolution offered by the honorable senator proposes to admit the state of California with a provision prohibiting slavery in territory which embraces all our possessions on the Pacific. It is true, there may be a new regulation of the boundary hereafter; but if there were to be such a regulation, why was it not embraced in this resolution? As no boundary is mentioned, we have a right to presume that the boundary established by the constitution of California was to be received as the established boundary. What concession, then, is it from the north, that we admit a state thus prohibiting slavery, embracing the whole of our possessions on the Pacific coast, according to these resolutions? As to the resolution relating to New Mexico and Deseret, if it had simply contained the provision that a constitutional government shall be established there, without any mention of slavery whatever, it would have been well enough. But, inasmuch as it is affirmed that slavery does not now exist in these territories, does it not absolutely preclude its admission there? and the resolutions might just as well affirm that slavery should be prohibited in these territories. The senator from Alabama, if I understood him aright, maintains that the proposition is of the same import as the Wilmot proviso; and, in view of these facts, I would ask, is there anything conceded to us of the south?"

Mr. Butler, of South Carolina, said: "Perhaps our northern brethren ought to understand that all the compromises that have been made, have been by concessions—acknowledged concessions—on the part of the south. When other compromises are proposed, that require new concessions on their part, whilst none are exacted on the other, the issue, at least, should be presented for their consideration before they come to the decision of their great question. If I understand it, the senator from Kentucky's whole proposition of compromise is nothing more than this: That California is already disposed of, having formed a state constitution, and that territorial governments shall be organized for Deseret and New Mexico, under which, by the operation of laws already existing, a slaveholding population could not carry with them, or own slaves there. What is there in the nature of a compromise here, coupled, as it is, with the proposition that by the existing laws in the territories, it is almost certain that slaveholders cannot, and have no right to go there with their property? What is there in the nature of a compromise here? I am willing, however, to run the risks, and am ready to give to the territories the governments they require. I shall always think, that under a constitution giving equal rights to all parties, the slaveholding people, as such, can go to these territories, and retain their property there. But, if we adopt this proposition of the senator from Kentucky, it is clearly on the basis that slavery shall not go there.

"I do not understand the senator from Mississippi (Mr. Davis) to maintain the proposition, that the south asked or desired a law declaring that slavery should go there, or that it maintained the policy even that it was the duty of congress to pass such a law. We have only asked, and it is the only compromise to which we will submit, that congress shall withhold the hand of violence from the territories. The only way in which this question can be settled is, for gentlemen from the north to withdraw all their opposition to the territorial governments, and not insist on their slavery prohibition. The Union is then safe enough. Why, then, insist on a compromise, when those already made are sufficient for the peace of the north and south, if faithfully observed? These propositions are in the name of a compromise, when none is necessary."

Mr. Benton said, "it had been affirmed and denied that slavery had been abolished in Mexico. He affirmed its abolition, and read copious extracts from the laws and constitution of Mexico, in proof of the affirmation. Slavery having been abolished by Mexican law before we acquired the countries, the Wilmot proviso in relation to these countries was a thing of nothing—an empty provision. He said, also, that African slavery never had existed in Mexico in the form in which it existed in the states of this Union; and that, if the Mexican law was now in force in New Mexico and California, no slaveholder from the Union would carry a slave thither, except to set him free. The policy of this country was to discourage emancipation; that of Mexico had been to promote it. This was shown by numerous quotations of the laws of Mexico. Slavery was defined by Spanish law to be 'the condition of a man who is the property of another against natural right.' Therefore, not being derived from nature, or divine law, but existing only by positive enactment, it had no countenance from Spanish law. He affirmed these three points: 1. Slavery was abolished in California and New Mexico before we got them. 2. Even if not abolished, no person would carry a slave to those countries to be held under such law. 3. Slavery could not exist there, except by positive law yet to be passed. According to this exposition, the proviso would have no more effect there than a piece of blank paper pasted on the statute book."

Mr. Calhoun said "the Union was in danger. The cause of this danger was the discontent at the south. And what was the cause of this discontent? It was found in the belief which prevailed among them that they could not, consistently with honor and safety, remain in the Union. And what had caused this belief? One of the causes was the long-continued agitation of the slave question at the north, and the many aggressions they had made on the rights of the south. But the primary cause was in the fact, that the equilibrium between the two sections at the time of the adoption of the constitution had been destroyed. The first of the series of acts by which this had been done, was the ordinance of 1787, by which the south had been excluded from all the northwestern region. The next was the Missouri compromise, excluding them from all the Louisiana territory north of 36 degrees 30 minutes, except the state of Missouri; in all 1,238,025 square miles, leaving to the south the southern portion of the original Louisiana territory, with Florida; to which had since been added the territory acquired with Texas; making in all but 609,023 miles. And now the north was endeavoring to appropriate to herself the territory recently acquired from Mexico, adding 526,078 miles to the territory from which the south was if possible to be excluded. Another cause of the destruction of this equilibrium was our system of revenue, (the tariff,) the duties falling mainly upon the southern portion of the Union, as being the greatest exporting states, while more than a due proportion of the revenue had been disbursed at the north.

But while these measures were destroying the equilibrium between the two sections, the action of the government was leading to a radical change in its character. It was maintained that the government itself had the right to decide, in the last resort, as to the extent of its powers, and to resort to force to maintain the power it claimed. The doctrines of General Jackson's proclamation, subsequently asserted and maintained by Mr. Madison, the leading framer and expounder of the constitution, were the doctrines which, if carried out, would change the character of the government from a federal republic, as it came from the hands of its framers, into a great national consolidated democracy.

Mr. Calhoun also spoke of the anti-slavery agitation, which, if not arrested, would destroy the Union; and he passed a censure upon congress for receiving abolition petitions. Had congress in the beginning adopted the course which he had advocated, which was to refuse to take jurisdiction, by the united voice of all parties, the agitation would have been prevented. He charged the north with false professions of devotion to the Union, and with having violated the constitution. Acts had been passed in northern states to set aside and annul the clause of the constitution which provides for delivering up fugitive slaves. The agitation of the slavery question, with the avowed purpose of abolishing slavery in the states, was another violation of the constitution. And during the fifteen years of this agitation, in not a single instance had the people of the north denounced these agitators. How then could their professions of devotion to the Union be sincere?

Mr. Calhoun disapproved both the plan of Mr. Clay and that of President

Taylor, as incapable of saving the Union. He would pass by the former without remark, as Mr. Clay had been replied to by several senators. The executive plan could not save the Union, because it could not satisfy the south that it could safely or honorably remain in the Union. It was a modification of the Wilmot proviso, proposing to effect the same object, the exclusion of the south from the new territory. The executive proviso was more objectionable than the Wilmot. Both inflicted a dangerous wound upon the constitution, by depriving the southern states of equal rights, as joint partners, in these territories; but the formerinflicted others equally great. It claimed for the inhabitants the right to legislate for the territories, which belonged to congress. The assumption of this right was utterly unfounded, unconstitutional, and without example. Under this assumed right, the people of California had formed a constitution and a state government, and appointed senators and representatives. If the people as adventurers had conquered the territory and established their independence, the sovereignty of the country would have been vested in them. In that case, they would have had the right to form a state government; and afterward they might have applied to congress for admission into the Union. But the United States had conquered and acquired California; therefore, to them belonged the sovereignty, and the powers of government over the territory. Michigan was the first case of departure from the uniform rule of acting. Hers, however, was a slight departure from established usage. The ordinance of 1787 secured to her the right of becoming a state when she should have 60,000 inhabitants. Congress delayed taking the census. The people became impatient; and after her population had increased to twice that number, they formed a constitution without waiting for the taking of the census; and congress waived the omission, as there was no doubt of the requisite number of inhabitants. In other cases there had existed territorial governments.

Having shown how the Union could not be saved, he then proceeded to answer the question how it could be saved. There was but one way certain. Justice must be done to the south, by a full and final settlement of all the questions at issue. The north must concede to the south an equal right to the acquired territory, and fulfill the stipulations respecting fugitive slaves; must cease to agitate the slave question, and join in an amendment of the constitution, restoring to the south the power she possessed of protecting herself, before the equilibrium between the two sections had been destroyed by the action of the government."

Mr. Webster, on the 7th of March, spoke at length on the resolutions of Mr. Clay, and in reply to Mr. Calhoun. In the course of his history of the slave question in this country, he remarked, "that a change had taken place since the adoption of the constitution. Both sections then held slavery to be equally an evil, moral and political. It was inhuman and cruel; it weakened the social fabric, and rendered labor less productive. The eminent men of the south then held it to be an evil, a blight, a scourge, and a curse. The framers of the constitution, in considering how to deal with it, concluded that it could not be continued if the importation of slaves should cease. The prohibition of the importation after twenty years was proposed : a term which some southern gentlemen, Mr. Madison for one, thought too long. The word 'slaves' was not allowed in the constitution; Mr. Madison was opposed to it; he did not wish to see it recognized in that instrument, that there could be property in men. The ordinance of 1787 also received the unanimous support of the south; a measure which Mr. Calhoun had said was the first in a series of measures which had enfeebled that section.

Soon after this, the age of cotton came. The south wanted land for its cultivation. Mr. Calhoun had observed that there had always been a majority in favor of the north. If so, the north had acted very liberally or very weakly; for they had seldom exercised their power. The truth was, the general lead in politics for three-fourths of the time had been southern lead. In 1802, a great cotton region, now embracing all Alabama, had been obtained from Georgia by the general government. In 1803, Louisiana was purchased, out of which several large slaveholding states had been formed. In 1819, Florida was ceded, which also had come in as slave territory. And lastly, Texas—great, vast, illimitable Texas—had been admitted as a slave state. In this, the senator himself, as secretary of state, and the late secretary of the treasury, then senator, had taken the lead. They had done their work thoroughly; having procured a stipulation for four new states to be formed out of that state ; and all south of the line 36° 30′ might be admitted with slavery. Even New England had aided in this measure. Three-fourths of liberty-loving Connecticut in the other house, and one-half in this, had supported it. And it had one vote from each of the states of Massachusetts and Maine.

Mr. Webster said he had repeatedly expressed the dertermination to vote for no acquisition, or cession, or annexation, believing we had territory enough. But Texas was now in with all her territories, as a slave state, with a pledge that, if divided into many states, those south of 36° 30′ might come in as slaves states; and he, for one, meant to fulfill the obligation. As to California and New Mexico, he held that slavery was effectually excluded from those territories by a law even superior to that which admits and sanctions it in Texas—he meant the law of nature. The physical geography of the country would forever exclude African slavery there; and it needed not the application of a proviso. If the question was now before the senate, he would not vote to add a prohibition—to reäffirm an ordinance of nature, nor reënact the will of God If they were making a government for New Mexico, and a Wilmot proviso were proposed, he would treat it as Mr. Polk had treated it in the Oregon bill. Mr. Polk was opposed to it; but some government was necessary, and he signed the bill, knowing that the proviso was entirely nugatory.

Both the north and the south had grievances. The south justly complained that individuals and legislatures of the north refused to perform their constitutional duties in regard to returning fugitive slaves. Members of the northern legislatures were bound by oath to support the constitution of the United States ; and the clause requiring the delivery of fugitive slaves was as binding as any other. Complaints had also been made against certain resolutions emanating from legislatures at the north on the subject of slavery in the district, and sometimes even in regard to its abolition in the states. Abolition societies were another subject of complaint. These societies had done nothing useful; but they had produced mischief by their interference with the south. He referred to the debate in the Virginia legislature in 1832, when the subject of gradual abolition was freely discussed. But since the agitation of this question, the bonds of the slave had been more firmly riveted. Again, the violence of the press was complained of. But wherever the freedom of the press existed, there always would be foolish and violent paragraphs, as there were foolish and violent speeches in both houses of congress. He thought, however, the north had cause for the same complaint of the south. But of these grievances of the south, one only was within the redress of the government; that was the want of proper regard to the constitutional injunction for the delivery of fugitive slaves.

The north complained of the south, that, when the former, in adopting the constitution, recognized the right of representation of the slaves, it was under a state of sentiment different from that which now existed. It was generally hoped and believed, that the institution would be gradually extinguished; instead of which, it was now to be cherished, and preserved, and extended; and for this purpose, the south was constantly demanding new territory. A southern senator had said that the condition of the slaves was preferable to that of the laboring population of the north. Said Mr. Webster: Who are the north? Five-sixths of the whole property of the north is in the hands of laborers, who cultivate their own farms, educate their children, and provide the means of independence. Those who were not freeholders, earned wages, which, as they were accumulated, were turned into capital.

Another grievance at the north was, that their free colored citizens employed on vessels arriving at southern ports, were taken on shore by the municipal authorities, and imprisoned till the vessel was ready to sail. This was inconvenient in practice; and was deemed unjustifiable, oppressive, and unconstitutional. It was a great grievance. So far as these grievances had their foundation in matters of law, they could and ought to be redressed; and so far as they rested in matters of opinion, in mutual crimination and recrimination, we could only endeavor to allay the agitation, and cultivate a better feeling between the south and the north.

Mr. Webster expressed great pain at hearing secession spoken of as a possible event. Said he: Secession! Peaceable secession! Sir, your eyes and mine are never destined to see that miracle. Who is so foolish—I beg every body's pardon—as to expect to see any such thing? There could be no such thing as peaceable secession—a concurrent agreement of the members of this great republic to separate? Where is the line to be drawn? What states are to secede? Where is the flag of the republic to remain? What is to become of the army?—of the navy?—of the public lands? How is each of the states to defend itself? To break up this great government! to dismem-

37

ber this great country! to astonish Europe with an act of folly, such as
Europe for two centuries has never beheld in any government! No, sir! no,
sir! There will be no secession. Gentlemen are not serious when they talk
of secession."

Mr. Clay's resolutions, and also those submitted by Mr. Bell, were referred
on the 19th of April to a select committee of thirteen. The members of the
committee were elected by ballot: Henry Clay, chairman, Bell, Berrien,
Downs, King, Mangum and Mason, from slave states; Cass, Webster, Dickinson, Phelps, Cooper and Bright, from free states. On the 8th of May, Mr.
Clay, from the committee, made the following report:

"The senate's committee of thirteen, to whom were referred various resolutions relating to California, to other portions of the territory recently acquired
by the United States from the republic of Mexico, and to other subjects connected with the institution of slavery, have, according to order, had these resolutions and subjects under consideration, and beg leave to submit the following
report: The committee entered on the discharge of their duties with a deep
sense of their great importance, and with earnest and anxious solicitude to arrive at such conclusions as might be satisfactory to the senate and to the country. Most of the matters referred have not only been subjected to extensive
and serious public discussions throughout the country, but to a debate in the
senate itself, singular for its elaborateness and its duration; so that a full exposition of all those motives and views which, on several subjects confided to
the committee, have determined the conclusions at which they have arrived,
seems quite unnecessary. They will, therefore, restrict themselves to a few
general observations, and to some reflections which grow out of those subjects.

"Out of our recent territorial acquisitions, and in connection with the institution of slavery, questions most grave sprung, which, greatly dividing and
agitating the people of the United States, have threatened to disturb the harmony, if not to endanger the safety of the Union. The committee believe it
to be highly desirable and necessary speedily to adjust all those questions, in a
spirit of concord, and in a manner to produce, if practicable, general satisfaction. They think it would be unwise to leave any of them open and unsettled,
to fester in the public mind, and to prolong, if not aggravate, the existing agitation. It has been their object, therefore, in this report, to make such proposals and recommendations as would accomplish a general adjustment of all
these questions.

"Among the subjects referred to the committee which command their first attention, are the resolutions offered to the senate by the senator from Tennessee,
Mr. Bell. By a provision in the resolution of congress annexing Texas to the
United States, it is declared that 'new states of convenient size, not exceeding
four in number, by the consent of said state, be formed out of *' territory
thereof, which shall be *entitled to admission*, under the provisions of the federal constitution; and such states as may be formed out of that portion of said
territory lying south of 36° 30' north latitude, commonly known as the Mis-

souri compromise line, *shall be* admitted into the Union with or without slavery, as the people of each state asking admission may desire.'

"The committee were unanimously of opinion, that whenever one or more states, formed out of the territory of Texas, not exceeding four, having sufficient population, with the consent of Texas, may apply to be admitted into the Union, they are entitled to such admission, beyond all doubt, upon the clear, unambiguous, and absolute terms of the solemn compact contained in the resolution of annexation adopted by congress, and assented to by Texas. But, whilst the committee conceive that the right of admission into the Union of any new state, carved out of the territory of Texas, not exceeding the number specified, and under the conditions stated, cannot be justly controverted, the committee do not think that the formation of any new states should now originate with congress. The initiative, in conformity with the usage which has hitherto prevailed, should be taken by a portion of the people of Texas themselves, desirous of constituting a new state, with the consent of Texas. And in the formation of such new states, it will be for the people composing it to decide for themslves whether they will admit, or whether they will exclude slavery. And however they may decide that purely municipal question, congress is bound to acquiesce, and to fulfill in good faith the stipulations of the compact with Texas. The committee are aware that it has been contended that the resolution of congress annexing Texas was unconstitutional. At a former epoch of our country's history, there were those (and Mr. Jefferson, under whose auspices the treaty of Louisiana was concluded, was among them,) who believed that the states formed out of Louisiana could not be received into the Union without an amendment of the constitution. But the state of Louisiana, Missouri, Arkansas and Iowa have been all, nevertheless, admitted. And who would now think of opposing Minnesota, Oregon, or new states formed out of the ancient province of Louisiana, upon the ground of an alleged original defect of constitutional power? In grave national transactions, while yet in their earlier or incipent stages, differences may well exist; but when once they have been decided by a constitutional majority, and are consummated, or in a process of consummation, there can be no other safe and prudent alternative than to respect the decision already rendered, and to acquiesce in it. Entertaining these views, a majority of the committee do not think it necessary or proper to recommend, at this time, or prospectively, any new state or states to be formed out of the territory of Texas. Should any such state be hereafter formed, and present itself for admission into the Union, whether with or without the establishment of slavery, it cannot be doubted that congress will admit it, under the influence of similar considerations, in regard to new states formed of or out of New Mexico and Utah, with or without the institution of slavery, according to the constitutions and judgment of the people who compose them, as to what may be best to promote their happiness.

"In considering the question of the admission of California as a state into the Union, a majority of the committee conceive that any irregularity, by which that state was organized without the previous authority of any act of congress, ought to be overlooked, in consideration of the omission by congress to establish any territorial government for the people of California, and the consequent necessity which they were under to create a government for themselves, best adapted to their own wants.   There are various instances, prior to the case of California, of the admission of new states into the Union without any previous authorization by congress.   The sole condition required by the constitution of the United States, in respect to the admission of a new state, is, that its constitution shall be republican in form.   California presents such a constitution; and there is no doubt of her having a greater population than that which, according to the practice of the government, has been heretofore deemed sufficient to receive a new state into the Union.

"In regard to the proposed boundaries of California, the committee would have been glad if there existed more full and accurate geographical knowledge of the territory which these boundaries include.   There is reason to believe that, large as they are, they embrace no very disproportionate quantity of land adapted to cultivation.   And it is known that they contain extensive ranges of mountains, deserts of sand, and much unproductive soil.   It might have been, perhaps, better to have assigned to California a more limited front on the Pacific; but even if there had been reserved, on the shore of that ocean, a portion of the boundary which it presents, for any other state or states, it is not very certain that an accessible interior of sufficient extent could have been given to them to render an approach to the ocean, through their own limits, of very great importance.

"A majority of the committee think that there are many and urgent concurring considerations in favor of admitting California, with the proposed boundaries, and of securing to her at this time the benefits of a state government. If, hereafter, upon an increase of her population, a more thorough exploration of her territory, and an ascertainment of the relations which may arise between the people occupying its various parts, it should be found conducive to their convenience and happiness to form a new state out of California, we have every reason to believe, from past experience, that the question of its admission will be fairly considered and justly decided.

"A majority of the committee, therefore, recommend to the senate the passage of the bill reported by the committee on territories, for the admission of California as a state into the Union.   To prevent misconception, the committee also recommend that the amendment reported by the same committee to the bill be adopted, so as to leave incontestable the right of the United States to the public domain and other public property of California.

"Whilst a majority of the committee believe it to be necessary and proper, under actual circumstances, to admit California, they think it quite as necessary and proper to establish governments for the residue of the territory derived from Mexico, and to bring it within the pale of the federal authority.   The remoteness of that territory from the seat of the general government; the dispersed state of its population; the variety of races—pure and mixed—of which it consists; the ignorance of some of the races of our laws, language, and habits; their exposure to inroads and wars of savage tribes ; and the solemn stipulations of the treaty by which we acquired dominion over them—impose upon the United States the imperative obligation of extending to them protection, and of providing for them government and laws suited to their condition. Congress will fail in the performance of a high duty, if it do not give, or attempt to give to them, the benefit of such protection, government, and laws. They are not now, and for a long time to come may not be, prepared for state government. The territorial form, for the present, is best suited to their condition. A bill has been reported by the committee on territories, dividing all the territory acquired from Mexico, not comprehended within the limits of California, into two territories, under the names of New Mexico and Utah, and proposing for each a territorial government.

"The committee recommend to the senate the establishment of those territorial governments; and, in order more certainly to secure that desirable object, they also recommend that the bill for their establishment be incorporated in the bill for the admission of California, and that, united together, they both be passed.

"The combination of the two measures in the same bill is objected to on various grounds. It is said that they are incongruous, and have no necessary connection with each other. A majority of the committee think otherwise. The object of both measures is the establishment of a government suited to the conditions, respectively, of the proposed new state and of the new territories. Prior to their transfer to the United States, they both formed a part of Mexico, where they stood in equal relations to the government of that republic. They were both ceded to the United States by the same treaty. And, in the same article of that treaty, the United States engaged to protect and govern both. Common in their origin, common in their alienation from one foreign government to another, common in their wants of good government, and conterminous in some of their boundaries, and alike in many particulars of physical condition, they have nearly every thing in common in the relation in which they stand to the rest of the Union. There is, then, a general fitness and propriety in extending the parental care of government to both in common. If California, by a sudden and extraordinary augmentation of population, has advanced so rapidly as to mature for herself a state government, that furnishes no reason why the less fortunate territories of New Mexico and Utah should be abandoned and left ungoverned by the United States, or should be disconnected with California, which, although she has organized for herself a state government, must, legally and constitutionally, be regarded as a territory until she is actually admitted as a state into the Union.

" It is further objected that, by combining the two measures in the same bill, members who may be willing to vote for one, and unwilling to vote for the other, would be placed in an embarrassing condition. They would be constrained, it is urged, to take or reject both. On the other hand, there are other members who would be willing to vote for both united, but would feel themselves constrained to vote against the California bill if it stood alone. Each

party finds in the bill which it favors something which commends it to acceptance, and in the other something which it disapproves.   The true ground,
therefore, of the objection to the union of the measures is not any want of af-
finity between them, but because of the favor or disfavor with which they are
respectively regarded.   In this conflict of opinion, it seems to a majority of
the committee that a spirit of mutual concession enjoins that the two measures should be connected together—the effect of which will be, that neither
opinion will exclusively triumph, and that both may find, in such an amicable
arrangement, enough of good to reconcile them to the acceptance of the combined measure.   And such a course of legislation is not at all unusual.   Few
laws have ever passed in which there were not parts to which exception was
taken.   It is inexpedient, if not impracticable, to separate these parts, and embody them in distinct bills, so as to accommodate the diversity of opinion which
may exist.   The constitution of the United States contained in it a great variety of provisions, to some of which serious objection was made in the convention which formed it, by different members of that body ; and, when it was
submitted to the ratification of the states, some of them objected to some
parts, and others to other parts, of the same instrument.   Had these various
parts and provisions been separately acted on in the convention, or separately
submitted to the people of the United States, it is by no means certain that
the constitution itself would ever have been adopted or ratified.   Those who
did not like particular provisions found compensation in other parts of it.   And
in all cases of constitution and laws, when either is presented as a whole, the
question to be decided is, whether the good which it contains is not of greater
amount, and capable of neutralizing anything objectionable in it.   And, as
nothing human is perfect, for the sake of that harmony so desirable in such a
confederacy as this, we must be reconciled to secure as much as we can of what
we wish, and be consoled by the reflection that what we do not exactly like is
a friendly concession, and agreeable to those who, being united with us in a
common destiny, it is desirable should always live with us in peace and concord.

" A majority of the committee have, therefore, been led to the recommendation to the senate that the two measures be united.   The bill for establishing
the two territories, it will be observed, omits the Wilmot proviso on the one
hand, and, on the other, makes no provision for the introduction of slavery into
any part of the new territories.

" That proviso has been the fruitful source of distraction and agitation.   If
it were adopted and applied to any territory, it would cease to have any obligatory force as soon as such territory were admitted as a state into the Union.
There was never any occasion for it to accomplish the professed object with
which it was originally offered.   This has been clearly demonstrated by the
current of events.   California, of all the recent territorial acquisitions from
Mexico, was that in which, if anywhere within them, the introduction of slavery
was most likely to take place ; and the constitution of California, by the unanimous vote of her convention, has expressly interdicted it.   There is the high-

est degree of probability that Utah and New Mexico will, when they come to be admitted as states, follow the example. The proviso is, as to all those regions in common, a mere abstraction. Why should it be any longer insisted on ? Totally destitute as it is of any practical import, it has, nevertheless, had the pernicious effect to excite serious, if not alarming consequences. It is high time that the wounds which it has inflicted should be healed up and closed. And, to avoid, in all future time, the agitations which must be produced by the conflict of opinion on the slavery question, existing as this institution does in some of the states, and prohibited as it is in others, the true principle which ought to regulate the action of congress in forming territorial governments for each newly-acquired domain, is to refrain from all legislation on the subject in the territory acquired, so long as it retains the territorial form of government—leaving it to the people of such territory, when they have attained to the condition which entitles them to admission as a state, to decide for themselves the question of the allowance or prohibition of domestic slavery. The committee believe that they express the anxious desire of an immense majority of the people of the United States, when they declare that it is high time that good feeling, harmony, and fraternal sentiment should be again revived, and that the government should be able once more to proceed in its great operations to promote the happiness and prosperity of the country, undisturbed by this distracting cause.

" As for California—far from seeing her sensibility affected by her being associated with other kindred measures—she ought to rejoice and be highly gratified that, in entering into the Union, she may have contributed to the tranquility and happiness of the great family of states, of which, it is to be hoped, she may one day be a distinguished member.

" The committee beg leave next to report on the subject of the northern and western boundary of Texas. On that question a great diversity of opinion has prevailed. According to one view of it, the western limit of Texas was the Nueces ; according to another, it extended to the Rio Grande, and stretched from its mouth to its source. A majority of the committee having come to the conclusion of recommending an amicable adjustment of the boundary with Texas, abstain from expressing any opinion as to the true and legitimate western and northern boundary of that state. The terms proposed for such an adjustment are contained in the bill herewith reported, and they are, with inconsiderable variation, the same as that reported by the committee on territories.

"According to these terms, it is proposed to Texas that her boundary be recognized to the Rio Grande, and up that river to the point commonly called El Paso, and thence running up that river twenty miles, measured thereon by a straight line, and thence eastwardly to a point where the hundredth degree of west longitude crosses Red River; being the southwest angle in the line designated between the United States and Mexico, and the same angle in the line of the territory set apart for the Indians by the United States.

" If this boundary be assented to by Texas, she will be quieted to that extent in her title. And some may suppose that, in consideration of this concession by the United States, she might, without any other equivalent, relinquish any claim she has beyond the proposed boundary; that is, any claim to any part of New Mexico. But, under the influence of sentiments of justice and great liberality, the bill proposes to Texas, for her relinquishment of any such claim, a large pecuniary equivalent. As a consideration for it, and considering that a portion of the debt of Texas was created on a pledge to her creditors of the duties on foreign imports, transferred by the resolution of annexation to the United States, and now received and receivable in her treasury, a majority of the committee recommend the payment of the sum of —— millons of dollars to Texas, to be applied in the first instance to the extinction of that portion of her debt for the reimbursement of which the duties on foreign imports were pledged as aforesaid, and the residue in such manner as she may direct. The sum is to be paid by the United States, in a stock, to be created, bearing five per cent. interest annually, payable half-yearly, at the treasury of the United States, and the principal reimbursable at the end of fourteen years.

"According to an estimate which has been made, there are included in the territory to which it is proposed that Texas shall relinquish her claim, embracing that part of New Mexico lying east of the Rio Grande, a little less than 124,933 square miles, and about 79,957,120 acres of land. From the proceeds of the sale of this land, the United States may ultimately be reimbursed a portion, if not the whole, of the amount of what is thus proposed to be advanced to Texas.

"It cannot be anticipated that Texas will decline to accede to these liberal propositions; but if she should, it is to be distinctly understood that the title of the United States to any territory acquired from Mexico, east of the Rio Grande, will remain unimpared, and in the same condition as if the proposals of adjustment now offered had never been made.

"A majority of the committee recommend to the senate that the section containing these proposals to Texas shall be incorporated into the bill embracing the admission of California as a state, and the establishment of territorial governments for Utah and New Mexico. The definition and establishment of the boundary between New Mexico and Texas have an intimate and necessary connection with the establishment of a territorial government for New Mexico. To form a territorial government for New Mexico, without prescribing the limits of the territory, would leave the work imperfect and incomplete, and might expose New Mexico to serious controversy, if not dangerous collisions, with the state of Texas. And most, if not all, of the considerations which unite in favor of combining the bill for the admission of California as a state and the territorial bills, apply to the boundary question of Texas. By the union of the three measures, every question of difficulty and division which has arisen out of the territorial acquisition from Mexico, will, it is hoped, be adjusted, or placed in a train of satisfactory adjustment. The committee, availing themselves of the arduous and valuable labors of the committee on territories, report a bill, herewith annexed, (marked A,) embracing those three measures, the passage of which, uniting them together, they recommend to the senate.

"The committee will now proceed to the consideration of, and to report upon the subject of persons owing service or labor in one state escaping into another. The text of the constitution is quite clear : "No person held to labor or service in one state, *under the laws thereof*, escaping into another, shall, in consequence of any law or regulation threin, be discharged from such service or labor, but *shall be delivered up* on the claim of the party to whom such service or labor is due." Nothing can be more explicit than this language ; nothing more manifest than the right to demand, and the obligation to deliver up to the claimant, any such fugitive. And the constitution addresses itself alike to the states composing the Union and to the general government. If, indeed, there were any difference in the duty to enforce this portion of the constitution between the states and the federal government, it is more clear that it is that of the former than of the latter. But it is the duty of both. It is well known and incontestable that citizens of slaveholding states encounter the greatest difficulty in obtaining the benefit of this provision of the constitution.

"The attempt to recapture a fugitive is almost always the subject of great irritation and excitement, and often leads to most unpleasant, if not perilous collisions. An owner of a slave, it is quite notorious, cannot pursue his property, for the purpose of its recovery, in some of the states, without iminent personal hazard. This is a deplorable state of things, which ought to be remedied. The law of 1793 has been found wholly ineffectual, and requires more stringent enactments. There is especially a deficiency in the number of public functionaries authorized to afford aid in the seizure and arrest of fugitives. Various states have declined to afford aid and coöperation in the surrender of fugitives from labor, as the committee believe, from a misconception of their duty, arising under the constitution of the United States. It is true that a decision of the supreme court of the United States has given countenance to them in witholding their assistance. But the committee cannot but believe that the intention of the supreme court has been misunderstood. They cannot but think that that court merely meant that laws of the several states, which created obstacles in the way of the recovery of fugitives, were not authorized by the constitution, and not that the state laws affording facilities in the recovery of fugitives were forbidden by that instrument. The non-slaveholding states, whatever sympathies any of their citizens may feel for persons who escape from other states, cannot discharge themselves from an obligation to enforce the constitution of the United States. All parts of the instrument being dependent upon, and connected with each other, ought to be fairly and justly enforced. If some states may seek to exonerate themselves from one portion of the constitution, other states may endeavor to evade the performance of the other portions of it ; and thus the instrument, in some of the most important provisions, might become inoperative and invalid.

"But, whatever may be the conduct of individual states, the duty of the general government is perfectly clear. That duty is, to amend the existing law, and provide an effectual remedy for the recovery of fugitives from service or labor. In devising such a remedy, congress ought, whilst, on the one hand, securing to the owner the fair restoration of his property, effectually to guard, on the other, against any abuses in the application of that remedy.

"In all cases of arrest, within a state, of persons charged with offenses; in all cases of the pursuit of fugitives from justice from one state to another state; in all cases of extradition, provided for by treaties between foreign powers, the proceeding uniformly is summary. It has never been thought necessary to apply, in cases of that kind, the form and ceremonies of a final trial. And, when that trial does take place, it is in the state or country from which the party has fled, and not in that in which he has found refuge. By the express language of the constitution, whether the fugitive is held to service or labor, or not, is to be determined *by the laws of the state from which he fled;* and, consequently, it is most proper that the tribunals of that state should expound and administer its own laws. If there have been any instances of abuse in the erroneous arrest of fugitives from service or labor, the committee have not obtained knowledge of them. They believe that none have occurred, and that such are not likely to occur. But, in order to guard against the possibility of their occurrence, the committee have prepared, and herewith report a section, (marked B,) to be offered to the fugitive bill now before the senate. According to this section, the owner of a fugitive from service or labor is, when practicable, to carry with him to the state in which the person is found a record from a competent tribunal, adjudicating the fact of elopement and slavery, with a general description of the fugitive. This record, properly attested and certified under the official seal of the court, being taken to the state where the person owing service or labor is found, is to be held competent and sufficient evidence of the facts which had been adjudicated, and will leave nothing more to be done than to identify the fugitive.

"Numerous petitions have been presented praying for a trial by jury, in the case of arrest of fugitives from service or labor in the non-slaveholding states. It has been already shown that this would be entirely contrary to practice and uniform usage in all similar cases. Under the name of a popular and cherished institution—an institution, however, never applied in cases of preliminary proceeding, and only in cases of final trial—there would be a complete mockery of justice, so far as the owner of the fugitive is concerned. If the trial by jury be admitted, it would draw after it its usual consequences; of continuance from time to time, to bring evidence from distant places; of second or new trials, in cases where the jury is hung, or the verdict set aside; and of revisals of the verdict and conduct of the juries by competent tribunals. During the progress of all these dilatory and expensive proceedings, what security is there as to the custody and forthcoming of the fugitive upon their termination? And if, finally, the claimant should be successful, contrary to what happens in ordinary litigation between free persons, he would have to bear all the burdens and expenses of the litigation, without indemnity, and would learn, by sad experience, that he had by far better abandoned his right in the first instance, than to establish it at such unremunerated cost and heavy sacrifice.

"But, whilst the committee conceive that a trial by jury in a state where a fugitive from service or labor is recaptured, would be a virtual denial of justice to the claimant of such fugitive, and would be tantamount to a positive refusal to execute the provision of the constitution, the same objections do not apply to such a trial in the state from which he fled. In the slaveholding states, full justice is administered, with entire fairness and impartiality, in cases of all actions for freedom. The person claiming his freedom is allowed to sue in *forma pauperis;* counsel is assigned him; time is allowed him to collect his witnesses and to attend the sessions of the court; and his claimant is placed under bond and security, or is divested of the possession during the progress of the trial, to insure the enjoyment of these privileges; and, if there be any leaning on the part of courts and juries, it is always to the side of the claimant for freedom.

"In deference to the feelings and prejudices which prevail in non-slaveholding states, the committee propose such a trial in the state from which the fugitive fled, in all cases where he declares to the officer giving the certificate for his return that he has a right to his freedom. Accordingly, the committee have prepared, and report herewith, (marked C,) two sections which they recommend should be incorporated in the fugitive bill, pending in the senate. According to these sections, the claimant is placed under bond, and required to return the fugitive to that county in the state from which he fled, and there to take him before a competent tribunal, and allow him to assert and establish his freedom, if he can, affording to him for that purpose all needful facilities.

"The committee indulge the hope that if the fugitive bill, with the proposed amendments, shall be passed by congress, it will be effectual to secure the recovery of all fugitives from service or labor, and it will remove all causes of complaint which have hitherto been experienced on that irritating subject. But if, in its practical operation, it shall be found insufficient, and if no adequate remedy can be devised for the restoration to their owners of fugitive slaves, those owners shall have a just title to indemnity out of the treasury of the United States.

"It remains to report upon the resolutions in relation to slavery and the slave-trade in the District of Columbia. Without discussing the power of congress to abolish slavery within the district, in regard to which a diversity of opinion exists, the committee are of opinion that it ought not to be abolished. It could not be done without indispensable conditions which are not likely to be agreed to. It could not be done without exciting great apprehension and alarm in the slave states. If the power were exercised within this district, they would apprehend that, under some pretext or another, it might hereafter be attempted to be exercised within the slaveholding states. It is true that, at present, all such power within those states is almost unanimously disavowed and disclaimed in the free states. But experience in public affairs has too often shown that where there is a desire to do a particular thing, the power to accomplish it, sooner or later, will be found or assumed.

" Nor does the number of slaves within the district make the abolition of slavery an object of any such consequence as appears to be attached to it in some parts of the Union. Since the retrocession of Alexandria county to Virginia, on the south side of the Potomac, the district now consists only of Washington county, on the north side of that river; and the returns of the decenary enumeration of the people of the United States show a rapidly progressing decrease in the number of slaves in Washington county. According to the census of 1830, the number was 4,505; and in 1840 it was reduced to 3,320; showing a reduction in ten years of nearly one-third. If it should continue in the same ratio, the number, according to the census now about to be taken, will be only a little upward of two thousand.

"But a majority of the committee think differently in regard to the slave trade within the district. By that trade is meant the introduction of slaves from adjacent states into the district, for sale, or to be placed in depot for the purpose of subsequent sale or transportation to other and distant markets. That trade, a majority of the committee are of opinion, ought to be abolished. Complaints have always existed against it, no less on the part of members of congress from the south than on the part of members from the north. It is a trade sometimes exhibiting revolting spectacles, and one in which the people of the district have no interest, but, on the contrary, are believed to be desirous that it should be discontinued. Most, if not all, of the slaveholding states have, either in their constitutions or by penal enactments, prohibited a trade in slaves as merchandise within their respective jurisdictions. Congress, standing in regard to this district, on this subject, in a relation similar to that of the state legislatures to the people of the states, may safely follow the example of the states. The committee have prepared, and herewith report, a bill for the abolition of that trade (marked D), the passage of which they recommend to the senate. This bill has been framed after the model of what the law of Maryland was when the general government was removed to Washington.

"The views and recommendations contained in this report may be recapitulated in a few words:

"1. The admission of any new state or states formed out of Texas to be postponed until they shall hereafter present themselves to be received into the Union, when it will be the duty of congress fairly and faithfully to execute the compact with Texas, by admitting such new state or states.

"2. The admission forthwith of California into the Union, with the boundaries which she has proposed.

"3. The establishment of territorial governments, without the Wilmot proviso, for New Mexico and Utah, embracing all the territory recently acquired by the United States from Mexico, not contained in the boundaries of California.

"4. The combination of these two last mentioned measures in the same bill.

"5. The establishment of the western and northern boundaries of Texas, and the exclusion from her jurisdiction of all New Mexico, with the grant to Texas of a pecuniary equivalent; and the section for that purpose to be incorporated in the bill admitting California and establishing territorial governments for Utah and New Mexico.

"6. More effectual enactments of law to secure the prompt delivery of persons bound to service or labor in one state, under the laws thereof, who escape into another state; and,

"7. Abstaining from abolishing slavery; but, under a heavy penalty, prohibiting the slave-trade in the District of Columbia.

" If such of these several measures as require legislation should be carried out by suitable acts of congress, all controversies to which our late territorial acquisitions have given rise, and all existing questions connected with the institution of slavery, whether resulting from those acquisitions, or from its existence in the states and the District of Columbia, will be amicably settled and adjusted, in a manner, it is confidently believed, to give general satisfaction to an overwhelming majority of the people of the United States. Congress will have fulfilled its whole duty in regard to the vast country which, having been ceded by Mexico to the United States, has fallen under their dominion. It will have extended to it protection, provided for its several parts the inestimable blessing of free and regular government, adapted to their various wants, and placed the whole under the banner and the flag of the United States. Meeting courageously its clear and entire duty, congress will escape the unmerited reproach of having, from considerations of doubtful policy, abandoned to an undeserved fate territories of boundless extent, with a sparse, incongruous, and alien, if not unfriendly population, speaking different languages, and accustomed to different laws, whilst that population is making irresistible appeals to the new sovereignty to which they have been transferred for protection, for government, for law, and for order.

" The committee have endeavored to present to the senate a comprehensive plan of addjustment, which, removing all causes of existing excitement and agitation, leaves none open to divide the country and disturb the general harmony. The nation has been greatly convulsed, not by measures of general policy, but by questions of a sectional character, and, therefore, more dangerous, and more to be deprecated. It wants repose. It loves and cherishes the Union. And it is most cheering and gratifying to witness the outbursts of deep and abiding attachment to it, which have been exhibited in all parts of it, amidst all the trials through which we have passed, and are passing. A people so patriotic as those of the United States, will rejoice in an accommodation of all troubles and difficulties by which the safety of the Union might have been brought into the least danger. And, under the blessing of that Providence who, amidst all vicissitudes, has never ceased to extend to them His protecting care, His smiles, His blessings, they will continue to advance in population, power, and prosperity, and work out triumphantly the glorious problem of man's capacity for self-government."

The debate on the principal bill reported, continued in the senate until July. The grouping of so many subjects in one bill gave it the name of "the omnibus." In its passage through the senate it had been trimmed down by amendments, so that but a small portion of the original remained, and it passed only as "a bill to provide for the territorial government of Utah." It was sent to the house, where it was received with merriment. Its dismemberment was called "upsetting the omnibus." Subsequently, all the bills originally included in Mr. Clay's omnibus were passed. California was admitted as a free state; the territory of New Mexico organized; the boundary of Texas established; the territory of Utah organized. The bill also to abolish the slave-trade in the District of Columbia, and the fugitive slave law were passed. These acts are substantially as follows:

ADMISSION OF CALIFORNIA.

Whereas, the people of California have presented a constitution and asked admission into the Union, which constitution was submitted to congress by the President of the United States, by message, dated February 13th, 1850, which, on due examination, is found to be republican in its form of government—

Be it enacted by the senate and house of representatives of the United States of America in congress assembled, That the state of California shall be one, and is hereby declared to be one, of the United States of America, and admitted into the Union on an equal footing with the original states, in all respects whatever.

Sec. 2. *And be it further enacted,* That until the representatives in congress shall be apportioned according to an actual enumeration of the inhabitants of the United States, the state of California shall be entitled to two representatives in congress.

Sec. 3. *And be it further enacted,* That the said state of California is admitted into the Union upon the express condition that the people of said state, through their legislature or otherwise, shall never interfere with the primary disposal of the public lands within its limits, and shall pass no law, and do no act, whereby the title of the United States to, and right to dispose of, the same, shall be impaired or questioned; and they shall never lay any tax or assessment of any description whatsoever on the public domain of the United States; and in no case shall non-resident proprietors, who are citizens of the United States, be taxed higher than residents; and that all the navigable waters within the said state shall be common highways, and for ever free, as well to the inhabitants of said state as to the citizens of the United States, without any tax, duty, or impost therefor; provided, that nothing herein contained shall be construed as recognizing or rejecting the propositions tendered by the people of California as articles of compact in the ordinance adopted by the convention which formed the constitution of that state.

Approved, September 9, 1850.

THE TEXAS BOUNDARY.

Be it enacted by the senate and house of representatives of the United States of America in congress assembled, That the following propositions shall be, and the same hereby are, offered to the state of Texas; which, when agreed to by the said state, in an act passed by the general assembly, shall be binding and obligatory upon the United States, and upon the said state of Texas; provided, that said agreement by the said general assembly shall be given on or before the first day of December, eighteen hundred and fifty.

First.—The state of Texas will agree that her boundary on the north shall commence at the point at which the meridian of one hundred degrees west from Greenwich is intersected by the parallel of thirty-six degrees and thirty minutes north latitude, and shall run from said point due west to the meridian of one hundred and three degrees west from Greenwich; hence her boundary shall run due south to the thirty-second degree of north latitude; thence on the said parallel of thirty-two degrees of north latitude to the Rio Bravo del Norte; and thence with the channel of said river to the gulf of Mexico.

Second.—The state of Texas cedes to the United States all her claims to territories exterior to the limits and boundaries which she agrees to establish by the first article of this agreement.

Third.—The state of Texas relinquishes all claim upon the United States for liability for the debts of Texas, and for compensation or indemnity for the surrender to the United States of her ships, forts, arsenals, custom-houses, custom-house revenue, arms and munitions of war, and public buildings, with their sites, which became the property of the United States at the time of the annexation.

Fourth.—The United States, in consideration of said establishment of boundaries, cession of claims to territory, and relinquishment of claims, will pay to the state of Texas the sum of ten millions of dollars, in a stock bearing five per cent. interest, and redeemable at the end of fourteen years, the interest payable half-yearly at the treasury of the United States.

Fifth.—Immediately after the president of the United States shall have been furnished with an authentic copy of the act of the general assembly of Texas, accepting these propositions, he shall cause the stock to be issued in favor of the state of Texas, as provided for in the fourth article of this agreement.

Provided also, That no more than five millions of said stock shall be issued until the creditors of the state, holding bonds and other certificates of stock of Texas, for which duties on imports were specially pledged, shall first file, at the treasury of the United States, releases of all claims against the United States for or on account of said bonds or certificates, in such form as shall be prescribed by the secretary of the treasury, and approved by the president of the United States.

ORGANIZATION OF NEW MEXICO.

The second section of the "act for the organization of New Mexico," enacts that all that portion of the territory of the United States bounded as follows, to wit: beginning at a point on the Colorado river where the boundary line of the republic of Mexico crosses the same; thence eastwardly with the said boundary line to the Rio Grande; thence following the main channel of said river to the parallel of the thirty-second degree of north latitude; thence eastwardly with said degree to its intersection with the one hundred and third degree of longitude west from Greenwich; thence north with said degree of longitude to the parallel of the thirty-eight degree of north latitude; thence west with said parallel to the summit of the Sierra Madre; thence south with the crest of said mountains to the thirty-seventh parallel of north latitude; thence west with the said parallel to its intersection with the boundary line of the state of California; thence with the said boundary line to the place of beginning, be, and the same is hereby, erected into a temporary government by the name of the territory of New Mexico; provided, that nothing in this act contained shall be construed to inhibit the government of the United States from dividing said territory into two or more territories, in such manner and at such times as congress shall deem convenient and proper, or from attaching any portion thereof to any other territory or state; provided further, that when admitted as a state, the said territory, or any portion of the same, shall be received into the Union, with or without slavery, as their constitution may prescribe at the time of their admission.

The eighteenth section enacts, that the provisions of this act be suspended until the boundary between the United States and the state of Texas shall be adjusted; and when such adjustment shall have been effected, the president of the United States shall issue his proclamation, declaring this act to be in full force and operation, and shall proceed to appoint the officers herein provided to be appointed for the said territory.

UTAH TERRITORIAL GOVERNMENT.

The act to establish a territorial government for Utah provides: That all that part of the territory of the United States included within the following limits, to wit: bounded on the west by the state of California, on the north by the territory of Oregon, on the east by the summit of the Rocky mountains, and on the south by the thirty-seventh parallel of north latitude, be, and the same is hereby, created into a temporary government, by the name of the territory of Utah; and, when admitted as a state, the said territory, or any portion of the same, shall be received into the Union, with or without slavery, as their constitution may prescribe at the time of their admission; provided, that nothing in this act contained shall be construed to prohibit the government of the United States from dividing said territory into two or more territories, in such manner and at such time as congress shall deem convenient and proper, or from attaching any portion of said territory to any other state or territory of the United States.

The act proceeds to provide for the appointment of a territorial governor, secretary, marshal, judges, &c., and for the election of a council of thirteen, and a house of representatives of twenty-six members; also for a delegate in congress. All recognized citizens to be voters.

The governor shall receive an annual salary of fifteen hundred dollars as governor, and one thousand dollars as superintendent of Indian affairs. The chief justice and associate justices shall each receive an annual salary of eighteen hundred dollars. The secretary shall receive an annual salary of eighteen hundred dollars. The said salaries shall be paid quarter-yearly, at the treasury of the United States. The members of the legislative assembly shall be entitled to receive each three dollars per day during their attendance at the sessions thereof, and three dollars each for every twenty miles' travel in going to and returning from said sessions, estimated according to the nearest usually traveled route.

That the legislative power of said territory shall extend to all rightful subjects of legislation, consistent with the constitution of the United States and the provisions of this act; but no law shall be passed interfering with the primary disposal of the soil; no tax shall be imposed upon the property of the United States; nor shall the lands or other property of non-residents be taxed higher than the lands or other property of residents. All the laws passed by the legislative assembly and governor shall be submitted to the congress of the United States, and, if disapproved, shall be null and of no effect.

That the constitution and laws of the United States are hereby extended over, and declared to be in force in, said territory of Utah, so far as the same, or any provision thereof, may be applicable.

The debates upon the bills in both houses were animated and interesting. Mr. Seward, of New York, touched upon the principal topics embraced in the general questions of slavery, as presented at this session, as follows:

"But it is insisted that the admission of California shall be attended by a *compromise* of questions which have arisen out of *slavery!*

I am opposed to any such compromise, in any and all the forms in which it has been proposed; because, while admitting the purity and the patriotism of all from whom it is my misfortune to differ, I think all legislative compromises, which are not absolutely necessary, radically wrong and essentially vicious. They involve the surrender of the exercise of judgment and conscience on distinct and separate questions, at distinct and separate times, with the indispensable advantages it affords for ascertaining truth. They involve a relinquishment of the right to reconsider in future the decisions of the present, on questions prematurely anticipated. And they are acts of usurpation as to future questions of the province of future legislators.

Sir, it seems to me as if slavery had laid its paralyzing hand upon myself, and the blood were coursing less freely than its wont through my veins, when I endeavor to suppose that such a compromise has been effected, and that my utterance for ever is arrested upon all the great questions—social, moral, and political—arising out of a subject so important, and yet so incomprehensible.

What am I to receive in this compromise? Freedom in California. It is well; it is a noble acquisition; it is worth a sacrifice. But what am I to give as an equivalent? A recognition of the claim to perpetuate slavery in the District of Columbia; forbearance toward more stringent laws concerning the arrest of persons suspected of being slaves found in the free states; forbearance from the *proviso* of freedom in the charters of new territories. None of the plans of compromise offered demand less than two, and most of them insist on all of these conditions. The equivalent, then, is some portion of liberty, some portion of human rights in one region for liberty in another region. But California brings gold and commerce as well as freedom. I am, then, to sur-

38

render some portion of human freedom in the District of Columbia, and in East California and New Mexico, for the mixed consideration of liberty, gold, and power on the Pacific coast. But, sir, if I could overcome my repugnance to compromises in general, I should object to this one, on the ground of the *inequality* and *incongruity* of the interests to be compromised. Why, sir, according to the views I have submitted, California ought to come in, and and must come in, whether slavery stand or fall in the District of Columbia; whether slavery stand or fall in New Mexico and Eastern California; and even whether slavery stand or fall in the slave states. California ought to come in, being a free state; and, under the circumstances of her conquest, her compact, her abandonment, her justifiable and necessary establishment of a constitution, and the inevitable dismemberment of the empire consequent upon her rejection, I should have voted for her admission even if she had come as a slave state. California ought to come in, and must come in at all events. It is, then, an independent, a paramount question. What, then, are these questions arising out of slavery, thus interposed, but collateral questions? They are unnecessary and incongruous, and therefore false issues, not introduced designedly, indeed, to defeat that great policy, yet unavoidably tending to that end.

Mr. Foote. Will the honorable senator allow me to ask him if the senate is to understand him as saying that he would vote for the admission of California if she came here seeking admission as a slave state.

Mr. Seward. I reply, as I said before, that even if California had come as a slave state, yet coming under the extraordinary circumstances I have described and in view of the consequences of a dismemberment of the empire, consequent upon her rejection, I should have voted for her admission, even though she had come as a slave state. But I should not have voted for her admission otherwise.

I remark, in the next place, that consent on my part would be disingenuous and fraudulent, because the compromise would be unavailing. It is now avowed by the honorable senator from South Carolina, (Mr. Calhoun,) that nothing will satisfy the slave states but a compromise that will convince them that they can remain in the Union consistently with their honor and their safety. And what are the concessions which will have that effect? Here they are, in the words of that senator:

'The north must do justice by conceding to the south an equal right in the acquired territory, and do her duty by causing the stipulations relative to fugitive slaves to be faithfully fulfilled—cease the agitation of the slave question—and provide for the insertion of a provision in the constitution by an amendment, which will restore to the south in substance the power she possessed of protecting herself, before the equilibrium between the sections was destroyed by the action of this government.'

These terms amount to this: that the free states having already, or although they may hereafter have, majorities of population, and majorities in both houses of congress, shall concede to the slave states, being in a minority in both, the unequal advantage of an equality. That is, that we shall alter the constitution so as to convert the government from a national democracy, operating by a constitutional majority of voices, into a federal alliance, in which the minority shall have a veto against the majority. And this would be nothing less than to return to the original articles of confederation.

· Nor would success attend any of the details of this compromise. And, first, I advert to the proposed alteration of the law concerning fugitives from service or labor. I shall speak on this, as on all subjects, with due respect, but yet frankly, and without reservation. The constitution contains only a compact, which rests for its execution on the states. Not content with this, the slave states induced legislation by congress ; and the supreme court of the United States have virtually decided that the whole subject is within the province of congress, and exclusive of state authority. Nay, they have decided that slaves are to be regarded, not merely as persons to be claimed, but as property and chattels, to be seized without any legal authority or claim whatever. The compact is thus subverted by the procurement of the slave states. With what reason, then, can they expect the states *ex gratia* to reässume the obligations from which they caused those states to be discharged ? I say, then, to the slave states, you are entitled to no more stringent laws ; and that such laws would be useless. The cause of the inefficiency of the present statute is not at all the leniency of its provisions. It is a law that deprives the alleged refugee from a legal obligation not assumed by him, but imposed upon him by laws enacted before he was born, of the writ of *habeas corpus*, and of any certain judicial process of examination of the claim set up by his pursuer, and finally degrades him into a chattel which may be seized and carried away peaceably wherever found, even although exercising the rights and responsibilities of a free citizen of the commonwealth in which he resides, and of the United States—a law which denies to the citizen all the safeguards of personal liberty, to render less frequent the escape of the bondman. And since complaints are so freely made against the one side, I shall not hesitate to declare that there have been even greater faults on the other side. Relying on the perversion of the constitution which makes slaves mere chattels, the slave states have applied to them the principles of the criminal law, and have held that he who aided the escape of his fellow-man from bondage was guilty of a larceny in stealing him. I speak of what I know. Two instances came within my own knowledge, in which governors of slave states, under the provision of the constitution relating to fugitives from justice, demanded from the governor of a free state the surrender of persons as thieves whose alleged offenses consisted in constructive larceny of the rags that covered the persons of female slaves, whose attempt at escape they permitted or assisted. We deem the principle of the law for the recapture of fugitives. as thus expounded, therefore, unjust, unconstitutional, and immoral ; and thus, while patriotism withholds its approbation, the consciences of our people condemn it.

Another feature in most of these plans of compromise is a bill of peace for slavery in the District of Columbia ; and this bill of peace we cannot grant. We of the free states are, equally with you of the slave states, responsible for the existence of slavery in this district, the field exclusively of our common legislation. I regret that, as yet, I see little reason to hope that a majority in favor of emancipation exists here. The legislature of New York—from whom, with great deference, I dissent—seems willing to accept now the extinction of the slave-trade, and waive emancipation But we shall assume the whole responsibility, if we stipulate not to exercise the power hereafter when a majority shall be obtained. Nor will the plea with which you would furnish us be of any avail. If I could understand so mysterious a paradox myself, I never should be able to explain, to the apprehension of the people whom I represent, how it was that an absolute and express power to legislate in all cases over the District of Columbia, was embarrassed and defeated by an implied condition not to legislate for the abolition of slavery in this district. Sir, I shall vote for that measure, and am willing to appropriate any means necessary to carry it into execution. And, if I shall be asked what I did to embellish the capital of my country, I will point to her freedmen, and say, these are the monuments of my munificence!

I come now to notice the suggested *compromise of the boundary between Texas and New Mexico.* This is a judicial question in its nature, or at least a question of legal right and title. If it is to be compromised at all, it is due to the two parties, and to national dignity as well as to justice, that it be kept separate from compromises proceeding on the ground of expediency, and be settled by itself alone.

I take this occasion to say, that while I do not intend to discuss the questions alluded to in this connection by the honorable and distinguished senator from Massachusetts, I am not able to agree with him in regard to the alleged obligation of congress to admit four new slave states, to be formed in the state of Texas. There are several questions arising out of that subject, upon which I am not prepared to decide now, and which I desire to reserve for future consideration. One of these is, whether the article of annexation does really deprive congress of the right to exercise its choice in regard to the sub-division of Texas into four additional states. It seems to me by no means so plain a question as the senator from Massachusetts assumed, and that it must be left to remain an open question, as it is a great question, whether congress is not a party whose future consent is necessary to the formation of new states out of Texas.

Mr. Webster. Supposing congress to have the authority to fix the number and time of election, and apportionment of representatives, &c., the question is, whether, if new states are formed out of Texas, to come into this union, there is not a solemn pledge by law that they have a right to come in as slave states?

Mr. Seward. When the states are once formed, they have the right to come in as free or slave states, according to their own choice; but what I insist is, that they cannot be formed at all without the consent of congress, to be hereafter given, which consent congress is not obliged to give. But I pass that question for the present, and proceed to say that I am not prepared to admit that the article of the annexation of Texas is itself constitutional. I find no authority in the constitution of the United States for the annexation of foreign countries by a resolution of congress, and no power adequate to that purpose but the treaty-making power of the president and the senate. Entertaining this view, I must insist that the constitutionality of the annexation of Texas itself shall be cleared up before I can agree to the admission of any new states to be formed within Texas.

Mr. Foote. Did I not hear the senator observe that he would admit California, whether slavery was or was not precluded from these territories?

Mr. Seward. I said I would have voted for the admission of California even as a slave state, under the extraordinary circumstances which I have before distinctly described. I say that now; but I say also, that before I would agree to admit any more states from Texas, the circumstances which render such an act necessary must be shown, and must be such as to determine my obligation to do so; and that is precisely what I insist cannot be settled now. It must be left for those to whom the responsibility will belong.

Mr. President, I understand, and I am happy in understanding, that I agree with the honorable senator from Massachusetts, that there is no obligation upon congress to admit four new slave states out of Texas, but that congress has reserved her right to say whether those states shall be formed and admitted or not. I shall rely on that reservation. I shall vote to admit no more slave states, unless under circumstances absolutely compulsory—and no such case is now foreseen.

Mr. Webster. What I said was, that if the states hereafter to be made out of Texas choose to come in as slave states, they have a right so to do.

Mr. Seward. My position is, that they have not a right to come in at all, if congress rejects their institu.ions. The sub-division of Texas is a matter optional with both parties, Texas and the United States.

Mr. Webster. Does the honorable senator mean to say that congress can hereafter decide whether they shall be slave or free states?

Mr. Seward. I mean to say that congress can hereafter decide whether any states, slave or free, can be framed out of Texas. If they should never be framed out of Texas, they never could be admitted.

Another objection arises out of the principle on which the demand for compromise rests. That principle assumes a classification of the states as northern and southern states, as it is expressed by the honorable senator from South Carolina, (Mr. Calhoun,) but into slave states and free states, as more directly expressed by the honorable senator from Georgia, (Mr. Berrien.) The argument is, that the states are severally equal, and that these two classes were equal at the first, and that the constitution was founded on that equilibrium; that the states being equal, and the classes of the states being equal in rights, they are to be regarded as constituting an association in which each state, and each of these classes of states, respectively, contribute in due proportions; that the new territories are a common acquisition, and the people of these several states and classes of states have an equal right to participate in them, respectively; that the right of the people of the slave states to emigrate to the territories with their slaves as property is necessary to afford such a participation on their part, inasmuch as the people of the free states emigrate into the same territories with their property. And the argument deduces from this right the principle that, if congress exclude slavery from any part of this new domain, it would be only just to set off a portion of the domain—some say south of 36° 30′, others south of 34°—which should be regarded at least as free to slavery, and to be organized into slave states.

Argument ingenious and subtle, declamation earnest and bold, and persuasion gentle and winning as the voice of the turtle dove when it is heard in the land, all alike and altogether have failed to convince me of the soundness of this principle of the proposed compromise, or of any one of the propositions on which it is attempted to be established.

The constitution does not *expressly* affirm anything on the subject; all that it contains is two incidental allusions to slaves. These are, first, in the provision establishing a ratio of representation and taxation; and, secondly, in the provision relating to fugitives from labor. In both cases, the constitution designedly mentions slaves, not as slaves, much less as chattels, but as *persons*. That this recognition of them as persons was designed is historically known, and I think was never denied.

I deem it established that the constitution does not recognize property in man, but leaves that question, as between the states, to the law of nature and of nations. That law, as expounded by Vattel, is founded on the reason of things. When God had created the earth, with its wonderful adaptations, He gave dominion over it to man, absolute human dominion. The title of that dominion, thus bestowed, would have been incomplete, if the Lord of all terrestrial things could himself have been the property of his fellow-man.

But there is yet another aspect in which this principle must be examined. It regards the domain only as a possession, to be enjoyed either in common or by partition by the citizens of the old states. It is true, indeed, that the national domain is ours. It is true it was acquired by the valor and with the wealth of the whole nation. But we hold no arbitrary authority over it. We hold no arbitrary authority over anything, whether acquired lawfully or seized by usurpation. The constitution regulates our stewardship; the constitution devotes the domain to union, to justice, to defense, to welfare, and to liberty.

But there is a higher law than the constitution, which regulates our authority over the domain, and devotes it to the same noble purposes. The territory is a part, no inconsiderable part, of the common heritage of mankind, bestowed upon them by the Creator of the Universe. We are his stewards, and must so discharge our trust as to secure in the highest degree their happiness.

It remains only to remark that our own experience has proved the dangerous influence and tendency of slavery. All our apprehensions of dangers, present and future, begin and end with slavery. If slavery, limited as it yet is, now threatens to subvert the constitution, how can we, as wise and prudent statesmen, enlarge its boundaries and increase its influence, and thus increase already impending dangers? Whether, then, I regard merely the welfare of the future inhabitants of the new territories, or the security and welfare of the whole people of the United States, or the welfare of the whole family of mankind, I cannot consent to introduce slavery into any part of this continent which is now exempt from what seems to me so great an evil. These are my reasons for declining to compromise the question relating to slavery as a condition of the admission of California.

In acting upon an occasion so grave as this, a respectful consideration is due to the arguments, founded on extraneous considerations, of senators who commend a course different from that which I have preferred. The first of these arguments is, that congress has no power to legislate on the subject of slavery within the territories.

Sir, congress *may* admit new states; and since congress may admit, it follows that congress may *reject* new states. The discretion of congress in admitting is absolute, except that, when admitted, the state must be a republican state, and must be a STATE; that is, it shall have the constitutional form and powers of a state. But the greater includes the less, and therefore congress may impose *conditions* of admission not inconsistent with those fundamental powers and forms. Boundaries are such. The reservation of the public domain is such. The right to divide is such. The ordinance excluding slavery is such a condition. The organization of a territory is ancillary or preliminary; it is the inchoate, the *initiative* act of admission, and is performed under the clause granting the powers necessary to execute the express powers of the constitution.

The next of this class of arguments is, that the inhibition of slavery in the new territories is *unnecessary ;* and when I come to this question, I encounter the loss of many who lead in favor of the admission of California. The argument is, that the *proviso is unnecessary.* I answer, then, there can be no error in insisting upon it. But why is it unnecessary? It is said, *first,* by reason of *climate.* I answer, if this be so, why do not the representatives of the slave states concede the proviso? They deny that the climate prevents the introduction of slavery. Then I will leave nothing to a contingency. But, in truth, I think the weight of the argument is against the proposition. Is there any climate where slavery has not existed? It has prevailed all over Europe, from sunny Italy to bleak England, and is existing now, stronger than in any other land, in ice-bound Russia. But it will be replied that this is not African slavery. I rejoin, that only makes the case the stronger. If this vigorous Saxon race of ours was reduced to slavery while it retained the courage of semi-barbarism in its own high northern latitude, what security does climate afford against the transplantation of the more gentle, more docile, and already enslaved and debased African to the genial climate of New Mexico and eastern California?

Sir, there is no climate uncongenial to slavery. It is true it is less productive than free labor in many northern countries. But so it is less productive than free white labor in even tropical climates. Labor is in quick demand in all new countries. Slave labor is cheaper than free labor, and it would go first into new regions; and wherever it goes it brings labor into dishonor, and therefore free white labor avoids competition with it. Sir, I might rely on climate if I had not been born in a land where slavery existed—and this land was all of it north of the fortieth parallel of latitude; and if I did not know the struggle it has cost, and which is yet going on, to get complete relief from the institution and its baleful consequences. I desire to propound this question to those who are now in favor of dispensing with the Wilmot proviso : Was the ordinance of 1787 necessary or not ? Necessary, we all agree. It has received too many elaborate eulogiums to be now decried as an idle and superfluous thing. And yet that ordinance extended the inhibition of slavery from the thirty-seventh to the fortieth parallel of north latitude. And now we are told that the inhibition named is unnecessary anywhere north of 36° 30′ ! We are told that we may rely upon the laws of God, which prohibit slave labor north of that line, and that it is absurd to reënact the laws of God. Sir, there is no human enactment which is just that is not a reënactment of the law of God. The constitution of the United States and the constitutions of all the states are full of such reënactments. Wherever I find a law of God or a law of nature disregarded, or in danger of being disregarded, there I shall vote to reäffirm it, with all the sanction of the civil authority. But I find no authority for the position that climate prevents slavery anywhere. It is the indolence of mankind in any climate, and not any natural necessity, that introduces slavery in any climate.

It is insisted that the diffusion of slavery will not increase its evils. The argument seems to me merely specious, and quite unsound. I desire to propose one or two questions in reply to it. Is slavery stronger or weaker in these United States, from its diffusion into Missouri ? Is slavery weaker or stronger in these United States, from the exclusion of it from the northwest territory ? The answers to these questions will settle the whole controversy.

And this brings me to the great and all-absorbing argument that the Union is in danger of being dissolved, and that it can only be saved by compromise. I do not know what I would not do to save the Union ; and therefore I shall bestow upon this subject a very deliberate consideration. I do not overlook the fact that the entire delegation from the slave states, although they differ in regard to the details of the compromise proposed, and perhaps in regard to the exact circumstances of the crisis, seem to concur in this momentous warning. Nor do I doubt at all the patriotic devotion to the Union which is expressed by those from whom this warning proceeds. And yet, sir, although such warnings have been uttered with impassioned solemnity in my hearing every day for near three months, my confidence in the Union remains unshaken. I think they are to be received with no inconsiderable distrust, because they are uttered under the influence of a controlling interest to be secured, a paramount object to be gained ; and that is an equilibrium of power in the republic.

Sir, in any condition of society there can be no revolution without a cause, an adequate cause. What cause exists here ? We are admitting a new state ;

but there is nothing new in that: we have already admitted seventeen before. But it is said that the slave states are in danger of losing political power by the admission of the new state. Well, sir, is there anything new in that? The slave states have always been losing political power, and they always will be while they have any to lose. At first, twelve of the thirteen states were slave states; now only fifteen out of the thirty are slave states. Moreover, the change is constitutionally made, and the government was constructed so as to permit changes of the balance of power, in obedience to changes of the forces of the body politic. Danton used to say, "It's all well while the people cry Danton and Robespierre; but wo for me if ever the people learn to say, Robespierre and Danton!" That is all of it, sir. The people have been accustomed to say, "the south and the north;" they are only beginning now to say, "the north and the south."

Sir, when the founders of the republic of the south come to draw those fearful lines, they will indicate what portions of the continent are to be broken off from their connection with the Atlantic, through the St. Lawrence, the Hudson, the Delaware, the Potomac, and the Mississippi; what portion of this people are to be denied the use of the lakes, the railroads, and the canals, now constituting common and customary avenues of travel, trade, and social intercourse; what families and kindred are to be separated, and converted into enemies; and what states are to be the scenes of perpetual border warfare, aggravated by interminable horrors of servile insurrection. When those portentous lines shall be drawn, they will disclose what portion of this people is to retain the army and the navy, and the flag of so many victories; and on the other hand, what portion of the people is to be subjected to new and onerous imposts, direct taxes, and forced loans, and conscriptions, to maintain an opposing army, an opposing navy, and the new and hateful banner of sedition. Then the projectors of the new republic of the south will meet the question—and they may well prepare now to answer it—What is all this for? What intolerable wrong, what unfraternal injustice, have rendered these calamities unavoidable? What gain will this unnatural revolution bring to us? The answer will be: All this is done to secure the institution of African slavery.

But you insist on a guaranty against the abolition of slavery in the District of Columbia, or war. Well, when you shall have declared war against us, what shall hinder us from immediately decreeing that slavery shall cease within the national capital?

You say that you will not submit to the exclusion of slaves from the new territories. What will you gain by resistance? Liberty follows the sword, although her sway is one of peace and beneficence. Can you propagate slavery then by the sword?

You insist that you cannot submit to the freedom with which slavery is discussed in the free states. Will war—a war for slavery—arrest or even moderate that discussion? No, sir; that discussion will not cease; war will only inflame it to a greater height. It is a part of the eternal conflict between truth and error—between mind and physical force—the conflict of man against the obstacles which oppose his way to an ultimate and glorious destiny. It will go on until you shall terminate it in the only way in which any state or nation has ever terminated it—by yielding to it—yielding in your own time, and in your own manner indeed, but nevertheless yielding to the progress of emancipation. You will do this, sooner or later, whatever may be your opinion now; because nations which were prudent and humane, and wise as you are, have done so already.

Sir, the slave states have no reason to fear that this inevitable change will go too far or too fast for their safety or welfare. It cannot well go too fast or too far, if the only alternative is a war of races.

But it cannot go too fast. Slavery has a reliable and accommodating ally in a party in the free states, which, though it claims to be, and doubtless is in many respects, a party of progress, finds its sole security for its political power in the support and aid of slavery in the slave states. Of course, I do not include in that party those who are now coöperating in maintaining the cause of freedom against slavery. I am not of that party of progress which in the north thus lends its support to slavery. But it is only just and candid that I should bear witness to its fidelity to the interests of slavery.

Slavery has, moreover, a more natural alliance with the aristocracy of the north and with the aristocracy of Europe. So long as slavery shall possess the cotton-fields, the sugar-fields, and the rice-fields of the world, so long will commerce and capital yield it toleration and sympathy. Emancipation is a democratic revolution. It is capital that arrests all democratic revolutions. It was capital that, so recently, in a single year, rolled back the tide of revolution from the base of the Carpathian mountains, across the Danube and the Rhine, into the streets of Paris. It is capital that is rapidly rolling back the throne of Napoleon into the chambers of the Tuilleries.

Slavery has a guaranty still stronger than these in the prejudices of caste and color, which induce even large majorities in all the free states to regard sympathy with the slave as an act of unmanly humiliation and self-abasement, although philosophy meekly expresses her distrust of the asserted natural superiority of the white race, and confidently denies that such a superiority, if justly claimed, could give a title to oppression.

There remains one more guaranty—one that has seldom failed you, and will seldom fail you hereafter. New states cling in closer alliance than older ones to the federal power. The concentration of the slave power enables you for long periods to control the federal government with the aid of the new states. I do not know the sentiments of the representatives of California; but, my word for it, if they should be admitted on this floor to-day, against your most obstinate opposition, they would, on all questions really affecting your interests, be found at your side.

There are many well-disposed persons who are alarmed at the occurrence of any such disturbance. The failure of a legislative body to organize is to their apprehension a fearful omen, and an extra-constitutional assemblage to consult upon public affairs is with them cause for desperation. Even senators speak of the Union as if it existed only by consent, and, as it seems to be implied, by the assent of the legislatures of the states. On the contrary, the Union was not founded in voluntary choice, nor does it exist by voluntary consent.

A union was proposed to the colonies by Franklin and others, in 1754; but such was their aversion to an abridgment of their own importance, respectively, that it was rejected even under the pressure of a disastrous invasion by France.

A union of choice was proposed to the colonies in 1775 ; but so strong was their opposition, that they went through the war of independence without having established more than a mere council of consultation.

But with independence came enlarged interests of agriculture—absolutely new interests of manufactures—interests of commerce, of fisheries, of navigation, of common domain, of common debts, of common revenues and taxation, of the administration of justice, of public defense, of public honor ; in short, interests of common nationality and sovereignty—interests which at last compelled the adoption of a more perfect union—a national government.

The genius, talents, and learning of Hamilton, Jay, and of Madison, surpassing, perhaps, the intellectual power ever exerted before for the establishment of a government, combined with the serene but mighty influence of Washington, were only sufficient to secure the reluctant adoption of the constitution that is now the object of all our affections and of the hopes of mankind. No wonder that the conflicts in which that constitution was born, and the almost desponding solemnity of Washington, in his farewell address, impressed his countrymen and mankind with a profound distrust of its perpetuity ! No wonder that while the murmurs of that day are yet ringing in our ears, we cherish that distrust, with pious reverence, as a national and patriotic sentiment.

I have heard somewhat here, and almost for the first time in my life, of divided allegiance—of allegiance to the south and to the Union. Sir, if sympathies with state emulation and pride of achievement could be allowed to raise up another sovereign to divide the allegiance of a citizen of the United States, I might recognize the claims of the state to which, by birth and gratitude, I belong—to the state of Hamilton and Jay, of Schuyler, of the Clintons, and of Fulton—the state which, with less than two hundred miles of natural navigation connected with the ocean, has, by her own enterprise, secured to herself the commerce of the continent, and is steadily advancing to the command of the commerce of the world. But for all this I know only one country and one sovereign—the United States of America and the American people. And such as my allegiance is, is the loyalty of every other citizen of the United States. As I speak, he will speak when his time arrives. He knows no other country and no other sovereign. He has life, liberty, property, and precious affections, and hopes for himself and for his posterity, treasured up in the ark of the Union. He knows as well and feels as strongly as I do, that this government is his own government; that he is a part of it; that it was established for him, and that it is maintained by him ; that it is the only truly wise, just, free, and equal government that has ever existed; that no other government could be so wise, just, free and equal ; and that it is safer and more beneficent than any which time or change could bring into its place.

You may tell me, sir, that although all this may be true, yet the trial of faction has not yet been made. Sir, if the trial of faction has not been made, it has not been because faction has not always existed, and has not always menaced a trial, but because faction could find no fulcrum on which to place the lever to subvert the Union, as it can find no fulcrum now; and in this is my confidence. I would not rashly provoke the trial; but I will not suffer a fear, which I nave not, to make me compromise one sentiment, one principle of truth or justice, to avert a danger that all experience teaches me is purely chimerical. Let, then, those who distrust the Union make compromises to save it. I shall not impeach their wisdom, as I certainly cannot their patriotism; but, indulging no such apprehensions myself, I shall vote for the admission of California into the Union directly, without conditions, without qualifications, and without compromise."

Mr. Cass, on the 13th of March, expressed his views at some length. A part of his speech was in reply to certain remarks of Mr. Calhoun and Mr. Seward. He agreed with what had been said by Mr. Clay; and he would vote for the proposed reference of the resolutions, indeed for almost any proposition likely to bring this country into harmony upon this perplexing question. He thought the country was under lasting obligations to Mr. Foote for his efforts to terminate the existing difficulties. For Mr. Calhoun, he expressed deep sympathy, but dissented from parts of his speech, which, he thought, contained a strange collection and collocation of facts, followed by strange conclusions. The sombre hue which pervaded his speech, he imagined, was owing to its having been prepared in the recesses of a sick chamber. [Mr. Calhoun, too feeble to address the senate, had written his speech, which had been read by Mr. Mason, of Virginia].

Mr. Cass took exception to an expression of Mr. Calhoun, calling Washington "the illustrious southerner." "Our Washington—the Washington of our whole country—receives in this senate, the epithet of 'southerner,' as if that great man, whose distinguished characteristic was his attachment to his country, and his whole country, who was so well known, and who, more than any one, deprecated all sectional feeling and all sectional action—loved Georgia better than he loved New Hampshire, because he happened to be born on the southern bank of the Potomac. I repeat, sir, that I heard with great pain, that expression from the distinguished senator form South Carolina.

We have been three months here, and what have we done? Nothing. We have not passed a single law of the least national importance. We have occupied the whole time by the discussion of this question, and no practical result has been attained; and present appearances do not indicate that such a result is near. But, though we have done nothing, we have ascertained that some things can not be done. We have ascertained (I think I may say with certainty) that no Wilmot proviso can be passed through this congress. That measure is dead. It is the latest, and I hope it is the last attempt that will be made to interfere with the right of self-government within the limits of this republic. I think we may also say, that no Missouri compromise line can pass,

and that no one expects or desires that it should pass. Mr. President, what **was** the compromise line ? Allow me to read the law which established it :

"Sec. 8. And be it further enacted, That in all that territory ceded by France to the United States, under the name of Louisiana, which lies north of 36° and 30′ north latitude, not included within the limits of the state contemplated by this act, slavery and involuntary servitude, otherwise than in the punishment of crimes, whereof the parties shall have been duly convicted, shall be, and is hereby, forever prohibited."

Now, sir, what is that provision ? It is intervention north of the line of 36° 30′, and non-intervention south of that line. Why, sir, there is not one southern senator on this floor, and not one southern member of the other house, nor indeed a southern man who understands the subject, who would accept that line as a proper settlement of this question. Why, sir, the whole doctrine of equal rights and of non-intervention is taken away by it at once. Why, sir putting out of view the constitutional objections to such an arrangement, it gives the south nothing, while it prohibits the people north of 36° 30′ from exercising their own will upon the subject. The true doctrine of non-intervention leaves the whole question to the people, and does not divide their right of decision by a parallel of latitude. If they choose to have slavery north of that line, they can have it. Is there a senator on this floor who would accept of a proposition to apply the principle of non-intervention to a part of the territory, leaving to the people of the other portion to do as they please ? No, sir ; there is not a southern senator here who would vote for it. I will tell you what would be voted for, has already been announced—a law declaratory, mandatory, or permissory, for the establishment of slavery south of the line of 36° 30′. The distinguished senator from South Carolina might be willing to accept a declaration that slavery does now exist, or that it shall exist, or may exist, south of a certain line ; but I take it for granted that no senator from the south would be willing to abandon the ground of non-intervention, without some provision like that. Well, then, Mr. President, if these things are impossible—if they cannot be done—it remains to inquire what it is in our power to do. My own opinion is, sir, that we should take up the bill for the recapture of fugitive slaves, reported by the judiciary committee. I am disposed to suspend all our discussions, and to lay aside all other business, with a view to act upon that bill, without unnecessary delay, and to pass it in such a form as would be acceptable to a majority of this body. That is a point upon which the south feels most acutely, and in regard to which it has the most serious cause of complaint. I have heard but one man in this body deny the existence of this evil, or the justice and necessity of providing an adequate remedy. If I understand the senator from New York, (Mr. Seward,) he intimated his belief that it was immoral to carry into effect the provision of the constitution for the recapture of fugitive slaves. That, sir, is a very strange view of the duties of a senator in this body. No man should come here who believes that ours is an immoral constitution ; no man should come here, and, by the solemn sanction of an oath, promise to support an immoral constitution. No man is compelled to take an oath to support it. He may live in this country, **and** believe what he chooses with regard to the constitution; but he has no right, as an honest man, to seek office, and obtain it, and then talk about its being so immoral that he can not fulfill its obligations. It is the duty of every man, who has sworn to support the constitution, fairly to carry its provisions into effect; and no man can stand up before his fellow-citizens and maintain any other doctrine, whatever reasons he may urge in his vindication. In one of the most disingenuous portions of the speech of the honorable senator from New York (Mr. Seward)—which itself was one of the most disingenuous I have ever heard—he speaks of "slavery having a reliable and accommodating ally in a party in the free states," and he says he "bears witness to its fidelity to the interests of slavery."

Now, I ask the senator from New York, if he believes there is a man in this senate from the north, whose course is influenced by his fidelity to slavery; and if he does, what right he has to cast odium upon gentlemen who are associated with him in the high duties which belong to his position?

Mr. Seward. The senator addresses a question to me, and I rise for no other purpose than to answer it. I think it was Mr. Jefferson who said that the natural ally of slavery in the south was the democracy of the north.

A senator. It was Mr. Buchanan.

Mr. Seward. I have heard it attributed to Mr. Jefferson. However this may be, I believe it. I assail the motives of no senator. I am not to be drawn into personal altercations by any interrogatories addressed to me. I acknowledge the patriotism, the wisdom, the purity of every member of this body. I never have assailed the motives of honorable senators in any instance, I never shall. When my own are assailed, I stand upon my own position. My life and acts must speak for me. I shall not be my own defender or advocate.

Mr. Cass concluded his speech the next day. He said: I was remarking yesterday, when I resigned the floor, that there were certain things we could not accomplish, and others that, with equal certainty, we might take for granted we could do. Among the latter, was the bill providing for the recapture of fugitive slaves; and another object, which I trust will be accomplished, is the providing of a government for the new territories. I think it essential to calm this agitation, and so long as these territories are left without a government, so long will the present state of things continue, and this agitation be kept up, which is so harassing to the tranquility, and dangerous to the peace of the Union. That a law may be passed authorizing the people of the territories to govern themselves, without any Wilmot proviso being attached to it, is my wish and my hope. Sir, we cannot stand before the country, and before the world, and object to the admission of California on the ground that has been urged. The objection is not to her boundaries, though that topic has been much debated. I myself was at first startled at the boundary claimed, stretching as it does along the coast of the Pacific one thousand miles—a much greater extent than any one state in the Union ought to possess. But the country between the ocean and the sea is a narrow one, and east of the mountains is a desert, and in proportion to its extent, the quantity of arable land is small. Be the boundaries as they may, it is not probable that its population will ever be as great as that of some of the other states of this Union. And if its southern boundary were to stop at the mountains, there would be left between them and the Mexican possessions a small district of country, which would have to remain for an indefinite period, perhaps forever, in a colonial condition. The senator from South Carolinia, (Mr. Calhoun,) who I regret to see is not in his seat to-day, does not assume this ground as an objection to the admission of California. That objection rests upon her present position and mode of application; because she has established a government of her own without passing through territorial process, and comes here of her own accord, and asks admission into this Union. This ground of objection cannot be maintained in this age of the world, before the people of this country, and, I may add, the people of Christendom. There are two positions I have always maintained with reference to this subject—first, that congress, under the constitution, has no right to establish governments for the territories; secondly, that under no circumstances have they the right to pass any law to regulate the internal affairs of the people inhabiting them. The first may be a matter of necessity; and when the necessity exists, if a senator votes for it, he votes upon his own responsibility to his constituents. If they believe the necessity and support him, he is safe, but if not, he must fall. If I had voted under such circumstances, I must have looked to my constituents for my justification; but under no circumstances could I have voted for any law interfering with the internal concerns of the people of a territory. No necessity requires it; there is no necessity which would justify it

Mr. Chase. Did I understand the senator as saying, that in voting for a bill to establish a government in the territories he would assume the exercise of any authority not given in the constitution?

Mr. Cass. The honorable senator will undoubtedly recollect, that in a historical document called the Nicholson letter, which subsequent circumstances have made somewhat important, I distinctly stated my views upon this subject, and those views have remained unchanged to the present hour. I maintained that no power is given by the constitution to establish territorial governments, but that where an imperious necessity exists for such a measure, the legislator who yields to it must look to his constituents for his justification.

Mr. Chase. I understood the senator to say that there was no such authority given by the constitution?

Mr. Cass. I said, that if we do an act not authorized by the constitution, under a pressure of necessity, that act must be done upon our own responsibility; and I refer the gentleman to the authority of Mr. Madison, who justified the action of the congress of the confederation, on the subject of territories, upon this ground—and upon this alone. If the gentleman will take the trouble to look at my speech on the Wilmot proviso, he will find my views on this point distinctly laid down. What is the objection in principle to the admission of California? Allow me to say, that great political rights and movements,

in this age of the world, are not to be determined by mere abstract or specula-
tive opinions. There is no want of heavy books in the world, which treat of
political science; but you need not go to them to ascertain the rights of men—
either individuals or in communities; if you do, you will lose yourself groping
in a labyrinth, and where no man can follow you. If there are rights of sovereignty, there may be wrongs of sovereignty; and this truth should be held
in everlasting remembrance. And this is the case with regard to California.
We have rights, and we have duties; and if the former are sacred, the latter
should be sacred also. One of these duties we have neglected to perform;
and we are told by gentlemen who have spoken here, that when a state wishes
admission into the Union, she should come to the door of congress and knock
for admission. California has thus come and knocked; but no door is open to
her. and she is to be told, "go back and wait till we are ready." There is
but one door through which you can enter, and that door we keep shut. You
must pass through a territorial government; but that government we have
neglected to give you, and we are probably as far from establishing it as ever.
And such is the paternal regard we manifest toward one hundred thousand
American citizens, who are upholding the flag of our country on the distant
shores of the Pacific.

CHAPTER XXXI.

Repeal of Missouri Compromise.—Kansas and Nebraska Organized.

The platforms, slavery agitation repudiated by both parties.—Mr. Pierce's Inaugural and
Message denounce agitation.—Session of 1853–4:—the storm bursts forth.—Proposition to repeal the Missouri Compromise.—Kansas-Nebraska bill.—Mr. Douglas' defense of the bill—Mr. Chase's reply—Remarks of Houston, Cass, Seward, and others.
—Passage of the bill in the house.—Passed by senate, and approved.—The territories
organized.

THE democratic convention to nominate candidates for the presidency and
vice-presidency was held in Baltimore, June 1, 1852. Franklin Pierce, of New
Hampshire, received the nomination on the 49th ballot. The whig convention
met in the same city on the 16th of June, and nominated General Scott on the
53d ballot. Upon the subject of slavery, the platforms of the two conventions
agree. The democratic convention declared:

"That congress has no power under the constitution to interfere with or
control the domestic institutions of the several states, and that such states are
the sole and proper judges of every thing appertaining to their own affairs,
not prohibited by the constitution; that all efforts of the abolitionists, or others, made to induce congress to interfere with questions of slavery, or to take
incipient steps in relation thereto, are calculated to lead to the most alarming

and dangerous consequences; and that all such efforts have an inevitable tendency to diminish the happiness of the people, and endanger the stability and permanency of the Union, and ought not to be countenanced by any friend of our political institutions.

"That the foregoing proposition covers, and was intended to embrace the whole subject of slavery agitation in congress; and therefore the democratic party of the Union, standing on this national platform, will abide by and adhere to a faithful execution of the *acts known as the compromise measures settled by the last congress—the act for reclaiming fugitives from service or labor included; which act being designed to carry out an express provision of the constitution, can not with fidelity thereto be repealed, nor so changed as to destroy or impair its efficiency.

"That the democratic party will resist all attempts at renewing, in congress or out of it, the agitation of the slavery question, under whatever shape or color the attempt may be made."

The whig convention made the following declaration:

"That the series of acts of the thirty-first congress—the act known as the fugitive slave law included—are received and acquiesced in by the whig party of the United States, as a settlement in principle and substance of the dangerous and exciting question which they embrace; and so far as they are concerned, we will maintain them and insist on their strict enforcement, until time and experience shall demonstrate the necessity of further legislation, to guard against the evasion of the laws on the one hand, and the abuse of their powers on the other, not impairing their present efficiency; and we deprecate all further agitation of the question thus settled, as dangerous to our peace; and will discountenance all efforts to continue or renew such agitation whenever, wherever, or however the attempt may be made; and we will maintain this system as essential to the nationality of the whig party of the Union."

The presidential contest resulted in the election of Mr. Pierce. The "slavery question" was now dead and buried—the democratic party planted itself upon the grave to "resist all attempts" at disturbing the body—the whigs stood by to "discountenance all efforts" at resurrection, "whenever, wherever or however the attempt may be made."

Mr. Pierce was inaugurated on the 4th of March, 1853. In his inaugural address he said: "I believe that involuntary servitude is recognized by the constitution. I believe that the states where it exists are entitled to efficient remedies to enforce the constitutional provisions. I hold that the compromise measures of 1850 are strictly constitutional, and to be unhesitatingly carried into effect." "And now," said Mr. Pierce, "I fervently hope that the question is at rest, and that no sectional, or ambitious, or fanatical excitement may again threaten the durability" of its repose.

Congress convened on the 5th of December, 1853. On the next day the President communicated his message. The dead and buried slavery question was again alluded to; and he declared his fixed purpose to leave undisturbed, "a subject which had been set at rest by the deliberate judgment of the peo-

39

ple." That "this repose is to suffer no shock during my official term, if I have power to avert it, those who placed me here may be assured."

Notwithstanding the legislation of 1850, the platforms of the political parties, and the asseverations of the president, the "shock" came. As Mr. Chase described it, "the rattling thunder broke from a cloudless firmament, and the storm burst forth in fury." But this time the agitation was not to be confined to the floor of congress—the "people" were invited to take a part in it.

On the 15th of December, 1853, Mr. Dodge, of Iowa, submitted to the senate a bill to organize the territory of Nebraska, which was referred to the committee on territories, and subsequently reported by Mr. Douglas of said committee with amendments. The following is the accompanying report:

"The principal amendments which your committee deem it their duty to commend to the favorable action of the senate, in a special report, are those in which the principles established by the compromise measures of 1850, so far as they are applicable to territorial organizations, are proposed to be affirmed and carried into practical operation within the limits of the new territory.

"The wisdom of those measures is attested, not less by their salutary and beneficial effects, in allaying sectional agitation and restoring peace and harmony to an irritated and distracted people, than by the cordial and almost universal approbation with which they have been received and sanctioned by the whole country. In the judgment of your committee, those measures were intended to have a far more comprehensive and enduring effect than the mere adjustment of difficulties arising out of the recent acquisition of Mexican territory. They were designed to establish certain great principles, which would not only furnish adequate remedies for existing evils, but, in all time to come, avoid the perils of similar agitation, by withdrawing the question of slavery from the halls of congress and the political arena, and committing it to the arbitration of those who were immediately interested in, and alone responsible for its consequences. With a view of conforming their action to what they regard as the settled policy of the government, sanctioned by the approving voice of the American people, your committee have deemed it their duty to incorporate and perpetuate, in their territorial bill, the principles and spirit of those measures. If any other considerations were necessary to render the propriety of this course imperative upon the committee, they may be found in the fact that the Nebraska country occupies the same relative position to the slavery question, as did New Mexico and Utah, when those territories were organized.

"It was a disputed point, whether slavery was prohibited by law in the country acquired from Mexico. On the one hand, it was contended, as a legal proposition, that slavery, having been prohibited by the enactments of Mexico, according to the laws of nations, we received the country with all its local laws and domestic institutions attached to the soil, so far as they did not conflict with the constitution of the United States; and that a law either protecting or prohibiting slavery, was not repugnant to that instrument, as was evidenced by the fact that one half of the states of the Union tolerated, while the other half prohibited, the institution of slavery. On the other hand, it was insisted that, by virtue of the constitution of the United States, every citizen had a right to remove to any territory of the Union, and carry his property with him under the protection of law, whether that property consisted of persons or things. The difficulties arising from this diversity of opinion, were greatly aggravated by the fact that there were many persons on both sides of the legal controversy, who were unwilling to abide the decision of the courts on the legal matters in dispute; thus, among those who claimed that the Mexican laws were still in force, and, consequently, that slavery was already prohibited in those territories by valid enactment, there were many who insisted upon congress making the matter certain, by enacting another prohibition. In like manner, some of those who argued that Mexican law had ceased to have any binding force, and that the constitution tolerated and protected slave property in those territories, were unwilling to trust the decision of the courts upon the point, and insisted that congress should, by direct enactment, remove all legal obstacles to the introduction of slaves into those territories.

"Such being the character of the controversy in respect to the territory acquired from Mexico, a similar question has arisen in regard to the right to hold slaves in the territory of Nebraska, when the Indian laws shall be withdrawn, and the country thrown open to emigration and settlement. By the 8th section of 'an act to authorize the people of Missouri territory to form a constitution and state government, and for the admission of such state into the Union on an equal footing with the original states, and to prohibit slavery in certain territories,' approved March 6th, 1820, it was provided, 'that in all that territory ceded by France to the United States under the name of Louisiana, which lies north of 36° 30' north latitude, not included within the limits of the state contemplated by this act, slavery and involuntary servitude, otherwise than in the punishment of crimes whereof the parties shall have been duly convicted, shall be, and are hereby, prohibited; provided always, that any person escaping into the same, from whom labor or service is lawfully claimed in any state or territory of the United States, such fugitive may be lawfully reclaimed, and conveyed to the persons claiming his or her labor or services as aforesaid.'

"Under this section, as in the case of the Mexican law in New Mexico and Utah, it is a disputed point whether slavery is prohibited in Nebraska country by *valid* enactment. The decision of this question involves the constitutional power of congress to pass laws prescribing and regulating the domestic institutions of the various territories of the Union. In the opinion of those eminent statesmen who hold that congress is invested with no rightful authority to legislate upon the subject of slavery in the territories, the 8th section of the act preparatory to the admission of Missouri is null and void; while the prevailing sentiment in large portions of the Union sustains the doctrine that the constitution of the United States secures to every citizen an inalienable right to move into any of the territories with his property, of whatever kind and description, and to hold and enjoy the same under the sanction of law. Your committee do not feel themselves called upon to enter upon the discussion of these controverted questions. They involve the same grave issues which produced the agitation, the sectional strife, and the fearful struggle of 1850. As congress deemed it wise and prudent to refrain from deciding the matters in controversy then, either by affirming or repealing the Mexican laws, or by an act declaratory of the true intent of the constitution, and the extent of the protection afforded by it to slave property in the territories, so your committee are not prepared to recommend a departure from the course pursued on that memorable occasion, either by affirming or repealing the 8th section of the Missouri act, or by any act declaratory of the meaning of the constitution in respect to the legal points in dispute.

"Your committee deem it fortunate for the peace of the country, and the security of the Union, that the controversy then resulted in the adoption of the compromise measures, which the two great political parties, with singular unanimity, have affirmed as a cardinal article of their faith, and proclaimed to the world as a final settlement of the controversy and an end of the agitation. A due respect, therefore, for the avowed opinions of senators, as well as a proper sense of patriotic duty, enjoins upon your committee the propriety and necessity of a strict adherence to the principles, and even a literal adoption of the enactments of that adjustment, in all their territorial bills, so far as the same are not locally inapplicable. Those enactments embrace, among other things less material to the matters under consideration, the following provisions :

"When admitted as a state, the said territory, or any portion of the same, shall be received into the Union, with or without slavery, as their constitution may prescribe at the time of their admission.

"That the legislative power and authority of said territory shall be vested in the governor and legislative assembly.

"That the legislative power of said territory shall extend to all rightful subjects of legislation, consistent with the constitution of the United States, and the provisions of this act ; but no law shall be passed interfering with the primary disposal of the soil ; no tax shall be imposed upon the property of the United States ; nor shall the lands or other property of non-residents be taxed higher than the lands or other property of residents.

"Writs of error and appeals from the final decisions of said supreme court shall be allowed, and may be taken to the supreme court of the United States in the same manner and under the same regulations as from the circuit courts of the United States, where the value of the property or amount in controversy, to be ascertained by the oath or affirmation of either party, or other competent witness, shall exceed one thousand dollars ; except only that, in all cases involving title to slaves, the said writs of error or appeals shall be allowed and decided by the said supreme court, without regard to the value of the matter, property, or title in controversy : and except also, that a writ of error or appeal shall also be allowed to the supreme court of the United States from the decisions of the said supreme court by this act, or any judge thereof, or of the district courts created by this act, or of any judge thereof, upon any writ of *habeas corpus* involving the question of personal freedom ; and each of the said district courts shall have and exercise the same jurisdiction, in all cases arising under the constitution and laws of the United States, as is vested in the circuit and district courts of the United States ; and the said supreme and district courts of the said territory, and the respective judges thereof, shall and may grant writs of *habeas corpus*, in all cases in which the same are granted by the judges of the United States in the District of Columbia.

" To which may be added the following proposition affirmed by the act of 1850, known as the fugitive slave law :

" That the provisions of the ' act respecting fugitives from justice, and persons escaping from the service of their masters,' approved February 12, 1793, and the provisions of the act to amend and supplementary to the aforesaid act, approved September 18, 1850, shall extend to, and be in force in, all the organized territories, as well as in the various states of the Union.

" From these provisions, it is apparent that the compromise measures of 1850 affirm, and rest upon, the following propositions :

" *First.*—That all questions pertaining to slavery in the territories, and the new states to be formed therefrom, are to be left to the decision of the people residing therein, by their appropriate representatives, to be chosen by them for that purpose.

" *Second.*—That ' all cases involving title to slaves,' and ' questions of personal freedom,' are to be referred to the adjudication of the local tribunals, with the right of appeal to the supreme court of the United States.

" *Third.*—That the provision of the constitution of the United States, in respect to fugitives from service, is to be carried into faithful execution in all ' the original territories,' the same as in the states.

" The substitute for the bill which your committee have prepared, and which is commended to the favorable action of the senate, proposes to carry these propositions and principles into practical operation, in the precise language of the compromise measures of 1850."

Some doubts having been expressed whether the amendments repealed the Missouri compromise, a special report was made, January 4th, 1854, so amending the bill as to leave no doubt upon that subject. The report which proposed to open to slavery all the vast territory secured to freedom by the Missouri compromise, startled the nation from its "repose," and produced an agitation that had never been equaled.

On the 16th January, Mr. Dixon, of Kentucky, gave notice of an amendment directly and plainly repealing the Missouri compromise.

The debate on the bill was opened by Mr. Douglas, on the 30th of January. In justification of his proposition to leave the whole territory open to slavery, he insisted that the Missouri compromise had been repealed. One of the grounds upon which this declaration was founded, was the action of congress in 1848, after the acquisition of territory from Mexico, when the senate voted into a bill a provision to extend the Missouri compromise line westward to the

Pacific ocean; which provision was defeated in the house. This defeat of that proposition Mr. D. construed into an abandonment of the compromise. It was this defeat of that compromise that created the struggle of 1850, and the necessity for making the new compromise of that year; the leading feature of which was non-intervention by congress as to slavery in the territories—leaving the question to be settled by the people therein. It was of universal application—to the country both north and south of 36° 30′.

Mr. Douglas said "the legal effect of this bill, if passed, was neither to legislate slavery into nor out of these territories, but to leave the people to do as they pleased. And why should any man, north or south, object to this principle? It was by the operation of this principle, and not by any dictation from the federal government, that slavery had been abolished in half of the twelve states in which it existed at the time of the adoption of the constitution."

In regard to Utah and New Mexico, Mr. D. said: "In 1850, we who resisted any attempt to force institutions upon the people of those territories inconsistent with their wishes and the right to decide for themselves, were denounced as slavery propagandists. Every one of us who was in favor of the compromise measures of 1850 was arraigned for having advocated a principle purposing to introduce slavery into those territories, and the people were told, and made to believe, that, unless we prohibited it by act of congress, slavery would necessarily and inevitably be introduced into these territories.

"Well, sir, we did establish the territorial governments of Utah and New Mexico without any prohibition. We gave to these abolitionists a full opportunity of proving whether their predictions would prove true or false. Years have rolled round, and the result is before us. The people there have not passed any law recognizing, or establishing, or introducing, or protecting slavery in the territories.

"I do not like, I never did like, the system of legislation on our part, by which a geographical line, in violation of the laws of nature, and climate, and soil, and of the laws of God, should be run to establish institutions for a people contrary to their wishes; yet, out of a regard for the peace and quiet of the country, out of respect for past pledges, and out of a desire to adhere faithfully to all compromises, I sustained the Missouri compromise so long as it was in force, and advocated its extension to the Pacific ocean. Now, when that has been abandoned, when it has been superseded, when a great principle of self-government has been substituted for it, I choose to cling to that principle, and abide in good faith, not only by the letter, but by the spirit of the last compromise.

"Sir, I do not recognize the right of the abolitionists of this country to arraign me for being false to sacred pledges, as they have done in their proclamations. Let them show when and where I have ever proposed to violate a compact. I have proved that I stood by the compact of 1820 and 1845, and proposed its continuance and observance in 1848. I have proved that the free-soilers and abolitionists were the guilty parties who violated that compromise then. I should like to compare notes with these abolition confederates about adherence to compromises. When did they stand by or approve of any one that was ever made ?

" Did not every abolitionist and free-soiler in America denounce the Missouri compromise in 1820 ? Did they not for years hunt down ravenously, for his blood, every man who assisted in making that compromise ? Did they not in 1845, when Texas was annexed, denounce all of us who went for the annexation of Texas and for the continuation of the Missouri compromise line through it ? Did they not, in 1848, denounce me as a slavery propagandist for standing by the principles of the Missouri compromise, and proposing to continue it to the Pacific ocean ? Did they not themselves violate and repudiate it then ? Is not the charge of bad faith true as to every abolitionist in America, instead of being true as to me and the committee, and those who advocate this bill ?

" They talk about the bill being a violation of the compromise measures of 1850. Who can show me a man in either house of congress who was in favor of those compromise measures in 1850, and who is not now in favor of leaving the people of Nebraska and Kansas to do as they please upon the subject of slavery, according to the principle of my bill ? Is there one ? If so, I have not heard of him. This tornado has been raised by abolitionists, and abolitionists alone. They have made an impression upon the public mind, in the way in which I have mentioned, by a falsification of the law and the facts ; and this whole organization against the compromise measures of 1850 is an abolition movement. I presume they had some hope of getting a few tender-footed democrats into their plot ; and, acting on what they supposed they might do, they sent forth publicly to the world the falsehood that their address was signed by the senators and a majority of the representatives from the state of Ohio ; but when we come to examine signatures, we find no one whig there, no one democrat there ; none but pure, unmitigated, unadulterated abolitionists."

On the 3d of February, Mr. Chase, senator from Ohio, moved to strike out from the bill the words, " was superseded by the principles of the legislation of 1850, commonly called the compromise measures, and," so that the clause would read : " That the constitution, and all laws of the United States which are not locally inapplicable, shall have the same force and effect within the said territory of Nebraska as elsewhere within the United States, except the eighth section of the act preparatory to the admission of Missouri into the Union, approved March 6, 1820, which is hereby declared inoperative."

Mr. Chase then proceeded to reply to Mr. Douglas : " Mr. President, I had occasion, a few days ago, to expose the utter groundlessness of the personal charges made by the senator from Illinois (Mr. Douglas) against myself and the other signers of the independent democratic appeal. I now move to strike from this bill a statement which I will to-day demonstrate to be without any foundation in fact or in history. I intend afterwards to move to strike out the whole clause annulling the Missouri prohibition.

" A few days only have elapsed since the congress of the United States assembled in this capitol. Then no agitation seemed to disturb the political elements. Two of the great political parties of the country, in their national conventions, had announced that slavery agitation was at an end, and that henceforth that subject was not to be discussed in congress or out of congress. The president, in his annual message, had referred to this state of opinion, and had declared his fixed purpose to maintain, as far as any responsibility attached to him, the quiet of the country.

"The agreement of the two old political parties, thus referred to by the chief magistrate of the country, was complete, and a large majority of the American people seemed to acquiesce in the legislation of which he spoke. A few of us, indeed, doubted the accuracy of these statements, and the permanency of this repose. We never believed that the acts of 1850 would prove to be a permanent adjustment of the slavery question. But, sir, we only represented a small, though vigorous and growing party in the country. Our number was small in congress. By some we were regarded as visionaries—by some as factionists; while almost all agreed in pronouncing us mistaken. And so, sir, the country was at peace. As the eye swept the entire circumference of the horizon and upward to mid-heaven, not a cloud appeared; to common observation there was no mist or stain upon the clearness of the sky. But suddenly all is changed; rattling thunder breaks from the cloudless firmament. The storm bursts forth in fury. And now we find ourselves in the midst of an agitation, the end and issue of which no man can foresee.

"Now, sir, who is responsible for this renewal of strife and controversy? Not we, for we have introduced no question of territorial slavery into congress—not we, who are denounced as agitators and factionists. No, sir: the quietists and the finalists have become agitators; they who told us that all agitation was quieted, and that the resolutions of the political conventions put a final period to the discussion of slavery. This will not escape the observation of the country. It is *slavery* that renews the strife. It is slavery that again wants room. It is slavery with its insatiate demand for more slave territory and more slave states. And what does slavery ask for now? Why, sir, it demands that a time-honored and sacred compact shall be rescinded—a compact which has endured through a whole generation—a compact which has been universally regarded as inviolable, north and south—a compact, the constitutionality of which few have doubted, and by which all have consented to abide.

"It will not answer to violate such a compact without a pretext. Some plausible ground must be discovered or invented for such an act, and such a ground is supposed to be found in the doctrine which was advanced the other day by the senator from Illinois, that the compromise acts of 1850 'superseded' the prohibition of slavery north of 36° 30', in the act preparatory for the admission of Missouri. Ay, sir, 'superseded' is the phrase—'superseded by the principles of the legislation of 1850, commonly called the compromise measures.'

"It is against this statement, untrue in fact, and without foundation in history, that the amendment which I have proposed is directed During the long discussion of the compromise measures in 1850, it was never suggested that they were to supersede the Missouri prohibition. At the last session, a Nebraska bill passed the house, came to the senate, and was reported on by Mr. Douglas, who also made a speech in its favor; and in all there was not a word about repeal by supersedure. The senator from Missouri, (Mr. Atchison,) had also spoken upon the bill, and had distinctly declared that the Missouri prohibition was not and could not be repealed." An extract was here read from the speech of this senator, of which this is a part :

'I have always been of opinion that the first great error committed in the political history of this country was the ordinance of 1787, rendering the northwest territory free territory. The next great error was the Missouri compromise. But they are both irremediable. There is no remedy for them. We must submit to them. I am prepared to do it. It is evident that the Missouri compromise cannot be repealed. So far as that question is concerned, we might as well agree to the admission of this territory now as next year, or five or ten years hence.'

"Now, sir, when was this said? It was on the morning of the 4th of March, just before the close of the last session, when that Nebraska bill, reported by the senator from Illinois, which proposed no repeal, and suggested no supersedure, was under discussion. I think, sir, that all this shows pretty clearly that up to the very close of the last session of congress, nobody had ever thought of a repeal by supersedure. Then what took place at the commencement of the present session? The senator from Iowa, early in December, introduced a bill for the organization of Nebraska. I believe it was the same bill that was under discussion here at the last session, line for line, and word for word. If I am wrong, the senator will correct me. Did the senator from Iowa then entertain the idea that the Missouri prohibition had been superseded? No, sir; neither he or any other man here, so far as could be judged from any discussion, or statement, or remark, had received this notion."

Mr. C. then referred to Mr. Douglas' own report of the 4th of January last, made only thirty days ago. "Nor did this report express the opinion that the compromise acts of 1850 had superseded the Missouri prohibition. The committee said that some affirmed and others denied that the Mexican laws prohibiting slavery in the territory acquired from Mexico, were still in force there ; and they said that the territorial compromise acts stood clear of these questions. They simply provided 'that the states organized out of these territories might come in with or without slavery as they should elect, but did not affect the question whether slaves could or could not be introduced before the organization of state governments. That question was left to judicial decision.'

"So in respect to the Nebraska territory. There were southern men who contended they would, by virtue of the constitution, take their slaves thither, and hold them there, notwithstanding the Missouri prohibition, while a majority of the American people, north and south, believed that prohibition constitutional and effectual. But did the committee propose to repeal it, or suggest that it had been superseded? No. They said they did 'not feel themselves called upon to enter into the discussion of these controverted questions. Congress deemed it wise and prudent to refrain from deciding the matters in controversy then, either by affirming or repealing the Mexican laws, or by an act declaratory of the true intent of the constitution and the extent of the protection afforded by it to slave property in the territories; so your committee are not prepared now to recommend a departure from the course pursued on that memorable occasion, either by affirming or repealing the eighth section of the Missouri act, or by any act declaratory of the meaning of the constitution in respect to the legal points in dispute.'

" Mr. President, here are very remarkable facts. The committee on territories declared that it was not wise, that it was not prudent, that it was not right to renew the old controversy, and to rouse agitation. They declared that they would abstain from any recommendation of a repeal of the prohibition, or of any provision declaratory of the construction of the constitution in respect to the legal points in dispute."

Mr. Chase traced the progress of the committee's bill. "As published January 7th, it contained twenty sections. On the 10th, it was published again: it then had twenty-one sections. The omission of the last section was alleged to be a clerical error. It was, he said, a singular fact that this twenty-first section was not in harmony with the committee's report. It in effect repealed the Missouri prohibition, which the committee, in their report, declared ought not to be done. Was it possible that this was a mere clerical error?

"But the addition of this section did not help the bill. It declared, among other things, that the question of slavery in the territories and in the states to be formed therefrom, was to be left to the decision of the people through their representatives. But this did not meet the approbation of the southern gentlemen, who claimed the right to take their slaves into the territories, notwithstanding any prohibition either by congress or by a territorial legislature. It was not enough that the committee had abandoned their report, and added this twenty-first section in direct contravention of its reasonings and principles; the section must itself be abandoned and the repeal of the Missouri prohibition placed in a shape which would not deny the slaveholding claim. He next alluded to the amendment of the senator from Kentucky, which came square up to repeal and to the claim. The amendment probably produced some fluttering and some consultation. It met the views of southern senators, and probably determined the shape which the bill had assumed. For it was just seven days after the amendment had been offered by senator Dixon, that a fresh amendment was reported from the committee on territories, in the shape of a new bill, enlarged to forty sections. This new bill cuts off from the proposed territory half a degree of latitude on the south, and divides the residue into two territories." This new bill thus provided for the repeal of the Missouri prohibition:

" The constitution and all laws of the United States which are not locally inapplicable, shall have the same force and effect within the said territory of Nebraska as elsewhere within the United States, except the eighth section of the act preparatory to the admission of Missouri into the Union, approved March 6, 1820, which was superseded by the principles of the legislation of 1850, commonly called the compromise measures, and is therefore declared inoperative.'

" Doubtless, Mr. President, this provision operates as a repeal of the prohibition. The senator from Kentucky was right when he said it was in effect the equivalent of his amendment. Those who are willing to break up and destroy the old compact of 1820, can vote for this bill with full assurance that such will be its effect. But I appeal to them not to vote for this supersedure clause. I ask them not to incorporate into the legislation of the country a declaration which every one knows to be wholly untrue. I have said that this doctrine of supersedure is new. I have now proved that it is a plant of but ten day's growth. It was never seen or heard of until the 23d day of January, 1854. It was upon that day that this tree of Upas was planted: we already see its poisonous fruits.

"The provision I have quoted abrogates the Missouri prohibition. It asserts no right in the territorial legislature to prohibit slavery. The senator from Illinois, in his speech, was very careful to assert no right of legislation in a territorial legislature, except subject to the restrictions and limitations of the constitution. We know well enough what the understanding or claim of southern gentlemen is in respect to these limitations and restrictions. They insist that by them every territorial legislature is absolutely precluded from all power of legislation for the prohibition of slavery. I warn gentlemen who propose to support this bill, that their votes for this provision will be regarded as admitting this claim."

Having thus endeavored to prove that the doctrine that the Missouri compromise had been superseded by the acts of 1850, was new, Mr. Chase attempted to prove it unfounded. Mr. Douglas had charged as a misrepresentation, the statement in the appeal of the independent democrats, that the acts of 1850 were intended to apply to the territory acquired from Mexico only; and that they did not touch the existing exclusion of slavery from what was now called Nebraska. Mr. Chase referred to the report of the committee of thirteen in 1850, which distinctly stated that the compromise measures applied to the newly acquired territory, and he appealed to Gen. Cass, who sat near him, whether any thing had been said in the committee of thirteen, or elsewhere, which indicated a purpose to apply them to any other territory. (Mr. Cass remained silent.) Mr. C. therefore assumed that he was correct; and he proceeded at length in attempting to disprove the assertion of Mr. Douglas, that the Missouri compromise had been superseded. He said :

"But the senator from Illinois says that the territorial compromise acts did in fact apply to other territory than that acquired from Mexico. How does he prove that ? He says that a part of the territory was acquired from Texas. But this very territory which he says was acquired from Texas, was first acquired first from Mexico. After Mexico ceded it to the United States, Texas claimed that that cession inured to her benefit. That claim only was relinquished to the United States. The case, then, stands thus : we acquired the territory from Mexico ; Texas claimed it, but gave up her claim. This certainly does not disprove the assertion that the territory was acquired from Mexico, and as certainly it does not sustain the senator's assertion that it was acquired from Texas.

"The senator next tells the senate and the country, that by the Utah act, there was included in the territory of Utah a portion of the old Louisiana acquisition, covered by the Missouri prohibition, which prohibition was annulled as to that portion by the provisions of that act. Every one at all acquainted with our public history knows that the dividing line between Spain and the United States extended due north from the source of the Arkansas to the 42d parallel of north latitude. That arbitrary line left within the Louisiana acquisition a little valley in the midst of rocky mountains, where several branches of the Grand river, one of the affluents of the Colorado, take their rise. Here is the map. Here spreads out the vast territory of Utah, more than one hundred and eighty-seven thousand square miles. Here is the little spot, hardly a pin's point upon the map, which I cover with the tip of my little finger, which, according to the boundary fixed by the territorial bill, was cut off from the Louisiana acquisition and included in Utah. The account given of it in the senator's speech would lead one to suppose that it was an important part of the Louisiana acquisition. It is, in fact, not of the smallest consequence. There are no inhabitants there. It was known that the Rocky Mountain range was very near the arbitrary line fixed by the treaty, and nobody ever dreamed that the adoption of that range as the eastern boundary of Utah would abrogate the Missouri prohibition. The senator reported that boundary line. Did he tell the senate or the country that its establishment would have that effect? No, sir ; never. The assertion of the senator that a ' close examination of the Utah act clearly establishes the fact that it was the intent, as well as the legal effect of the compromise measures of 1850 to supersede the Missouri compromise, and all geographical and territorial lines,' is little short of preposterous. There was no intent at all, except to make a convenient eastern boundary to Utah, and no legal effect at all upon the Louisiana acquisition, except to cut off from it the little valley of the Middle Park."

Mr. Douglas had charged the signers of the appeal with misrepresentation in assuming that it was the policy of the fathers of the republic to prohibit slavery in all the territories ceded by the old states to the Union. Mr. Chase commenced with a reference to the sentiments of Jefferson, and traced the history of the action of the government on the subject, through a long period of years, in vindication of the statement controverted by Mr. Douglas.

Mr. Chase's amendment was negatived, 13 to 30.

Mr. Houston advocated the rights of the Indians included within the territories, who were to be disturbed by this bill. He adverted to the pledges made to them from time to time, and especially the assurance given them in the treaty of 1835, that their lands beyond the Mississippi should never, without their consent, be included within the territorial limits or jurisdiction of any state or territory. He objected to the bill on other grounds. There was no necessity for joining three such important subjects. The organization of Nebraska without a sufficient population to warrant it, nearly all being Indian territory; the organization of Kansas, entirely held and occupied by Indians; and the repeal of the Missouri compromise, an important consideration for the American people, were all placed in this omnibus shape, and presented for action. He had on former occasions supported the Missouri compromise, assisted by the south, because they regarded it as a solemn compact. Texas, he said, had been admitted upon that principle. It was an express condition of her admission, that in all new states formed out of her territory north of 36° 30′, slavery should be prohibited.

Mr. H. said he had voted for the compromise of 1850; but he did not suppose that he was voting to repeal the Missouri compromise. He regarded it as a final settlement of this mooted question, this source of agitation. Great trials and emergencies, he feared, would arise between the north and the south. The south was in a minority; she could not be otherwise. If she should accede to the violation of a compact so sacred as this, she would set an example that would be followed when she did not desire it. He averred that he would resist every attempt to infringe or repeal the Missouri compromise.

On the 15th of February, the question was taken on the substitute of the committee reported by Mr. Douglas, to strike out the words which declared the Missouri compromise to be superseded by that of 1850, and to insert the provision declaring the Missouri compromise inconsistent with the principles of non-intervention of congress with slavery in the states and territories as recognized by the legislation of 1850, and inoperative and void; and declaring the people free to regulate their domestic institutions in their own way, subject only to the constitution of the United States. The substitute was adopted, 35 to 10.

Mr. Cass expressed his regret that this question of the repeal of the Missouri compromise, which opened all the disputed points connected with the subject of congressional action upon slavery in the territories, had again been brought before the senate. The advantages to result from the measure would not outweigh the injury which the ill-feeling accompanying the discussion would produce. Nor would the south derive any benefit from it, as no human power could establish slavery in the regions defined by these bills. He was, however, in favor of the amendment of the committee which declared that the people, whether in the territories, or in the states to be formed from them, were free to regulate their domestic institutions in their own way, subject only to the constitution of the United States.

Mr. Cass, in the course of his speech, replied to the complaints that the south was excluded from, and robbed of the territories, and that they were appropriated to the north. While he repeated the opinion that congress was not authorized to restrain a person, by legal enactment, from taking slaves into any territory of the United States, he maintained that the prohibition of slavery by local legislation was *not* an exclusion of the south more than the north, as a slaveholder and a non-slaveholder could go into such territory on equal terms; and he denied the charge of the south, that congress, by admitting a state whose constitution interdicts slavery, is responsible for that act.

In relation to the power of congress over the territories, he contended that the power granted by the constitution to regulate and "dispose of the territory and other property of the United States," meant simply the power to dispose of the public lands, as property, and did not include the power of life and death over the inhabitants.

The bill was further discussed until March 2d, when the vote was taken on Mr. Chase's amendment, to allow the people of the territory, through their representatives, to prohibit slavery, which was rejected by a vote of 36 to 10. Mr. Badger's amendment, "that nothing herein contained shall be construed to revive or put in force any law or regulation which may have existed prior to the act of March 6th, 1820, either protecting, establishing, prohibiting or abolishing slavery," was carried, yeas, 35; nays, 6.

On the 3d of March, the bill was put upon its final passage, when a long and earnest debate ensued. Mr. Seward addressed the senate at a late hour, as follows:

Mr. PRESIDENT :—I rise with no purpose of further resisting or even delaying the passage of this bill. Let its advocates have only a little patience, and they will soon reach the object for which they have struggled so earnestly and so long. The sun has set for the last time upon the guaranteed and certain liberties of all the unsettled and unorganized portions of the American continent that lie within the jurisdiction of the United States. To-morrow's sun will rise in dim eclipse over them. How long that obscuration shall last, is known only to the Power that directs and controls all human events. For myself, I know only this—that now no human power will prevent its coming on, and that its passing off will be hastened and secured by others than those now here, and perhaps by only those belonging to future generations.

Sir, it would be almost factious to offer further resistance to this measure here. Indeed, successful resistance was never expected to be made in this hall. The senate floor is an old battle ground, on which have been fought many contests, and always, at least since 1820, with fortune adverse to the cause of equal and universal freedom. We were only a few here who engaged in that cause in the beginning of this contest. All that we could hope to do—all that we did hope to do—was to organize and to prepare the issue for the house of representatives, to which the country would look for its decision as authoritative, and to awaken the country that it might be ready for the appeal which would be made, whatever the decision of congress might be. We are no stronger now. Only fourteen at the first, it will be fortunate if, among the ills and accidents which surround us, we shall maintain that number to the end.

We are now on the eve of the consummation of a great national transaction—a transaction which will close a cycle in the history of our country—and it is impossible not to desire to pause a moment and survey the scene around us, and the prospect before us. However obscure we may individually be, our connection with this great transaction will perpetuate our names for the praise or for the censure of future ages, and perhaps in regions far remote. If, then, we had no other motive for our actions but that of an honest desire for a just fame, we could not be indifferent to that scene and that prospect. But individual interests and ambition sink into insignificance in view of the interests of our country and of mankind. These interests awaken, at least in me, an intense solicitude.

It was said by some in the beginning, and it has been said by others later in this debate, that it was doubtful whether it would be the cause of slavery or the cause of freedom that would gain advantages from the passage of this bill. I do not find it necessary to be censorious, nor even unjust to others, in order that my own course may be approved. I am sure that the honorable senator from Illinois, [Mr. Douglas,] did not mean that the slave states should gain an advantage over the free states; for he disclaimed it when he introduced the bill. I believe in all candor, that the honorable senator from Georgia, [Mr. Toombs,] who comes out at the close of the battle as one of the chiefest leaders of the victorious party, is sincere in declaring his own opinion that the slave states will gain no unjust advantage over the free states, because he disclaims it as a triumph in their behalf. Notwithstanding all this, however, what has occurred here and in the country, during this contest, has compelled a conviction that slavery will gain something, and freedom will endure a severe, though I hope not an irretrievable, loss. The slaveholding states are passive, quiet, content, and satisfied with the prospective boon, and the free states are excited and alarmed with fearful forebodings and apprehensions. The impatience for the speedy passage of the bill, manifested by its friends, betrays a knowledge that this is the condition of public sentiment in the free states. They thought in the begining that it was necessary to guard the measure by inserting the Clayton amendment, which would exclude unnaturalized foreign inhabitants of the territories from the right of suffrage. And now they seem willing with almost perfect unanimity, to relinquish that safe-guard, rather than to delay the adoption of the principal measure for at most a year, perhaps for only a week or a day. Suppose that the senate should adhere to that condition, which so lately was thought so wise and so important—what then ? The bill could only go back to the house of representatives, which must either yield or insist ! In the one case or in the other, a decision in favor of the bill would be secured ; for even if the house should disagree, the senate would have time to recede. But the majority will hazard nothing, even on a prospect so certain as this. They will recede at once, without a moment's further struggle, from the condition, and thus secure the passage of this bill now, to-night. Why such haste ? Even if the question were to go to the country before a final decision here, what would there be wrong in that ? There is no man living who will say that the country anticipated, or that *he* anticipated, the agitation of this measure in congress, when this congress was elected, or even when it assembled in December last.

Under such circumstances, and in the midst of agitation, and excitement, and debates, it is only fair to say, that certainly the country has not decided in favor of the bill. The refusal, then, to let the question go to the country is a conclusive proof that the slave states, as represented here, expect from the passage of this bill what the free states insist that they will lose by it—an advantage, a material advantage, and not a mere abstraction. There are men in the slaves states, as in the free states, who insist always too pertinaciously upon mere abstractions. But that is not the policy of the slave states to-day. They are in earnest in seeking for, and securing, an object, and an important one. I believe they are going to have it. I do not know how long the advantage gained will last, nor how great or comprehensive it will be. Every senator who agrees with me in opinion must feel as I do—that under such circumstances he can forego nothing that can be done decently, with due respect to difference of opinion, and consistently with the constitutional and settled rules of legislation, to place the true merits of the question before the country. Questions sometimes occur which seem to have two right sides. Such were the questions that divided the English nation between Pitt and Fox—such the contest between the assailant and the defender of Quebec. The judgment of the world was suspended by its sympathies, and seemed ready to descend in favor of him who should be most gallant in conduct. And so, when both fell with equal chivalry on the same field, the survivors united in raising a common monument to the glorious but rival memories of Wolfe and Montcalm. But this contest involves a moral question. The slave states so present it. They maintain that African slavery is not erroneous, not unjust, not inconsistent with the advancing cause of human nature. Since they so regard it, I do not expect to see statesmen representing those states indifferent about a vindication of this system by the congress of the United States. On the other hand, we of the free states regard slavery as erroneous, unjust, oppressive, and therefore absolutely inconsistent with the principles of the American constitution and government. Who will expect us to be indifferent to the decisions of the American people and of mankind on such an issue?

Again: there is suspended on the issue of this contest the political equilibrium between the free and the slave states. It is no ephemeral question, no idle question, whether slavery shall go on increasing its influence over the central power here, or whether freedom shall gain the ascendency. I do not expect to see statesmen of the slave states indifferent on so momentous a question, and as little can it be expected that those of the free states will betray their own great cause. And now it remains for me to declare, in view of the decision of this controversy so near at hand, that I have seen nothing and heard nothing during its progress to change the opinions which at the earliest proper period I deliberately expressed. Certainly, I have not seen the evidence then promised, that the free states would acquiesce in the measure. As certainly, too, I may say that I have not seen the fulfillment of the promise that the history of the last thirty years would be revised, corrected, and amended, and that it would then appear that the country, during all that period, had been resting in prosperity, and contentment, and peace, not upon a valid, constitutional, and irrevocable compromise between the slave states and the free states, but upon an unconstitutional and false, and even infamous, act of congressional usurpation.

On the contrary, I am now, if possible, more than ever satisfied that, after all this debate, the history of the country will go down to posterity just as it stood before, carrying to them the everlasting facts, that until 1820 the congress of the United States legislated to prevent the introduction of slavery into new territories whenever that object was practicable ; and that in that year they so far modified that policy, under alarming apprehensions of civil convulsion, by a constitutional enactment in the character of a compact, as to admit Missouri a new slave state, but upon the express condition, stipulated in favor of the free states, that slavery should forever be prohibited in all the residue of the existing and unorganized territories of the United States lying north of the parallel 36° 30' north latitude.   Certainly, I find nothing to win my favor toward the bill in the proposition of the senator from Maryland, [Mr. Pearce,] to restore the Clayton amendment, which was struck out in the house of representatives.   So far from voting for that proposition, I shall vote against it now, as I did when it was under consideration here before, in accordance with the opinion adopted as early as any political opinions I ever had, and cherished as long, that the right of suffrage is not a mere conventional right, but an inherent natural right, of which no government can rightly deprive any adult man who is subject to its authority, and obligated to its support.

I hold, moreover, sir that inasmuch as every man is, by force of circumstances beyond his own control, a subject of government somewhere, he is, by the very constitution of human society, entitled to share equally in the conferring of political power on those who wield it, if he is not disqualified by crime; that in a despotic government he ought to be allowed arms, in a free government the ballot or the open vote, as a means of self-protection against unendurable oppression.   I am not likely, therefore, to restore to this bill an amendment which would deprive it of an important feature imposed upon it by the house of representatives, and that one, perhaps, the only feature that harmonizes with my own convictions of justice.   It is true that the house stipulates such suffrage for white men as a condition for opening the territory to the possible proscription and slavery of the African.   I shall separate them.   I shall vote for the former and against the latter, glad to get universal suffrage for white men, if only that can be gained now, and working right on, full of hope and confidence, for the prevention or the abrogation of slavery in the territories hereafter.

Sir, I am surprised at the pertinacity with which the honorable senator from Delaware, mine ancient and honorable friend, [Mr. Clayton,] perseveres in opposing the granting of the right of suffrage to the unnaturalized foreigner in

40

the territories. Congress cannot deny him that right. Here is the third article of that convention by which Louisiana, including Kansas and Nebraska, was ceded to the United States:

"The inhabitants of the ceded territory shall be incorporated in the Union of the United States, and admitted as soon as possible, according to the principles of the federal constitution, to the enjoyment of the rights, privileges, and immunities of citizens of the United States; and in the mean time they shall be maintained and protected in the free enjoyment of their liberty, property, and the religion they profess."

The inhabitants of Kansas and Nebraska are citizens already, and by force of this treaty must continue to be, and as such to enjoy the right of suffrage, whatever laws you may make to the contrary. My opinions are well known, to wit: that slavery is not only an evil, but a local one, injurious and ultimately pernicious to society, wherever it exists, and in conflict with the constitutional principles of society in this country. I am not willing to extend nor to permit the extension of that local evil into regions now free within our empire. I know that there are some who differ from me, and who regard the constitution of the United States as an instrument which sanctions slavery as well as freedom. But if I could admit a proposition so incongruous with the letter and spirit of the federal constitution, and the known sentiments of its illustrious founders, and so should conclude that slavery was national, I must still cherish the opinion that it is an evil; and because it is a national one, I am the more firmly held and bound to prevent an increase of it, tending, as I think it manifestly does, to the weakening and ultimate overthrow of the constitution itself, and therefore to the injury of all mankind. I know there have been states which have endured long, and achieved much, which tolerated slavery; but that was not the slavery of caste, like African slavery. Such slavery tends to demoralize equally the subjected race and the superior one. It has been the absence of such slavery from Europe that has given her nations their superiority over other countries in that hemisphere. Slavery, wherever it exists, begets fear, and fear is the parent of weakness. What is the secret of that eternal, sleepless anxiety in the legislative halls, and even at the firesides of the slave states, always asking new stipulations, new compromises and abrogation of compromises, new assumptions of power and abnegations of power, but fear? It is the apprehension that, even if safe now, they will not always or long be secure against some invasion or some aggression from the free states. What is the secret of the humiliating part which proud old Spain is acting at this day, trembling between alarms of American intrusion into Cuba on one side, and British dictation on the other, but the fact that she has cherished slavery so long, and still cherishes it, in the last of her American colonial possessions? Thus far Kansas and Nebraska are safe, under the laws of 1820, against the introduction of this element of national debility and decline. The bill before us, as we are assured, contains a great principle, a glorious principle; and yet that principle, when fully ascertained, proves to be nothing less than the subversion of that security, not only within the territories of Kansas and Nebraska, but within all the other present and future territories of the United States. Thus it it is quite clear that it is not a principle alone that is involved, but that those who crowd this measure with so much zeal and earnestness must expect that either freedom or slavery shall gain something by it in those regions. The case, then, stands thus in Kansas and Nebraska: freedom may lose, but certainly can gain nothing; while slavery may gain, but as certainly can lose nothing.

So far as I am concerned, the time for looking on the dark side has passed. I feel quite sure that slavery at most can get nothing more than Kansas; while Nebraska—the wider northern region—will, under existing circumstances, escape, for the reason that its soil and climate are uncongenial with the staples of slave culture—rice, sugar, cotton, and tobacco. Moreover, since the public attention has been so well and so effectually directed toward the subject, I cherish a hope that slavery may be prevented even from gaining a foothold in Kansas. Congress only gives consent, but it does not and cannot introduce slavery there. Slavery will be embarrassed by its own overgrasping spirit. No one, I am sure, anticipates the possible reëstablishment of the African slave-trade. The tide of emigration to Kansas is therefore to be supplied there solely by the domestic fountain of slave production. But slavery has also other regions besides Kansas to be filled from that fountain. There are all of New Mexico and all of Utah already within the United States; and then there is Cuba that consumes slave labor and life as fast as any one of the slaveholding states can supply it; and besides these regions, there remains all of Mexico down to the Isthmus. The stream of slave labor flowing from so small a fountain, and broken into several divergent channels, will not cover so great a field; and it is reasonably to be hoped that the part of it nearest to the North Pole will be the last to be inundated. But African slave emigration is to compete with free emigration of white men, and the source of this latter tide is as ample as the civilization of the two entire continents. The honorable senator from Delaware mentioned, as if it were a startling fact, that twenty thousand European immigrants arrived in New York in one month. Sir, he has stated the fact with too much moderation. On my return to the capital a day or two ago, I met twelve thousand of these emigrants who had arrived in New York on one morning, and who had thronged the churches on the following Sabbath, to return thanks for deliverence from the perils of the sea, and for their arrival in the land, not of slavery, but of liberty. I also thank God for their escape, and for their coming. They are now on their way westward, and the news of the passage of this bill preceding them, will speed many of them towards Kansas and Nebraska. Such arrivals are not extraordinary—they occur almost every week; and the immigration from Germany, from Great Britian, and from Norway, and from Sweden, during the European war, will rise to six or seven hundred thousand souls in a year. And with this tide is to be mingled one rapidly swelling from Asia and from the islands of the south seas. All the immigrants under this bill, as the house of representatives overruling you have ordered, will be good, loyal, liberty-loving, slavery-fearing citizens. Come on, then, gentlemen of the slave states. Since there is no escaping your challenge, I accept it in behalf of the cause of freedom. We will engage in competition for the virgin soil of Kansas, and God give the victory to the side which is stronger in numbers as it is in right.

There are, however, earnest advocates of this bill, who do not expect, and who, I suppose, do not desire that slavery shall gain possession of Nebraska. What do they expect to gain? The honorable senator from Indiana (Mr. Pettit) says that by thus obliterating the Missouri compromise restriction, they will gain a *tabula rasa*, on which the inhabitants of Kansas and Nebraska may write whatever they will. This is the great principle of the bill, as he understands it. Well, what gain is there in that? You obliterate a constitution of freedom. If they write a new constitution of freedom, can the new be better than the old? If they write a constitution of slavery, will it not be a worse one? I ask the honorable senator that. But the honorable senator says that the people of Nebraska will have the privilege of establishing institutions for themselves. They have now the privilege of establishing free institutions. Is it a privilege, then, to establish slavery? If so, what a mockery are all our constitutions, which prevent the inhabitants from capriciously subverting free institutions and establishing institutions of slavery! Sir, it is a sophism, a subtlety, to talk of conferring upon a country, already secure in the blessings of freedom, the power of self-destruction.

What mankind everywhere want, is not the removal of the constitutions of freedom which they have, that they may make at their pleasure constitutions of slavery or freedom, but the privilege of retaining constitutions of freedom when they already have them, and the removal of constitutions of slavery when they have them, that they may establish constitutions of freedom in their place. We hold on tenaciously to all existing constitutions of freedom. Who denounces any man for diligently adhering to such constitutions? Who would dare to denounce any one for disloyalty to our existing constitutions, if they were constitutions of despotism and slavery? But it is supposed by some that this principle is less important in regard to Kansas and Nebraska than as a general one—a general principle applicable to all other present and future territories of the United States. Do honorable senators then indeed suppose they are establishing a principle at all? If so, I think they egregiously err, whether the principle is either good or bad, right or wrong. They are not establishing it, and cannot establish it in this way. You subvert one law capriciously by making another law in its place. That is all. Will your law have any more weight, authority, solemnity, or binding force on future congresses than the first had? You abrogate the law of your predecessors—others will have equal power and equal liberty to abrogate yours. You allow no barriers around the old law, to protect it from abrogation. You erect none around your new law, to stay the hand of future innovators.

On what ground do you expect the new law to stand? If you are candid, you will confess that you rest your assumptions on the ground that the free states will never agitate repeal, but always *acquiesce*. It may be that you are right. I am not going to predict the course of the free States. I claim no authority to speak for them, and still less to say what they will do. But I may venture to say, that if they shall not repeal this law it will not be because they are not strong enough to do it. They have power in the house of representatives greater than that of the slave states, and, when they choose to exercise it, a power greater even here in the senate. The free States are not dull scholars, even in practical political strategy. When you shall have taught them that a compromise law establishing freedom can be abrogated, and the Union nevertheless stand, you will have let them into another secret, namely : that a law permitting or establishing slavery can be repealed, and the Union nevertheless remain firm. If you inquire why they do not stand by their rights and their interests more firmly, I will tell you to the best of my ability. It is because they are conscious of their strength, and, therefore, unsuspecting and slow to apprehend danger. The reason why you prevail in so many contests, is because you are in perpetual fear.

There cannot be a convocation of abolitionists, however impracticable, in Faneuil Hall or the Tabernacle, though it consists of men and women who have separated themselves from all effective political parties, and who have renounced all political agencies, even though they resolve that they will vote for nobody, not even for themselves, to carry out their purposes, and though they practice on that resolution, but you take alarm, and your agitation renders necessary such compromises as those of 1820 and of 1850. We are young in the arts of politics; you are old. We are strong; you are weak. We are, therefore, over-confident, careless, and indifferent; you are vigilant and active. These are traits that redound to your praise. They are mentioned not in your disparagement. I say only that there may be an extent of intervention, of aggression on your side, which may induce the north, at some time, either in this or some future generation, to adopt your tactics and follow your example. Remember now, that by unanimous consent, this new law will be a repealable statute, exposed to all the chances of the Missouri compromise. It stands an infinitely worse chance of endurance than that compromise did.

The Missouri compromise was a transaction which wise, learned, patriotic statesmen agreed to surround and fortify with the principles of a compact for mutual considerations, passed and executed, and therefore, although not irrepealable in fact, yet irrepealable in honor and conscience, and down at least until this very session of the congress of the United States, it has had the force and authority not merely of an act of congress, but of a covenant between the free states and slave states, scarcely less sacred than the constitution itself. Now, then, who are your contracting parties in the law establishing governments in Kansas and Nebraska, and abrogating the Missouri compromise ? What are the equivalents in this law ? What has the north given, and what has the south got back, that makes this a contract ? Who pretends that it is anything more than an ordinary act of ordinary legislation ? If, then, a law which has all the forms and solemnities recognized by common consent as a compact, and is covered with traditions, cannot stand amid this shuffling of the balance between the free states and the slave states, tell me what chances this new law that you are passing will have ?

You are, moreover, setting a precedent which abrogates all compromises. Four years ago you obtained the consent of a portion of the free tates— enough to render the effort at immediate repeal or resistance alike impossible—to what we regard as an unconstitutional act for the surrender of fugitive slaves. That was declared by the common consent of the persons acting in the name of the two parties, the slave states and the free states in congress, an irrepealable law—not even to be questioned, although it violated the constitution. In establishing this new principle, you expose that law also to the chances of repeal. You not only so expose the fugitive slave law, but there is no solemnity about the articles for the annexation of Texas to the United states, which does not hang about the Missouri compromise, and when you have shown that the Missouri compromise can be repealed, then the articles for the annexation of Texas are subject to the will and pleasure and the caprice of a temporary majority in congress. Do you, then, expect that the free states are to observe compacts, and you to be at liberty to break them; that they are to submit to laws and leave them on the statute-book, however unconstitutional and however grievous, and that you are to rest under no such obligation ? I think it is not a reasonable expectation. Say, then, who from the north will be bound to admit Kansas, when Kansas shall come in here, if she shall come as a slave state ?

The honorable senator from Georgia (Mr. Toombs)—and I know he is as sincere as he is ardent—says if he shall be here when Kansas comes as a free state, he will vote for her admission. I doubt not that he would; but he will not be here, for the very reason, if there be no other, that he would vote that way. When Oregon or Minnesota shall come here for admission—within one year, or two years, or three years from this time—we shall then see what your new principle is worth in its obligation upon the slaveholding states. No ; you establish no principle, you only abrogate a principle which was established for your own security as well as ours ; and while you think you are abnegating and resigning all power and all authority on this subject into the hands of the people of the territories, you are only getting over a difficulty in settling this question in the organization of two new territories, by postponing it till they come here to be admitted as states, slave or free.

Sir, in saying that your new principle will not be established by this bill, I reason from obvious, clear, well-settled principles of human nature. Slavery and freedom are antagonistical elements of this country. The founders of the constitution framed it with a knowledge of that antagonism, and suffered it to continue, that it might work out its own ends. There is a commercial antagonism, an irreconcilable one, between the systems of free labor and slave labor. They have been at war with each other ever since the government was established, and that war is to continue forever. The contest, when it ripens between these two antagonistic elements, is to be settled somewhere ; it is to be settled in the seat of central power, in the federal legislature. The constitution makes it the duty of the central government to determine questions, as often as they shall arise, in favor of one or the other party, and refers the decision of them to the majority of the votes in the two houses of congress. It will come back here, then, in spite of all the efforts to escape from it.

This antagonism must end either in a separation of the antagonistic parties— the slaveholding states and the free states—or, secondly, in the complete establishment of the influence of the slave power over the free—or else, on the other hand, in the establishment of the superior influence of freedom over the interests of slavery. It will not be terminated by a voluntary secession of either party. Commercial interests bind the slave states and the free states together in links of gold that are riveted with iron, and they cannot be broken by passion or by ambition. Either party will submit to the ascendency of the other, rather than yield the commercial advantages of this Union. Political ties bind the Union together—a common necessity, and not merely a common necessity, but the common interests of empire—of such empire as the world has never before seen. The control of the national power is the control of the great western continent; and the control of this continent is to be, in a very few years, the controlling influence in the world. Who is there north, that hates slavery so much, or who south, that hates emancipation so intensely, that he can attempt, with any hope of success, to break a Union thus forged and welded together? I have always heard, with equal pity and disgust, threats of disunion in the free states, and similar threats in the slaveholding states. I know that men may rave in the heat of passion, and under great political excitement; but I know that when it comes to a question whether this Union shall stand, either with freedom or with slavery, the masses will uphold it, and it will stand until some inherent vice in its constitution, not yet disclosed, shall cause its dissolution. Now, entertaining these opinions, there are for me only two alternatives, viz : either to let slavery gain unlimited sway, or so to exert what little power and influence I may have, as to secure, if I can, the ultimate predominance of freedom.

In doing this, I do no more than those who believe the slave power is rightest, wisest, and best, are doing, and will continue to do, with my free consent, to establish its complete supremacy. If they shall succeed, I still shall be, as I have been, a loyal citizen. If we succeed, I know they will be loyal also, because it will be safest, wisest, and best for them to be so. The question is one, not of a day, or of a year, but of many years, and, for aught I know, many generations. Like all other great political questions, it will be attended sometimes by excitement, sometimes by passion, and sometimes, perhaps, even by faction ; but it is sure to be settled in a constitutional way, without any violent shock to society, or to any of its great interests. It is, moreover, sure to be settled rightly ; because it will be settled under the benign influences of republicanism and Christianity, according to the principles of truth and justice, as ascertained by human reason. In pursuing such a course, it seems to me obviously as wise as it is necessary to save all existing laws and constitutions which are conservative of freedom, and to permit, as far as possible, the establishment of no new ones in favor of slavery; and thus to turn away the thoughts of the states which tolerate slavery, from political efforts to perpetuate what in its nature cannot be perpetual, to the more wise and benign policy of emancipation.

This, in my humble judgment, is the simple, easy path of duty for the American statesman. I will not contemplate that other alternative—the greater ascendency of the slave power. I believe that if it shall ever come, the voice of freedom will cease to be heard in these halls, whatever may be the evils and dangers which slavery shall produce. I say this without disrespect for representatives of slave states, and I say it because the rights of petition and of debate on that are effectually suppressed—necessarily suppressed—in all the slave states, and because they are not always held in reverence, even now, in the two houses of congress. When freedom of speech on a subject of such vital interest shall have ceased to exist in congress, then I shall expect to see slavery not only luxuriating in all new territories, but stealthily creeping even into the free states themselves. Believing this, and believing, also, that complete responsibility of the government to the people is essential to public and private safety, and that decline and ruin are sure to follow always in the train of slavery, I am sure that this will be no longer a land of freedom and constitutional liberty when slavery shall have thus become paramount.

Sir, I have always said that I should not despond, even if this fearful measure should be effected; nor do I now despond. Although, reasoning from my present convictions, I should not have voted for the compromise of 1820, I have labored, in the very spirit of those who established it, to save the landmark of freedom which it assigned. I have not spoken irreverently even of the compromise of 1850, which, as all men know, I opposed earnestly and with diligence. Nevertheless, I have always preferred the compromises of the constitution, and have wanted no others. I feared all others. This was a leading principle of the great statesman of the south, (Mr. Calhoun). Said he :

" I see my way in the constitution ; I cannot in a compromise. A compromise is but an act of congress. It may be overruled at any time. It gives us no security. But the constitution is stable. It is a rock on which we can stand, and on which we can meet our friends from the non-slaveholding states. It is a firm and stable ground, on which we can better stand in opposition to fanaticism than on the shifting sands of compromise. Let us be done with compromises. Let us go back and stand upon the constitution."

I stood upon this ground in 1850, defending freedom upon it as Mr. Calhoun did in defending slavery. I was overruled then, and I have waited since without proposing to abrogate any compromises.

It has been no proposition of mine to abrogate them now ; but the proposition has come from another quarter—from an adverse one. It is about to prevail. The shifting sands of compromise are passing from under my feet, and they are now, without agency of my own, taking hold again on the rock of the constitution. It shall be no fault of mine if they do not remain firm. This seems to me auspicious of better days and wiser legislation. Through all the darkness and gloom of the present hour, bright stars are breaking, that inspire me with hope, and excite me to perseverance. They show that the day of compromises has past forever, and that henceforward all great questions between freedom and slavery legitimately coming here—and none other can come—shall be decided, as they ought to be, upon their merits, by a fair exercise of legislative power, and not by bargains of equivocal prudence, if not of doubtful morality.

The house of representatives has, and it always will have, an increasing majority of members from the free states. On this occasion, that house has not been altogether faithless to the interests of the free states; for, although it has taken away the charter of freedom from Kansas and Nebraska, it has, at the same time, told this proud body, in language which compels acquiescence, that in submitting the question of its restoration, it would submit it not merely to interested citizens, but to the alien inhabitants of the territories also. So the great interests of humanity are, after all, thanks to the house of representatives, and thanks to God, submitted to the voice of human nature.

Sir, I see one more sign of hope. The great support of slavery in the south has been its alliance with the democratic party of the north. By means of that alliance, it obtained paramount influence in this government about the year 1800, which from that time to this, with but few and slight interruptions, it has maintained. While democracy in the north has thus been supporting slavery in the south, the people of the north have been learning more profoundly the principles of republicanism and of free government. It is an extraordinary circumstance, which you, sir, the present occupant of the chair, (Mr. Stuart,) I am sure will not gainsay, that at this moment, when there seems to be a more complete divergence of the federal government in favor of slavery than ever before, the sentiment of universal liberty is stronger in all free states than it ever was before. With that principle, the present democratic party must now come into a closer contest. Their prestige of democracy is fast waning, by reason of the hard service which their alliance with their slaveholding brethren has imposed upon them. That party perseveres, as indeed it must, by reason of its very constitution, in that service, and thus comes into closer conflict with elements of true democracy, and for that reason is destined to lose, and is fast losing, the power which it has held so firmly and long. That power will not be restored until the principle established here now shall be reversed, and a constitution shall be given, not only to Kansas and Nebraska, but also to every other national territory, which will be not a *tabula rasa*, but a constitution securing equal, universal, and perpetual freedom.

Mr. Douglas closed the debate; the vote was taken, and the bill passed; yeas 37, nays 14.

In the house, a bill had been reported on the 31st of January, by Richardson, of Illinois, for which, on the 8th of May, he offered as a substitute the senate bill, leaving out Clayton's amendment. On the 22d the substitute was adopted, and finally passed by a vote of 113 yeas to 100 nays, as follows:

Representatives from free states in favor of the bill.....................44
Representatives from slave states in favor of the bill...................69

— 113

Representatives from free states against the bill........................91
Representatives from slave states against the bill......................9

— 100

The bill was sent to the senate, passed, and being approved by the president, became a law, under the title of "An act to organize the territories of Kansas and Nebraska."

COPY OF THE ACT.

Be it enacted by the senate and house of representatives of the United States of America in congress assembled, That all that part of the territory of the United States included within the following limits, except such portions thereof as are hereinafter expressly exempted from the operations of this act, to wit: beginning at a point in the Missouri river where the fortieth parallel of north latitude crosses the same; thence west on said parallel to the east boundary of the territory of Utah on the summit of the Rocky Mountains; thence on said summit northward to the forty-ninth parallel of north latitude; thence east on said parallel to the western boundary of the territory of Minnesota; thence southward on said boundary to the Missouri river; thence down the main channel of said river to the place of beginning, be, and the same is hereby created into a temporary government by the name of the territory of Nebraska; and when admitted as a state or states, the said territory, or any portion of the same, shall be received into the Union with or without slavery, as their constitution may prescribe at the time of their admission; provided, that nothing in this act contained shall be construed to inhibit the government of the United States from dividing said territory into two or more territories, in such manner and at such times as congress shall deem convenient and proper, or from attaching any portion of said territory to any other state or territory of the United States: provided further, that nothing in this act contained shall be construed to impair the rights of person or property now pertaining to the Indians in said territory, so long as such rights shall remain unextinguished by treaty between the United States and such Indians, or to include any territory which, by treaty with any Indian tribe, is not, without the consent of said tribe, to be included within the territorial limits or jurisdiction of any state or territory; but all such territory shall be excepted out of the boundaries, and constitute no part of the territory of Nebraska, until said tribe shall signify their assent to the president of the United States to be included within the said territory of Nebraska, or to affect the authority of the government of the United States to make any regulations respecting such Indians, their lands, property, or other rights, by treaty, law, or otherwise, which it would have been competent to the government to make if this act had never passed.

SEC. 2. That the executive power and authority in and over said territory of Nebraska shall be vested in a governor, who shall hold his office for four years, and until his successor shall be appointed and qualified, unless sooner removed by the president of the United States. The governor shall reside within said territory, and shall be commander-in-chief of the militia thereof. He may grant pardons and respites for offenses against the laws of said territory, and reprieves for offenses against the laws of the United States, until the decision of the president can be made known thereon; he shall commission all officers who shall be appointed to office under the laws of the said territory, and shall take care that the laws be faithfully executed.

Sec. 3. That there shall be a secretary of said territory, who shall reside therein, and hold his office for five years, unless sooner removed by the president of the United States; he shall record and preserve all the laws and proceedings of the legislative assembly hereinafter constituted, and all the acts and proceedings of the governor in his executive dapartment; he shall transmit one copy of the laws and journals of the legislative assembly, within thirty days after the end of each session, and one copy of the executive proceedings and official correspondence semi-annually on the first days of January and July in each year, to the president of the United States, and two copies of the laws to the president of the senate and to.the speaker of the house of representatives, to be deposited in the libraries of congress; and, in case of the death, removal, resignation, or absence of the governor from the territory, the secretary shall be, and he is hereby authorized and required to execute and perform all the powers and duties of the governor during such vacancy or absence, or until another governor shall be duly appointed and qualified to fill such vacancy.

Sec. 4. That the legislative power and authority of said territory shall be vested in the governor and a legislative assembly. The legislative assembly shall consist of a council and house of representatives. The council shall consist of thirteen members, having the qualifications of voters as hereinafter prescribed, whose term of service shall continue two years. The house of representatives shall, at its first session, consist of twenty-six members, possessing the same qualifications as prescribed for members of the council, and whose term of service shall continue one year. The number of representatives may be increased by the legislative assembly, from time to time, in proportion to the increase of qualified voters; provided, that the whole number shall never exceed thirty-nine; an apportionment shall be made as nearly equal as practicable, among the several counties or districts, for the election of the council and representatives, giving to each section of the territory representation in the ratio of its qualified voters as nearly as may be. And the members of the council and of the house of representatives shall reside in, and be inhabitants of, the district or county, or counties, for which they may be elected, respectively. Previous to the first election, the governor shall cause a census, or enumeration of the inhabitants and qualified voters of the several counties and districts of the territory, to be taken by such persons and in such mode as the governor shall designate and appoint; and the persons so appointed shall receive a reasonable compensation therefor. And the first election shall be held at such times, and places, and be conducted in such manner, both as to the persons who shall superintend such election, and the returns thereof, as the governor shall appoint and direct; and he shall at the same time declare the number of members of the council and house of representatives to which each of the counties or districts shall be entitled under this act. The persons having the highest number of legal votes in each of said council districts for members of the council, shall be declared by the governor to be duly elected to the council; and the persons having the highest number of legal votes for the house of representatives, shall be declared by the governor to be duly elected members of said house; provided, that in case two or more persons voted for shall have an equal number of votes, and in case a vacancy shall otherwise occur in either branch of the legislative assembly, the governor shall order a new election; and the persons thus elected to the legislative assembly shall meet at such place and on such day as the governor shall appoint; but thereafter, the time, place, and manner of holding and conducting all elections by the people, and the apportioning the representation in the several counties or districts to the council and house of representatives, according to the number of qualified voters, shall be prescribed by law, as well as the day of the commencement of the regular sessions of the legislative assembly; provided, that no session in any one year shall exceed the term of forty days, except the first session, which may continue sixty days.

Sec. 5. That every free white male inhabitant above the age of twenty-one years, who shall be an actual resident of said territory, and shall possess the qualifications hereinafter prescribed, shall be entitled to vote at the first election, and shall be eligible to any office within the said territory; but the qualifications of voters, and of holding office, at all subsequent elections, shall be such as shall be prescribed by the legislative assembly; provided, that the right of suffrage and of holding office shall be exercised only by citizens of the United States and those who shall have declared on oath their intention to become such, and shall have taken an oath to support the constitution of the United States and the provisions of this act: and provided further, that no officer, soldier, seaman, or marine, or other person in the army or navy of the United States, or attached to troops in the service of the United States, shall be allowed to vote or hold office in said territory, by reason of being on service therein.

Sec. 6. That the legislative power of the territory shall extend to all rightful subjects of legislation consistent with the constitution of the United States and the provisions of this act; but no law shall be passed interfering with the primary disposal of the soil; no tax shall be imposed upon the property of the United States; nor shall the lands or other property of non-residents be taxed higher than the lands or other property of residents. Every bill which shall have passed the council and house of representatives of the said territory, shall, before it become a law, be presented to the governor of the territory; if he approve, he shall sign it; but if not, he shall return it, with his objections, to the house in which it originated, who shall enter the objections at large on their journal, and proceed to reconsider it. If, after such reconsideration, two-thirds of that house shall agree to pass the bill, it shall be sent, together with the objections, to the other house, by which it shall likewise be reconsidered, and if approved by two-thirds of that house, it shall become a law. But in all such cases the votes of both houses shall be determined by yeas and nays, to be entered on the journal of each house respectively. If any bill shall not be returned by the governor within three days (Sundays excepted) after it shall have been presented to him, the same shall be a law in like manner as if he had signed it, unless the assembly, by adjournment, prevent its return, in which case it shall not be a law.

SEC. 7. That all township, district, and county officers, not herein otherwise provided for, shall be appointed or elected, as the case may be, in such manner as shall be provided by the governor and legislative assembly of the territory of Nebraska. The governor shall nominate, and, by and with the advice and consent of the legislative council, appoint all officers not herein otherwise provided for; and in the first instance the governor alone may appoint all said officers, who shall hold their offices until the end of the first sesssion of the legislative assembly; and shall lay off the necessary districts for members of the council and house of representatives, and all other officers.

SEC. 8. That no member of the legislative assembly shall hold, or be appointed to, any office which shall have been created, or the salary or emoluments of which shall have been increased, while he was a member, during the term for which he was elected, and for one year after the expiration of such term; but this restriction shall not be applicable to members of the first legislative assembly; and no person holding a commission or appointment under the United States, except postmasters, shall be a member of the legislative assembly, or shall hold any office under the government of said territory.

SEC. 9. That the judicial power of said territory shall be vested in a supreme court, district courts, probate courts, and in justices of the peace. The supreme court shall consist of a chief justice and two associate justices, any two of whom shall constitute a quorum, and who shall hold a term at the seat of government of said territory annually, and they shall hold their offices during the period of four years, and until their successors shall be appointed and qualified. The said territory shall be divided into three judicial districts, and a district court shall be held in each of said districts by one of the justices of the supreme court, at such times and places as may be prescribed by law; and the said judges shall, after their appointments, respectively, reside in the district which shall be assigned them. The jurisdiction of the several courts herein provided for, both appellate and original, and that of the probate courts and of justices of the peace, shall be as limited by law; provided, that justices of the peace shall not have jurisdiction of any matter in controversy when the title or boundaries of land may be in dispute, or where the debt or sum claimed shall exceed one hundred dollars; and the said supreme and district courts, respectively, shall possess chancery as well as common law jurisdiction. Each district court, or the judge thereof, shall appoint its clerk, who shall also be the register in chancery, and shall keep his office at the place where the court may be held. Writs of error, bills of exception, and appeals shall be allowed in all cases from the final decision of said district courts to the supreme court, under such regulations as may be prescribed by law; but in no case removed to the supreme court shall trial by jury be allowed in said court. The supreme court, or the justices thereof, shall appoint its own clerk, and every clerk shall hold his office at the pleasure of the court for which he shall have been appointed. Writs of error, and appeals from the final decision of said supreme court, shall be allowed, and may be taken to the supreme court of the United States, in the same manner and under the same regulations as from the circuit courts of the United States, where the value of the property, or the amount in controversy, to be ascertained by the oath or affirmation of either party, or other competent witness, shall exceed one thousand dollars; except only that in all cases involving title to slaves, the said writs of error or appeals shall be allowed and decided by the said supreme court, without regard to the value of the matter, property, or title in controversy; and except also that a writ of error or appeal shall also be allowed to the supreme court of the United States, from the decisions of the said supreme court created by this act, or of any judge thereof, or of the district courts created by this act, or of any judge thereof, upon any writ of habeas corpus, involving the question of personal freedom; provided, that nothing herein contained shall be construed to apply to or affect the provisions of the "act respecting fugitives from justice, and persons escaping from the service of their masters," approved February 12th, 1793, and the "act to amend and supplementary to the aforesaid act," approved September 18th, 1850; and each of the said district courts shall have and exercise the same jurisdiction in all cases arising under the constitution and laws of the United States, as is vested in the circuit and district courts of the United States; and the said supreme and district courts of the said territory, and the respective judges thereof, shall and may grant writs of habeas corpus in all cases in which the same are granted by the judges of the United States in the District of Columbia; and the first six days of every term of said courts, or so much thereof as shall be necessary, shall be appropriated to the trial of causes arising under the said constitution and laws, and writs of error and appeal in all such cases shall be made to the supreme court of said territory, the same as in other cases. The said clerk shall receive in all such cases the same fees which the clerks of the district courts of Utah territory now receive for similar services.

SEC. 10. That the provisions of an act entitled "an act respecting fugitives from justice, and persons escaping from the service of their masters," approved February 12th, 1793, and the provisions of the act entitled "an act to amend, and supplementary to, the aforesaid act," approved September 18th, 1850, be, and the same are hereby, declared to extend to, and be in full force within, the limits of said territory of Nebraska.

SEC. 11. That there shall be appointed an attorney for said territory, who shall continue in office for four years, and until his successor shall be appointed and qualified, unless sooner removed by the president, and who shall receive the same fees and salary as the attorney of the United States for the present territory of Utah. There shall also be a marshal for the territory appointed, who shall hold his office for four years, and until his successor shall be appointed and qualified, unless sooner removed by the president, and who shall execute all processes issuing from the said courts when exercising their jurisdiction as circuit and district courts of the United States; he shall perform the duties, be subject to the same regulations and penalties, and be entitled to the same fees as the marshal of the district court of the United States for the present territory of Utah, and shall, in addition, be paid two hundred dollars annually as a compensation for extra services.

SEC. 12. That the governor, secretary, chief justice, and associate justices, attorney and marshal, shall be nominated, and, by and with the advice and consent of the senate, appointed by the President of the United States. The governor and secretary to be appointed as aforesaid, shall, before they act as such, respectively take an oath or affirmation by the laws now in force therein, or before the chief justice or some associate justice of the supreme court of the United States, to support the constitution of the United States, and faithfully to discharge the duties of their respective offices, which said oaths, when so taken, shall be certified by the person by whom the same shall have been taken; and such certificates shall be received and recorded by the said secretary among the executive proceedings; and the chief justice and associate justices, and all other civil officers in said territory, before they act as such, shall take a like oath or affirmation before the said governor or secretary, or some judge or justice of the peace of the territory who may be duly commissioned and qualified, which said oath or affirmation shall be certified and transmitted by the person taking the same to the secretary, to be by him recorded as aforesaid; and afterwards the like oath or affirmation shall be taken, certified, and recorded, in such manner and form as may be prescribed by law. The governor shall receive an annual salary of two thousand five hundred dollars. The chief justice and associate justices shall receive an annual salary of two thousand dollars. The secretary shall receive an annual salary of two thousand dollars. The said salaries shall be paid quarter-yearly, from the dates of the respective appointments, at the treasury of the United States; but no such payment shall be made until said officers shall have entered upon the duties of their respective appointments. The members of the legislative assembly shall be entitled to receive three dollars each per day during their attendance at the sessions thereof, and three dollars each for every twenty miles' travel in going to, and returning from, the said sessions, estimated according to the nearest usually traveled route; and an additional allowance of three dollars shall be paid to the presiding officer of each house for each day he shall so preside. And a chief clerk, one assistant clerk, a sergeant-at-arms, and door-keeper may be chosen for each house; and the said chief clerk shall receive four dollars per day, and the said other officers three dollars per day, during the session of the legislative assembly; but no other officer shall be paid by the United States; provided, that there shall be but one session of the legislature annually, unless, on an extraordinary occasion, the governor shall think proper to call the legislature together. There shall be appropriated, annually, the usual sum, to be expended by the governor to defray the contingent expenses of the territory, including the salary of a clerk of the executive department; and there shall also be appropriated annually, a sufficient sum, to be expended by the secretary of the territory, and upon an estimate to be made by the secretary of the treasury of the United States, to defray the expenses of the legislative assembly, the printing of the laws, and other incidental expenses; and the governor and secretary of the territory shall, in the disbursement of all moneys intrusted to them, be governed solely by the instructions of the secretary of the treasury of the United States, and shall, semi-annually, account to the said secretary for the manner in which the aforesaid moneys shall have been expended; and no expenditure shall be made by said legislative assembly for objects not specially authorized by the acts of congress making the appropriations, nor beyond the sum thus appropriated for such objects.

SEC. 13. That the legislative assembly of the territory of Nebraska shall hold its first session at such time and place in said territory as the governor thereof shall appoint and direct; and at said first session, or as soon thereafter as they shall deem expedient, the governor and legislative assembly shall proceed to locate and establish the seat of government for said territory at such place as they may deem eligible; which place, however, shall thereafter be subject to be changed by the said governor and legislative assembly.

SEC. 14. That a delegate to the house of representatives of the United States, to serve for the term of two years, who shall be a citizen of the United States, may be elected by the voters qualified to elect members of the legislative assembly, who shall be entitled to the same rights and privileges as are exercised and enjoyed by the delegates from the several other territories of the United States to the said house of representatives; but the delegate first elected shall hold his seat only during the term of the congress to which he shall be elected. The first election shall be held at such time and places, and be conducted in such manner, as the governor shall appoint and direct; and at all subsequent elections, the times, places, and manner of holding the elections shall be prescribed by law. The person having the greatest number of votes shall be declared by the governor to be duly elected, and a certificate thereof shall be given accordingly. That the constitution and all the laws of the United States which are not locally inapplicable, shall have the same force and effect within the said territory of Nebraska as elsewhere within the United States, except the eighth section of the act preparatory to the admission of Missouri into the Union, approved March 6th, 1820, which, being inconsistent with the principle of non-intervention by congress with slavery in the states and territories, as recognized by the legislation of 1850, commonly called the compromise measures, is hereby declared inoperative and void; it being the true intent and meaning of this act not to legislate slavery into any territory or state, nor to exclude it therefrom, but to leave the people thereof perfectly free to form and regulate their domestic institutions in their own way, subject only to the constitution of the United States; provided, that nothing herein contained shall be construed to revive or put in force any law or regulation which may have existed prior to the act of 6th of March, 1820, either protecting, establishing, prohibiting or abolishing slavery.

SEC. 15. That there shall hereafter be appropriated, as has been customary for the territorial governments, a sufficient amount, to be expended under the direction of the said governor of the territory of Nebraska, not exceeding the sums heretofore appropriated for similar objects, for the erection of suitable public buildings at the seat of government, and for the purchase of a library to be kept at the seat of government for the use of the governor, legislative assembly, judges of the supreme court, secretary, marshal, and attorney of said territory, and such other persons, and under such regulations as shall be prescribed by law.

SEC. 16. That when the lands in the said territory shall be surveyed under the direction of the government of the United States, preparatory to bringing the same into market, sections numbered sixteen and thirty-six, in each township in said territory, shall be, and the same are herby, reserved for the purpose of being applied to schools in said territory, and in the states and territories hereafter to be erected out of the same.

SEC. 17. That, until otherwise provided by law, the governor of said territory may define the judicial districts of said territory, and assign the judges who may be appointed for said territory to the several districts ; and also appoint the times and places for holding courts in the several counties or subdivisions in each of said judicial districts by proclamation, to be issued by him ; but the legislative assembly, at their first, or any subsequent session, may organize, alter, or modify such judicial districts, and assign the judges, and alter the times and places of holding the courts, as to them shall seem proper and convenient.

SEC. 18. That all officers to be appointed by the president, by and with the advice and consent of the senate, for the territory of Nebraska, who, by virtue of the provisions of any law now existing, or which may be enacted during the present congress, are required to give security for moneys that may be intrusted with them for disbursements, shall give such security, at such time and place, and in such manner as the secretary of the treasury may prescribe.

SEC. 19. That all that part of the territory of the United States included within the following limits, except such portions thereof as are hereinafter expressly exempted from the operations of this act, to wit : beginning at a point on the western boundary of the state of Missouri, where the thirty-seventh parallel of north latitude crosses the same ; thence west on said parallel to the eastern boundary of New Mexico ; thence north on said boundary to latitude thirty-eight ; thence following said boundary westward to the east boundary of the territory of Utah, on the summit of the Rocky mountains ; thence northward on said summit to the fortieth parallel of latitude ; thence east on said parallel to the western boundary of the state of Missouri ; thence south with the western boundary of said state to the place of beginning, be, and the same is hereby, created into a temporary government by the name of the territory of Kansas ; and when admitted as a state or states, the said territory, or

41

any portion of the same, shall be received into the Union with or without slavery, as their constitution may prescribe at the time of their admission; provided, that nothing in this act contained shall be construed to inhibit the government of the United States from dividing said territory into two or more territories, in such manner and at such times as congress shall deem convenient and proper, or from attaching any portion of said territory to any other state or territory of the United States; provided further, that nothing in this act contained shall be so construed as to impair the rights of persons or property now pertaining to the Indians in said territory, so long as such rights shall remain unextinguished by treaty between the United States and such Indians, or to include any territory which, by treaty with any Indian tribe, is not, without the consent of said tribe, to be included within the territorial limits or jurisdiction of any state or territory; but all such territory shall be excepted out of the boundaries, and constitute no part of the territory of Kansas, until said tribe shall signify their assent to the president of the United States to be included within the said territory of Kansas, or to affect the authority of the government of the United States to make any regulation respecting such Indians, their lands, property, or other rights, by treaty, law, or otherwise, which it would have been competent to the government to make if this act had never passed.

[The next seventeen sections substantially repeat the foregoing, save that their provisions apply to Kansas instead of Nebraska. The final section refers to both territories, as follows:]

SEC. 37. And be it further enacted, that all treaties, laws, and other engagements made by the government of the United States with the Indian tribes inhabiting the territories embraced within this act, shall be faithfully and rigidly observed, notwithstanding anything contained in this act; and that the existing agencies and superintendencies of said Indians be continued with the same powers and duties which are now prescribed by law, except that the President of the United States may, at his discretion, change the location of the office of superintendent.

CHAPTER XXXII.

Affairs of Kansas.—Congressional Proceedings.

Session of 1855–6.—The President's special message referred.—Report of committee by Mr. Douglas.—Emigrant Aid Societies.—Minority report by Mr. Collamer.—Special Committee of the House sent to Kansas to investigate affairs.—Report of the Committee.—Armed Missourians enter the territory and control the elections.—Second foray of armed Missourians.—Purposes of Aid Societies defended.—Mob violence.—Legislature assembles at Pawnee.—Its acts.—Topeka Constitutional Convention.—Free State Constitution framed.—Adopted by the people.—Election for State officers.—Topeka legislature.—The Wakerusa war.—Outrages upon the citizens.—Robberies and murders.—Lawrence attacked.—Free state constitution submitted to Congress.—Bill to admit Kansas under free state constitution passes the house.—Douglas' bill before the senate.—Trumbull's propositions rejected.—Amendments proposed by Foster, Collamer, Wilson and Seward rejected.—Bill passed by senate.—Dunn's bill passed by house.—Appropriation bills.—Proviso to army bill.—Session terminates.—Extra session.—President stands firm, house firmer, senate firmest.—The army bill passed without the proviso.

THE thirty-fourth session of congress convened at the capitol on the 3d of December, 1855. Nine weeks were spent in unsuccessful attempts to organize by the choice of a speaker. The plurality rule was finally adopted, and on the one hundred and thirty-third ballot, Nathaniel P. Banks, republican, was chosen by a vote of 103 to 100.

A history of the events which followed the organization of Kansas under the provisions of the act, may be gathered from the following extracts from official documents. On the 24th of January, 1856, President Pierce transmitted the following special message to congress on the affairs of Kansas:

MESSAGE OF THE PRESIDENT.

Circumstances have occurred to disturb the course of governmental organization in the territory of Kansas, and produce there a condition of things which renders it incumbent on me to call your attention to the subject, and urgently recommend the adoption by you of such measures of legislation as the grave exigencies of the case appear to require.

A brief exposition of the circumstances referred to, and of their causes, will be necessary to the full understanding of the recommendations which it is proposed to submit.

The act to organize the territories of Nebraska and Kansas was a manifestation of the legislative opinion of congress on two great points of constitutional construction: One, that the designation of the boundaries of a new territory, and provision for its political organization and administration as a territory, are measures which of right fall within the powers of the general government; and the other, that the inhabitants of any such territory, considered as an inchoate state, are entitled, in the exercise of self-government, to determine for themselves what shall be their own domestic institutions, subject only to the constitution and the laws duly enacted by congress under it, and to the power of the existing states to decide, according to the provisions and principles of the constitution, at what time the territory shall be received as a state into the Union. Such are the great political rights which are solemnly declared and affirmed by that act.

Based upon this theory, the act of congress defined for each territory the outlines of republican government, distributing public authority among the lawfully created agents—executive, judicial and legislative—to be appointed either by the general government or by the territory. The legislative functions were entrusted to a council and a house of representatives, duly elected and empowered to enact all the local laws which they might deem essential to their prosperity, happiness and good government. Acting in the same spirit, congress also defined the persons who were in the first instance to be considered as the people of each territory ; enacting that every free white male inhabitant of the same above the age of twenty-one years, being an actual resident thereof, and possessing the qualifications hereafter described, should be entitled to vote at the first election, and be eligible to any office within the territory ; but that the qualifications of voters and holding office at all subsequent elections should be such as might be prescribed by the legislative assembly ; provided, however, that the right of suffrage and of holding office should be exercised only by citizens of the United States, and those who should have declared on oath their intention to become such, and have taken an oath to support the constitution of the United States and the provisions of the act ; and provided further, that no officer, soldier, seaman or marine, or other person in the army or navy of the United States, or attached to troops in their service, should be allowed to vote or hold office in either territory by reason of being on service therein.

Such of the public officers of the territories as, by the provisions of the act, were to be appointed by the general government, including the governors, were appointed and commissioned in due season—the law having been enacted on the 30th of May, 1854, and the commission of the governor of the territory of Nebraska being dated on the 2d day of August, 1854, and of the territory of Kansas on the 29th day of June, 1854.

Among the duties imposed by the act upon the governors, was that of directing and superintending the political organization of the respective territories. The governor of Kansas was required to cause a census or enumeration of the inhabitants and qualified voters of the several counties and districts of the territory to be taken, by such persons and in such mode as he might designate and appoint ; to appoint and direct the time and places of holding the first elections, and the manner of conducting them, both as to the persons to superintend such elections, and the returns thereof ; to declare the number of the members of the council and house of representatives for each county or district ; to declare what persons might appear to be duly elected ; and to appoint the time and place of the first meeting of the legislative assembly. In substance, the same duties were devolved on the governor of Nebraska.

While, by this act, the principle of constitution for each of the territories was one and the same, and the details of organic legislation regarding both were as nearly as could be identical, and while the territory of Nebraska was tranquilly and successfully organized in the due course of law, and its first legislative assembly met on the 16th of January, 1855, the organization of Kansas was long delayed, and has been attended with serious difficulties and embarrassments, partly the consequence of local mal-administration, and partly of the unjustifiable interference of the inhabitants of some of the states, foreign by residence, interests and rights to the territory.

The governor of the territory of Kansas did not reach the designated seat of his government until the 7th of the ensuing October, and even then failed to make the first step in its legal organization—that of ordering the census or enumeration of its inhabitants—until so late a day that the election of the members of the legislative assembly did not take place until the 30th of March, 1855, nor its meeting until the 2d of July, 1855; so that, for a year after the territory was constituted by the act of congress, and the officers to be appointed by the federal executive had been commissioned, it was without a complete government, without any legislative authority, without local law, and, of course, without the ordinary guarantees of peace and public order.

In other respects, the governor, instead of exercising constant vigilance and putting forth all his energies to prevent or counteract the tendencies to illegality which are prone to exist in all imperfectly-organized and newly-associated communities, allowed his attention to be diverted from official obligation by other objects, and himself sat an example of the violation of law in the performance of acts which rendered it my duty, in the sequel, to remove him from the office of chief executive magistrate of the territory.

Before the requisite preparation was accomplished for election of a territorial legislature, an election for delegate to congress had been held in the territory on the 29th day of November, 1854, and the delegate took his seat in the house of representatives without challenge. If arrangements had been perfected by the governor so that the election for members of the legislative assembly might be held in the several precincts at the same time as for delegate to congress, any question appertaining to the qualification of the persons voting as people of the territory, would have passed necessarily and at once under the supervision of congress, as the judge of the validity of the return of the delegate, and would have been determined before conflicting passions had become inflamed by time, and before opportunity could have been afforded for systematic interference of the people of individual states.

This interference, in so far as concerns its primary causes and its immediate commencement, was one of the incidents of that pernicious agitation on the subject of the condition of the colored persons held to service in some of the states, which has so long disturbed the repose of our country, and excited individuals, otherwise patriotic and law-abiding, to toil with misdirected zeal in the attempt to propagate their social theories by the perversion and abuse of the powers of congress.

The persons and parties whom the tenor of the act to organize the territories of Nebraska and Kansas thwarted in the endeavor to impose, through the agency of congress, their particular views of social organization on the people of the future new states, now perceiving that the policy of leaving the inhabitants of each state to judge for themselves in this respect was ineradicably rooted in the convictions of the people of the Union, then had recourse, in the pursuit of their general object, to the extraordinary measure of propagandist colonization of the territory of Kansas, to prevent the free and natural action of its inhabitants in its internal organization, and thus to anticipate or to force the determination of that question in this inchoate state.

With such views, associations were organized in some of the states, and their purpose was proclaimed through the press in language extremely irritating and offensive to those of whom the colonists were to become the neighbors.   Those designs and acts had the necessary consequence to awaken emotions of intense indignation in states near to the territory of Kansas, and especially in the adjoining state of Missouri, whose domestic peace was thus the most directly endangered; but they are far from justifying the illegal and reprehensible counter-movements which ensued.

Under these inauspicious circumstances, the primary elections for members of the legislative assembly were held in most, if not all, of the precincts, at the time and the places and by the persons designated and appointed by the governor, according to law.

Angry accusations that illegal votes had been polled, abounded on all sides, and imputations were made both of fraud and violence.   But the governor, in the exercise of the power and the discharge of the duty conferred and imposed by law on him alone, officially received and considered the returns; declared a large majority of the members of the council and the house of representatives "duly elected;" withheld certificates from others because of alleged illegality of votes; appointed a new election to supply the place of the persons not certified; and thus, at length, in all the forms of statute, and with his own official authentication, complete legality was given to the first legislative assembly of the territory.

Those decisions of the returning-officers and of the governor are final, except that by the parliamentary usage of the country applied to the organic law, it may be conceded that each house of the assembly must have been competent to determine, in the last resort, the qualifications and the election of its members.   The subject was, by its nature, one appertaining exclusively to the jurisdiction of the local authorities of the territory.   Whatever irregularities may have occurred in the elections, it seems too late now to raise that question as to which, neither now nor at any previous time, has the least possible legal authority been possessed by the President of the United States.   For all present purposes, the legislative body, thus constituted and elected, was the legitimate assembly of the territory.

Accordingly, the governor, by procalmation, convened the assembly thus elected to meet at a place called Pawnee City.   The two houses met, and were duly organized in the ordinary parliamentary form; each sent to and received from the governor the official communications usual on such occasions; an elaborate message opening the session was communicated by the governor, and the general business of legislation was entered upon by the legislative assembly.

But, after a few days, the assembly resolved to adjourn to another place in the territory. A law was accordingly passed, against the consent of the governor, but in due form otherwise, to remove the seat of government temporarily to the "Shawnee Manual-labor School" (or mission,) and thither the assembly proceeded. After this, receiving a bill for the establishment of a ferry at the town of Kickapoo, the governor refused to sign it, and, by special message, assigned for reason of refusal, not anything objectionable in the bill itself, nor any pretense of the illegality or incompetency of the assembly as such, but only the fact that the assembly had, by its act, transferred the seat of government temporarily from Pawnee City to Shawnee Mission. For the same reason he continued to refuse to sign other bills, until, in the course of a few days, he, by official message, communicated to the assembly the fact that he had received notification of the termination of his functions as governor, and that the duties of the office were legally devolved on the secretary of the territory; thus to the last recognizing the body as a duly-elected and constituted legislative assembly.

It will be perceived that if any constitutional defect attached to the legislative acts of the assembly, it is not pretended to consist in irregularity of election or want of qualification of the members, but only in the change of its place of session. However trivial the objection may seem to be, it requires to be considered, because upon it is founded all that superstructure of acts, plainly against law, which now threatens the peace not only of the territory of Kansas, but of the Union.

Such an objection to the proceedings of the legislative assembly was of exceptionable origin, for the reason that, by the express terms of the organic law, the seat of government of the territory was "located temporarily at Fort Leavenworth;" and yet the governor himself remained there less than two months, and of his own discretion transferred the seat of government to the Shawnee Mission, where it in fact was at the time the assembly were called to meet at Pawnee City. If the governor had any such right to change temporarily the seat of government, still more had the legislative assembly. The objection is of exceptional origin for the further reason that the place indicated by the governor, without having an exclusive claim of preference in itself, was a proposed town-site only, which he and others were attempting to locate unlawfully upon land within a military reservation, and for participation in which illegal act the commander of a post, a superior officer of the army, has been dismissed by sentence of court-martial.

Nor is it easy to see why the legislative assembly might not with propriety pass the territorial act transferring its sittings to the Shawnee Mission. If it could not, that must be on account of some prohibitory or incompatible provision of act of congress. But no such provision exists. The organic act, as already quoted, says "the seat of government is hereby located temporarily at Fort Leavenworth;" and it then provides that certain of the public buildings there "may be occupied and used under the direction of the governor and legislative assembly." These expressions might possibly be construed to imply that when, in a previous section of the act, it was enacted that "the first legislative assembly shall meet at such place and on such day as the governor shall appoint," the word "place" means place at Fort Leavenworth, not place anywhere in the territory. If so, the governor would have been the first to err in this matter, not only in himself having removed the seat of government to the Shawnee Mission, but in again removing it to Pawnee City. If there was any departure from the letter of the law, therefore, it was his in both instances.

But, however this may be, it is most unreasonable to suppose that by the terms of the organic act, congress intended to do impliedly what it has not done expressly—that is, to forbid to the legislative assembly the power to choose any place it might see fit as the temporary seat of its deliberations. That is proved by the significant language of one of the subsequent acts of congress on the subject, that of March 3, 1855, which, in making appropriation for public buildings of the territory, enacts that the same shall not be expended "until the legislature of said territory shall have fixed by law the permanent seat of government." Congress, in these expressions, does not profess to be granting the power to fix the permanent seat of government, but recognizes the power as one already granted. But how ? Undoubtedly by the comprehensive provision of the organic act itself, which declares that "the legislative power of the territory shall extend to all rightful subjects of legislation consistent with the constitution of the United States and the provisions of this act." If, in view of this act, the legislative assembly had the large power to fix the permanent seat of government at any place in its discretion, of course by the same enactment it had the less and the included power to fix it temporarily.

Nevertheless, the allegation that the acts of the legislative assembly were illegal by reason of this removal of its place of session, was brought forward to justify the first great movement in disregard of law within the territory. One of the acts of the legislative assembly provided for the election of a delegate to the present congress, and a delegate was elected under that law. But, subsequently to this, a portion of the people of the territory proceeded, without authority of law, to elect another delegate.

Following upon this movement was another and more important one of the same general character. Persons confessedly not constituting the body politic, or all the inhabitants, but merely a party of the inhabitants, and without law, have undertaken to summon a convention for the purpose of transforming the territory into a state, and have framed a constitution, adopted it, and under it elected a governor and other officers, and a representative to congress.

In extenuation of these illegal acts, it is alleged that the state of California, Michigan, and others, were self-organized, and as such were admitted into the Union, without a previous enabling act of congress. It is true that, while in a majority of cases a previous act of congress has been passed to authorize the territory to present itself as a state, and that this is deemed the most regular course, yet such an act has not been held to be indispensable, and in some cases the territory has proceeded without it, and has nevertheless been admitted into the Union as a state. It lies with congress to authorize beforehand, or to confirm afterward, in its discretion; but in no instance has a state been admitted upon the application of persons acting against authorities duly constituted by act of congress. In every case it is the people of the territory, not a party among them, who have the power to form a constitution and ask for admission as a state. No principle of public law, no practice or precedent under the constitution of the United States, no rule of reason, right, or common sense, confers any such power as that now claimed by a mere party in the territory. In fact, what has been done is of revolutionary character. It is avowedly so in motive and in aim as respects the local law of the territory. It will become treasonable insurrection if it reach the length of organized resistance by force to the fundamental or any other federal law, and to the authority of the general government.

In such an event, the path of duty for the executive is plain. The constitution requiring him to take care that the laws of the United States be faithfully executed, if they be opposed in the territory of Kansas, he may and should place at the disposal of the marshal any public force of the United States which happens to be within the jurisdiction, to be used as a portion of the *posse comitatus;* and, if that do not suffice to maintain order, then he may call forth the militia of one or more states for that object, or employ for the same object any part of the land or naval force of the United States. So also if the obstruction be to the laws of the territory, and it be duly presented to him as a case of insurrection, he may employ for its suppression the military of any state, or the land or naval force of the United States. And if the territory be invaded by the citizens of other states, whether for the purpose of deciding elections or for any other, and the local authorities find themselves unable to repel or withstand it, they will be entitled to, and upon the fact being fully ascertained, they shall most certainly receive, the aid of the general government.

But it is not the duty of the President of the United States to volunteer interposition by force to preserve the purity of elections either in a state or territory. To do so would be subversive of public freedom. And whether a law be wise or unwise, just or unjust, is not a question for him to judge. If it be constitutional—that is, if it be the law of the land—it is his duty to cause it to be executed, or to sustain the authorities of any state or territory in executing it in opposition to all insurrectionary movements.

Our system affords no justification of revolutionary acts; for the constitutional means of relieving the people of unjust administration and laws, by a change of public agents and by repeal, are ample, and more prompt and effective than illegal violence. These constitutional means must be scrupulously guarded—this great prerogative of popular sovereignty sacredly respected.

It is the undoubted right of the peaceable and orderly people of the territory of Kansas to elect their own legislative body, make their own laws, and regulate their own social institutions, without foreign or domestic molestation. Interference, on the one hand, to procure the abolition or prohibition of slave-labor in the territory, has produced mischievous interference on the other for its maintenance or introduction. One wrong begets another. Statements entirely unfounded or grossly exaggerated, concerning events within the territory, are sedulously diffused through remote states to feed the flame of sectional animosity there; and the agitators there exert themselves indefatigably in return to encourage and stimulate strife within the territory.

The inflammatory agitation, of which the present is but a part, has for twenty years produced nothing save unmitigated evil, north and south. But for it the character of the domestic institutions of the future new state would have been a matter of too little interest to the inhabitants of the contiguous states, personally or collectively, to produce among them any political emotion. Climate, soil, production, hopes of rapid advancement, and the pursuit of happiness on the part of settlers themselves, with good wishes but with no interference from without, would have quietly determined the question which is at this time of such disturbing character.

But we are constrained to turn our attention to the circumstances of embarrassment as they now exist. It is the duty of the people of Kansas to discountenance every act or purpose of resistance to its laws. Above all, the emergency appeals to the citizens of the states and especially of those contiguous to the territory, neither by intervention of non-residents in elections, nor by unauthorized military force, to attempt to encroach upon or usurp the authority of the inhabitants of the territory.

No citizen of our country should permit himself to forget that he is a part of its government, and entitled to be heard in the determination of its policy and its measures; and that, therefore, the highest considerations of personal honor and patriotism require him to maintain, by whatever of power or influence he may possess, the integrity of the laws of the republic.

Entertaining these views, it will be my imperative duty to exert the whole power of the federal executive to support public order in the territory; to vindicate its laws, whether federal or local, against all attempts of organized resistance; and so to protect its people in the establishment of their own institutions, undisturbed by encroachment from without, and in the full enjoyment of the rights of self-government assured to them by the constitution and the organic act of congress.

Although serious and threatening disturbances in the territory of Kansas, announced to me by the governor, in December last, were speedily quieted without the effusion of blood, and in a satisfactory manner, there is, I regret to say, reason to apprehend that disorders will continue to occur there, with increasing tendency to violence, until some decisive measures be taken to dispose of the question itself which constitutes the inducement or occasion of internal agitation and of external interference.

This, it seems to me, can best be accomplished by providing that, when the inhabitants of Kansas may desire it, and shall be of sufficient numbers to constitute a state, a convention of delegates, duly elected by the qualified voters, shall assemble to frame a constitution, and thus to prepare, through regular and lawful means, for its admission into the Union as a state. I respectfully recommend the enactment of a law to that effect.

I recommend, also, that a special appropriation be made to defray any expense which may become requisite in the execution of the laws or the maintenance of public order in the territory of Kansas.

This message of the president was referred to the committee on territories in the senate, and on the 12th of March, Mr. Douglas, from the committee, made an elaborate report, from which we have room only for a few extracts. Mr. Douglas attributed the origin of the difficulties in Kansas to the emigrant aid societies :

EXTRACTS FROM REPORT OF MR. DOUGLAS.

Your committee deem this an appropriate occasion to state briefly, but distinctly, the principles upon which new states may be admitted and territories organized under the authority of the constitution of the United States.

The constitution (section 3, article 4) provides that "new states may be admitted by the congress into this Union."

Section 8, article 1 : "Congress shall have power to make all laws which shall be necessary and proper for carrying into execution the foregoing powers and all other powers vested by this constitution in the government of the United States, or in any department or office thereof."

10th amendment : "The powers not delegated to the United States by the constitution, nor prohibited by it to the states, are reserved to the states respectively, or to the people."

A state of the federal Union is a sovereign power, limited only by the constitution of the United States.

The limitations which that instrument has imposed are few, specific, and uniform—applicable alike to all the states, old and new. There is no authority for putting a restriction upon the sovereignty of a new state which the constitution has not placed on the original states. Indeed, if such a restriction could be imposed on any state, it would instantly cease to be a *state* within the meaning of the federal constitution, and, in consequence of the inequality, would assimilate to the condition of a province or dependency. Hence, equality among all the states of the Union is a fundamental principle in our federative system—a principle embodied in the constitution, as the basis upon which the American Union rests.

African slavery existed in all the colonies, under the sanction of the British government, prior to the declaration of independence. When the constitution of the United States was adopted, it became the supreme law and bond of union between twelve slaveholding states and one non-slaveholding state. Each state reserved the right to decide the question of slavery for itself—to continue it as a domestic institution so long as it pleased, and to abolish it when it chose.

In pursuance of this reserved right, six of the original slaveholding states have since abolished and prohibited slavery within their limits respectively, without consulting congress or their sister states; while the other six have retained and sustained it as a domestic institution which, in their opinion, had become so firmly engrafted on their social systems that the relation between the master and slave could not be dissolved with safety to either. In the mean time eighteen new states have been admitted into the Union, in obedience to the federal constitution, on an equal footing with the original states, including, of course, the right of each to decide the question of slavery for itself. In deciding this question, it has so happened that nine of these new states have abolished and prohibited slavery, while the other nine have retained and regulated it. That these new states had at the time of their admission, and still retain, an equal right under the federal constitution with the original states, to decide all questions of domestic policy for themselves, including that of African slavery, ought not to be seriously questioned, and certainly cannot be successfully controverted.

They are all subject to the same supreme law, which, by the consent of each, constitutes the only limitation upon their sovereign authority.

Since we find the right to admit new states enumerated among the powers expressly delegated in the constitution, the question arises, whence does congress derive authority to organize temporary government for the territories preparatory to their admission into the Union on an equal footing with the original states? Your committee are not prepared to adopt the reasoning which deduces the power from that other clause of the constitution, which says:

"Congress shall have power to dispose of and make all needful rules and regulations respecting the territory or other property belonging to the United States."

The language of this clause is much more appropriate when applied to property than to persons. It would seem to have been employed for the purpose of conferring upon congress the power of disposing of the public lands and *other property belonging to the United States*, and to make all needful rules and regulations for that purpose, rather than to govern the people who might purchase those lands from the United States and become residents thereon. The word "territory" was an appropriate expression to designate that large area of public lands of which the United States had become the owner by virtue of the revolution and the cession by the several states. The additional words, " or other property belonging to the United States," clearly shows that the term "territory" was used in its ordinary geographical sense, to designate the public domain, and not as descriptive of the whole body of the people constituting a distinct political community, who have no representation in congress, and consequently no voice in making the laws upon which all their rights and liberties would depend, if it were conceded that congress had the general and unlimited power to make all "needful rules and regulations concerning" their internal affairs and domestic concerns. It is under this clause of the constitution, and from this alone, that congress derives authority to provide for the survey of the public lands, for securing preëmption rights to actual settlers, for the establishment of land offices in the several states and territories, for exposing the lands to private and public sale, for issuing patents and confirming titles, and, in short, for making all needful rules and regulations for protecting and disposing of the public domain and other property belonging to the United States.

These needful rules and regulations may be embraced, and usually are found in general laws applicable alike to states and territories, wherever the United States may be the owner of the lands or other property to be regulated or disposed of. It can make no difference, under this clause of the constitution, whether the "territory or other property belonging to the United States," shall be situated in Ohio or Kansas, in Alabama or Minnesota, in California or Oregon. The power of congress to make needful rules and regulations is the same in the states and the territories, to the extent that the title is vested in the United States. Inasmuch as the right of legislation in such cases rests exclusively upon the fact of ownership, it is obvious it can extend only to the tracts of land to which the United States possess the title, and must cease in respect to each tract the instant it becomes private property by purchase from the United States. It will scarcely be contended that congress possesses the power to legislate for the people of those states in which public lands may be located, in respect to their internal affairs and domestic concerns, merely because the United States may be so fortunate as to own a portion of the territory and other property within the limits of those states. Yet it should be borne in mind that this clause of the constitution confers upon congress the same power to make needful rules and regulations in the states as it does in the territories, concerning the territory or other property belonging to the United States.

In view of these considerations, your committee are not prepared to affirm that congress derives authority to institute governments for the people of the territories, from that clause of the constitution which confers the right to make needful rules and regulations concerning the territory or other property belonging to the United States ; much less can we deduce the power from any supposed necessity, arising outside of the constitution and not provided for in that instrument. The federal government is one of delegated and limited powers, clothed with no rightful authority which does not result directly and necessarily from the constitution. Necessity, when experience shall have clearly demonstrated its existence, may furnish satisfactory reasons for enlarging the authority of the federal government, by amendments to the constitution, in the mode prescribed in that instrument; but cannot afford the slightest excuse for the assumption of powers not delegated, and which, by the tenth amendment, are expressly "reserved to the states respectively, or to the people." Hence, before the power can be safely exercised, the right of congress to organize territories, by instituting temporary governments, must be traced directly to some provision of the constitution conferring the authority in express terms, or as a means necessary and proper to carry into effect some one or more of the powers which are specifically delegated. Is not the organization of a territory eminently necessary and proper as a means of enabling the people thereof to form and mould their local and domestic institutions, and establish a state government under the authority of the constitution, preparatory to its admission into the Union ? If so, the right of congress to pass the organic act for the temporary government is clearly included in the provision which authorizes the admission of new states. This power, however, being an incident to an express grant, and resulting from it by necessary implication, as an appropriate means for carrying it into effect, must be exercised in harmony with the nature and objects of the grant from which it is deduced. The organic act of the territory, deriving its validity from the power of congress to admit new states, must contain no provision or restriction which would destroy or impair the equality of the proposed state with the original states, or impose any limitation upon its sovereignty which the constitution has not placed on all the states. So far as the organization of a territory may be necessary and proper as a means of carrying into effect the provision of the constitution for the admission of new states, and when exercised with reference only to that end, the power of congress is clear and explicit; but beyond that point the authority cannot extend, for the reason that all "powers not delegated to the United States by the constitution, nor prohibited by it to the states, are reserved to the states respectively, or to the people." In other words, the organic act of the territory, conforming to the spirit of the grant from which it receives its validity, must leave the people entirely free to form and regulate their domestic institutions and internal concerns in their own way, subject only to the constitution of the United States, to the end that when they attain the requisite population, and establish a state government in conformity to the federal constitution, they may be admitted into the Union on an equal footing with the original states in all respects whatsoever.

The act of congress for the organization of the territories of Kansas and Nebraska was designed to conform to the spirit and letter of the federal constitution, by preserving and maintaining the fundamental principles of equality among all the states of the Union, notwithstanding the restriction contained in the 8th section of the act of March 6, 1820, (preparatory to the admission of Missouri into the Union,) which assumed to deny to the people forever the right to settle the question of slavery for themselves, provided they should make their homes and organize states north of thirty-six degrees and thirty minutes north latitude. Conforming to the cardinal principles of state equality and self-government, in obedience to the constitution, the Kansas-Nebraska act declared, in the precise language of the compromise measures of 1850, that, "when admitted as a state, the said territory, or any portion of the same, shall be received into the Union, with or without slavery, as their constitution may prescribe at the time of their admission." Again, after declaring the 8th section of the Missouri act (sometimes called the Missouri compromise, or Missouri restriction) inoperative and void, as being repugnant to these principles, the purpose of congress, in passing this act, is declared in these words : "It being the true intent and meaning of this act not to legislate slavery into any state or territory, nor to exclude it therefrom, but to leave the people thereof perfectly free to form and regulate their domestic institutions in their own way, subject only to the constitution of the United States."

Immediately after the passage of the act, combinations were entered into in some portions of the Union to control the political destinies, and form and regulate the domestic institutions, of those territories and future states, through the machinery of emigrant aid societies. In order to give consistency and efficiency to the movement, and surround it with the color of legal authority, an act of incorporation was procured from the legislature of the state of Massachusetts, in which it was provided, in the first section, that twenty persons therein named, and their "associates, successors, and assigns, are hereby made a corporation, by the name of the Massachusetts Emigrant Aid Company, for the purpose of assisting emigrants to settle in the west." The second section limited the capital stock of the company to five millions of dollars, and authorized the whole to be invested in real and personal estate, with the proviso that "the said corporation shall not hold real estate in this commonwealth, (Massachusetts) to an amount exceeding twenty thousand dollars." Although the act of incorporation does not distinctly declare that the company was formed for the purpose of controlling the domestic institutions of the territory of Kansas, and forcing it into the Union with a prohibition of slavery in her constitution, regardless of the rights and wishes of the people as guarantied by the constitution of the United States, and secured by their organic law, yet the whole history of the movement, the circumstances in which it had its origin, and the professions and avowals of all engaged in it, render it certain and undeniable that such was its object.

To remove all doubt upon this point, your committee present a few extracts from a pamphlet published by the company:

"For the purpose of answering numerous communications concerning the plan of operations of the Emigrant Aid Company, and the resources of Kansas territory, which it is proposed now to settle, the secretary of the company has deemed it expedient to publish the following definite information in regard to this particular: * *

"For these purposes it is recommended, 1st. That the trustees contract immediately with some one of the competing lines of travel for the conveyance of 20,000 persons from Massachusetts to that place in the west which the trustees shall select for their first settlement." * * * * *

"It is recommended that the company's agents locate and take up for the company's benefit, the sections of land in which the boarding-houses and mills are located, and no others. And further, whenever the territory shall be organized as a free state, the trustees shall dispose of all its interests there, replace by the sales the money laid out, declare a dividend to the stockholders, and that they then select a new field, and make similar arrangements for the settlement and organization of another free state of this Union." * * * * *

"With the advantages attained by such a system of effort, the territory selected as the scene of operations would, it is believed, be filled up with free inhabitants." *

"There is reason to suppose several thousand men of New England origin propose to emigrate under the auspices of some such arrangement, this very summer. Of the whole emigration from Europe, amounting to some 400,000 persons, there can be no difficulty in inducing some thirty or forty thousand to take the same direction." * *

"Especially will it prove an advantage to Massachusetts, if she create the new state by her foresight, supply the necessities of its inhabitants, and open in the outset communications between their homes and her ports and factories."

"It determines in the right way the institutions of the unsettled territories, in less time than the discussion of them has required in congress." * *

This movement is justified by those who originated and control the plan, upon the ground that the persons whom they sent to Kansas were free men, who, under the constitution and laws, had a perfect right to emigrate to Kansas or any other territory; that the act of emigration was entirely voluntary on their part; and when they arrived in the territory as actual settlers, they had as good a right as any other citizens to vote at the elections, and participate in the control of the government of the territory. This would undoubtedly be true in a case of ordinary emigration, such as has filled up our new states and territories, where each individual has gone, on his own account, to improve his condition and that of his family. But it is a very different thing where a state creates a vast moneyed corporation for the purpose of controlling the domestic institutions of a distinct political community fifteen hundred miles distant, and sends out the emigrants only as a means of accomplishing its paramount political objects. When a powerful corporation, with a capital of five millions of dollars invested in houses and lands, in merchandise and mills, in cannon and rifles, in powder and lead—in all the implements of art, agriculture, and war, and employing a corresponding number of men, all under the management and control of non-resident directors and stockholders, who are authorized by their charter to vote by proxy to the extent of fifty votes each, enters a distant and sparsely settled territory with the fixed purpose of wielding all its power to control the domestic institutions and political destinies of the territory, it becomes a question of fearful import, how far the operations of the company are compatible with the rights and liberties of the people. Whatever may be the extent or limit of congressional authority over the territories, it is clear that no individual state has the right to pass any law or authorize any act concerning or affecting the territories, which it might not enact in reference to any other state.

When the emigrants sent out by the Massachusetts Emigrant Aid Company, and their affiliated societies, passed through the state of Missouri in large numbers on their way to Kansas, the violence of their language, and the unmistakable indications of their determined hostility to the domestic institutions of that state, created apprehensions that the object of the company was to abolitionize Kansas as a means of prosecuting a relentless warfare upon the institution of slavery within the limits of Missouri. These apprehensions increased and spread with the progress of events, until they became the settled convictions of the people of that portion of the state most exposed to the danger by their proximity to the Kansas border. The natural consequence was, that immediate steps were taken by the people of the western counties of Missouri to stimulate, organize, and carry into effect a system of emigration similar to that of the Massachusetts Emigrant Aid Company, for the avowed purpose of counteracting the effects, and protecting themselves and their domestic institutions from the consequences of that company's operations.

The material difference in the character of the two rival and conflicting movements consists in the fact that the one had its origin in an aggressive, and the other in a defensive policy. The one was organized in pursuance of the provisions and claiming to act under the authority of a legislative enactment of a distant state, whose internal prosperity and domestic security did not depend upon the success of the movement; while the other was the spontaneous action of the people living in the immediate vicinity of the theatre of operations, excited by a sense of common danger to the necessity of protecting their own firesides from the apprehended horrors of servile insurrection and intestine war. Both parties, conceiving it to be essential to the success of their respective plans that they should be upon the field of operations prior to the first election in the territory, selected principally young men, persons unencumbered by families, and whose conditions in life enabled them to leave at a moment's warning, and move with great celerity, to go at once, and select and occupy the most eligible sites and favored locations in the territory, to be held by themselves and their associates who should follow them. For the successful prosecution of such a scheme, the Missourians, who lived in the immediate vicinity, possessed peculiar advantages over their rivals from the more remote portions of the Union. Each family could send one of its members across the line to mark out his claim, erect a cabin, and put in a small crop, sufficient to give him as valid a right to be deemed an actual settler and qualified voter as those who were being imported by the emigrant aid societies. In an unoccupied territory, where the lands have not been surveyed, and where there were no marks or lines to indicate the boundaries of sections and quarter-sections, and where no legal title could be had until after the surveys should be made, disputes, quarrels, violence, and bloodshed might have been expected as the natural and inevitable consequences of such extraordinary systems of emigration, which divided and arrayed the settlers into two great hostile parties, each having an inducement to claim more than was his right, in order to hold it for some new comer of his own party, and at the same time prevent persons belonging to the opposite party from settling in the neighborhood. As a result of this state of things, the great mass of emigrants from the northwest and from other states who went there on their own account, with no other object and influence, by no other motives than to improve their condition and secure good homes for their families, were compelled to array themselves under the banner of one of these hostile parties, in order to insure protection to themselves and their claims against the aggressions and violence of the other.

Your committee have not considered it any part of their duty to examine and review each enactment and provision of the large volume of laws adopted by the legislature of Kansas upon almost every rightful subject of legislation, and affecting nearly every relation and interest in life, with a view either to their approval or disapproval by congress, for the reason that they are local

42

laws, confined in their operation to the internal concerns of the territory, the control and management of which, by the principles of the federal constitution, as well as by the terms of the Kansas-Nebraska act, are confided to the people of the territory, to be determined by themselves through their representatives in their local legislature, and not by the congress, in which they have no representatives to give or withhold their assent to the laws upon which their rights and liberties may all depend. Under these laws marriages have taken place, children have been born, deaths have occurred, estates have been distributed, contracts have been made, and rights have accrued which it is not competent for congress to divest. If there can be a doubt in respect to the validity of these laws, growing out of the alleged irregularity of the election of the members of the legislature, or the lawfulness of the place where its sessions were held, which it is competent for any tribunal to inquire into with a view to its decision at this day, and after the series of events which have ensued, it must be a judicial question, over which congress can have no control, and which can be determined only by the courts of justice, under the protection and sanction of the constitution.

When it was proposed in the last congress to annul the acts of the legislative assembly of Minnesota, incorporating certain railroad companies, this committee reported against the proposition, and, instead of annulling the local legislation of the territory, recommended the repeal of that clause of the organic act of Minnesota which reserves to congress the right to disapprove its laws. That recommendation was based on the theory that the people of the territory, being citizens of the United States, were entitled to the privilege of self-government in obedience to the constitution; and if, in the exercise of this right, they had made wise and just laws, they ought to be permitted to enjoy all the advantages resulting from them; while, on the contrary, if they had made unwise and unjust laws, they should abide the consequences of their own acts until they discovered, acknowledged, and corrected their errors.

It has been alleged that gross misrepresentations have been made in respect to the character of the laws enacted by the legislature of Kansas, calculated, if not designed, to prejudice the public mind at a distance against those who enacted them, and to create the impression that it was the duty of congress to interfere and annul them. In view of the violent and insurrectionary measures which were being taken to resist the laws of the territory, a convention of delegates, representing almost every portion of the territory of Kansas, was held at the city of Leavenworth on the 14th of November, 1855, at which men of all shades of political opinions, "whigs, democrats, pro-slavery men, and free state men, all met and harmonized together, and forgot their former differences in the common danger that seemed to threaten the peace, good order, and prosperity of this community." This convention was presided over by the governor of the territory, assisted by a majority of the judges of the supreme court; and the address to the citizens of the United States, among other distinguished names, bears the signatures of the United States district attorney and marshal for the territory.

It is but reasonable to assume that the interpretation which these function-aries have given to the acts of the Kansas legislature in this address will be observed in their official exposition and execution of the same. In reference to the wide-spread perversions and misrepresentations of those laws, this ad-dress says:

"The laws passed by the legislature have been most grossly misrepresented, with the view of prejudicing the public against that body, and as an excuse for the revolutionary movements in this territory. The limits of this address will not permit a correction of all these misrepresentations; but we will notice some of them, that have had the most wide-spead circulation.

"It has been charged and widely circulated that the legislature, in order to perpetuate their rule, had passed a law prescribing the qualifications of voters, by which it is de-clared 'that any one may vote who will swear allegiance to the fugitive slave law, the Kansas and Nebraska bill, and pay one dollar.' Such is declared to be the evidence of citizenship, such the qualification of voters. In reply to this, we say that no such law was ever passed by the legislature. The law prescribing the qualification of voters ex-pressly provides that, to entitle a person to vote, he must be twenty-one years of age, an actual inhabitant of this territory, and of the county or district in which he offers to vote, and shall have paid a territorial tax. There is no law requiring him to pay a dol-lar-tax as a qualification to vote. He must pay a tax it is true, [and this is by no means an unusual requirement in the states;] but whether this tax is levied on his personal or real property, his money at interest, or is a poll-tax, makes no difference; the payment of any territorial tax entitles the person to vote, provided he has the other qualifications provided by law. The act seems to be carefully drawn with the view of excluding all illegal and foreign votes. The voter must be an inhabitant of the territory, and of the county or district in which he offers to vote, and he must have paid a territorial tax. The judges and clerks are required to be sworn, and to keep duplicate poll-boxes; and ample provision is made for contesting elections, and purging the polls of the illegal votes. It is difficult to see how a more guarded law could be framed, for the purpose of protecting the purity of elections and the sanctity of the ballot-box. The law does not require the voter to swear to support the fugitive slave law, or the Kansas and Nebraska bill, unless he is challenged; in that case, he is required to take an oath to support each of these laws. As to the dollar law, [so called,] it is merely a poll-tax, and has no more connection with the right of suffrage than any other tax levied by the territorial authority, and is to be paid whether the party votes or not. It is a mere temporary measure, having no force beyond this year, and was resorted to as such to supply the territorial treasury with the necessary means to carry on the government.

"It has also been charged against the legislature that they elected all of the officers of the territory for six years. This is without any foundation. They elected no officer for six years; and the only civil officers they retain the election of, that occurs to us at present, are the auditor and treasurer of state, and the district attorneys, who hold their offices for four, and not six years. By the organic act, the commissions issued by the governor to the civil officers of the territory all expired on the adjournment of the legis-lature. To prevent a failure in the local administration, and from necessity, the legisla-ture made a number of temporary appointments, such as probate judge, and two county commissioners, and a sheriff of each county. The probate judge and county commis-sioners constitute the tribunal for the transaction of county business, and are invested with the power to appoint justices of the peace, constables, county surveyor, recorder, and clerk, etc. Probate judges, county commissioners, sheriffs, etc., are all temporary appointments, and are made elective by the people at the first annual election in 1857. The legislature could not have avoided making some temporary appointments. No election could have been held without them. There were no judges, justices of the peace, or other officers to conduct an election of any kind, until appointed by the legislature. It was the exercise of a power which the first legislative assembly in every territory must of necessity exercise, in order to put the local government in motion. We see nothing in this to justify revolution or a resort to force. The law for the protection of slave property has also been much misunderstood. The right to pass such a law is expressly stated by Governor Reeder in his inaugural message, in which he says: 'A territorial legislature may undoubtedly act upon the question to a limited and partial extent, and may temporarily prohibit, tolerate or regulate slavery in the territory, and in an absolute or modified form, with all the force and effect of any other legislative act, binding until repealed by the same power that enacted it.' There is nothing in the act itself, as has been charged, to prevent a free discussion of the subject of slavery. Its bearing on society, its morality or expediency, or whether it would be politic or impolitic to make this a slave state, can be discussed here as freely as in any state in this Union, without infringing any of the provisions of the law. To deny the right of a person to hold slaves under the law in this territory is made penal; but beyond this, there is no restriction to the discussion of the slavery question, in any aspect in which it is capable of being considered. We do not wish to be understood as approving of all the laws passed by the legislature; on the contrary, we would state that there are some that we do not approve of, and which are condemned by public opinion here, and which will, no doubt, be repealed or modified at the meeting of the next legislature. But this is nothing more than what frequently occurs, both in the legislation of congress and of the various state legislatures. The remedy for such evils is to be found in public opinion, to which, sooner or later, in a government like ours, all laws must conform."

A few days after Governor Reeder dissolved his official relation with the legislature, on account of the removal of the seat of government, and while that body was still in session, a meeting was called by "many voters," to assemble at Lawrence on the 14th or 15th of August, 1855, "to take into consideration the propriety of calling a territorial convention, preliminary to the formation of a state government, and other subjects of public interest." At that meeting the following preamble and resolutions were adopted with but one dissenting voice:

"Whereas, the people of Kansas territory have been since its settlement, and now are, without any law-making power: therefore,

"Be it resolved, that we, the people of Kansas territory, in mass meeting assembled, irrespective of party distinctions, influenced by a common necessity, and greatly desirous of promoting the common good, do hereby call upon and request all bona fide citizens of Kansas territory, of whatever political views and predilections, to consult together in their respective election districts, and in mass convention or otherwise, elect three delegates for each representative of the legislative assembly, by proclamation of Governor Reeder of date 10th March, 1855; said delegates to assemble in convention at the town of Topeka, on the 19th day of September, 1855, then and there to consider and determine upon all subjects of public interest, and particularly upon that having reference to the speedy formation of a state constitution, with an intention of an immediate application to be admitted as a state into the Union of the United States of America."

This meeting, so far as your committee have been able to ascertain, was the first step in that series of proceedings which resulted in the adoption of a constitution and state government, to be put in operation on the 4th of the present

month, in subversion of the territorial government established under the authority of congress. The right to set up the state government in defiance of
the constituted authorities of the territory, is based on the assumption "that
the people of Kansas territory have been since its settlement, and now are,
without any law-making power;" in the face of the well-known fact, that the
territorial legislature were then in session, in pursuance of the proclamation of
Governor Reeder, and the organic law of the territory. On the 5th of September, a "territorial delegate convention" assembled at the Big Springs, "to
take into consideration the present exigencies of political affairs," at which,
among others, the following resolutions were adopted:

"Resolved, That this convention, in view of its recent repudiation of the acts of the
so-called Kansas legislative assembly, respond most heartily to the call made by the
people's convention of the 14th ultimo, for a delegate convention of the people of Kansas, to be held at Topeka, on the 19th instant, to consider the propriety of the formation
of a state constitution, and such matters as may legitimately come before it.

"Resolved, That we owe no allegiance or obedience to the tyranical enactments of
this spurious legislature; that their laws have no validity or binding force upon the
people of Kansas; and that every freeman among us is at full liberty, consistently with
his obligations as a citizen and a man, to defy and resist them if he choose so to do.

"Resolved, That we will endure and submit to these laws no longer than the best interests of the territory require, as the least of two evils, and will resist them to a bloody
issue as soon as we ascertain that peaceable remedies shall fail, and forcible resistance
shall furnish any reasonable prospect of success; and that in the mean time we recommend to our friends through the territory, the organization and discipline of volunteer
companies, and the procurement and preparation of arms."

With the view to a distinct understanding of the meaning of so much of
this resolution as relates to the "organization and discipline of volunteer companies, and the procurement and preparation of arms," it may be necessary to
state, that there was at that time existing in the territory a secret military organization, which had been formed for political objects prior to the alleged invasion, at the election on the 30th of March, and which held its first "grand
encampment at Lawrence, February 8th, 1855." Your committee have been
put in possession of a small printed pamphlet, containing the "constitution
and ritual of the grand encampment and regiments of Kansas legion of Kansas territory, adopted April 4th, 1855," which, during the recent disturbances
in that territory, was taken on the person of one George F. Warren, who attempted to conceal and destroy the same by thrusting it into his mouth, and
biting and chewing it. Although somewhat mutilated by the "tooth prints,"
it bears internal evidence of being a genuine document, authenticated by the
original signature of "G. W. Hutchinson, grand general," and "J. K. Good-
win, grand quartermaster."

The constitution consists of six articles, regulating the organization of the
"Grand Encampment," which is "composed of representatives elected from
each subordinate regiment existing in the territory, as hereafter provided. The
officers of the Grand Encampment shall consist of a grand general, grand vice-

general, grand quartermaster, grand paymaster, grand aid, two grand sentinels, and grand chaplain.

"The Grand Encampment shall make all nominations for territorial officers at large, and immediately after such nominations shall have been made, the grand general shall communicate the result to every regiment in the territory."

The "opening ceremony" of the subordinate encampment is as follows :

"The colonel, lieutenant colonel, quartermaster, paymaster, aid, and sentinels, being in their respective places, the regiment shall be called and thus addressed by the colonel : Fellow-soldiers in the free-state army: The hour has arrived when we must resume the duties devolving upon us. Let us each, with a heart devoted to justice, patriotism, and liberty, attend closely to all the regulations laid down for our government and action ; each laboring to make this review pleasant and profitable to ourselves and a blessing to our country. Aid, are the sentinels at their posts, with closed doors ?

"Aid. They are.

"Colonel. Aid, you will now review the troops in the regiment's pass word.

"Aid. (After examination.) I have examined them personally, and find each correct.

"Colonel. I pronounce this regiment arrayed and ready for service."

Then follows the process of initiating new recruits, who are properly vouched for by members of the order, the preliminary obligations to observe secrecy, the catechism to which the candidate is subjected, and the explanations of the colonel in respect to the objects of the order, which are thus stated : "First, to secure to Kansas the blessing and prosperity of being a free state; and, secondly, to protect the ballot-box from the LEPROUS TOUCH OF UNPRINCIPLED MEN." These and all other questions being satisfactorily answered, the final oath is thus administered : "With these explanations upon our part, we shall ask of you that you take with us an obligation, placing yourself in the same attitude as before.

OBLIGATION.

"I, ———— ————, in the most solemn manner, here in the presence of Heaven and these witnesses, bind myself that I will never reveal, nor cause to be revealed, either by word, look, or sign, by writing, printing, engraving, painting or in any manner whatsoever, anything pertaining to this institution, save to persons duly qualified to receive the same. I will never reveal the nature of the organization, the place of meeting, the fact that any person is a member of the same, or even the existence of the organization, except to persons legally qualified to receive the same. Should I at any time withdraw, or be suspended or expelled from this organization, I will keep this obligation to the end of life. If any books, papers or moneys belonging to this organization be entrusted to my care or keeping, I will faithfully and completely deliver up the same to my successor in office, or any one legally authorized to receive them. I will never knowingly propose a person for membership in this order who is not in favor of making Kansas a free state, and whom I feel satisfied will use his entire influence to bring about this result. I will support, maintain, and abide by any honorable movement made by the organization to secure this great end, which will not conflict with the laws of the country and the constitution of the United States. I will unflinchingly vote for and support the candidates nominated by this organization in preference to any and all others.

"To all of this obligation I do most solemnly promise and affirm, binding myself under the penalty of being expelled from this organization, of having my name published to the several territorial encampments as a perjurer before Heaven, and a traitor to my country, of passing through life, scorned and reviled by man, frowned on by devils, forsaken by angels, and abandoned by God."

Your committee have deemed it important to give the outline of the "constitution and ritual of the grand encampment and regiments of the Kansas legion," as constituting the secret organization, political and military, in obedience to which the public demonstrations have been made to subvert the authority of the territorial government established by congress, by setting up a state government, either with or without the assent of congress, as circumstances should determine. The indorsement of this military organization, and the recommendation by the Big Springs convention for "the procurement and preparation of arms," accompanied with the distinct declaration that "we will resist them [the laws enacted by the Kansas legislature] to a bloody issue, as soon as we ascertain that peaceable remedies shall fail, and forcible resistance shall furnish any reasonable prospect of success," would seem to admit of no other interpretation than that, in the event that the courts of justice shall sustain the validity of those laws, and congress shall refuse to admit Kansas as a state with the constitution to be formed at Topeka, they will set up an independent government in defiance of the federal authority.

The same purpose is clearly indicated by the other proceedings of this convention, in which it is declared that "we with scorn repudiate the election law, so called," and nominate governor Reeder for congress, to be voted for on a different day from that authorized by law, at an election to be held by judges and clerks not appointed in pursuance of any legal authority, and not to be sworn by any person authorized by law to administer oaths; and the returns to be made, and result proclaimed, and certificate granted, in a mode and by persons not permitted to perform these acts by any law, in or out of the territory.

In accepting the nomination, governor Reeder addressed the convention as follows; and, among other things, said:

"In giving him this nomination in this manner, they had strengthened his arms to do their work, and, in return, he would now pledge to them a steady, unflinching pertinacity of purpose, never-tiring industry, dogged perseverance, and, in all the abilities with which God has endowed him, to the righting of their wrongs, and the final triumph of their cause. He believed, from the circumstances which had for the last eight months surrounded him, and which had, at the same time, placed in his possession many facts, and bound him, heart and soul, to the oppressed voters of Kansas, that he could do much towards obtaining a redress of their grievances.

"He said that, day by day a crisis was coming upon us; that, in after times, this would be to posterity a turning-point, a marked period, as are to us the opening of the revolution, the adoption of the Declaration of Independence, and the era of the alien and sedition laws; that we should take each carefully, so that each be a step of progress, and so that no violence be done to the tie which binds the American people together. He alluded to the unprecedented

tyranny under which we are and have been; and said that, if any one supposed that institutions were to be imposed by force upon a free and enlightened
people, they never knew, or had forgotten, the history of our fathers. American citizens bear in their breasts too much of the spirit of other and trying
days, and have lived too long amid the blessings of liberty, to submit to oppression from any quarter; and the man who having once been free, could
tamely submit to tyranny, was fit to be a slave.

"He urged the free state men of Kansas to forget all minor issues, and pursue determinedly the one great object, never swerving, but steadily pressing on
as did the wise men who followed the star to the manger, looking back only
for fresh encouragement. He counseled that peaceful resistance be made to
the tyrannical and unjust laws of the spurious legislature; that appeals to the
courts, to the ballot box, and to congress, be made for relief from this oppressive load; that violence should be deprecated as long as a single hope of
peaceable redress remained; but if, at last, all these should fail—if, in the
proper tribunals, there is no hope for our dearest rights, outraged and profan-
ed—if we are still to suffer, that corrupt men may reap harvests watered by
our tears—then there is one more chance for justice. God has provided, in
the eternal frame of things, redress for every wrong; and there remains to
us still the steady eye and the strong arm, and we must conquer, or mingle the
bodies of the oppressors with those of the oppressed upon the soil which the
Declaration of Independence no longer protects. But he was not at all apprehensive that such a crisis would ever arrive. He believed that justice
might be found far short of so dreadful an extremity; and, even should an
appeal to arms come, it was his opinion, that if we are well prepared, that
moment the victory is won."

In pursuance of the recommendation of the mass meeting held at Lawrence
on the 14th of August, and indorsed by the convention held at the Big Springs
on the 5th and 6th of September, a convention was held at Topeka, on the
19th and 20th of September, at which it was determined to hold another convention at the same place on the fourth Tuesday of October, for the purpose
of forming a constitution and state government; and to this end such proceedings were had as were deemed necessary for giving the notices, conducting the
election of delegates, making the returns, and assembling the convention.
With regard to the regularity of these proceedings, your committee see no
necessity for further criticism than is to be found in the fact that it was the
movement of a political party instead of the whole body of the people of
Kansas, conducted without the sanction of law, and in defiance of the constituted authorities, for the avowed purpose of overthrowing the territorial government established by congress.

The election for all these officers were held at the time specified; and on
the fourth day of the present month, the new government was to have been
put in operation, in conflict with the territorial government established by congress, and for the avowed purpose of subverting and overthrowing the same,

without reference to the action of congress upon their application for admission into the Union.

Your committee are not aware of any case in the history of our own country, which can be fairly cited as an example, much less a justification, for these extraordinary proceedings. Cases have occurred in which the inhabitants of particular territories have been permitted to form constitutions, and take the initiatory steps for the organization of state governments, preparatory to their admission into the Union, without obtaining the previous assent of congress ; but in every instance the proceeding has originated with, and been conducted in subordination to, the authority of the local governments established or recognized by the government of the United States. Michigan, Arkansas, Florida, and California, are sometimes cited as cases in point.

In tracing, step by step, the origin and history of these Kansas difficulties, your committee have been profoundly impressed with the significant fact, that each one has resulted from an attempt to violate or circumvent the principles and provisions of the act of congress for the organization of Kansas and Nebraska. The leading idea and fundamental principle of the Kansas-Nebraska act, as expressed in the law itself, was *to leave the actual settlers and bonafide inhabitants of each territory "perfectly free to form and regulate their domestic institutions in their own way, subject only to the constitution of the United States."* While this is declared to be "the true intent and meaning of the act," those who were opposed to allowing the people of the territory, preparatory to their admission into the Union as a state, to decide the slavery question for themselves, failing to accomplish their purpose in the halls of congress, and under the authority of the constitution, immediately resorted, in their respective states, to unusual and extraordinary means to control the political destinies and shape the domestic institutions of Kansas, in defiance of the wishes, and regardless of the rights, of the people of that territory, as guarantied by their organic law. Combinations, in one section of the Union, to stimulate an unnatural and false system of emigration, with the view of controlling the elections, and forcing the domestic institutions of the territory to assimilate to those of the non-slaveholding states, were followed, as might have been foreseen, by the use of similar means in the slaveholding states, to produce directly the opposite result. To these causes, and to these alone, in the opinion of your committee, may be traced the origin and progress of all the controversies and disturbances with which Kansas is now convulsed.

If these unfortunate troubles have resulted, as natural consequences, from unauthorized and improper schemes of foreign interference with the internal affairs and domestic concerns of the territory, it is apparent that the remedy must be sought in a strict adherence to the principles, and rigid enforcement of the provisions, of the organic law. In this connection, your committee feel sincere satisfaction in commending the messages and proclamation of the president of the United States, in which we have the gratifying assurance that the supremacy of the laws will be maintained ; that rebellion will be crushed ; that insurrection will be suppressed ; that aggressive intrusion for the purpose of deciding elections, or any other purpose, will be repelled; that unauthorized intermeddling in the local concerns of the territory, both from adjoining and distant states, will be prevented; that the federal and local laws will be vindicated against all attempts of organized resistance; and that the people of the territory will be protected in the establishment of their own institutions, undisturbed by encroachments from without, and in the full enjoyment of the rights of self-government assured to them by the constitution and the organic law.

In view of these assurances, given under the conviction that the existing laws confer all authority necessary to the performance of these important duties, and that the whole available force of the United States will be exerted to the extent required for their performance, your committee repose in entire confidence that peace, and security, and law, will prevail in Kansas. If any further evidence were necessary to prove that all the collisions and difficulties in Kansas were produced by the schemes of foreign interference which have been developed in this report, in violation of the principles and in evasion of the provisions of the Kansas-Nebraska act, it may be found in the fact that in Nebraska, to which the emigrant-aid societies did not extend their operations, and into which the stream of emigration was permitted to flow in its usual and natural channels, nothing has occurred to disturb the peace and harmony of the territory, while the principle of self-government, in obedience to the constitution, has had fair play, and is quietly working out its legitimate results.

It now only remains for your committee to respond to the two specific recommendations of the president, in his special message.

In compliance with the first recommendation, your committee ask leave to report a bill authorizing the legislature of the territory to provide by law for the election of delegates by the people, and the assembling of a convention to form a constitution and state government preparatory to their admission into the Union on an equal footing with the original states, so soon as it shall appear, by a census to be taken under the direction of the governor, by the authority of the legislature, that the territory contains ninety-three thousand four hundred and twenty inhabitants—that being the number required by the present ratio of representation for a member of congress.

In compliance with the other recommendation, your committee propose to offer to the appropriation bill an amendment appropriating such sum as shall be found necessary, by the estimates to be obtained, for the purpose indicated in the recommendation of the president.

All of which is respectfully submitted to the senate by your committee.

Mr. Collamer, of Vermont, the minority member of said committee, submitted the following

MINORITY REPORT.

Thirteen of the present prosperous states of this Union passed through the period of apprenticeship or pupilage of territorial training, under the guardianship of congress, preparatory to assuming their proud rank of manhood as sovereign and independent states. This period of their pupilage was, in every case, a period of the good offices of parent and child, in the kind relationship sustained between the national and the territorial government, and may be remembered with feelings of gratitude and pride. We have fallen on different times. A territory of our government is now convulsed with violence and discord, and the whole family of our nation is in a state of excitement and anxiety. The national executive power is put in motion, the army in requisition, and congress is invoked for interference.

In this case, as in all others of difficulty, it becomes necessary to inquire what is the true *cause* of existing trouble, in order to apply effectual cure. It is but temporary palliatives to deal with the external and more obvious manifestations and developments, while the real, procuring cause lies unattended to, and uncorrected, and unremoved.

It is said that organized opposition to law exists in Kansas. That, if existing, may probably be suppressed by the president, by the use of the army; and so, too, may invasions by armed bodies from Missouri, if the executive be sincere in its efforts; but when this is done, while the cause of trouble remains, the results will continue with renewed and increased developments of danger.

Let us, then, look fairly and undisguisedly at this subject, in its true character and history. Wherein does this Kansas territory differ from all our other territories, which have been so peacefully and successfully carried through, and been developed into the manhood of independent states? Can that difference account for existing troubles? Can that difference, as a cause of trouble, be removed?

The first and great point of difference between the territorial government of Kansas and that of the thirteen territorial governments before mentioned, consists in the subject of slavery—the undoubted cause of present trouble.

The action of congress in relation to all those thirteen territories was conducted on a uniform and prudent principle, to wit: to settle, by a clear provision, the law in relation to the subject of slavery to be operative in the territory, while it remained such; not leaving it in any one of those cases to be a subject of controversy within the same, while in the plastic gristle of its youth. This was done by congress in the exercise of the same power which moulded the form of their organic laws, and appointed their executive and judiciary, and sometimes their legislative officers. It was the power provided in the constitution, in these words: "Congress shall have power to dispose of and make all needful rules and regulations respecting the territory or other property belonging to the United States." Settling the subject of slavery while the country remained a territory, was no higher exercise of power in congress than the regulation of the functions of the territorial government, and actually appointing its principal functionaries. This practice commenced with this national government, and was continued, with uninterrupted uniformity, for more than *sixty* years. This practical contemporaneous construction of the constitutional *power* of this government is too clear to leave room for doubt, or opportunity for skepticism. The peace, prosperity, and success which attended this course, and the results which have ensued, in the formation and admission of the thirteen states therefrom, are most conclusive and satisfactory evidence, also, of the wisdom and prudence with which this *power* was *exercised*. Deluded must be that people who, in the pursuit of plausible theories, become deaf to the lessons, and blind to the results, of their own experience.

Let us next inquire by what rule of uniformity congress was governed, in the exercise of this power of determining the condition of each territory as to slavery, while remaining a territory, as manifested in those thirteen instances. An examination of our history will show that this was not done from time to time by agitation and local or party triumphs in congress. The rule pursued was uniform and clear; and whoever may have lost by it, peace and prosperity have been gained. That rule was this:

Where slavery was actually existing in a country to any considerable or general extent, it was (though somewhat modified as to further importation in some instances, as in Mississippi and Orleans territories) suffered to remain. The fact that it had been taken and existed there, was taken as an indication of its adaptation and local utility. Where slavery did not in fact exist to any appreciable extent, the same was, by congress, expressly prohibited; so that in either case the country settled up without difficulty or doubt as to the character of its institutions. In no instance was this difficult and disturbing subject left to the people who had and who might settle in the territory, to be there an everlasting bone of contention, so long as the territorial government should continue. It was ever regarded, too, as a subject in which the whole country had an interest, and, therefore, improper for local legislation.

And though whenever the people of a territory come to form their own organic law, as an independent state, they would, either before or after their admission as a state, form and mould their institutions, as a sovereign state, in their own way, yet it must be expected, and has always proved true, that the state has taken the character her pupilage has prepared her for, as well in respect to slavery as in other respects. Hence, six of the thirteen states are free states, because slavery was prohibited in them by congress while territories, to wit: Ohio, Indiana, Illinois, Michigan, Wisconsin, and Iowa. Seven of the thirteen are slaveholding states, because slavery was allowed in them by congress while they were territories, to wit: Tennessee, Alabama, Mississippi, Florida, Louisiana, Arkansas, and Missouri.

On the 6th of March, A. D. 1820, was passed by congress the act preparatory to the admission of the state of Missouri into the Union. Much controversy and discussion arose on the question whether a prohibition of slavery within said state should be inserted, and it resulted in this: that said state should be admitted without such prohibition, but that slavery should be *forever prohibited* in the rest of that country ceded to us by France lying north 36° 30′ north latitude, and it was so done. This contract is known as the Missouri compromise. Under this arrangement Missouri was admitted as a slaveholding state, the same having been a slaveholding territory. Arkansas, south of the line, was formed into a territory, and slavery allowed therein, and afterwards admitted as a slaveholding state. Iowa was made a territory, north of the line, and, under the operation of the law, was settled up without slaves and admitted as a free state. The country now making the territories of Kansas and Nebraska, in 1820 was almost or entirely uninhabited, and lay north of said line, and whatever settlers entered the same before 1854 did so under that law, forever forbidding slavery therein.

In 1854 congress passed an act establishing two new territories—Nebraska and Kansas—in this region of country, where slavery had been prohibited for more than thirty years; and instead of leaving said law against slavery in operation, or prohibiting or expressly allowing or establishing slavery, congress left the subject in said territories to be discussed, agitated and legislated on, from time to time, and the elections in said territories to be conducted with reference to that subject, from year to year, so long as they should remain territories; for whatever laws might be passed by the territorial legislatures on this subject, must be subject to change or repeal by those of the succeeding years. In most former territorial governments, it was provided by law that their laws were subject to the revision of congress, so that they would be made with caution. In these territories that was omitted.

The provision in relation to slavery in Nebraska and Kansas is as follows: "The eighth section of the act preparatory to the admission of Missouri into the Union (which being inconsistent with the principle of non-intervention by congress with slavery in the states and territories, as required by the legislation of 1850, commonly called the compromise measures) is hereby declared *inoperative and void*; it being the true intent and meaning of this act not to legislate slavery into said territory or state, nor to exclude it therefrom, but to leave the people thereof *perfectly free* to form and regulate their domestic institutions in their own way, subject only to the constitution of the United States; provided, that nothing herein contained shall be construed to revive or put in force any law or regulation which may have existed prior to the act of 6th March, 1820, either protecting, establishing, prohibiting, or abolishing slavery."

Thus it was promulgated to the people of this whole country that here was a clear field for competition—an open course for the race of rivalship; the goal of which was the ultimate establishment of a sovereign state; and the prize, the reward of everlasting liberty and its institutions on the one hand, or the perpetuity of slavery and its concomitants on the other. It is the obvious duty of this government, while this law continues, to see this manifesto faithfully, and honorably, and honestly performed, even though its particular supporters may see cause of a result unfavorable to their hopes.

It is further to be observed, that in the performance of this novel experiment, it was provided that all white men who became inhabitants in Kansas were entitled to vote without regard to their time of residence, usually provided in other territories. Nor was this right of voting confined to American citizens, but included all such aliens as had declared, or would declare, on oath, their intention to become citizens. Thus was the proclamation to the world to become inhabitants of Kansas, and enlist in this great enterprise, by the force of numbers, by vote, to decide for it the great question. Was it to be expected that this great proclamation for the political tournament would be listened to with indifference and apathy ? Was it prepared and presented in that spirit ? Did it relate to a subject on which the people were cool or indifferent ? A large part of the people of this country look on domestic slavery as " only evil, and that continually," alike to master and to slave, and to the community; to be left alone to the management or enjoyment of the people of the states where it exists, but not to be extended, more especially as it gives, or may give, political supremacy to a minority of the people of this country in the United States government. On the other hand, many of the people of another part of the United States regard slavery, if not in the abstract a blessing, at least as now existing a condition of society best for both white and black, while they exist together; while others regard it as no evil, but as the highest state of social condition. These consider that they cannot, with safety to their interests, permit political ascendency to be largely in the hands of those unfriendly to this peculiar institution. From these conflicting views, long and violent has been the controversy, and experience seems to show it interminable.

Many, and probably a large majority of this nation, lovers of quiet, entertained the hope that, after 1850, the so-called compromise measures, even though not satisfactory to the free states, would be kept by their supporters, and made by them what they were professed to be, a finality on the subject of the extent and limitations of slave territory; more especially after the assurances contained in the inaugural address of President Pierce. This hope was fortified with the consideration that at that time congress had, by different provisions, settled by law the condition of freedom or slavery for all the territory of the United States. These hopes have been disappointed, and from this very provision for repose has been extracted a *principle* for disturbing the condition of things on which its foundation of finality rested—that is, the permanence and continuance of the then existing condition of legal provisions. The establishment of the territorial governments for Utah and New Mexico, without a prohibition of slavery, was sustained by many on the ground that no such provision was required for its exclusion, as the condition of the country and its laws were a sufficient barrier; and therefore they sustained them, because it would complete the series, and finish the provisions as to slavery in all our territory, and make an end of controversy on that subject : yet, in 1854, it was insisted by the friends and supporters of the laws of 1850, and it is actually asserted in the law establishing the territorial government of Kansas, that the laws for new Mexico and Utah, being of the compromise measures, adopt and contain a principle utterly at war with their great and professed object of finality ; and that, instead of completing and ending the provisions of congressional action for the territories as to slavery, it really declared a principle which *unsettled* all those where slavery had been prohibited, and rendered it proper, and only proper, to declare such prohibitions all "inoperative and void." The spirit and feeling which thus perverted those compromise laws, and made them the direct instrument of renewed disturbance, could not be expected then to leave the result to the decision of the people of Kansas with entire inactivity and indifference.

The slaveholding states, in 1820, secured the admission of Missouri as a slaveholding state, and all the region south of 36° 30' to the same purpose, by agreeing and enacting that all north of that line should be *forever free;* and by this they obtained only a sufficient number of votes from the free states, as counted with theirs, to adopt it. In 1850 they agreed that if Utah and New Mexico were made territories, without a prohibition of slavery, it would, with the laws already made for the rest of our territory, settle forever the whole subject. This proposition, for such a termination, also secured votes from the free states enough, with their own from the slaveholding states, to adopt it. In 1854, in utter disregard of these repeated contracts, both these arrangements were broken, and both these compromises disregarded, and all their provisions for freedom declared inoperative and void, by the vote of the slaveholding states, with a very few honorable exceptions, and a minority of the votes of the free states. After this extraordinary and inexcusable proceeding, it was not to be expected that the people of the slaveholding states would take no active measures to secure a favorable result by votes in the territory of Kansas. Neither could it be expected that the people of the free states, who regarded the act of 1854 as a double breach of faith, would sit down and make no effort, by legal means, to correct it.

It has been said that the repeal of this provision of the Missouri compromise, and breach of the compromise of 1850, should not be regarded as a measure of the slaveholding states, because it was presented by a senator from a free state.

The actions or votes of one or more individual men cannot give character to, or be regarded as fixing a measure on, their section or party. The only true or honest mode of determining whether any measure is that of any section or party, is to ascertain whether the *majority* of that section or party voted for it. Now, a large majority—indeed, the whole, with a few rare exceptions—of the representatives from the slaveholding states voted for that repeal. On the other hand, a majority of the representatives from the free states voted against it.

This subject of slavery in the territories, which has voilently agitated the country for many years, and which has been attempted to be settled twice by compromise, as before stated, does not remain settled. The Missouri compromise and the supposed finality by the acts of 1850, are scattered and dissolved by the votes of the slaveholding states; and it is not to be disguised that this uncalled for and disturbing measure has produced a spirit of resentment, from a feeling of its injustice, which, while the cause continues, will be difficult to allay.

This subject, then, which congress has been unable to settle in any such way as the slave states will sustain, is now turned over to those who have or shall become inhabitants of Kansas to arrange; and all men are invited to participate in the experiment, regardless of their character, political or religious views, or place of nativity.

Now, what is the *right* and the *duty* of the people of this country in relation to this matter? Is it not the right of all who believe in the blessings of slaveholding, and regard it as the best condition of society, either to go to Kansas *as inhabitants*, and by their votes to help settle this good condition of that territory; or if they cannot so go and settle, is it not their duty, by all lawful means in their power, to promote this object by inducing others like-minded to go? This *right* becomes a *duty* to all who follow their convictions. All who regard an establishment of slavery in Kansas as best for that territory, or as necessary to their own safety by the political weight it gives in the national government, should use all lawful means to secure that result; and clearly, the inducing men to go there to become permanent inhabitants and voters, and to vote as often as the elections occur in favor of the establishment of slavery, and thus control the elections, and preserve it a slave state forever, is neither unlawful nor censurable. It is, and would be highly praiseworthy and commendable, because it is using lawful means to carry forward honest convictions of public good. All lawfully-associated effort to that end is equally commendable. Nor will the application of opprobrious epithets, and calling it *propagandism*, change its moral or legal character, from whatever quarter or source, official or otherwise, such epithets may come. Neither should they deter any man from peaceably performing his duty by following his honest convictions.

On the other hand, all those who have seen and realized the blessings of universal liberty, and believe that it can only be secured and promoted by the prohibition of domestic slavery, and that the elevation of honest industry can never succeed where servitude makes labor degrading, should, as in duty bound, put forth all reasonable exertions to advance this great object, by lawful means, whenever permitted by the laws of their country. When, therefore, Kansas was presented, by law, as an open field for this experiment, and all were invited to enter, it became the right and duty of all such as desired, to go there as inhabitants for the purpose, by their numbers and by their votes lawfully cast, from time to time, to carry or control, in a legal way, the elections there for this object. This could only be lawfully effected by permanent residence, and continued and repeated effort, during the continuance of the territorial government, and permanently remaining there to form and preserve a free state constitution. All those who entertained the same sentiments, but were not disposed themselves to go, had the right and duty to use all lawful means to encourage and promote the object. If the purpose could be best effected by united efforts, by voluntary associations or corporations, or by state assistance, as proposed in some southern states, it was all equally lawful and laudable. This was not the officious intermeddling with the internal affairs of another nation, or state, or the territory of another people. The territory is the property of the nation, and is, professedly, open to the settlement and the institutions of every part of the United States. If lawful means, so extensive as to be effectual, were used to people it with a majority of inhabitants opposed to slavery, is now considered as a violation of, or an opposition to the law establishing the territory, then the declarations and provisions of that law were but a premeditated delusion, which not only allowed such measures, but actually invited them, by enacting that the largest number of the settlers should determine the condition of the country; thus inviting efforts for numbers. Such an invitation must have been expected to produce such efforts on both sides.

It now becomes necessary to inquire what has in fact taken place. If violence has taken place as the natural, and perhaps unavoidable, consequences of the nature of the experiment, bringing into dangerous contact and collision inflammable elements, it was the vice of a mistaken law, and immediate measures should be taken by congress to correct such law. If force and violence have been substituted for peaceful measures there, legal provisions should be made and executed to correct all the wrong such violence has produced, and to prevent their recurrence, and thus secure a fair fulfillment of the experiment by peaceful means, as originally professed and presented in the law.

A succient statement of the origin and progress of the material events in Kansas is this: After the passage of this law, establishing the territory of Kansas, a large body of settlers rapidly entered into said territory with a view to permanent inhabitancy therein. Most of these were from the free states of the west and north, who probably intended by their votes and influence to establish there a free state, agreeable to the law which invited them. Some part of those from the northern states had been encouraged and aided in this enterprise by the Emigrant Aid Society formed in Massachusetts, which put forth some exertions in this laudable object, by open and public measures, in providing facilities for transportation to all peaceable citizens who desired to become permanent settlers in said territory, and providing therein hotels, mills, etc., for the public accomodation of that new country.

The governor of Kansas, having, in pursuance of law, divided the territory into districts, and procured a census thereof, issued his proclamation for the election of a legislative assembly therein, to take place on the 30th day of March, 1855, and directed how the same should be conducted, and the returns made to him agreeable to the law establishing said territory. On the day of election, large bodies of armed men from the state of Missouri appeared at the polls in most of the districts, and by most violent and tumultuous carriage and demeanor overawed the defenseless inhabitants, and by their own votes elected a large majority of the members of both houses of said assembly. On the returns of said election being made to the governor, protests and objections were made to him in relation to a part of said districts; and, as to them, he set aside such, and such only, as by the returns appeared to be bad. In relation to others, covering, in all, a majority of the two houses, equally vicious in fact, but apparently good by formal returns, the inhabitants thereof, borne down by said violence and intimidation, scattered and discouraged, and laboring under apprehensions of personal violence, refrained and desisted from presenting any protest to the governor in relation thereto; and he, then uninformed in relation thereto, issued certificates to the members who appeared by said formal returns to have been elected.

In relation to those districts which the governor so set aside, orders were by him issued for new elections. In one of these districts the same proceedings were repeated by men from Missouri, and in others not, and certificates were issued to the persons elected.

This legislative assembly, so elected, assembled at Pawnee, on the second day of July, 1855, that being the time and place for holding said meeting, as fixed by the governor, by authority of law. On assembling, the said houses proceeded to set aside and reject those members so elected on said second election, except in the district where the men from Missouri had, at said election, chosen the same persons they had elected at the said first election, and they admitted all of the said first elected members.

A legislative assembly, so created by military force, by a foreign invasion, in violation of the organic law, was but a usurpation. No act of its own, no act or neglect of the governor, could legalize or sanctify it. Its own decisions as to its own legality are like its laws, but the fruits of its own usurpation, which no governor could legitimate.

They passed an act altering the place of the temporary seat of government to the Shawnee Mission, on the border of, and in near proximity to Missouri. This act the governor regarded as a violation of the organic law establishing the territory, which fixed the temporary seat of government, and prohibited the legislative assembly from doing anything inconsistent with said act. He, therefore, and for that cause, vetoed said bill; but said assembly repassed the same by a two-thirds majority, notwithstanding said veto, and removed to said Shawnee Mission. They then proceeded to pass laws, and the governor, in writing, declined further to recognize them as a legitimate assembly, sitting at that place. They continued passing laws there from the 16th day of July to the 31st day of August, 1855.

On the 15th day of August, the governor of said territory was dismissed from office, and the duties devolved upon the secretary of the territory; and, how many of the laws passed with his official approbation does not appear, the laws as now presented being without date or authentication.

As by the law of congress organizing said territory it was expressly provided that the people of the territory were to be "left perfectly free to form and regulate their domestic institutions in their own way," and among these institutions slavery is included, it was, of course, implied that that subject was to be open and free to public and private discussion in all its bearings, rights, and relationships. Among these must, of course, be the question, what was the state of *the existing laws*, and the modifications that might be required on that subject? The law had declared that its "true intent and meaning was not to legislate slavery into the territory, or exclude it therefrom." This would, of course, leave to that people the inquiry, what, then, are the existing rights under the constitution? Can slaves be holden in the absence of any law on the subject? This question, about which so much difference of opinion exists, and which congress and the courts have never settled, was thus turned over to the people there, to discuss and settle for themselves.

This territorial legislature, so created by force from Missouri, utterly refused to permit discussion on the subject; but, assuming that slavery already existed there, and that neither congress nor the people in the territory, under the authority of congress, had or could prohibit it, passed a law which, if enforced, utterly prohibits all *discussion* of the question. The eleventh and twelfth sections of that act are as follows :

" SEC. 11. If any person print, write, introduce into, publish or circulate, or cause to be brought into, printed, written, published or circulated, or shall knowingly aid or assist in bringing into, printing, publishing or circulating within this territory, any book, paper, pamphlet, magazine, hand-bill or circular, containing any statements, arguments, opinions, sentiments, doctrines, advice or inuendo, calculated to promote a disorderly, dangerous or rebellious disaffection among the slaves in this territory, or to induce such slaves to escape from the service of their masters or to resist their authority, he shall be guilty of a felony, and be punished by imprisonment and hard labor for a term not less than five years.

" SEC. 12. If any free person, by speaking or by writing, assert or maintain that persons have not the right to hold slaves in this territory, or shall introduce into this territory, print, publish, write, circulate, or cause to be introduced into this territory, written, printed, published or circulated in this territory, any book, paper, magazine, pamphlet or circular, containing any denial of the right of persons to hold slaves in this territory, such person shall be deemed guilty of felony, and punished by imprisonment at hard labor for a term of not less than two years."

And further providing, that no person " conscientiously opposed to holding slaves " shall sit as a juror in the trial of any cause founded on a breach of the foregoing law. They further provided, that all officers and attorneys should be sworn not only to support the constitution of the United States, but also to support and sustain the organic law of the territory, and the fugitive slave laws; and that any person offering to vote shall be presumed to be entitled to vote until the contrary is shown, and if any one, when required, shall refuse to take oath to sustain the fugitive-slave laws, he shall not be permitted to vote. Although they passed a law that none but an inhabitant, who had paid a tax, should vote, yet they required no *time of residence* necessary, and provided for the immediate payment of a poll-tax; so providing, in effect, that on the eve of an election the people of a neighboring state could come in, in unlimited numbers, and, by taking up a residence of a day or an hour, pay a poll-tax, and thus become legal voters, and then, after voting, return to their own state. They thus, in practical effect, provided for the people of Missouri to control elections at their pleasure, and permitted such only of the real inhabitants of the territory to vote as are friendly to the holding of slaves.

They permitted no election of any of the officers in the territory to be made by the people thereof, but created the offices and filled them, or appointed officers to fill them for long periods, and provided that the next annual election should be holden in October, 1856, and the assembly to meet in January, 1857 ; so that none of these laws could be changed, until the lower house might be changed, in 1856 ; but the council, which is elected for two years, could not be changed so as to allow a change of the laws or officers until the session of 1858, however much the inhabitants of the territory might desire it.

These laws, made by an assembly created by a foreign force, are but a manifestation of the spirit of oppression which was the parent of the whole transaction. No excuse can be found for it in the pretense that the inhabitants had carried with them into said territory a quantity of Sharp's rifles—first, because that, if true, formed no excuse ; secondly, it is untrue, as their Sharp's rifles were only obtained afterwards, and entirely for the purpose of self-defense, the necessity for which, this invasion and other acts of violence and threats clearly demonstrated. These laws were obviously made to oppress and drive out all who were inclined to the exclusion of slavery ; and if they remained, to silence them on this subject, and subject them to the will and control of the people of Missouri. These are the laws which the president says must be enforced by the army and the whole power of the nation. The people of Kansas, thus invaded, subdued, oppressed, and insulted, seeing their territorial government (such only in form) perverted into an engine to crush them in the dust, and to defeat and destroy the professed object of their organic law, by depriving them of the "*perfect freedom*" therein provided, and finding no ground to hope for rights in that organization, they proceeded, under the guaranty of the United States constitution, "peaceably to assemble to petition the government for the redress of (their) grievances." They saw no earthly source of relief but in the formation of a state government by the people, and the acceptance and ratification thereof by congress.

In this view of the subject, in the first part of August, 1855, a call was published in the public papers for a meeting of the citizens of Kansas, irrespective of party, to meet at Lawrence, in said territory, on the 15th of said August, to take into consideration the propriety of calling a convention of the people of the whole territory, to consider that subject. That meeting was held on the 15th day of August last, and it proceeded to call such convention of delegates to be elected and to assemble at Topeka, in said territory, on the 19th day of September, 1855, not to form a constitution, but to consider the propriety of calling, formally, a convention for that purpose.

The meeting was duly held, and resulted in the call for a constitutional convention.

Delegates were elected agreeably to a proclamation issued, and they met at Topeka on the fourth Tuesday in October, 1855, and formed a constitution, which was submitted to the people, and was ratified by them by vote in the districts. An election of state officers and members of the state legislature has been had, and a representative to congress elected, and it is intended to proceed to the election of senators, with the view to present the same, with the constitution, to congress for admission into the Union.

It now becomes proper to inquire what should be done by congress ; for we are informed by the president, in substance, that he has no power to correct a usurpation, and that the laws, even though made by usurped authority, must be by him enforced and executed, even with military force. The measures of redress should be applied to the true cause of the difficulty. This obviously lies in the repeal of the clause for freedom in the act of 1820, and therefore the true remedy lies in the entire repeal of the act of 1854, which effected it. Let this be done with frankness and magnanimity, and Kansas be organized anew, as a free territory, and all will be put right.

Treating this grievance in Kansas with ingenious excuses, with neglect or contempt, or riding over the oppressed with an army, and dragooning them into submission, will make no satisfactory termination. Party success may at times be temporarily secured by adroit devices, plausible pretenses, and partisan address; but the permanent preservation of this Union can be maintained only by frankness and integrity. Justice may be denied where it ought to be granted; power may perpetuate that vassalage which violence and usurpation have produced; the subjugation of white freemen may be necessary, that African slavery may succeed; but such a course must not be expected to produce peace and satisfaction in our country, so long as the people retain any proper sentiment of justice, liberty, and law.

On the 19th of March, the house of representatives passed a resolution providing for a committee of three members of the house, to be sent to Kansas, to inquire into and collect evidence in regard to the troubles in that territory, and to report the same to the house. William A. Howard, of Michigan, John Sherman, of Ohio, and Mordecai Oliver, of Missouri, were appointed the committee of investigation. These gentlemen proceeded to Kansas and spent several weeks in taking testimony, which, when printed, formed a volume of twelve hundred pages. Our limits confine us to such extracts from the report as will furnish a brief history of the events in the territory subsequent to its organization.

EXTRACTS FROM REPORT OF INVESTIGATING COMMITTEE.

Your committee deem it their duty to state, as briefly as possible, the principal facts proven before them. When the act to organize the territory of Kansas was passed on —— day of May, 1854, the greater portion of its eastern border was included in Indian reservations not open for settlement, and there were but few white settlers in any portion of the territory. Its Indian population was rapidly decreasing, while many emigrants from different parts of our country were anxiously waiting the extinction of the Indian title, and the establishment of a territorial government, to seek new homes in its fertile prairies. It cannot be doubted that if its condition as a free territory had been left undisturbed by congress, its settlement would have been rapid, peaceful, and prosperous. Its climate, soil, and its easy access to the older settlements would have made it the favored course for the tide of emigration constantly flowing to the West, and by this time it would have been admitted into the Union as a free state, without the least sectional excitement. If so organized, none but the kindest feelings could have existed between it and the adjoining state. Their mutual interests and intercourse, instead of, as now, endangering the harmony of the Union, would have strengthened the ties of national brotherhood. The testimony clearly shows, that before the proposition to repeal the Missouri compromise was introduced into congress, the people of western Missouri appeared indifferent to the prohibition of slavery in the territory, and neither asked nor desired its repeal.

When, however, the prohibition was removed by the action of congress, the aspect of affairs entirely changed. The whole country was agitated by the reöpening of a controversy which conservative men in different sections hoped had been settled, in every state and territory, by some law beyond the danger of repeal. The excitement which has always accompanied the ,discussion of the slavery question was greatly increased by the hope on the one hand of extending slavery into a region from which it had been excluded by law, and on the other by a sense of wrong done by what was regarded as a dishonor of a national compact. This excitement was naturally transferred into the border counties of Missouri and the territory, as settlers favoring free or slave institutions moved into it. A new difficulty soon occurred. Different constructions were put upon the organic law. It was contended by the one party that the right to hold slaves in the territory existed, and that neither the people nor the territorial legislature could prohibit slavery—that the power was alone possessed by the people when they were authorized to form a state government. It was contended that the removal of the restriction virtually established slavery in the territory. This claim was urged by many prominent men in western Missouri, who actively engaged in the affairs of the territory. Every movement, of whatever character, which tended to establish free institutions, was regarded as an interference with their rights.

Within a few days after the organic law passed, and as soon as its passage could be known on the border, leading citizens of Missouri crossed into the territory, held squatter meetings, and then returned to their homes. Among their resolutions are the following :

"That we will afford protection to no abolitionist as a settler of this territory."
"That we recognize the institution of slavery as already existing in this territory, and advise slaveholders to introduce their property as early as possible."

Similar resolutions were passed in various parts of the territory, and by meetings in several counties of Missouri. Thus the first effect of the repeal of the restriction against slavery was to substitute the resolves of squatter meetings, composed almost exclusively of citizens of a single state, for the deliberate action of congress, acquiesced in for thirty-five years.

This unlawful interference has been continued in every important event in the history of the territory ; *every election* has been controlled not by the actual settlers, but by citizens of Missouri, and as a consequence every officer in the territory, from constables to legislators, except those appointed by the president, owe their positions to non-resident voters. None have been elected by the settlers, and your committee have been unable to find that any political power whatever, however unimportant, has been exercised by the people of the territory.

In October, A. D. 1854, Gov. A. H. Reeder and the other officers appointed by the president, arrived in the territory. Settlers from all parts of the country were moving in in great numbers, making their claims and building their cabins. About the same time, and before any election was or could be held in the territory, a secret political society was formed in the state of Missouri. It was known by different names, such as "Social Band," "Friends' Society," "Blue Lodge," "The Sons of the South." Its members were bound together by secret oaths, and they had passwords, signs, and grips, by which they were known to each other. Penalties were imposed for violating the rules and secrets of the order. Written minutes were kept of the proceedings of the lodges, and the different lodges were connected together by an effective organization. It embraced great numbers of the citizens of Missouri, and was extended into other slave states and into the territory. Its avowed purpose was not only to extend slavery into Kansas, but also into other territory of the United States, and to form a union of all the friends of that institution. Its plan of operating was to organize and send men to vote at the elections in the territory, to collect money to pay their expenses, and, if necessary, to protect them in voting. It also proposed to induce pro-slavery men to emigrate into the territory, to aid and sustain them while there, and to elect none to office but those friendly to their views. This dangerous society was controlled by men who avowed their purpose to extend slavery into the territory at all hazards, and was altogether the most effective instrument in organizing the subsequent armed invasions and forays. In its lodges in Missouri the affairs of Kansas were discussed, the force necessary to control the election was divided into bands, and leaders selected, means were collected, and signs and badges were agreed upon.

The first election was for a delegate to congress. It was appointed for the 29th of November, 1854. The governor divided the territory into seventeen election districts; appointed judges and prescribed proper rules for the election. In the Ist, IIId, VIIIth, IXth, Xth, XIIth, XIIIth, and XVIIth districts, there appears to have been but little if any fraudulent voting.

The election in the IId district was held at the village of Douglas, nearly fifty miles from the Missouri line. On the day before the election, large companies of men came into the district in wagons and on horseback, and declared that they were from the state of Missouri, and were going to Douglas to vote. On the morning of the election they gathered around the house where the election was to be held. Two of the judges appointed by the governor did not appear, and other judges were elected by the crowd. All then voted. In order to make a pretense of right to vote, some persons of the company kept a pretended register of squatter claims, on which any one could enter his name and then assert he had a claim in the territory. A citizen of the district who was himself a candidate for delegate to congress, was told by one of the strangers that he would be abused and probably killed if he challenged a vote. He was seized by the collar, called a d——d abolitionist, and was compelled to seek protection in the room with the judges. About the time the polls were closed, these strangers mounted their horses and got into their wagons and cried out— "All aboard for Westport and Kansas City." A number were recognized as residents of Missouri, and among them was Samuel H. Woodson, a leading lawyer of Independence. Of those whose names are on the poll-books, 35 were resident settlers and 226 were non-residents.

The election in the IVth district was held at Dr. Chapman's, over 40 miles from the Missouri state line. It was a thinly-settled region, containing but 47 votes in February, 1855, when the census was taken. On the day before the election, from 100 to 150 citizens of Cass and Jackson counties, Mo., came into the district, declaring their purpose to vote, and that they were bound to make Kansas a slave state, if they did it at the point of the sword. Persons of the party on the way drove each a stake in the ground and called it a claim—and in one case several names were put on one stake. The party of strangers camped all night near where the election was to be held, and in the morning were at the election-polls and voted. One of their party got drunk, and to get rid of Dr. Chapman, a judge of the election, they sent for him to come and see a sick man, and in his absence filled his place with another judge, who was not sworn. They did not deny or conceal that they were residents of Missouri, and many of them were recognized as such by others. They declared that they were bound to make Kansas a slave state. They insisted upon their right to vote in the territory if they were in it one hour. After the election, they again returned to their homes in Missouri, camping over night on the way.

We find upon the poll-books 161 names; of these not over 30 resided in the territory; 131 were non-residents.

But few settlers attended the election in the Vth district, the district being large and the settlement scattered. 82 votes were cast; of these between 20 and 30 were settlers, and the residue were citizens of Missouri. They passed into the territory by way of the Santa Fe road and by the residence of Dr. Westfall, who then lived on the western line of Missouri. Some little excitement arose at the polls as to the legality of their voting, but they did vote for General Whitfield, and said they intended to make Kansas a slave state—and that they had claims in the territory. Judge Teazle, judge of the court in Jackson county, Missouri, was present, but did not vote. He said he did not intend to vote, but came to see that others voted After the election, the Missourians returned the way they came.

The election in the VIth district was held at Fort Scott, in the southeast part of the territory and near the Missouri line. A party of about one hundred men, from Cass and the counties in Missouri south of it, went into the territory, traveling about 45 miles, most of them with their wagons and tents, and camping out. They appeared at the place of election. Some attempts were made to swear them, but two of the judges were prevailed upon not to do so, and none were sworn, and as many as chose voted. There were but few resident voters at the polls. The settlement was sparse—about 25 actual settlers voted out of 105 votes cast, leaving 80 illegal votes. After the voting was over the Missourians went to their wagons and commenced leaving for home. The most shameless fraud practiced upon the rights of the settlers at this election was in the VIIth district. It is a remote settlement, about 75 miles from the Missouri line, and contained in February, A. D. 1855, three months afterwards, when the census was taken, about 53 voters; and yet the poll-books show that 604 votes were cast. The election was held at the house of Frey McGee, at a place called "110." But few of the actual settlers were present at the polls. A witness who formerly resided in Jackson county, Missouri, and was well acquainted with the citizens of that county, says that he saw a great many wagons and tents at the place of election, and many individuals he knew from Jackson county. He was in their tents and conversed with some of them, and they told him they had come with the intention of voting. He went to the polls intending to vote for Flennekin, and his ticket being of a different color from the rest, his vote was challenged by Frey McGee, who had been appointed one of the judges but did not serve. Lemuel Ralstone, a citizen of Missouri, was acting in his place. The witness then challenged the vote of a young man by the name of Nolan, whom he knew to reside in Jackson county. Finally the thing was hushed up, as the witness had a good many friends there from that county, and it might lead to a fight if he challenged any more votes. Both voted, and then went down to their camp. He there saw many of his old acquaintances whom he knew had voted at the election in August previous in Missouri, and who still resided in that state. By a careful comparison of the poll-lists with the census-rolls, we find but 12 names on the poll-book who were voters when the census was taken three months afterwards, and we are satisfied that not more than 20 legal votes could have been polled at that election. The only residents who are known to have voted are named by the witness, and are 13 in number—thus leaving 584 illegal votes cast in a remote district, where the settlers within many miles were acquainted with each other.

The total number of white inhabitants in the XIth district in the month of February, A. D. 1855, including men, women, and children, was 36, of whom 24 were voters—yet the poll-lists in this district show that 245 votes were cast at this election. For reasons stated hereafter in regard to the election on the 30th of March, your committee were unable to procure the attendance of witnesses from this district. From the records, it clearly appears that the votes cast could not have been by lawful resident voters. The best test, in the absence of direct proof, by which to ascertain the number of legal votes cast, is by a comparison of the census-roll with the poll-book—by which it appears that but 7 resident settlers voted, and 238 votes were illegally and fraudulently given.

The election in the XIVth district was held at the house of Benjamin Harding, a few miles from the town of St. Joseph, Missouri. Before the polls were opened, a large number of citizens of Buchanan county, Missouri, and among them many of the leading citizens of St. Joseph, were at the place of voting, and made a majority of the company present. At the time appointed by the governor for opening the polls, two of the judges were not there, and it became the duty of the legal voters present to select other judges. The judge who was present suggested the name of Mr. Waterson as one of the judges, but the crowd voted down the proposition. Some discussion then arose as to the right of non-residents to vote for judges, during which Mr. Bryant was nominated and elected by the crowd. Some one nominated Colonel John Scott as the other judge, who was then and is now a resident of St. Joseph. At that time he was the city attorney of that place, and so continued until this spring, but he claimed that the night before he had come to the house of Mr. Bryant, and had engaged boarding for a month, and considered himself a resident of Kansas on that ground. The judges appointed by the governor refused to put the nomination of Colonel Scott to vote, because he was not a resident. After some discussion, Judge Leonard, a citizen of Missouri, stepped forward and put the vote himself; and Mr. Scott was declared by him as elected by the crowd, and served as a judge of election that day. After the election was over he returned to St. Joseph, and never since has *resided* in the territory. It is manifest that this election of a non-resident lawyer as a judge was imposed upon the settlers by the citizens of the state. When the board of judges was thus completed, the voting proceeded, but the effect of the rule adopted by the judges allowed many, if not a majority, of the non-residents to vote. They claimed that their presence on the ground, especially when they had a *claim* in the territory, gave them a right to vote—under that construction of the law they readily, when required, swore they were "residents" and then voted. By this evasion, as near as your committee can ascertain from the testimony, as many as 50 illegal votes were cast in this district out of 153, the whole number polled.

The election in the XVth district was held at Penseman's, on Stranger Creek, a few miles from Weston, Missouri. On the day of the election a large number of citizens of Platte county, but chiefly from Weston and Platte city, came in small parties, in wagons and on horseback, to the polls. Among them were several leading citizens of that town, and the names of many of them are given by the witnesses. They generally insisted upon their right to vote, on the ground that every man having a claim in the territory could vote, no matter where he lived. All voted who chose. No man was challenged or sworn. Some of the residents did not vote. The purpose of the strangers voting was declared to be to make Kansas a slave state. We find by the poll-books that 306 votes were cast—of these we find but 57 are on the census-rolls as legal voters in February following. Your committee is satisfied from the testimony that not over 100 of those who voted had any right so to do, leaving at least 206 illegal votes cast.

The election in the XVIth district was held at Leavenworth. It was then a small village of three or four houses, located on the Delaware Reservation. There were but comparatively few settlers then in the district, but the number rapidly increased afterward. On the day before and on the day of election, a great many citizens of Platte, Clay, and Ray counties crossed the river—most

of them camping in tents and wagons about the town, "like a camp-meeting."
They were in companies or messes of ten to fifteen in each, and numbered in
all several hundred. They brought their own provisions and cooked it themselves, and were generally armed. Many of them were known by the witnesses,
and their names given, and their names are found upon the poll-books. Among
them were several persons of influence where they resided in Missouri, who
held, or had held, high official positions in that state. They claimed to be
residents of the territory, from the fact that they were then present and insisted
upon the right to vote, and did vote. Their avowed purpose in doing so was
to make Kansas a slave state. These strangers crowded around the polls, and
it was with great difficulty that the settlers could get to the polls. One resident attempted to get to the polls in the afternoon, but was crowded out and
pulled back. He then went outside of the crowd and hurrahed for General
Whitfield, and some of those who did not know him said, "that's a good pro-
slavery man," and lifted him up over their heads so that he crawled on their
heads and put in his vote. A person who saw from the color of his ticket
that it was not for General Whitfield, cried out, "He is a damned abolitionist—let him down;" and they dropped him. Others were passed to the polls
in the same way, and others crowded up the best way they could. After this
mockery of an election was over, the non-residents returned to their homes in
Missouri. Of the 312 votes cast, not over 150 were by legal voters.

Thus your committee find that in this the first election in the territory, a
very large majority of votes were cast by citizens of the state of Missouri, in
violation of the organic law of the territory.

In January and February, 1855, the governor caused an enumeration to be
taken of the inhabitants and qualified voters in the territory. There were
2,905 voters; 8,501 inhabitants.

On the day the census was completed, the governor issued his proclamation
for an election to be held on the 30th of March, A. D. 1855, for members of the
legislative assembly of the territory. By an organized movement in Missouri,
which extended from Andrew county on the north to Jasper county in the
south, and as far eastward as Boone and Cole counties, companies of men were
arranged in regular parties and sent *into every council district in the territory, and into every representative district* but one. The numbers were so
distributed as to control the election in each district. They went to vote, and
with the avowed design to make Kansas a slave state. They were generally
armed and equipped, carried with them their own provisions and tents, and so
marched into the territory. The details of this invasion, from the mass of the
testimony taken by your committee, are so voluminous that we can here state
but the leading facts elicited. If the governor's proclamation had been observed, a just and fair election would have resulted.

The company of persons who marched into Lawrence district, collected in
Ray, Howard, Carroll, Boone, La Fayette, Randolph, Saline, and Cass counties, in the state of Missouri. Their expenses were paid—those who could

not come contributing provisions, wagons, etc. Provisions were deposited for those who were expected to come to Lawrence, in the house of William Lykins, and were distributed among the Missourians after they arrived there. The evening before and the morning of the day of election, about 1,000 men from the above counties arrived at Lawrence, and encamped in a ravine a short distance from town, near the place of voting. They came in wagons—of which there were over one hundred—and on horseback, under the command of Col. Samuel Young, of Boone county, Missouri, and Claibourne F. Jackson, of Missouri. They were armed with guns, rifles, pistols, and bowie-knives, and had tents, music, and flags with them. They brought with them two pieces of artillery loaded with musket-balls. On their way to Lawrence, some of them met Mr. N. B. Blanton, who had been appointed one of the judges of election by Gov. Reeder, and after learning from him that he considered it his duty to demand an oath from them as to their place of residence, first attempted to bribe, and then threatened him with hanging, in order to induce him to dispense with that oath. In consequence of these threats, he did not appear at the polls the next morning to act as judge.

The evening before the election, while in camp, the Missourians were called together at the tent of Captain Claibourne F. Jackson, and speeches were made to them by Col. Young and others, calling for volunteers to go to other districts where there were not Missourians enough to control the election, and there were more at Lawrence than were needed there. Many volunteered to go, and the morning of the election, several companies, from 150 to 200 men each, went off to Tecumseh, Hickory Point, Bloomington, and other places. On the morning of the election, the Missourians came over to the place of voting from their camp, in bodies of one hundred at a time. Mr. Blanton not appearing, another judge was appointed in his place—Col. Young claiming that, as the people of the territory had two judges, it was nothing more than right that the Missourians should have the other one, to look after their interests; and Robert E. Cummins was elected in Blanton's stead, because he considered that every man had a right to vote if he had been in the territory but an hour. The Missourians brought their tickets with them; but not having enough, they had three hundred more printed in Lawrence on the evening before and the day of election. They had white ribbons in their button-holes to distinguish themselves from the settlers.

When the voting commenced, the question of the legality of the vote of a Mr. Page was raised. Before it was decided, Col. Samuel Young stepped up to the window where the votes were received, and said he would settle the matter. The vote of Mr. Page was withdrawn, and Col. Young offered to vote. He refused to take the oath prescribed by the governor, but swore he was a resident of the territory, upon which his vote was received. He told Mr. Abbott, one of the judges, when asked if he intended to make Kansas his future home, that it was none of his business; that if he were a resident then, he should ask no more. After his vote was received, Col. Young got up in the window-sill and announced to the crowd that he had been permitted to vote, and they could all come up and vote. He told the judges that there was no use in swearing the others, as they would all swear as he had done. After the other judges concluded to receive Col. Young's vote, Mr. Abbott resigned as judge of election, and Mr. Benjamin was elected in his place.

The polls were so much crowded until late in the evening, that, for a time, when the men had voted, they were obliged to get out by being hoisted up on the roof of the building where the election was being held, and pass out over the house. Afterward a passage-way through the crowd was made by two lines of men being formed, through which the voters could get up to the polls. Col. Young asked that the old men be allowed to go up first and vote, as they were tired with the traveling, and wanted to get back to camp.

The Missourians sometimes came up to the polls in procession, two by two, and voted.

During the day the Missourians drove off the ground some of the citizens, Mr. Stevens, Mr. Bond, and Mr. Willis. They threatened to shoot Mr. Bond, and a crowd rushed after him threatening him, and as he ran from them some shots were fired at him as he jumped off the bank of the river and made his escape. The citizens of the town went over in a body, late in the afternoon, when the polls had become comparatively clear, and voted.

Before the voting had commenced, the Missourians said, if the judges appointed by the governor did not receive their votes, they would choose other judges. Some of them voted several times, changing their hats or coats and coming up to the window again. They said they intended to vote first, and after they had got through, then the others could vote. Some of them claimed a right to vote under the organic act, from the fact that their mere presence in the territory constituted them residents, though they were from Wisconsin, and had homes in Missouri. Others said they had a right to vote, because Kansas belonged to Missouri, and people from the east had no right to settle in the territory and vote there. They said they came to the territory to elect a legislature to suit themselves, as the people of the territory and persons from the east and north wanted to elect a legislature that would not suit them. They said they had a right to make Kansas a slave state, because the people of the north had sent persons out to make it a free state. Some claimed that they had heard that the emigrant aid society had sent men out to be at the election, and they came to offset their votes; but the most of them made no such claim. Col. Young said he wanted the citizens to vote in order to give the election some show of fairness. The Missourians said there would be no difficulty if the citizens did not interfere with their voting, but they were determined to vote—peaceably, if they could, but vote any how. They said each one of them was prepared for eight rounds without loading, and would go the ninth round with the butcher-knife. Some of them said that by voting in the territory, they would deprive themselves of the right to vote in Missouri for twelve months afterward. The Missourians began to leave the afternoon of the day of election, though some did not go home until the next morning. In many cases, when a wagon-load had voted, they immediately started for home. On their way home, they said if Gov. Reeder did not sanction the election, they would hang him.

The citizens of the town of Lawrence, as a general thing were not armed on the day of election, though some had revolvers, but not exposed, as were the arms of the Missourians. They kept a guard about the town, the night after the election, in consequence of the threats of the Missourians, in order to protect it. The pro-slavery men of the district attended the nominating conventions of the free-state men, and voted for, and secured the nominations of, the men they considered the most obnoxious to the free-state party, in order to cause dissension in that party.

Quite a number of settlers came into the district before the day of election, and after the census was taken. According to the census returns, there were then in the district 369 legal voters. Of those whose names are on the census returns, 177 are to be found on the poll-books of the 30th of March, 1855. Messrs. Ladd, Babcock, and Pratt testify to 55 names on the poll books of persons they knew to have settled in the district after the census was taken and before the election. A number of persons came into the territory in March, before the election, from the northern and eastern states, intending to settle, who were in Lawrence on the day of election. At that time, many of them had selected no claims, and had no fixed place of residence. Such were not entitled to vote. Many of them became dissatisfied with the country. Others were disappointed in its political condition, and the price and demand for labor, and returned. Whether any such voted at the election, is not clearly shown, but from the proof, it is probable that in the latter part of the day, after the great body of the Missourians had voted, some did go to the polls. The number was not over fifty. These voted the free-state ticket. The whole number of names appearing on the poll-list is 1034. After full examination, we are satisfied that not over 232 of these were legal voters, and 802 were non-resident and illegal voters. This district is strongly in favor of making Kansas a free state, and there is no doubt but that the free-state candidates would have been elected by large majorities, if none but the actual settlers had voted. At the preceding election in November, 1854, when none but legal votes were polled, general Whitfield, who received the full strength of the pro-slavery party, got but 46 votes.

In Bloomington district, on the morning of the election, the judges appointed by the governor appeared and opened the polls. Their names were Harrison Burson, Nathaniel Ramsay, and Mr. Ellison. The Missourians began to come in early in the morning, some 500 or 600 of them, in wagons and in carriages, and on horseback, under the lead of Samuel J. Jones, then postmaster of Westport, Missouri, Claibourne F. Jackson, and Mr. Steely, of Independence, Missouri. They were armed with double-barreled guns, rifles, bowie-knives and pistols, and had flags hoisted. They held a sort of informal election, off at one side, at first for governor of Kansas, and shortly afterwards announced Thomas Johnson, of Shawnee Missions, elected governor. The polls had been opened but a short time, when Mr. Jones marched with the crowd up to the window and demanded that they should be allowed to vote without swearing as to their residence. After some noisy and threatening talk, Claibourne F. Jackson addressed the crowd, saying they had come there to vote, that they had a right to vote if they had been there but five minutes, and he was not willing to go home without voting; which was received with cheers. Jackson then called upon them to form into little bands of fifteen or twenty, which they did, and went to an ox wagon filled with guns, which were distributed among them, and proceeded to load some of them on the ground. In pursuance of Jackson's request, they tied white tape or ribbon in their buttonholes to distinguish them from the "abolitionists." They again demanded that the judges should resign, and on their refusing to do so, smashed in the window, sash and all, and presented their pistols and guns to them, threatening to shoot them. Some one on the outside cried out to them not to shoot, as there were pro-slavery men in the room with the judges. They then put a pry under the corner of the house, which was a log house, and lifted it up a few inches and let it fall again, but desisted upon being told there were pro-slavery men in the house. During this time the crowd repeatedly demanded to be allowed to vote without being sworn, and Mr. Ellison, one of the judges, expressed himself willing, but the other two judges refused; thereupon a body of men, headed by "Sheriff Jones," rushed into the judges' room with cocked pistols and drawn bowie-knives in their hands, and approached Burson and Ramsay. Jones pulled out his watch, and said he would give them five minutes to resign in, or die. When the five minutes had expired and the judges *did not* resign, Jones said he would give them another minute, and no more. Ellison told his associates that if they did not resign, there would be one hundred shots fired in the room in less than fifteen minutes; and then snatching up the ballot-box, ran out into the crowd, holding up the ballot-box and hurrahing for Missouri. About that time Burson and Ramsay were called out by their friends, and not suffered to return. As Mr. Burson went out, he put the ballot poll-books in his pocket, and took them with him; and as he was going out, Jones snatched some papers away from him, and shortly afterward came out himself holding them up, crying "hurrah for Missouri." After he discovered they were not the poll-books, he took a party of men with him and started off to take the poll-books from Burson. Mr. Burson saw them coming, and he gave the books to Mr. Umberger, and told him to start off in another direction, so as to mislead Jones and his party. Jones and his party caught Mr. Umberger, took the poll-books away from him, and Jones took him up behind him on a horse, and carried him back a prisoner. After Jones and his party had taken Umberger back, they went to the house of Mr. Ramsay and took judge John A. Wakefield prisoner, and carried him to the place of election, and made him get up on a wagon and make them a speech; after which they put a white ribbon in his button-hole and let him go. They then chose two new judges, and proceeded with the election.

They also threatened to kill the judges if they did not receive their votes without swearing them, or else resign. They said no man should vote who would submit to be sworn—that they would kill any one who would offer to do so—"shoot him," "cut his guts out," etc. They said no man should vote this day unless he voted an open ticket, and was "all right on the goose," and that if they could not vote by fair means, they would by foul means. They said they had as much right to vote, if they had been in the territory two minutes, as if they had been there for two years, and they would vote. Some of the citizens who were about the window, but had not voted when the crowd of Missourians marched up there, upon attempting to vote, were driven back by the mob, or driven off. One of them, Mr. J. M. Marcy, was asked if he would take the oath, and upon his replying that he would if the judges required it, he was dragged through the crowd away from the polls, amid cries of "kill the d—d nigger thief," "cut his throat," "tear his heart out," etc. After they got him to the outside of the crowd, they stood around him with cocked pistols and drawn bowie-knives, one man putting a knife to his heart, so that it touched him, another holding a cocked pistol to his ear, while another struck at him with a club. The Missourians said they had a right to vote if they had been in the territory but five minutes. Some said they had been hired to come there and vote, and get a dollar a day, and by G—d, they would vote or die there.

They said the 30th of March was an important day, as Kansas would be made a slave state on that day. They began to leave in the direction of Missouri in the afternoon, after they had voted, leaving some thirty or forty around the house where the election was held, to guard the polls until after the election was over. The citizens of the territory were not around, except those who took part in the mob, and a large portion of them did not vote; 341 votes were polled there that day, of which but some thirty were citizens. A protest against the election was made to the governor. The returns of the election made to the governor were lost by the committee of elections of the legislature at Pawnee. The duplicate returns left in the ballot-box were taken by F. E. Laley, one of the judges elected by the Missourians, and were either lost or destroyed in his house, so that your committee have been unable to institute a comparison between the poll-lists and census returns of this district. The testimony, however, is uniform, that not over thirty of those who voted there that day were entitled to vote, leaving 311 illegal votes. We are satisfied from the testimony that had the actual settlers alone voted, the free-state candidates would have been elected by handsome majorities.

On the 28th of March, persons from Clay, Jackson and Howard counties, Missouri, began to come into Tecumseh district, in wagons, carriages, and on horseback, armed with guns, bowie-knives and revolvers; and with threats, encamped close by the town, and continued coming until the day of election. The night before the election 200 men were sent for from the camp of Missourians at Lawrence. On the morning of the election, before the polls were opened, some 300 or 400 Missourians and others were collected in the yard about the house of Thomas Stinson, where the election was to be held, armed with bowie-knives, revolvers and clubs. They said they came to vote, and whip the d——d Yankees, and would vote without being sworn. Some said they came to have a fight and wanted one. Colonel Samuel H. Woodson, of Independence, Missouri, was in the room of the judges when they arrived, preparing poll-books and tally-lists, and remained there during their attempts to organize. The room of the judges was also filled by many of the strangers. The judges could not agree concerning the oath to be taken by themselves, and the oath to be administered to the voters, Mr. Burgess wishing to administer the oath prescribed by the governor and the other two judges opposing it. During this discussion between the judges, which lasted some time, the crowd outside became excited and noisy, threatening and cursing Mr. Burgess, the free-state judge. Persons were sent, at different times, by the crowd outside, into the room where the judges were, with threatening messages, especially against Mr. Burgess, and at last ten minutes were given them to organize in or leave; and as the time passed, persons outside would call out the number of minutes left, with threats against Burgess, if he did not agree to organize. At the end of that time, the judges not being able to organize, left the room and the crowd proceeded to elect nine judges and carry on the election. The free-state men generally left the ground without voting, stating that there was no use in their voting there. The polls were so crowded during the first part of the day that the citizens could not get up to the window to vote. Threats were made against the free-state men. In the afternoon the reverend Mr. Gispatrick was attacked and driven off by the mob. A man, by some called "Texas," made a speech to the crowd, urging them to vote and to stay on the ground till the polls were closed, for fear the abolitionists would come there in the afternoon and overpower them, and thus they would loose all their trouble.

For some days prior to the election, companies of men were organized in Jackson, Cass, and Clay counties, Mo., for the purpose of coming to the territory and voting in the Vth district. The day previous to the election, some 400 or 500 Missourians, armed with guns, pistols, and knives, came into the territory and camped, some at Bull Creek, and others at Potawatamie Creek. Their camps were about sixteen miles apart. On the evening before the election, Judge Hamilton, of the Cass county court, Mo., came from the Potawatamie Creek camp to Bull Creek for sixty more Missourians, as they had not enough there to render the election certain, and about that number went down there with him. On the evening before the election, Dr. B. C. Westfall was elected to act as one of the judges of election in the Bull Creek precinct, in place of one of the judges appointed by the governor, who, it was said, would not be there the next day. Dr. Westfall was at that time a citizen of Jackson county, Mo. On the morning of the election, the polls for Bull Creek precinct were opened, and, without swearing the judges, they proceeded to receive the votes of all who offered to vote. For the sake of appearance, they would get some one to come to the window and offer to vote, and when asked to be sworn, he would pretend to grow angry at the judges, and would go away, and his name would be put down as having offered to vote, but "rejected, refusing to be sworn." This arrangement was made previously, and per-

44

fectly understood by the judges. But few of the residents of the district were present at the election, and only thirteen voted. The number of votes cast in the precinct was 393.

One Missourian voted for himself and then voted for his little son, but 10 or 11 years old. Col. Coffer, Henry Younger, and Mr. Lykins, who were voted for and elected to the legislature, were residents of Missouri at the time. Col. Coffer subsequently married in the territory. After the polls were closed, the returns were made, and a man, claiming to be a magistrate, certified on them that he had sworn the judges of election before opening the polls. In the Potawatamie precinct, the Missourians attended the election, and after threatening Mr. Chesnut, the only judge present appointed by the governor, to induce him to resign, they proceeded to elect two other judges—one a Missourian and the other a resident of another precinct of that district. The polls were then opened, and all the Missourians were allowed to vote without being sworn.

After the polls were closed, and the returns made out for the signature of the judges, Mr. Chesnut refused to sign them, as he did not consider them correct returns of legal voters.

Col. Coffer, a resident of Missouri, but elected to the Kansas legislature from that district at that election, endeavored with others to induce Mr. Chesnut by threats to sign the returns, which he refused to do, and left the house. On his way home, he was fired at by some Missourians, though not injured. There were three illegal to one legal vote given there that day. At the Big Layer precinct, the judges appointed by the governor met at the time appointed, and proceeded to open the polls, after being duly sworn. After a few votes had been received, a party of Missourians came into the yard of the house where the election was held, and, unloading a wagon filled with arms, stacked their guns in the yard, and came up to the window and demanded to be admitted to vote. Two of the judges decided to receive their votes, whereupon the third judge, Mr. J. M. Arthur, resigned, and another was chosen in his place. Col. Young, a citizen of Missouri, but a candidate for, and elected to, the territorial legislative council, was present and voted in the precinct. He claimed that all Missourians who were present on the day of election were entitled to vote. But thirty or forty of the citizens of the precinct were present, and many of them did not vote. At the Little Sugar precinct, the election seemed to have been conducted fairly, and there a free state majority was polled. From the testimony, the whole district appears to have been largely free state, and had none but actual settlers voted, the free state candidates would have been elected by a large majority. From a careful examination of the testimony and the records, we find that from 200 to 225 legal votes were polled out of 885, the total number given in the precincts of the Vth district. Of the legal votes cast, the free state candidates received 152.

A company of citizens from Missouri, mostly from Bates county, came into the VIth district the day before the election, some camping and others putting up at the public house. They numbered from 100 to 200, and came in wagons and on horseback, carrying their provisions and tents with them, and were generally armed with pistols. They declared their purpose to vote, and claimed the right to do so. They went to the polls generally in small bodies, with tickets in their hands, and many, if not all, voted. In some cases, they declared that they had voted, and gave their reasons for so doing. Mr. Anderson, a pro-slavery candidate for the legislature, endeavored to dissuade the non-residents from voting, because he did not wish the election contested. This person, however, insisted upon voting, and upon his right to vote, and did so. No one was challenged or sworn, and all voted who desired to. Out of 350 votes cast, not over 100 were legal, and but 64 of these named in the census taken one month before by Mr. Barber, the candidate for council, voted. Many of the free state men did not vote, but your committee is satisfied that, of the legal votes cast, the pro-slavery candidates received a majority. Mr. Anderson, one of these candidates, was an unmarried man, who came into the district from Missouri a few days before the election, and boarded at the public house until the day after the election. He then took with him the poll-lists, and did not return to Fort Scott until the occasion of a barbecue the week before the election of October 1, 1855. He voted at that election, and after it, left, and has not since been in the district. S. A. Williams, the other pro-slavery candidate, at the time of the election had a claim in the territory, but his legal residence was not there until after the election.

From two to three hundred men, from the state of Missouri, came in wagons or on horseback to the election ground at Switzer's Creek, in the VIIth district, and encamped near the polls, on the day preceding the election. They were armed with pistols and other weapons, and declared their purpose to vote, in order to secure the election of pro-slavery members. They said they were disappointed in not finding more Yankees there, and that they had brought more men than were necessary to counterbalance their vote. A number of them wore badges of blue ribbon, with a motto, and the company were under the direction of leaders. They declared their intention to conduct themselves peacefully, unless the residents of the territory attempted to stop them from voting. Two of the judges of election appointed by Gov. Reeder refused to serve, whereupon two others were appointed in their stead by the crowd of Missourians who surrounded the polls. The newly-appointed judges refused to take the oath prescribed by Gov. Reeder, but made one to suit themselves.

The election in the XIIth district was conducted fairly. No complaint was made that illegal votes were cast.

Previous to the day of election, several hundreds of Missourians from Platte, Clay, Boone, Clinton, and Howard counties, came into the XIIIth district in wagons and on horseback, and camped there. They were armed with guns, revolvers, and bowie-knives, and had badges of hemp in their button-holes and elsewhere about their persons. They claimed to have a right to vote, from the fact that they were there on the ground, and had, or intended to make, claims in the territory, although their families were in Missouri.

The judges appointed by the governor opened the polls, and some persons offered to vote, and when their votes were rejected on the ground that they were not residents of the district, the crowd threatened to tear the house down if the judges did not leave. The judges then withdrew, taking the poll-books with them. The crowd then proceeded to select other persons to act as judges, and the election went on. Those persons voting who were sworn were asked if they considered themselves residents of the district, and if they said they did, they were allowed to vote. But few of the residents were present and voted, and the free state men, as a general thing, did not vote.

Several hundred Missourians from Buchanan, Platte, and Andrew counties, Mo., including a great many of the prominent citizens of St. Joseph, came into the XIVth district the day before and on the day of election, in wagons and on horseback, and encamped there. Arrangements were made for them to cross the ferry at St. Joseph free of expense to themselves. They were armed with bowie-knives and pistols, guns and rifles. On the morning of the election, the free state candidates resigned in a body, on account of the presence of the large number of armed Missourians, at which the crowd cheered and hurrahed. Gen. B. F. Stringfellow was present, and was prominent in promoting the election of the pro-slavery ticket, as was also the Hon. Willard P. Hall, and others of the most prominent citizens of St. Joseph, Mo. But one of the judges of election, appointed by the governor, served on that day, and the crowd chose two others to supply the vacancies.

The evening before the election, some two hundred or more Missourians from Platte, Buchanan, Saline, and Clay counties, Mo., came into the Doniphan precinct, with tents, music, wagons, and provisions, and armed with guns, rifles, pistols, and bowie-knives, and encamped about two miles from the place of voting. They said they came to vote, to make Kansas a slave state, and intended to return to Missouri after they had voted.

On the morning of the election, the judges appointed by the governor would not serve, and others were appointed by the crowd. The Missourians were allowed to vote without being sworn—some of them voting as many as eight or nine times; changing their hats and coats, and giving in different names each time. After they had voted, they returned to Missouri. The free state men generally did not vote, though constituting a majority in the precinct. Upon counting the ballots in the box and the names on the poll-lists, it was found that there were too many ballots, and one of the judges of election took out ballots enough to make the two numbers correspond.

The election in the XVth district was held in the house of a Mr. Hayes. On the day of election, a crowd of from 400 to 500 men collected around the polls, of which the great body were citizens of Missouri. One of the judges of election, in his testimony, states that the strangers commenced crowding around the polls, and that then the residents left. Threats were made before and during the election day that there should be no free state candidates, although there were nearly or quite as many free state as pro-slavery men resident in the district. Most of the crowd were drinking and carousing, cursing

the abolitionists and threatening the only free state judge of election.   A majority of those who voted wore hemp in their button-holes, and their pass-
word was, "all right on the hemp."   Many of the Missourians were known,
and are named by the witnesses.   Several speeches were made by them at the
polls, and among those who spoke were Major Oliver, one of your committee,
Col. Burns, and Lalan Williams, of Platte county.   Major Oliver urged upon
all present to use no harsh words, and expressed the hope that nothing would
be said or done to harm the feelings of the most sensitive on the other side.
He gave some grounds, based on the Missouri compromise, in regard to the
right of voting, and was understood to excuse the Missourians for voting.
Your committee are satisfied that he did not vote.   Col. Burns recommended
all to vote, and he hoped none would go home without voting.   Some of the
pro-slavery residents were much dissatisfied at the interference with their rights
by the Missourians, and for that reason—because reflection convinced them that
it would be better to have Kansas a free state—they "fell over the fence."
The judge requested the voters to take an oath that they were actual residents.
They objected at first, some saying they had a claim, or "I am here."   But
the free state judge insisted upon the oath, and his associates, who at first were
disposed to waive it, coincided with him, and the voters all took it after some
grumbling.   One said he cut him some poles and laid them in the shape of a
square, and that made him a claim ; and another said that he had cut him a
few sticks of wood, and that made him a claim.

For some time previous to the election, meetings were held and arrangements made in Missouri to get up companies to come over to the territory and
vote, and the day before and on the day of election, large bodies of Missourians from Platte, Clay, Ray, Charlton, Carrol, Clinton, and Saline counties,
Missouri, came into the XVIth district and camped there.   They were armed with
pistols and bowie-knives, and sum with guns and rifles, and had badges of
hemp in their button-holes and elsewhere about their persons.

On the morning of the election there were from 1,000 to 1,400 persons
present on the ground.   Previous to the election, the Missourians endeavored
to persuade the free state judges to resign by making threats of personal violence to them, one of whom resigned on the morning of election, and the
crowd chose another to fill his place.   But one of the judges, the free state
judge, would take the oath prescribed by the governor, the other two deciding
that they had no right to swear any one who offered to vote, but that all on
the ground were entitled to vote.   The only votes refused were some Delaware
Indians, some 30 Wyandot Indians being allowed to vote.

One of the free state candidates withdrew in consequence of the presence of
the Missourians, amid cheering and acclamations by the Missourians.   During
the day, the steamboat New Lucy came down from Western Missouri, with a
large number of Missourians on board, who voted and then returned on the
boat.

The Missourians gave as a reason for their coming over to vote, that the
north had tried to force emigration into the territory, and they wanted to coun-

teract that movement. Some of the candidates and many of the Missourians took the ground that, under the Kansas-Nebraska act, all who were on the ground on the day of election were entitled to vote, and others, that laying out a town, staking a lot, or driving down stakes, even on another man's claim, gave them a right to vote. And one of the members of the council, R. R. Rees, declared in his testimony that he who should put a different construction upon the law must be either a knave or a fool.

The free state men generally did not vote at that election; and no newly arrived eastern emigrants were there. The free state judge of election refused to sign the returns until the words "by lawful resident voters" were stricken out, which was done, and the returns made in that way. The election was contested, and a new election ordered by Governor Reeder for the 22d of May.

The testimony is divided as to the relative strength of parties in this district. The whole number of voters in the district, according to the census returns, was 385; and according to a very carefully prepared list of voters, prepared for the pro-slavery candidates and other pro-slavery men, a few days previous to the election, there were 305 voters in the district, including those who had claims but did not live on them. The whole number of votes cast was 964. Of those named in the census, 106 voted. Your committee, upon careful examination, are satisfied that there were not over 150 legal votes cast, leaving 814 illegal votes.

The election in the XVIIth district seems to have been fairly conducted, and not contested at all. In this district the pro-slavery party had the majority.

Previous to the election, Gen. David R. Atchison, of Platte City, Mo., got up a company of Missourians, and passing through Weston, Mo., went over into the territory. He remained all night, and then exhibited his arms, of which he had an abundance. He proceeded to the Nemohaer (XVIIIth) district. On his way, he and his party attended a nominating convention in the XIVth district, and proposed and caused to be nominated a set of candidates in opposition to the wishes of the pro-slavery residents of the district. At that convention he said that there were 1,100 men coming over from Platte county, and if that wasn't enough they could send 5,000 more—that they came to vote, and would vote or kill every G—d d—d abolitionist in the territory.

On the day of election, the Missourians under Atchison, who were encamped there, came up to the polls in the XVIIIth district, taking the oath that they were residents of the district. The Missourians were all armed with pistols or bowie-knives, and said there were 60 in their company. But 17 votes given on that day were given by residents of the district. The whole number of votes was 62.

Your committee report the following facts not shown by the tables: Of the twenty-nine hundred and five voters named in the census-rolls, eight hundred and thirty-one are found on the poll-books. Some of the settlers were prevented from attending the election by the distance of their homes from the polls; but the great majority were deterred by the open avowal that large bodies of armed Missourians would be at the polls to vote, and by the fact that they did so appear and control the election. The same causes deterred the free state settlers from running candidates in several districts, and in others induced the candidates to withdraw.

The poll-books of the IId and VIIIth districts were lost; but the proof is quite clear that, in the IId district, there were thirty, and in the VIIIth distrrict thirty-eight legal votes, making a total of eight hundred and ninety-eight legal voters of the territory, whose names are on the census returns; and yet the proof, in the state in which we are obliged to present it, after excluding illegal votes, leaves the total vote of 1,310, showing a discrepancy of 412. The discrepancy is accounted for in two ways: first, the coming in of settlers before the March election, and after the census was taken, or settlers who were omitted in the census; or secondly, the disturbed state of the territory while we were investigating the elections in some of the districts, thereby preventing us from getting testimony in relation to the names of legal voters at the time of election.

If the election had been confined to the actual settlers, undeterred by the presence of non-residents, or the knowledge that they would be present in numbers sufficient to out-vote them, the testimony indicates that the council would have been composed of seven in favor of making Kansas a free state, elected from the Ist, IId, IIId, IVth, and VIth council districts. The result in the VIIIth and Xth, electing three members, would have been doubtful, and the Vth, VIIth, and IXth would have elected three pro-slavery members.

Under like circumstances, the house of representatives would have been composed of fourteen members in favor of making Kansas a free state, elected from the IId IIId, IVth, Vth, VIIth, VIIIth, IXth, and Xth representative districts.

The result in the XIIth and XIVth representative districts, electing five members, would have been doubtful, and the Ist, VIth, XIth, and XVth districts would have elected seven pro-slavery members.

By the election, as conducted, the pro-slavery candidates in every district but the VIIIth representative district, received a majority of the votes; and several of them, in both the council and the house, did not "reside in," and were not "inhabitants of" the district for which they were elected, as required by the organic law. By that act it was declared to be the true intent and meaning of this act to leave the people thereof perfectly free to form and regulate their domestic institutions in their own way, subject to the constitution of the United States.

So careful was congress of the right of popular sovereignty, that to secure it to the people, without a single petition from any portion of the country, they removed the restriction against slavery imposed by the Missouri compromise. And yet this right, so carefully secured, was thus by force and fraud overthrown by a portion of the people of an adjoining state.

The striking difference between this republic and other republics on this continent, is not in the provisions of constitutions and laws, but that here changes in the administration of those laws have been made peacefully and quietly through the ballot-box. This invasion is the first and only one in the history of our government, by which an organized force from one state has elected a legislature for another state or territory, and as such it should have been resisted by the whole executive power of the national government.

Your committee are of the opinion that the constitution and laws of the United States have invested the president and governor of the territory with ample power for this purpose. They could only act after receiving authentic information of the facts, but when received, whether before or after the certificates of election were granted, this power should have been exercised to its fullest extent. It is not to be tolerated that a legislative body thus selected should assume or exercise any legislative functions; and their enactments should be regarded as null and void; nor should the question of its legal existence as a legislative body be determined by itself, as that would be allowing the criminal to judge of his own crime. In section twenty-two of the organic act, it is provided that "the persons having the highest number of legal votes in each of said council districts for members of the council, shall be declared by the governor to be duly elected to the council, and the persons having the highest number of legal votes for the house of representatives, shall be declared by the governor duly elected members of said house." The proclamation of the governor required a verified notice of a contest, when one was made, to be filed with him within four days after the election. Within that time he did not obtain information as to force or fraud in any except the following districts, and in these there were material defects in the returns of election. Without deciding upon his power to set aside elections for force and fraud, they were set aside for the following reasons:

In the Ist district, because the words "by lawful resident voters," were stricken from the returns.

In the IId district, because the oath was administered by G. W. Taylor, who was not authorized to administer an oath.

In the IIId district, because material erasures from the printed form of the oath were purposely made.

In the IVth district, for the same reason.

In the VIIth district, because the judges were not sworn at all.

In the XIth district, because the returns show the election to have been held *viva voce* instead of by ballot.

In the XVIth district, because the words "by lawful residence" were stricken from the returns.

Although the fraud and force in other districts were equally great as in these, yet as the governor had no information in regard to them, he issued certificates according to the returns.

Your committee here felt it to be their duty not only to inquire into and collect evidence in regard to force and fraud attempted and practiced at the elections in the territory, but also into the facts and pretexts by which this force and fraud has been excused and justified; and for this purpose, your committee have allowed the declarations of non-resident voters to be given as evidence in their own behalf; also the declarations of all those who came up the Missouri river as emigrants, in March, 1855, whether they voted or not, and whether they came into the territory at all or not; and also the rumors which were circulated among the people of Missouri previous to the election. The great body of the testimony taken at the instance of the sitting delegate is of this character.

When the declarations of parties passing up the river were offered in evidence, your committee received them upon the distinct statement that they would be excluded unless the persons making the declarations were by other proof shown to have been connected with the elections. This proof was not made, and therefore much of this class of testimony is incompetent by the rules of law, but is allowed to remain as tending to show the cause of the action of the citizens of Missouri.

The alleged causes of the invasion of March, 1855, are included in the following charges :

I. That the New England Aid Society of Boston was then importing into the territory large numbers of men merely for the purpose of controlling the elections. That they came without women, children, or baggage, went into the territory, voted, and returned again.

II. That men were hired in the eastern or northern states, or induced to go into the territory solely to vote, and not to settle, and by so doing to make it a free state.

III. That the governor of the territory purposely postponed the day of election to allow this emigration to arrive, and notified the emigrant aid society, and persons in the eastern states, of the day of election, before he gave notice to the people of Missouri and the territory.

That these charges were industriously circulated; that grossly exaggerated statements were made in regard to them; that the newspaper press and leading men in public meetings in western Missouri, aided in one case by a chaplain of the United States army, gave currency and credit to them, and t us excited the people, and induced many well-meaning citizens of Missouri to march into the territory to meet and repel the alleged eastern paupers and abolitionists, is fully proven by many witnesses.

But these charges are not sustained by the proof.

In April, 1854, the general assembly of Massachusetts passed an act entitled " An act to incorporate the Massachusetts Emigrant Aid Society." The object of the society, as declared in the first section of this act, was "for the purpose of assisting emigrants to settle in the west." The moneyed capital of the corporation was not to exceed five millions of dollars; but no more th n four per cent. could be assessed during the year 1854, and no more than en per cent. in any one year thereafter. No organization was perfected, or proceedings had, under this law.

On the 24th of July, 1854, certain persons in Boston, Massachusetts, concluded articles of agreement and association for an emigrant aid society. The purpose of this association was declared to be "assisting emigrants to settle in the west." Under these articles of association, each stockholder was individually liable. To avoid this difficulty, an application was made to the general assembly of Massachusetts for an act of incorporation, which was granted. On the 21st day of February, 1855, an act was passed to incorporate the New England Emigrant Aid Company. The purposes of this act were declared to be "directing emigration westward, and aiding and providing accommodation for the emigrants after arriving at their place of destination." The capital stock of the corporation was not to exceed one million of dollars. Under this charter a company was organized.

Your committee have examined some of its officers and a portion of its circulars and records to ascertain what has been done by it. The public attention, at that time, was directed to the territory of Kansas, and emigration naturally tended in that direction. To ascertain its character and resources, this company sent its agent into it, and the information thus obtained was published. The company made arrangements with various lines of transportation to reduce the expense of emigration into the territory, and procured tickets at the reduced rates. Applications were made to the company by persons desiring to emigrate, and when they were numerous enough to form a party of convenient size, tickets were sold to them at the reduced rates. An agent acquainted with the route was selected to accompany them. Their baggage was checked, and all trouble and danger of loss to the emigrant in this way avoided.

Under these arrangements, companies went into the territory in the fall of 1854, under the articles of association referred to. The company did not pay any portion of the fare, or furnish any real or personal property to the emigrant. The company during 1855 sent into the territory from eight to ten saw-mills, purchased one hotel in Kansas City, which they subsequently sold, built one hotel at Lawrence, and owned one other building in that place. In some cases, to induce them to make improvements, town lots were given to them by town associations in this territory. They held no property of any other kind or description. They imposed no condition upon their emigrants, and did not inquire into their political, religious, or social opinions. The total amount expended by them, including the salaries of their agents and officers, and the expenses incident to all organizations, was less than $100,000.

Their purposes, as far as your committee can ascertain, were lawful, and contributed to supply those wants most experienced in the settlement of a new country.

The only persons or company who emigrated into the territory under the auspices of the emigrant aid society in 1855, prior to the election in March, was a party of 159 persons, who came under the charge of Charles Robinson.

In this party there were 67 women and children. They came as actual settlers, intending to make their homes in the territory, and for no other purpose. They had about their persons but little baggage; usually sufficient clothing in a carpet-sack for a short time. Their personal effects, such as clothing, furniture, etc., was put into trunks and boxes; and for convenience in selecting and cheapness in transporting, was marked "Kansas party baggage, care B. Slater, St. Louis." Generally this was consigned as freight, in the usual way, to the care of a commission merchant. This party had, in addition to the usual allowance of one hundred pounds to each passenger, a large quantity of baggage, on which the respective owners paid the usual extra freight. Each passenger or party paid his or their own expenses; and the only benefit they derived from the society, not shared by all the people of the territory, was the reduction of about $7 in the price of the fare, the convenience of traveling in a company instead of alone, and the cheapness and facility of transporting their freight through regular agents. Subsequently, many emigrants, being either disappointed with the country or its political condition, or deceived by the statements made by the newspapers and by the agents of the society, became dissatisfied, and returned, both before and after the election, to their old homes. Most of them are now settlers in the territory. Some few voted at the election in Lawrence, but the number was small. The names of these emigrants have been ascertained, and —— of them were found upon the poll-books. This company of peaceful emigrants, moving with their household goods, was distorted into an invading horde of pauper abolitionists, who were, with others of a similar character, to control the domestic institutions of the territory, and then overturn those of a neighboring powerful state.

In regard to the second charge: There is no proof that any man was either hired or induced to come into the territory from any free state, merely to vote. The entire emigration in March, 1855, is estimated at 500 persons, including men, women, and children. They came on steamboats up the Missouri river, in the ordinary course of emigration. Many returned for causes similar to those before stated; but the body of them are now residents. The only persons of those who were connected by proof with the election, were some who voted at the Big Blue precinct in the Xth district, and at Pawnee in the IXth district. Their purpose and character are stated in a former part of this report.

The third charge is entirely groundless.

Your committee are satisfied that these charges were made the mere pretext to induce an armed invasion into the territory, as a means to control the election and establish slavery there.

The real purpose is avowed and illustrated by the testimony and conduct of Col. John Scott, of St. Joseph, Missouri, who acted as the attorney for the sitting delegate before your committee. The following is an extract from his deposition:

"It is my intention, and the intention of a great many other Missourians now resident in Missouri, whenever the slavery issue is to be determined upon by the people of this territory in the adoption of the state constitution, to remove to this territory in time to acquire the right to become legal voters upon that question. The leading purpose of our intended removal to the territory is to determine the domestic institutions of this territory, when it comes to be a state, and we would not come but for that purpose, and would never think of coming here but for that purpose. I believe there are a great many in Missouri who are so situated."

The invasion of March 30th left both parties in a state of excitement, tending directly to produce violence. The successful party was lawless and reckless, while assuming the name of the "law and order" party. The other party, at first surprised and confounded, was greatly irritated, and some resolved to prevent the success of the invasion. In some districts protests were sent to the governor; in others this was prevented by threats; in others, by the want of time, only four days being allowed by the proclamation for this purpose; and in others, by the belief that a new election would bring a new invasion. About the same time all classes of men commenced bearing deadly weapons about their person, a practice which has continued to this time. Under these circumstances, a slight or accidental quarrel produced unusual violence, and lawless acts became frequent. This evil condition of the public mind was further increased by acts of violence in Western Missouri, where, in April, a newspaper press called "The Parkville Luminary" was destroyed by a mob.

About the same time, Malcolm Clark assaulted Cole McCrea, at a squatter meeting in Leavenworth, and was shot by McCrea, in alleged self-defense.

On the 17th day of May, William Phillips, a lawyer of Leavenworth, was first notified to leave, and upon his refusal, was forcibly seized, taken across the river, and carried several miles into Missouri, and then tarred and feathered, and one side of his head shaved, and other gross indignities put upon his person.

Previous to the outrage, a public meeting was held, at which resolutions were unanimously passed, looking to unlawful violence, and grossly intolerant in their character. The right of free speech upon the subject of slavery was characterized as a disturbance of the peace and quiet of the community, and as "circulating incendiary sentiments." They say "to the peculiar friends of northern fanatics," "go home and do your treason where you may find sympathy." Among other resolves is the following:

"Resolved, That the institution of slavery is known and recognized in this territory; that we repel the doctrine that it is a moral and political evil, and we hurl back with scorn upon its slanderous authors the charge of inhumanity; and we warn all persons not to come to our peaceful firesides to slander us, and sow the seeds of discord between the master and the servant; for, as much as we deprecate the necessity to which we may be driven, we cannot be responsible for the consequences."

A committee of vigilance of thirty men was appointed, "to observe and report all such persons as shall, * * * * by the expression of abolition sentiments, produce disturbance to the quiet of the citizens, or danger to their domestic relations; and all such persons so offending, shall be notified, and made to leave the territory."

The meeting was "ably and eloquently addressed by Judge Lecompte, Col. J. N. Burns, of Western Missouri, and others." Thus the head of the judiciary in the territory, not only assisted at a public and bitterly partisan meeting, whose direct tendency was to produce violence and disorder, but before any law is passed in the territory, he prejudges the character of domestic institutions, which the people of the territory were, by their organic law, "left perfectly free to form and regulate in their own way."

On this committee were several of those who held certificates of election as members of the legislature; some of the others were then and still are residents of Missouri; and many of the committee have since been appointed to the leading offices in the territory, one of which is the sheriffalty of the county. Their first act was that of mobbing Phillips.

Subsequently, on the 25th of May, A. D. 1855, a public meeting was held, at which R. R. Rees, a member elect of the council, presided. The following resolutions, offered by Judge Payne, a member elect of the house, were unanimously adopted:

"Resolved, That we heartily indorse the action of the committee of citizens that shaved, tarred and feathered, rode on a rail, and had sold by a negro, Wm. Phillips, the moral perjurer.

"Resolved, That we return our thanks to the committee for faithfully performing the trust enjoined upon them by the pro-slavery party.

"Resolved, That the committee be now discharged.

"Resolved, That we severely condemn those pro-slavery men who, from mercenary motives, are calling upon the pro-slavery party to submit without further action.

"Resolved, That in order to secure peace and harmony to the community, we now solemnly declare that the pro-slavery party will stand firmly by and carry out the resolutions reported by the committee appointed for that purpose on the memorable 30th."

The act of moral perjury here referred to, is the swearing by Phillips to a truthful protest in regard to the election of March 30, in the XVIth district.

The members receiving their certificates of the governor as members of the general assembly of the territory, met at Pawnee, the place appointed by the governor, on the 2d of July, A. D. 1855. Their proceedings are stated in three printed books, herewith submitted, entitled respectively, "The Statutes of the Territory of Kansas;" "The Journal of the Council of the Territory of Kansas;" and "The Journal of the House of Representatives of the Territory of Kansas."

Your committee do not regard their enactments as valid laws. A legislature thus imposed upon a people, cannot affect their political rights. Such an attempt to do so, if successful, is virtually an overthrow of the organic law, and reduces the people of the territory to the condition of vassals to a neighboring state. The great body of the general laws are exact transcripts from the Missouri code. To make them in some cases conform to the organic act, separate acts were passed, defining the meaning of words. Thus the word "state" is to be understood as meaning "territory;" the word "county court" shall be considered to mean the board of commissioners transacting county business, or the probate court, according to the intent thereof. The words "circuit court" to mean "district court."

The material differences in the Missouri and Kansas statutes are upon the following subjects : The qualifications of voters and of members of the legislative assembly ; the official oath of all officers, attorneys, and voters ; the mode of selecting officers, and their qualifications ; the slave code, and the qualifications of jurors.

Upon these subjects the provisions of the Missouri code are such as are usual in many of the states. But by the "Kansas statutes," every office in the territory, executive and judicial, was to be appointed by the legislature, or by some officer appointed by it. These appointments were not merely to meet a temporary exigency, but were to hold over two regular elections, and until after the general election in October, 1857, at which the members of the new council were to be elected. The new legislature is required to meet on the first Monday in January, 1858. Thus, by the terms of these "laws," the people have no control whatever over either the legislative, the executive, or the judicial departments of the territorial government until a time before which, by the natural progress of population, the territorial government will be superseded by a state government.

No session of the legislature is to be held during 1856, but the members of the house are to be elected in October of that year. A candidate, to be eligible at this election, must swear to support the fugitive slave law, and each judge of election, and each voter, if challenged, must take the same oath. The same oath is required of every officer elected or appointed in the territory, and of every attorney admitted to practice in the courts.

A portion of the militia is required to muster on the day of election. "Every free white male citizen of the United States, and every free male Indian, who is made a citizen by treaty or otherwise, and over the age of twenty-one years, and who shall be an inhabitant of the territory, and of the county and district in which he offers to vote, and shall have paid a territorial tax, shall be a qualified elector for all elective offices." Two classes of persons were thus excluded, who by the organic act were allowed to vote, viz : those who would not swear to the oath required, and those of foreign birth who had declared on oath their intention to become citizens. Any man of proper age who was in the territory on the day of election, and who had paid one dollar as a tax to the sheriff, who was required to be at the polls to receive it, could vote as an "inhabitant," although he had breakfasted in Missouri, and intended to return there for supper. There can be no doubt that this unusual and unconstitutional provision was inserted to prevent a full and fair expression of the popular will in the election of members of the house, or to control it by non-residents.

All jurors are required to be selected by the sheriff, and "no person who is conscientiously opposed to the holding of slaves, or who does not admit the right to hold slaves in the territory, shall be a juror in any cause " affecting the right to hold slaves, or relating to slave property.

The slave code, and every provision relating to slaves, are of a character intolerant and unusual, even for that class of legislation. The character and conduct of the men appointed to hold office in the territory contributed very much to produce the events which followed. Thus, Samuel J. Jones was appointed sheriff of the county of Douglas, which included within it the Ist and IId election districts. He had made himself peculiarly obnoxious to the settlers by his conduct on the 30th of March, in the IId district, and by his burning the cabins of Joseph Oakley and Samuel Smith.

While these enactments of the alleged legislative assembly were being made, a movement was instituted to form a state government, and apply for admission into the Union as a state. The first general meeting was held in Lawrence on the 15th of August, 1855. The following preamble and resolutions were then passed:

"WHEREAS, The people of Kansas have been, since its settlement, and now are, without any law-making power; therefore, be it

"Resolved, That we, the people of Kansas territory, in mass meeting assembled, irrespective of party distinctions, influenced by common necessity, and greatly desirous of promoting the common good, do hereby call upon and request all bona fide citizens of Kansas territory, of whatever political views or predilections, to consult together in their respective election districts, and in mass convention or otherwise, elect three delegates for each representative to which said election district is entitled in the house of representatives of the legislative assembly, by proclamation of Governor Reeder, of date 19th of March, 1855; said delegates to assemble in convention at the town of Topeka, on the 19th day of September, 1855, then and there to consider and determine upon all subjects of public interest, and particularly upon that having reference to the speedy formation of a state constitution, with an intention of an immediate application to be admitted as a state into the Union of the United States of America."

Other meetings were held in various parts of the territory, which indorsed the action of the Lawrence meeting, and delegates were selected in compliance with its recommendations.

They met at Topeka on the 19th day of September, 1855. By their resolutions they provided for the appointment of an executive committee to consist of seven persons, who were required to "keep a record of their proceedings, and shall have a general superintendence of the affairs of the territory, so far as regards the organization of the state government." They were required to take steps for an election to be held on the second Tuesday of the October following, under regulations imposed by that committee, "for members of a convention to form a constitution, adopt a bill of rights for the people of Kansas, and take all needful measures for organizing a state government, preparatory to the admission of Kansas into the Union as a state." The rules prescribed were such as usually govern elections in most of the states of the Union, and in most respects were similar to those contained in the proclamation of Gov. Reeder for the election of March 30, 1855.

The executive committee, appointed by that convention, accepted their appointment, and entered upon the discharge of their duties by issuing a proclamation addressed to the legal voters of Kansas, requesting them to meet at their several precincts, at the time and places named in the proclamation, then and there to cast their ballots for members of a constitutional convention, to meet at Topeka on the 4th Tuesday of October then next.

The proclamation designated the places of elections, appointed judges, recited the qualifications of voters and the apportionment of members of the convention.

After this proclamation was issued, public meetings were held in every district in the territory, and in nearly every precinct. The state movement was a general topic of discussion throughout the territory, and there was but little opposition exhibited to it. Elections were held at the time and places designated, and the returns were sent to the executive committee.

The result of the election was proclaimed by the executive committee, and the members elect were required to meet on the 23d day of October, 1855, at Topeka. In pursuance of this proclamation and direction, the constitutional convention met at the time and place appointed, and formed a state constitution. A memorial to congress was also prepared, praying for the admission of Kansas into the Union under the constitution. The convention also provided that the question of the adoption of the constitution and other questions be submitted to the people, and required the executive committee to take the necessary steps for that purpose.

Accordingly, an election was held for that purpose on the 15th day of December, 1855, in compliance with the proclamation issued by the executive committee. The returns of this election were made to the executive committee, exhibiting the following result: For the adoption of the constitution, 1731; against it, 46.

The executive committee then issued a proclamation reciting the results of the election of the 15th of December, and at the same time provided for an election to be held on the 15th day of January, 1856, for state officers and members of the general assembly of the state of Kansas. The result of this election was announced by a proclamation by the executive committee.

In accordance with the constitution thus adopted, the members of the state legislature and most of the state officers met on the day and at the place designated by the state constitution, and took the oath therein prescribed.

After electing United States senators, passing some preliminary laws, and appointing a codifying committee and preparing a memorial to congress, the general assembly adjourned to meet on the 4th day of July, 1856.

The laws passed were all conditional upon the admission of Kansas as a state into the Union. These proceedings were regular, and, in the opinion of your committee, the constitution thus adopted fairly expresses the will of the majority of the settlers. They now await the action of congress upon their memorial.

These elections, whether they were conducted in pursuance of law or not, were not illegal.

Whether the result of them is sanctioned by the action of congress, or they are regarded as the mere expression of a popular will, and congress should re fuse to grant the prayer,of the memorial, that cannot affect their legality. The right of the people to assemble and express their political opinion in any form, whether by means of an election or a convention, is secured to them by the constitution of the United States. Even if the elections are to be regarded as the act of a party, whether political or otherwise, they were proper, in accordance with examples, both in states and territories.

The elections, however, were preceded and followed by acts of violence on the part of those who opposed them, and those persons who approved and sustained the invasion from Missouri were peculiarly hostile to these peaceful movements preliminary to the organization of a state government. Instances of this violence will be referred to hereafter.

In the fall of 1855, there sprang out of the existing discords and excitement in the territory two secret free state societies. They were defensive in their character, and were designed to form a protection to their members against unlawful acts of violence and assault. One of the societies was purely of a local character, and was confined to the town of Lawrence. Very shortly after its organization, it produced its desired effect, and then went out of use and ceased to exist. Both societies were cumbersome, and of no utility except to give confidence to the free state men, and enable them to know and aid each other in contemplated danger. So far as the evidence shows, they led to no act of violence in resistance to either real or alleged laws.

On the 21st day of November, 1855, F. M. Coleman, a pro-slavery man, and Charles W. Dow, a free-state man, had a dispute about the division line between their respective claims. Several hours afterward, as Dow was passing from a blacksmith's shop towards his claim, and by the cabin of Coleman, the latter shot Dow with a double-barreled gun loaded with slugs. Dow was unarmed. He fell across the road and died immediately. This was about 1 o'clock P. M. His dead body was allowed to lie where it fell until after sundown, when it was conveyed by Jacob Branson to his house, at which Dow boarded. The testimony in regard to this homicide is voluminous, and shows clearly that it was a deliberate murder by Coleman, and that Harrison Buckely and a Mr. Hargous were accessories to it. The excitement caused by it was very great among all classes of the settlers. On the 26th, a large meeting of citizens was held at the place where the murder was committed, and resolutions passed that Coleman should be brought to justice. In the meantime Coleman had gone to Missouri, and then to governor Shannon, at Shawnee Mission, in Johnson county. He was there taken into custody by S. J. Jones, then acting as sheriff. No warrant was issued or examination had. On the day of the meeting at Hickory Point, Harrison Bradley procured a peace warrant against Jacob Branson, which was placed in the hands of Jones. That same evening, after Branson had gone to bed, Jones came to his cabin with a party of about 25 persons, among whom were Hargous and Buckley—burst open the door and saw Branson in bed. He then drew his pistol, cocked it, and presented it to Branson's breast, and said, "You are my prisoner, and if you move I will blow you through." The others cocked their guns and gathered round him, and took him prisoner. They all mounted and went to Buckley's house. Af-

45

ter a time they went on a circuitous route towards Blanton's bridge, stopping to "drink" on the way. As they approached the bridge, there were 13 in the party, several having stopped. Jones rode up to the prisoner, and among other things, told him he had "heard there were 100 men at your house to-day," and "that he regretted they were not there, and that they were cheated out of their sport." In the meantime the alarm had been given in the neighborhood of Branson's arrest, and several of the settlers, among whom were some who had attended the meeting at Hickory Point that day, gathered together. They were greatly excited; the alleged injustice of such an arrest of a quiet settler, under a peace warrant by "sheriff Jones," aided by two men believed to be accessory to a murder, and who were allowed to be at large, exasperated them, and they proceeded as rapidly as possible by a nearer route than that taken by Jones, and stopped near the house of J. S. Abbott, one of them. They were on foot as Jone's party approached on a canter. The rescuers suddenly formed across the road in front of Jones and his party. Jones halted, and asked, "what's up?" The reply was, "that's what we want to know. What's up?" Branson said, "they have got me a prisoner." Some one in the rescuing party told him to come over to their side. He did so, and dismounted, and the mule he rode was driven over to Jone's party; Jones then left. Of the persons engaged in this rescue, three were from Lawrence, and had attended the meeting. Your committee have deemed it proper to detail the particulars of this rescue, as it was made the groundwork of what is known as the Wakerusa war. On the same night of the rescue the cabins of Coleman and Buckley were burned, but by whom, is left in doubt by the testimony.

On the morning of the rescue of Branson, Jones was at the village of Franklin, near Lawrence. The rescue was spoken of in the presence of Jones, and more conversation passed between two others in his presence, as to whether it was most proper to send for assistance to colonel Boon in Missouri, or to governor Shannon. Jones wrote a dispatch and handed it to a messenger. As soon as he started, Jones said: "That man is taking my dispatch to Missouri, and by G—d I'll have revenge before I see Missouri." A person present, who was examined as a witness, complained publicly that the dispatch was not sent to the governor; and within half an hour one was sent to the governor by Jones, through Hargous. Within a few days, large numbers of men from the state of Missouri gathered and encamped on the Wakarusa. They brought with them all the equipments of war. To obtain them, a party of men under the direction of Judge T. V. Thompson broke into the United States arsenal and armory at Liberty, Missouri, and after a forcible detention of captain Leonard (then in charge,) they took the cannon, muskets, rifles, powder, harness, and in deed all the materials and munitions of war they desired, some of which have never been returned or accounted for.

The chief hostility of this military foray was against the town of Lawrence, and this was especially the case with the officers of the law.

Your committee can see in the testimony no reason, excuse or palliation for this feeling. *Up to this time no warrant or proclamation of any kind had* .

been in the hands of any officer against any citizen of Lawrence. No arrest had been attempted, and no writ resisted in that town. The rescue of Branson sprang out of a murder committed thirteen miles from Lawrence, in a detached settlement, and neither the town nor its citizens extended any protection to Branson's rescuers. On the contrary, two or three days after the rescue, S. N. Wood, who claimed publicly to be one of the rescuing party, wished to be arrested for the purpose of testing the territorial laws, and walked up to sheriff Jones and shook hands with him, and exchanged other courtesies. He could have been arrested without any difficulty, and it was his design, when he went to Mr. Jones, to be arrested, but no attempt was made to do so.

It is obvious that the only cause of this hostility is the known desire of the citizens of Lawrence to make Kansas a free state, and their repugnance to laws imposed upon them by non-residents.

Your committee do not propose to detail the incidents connected with this foray. Fortunately for the peace of the country, a direct conflict between the opposing forces was avoided by an amicable arrangement. The losses sustained by the settlers in property taken and time and money expended in their own defense, added much to the trials incident to a new settlement. Many persons were unlawfully taken and detained—in some cases, under circumstances of gross cruelty. This was especially so in the arrest and treatment of doctor G. A. Cutter and G. F. Warren. They were taken without cause or warrant, 60 miles from Lawrence, and when doctor Cutter was quite sick. They were compelled to go to the camp at Lawrence, were put into the custody of "Sheriff Jones," who had no process to arrest them—they were taken into a small room kept as a liquor shop, which was open and very cold. That night Jones came in with others, and went to "playing poker at twenty-five cents ante." The prisoners were obliged to sit up all night, as there was no room to lie down when the men were playing. Jones insulted them frequently, and told one of them he must either "tell or swing." The guard then objected to this treatment of the prisoners, and Jones desisted. G. F. Warren thus describes their subsequent conduct:

"They then carried us down to their camp; Kelly, of *The Squatter Sovereign,* who lives in Atchison, came round and said he thirsted for blood, and said he should like to hang us on the first tree. Cutter was very weak, and that excited him so that he became delirious. They sent for three doctors, who came. Doctor Stringfellow was one of them. They remained there with Cutter until after midnight, and then took him up to the office, as it was very cold in camp."

During the foray, either George W. Clark or Mr. Burns murdered Thomas Barber, while the latter was on the highway on his road from Lawrence to his claim. Both fired at him, and it is impossible from the proof to tell whose shot was fatal. The details of this homicide are stated by an eye witness.

Among the many acts of lawless violence which it has been the duty of your committee to investigate, this invasion of Lawrence is the most defenseless. A comparison of the facts proven, with the official statement of the officers of the government, will show how groundless were the pretexts which gave rise to it. A community in which no crime had been committed by any of its members, against none of whom had a warrant been issued or a complaint made, who had resisted no process in the hands of a real or pretended officer, was threatened with destruction in the name of "law and order," and that, too, by men who marched from a neighboring state with arms obtained by force, and who, in every stage of their progress, violated many laws, and among others the constitution of the United States.

The chief guilt of it must rest on Samuel J. Jones. His character is illustrated by his language at Lecompton, where peace was made : " He said major Clark and Burns both claimed the honor of killing that d—d abolitionist, and he did'nt know which ought to have it. If Shannon had'nt been a d—d old fool, that peace would never have been declared. He would have wiped Lawrence out. He had men and means enough to do it."

Shortly after the retreat of the forces from before Lawrence, the election upon the adoption of the state constitution was held at Leavenworth city, on the 15th of December, 1855. While it was proceeding quietly, about noon, Charles Dunn, with a party of others, smashed in the window of the building in which the election was being held, and then jumped into the room where the judges of election were sitting, and drove them off. One of the clerks of election snatched up the ballot-box and followed the judges, throwing the box behind the counter of an adjoining room through which he passed on his way out. As he got to the street door, Dunn caught him by the throat, and pushed him up against the side of the building, and demanded the ballot-box.

Then Dunn and another person struck him in the face, and he fell into the mud, the crowd rushed on him and kicked him on the head and in his sides. In this manner the election was broken up, Dunn and his party obtaining the ballot-box and carrying it off.

To avoid a similar outrage at the election for state officers, etc., to be held on the 15th of January, 1856, the election for Leavenworth district was appointed to be held at Easton, and the time postponed until the 17th day of January, 1856. On the way to the election, persons were stopped by a party of men at a grocery, and their guns taken from them. During the afternoon, parties came up to the place of election and threatened to destroy the ballot-box, and were guilty of other insolent and abusive conduct. After the polls were closed, many of the settlers being apprehensvie of an attack, were armed in the house where the election had been held until the next morning. Late that night Stephen Sparks, with his son and nephew, started for home, his route running by the store of a Mr. Dawson, where a large party of armed men had collected. As he approached, these men demanded that he should surrender, and gathered about him to enforce the demand. Information was carried by a man in the company of Mr. Sparks to the house where the election had been held. R. P. Brown and a company of men immediately went down to relieve Mr. Sparks, and did relieve him when he was in imminent danger. Mr. Sparks then started back with Mr. Brown and his party, and while on their

way were fired on by the other party.   They returned the fire, and an irregular
fight then ensued, in which a man by the name of Cook, of the pro-slavery
party, received a mortal wound, and two of the free state prrty were slightly
wounded.

Mr. Brown, with seven others who had accompanied him from from Leavenworth, started on their return home.   When they had proceeded part of the
way, they were stopped and taken prisoners by a party of men called the
Kickapoo Rangers, under the command of captain John W. Martin.   They
were disarmed and taken back to Easton, and put in Dawson's store.   Brown
was separated from the rest of his party, and taken into the office of E. S.
Trotter.   By this time several of Martin's party and some of the citizens of
the place had become intoxicated, and expressed a determination to kill Brown.
Captain Martin was desirous, and did all in his power to save him.   Several
hours were spent in discussing what should be done with Brown and his
party.   In the meantime, without the knowledge of his party, captain Martin
liberated all of Brown's party but himself, and aided them in their escape.
The crowd repeatedly tried to get into the room where Brown was, and at one
time succeeded, but were put out by Martin and others.   Martin, finding that
further effort on his part to save Brown was useless, left and went home.   The
crowd then got possession of Brown and finally butchered him in cold blood.
The wound of which he died was inflicted with a hatchet by a man by the
name of Gibson.   After he had been mortally wounded, Brown was sent home
with Charles Dunn, and died that night.   No attempt was made to arrest and
punish the murderers of Brown.   Many of them were well-known citizens, and
some of them were officers of the law.   On the next grand jury that set in
Leavenworth county, the sheriff summoned several of the persons implicated in
this murder.   One of them was M. P. Rively, at that time treasurer of the county.
He has been examined as a witness before us.   The reason he gives why no
indictments were found is, "they killed one of the pro-slavery men, and the
pro-slavery men killed one of the others, and I thought it was about mutual."
The same grand jury, however, found bills of indictment against those who
acted as judges of the free-state election.   Rively says, "I know our utmost
endeavors were made to find out who acted as judges and clerks on the 17th
of January last, and at all the bogus elections held by the abolitionists here.
We were very anxious to find them out, as we thought them acting illegally."

Your committee, in their examination, have found that in no case of crime
or homicide, mentioned in the report or in the testimony, has any indictment
been found against the guilty party, except in the homicide of Clark by Mc-
Crea, McCrea being a free state man.

Your committee did not deem it within their power or duty to take testimony as to events which have transpired since the date of their appointment;
but as some of the events tended seriously to embarrass, hinder, and delay their
investigations, they deem it proper here to refer to them.   On their arrival in
the territory, the people were arrayed in two hostile parties.   The hostility of
them was continually increased during our stay in the territory, by the arrival

of armed bodies of men, who, from their equipments, came not to follow the peaceful pursuits of life, but armed and organized into companies, apparently for war—by the unlawful detention of persons and property while passing through the state of Missouri, and by frequent forcible seizures of persons and property in the territory without legal warrant. Your committee regret that they were compelled to witness instances of each of these classes of outrages. While holding their session at Westport, Mo., at the request of the sitting delegate, they saw several bodies of armed men, confessedly citizens of Missouri, march into the territory on forays against its citizens, but under the pretense of enforcing the enactments before referred to. The wagons of emigrants were stopped in the highways, and searched without claim or legal powers, and in some instances all their property taken from them. In Leavenworth City, leading citizens were arrested at noonday in our presence, by an armed force, without any claim of authority, except that derived from a self-constituted committee of vigilance, many of whom were executive and legislative officers. Some were released on promising to leave the territory, and others, after being detained for a time, were formally notified to leave, under the severest penalties. The only offense charged against them was their political opinions, and no one was thus arrested for alleged crime of any grade. There was no resistance to these lawless acts by the settlers, because, in their opinion, the persons engaged in them would be sustained and reïnforced by the citizens of the populous border counties of Missouri, from whence they were only separated by the river. In one case witnessed by your committee, an application for the writ of habeas corpus was prevented by the urgent solicitation of pro-slavery men, who insisted that it would endanger the life of the prisoner to be discharged under legal process.

While we remained in the territory, repeated acts of outrage were committed upon the quiet, unoffending citizens, of which we received authentic intelligence. Men were attacked on the highway, robbed, and subsequently imprisoned. Men were seized and searched, and their weapons of defense taken from them without compensation. Horses were frequently taken and appropriated. Oxen were taken from the yoke while plowing, and butchered in the presence of their owners. One young man was seized in the streets of the town of Atchison, and under circumstances of gross barbarity was tarred and cottoned, and in that condition was sent to his family. All the provisions of the constitution of the United States, securing persons and property, are utterly disregarded. The officers of the law, instead of protecting the people, were in some instances engaged in these outrages, and in no instance did we learn that any man was arrested, indicted, or punished for any of these crimes. While such offenses were committed with impunity, the laws were used as a means of indicting men for holding elections, preliminary to framing a constitution and applying for admission into the Union as the state of Kansas. Charges of high treason were made against prominent citizens upon grounds which seem to your committee absurd and ridiculous, and under these charges they are now held in custody and are refused the privilege of bail. In several cases, men were arrested in the state of Missouri while passing on their lawful business through the state, and detained until indictments could be found in the territory.

These proceedings were followed by an offense of still greater magnitude. Under color of legal process, a company of about 700 armed men, the great body of whom your committee are satisfied were not citizens of the territory, marched into the town of Lawrence under Marshal Donaldson and S. J. Jones, officers claiming to act under the law, and bombarded and then burned to the ground a valuable hotel and one private house; destroyed two printing-presses and material; and then, being released by the officers, whose posse they claim to be, proceeded to sack, pillage, and rob houses, stores, trunks, etc., even to the clothing of women and children. Some of the letters thus unlawfully taken were private ones, written by the contesting delegate, and they were offered in evidence. Your committee did not deem that the persons holding them had any right thus to use them, and refused to be made the instruments to report private letters thus obtained.

This force was not resisted, because it was collected and marshaled under the forms of law. But this act of barbarity, unexampled in the history of our government, was followed by its natural consequences. All the restraints which American citizens are accustomed to pay even to the appearance of law, were thrown off; one act of violence led to another; homicides became frequent. A party under H. C. Pate, composed chiefly of citizens of Missouri, were taken prisoners by a party of settlers; and while your committee were at Westport, a company, chiefly of Missourians, accompanied by the acting delegate, went to relieve Pate and his party, and a collision was prevented by the United States troops. Civil war has seemed impending in the territory. Nothing can prevent so great a calamity but the presence of a large force of United States troops, under a commander who will with prudence and discretion quiet the excited passions of both parties, and expel with force the armed bands of lawless men coming from Missouri and elsewhere, who, with criminal pertinacity, infest that territory.

In some cases, and as to one entire election district, the condition of the country prevented the attendance of witnesses, who were either arrested or detained while obeying our process, or deterred from so doing. The sergeant-at-arms who served the processes upon them was himself arrested and detained for a short time by an armed force, claiming to be a part of the posse of the marshal, but was allowed to proceed upon an examination of his papers, and was furnished with a pass signed by "Warren D. Wilkes, of South Carolina." John Upton, another officer of the committee, was subsequently stopped by a lawless force on the borders of the territory, and after being detained and treated with great indignity, was released. He also was furnished with a pass signed by two citizens of Missouri, and addressed to "pro-slavery men." By reason of these disturbances, we were delayed in Westport, so that while in session there, our time was but partially occupied.

But the obstruction which created the most serious embarrassment to your committee was the attempted arrest of Gov. Reeder, the contesting delegate, upon a writ of attachment issued against him by Judge Lecompte to compel his attendance as a witness before the grand jury of Douglas county. William Fane, recently from the state of Georgia, and claiming to be the deputy marshal, came into the room of the committee while Gov. Reeder was examining a witness before us, and producing the writ, required Gov. Reeder to attend him.   Subsequent events have only strengthened the conviction of your committee that this was a wanton and unlawful interference by the judge who issued the writ, tending greatly to obstruct a full and fair investigation. Gov. Reeder and Gen. Whitfield alone were possessed of that local information which would enable us to elicit the whole truth, and it was obvious to every one that any event which would separate either of them from the committee would necessarily hinder, delay, and embarrass it. Gov. Reeder claimed that, under the circumstances in which he was placed, he was privileged from arrest except for treason, felony, or breach of the peace. As this was a question of privilege, proper for the courts, or for the privileged person alone to determine on his peril, we declined to give him any protection or take any action in the matter.   He refused to obey the writ, believing it to be a mere pretense to get the custody of his person, and fearing, as he alleged, that he would be assassinated by lawless bands of men then gathering in and near Lecompton. He then left the territory.

Subsequently, H. Miles Moore, an attorney in Leavenworth City, but for several years a citizen of Westport, Mo., kindly furnished the committee information as to the residence of persons voting at the elections, and in some cases examined witnesses before us.   He was arrested on the streets of that town by an armed band of about thirty men, headed by W. D. Wilkes, without any color of authority, confined, with other citizens, under a military guard for twenty-four hours, and then notified to leave the territory. His testimony was regarded as important, and upon his sworn statement that it would endanger his person to give it openly, the majority of your committee deemed it proper to examine him *ex parte*, and did so.

By reason of these occurrences, the contestant, and the party with and for whom he acted, were unrepresented before us during a greater portion of the time, and your committee were required to ascertain the truth in the best manner they could.

Your committee report the following facts and conclusions as established by the testimony :

First : That each election in the territory, held under the organic or alleged territorial law, has been carried on by organized invasions from the state of Missouri, by which the people of the territory have been prevented from exercising the rights secured to them by the organic law.

Second : That the alleged territorial legislature was an illegally constituted body, and had no power to pass valid laws, and their enactments are, therefore, null and void.

Third : That these alleged laws have not, as a general thing, been used to protect persons and property and to punish wrong, but for unlawful purposes.

Fourth : That the election under which the sitting delegate, John W. Whitfield, holds his seat, was not held in pursuance of any valid law, and that it should be regarded only as the expression of the choice of those resident citizens who voted for him.

Fifth : That the election under which the contesting delegate, Andrew H. Reeder, claims his seat, was not held in pursuance of law, and that it should be regarded only as the expression of the choice of the resident citizens who voted for him.

Sixth : That Andrew H. Reeder received a greater number of votes of resident citizens than John W. Whitfield, for delegate.

Seventh : That in the present condition of the territory, a fair election cannot be held without a new census, a stringent and well-guarded election law, the selection of impartial judges, and the presence of United States troops at every place of election.

Eighth : That the various elections held by the people of the territory preliminary to the formation of the state government, have been as regular as the disturbed condition of the territory would allow ; and that the constitution passed by the convention held in pursuance of said elections, embodies the will of a majority of the people.

As it is not the province of your committee to suggest remedies for the existing troubles in the territory of Kansas, they content themselves with the foregoing statement of facts.

All of which is respectfully submitted.
WM. A. HOWARD,
JOHN SHERMAN.

The free state constitution,* framed at Topeka, as set forth in the foregoing report, was duly submitted to congress, and referred, in both houses, to the committees on territories ; but the accompanying memorial from the free state legislature, setting forth the grounds of the application, and praying for admission as a state, was rejected by the senate on the allegation that material changes had been made in it since it left Kansas. The senate also rejected repeated motions to accept the constitution and admit Kansas as a free state ; but sixteen senators being found in favor of such admission.

In the house, the majority of the committee on territories reported in favor of the admission of Kansas, under the aforesaid constitution, as a free state ; and after debate, the previous question thereon was ordered on the 28th of June by a vote of 98 ayes to 63 noes. Previous to this, Mr. Stephens, of Georgia, had proposed, as an amendment or substitute, a radically different bill, contemplating the appointment by the president and senate of five commissioners, who should repair to Kansas, take a census of the inhabitants and legal voters, and thereupon proceed to apportion, during the month of September, 1856, the delegates (52) to form a constitutional convention, to be

---

* ARTICLE I. SEC. 6. There shall be no slavery in this state, nor involuntary servitude, unless for the punishment of crime.

elected by the legal voters aforesaid; said delegates to be chosen on the day of the presidential election (Tuesday, November 4th, 1856,) and to assemble in convention on the first Monday in December, 1856, to form a state constitution. The bill proposed, also, penalties for illegal voting at said election.

To this substitute bill, Mr. Dunn, of Indiana, proposed the following amendment, to come in at the end as an additional section:

SEC. 18. *And be it further enacted,* That so much of the fourteenth section and of the thirty-second section of the act passed at the first session of the thirty-third congress, commonly called the Kansas and Nebraska act, as reads as follows: "Except the eighth section of the act preparatory to the admission of Missouri into the Union, approved March 6th, 1820, which, being inconsistent with the principles of non-intervention by congress with slavery in the states and territories, as recognized by the legislation of 1850, commonly called the compromise measures, is hereby declared inoperative and void; it being the true intent and meaning of the act not to legislate slavery into any state or territory, or to exclude it therefrom, but to leave the people thereof perfectly free to form and regulate their domestic institutions in their own way, subject only to the constitution of the United States; provided, that nothing herein contained shall be construed to revive or put in force any law or regulation which may have existed prior to the act of 6th March, 1820, either protecting, establishing, prohibiting, or abolishing slavery," be, and the same is hereby repealed; provided, that any person or persons lawfully held to service within either of the territories named in said act shall be discharged from such service, if they shall not be removed and kept out of said territories within twelve months from the passage of this act.

This amendment to the Stephens substitute was carried by a vote of 109 to 102, and the bill, thus amended by its adversaries, was abandoned by its friends and received but two votes, Dunn, of Indiana, and Harrison, of Ohio.

Mr. Jones, of Tennessee, now moved that the bill reported by the committee do lie on the table, which was defeated by a vote of yeas, 106; nays, 107. The house now refused to adjourn by a vote of 106 to 102; and after a long struggle, the final question was reached and the bill *rejected,* by a vote of 107 to 106. On the 1st of July, Mr. Barclay, of Pennsylvania, moved a reconsideration of the preceding vote by which the free Kansas bill had been rejected. The reconsideration was carried on the 3d of July, by a vote of 101 to 99. The previous question on the passage of the bill was then ordered, and the bill was finally *passed,* yeas, 99; nays, 97.

On the 30th of June, Mr. Douglas reported to the senate on several bills submitted by Messrs. Clayton, Toombs and others for the pacification of the Kansas troubles, as also against Governor Seward's proposition to admit Kansas as a free state under the Topeka constitution. Mr. Collamer, being the minority of the territorial committee, made a counter report. Mr. Douglas gave notice that he would ask for a final vote on the 3d of July. The bill was debated on the 1st and 2d of July, and the following night, the majority resisting all motions to adjourn. An amendment, moved by Mr. Adams, of

Mississippi, striking out so much of the bill as secured the right of suffrage in the proposed reörganization of Kansas to alien residents who shall have declared their intention to become citizens, and renounced all allegiance to foreign governments, was adopted by a vote of 22 to 16.   Sometime in the morning of July 3d, the following amendment, reduced to shape by Mr. Geyer, of Missouri, was added to the 18th section of the bill, by a vote of 40 to 3 :

"No law shall be made or have force or effect in said territory [of Kansas] which shall require any attestation or oath to support any act of congress or other legislative act, as a qualification for any civil office, public trust, or for any employment or profession, or to serve as juror, or vote at any election, or which shall impose any tax upon, or condition ·to, the exercise of the right of suffrage, by any qualified voter, or which shall restrain or prohibit the free discussion of any law or subject of legislation in the said territory, or the free expression of opinion thereon by the people of said territory."

Mr. Trumbull, of Illinois, moved the following :

"*And be it further enacted,* That it was the true intent and meaning of the 'act to organize the territory of Nebraska and Kansas,' not to legislate slavery into Kansas, nor to exclude it therefrom, but to leave the people thereof perfectly free through their territorial legislature to regulate the institution of slavery in their own way, subject only to the constitution of the United States; and that, until the territorial legislature acts upon the subject, the owner of a slave in one of the states has no right or authority to take such slave into the territory of Kansas, and there hold him as a slave; but every slave taken to the territory of Kansas by his owner for the purposes of settlement is hereby declared to be free, unless there is some valid act of a duly constituted legislative assembly of said territory, under which he may be held as a slave."

The yeas and nays being ordered, the proposition was voted down; yeas, 9; nays, 34.   Mr. Trumbull then proposed the following :

"*And be it further enacted,* That the provision in the 'act to organize the territory of Nebraska and Kansas,' which declares it to be 'the true intent and meaning' of said act 'not to legislate slavery into any territory or state, nor to exclude it therefrom, but to leave the people thereof perfectly free to form and regulate their domestic institutions in their own way, subject only to the constitution of the United States,' was intended to, and does, confer upon, or leave to, the people of the territory of Kansas full power, at any time, through its territorial legislature, to exclude slavery from said territory or to recognize and regulate it therein."

This was also voted down; yeas, 11; nays, 34.   Mr. Trumbull then submitted the following :

"*And be it further enacted,* That all the acts and proceedings of all and every body of men heretofore assembled in said territory of Kansas, and claiming to be a legislative assembly thereof, with authority to pass laws for the government of said territory, are hereby declared to be utterly null and void. And no person shall hold any office, or exercise any authority or jurisdiction in said territory, under or by virtue of any power or authority derived from such legislative assembly; nor shall the members thereof exercise any power or authority as such."

This, too, was voted down; yeas, 11; nays, 36. Mr. Foster, of Connecticut, moved the following amendment:

And be it further enacted, That, until the inhabitants of said territory shall proceed to hold a convention to form a state constitution according to the provisions of this act, and so long as said territory remains a territory, the following sections contained in chapter one hundred and fifty-one, in the volume transmitted to the senate by the President of the United States, as containing the laws of Kansas, be, and the same are hereby, declared to be utterly null and void, viz.:

"SEC. 12. If any free person, by speaking or by writing, assert or maintain that persons have not the right to hold slaves in this territory, or shall introduce into this territory any book, paper, magazine, pamphlet, or circular, containing any denial of the right of persons to hold slaves in this territory, such person shall be deemed guilty of felony, and punished by imprisonment at hard labor for a term of not less than two years.

"SEC. 13. No person who is conscientiously opposed to holding slaves, or who does not admit the right to hold slaves in this territory, shall sit as a juror on the trial of any prosecution for the violation of any one of the sections of this act."

This was rejected, as superfluous, or covered by the amendment of Mr. Geyer; yeas, 13; nays, 32. Mr. Collamer, of Vermont, proposed the following:

And be it further enacted, That until the people of said territory shall form a constitution and state government, and be admitted into the Union under the provisions of this act, there shall be neither slavery or involuntary servitude in said territory, otherwise than in punishment of crimes, whereof the party shall have been duly convicted; provided always, that any person escaping into the same, from whom labor or service is lawfully claimed in any state, such fugitive may be lawfully reclaimed and conveyed to the person claiming his or her service or labor as aforesaid.

This was voted down; yeas, 10; nays, 35. Mr. Wilson, of Massachusetts, moved that the whole bill be stricken out, and another inserted instead, repealing all the territorial laws of Kansas. This was rejected; yeas, 8; nays, 35. Mr. Seward moved to strike out the whole bill, and insert instead one admitting Kansas as a free state under the Topeka constitution. Lost, yeas, 11; nays, 36. The bill was now reported as amended, and the amendment made in committee of the whole concurred in. At 8 o'clock in the morning, the bill was ordered to be engrossed and read a third time, and on the question of its final passage the vote stood, yeas, 33; nays, 12. The bill was then sent to the house. The title is as follows: "An act to authorize the people of the territory of Kansas to form a constitution and state government preparatory to their admission into the Union on an equal footing with the original states."

This bill was never acted on in the house, but lay on the speaker's table when the session terminated on the 18th of August.

In the senate, on the 8th of July, Mr. Douglas reported back from the committee on territories the house bill to admit Kansas as a state, with an amendment, striking out all after the enacting clause, and inserting instead the senate bill above referred to. Mr. Hale, of New Hampshire, moved to amend this substitute by providing that all who migrate to the territory prior to July 4th, 1857, shall be entitled to vote in determining the character of the institutions of Kansas. Mr. Trumbull, of Illinois, moved that all the territorial laws of Kansas be repealed and the territorial officers dismissed. Mr. Collamer, of Vermont, proposed an amendment prohibiting slavery in all that portion of the Louisiana purchase north of 36° 30′, not included in the territory of Kansas. These propositions were severally rejected, and the substitute reported by Mr. Douglas agreed to. This amendment was, however, never acted upon by the house.

In the house, on the 29th of July, Mr. Dunn, of Indiana, called up a bill "to reörganize the territory of Kansas and for other purposes," which he had originally proposed as a substitute for the before-mentioned senate bill. The two last sections of Mr. Dunn's bill are as follows:

SEC. 24. *And be it further enacted,* That so much of the fourteenth section, and also so much of the thirty-second section, of the act passed at the first session of the thirty-third congress, commonly known as the Kansas-Nebraska act, as reads as follows, to wit: "Except the eighth section of the act preparatory to the admission of Missouri into the Union, approved March 6th, 1820, which, being inconsistent with the principle of non-intervention by congress with slavery in the states and territories as recognized by the legislation of 1850, commonly called the compromise measures, is hereby declared inoperative and void; it being the true intent and meaning of this act not to legislate slavery into any territory or state, nor to exclude it therefrom, but to leave the people thereof perfectly free to form and regulate their domestic institutions in their own way, subject only to the constitution of the United States'; provided, that nothing herein contained shall be construed to revive or put in force any law or regulation which may have existed prior to the act of 6th March, 1820, either protecting, establishing, prohibiting, or abolishing slavery," be, and the same is hereby repealed, and the said eighth section of said act of the 6th of March, 1820, is hereby revived and declared to be in full force and effect within the said territories of Kansas and Nebraska; provided, however, that any person lawfully held to service in either of said territories shall not be discharged from such service by reason of such repeal and revival of said eighth section, if such person shall be permanently removed from such territory or territories prior to the 1st day of January, 1858; and any child or children born in either of said territories, of any female lawfully held to service, if in like manner removed without said territories before the expiration of that date, shall not be, by reason of anything in this act, emancipated from any service it might have owed had this act never been passed; and provided further, that any person lawfully held to service in any other state or territory of the United States, and escaping into either the territory of Kansas or Nebraska, may be reclaimed and removed to the person or place where such service is due, under any law of the United States which shall be in force upon the subject.

Sec. 25. *And be it further enacted*, That all other parts of the aforesaid Kansas-Nebraska act which relate to the said territory of Kansas, and every other law or usage having, or which is pretended to have, any force or effect in said territory in conflict with the provisions or the spirit of this act, except such laws of congress and treaty stipulations as relate to the Indians, are hereby repealed, and declared void.

Mr. Dunn moved to strike out a bill previously introduced by Mr. Grow, repealing all the acts of the alleged territorial legislature of Kansas, and the insertion of his own as a substitute. This motion prevailed; and Mr. Dunn moved the previous question on ordering this bill to be engrossed and read a third time, which prevailed, and the bill passed, yeas, 88; nays, 74. This bill was not acted upon by the senate.

When the annual appropriation bills came before congress, the house affixed to several of them provisos respecting the obnoxious acts of the territorial legislature of Kansas; these were resisted by the senate, and finally given up by the house save one, appropriating $20,000 for the pay and expenses of the *next* territorial legislature. This the senate gave up, and thus secured the passage of the civil appropriation bill. The army bill remained unpassed when the session terminated, as the two houses could not agree on a proviso forbidding the employment of the army to enforce the acts of the Kansas Shawnee-Mission legislature. In this state of affairs, the president issued his proclamation, convening an extra session, August 21st, three days after the termination of the former session. A quorum was present, and the house repassed the army bill with the same proviso attached, which proviso was again struck out by the senate, and reïnserted by the house. The senate insisted on its disagreement, and the house decided to adhere to its proviso by a close vote. The senate also voted to adhere. Mr. Clayton, in the senate, proposed a committee of conference, which was objected to. Mr. Campbell in the house made the same proposition, which was likewise objected to. The struggle continued until the 30th, when the house again passed the army bill with the proviso modified. This gave no better satisfaction to the senate. It was struck out, and the bill returned to the house, which finally concurred in the senate amendment by a vote of 101 yeas to 97 nays. The use of the army in Kansas was left at the president's discretion.

CHAPTER XXXIII.

HISTORY OF THE TROUBLES IN KANSAS, CONTINUED.

Judge Lecompte's charge to Grand Jury—Presentments.—Official correspondence.—Attack on Lawrence.—Free State bands organized—attack pro-slavery settlements.—Fights at Palmyra, Franklin, and Ossawattamie.—Murders.—Shannon removed.—Atchison's army retreat.—Geary appointed governor.—Deplorable condition of the territory.—Letter to Secretary Marcy.—Inaugural address and proclamations.—Atchison's call upon the South.—Woodson's proclamation.—Armed bands enter the territory.—Lawrence doomed to destruction.—Gov. Geary's decisive measures.—Army dispersed and Lawrence saved.—Hickory Point—capture of Free State company.—Dispatch to Secretary Marcy.—Murder of Buffum.—Geary and Lecompte in collision.—Official documents.—The Judiciary.—Rumors of Lane's army.—Redpath's company captured—released by governor.—Capture of Eldridge's company.—Official correspondence.—Assembling of Topeka legislature—Members arrested.—Territorial Legislative Assembly convened.—Inaugural—Vetoes of the governor.—The "Census Bill"—its provisions for forming State Constitution.—Constitution not to be submitted to the people.—Gov. Geary's proposition rejected.—He vetoes the bill—Bill passed.—Disturbances in the capital.—Geary's requisition for U. S. troops refused.—His application for money refused.—Difficulties of his situation—he resigns—his farewell address.—Robert J. Walker appointed his successor.—Secretary Stanton.—Fraudulent apportionment.—Walker's Inaugural—his recommendation to have Constitution submitted to the people.—This measure denounced at the South.—Convention assembles September, 1857.—Adjourns to October 26th, 1857.

As the legislation of congress at the session of 1856–7 on the affairs of Kansas produced no definite results, the details are omitted, and other sources than congressional documents sought for information relative to events in the territory. We will now take a look at the internal affairs of Kansas, in order to see how "the people" behave when they are "left entirely free to settle their internal affairs in their own way." The report of the congressional committee, given in the previous chapter, furnishes a history of events down to the summer of 1856. On the 5th of May of that year, Judge Lecompte, the judicial head of the territory, delivered a charge to the grand jury of Douglas county, from which we make an extract :

"This territory was organized by an act of congress, and so far its authority is from the United States. It has a legislature elected in pursuance of that organic act. This legislature, being an instrument of congress, by which it governs the territory, has passed laws ; these laws, therefore, are of United States authority and making, and all that resist these laws, resist the power and authority of the United States, and are, therefore, guilty of high treason. Now, gentlemen, if you find that any persons *have* resisted these laws, then must you, under your oaths, find bills against such persons for high treason. If you find that no such resistance has been made, but that combinations have been formed for the purpose of resisting them, and individuals of influence and notoriety have been aiding and abetting in such combinations, then must you still find bills for constructive treason, as the courts have decided that to constitute treason the blow need not be struck, but only the *intention* be made evident."

The grand jury accordingly made a presentment, as follows :

"The grand jury, sitting for the adjourned term of the first district court in and for the county of Douglas, in the territory of Kansas, beg leave to report to the honorable court that, from evidence laid before them, showing that the newspaper known as The Herald of Freedom, published at the town of Lawrence, has from time to time issued publications of the most inflammatory and seditious character, denying the legality of the *territorial authorities*, addressing and commanding forcible resistance to the same, demoralizing the popular mind, and rendering life and property unsafe, even to the extent of advising assassination as a last resort :

" Also, that the paper known as The Kansas Free State has been similarly engaged, and has recently reported the resolutions of a public meeting in Johnson county, in this territory, in which resistance to the *territorial laws*, even unto blood, has been agreed upon ; and that we respectfully recommend their abatement as a nuisance. Also, that we are satisfied that the building known as the ' Free State Hotel,' in Lawrence, has been constructed with the view to military occupation and defense, regularly parapeted and port-holed for the use of cannon and small arms, and could only have been designed as a stronghold of resistance to law, thereby endangering the public safety, and encouraging rebellion and sedition in this country ; and respectfully recommend that steps may be taken whereby this nuisance may be removed.

" OWEN C. STEWART, Foreman."

In order to accomplish the objects of this presentment, a number of writs were made out and placed in the hands of the marshal for the arrest of prominent citizens of that place. Although it is asserted that no attempts were made to resist the marshal's deputies in serving these writs, the marshal, on the 11th of May, issued the following proclamation :

" TO THE PEOPLE OF KANSAS TERRITORY :

" Whereas, certain judicial writs of arrest have been directed to me by the first district court of the United States, etc., to be executed within the county of Douglas ; and whereas, an attempt to execute them by the United States deputy marshal was evidently resisted by a large number of the citizens of Lawrence, and as there is every reason to believe that any attempt to execute these writs will be resisted by a large body of armed men ; now, therefore, the law-abiding citizens of the territory are commanded to be and appear at Lecompton, as soon as practicable, and in numbers sufficient for the execution of the law.

" Given under my hand, this 11th day of May, 1856.

" I B. DONALSON,
" *United States Marshal for Kansas Territory.*"

Previous to the publication of this proclamation, Buford's Alabama, South Carolina, and Georgia regiment, and other armed bands, had taken up positions in the vicinity of Lawrence, who were not only committing depredations upon the property of the settlers, but were intercepting, robbing, and imprisoning travelers on the public thoroughfares, and threatening to attack the town, in consequence of which a meeting was held, and a committee appointed to address Gov. Shannon, stating the facts in gentle terms, and asking his protection against such bands by the United States troops at his disposal.

To this respectful application the committee received the following reply:

"GENTLEMEN: Your note of the 11th inst. is received, and, in reply, I have to state that there is no force around or approaching Lawrence, except the legally constituted posse of the United States marshal and sheriff of Douglas county, each of whom, I am informed, have a number of writs in their hands for execution against persons now in Lawrence. I shall in no way interfere with either of these officers in the discharge of their official duties.

"If the citizens of Lawrence submit themselves to the territorial laws, and aid and assist the marshal and sheriff in the execution of processes in their hands, as all good citizens are bound to do when called on, they, or all such, will entitle themselves to the protection of the law. But so long as they keep up a military or armed organization to resist the territorial laws and the officers charged with their execution, I shall not interpose to save them from the legitimate consequences of their illegal acts.

"I have the honor to be yours, with great respect,

"WILSON SHANNON."

Still desirous of averting the impending difficulties, the citizens of Lawrence held another meeting on the 13th, when the following preamble and resolution were adopted, copies of which were immediately forwarded to Marshal Donalson and Governor Shannon:

"Whereas, by a proclamation to the people of Kansas territory, by I. B. Donalson, United States Marshal for said territory, issued on the 11th day of May, 1856, it is alleged that 'certain judicial writs of arrest have been directed to him by the first district court of the United States, etc., to be executed within the county of Douglas, and that an attempt to execute them by the United States deputy marshal was violently resisted by a large number of the citizens of Lawrence, and that there is every reason to believe that any attempt to execute said writs will be resisted by a large body of armed men'; therefore,

"Resolved, by this public meeting of the citizens of Lawrence, held this thirteenth day of May, 1856, that the allegations and charges against us, contained in the aforesaid proclamation, are wholly untrue in fact, and the conclusion which is drawn from them. The aforesaid deputy marshal was resisted in no manner whatever, nor by any person whatever, in the execution of said writs, except by him whose arrest the said deputy marshal was seeking to make. And that we now, as we have done heretofore, declare our willingness and determination, without resistance, to acquiesce in the service upon us of any judicial writs against us by the United States deputy marshal for Kansas territory, and will furnish him with a posse for that purpose, if so requested; but that we are ready to resist, if need be, unto death, the ravages and desolation of an invading mob.   J. A. WAKEFIELD, President."

On the 14th, still another meeting was held at Lawrence, and a letter, signed

46

by a large and respectable committee appointed for that purpose, was sent to the marshal, in which it was affirmed "that no opposition will now, or at any future time, be offered to the execution of any legal process by yourself, or any person acting for you. We also pledge ourselves to assist you, if called upon, in the execution of any legal process.

"We declare ourselves to be order-loving and law-abiding citizens; and only await an opportunity to testify our fidelity to the laws of the country, the constitution, and the Union.

"We are informed, also, that those men collecting about Lawrence openly declare that it is their intention to destroy the town and drive off the citizens. Of course we do not believe you give any countenance to such threats; but, in view of the excited state of the public mind, we ask protection of the constituted authorities of the government, declaring ourselves in readiness to coöperate with them for the maintenance of the peace, order, and quiet of the community in which we live."

In reply to this, the marshal sends a lengthy communication, which he closes with these words :

"You say you call upon the constituted authorities of the government for protection. This, indeed, sounds strange from a large body of men armed with Sharpe's rifles, and other implements of war, bound together by oaths' and pledges, to resist the laws of the government they call on for protection. All persons in Kansas territory, without regard to location, who honestly submit to the constituted authorities, will ever find me ready to aid in protecting them; and all who seek to resist the laws of the land, and turn traitors to their country, will find me aiding and enforcing the laws, if not as an officer, as a citizen."

Whilst these documents were passing, the roads were blockaded by the marshal's posse of southern volunteers, upon which no man without a passport could safely venture. Captain Samuel Walker, who had carried one of the above-mentioned letters to Lecompton, was fired upon on his return to Lawrence. Mr. Miller, who with two others had gone up to negotiate with the governor for an amicable adjustment of the pending troubles, was taken prisoner by a detachment of Buford's South Carolinians near Lecompton, who, knowing him to have been from their own state, tried him for treason and sentenced him to be hung. He contrived, somehow, to get away with the loss of his horse and purse. Mr. Weaver, a sergeant-at-arms of the congressional committee, was arrested while in the discharge of his duty, and carried across the Kansas river, to the South Carolinian camp, where, after a critical examination of his papers, he was discovered to be in the service of the United States, and released, the officer in command giving him a pass, and kindly advising him to answer promptly, if challenged, otherwise he might be shot. Outrages of this kind became so frequent that all travel was at last suspended.

On the 17th of May, the citizens of Lawrence, through a committee, again addressed the United States marshal in the words of the following letter :

"I. B. DONALSON, U. S. MARSHAL OF K. T.

"Dear Sir : We desire to call your attention, as citizens of Kansas, to the fact that a large force of armed men have collected in the vicinity of Lawrence, and are engaged in committing depredations upon our citizens; stopping wagons, arresting, threatening and robbing unoffending travelers on the highway, breaking open boxes of merchandise and appropriating the contents; have slaughtered cattle, and terrified many of the women and children.

"We also learned from governor Shannon, 'that there are no armed forces in the vicinity of this place but the regular constituted militia of the territory; this is to ask if you recognize them as your *posse*, and feel responsible for their acts. If you do not, we hope and trust you will prevent a repetition of such acts, and give peace to the settlers." Signed by the citizens.

To this communication no reply was given. "In the meantime, preparations were going forward, and vigorously prosecuted, for the sacking of Lawrence.* The pro-slavery people were to 'wipe out' this ill-fated town under authority of law. They had received the countenance of the president—the approbation of the chief-justice—the favorable presentment of the grand jury—the concurrence of the governor—the orders of the marshal,—and were prepared to consummate their purpose with the arms of the government, in the hands of a militia force gathered from the remotest sections of the Union. They concentrated their troops in large numbers around the doomed city, stealing, or, as they termed it, 'pressing into the service,' all the horses they could find belonging to free-state men, whose cattle were also slaughtered, without remuneration, to feed the marshal's forces; and their stores and dwellings broken open and robbed of arms, provisions, blankets and clothing. The marshal's army had a host of commanders. There was general Atchison, with the Missouri Platte county rifles, and two pieces of artillery; captain Dunn, with the Kickapoo Rangers; general Stringfellow, and colonel Abel, his law-partner, aided by doctor John H. Stringfellow, and Robert S. Kelly, editors of the *Squatter Sovereign*, with the forces from Doniphan, Atchison and Leavenworth; colonel Boone, with sundry aids, at the head of companies from Westport, Liberty and Independence; colonels Wilkes and Buford, with the Carolinians, Georgians and Mississippians; colonel H. T. Titus, in command of the Douglas county militia; and many others too numerous to mention. On the 19th of May, while these forces were collecting for the destruction of Lawrence, a young man from Illinois, named Jones, had been to a store near Blanton's bridge, to purchase flour, when he was attacked by two of the marshal's party, who were out as scouts. To escape these men, Jones dismounted and entered the store, into which they followed, and there abused him. He again mounted his horse and started for home, the others following, and swearing that the d—d abolitionist should not escape. When near the bridge, they leveled their guns (United States muskets,) and fired. Jones fell mortally wounded, and soon expired. On the following morning, several young men, hearing of this transaction, left Lawrence to visit the scene of the tragedy. One of these was named Stewart, who had but recently arrived from the

*Gihon's History of Kansas.

state of New York. They had gone about a mile and a half, when they met two men, armed with Sharpe's rifles. Some words passed between them, when the two strangers raised their rifles, and, taking deliberate aim at Stewart, fired. One of the balls entered his temple. The work of death was instantly accomplished. Soon after sunrise, on the morning of the 21st, an advanced guard of the marshal's army consisting of about 200 horsemen, appeared on the top of Mount Oread, on the outskirts of Lawrence, where their cannon had been stationed late on the preceding night. The town was quiet, and the citizens had determined to submit without resistance to any outrage that might be perpetrated. About seven o'clock, doctor Robinson's house, which stood on the side of the hill, was taken possession of, and used as the head quarters of the invaders. At eight o'clock, the main body of the army posted themselves on the outer edge of the town. Deputy marshal Fain, with ten men, entered Lawrence, and, without molestation, served the writs in his possession, and arrested judge G. W. Smith and G. W. Deitzler. Fain and his companions dined at the free-state hotel, and afterwards returned to the army on Mount Oread. The marshal then dismissed his monster posse, telling them he had no further use for them. It was three o'clock in the afternoon, when sheriff Jones rode rapidly into Lawrence, at the head of twenty-five mounted men; and as he passed along the line of the troops, he was received with deafening shouts of applause. His presence was the signal for action, and a sanction for the outrages that ensued. Atchison addressed his forces, and then marched the whole column to within a short distance of the hotel, where they halted. Jones now informed colonel Eldridge, the proprietor, that the hotel must be destroyed; he was acting under orders; he had writs issued by the first district court of the United States to destroy the free-state Hotel, and the offices of the *Herald of Freedom* and *Free Press*. The grand jury at Lecompton had indicted them as nuisances, and the court had ordered them to be destroyed. He gave colonel Eldridge an hour and a half to remove his family and furniture, after which time the demolition commenced, and was prosecuted with an earnestness that would have done credit to a better cause. In the meantime the newspaper offices had been assailed, the presses broken to pieces, and these, with the type and other material, thrown into the Kansas river. Whilst the work of destruction was going on at the printing offices, the bombardment of the hotel, a strongly constructed three-story stone building, commenced. Kegs of gunpowder had been placed inside and the house fired in numerous places; and whilst the flames were doing their destructive work within, heavy cannon were battering against the walls without; and amid the crackling of the conflagration, the noise of falling walls and timbers, and the roar of the artillery, were mingled almost frantic yells of satisfaction. And then followed scenes of reckless pillage and wanton destruction in all parts of that ill-fated town. Stores were broken into and plundered of their contents. Bolts and bars were no obstacles to the entrance of drunken and infuriated men into private dwellings, from which most of the inhabitants had fled in terror. From these everything of value was stolen, and much that was useless to the marauders was destroyed. The closing act of this frightful drama was the burning of the house of doctor Robinson on the brow of Mount Oread. This was set on fire after the sun had gone down, and the bright light which its flames shed over the country illuminated the paths of the retreating army, as they proceeded towards their homes.

"After the sacking of Lawrence, parties of free-state men were organized and armed with the determination to continue the war which had now begun in earnest. Some of these committed depredations upon their political opponents under the pretense of recovering horses and other property of which themselves and neighbors had been robbed. They attacked the pro-slavery men in the roads and at their dwellings, and committed most flagrant outrages. These organizations and their actions were condemned by the prominent and more respectable portions of the free-state party, and very few of the actual settlers of the territory had any lot or part in their proceedings. They were chiefly composed of men of desperate fortunes, who were actuated in many instances as much by a disposition to plunder as from a spirit of retaliation and revenge for insults and injuries they had received. A detachment of one of these parties, eight in number, secreted themselves in a ravine near the Santa Fe road, where they laid in wait for a company of eighteen pro-slavery men who they had understood were coming in that direction on a marauding expedition, and as they approached, a fire was poured into them from their ambushed enemies, killing three and wounding several more. The remainder, not knowing the strength of their assailants, fled in dismay. Other instances of the kind were constantly occurring. Indeed, it seems as though each party was determined to vie with the other in the number of outrages it could commit. Captain John Brown, who lived near Ossawattomie, was the leader of one of these free-state guerilla bands. He was a Vermonter by birth, an old soldier, and had served through the war of 1812. He was a resolute, determined and brave old man; but fierce, passionate, revengeful and inexorable. His hatred for the border-ruffians had reached so high a degree, that he could emulate the worst of them in acts of cruelty, whilst not one of them was his equal as a tactician, or possessed as much courage and daring. Hence his name soon became a terror, and not a few unsuccessful attempts were made to effect his capture. Brown is said to have been the leader of a band, who on the night of the 26th of May, attacked a pro-slavery settlement at Pottawattomie, and cruelly murdered a Mr. Doyle and his two sons, Mr. Wilkinson and Wm. Sherman. The excuse given for this act is, that the persons killed were there assembled to assassinate and burn the houses of certain free-state men, whom they had notified to quit the neighborhood. These five men were seized and disarmed, a sort of trial was had, and in conformity with the sentence passed, were shot in cold blood. This was doubtless an act of retaliation for the work done but a few days before at Lawrence. Captain H. C. Pate, who was in command of a predatory band of about sixty Missourians, called 'Shannon's Sharp Shooters,' resolved to capture Capt. John Brown, and with this intent visited Ossawattomie on the last day of May. Brown was absent, and Captain Pate succeeded without resistance, in taking prisoners two of his sons, whom he found engaged in their peaceful occupations. Captain Pate's men burned the store of a German named Winer, who was supposed to have been in the Pottawatomie affair, and also the house of young John Brown, the Captain's son. After committing these and other depredations upon the free-state settlers, the most of whose houses they entered and robbed, Pate and his company left the place, taking with them their prisoners. These they delivered to a company of United States dragoons, whom they found encamped on the Middle Ottawa Creek. When Captain Brown learned of the visit of Pate, he gathered a company of about thirty men, and hastening in pursuit, overtook him on the 2d of June, near Palmyra, about fifteen miles from Lawrence. Pate was encamped when Brown appeared, and having been informed of his approach, had fortified his camp by drawing together some heavy wagons. Brown soon made his arrangements, and notwithstanding the disparity of their forces, commenced the attack, when a spirited battle ensued. This lasted about three hours, when Captain Pate sent out a flag of truce, and unconditionally surrendered. Some of his men had ridden off during the fight, as was also the case with some of Brown's command. Several were severely wounded on both sides, but none were killed. Brown took thirty-one prisoners, a large number of horses, some wagons, arms, munitions, and a considerable amount of plunder that had been seized at various places by Pate's men. Soon after the surrender of Pate, Brown was reinforced by Captain Abbott, with a company of fifty men from the Wakarusa, who had come to his assistance. Whilst Brown was in pursuit of Captain Pate with the free-state men from Ossawattomie, other parties from Lawrence and the Wakarusa were planning an attack on Franklin, where a number of the pro-slavery rangers had remained, since the sacking of Lawrence. Franklin is about four miles from the latter town, near the Wakarusa, and on the road to Westport. It was a sort of Missouri headquarters, where the forces were accustomed to assemble whenever a descent upon Lawrence was contemplated. Having settled the preliminaries to their satisfaction, a company of the attacking party entered Franklin about two o'clock on the morning of June 4th. The night was extremely dark, and everything in and about the town was wrapped in the most profound stillness. Yet the pro-slavery forces had been apprised of the intended visit, and were prepared to give the intruders a warm reception. The latter, numbering about fifteen men, proceeded directly to the guard-house and demanded a surrender, which was answered by the discharge of a cannon planted in the door, that had been loaded heavily with every imaginable sort of missile that could be crammed into its muzzle. The noise of the explosion was like the loud roar of thunder in the very midst of the town. Fortunately for the assailants, the gun was not properly pointed, and its infernal contents passed harmless over their heads. Then came on the battle. A volley from the Sharpe's rifles of the free-state men was poured into the guard-room door, simultaneously with which, many shots came down from the neighboring houses. The attacking party threw themselves upon the ground, and without any regular order, kept up a random fire as rapidly as they could load their pieces, their enemies constantly returning their shots. In the meantime, reinforcements entered the town, but in consequence of the extreme darkness and the uncertainty of the positions of the contending forces, they could take no part in the fight, not being able to distinguish their foes from their friends. They nevertheless made the best of their time, having broken into the stores and loaded their wagon, which had been brought for the purpose, with ammunition, rifles, guns, provisions and such other articles as they desired, the greater part of which were Buford's stores, previously captured from free-state people. The firing continued on both sides until nearly daylight, when the pro-slavery men retired, leaving their enemies in possession of the town. In this affair a pro-slavery man named Teschmaker was killed, and three or four wounded. One man had his ear shot off. The assailants received no injury whatever. One remarkable feature in all these Kansas battles, is, that although many persons were sometimes engaged, who fought with passions inflamed to the most violent pitch, the loss on either side was almost invariably quite insignificant. Those who suffered death were generally murdered, not in the heat of battle, but deliberately and in cold blood, when the fights were over. General Whitfield, in the meantime, had collected a large force, chiefly from Jackson county, Mo., with which, accompanied by General Reid, and other prominent members of his party, professedly to relieve Captain Pate, and attack and capture Brown, he entered the territory and encamped near Palmyra. Whilst this army was assembling, the free-state bands were also concentrating and moving towards the same neighborhood. These latter, says one of their own writers, ' were a harum-scarum set, as brave as steel, mostly mere boys, and did not consider it a sin to ' press ' a pro-slavery man's horse. At various times they have made more disturbance than all other free-state men together. They were under no particular restraint, and did not recognise any authority—military, civil, or otherwise—any further than suited their convenience. While they went around the country skirmishing, and carrying on the war against the pro-slavery men on their own hook, and in their own time and way, they were at the same time quite willing to lend a hand in more systematic and important fighting when there was an opportunity. These boys have been most bitterly maligned, and the free state men, or conservative free-state men, were not slow to denounce them. Resolutions were passed by the sensitively moral free-state people, or the *sensitively timid*, declaring that these daring young guerillas were a nuisance, and that they, the conservative class, did not wish to be held responsible for them. To all this moralizing these young braves turned up their noses, ironically recommending all who were too cowardly to fight to ' keep right on the record.' For their own part they regarded the war as begun, and would wage it against the pro-slavery men as the pro-slavery men waged it against their free-state friends.' This was the state of affairs near Hickory Point on the morning of the 5th of June. Whitfield was encamped behind Palmyra with near three hundred men. The free-state camps mustered, on mustering on that day, were about two hundred strong, and two companies were marching from Topeka with fifty more, who arrived the day after. The governor, in view of this condition of things, issued a proclamation on the 4th, 'commanding all persons belonging to military companies unauthorized by law to disperse, otherwise they would be dispersed by United States troops.' Col. Sumner, at the head of a large force of dragoons, proceeded towards Hickory Point to enforce the order. He went directly to the camp of Brown, on Ottawa Creek, who consented to disband, but not until he was assured that Whitfield's army should be dispersed. Pate and the other prisoners were then set at liberty, and their horses, arms and other property restored. Captain Pate received a severe rebuke for invading the territory without authority, and especially for being in possession of the United States arms. Col. Sumner next visited the camp of Whitfield, who promised to return with his men to Missouri, and at once moved down the Santa Fe road, and encamped about five miles below Palmyra on the Black Jack. Early on the following morning, June 6th, this army separated into two divisions, one-half of it under General Reid, with Captain Pate, Bell, Jenigen, and other prominent leaders, moving towards Ossawattomie, whilst the others under Whitfield, started for Westport. They had, in their march on the day previous, taken several prisoners, and before they divided, held a court among themselves and tried one of these, a free-state man named Cantral, whom they sentenced to death, carried into a deep ravine near by, and shot. The executioner in this case is said to have been a man named Forman, of Pate's company, belonging to Westport, Missouri. On the 7th, Reid, with one hundred and seventy men, marched into Ossawattomie, and without resistance, entered each house, robbing it of everything of value. There were but few men in the town, and the women and children were treated with the utmost brutality. Stores and dwellings were alike entered and pillaged. Trunks, boxes, and desks were broken open, and their contents appropriated or destroyed. Even rings were rudely pulled from the ears and fingers of the women, and some of the apparel from their persons. The liquor found was freely drunk, and served to incite the plunderers to increased violence in the prosecution of their mischievous work. Having completely stripped the town, they set fire to several houses, and then beat a rapid retreat, carrying off a number of horses, and loudly urging each other to greater haste, as 'the d—d abolitionists were coming!' There are hundreds of well authenticated accounts of the cruelties practiced by this horde of ruffians, some of them too shocking and disgusting to relate, or to be accredited if told. The tears and shrieks of terrified women failed to touch a chord of mercy, and the mutilated bodies of murdered men, hanging upon the trees, or left to rot upon the prairies or in the deep ravines, or furnish food for vultures and wild beasts, told frightful stories of brutal ferocity."

An Indian agent named Gay, was traveling in the vicinity of Westport, and was stopped by a party of Buford's men, who asked if he was in favor of making Kansas a free state. He promptly answered in the affirmative, and was instantly shot dead. Whilst these events were transpiring on the south side of the Kansas river, Col. Wilkes, Captain Emory, and other prominent pro-slavery men, were actively employed in persecuting the free-state citizens of Leavenworth. Notices were served on them to quit the city; some were violently seized and imprisoned, and still others carried to the levee, having been deprived of all their property and the greater part of their clothing, placed on board of steamers, and thus compelled to leave the country. At the same time the steamboats coming up the river continued to be boarded at every stopping place, the free-state passengers insulted, their trunks broken open and robbed, and their arms taken from them; after which they were put upon return boats, and forced to go back.

In August, 1856, the troubles in the territory reached their culminating point. The free state immigrants had opened a new route into the territory through Nebraska and Iowa, and large and well-armed companies came pouring in, many of them of irreproachable character, who came to the relief of the oppressed; and others of desperate fortunes, eager to take part in the disturbances, from a spirit of revenge or a love of the excitement; and still others, perhaps for the sole purpose of plunder. These bands were generally under the direction of Lane, Redpath, Perry, and other prominent free state leaders. The pro-slavery marauders south of the Kansas river had established and fortified themselves at the town of Franklin; at a fort thrown up near Osawattomie; at another on Washington Creek, twelve miles from Lawrence; and at Col. Titus' house, on the border of Lecompton. From these strongholds they would sally forth, "press" horses and cattle, intercept the mails, rob stores and dwellings, plunder travellers, burn houses, and destroy crops. The fort near Osawattomie, in consequence of outrages committed in the neighborhood, and at the solicitation of the settlers, was attacked by a company of free state men from Lawrence, on the 5th of August. A party of Georgians who held this position, upon the approach of the enemy, fled without firing a gun, leaving behind a large quantity of plunder. The fort was then taken and demolished. The defeated party retreated to the fort at Washington Creek, and thence continued their depredations upon the neighboring inhabitants. On the 11th, the people of Lawrence sent Major D. S. Hoyt, a peaceable man, who was greatly respected, to this camp to endeavor to make some sort of amicable arrangement with Col. Treadwell, the commander. On his way home he was waylaid and shot, his body being fairly riddled with bullets. This news so enraged the people of Lawrence, that on the 12th they attacked the pro-slavery post at Franklin. The enemy was strongly fortified in a block-house, and had one brass six-pounder. This battle lasted three hours, and was conducted with great spirit on both sides. The free state men, at length, drew a wagon load of hay against the house, and were about to set it on fire, when the inmates cried for quarter. They then threw down their arms and fled. In this engagement the free state men had one killed and six wounded. The other side had four severely wounded, one of them mortally. The cannon taken was one that had been used to batter down the walls of the Lawrence hotel. A general panic seized the Missouri and other southern intruders, on learning these repeated free state successes. On the 15th, the Georgian camp at Washington

Creek broke up in great confusion, its occupants flying in hot haste as the Lawrence forces approached. This fort was entered without resistance ; large quantities of provisions and goods taken at Lawrence were recovered ; the building was set on fire and entirely consumed. The next blow was struck at Col. Titus' fortified house, near Lecompton. Lecompton was the stronghold of the pro-slavery party. It was the capital of the territory, the headquarters of Governor Shannon, and within two miles of the house of Titus, a large force of United States dragoons was encamped. Captain Samuel Walker, a Pennsylvanian, commanded the attacking army. With about four hundred men and one brass six-pounder, he took up a position upon an elevated piece of ground near the house, soon after sunrise on the morning of the 16th of August. The fight, which was a spirited one, immediately commenced, and resulted in the capture of Titus, Capt. William Donaldson (who also had rendered himself notorious at the sacking of Lawrence and elsewhere), and of eighteen others. Five prisoners, previously taken by Titus' party, were released, one of whom had been sentenced to be shot that very day. One of his men was killed in this engagement, and several others wounded. Titus was shot in the shoulder and hand. Walker's cannon was loaded with slugs and balls cast from the type of the *Herald of Freedom*, fished out of the Kansas river, where it had been thrown on the day that Lawrence was sacked. Walker set fire to the house of Titus, which was completely destroyed, and carried his prisoners to Lawrence. On the 17th of August, Governor Shannon, Dr. Rodrique, and Major Sedgwick visited Lawrence, as a committee from Lecompton, to make a treaty. It was agreed that no more arrests should be made of free state people under the territorial laws ; that five free state men arrested after the attack on Franklin, should be set at liberty ; and that the howitzer taken by Jones from Lawrence, should be restored. On the 17th, a shocking affair occured in the neighborhood of Leavenworth. Two ruffians sat at a table in a low groggery, imbibing potations of whiskey. One of them, named Fugert, belonging to Atchison's band, bet his companion six dollars against a pair of boots, that he would go out, and in less than two hours bring in the scalp of an abolitionist. He went into the road, and meeting a Mr. Hoppe, who was in his carriage, just returning to Leavenworth from a visit to Lawrence, where he had conveyed his wife, Fugert deliberately shot him ; then taking out his bowie-knife, whilst his victim was still alive, he cut and tore off the scalp from his quivering head. Leaving the body of Hoppe lying in the road, he elevated his bloody trophy upon a pole, and paraded it through the streets of Leavenworth. This murderer was afterwards arrested, tried before Judge Lecompte, and acquitted.

Governor Shannon receiving official notice of his removal, Secretary Woodson took charge of the government. He forthwith issued a proclamation, declaring the territory in a state of rebellion and insurrection, and called for help from Missouri, to drive out and exterminate the destroyers of the public peace. Atchison and Stringfellow soon responded to this call, and concentrated an army of eleven hundred men at Little Santa Fe, on the Missouri border. A detachment of Atchison's army, under Gen. Reid, numbering about three hundred men, with one piece of artillery, attacked Osawattomie on the 30th of August. Brown was in command at the time, and, having only between thirty and forty men, he retreated to the timber on the river or creek known as Marias Des Cygnes. The battle which ensued lasted about three hours, Brown having a decided advantage. He was overpowered, however, by superior numbers, and driven to the river, in crossing which he suffered some loss from the enemy. After the retreat of Brown, Reid's forces burned some twenty or thirty houses, robbed the post office and stores, took possession of all the horses, cattle, and wagons in town, and committed many other depredations. They found a man named Garrison concealed in the woods, whom they killed, and wounded another by the name of Cutter, whom they supposed to be dead, but who has since recovered. A Mr. Williams, a pro-slavery man, was murdered by them in mistake.

On the day of the battle at Osawattomie, Lane, with about three hundred men, marched in pursuit of Atchison, who was encamped with the main body of his army on Bull Creek. Atchison would not stop to fight, but retreated into Missouri, and Lane on the following day returned to Lawrence. Whilst these things were occurring, a party of pro-slavery men entered the Quaker Mission, on the Lawrence road, near Westport, plundered it of everything worth carrying away, and brutally treated the occupants. At the same time, Woodson's "territorial militia," were amusing themselves by burning the houses of the free state settlers between Lecompton and Lawrence. Seven buildings were destroyed, among which were the dwellings of Capt. Walker and Judge Wakefield. Because of these outrages, and the seizure of some free state prisoners, Lane, with a large force, proceeded to Lecompton, on September 4th, and before any intimation was received by the citizens, his cannon was frowning upon their houses from the summit of Court House hill. Gen. Richardson, who was in command of the pro-slavery forces, refused to defend the town, having no confidence in the courage of the inhabitants, who were flying in all directions, in confusion and alarm, and he therefore resigned his commission. Gen. Marshall being next in command, held a parley with Lane, who demanded the liberation of free state prisoners. This was agreed to. Lane returned to Lawrence, and the next day the prisoners came down with an escort of United States dragoons. At Leavenworth and vicinity, outrages had been renewed, and were being committed, if possible, with increased ferocity. As Governor Shannon afterwards remarked, "the roads were literally strewn with dead bodies." A United States officer discovered a number of slaughtered men, thirteen, it is stated, lying unburied, who had been seized and brained, some of them being shot in the forehead, and others down through the top of the skull, whilst some were cut with hatchets, and their bodies shockingly and disgustingly mutilated. On the first of September, Capt. Frederick Emory, a United States mail contractor, rendered himself conspicuous in Leavenworth, at the head of a band of ruffians, mostly from Western Missouri. They entered houses, stores, and dwellings of free state people, and, in the name of "law and order," abused and robbed the occupants, and drove them out into the roads, irrespective of age, sex, or condition. Under pretence of searching for arms, they approached the house of William Phillips, the lawyer who had previously been tarred and feathered and carried to Missouri. Phillips, supposing he was to be subjected to a similar outrage, and resolved not to submit to the indignity, stood upon his defence. In repelling the assaults of the mob, he killed two of them, when the others burst into the house, and poured a volley of balls into his body, killing him instantly, in the presence of his wife and another lady. His brother, who was also present, had an arm badly broken with bullets, and was compelled to submit to an amputation. Fifty of the free state prisoners were then driven on board the Polar Star, bound for St. Louis On the next day a hundred more were embarked by Emory and his men, on the steamboat Emma.

In July, 1856, Col. John W. Geary, of Pennsylvania, was appointed by the president governor of the territory. His appointment was confirmed unanimously by the senate. In September, he started for Kansas, and on the 6th of that month he held a consultation at Jefferson City with Governor Price, of Missouri, relative to the affairs of the territory, and to whom he unfolded his plans. Measures mutually approved were adopted to clear the Missouri river for the unobstructed transit of free state emigrants to Kansas. On Sunday, the 7th, Gov. Geary arrived at Glasgow, in Missouri. In company with the governor was his private secretary, J. H. Gihon, who, since his return, has published a history of the proceedings in the territory during the administration of Gov. Geary. "On approaching the town of Glasgow," says Mr. Gihon, "a most stirring scene was presented. The entire population of the city and surrounding neighborhood was assembled upon the high bank overlooking the river, and all appeared to be laboring under a state of extraordinary excitement. Whites and blacks—men, women, and children, of all ages, were crowded together in one confused mass, or hurrying hither and yon, as though some terrible event was about to transpire. A large brass-field-piece was mounted in a prominent position, and ever and anon belched forth a fiery flame and deafened the ear with its thundering warlike sounds. When the Keystone touched the landing, a party of about sixty, comprising Captain Jackson's company of Missouri volunteers for the Kansas militia, descended the hill, dragging their cannon with them, and ranged themselves along the shore ; the captain, after numerous attempts, failing to get them into what might properly be termed a line. He got them into as good a military position as possible, by backing them up against the foot of the hill. They were as raw and undisciplined a set of recruits as ever shouldered arms. Their ages varied, through every gradation, from the smooth-faced half-grown boy to the gray-bearded old man; whilst their dresses, which differed as much as their ages, gave unmistakable evidences that they belonged to any class of society except that usually termed respectable. Each one carried some description of fire-arm, not two of which were alike. There were muskets, carbines, rifles, shot-guns, and pistols of every size, quality, shape, and style. Some of them were in good condition, but others were never intended for use, and still others unfit to shoot robins or tomtits.

"Whilst these parting ceremonies were being performed, a steamboat, bound down the river, and directly from Kansas, came alongside the Keystone. Ex-governor Shannon was a passenger, who, upon learning the close proximity of Gov. Geary, sought an immediate interview with him. The ex-governor was greatly agitated. He had fled in haste and terror from the territory, and seemed still to be laboring under an apprehension for his personal safety. His description of Kansas was suggestive of everything that is frightful and horrible. Its condition was deplorable in the extreme. The whole territory was in a state of insurrection, and a destructive civil war was devastating the country. Murder ran rampant, and the roads were everywhere strewn with the bodies of slaughtered men. No language can exaggerate the awful picture that was drawn ; and a man of less nerve than Gov. Geary, believing it not too highly colored, would instantly have taken the backward track, rather than rush upon the dangers so eloquently and fearfully portrayed.

"During this interview, Captain Jackson embarked his company, cannon, wagons, arms and ammunition on board the Keystone, and soon after, she was again on her way. Opportunities now occurred for conversation with the volunteers. Very few of them had any definite idea of the nature of the enterprise in which they had embarked. The most they seemed to understand about the matter was, that they were to receive so much per diem for going to Kansas to hunt and kill abolitionists. They seemed to apprehend no danger to themselves, as they had been told the abolitionists would not fight ; but being overawed by the numbers and warlike appearance of their adversaries, would escape as rapidly as possible out of the territory, leaving behind them any quantity of land, horses, clothing, arms, goods and chattels, all of which was to be divided among the victors.

"The Keystone no sooner touched the shore at Kansas City, than she was boarded by half a dozen or more of the leading ruffians, who dashed through the cabins and over the decks, inspecting the passengers and the state-rooms to satisfy themselves that no abolitionists were on board. She remained at Kansas City only long enough for Captain Jackson to land his company with its paraphernalia of war, and to undergo a thorough inspection of the border ruffian inquisitors, when she proceeded up the river for Fort Leavenworth. She left Kansas City late on the evening of the 8th, and soon after day-break of the 9th, reached the landing at Leavenworth City, three miles below the fort. Here was given another exhibition of the wretched condition of the country and deplorable spirit of the times. In front of the grog-shops, and these comprised nearly every house on the river front ; on piles of wood, lumber, and stone ; upon the heads of whiskey barrels ; at the corners of the streets ; and upon the river bank — lounged, strolled, and idled, singly or in squads, men and boys clad in the ruffian attire, giving sure indication that no useful occupation was being pursued, and that vice, confusion, and anarchy had undivided and undisputed possession of the town. Armed horsemen were dashing about in every direction, the horses' feet striking fire from the stones beneath, and the sabres of the riders rattling by their sides. The drum and fife disturbed the stillness of the morning, and volunteer companies were on parade and drill, with all the habiliments and panoply of war. The town was evidently under a complete military rule, and on every side were visible indications of a destructive civil strife."

Previous to Gov. Geary's departure from Fort Leavenworth for Lecompton, the capital of the territory, he addressed a communication to the Hon. Wm. L. Marcy, secretary of state of the United States, in which he describes the condition of the territory at the time of his arrival:

"FORT LEAVENWORTH, Kansas Territory, }
"September 9, 1856. }

"HON. WM. L. MARCY:

"Dear Sir: I arrived here this morning, and have passed the day mostly in consultation with Gen. P. F. Smith, in relation to the affairs of the territory, which, as I am now on the spot, I begin more clearly to understand. It is no exaggeration to say that the existing difficulties are of a far more complicated character than I had anticipated.

"I find that I have not simply to contend against bands of armed ruffians and brigands, whose sole aim and end is assassination and robbery—infatuated adherents and advocates of conflicting political sentiments and local institutions—and evil-disposed persons, actuated by a desire to obtain elevated positions; but worst of all, against the influence of men who have been placed in authority, and have employed all the destructive agents around them to promote their own personal interests, at the sacrifice of every just, honorable, and lawful consideration.

"I have barely time to give you a brief statement of facts as I find them. The town of Leavenworth is now in the hands of armed bodies of men, who, having been enrolled as militia, perpetrate outrages of the most atrocious character under shadow of authority from the territorial government. Within a few days, these men have robbed and driven from their homes unoffending citizens; have fired upon and killed others in their own dwellings; and stolen horses and property under the pretense of employing them in the public service. They have seized persons who had committed no offense; and after stripping them of all their valuables, placed them on steamers, and sent them out of the territory. Some of these bands, who have thus violated their rights and privileges, and shamefully and shockingly misused and abused the oldest inhabitants of the territory, who had settled here with their wives and children, are strangers from distant states, who have no interest in, nor care for the welfare of Kansas, and contemplate remaining here only so long as opportunities for mischief and plunder exist.

"The actual pro-slavery settlers of the territory are generally as well-disposed persons as are to be found in most communities. But there are among them a few troublesome agitators, chiefly from distant districts, who labor assiduously to keep alive the prevailing sentiment.

"It is also true that among the free-soil residents are many peaceable and useful citizens; and if uninfluenced by aspiring demagogues, would commit no unlawful act. But many of these, too, have been rendered turbulent by officious meddlers from abroad. The chief of these is Lane, now encamped and fortified at Lawrence, with a force, it is said, of fifteen hundred men. They are suffering for provisions, to cut off the supplies of which, the opposing faction is extremely watchful and active.

"In isolated or country places, no man's life is safe. The roads are filled with armed robbers, and murders for mere plunder are of daily occurrence. Almost every farm-house is deserted, and no traveler has the temerity to venture upon the highway without an escort.

"Such is the condition of Kansas, faintly pictured. It can be no worse. Yet I feel assured that I shall be able ere long to restore it to peace and quiet. To accomplish this, I should have more aid from the general government. The number of United States troops here is too limited to render the needed services. Immediate reinforcements are essentially necessary; as the excitement is so intense, and citizens generally are so much influenced by their political prejudices, that members of the two great factions cannot be induced to act in unison, and therefore cannot be relied upon. As soon, however, as I can succeed in disbanding a portion of those now in service, I will from time to time cause to be enrolled as many of the *bona fide* inhabitants as exigencies may seem to require. In the meantime, the presence of additional government troops will exert a moral influence that cannot be obtained by any militia that can here be called into requisition.

"In making the foregoing statements, I have endeavored to give the truth, and nothing but the truth. I deem it important that you should be apprised of the actual state of the case; and whatever may be the effect of such relations, they will be given, from time to time, without extenuation.

"I shall proceed early in the morning to Lecompton, under an escort furnished by Gen. Smith, where I will take charge of the government, and whence I shall again address you at an early moment.

"Very respectfully, your obedient servant,
"Jno. W. Geary,
"*Governor of Kansas.*"

Governor Geary proceeded forthwith to Lecompton, the capital of the territory. This town is situated on the Kansas river, about fifty miles from its junction with the Missouri, and contained at that time about thirty houses. Some $50,000 had been appropriated by congress for public buildings. No free-state man was permitted to live in the place. At Lecompton, Governor Geary issued his inaugural address.

GOVERNOR GEARY'S INAUGURAL.

"Fellow-Citizens:—I appear among you a stranger to most of you, and for the first time have the honor to address you, as the governor of the territory of Kansas. The position was not sought by me; but was voluntarily tendered by the present chief magistrate of the nation. As an American citizen, deeply conscious of the blessings which ever flow from our beloved Union, I did not consider myself at liberty to shrink from any duties, however delicate and onerous, required of me by my country.

"With a full knowledge of all the circumstances surrounding the executive office, I have deliberately accepted it, and as God may give me strength and ability, I will endeavor faithfully to discharge its varied requirements. When I received my commission I was solemnly sworn to support the constitution of the United States, and to discharge my duties as governor of Kansas with fidelity. By reference to the act for the organization of this territory, passed by congress on the 30th day of March, 1854, I find my duties more particularly defined. Among other things, I am 'to take care that the laws be faithfully executed.'

"The constitution of the United States and the organic law of the territory, will be the lights by which I will be guided in my official career.

"A careful and dispassionate examination of our organic act will satisfy any reasonable person that its provisions are eminently just and beneficial. If this act has been distorted to unworthy purposes, it is not the fault of its provisions. The great leading feature of that act is the right therein conferred upon the actual and *bona fide* inhabitants of this territory 'in the exercise of self-government, to determine for themselves what shall be their domestic institutions, subject only to the constitution and the laws duly enacted by congress, under it.' The people, accustomed to self-government in the states from whence they came, and having removed to this territory with the *bona fide* intention of making it their future residence, were supposed to be capable of creating their own municipal government, and to be the best judges of their own local necessities and institutions. This is what is termed *"popular sovereignty."* By this phrase we simply mean the right of the majority of the people of the several states and territories, being qualified electors, to regulate their own domestic concerns, and to make their own municipal laws. Thus understood, this doctrine underlies the whole system of republican government. It is the great right of self-government, for the establishment of which our ancestors, in the stormy days of the revolution, pledged 'their lives, their fortunes and their sacred honor.'

"A doctrine so eminently just should receive the willing homage of every American citizen. When legitimately expressed, and duly ascertained, the will of the majority must be the imperative rule of civil action for every law abiding citizen. This simple, just rule of action has brought order out of chaos, and by a progress unparalleled in the history of the world, has made a few feeble, infant colonies, a giant confederated republic.

"No man, conversant with the state of affairs now in Kansas, can close his eyes to the fact that much civil disturbance has for a long time past existed in this territory. Various reasons have been assigned for this unfortunate state of affairs, and numerous remedies have been proposed.

"The house of representatives of the United States have ignored the claims of both gentlemen claiming the legal right to represent the people of this territory in that body. The Topeka constitution, recognized by the house, has been repudiated by the senate. Various measures, each in the opinion of its respective advocates, suggestive of peace to Kansas, have been alternately proposed and rejected. Men, *outside of the territory*, in various sections of the Union, influenced by reasons best known to themselves, have endeavored to stir up internal strife, and to array brother against brother.

" In this conflict of opinion, and for the promotion of most unworthy purposes, Kansas is left to suffer, her people to mourn, and her prosperity is endangered.

" Is there no remedy for these evils? Cannot the wounds of Kansas be healed, and peace restored to all her borders ?

" Men of the north—men of the south—of the east, and of the west, *in Kansas*, you, and you only, have the remedy in your own hands. Will you not suspend fratricidal strife? Will you not cease to regard each other as enemies, and look upon one another as the children of a common mother, and come and reason together ?

" Let us banish all *outside influences* from our deliberations, and assemble around our council board with the constitution of our country and the organic law of this territory, as the great charts for our guidance and direction. The *bona fide* inhabitants of the territory *alone* are charged with the solemn duty of enacting her laws, upholding her government, maintaining peace, and laying the foundation for a future commonwealth.

" On this point let there be a perfect unity of sentiment. It is the first great step towards the attainment of peace. It will inspire confidence amongst ourselves and insure the respect of the whole country. Let us show ourselves worthy and capable of self-government.

" Do not the inhabitants of this territory better understand what domestic institutions are suited to their condition—what laws will be most conducive to their prosperity and happiness, than the citizens of distant, or even neighboring states? This great right of regulating our own affairs and attending to our own business, without any interference from others, has been guaranteed to us by the law which congress has made for the organization of this territory. This right of self-government—this privilege guaranteed to us by the organic law of our territory, I will uphold with all my might, and with the entire power committed to me.

" In relation to any changes of the laws of the territory which I may deem desirable, I have no occasion now to speak; but these are subjects to which I shall direct public attention at the proper time.

" The territory of the United States is the *common property* of the several states, or of the people thereof. This being so, no obstacle should be interposed to the free settlement of this common property, while in a territorial condition.

" I cheerfully admit that the people of this territory, under the organic act, have the absolute right of making their own municipal laws. And from citizens who deem themselves agrieved by recent legislation, I would invoke the

47

utmost forbearance, and point out to them a sure and peaceable remedy. You have the right to ask the next legislature to revise any and all laws; and in the meantime, as you value the peace of the territory and the maintenance of future laws, I would earnestly ask you to refrain from all violations of the present statutes.

"I am sure that there is patriotism sufficient in the people of Kansas to induce them to lend a willing obedience to law. All the provisions of the constitution of the United States must be sacredly observed—all the acts of congress, having reference to this territory, must be unhesitatingly obeyed, and the decisions of our courts respected. It will be my *imperative* duty to see that these suggestions are carried into effect. In my official action here, I will do justice at all hazards. Influenced by no other considerations than the welfare of the whole people of this territory, I desire to know no party, no section, no north, no south, no east, no west—nothing but Kansas and my country.

"Fully conscious of my great responsibilities in the present condition of Kansas, I must invoke your aid, and solicit your generous forbearance. Your executive officer can do little without the aid of the people. With a firm reliance upon divine providence, to the best of my ability, I shall promote the interests of the citizens of this territory, not merely collectively, but individually, and I shall expect from them, in return, that cordial aid and support, without which the government of no state or territory can be administered with beneficent effect.

Let us all begin anew. Let the past be buried in oblivion. Let all strife and bitterness cease. Let us all honestly devote ourselves to the true interests of Kansas; develop her rich agricultural and mineral resources; build up manufacturing enterprises; make public roads and highways; prepare amply for the education of our children; devote ourselves to all the arts of peace; and make our territory the sanctuary of those cherished principles which protect the inalienable rights of the individual, and elevate states in their sovereign capacities.

"Then shall peaceful industry soon be restored; population and wealth will flow upon us; 'the desert will blossom as the rose;' and the state of Kansas will soon be admitted into the Union, the peer and pride of her elder sisters.

"JOHN W. GEARY."

Simultaneously with this address, developing the policy by which his official action was to be guided and controlled, the governor published the following proclamations:—

PROCLAMATION.

"WHEREAS, A large number of volunteer militia have been called into the service of the territory of Kansas, by authority of the late acting governor, for the maintenance of order, many of whom have been taken from occupations or business, and deprived of their ordinary means of support and of their domestic enjoyments; and

"WHEREAS, The employment of militia is not authorized by my instructions from the general government, except upon requisition of the commander of the military department in which Kansas is embraced; and

"WHEREAS, An authorized regular force has been placed at my disposal, sufficient to insure the execution of the laws that may be obstructed by combinations too powerful to be suppressed by the ordinary course of judicial proceedings; now

"*Therefore*, I, JOHN W. GEARY, governor of the territory of Kansas, do issue this, my proclamation, declaring that the services of such volunteer militia are no longer required; and hereby order that they be immediately discharged. The secretary and adjutant-general of the territory will muster out of service each command at its place of rendezvous.

"And I command all bodies of men, combined, armed and equipped with munitions of war, without authority of the government, instantly to disband or quit the territory, as they will answer the contrary at their peril.

"In testimony whereof, I have hereunto set my hand, and affixed the seal of the territory of Kansas.

"Done at Lecompton, this eleventh day of September, in the year of our Lord one thousand eight hundred and fifty-six.   JOHN W. GEARY,
Governor of Kansas Territory."

"WHEREAS, It is the true policy of every state or territory to be prepared for any emergency that may arise from internal dissension or foreign invasion:

"*Therefore*, I, John W. Geary, governor of the territory of Kansas, do issue this my proclamation, ordering all free male citizens, qualified to bear arms, between the ages of eighteen and forty-five years, to enrol themselves, in accordance with the act to organize the militia of the territory, that they may be completely organized by companies, regiments, brigades, or divisions, and hold themselves in readiness, to be mustered, by my order, into the service of the United States, upon requisition of the commander of the military department in which Kansas is embraced, for the suppression of all combinations to resist the laws, and for the maintenance of public order and civil government.

"In testimony whereof, I have hereunto set my hand, and affixed the seal of the territory of Kansas.

"Done at Lecompton, this eleventh day of September, in the year of our Lord one thousand eight hundred and fifty-six.   JOHN W. GEARY,
Governor of Kansas Territory."

When Governor Geary's appointment was first announced in Kansas, it was generally understood that he would not affiliate with either party, but would use his endeavors to carry out the doctrine of popular sovereignty. Measures were immediately set on foot, by the pro-slavery party, to frustrate his plans, by gathering an army in Missouri and other slave states, with which to overrun the territory, and drive out the free state people. An address was issued for circulation in the slave states, calling for assistance, and signed by Atchison, Stringfellow, Reid, Doniphan, and others. From this address we extract the following :

"We have asked the appointment of a successor who was acquainted with our condition; who, a citizen of the territory, identified with its interests, familiar with its history, would not be prejudiced or misled by the falsehoods which have been so systematically fabricated against us—one who, heretofore a resident as he is a native of a non-slaveholding state, is yet not a slaveholder, but has the capacity to appreciate, and the boldness and integrity requisite faithfully to discharge his duty, regardless of the possible effect it might have upon the election of some petty politician in a distant state.

"In his stead we have one appointed who is ignorant of our condition, a stranger to our people; who we have too much cause to fear will, if no worse, prove no more efficient to protect us than his predecessors.

"With, then, a government which has proved imbecile—has failed to enforce the laws for our protection—with an army of lawless banditti overrunning our country—what shall we do ?

"Though we have full confidence in the integrity and fidelity of Mr. Woodson, now acting as governor, we know not at what moment his authority will be superseded. We cannot await the convenience, in coming, of our newly appointed governor. We cannot hazard a second edition of imbecility or corruption.

"We must act at once and effectively. These traitors, assassins, and robbers must be punished; must now be taught a lesson they will remember.

"We wage no war upon men for their opinions; have never attempted to exclude any from settling among us; we have demanded only that all should *alike* submit to the law. To all such we will afford protection, whatever be their political opinions. But Lane's army and its allies must be expelled from the territory. Thus alone can we make safe our persons and property—thus alone can we bring peace to our territory.

"To do this we will need assistance. Our citizens unorganized, many of them unarmed, for they came not as soldiers—though able heretofore to assemble a force sufficient to compel the obedience of the rebels, now that they have been strengthened by this invading army, thoroughly drilled, perfectly equipped, mounted, and ready to march at a moment's notice, to attack our defenceless settlements—may be overpowered. Should we be able even to vanquish this additional force, we are threatened with a further invasion of like character through Iowa and Nebraska.

"This is no mere local quarrel; no mere riot; but it is a war! a war waged by an army! a war professedly for our extermination. It is no mere resistance to the laws; no simple rebellion of our citizens, but a war of invasion—the army a foreign army—properly named the 'army of the north.'

"It is then not only the right but the duty of all good citizens of Missouri and every other state, to come to our assistance, and enable us to expel these invaders.

"Mr. Woodson, since the resignation of Governor Shannon, in the absence of Governor Geary, has fearlessly met the responsibilities of the trust forced upon him, has proclaimed the existence of the rebellion, and called on the militia of the territory to assemble for its suppression.

"We call on you to come! to furnish us assistance in men, provisions, and munitions, that we may drive out the 'army of the north,' who would subvert our government and expel us from our homes.

"Our people though poor, many of them stripped of their all, others harassed by these fiends, so that they have been unable to provide for their families, are yet true men; will stand with you shoulder to shoulder in defence of rights, of principles in which you have a common if not deeper interest than they.

"By the issue of this struggle is to be decided whether law or lawlessness shall reign in our country. If we are vanquished you too will be victims. Let not our appeal be in vain!"

Before Governor Geary's arrival, Secretary Woodson, the acting governor of the territory after the flight of Shannon, issued the following proclamation. This was issued at a time when Woodson was aware that Geary was on his way to the territory:

"PROCLAMATION.

"WHEREAS, satisfactory evidence exists that the territory of Kansas is infested with large bodies of armed men, many of whom have just arrived from the states, combined and confederated together, and amply supplied with the munitions of war, under the direction of a common head, with a thorough military organization, who have been and are still engaged in murdering law-abiding citizens of the territory, driving others from their homes, and compelling them to flee to the states for protection, capturing and holding others as prisoners of war, plundering them of their property, and in some instances burning down their houses and robbing United States post offices, and the local militia of the arms furnished them by the government, in open defiance and contempt of the laws of the territory, and of the constitution and laws of the United States, and of civil and military authority thereof—all for the purpose of subverting, by force and violence, the government established by law of congress in this territory.

"Now, therefore, I, Daniel Woodson, acting governor of the territory of Kansas, do hereby issue my proclamation declaring the said territory to be in a state of open insurrection and rebellion; and I do hereby call upon all law-abiding citizens of the territory to rally to the support of their country and its laws, and require and command all officers, civil and military, and all other citizens of the territory, to aid and assist by all means in their power, in putting down the insurrectionists, and bringing to condign punishment all persons engaged with them, to the end of assuring immunity from violence, and full protection to the persons, property, and civil rights to all peaceable and law-abiding inhabitants of the territory.

"In testimony whereof, I have hereunto set my hand and caused to be attached the seal of the territory of Kansas.

"Done at the city of Lecompton, this twenty-fifth day of August, in the year of our Lord eighteen hundred and fifty-six, and of the independence of the United States the eightieth.

"DANIEL WOODSON, Acting Governor, K. T."

Private letters were written by the acting governor to parties in Missouri, calling for men, money, and the munitions of war, to carry out the purposes of the pro-slavery party. The address, the proclamation, and the letters had the effect of calling into the territory large numbers of armed men, chiefly from Missouri, with passions highly inflamed, and prepared for a war of extermination against the free state settlements. Such was the state of affairs on the arrival of governor Geary at Lecompton.

In accordance with his proclamation, he forthwith proceeded to disband all the armed bodies in the territory which had been collected under the authority of secretary Woodson, and to this end he issued the following orders to the proper military officers; and on the same day sent the following dispatch to secretary Marcy:

"EXECUTIVE DEPARTMENT, LECOMPTON, K. T.,
September 12, 1856.

"ADJT.-GEN. H. J. STRICKLER:

"DEAR SIR: You will proceed without a moment's delay to disarm and disband the present organized militia of the territory, in accordance with the instructions of the president, and the proclamations which I have issued, copies of which you will find enclosed. You will also take care to have the arms belonging to the territory deposited in a place of safety and under proper accountability.   "Yours, &c.,   JNO. W. GEARY,
"Governor of Kansas Territory."

EXECUTIVE DEPARTMENT, LECOMPTON, K. T.,
September 12, 1856.

"INSPECTOR-GEN. THOS. J. B. CRAMER:

"SIR: You will take charge of the arms of the territory of Kansas, now in the hands of the militia about to be disbanded and mustered out of the service by the adjutant-general. You will also carefully preserve the same agreeably to the 15th section of the act of assembly, to organize, discipline, and govern the militia of the territory.

"Yours, &c.,   JNO. W. GEARY,
"Governor of Kansas Territory."

"EXECUTIVE OFFICE, LECOMPTON, K. T.,
September 12, 1856.

"HON. WM. L. MARCY,
"Secretary of State, Washington, D. C.

"MY DEAR SIR: I arrived here late on the night of the 10th inst., having crossed from Fort Leavenworth with an escort furnished me by General Smith. On the road, I witnessed numerous evidences of the atrocities that are being committed by the bands of marauders that infest the country. In this place everything is quiet; which is attributable to the presence of a large force of United States troops. The trial of the United States prisoners was to have taken place on the day of my arrival; but in consequence of the absence of the district attorney, and the non-appearance of witnesses, it was deferred until the next regular term of court, Judge Lecompte admitting the prisoners to bail in the sum of five thousand dollars each. They departed on the same day for Lawrence, where Lane still continues in force.

"Accompanying this you will find printed copies of my inaugural address, and my first proclamations, which will exhibit the policy I have thus far thought proper to pursue.

"I have determined to dismiss the present organized militia, after consultation with and by the advice of General Smith; and for the reasons that they were not enrolled in accordance with the laws; that many of them are not citizens of the territory; that some of them were committing outrages under the pretence of serving the public; and that they were unquestionably perpetuating, rather than diminishing, the troubles with which the territory is agitated.

"I have also, as you will see, taken the proper steps to enroll the militia of the territory, agreeably to the act of assembly, and to your instructions of September 2d. I trust that the militia, thus organized, may be rendered serviceable to the government. It is probable also that these proclamations may have the tendency to disband the free state organizations at Lawrence.

"Nothing of material importance has occurred, or come under my notice, since I last addressed you. I shall continue to keep you apprised of all matters that I may deem of sufficient interest to communicate.

"As there is no telegraphic communication nearer than Boonville, I am compelled to trust my dispatches to the mails, which are now in this region somewhat uncertain.

"Most truly and respectfully, your obedient servant,

"JNO. W. GEARY."

At the time of writing the above, the strength, movements and designs of the Missouri army were unknown to Governor Geary; but soon afterwards their plans and operations began to be developed. Shortly after midnight, on the morning of September 13th, the governor received a messenger bearing the following dispatch:

"HEAD QUARTERS, MISSION CREEK, K. T ,
"11th September, 1856.

"To HIS EXCELLENCY, J. W. GEARY,
"*Governor of Kansas Territory.*

"SIR: In obedience to the call of Acting-Governor Woodson, I have organized a militia force of about eight hundred men who are now in the field, ready for duty, and impatient to act. Hearing of your arrival, I beg leave to report them to you for orders. Any communication forwarded to us, will find us encamped at or near this point.

"I have the honor to be, respectfully, your obedient servant,

"WM. A. HEISKILL,

"*Brig. Gen. Com. 1st Brig., Southern Division, Kansas Militia.*
"By order: L. A. MACLEAN, Adjutant."

Not more than an hour after the receipt of the foregoing, a second messenger arrived, himself almost exhausted with a long and fast ride, and his horse nearly broken down, and presented the following:

"HEAD QUARTERS, MISSION CAMP,
"12th September, 1856.

"To HIS EXCELLENCY, J. W. GEARY,
"*Governor of Kansas Territory.*

"SIR: Yesterday I had the honor to report to you my command of the Kansas Militia, then about eight hundred strong, which was dispatched via Leavenworth. In case it may not have reached you, I now report one thousand men as territorial militia, called into the field by proclamation of Acting-Governor Woodson, and subject tô your orders.

"I have the honor to be, respectfully, your obedient servant,

"WM. A. HEISKILL,

"*Brig. Gen. Com. 1st Brig. Southern Division, Kansas Militia.*
"By order: L. A. MCLEAN, Adjutant."

Without a moment's hesitation, the governor determined at once to disband these troops and send them back to their homes; and he accordingly answered the dispatches of General Heiskell, as follows:

"EXECUTIVE OFFICE, LECOMPTON, K. T.,
"September 12, 1856, 1½ o'clock.

"BRIG. GEN. WM. A. HEISKELL:

"SIR: Your first and second dispatches have been received. I will communicate with you through the person of either the secretary of the territory, or the adjutant-general, as soon as he can reach your camp, he starting from this place at an early hour this morning.

"Very respectfully yours,

JNO. W. GEARY,
"*Governor of Kansas Territory.*

Whilst the foregoing was being written, a message was received from a special agent of the governor, dated at Lawrence, in which he says:

"I arrived here a few moments ago, and distributed the address and proclamations, and found the people prepared to repel a contemplated attack from the forces coming from Missouri. Reports are well authenticated, in the opinion of the best men here, that there are within six miles of this place a large number of men—three hundred have been seen. * * At this moment one of the scouts came in, and reports the forces marching against them at Franklin, three miles off, and all have flown to their arms to meet them."

This message was enclosed with the following dispatch, and sent immediately to Colonel Cook, commanding United States forces near Lecompton:

"EXECUTIVE OFFICE, LECOMPTON, K. T.,
Sept. 13, 1856, at 1½ o'clock, A. M.

"COL. P. ST. GEORGE COOK:

"DEAR SIR: The accompanying dispatch, just received from Lawrence, gives sufficient reason to believe that trouble of a serious character is likely to take place there. Mr. Adams, the writer of the dispatch, is a special agent whom I sent down last evening to ascertain the state of affairs. I think you had better send *immediately* to Lawrence a force sufficient to prevent bloodshed, as it is my orders from the president to use every possible means to prevent collisions between belligerent troops. If desirable, I will accompany the forces myself, and should be glad to have you go along.

"Truly yours,   JNO. W. GEARY,
"*Governor of Kansas Territory.*"

Colonel Cook, with three hundred mounted soldiers and four pieces of artillery, started immediately for Lawrence, accompanied by Governor Geary. On their arrival they learned that the danger was not imminent. The citizens of Lawrence were under arms and the town fortified at every point. The governor assembled the inhabitants, cautioned them against the commission of any unlawful acts, and promised them his protection in case they were attacked. He was immediately recalled to Lecompton with the troops in consequence of troubles in that neighborhood. Upon his arrival he found his office thronged with people excited by the intelligence that Lane meditated an attack upon the pro-slavery settlements of Hickory Point, Osawkee and the neighborhood; some of the inhabitants of those places having fled in terror to Lecompton. Affidavits were made of outrages committed and handed to the governor, upon the receipt of which he made the following requisition upon Colonel Cook:

"EXECUTIVE DEPARTMENT, LECOMPTON, K. T.,
September 14th, 1856.

"COL. P. ST. G. COOK:

"DEAR SIR: You will perceive by the accompanying affidavit, and from verbal statements that will be made to you by Dr. Tebbs, that a desperate state of affairs is existing at Osawkee and its vicinity, which seems to require some action at our hands. I strongly recommend that you send a force, such as you can conveniently spare, to visit that neighborhood, at the earliest moment. If such a force cannot succeed in arresting the perpetrators of the outrages already committed, and of which complaint has been made in due form, it may at least tend to disperse or drive off the band or bands of marauders who are threatening the lives and property of peaceable citizens. The deputy marshall will accompany such troops as you may judge expedient to detail on this service.   "Very respectfully and truly yours,   JNO. W. GEARY,
"*Governor of Kansas Territory.*"

A detachment of dragoons was forthwith dispatched by Colonel Cook to pursue the marauders and protect the neighborhood. At midnight they fell in with a party of armed men and took one hundred of them prisoners without resistance. They were mostly mounted, and heavily armed, and had with them a brass field-piece and several wagons, all of which were captured and taken to Lecompton They were said to be a detachment of forces of General Lane, under command of Captain Harvey, and were on their way from Lawrence to join a large body from Topeka. They had been engaged in an affray at Hickory Point. One of the leaders, on being asked if they had not read the governor's proclamation, wittily replied, "Oh yes, and before we commenced our fire upon the border ruffians, we read the proclamation to them, and commanded them to surrender in the name of the governor." These prisoners were taken to a dilapidated house in Lecompton and guarded by a company of militia under command of Colonel Titus. Here they suffered for the want of food, clothing and bedding; overrun with vermin, and exposed to constant insults from the guards. At the October term of the district court, some were acquitted and others convicted of manslaughter. These were sentenced to terms of confinement varying from five to ten years of hard labor, and to wear a ball and chain. As sheriff Jones had not been permitted by the verdict to hang the prisoners, he was exceedingly anxious to apply the ball and chain, and wrote to Governor Geary that "It is indipensably necessary that balls and chains should be furnished, and understanding that the same can be procured by your application to General Smith, I will request that you will procure and have them sent over at the earliest day possible." To this application the governor replied that "General Smith has no balls and chains for the purpose—nor is it deemed advisable to procure any." The governor immediately remitted that portion of their sentence requiring the ball and chain, as being "cruel and unusual, and especially inappropriate." The prisoners were subsequently placed under the charge of Captain Hampton, Master of Convicts, an office created by an act of the territorial legislature. They were treated with a kindness and consideration by that generous hearted Kentuckian, which called down upon him the vengeance of the leading members of his party, and his removal by the governor was demanded. The prisoners were subsequently pardoned by Governor Geary.

While the governor was attending to the troubles at Hickory Point, a large army was gathering on the Wakarusa preparatory to an attack on Lawrence. As these men styled themselves the territorial militia and were called into service by Woodson, the governor immediately commanded that officer to take with him adjutant-general Strickler with an escort of United States troops and disband the forces he had assembled. But Woodson discovered that he had raised a storm which he could not control. Mr. Adams, who accompanied Woodson to the camp, sent the following dispatch to the governor:

"HIS EXCELLENCY, GOVERNOR GEARY:

"Sir: I went as directed to the camp of the militia, and found at the town of Franklin, three miles from this place, encamped three hundred men, with four pieces of artillery. One mile to the right, on the Wakarusa, I found a very large encampment of three hundred tents and wagons. They claim to have two thousand five hundred men; and from the appearance of the camp, I have no doubt they have that number. General Reid is in command. I saw and was introduced to General Atchison, Col. Titus, Sheriff Jones, General Richardson, etc. The proclamations were distributed.

" Secretary Woodson and General Strickler had not, up to the time I left, delivered their orders, but were about doing so as soon as they could get the officers together.

" The outposts of both parties were fighting about an hour before sunset. One man killed of the militia, and one house burned at Franklin.

" There were but few people at Lawrence, most of them having gone to their homes after your visit here.

" I reported these facts to the officer in command here, and your prompt action has undoubtedly been the means of preventing the loss of blood and saving valuable property.

" Secretary Woodson thought you had better *come* to the camp of the militia as soon as you can. I think a prompt visit would have a good effect. I will see you as you come this way, and communicate with you more fully.

" Very respectfully, your obedient servant,
" THEODORE ADAMS."

Before this dispatch reached Lecompton, the governor had departed with three hundred United States mounted troops and a battery of light artillery, and riding speedily, arrived at Lawrence early in the evening of the 14th, where he found matters precisely as described. Skillfully stationing his troops outside the town, in commanding positions, to prevent a collision between the invading forces from Missouri and the citizens, he entered Lawrence alone, and there he beheld a sight which a writer has thus eloquently described:

" About three hundred persons were found in arms, determined to sell their lives at the dearest price to their ruffian enemies. Among these were many women, and children of both sexes, armed with guns and otherwise accoutred for battle. They had been goaded to this by the courage of despair. Lawrence was to have been their Thermopylæ, and every other free town would have proved a Saragossa. When men determine to die for the right, a hecatomb of victims grace their immolation; but when women and children betake themselves to the battle-field, ready to fight and die with their husbands and fathers, heroism becomes the animating principle of every heart, and a giant's strength invigorates every arm. Each drop of blood lost by such warriors becomes a dragon's tooth, which will spring from the earth, in all the armor of truth and justice, to exact a fearful retribution. Had Lawrence been destroyed, and her population butchered, the red right hand of vengeance would have gleamed over the entire south, and the question of slavery have been settled by a bloody and infuriated baptism. There are such examples in history, and mankind have lost none of their impulses or human emotions.

" Gov. Geary addressed the armed citizens of Lawrence, and when he assured them of his and the law's protection, they offered to deposit their arms at his feet and return to their respective habitations. He bid them go to their homes in confidence, and to carry their arms with them, as the constitution of the Union guaranteed that right; but to use those arms only in the last resort to protect their lives and property, and the chastity of their females. They obeyed the governor and repaired to their homes."

On the morning of the 15th of September, the governor, having left the United States troops to protect the town of Lawrence, proceeded alone to the camp of the invading army, then within three miles, and drawn up in order of battle. The scene that was presented is thus described by the governor's private secretary: "The militia had taken a position upon an extensive and beautiful plain near the junction of the Wakarusa with the Kansas river. On one side towered a lofty hill, known as the Blue Mound, and on the other Mount Oread showed its fortified summit. The town of Franklin, from its elevated site, looked down upon the active scene, while beyond, in a quiet vale, the more flourishing city of Lawrence reposed as though unconscious of its threatened doom. The waters of the Kansas river might be seen gliding rapidly toward the Missouri, and the tall forest trees which line its banks, plainly indicated the course of the Wakarusa. The red face of the rising sun was just peering over the top of the Blue Mound, as the governor, with his strange escort of three hundred mounted men, with red shirts and odd-shaped hats, descended upon the Wakarusa plain. There, in battle array, were ranged at least three thousand armed and desperate men. They were not dressed in the usual habiliments of soldiers; but in every imaginable costume that could be obtained in that western region. Scarcely two presented the same appearance, while all exhibited a ruffianly aspect. Most of them were mounted, and manifested an unmistakable disposition to be at their bloody work. In the background stood at least three hundred army tents and as many wagons, while here and there a cannon was planted ready to aid in the anticipated destruction. Among the banners floated black flags to indicate the design that neither age, sex, nor condition would be spared in the slaughter that was to ensue. The arms and cannon also bore the black indices of extermination.

"In passing along the lines, murmurs of discontent and savage threats of assassination fell upon the governor's ears; but heedless of these, and regardless, in fact, of everything but a desire to avert the calamity that was impending, he fearlessly proceeded to the quarters of their leader.

"This threatening army was under the command of General John W. Reid, then and now a member of the Missouri legislature, assisted by ex-senator Atchison, General B. F. Stringfellow, General L. A. Maclean, General J. W. Whitfield, General George W. Clarke, Generals Wm. A. Heiskell, Wm. H. Richardson, and F. A. Marshal, Colonel H. T. Titus, Captain Frederick Emory, and others of similar character.

"Gov. Geary at once summoned the officers together, and addressed them at length and with great feeling. He depicted in a forcible manner the improper position they occupied, and the untold horrors that would result from the consummation of their cruel designs: that if they persisted in their mad career, the entire Union would be involved in a civil war, and thousands and tens of thousands of innocent lives be sacrificed. To Atchison, he especially addressed himself, telling him that when he last saw him, he was acting as vice-president of the nation and president of the most dignified body of men in the world, the senate of the United States; but now with sorrow and pain he saw him leading on to a civil and disastrous war an army of men, with uncontrollable passions, and determined upon wholesale slaughter and destruction. He concluded his remarks by directing attention to his proclamation, and ordered the army to be disbanded and dispersed. Some of the more judicious of the officers were not only willing, but anxious to obey this order; whilst others, resolved upon mischief, yielded a very reluctant assent. General Clarke said he was for pitching into the United States troops, if necessary, rather than abandon the objects of the expedition. General Maclean didn't see any use of going back until they had whipped the d—d abolitionists. Sheriff Jones was in favor, now they had a sufficient force, of 'wiping out' Lawrence and all the free state towns. And these and others cursed Gov. Geary in not very gentle expressions for his untimely interference with their well-laid plans. They, however, obeyed the order, and retired, not as good and law-loving citizens, but as bands of plunderers and destroyers, leaving in their wake ruined fortunes, weeping eyes, and sorrowing hearts."

On the 16th of September, the governor dispatched the following letter to Secretary Marcy:

"EXECUTIVE DEPARTMENT, Lecompton, K. T., }
"September 16, 1856. }

" HON. WM. L. MARCY, Secretary of State:

" My Dear Sir: My last dispatch was dated the 12th instant, in which I gave you a statement of my operations to that date. Since then, I have had business of the deepest importance to occupy every moment of my attention, and to require the most constant watchfulness and untiring energy. Indeed, so absolutely occupied is all my time, that I scarcely have a minute to devote to the duty of keeping you apprised of the true condition of this territory. I have this instant returned from an expedition to Lawrence and the vicinity, and am preparing to depart almost immediately for other sections of the territory, where my presence is demanded.

" After having issued my address and proclamations in this city, copies of which have been forwarded to you, I sent them, with a special messenger, to Lawrence, twelve miles to the eastward, where they were made known to the citizens on the 12th instant. The people of that place were alarmed with a report that a large body of armed men, called out under the proclamation of the late acting-governor Woodson, were threatening them with an attack, and they were making the necessary preparations for resistance. So well authenticated seemed their information, that my agent forwarded an express by a United States trooper, announcing the fact, and calling upon me to use my power to prevent the impending calamity. This express reached me at half-past one o'clock, on the morning of the 13th instant. I immediately made a requisition upon Colonel Cook, commander of the United States forces stationed at this place, for as many troops as could be made available, and in about an hour was on my way towards Lawrence, with three hundred mounted men, including a battery of light artillery. On arriving at Lawrence, we found the danger had been exaggerated, and that there was no immediate necessity for the intervention of the military. The moral effect of our presence, however, was of great avail. The citizens were satisfied that the government was disposed to render them all needed protection, and I received from them the assurance that they would conduct themselves as law-abiding and peace-loving men. They voluntarily offered to lay down their arms, and enrol themselves as territorial militia, in accordance with the terms of my proclamations. I returned the same day with the troops, well satisfied with the result of my mission.

"During the evening of Saturday, the 13th, I remained at my office, which was constantly crowded with men uttering complaints concerning outrages that had been and were being committed upon their persons and property. These complaints came in from every direction, and were made by the advocates of all the conflicting political sentiments with which the territory has been agitated; and they exhibited clearly a moral condition of affairs, too lamentable for any language adequately to describe. The whole country was evidently infested with armed bands of marauders, who set all law at defiance, and traveled from place to place, assailing villages, sacking and burning houses, destroying crops, maltreating women and children, driving off and stealing cattle and horses, and murdering harmless men in their own dwellings and on the public highways. Many of these grievances needed immediate redress; but unfortunately the law was a dead letter, no magistrate or judge being at hand to take an affidavit or issue a process, and no marshal or sheriff to be found, even had the judges been present to prepare them, to execute the same.

"The next day, Sunday, matters grew worse and worse. The most positive evidence reached me that a large body of armed and mounted men were devastating the neighborhoods of Osawkee and Hardtville, commonly called Hickory Point. Being well convinced of this fact, I determined to act upon my own responsibility, and immediately issued an order to Colonel Cook for a detachment of his forces, to visit the scene of disturbance. In answer to this requisition, a squadron of eighty-one men were detached, consisting of companies C. and H. 1st cavalry, Captains Wood and Newby, the whole under command of Captain Wood. This detachment left the camp at two o'clock, P. M., with instructions to proceed to Osawkee and Hickory Point, the former twelve, and the latter eighteen miles to the northward of Lecompton. It was accompanied by a deputy marshal.

"In consequence of the want of proper facilities for crossing the Kansas river, it was late in the evening before the force could march. After having proceeded about six miles, intelligence was brought to Captain Wood, that a large party of men, under command of a person named Harvey, had come over from Lawrence, and made an attack upon a log house at Hickory Point, in which a number of the settlers had taken refuge. The assault commenced about eleven o'clock in the morning, and continued six hours. The attacking party had charge of a brass four-pounder,.the same that was taken by Colonel Doniphan at the battle of Sacramento. This piece had been freely used in the assault, but without effecting any material damage. As far as has yet been ascertained, but one man was killed, and some half-dozen wounded.

"About eleven o'clock in the evening, Captain Wood's command met a party of twenty-five men, with three wagons, one of which contained a wounded man. These he ascertained to be a portion of Harvey's forces, who had been engaged in the assault at Hickory Point, and who were returning to Lawrence. They were immediately arrested, without resistance, disarmed, and held as prisoners. Three others were soon after arrested, who also proved to be a portion of Harvey's party.

"When within about four miles of Hickory Point, Captain Wood discovered a large encampment upon the prairie, near the road leading to Lawrence. It was the main body of Harvey's men, then under command of a man named Bickerton, Harvey having left after the attack on Hickory Point. The party was surprised and captured.

"After securing the prisoners, Captain Wood returned to Lecompton, which place he reached about day-break, on Monday, the 15th instant, bringing with him one hundred and one prisoners, one brass field-piece, seven wagons, thirty-eight United States muskets, forty-seven Sharpe's rifles, six hunting rifles, two shot guns, twenty revolving pistols, fourteen bowie-knives, four swords, and a large supply of ammunition for artillery and small arms.

"Whilst engaged in making preparations for the foregoing expedition, several messengers reached me from Lawrence, announcing that a powerful army was marching upon that place, it being the main body of the militia called into service by the proclamation of Secretary Woodson, when acting-governor.

"Satisfied that the most prompt and decisive measures were necessary to prevent the sacrifice of many lives, and the destruction of one of the finest and most prosperous towns in the territory, and avert a state of affairs which must have inevitably involved the country in a most disastrous civil war, I dispatched the following order to Colonel Cook :

"'Proceed at all speed with your command to Lawrence, and prevent a collision, if possible, and leave a portion of your troops there for that purpose.'

"Accordingly, the entire available United States force was put in motion, and reached Lawrence at an early hour in the evening. Here, the worst apprehensions of the citizens were discovered to have been well founded. Twenty-seven hundred men, under command of Generals Heiskell, Reid, Atchison, Richardson, Stringfellow, and others, were encamped on the Wakarusa, about four miles from Lawrence, eager and determined to exterminate that place and all its inhabitants. An advanced party of three hundred men had already taken possession of Franklin, one mile from the camp, and three miles from Lawrence, and skirmishing parties had begun to engage in deadly conflict.

"Fully appreciating the awful calamities that were impending, I hastened with all possible dispatch to the encampment, assembled the officers of the militia, and in the name of the President of the United States, demanded suspension of hostilities. I had sent in advance, the secretary and adjutant-general of the territory, with orders to carry out the spirit and letter of my proclamations; but up to the time of my arrival, these orders had been unheeded, and I could discover but little disposition to obey them. I addressed the officers in council at considerable length, setting forth the disastrous consequences of such a demonstration as was contemplated, and the absolute necessity of more lawful and conciliatory measures to restore peace, tranquility, and prosperity to the country. I read my instructions from the president, and convinced them that my whole course of procedure was in accordance therewith, and called upon them to aid me in my efforts, not only to carry out those instructions, but to support and enforce the laws, and the constitution of the United States. I am happy to say that a more ready concurrence in my views was met, than I had at first any good reason to expect. It was agreed that the terms of my proclamation should be carried out by the disbandment of the militia; whereupon the camp was broken up, and the different commands separated, to repair to their respective homes.

"The occurrences, thus related, are already exerting a beneficent influence; and although the work is not yet accomplished, I do not despair of success in my efforts to satisfy the government that I am worthy of the high trust which has been reposed in me. As soon as circumstances will permit, I shall visit, in person, every section of the territory, where I feel assured that my presence will tend to give confidence and security to the people.

"In closing, I have merely to add, that unless I am more fully sustained hereafter by the civil authorities, and serious difficulties and disturbances continue to agitate the territory, my only recourse will be to martial law, which I must needs proclaim and enforce.

"Very respectfully, &c., JNO. W. GEARY,
"Governor of Kansas Territory."

The dismissal of the Missouri invaders, the arrest of Harvey's party, and the departure of Col. Lane (which took place about this time) from the territory, were followed with the most beneficial effects. The prompt, bold, rapid, and decisive movements of the governor struck the numerous predatory bands with terror, and they either dispersed, or fled the country; and a happier condition of things began to be apparent on every hand.

The management of the judicial affairs of the territory now merit some notice. A portion of the disbanded army, called the Kickapoo Rangers, took the road to Lecompton, and when within a few miles of that place they halted by a field where a poor lame man by the name of David C. Buffum was at work. Some of the party entered the field, and after robbing the man of his horses, one of them shot him in the abdomen, from which wound he afterwards died. Almost immediately after the commission of this crime, Governor Geary, accompanied by Judge Cato, arrived on the spot, and found the wounded man weltering in blood. The governor directed Judge Cato to take an affidavit of the unfortunate man's dying words, who, writhing in agony, exclaimed: "Oh, this was a most unprovoked and horrid murder! They asked me for my horses, and I plead with them not to take them. I told them that I was a cripple—a poor lame man—that I had an aged father, a deaf and dumb brother, and two sisters, all depending upon me for a living, and my horses were all I had with which to procure it. One of them said I was a God d—d abolitionist, and seizing me by the shoulder with one hand, he shot me with a pistol that he held in the other. I am dying; but my blood will call to Heaven for vengeance, and this horrible deed will not go unpunished. I die a martyr to the cause of freedom, and my death will do much to aid that cause." The governor was affected to tears. He had been on many a battle-field, and had been familiar with suffering and death; but, says he, "I never witnessed a scene that filled my mind with so much horror. There was a peculiar significance in the looks and words of that poor dying man that I never can forget; for they seemed to tell me that I could have no rest until I brought his murderer to justice. And I resolved that no means in my power should be spared to discover, arrest and punish the author of that most villanous butchery."

On his arrival at Lecompton, the governor immediately had a warrant drawn and placed in the hands of the United States marshal, for the arrest of the murderer, for the execution of which warrant the whole of the United States force was at his disposal. Several days elapsed and no return was made, nor had any disposition been discovered to effect the governor's wishes in the matter. The governor, besides offering a reward of five hundred dollars for the arrest of the murderer, employed secret agents to visit that portion of Missouri in which the Rangers resided, and, by making cautious inquiries, to obtain some clue to the perpetrators of the deed. The murderer was discovered in the person of Charles Hays, a resident of Atchison county, Missouri. A new warrant was issued for his arrest, and he was brought to Lecompton. A grand jury, composed entirely of pro-slavery men, on hearing the overwhelming testimony, found a true bill, and committed him for trial. At this time free-state men were seized almost daily by the officers, and thrust into prison, and bail utterly refused by the pro-slavery magistrates. Much to the astonishment and indignation of Governor Geary, he was informed that Judge Lecompte had admitted the murderer of Buffum to bail, and that Sheriff Jones, a man notoriously not worth a cent, was on his bail-bond. The governor boldly pronounced the action of the chief justice in dismissing the murderer of Buffum as a "judicial outrage," and proceeded to treat it as a nullity by issuing the following warrant:

"Executive Department, K. T., }
"Lecompton, Nov. 10, 1856. }

"I. B. Donelson, Esq., Marshal of Kansas Territory:

"Sir: An indictment for murder in the first degree having been duly found by the grand jury of the territory against Charles Hays, for the murder of a certain David C. Buffum, in the county of Douglas, in this territory, and the

48

said Charles Hays having been discharged upon bail, as I consider in violation of law, and greatly to the endangering of the peace of this territory :

"This is therefore to authorize and command you to reärrest the said Charles Hays, if he be found within the limits of this territory, and safely to keep him until he is duly discharged by a jury of his country, according to law.

"Given under my hand and seal, at the city of Lecompton, the day and year first above written.   "JNO. W. GEARY,
                              "*Governor of Kansas Territory.*"

This warrant was handed to Marshal Donelson, who, however, declined to execute it, saying he would take time to consider the matter. The governor made out a duplicate warrant, and placed it in the hands of Col. Titus, with orders to take a file of men and execute it without delay. The murderer was promptly reärrested, and remained in the custody of Col. Titus, until, during the absence of the governor from the city, he was again discharged by Judge Lecompte on a writ of habeas corpus, as shown in the subjoined letter of Col. Titus:

"LECOMPTON, Nov. 21, 1856.
"HIS EXCELLENCY, JOHN W. GEARY,
          "Governor of Kansas Territory :

"Sir : I have the honor to state that during your recent absence from this place, a writ of habeas corpus, issued by Chief Justice Lecompte, was served upon me, by which I was commanded to produce the body of Charles Hays before him, with the cause of his detainer:

"That in obedience to the writ, I caused the body of Hays to be produced before Judge Lecompte, and returned as cause of his detention the finding by the grand jury of a true bill of indictment against him for murder in the first degree, committed upon the person of one David C. Buffum, together with your warrant, commanding the reärrest of said Hays and his detention until his discharge by a jury of his country according to law.

"I have further to state that Judge Lecompte discharged the said Hays from my custody notwithstanding my return, and that he is now at large. I have the honor to remain your obedient servant,   "H. T. TITUS."

The governor did not attempt to interfere with the writ of habeas corpus, but forwarded to the president and secretary his executive minutes, containing a history of the circumstances, and showing the necessity of a less partial judiciary in order to preserve the peace of the territory. Judge Lecompte also wrote a letter to Washington. The following correspondence ensued between the secretary of state and the governor :

                    "DEPARTMENT OF STATE, }
                    "WASHINGTON, 4th February, 1857. }
"To JOHN W. GEARY, ESQ., Governor of Kansas, Lecompton :

"Sir : The original letter of which the inclosed is a copy, was brought to the notice of the president, a few days since, by Hon. James A. Pearce, of the

United States Senate. The discrepancies between the statements of this letter and those contained in your official communication of the 19th of September, are such that the president directs me to inclose you a copy for explanation.

"I am, sir, respectfully, your obedient servant,

"W. L. MARCY."

"EXECUTIVE DEPARTMENT, Kansas Territory,}
" LECOMPTON, February 20th, 1857. }

" HON. WM. L. MARCY, Secretary of State:

" Sir: Your dispatch of the 4th instant, inclosing me a copy of Judge Lecompte's letter in the Hays case, and calling my attention 'to discrepancies between the statements of that letter, and those contained in your (my) official communication of 19th of September last,' and requesting 'explanation,' was received by the last mail.

" In reply, I have simply to state, that 'what I have written, I have written,' and I have nothing further to add, alter or amend on this subject.

" My executive minutes, faithfully chronicling my official actions, and the policy which dictated them at the time they occurred, and my various dispatches to the government, contain but the simple truth, told without fear, favor, or affection, and I will esteem it a favor to have them all published for the inspection of the country.   " Your obedient servant,

" JNO. W. GEARY,

" *Governor of Kansas Territory.*"

The president made a show of removing Lecompte, by nominating Mr. Harrison, of Kentucky, to the senate, without issuing a writ of supersedas. This enabled the senate to withhold their confirmation of Harrison's appointment, and Judge Lecompte remained in office.

During the latter part of September, information was received by Governor Geary that Colonel Lane, with a force of a thousand men and several pieces of artillery, was preparing to enter Kansas by way of Nebraska. A detachment of troops, accompanied by deputy marshal Preston, was immediately sent to the northern frontier. They arrested Captain James Redpath and 130 men, who had entered the territory armed, equipped and organized, and escorted them to Lecompton. Redpath, in an interview with the governor, convinced him that the prisoners were a company of peaceable immigrants, and they were accordingly released.

Another representation was made to the governor, that Redpath's party was but an advanced guard of the forces of Lane, who had contracted with the ferryman at Nebraska City, for the transit of 700 men and three pieces of cannon. Three hundred dragoons under Colonels Cook and Johnson were forthwith dispatched to intercept their passage.

On the 1st of October a deputation waited upon the governor, stating that they had been sent by General Pomeroy and Colonels Eldridge and Perry, who were escorting three hundred immigrants into the territory by way of Nebraska; that they did not come to disturb the peace, but as bona fide settlers with agricultural implements; that they did not wish to enter the territory, in its present disturbed state without notifying the governor. In reply, the governor informed his visitors that he was determined no armed bodies of men, with cannon and munitions of war, should enter the territory to the terror of peaceable citizens; that there was no further occasion for such demonstrations; that he would, on the other hand, welcome all immigrants who should come for peaceful and lawful purposes; that he would furnish them a safe escort, and guarantee them protection. He then gave the deputation a letter directing all military commanders to give Colonel Eldridge's party a safe escort, should they be, as represented, a party of peaceable immigrants.

Shortly afterwards the governor received the following dispatch from Col. Cook, by the hands of deputy marshal Preston.

"Head-quarters, Camp near Nebraska River, }
"Kansas Territory, October 10, 1856. }

"His Excellency, J. W. Geary,

"Governor of Kansas Territory.

Sir: Colonel Preston, deputy marshal, has arrested, with my assistance, and disarmed, a large body of *professed* immigrants, being entirely provided with arms and munitions of war; amongst which, two officer's and sixty-one private's *sabres*, and many boxes of new saddles. Agreeably to your requisition of September 26th, I send an escort to conduct them, men, arms, and munitions of war, to appear before you at the capitol. Colonel Preston will give you the details.

I have the honor to be, with high respect, your obedient servant,

P. St. George Cook,
Lieutenant Colonel 2d Dragoons, Comm'g in the Field."

From the letter of Governor Geary to Secretary Marcy, dated October 15th, we gather the particulars of this arrest. He says:

"Colonel Wm. S. Preston, a deputy U. S. Marshal, who had accompanied Colonel Cook and his command to the northern frontier to look after a large party of professed immigrants who were reported to be about invading the territory in that quarter in warlike array and for hostile purposes, returned to Lecompton on the 12th instant.

"He informed me that he had caused to be arrested, an organized band, consisting of about two hundred and forty persons, among whom were a very few women and children, comprising some seven families.

"This party was regularly formed in military order, and were under the command of General Pomeroy, Colonels Eldridge and Perry, and others. They had with them twenty wagons, in which was a supply of new arms, mostly muskets and sabres, and a lot of saddles, &c., sufficient to equip a battalion, consisting one-fourth of cavalry and the remainder of infantry. Besides these arms, the immigrants were provided with shot-guns, rifles, pistols, knives, &c., sufficient for the ordinary uses of persons traveling in Kansas, or any other of the western territories. From the reports of the officers, I learn they had with them neither oxen, household furniture, mechanics' tools, agricultural implements, nor any of the necsseary appurtenances of peaceful settlers.

"These persons entered the territory on the morning of the 10th instant, and met Colonel Cook's command a few miles south of the territorial line. Here the deputy-marshal questioned them as to their intentions, the contents of their wagons, and such other matters as he considered necessary in the exercise of his official duties. Not satisfied with their answers, and being refused the privilege of searching their effects, he felt justified in considering them a party organized and armed in opposition to my proclamation of the 11th of September. After consultation with Colonel Cook and other officers of the army, who agreed with him in regard to the character of the immigrants, he directed a search to be made, which resulted in the discovery of the arms already mentioned.

"An escort was offered them to Lecompton, that I might examine them in person, and decide as to their intentions, which they refused to accept. Their superfluous arms were then taken in charge of the troops, and the entire party put under arrest—the families, and all others, individually, being permitted to retire from the organization, if so disposed. Few availed themselves of this privilege.

"But little delay, and less annoyance, was occasioned them by these proceedings. Every thing that circumstances required or permitted was done for the comfort and convenience of the prisoners. Their journey was facilitated rather than retarded. They were accompanied by a squadron of United States dragoons, in command of Major H. H. Sibley. A day's rations were dealt out to them, and they were allowed to pursue the route themselves had chosen.

"Being apprised of the time at which they would probably arrive at Topeka, I forwarded orders for their detention on the northern side of the river, near that place, where, as I promised, I met them on the morning of the 14th instant.

"I addressed these people in their encampment, in regard to the present condition of the territory, the suspicious position they occupied, and the reprehensible attitude they had assumed. I reminded them that there was no possible necessity or excuse for the existence of large armed organizations at present in the territory. Everything was quiet and peaceful. And the very appearance of such an unauthorized and injudicious array as they presented, while it could do no good, was calculated, if not intended, to spread anew distrust and consternation through the territory, and rekindle the fires of discord and strife that had swept over the land, ravaging and desolating everything that lay in their destructive path.

"Their apology for an evident disregard of my proclamation, was, that they had made arrangements to emigrate to Kansas when the territory was not only disturbed by antagonistic political parties, armed for each other's destruction, but when numerous bands of marauders, whose business was plunder and assassination, infested all the highways, rendering travel extremely hazardous, even though every possible means for self-protection were employed.

"After showing the necessity of so doing, I insisted on the immediate disbandment of this combination, which was agreed to with great alacrity. The majority of the men were evidently gratified to learn that they had been deceived in relation to Kansas affairs, and that peace and quiet, instead of strife and contention, were reigning here. My remarks were received with frequent demonstrations of approbation, and at their close the organization was broken up, its members dispersing in various directions. After they had been dismissed from custody, and the fact was announced to them by Major Sibley, their thankfulness for his kind treatment to them while under arrest was acknowledged by giving him three hearty and enthusiastic cheers."

Soon after the letter, from which the foregoing is extracted, was forwarded to Washington, the following statement from the leaders of the party in question was received by Governor Geary:

"TOPEKA, KANSAS TERRITORY,
"October 14, 1856.

"His EXCELLENCY, JOHN W. GEARY,

"Governor of Kansas Territory:

"Dear Sir: We, the undersigned, conductors of an emigrant train, who entered the terrritory on the 10th instant, beg leave to make the following statement of facts, which, if required, we will attest upon our oaths.

"1st. Our party numbered from two hundred to three hundred persons, in two separate companies; the rear company, which has not yet arrived, being principally composed of families, with children, who left Mount Pleasant, Iowa, three days after this train which has arrived to-day.

"2d. We are all actual, *bona fide* settlers, intending, so far as we know, to become permanent inhabitants.

"3d. The blockading of the Missouri river to free-state emigrants, and the reports which reached us in the early part of September, to the effect that armed men were infesting and marauding the northern portions of Kansas, were the sole reasons why we came in a company and were armed.

"4th. We were stopped near the northern line of the territory by the United States troops, acting, as we understood, under the orders of one Preston, deputy United States marshal, and after stating to the officers who we were and what we had, they commenced searching our wagons (in some instances breaking open trunks, and throwing bedding and wearing apparel on the ground in the rain,) taking arms from the wagons, wresting some private arms from the hands of men, carrying away a lot of sabres belonging to a gentleman in the territory, as also one and a half kegs of powder, purcussion caps, and some cartridges; in consequence of which we were detained about two-thirds of a day, taken prisoners and are now presented to you.

"All we have to say is, that our mission to this territory is entirely peaceful. We have no organization, save a police organization for our own regulation and defense on the way. And coming in that spirit to this territory, we claim the rights of American citizens to bear arms, and to be exempt from unlawful search and seizure.

"Trusting to your integrity and impartiality, we have confidence to believe that our property will be restored to us, and that all that has been wrong will be righted.

"We here subscribe ourselves, cordially and truly, your friends and fellow-citizens,
"S. W. ELDRIDGE, Conductor,
"SAMUEL C. POMEROY,
"JOHN A. PERRY,
"ROBERT MORROW,
"EDWARD DANIELS,
"RICHARD RAELF."

During the latter part of October, the governor made a tour of observation through the southern and western portions of the territory, and on his return addressed the following letter to Secretary Marcy, which will explain the state of affairs at that time:

"EXECUTIVE DEPARTMENT, K. T.,
Lecompton, Nov. 7, 1856.

"HON. WM. L. MARCY, *Secretary of State:*

"SIR: I have just returned to this place, after an extended tour of observation through a large portion of this territory. I left Lecompton on the 17th ult., *via* Lawrence, Franklin, Wakarusa Creek, Hickory Point, Ottawa Creek, Osawattomie, Bull Creek, Paoli, Potawattomie, North and South Middle Creeks, Big and Little Sugar Creeks, and Sugar Mound, passing westward along the California and Santa Fe road to Fort Riley; thence down the Kansas river, *via* Pawnee, Riley City, Manhattan, Waubonsee, Baptist Mission, Topeka, Tecumseh, and other places. I also visited, at their houses, as many citizens as I conveniently could, and addressed various bodies of people, as I have reason to believe, with beneficial results.

"During this tour I have obtained much valuable information relative to affairs in Kansas, and made myself familiar with the wants and grievances of the people, which will enable me to make such representations to the next legislature and the government at Washington, as will be most conducive to the public interests. The general peace of the territory remains unimpaired; confidence is being gradually and surely restored; business is resuming its ordinary channels; citizens are preparing for winter; and there is a readiness among the good people of all parties to sustain my administration.

"Very respectfully, your obed't servt., JNO. W. GEARY,
"*Governor of Kansas Territory.*"

On the 31st December, 1856, the governor again addressed Secretary Marcy as follows, in regard to the condition of the territory at that period:

"In reviewing, on this, the last evening of the year, the events of the past four months, and contrasting the disturbed condition of affairs upon my advent with the present tranquil and happy state of things, which has held its sway for the last three months, I must congratulate the administration and the country upon the auspicious results. Crime, so rife and daring at the period of my arrival, is almost entirely banished. I can truthfully assure you, that in proportion to her population and extent, less crime is now being committed in Kansas than in any other portion of the United States."

The 6th of January, 1857, was the day appointed for the meeting of the free state legislature at Topeka. As apprehensions were entertained as to the results of this meeting, the governor had taken precautions against any evil consequences; but there were persons about Lecompton who were unwilling to trust the management of the affair to the governor. A writ for the arrest of the Topeka legislators had been quietly issued by Judge Cato, on the oath of Sheriff Jones, which was served by deputy marshall Pardee—Jones being present—on the members assembled, who yielded themselves prisoners without resistance, much to the disappointment of the sheriff and his coädjutors. The prisoners were conveyed to Tecumseh, where they received a hearing before Judge Cato, who liberated them on their own recognizance. They were, of course, never brought to trial, the district attorney entering *nolle prosequies* in theirs, as in all other cases of free state treason prisoners.

The territorial legislative assembly met at Lecompton on the 12th of January, and was duly organized. A committee was appointed to wait upon the governor, and apprise him of the organization. On the following morning his message was read before both houses.

MESSAGE.

GENTLEMEN OF THE COUNCIL AND OF THE HOUSE OF REPRESENTATIVES:

The All-Wise and beneficent Being, who controls alike the destinies of individuals and of nations, has permitted you to convene, this day, charged with grave responsibilities.

The eyes, not only of the people of Kansas, but of the entire Union, are upon you, watching with anxiety the result of your deliberations, and of our joint action in the execution of the delicate and important duties devolving upon us.

Selected at a critical period in the history of the country, to discharge the executive functions of this territory, the obligations I was required to assume were of the most weighty importance. And when I came seriously to contemplate their magnitude, I would have shrunk from the responsibility, were it not for an implicit reliance upon Divine aid, and a full confidence in the virtue, zeal and patriotism of the citizens, without which the wisest executive suggestions must be futile and inoperative.

To you, legislators, invested with sovereign authority, I look for that hearty coöperation which will enable us successfully to guide the ship of state through the troubled waters, into the haven of safety. It is with feelings of profound gratitude to Almighty God, the bounteous Giver of all good, I have the pleasure of announcing, that after the bitter contest of opinion through which we have recently passed, and which has unfortunately led to fratricidal strife, that peace, which I have every reason to believe to be permanent, now reigns throughout the territory, and gladdens, with its genial influences, homes and hearts which but lately were sad and desolate; that the robber and the murderer have been driven from our soil; that burned cabins have been replaced by substantial dwellings; that a feeling of confidence and kindness has taken the place of distrust and hate; that all good citizens are disposed to deplore the errors and excesses of the past, and unite with fraternal zeal in repairing its injuries; and that this territory, unsurpassed by any portion of the continent for the salubrity of its climate and the fertility of its soil, its mineral and agricultural wealth, its timber-fringed streams and fine quarries of building stone, has entered upon a career of unparalleled prosperity.

To maintain the advance we have made, and realize the bright anticipations of the future; to build up a model commonwealth, enriched with all the treasures of learning, of virtue and religion, and make it a choice heritage for our children and generations yet unborn, let me, not only as your executive, but as a Kansan, devoted to the interests of Kansas, and animated solely by patriotic purposes, with all earnestness invoke you, with one heart and soul, to pursue so high and lofty a course in your deliberations, as, by its moderation and justice, will commend itself to the approbation of the country, and command the respect of the people.

This being the first occasion offered me to speak to the legislative assembly, it is but proper, and in accordance with general usage, that I should declare the principles which shall give shape and tone to my administration. These principles, without elaboration, I will condense into the narrowest compass.

"Equal and exact justice" to all men, of whatever political or religious persuasion; peace, comity, and friendship with neighboring states and territories, with a sacred regard for state rights, and reverential respect for the integrity and perpetuity of the Union; a reverence for the federal constitution as the concentrated wisdom of the fathers of the republic, and the very ark of our political safety; the cultivation of a pure and energetic nationality, and the development of an excellent and intensely vital patriotism; a jealous regard for the elective franchise, and the entire security and sanctity of the ballot-box; a firm determination to adhere to the doctrines of self-government and popular sovereignty, as guaranteed by the organic law; unqualified submission to the will of the majority; the election of all officers by the people themselves; the supremacy of the civil over the military power; strict economy in public expenditures, with a rigid accountability of all public officers; the preservation of the public faith, and a currency based upon, and equal to, gold and silver; free and safe immigration from every quarter of the country; the cultivation of the proper territorial pride, with a firm determination to submit to no invasion of our sovereignty; the fostering care of agriculture, manufactures, mechanic arts, and all works of internal improvement; the liberal and free education of all the children of the territory; entire religious freedom; a free press, free speech, and the peaceable right to assemble and discuss all questions of public interest; trial by jurors impartially selected; the sanctity of the habeas corpus; the repeal of all laws inconsistent with the constitution of the United States and the organic act, and the steady administration of the government so as best to secure the general welfare.

These sterling maxims, sanctioned by the wisdom and experience of the past, and the observance of which has brought our country to so exalted a position among the nations of the earth, will be steady lights by which my administration shall be guided.

A summary view of the state of the territory upon my advent, with an allusion to some of my official acts, may not be inappropriate to this occasion, and may serve to inspire your counsels with that wisdom and prudence, by a contemplation of the frightful excesses of the past, so essential to the adoption of measures to prevent their recurrence, and enable you to lay the broad and solid foundations of a future commonwealth which may give protection and happiness to millions of freemen.

It accords not with my policy or intentions to do the least injustice to any citizen or party of men in this territory or elsewhere. Pledged to do "equal and exact justice" in my executive capacity, I am inclined to throw the veil of oblivion over the errors and outrages of the period antecedent to my arrival, except so far as reference to them may be necessary for substantial justice, and to explain and develope the policy which has shed the benign influences of peace upon Kansas, and which, if responded to by the legislature in a spirit of kindness and conciliation, will contribute much to soothe those feelings of bitterness and contention which in the past brought upon us such untold evils.

I arrived at Fort Leavenworth on the ninth day of September last, and immediately assumed the executive functions. On the eleventh, I issued my inaugural address, declaring the general principles upon which I intended to administer the government. In this address, I solemnly pledged myself to support the constitution of the United States, and to discharge my duties as governor of Kansas with fidelity; to sustain all the provisions of the organic act, which I pronounced to be "eminently just and beneficial;" to stand by the doctrine of popular sovereignty, or the will of the majority of the actual *bona fide* inhabitants, when legitimately expressed, which I characterized "the imperative rule of civil action for every law-abiding citizen." The gigantic evils under which this territory was groaning were attributed to outside influences, and the people of Kansas were earnestly invoked to suspend unnatural strife; to banish all extraneous and improper influences from their deliberations; and in the spirit of reason and mutual conciliation to adjust their own differences. Such suggestions in relation to modifications of the present statutes as I deemed for the public interests, were promised at the proper time. It was declared that this territory was the common property of the people of the several states, and that no obstacle should be interposed to its free settlement, while in a territorial condition, by the citizens of every state of the Union. A just territorial pride was sought to be infused; a pledge was solemnly given to know no party, no section, nothing but Kansas and the Union; and the people were earnestly invoked to bury the past in oblivion, to suspend hostilities and refrain from the indulgence of bitter feeling; to begin anew; to devote themselves to the true and substantial interests of Kansas; develope her rich agricultural resources; build up manufactures; make public roads and other works of internal improvement; prepare amply for the education of their children; devote themselves to all the arts of peace, and make this territory the sanctuary of those cherished principles which protect the inalienable rights of the individual, and elevate states in their sovereign capacities.

The foregoing is a brief summary of the principles upon which my administration was commenced. I have steadily adhered to them, and time and trial have but served to strengthen my convictions of their justice.

Coincident with my inaugural were issued two proclamations, the one, disbanding the territorial militia, composed of a mixed force of citizens and others, and commanding "all bodies of men, combined, armed and equipped with munitions of war, without authority of the government, instantly to disband or quit the territory, as they would answer the contrary at their peril." The other, ordering "all free male citizens qualified to bear arms, between the ages of eighteen and forty-five years, to enroll themselves, that they might be completely organized by companies, regiments, brigades, and divisions, and hold themselves in readiness to be mustered, by my order, into the service of the United States, upon a requisition of the commander of the military department in which Kansas is embraced, for the suppression of all unlawful combinations, and for the maintenance of public order and civil government."

The policy of these proclamations is so evident, and their beneficial effects have been so apparent, as to require no vindication.

The territory was declared by the acting-governor to be in a state of insurrection; the civil authority was powerless—entirely without capacity to vindicate the majesty of the law and restore the broken peace; the existing difficulties were of a far more complicated character than I had anticipated; predatory bands, whose sole aim, unrelieved by the mitigation of political causes, was assassination, arson, plunder, and rapine, had undisturbed possession of some portions of the territory, while every part of it was kept in constant alarm and terror by the advocates of political sentiments, uniting, according to their respective sympathies, in formidable bodies of armed men, completely equipped with munitions of war, and resolved upon mutual extermination as the only hope of peace; unoffending and peaceable citizens were driven from their homes; others murdered in their own dwellings, which were given to the flames; that sacred respect for woman which has characterized all civilized nations, seemed in the hour of mad excitement to be forgotten; partisan feeling, on all sides, intensely excited by a question which inflamed the entire nation, almost closed the minds of the people against me; idle and mendacious rumors, well calculated to produce exasperation and destroy confidence, were everywhere rife; the most unfortunate suspicions prevailed; in isolated country places no man's life was safe; robberies and murders were of daily occurrence; nearly every farm-house was deserted; and no traveler could safely venture on the highway without an escort. This state of affairs was greatly aggravated by the interference of prominent politicians outside of the territory. The foregoing is but a faint outline of the fearful condition of things which ruled Kansas and convulsed the nation. The full picture will be drawn by the iron pen of impartial history, and the actors in the various scenes will be assigned their true positions.

I came here a stranger to your difficulties, without prejudice, with a solemn sense of my official obligations, and with a lofty resolution to put a speedy termination to events so fraught with evil, and which, if unchecked, would have floated the country into the most bloody civil war.

Hesitation, or partisan affiliations, would have resulted in certain failure, and only served further to complicate affairs. To restore peace and order, and relieve the people from the evils under which they were laboring, it was necessary that an impartial, independent, and just policy should be adopted, which would embrace in its protection all good citizens, without distinction of party, and sternly punish all bad men who continued to disturb the public tranquility. Accordingly, my inaugural address and proclamations were immediately circulated among the people, in order that they might have early notice of my intentions.

On the fourteenth day of September, reliable information was received that a large body of armed men were marching to attack Hickory Point, on the north side of the Kansas river. I immediately dispatched a squadron of United States dragoons, with instruction to capture and bring to this place any persons whom they might find acting in violation of my proclamation. In pursuance of these instructions, one hundred and one prisoners were taken, and committed for trial.

While a portion of the army was performing this duty, I was advised that a large body of men was approaching the town of Lawrence, determined upon its destruction. I at once ordered three hundred United States troops to that place, and repaired there in person. Within four miles of Lawrence, I found a force of twenty-seven hundred men, consisting of citizens of this territory and other places, organized as territorial militia, under a proclamation of the late acting governor. I disbanded this force, ordering the various companies composing it, to repair to their respective places of rendezvous, there to be mustered out of service. My orders were obeyed; the militia retired to their homes; the effusion of blood was prevented; the preservation of Lawrence effected; and a great step made towards the restoration of peace and confidence.

To recount my various official acts, following each other in quick succession under your immediate observation, would be a work of supererogation, and would occupy more space than the limits of an executive message would justify. My executive minutes, containing a truthful history of my official transactions, with the policy which dictated them, have been forwarded to the general government, and are open to the inspection of the country.

In relation to any alterations or modifications of the territorial statutes which I might deem advisable, I promised in my inaugural address to direct public attention at the proper time. In the progress of events, the time has arrived, and you are the tribunal to which my suggestions must be submitted. On this subject I bespeak your candid attention, as it has an inseparable connection with the prosperity and happiness of the people.

It has already been remarked that the territories of the United State are the common property of the citizens of the several states. It may be likened to a joint ownership in an estate, and no condition should be imposed or restrictions placed upon the equal enjoyment of the benefits arising therefrom, which will do the least injustice to any of the owners, or which is not contemplated in the tenure by which it is held, which is no less than the constitution of the United States, the sole bond of the American Union. This being the true position, no obstacle should be interposed to the free, speedy, and general settlement of this territory.

The durability and imperative authority of a state constitution, when the interests of the people require a state government, and a direct popular vote is necessary to give it sanction and effect, will be the proper occasion, once for all, to decide the grave political questions which underlie a well regulated commonwealth.

Let this, then, be the touchstone of your deliberations. Enact no law which will not clearly bear the constitutional test; and if any laws have been passed which do not come up to this standard, it is your solemn duty to sweep them from the statute book.

The territorial government should abstain from the exercise of authority not clearly delegated to it, and should permit all doubtful questions to remain in abeyance until the formation of a state constitution.

On the delicate and exciting question of slavery, a subject which so peculiarly engaged the attention of congress at the passage of our organic act, I cannot too earnestly invoke you to permit it to remain where the constitution of the United States and that act place it, subject to the decision of the courts upon all points arising during our present infant condition.

The repeal of the Missouri line, which was a restriction on popular sovereignty, anew consecrated the great doctrine of self-government, and restored to the people their full control over every question of interest to themselves, both north and south of that line.

Justice to the country and the dictates of sound policy require that the legislature should confine itself to such subjects as will preserve the basis of entire equality; and when a sufficient population is here, and they choose to adopt a state government, that they shall be "perfectly free," without let or hindrance, to form all their domestic institutions "in their own way," and to dictate that form of government which in their deliberate judgment may be deemed proper.

Any attempt to incite servile insurrection and to interfere with the domestic institutions of sovereign states, is extremely reprehensible, and shall receive no countenance from me. Such intervention can result in no good, but is pregnant with untold disasters. Murder, arson, rapine, and death follow in its wake, while not one link in the fetters of the slave is weakened or broken, or any amelioration in his condition secured. Such interference is a direct invasion of state rights, only calculated to produce irritation and estrangement. Every dictate of self-respect—every consideration of state equality—the glories of the past and the hopes of the future—all, with soul-stirring eloquence, constrain us to cultivate a reverential awe for the constitution as the sheet-anchor of our safety, and bid us, in good faith, to carry out all its provisions.

Many of the statutes are excellent, and suited to our wants and condition, but in order that they may receive that respect and sanction which is the vital principle of all law, let such be abolished as are not eminently just and will not receive the fullest approbation of the people. I trust you will test them all by the light of the general and fundamental principles of our government, and that all that will not bear this ordeal, be revised, amended, or repealed. To some of them which strike my mind as objectionable, your candid and special attention is respectfully invited.

By carefully comparing the organic act, as printed in the statutes, with a certified copy of the same from the department of state, important discrepancies, omissions and additions will be discovered. I therefore recommend the appointment of a committee, to compare the printed statutes with the original rolls on file in the secretary's office, to ascertain whether the same liberty has been taken with the act under which they were made.

Of the numerous errors discovered by me in the copy of the organic act as printed in the statutes, I will refer to one in illustration of my meaning. In the 29th section, defining the executive authority, will be found the following striking omission—"against the laws of said territory, and reprieves for offenses." This omission impairs the executive authority, and deprives the governor of the pardoning power for offenses committed "against the laws of the territory," which congress, for the wisest and most humane reasons, has conferred upon him.

The organic act requires every bill to be presented to the governor, and demands his signature, as the evidence of his approval, before it can become a law. The statutes are defective in this respect, as they do not contain the date of approval, nor the proper evidence of that fact, by having the governor's signature.

Your attention is invited to chapter 30, in relation to county boundaries. The boundary of Douglas county is imperfect, and in connection with Shawnee county, is an absurdity for both counties. The boundary lines for all the counties should be absolutely established.

Chapter 44, establishing the probate court, also requires attention. The act is good generally, so far as it relates to the organization and duties of the court. But all provisions in this and other acts, vesting the appointment of probate judges, county commissioners, and other public officers, in the legislative assembly, should at once be repealed, and the unqualified right of election conferred upon the people, whose interests are immediately affected by the acts of those officials. The free and unrestricted right of the people to select all their own agents, is a maxim so well settled in political ethics, and springs so legitimately from the doctrines of self-government, that I need only to allude to the question to satisfy every one of its justice. The "people must be perfectly free" to regulate their own business in their own way; and when the voice of the majority is fairly expressed, all will bow to it as the voice of God. Let the people, then, rule in everything. I have every confidence in the virtue, intelligence, and "sober thought" of the toiling millions. The deliberate popular judgment is never wrong. When, in times of excitement, the popular mind may be temporarily obscured from the dearth of correct information or the mists of passion, the day of retribution and justice speedily follows, and a summary reversal is the certain result. Just and patriotic sentiment is a sure reliance for every honest public servant. The sovereignty of the people must be maintained.

Section 15th of this act allows writs of habeas corpus to be issued by the probate judge, but leaves him no authority to hear the case and grant justice; but refers the matter to the "next term of the district court." The several terms of the district court are at stated periods, and the provision alluded to amounts to a denial of justice and a virtual suspension of "the great writ of liberty," contrary to the letter and spirit of the constitution of the United States.

Many provisions of chapter 66, entitled "Elections," are objectionable. Section 11th, requiring certain "test oaths" as pre-requisites to the right of suffrage, is wrong, unfair, and uneqal upon the citizens of different sections of the Union. It is exceedingly invidious to require obedience to any special enactment. The peculiar features of these test oaths should be abolished, and all citizens presumed to be law-abiding and patriotic until the contrary clearly appears. Sworn obedience to particular statutes has seldom secured that object. Justice will ever commend itself to the support of all honest men, and the surest means of insuring the ready execution of law, is to make it so pre-eminently just, equal and impartial as to command the respect of those whom it is intended to affect.

Section 36th deprives electors of the great safeguard of the purity and in-dependence of the elective franchise : I mean the right to vote by ballot; and after the first day of November, 1856, requires all voting to be *viva voce*. This provision, taken in connection with section 9th, which provides that "if all the votes offered cannot be taken before the hour appointed for closing the polls, the judges shall by public proclamation, adjourn such election until the following day, when the polls shall again be opened, and the election continued as before," &c., offers great room for fraud and corruption. Voting *viva voce*, the condition of the poll can be ascertained at any moment. If the parties having the election officers are likely to be defeated, they have the option of adjourning for the purpose of drumming up votes ; or in the insane desire of victory, may be tempted to resort to other means even more reprehensible. The right of voting by ballot is now incorporated into the constitutions of nearly all the states, and is classed with the privileges deemed sacred. The arguments in its favor are so numerous and overwhelming that I have no hesitation in recommending its adoption. The election law should be carefully examined, and such guards thrown around it as will most effectually secure the sanctity of the ballot-box and preserve it from the taint of a single illegal vote. The man who will deliberately tamper with the elective franchise and dare to offer an illegal vote, strikes at the foundation of justice, undermines the pillars of society, applies the torch to the temple of our liberties, and should receive severe punishment. As a qualification for voting, a definite period of actual inhabitancy in the territory, to the exclusion of a home elsewhere, should be rigidly prescribed. No man should be permitted to vote upon a floating residence. He should have resided within the territory for a period of not less than ninety days, and in the district where he offers to vote at least ten days immediately preceding such election. All the voters should be registered and published for a certain time previous to the election. False voting should be severely punished, and false swearing to receive a vote visited with the pains and penalties of perjury.

In this connection your attention is also invited to chapter 92, entitled "Jurors." This chapter leaves the selection of jurors to the absolute discretion of the marshal, sheriff, or constable, as the case may be, and affords great room for partiality and corruption. The names of all properly qualified citizens, without party distinction, should be thrown into a wheel or box, and at stated periods, under the order of the courts, jurors should be publicly drawn by responsible persons. Too many safeguards cannot be thrown around the right of trial by jury, in order that it may still continue to occupy that cherished place in the affections of the people so essential to its preservation and sanctity.

Some portions of chapter 110, "Militia," infringes the executive prerogative, impairs the governor's usefulness, and clearly conflicts with the organic act. This act requires the executive to reside in the territory, and makes him "commander-in-chief of the militia." This power must be vested some place, and is always conferred upon the chief magistrate. Section 26 virtually confers this almost sovereign prerogative "upon any commissioned officer," and permits him, "whenever and as often as any invasion or danger may come to his knowledge, to order out the militia or volunteer corps, or any part thereof, under his command, for the defense of the the territory," &c.; thus almost giving "any commissioned officer" whatever, at his option, the power to involve the territory in war.

Section 12 provides for a general militia training on the first Monday of October, the day fixed for the general election. This is wrong, and is well calculated to incite to terrorism. The silent ballots of the people, unawed by military display, should quietly and definitely determine all questions of public interest.

The other sections of the law, requiring the appointment of field and commissioned officers, should be repealed. All officers should derive their authority directly from their respective commands, by election. To make the military system complete and effective, there must be entire subordination and unity running from the commander-in-chief to the humblest soldier, and one spirit must animate the entire system.

The 122d chapter, in relation to "patrols," is unnecessary. It renders all other property liable to heavy taxation for the protection of slave property; thus operating unequally upon citizens, and is liable to the odious charge of being a system of espionage, as it authorizes the patrols, an indefinite number of whom may be appointed, to visit not only negro quarters, but "any other places" suspected of unlawful assemblages of slaves.

Chapter 131, "Preëmption," squanders the school fund, by appropriating the school sections contrary to the organic act, which provides "that sections numbered sixteen and thirty-six, in each township in Kansas territory, shall be, and the same are hereby reserved for the purpose of being applied to schools in said territory, and in the states and territories to be erected out of the same;" contravenes the United States preëmption laws, which forbid trafficking in claims, and holding more than one claim; and directs the governor to grant patents for lands belonging to the United States, and only conditionally granted to the territory. This act is directly calculated to destroy the effect of a munificent grant of land by congress for educational purposes. The territory is the trustee of this valuable gift, and posterity has the right to demand of us that this sacred trust shall remain unimpaired, in order that the blessings of free education may be shed upon our children.

Every state should have the best educational system which an intelligent government can provide. The physical, moral and mental faculties should be cultivated in harmonious unison, and that system of education is the best which will effect these objects. Congress has already provided for the support of common schools. In addition to this, I would recommend the legislature to ask congress to donate land lying in this territory for the establishment of a university, embracing a normal, agricultural and mechanical school. A university, thus endowed, would be a blessing to our people; disseminate useful and scientific intelligence; provide competent teachers for our primary schools; and furnish a complete system of education adequate to our wants in all the departments of life.

The subject of roads, bridges and highways, merits your especial attention. Nothing adds more to comfort, convenience, prosperity and happiness, and more greatly promotes social intercourse and kind feeling, than easy and convenient inter-communication. Roads should be wide and straight, and the various rivers and ravines substantially bridged.

Railroads should be encouraged; and in granting charters, the legislature should have in view the interests of the whole people. The prosperity of the territory is intimately connected with the early and general construction of the rapid and satisfactory means of transit.

While on the subject of internal improvement, I would call to your notice and solicit for it your serious consideration, the opening, at the earliest period, of a more easy means of communication with the seaboard than any we at present enjoy. One great obstacle to our prosperity is the immense distance

49

of Kansas from all the great maritime depots of the country by any of the
routes now traveled. This can be removed by the construction of a railway,
commencing at an appropriate place in this territory, and running southwardly
through the Indian territory and Texas, to the most eligible point on the Gulf
of Mexico. The entire length of such a road would not exceed six hundred
miles, much less than half the distance to the Atlantic, and at an ordinary
speed of railroad travel could be traversed in less than twenty-four hours. It
would pass through a country remarkable for beauty of scenery, fertility of
soil and salubrity of climate, and which has properly been styled "the Eden
of the world;" and would open up new sources of wealth superior to any that
have yet been discovered on the eastern division of the continent. It would
place Kansas, isolated as she now is, in as favorable a position for commercial
enterprises as very many of the most populous states in the Union, and furnish
her a sure, easy and profitable market for her products, as well as a safe, expeditious and economical means of obtaining all her needed supplies at every
season of the year. You will not fail at once to perceive the importance of
this suggestion. Not only Kansas and Nebraska, but the entire country
west of the Mississippi, will be vastly benefited by its adoption. The advantages to Texas would be incalculable. And should you be favorably impressed
with the feasibility of the plan, I would advise that you communicate, in your
legislative capacity, with the legislature of that state, and that also of the territory of Nebraska, in regard to the most effectual measures for its speedy accomplishment.

Chapter 149, permitting settlers to hold three hundred and twenty acres of
land, is in violation of the preëmption laws, and leads to contention and litigation.

Chapter 151, relating to "slaves," attacks the equality which underlies the
theory of our territorial government; and destroys the freedom of speech, and
the privileges of public discussion, so essential to uncloak error, and enable the
people properly to mould their institutions in their own way. The freedom of
speech and press, and the right of public discussion upon all matters affecting
the interest of the people, are the great constitutional safeguards of popular
rights, liberty and happiness.

The act in relation to a territorial library, makes the auditor ex-officio libra-
rian, and gives him authority to audit his own accounts. These offices should
be distinct, as their duties conflict.

The congressional appropriation for a territorial library has been expended
in the purchase of a very valuable collection of books.

Time and space will not permit me to point out all the inconsistencies and
incongruities found in the Kansas statutes. Passed, as they were, under the
influence of excitement, and in too brief a period to secure mature deliberation, many of them are open to criticism and censure, and should pass under
your careful revision, with a view to modification or repeal. Some which have
been most loudly complained of have never been enforced. It is a bad principle to suffer dead-letter laws to deface the statute book. It impairs salutary

reverence for law, and excites in the popular mind a questioning of all law, which leads to anarchy and confusion. The best way is to leave no law on the statute book which is not uniformly and promptly to be administered with the authority and power of the government.

In traveling through the territory, I have discovered great anxiety in relation to the damages sustained during the past civil disturbances, and everywhere the question has been asked as to whom they should look for indemnity. These injuries—burning houses, plundering fields, and stealing horses and other property—have been a fruitful source of irritation and trouble, and have impoverished many good citizens. They cannot be considered as springing from purely local causes, and as such, the subjects of territorial redress. Their exciting cause has been outside of this territory, and the agents in their perpetration have been the citizens of nearly every state in the Union. It has been a species of national warfare waged upon the soil of Kansas; and it should not be forgotten that both parties were composed of men rushing here from various sections of the Union; that both committed acts which no law can justify; and the peaceable citizens of Kansas have been the victims. In adjusting the question of damages, it appears proper that a broad and comprehensive view of the subject should be taken; and I have accordingly suggested to the general government the propriety of recommending to congress the passage of an act providing for the appointment of a commissioner, to take testimony and report to congress for final action, at as early a day as possible.

There is not a single officer in the territory amenable to the people or to the governor; all having been appointed by the legislature, and holding their offices until 1857. This system of depriving the people of the just exercise of their rights, cannot be too strongly condemned.

A faithful performance of duty should be exacted from all public officers.

As the executive, I desire that the most cordial relations may exist between myself and all other departments of the government.

Homesteads should be held sacred. Nothing so much strengthens a government as giving its citizens a solid stake in the country. I am in favor of assuring to every industrious citizen one hundred and sixty acres of land.

The money appropriated by congress for the erection of our capitol has been nearly expended. I have asked for an additional appropriation of fifty thousand dollars, which will scarcely be sufficient to complete the building upon the plan adopted by the architect.

Where crime has been so abundant, the necessity for a territorial penitentiary is too evident to require elaboration, and I have therefore suggested a congressional appropriation for that purpose.

The Kansas river, the natural channel to the west, which runs through a valley of unparalleled fertility, can be made navigable as far as Fort Riley, a distance of over one hundred miles, and congress should be petitioned for aid to accomplish this laudable purpose. Fort Riley has been built, at an expense exceeding five hundred thousand dollars, with the expectation that the river was navigable to that place, and doubtless the general government will readily unite with this territory to secure this object.

A geological survey, developing the great mineral resources of this territory, is so necessary as merely to require notice. Provision for this useful work should immediately be made.

The early disposal of the public lands and their settlement will materially advance our substantial prosperity. Great anxiety prevails among the settlers to secure titles to their lands The facilities for this purpose, by but one land-office in the territory, are inadequate to the public wants, and I have consequently recommended the establishment of two or more additional land-offices in such positions as will best accommodate the people.

After mature consideration, and from a thorough conviction of its propriety, I have suggested large congressional appropriations. The coming immigration, attracted by our unrivaled soil and climate, will speedily furnish the requisite population to make a sovereign state. Other territories have been for years the recipients of congressional bounty, and a similar amount of money and land bestowed upon them during a long period, should at once be given to Kansas, as, like the Eureka state, she will spring into full life, and the prosperity of the territory, and the welfare and protection of the people coming here from every state of the Union, to test anew the experiment of republican government, require ample and munificent appropriations.

As citizens of a territory, we are peculiarly and immediately under the protecting influence of the Union, and, like the inhabitants of the states comprising it, feel a lively interest in all that concerns its welfare and prosperity. Within the last few years, sundry conflicting questions have been agitated throughout the country, and discussed in a spirit calculated to impair confidence in its strength and perpetuity, and furnish abundant cause for apprehension and alarm. These questions have mostly been of a local or sectional character, and as such should never have acquired general significance or importance. All American citizens should divest themselves of selfish considerations in relation to public affairs, and in the spirit of patriotism make dispassionate inquisition into the causes which have produced much alienation and bitterness among men whom the highest considerations require should be united in the bonds of fraternal fellowship. All Union-loving men should unite upon a platform of reason, equality, and patriotism. All sectionalism should be annihilated. All sections of the Union should be harmonized under a national, conservative government, as during the early days of the republic. The value of the Union is beyond computation, and no respect is due to those who will even dare to calculate its value. One of our ablest statesmen has wisely and eloquently said, "Who shall assign limits to the achievements of free minds and free hands under the protection of this glorious Union? No treason to mankind since the organization of society would be equal in atrocity to that of him who would lift his hand to destroy it. He would overthrow the noblest structure of human wisdom, which protects himself and his fellow man. He would stop the progress of free government, and involve his country either in anarchy or despotism. He would extinguish the fire of liberty which warms and animates the hearts of happy millions, and invites all the nations of the earth to imitate our example."

The soldier-president, whose exploits in the field were only equaled by his wisdom in the cabinet, with that singular sagacity which has stamped with the seal of prophecy all his foreshadowings, has repudiated, as morbid and unwise, that philanthropy which looks to the amalgamation of the American with any inferior race. The white man, with his intellectual energy, far-reaching science, and indomitable perseverance, is the peculiar object of my sympathy, and should receive the especial protection and support of government. In this territory there are numerous "Indian reserves," of magnificent extent and choice fertility, capable of sustaining a dense civilized population, now held unimproved by numerous Indian tribes. These tribes are governed by Indian agents, entirely independent of the executive of this territory, and are, indeed, governments within a government. Frequent aggressions upon these reserves are occurring, which have produced collisions between the Indian agents and the settlers, who appeal to me for protection. Seeing so much land unoccupied and unimproved, these enterprising pioneers naturally question the policy which excludes them from soil devoted to no useful or legitimate purpose. Impressed with the conviction that the large Indian reserves, if permitted to remain in their present condition, cannot fail to exercise a blighting influence on the prosperity of Kansas, and result in great injury to the Indians themselves, I shall be pleased to unite with the legislature in any measures deemed advisable, looking to the speedy extinguishment of the Indian title to all surplus land lying in this territory, so as to throw it open for settlement and improvement.

For official action, I know no better rule than a conscientious conviction of duty—none more variable than the vain attempt to conciliate temporary prejudice. Principles and justice are eternal, and if tampered with, sooner or later the sure and indignant verdict of popular condemnation against those who are untrue to their leadings, will be rendered. Let us not be false to our country, our duty, and our constituents. The triumph of truth and principle, not of partisan and selfish objects, should be our steady purpose—the general welfare, and not the interests of the few, our sole aim. Let the past, which few men can review with satisfaction, be forgotten. Let us not deal in criminations and recriminations; but, as far as possible, let us make restitution and offer regrets for past excesses. The dead, whom the madness of partisan fury has consigned to premature graves, cannot be recalled to life; the insults, the outrages, the robberies and murders, "enough to stir a fever in the blood of age," in this world of imperfection and guilt, can never be fully atoned for or justly punished. The innocent blood, however, shall not cry in vain for redress, as we are promised by the great Executive of the Universe, whose power is almighty and whose knowledge is perfect, that he "will repay."

"To fight in a just cause and for our country's glory, is the best office of the best of men." Let "justice be the laurel" which crowns your deliberations;

let your aims be purely patriotic, and your sole purpose the general welfare and the substantial interests of the whole people. If we fix our steady gaze upon the constitution and the organic act as " the cloud by day and the pillar of fire by night," our footsteps will never wander into any unknown or forbidden paths. Then will this legislative assembly be as a beacon light, placed high in the pages of our history, shedding its luminous and benign influence to the most remote generations; its members will be remembered with veneration and respect as among the early fathers of the magnificent commonwealth, which, in the not distant future, will overshadow with its protection a population of freemen unsurpassed by any state in this beloved Union for intelligence, wealth, religion, and all the elements which make and insure the true greatness of a nation; the present citizens of Kansas will rejoice in the benefits conferred; the mourning and gloom, which too long, like a pall, have covered the people, will be dispersed by the sunshine of joy with which they will hail the advent of peace founded upon justice; we will enter upon a career of unprecedented prosperity; good feeling and confidence will prevail; the just rule of action which you are about to establish, will be recognized; the entire country, now watching your deliberations with momentous interest, will award you their enthusiastic applause; and above and over all, you will have the sanction of your own consciences, enjoy self-respect, and meet with Divine approbation, without which all human praise is worthless and unavailing.   JNO. W. GEARY.

Lecompton, K. T., Jan. 12, 1857.

One of the first proceedings of the members of this body was to hold a secret meeting, at which it was resolved, that should any act be vetoed by the governor, there should be a mutual agreement to disregard the veto, and pass the act by a two-third vote, which was strictly adhered to. The governor attempted to arrest several bills by his veto, but to no purpose. A bill was passed, which was intended as an indorsement of the conduct of Judge Lecompte in admitting the murderer Hays to bail, and giving to any district judge authority to bail all persons charged with any crime whatsoever, whether previously considered bailable or not. This the governor vetoed, giving his reasons as follows, but the bill was passed by an almost unanimous vote:

To the Council and House of Representatives of Kansas Territory:

GENTLEMEN:—The bill "to authorize Courts and Judges to admit to bail in certain cases," has been carefully examined, and notwithstanding my earnest desire to agree with the legislature, I am compelled to return it without approval, for the following reasons:

The doctrine that the more certain the punishment of crime is made, the greater will be the restraints upon the evil passions of wicked men, has been established in all civilized communities, and approved by the wisdom and experience of every age of the world; and had we no other evidence of its truth, more than sufficient has been furnished in the disturbances and outrages which have so recently occurred in the territory of Kansas; for no one can be insensible of the fact, that the impunity that has here been given to crime, has been the cause of many of the offenses that have been committed. Had but a few of the early agitators, and defiants of law, been brought to punishment, the subsequent events, which every good citizen deplores and condems, would never have occurred.

It is of the utmost importance to the safety of society that the laws should be rendered as stringent, and their execution as certain as possible; especially as regards the crime of wilful and deliberate murder. Such an offense should be guarded against with the utmost care. No door whatever should be opened for the escape of the criminal. Once in the hands of the proper authorities, he should there be secured until the ends of justice are effected. The man whose life has been forfeited to the law, will stop at no means within the range of human possibility to accomplish his escape; for "what will a man not give in exchange for his life?"

The act under consideration makes it comparatively easy for the most notorious criminal to escape the punishment his crimes have merited. Any judge of a district court is thereby allowed to set him at liberty on bail. The bill does not even establish the amount of bail required. This, as well as the propriety of bailing, is left to the discretion of the court or of the district judge. Were the bill passed expressly to tamper with and corrupt the judiciary, it could not have been more effectual. All human beings are fallible, and it is a sound principle to throw in their way to err, as few temptations as possible. No judge, who has a proper regard for his own reputation, can desire the passage of a law which will render him liable to invidious imputations. If this bill becomes a law, appeals will be made to the district judge to bail every person charged with the crime of murder, and the strongest inducements will be offered to influence his action. Should he refuse to accede to the wishes of the individual accused, or his importunate friends, he will subject himself to the charge of some unjust bias; while, on the other hand, should he yield to such importunities, he is almost certain of being charged with bribery and corruption; and violence towards himself might ensue in either case. The judge, therefore, would prefer to avoid the additional responsibility which this bill imposes.

But apart from this, one tendency of the act is to corrupt the judiciary. It will not do to affirm that this is impossible. It has frequently been done to such an extent as to endanger the safety of communities, and even incite to anarchy, with all its fearful consequences. The intention of the laws have been so disregarded, that the people, in self-defense, have repudiated the courts, and in opposition to all legislative enactments, have taken upon themselves the administration of justice. Indeed, in every instance where "lynch law" has been resorted to, the excuse given by the people has been founded on the laxity of the courts, or the inefficiency or corruption of the judiciary.

This want of confidence in the authorities regularly constituted for the execution of justice upon persons charged with heinous crimes, produced those terrible excitements in California, consequent upon the organization of the memorable "Vigilance Committee."

It is to be hoped that a similar condition of things may never transpire in Kansas, though it may well be anticipated, if murder is permitted by the courts to be perpetrated with impunity. The murmurings on this subject are even now loud and almost universal. Some of our best citizens have been stricken down by the hand of the assassin, whose blood has cried in vain upon the legal tribunals for justice. And although many have fallen victims to this atrocious crime, not one of its numerous perpetrators has yet suffered the just penalty of the law. The murderer, his hands still reeking with human gore, walks unmolested in our midst, laughing to scorn the laws which condemn him to an ignominious death.

Let the law contemplated in this bill be adopted, and this evil, already sufficiently deplorable, will be rendered far worse. The slight restraints now held upon the vicious, will be almost entirely removed. No good citizens can venture in the streets or upon the highways, with a proper feeling of security. The personal safety of all who are well disposed, will be constantly endangered. The odious practice of bearing concealed weapons for self-defense will become general, and the most disastrous results willl follow. Every man, conscious of the uncertainty of punishment by the courts, will take the law in his own hands, and the slayer of one individual will fall a victim to the retaliatory vengeance of another. Or should he be brought before a judge or court, and liberated upon bail, an offended people will arise in their majesty, and prevent his escape by the infliction of summary punishment.

The fact that bail has been given, will have no tendency to prevent these results; for no one can have confidence in the security furnished by such bail as a deliberate murderer can obtain. The person who will step in between him and the execution of justice, must himself be destitute of those feelings and sentiments which will render him worthy the confidence of peace-loving citizens. Or even were it otherwise, and the murderer is substantially bailed by a wealthy relative or friend, the only object in the whole transaction is the criminal's escape; for any amount of property, under such circumstances, will be forfeited to preserve his life. But in the majority of the cases the bail is entirely worthless, and its being admitted by a court or judge is equivalent to the murderer's discharge; for no one who is conscious of a conviction that will condemn him to death, will ever present himself for trial. If he has wealth, he can purchase sureties; and if he has not, he may obtain the aid of those who are worthless, or if possessed of the property to which they swear, may dispose of it at pleasure, and thus defraud the territory as well as justice. Bail-bonds, as now given, are of little value even in trivial cases; for when forfeited the amount is seldom collected. To make them of any avail, a lien should immediately be created on the lands of the persons acknowledging them, " and the execution issued by virtue of a judgment thereon, may rightly command the taking and sale of the lands, of which defendant was seized at the time the recognizance was acknowledged." Were this rule of law adopted, there would be some value in a bail-bond, and fewer persons would be found willing to execute it. But as the law now rests in this territory, a criminal may be bailed to-day upon what is apparently tangible security, and to-morrow, both himself and sureties dispose of all their property, and unmolested and quietly depart to another region, and thus the matter ends. In the majority of instances, therefore, the taking of bail in criminal cases only tends to defeat the ends of justice, and in every case of absolute premeditated murder, where the proof is clear, or sufficient to convict, is tatamount to an acquittal of the criminal.

The fact that we have no sufficient prisons for the safe-keeping of the murderer, affords no argument for the passage of the bill. This want can soon be supplied, and it will be better far to commence the work at once, than to adopt a law which must remove the almost only restraint that now exists upon murderous inclinations and passions. There is no necessity for deliberate murderers to be set free, on bail or otherwise, for want of a prison to keep them in lengthy confinement. Frequent sessions of the courts, early trials, and speedy executions, will dispose of such cases, and give to the people confidence in the judiciary and the laws, and a sense of security of which they have so long been deprived.

Remove or weaken any one of the safeguards we now possess against criminals and crime, and the peace we enjoy must measurably be shaken. Hence it becomes a subject of the utmost importance, not only to guard against such a result, but to adopt, if possible, laws which will strengthen the general confidence, by making the barriers to the escape of the criminal even more firm and impassable.

Let it be established and universally known, that "though hand joined in hand, the guilty shall not go unpunished;" that the blood-stained murderer, once in the hands of the authorities, shall have no possibility or hope of escape; that he who wilfully and deliberately sheds the blood of his fellow-man shall surely suffer the penalty by which his life is forfeit, and our laws will be more respected, fewer crimes will be committed, and the community will repose in far greater security and peace.   JOHN W. GEARY.

Lecompton, K. T., January 22d, 1857.

It was during this session that an attempt was made to assassinate the governor, by one Sherrard, whom the governor had refused to commission as a sheriff. A few days after Sherrard was himself shot down, in a melee at a public meeting in Lecompton, by a man whom he had assaulted.

The most important act of this legislature was the passage of the "Census Bill." On the part of the free state men, this bill was objected to on the ground that it would deprive many citizens of the elective franchise who had temporarily left the territory, and could not return early in March, as the river would not then be navigable.

It provides for the taking of a census, preparatory to an election to be held in June, 1857, for delegates to a convention to frame a state constitution, to be presented to the next congress for its approval. No citizen to be allowed to vote who was not in the territory on or before the 15th of March. "The census-takers and judges of election were the sheriffs and other officers appointed by the pro-slavery party. By this arrangement, hundreds of free state men who had been forcibly driven from their claims and homes, and who would not return so early as the 15th of March, were disfranchised, as well as the thousands who would become citizens of the territory before the day of election. Under these regulations the free state party concluded to take no part in the elections. There was a clause in the bill, intended for their intimidation, that the voting should be *viva voce*. Another feature of the bill was, that, although it was framed to defraud the free state citizens of their rights, it required them to pay a tax to assist in the accomplishment of the fraud.

"Governor Geary, before the passage of the bill, sent for the chairmen of the committees of the two branches of the legislature, and informed them that if they would consent to add a clause referring the constitution that might be framed by the convention TO THE CITIZENS OF THE TERRITORY FOR THEIR SANCTION OR REJECTION, before its being submitted to congress, he would waive all other objections and give it his approval. They replied to him, that the suggestion had already been fully discussed, and could not be adopted, as it would *defeat the only object of the act, which was to secure, beyond any possibility of failure, the territory of Kansas to the south as a slave state.* They had already, in anticipation of the passage of the bill, so apportioned the territory, that the accomplishment of this grand object was placed beyond the reach of any contingency.* The bill passed both houses, and was sent to the governor, who returned it with the following objections :

GENTLEMEN OF THE COUNCIL OF KANSAS TERRITORY :

After mature consideration of the bill entititled "an act to provide for the taking of a census, and election for delegates to convention," I am constrained to return the same without my approval.

Passing over other objections, I desire to call your serious attention to a material omission in the bill.

I refer to the fact that the legislature has failed to make any provision to submit the constitution, when framed, to the consideration of the people, for their ratification or rejection.

The position that a convention can do no wrong, and ought to be invested with sovereign power, and that its constituents have no right to judge of its acts, is extraordinary and untenable.

The history of state constitutions, with scarcely an exception, will exhibit a uniform and sacred adherence to the salutary rule of popular ratification.

The practice of the federal and state governments, in the adoption of their respective constitutions, exhibiting the wisdom of the past, will furnish us with a safe and reliable rule of action.

The federal constitution was first proposed by a convention of delegates from twelve states, assembled in Philadelphia. This constitution derived no authority from the first convention. It was submitted to the various states, fully discussed in all its features, and concurred in by the people of the states

---

* Dr. Gihon's History of Kansas.

in convention assembled; and that concurrence armed it with power and invested it with dignity. Article seventh of the constitution makes the ratification of nine states, three-fourths of the number represented in the convention, essential to its adoption.

In the adoption, not only of the federal constitution, but of nearly all the state constitutions, the popular ratification was made essential; and all amendments to those of most of the states are required to pass two legislatures, and then be submitted to the people for their approval.

In Kentucky, especially, all amendments to the constitution must pass two legislatures, and for two years be submitted to the vote of the people, upon the question of convention or no convention, on the specific amendments proposed.

Treaties made by ambassadors are not binding until duly ratified by their respective governments, whose agents they are.

Members of the legislature or of conventions are but the agents of the people, who have an inherent right to judge of the acts of their agents, and to condemn or approve them, as in their deliberate judgment they may deem proper.

The fundamental law of a commonwealth, so inseparably connected with the happiness and prosperity of the citizens, cannot be too well discussed, and cannot pass through too many ordeals of popular scrutiny.

What delegates to conventions may do or what omit, cannot be known until they have assembled and developed their action. If the whole power be vested in them without recourse over to the people, there is no guarantee that the popular wishes will be fairly and fully expressed.

Although the people may have voted for a convention to form a state constitution, yet they have by no just rule of construction voted away the usual and universal right of ratification.

Special instructions, covering every point arising in the formation of a constitution, cannot be given in the elections preliminary to a convention; and it is, therefore, proper that the action of the convention, necessarily covering new ground, should be submitted to the people for their consideration.

The practical right of the people to ordain and establish governments, is found in the expressive and beautiful preamble to the federal constitution: "We the people," &c., "do ordain and establish this constitution."

Let the constitution of Kansas be ratified and established by the solemn vote of the people, surrounded by such safeguards as will insure a fair and unbiased expression of the actual *bona fide* citizens, and it will remain inviolably fixed in the affections of the people.

In his report upon the Toombs bill, its distinguished author thus logically enumerates the various steps in the formation of a constitution: "The preliminary meetings; the calling of the convention; the appointment of delegates; the assembling of the convention; the formation of the constitution; *the voting on its ratification;* the election of officers under it."

In the same report, the author most justly remarks: "Whenever a constitution shall be formed in any territory, preparatory to its admission into the Union as a state, justice, the genius of our institutions, the whole theory of our republican system, imperatively demand that *the voice of the people shall be fairly expressed, and their will embodied in that fundamental law,* without fraud or violence, or intimidation, or any other improper or unlawful influence, and subject to no other restrictions than those imposed by the constitution of the United States."

The voice of the people fairly expressed, and its embodiment in the fundamental law, should be the earnest desire of every citizen of a republic.

But how can the voice of a people be fairly expressed, and their will be embodied in the organic law, unless that law, when made, be submitted to them to determine whether it is their will which the convention has proclaimed ?

The leading idea and fundamental principle of our organic act, as expressed in the law itself, was to leave the actual *bona fide* inhabitants of the territory "perfectly free to form and regulate their domestic institutions in their own way." The act confers almost unlimited power upon the people, and the only restriction imposed upon its exercise is the constitution of the United States.

The great principle, then, upon which our free institutions rest, is the unqualified and absolute sovereignty of the people, and constituting, as that principle does, the most positive and essential feature in the great charter of our liberties, so it is better calculated than any other to give elevation to our hopes and dignity to our actions. So long as the people feel that the power to alter the form or change the character of the government abides in them, so long will they be impressed with the sense of security and dignity which must ever spring from the consciousness that they hold within their own hands a remedy for every political evil—a corrective for every governmental abuse and usurpation.

" This principle must be upheld and maintained, at all hazards and at every sacrifice—maintained in all the power and fulness—in all the breadth and depth of its utmost capacity and signification. It is not sufficient that it be acknowledged as a mere abstraction, or theory, or doctrine; but as a practical, substantial, living reality, vital in every part."

The idea of surrendering the sovereignty of the territories, the common property of the people of the several states, into the hands of the few who first chanced to wander into them, is, to me, a political novelty. Is it just that the territories should exercise the rights of sovereign states until their condition and numbers become such as to entitle them to be admitted into the Union on an equality with the original states ?

In speaking of the proper construction of the organic act, its distinguished author remarks: " The act recognizes the rights of the people thereof, while a territory, to form and regulate their own domestic institutions in their own way, subject only to the constitution of the United States, and to be received into the Union, *as soon as they should attain the requisite number of inhabitants, on an equal footing with the original states in all respects whatever.*"

In the report before alluded to, the author says : " The point upon which your committee have entertained the most serious and grave doubts in regard to the propriety of indorsing this proposition, relates to the fact that, in the absence of any census of the inhabitants, there is reason to apprehend that the territory does not contain sufficient population to entitle them to demand admission under the treaty with France, if we take the ratio of representation for a member of congress as the rule."

In accordance with the foregoing views, I remarked in my first message to your body, that "the durability and imperative authority of a state constitution, when the interests of the people require a state government, *and a direct popular vote is necessary to give it sanction and effect*, will be the proper occasion, once for all, to decide the grave political questions which underlie a well-regulated commonwealth." And in another portion of the same message, I said : "Justice to the country and the dictates of sound policy, require that the legislature should confine itself to such subjects as will preserve the basis of entire equality ; and *when a sufficient population is here*, and they choose to adopt a state government, that they shall be 'perfectly free,' without let or hindrance, to form all their domestic institutions in their own way, and to dictate that form of government, which, in their deliberate judgment, may be deemed proper."

The expressions, "requisite number of inhabitants," "sufficient population," and others, of similar import, can have no other meaning than that given them by our leading statesmen, and by the common judgment of the country, to wit : "the ratio of representation for a member of congress."

The present ratio for a member of congress is 93,420 inhabitants. What, then, is the present population of Kansas ; or what will it be on the 15th of March next ? as after that time, no person arriving in the territory can vote for a member of the convention under the provisions of this bill.

At the last October election, the whole vote polled for delegate to congress was four thousand two hundred and seventy-six (4276) ; while the vote in favor of a convention to frame a state constitution, was but two thousand six hundred and seventy (2670).

It is a well known fact, to every person at all conversant with the circumstances attending the last election, that the question of a state government entered but little into the canvas, and the small vote polled for a convention is significantly indicative of the popular indifference on the subject.

No one will claim that 2670 is a majority of the voters of this territory, though it is a majority of those voting, and it is conceded that those not voting are bound by the act of those who did.

The bill under consideration seems to be drawn from the bill known as the Toombs' bill ; but in several respects it differs from that bill, and in these particulars it does not furnish equal guarantees for fairness and impartiality. The former secured the appointment of five impartial commissioners to take and correct the census, to make a partial apportionment among the several counties, and generally to superintend all the preliminaries so as to secure a fair election, while by the present bill all these important duties are to be performed by probate judges and sheriffs, elected by and owing allegiance to a party. It differs in other important particulars. The bill of Mr. Toombs conferred valuable rights and privileges upon this territory, and provided means to pay the expenses of the convention ; while this bill does neither.

If we are disposed to avail ourselves of the wisdom of the past, we will pause some time before we throw off our territorial condition, under present circumstances, by the adoption of a state government.

The state of Michigan remained a territory for five years after she had the requisite population, and so with other states ; and when they were admitted, they were strong enough in all the elements of material wealth to be self-supporting. And hence they knocked at the door of the Union with that manly confidence which spoke of equality and self-reliance.

California was admitted under peculiar and extraordinary circumstances. Her rich mines of the precious metals attracted a teeming population to her shores, and her isolated position from the parent government, with her superabundant wealth, at once suggested the experiment of self-government ; and at the time of her state constitution, ratified by the vote of the people, the population of California entitled her to two representatives in congress.

I observe by the message of the governor of Minnesota, that the population of that thriving territory exceeds 180,000. The taxable property amounts to between thirty and thirty-five millions of dollars. And in view of these facts, and of the large increase of agricultural products, cash capital, etc., the governor favors a change from a territorial to a state government. To this end he suggests that a convention be called *to form* a constitution ; that an act be passed for the taking of a census in April, and for such other preliminary steps as are necessary ; and that if the constitution be "*ratified by the people*" at the next October election, it shall be presented to congress in December following.

These facts furnish an additional argument why the constitution should be submitted to the people, as the majority, preferring a territorial government, and thinking a state government premature, may desire to avail themselves of that opportunity to vote against any state constitution whatever.

Burthened with heavy liabilities ; without titles to our lands ; our public buildings unfinished ; our jails and court-houses not erected ; without money even to pay the expenses of a convention ; and just emerging from the disastrous effects of a bitter civil feud ; it seems unwise for a few thousand people, scarcely sufficient to make a good county, to discard the protecting and fostering care of a government, ready to assist us with her treasures and to protect us with her armies. JNO. W. GEARY,
Governor of Kansas Territory.

Notwithstanding the veto of the governor, the bill passed both branches of the assembly by an almost unanimous vote, and without discussion. The proslavery party now exulted in the certain prospect of making Kansas a slave state. The time of the meeting of the convention was fixed for September. It was stated to Gov. Geary, as a part of the plan, that a constitution would be framed in which no reference would be made to the subject of slavery ; but, says Dr. Gihon, "the pretended merit of this scheme will disappear as soon as it is understood that slavery already exists in the territory by statute ; and although no mention of it be made in the constitution, it will still remain an established institution of the new state." The legislative assembly adjourned on the 21st of February.

During the sitting of this legislature, there were so many disturbances of the public peace in Lecompton, that the peaceful citizens called upon the governor to send for a detachment of the United States troops to protect them. A messenger was accordingly dispatched to Fort Leavenworth with the following requisition :

"EXECUTIVE DEPARTMENT, Kansas Territory,
"February 9, 1857.

"MAJOR-GENERAL PERSIFER F. SMITH,

"Commanding Department of the West :

"Dear Sir : There are certain persons present in Lecompton, who are determined, if within the bounds of possibility, to bring about a breach of the peace. During the last few days, a number of persons have been grossly insulted ; and to-day an insult has been offered to myself. A person named Sherrard, who some days ago had been appointed sheriff of Douglas county, which appointment was strongly protested against by a respectable number of the citizens of the county, and I had deferred commissioning him. This, it appears, gave mortal offense to Sherrard, and he has made up his mind to *assassinate* me. This may lead to *trouble*. It must be prevented, and that by immediate action. I require, therefore, two additional companies of dragoons to report to me with the least possible delay. *I think this is absolutely necessary, and I trust you will immediately comply with my request.* I write in great haste, as the messenger is about leaving.

"I wish you would keep an eye upon Leavenworth City, as I hear of troublesome indications there. I am confident that there is a conspiracy on foot to disturb the peace, and various pretexts *will be*, and have been used to accomplish this fell purpose.

"I am perfectly cool, and intend to keep so ; but I am also more vigilant than ever.   Very truly, your friend,

"JNO. W. GEARY."

Much to the astonishment of the governor, Gen. Smith refused to comply with this requisition, partly on the ground that "probable breaches of the peace did not authorize the employment of troops," and partly, that the forces under his command had "just been designated *by the secretary of war* for other service."

When Gov. Geary was sent to Kansas, he was authorized to use the regular forces "at his discretion" to "preserve the peace," and be governed by "the exigencies of affairs as they should be presented to *him* on the spot."

Previous to this, the governor had applied to the department at Washington for a draft of two thousand dollars to meet the contingent expenses of the government of Kansas. He received, in reply, a statement that "the president had no authority to advance for the contingent expenses of the government of Kansas any amount whatever."

It is evident that the just and equitable administration of Gov. Geary received no approval at Washington. Yet he persevered even after the sword and the purse had been withdrawn from him, in maintaining the peace of the territory. "It could have been," says Dr. Gihon, the historian of Kansas, "nothing less than an enlarged patriotism that caused him to retain so long the most thankless and unprofitable office in the nation. For months he had labored for the public good with untiring energy, not even taking time for needed rest and sleep; deprived of all the usual comforts of life; occupying a log house, and very often unable to obtain wholesome food; vexed and harassed hourly with the complaints of an abused people; constant drafts being made by persons whom he was compelled to employ, upon his pecuniary resources; required to pay the militia called into the service by the president himself, from his own private funds; every federal officer in the territory conspiring to embarrass his administration; his mails overhauled and their contents examined by government officials; surrounded with organized bands of assassins; and without a word of comfort or a particle of aid from the general government, he still continued, with fidelity, zeal, and unflagging energy, to discharge the arduous duties of his station."

Finally, upon the incoming of a new administration at Washington, Governor Geary forwarded to the new president the following letter of resignation:

> EXECUTIVE DEPARTMENT, K. T. }
> Lecompton, March 4, 1857. }

HIS EXCELLENCY, JAMES BUCHANAN,
>   President of the United States:

Dear Sir: Please accept my resignation as governor of Kansas Territory, to take effect on the 20th of the present month, by which time you will be enabled to select and appoint a proper successor.

With high respect, your friend and obedient servant,

>   JOHN W. GEARY.

Previous to leaving the territory, the governor issued the following farewell address:

To the People of Kansas Territory:

Having determined to resign the executive office, and retire again to the quiet scenes of private life and the enjoyment of those domestic comforts of which I have so long been deprived, I deem it proper to address you on the occasion of my departure.

The office from which I now voluntarily withdraw, was unsought by me, and at the time of its acceptance was by no means desirable. This was quite evident, from the deplorable moral, civil and political condition of the territory—the discord, contention and deadly strife which then and there prevailed; and the painful anxiety with which it was regarded by patriotic citizens in every portion of the American Union. To attempt to govern Kansas at such a period and under such circumstances, was to assume no ordinary responsibilities. Few men could have desired to undertake the task, and none would have been so presumptuous, without serious forebodings as to the result. That I should have hesitated, is no matter of astonishment to those acquainted with the facts; but that I accepted the appointment, was a well-grounded source of regret to many of my well-tried friends, who looked upon the enterprise as one that could terminate in nothing but disaster to myself. It was not supposed possible that order could be brought, in any reasonable space of time, and with the means at my command, from the existing chaos.

Without descanting upon the feelings, principles and motives which prompted me, suffice it to say, that I accepted the president's tender of the office of governor. In doing so, I sacrificed the comforts of a home, endeared by the strongest earthly ties and most sacred associations, to embark in an undertaking which presented at the best but a dark and unsatisfactory prospect. I reached Kansas and entered on the discharge of my official duties in the most gloomy hour of her history. Desolation and ruin reigned on every hand. Homes and firesides were deserted. The smoke of burning dwellings darkened the atmosphere. Women and children, driven from their habitations, wandered over the prairies and through the woodlands, or sought refuge and protection even among the Indian tribes. The highways were infested with numerous predatory bands, and the towns were fortified and garrisoned by armies of conflicting partisans, each excited almost to frenzy, and determined upon mutual extermination. Such was, without exaggeration, the condition of the territory at the period of my arrival. Her treasury was bankrupt. There were no pecuniary resources within herself to meet the exigencies of the time. The congressional appropriations, intended to defray the expenses of a year, were insufficient to meet the demands of a fortnight. The laws were null, the courts virtually suspended, and the civil arm of the government almost entirely powerless. Action—prompt, decisive, energetic action—was necessary. I at once saw what was needed, and without hesitation gave myself to the work. For six months I have labored with unceasing industry. The accustomed and needed hours for sleep have been employed in the public service. Night and day have official duties demanded unremitting attention. I have had no proper leisure moments for rest or recreation. My health has failed under the pressure. Nor is this all; to my own private purse, without assurance of reimbursement, have I resorted in every emergency for the required funds. Whether these arduous services and willing sacrifices have been beneficial to Kansas and my country, you are abundantly qualified to determine.

That I have met with opposition, and even bitter vituperation and vindictive malice, is no matter for astonishment. No man has ever yet held an important or responsible post in our own or any other country and escaped censure. I should have been weak and foolish indeed, had I expected to pass through the fiery ordeal entirely unscathed, especially as I was required, if not to come in conflict with, at least to thwart evil machinations, and hold in restraint wicked

50

passions, or rid the territory of many lawless, reckless and desperate men. Beside, it were impossible to come in contact with the conflicting interests which governed the conduct of many well-disposed persons, without becoming an object of mistrust and abuse. While from others, whose sole object was notoriously personal advancement at any sacrifice of the general good and at every hazard, it would have been ridiculous to anticipate the meed of praise for disinterested action ; and hence, however palpable might have been my patriotism, however just my official conduct, or however beneficial its results, I do not marvel that my motives have been impugned and my integrity maligned. It is, however, so well known, that I need scarcely record the fact, that those who have attributed my labors to a desire for gubernatorial or senatorial honors, were and are themselves the aspirants for those high trusts and powers, and foolishly imagined that I stood between them and the consummation of their ambitious designs and high-towering hopes.

But whatever may be thought or said of my motives or desires, I have the proud consciousness of leaving this scene of my severe and anxious toil with clean hands, and the satisfactory conviction that He who can penetrate the inmost recesses of the heart, and read its secret thoughts, will approve my purposes and acts. In the discharge of my executive functions, I have invariably sought to do equal and exact justice to all men, however humble or exalted. I have eschewed all sectional disputations, kept aloof from all party affiliations, and have alike scorned numerous threats of personal injury and violence, and the most flattering promises of advancement and reward. And I ask and claim nothing more for the part I have acted than the simple merit of having endeavored to perform my duty. This I have done at all times, and upon every occasion, regardless of the opinions of men, and utterly fearless of consequences. Occasionally I have been forced to assume great responsibilities, and depend solely upon my own resources to accomplish important ends; but in all such instances, I have carefully examined surrounding circumstances, weighed well the probable results, and acted upon my own deliberate judgment ; and in now reviewing them, I am so well satisfied with the policy uniformly pursued, that were it to be done over again, it should not be changed in the slightest particular.

In parting with you, I can do no less than give you a few words of kindly advice, and even of friendly warning. You are well aware that most of the troubles which lately agitated the territory, were occasioned by men who had no especial interest in its welfare. Many of them were not even residents ; whilst it is quite evident that others were influenced altogether in the part they took in the disturbances by mercenary or other personal considerations. The great body of the actual citizens are conservative, law-abiding and peace-loving men, disposed rather to make sacrifices for conciliation and consequent peace, than to insist for their entire rights, should the general good thereby be caused to suffer. Some of them, under the influence of the prevailing excitement and misguided opinions, were led to the commission of grievous mistakes, but not with the deliberate intention of doing wrong.

A very few men, resolved upon mischief, may keep in a state of unhealthy excitement and involve in fearful strife an entire community. This was demonstrated during the civil commotions with which the territory was convulsed. While the people generally were anxious to pursue their peaceful callings, small combinations of crafty, scheming and designing men succeeded, from pure selfish motives, in bringing upon them a series of most lamentable and destructive difficulties. Nor are they satisfied with the mischief already done. They never desired that the present peace should be effected; nor do they intend that it shall continue if they have the power to prevent it. In the constant croakings of disaffected individuals in various sections, you hear only the expressions of evil desires and intentions. Watch, then, with a special, jealous and suspicious eye those who are continually indulging surmises of renewed hostilities. They are not the friends of Kansas, and there is reason to fear that some of them are not only enemies of this territory but of the Union itself. Its dissolution is their ardent wish, and Kansas has been selected as a fit place to commence the accomplishment of a most nefarious design. The scheme has thus far been frustrated; but it has not been abandoned. You are entrusted, not only with the guardianship of this territory, but the peace of the Union, which depends upon you in a greater degree than you may at present suppose.

You should, therefore, frown down every effort to foment discord, and especially to array settlers from different sections of the Union in hostility against each other. All true patriots, whether from the north or south, the east or west, should unite together for that which is and must be regarded as a common cause, the preservation of the Union; and he who shall whisper a desire for its dissolution, no matter what may be his pretensions, or to what faction or party he claims to belong, is unworthy of your confidence, deserves your strongest reprobation, and should be branded as a traitor to his country. There is a voice crying from the grave of one whose memory is dearly cherished in every patriotic heart, and let it not cry in vain. It tells you that this attempt at dissolution is no new thing; but that, even as early as the days of our first president, it was agitated by ambitious aspirants for place and power. And if the appeal of a still more recent hero and patriot was needed in his time, how much more applicable is it now, and in this territory!

"The possible dissolution of the Union," he says, "has at length become an ordinary and familiar subject of discussion. Has the warning voice of Washington been forgotten? or have designs already been formed to sever the Union? Let it not be supposed that I impute to all of those who have taken an active part in these unwise and unprofitable discussions, a want of patriotism or of public virtue. The honorable feelings of state pride and local attachments find a place in the bosoms of the most enlightened and pure. But while such men are conscious of their own integrity and honesty of purpose, they ought never to forget that the citizens of other states are their political brethren; and that, however mistaken they may be in their views, the great body of them are equally honest and upright with themselves. Mutual suspicions and reproaches may, in time, create mutual hostility, and artful and designing men will always be found who are ready to foment these fatal divisions, and to inflame the natural jealousies of different sections of the country. The history of the world is full of such examples, and especially the history of republics."

When I look upon the present condition of the territory, and contrast it with what it was when I first entered it, I feel satisfied that my administration has not been prejudicial to its interests. On every hand, I now perceive unmistakable indications of welfare and prosperity. The honest settler occupies his quiet dwelling, with his wife and children clustering around him, unmolested, and fearless of danger. The solitary traveler pursues his way unharmed over every public thoroughfare. The torch of the incendiary has been extinguished, and the cabins which were destroyed, have been replaced by more substantial buildings. Hordes of banditti no longer lie in wait in every ravine for plunder and assassination. Invasions of hostile armies have ceased, and infuriated partisans, living in our midst, have emphatically turned their swords into plowshares, and their spears into pruning-hooks. Laborers are everywhere at work—farms are undergoing rapid improvements—merchants are driving a thriving trade, and mechanics pursuing with profit their various occupations. Real estate, in town and country, has increased in value almost without precedent, until in some places it is commanding prices that never could have been anticipated. Whether this healthy and happy change is the result solely of my executive labors, or not, it certainly has occurred during my administration. Upon yourselves must mainly depend the preservation and perpetuity of the present prosperous condition of affairs. Guard it with unceasing vigilance, and protect it as you would your lives. Keep down that party spirit, which, if permitted to obtain the mastery, must lead to desolation. Watch closely, and condemn in its infancy, every insidious movement that can possibly tend to discord and disunion. Suffer no local prejudices to disturb the prevailing harmony. To every appeal to these, turn a deaf ear, as did the Savior of men to the promptings of the deceiver. Act as a united band of brothers, bound together by one common tie. Your interests are the same, and by this course alone can they be maintained. Follow this, and your hearts and homes will be made light and happy by the richest blessings of a kind and munificent Providence.

To you, the peaceable citizens of Kansas, I owe my grateful acknowledgments for the aid and comfort your kind assurances and hearty coöperation have afforded in many dark and trying hours. You have my sincerest thanks, and my earnest prayers that you may be abundantly rewarded of heaven.

To the ladies of the territory—the wives, mothers, sisters and daughters of the honest settlers—I am also under a weight of obligation. Their pious prayers have not been raised in vain, nor their numerous assurances of confidence in the policy of my administration failed to exert a salutary influence.

And last, though not the least, I must not be unmindful of the noble men who form the military department of the west. To Gen. Persifer F. Smith, and the officers acting under his command, I return my thanks for many vuluable services. Although from different parts of the Union, and naturally imbued with sectional prejudices, I know of no instance in which such prejudices have been permitted to stand in the way of a faithful, ready, cheerful and energetic discharge of duty. Their conduct in this respect is worthy of universal commendation, and presents a bright example for those executing the civil power. The good behavior of all the soldiers who were called upon to assist me, is, in fact, deserving of especial notice. Many of these troops, officers and men, had served with me on the fields of Mexico against a foreign foe, and it is a source of no little satisfaction to know that the laurels there won have been further adorned by the praiseworthy alacrity with which they aided to allay a destructive fratricidal strife at home.

With a firm reliance in the protecting care and overruling providence of that Great Being who holds in his hand the destinies alike of men and of nations, I bid farewell to Kansas and her people, trusting that whatever events may hereafter befall them, they will, in the exercise of His wisdom, goodness and power, be so directed as to promote their own best interest and that of the beloved country of which they are destined to form a most important part.

JNO. W. GEARY.

Lecompton, March 10, 1857.

The Hon. Robert J. Walker, of Mississippi, was appointed successor to Governor Geary, and Frederick P. Stanton was appointed Secretary. Stanton proceeded to Kansas as acting governor, and immediately issued an address, the main features of which were afterwards incorporated in the inaugural of Governor Walker. The first official act of the secretary was to make an apportionment of delegates to the convention to frame a state constitution. In regard to this apportionment it is stated, that "out of thirty-six counties, as organized by the authorities, only twenty-one have even a nominal representation. The census has only been taken in ten of these, and in only some portions of these ten. In six of these twenty-one counties thus reported, no census was taken, but a list of voters was taken from their old poll-books; this having been done after the time for taking the census had expired. The other five are counties forming parts of districts which are mentioned because they are connected with others; but in these no census was taken, and no former vote or representation on account of former vote, has been allowed. By this apportionment three-fifths of the settled counties of the territory are allowed no representation. In these there are at least two-fifths of the people in the whole territory, and including the emigration of this spring, one half.

"There are twenty counties to the south of the Kansas river, lying in a great solid mass, and filled with free state towns and settlements, teeming with active life and industry; in one-half of them the great majority of claims are taken, and all are about as well settled as the majority of counties in most of the western states, and the whole of these are left without a particle of representation by this proclamation."

Governor Walker reached Kansas on the 25th of May, and a few days after he issued his inaugural address at Lecompton. This document was intended to conciliate both political parties.

GOVERNOR WALKER'S INAUGURAL.

FELLOW-CITIZENS OF KANSAS: At the earnest request of the president of the United States, I have accepted the position of governor of the territory of Kansas. The president, with the cordial concurrence of all his cabinet, expressed to me the conviction that the condition of Kansas was fraught with imminent peril to the Union, and asked me to undertake the settlement of that momentous question, which has introduced discord and civil war throughout your borders, and threatens to involve you and our country in the same common ruin. This was a duty thus presented, the performance of which I could not decline consistently with my view of the sacred obligation which every citizen owes to his country.

The mode of adjustment is provided in the act organizing your territory—namely, by the people of Kansas, who, by a majority of their own votes, must decide this question for themselves in forming their state constitution.

Under our practice, the preliminary act of framing a state constitution is uniformly performed through the instrumentality of a convention of delegates chosen by the people themselves. That convention is now about to be elected by you under the call of the territorial legislature, created and still recognized by the authority of congress, and clothed by it, in the comprehensive language of the organic law, with full power to make such an enactment. The territorial legislature, then, in assembling this convention, were fully sustained by the act of congress, and the authority of the convention is distinctly recognized in my instructions from the President of the United States. Those who oppose this course cannot aver the alleged irregularity of the territorial legislature, whose laws in town and city elections, in corporate franchises, and on all other subjects but slavery, they acknowledge by their votes and acquiescence. If that legislature was invalid, then are we without law or order in Kansas; without town, city, or county organization; all legal and judicial transactions are void, all titles null, and anarchy reigns throughout our borders.

It is my duty, in seeing that all constitutional laws are executed, to take care, as far as practicable, that this election of delegates to the convention shall be free from fraud or violence, and that they shall be protected in their deliberations.

The people of Kansas, then, are invited by the highest authority known to the constitution to participate freely and fairly in the election of delegates to frame a constitution and state government. The law has performed its entire appropriate function when it extends to the people the right of suffrage, but it cannot compel the performance of that duty. Throughout our whole union, however, and wherever free government prevails, those who abstain from the exercise of the right of suffrage authorize those who do vote to act for them in that contingency, and the absentees are as much bound under the law and the constitution, where there is no fraud or violence, by the act of the majority of those who do vote, as although all had participated in the election. Otherwise, as voting must be voluntary, self-government would be impracticable, and monarchy or despotism would remain as the only alternative.

You should not console yourselves, my fellow-citizens, with the reflection that you may, by a subsequent vote, defeat the ratification of the constitution. Although *most anxious to secure to you the exercise of that great constitutional right*, and believing that the convention is the servant, and not the master of the people, yet I have no power to dictate proceedings to that body. I cannot doubt, however, the course they will adopt on this subject. But why incur the hazard of the preliminary formation of a constitution by a minority, as alleged by you, when a majority, by their own votes, could control the forming of that instrument?

But it is said that the convention is not legally called, and that the election will not be freely and fairly conducted. The territorial legislature is the power ordained for this purpose by the congress of the United States; and in opposing it you resist the authority of the federal government. That legislature was called into being by the congress of 1854, and is recognized in the very latest congressional legislation. It is recognized by the present chief magistrate of the Union, just chosen by the American people, and many of its acts are now in operation here by universal assent. As the governor of the territory of Kansas, I must support the laws and the constitution; and I have no other alternative under my oath but to see that all constitutional laws are fully and fairly executed.

I see in this act, calling the convention, no improper or unconstitutional restrictions upon the right of suffrage. I see in it no test-oath or other similar provisions objected to in relation to previous laws, but clearly repealed as repugnant to the provisions of this act, so far as regards the election of delegates to this convention. It is said that a fair and full vote will not be taken. Who can safely predict such a result? Nor is it just for a majority, as they allege, to throw the power into the hands of a minority, from a mere apprehension— I trust entirely unfounded—that they will not be permitted to exercise the right of suffrage. If, by fraud or violence, a majority should not be permitted to vote, there is a remedy, it is hoped, in the wisdom and justice of the convention itself, acting under the obligations of an oath, and a proper responsibility to the tribunal of public opinion. There is a remedy, also, if such facts can be demonstrated, in the refusal of congress to admit a state into the union under a constitution imposed by a minority upon a majority by fraud or violence. Indeed, I cannot doubt that the convention, after having framed a state constitution, will submit it for ratification or rejection, by a majority of the then actual *bona fide* resident settlers of Kansas.

With these views, well known to the president and cabinet, and approved by them, I accepted the appointment of governor of Kansas. My instructions from the president, through the secretary of state, under date of the 30th of

March last, sustain " the regular legislature of the territory " in "assembling a convention to form a constitution ;" and they express the opinion of the president that " when such a constitution shall be submitted to the people of the territory, they must be protected in the exercise of their right of voting for or or against that instrument; and the fair expression of the popular will must not be interrupted by fraud or violence."

I repeat, then, as my clear conviction, that *unless the convention submit the constitution to the vote of all the actual resident settlers of Kansas, and the election be fairly and justly conducted, the constitution will be, and ought to be, rejected by congress.*

There are other important reasons why you should participate in the election of delegates to this convention. Kansas is to become a new state, created out of the public domain, and will designate her boundaries in the fundamental law. To most of the land within her limits the Indian title, unfortunately, is not yet extinguished, and this land is exempt from settlement, to the grievous injury of the people of the state. Having passed many years of my life in a new state, and represented it for a long period in the senate of the United States, I know the serious incumbrance arising from large bodies of lands within a state to which the Indian title is not extinguished. Upon this subject the convention may act by such just and constitutional provisions as will accelerate the extinguishment of Indian title.

There is, furthermore, the question of railroad grants made by congress to all the new states but one, (where the routes could not be agreed upon,) and within a few months past, to the flourishing territory of Minnesota. This munificent grant of four millions and a half of acres was made to Minnesota, even in advance of her becoming a state, under the auspices of her present distinguished executive, and will enable our sister state of the northwest speedily to unite her railroad system with ours.

Kansas is undoubtedly entitled to grants similar to those just made to Minnesota, and upon this question the convention may take important action.

These, recollect, are grants by congress, not to companies, but to states. Now, if Kansas, like the state of Illinois, in granting hereafter these lands to companies to build these roads, should reserve, at least, the seven per cent. of their gross annual receipts, it is quite certain that so soon as these roads are constructed, such will be the large payments into the treasury of our state that there will be no necessity to impose in Kansas any state tax whatever, especially if the constitution should contain wise provisions against the creation of state debts.

The grant to the state of Illinois for the Illinois Central Railroad, passed under the wise and patriotic auspices of her distinguished senator, was made before the pernicious system lately exposed in Washington had invaded the halls of congress; and, therefore, that state, unlike most others which obtained recent grants, was enabled to make the great reservation for the benefit of the state. This constitutes of itself a conclusive reason why these railroad grants should be reserved in the ordinance accompanying our state constitutions, so that our state might have the whole benefit of the grant, instead of large portions being given to agents appointed to obtain these grants by companies substantially in many cases for their own benefit, although in the name of the state.

There is another reason why these railroad grants should thus be reserved in our ordinance.

It is to secure these lands to the state before large bodies of them are engrossed by speculators, especially along the contemplated lines of railroads. In no case should these reservations interfere with the preëmption rights reserved to settlers, or with school sections.

These grants to states, as is proved by the official documents, have greatly augmented the proceeds of the sales of the public lands, increasing their value, accelerating their sale and settlement, and bringing enhanced prices to the government, whilst greatly benefiting the lands of the settler by furnishing him new markets and diminished cost of transportation. On this subject, Mr. Buchanan, always the friend of the new states, in his recent inaugural, uses the following language:

" No nation in the tide of time has ever been blessed with so rich and noble an inheritance as we enjoy in the public lands. In administering this important trust, whilst it may be wise to grant portions of them for improvement of the remainder, yet we should never forget that it is our cardinal policy to reserve the lands as much as may be for actual settlers; and this at moderate prices. We shall thus not only best promote the prosperity of the new states by furnishing them a hardy and independent race of honest and industrious citizens, but shall secure homes for our children and our children's children, as well as those exiled from foreign shores, who may seek in this country to improve their condition and enjoy the blessings of civil and religious liberty."

Our American railoads, now exceeding twenty-four thousand miles completed, have greatly advanced the power, prosperity, and progress of the country, whilst linking it together in bonds of ever-increasing commerce and intercourse, and tending by these results, to soften or extinguish sectional passions and prejudice, and thus perpetuate the union of the states. This system it is clearly the interest of the whole country shall progress until the states west of the Mississippi shall be intersected, like those east of that river, by a network of railroads, until the whole, at various points, shall reach the shores of the Pacific. The policy of such grants by congress is now clearly established; and whatever doubts may have prevailed in the minds of a few persons as to the constitutionality of such grants, when based only upon the transfer of a portion of the public domain, in the language of the inaugural of the president, "*for the improvement of the remainder*," yet when they are made, as now proposed in the ordinance accompanying our constitution, in consideration of our relinquishing the right to tax the public lands, such grants become, in fact, sales for ample equivalents, and their constitutionality is placed beyond all doubt or controversy. For this reason, also, and in order that these grants may be made for ample equivalents, and upon grounds of clear, constitutional authority, it is most wise that they should be included in our ordinance, and take effect by compact when the state is admitted into the Union. If my will could have prevailed as regards the public lands, as indicated in my public career, and especially in the bill presented by me, as chairman of the committee on public lands, to the senate of the United States, which passed that body, but failed in the house, I would authorize no sales of these lands except for settlement and cultivation, reserving not merely a preëmption, but a homestead of a quarter-section of land in favor of every actual settler, whether coming from other states or emigrating from Europe. Great and populous states would thus rapidly be added to the confederacy, until we should soon have one unbroken line of states from the Atlantic to the Pacific, giving immense additional power and security to the Union, and facilitating intercourse between all its parts. This would be alike beneficial to the old and to the new states. To the working-men of the old states, as well as of the new, it would be of incalculable advantage, not merely by affording them a home in the west, but by maintaining the wages of labor, by enabling the working classes to emigrate and become cultivators of the soil, when the rewards of daily toil should sink below a fair remuneration. Every new state, besides, adds to the customers of the old states, consuming their manufactures, employing their merchants, giving business to their vessels and canals, their railroads and cities, and a powerful impulse to their industry and prosperity. Indeed, it is the growth of the mighty west which has added, more than all other causes combined, to the power and prosperity of the whole country, whilst at the same time, through the channels of business and commerce, it has been building up immense cities in the eastern, Atlantic, and middle states, and replenishing the federal treasury with large payments from the settlers upon the public lands, rendered of real value only by their labor; and thus, from increased exports, bringing back augmented imports, and soon largely increasing the revenue of the government from that source also.

Without asking anything new from congress, if Kansas can receive, on coming into the Union, all the usual grants, and use them judiciously, she can not only speedily cover herself with a network of railroads, but, by devoting all the rest to purposes of education, she would soon have a complete system of common schools, with normal schools, free academies, and a great university, in all of which tuition should be free to all our people. In that university the mechanic arts, with model workshops, and all the sciences should be taught, and especially agriculture in connection with a model farm.

Although you ask nothing more in your ordinance than has already been granted to the other new states, yet in view of the sacrifice of life and property incurred by the people of Kansas, in establishing here the great principles of state and popular sovereignty, and thus perpetuating the Union, congress, doubtless, will regard with indulgent favor the new state of Kansas, and will welcome her into the Union with joyful congratulations and a most liberal policy as to the public domain.

The full benefit of that great measure, the graduation and reduction of the price of the public lands in favor only of settlers and cultivators, so often urged by me in the senate and in the treasury department, and finally adopted by congress, should also be secured in our ordinance. Having witnessed in new states the deep injury inflicted upon them by large bodies of their most fertile land being monopolized by speculators, I suggest, in accordance with the public policy ever advocated by me, that our entire land tax, under the constitution, for the next twenty years should be confined exclusively to unoccupied land—whether owned by residents or non-residents—as one of the best means of guarding against a monopoly of our choice lands by speculators. I desire, in fact, to see our convention exercise the whole constitutional power of a state, to guard our rights and interests, and especially to protect the settlers and cultivators against the monopoly of our public domain by speculators.

As regards the school lands of the new states, the following views will be found in my reports of the 8th of December, 1847, and 9th of December, 1848, as secretary of the treasury of the United States:

"The recommendation contained in my last report for the establishment of ports of entry in Oregon, and the extension there of our revenue laws, is again respectfully presented to the consideration of congress, together with donations of farms to settlers and emigrants, and the grant of a school section in the center of every quarter of a township, which would bring the school-house within a point not exceeding a mile and a half in distance from the most remote inhabitants of such quarter township."

And again: "My last report recommended the grant of one section of land for schools in every quarter township in Oregon. * * * * * Congress, to some extent, adopted this recommendation by granting two school sections in each township, instead of one, for education in Oregon; but it is respectfully suggested that even thus extended the grant is still inadequate in amount, whilst the location is inconvenient, and too remote for a school which all can attend. The subject is again presented to the attention of congress, with the recommendation that it shall be extended to California and New Mexico, and also to all the other new states and territories containing the public domain."

Acting upon the first of these recommendations, but not carrying them fully into effect, congress doubled the school section grants—an advance upon the former system. But, in my judgment, the benefits intended will never be fully realized until four school sections, instead of two, are granted in every township, locating the school section in the center of every quarter township; thus, by only doubling the school sections, causing every section of the public domain in the new states to adjoin a school section, which would add immensely to the value of the public lands, whilst, at the same time, affording an adequate fund not only for the establishment of common schools in every township, but of high schools, normal schools, and free academies, which, together with the five per cent. fund and university grant before referred to, would place Kansas in a few years, in point of science and education, in the front rank of the states of the American Union and of the world. This is a subject always regarded by me with intense interest, inasmuch as my highest hope of the perpetuity of our Union, and of the continued success of self-government, is based upon the progressive education and enlightenment of the people, enabling them fully to comprehend their own true interests, the incalculable advantages of our Union, the exemption from the power of demagogues, the control of sectional passions and prejudice, the progress of the arts and sciences, and the accumulation of knowledge, which is every day more and more becoming real power, and which will advance so much the great interests of our whole country.

These noble grants for schools and education in some of the new states have not produced all the advantages designed, for want of adequate checks and guards against improvident legislation; but I trust that the convention, by a distinct constitutional provision, will surround these lands with such guarantees, legislative, executive, judicial, and popular, as to require the combined action of the whole under the authority of the legislature in the administration of a fund so sacred.

It will be observed that these school sections and the five per cent. fund, or their equivalent, have always been made good to the new states by congress, whether the lands were sold in trust, for Indians, or otherwise.

Upon looking at the location of Kansas, equidistant from north to south, and from the Atlantic to the Pacific, I find, that, within reasonable boundaries, she would be the central state of the American Union. On the north lies the Nebraska territory, soon to become a state; on the south the great and fertile southwestern Indian territory, soon, I hope, to become a state also. To the boundary of Kansas run nearly all the railroads of Missouri, whilst westward, northward, and southward, these routes continued through Kansas would connect her directly with Puget Sound, the mouth of the Oregon river, and San Francisco. The southern boundary of Kansas is but five hundred miles from the Gulf of Mexico, and the same railroad through the great southwestern Indian territory and Texas would connect her with New Orleans, with Galveston, with all the roads of Arkansas, and through Texas to San Francisco, and other points upon the Pacific; northward and eastward our lines would connect with the roads of Iowa, Illinois, Wisconsin, Nebraska, and the lakes of the north.

It is the people of Kansas who, in forming their state constitution, are to declare the terms on which they propose to enter the Union. Congress can not compel the people of the territory to enter the Union as a state, or change, without their consent, the constitution framed by the people. Congress, it is true, may for constitutional reasons refuse admission, but the state alone, in forming her constitution, can prescribe the terms on which she will enter the Union. This power of the people of a territory in forming a state constitution is one of vital importance, especially in the states carved out of the public domain. Nearly all the lands of Kansas are public lands, and most of them are occupied by Indian tribes. These lands are the property of the federal government, but their right is exclusively that of a proprietor, carrying with it no political power.

Although the states cannot tax the constitutional functions of the federal government, they may assess its real estate within the limits of the state. Thus, although a state cannot tax the federal mint or custom houses, yet it may tax the ground on which they stand, unless exempted by state authority. Such is the well-settled doctrine of the supreme court of the United States. In 1838, Judge McLean, of the supreme court of the United States, made the following decision :

"It is true, the United States held the proprietary right under the act of cession, and also the right of sovereignty until the state government was established ; but the mere proprietary right, if it exists, gives no right of sovereignty. The United States may own land within a state, but political jurisdiction does not follow this ownership. Where jurisdiction is necessary, as for forts and arsenals, a cession of it is obtained from the state. Even the lands of the United States within the state are exempted from taxation by compact."

By the recent decision of the supreme court of the United States, so justly favorable to the rights and interest of the new states, especially those formed out of the territory acquired, like Kansas, since the adoption of the constitution, it is clear that the ownership of the public lands of such territory is viewed by the court exclusively as a proprietary right, carrying with it no political power or right of eminent domain, and affecting in no way the exercise of any of the soveereign attributes of state authority. When Kansas becomes a state, with all the attributes of state sovereignty coëxtensive with her limits, among these must be the taxing power, which is an inherent element of state authority. I do not dispute the title of the government to the public lands of Kansas, but I do say this right is that of an owner only, and that, when Kansas becomes a state, the public lands are subject to taxation by state authority, like those of any individual proprietor, unless that power is relinquished by the state in the ordinance, assuming the form of a compact, by which the state is admitted into the Union.

This relinquishment of the taxing power as to the public lands, so important to the general government, and which has heretofore been exacted by congress on their own terms from all the new states, is deeply injurious to a state, depriving her almost entirely of the principal recourse of a new state by taxation to support her government. Now that this question is conclusively settled by the supreme court of the United States, as a consequence of their recent decision, it is proper for the state, in making this relinquishment of the right to tax the public lands, to annex the conditions on which she consents to such exemption. This should be done in the constitution upon terms just to Kansas and to the federal government.

Should Kansas relinquish the right of taxing the public lands for an equivalent, she should, in my judgment, although sustained by irresistible conclusions from the decision of the supreme court of the United States, and sound constitutional views of state rights, place the question in its strongest form, by asking nothing more than has been granted to the other new states, including the grants for education, railroads, etc. She will thus give the highest proof that she is not governed by sordid views, and that she means to exact nothing from congress that is unjust or unusual.

I cannot too earnestly impress upon you the necessity of removing the slavery agitation from the halls of congress and presidential conflicts. It is conceded that congress has no power to interfere with slavery in the states where it exists; and if it can now be established, as is clearly the doctrine of the constitution, that congress has no authority to interfere with the people of a territory on this subject, in forming a state constitution, the question must be removed from congressional and presidential elections.

This is the principle affirmed by congress in the act organizing this territory, ratified by the people of the United States in the recent election, and maintained by the late decision of the supreme court of the United States. If this principle can be carried into successful operation in Kansas—that her people shall determine what shall be her social institutions—the slavery question must be withdrawn from the halls of congress, and from our presidential conflicts, and the safety of the Union be placed beyond all peril; whereas, if the principle should be defeated here, the slavery agitation must be renewed in all elections throughout the country, with increasing bitterness, until it shall eventually overthrow the government.

It is this agitation which, to European powers, presents the only hope of subverting our free institutions, and, as a consequence, destroying the principle of self-government throughout the world. It is this hope that has already inflicted deep injury upon our country, exciting monarchical or despotic interference with our domestic as well as foreign affairs, and inducing their interposition, not only in our elections, but in diplomatic intercourse, to arrest our progress, to limit our influence and power, depriving us of great advantages in peaceful territorial expansion, as well as in trade with the nations of the world.

Indeed, when I reflect upon the hostile position of the European press during the recent election, and their exulting predictions of the dissolution of our Union as a consequence of the triumph of a sectional candidate, I cannot doubt that the peaceful and permanent establishment of these principles, now being subjected to their final test in Kansas, will terminate European opposition to all those measures which must so much increase our commerce, furnish new markets for our products and fabrics, and by conservative, peaceful progress, carry our flag and the empire of our constitution into new and adjacent regions indispensable as a part of the Union to our welfare and security, adding coffee, sugar, and other articles to our staple exports, whilst greatly reducing their price to the consumer.

Nor is it only in our foreign intercourse that peace will be preserved and our prosperity advanced by the accepted fact of the permanence of our government, based upon the peaceful settlement of this question in Kansas, but at home the same sentiment will awaken renewed confidence in the stability of our institutions, give a new impulse to all our industry, and carry us onward in a career of progress and prosperity exceeding even our most sanguine expectations; a new movement of European capital will flow in upon us for permanent investment, and a new exodus of the European masses, aided by the preëmption principle, carry westward the advancing column of American states in one unbroken phalanx to the Pacific.

And let me ask you, what possible good has been accomplished by agitating in congress and in presidential conflicts the slavery question? Has it emancipated a single slave, or improved their condition? Has it made a single state free where slavery otherwise would have existed? Has it accelerated the disappearance of slavery from the more northern of the slaveholding states, or accomplished any practical good whatever? No, my fellow-citizens, nothing but unmitigated evil has already ensued, with disasters still more fearful impending for the future, as a consequence of this agitation.

There is a law more powerful than the legislation of man—more potent than passion or prejudice—that must ultimately determine the location of slavery in this country; it is the isothermal line; it is the law of the thermometer, of latitude or altitude, regulating climate, labor, and productions, and, as a consequence, profit and loss. Thus even upon the mountain heights of the tropics slavery can no more exist than in northern latitudes, because it is unprofitable, being unsuited to the constitution of that sable race transplanted here from the equatorial heats of Africa. Why is it that in the Union slavery recedes from the north and progresses south? It is this same great climatic law now operating for or against slavery in Kansas. If, on the elevated plains of Kansas, stretching to the base of our American alps—the Rocky mountains—and including their eastern crest, crowned with perpetual snow, from which sweep over her open prairies those chilling blasts, reducing the average range of the thermometer here to a temperature nearly as low as that of New England, should render slavery unprofitable here, because unsuited to the tropical constitution of the negro race, the law above referred to must ultimately determine that question here, and can no more be controlled by the legislation of man than any other moral or physical law of the Almighty. Especially must this law operate with irresistible force in this country, where the number of slaves is limited, and cannot be increased by importation, where many millions of acres of sugar and cotton lands are still uncultivated, and, from the ever-augmenting demand, exceeding the supply, the price of those great staples has nearly doubled, demanding vastly more slave labor for their production.

If, from the operation of these causes, slavery should not exist here, I trust it by no means follows that Kansas should become a state controlled by the treason and fanaticism of abolitionism. She has, in any event, certain constitutional duties to perform to her sister states, and especially to her immediate neighbor—the slaveholding state of Missouri. Through that great state, by rivers and railroads, must flow, to a great extent, our trade and intercourse, our imports and exports. Our entire eastern front is upon her border; from Missouri come a great number of her citizens; even the farms of the two states are cut up by the line of the state boundary, part in Kansas, part in Missouri; her citizens meet us in daily intercourse; and that Kansas should become hostile to Missouri, an asylum for her fugitive slaves, or a propagandist of abolition treason, would be alike inexpedient and unjust, and fatal to the continuance of the American Union.   In any event, then, I trust that the constitution of Kansas will contain such clauses as will forever secure to the state of Missouri the faithful performance of all constitutional guarantees, not only by federal, but by state authority, and the supremacy within our limits of the authority of the supreme court of the United States on all constitutional questions be firmly established.

Upon the south, Kansas is bounded by the great southwestern Indian territory. This is one of the most salubrious and fertile portions of this continent. It is a great cotton-growing region, admirably adapted by soil and climate for the products of the south, embracing the valleys of the Arkansas and Red rivers, adjoining Texas on the south and west, and Arkansas on the east, and it ought speedily to become a state of the American Union.   The Indian treaties will constitute no obstacle any more than precisely similar treaties did in Kansas ; for their lands, valueless to them, now for sale, but which, sold with their consent and for their benefit, like the Indian land of Kansas, would make them a most wealthy and prosperous people ; and their consent, on these terms, would be most cheerfully given.   This territory contains double the area of the state of Indiana, and, if necessary, an adequate portion of the western and more elevated part could be set apart exclusively for these tribes, and the eastern and larger portion be formed into a state, and its lands sold for the benefit of these tribes, (like the Indian lands of Kansas,) thus greatly promoting all their interests.   To the eastern boundary of this region on the state of Arkansas, run the railroads of that state ; to her southern limits come the great railroads from Louisiana and Texas, from New Orleans and Galveston, which will ultimately be joined by railroads from Kansas, leading through this Indian territory, connecting Kansas with New Orleans, the Gulf of Mexico, and with the Southern Pacific railroad, leading through Texas to San Francisco.

It is essential to the true interests not only of Kansas, but of Louisiana, Texas, and Arkansas, Iowa and Missouri, and the whole region west of the Mississippi, that this conterminous southwestern Indian territory should speedily become a state, not only to supply us with cotton, and receive our products in return, but as occupying the area over which that portion of our railroads should run which connect us with New Orleans and Galveston, and by the southern route with the Pacific.   From her central position, through or connected with Kansas, must run the central, northern, and southern routes to the Pacific ; and with the latter, as well as with the Gulf, the connection can only be secured by this southwestern territory becoming a state, and to this Kansas should direct her earnest attention as essential to her prosperity.

Our country and the world are regarding with profound interest the struggle now impending in Kansas.   Whether we are competent to self-government— whether we can decide this controversy peacefully for ourselves by our own votes, without fraud or violence—whether the great principles of self-government and state sovereignty can be carried here into successful operation—are the questions now to be determined, and upon the plains of Kansas may now be fought the last great and decisive battle, involving the fate of the Union, of state sovereignty, of self-government, and the liberties of the world. If, my fellow-citizens, you could, even for a brief period, soften or extinguish sectional passions or prejudice, and lift yourselves to the full realization of the momentous issues intrusted to your decision, you would feel that no greater responsibility was ever devolved upon any people. It is not merely, shall slavery exist in or disappear from Kansas? but, shall the great principles of self government and state sovereignty be maintained or subverted? State sovereignty is mainly a practical principle, in so far as it is illustrated by the great sovereign right of the majority of the people, in forming a state government, to adopt their own social institutions; and this principle is disregarded whenever such decision is subverted by congress, or overthrown by external intrusion, or by domestic fraud or violence. All those who oppose this principle are the enemies of state rights, of self-government, of the constitution and the Union. Do you love slavery so much, or hate it so intensely, that you would endeavor to establish or exclude it by fraud or violence, against the will of the majority of the people? What is Kansas, with or without slavery, if she should destroy the rights and union of the states? Where would be her schools, her free academies, her colleges and university, her towns and cities, her railroads, farms, and villages, without the Union, and the principles of self-government? Where would be her peace and prosperity, and what the value of her lands and property? Who can decide this question for Kansas, if not the people themselves? And if they cannot, nothing but the sword can become the arbiter.

On the one hand, if you can and will decide peacefully this question yourselves, I see for Kansas an immediate career of power, progress, and prosperity, unsurpassed in the history of the world. I see the peaceful establishment of our state constitution, its ratification by the people, and our immediate admission into the Union; the rapid extinguishment of the Indian title, and the occupancy of those lands by settlers and cultivators; the diffusion of universal education; preëmptions for the actual settlers; the state rapidly intersected by a network of railroads; our churches, schools, colleges, and university carrying westward the progress of law, religion, liberty, and civilization; our towns, cities, and villages prosperous and progressing; our farms teeming with abundant products, and greatly appreciated in value; and peace, happiness, and prosperity smiling throughout our borders. With proper clauses in our constitution, and the peaceful arbitrament of this question, Kansas may become the model state of the American Union. She may bring down upon us from north to south, from east to west, the praises and blessings of every patriotic American, and of every friend of self-government throughout the world. She may record her name on the proudest page of the history of our country and of the world, and as the youngest and last-born child of the American Union, all will hail and regard her with respect and affection.

On the other hand, if you cannot thus peacefully decide this question, fraud,

51

violence, and injustice will reign supreme throughout our borders, and we will have achieved the undying infamy of having destroyed the liberty of our country and of the world. We will become a byword of reproach and obloquy; and all history will record the fact that Kansas was the grave of the American Union. Never was so momentous a question submitted to the decision of any people; and we cannot avoid the alternative now placed before us of glory or of shame.

May that overruling Providence who brought our forefathers in safety to Jamestown and Plymouth—who watched over our colonial pupilage—who convened our ancestors in harmonious councils on the birthday of American independence—who gave us Washington, and carried us successfully through the struggles and perils of the revolution—who assembled, in 1787, that noble band of patriots and statesmen from north and south who framed the federal constitution—who has augmented our numbers from three millions to thirty millions, has carried us from the eastern slope of the Alleghanies through the great valleys of the Ohio, Mississippi, and Missouri, and now salutes our standard on the shores of the Pacific—rouse in our hearts a love of the whole Union, and a patriotic devotion to the whole country. May it extinguish or control all sectional passions and prejudice, and enable us to conduct to a successful conclusion the great experiment of self-government now being made within your boundaries.

Is it not infinitely better that slavery should be abolished or established in Kansas, rather than that we should become slaves and not permitted to govern ourselves? Is the absence or existence of slavery in Kansas paramount to the great questions of state sovereignty, of self-government, and of the Union? Is the sable African alone entitled to your sympathy and consideration, even if he were happier as a freeman than as a slave, either here or in St. Domingo, or the British West Indies or Spanish America, where the emancipated slave has receded to barbarism, and approaches the lowest point in the descending scale of moral, physical, and intellectual degradation? Have our white brethren of the great American and European race no claims upon our attention? Have they no rights or interests entitled to regard and protection? Shall the destiny of the African in Kansas exclude all considerations connected with our own happiness and prosperity? And is it for the handful of that race now in Kansas, or that may be hereafter introduced, that we should subvert the Union and the great principles of self-government and state sovereignty, and imbrue our hands in the blood of our countrymen! Important as this African question may be in Kansas, and which it is your solemn right to determine, it sinks into insignificance compared with the perpetuity of the Union and the final successful establishment of the principles of state sovereignty and free government. If patriotism, if devotion to the constitution and love of the Union, should not induce the minority to yield to the majority on this question, let them reflect that in no event can the minority successfully determine this question permanently, and that in no contingency will congress admit Kansas as a slave or free state unless a majority of the people of Kansas shall first have fairly and freely decided this question for themselves by a direct vote on the adoption of the constitution, excluding all fraud or violence. The minority, in resisting the will of the majority, may involve Kansas again in civil war; they may bring upon her reproach and obloquy, and destroy her progress and prosperity; they may keep her for years out of the Union, and, in the whirlwind of agitation, sweep away the government itself; but Kansas never can be brought into the Union with or without slavery except by a previous solemn decision, fully, freely, and fairly made by a majority of her people in voting for or against the adoption of her state constitution. Why, then, should this just, peaceful, and constitutional mode of settlement meet with opposition from any quarter? Is Kansas willing to destroy her own hopes of prosperity, merely that she may afford political capital to any party, and perpetuate the agitation of slavery throughout the Union? Is she to become a mere theme for agitators in other states, the theatre on which they shall perform the bloody drama of treason and disunion? Does she want to see the solemn acts of congress, the decision of the people of the Union in the recent election, the legislative, executive, and judicial authorities of the country all overthrown, and revolution and civil war inaugurated throughout her limits? Does she want to be "bleeding Kansas" for the benefit of political agitators, within or out of her limits? or does she prefer the peaceful and quiet arbitrament of this question for herself? What benefit will the great body of the people of Kansas derive from these agitations? They may, for a brief period, give consequence and power to political leaders and agitators, but it is at the expense of the happiness and welfare of the great body of the people of this territory.

Those who oppose slavery in Kansas do not base their opposition upon any philanthropic principles, or any sympathy for the African race; for in their so-called constitution, framed at Topeka, they deem that entire race so inferior and degraded as to exclude them all forever from Kansas, whether they be bond or free—thus depriving them of all rights here, and denying even that they can be citizens of the United States; for, if they are citizens, they could not constitutionally be excluded from Kansas. Yet such a clause, inserted in the Topeka constitution, was submitted by that convention for the vote of the people, and ratified here by an overwhelming majority of the anti-slavery party. This party, here, therefore, has, in the most positive manner, affirmed the constitutionality of that portion of the recent decision of the supreme court of the United States, declaring that Africans are not citizens of the United States.

This is the more important, inasmuch as this Topeka constitution was ratified with this clause inserted by the entire republican party in congress—thus distinctly affirming the recent decision of the supreme court of the Union, that Africans are not citizens of the United States; for if citizens, they may be elected to all offices, state and national, including the presidency itself; they must be placed upon a basis of perfect equality with the whites, serve with them in the militia, on the bench, the legislature, the jury-box, vote in all elections, meet us in social intercourse, and intermarry freely with the whites. This doctrine of the perfect equality of the white with the black, in all respects whatsoever, social and political, clearly follows from the position that Africans are citizens of the United States. Nor is the supreme court of the Union less clearly vindicated by the position now assumed here by the published creed of this party, that the people of Kansas, in forming their state constitution, (and not congress,) must decide this question of slavery for themselves. Having thus sustained the court on both the controverted points decided by that tribunal, it is hoped they will not approve the anarchical and revolutionary proceedings in other states, expunging the supreme court from our system by depriving it of the great power for which it was created, of expounding the constitution. If that be done, we can have in fact no unity of government or fundamental law, but just as many ever-varying constitutions as passion, prejudice, and local interests may from time to time prescribe in the thirty-one states of the Union.

I have endeavored heretofore faintly to foreshadow the wonderful prosperity which would follow at once in Kansas the peaceful and final settlement of this question. But, if it should be in the power of agitators to prevent such a result, nothing but ruin will pervade our territory. Confidence will expire and law and order will be subverted. Anarchy and civil war will be reïnaugurated among us. All property will greatly depreciate in value. Even the best farms will become almost worthless. Our towns and cities will sink into decay. Emigration to our territory will cease. A mournful train of returning settlers, with ruined hopes and blasted fortunes, will leave our borders. All who have purchased property at present prices will be sacrificed, and Kansas will be marked by universal ruin and desolation.

Nor will the mischief be arrested here. It will extend into every other state. Despots will exult over the failure here of the great principles of self-government, and the approaching downfall of our confederacy. The pillars of the union will rock upon their base, and we may close the next presidential conflict amid the scattered fragments of the constitution of our once happy and united people. The banner of the stars and stripes, the emblem of our country's glory, will be rent by contending factions. We shall no longer have a country. The friends of human liberty in other realms will shrink despairing from the conflict. Despotic power will resume its sway throughout the world, and man will have tried in vain the last experiment of self-government. The architects of our country's ruin, the assassins of her peace and prosperity, will share the same common ruin of all our race. They will meet, whilst living, the bitter curses of a ruined people, whilst history will record as their only epitaph: *These were the destroyers of the American Union, of the liberties of their country and the world.*

But I do not despair of the republic. My hope is in the patriotism and intelligence of the people; in their love of country, of liberty, and of the Union. Especially is my confidence unbounded in the hardy pioneers and settlers of the west. It was such settlers of a new state devoted to the constitution and the Union, whom I long represented in the senate of the United States, and whose rights and interests it was my pride and pleasure there, as well as in the treasury department, to protect and advocate. It was men like these whose rifles drove back the invader from the plains of Orleans, and planted the stars and stripes upon the victorious fields of Mexico. These are the men whom gold cannot corrupt nor foes intimidate. From their towns and villages, from their farms and cottages, spread over the beautiful prairies of Kansas, they will come forward now in defense of the constitution and the Union. These are the glorious legacy they received from our fathers, and they will transmit to their children the priceless heritage. Before the peaceful power of their suffrage this dangerous sectional agitation will disappear, and peace and prosperity once more reign throughout our borders. In the hearts of this noble band of patriotic settlers, the love of their country and of the Union is inextinguishable. It leaves them not in death, but follows them into that higher realm, where, with Washington and Franklin, and their noble compatriots, they look down with undying affection upon their country, and offer up prayers that the Union and the constitution may be perpetual. For, recollect, my fellow-citizens, that it is the constitution that makes the Union, and unless that immortal instrument, bearing the name of the Father of his Country, shall be maintained entire in all its wise provisions and sacred guarantees, our free institutions must perish.

My reliance also is unshaken upon the same overruling Providence which has carried us triumphantly through so many perils and conflicts, which has lifted us to a height and power of prosperity unexampled in history, and, if we shall maintain the constitution and the Union, points us to a future more glorious and sublime than mind can conceive or pen describe. The march of our country's destiny, like that of His first chosen people, is marked by the foot-prints of the steps of God. The constitution and the Union are "the cloud by day, and the pillar of fire by night," which will carry us safely, under his guidance, through the wilderness and bitter waters, into the promised and ever-extending fields of our country's glory. It is his hand which beckons us onward in the pathway of peaceful progress and expansion, of power and renown, until our continent, in the distant future, shall be covered by the folds of the American banner, and, instructed by our example, all the nations of the world, through many trials and sacrifices, shall establish the great principles of our constitutional confederacy of free and sovereign states.

R. J. WALKER.

The suggestion of Governor Walker to refer the constitution then to be framed back to the people of Kansas for their ratification or rejection, met with most decided condemnation, not only by the pro-slavery party in Kansas, but by the southern press generally. The Charleston *Mercury* said: "Now we hold that the submitting of the constitution soon to be framed by the people of Kansas in convention assembled, back again to the people individually, for ratification, is a work of supererogation—a matter to be done or not, entirely to the discretion of the convention, as a thing of contingent expediency only, and not by any means a thing of necessity. And we cannot but look upon this suggestion of Mr. Stanton, however coupled with declarations of southern feeling, and the determination expressed by Governor Walker, as partaking of the nature of official dictation, and being, in fact, a violation of the promised neutrality—an insidious and high-handed breach of faith towards the south and southern men in Kansas. We, therefore, desire in the outset to stamp this game as it deserves, and to protest against all attempts to influence the action of the convention from without, whether coming from the territorial officers appointed by the president, or the free-soil schemers of New York and Boston. The real object and end is under the guise of fair words to the south to make a free state of Kansas."

The Richmond *South* said : "Upon the new plan which Governor Walker promulgates for the settlement of the Kansas difficulty, we cannot venture an opinion before we scrutinize it in detail. There is one point, however, upon which we can give an instant and emphatic judgment; and that is, the proposition to submit the constitution of Kansas to a popular vote. The convention can do nothing for which there is not an express authority in the law ; and as there is neither an express or implied authority in the law to submit the constitution of Kansas to the vote of the inhabitants of the territory, the step would be an illegal and invalid usurpation of power. The proposition is too plain to allow of controversy. Submit it to any lawyer in the land, from Chief Justice Taney or Reverdy Johnson to the poorest pettifogger in the most obscure country village, and the instant answer will be that the convention in Kansas has no right to submit the constitution to a popular vote. The journals of the north concede the point, and declaim against the law calling the convention on the ground that it makes no provision for a popular vote on the constitution. Why then does Governor Walker raise the question ? It is especially surprising that he should assume an undeniably untenable position."

Such is a brief history of the troubles in Kansas down to the summer of 1857. The constitutional convention met at Lecompton in September, was duly organized, and then adjourned to meet again on the 25th of October.

CHAPTER XXXIV.

STATISTICAL TABLES CONSTRUCTED FROM THE CENSUS OF 1850.

TERRITORY—Area of Free States ; area of Slave States.—POPULATION—Free colored in Free States: Free colored in Slave States ; Slaves.—Amalgamation ; Mulattoes of Free States; Mulattoes of Slave States ; Proportion to Whites.—Manumitted Slaves ; Fugitive Slaves; Occupation of Slaves ; Number of Slave Holders ; Proportion to Non-Slave Holders.—REPRESENTATION—Number of Representatives from Slave States.—Number of Representatives from Free States ; Basis in numbers and classes.—MORAL AND SOCIAL—Churches, Church Property, Colleges, Public Schools, Private Schools ; Number of Pupils ; Annual Expenditure ; Persons who cannot read and write : Lands appropriated by General Government for Education ; Periodical Press : Libraries.—CHARITIES—Pauperism in Free States ; in Slave States.—CRIMINALS—Number of Prisoners.—AGRICULTURE—Value of Farms and Implements in Free and Slave States.—MANUFACTURES, MINING, MECHANIC ARTS—Capital invested: Annual Product.—RAIL ROADS AND CANALS—Number of Miles; Cost.—TOTAL REAL AND PERSONAL ESTATE.—Value of Real Estate in Free States ; in Slave States: value of Personal in Free States ; in Slave States, including and excluding Slaves.—Miscellaneous.

THE United States consist at the present time of thirty-one independent states, and eight organized territories, including the District of Columbia.

TERRITORY.

AREA IN SQUARE MILES OF THE FREE STATES.

California	155,980	New Hampshire	9,280
Connecticut	4,674	New York	47,000
Illinois	55,405	New Jersey	8,320
Indiana	33,809	Ohio	39,964
Iowa	50,914	Pennsylvania	46,000
Maine	31,766	Rhode Island	1,306
Massachusetts	7,800	Vermont	10,212
Michigan	56,243	Wisconsin	53,924

Total area of the Free States............612,597

AREA IN SQUARE MILES OF THE SLAVE STATES.

Alabama	50,722	Maryland	11,124
Arkansas	52,198	Mississippi	47,156
District of Columbia	60	Missouri	67,380
Delaware	2,120	North Carolina	50,704
Florida	59,268	South Carolina	29,385
Georgia	58,000	Tennessee	45,600
Kentucky	37,680	Texas	237,504
Louisiana	41,255	Virginia	61,352

Total area of the Slave States............851,500

Area of the thirty-one states in square miles.................... 1,464,105
Area of the territories in square miles........................... 1,472,061

POPULATION.

White population in the Free States	13,330,650
White population in the Slave States	6,222,418
Free colored population of Free States	196,016
Free colored population of Slave States	238,187
Slaves	3,204,313
Proportion of colored to white in Free States	1 to 68
Proportion of colored to white in Slave States	1 to 2

FREE COLORED IN FREE STATES.

California	962	New Hampshire	520
Connecticut	7,693	New York	49,069
Illinois	5,436	New Jersey	23,810
Indiana	11,262	Ohio	25,279
Iowa	333	Pennsylvania	53,626
Maine	1,356	Rhode Island	3,670
Massachusetts	9,064	Vermont	718
Michigan	2,583	Wisconsin	635
Total			196,016

FREE COLORED IN SLAVE STATES.

Alabama	2,265	Maryland	74,723
Arkansas	608	Mississippi	930
District of Columbia	10,059	Missouri	2,618
Delaware	18,733	North Carolina	27,463
Georgia	2,932	South Carolina	8,960
Florida	932	Tennessee	6,422
Kentucky	10,011	Texas	397
Louisiana	17,462	Virginia	54,333
Total			238,187

SLAVE POPULATION.

Alabama	342,844	Maryland	90,368
Arkansas	47,100	Mississippi	309,878
District of Columbia	3,687	Missouri	87,422
Delaware	2,290	North Carolina	288,548
Georgia	381,682	South Carolina	384,984
Florida	39,310	Tennessee	239,459
Kentucky	210,981	Texas	58,161
Louisiana	244,809	Virginia	472,528
Total			3,204,313

MULATTO POPULATION OF FREE STATES.

California	87	New Hampshire	184
Connecticut	1,798	New Jersey	3,697
Illinois	2,506	New York	8,139

Indiana	5,321	Ohio	14,265
Iowa	155	Pennsylvania	15,341
Maine	461	Rhode Island	731
Massachusetts	2,340	Vermont	206
Michigan	1,118	Wisconsin	297

Total _____ 56,646

MULATTO POPULATION OF SLAVE STATES.

	Free.	Slaves.	Total.
Alabama	1,698	21,605	23,303
Arkansas	407	6,361	6,768
District of Columbia	3,276	802	4,078
Delaware	1,648	83	1,731
Florida	703	3,022	3,725
Georgia	1,528	22,669	24,197
Kentucky	2,630	29,729	32,359
Louisiana	14,083	19,835	33,918
Maryland	13,614	7,889	21,503
Mississippi	635	19,730	20,365
Missouri	931	13,235	14,166
North Carolina	17,205	16,815	34,020
South Carolina	4,372	12,502	16,874
Tennessee	3,766	20,356	24,132
Texas	257	7,703	7,960
Virginia	35,476	44,299	79,775
Total	102,239	246,635	348,874

Mulatto population of Free States _____ _____ 56,646

Mulatto population of Slave States _____ Free, 102,239

Slave, 246,635 _____ 348,874

White population of Free States ____ 13,330,650

Mulatto population of Free States __ 56,646 _____ Proportion, 1 to 235

White population of Slave States ___ 6,222,418

Mulatto population of Slave States __ 348,874 _____ Proportion, 1 to 18

MANUMITTED AND FUGITIVE SLAVES IN 1850.

States.	Manumitted.	Fugitive.	States.	Manumitted	Fugitive.
Alabama	16	29	Missouri	50	60
Arkansas	1	21	Mississippi	6	41
Delaware	277	26	North Carolina	2	64
Florida	22	18	South Carolina	2	16
Georgia	19	89	Tennessee	45	70
Kentucky	152	96	Texas	5	29
Louisiana	159	90	Virginia	218	83
Maryland	493	279			
			Total	1,467	1,011

On the schedules 1,467 slaves are returned in 1850 as emancipated in the slaveholding states during the previous year. The number of slaves who had absconded during the year 1849–50, and had not been heard from, was 1,011 by the reports.

Proportion of Fugitive Slaves.......................... one in 3,200
Proportion of Manumitted Slaves..................... one in 2,200

In Maryland there was one fugitive in 320 slaves; in Virginia there was one in 5,695; in Missouri, one in 1,450; in Kentucky, one in 2,100; in Georgia, one in 2,700; and in Louisiana, one in 4,000.

Deaf and Dumb Slaves.................................. 531
Blind 1,387
Insane 327
Idiotic 1,182
                                                    _____
    Total 3,427

OCCUPATIONS OF SLAVES.

Residents of Towns.................................. 400,000
Rural.. 2,804,313

Of the latter class 2,500,000 are directly employed in agriculture, including males and females, and persons of all ages. Slaves under 10 and over 60 years of age are seldom employed industrially. These 2,500,000 are distributed between the great staples of the south in something like the following proportions, bearing in mind that large quantities of breadstuffs are produced in addition:

Hemp.. 60,000
Rice 125,000
Sugar 150,000
Tobacco 350,000
Cotton, &c... 1,815,000

NUMBER OF SLAVE HOLDERS.

Alabama	29,295	Maryland	16,040
Arkansas	5,999	Mississippi	23,116
District of Columbia	1,477	Missouri	19,185
Delaware	809	North Carolina	28,303
Florida	3,520	South Carolina	25,596
Georgia	38,456	Tennessee	33,864
Kentucky	38,385	Texas	7,747
Louisiana	20,670	Virginia	55,063
Total			347,525

Proportion of Slave Holders to Non-Slave Holders in the Slave States.

States.	Slave Holders.	Non-Slave Holders.
Alabama	29,295	397,219
Arkansas	5,999	156,190
District of Columbia	1,477	36,464
Delaware	809	70,360
Florida	3,520	43,683
Georgia	38,456	483,116
Kentucky	38,385	723,028
Louisiana	20,670	234,821
Maryland	16,040	401,903
Mississippi	23,116	272,602
Missouri	19,185	572,819
North Carolina	28,303	524,725
South Carolina	25,596	248,967
Tennessee	33,864	722,972
Texas	7,747	146,287
Virginia	55,063	839,737
	347,525	5,873,893

Representation in Congress.—Slave States.

States.	Slaves.	Free Colored.	White.	No. of. Reps.
Alabama	342,844	2,265	426,514	7
Arkansas	47,100	608	162,189	2
Delaware	2,290	18,073	71,169	1
Florida	39,310	932	47,203	1
Georgia	381,682	2,932	521,572	8
Kentucky	210,981	10,011	761,413	10
Louisiana	244,809	17,462	255,491	4
Maryland	90,368	74,723	417,943	6
Mississippi	309,878	930	295,718	5
Missouri	87,422	2,618	592,004	7
North Carolina	288,548	27,463	553,028	8
South Carolina	384,984	8,960	274,563	6
Tennessee	239,459	6,422	756,836	10
Texas	58,161	397	154,034	2
Virginia	472,528	54,333	894,800	13
	3,200,626	238,187	6,222,418	90

REPRESENTATION IN CONGRESS.—FREE STATES.

States.	Colored.	White.	No. of Reps.
California	962	91,635	2
Connecticut	7,693	363,099	4
Illinois	5,436	846,034	9
Indiana	11,262	977,154	11
Iowa	333	191,881	2
Maine	1,356	581,813	6
Massachusetts	9,064	985,450	11
Michigan	2,583	395,071	4
New Hampshire	520	317,456	3
New York	49,069	3,048,325	33
New Jersey	23,816	465,509	5
Ohio	25,279	1,955,050	21
Pennsylvania	53,626	2,258,160	25
Rhode Island	3,670	143,875	2
Vermont	718	313,402	3
Wisconsin	635	304,756	3
	196,016	13,330,650	144

Northern Representatives based on White Population _____ 142
Northern Representatives based on Colored Population _____ 2
Southern Representatives based on White Population _____ 68
Southern Representatives based on Free Colored Population _____ 2
Southern Representatives based on Slave Population _____ 20

Ratio of Representation for 1853, ____ 93,420

MORAL AND SOCIAL.

RELIGIOUS WORSHIP.

Slave States.	No. of Churches.	Value Church Property.	Church Accommodations.
Alabama	1,325	$1,131,616	440,155
Arkansas	362	89,315	60,226
District of Columbia	46	363,000	34,120
Delaware	180	340,345	55,741
Florida	177	165,400	44,960
Georgia	1,862	1,269,359	632,992
Kentucky	1,849	2,251,918	673,528
Louisiana	307	1,782,470	109,615
Maryland	909	3,947,884	379,465
Mississippi	1,016	755,542	294,104
Missouri	909	1,587,410	264,979
North Carolina	1,787	905,573	574,924
South Carolina	1,182	2,172,246	460,450
Tennessee	2,027	1,216,201	628,495
Texas	328	206,930	64,155
Virginia	2,386	2,860,876	858,086
Totals	16,652	$22,142,085	5,574,995

RELIGIOUS WORSHIP.

Free States.	No. of Churches.	Value Church Property.	Church Accommodations.
California	28	$ 267,800	10,020
Connecticut	734	3,555,194	307,299
Illinois	1,223	1,482,185	486,576
Indiana	2,035	1,529,585	709,655
Iowa	207	177,425	43,529
Maine	945	1,725,845	321,167
Massachusetts	1,447	10,206,184	692,828
Michigan	399	723,600	120,117
New Hampshire	626	1,405,786	237,417
New Jersey	814	3,680,936	345,733
New York	4,169	21,219,207	1,915,179
Ohio	3,939	5,793,099	1,457,769
Pennsylvania	3,596	11,586,315	1,576,245
Rhode Island	231	1,254,400	102,040
Vermont	599	1,216,125	234,534
Wisconsin	365	353,900	97,773
Totals	21,357	$65,167,586	8,647,881

EDUCATION.

SLAVE STATES.	COLLEGES.			PUBLIC SCHOOLS.			ACADEMIES AND PRIVATE SCHOOLS.		Total Annual Income in all schools.	Total number of scholars in all schools.
	No.	Pupils.	Total Annual Income.	No.	Pupils.	Total Annual Income.	No.	Pupils.		
Alabama	5	567	$41,255	1,152	28,380	$315,602	166	8,290	$164,165	37,237
Arkansas	3	150	3,100	353	8,493	43,763	90	2,407	27,937	11,050
District of Columbia	2	218	24,000	22	2,169	14,232	47	2,333	84,040	4,720
Delaware	2	144	17,200	194	8,970	43,861	65	2,011	47,832	11,125
Florida				69	1,878	22,386	34	1,251	13,089	3,129
Georgia	13	1,535	105,430	1,251	32,705	182,231	219	9,059	108,983	43,299
Kentucky	15	1,773	131,461	2,234	71,429	211,852	330	12,712	252,617	85,914
Louisiana	6	629	85,750	664	25,046	349,679	143	5,328	193,077	31,003
Maryland	13	1,127	113,714	898	33,101	218,836	223	10,787	232,341	45,025
Mississippi	11	862	42,400	782	18,746	254,159	171	6,628	73,717	26,236
Missouri	9	1,009	79,528	1,570	51,754	160,770	204	8,829	143,171	61,592
North Carolina	5	513	40,700	2,657	104,095	158,564	272	7,822	187,648	112,430
South Carolina	8	720	104,790	724	17,838	200,600	202	7,467	205,489	26,025
Tennessee	18	1,705	65,307	2,680	104,117	198,518	264	9,928	155,902	115,750
Texas	2	165	1,000	349	7,946	44,088	97	3,389	39,384	11,500
Virginia	12	1,343	159,790	2,930	67,353	314,625	317	9,068	234,372	77,764
Totals	124	12,460	1,015,126	18,529	584,430	2,733,766	2,842	107,309	2,163,764	703,889

EDUCATION.

Free States	Colleges			Public Schools			Academies and Private Schools			
	No.	Pupils.	Total Annual Income.	No.	Pupils.	Total Annual Income.	No.	Pupils.	Total Annual Income.	Total number of scholars in all schools.
California	----	----	----	2	49	$3,600	6	170	$14,270	219
Connecticut	4	738	$53,639	1,656	71,269	231,220	202	6,996	145,967	79,003
Illinois	6	442	13,300	4,052	125,725	349,712	83	4,244	40,488	130,411
Indiana	11	1,069	43,350	4,822	161,500	316,955	131	6,185	63,520	168,754
Iowa	3	100	2,000	740	29,556	51,492	33	1,111	7,980	30,767
Maine	3	282	14,000	4,042	192,815	315,436	131	6,648	51,187	199,745
Massachusetts	6	1,043	107,901	3,679	176,475	1,006,795	403	13,436	310,177	190,924
Michigan	3	308	14,000	2,714	110,455	167,806	37	1,619	24,947	112,382
New Hampshire	1	273	11,000	2,381	75,643	166,944	107	5,321	43,202	81,237
New Jersey	4	470	79,700	1,473	77,930	216,672	225	9,844	227,588	88,244
New York	18	2,673	148,258	11,580	675,221	1,472,657	887	49,328	810,332	727,222
Ohio	26	3,621	125,792	11,661	484,153	743,074	206	15,052	149,392	502,826
Pennsylvania	22	3,520	286,805	9,061	413,706	1,348,249	524	23,751	467,843	440,977
Rhode Island	1	283	23,000	416	23,130	100,481	46	1,601	32,748	25,014
Vermont	5	464	21,558	2,731	93,457	176,111	118	6,864	48,935	100,785
Wisconsin	2	75	4,700	1,423	58,817	113,133	58	2,723	18,796	61,615
Totals	114	15,361	949,003	62,433	2,769,763	6,780,337	3,197	154,893	2,457,372	2,940,125

Estimated Educational Income in Slave States _____ __ 6,819,808
Estimated Educational Income in Free States _____ 10,962,368

PERSONS OVER 20 YEARS OF AGE WHO CANNOT READ AND WRITE.

SLAVE STATES.	WHITES.	FREE COLORED.	WHITE & FREE COLORED.		
			Native.	Foreign.	Aggregate.
Alabama	33,757	235	33,853	139	33,902
Arkansas	16,819	116	16,908	27	16,935
District of Columbia	1,457	3,214	4,349	322	4,671
Delaware	4,536	5,645	9,777	404	10,181
Florida	3,859	270	3,834	295	4,129
Georgia	41,200	467	41,261	406	41,667
Kentucky	66,687	3,019	67,359	2,347	69,706
Louisiana	21,221	3,389	18,339	6,271	24,610
Maryland	20,815	21,062	38,426	3,451	41,877
Mississippi	13,405	.123	13,447	81	13,528
Missouri	36,281	497	34,917	1,861	36,778
North Carolina	73,566	6,857	80,083	340	80,423
South Carolina	15,684	880	16,460	104	16,564
Tennessee	77,522	1,097	78,114	505	78,619
Texas	10,525	58	8,095	2,488	10,583
Virginia	77,005	11,515	87,383	1,137	88,520
Totals	514,339	58,444	552,605	20,178	572,782

PERSONS OVER 20 YEARS OF AGE WHO CANNOT READ AND WRITE.

FREE STATES.	WHITES.	FREE COLORED.	WHITE & FREE COLORED.		
			Native.	Foreign.	Aggregate.
California	5,118	117	2,318	2,917	5,235
Connecticut	4,739	567	1,293	4,013	5,306
Illinois	40,054	1,229	35,336	5,947	41,283
Indiana	70,540	2,170	69,445	3,265	72,710
Iowa	8,120	33	7,076	1,077	8,153
Maine	6,147	135	2,134	4,148	6,282
Massachusetts	27,539	806	1,861	26,484	28,345
Michigan	7,912	369	5,272	3,009	8,281
New Hampshire	2,957	52	945	2,064	3,009
New Jersey	14,248	4,417	12,787	5,878	18,665
New York	91,293	7,429	30,670	68,052	98,722
Ohio	61,030	4,990	56,958	9,062	66,020
Pennsylvania	66,928	9,344	51,283	24,989	76,272
Rhode Island	3,340	*267	1,248	2,359	3,607
Vermont	6,189	51	616	5,624	6,240
Wisconsin	6,361	92	1,551	4,902	6,453
Totals	422,515	32,068	280,793	173,790	454,583

LANDS APPROPRIATED BY GENERAL GOVERNMENT FOR EDUCATIONAL PURPOSES TO JANUARY 1, 1854.

Slave States.	Acres for Schools.	Acres for Universities.
Missouri	1,199,139	23,040
Alabama	902,774	23,040
Mississippi	837,584	23,040
Louisiana	786,044	46,080
Arkansas	886,460	46,080
Florida	908,503	46,080
Tennessee	3,553,824*	------
Total	9,074,328	207,360

Free States.	Acres for Schools.	Acres for Universites.
Ohio	704,488	23,040
Indiana	650,317	23,040
Illinois	978,755	23,040
Michigan	1,067,397	46,080
Iowa	905,144	46,080
Wisconsin	958,648	46,080
California	6,719,324	46,080
Total	11,984,073	253,440

NEWSPAPER AND PERIODICAL PRESS.

Aggregate number of copies printed annually in Slave States.. 92,165,919

Aggregate number of copies printed annually in Free States... 334,146,081

LIBRARIES.

	Libraries.	Volumes.
Libraries other than Private in Slave States...	722	742,794
Libraries other than Private in Free States....	14,902	3,382,217

These Libraries include Public, School, Sunday School, College and Church.

---

* Forty thousand dollars of proceeds to be applied to establish and support a College.

52

STATISTICAL TABLES.

CHARITIES.

PAUPERISM.—WHOLE NUMBER OF PERSONS JUNE 1, 1850.

Slave States.	Native.	Foreign.	Total.
Alabama	306	9	315
Arkansas	67	-----	67
Delaware	240	33	273
Florida	58	4	62
Georgia	825	29	854
Kentucky	690	87	777
Louisiana	76	30	106
Maryland	1,681	320	2,001
Mississippi	245	12	257
Missouri	251	254	505
North Carolina	1,567	13	1,580
South Carolina	1,113	180	1,293
Tennessee	577	14	594
Texas	4	----	4
Virginia	4,356	102	4,458
Totals	**12,056**	**1,087**	**13,143**

Free States.	Native.	Foreign.	Total
California	----	-----	-----
Connecticut	1,463	281	1,744
Illinois	279	155	434
Indiana	446	137	583
Iowa	27	17	44
Maine	3,209	326	3,535
Massachusetts	4,059	1,490	5,549
Michigan	248	181	429
New Hampshire	1,998	186	2,184
New Jersey	1,339	239	1,578
New York	5,755	7,078	12,833
Ohio	1,254	419	1,673
Pennsylvania	2,654	1,157	3,811
Rhode Island	492	204	696
Vermont	1,565	314	1,879
Wisconsin	72	166	238
Totals	**24,860**	**12,350**	**37,210**

CRIMINAL STATISTICS.

SLAVE STATES.—Number in State Prisons and Penitentiaries :

Whites—Native 988
Foreign 370
Colored, including slaves.. 323 ....Total.... 1,681

FREE STATES.—Number in State Prisons and Penitentiaries:

Whites—Native 2,271

Foreign 1,129

Colored .... 565 ....Total.... 3,965

INDUSTRY.
FARMING LANDS AND IMPROVEMENTS.

SLAVE STATES.	Cash value of Farms and Plantations.	Value of Farming Implements and Machinery.
Alabama	$64,323,224	$5,125,663
Arkansas	15,265,245	1,601,296
District of Columbia...........	1,730,460	40,220
Delaware	18,880,031	510,279
Florida.....................	6,323,109	658,795
Georgia	95,753,445	5,894,150
Kentucky	155,021,262	5,169,037
Louisiana...................	75,814,398	11,576,938
Maryland	87,178,545	2,463,443
Mississippi	54,738,634	5,762,927
Missouri....................	63,225,543	3,981,525
North Carolina	67,891,766	3,931,532
South Carolina	82,431,684	4,136,354
Tennessee..................	97,851,212	5,360,210
Texas	16,550,008	2,151,704
Virginia	216,401,543	7,021,762
Totals.........	$1,119,380,109	$65,386,045

FARMING LANDS AND IMPROVEMENTS.

FREE STATES.	Cash value of Farms and Plantations.	Value of Farming Implements and Machinery.
California..	$3,874,041	$103,483
Connecticut	72,726,422	1,892,541
Illinois	96,133,290	6,405,561
Indiana.....................	136,385,173	6,704,444
Iowa	16,657,567	1,172,869
Maine......................	54,861,748	2,284,557
Massachusetts	109,076,347	3,209,584
Michigan	51,872,446	2,891,371
New Hampshire	55,245,997	2,314,125
New Jersey	120,237,511	4,425,503
New York	554,546,642	22,084,926
Ohio.......................	358,758,603	12,750,585
Pennsylvania	407,876,099	14,722,541
Rhode Island...............	17,070,802	497,201
Vermont	63,367,227	2,739,282
Wisconsin	28,528,563	1,641,568
Totals.........	$2,147,218,478	$85,840,141

MANUFACTURES, MINING AND MECHANIC ARTS.

SLAVE STATES.	Capital Invested.	Raw Material used.	Annual Product.
Alabama	$3,450,606	$2,224,960	$4,528,878
Arkansas	324,065	268,564	607,436
District of Columbia	888,965	1,339,146	2,493,008
Delaware	2,978,945	2,864,607	4,649,296
Florida	547,060	220,611	668,335
Georgia	5,460,483	3,404,917	7,086,525
Kentucky	12,350,734	12,170,225	24,588,483
Louisiana	5,318,074	2,958,988	7,320,948
Maryland	14,753,143	17,326,734	32,477,702
Mississippi	1,833,420	1,290,271	2,972,038
Missouri	9,079,695	12,446,738	23,749,265
North Carolina	7,252,225	4,805,463	9,111,245
South Carolina	6,056,865	2,809,534	7,063,513
Tennessee	6,975,279	4,900,952	9,728,438
Texas	539,290	394,642	1,165,538
Virginia	18,109,993	18,103,433	29,705,387
Totals	$95,918,842	$87,529,785	$167,906,035

MANUFACTURES, MINING AND MECHANIC ARTS.

FREE STATES.	Capital Invested.	Raw Material used.	Annual Product.
California	$1,006,197	$1,201,154	$12,862,522
Connecticut	23,890,348	23,589,397	45,110,102
Illinois	6,385,387	8,915,173	17,236,073
Indiana	7,941,602	10,214,337	18,922,651
Iowa	1,292,875	2,356,881	3,551,783
Maine	14,700,452	13,555,806	24,664,135
Massachusetts	83,357,642	85,856,771	151,137,145
Michigan	6,534,250	6,105,561	10,976,894
New Hampshire	18,242,114	12,745,466	23,164,503
New Jersey	22,184,730	21,992,186	39,713,586
New York	99,904,405	134,655,674	237,597,249
Ohio	29,019,538	34,677,937	62,647,259
Pennsylvania	94,473,810	87,206,377	155,044,910
Rhode Island	12,923,176	13,183,889	22,093,258
Vermont	5,001,377	4,173,552	8,570,920
Wisconsin	3,382,148	5,414,931	9,293,068
Totals	$431,290,351	$467,125,253	$845,430,428

RAIL ROADS AND CANALS IN 1854.

	Miles of Canals.	Miles of Railroads.	Cost of Railroads.
Slave States	1,116	4,212	$92,620,204
Free States	3,682	13,105	$396,980,924

REAL AND PERSONAL ESTATE.

Slave States.	Real Estate	Personal Estate including Slaves.	Total.
Alabama	$78,870,718	$162,463,705	$241,334,423
Arkansas	17,372,524	19,056,151	36,428,675
District of Columbia	14,409,413	1,774,342	16,183,755
Delaware	14,486,595	1,410,275	15,896,870
Florida	7,924,588	15,274,146	23,198,734
Georgia	121,619,739	213,490,486	335,110,225
Kentucky	177,013,407	114,374,147	291,387,554
Louisiana	176,623,654	49,832,464	226,456,118
Maryland	139,026,610	69,536,956	208,563,566
Mississippi	65,171,438	143,250,729	208,422,167
Missouri	66,802,223	36,793,240	98,595,463
North Carolina	71,702,740	140,368,673	212,071,413
South Carolina	105,737,492	178,130,217	283,867,709
Tennessee	107,981,793	87,299,565	195,281,358
Texas	28,149,671	25,414,000	53,563,671
Virginia	252,105,824	130,198,429	383,304,253
Totals	$1,444,998,429	$1,383,667 525	$2,828,665,954

REAL AND PERSONAL ESTATE.

Free States.	Real Estate.	Personal Estate.	Total.
California	$16,347,442	$5,575,731	$21,923,173
Connecticut	96,412,947	22,675,725	119,088,672
Illinois	81,524,835	33,257,810	114,782,645
Indiana	112,947,740	39,922,659	152,870,399
Iowa	15,672,332	6,018,310	21,690,642
Maine	64,336,119	32,463,434	96,799,553
Massachusetts	349,129,932	201,976,892	551,106,824
Michigan	25,580,371	5,296,852	30,877,223
New Hampshire	67,839,108	27,412,488	95,251,596
New Jersey	153,151,619	30,000,000	183,151,619
New York	564,649,649	150,719,379	715,369,028
Ohio	337,521,075	96,351,557	433,872,632
Pennsylvania	427,865,660	72,410,191	500,275,851
Rhode Island	54,358,231	23,400,743	77,758,974
Vermont	57,320,369	15,660,114	72,980,483
Wisconsin	22,468,442	4,257,083	26,715,525
Totals	$2,447,115,871	$9767,398,968	$3,214,514,839

Value of Real Estate in Free States $2,447,115,871
Value of Real Estate in Slave States 1,444,998,429

Value of Personal Estate in Free States $767,398,968
Value of Personal Estate in Slave States including Slaves.. 1,383,667,525
Value of Personal Estate in Slave States excluding Slaves. 422,373,625

Total value of Real and Personal Estate in Free States $3,214,514,839
Total value of Real and Personal Estate in Slave States including Slaves $2,828,665,954
Total value Real and Personal Estate in Slave States excluding Slaves $1,867,372,054

Estimated average value of Slaves, in above calculation, $300.

SLAVE LABOR PRODUCTS IN 1850.

Cotton	$98,603,720
Tobacco	13,982,686
Cane Sugar	12,378,850
Hemp	5,000,000
Rice	4,000,000
Molasses	2,540,179
	$136,505,435

SLAVE POPULATION IN AMERICA.

In United States	3,204,313
" Brazil	3,250,000
" Spanish Colonies	900,000
" Dutch Colonies	85,000
" South American Republics	140,000

APPENDIX.

SUPREME COURT OF THE UNITED STATES.

CASE OF DRED SCOTT vs. SANDFORD.

THE Supreme Court of the United States, at the December term, in 1856, gave its decision in what is popularly known as the "Dred Scott case." This case involved not only private rights but constitutional principles of the highest importance. In reference to the questions involved, Judge Daniel declared, that since the establishment of the several communities now constituting the states of this confederacy, there never had been submitted to any tribunal within its limits, questions surpassing in importance those submitted in this case to the consideration of the court. Judge Wayne remarked, that there had become such a difference of opinion in respect to the questions presented that the peace and harmony of the country required the settlement of them by judicial decision.

STATEMENT OF THE CASE.

This case, Dred Scott vs. Sandford, was brought up by writ of error from the circuit court of the United States for the district of Missouri. It was an action for trespass vi et armis instituted in the circuit court by Scott against Sandford.

Prior to the institution of the present suit, an action was brought by Scott for his freedom in the circuit court of St. Louis county, (state court,) where there was a verdict and judgment in his favor. On a writ of error to the supreme court of the state, the judgment below was reversed, and the case remanded to the circuit court, where it was continued to await the decision of the case now in question.

The declaration of Scott contained three counts; one, that Sandford had assaulted the plaintiff; one, that he had assaulted Harriet Scott, his wife; and one, that he had assaulted Eliza Scott and Lizzie Scott, his children.

Sandford appeared and filed the following plea: "And the said John F. A. Sandford, in his own proper person, comes and says that this court ought not to have or take further cognizance of the action aforesaid, because he says that said cause of action, and each and every of them, (if any such have accrued to the said Dred Scott,) accrued to the said Dred Scott out of the jurisdiction of this court, and exclusively within the jurisdiction of the courts of the state of Missouri, for that, to wit: the said plaintiff, Dred Scott, is not a citizen of the state of Missouri, as alleged in his declaration, because he is a negro of African descent; his ancestors were of pure African blood, and were brought into this country and sold as negro slaves, and this the said Sandford is ready to verify. Wherefore, he prays judgment whether this court can or will take further cognizance of the action aforesaid."

To this plea there was a demurrer in the usual form, which was argued ... April, 1854, when the court gave judgment that the demurrer should be sustained.

In May, 1854, the defendant, in pursuance of an agreement between counsel, and with the leave of the court, pleaded in bar of the action: 1. Not guilty. 2. That the plaintiff was a negro slave, the lawful property of the defendant, and, as such, the defendant gently laid his hands upon him, and thereby had only restrained him, as the defendant had a right to do. 3. That with respect to the wife and daughters of the plaintiff, in the second and third counts of the declaration mentioned, the defendant had, as to them, only acted in the same manner, and in virtue of the same legal right.

In the first of these pleas, the plaintiff joined issue; and to the second and third, filed replications alleging that the defendant, of his own wrong and without the cause in his second and third pleas alleged, committed the trespasses, &c. The counsel then filed the following agreed statement of facts, viz:

In the year 1834, the plaintiff was a negro slave belonging to Dr. Emerson, who was a surgeon in the army of the United States. In that year, 1834, said Dr. Emerson took the plaintiff from the state of Missouri to the military post at Rock Island, in the state of Illinois, and held him there as a slave until the month of April or May, 1836. At the time last mentioned, said Dr. Emerson removed the plaintiff from said military post at Rock Island to the military post at Fort Snelling, situate on the west bank of the Mississippi river, in the territory known as Upper Louisiana, acquired by the United States of France, and situated north of the latitude of thirty-six degrees thirty minutes north, and north of the state of Missouri. Said Dr. Emerson held the plaintiff in slavery at said Fort Snelling, from said last mentioned date until the year 1838.

In the year 1835, Harriet, who is named in the second count of the plaintiff's declaration, was the negro slave of Major Taliaferro, who belonged to the army of the United States. In that year, 1835, said Major Taliaferro took said Harriet to said Fort Snelling, a military post, situated as hereinbefore stated, and kept her there as a slave until the year 1836, and then sold and delivered her as a slave at said Fort Snelling unto the said Dr. Emerson hereinbefore named. Said Dr. Emerson held said Harriet in slavery at said Fort Snelling until the year 1838.

In the year 1836, the plaintiff and said Harriet, at said Fort Snelling, with the consent of said Dr. Emerson, who then claimed to be their master and owner, intermarried, and took each other for husband and wife. Eliza and Lizzie, named in the third count of the plaintiff's declaration, are the fruit of that marriage. Eliza is about fourteen years old, and was born on board the Steamboat Gipsey, north of the north line of the state of Missouri, and upon the river Mississippi. Lizzie is about seven years old, and was born in the state of Missouri, at the military post called Jefferson Barracks.

In the year 1838, said Dr. Emerson removed the plaintiff and said Harriet and their said daughter Eliza, from said Fort Snelling to the state of Missouri, where they have ever since resided.

Before the commencement of this suit, said Dr. Emerson sold and conveyed the plaintiff, said Harriet, Eliza and Lizzie, to the defendant, as slaves, and the defendant has ever since claimed to hold them and each of them as slaves.

At the time mentioned in the plaintiff's declaration, the defendant, claiming to be owner as aforesaid, laid his hands upon said plaintiff, Harriet, Eliza and Lizzie, and imprisoned them, doing, in this respect, however, no more than what he might lawfully do if they were of right his slaves at such times.

It is agreed that Dred Scott brought suit for his freedom in the circuit court of St. Louis county; that there was a verdict and judgment in his favor; that on a writ of error to the supreme court, the judgment below was reversed, and the same remanded to the circuit court, where it has been continued to await the decision of this case.

In May, 1854, the cause went before a jury, who found the following verdict, viz: "As to the first issue joined in this case, we of the jury find the defendant not guilty; and as to the issue secondly above joined, we of the jury find that before and at the time when, &c., in the first count mentioned, the said Dred Scott was a negro slave, the lawful property of the defendant; and as to the issue thirdly above joined, we, the jury, find that before and at the time when, &c., in the second and third counts mentioned, the said Harriet, wife of said Dred Scott, and Eliza and Lizzie, the daughters of the said Dred Scott, were negro slaves, the lawful property of the defendant." Whereupon the court gave judgment for the defendant. After an ineffectual motion for a new trial, the plaintiff filed the following bill of exceptions:

On the trial of this cause by the jury, the plaintiff, to maintain the issues on his part, read to the jury the following agreed statement of facts, (see agreement above.) No further testimony was given to the jury by either party. Thereupon the plaintiff moved the court to give to the jury the folowing instruction, viz: "That upon the facts agreed to by the parties, they ought to find for the plaitiff. The court refused to give such instruction to the jury, and the plaintiff, to such refusal, then and there duly excepted."

The court then gave the following instruction to the jury, on motion of the defendant: "The jury are instructed, that upon the facts in this case, the law is with the defendant." The plaintiff excepted to this instruction. Upon these exceptions, the case came up to the supreme court.

APPENDIX.

DECISION OF THE COURT.

I.

1. Upon a writ of error to the Circuit Court of the United States, the transcript of the record of all the proceedings in the case is brought before this court, and is open to its inspection and revision.

2. When a plea to the jurisdiction, in abatement, is overruled by the court upon demurrer, and the defendant pleads in bar, and upon these pleas the final judgment of the court is in his favor—if the plaintiff brings a writ of error, the judgment of the court upon the plea in abatement is before this court, although it was in favor of the plaintiff—and if the court erred in overruling it, the judgment must be reversed, and a mandate issued to the Circuit Court to dismiss the case for want of jurisdiction.

3. In the Circuit Courts of the United States, the record must show that the case is one in which, by the constitution and laws of the United States, the court had jurisdiction—and if this does not appear, and the court gives judgment either for plaintiff or defendant, it is error, and the judgment must be reversed by this court—and the parties cannot by consent waive the objection to the jurisdiction of the Circuit Court.

4. A free negro of the African race, whose ancestors were brought to this country and sold as slaves, is not a " citizen " within the meaning of the Constitution of the United States.

5. When the Constitution was adopted, they were not regarded in any of the States as members of the community which constituted the State, and were not numbered among its "people or citizens." Consequently, the special rights and immunities guaranteed to citizens do not apply to them. And not being " citizens " within the meaning of the Constitution, they are not entitled to sue in that character in a court of the United States, and the Circuit Court has not jurisdiction in such a suit.

6. The only two clauses in the Constitution which point to this race, treat them as persons whom it was morally lawful to deal in as articles of property and to hold as slaves.

7. Since the adoption of the Constitution of the United States, no State can by any subsequent law make a foreigner or any other description of persons citizens of the United States, nor entitle them to the rights and privileges secured to citizens by that instrument.

8. A state, by its laws passed since the adoption of the Constitution, may put a foreigner or any other description of persons upon a footing with its own citizens, as to all the rights and privileges enjoyed by them within its dominion and by its laws. But that will not make him a citizen of the United States, nor entitle him to sue in its courts, nor to any of the privileges and immunities of a citizen in another state.

9. The change in public opinion and feeling in relation to the African race, which has taken place since the adoption of the Constitution, cannot change its construction and meaning, and it must be construed and administered now according to its true meaning and intention when it was formed and adopted

10. The plaintiff having admitted, by his demurrer to the plea in abatement, that his ancestors were imported from Africa and sold as slaves, he is not a citizen of the state of Missouri according to the Constitution of the United States, and was not entitled to sue in that character in the Circuit Court.

11. This being the case, the judgment of the court below, in favor of the plaintiff on the plea in abatement, was erroneous.

II.

1. But if the plea in abatement is not brought up by this writ of error, the objection to the citizenship of the plaintiff is still apparent on the record, as he himself, in making out his case, states that he is of African descent, was born a slave, and claims that he and his family became entitled to freedom by being taken, by their owner, to reside in a territory where slavery is prohibited by act of congress—and that, in addition to this claim, he himself became entitled to freedom by being taken to Rock Island, in the state of Illinois—and being free when he was brought back to Missouri, he was by the laws of that state a citizen.

2. If, therefore, the facts he states do not give him or his family a right to freedom, the plaintiff is still a slave, and not entitled to sue as a "citizen," and the judgment of the Circuit Court was erroneous on that ground also, without any reference to the plea in abatement.

3. The Circuit Court can give no judgment for plaintiff or defendant in a case where it has not jurisdiction, no matter whether there be a plea in abatement or not. And unless it appears upon the face of the record, when brought here by writ of error, that the Circuit Court had jurisdiction, the judgment must be reversed.

4. When the record, as brought here by writ of error, does not show that the Circuit Court had jurisdiction, this court has jurisdiction to revise and correct the error, like any other error in the court below. It does not and cannot dismiss the case for want of jurisdiction here; for that would leave the erroneous judgment of the court below in full force, and the party injured without remedy. But it must reverse the judgment, and, as in any other case of reversal, send a mandate to the Circuit Court to conform its judgment to the opinion of this court.

5. The difference of the jurisdiction in this court in the cases of writs of error to state courts and to Circuit Courts of the United States, pointed out; and the mistakes made as to the jurisdiction of this court in the latter case, by confounding it with its limited jurisdiction in the former.

6. If the court reverses a judgment upon the ground that it appears by a particular part of the record that the Circuit Court had not jurisdiction, it does not take away the jurisdiction of this court to examine into and correct, by a reversal of the judgment, any other errors, either as to the jurisdiction or any other matter, where it appears from other parts of the record that the Circuit Court had fallen into error. On the contrary, it is the daily and familiar practice of this court to reverse on several grounds, where more than one error ap-

pears to have been committed. And the error of a Circuit Court in its jurisdiction stands on the same ground, and is to be treated in the same manner as any other error upon which its judgment is founded.

7. The decision, therefore, that the judgment of the Circuit Court upon the plea in abatement is erroneous, is no reason why the alleged error apparent in the exception should not also be examined, and the judgment reversed on that ground also, if it discloses a want of jurisdiction in the Circuit Court.

8. It is often the duty of this court, after having decided that a particular decision of the Circuit Court was erroneous, to examine into other alleged errors, and to correct them if they are found to exist. And this has been uniformly done by this court, when the questions are in any degree connected with the controversy, and the silence of the court might create doubts which would lead to further and useless litigation.

III.

1. The facts upon which the plaintiff relies, did not give him his freedom, and make him a citizen of Missouri.

2. The clause in the Constitution authorizing congress to make all needful rules and regulations for the government of the territory and other property of the United States, applies only to territory within the chartered limits of some one of the states when they were colonies of Great Britain, and which was surrendered by the British government to the old confederation of the states in the treaty of peace. It does not apply to territory acquired by the present federal government, by treaty or conquest, from a foreign nation.

The case of the American and Ocean Insurance Companies v. Canter (1 Peters, 511) referred to and examined, showing that the decision in this case is not in conflict with that opinion, and that the court did not, in the case referred to, decide upon the construction of the clause of the constitution above mentioned, because the case before them did not make it necessary to decide the question.

3. The United States, under the present constitution, cannot acquire territory to be held as a colony, to be governed at its will and pleasure. But it may acquire terrritory, which, at the time, has not a population that fits it to become a state, and may govern it as a territory until it has a population which, in the judgment of Congress, entitles it to be admitted as a state of the Union.

4. During the time it remains a territory, Congress may legislate over it within the scope of its constitutional powers in relation to citizens of the United States—and may establish a territorial government—and the form of this local government must be regulated by the discretion of Congress—but with powers not exceeding those which Congress itself, by the constitution, is authorized to exercise over citizens of the United States, in respect to their rights of persons or rights of property.

IV.

1. The territory thus acquired, is acquired by the citizens of the United States for their common and equal benefit, through their agent and trustee, the fede-

ral government. Congress can exercise no power over the rights of persons or property of a citizen in the territory which is prohibited by the constitution. The government and the citizen, whenever the territory is open to settlement, both enter it with their respective rights defined and limited by the constitution.

2. Congress has no right to prohibit the citizens of any particular state or states from taking up their home there, while it permits citizens of other states to do so. Nor has it a right to give privileges to one class of citizens which it refuses to another. The territory is acquired for their equal and common benefit—and if open to any, it must be open to all upon equal and the same terms.

3. Every citizen has a right to take with him into the territory any article of property which the constitution of the United States recognizes as property.

4. The constitution of the United States recognizes slaves as property, and pledges the federal government to protect it. And Congress cannot exercise any more authority over property of that description than it may constitutionally exercise over property of any other kind.

5. The act of Congress, therefore, prohibiting a citizen of the United States from taking with him his slaves when he removes to the territory in question to reside, is an exercise of authority over private property which is not warranted by the constitution—and the removal of the plaintiff, by his owner, to that territory, gave him no title to freedom.

V.

1. The plaintiff acquired no title to freedom by being taken, by his owner, to Rock Island, in Illinois, and brought back to Missouri. This court has heretofore decided that the *status* or condition of a person of African descent depended on the laws of the state in which he resided.

2. It has been settled by the decisions of the highest court in Missouri, that, by the laws of that state, a slave does not become entitled to his freedom where the owner takes him to reside in a state where slavery is not permitted, and afterwards brings him back to Missouri.

Conclusion. It follows that it is apparent upon the record that the court below erred in its judgment on the plea in abatement, and also erred in giving judgment for the defendant, when the exception shows that the plaintiff was not a citizen of the United States. And as the Circuit Court had no jurisdiction, either in the case stated in the plea in abatement, or in the one stated in the exception, its judgment in favor of the defendant is erroneous, and must be reversed.

ANALYSIS OF THE DRED SCOTT DECISION.

It was held by seven judges (M'Lean and Curtis dissenting) that the record showed on the part of Scott a disability to maintain his suit. Of these judges, Taney, Wayne and Daniel held that the fact set forth in the plea in abatement in the court below, and admitted in the demurrer, "that the plaintiff was a negro of African descent, whose ancestors were of pure African blood, and who were brought into this country and sold as slaves," showed him not to be a citizen of the United States, and therefore disqualified to sue in a United States Court; and that the suit ought, on that ground, to be remanded to be dismissed for want of jurisdiction. Grier and Campbell (making with the other three a majority of the court) concurred in this remanding for dismissal, and such was the judgment of the court. Both Grier and Campbell based themselves, however, not on the plea in abatement, but on the fact apparent, as they thought, in the agreed statement of facts which made a part of the record, that Scott was a slave, and on that ground disqualified to sue, and they both seemed to think that the more regular course would be to confirm the judgment of the court below. Such a confirmation of the judgment of the court below, Nelson and Catron held to be the only proper course, thus siding, so far as the question of jurisdiction was concerned, with Curtis and McLean, while even Grier (making up, with the other four, a majority of the court) went so far as to admit that the record showed a *prima facie* case of jurisdiction.

McLean and Catron held, that as there was no appeal from the judgment of the Circuit Court on the plea in abatement, the question of jurisdiction was not before the court. Taney, Wayne, Daniel and Curtis held, *per contra*, that, as the courts of the United States were of limited jurisdiction, the question of jurisdiction was always in order. Grier, Nelson and Campbell were silent on this point.

Three judges—Taney, Wayne and Daniel—held that, although the court below had no jurisdiction, and the case must be dismissed on that ground, it was still competent for the Supreme Court to give an opinion on the merits of the case, and on all the questions therein involved. McLean and Curtis dissented from this view. In their opinion, any doctrines laid down under such circumstances must be regarded as extra-judicial. They based their right of going into the merits on the assumption that the court below had jurisdiction, a view in which they were sustained by Catron and Grier. Nelson and Campbell, as they had avoided any expression of opinion on the question of jurisdiction, did the same on this question of judicial propriety; but Nelson, by confining himself, in his opinion, to the single point of the revival of Scott's condition of slavery by his return to Missouri, seemed to concur in the view of judicial propriety taken by McLean and Curtis.

Three judges—Taney, Wayne and Daniel—held that a negro of African descent was incapable of being a citizen of the United States, or even of suing as such in a federal court. From this doctrine McLean and Curtis expressly dissented, while Nelson, Grier, Campbell and Catron avoided any expression of opinion upon it.

Taney, Wayne, Daniel and Campbell held that the constitution conferred no power on Congress to legislate for the territories, the power to make all needful rules and regulations being confined solely to the disposition of lands as property, and even that authority being limited to the territories belonging to the United States (i. e. the territory northwest of the Ohio) when the constitution was made. They, however, seemed to admit a certain power of legislation in Congress, based on the fact of acquisition and growing out of the necessity of the case. McLean, Catron and Curtis held, on the other hand, that under authority to make needful rules and regulations, as well as by the necessity of the case, Congress had a full power of legislation for the territories, limited only by the general restraints upon its legislative power contained in the constitution. Nelson expressed no opinion on this point; nor did Grier, except the implication in favor of the first view from his joining in pronouncing the Missouri prohibition of 1820 unconstitutional, though on what particular ground he held it to be so does not appear.

Taney, Wayne, and Daniel held that the ordinance of 1787, though good and binding under the confederation, expired with the confederation, and that the act of Congress passed to confirm it was void, because Congress had no power to legislate for the territories. M'Lean, Catron, and Curtis held, *per contra*, that the reënactment of the ordinance of 1787 was a valid exercise of the power of Congress; while Campbell admitted—and in this Catron concurred with him (Daniel *contra*, the others silent)—that the ordinance of 1787, having been agreed to by Virginia, became thereby a part of the compact of cession permanently binding on the parties, and was so regarded by the convention that framed the constitution.

Five judges, a majority of the court—Taney, Wayne, Daniel, Campbell, and Grier—held that the Missouri prohibition of 1820 was unconstitutional and void; while Catron argued that it was void because it conflicted with the French treaty for the cession of Louisiana. M'Lean and Curtis held the prohibition constitutional and valid. Nelson silent.

Five judges—Taney, Wayne, Daniel, Campbell, and Catron—a majority of the court, held that slaves were property in a general sense, as much so as cattle, or at least were so recognized by the constitution of the United States; and as such might be carried into territories, notwithstanding any congressional prohibition. M'Lean and Curtis held, *per contra*, that slaves are recognized property only locally and by the laws of particular states, being out of those states not property, nor even slaves, except in the single case of fugitives. Grier and Nelson silent.

It was held by six judges—Taney, Wayne, Daniel, Campbell, Catron, and Nelson—that, whatever claim to freedom Scott might have had (if any, which most of them denied,) he lost it by his return to Missouri. This opinion, on the part of Taney, Wayne, and Daniel, was based solely on the law of Missouri, as recently laid down by the Supreme Court of that state. Nelson and Catron based it on what they thought the prevailing current of legal decision on the subject; and Campbell on the fact that no sufficient domicil, either in slave or master, appeared in Illinois or Minnesota. M'Lean and Curtis held, *per contra*, that Scott had been made free by his residence in Illinois and Minnesota, and that the rules of international law respecting the emancipation of slaves by residence were a part of the law of Missouri, which law had been improperly departed from and set at nought by the Missouri decision in the plaintiff's case; and that, on questions depending not on any statute or local usage, but on principles of universal jurisprudence, the decisions of state courts are not conclusive on the United States courts as to the laws of the states.

Seven judges (M'Lean and Curtis dissenting) held that by the facts on the record, it appeared that Scott was a slave, notwithstanding his residence in Illinois and Minnesota.

It appears from this analysis that only the following points commanded a majority of voices, and can be considered as having been ruled in this case :

1. That Scott was a slave notwithstanding his residence in Illinois and Minnesota. Seven judges to two.

2. That the Missouri prohibition of 1820 was unconstitutional and void. Five judges against two ; one silent, and one holding it void but not unconstitutional.

3. That, under the constitution of the United States, slaves are as much property as horses. Five judges, all slaveholders, against two non-slaveholders, the two other non-slaveholders being silent.

The question whether any power of legislation over the territories is given to Congress, by the power to make needful rules and regulations, is left undecided, four judges denying any such power, three maintaining it, Nelson silent, and Grier *in nubibus.*